Financial Management

A Modelling Approach Using Spreadsheets

Financial Management

A Modelling Approach Using Spreadsheets

George Diacogiannis
Piraeus University

McGRAW-HILL BOOK COMPANY

London · New York · St Louis · San Francisco · Auckland
Bogotá · Caracas · Lisbon · Madrid · Mexico
Milan · Montreal · New Delhi · Panama · Paris · San Juan
São Paulo · Singapore · Sydney · Tokyo · Toronto

Published by
McGRAW-HILL Book Company Europe
Shoppenhangers Road, Maidenhead, Berkshire, SL6 2QL, England
Telephone 0628 23432
Fax 0628 770224

British Library Cataloguing in Publication Data
Diacogiannis, George
Financial Management: Modelling Approach
Using Spreadsheets
I. Title
658.15

ISBN 0-07-707730-X

Library of Congress Cataloging-in-Publication Data
Diacogiannis, George
Financial management: a modelling approach using spreadsheets /
George P. Diacogiannis.
p. cm.
Includes bibliographical references and index.
ISBN 0-07-707730-X
1. Business enterprises—Finance—Data processing.
2. Corporations—Finance—Data processing. 3. Lotus 1-2-3 (Computer file)
4. Electronic spreadsheets. I. Title.
HG4012.5.D5 1993
658.15′0285′5369—dc20 93-983
CIP

12345 BP 97654

Typeset at Alden Press Limited, Oxford and Northampton
and printed and bound in Great Britain by The Bath Press, Avon

To Ruth
Pantoleon Markos and
my parents

Contents

	Preface	**xv**
	Acknowledgements	**xix**
1	**INTRODUCTION: MODELS AND FINANCIAL MANAGEMENT**	**1**
	Analog models and financial management	1
	Mathematical models and financial management	3
	Spreadsheet-based financial modelling process	10
	Advantages of financial modelling using spreadsheets	16
	Remarks related to the models used in financial management	17
	References and bibliography	20
2	**THE ROLE OF FINANCIAL MANAGEMENT**	**21**
	Nature of financial management	21
	The basic assumptions in financial management	22
	Factors affecting the firm's ordinary share market price	28
	The evolution of financial management	31
	Financial management and other disciplines	31
	The role of financial director	32
	The agency problem	33
	The objective of the firm in practice	33
	Overview of the present work	35
	Summary	36
	Questions for discussion	37
Appendix 2A	Types of business organizations in the private sector	38
Appendix 2B	Frequency distributions	42
	References and bibliography	47
3	**TIME VALUE OF MONEY**	**48**
	Basic concepts, definitions and examples	48
	Future value	49
	Present value	59
	Using future and present values in practice	68
	Summary	78
	Questions for discussion	79
Appendix 3A	The equation of the future value of a single payment under continuous compounding	81

Appendix 3B	Describing data using statistical measures	82
	References and bibliography	91
4	**FINANCIAL ANALYSIS**	**92**
	Basic concepts, definitions and examples	92
	The accounting model	94
	Financial ratio analysis	102
	Cash flow statement	113
	Financial forecasting	117
	Summary	120
	Questions for discussion	121
Appendix 4A	An alternative format of balance sheet	123
Appendix 4B	Depreciation methods	123
Appendix 4C	Simple linear regression analysis using Lotus 1-2-3	126
Appendix 4D	Forecasting sales	131
	References and bibliography	134
5	**CAPITAL BUDGETING UNDER CONDITIONS OF CERTAINTY**	**135**
	Basic concepts, definitions and examples	135
	Importance of making sound capital budgeting decisions	137
	The capital budgeting process	137
	Initial investment	139
	Estimating the profits associated with a new project	141
	Estimating the future net cash flows of a project	142
	Capital budgeting methods	146
	Ranking mutually exclusive projects	164
	The theory of Fisher	169
	Capital budgeting methods used in practice	180
	Summary	182
	Questions for discussion	183
Appendix 5A	The British corporation tax system	185
Appendix 5B	The covariance between two variables	188
	References and bibliography	191
6	**ADVANCED CAPITAL BUDGETING TOPICS**	**193**
	Capital budgeting and inflation	193
	Leasing	198
	Capital rationing	202
	Summary	207
	Questions for discussion	207
Appendix 6A	Linear programming	209
Appendix 6B	The correlation coefficient	214
	References and bibliography	217

7	**INCORPORATION OF RISK INTO CAPITAL BUDGETING DECISIONS**	**218**
	Basic concepts, definitions and examples	218
	Informal methods	220
	Indirect methods for incorporating risk into capital budgeting	221
	The probability distribution method	225
	Sensitivity analysis	232
	Simulation analysis	238
	Decision trees	244
	The use of risk assessment methods in practice	247
	Summary	249
	Questions for discussion	250
Appendix 7A	Calculating the certainty equivalent coefficients	252
Appendix 7B	The normal distribution	254
	References and bibliography	256
8	**PORTFOLIO THEORY**	**258**
	Basic concepts, definitions and examples	258
	Security analysis	260
	Portfolio analysis	271
	Portfolio selection	279
	Generalizing the results	279
	Naive diversification and diversification across industries	282
	The modified efficient frontier	284
	Summary	292
	Questions for discussion	293
Appendix 8A	Calculating historical rates of return for Marks and Spencer plc	296
Appendix 8B	Portfolio risk and the effects of diversification	298
Appendix 8C	Matrices	300
Appendix 8D	Expressing portfolio return and risk using a matrix notation	305
Appendix 8E	Mean–standard deviation indifference curves	307
Appendix 8F	The studentized range test for normality	310
	References and bibliography	312
9	**ASSET PRICING MODELS**	**314**
	Basic concepts, definitions and examples	314
	The capital market line	316
	The capital asset pricing model	320
	The two-factor capital asset pricing model	324
	Capital asset pricing model: the empirical evidence	326
	The problem of testing the CAPM: Roll's critique	329
	The arbitrage pricing model	331
	Forms of the efficient market hypothesis	336
	Empirical tests of the efficient market hypothesis	342
	Summary	349
	Questions for discussion	350

Appendix 9A	Proving the capital market line and capital asset pricing model	353
Appendix 9B	The single index model	355
Appendix 9C	Multiple linear regression analysis	364
	References and bibliography	366
10	**MANAGEMENT OF WORKING CAPITAL**	**370**
	Basic concepts, definitions and examples	371
	Working capital ratios	373
	The risk–return trade-off	374
	Managing cash	379
	Cost-balancing models for managing cash	380
	Managing marketable securities	386
	Characteristics of marketable securities	387
	Yield on a marketable security	387
	The portfolio of marketable securities	388
	Models of marketable securities management	388
	Managing debtors	389
	Credit policy	389
	Credit analysis	398
	Managing stocks	398
	The economic order quantity model	399
	Extensions of the basic EOQ model	402
	Managing creditors	406
	Cost of credit	407
	Managing accruals	411
	Managing short-term borrowing	412
	Cost of short-term borrowing	413
	Summary	416
	Questions for discussion	418
Appendix 10A	Sampling methods	422
	References and bibliography	427
11	**VALUATION OF DEBENTURES AND PREFERENCE SHARES**	**429**
	Basic concepts, definitions and examples	430
	Valuation of debentures	431
	Returns on investments in debentures	434
	Gilt-edged securities	441
	Spot rates	446
	Sensitivity of debenture prices	447
	Inflation and interest rates	452
	Valuation of preference shares	456
	Summary	457
	Questions for discussion	458
Appendix 11A	Statistical inference: estimation	460
	References and bibliography	462

12	**THE DETERMINANTS OF REDEMPTION YIELDS**	**463**
	Risk on investment in debentures	463
	The term structure of interest rates	466
	Hypotheses of the term structure of interest rates	469
	Duration	481
	Summary	487
	Questions for discussion	488
Appendix 12A	Sensitivity of duration to changes in term to maturity and coupon rate with 1-2-3	489
Appendix 12B	Confidence intervals	491
	References and bibliography	493
13	**VALUATION OF ORDINARY SHARES**	**494**
	Basic concepts, definitions and examples	494
	Valuation of ordinary shares	495
	Special cases of the *T*-period valuation model	502
	Estimating the growth rate in dividends per share	508
	The price/earnings ratio and the constant growth valuation model	516
	Estimating the value of a firm in practice	518
	Share price information	521
	Summary	524
	Questions for discussion	524
Appendix 13A	Proof of the equation $PV = D_1(1 - a^T)/(r_0 - g)$	526
Appendix 13B	Confidence intervals for standard deviations	527
	References and bibliography	528
14	**THE COST OF CAPITAL**	**529**
	Basic concepts, definitions and examples	529
	Specific costs of capital	532
	Weighted average cost of capital	539
	Risk and weighted average cost of capital	542
	Marginal cost of capital	542
	Calculating the cost of capital in the real world	549
	Using the CAPM to calculate a firm's cost of capital	553
	Empirical evidence on the cost of capital	558
	Summary	559
	Questions for discussion	559
Appendix 14A	Inefficient market proxy and the cost of equity	561
Appendix 14B	Statistical inference: hypothesis testing	562
	References and bibliography	565
15	**GEARING AND CAPITAL STRUCTURE**	**567**
	Operating gearing	567
	Financial gearing	575
	Combined gearing	579
	Capital structure theories	583

	Capital structure theories with no taxes	584
	Capital structure theories with taxes	596
	The value of the firm with corporation and personal taxes	601
	Summary	607
	Questions for discussion	608
Appendix 15A	Deriving the measurement equations for DOG, DFG and DCG	611
Appendix 15B	Proofs for various equations	613
Appendix 15C	The cost of equity under corporation and personal taxes	614
Appendix 15D	Confidence intervals for a population's simple regression coefficients	615
	References and bibliography	618
16	**DIVIDEND POLICY**	**619**
	Basic concepts, definitions and examples	619
	Dividend policy theories	623
	Tax-differential theory	627
	Comparing three theories on dividends	629
	Dividend signalling approach	631
	Clientele effect	632
	Dividend policies	633
	Factors influencing dividend policy	638
	Dividend policy: empirical evidence	641
	Summary	644
	Questions for discussion	645
Appendix 16A	Scrip dividends and stock splits	647
Appendix 16B	Dividend policy theories	648
Appendix 16C	A statistical analysis of the dividends per share of Marks and Spencer	649
	References and bibliography	654
17	**MERGERS**	**656**
	Basic concepts, definitions and examples	656
	Motives for mergers	658
	Evaluating mergers	661
	The problem with the earnings per share in valuation of mergers	670
	Methodological issues	675
	Summary	685
	Questions for discussion	686
Appendix 17A	Database statistical functions	688
	References and bibliography	690
18	**OPTIONS**	**692**
	Basic concepts, definitions and examples	692
	The intrinsic value of an option	696
	Profits profiles of call and put options	697
	Properties of options	703
	Summary	712
	Questions for discussion	713

Appendix 18A	The runs test of randomness	715
	References and bibliography	718
19	**OPTION VALUATION MODELS**	**719**
	The Black and Scholes valuation formula	719
	Factors influencing option prices	724
	Extensions of the Black–Scholes model	727
	Index options	730
	Foreign currency options	732
	The use of options	732
	Alternatives to Black–Scholes option valuation model	738
	Empirical investigations on option pricing models	740
	Summary	743
	Questions for discussion	743
Appendix 19A	Calculating $N(d_j)$	746
Appendix 19B	Implicit volatility	749
Appendix 19C	One-Way sensitivity analysis of call prices	751
Appendix 19D	Proving Properties 1 and 2	753
Appendix 19E	Estimating the variance of continuously compounded rates of return	754
	References and bibliography	755
Appendix A	A history of spreadsheets and general comparisons	757
Appendix B	UK–USA equivalent terms	768
Appendix C	Glossary	769
Appendix D	Tables	779
Appendix E	Statistical references	797
Index		**798**

Preface

Before the advent of the microcomputer and the 'spreadsheet', skilled programmers were employed to provide the vital information that management required. Also, firms had to use up their scarce financial resources in acquiring the expensive mainframe computers.

The development of powerful and low-cost microcomputers has caused a revolution in the application of financial management techniques. With the advent of financial spreadsheet software, it is possible for managers to analyse financial management problems without extensive training in programming and without the need to rely on scarce computer personnel. The marriage of financial management with a spreadsheet provides a powerful tool which can be utilized to quantify, model, understand and interpret the results and to use them when making a decision.

Objectives and features of this book

This book is intended for people wanting to learn the essential approaches and concepts of modern financial management and the basic techniques of financial modelling with a spreadsheet. *Financial Management: A Modelling Approach Using Spreadsheets* pays considerable attention to the analysis of financial management problems and illustrates how to utilize the powerful features of a spreadsheet in order to enhance the benefits from such an analysis.

The unusual feature of the book is that it contains the following two units each of which could on its own stand as a book:

1 Approaches and concepts of financial management. Examples of financial management problems solved using Lotus 1-2-3.
2 A series of statistical approaches and concepts used in financial management.

The Contents illustrate the broad range of concepts and applications in this book. It is used extensively to show the potential of Lotus 1-2-3, including display facilities, sensitivity analysis, graphical representations (two-dimension and three-dimension—the latter performed with the aid of the Lotus add-on 3-D Graphics), statistical procedures, using 1-2-3 for risk analysis (for example, simulation analysis), use of various spreadsheet functions, database facilities and macros.

The book also presents and discusses various forecasting tools for financial analysis, mathematical proofs of financial models and the basic concepts of linear programming (mathematical proofs and a solution of the linear program model are included in the appendices).

Additionally, the book includes various figures which are used to summarize financial management concepts. Each of these figures is comprised of three parts: definition, calculation and interpretation. Also, summary figures of empirical results are presented in most of the 19 chapters. With the exception of Chapter 1, the chapters contain a complete set of questions related to the most important issues and methods in that chapter. Finally, when possible, real data is used.

Who can use this book?

This book is written to satisfy the needs of two particular groups of people:

- Finance and management undergraduate and postgraduate students who wish to learn the basic tools of financial analysis and techniques of financial modelling.
- Business executives who want to learn new skills, or refresh their skills, about the relevant methods of financial management and analyse problems by building and interpreting spreadsheet models.

What spreadsheet?

The solutions of the financial management problems are provided by using Lotus 1-2-3 (the models in this book can be used with both releases 2.1 and 2.2). These solutions can be easily adopted for other spreadsheets (for example, Excel, Quatro, etc.). Appendix A, at the end of the book, presents and compares the main features of four popular spreadsheets: Lotus 1-2-3, Excel, Supercalc 5 and Quatro. The book does assume a prior knowledge of Lotus 1-2-3, but you do not have to be an expert in the program. In each case, an explanation will show you how to create each spreadsheet.

How to use this book?

This book helps you to learn relevant concepts of modern financial management. Each concept is presented in a straightforward manner and it is illustrated by an example solved using Lotus 1-2-3. It will be very beneficial if you follow the steps below:

- Read a chosen concept thoroughly.
- Try to work through the solution of the example associated with the chosen concept and compare it with the one given in the book.
- Try to examine the impact of the various assumptions on the solution of your problem.

By using the various examples, you may find new financial applications for Lotus 1-2-3 (or another spreadsheet) and ways to speed quickly through the utilization of real-life complex spreadsheet financial applications.

Organization of this book

This book is organized into 19 chapters, and 5 general appendices. Most of the chapters have the following structure:

- A brief introduction

- Basic concepts, definitions and examples
- Discussion, examples and problems related to various approaches and concepts
- Empirical results
- Summary
- Questions for discussion
- References
- Appendix/appendices.

The general appendices are:

- A history of spreadsheets and general comparisons between four popular spreadsheets
- UK–USA equivalent terms
- Glossary
- Financial and statistical tables
- Statistical references.

Conventions used in this book

1 The first letter of each word in a spreadsheet command is capitalized (for example, `/Data Table 1`).
2 The names of spreadsheet functions always appear in capital letters (for example, `@SUM`).
3 Usually the contents of cells are displayed formatted.
4 Names of standard keyboard keys are enclosed in ⟨ ⟩, for example the Enter/return key is represented by ⟨Enter⟩.

Acknowledgements

I would like to express my appreciation to the students of Warwick Business School for providing a stimulating environment for the preparation of this book. I appreciate the suggestions and support of the following people, without, of course, holding them responsible for any deficiencies that remain in this book:

Panayiotis Athanasopoulos (Professor at Piraeus University)
Rob Bryer (Warwick Business School)
Edgar De Souza (Bath University)
Michalis Glezakos (Assistant Professor at Piraeus University)
Masood Javid (Warwick Business School)
Stewart Hodges (Professor at Warwick Business School)
Pui Man Leung (Warwick Business School)
Andreas Merikas (Assistant Professor at Piraeus University)
Stelios Saradidis (Professor at Piraeus University)
Mick Silver (Professor at Cardiff Business School)
Antony Steele (Professor at Warwick Business School)
Kostas Tassis (Bath College)
Yew Tiok Teh (Warwick Business School)
Nick Travlos (Associate Professor at Piraeus University)
Nicholas Webber (Warwick Business School)
Norman Strong (Manchester University)
Al Raitt

Special thanks are due to the staff at McGraw-Hill for their valuable assistance in the preparation of this manuscript and particularly the help of Brendan Lambon, editor in business, finance and economics.

Finally, I would like to express my deepest appreciation to my wife Ruth and my son Pantoleon whose sacrifices made this book possible.

Publisher's acknowledgements

The primary source for financial data is Datastream International. Datastream is the leading provider of historical financial information services worldwide.

We acknowledge the use of data from the London Business School's London Share Price Database and Risk Measurement Service. Potential subscribers to either should contact: The Financial Database Manager, Institute of Finance, London Business School, Sussex Place, Regents Park, London NW1 4SA.

1 Introduction: models and financial management

A model is a simplified representation of a real object or situation that facilitates the understanding and manipulation of the real thing. Models can be classified into three categories.

1 An iconic model is a physical replica of the real thing; a scale model for a shopping centre or an airport, or an aircraft simulator are examples of iconic models.
2 An analog model is a physical representation of objects or situations but it does not look like the real thing; for example, maps, a diagram showing the relationship between the financing decisions and objectives of a firm, profitability charts, and so on are analog models.
3 A mathematical model is a set of symbols and mathematical relationships that represent a real situation; for example, break-even analysis, maximizing the earnings per share of a firm, optimizing the use of financial resources, and so on can all be represented as mathematical models.

Financial management uses analog and mathematical models.

Analog models and financial management

Analog models such as graphs and charts can be used to:

1 Summarize large amounts of information. In many cases a graph can be used to illustrate numerical data from a large table of data or a data base. For example, a line graph can illustrate the daily changes of a share price over a period of two years, a bar graph can present the earnings per share of 100 firms, and so on. Likewise, a chart can be used to provide a visual image of information from a lengthy report. For example, a chart can illustrate the finance function within a firm or the capital budgeting process of a firm, and so on.
2 Enhance the understanding of complex situations. Building and studying a chart or a graph from a complex situation provides us with further understanding of the situation. For example, the environment of financial decision making is extremely complex (it contains taxes, regulations, financial institutions and highly competitive financial markets); a chart illustrating how the financial system fits together facilitates our understanding of the situation.
3 Make comparisons among financial items. A graph can be used to compare numerical financial data over time, or to facilitate comparisons among numerical financial items. For example, a graph can be used to illustrate the changes of profit after tax over time, or to compare the 1990 profit after tax and sales among the branches of an electrical firm, and so on.

4 Convey information that cannot be conveyed by a column of figures. A graph can help the reader to recognize patterns and trends that could otherwise be overlooked. For example, a graph can illustrate that the sales of a firm vary with the seasons.
5 Enhance the presentation of financial reports. Charts and graphs are always powerful tools for financial report presentations. They also force the presenter of a financial report to put it into a logical sequence.

Characteristics of an analog model

An analog model is comprised of the following:

1 An objective. The objective of a model must be clearly and concisely defined.
2 The assumptions of the model. Analog models are used to simplify reality and thus are based upon a number of abstractions and simplifications from reality. These assumptions must be simple and comprehensive. Simplicity is necessary to make the model workable and attractive. Comprehensiveness is required to provide a clear presentation of the real situation. The objective of the model developer is always to achieve a balance between simplicity and comprehensiveness in order to obtain a workable, easy to understand and realistic presentation.
3 The components of the model. The components of a chart are usually a set of labels included in geometrical symbols (for example, boxes, circles, and so on). Each label represents our thoughts about an event. For example, the discounted methods that can be used for the evaluation of capital projects include the net present value (NPV), the profitability index (PI) and the internal rate of return (IRR); then we can display NPV, PI and IRR in boxes and use them to prepare a chart.

   The components of a graph are the numerical data corresponding to the quantities under consideration. For example, assume that the yearly sales of a firm during 1985, 1986, 1987, 1988, 1989, 1990 and 1991 are £20,000, £30,000, £35,000, £38,000, £40,000, £45,000 and £49,000 respectively; then the sets of data (1985, 1986, 1987, 1988, 1989, 1990, 1991) and (£20,000, £30,000, £35,000, £38,000, £40,000, £45,000, £49,000) are the components of the graph.
4 The relationships between the model's components. The construction of an analog model consists of identifying and illustrating the relationships between its components. In charts these relationships are usually indicated by arrows which reflect the flow of the model's components (these arrows are referred to as branches or links). In graphs data is turned into pictures: namely, changes, comparisons, or relationships between the model's components are displayed by points, lines, bars, and so on.

Example 1.1 The functions of financial management

Suppose you wish to create a chart illustrating the financial management's functions and how they are related to the firm's objective assumed in this book (i.e. the maximization of the shareholders' wealth, see also Chapter 2).

The financial management's functions are:

- Examining the firm's financial position and looking ahead to future goals.
- Efficient allocation of funds to assets.
- Acquisition of funds and determination of the firm's capital structure.

The model under consideration is comprised of the following:

1 An objective. To provide a chart illustrating the financial management functions and the fact that these functions should be carried in such a way as to achieve the firm's objective.
2 The assumption of the model. The following assumptions are made:
   (a) The function of financial management can be classified into three groups.
   (b) The objective of the firm is to maximize shareholders' wealth.
   (c) The functions of financial management should be carried out in such a way as to maximize the shareholders' wealth.
3 The components of the model: The model's components are shown in Figure 1.1.

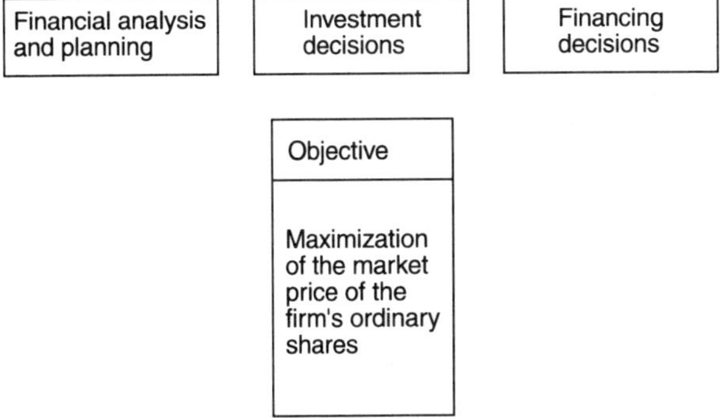

Figure 1.1. The components of an analog model

4 The relationships between the model's components: these are shown in Figure 1.2.

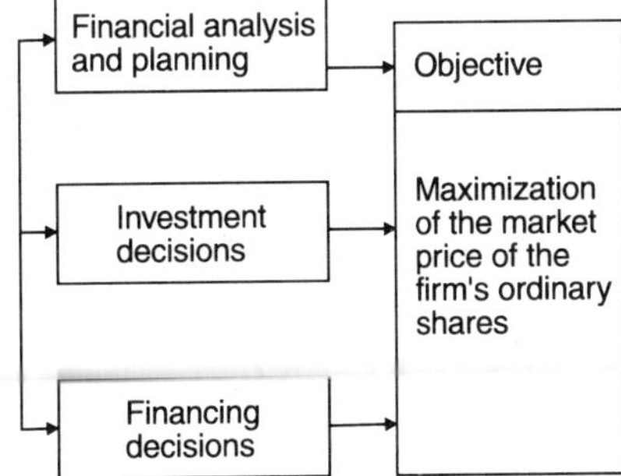

Figure 1.2. The financial management decisions and the objective of the firm

Many financial management analog models are composites of submodels. It is generally simpler to develop each of the submodels separately and then aggregate them into an overall model.

Mathematical models and financial management

Mathematical models are used in financial management for the following reasons:

1 Mathematical models are clear. The solution of a mathematical model can be viewed in terms of the approach used, the assumptions of the model, the components that are essential to the problem analysis (for example, the major

components of a model using the net present value for project evaluation are: useful life of investment, initial investment, periodic cash flows and discount rate) and the relationships between these components (for example, the net present value formula). Building and studying a model in such a way facilitates our understanding of the problem and solution.

2 There are standard mathematical models. In many cases an approach can be used with many different sets of numerical data and this approach can be developed into a standard function. For example, the evaluation of investment projects can be conducted by using discounted cash flow techniques such as the net present value and the internal rate of return. The variability of returns on shares can be measured by using the standard deviation; the relationship between different variables (with cross-sectional or time-series observations) can be investigated by employing the technique of regression analysis, and so on.

3 Mathematical models can be numerical models providing quantitative results. Many problems of financial management require quantitative results (for example, evaluation of investment project, valuation of shares, and so on). In many situations the comparison of quantitative results can be easy and accurate.

4 Many (numerical) mathematical models can be solved with the computer. Computer software can be viewed as a tool for solving (numerical) mathematical models. Much software providing ready-made models (for example, linear programming software) is available and other software is designed to facilitate the development of mathematical models (for example, electronic spreadsheets).

5 Mathematical models increase the user's understanding of decision making. Mathematical models improve the user's ability to gain insight into the situation in which a decision has to be made (for example, evaluating an investment project by using the net present value method) and helps him or her to understand the possible outcome of that decision (for example, accepting the investment project because its net present value is positive). Increasing the user's understanding of decision making can help him or her to make the best possible decisions.

6 Mathematical models bring into the open methods and their assumptions. Mathematical models bring into the open relationships and assumptions so that we can question their validity and reasonableness. In many instances, assumptions can be modified for constructing more accurate models and thus making better decisions. For example, dropping the assumption of certainty in the appraisal of investment projects and taking risk into account.

7 Mathematical models and the computer help to evaluate different alternatives. A mathematical model and the computer can be used to perform 'what if' analysis (that is, identify the model's components to which the numerical result of the model is sensitive and assess the extent of such sensitivity). For example, one can examine the sensitivity of a project's net present value to changes in the discount rate.

Many methods in the theory of financial management can be described with the aid of mathematical models and Figure 1.3 provides some examples discussed in the present work.

Modelling approach in problem-solving and decision-making processes

Using modelling (that is, making a mathematical description of a situation) facilitates the manipulation, understanding, experimentation and analysis of a financial management situation.

Method	Financial management area
Future value of cash flows	Personal and business investment decisions
Present values of cash flows	
Accounting profits	Business investment decisions under conditions of certainty
Payback period	
Discounted payback	
Accounting rate of return	
Net present value	
Profitability index	
Internal rate of return	
Capital rationing	Business investment decisions under conditions of risk
The risk-adjusted discount rate method	
The certainty equivalent method	
The probability distribution method	
Probability distributions	
Normal distribution	
Simulation analysis	
Sensitivity (or 'what if') analysis	
Decision trees	
Sources and applications of funds	Financial analysis and planning
Funds flow statement	
Changes in net working capital	
Working capital financial ratios	
Working capital policies	
The cost of ordinary shares	Measuring the firm's cost of capital and deciding about the composition of long-term liabilities and shareholders' funds
The cost of preference shares	
The cost of debentures	
The weighted average cost of capital	
The marginal cost of capital	
The net income approach	
The net operating income approach	
Modigliani and Miller approach	
The traditional approach	

Figure 1.3. Quantitative descriptions of methods discussed in this book

A modelling approach to a problem-solving process

A modelling approach used in a problem-solving process is comprised of the following stages:

1 Defining the problem. A clear and concise definition of the problem must be developed. The following are examples of clear definitions of problems:
   - **(a)** Analyse the current financial position of Marks and Spencer plc by comparing its 1990 financial ratios with the industry averages.
   - **(b)** Calculate the yearly changes in the net working capital of Marks and Spencer plc for the period 1983–88.
   - **(c)** Estimate the future sales, and cost of sales for Marks and Spencer plc by using the trend projection forecasting method.

2 Selecting/formulating a mathematical model.
   - **(a)** Assumptions and constraints of the model. Mathematical models are used to simplify reality and thus are based upon a number of abstractions and simplifications from reality. These assumptions must be simple

and comprehensive. The former usually results in making the model feasible, easy to understand and attractive. Comprehensiveness is required in order to obtain a realistic solution. The model developer's objective is always to achieve a balance between simplicity and comprehensiveness in order to obtain a workable, easy to understand and realistic solution.

The constraints of a model are the restrictions about the environment stating what cannot be done. For example, a firm may have to evaluate only three new financial plans.

(b) Variables and parameters of the model. A variable is a measurable quantity which can vary, or is subject to change; variables can be divided into controllable (or decision) variables, uncontrollable (or environmental) variables and result (or outcome) variables.

Controllable variables are factors that affect the outcome of the financial model and are determined by the model's developer; for example, the sale price of a new product of a firm can be a controllable variable. Uncontrollable variables are factors that affect the outcome of a financial situation beyond the control of the model developer; for example, corporate tax regulations, interest rates, number of units from a product a firm will sell are possible illustrations. It is important to recognize that the assumptions of the model can transfer controllable variables to uncontrollable in order to simplify the model.

A result variable is the variable to be measured in order to evaluate various solutions; for example the net present value of an investment project is a result variable. Intermediate variables are variables that relate controllable, uncontrollable and result variables. For example, assume that a model having as an objective to calculate the total assets of a firm on a specific point in time. Consider the following relationships:

(i) Fixed assets – Depreciation = Net fixed assets;
(ii) Stocks + Debtors + Cash = Current assets;
(iii) Net fixed assets + Current assets = Total assets.

In this case, the intermediate variables are net fixed assets and current assets. Finally, the parameters are measurable quantities that are inherent in the model, for example, financial ratios derived from the balance sheet of a firm are parameters of the balance sheet model.

(c) Mathematical relationships between the variables. The construction of a financial model consists of identifying the functional relationships between its variables. In most cases, relationships are expressed in equations and inequalities. Figure 1.4 provides an analog model illustrating the structure of a mathematical model.

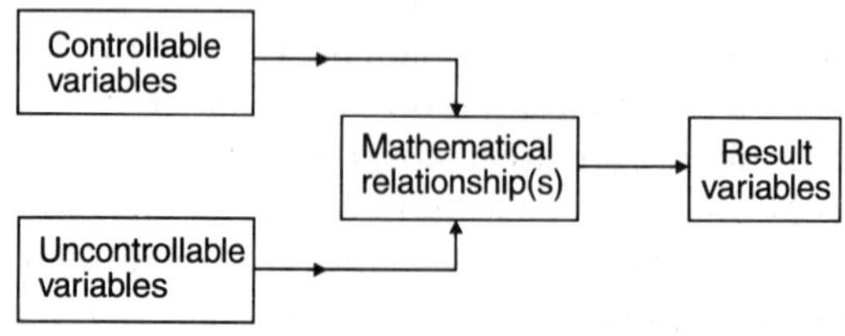

Figure 1.4. Structure of a mathematical model

3 Gathering relevant data. Models require data on their variables. For example, the calculation of the net present value of an investment project requires data on the life of the project, cash flows and discount rate.

4 Developing a solution to the problem. Use the data collected in the previous step together with the mathematical model's relationship(s) to obtain a numerical solution.

5 Testing the solution. Test the logic of the steps used to derive the solution and make sure that the data and mathematical relationship(s) used are accurate and valid. If the steps used are not logical, the data or relationship(s) are wrong, try to derive a solution again by defining a flow among steps, using the correct data, or relationship(s).

6 Analysing the results. Determine and analyse the implication of the solution. For example, suppose that a firm wishes to raise additional share capital by issuing 1,000,000 ordinary shares, however, this solution will temporarily deteriorate the earnings per share for the existing shareholders. The results can be analysed by conducting a sensitivity analysis. This analysis determines how sensitive is the solution to changes in the data or the model specification. For example, if a firm wishes to raise additional share capital, then you can examine the sensitivity of the earnings per share to changes in the number of new ordinary shares.

A modelling approach to a decision-making process

A modelling approach used in a decision-making process is comprised of the following stages:

1 Defining the problem and identify the objective(s) of the decision. A clear and concise definition of the problem must be developed and the objective(s) of the decision must be clearly identified. For example, the general problem of a firm to accept as many profitable investment projects as possible can be defined as maximize the total net present value of all projects under consideration, subject to the limited resources available to the firm. In this case, we assume that the single objective of the firm is to maximize the shareholders' wealth.

2 Identifying decision alternatives that are available and feasible. Consider decision alternatives (also called courses of action) available and feasible for the analysis. For example, a firm can consider to evaluate three new investment proposals by using the technique of the net present value.

3 Establishing criteria for the evaluation of the alternatives. A criterion is a logical method that can be utilized to select the alternative (or alternatives) that best satisfies the objectives of the decision under consideration. For example, a firm can accept investment projects that provide a positive net present value, support environmental protection and increase the welfare of its employees.

4 Gathering the relevant data. Relevant data can be quantitative (for example, future cash flows), or qualitative (for example, the results obtained from interviews with the firm's employees).

5 Evaluating alternatives and test the accuracy of your evaluation. Apply the mathematical model to the quantitative data available, or process the qualitative data into information that is valuable for decision making. Test the accuracy of your results.

6 Performing a selection of alternative(s). Decision alternatives can be broadly

classified as independent (that is, the selection of one does not eliminate the selection of the others) and mutually exclusive (that is, the selection of one eliminates the acceptance of the other). For example, the decision alternatives to buy a new computer machine and to buy new office equipment are independent; the decision alternatives to buy a new machine and to lease a new machine when only one machine is needed are mutually exclusive.

Use the results of the previous steps together with the established criteria to select the alternative (alternatives) that best satisfies the decision objective(s). For example, suppose the objective of a firm is to maximize the wealth of its shareholders, the firm has under consideration two investment projects providing a positive and a negative net present value, respectively. Under these conditions the firm will select the project with the positive net present value because it will increase its shareholders' wealth (we assume that the firm has enough funds for both projects).

7 Analysing the selection(s). Determine and analyse the implication of the solution. For example, a decision to accept a new project may require additional external sources of funds. Your selection can be further analysed by examining how sensitive is the solution to changes in the data or the model specification. For example, suppose you have selected a project with a positive net present value, then examine how sensitive is the net present value of the project to the changes of the discount rate.

Figure 1.5 illustrates the quantitative problem-solving process and the decision-making process.

Example 1.2 An example of the decision-making process.

We assume that the current date is 30 March 1988. Marks and Spencer plc has 2,659,000 ordinary shares. Assume that the firm is considering the following three alternative financial plans having similar risk levels:

Plan A Carry on operations without adopting new investment projects.
Plan B Adopt a new expansion investment and a new financing plan.
Plan C Adopt a new investment project.

Each financial plan is expected to increase the future profits of the firm and its future share price. We assume that the increase in the future profits will result in higher dividends per share. We want to identify the plan that maximizes the ordinary shareholders' wealth.

The anticipated effect on the company's share price for each plan is as follows:

Plan A: 151 pence Plan B: 154 pence Plan C: 148 pence

The present model is comprised of the following steps:

1 Definition of the problem and identification of the decision's objective. Identify among the three given plans that plan which maximizes the ordinary shareholders' wealth.
2 Identifying decision alternatives that are available and feasible. There are three alternatives which were identified previously.

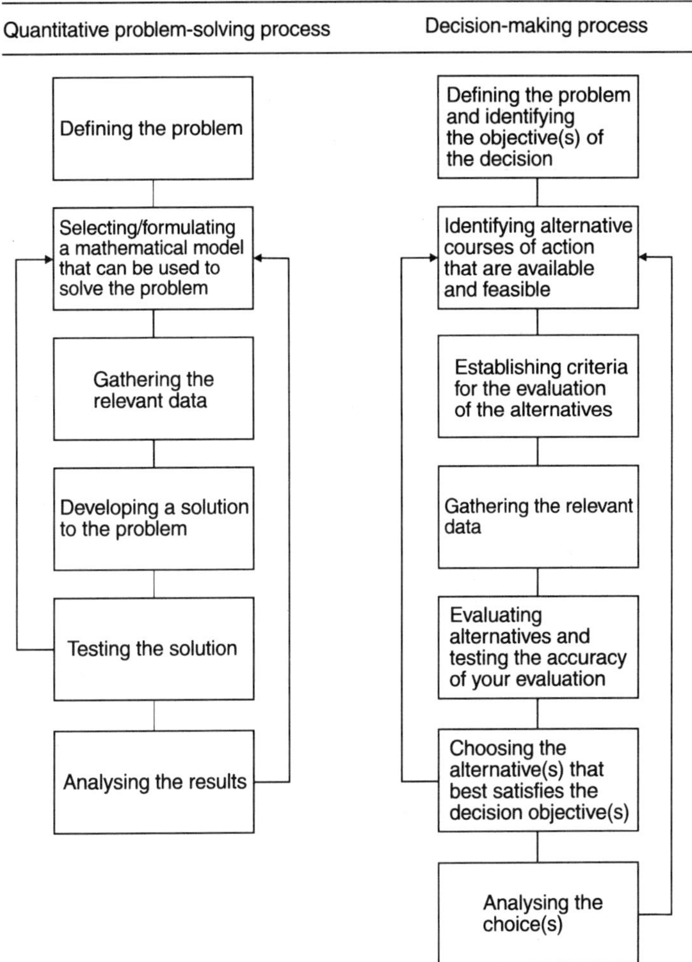

Figure 1.5. The quantitative problem-solving and decision-making processes

3 Establishing criteria for the evaluation of the alternatives. The following assumptions are made:

(**a**) There are only three available plans for the firm.
(**b**) The plans have similar levels of risk.
(**c**) The plan that maximizes the ordinary shareholders' wealth is identified.

The present model is based upon the following mathematical relationship:

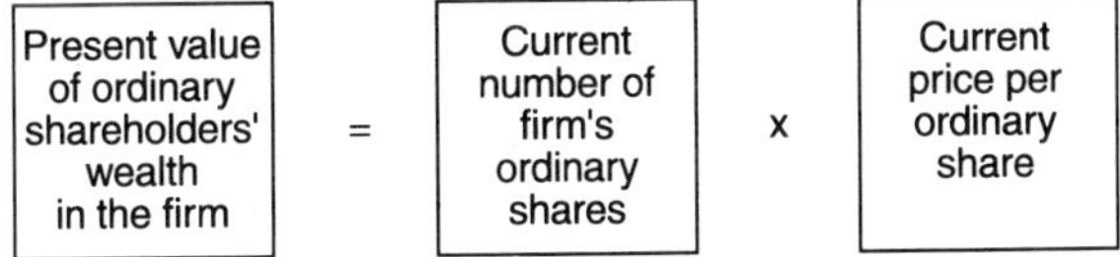

This model has a controllable variable, the current number of ordinary shares, an uncontrollable variable, the current marker price per ordinary share and a result variable, the present value of the ordinary shareholders' wealth in the firm. The criterion is to accept the plan that provides the highest possible value of the shareholders' wealth.

Figure 1.6. Calculating the current shareholders' wealth for each plan

	Plan A	Plan B	Plan C
Current number of ordinary shares ('000s)	2,659	2,659	2,659
Current price per share (p)	151	154	148
Current value of wealth (£'000s)	401,509	409,486	393,532

4 Gathering the relevant data. The quantitative data is given above.
5 Evaluating alternatives and test the accuracy of your evaluation (see Figure 1.6).
6 Performing a selection of alternative(s). A comparison of the results reveals that Plan B should be selected.
7 Analysing the selection(s). The analysis includes the consequences of accepting Plan B (for example, future capital structure, future dividend growth, and so on).

Spreadsheet-based financial modelling process

A spreadsheet is frequently referred as a personal 'modelling' tool because it enables the user to build a 'personal' model and carry out the modelling himself or herself. The user decides on the logic and data during the construction phase of the model. Additionally, the user validates the model by using it and expanding it if necessary. The series of phases for the creation of a spreadsheet-based financial model are as follows:

1 Initial view of the problem. This phase does not require a clear and concise definition of the problem, because a spreadsheet provides you with the facilities of revising and restructuring your model at any time. In some cases, it is recommended that you plan your model on a piece of paper (for example, if you are new to financial modelling with the spreadsheet).
2 Constructing an initial model. In this phase you are building an initial model by planning the logical steps in the model and using the necessary numerical data. Here you are developing a process for converting input data to output. The presentation style of the model is tailored to the individual. For example, when you develop a model that calculates the net present value of an investment project, you may decide to display all the input data before the solution of the problem. It is a good idea to separate the input data from the main calculation section of your model, where the data is employed for processing.
3 Testing the initial model. Once the initial construction of the model is completed, the model is tested. Testing involves using the model with different sets of data to determine whether it always produces correct results. If you have made an error (or errors) find it and then use the spreadsheet's facilities to correct it. Typical errors include: misreferenced cells, errors in a formula or function, a missed bracket in a lengthy formula or function. If your model needs a restructure alter your worksheet as necessary. Before going to the next phase review the learning achieved to this point.
4 Expanding further the model. This phase is devoted to the expansion of your model by using more data, modifying one or more of its initial assumptions, or providing a further development. The presentation style of the model is tailored to the model creator.

5 Testing the new expanded model. In this phase you test the expanded model by using it. If a restructure is required or a simplification of the model, alter your worksheet as necessary. If no errors exist and your model needs further expansion, review the learning achieved to this point and go back to phase 4. Before going back to phase 4 review the learning achieved to this point. If none of the foregoing is necessary, you have constructed your final version of the model. Review the learning achieved from using the modelling approach.

During the construction phase or testing phase remember the following three tips:

- Saving your spreadsheet is considered good computer practice, because this simple tip saves hours of time and discouragement.
- You can enhance the presentation of your worksheet; for example, format the contents of cells, allow more blank spaces when entries crowd into one another, underline titles, and so on.
- Document your financial model. This can be created by explaining the procedure required to use the model, showing how the model can be divided into various parts (called submodels) and how the submodels relate to one another. Documenting your model will be particularly valuable if you want to modify or update the model in the future. A brief documentation can be stored in a section of the spreadsheet that is separated form your work area or it can be saved as an independent lotus file.

Figure 1.7 summarizes the phases of a spreadsheet-based financial model.

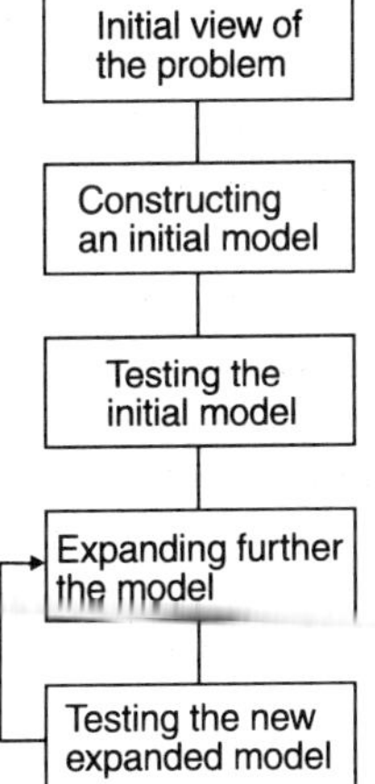

Figure 1.7. Spreadsheet-based financial modelling process

Example 1.3 An example of the spreadsheet-based financial modelling process

AD Computers plc is considering investing in a project with the following net cash flows: year 1: £1,802,000, year 2: £2,363,000, year 3: £2,517,000, year 4: £2,529,000 and year 5: £2,057,000. The project requires an initial investment of £7,000,000 and the firm has a required rate of return or discount rate of 12 per cent. How should AD computers evaluate the project?

The following procedure is adopted:

1 Initial view of the problem. Evaluating a new investment project.

2 Constructing an initial model. The initial model calculates the net present value (NPV) of the investment project. In this case, the variables are initial investment, net cash flows and discount rate. It is decided to choose an area of the worksheet in which all variables can be entered and displayed. The net present value will be displayed below the area of the variables. The initial model is presented in Figure 1.8. The mix of the logical steps and the numerical data is stated as follows:

(a) Enter the initial investment in cell B4.
(b) Enter the net cash flows in cells B5 . . B9.
(c) Enter the discount rate in cell B11.
(d) Calculate the net present value by using the financial function @NPV.

```
            A                 B          C          D          E          F          G
 1 CALCULATING THE NPV OF AN INVESTMENT PROJECT
 2
 3              YEAR     CASH FLOW
 4                 0      (7,000)
 5                 1       1,802
 6                 2       2,363
 7                 3       2,517
 8                 4       2,529
 9                 5       2,057
10
11 Discount Rate            12.0%
12                      ---------
13    NPV                  8,059
```

Figure 1.8. The initial model

3 Testing the initial model. In this phase the model must be checked to see if it correctly reflects what it is supposed to do. The solution depends on the input data and the equation of the net present value. We test the model by examining the impact on the solution of changing the input data. Firstly, we assume that the initial investment is £5,000,000 and the discount rate is 0 per cent. With the spreadsheet, package, making these changes will automatically cause the net present value figure to be recalculated and the new result stored (see Figure 1.9). We now assume an initial investment of £6,000,000 and a discount rate of 0 per cent (see Figure 1.10). Comparing Figures 1.9 and 1.10 we observe that the net present value figure is

```
            A                 B          C          D          E          F          G
 1 CALCULATING THE NPV OF AN INVESTMENT PROJECT
 2
 3              YEAR     CASH FLOW
 4                 0      (5,000)
 5                 1       1,802
 6                 2       2,363
 7                 3       2,517
 8                 4       2,529
 9                 5       2,057
10
11 Discount Rate             0.0%
12                      ---------
13    NPV                 11,268
```

Figure 1.9. Testing the initial model with a new data set

```
          A                  B        C         D         E         F         G
 1 CALCULATING THE NPV OF AN INVESTMENT PROJECT
 2
 3              YEAR    CASH FLOW
 4                 0     (6,000)
 5                 1      1,802
 6                 2      2,363
 7                 3      2,517
 8                 4      2,529
 9                 5      2,057
10
11 Discount Rate            0.0%
12                     ---------
13    NPV                 11,268
```

Figure 1.10. Testing the initial model with a second data set

```
          A                  B        C         D         E         F         G
 1 CALCULATING THE NPV OF AN INVESTMENT PROJECT
 2
 3              YEAR    CASH FLOW
 4                 0     (7,000)
 5                 1      1,802
 6                 2      2,363
 7                 3      2,517
 8                 4      2,529
 9                 5      2,057
10
11 Discount Rate           12.0%
12                     ---------
13    NPV                  1,059
```

Figure 1.11. The corrected solution

independent of the initial investment. This reveals the existence of an error in the net present value formula. Indeed we used the formula `@NPV(B11,B5..B9)` instead of using the formula `@NPV(B11,B5..B9)+B4`. The former calculates the present value of the project's future cash flows, while the latter computes the net present value of the project. The correct solution of the problem is shown in Figure 1.11.

Finally, it was decided to move the discount rate before the cash flows and to enhance the presentation of the worksheet as shown in Figure 1.12 (the following commands of 1-2-3 were used: /Move and /Copy). In this case, Lotus 1-2-3 automatically adjusts the cells used in the formula `@NPV`. The formula is now: `@NPV(B4,B9..B13)+B8`.

Up to this point you may have achieved the following benefits:

(a) Learning the concept of the net present value and understanding the result.
(b) Understanding the model's logic.
(c) Learning how to use the financial function `@NPV`.
(d) Learning how to test the model.

Finally, remember to save your spreadsheet often.

4 Expand the initial model. We wish to expand the model by calculating the profitability index (PI) of the investment project (see Figure 1.13).

5 Test the new expanded model. The expanded model shown in Figure 1.13 can be tested in a similar manner as shown in phase 3. After testing such a

```
               A                     B       C        D          E          F          G
 1 CALCULATING THE NPV OF AN INVESTMENT PROJECT
 2 ==============================================
 3
 4 Discount Rate ---->      12.0%
 5 ----------------------------
 6                YEAR   CASH FLOW|
 7 ----------------------------
 8                   0    (7,000)|
 9                   1     1,802
10                   2     2,363 |
11                   3     2,517
12                   4     2,529 |
13                   5     2,057
14                        ---------|
15  NPV ----------->       1,059
16 ============================|
```

Figure 1.12. Rearranging the data and enhancing the presentation of the model

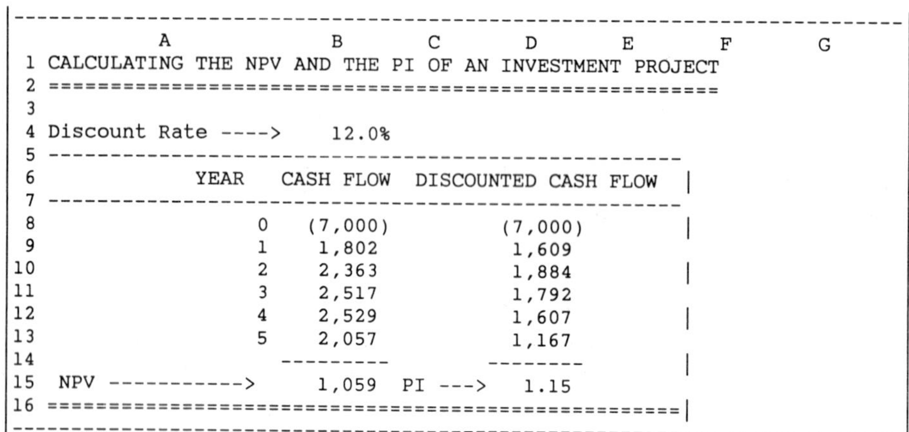

```
               A                     B       C        D          E          F          G
 1 CALCULATING THE NPV AND THE PI OF AN INVESTMENT PROJECT
 2 =========================================================
 3
 4 Discount Rate ---->      12.0%
 5 -------------------------------------------------------
 6                YEAR   CASH FLOW  DISCOUNTED CASH FLOW  |
 7 -------------------------------------------------------
 8                   0    (7,000)           (7,000)         |
 9                   1     1,802             1,609
10                   2     2,363             1,884          |
11                   3     2,517             1,792
12                   4     2,529             1,607          |
13                   5     2,057             1,167
14                        ---------          --------       |
15  NPV ----------->       1,059   PI --->    1.15
16 =======================================================|
```

Figure 1.13. Expanding the model by calculating the profitability index

model we found that its solution is correct. However, we decided to simplify the model (see Figure 1.14). The result of the following formula is stored in cell B16: `@NPV(B4,B9..B13)/(-B8)`.

Up to this point you may have achieved the following benefits:

(a) Learning the concept of the net present value and understanding the result.

(b) Learning the concept of the profitability index and understanding the result.

(c) Understanding the model's logic.

(d) Learning how to use the financial function `@NPV`.

(e) Learning how to test the model.

Finally, remember to save your spreadsheet often.

4a A new expansion of the model. We now wish to examine the effects of changing the discount rate on the net present value and the profitability index. The `/Data Table 1` command of Lotus 1-2-3 is designed for this purpose.

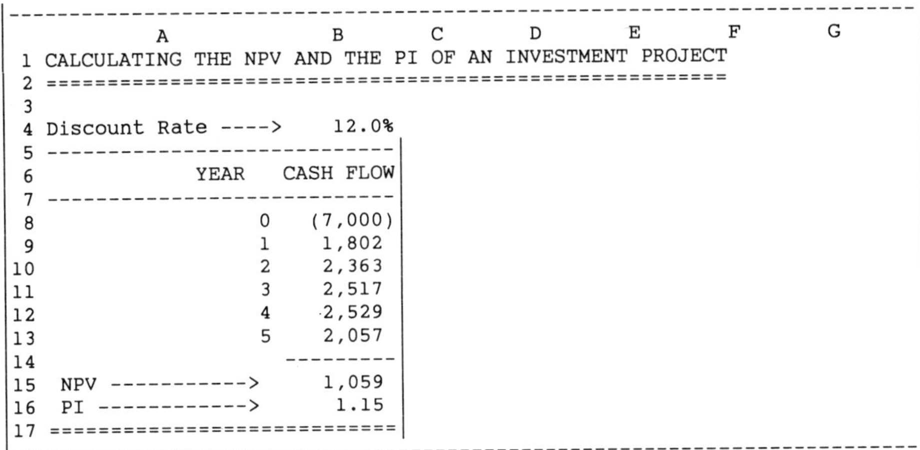

	A	B	C	D	E	F	G
1	CALCULATING THE NPV AND THE PI OF AN INVESTMENT PROJECT						
2	==						
3							
4	Discount Rate ---->	12.0%					
5	----------------------------						
6	YEAR	CASH FLOW					
7	----------------------------						
8	0	(7,000)					
9	1	1,802					
10	2	2,363					
11	3	2,517					
12	4	2,529					
13	5	2,057					
14		---------					
15	NPV ----------->	1,059					
16	PI ------------>	1.15					
17	============================						

Figure 1.14. Simplifying the expanded model shown in Figure 1.13

	A	B	C	D	E	F	G
1	CALCULATING THE NPV AND THE PI OF AN INVESTMENT PROJECT						
2	==						
3							
4	Discount Rate ---->	12.0%					
5	----------------------------			SENSITIVITY ANALYSIS			
6	YEAR	CASH FLOW	----------------------------				
7	----------------------------				+B15	+B16	
8	0	(7,000)		8%	1,951	1.28	
9	1	1,802		9%	1,714	1.24	
10	2	2,363		10%	1,487	1.21	
11	3	2,517		11%	1,268	1.18	
12	4	2,529		12%	1,059	1.15	
13	5	2,057		13%	857	1.12	
14		---------		14%	664	1.09	
15	NPV ----------->	1,059		15%	477	1.07	
16	PI ------------>	1.15		16%	298	1.04	
17	============================						

Figure 1.15. Expanding the model presented in Figure 1.14

In our case, the /Data Table 1 command uses a column (that is, D8 . . D16) containing various values of the discount rate and two formulas entered in cells E7 and F7, respectively (the /Range Format Text is used to assign the text format to the range E7 . . F7). The first formula +B15 stores in cell E7 the net present value via the formula stored in cell B15. Similarly, the second formula +B16 stores in cell F7 the profitability index via the formula stored in cell B16.

Select /Data Table 1, specify D7 . . F16 as the table range, and enter B4 as the input cell. Figure 1.15 shows the results.

5a Test the new expanded model. The results of the sensitivity table for a discount rate of 12 per cent are exactly the same as those stored in cells B15 and B16, respectively. Additionally, the net present value and the profitability index increase as the discount rate decreases. Finally, by changing the discount rate, stored in cell B4, from 12 per cent to 16 per cent we observe the same results as those stored in cells E16 and F16, respectively.

The modelling approach discussed in this example provides a basis for judging the situation of AD Computers plc analytically and it is intended to help you make a decision.

Up to this point you may have achieved the following benefits:

- Learning the concept of the net present value and understanding the result.
- Learning the concept of the profitability index and understanding the result.
- Understanding the model's logic.
- Learning how to use the financial function `@NPV`.
- Understanding the usefulness of 1-2-3's `/Data Table 1` command.
- Learning how to test the model.

Finally, save your spreadsheet.

Advantages of financial modelling using spreadsheets

The spreadsheet-based modelling approach can assist you in becoming more effective and productive in your job, because it provides the following benefits:

1 The modelling approach with a spreadsheet allows you to understand and learn the relevant financial concepts, because you have to work directly with the assumptions of the model, its components, the relationships between its components, tests of the model, expansion of the model, and the analysis of the results. Such a procedure enables you to determine how the results were obtained, helps in clarifying the method (or methods) used and provides more benefits as compared with studying the material of traditional textbooks.

2 The modelling approach with a spreadsheet can help you to examine more problems and the impact of changing the model's assumptions on the solution as compared to the evaluation and analysis of that situation using a pencil, an eraser and a calculator. For example, a spreadsheet can be utilized to calculate the future value of a lump sum and recalculate new results, in a split second, any time an assumption of the model is changed. This extremely useful feature produces one or more of the following benefits:
   - **(a)** It provides flexibility.
   - **(b)** It facilitates more experimentation.
   - **(c)** It allows a full understanding of the situation.
   - **(d)** It helps evaluating alternative plans.
   - **(e)** It aids the creation of new strategies.

3 Creating graphs using a spreadsheet offers an impressive way to communicate the results of data and information processing for the following reasons:
   - **(a)** They are professional-looking.
   - **(b)** They are easy (that is, menu driven) and fast to produce.
   - **(c)** They are interactive (provided that your computer has graphics capabilities).
   - **(d)** They can be easily edited.
   - **(e)** They can be saved on a disk for later use.
   - **(f)** They can represent vast amounts of data.
   - **(g)** They enhance the quality of the final financial management reports.
   - **(h)** They enhance the understanding of complex relationships.
   - **(i)** They are often more comprehensive than tables of numerical figures.
   - **(j)** They make comparisons of data more comprehensive.

(k) There exists a variation of graphs.
(l) Generally graph focus interest.
(m) They save time and effort in analysing data.
(n) Combinations of graphs (for example, a bar chart and a line) can be very effective.
(o) They help people to recall a situation.
(p) They allow you to perform a visual 'what if' analysis.

4 The modelling approach with a spreadsheet allows you to quantify, model, understand and evaluate complex financial situations—a task which is impossible to perform without the use of the spreadsheet. Practising financial modelling with a spreadsheet can uncover previously hidden relationships between the variables under consideration.

5 The modelling approach with a spreadsheet allows you to provide an effective and more accurate solution to a problem as compared to the case where you had to calculate the answer with a calculator. To do so, a spreadsheet offers you a collection of tools. For example, you can use in your analysis sensitivity tables, statistical techniques, forecasting techniques, mathematical techniques, visual representations of data, data base facilities, and so on. The flexibility, the enormous potential to create financial modelling and the ease of use of the spreadsheet have made it a 'decision support system' for managers.

Additionally, spreadsheets have various functions built in, which can save considerable time in computation.

6 A financial model created with a spreadsheet can have multiple uses which allow you to save considerable time in the future when that same model has to be used again. For example, you can create a model that calculates the present value of a lump sum, the present value of an annuity and the present value of an unequal series of cash flows.

7 Building financial models with a spreadsheet helps you to develop skills that are immediately transferable in everyday business situations.

8 The modelling approach with a spreadsheet help owners and managers of small businesses to utilize their resources more effectively.

9 In addition to the previous advantages, the modelling approach with a spreadsheet provides the following benefits:
(a) It is not necessary to rely on scarce computer specialists.
(b) Your data, ideas and methods used in the analysis remain confidential.
(c) You work in your own time and your own place.
(d) You develop skills for further learning in the area of spreadsheets (for example, you can learn to use for your analysis other software that works with your spreadsheet such as, 3-D Graphics).
(e) You can create professional spreadsheet applications.

Learning to build (and then actually building) effective models with a spreadsheet is a time-consuming task, because it requires frequent practice. This, however, is not a disadvantage when you know the benefits associated with the financial modelling approach.

Remarks related to the models used in financial management

The utilization of mathematical models and spreadsheets in financial analysis has increased rapidly in recent years. The area of financial management presents topics that are both challenging and in some instances technical. Building and studying a mathematical model provide us with further understanding of the real situation and facilitate the scientific experimentation and analysis of the situation. It is your choice to learn financial modelling, and if you are choosing to do so follow the proper steps outlined below.

1 *Financial modelling needs frequent practice* Like all learning, financial modelling needs frequent practice, so study the theory, use examples and case studies as frequently as you can until you have learnt and understood them. Note that a spreadsheet provides users with a wide range of tools for building a model, but training and practice are required to use them effectively.

 Financial modelling with a spreadsheet is not only for users with a strong technical background. Nevertheless, users without a technical background may need more practice than those who are familiar with quantitative concepts.

2 *The theory of finance and the spreadsheet-based modelling process provide the tools for practical problem solving* The mathematical models used by the theory of financial management constitute the common denominator for real financial situations. It is naive to believe that an issue involving a high level of quantitative exposition is a theoretical exercise. The most successful financial practitioner will be familiar with the fundamental concepts and theory of financial management in conjunction with their use. Today, the theory of financial management and the spreadsheet-based financial modelling process should be viewed as a carefully constructed methodology that provides you with powerful tools for improving your ability to make effective financial decisions.

3 *Adopt a step-by-step procedure for building financial models* A learning process starts with rough situations and then adopts a step-by-step procedure to improve your skills. Following a structured approach for building a model is of great value. It is better to build a model by yourself, understand it, and use it many times in the future than learn temporarily like a parrot the solutions of ten models.

Gross profit The profit remaining after subtracting the cost of goods sold from sales.
Current ratio The current ratio indicates the ability of the firm to pay its short-term liabilities as they come due with cash flows generated from its current assets. The current ratio is calculated by dividing the firm's current assets by its current liabilities.
Present value The value today of all future receipts.
Net present value for an investment project Total receipts (in today's values) total payments (in today's values).
Net present value criterion If total receipts (in today's value) exceed or are equal to the total payments (in today's values), then accept the project.

Figure 1.16. Example describing the mathematical relationships of a model

4 *Mathematical relationships and results can be described in simple terms* When you are working with mathematical models always use words to provide a simple description of the relationships in your model as well as the results of your model (examples are provided in Figure 1.16).

5 *Remember that mathematical relationships can have multi-uses* The theory of financial management is concerned with the evaluation of alternative future cash flows. Because the future is generally uncertain, the theory of financial

management evaluates risky cash flows over time. Two of the basic concepts of the financial management theory are: the time value of money and the return and risk characteristics of financial decisions.

(a) *The use of the present value concept.* The pound that will be received at some future date is worth less than a pound of today, because of the interest it could be earning in the meantime. Present value calculations are needed to show the current value of future cash flows. The present value formula can be used for the following cases:

- **(i)** Calculating the net present value of an investment project.
- **(ii)** Calculating the profitability index of an investment project.
- **(iii)** Calculating the internal rate of return of an investment project.
- **(iv)** Calculating the market value of an ordinary share.
- **(v)** Calculating the market value of a debenture.
- **(vi)** Calculating the cost of ordinary shares.
- **(vii)** Calculating the cost of debentures.

(b) *The use of return–risk measures.* Financial management uses some basic statistical concepts for measuring the risk and return associated with a project's cash flows, or with the rate of return observed from investing in financial assets (for example, shares, debentures, and so on). Assuming that the probability distribution of a financial random variable (for example, cash flow) is normal, the expected value (or mean) of the distribution measures return and the standard deviation of the distribution is commonly used to measure risk.

The expected return and risk concepts can be used in the following cases:

- **(i)** The expected return and risk associated with an investment project's cash flows.
- **(ii)** The expected return and risk associated with the probable values of net present value or internal rate of return.
- **(iii)** Security return and risk.
- **(iv)** Portfolio return and risk.
- **(v)** Business return and risk of a firm.
- **(vi)** Financial return and risk of a firm.
- **(vii)** Total return and risk of a firm.

6 *Discussion usually helps you to learn more* Try to spend some time to understand a situation. If you cannot see a solution, then discuss the problem with your colleagues. This discussion may be helpful in gaining further insight into the situation. When you have understood the problem, again discuss it with your colleagues—this discussion usually helps you to increase your learning.

7 *Never try to achieve perfection* Never aim for a perfect solution, because it does not exist in the real world. It is better, for example, to search for a good pen to write with instead of searching for the best pen in the world.

8 *Do not be afraid to use spreadsheets* Today, spreadsheets should be viewed as the most useful, powerful and flexible tools for financial analysis. A large number of individuals appear to have an aversion to investing the time necessary to learn how to utilize the spreadsheet's facilities to analyse financial management problems. You do not need to become a computer expert to use spreadsheets successfully for financial modelling. Some investment of time must be made in order to learn to use the spreadsheet properly and you might take longer to

create your first spreadsheet model than simply using paper, pencil, eraser and calculator (assuming that you are familiar with the use of the calculator). Soon you will realize that performing financial analysis with a spreadsheet is faster than your calculator, your results are more accurate and your analysis can be more extensive (for example, using sensitivity tables and graphical representations).

You should never be afraid to experiment on modelling with the spreadsheet—the more you use it, the more beneficial it will be in improving your ability to understand, manipulate and use financial models effectively. A lever can be used to increase your lifting power. The modelling approach with a spreadsheet can be considered as a similar tool enabling you to:

(a) increase your understanding of the essential of modern financial management;
(b) perform financial analysis faster than manual calculation;
(c) improve your skills in performing financial analysis effectively;
(d) utilize new powerful tools for financial analysis; and
(e) create new strategies.

References and bibliography

Ackoff, R. (1978) *The Art of Problem Solving—Accompanied by Ackoff's Fables*. John Wiley, New York.

Anderson, D.R., Sweeney, D.J. and Williams, T.A. (1982) *An Introduction to Management Sciences*, 3rd edn. West Publishing Company, St Paul.

Bierman, H., Bonini, C.P. and Hausman, W.H. (1981) *Quantitative Analysis for Business Decisions*, 6th edn. Richard D. Irwin, Homewood, Illinois.

Brightman, R.W. and Dimsdale, J.M. (1986) *Using Computers in an Information Age*. Delmar Publishers.

Davis, K.R. and McKeown, P.G. (1981) *Quantitative Models for Management*. Kent Publishing Company, Boston.

Hillier, F.S. and Lieberman, G.J. (1980) *Introduction to Operational Research*, 3rd edn. Holden-Day, San Francisco.

Rivett, P. (1980) *Model Building for Decision Analysis*. John Wiley, New York.

2 The role of financial management

This chapter includes:

- Defining financial management
- Functions of financial management
- The objective of financial management
- Other corporate objectives
- Factors affecting the firm's share price
- The objective of the firm in practice
- Using spreadsheets in financial management

Financial management concentrates on the process of making financial decisions in a way that maximizes the welfare and benefits of a firm's owners. The purpose of this chapter is to provide an introduction to the field of financial management. In this chapter we build an analog model that will help you to develop a progressive understanding of the different topics of financial management included in the present work as well as financial management as a whole. Such a model will be used throughout the book and it will be modified in every chapter to include the relevant concepts.

Nature of financial management

Finance can be defined as the money resources (that is, cash or credit) available to the firm for the operation of its key activities and the management of these money resources. For our purposes, financial management is defined as a process involving the acquisition of (limited) funds and their allocation among different investment opportunities in order to attain a desired objective. For instance, a firm can obtain funds via loans (for example, from a bank) or via issuing new shares and debentures. These funds can be allocated among different investment alternatives, for example, increasing stock levels, building a new plant, buying new equipment, and so on.

As an area of study, financial management is concerned with three essential functions

1 *Financial analysis and planning* Monitoring and planning the firm's financial performance.
2 *Investment* Determining and acquiring the most desirable mix of assets.
3 *Financing* Determining and utilizing the most desirable mix of methods for financing the firm's investments.

Financial analysis and planning involve the following:

- Evaluating the firm's current financial situation and operating results.
- Developing plans for new capital expenditures.
- Determining what resources are required for funding the firm's futures needs.

Financial analysis and planning is an important prerequisite to carrying out the investment and financial decisions of the firm. The investment and financing decisions can be either short term (that is, decisions usually having a duration of one year or less) or long term (that is, decisions usually lasting longer than a year). The short-term investment and financing decisions are concerned with the current assets and the current liabilities of the firm. The long-term investment and financing decisions deal with the firm's fixed assets and the capital employed (that is, shareholders' funds and long-term debt). Figure 2.1 shows a schematic representation of the financial management's decisions using the balance sheet.

Figure 2.1. A schematic representation of the financial management's decisions

	Investment	Financing
Long term	Fixed assets	Capital employed
Short term	Current assets	Current liabilities

Figure 2.2 summarizes the financial management's decisions.

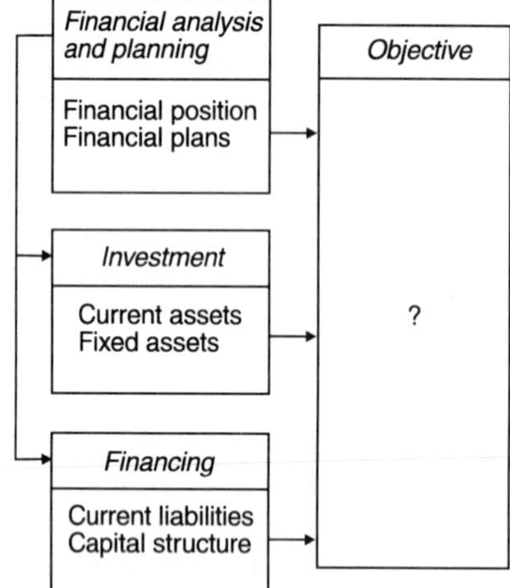

Figure 2.2. Decisions of financial management

The methods and concepts of financial management we discuss can be applied to all kinds of firms, but our focus here will be on limited liability business organizations rather than single proprietorships and partnerships. (Appendix 2A gives detailed descriptions of UK business organizations.)

The basic assumptions in financial management

Typical goals of firms include:

- Maximization of sales

- Maximization of profits
- Increasing market share
- Maximization of the existing ordinary shareholders' wealth
- Maximization of social responsibility
- Maintaining market share
- Survival of the firm
- Stabilization of prices
- Target return on investment
- Maximization of managerial salaries

etc.

The theory of financial management assumes that the major objective of the firm is to maximize the wealth of its existing ordinary shareholders. As the share price provides an indication of the owners' investment in the firm, the present value of the shareholders' wealth in the firm can be represented as follows:

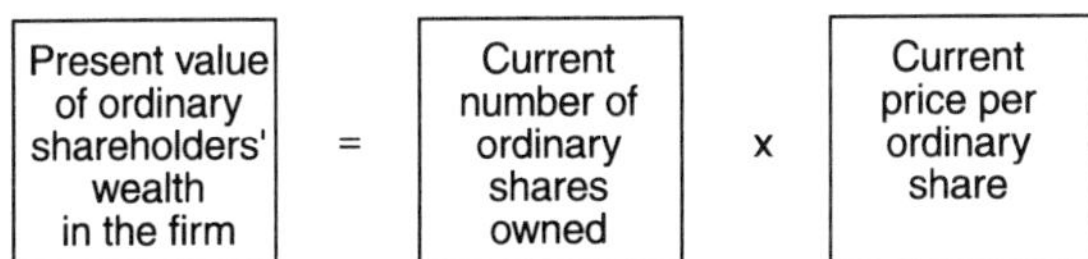

With regard to the previous definitions, Figure 2.3 summarizes the objective of financial management.

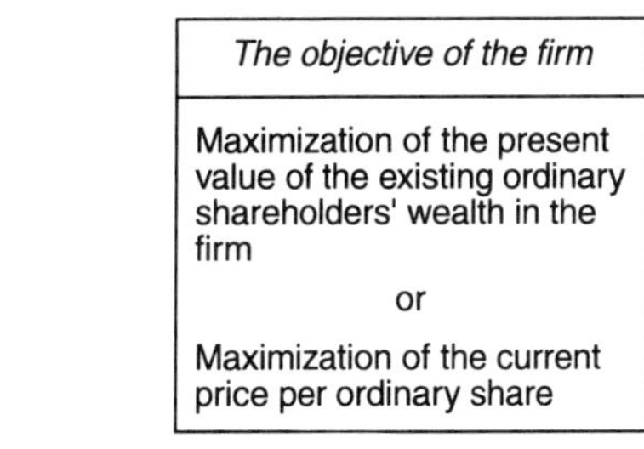

where

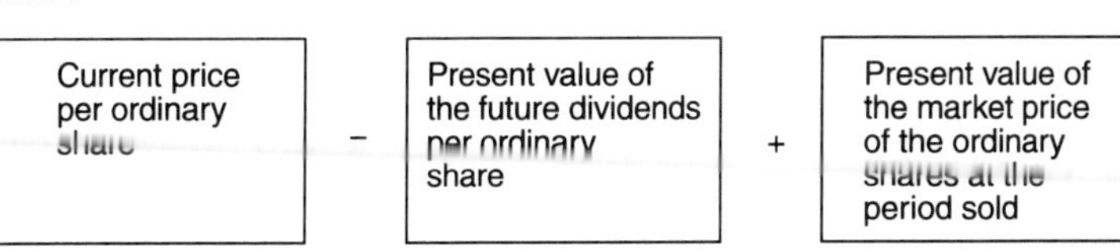

Figure 2.3. The financial management objective assumed in this work

Throughout this work the ordinary shareholders' wealth maximization objective will be assumed. Financial management can now be defined as a process of making investment and financing decisions that will maximize the current price of the firm's ordinary shares, given the number of shares outstanding (see Figure 2.4).

Example 2.1 Calculating the current value of shareholders' wealth for different investment plans

Marks and Spencer plc has currently 2,659,000 ordinary shares (the current time is March 1988). Assume that the company is considering three alternative financial plans each of which is expected to increase the future profits of the company and its future share price. Assume that the increase in the future

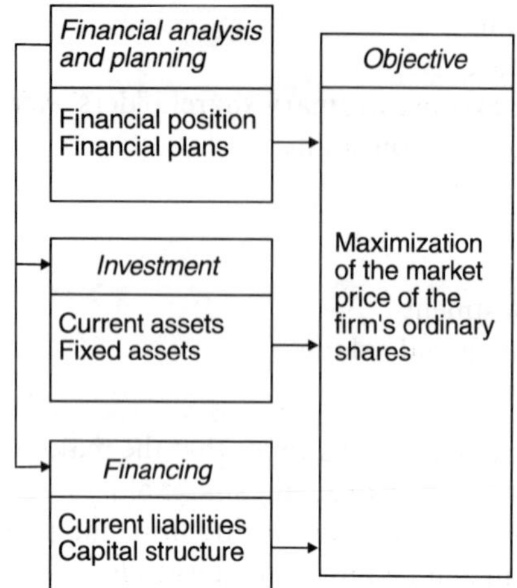

Fig. 2.4. The decisions and objective of the theory of financial management

profits implies that each year the company will pay out a higher dividend on each share. The plans have similar levels of risk. We want to identify the plan that maximizes the ordinary shareholders' wealth, where the wealth is defined in Figure 2.5. The three plans can be briefly described as follows:

Plan A Carry on operations without adopting new investment projects.
Plan B Adopt a new extension investment and a new financing plan.
Plan C Adopt a new investment project.

	A	B	C	D
1	THE THREE PLANS FOR MARKS AND SPENCER PLC			
2	==			
3				
4				
5		PLAN A	PLAN B	PLAN C
6				
7	Current No of Ordinary Shares (000s)	2,659	2,659	2,659
8	Current Price per Share (£)	1.51	1.54	1.48
9				
10	Current Value of Wealth (£000s)	4,015	4,095	3,935
11				

Fig. 2.5. Calculating the current value of the shareholders' wealth for each plan

The anticipated effect on the company's share price for each plan is:

Plan A: £1.51 Plan B: £1.54 Plan C: £1.48

A comparison of the results reveals that Plan B should be selected. There are several consequences of accepting Plan B, for example future capital structure, future dividend growth, and so on.

The ability to enter formulae into the cells makes the spreadsheet very powerful and useful. The spreadsheet does not record the result of a formula in the memory, instead it stores the formula which produces the result. So any time the contents of one cell that are referred to by the formula are changed, 1-2-3 can automatically change the formula's result.

Problems

1 Set up the worksheet shown in Figure 2.5 using a formula to calculate the current value of wealth.
2 Examine how the wealth of Plan B changes when the current price per share changes.
3 Graph the relationship between the current value of wealth and the current price per share.

Social responsibility

Social responsibility involves the achievement of social goals such as the welfare of employees, customers, support of community projects and protection of the environment. Some have argued that firms should act in a socially responsible manner rather than be concerned with the maximization of the ordinary shape price alone. There are two advantages of exercising social responsibility:

- It provides a substantial contribution to the welfare of the society.
- It receives a friendly reaction from the consumers which in turn may increase the sales of the firm.

The objective of social responsibility, however, has a drawback. If a firm attempts to live up to its social responsibility, its prices will have to increase to cover the additional costs. In a competitive environment, such a firm may experience lower sales and probably it will be forced to abandon its social responsibility commitments. As an alternative, the firm will operate with lower earnings, if it decides to keep the price of its products unchanged. This probably results in a lower share price. Does this mean that firms should not be engaged in social responsibility commitments? Not at all, most large firms maintain a certain level of social responsibility. Among those cases the following three are included:

1 Government authorities establish several rules of corporate behaviour (for example, product safety, automobile safety, pollution abatement, and so on).
2 Firms provide social responsibility on a voluntary basis.

Example 2.2 Social responsibility: the case of Marks and Spencer plc

The following paragraph has been extracted from the Chairman's Report of Marks and Spencer plc, 1988.

'Our involvement in community affairs stems from the belief that it is morally right and commercially important to promote a healthy business environment for our operations and to continue to the well-being of the society. In the first 10 years of our secondment programme over 90 people have been attached to specific projects involving job creation, enterprise agencies, youth training or charities. Our support of all these activities represented a total investment in the community last year of some £4.3m.'

3 Successful firms sell good quality products which satisfy the needs of the consumers.

It is very difficult to determine the exact balance between the maximization of the share price objective and the goal of social responsibility. However, one can argue that firms should provide a substantial contribution to the welfare of the social environment in which the objective of share price maximization could be pursued in a less persistent fashion.

Throughout this work, we shall assume that firms are share prices maximizers and operate subject to a certain level of social responsibility.

Wealth versus profit maximization

The wealth maximization objective is preferable to the profit maximization objective (frequently supported by economists) because (a) the profit maximization approach does not take into account a long-term emphasis; (b) profit maximization does not consider timing of returns; (c) profit maximization does not consider risk.

Profit maximization—a short-term strategy

Profit maximization can be achieved in the short term but such an approach may not always benefit the firm's shareholders. A short-term strategy could provide high profits in the current year, but lower profits or even losses in the long term

Example 2.3 Illustrating that the maximization of profit approach does not always benefit the firm's shareholders in the long term.

AD Computers plc has spent during the past few years a great deal of money to develop new products and improve its existing products, while BD Microsystems plc has invested little money in new product developments and improvements of its existing products. The short-term strategy of BD plc resulted in high profits for the current year (see Figure 2.6 where figures for profit and number of shares outstanding are in 000s) and a share price of £1.80. On the other hand, the long-term strategy of AD Computers resulted in lower profits for the current year and a share price of £2.80.

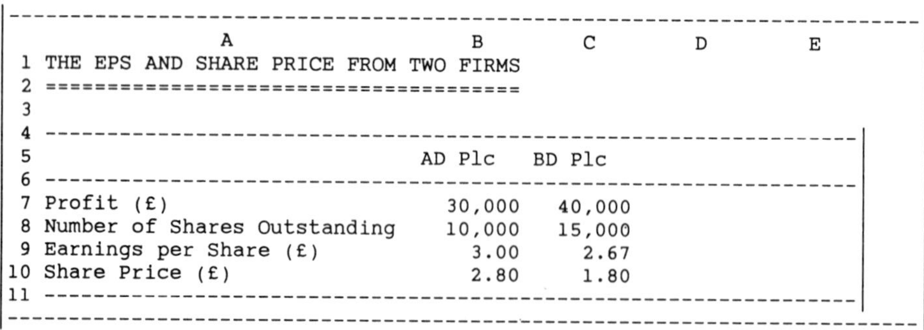

	A	B	C	D	E
1	THE EPS AND SHARE PRICE FROM TWO FIRMS				
2	======================================				
3					
4					
5		AD Plc	BD Plc		
6					
7	Profit (£)	30,000	40,000		
8	Number of Shares Outstanding	10,000	15,000		
9	Earnings per Share (£)	3.00	2.67		
10	Share Price (£)	2.80	1.80		
11					

Fig. 2.6. The earnings per share and share price for two firms

The price of BD Microsystems plc is lower than the price of AD Computers plc, because the market perceives that the profits of BD Microsystems will fall in the long run due to the low quality of its products. Thus, the short-term strategy adopted by AD Microsystems is not in the best interest of its shareholders.

Problems

1. Create the worksheet shown in Figure 2.6 (use the following formula to calculate the earnings per share: profit/number of shares outstanding).
2. Examine how the earnings per share figure changes when the profit or the number of shares outstanding changes.

Time value of money

The profit maximization approach does not consider the timing of returns. Profit maximization may fail as a criterion for decision making as it treats all future profits, irrespective of the timing, in the same manner. The profit maximization approach does not consider the time value of money in which earnings received today are more valuable than earnings received a year from now.

Example 2.4 Illustrating that the profit maximization approach does not consider the time value of money

Assume that a firm is considering two investment projects whose expected earnings per share (EPS) are listed in Figure 2.7. We assume that both projects cost the same and have the same level of risk. Project A is expected to generate £4.1 earnings per share in the first year and no profit in the next four years. Project B is expected to generate no earnings per share in the first year, earnings per share of £1.0 for the next three years and earnings per share of £1.5 in the fifth year.

THE EPS FROM TWO PROJECTS

Year	Project A	Project B
1	£4.1	£0.0
2	0.0	1.0
3	0.0	1.0
4	0.0	1.0
5	0.0	1.5
Total	£4.1	£4.5

Figure 2.7. The EPS from two alternative projects A and B over time

The profit maximization objective would favour project B over project A. This conclusion, however, does not consider the timing of the profit. If the timing of the profit is taken into account, project A is preferable since it provides its earnings per share earlier than project B. A pound received today is worth more than a pound received a year from now, because the current pound can be invested to earn a rate of return. This is known as time value of money and is elaborated in the next chapter.

The profit maximization approach does not consider risk

The profit maximization objective provides no real way for the firm to take into account the risk associated with various investment projects.

Example 2.5 Illustrating that the profit maximization approach does not consider the risk associated with investment projects.

Assume that a firm is considering two new investment projects with the same initial cost. Each project is expected to generate earnings per share over the next two years. For each year three possible values of earnings per share are predicted depending on three states of the economy—boom, normal and

	A	B	C	D	E	F	G
1	THE EPS FROM TWO PROJECTS UNDER DIFFERENT ECONOMIC CONDITIONS						
2	==						
3							
4	---						
5		Year	Boom(£)	Normal(£)	Recession(£)		
6	---						
7	PROJECT C	1	3	2	1		
8		2	3	2	1		
9							
10	PROJECT D	1	5	3	-1		
11		2	5	3	-1		
12	---						

Figure 2.8. Future EPS from two investment projects C and D

recession—as indicated in Figure 2.8. It can be seen that the earnings per share of project D are higher than the earnings per share of project B in a normal state of economy. However, earnings per share from project C lie between £1 and £3, while those from project D vary from £5 to −£1. Therefore, the degree of risk associated with project D is greater than that of C. Under these circumstances, many investors would prefer C to D. The profit maximization approach fails to recognize this.

Factors affecting the firm's ordinary share market price

Knowing that the goal of a firm should work towards the maximization of the market price of its shares, the question to consider is how to go about valuing a firm's ordinary shares. Theoretically, the following three factors can be used in determining the market price of a firm's shares:

1. The magnitude of the future cash flows to be received by its shareholders (that is, dividends, capital gains/losses). Shareholders prefer higher cash flows to lower ones, other things being the same.
2. The timing of those cash flows. Shareholders prefer to receive a pound today instead of receiving a pound one year later.
3. The risk associated with those cash flows. Shareholders prefer lower risk cash flows to those of greater risk, other things being equal.

The interaction of these three factors, as perceived by investors, affects the market price of the firm's ordinary shares. For example, if investors in aggregate perceive that lower cash flows will be received in the future, a delay of the receipt of the cash flows, or more risk associated with the future cash flows, their action will result in a deduction in the market price of the firm's ordinary shares. Changes in the opposite direction would result in an increase in the market price of the firm's shares. The objective of maximizing the wealth of the ordinary shareholders has the advantage of considering risk, time and other important factors from the existing shareholders' point of view. On the other hand, a firm cannot easily predict the market response to its potential decisions and this provides a limitation for the price maximization objective. In many cases, however, good managers can correctly assess the market's perception and they should direct the firm's decisions in such a way as to maximize its value.

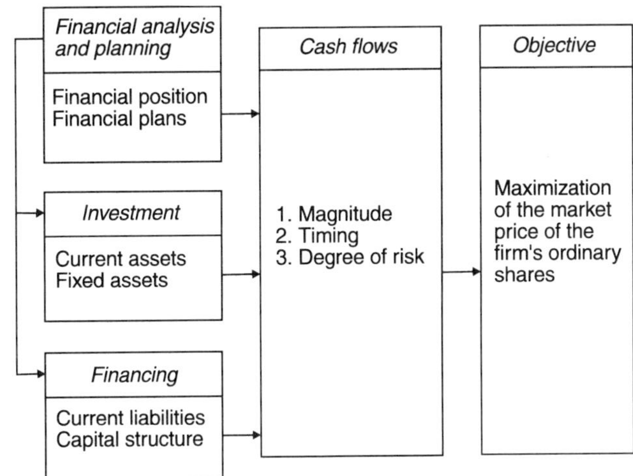

Figure 2.9. Three factors affecting the firm's share price

The concepts developed so far are best summarized in Figure 2.9.

There are also other factors affecting (indirectly or directly) a firm's share price. These can be classified as follows:

- Operating decisions, such as product mix, sales growth, marketing system, etc.
- External factors, such as exchange rates, oil prices, taxation structure, etc.

Figure 2.10 illustrates the financial management framework.

Example 2.6 The share price and the annual dividend per share of Marks and Spencer plc for the period 1985–89

Figure 2.11 shows graphically the month-by-month share price for Marks and Spencer plc from the period 1985 to 1989 (the actual numerical data is presented in Appendix 2B and is taken from the datastream). The largest price occurred in August 1987, with the smallest approximately two and a half years earlier in January 1985. The shares fell during the autumn 1987 crash and they recovered in the beginning of 1988. The latter half of 1988 saw a fall in price to 144.0 pence against a low of 171.0 pence in 1987. The shares recovered during 1989, the share price climbing rapidly to a peak of 220.5 pence in September 1989. An investment of £1 in Marks and Spencer shares in January 1985 would have grown to £1.68 by December 1989, an increase by 68 per cent.

Figure 2.12 presents the total dividend per share for each year in the period 1985–89. Over that five-year period Marks and Spencer's dividends per share (DPS) have risen from 3.4 to 5.6 pence, an increase of 64.7 per cent.

Problem

Use the 1-2-3 graphic facilities to present the Marks and Spencer's share price data shown in Appendix 2B.

The evolution of financial management

During 1900–50 the field of financial management was descriptive and emphasis was

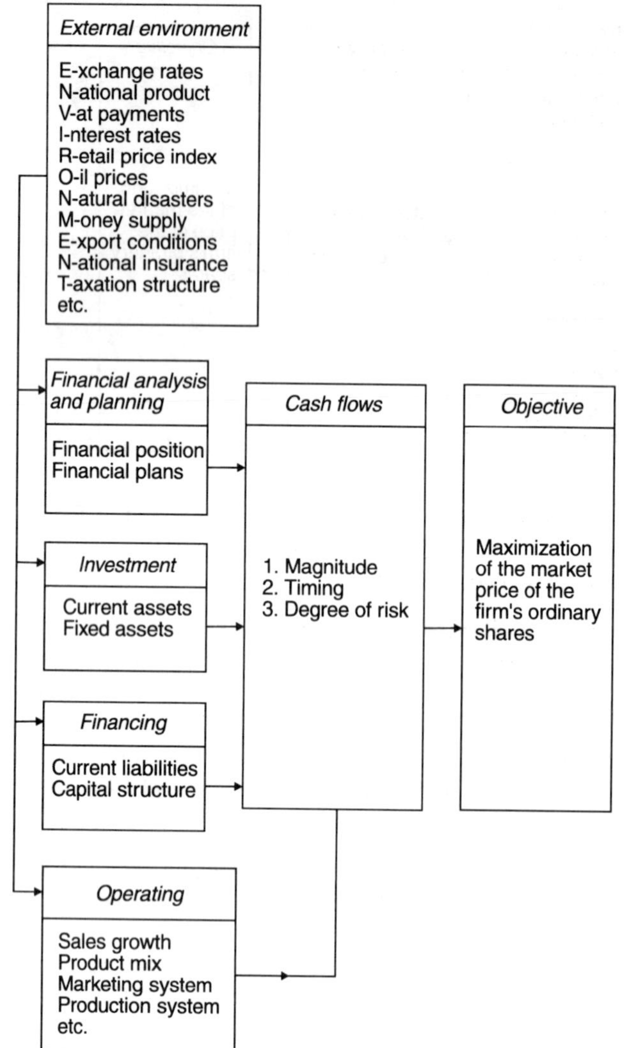

Figure 2.10. The financial management framework

mainly given to the firm's external financial operations (for example, raising funds in the capital market, mergers and consolidations, corporate failure, liquidation and reorganization, and so on). During the decade 1950–60 the financial management field changed significantly viewing primarily the internal management of the firm (for example, appraisal of investment projects, capital structure, dividend policy, and so on).

Developments in the field of financial management continued during the 1960s including the use of mathematical and statistical models (for example, risk analysis, capital market theory, external financing, and so on). During the decade of the 1970s financial management continued to expand mainly in the areas of risk analysis and valuation (for example, option valuation, the development of the arbitrage pricing model, and so on). Finally, during the 1980s there has been a dramatic increase in the application of computers to financial management decision making.

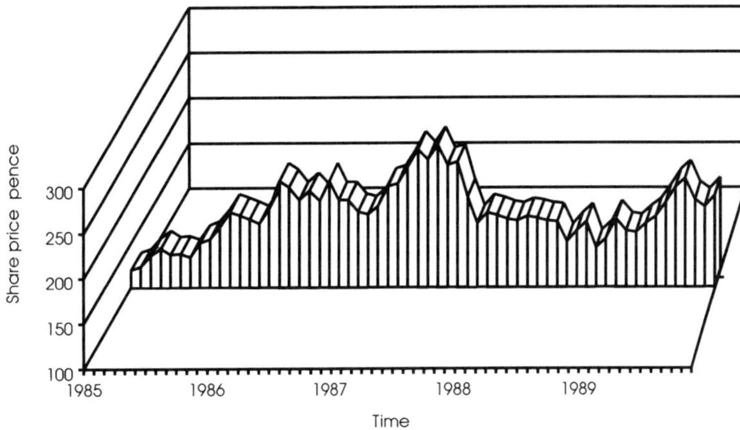

Figure 2.11.

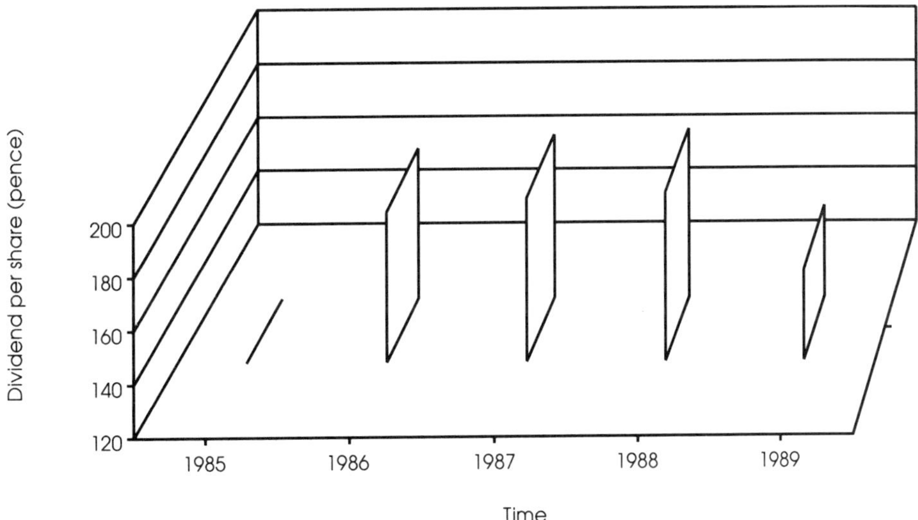

Figure 2.12

Financial management and other disciplines

Financial management uses accounting data (for example, balance sheet, profit and loss account statement, and so on) when making future resources allocation decisions concerning long-term and short-term investments. Monetary and fiscal policies influence financial decisions through product markets and financial markets. For example, the demand for new investments in fixed and current assets is low when interest rates are high and vice versa. Another example is that government taxing influences both investors and corporate income and hence the funds available for new investments. On the other hand, the financial decisions of firms have an impact on the nation's economic performance. For example, good investment decisions on fixed assets have a positive economic impact on the nation's gross national product. The discussion above reveals that the understanding of several economic concepts is very important for the understanding of sound financial management. Additionally, financial management utilizes microeconomic models, for example prices and costs models, when developing financial decision models.

Financial management employs quantitative techniques in analysing financial problems. For example, linear programming is used in solving capital rationing problems, forecasting analysis is utilized to project the future cash flows of investment projects, statistical analysis is employed to describe the behaviour of a firm's share price, and so on.

Financial management uses computer software in examining and analysing accounting and financial data. For example, spreadsheets can be used to calculate the cash flows associated with investment projects; statistical software can be employed to analyse the factors influencing share prices, and so on.

The role of financial director

In a large firm, the investment and financing decisions are seen as the responsibilities of the financial director, while the financial accountant's responsibilities are concerned with the preparation and analysis of the firm's financial statements. The titles of treasurer and controller are often used in large firms, the former can be compared to the financial director, the latter to the financial accountant.

There is not a universal pattern for the organization structure: it varies from firm to firm. Let us consider a typical large manufacturing firm having three departments: Manufacturing, Marketing and Finance. It is also assumed that the finance function is performed by the financial director and the accounting activities can be seen as the responsibility of the chief accountant.

Figure 2.13 presents a model illustrating the accounting and finance activities within the firm in a form of an organizational chart.

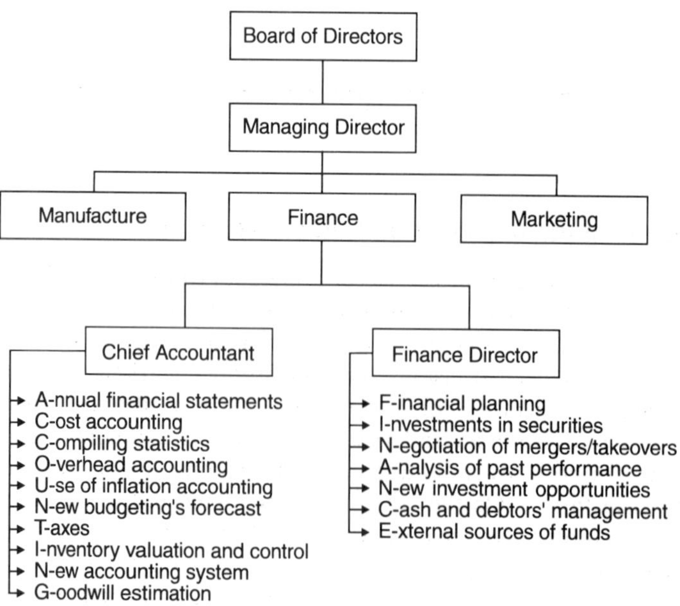

Figure 2.13. Accounting and finance functions within the firm

The agency problem

The managers of medium and large firms are the agents of the shareholders and their responsibility is to run the firm so as to maximize the price of its shares. A potential conflict of interest between managers and shareholders may arise when the managers are primarily concerned with their own welfare.

Example 2.7 An example of an agency problem

Assume a case where a firm is evaluating two profitable investment opportunities from which it can afford to accept only one. The first investment is expected to maximize the firm's share price but it is also considered to be highly risky. The second investment is considered to have moderate risk but the acceptance of it will not maximize the firm's share price. Assume that the firm's shareholders will accept the risk associated with the first investment (if the managers decide to proceed with it) and that the first investment is expected to produce low cash flows during its initial stage. If the managers of the firm realize that the acceptance of the first investment may cause them to lose their jobs, then they will proceed with the second investment, even though this decision is not in the best interest of the shareholders.

Other agency-related problems may arise because the managers require high salaries, or the use of luxurious offices and cars, and so on. The costs resulting when the managers and shareholders do not have identical interests are called agency costs. They include:

- Expenditure to monitor the actions of the managers, for example the costs associated with the internal audits of the firm's expenses.
- Expenditure to structure the organization so as to minimize the possibility for management to behave in a fashion that is not consistent with the maximization of the firm's share price.
- Bonding expenditures to ensure that management does not operate for personal benefit at the expense of the shareholders.

Competitive markets help reduce agency costs, but cannot eliminate them completely. For example, poor management may be reflected in a continuously low share price which in turn may provide the grounds for a hostile takeover by another firm. If a hostile takeover occurs, the managers of the acquired firm are most likely to lose their jobs.

Agency costs appear to be an obstacle to the objective of maximizing the firm's ordinary share price and thus shareholders should try to minimize them. There are several mechanisms which can be used by the shareholders in an effort to reduce the agency problem, including the following:

- The threat of firing.
- The payment of cash bonuses for achieving certain objectives.

The objective of the firm in practice

The theory of financial management is based upon the assumption that the objective of the firm is to maximize the market price of its shares. It is, therefore, of great importance to see how financial executives perceive this particular objective. From the results presented in Figure 2.14 it can be seen that the primary objective of (large or medium sized) firms is different from that assumed by the theory of financial management. This probably indicates that, in practice, the interest of the shareholders is not solely to maximize the market price of their shares or managers do not place first priority upon maximizing the share price. These findings reveal that the objective of maximizing share price is a normative one, because it specifies how financial decisions should be made and not what the firms actually do.

J.W. Petty, D.F. Scott and M.M. Bird
Year: 1971
Country: USA
Size of firms: large
Population: 500
Sample: 109

	% of times rank first	% of times rank third	% of times rank fifth
Maximize per cent return on asset investment	37	23	6
Maximize aggregate dollar earnings	15	18	13
Target earnings per share growth rate	36	19	0
Target share of the market	2	22	42
Maximize share price	11	18	40

Pike R.H.
Year: unknown
Country: UK
Size of firms: large
Population: 208
Sample: 122

	Very important (%)
Maximize percentage return on assets	58.4
Maximize earnings or earnings per share	43.8
Target share of the market	18.3
Maximize share price	17.9
Target earnings per share growth rate	12.3
Other	1.0

Diacogiannis G.P. and R. Lai
Year: 1988
Country: UK
Size of firms: medium sized
Population: 304
Sample: 95

	% out of 95
Maximize percentage return on assets	34
Maximize profits or earnings per share	11
Achieving target market share	33
Maximize share price	18
Achieving target earnings per share growth rate	65

Figure 2.14. The objective of the firm in practice

Overview of the present work

This work is divided into 19 chapters dealing with the investment and financing decisions of a firm (see Figure 2.15).

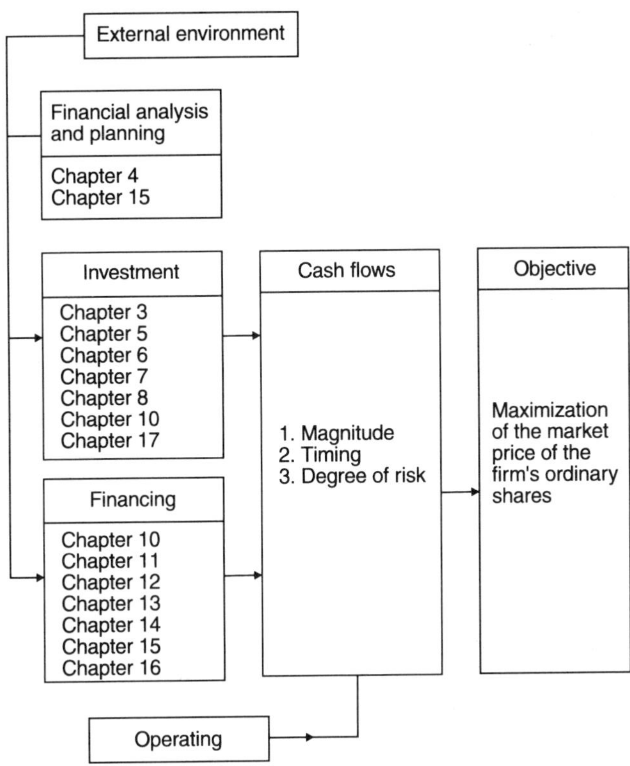

Chapter titles are as follows:

Chapter 3 Time value of money
Chapter 4 Financial analysis
Chapter 5 Capital budgeting under conditions of certainty
Chapter 6 Advanced capital budgeting topics
Chapter 7 Incorporation of risk into capital budgeting decisions
Chapter 8 Portfolio theory
Chapter 9 Asset pricing models
Chapter 10 Management of working capital
Chapter 11 Valuation of debentures and preference shares
Chapter 12 The determinants of redemption yields
Chapter 13 Valuation of ordinary shares
Chapter 14 The cost of capital
Chapter 15 Gearing and capital structure
Chapter 16 Dividend policy
Chapter 17 Mergers
Chapter 18 Options
Chapter 19 Option valuation models

Figure 2.15. Overview of present work

Summary

1 *Defining financial management* Financial management is a decision-making process involving how to raise and invest money in order to achieve a desired goal.

2 *Functions of financial management* The financial management process includes three functions:
(**a**) monitoring and planning the firm's financial position;
(**b**) allocating available funds on the best mix of assets;
(**c**) determining the most appropriate mix of funds required to finance the firm's investments.

3 *The objective of financial management* The functions of financial management should be performed in a way that achieves a desired objective. The theory of financial management assumes that the primary objective of the firm is to maximize the wealth of its shareholders. In a well-functioning competitive market, this objective is equivalent to maximizing the firm's current share price.

4 *Other corporate objectives* Other objectives such as profit maximization and social responsibility can be considered as possible objectives for the firm. Wealth maximization is preferred to profit maximization for the following three basic reasons:
(**a**) profit maximization tends to be a short-term approach and may ignore the long-run profitability of the firm, while shareholder wealth maximization considers wealth for a long run;
(**b**) it ignores the timing of profits, whereas shareholder wealth maximization tends to take into account the timing of benefits received from investment projects;
(**c**) profit maximization overlooks the risks associated with the future levels of profit, while shareholder wealth maximization takes into account the risks associated with investment alternatives. A firm should seek to maximize the wealth of its shareholders subject to the constraint of maintaining a certain level of social responsibility.

5 *Factors affecting the firm's share price* The price of a firm's shares is affected by factors within the firm and others that exist outside the firm. Theoretically, three factors can be used to determine a firm's share price, these are:
(**a**) the magnitude of the future cash flows to be received by shareholders;
(**b**) the timing of those cash flows;
(**c**) the risk associated with those cash flows.
Thus, a firm should be concerned with the impact its financial management decisions have on the magnitude, timing and riskiness of future cash flows.

6 *The objective of the firm in practice* Empirical evidence indicates that several objectives for financial management are more important than the shareholder wealth maximization objective. It seems that managers are more interested in profitability rather than seeking to maximize the shareholders' wealth. A possible explanation of those findings may be the separation of ownership and control in corporations.

7 *Using spreadsheets in financial management* Perhaps no other related discipline is as well suited for the spreadsheet as financial management. Spreadsheets have revolutionized the application of many financial management concepts and allow users to analyse financial problems without requiring an extensive training in programming.

Questions for discussion

1 For each term shown below provide a definition in your own words. Then check your responses against the definitions included in the chapter.

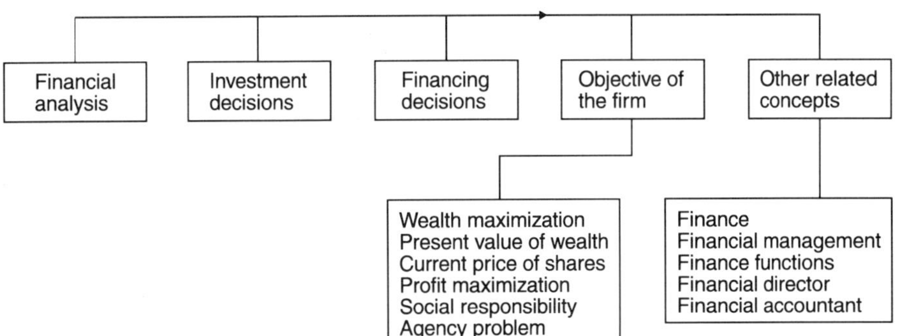

2 List examples of long-term assets in which funds can be invested by the firm. List examples of individual short-term and long-term sources of financing. Assume that you are the financial director of a firm of your choice. What are your responsibilities?

3 The theory of financial management assumes that the primary objective of a firm is to make and execute decisions in a way that maximizes its existing shareholders' wealth. The objective of maximizing profits is not necessarily consistent with the primary objective of the firm. Discuss.

4 Two other possible objectives of a firm are the following:
(a) maximization of market share;
(b) maximization of sales.
The firm should act so as to maximize existing shareholders' wealth rather than work towards either of these two objectives. Discuss.

5 Discuss the following statement:
'The decisions a firm makes result in cash flows and risks that jointly determine the share price of the firm in the market place.'

6 Financial management is closely related to other disciplines including accounting, economics, quantitative methods and computing. Explain the relationship between financial management and each of these disciplines.

7 Ian Kitchin, the financial director of A&C Electronics plc, sat at his desk reading a report given to him by the financial accountant Dave Johnson. The firm has an opportunity to invest in three projects and Kitchin will present to the board of directors the following day a document related to the nature, valuation and alternative ways of raising capital to finance those projects. The three projects are as follows: (a) starting the production of a large stereo television; (b) starting the production of a home entertainment system; (c) starting the production of cable television accessories.

The managers try to run the firm in the shareholders' best interest, namely, to maximize the owners' wealth within the firm. Additionally, they always assess any project in terms of its effect on the projected overall financial results of the firm. Since later summer 1987, A&C Electronic's shares have shown good growth and today are standing at the 362 pence level. At the meeting of the board, Kitchin explains that the acceptance of the first and third project will increase the shareholders' wealth more than any other combination and discusses two alternative ways of raising capital to finance the investments: (a) by 35 per cent loan and 65 per cent reserves; or (b) 65 per cent loan and 35 per cent reserves. The adoption of any of the two financing plans will not affect the ability of the firm to meet its target dividend payments.

Prepare a chart, similar to that shown in Figure 2.10 (see page 30) illustrating the financial management framework (use your own assumptions if necessary).

8 Choose either one of the following firms or supply your own choice and gather information related to its investment and financing activities over a period of three years.

Amstrad plc (*Financial Times* classification: Electronics)
Marks and Spencer plc (*Financial Times* classification: Drapery and Stores)
Rowntree plc (*Financial Times* classification: Food, Groceries, etc.)

Present a discussion of the relevant information in a form of a small report.

9 List examples of corporate objectives. Discuss the following statement: 'Empirical evidence indicates that several objectives for financial management are considered to be more important than the objective of wealth maximization.'

10 It is often argued that spreadsheets are powerful tools for enhancing the understanding and the analysis of a vast number of financial management problems and applications. Additionally, their graphic facilities enable users to analyse financial management concepts graphically and produce various types of graphs for use in reports and business presentations. Discuss.

11 How can spreadsheets be used to facilitate the application of the concepts discussed in this chapter?

Appendix 2A Types of business organizations in the private sector

Business organizations in the private sector are divided into two basic categories: unincorporated and incorporated.

Unincorporated

These are business organizations which do not have a separate legal entity from their owners. The two basic forms of unincorporated business are the single proprietorships or sole traders and the partnerships.

A single proprietorship is a business organization that has only one owner. Its main advantages and disadvantages are shown in Figure 2A.1.

Advantages	Disadvantages
1. Ease of formation and dissolution	1. Unlimited owner's personal liability for the firm's debt
2. Ownership of the whole business and its profits	2. Limited ability of raising funds
3. Complete control and freedom to manage the business	3. Lack of continuity
4. Privacy of accounts	4. Lack of managerial skills

Figure 2A.1. Advantages and disadvantages of a single proprietorship

A partnership is a business organization that has more than one owner. Figure 2A.2 presents in summary the principal advantages and disadvantages of the partnership.

Advantages	Disadvantages
1. Ease of formation	1. Unlimited owner's personal liability for the firm's debt
2. Greater specialization in management than the sole trader	2. Limited ability of raising funds (but less limited than that of single proprietorship)
3. Ability of partners to provide a combination of their financial resources	
4. Privacy of accounts	

Figure 2A.2. Advantages and disadvantages of a partnership

Incorporated

An incorporated business organization is a single body composed of a group of persons. It is recognized by the law as a legal personality separated from the persons who own it. A company limited by shares is an incorporated business organization where the liability of each shareholder is limited to any amount unpaid for his or her shares up to the full nominal value of the shares.

Companies limited by shares can be public limited companies or private limited companies. A public limited company (plc) is a company that can invite the public at large to subscribe for its shares and debentures. A private limited company (Ltd) can only sell its shares or debentures privately. The discussion that follows apply to all kinds of incorporated business organizations, but our focus will be on public limited companies. A public limited company has many similar rights and obligations as a person:

- It is 'born' when a group of parties together combine funds.
- It has its own identity in the eye of the law.
- It owns assets; it earns or loses money.
- It can 'grow' by investing money in assets.
- It can get 'married' to another corporation through a merger.
- It can 'die' after suffering from 'financial health' problems.

Birth

A company is established by its owners, called members or shareholders, in the expectation of making future earnings. Money contributed to start a company is in the form of share capital and loan capital (if this is required).

Share capital is divided into shares. For example, a company may have a share capital of £2m divided into 2 million shares of £1 each. A loan capital usually has a long-term nature and it pays interest (that is, the price paid for the use of the loan capital over time). Shares can be divided into several types including ordinary shares and preference shares. The former represents the larger class of shares, the owners of which possess the right to receive a part of the profits and assets of the company only after all other claims have been made (for example, paying interest, paying part of the profits to preference shareholders, and so on). Preference shares are those receiving a fixed payment (called preference dividends) before any other payment on ordinary shares has been made. A loan capital can take the form of debentures which are debt obligations offering a fixed income to the holders and having a claim on the firm's profits and assets before either preference or ordinary shares.

Investors buy shares in a public limited company with the expectation of future benefits. For each share, these benefits can be expressed as dividends per share (that is, amount of profits attributable to each ordinary share) and capital gains (that is, the increase in money value of the share, the gain will be obtained when the share is sold). For example, suppose an investor bought a share at £10 a year ago and today the market price of the share is £12; the investor's capital gain is £2. Likewise, a debenture holder can earn periodic interest and obtain a capital gain during the period held (money received less cost). Figure 2A.3 compares the three sources of finance.

	Ordinary	Preference	Debentures
Income	All profits after all other claims have been met	Fixed dividends	Periodic interest
Capital gains/losses	Yes	Yes	Yes
Ownership	Yes	No, normally	No
Priority of claims with regard to earnings and assets	Last in line behind preference shareholders	Priority over ordinary shareholders	Priority over all shareholders

Figure 2A.3. Comparing ordinary shares, preference shares and debentures

Identity

A company is treated as a legal person in the eyes of the law and can therefore sue and be sued in its own name. For example, a company that has exclusive rights of a computer software can sue an individual or another company if the latter uses the software without being authorized by the owner of the software.

Wealth

The share capital and the loan capital are used by a company to acquire physical assets (for example, buildings, land, and so on) and non-physical assets (for example, payments due from customers). These assets provide the company with the productive capacity to carry on its operations. A company uses its assets to produce goods or services for sales to customers. A profit is made when the selling value of the goods or services exceeds the costs associated with selling the goods or services.

Internal growth

Companies continually search for new investment opportunities and make a large number of capital investment decisions. A company's growth and development depend upon effective capital investment decisions (that is, investment decisions that meet its objectives). Sound capital investment decisions affect the firm's future profitability and frequently lead to the expansion of ongoing business, or the development of new products.

'Marriage'

A company can achieve an internal growth by expanding production, or by offering new types of products to the market. This is in contrast to external growth, which can be achieved by combining a company with another ongoing company. The more common reasons for merging include: growth in size or in the range of products, economies of scale, increased debt capacity, increased managerial skills and tax considerations.

Possible 'death'
Companies do not always grow. A company can experience various 'financial health' problems, such as poor profitability, the inability to meet its current financial obligations as they come due, and so on. If 'financial health' problems cannot be solved, eventually the company will be liquidated. The latter is the situation when the company has to sell its assets to pay its various claims and then ceases trading. Corporate collapse can be attributed to a number of factors including: poor management, overexpansion, an economic downturn, natural disasters, and so on.

Public limited companies wanting to raise capital are brought together with those parties having surplus funds in the financial market. Two major types of financial markets are:

- *Money markets* They are financial markets in which short-term debt securities are traded between interested parties (for example, financial institutions, governments, investors, and so on). A treasury bill provides an example of a money market instrument.
- *Capital markets* They are financial markets in which shares and long-term debt securities (for example, debentures) are traded among investors.

The advantages and disadvantages of a limited liability business organization are summarized in Figure 2A.4.

Figure 2A.4. Advantages and disadvantages of a limited liability company

Advantages	Disadvantages
1. The owners have limited (personal) liability for the firm's debt	1. Complicated and costly formation and resolution
2. Ability of raising funds through the sales of shares and debentures	2. Double taxation (the firm is taxed on its profits and the ordinary shareholders are taxed when dividends are paid)
3. Use of a professional management team	3. Reconciling the objectives of the owners and managers can be a difficult task

Among the public limited firms a very small number have joined the London Stock Exchange (an organized market where shares and long-term debt securities are bought and sold to the public at large). Figure 2A.5 summarizes the business organization of the private sector in the United Kingdom.

The environment of financial decision making is extremely complex, it contains taxes, regulations, financial institutions and highly competitive financial markets. Figure 2A.6 illustrates how the financial system fits together and facilitates our understanding of the situation.

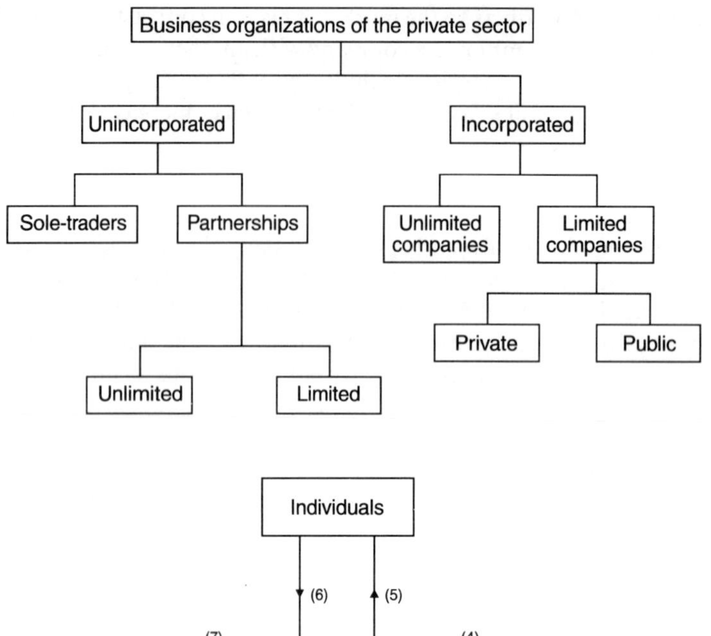

Figure 2A.5. The business organizations of the private sector in the United Kingdom

Individuals
(6)
(5)
(7)
(4)
Government
Firms
Financial institutions
(8)
(3)
(2)
(1)
Money and capital markets

(1) Funds are invested in money markets (for example, in government securities) or in securities of other firms.
(2) Funds are raised from capital markets (for example, share capital, loans, and so on).
(3) Funds are paid (for example, interest, payments of sum assured, and so on).
(4) Funds are invested (for example, loans, insurance, and so on).
(5) Funds are returned (for example, dividends, interest, and so on).
(6) Funds are paid for buying goods and services.
(7) Funds are paid (for example, taxes).
(8) Funds are returned (for example, interest).

Figure 2A.6. Fund flows among firms and other parties in the economy

Appendix 2B Frequency distributions

We can frequently obtain valuable information about a large set of data by grouping the data into a number of classes (or intervals). Figure 2B.1 shows 60 monthly observations for the share price of Marks and Spencer plc (prices are in pence). The significant characteristics of the data presented in Figure 2B.1 do not become apparent until individual prices have been distributed in a relatively few classes. For example, the price data of Marks and Spencer could be grouped into five classes. A class interval refers to the range of values included in a class. For example, 120p–160p is a class interval. The smallest value of the class interval is called the lower class limit and the largest value of the class interval is called the upper class limit. For example, the 120p–160p class has 120 as its lower class limit

	A	B	C	D	E	F	G	H
1	MONTHLY SHARE PRICE OF MARKS AND SPENCER PLC (1985-89)							
2	==========							
3								
4	----------							
5	Month	1985	1986	1987	1988	1989		
6	----------							
7	JAN	120.0	176.0	181.0	183.0	154.0		
8	FEB	124.0	171.0	190.0	180.0	176.0		
9	MAR	136.0	187.0	212.0	176.0	163.0		
10	APR	144.0	218.0	215.0	174.0	161.0		
11	MAY	137.0	211.0	233.0	179.0	171.0		
12	JUN	138.0	197.0	253.0	177.0	179.0		
13	JUL	134.0	207.0	241.0	174.0	194.0		
14	AUG	150.0	196.0	258.0	173.0	211.0		
15	SEP	154.0	218.0	235.0	150.5	220.5		
16	OCT	167.0	197.0	239.0	163.0	197.0		
17	NOV	184.0	197.0	200.0	173.0	189.0		
18	DEC	180.0	184.0	171.0	144.0	201.5		
19	----------							

Figure 2B.1. The share price of Marks and Spencer (January 1985 to December 1989)

and 160 as its upper class limit. If the classes of the distribution are all equal in size, their common class interval is known as the class interval of the distribution.

A frequency distribution shows the grouping of numerical data into specified class intervals and includes a count of the number of values in the data that fall into the class intervals. The number of values included in a class interval is called class frequency or simply frequency.

Example 2B.1 The frequency distribution of the share price of Marks and Spencer (January 1985–December 1989).

In order to create a frequency distribution of the share price of Marks and Spencer using 1-2-3, you must enter two sets of data. First, the monthly share prices and second the class limits (1-2-3 calls these class intervals bins). The frequency distribution is calculated with the aid of the command /`Data Distribution`. After issuing this command, 1-2-3 requires the 'value range', that is the range you want to group in the frequency distribution. In our case this range is B7..F18 (see Figure 2B.1). Then 1-2-3 will require the bin range, that is the range of the class limits. In this example the bin range is B25..B29 (see Figure 2B.2). After defining the bin range, 1-2-3 will display the distribution, see Figure 2B.2.

The bin range must be numeric and in ascending order. Each bin contains the values that are 'less than' or 'equal to' the corresponding bin value, but

	A	B	C	D	E	F	G	H
22	CREATING A FREQUENCY DISTRIBUTION FOR PRICE							
23	==========							
24								
25		120	1					
26		160	11					
27		200	33					
28		240	12					
29		280	3					
30			0					

Figure 2B.2. Frequency distribution for Figure 2B.1

greater than the next lowest bin value. Every time the distribution is executed an additional entry is appended to the output. This value represents the frequency of all values greater than the last interval of the bin range.

The frequency distribution shown in Figure 2B.2 presents the price data of Marks and Spencer in a more readily usable and understandable form revealing the following:

- Only for one month during the period January 1985–December 1989, was the price of Marks and Spencer's shares 120 pence or below.
- For 11 months during the same period the price was 160 pence or below but greater than 120 pence.
- For 33 months during the 60-month period the share price was 200 pence or lower but greater than 160 pence.
- For 12 months during the 60-month period the share was 240 pence or lower but greater than 200 pence.
- Finally, for three months during the same period the share price was 280 pence or lower but greater than 240 pence.

Some useful points

1 Avoid using overlapping classes; that is, each value in the data must fall in only one class.

2 Choose the number of classes and class limits so as to obtain no empty classes (that is, classes with frequencies greater than 0) within the range of your data.

3 When you use class intervals of the same size, the frequencies are not related to the sizes of the intervals. Using class intervals of the same size is desirable when you compare frequencies in a distribution.

4 The classes must be selected so as to cover the whole range of the data under consideration.

5 The number of classes in a frequency distribution is essentially arbitrary. As a rule of thumb, use from about 5 to about 20 classes. The exact number of classes is dependent on the nature, magnitude and range of the data. For example, for a small data set use a smaller number of classes while for a large data set use a larger number of classes.

Statisticians also employ a simple guide to determine the approximate number of classes in a frequency distribution:

> The number of classes in a frequency distribution should satisfy the inequality: $2^k < N < 2^{k+1}$, where k is the number of classes and N is the number of observations.

For example, if $N = 100$, then $2^6 = 64 < 100 < 2^7 = 128$, thus $k = 6$. However, note that such a rule should be used carefully.

Graphing a frequency distribution

A frequency distribution can be presented graphically by using the following type of graphs: a histogram, a frequency polygon and ogive.

A histogram is a graph in which each class in the distribution is represented by a vertical rectangle whose base corresponds to the class interval and whose height is

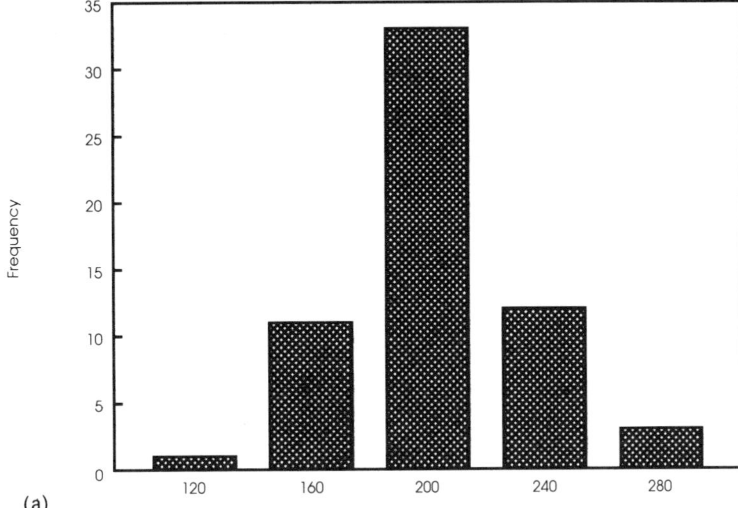

Figure 2B.3 Graphical representations of a frequency distribution

proportional to the frequency of that class. A frequency polygon is a graph showing a frequency distribution in which each pair of numbers (class mark, class frequency) is plotted as a point and then these points are connected with straight lines (a class mark is calculated by adding the lower and upper limits in a class and then dividing the result by 2). An ogive is a line graph used to graph a cumulative frequency distribution (the latter is a frequency distribution showing the number of observations in a data set that are 'less than' or 'more than' given values).

1-2-3 offers several types of graphs. A histogram can be created by using the bar graph type of 1-2-3. A frequency polygon or an ogive can be displayed by using the line graph type of 1-2-3.

Example 2B.2 A graphical presentation of the frequency distribution of the Marks and Spencer share

The frequency distribution shown in Figure 2B.2 can be presented graphically by using the types of graph shown in Figures 2B.3(a)–(d).

Problems

1 Group the Marks and Spencer share price presented in Figure 2B.1 into a frequency distribution having the following bins: 120, 140, 160, 180, 200, 220, 240 and 260. Discuss your results.

2 Draw a histogram of the distribution obtained in Problem 1.

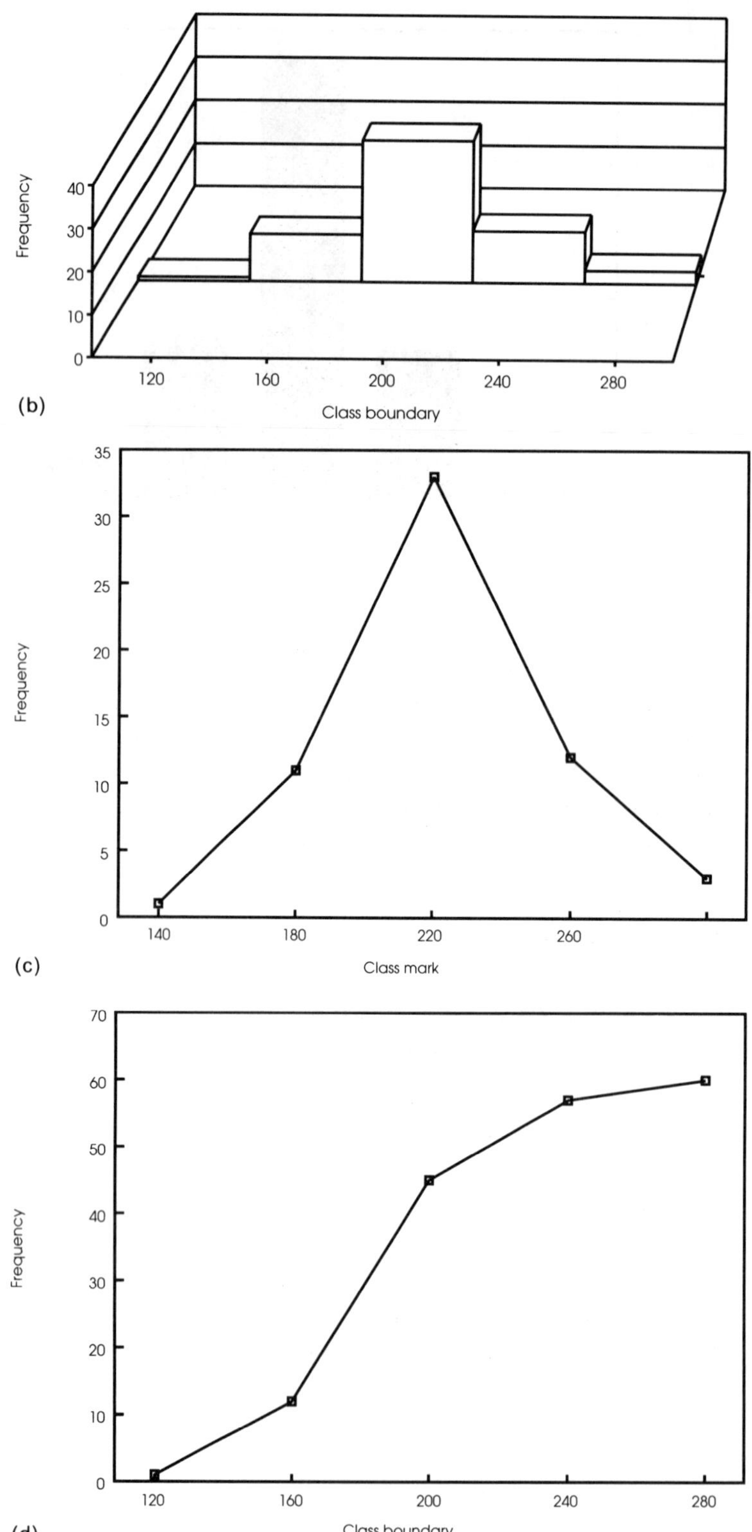

Figure 2B.3 (*continued*)

References and bibliography

Beranek, W. (1981) Research directions in finance, *Quarterly Review of Economics and Business*, Spring, 6–24.

Cooley, P.L. and Heck, J.L. (1981) Significant contributions to financial literature, *Financial Management*, Tenth Anniversary Issue, 13–33.

De Souza E., Diacogiannis, G. and Tomkins, C. (1990) An attempt to automate the teaching of accounting/financial management, *University Computing*, 12, 22–5.

Diacogiannis P.G. and Lai R. (1989). Survey on the investment and financing decisions of the companies in the USM, Warwick Paper in Management, No. 33, April.

Donaldson, G. (1963) Financial goals: Management versus stockholders, *Harvard Business Review*, May–June, 116–29.

Fama, E. (1980) Agency problems and the theory of the firm, *Journal of Political Economy*, April, 288–307.

Grossman, S.J. and Stiglitz J.E. (1977). On value maximisation and alternative objectives of the firm, *Journal of Finance*, May, 389–402.

Jensen, M. and Meckling, W.H. (1976) Theory of the firm: Managerial behaviour, agency costs and ownership structure, *Journal of Financial Economics*, October, 305–60.

Levy, H. and Sarnat, M. (1977) A pedagogic note on alternative formulations of the goal of the firm, *Journal of Business*, October, 526–8.

Lewellen, W.G. (1969) Management and ownership in the large firm, *Journal of Finance*, **24**, May, 299–322.

Norgaard, R.L. (1981) The evolution of business finance textbooks, *Financial Management*, Tenth Anniversary Issue, 34–45.

Petty, J.W., Scott, D.F. and Bird, M.M. (1975) The capital expenditure decision-making process of large corporations, *Engineering Economist*, Spring, 159–72.

Pike, R.H. (1985) Owner–manager conflict and the role of the payback method, *Accounting and Business Research*, Winter, 47–51.

Solomon, E. (1966) What should we teach in a course in business finance? *Journal of Finance*, May, 411–15.

Weston, J.F. (1981) Developments in financial theory, *Financial Management*, Tenth Anniversary Issue, 5–22.

3 Time value of money

This chapter includes:

- The present value topic
- The future value topic

In Chapter 2 we assumed that the objective of financial management is to maximize the market price of the firm's shares. Given this objective, the price of the firm's shares is dependent on three factors:

1 the expected size of the future cash flows to be received by the shareholders;
2 the timing of these cash flows;
3 the riskiness associated with these cash flows.

The second factor is considered because money has a time value. Shareholders prefer getting £1 today than £1 one year from now, since they can immediately invest £1 and earn a return one year later.

Understanding the time value of money is also important for the following reasons. First, firms and individual investors frequently deal with time value of money problems. Here are two examples:

1 An individual investor can use the future value concept to compute the amount to which a present sum of money will grow over time when deposited in a bank at a given interest rate.
2 A firm which borrows money from a bank can use the present value concept to calculate the periodic payment of its loan; it also provides the background information that is necessary for evaluating investment proposals as well as for evaluating new securities that a firm sells to investors.

This chapter deals with the concepts of the future and present values and their applications. Figure 3.1 presents the time value of money concept in relation to the framework for financial management introduced in Chapter 2.

Basic concepts, definitions and examples

In order to avoid complications we divided time into equally spaced periods (for example, years). The immediate present is referred to as period 0. Later time periods are referred to as periods 1, 2, 3, and so on. For example, assume that it is now 11 June 1988 and you will deposit into a savings account four payments of £300 each on 11 June 1989, 11 June 1990, 11 June 1991 and 11 June 1992. Then today becomes period 0, period 1 is the time that elapses from the end of period 0 to the last day of year 1,

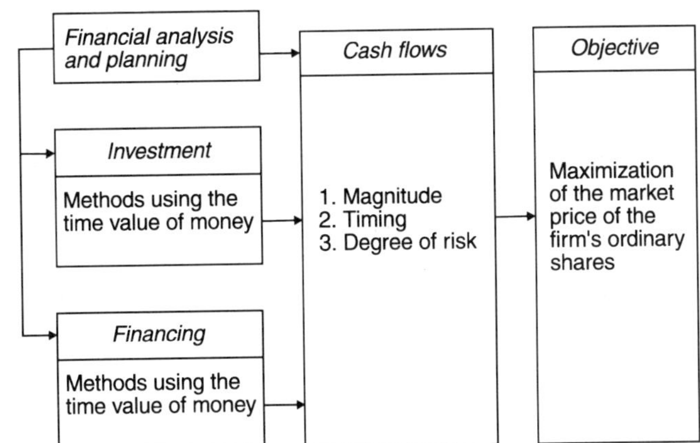

Figure 3.1. Relating the time value of money concept to the financial management framework introduced in Chapter 2

period 2 is the time that elapses from the last day of year 1 to the last day of year 2, and so on. The periods used in this example can be illustrated as follows:

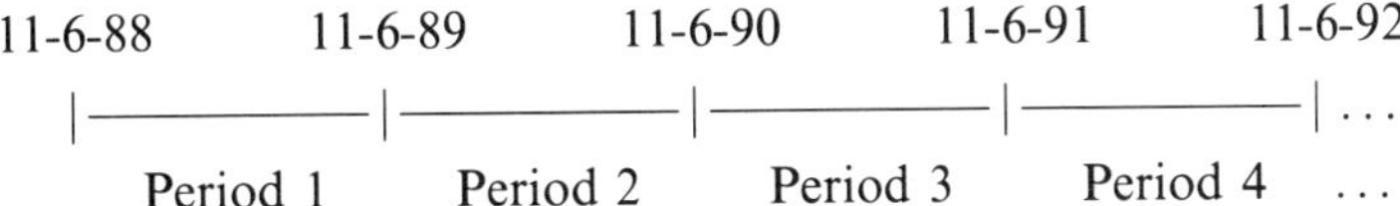

Money has a time value because a pound today is worth more than a pound one year from now. How much more is determined by three factors:

1. The time preference of the parties involved (for example, individual households, firms and so on).
2. The available investment opportunities of the parties involved.
3. The expected rate of inflation.

The time value of money is reflected in the interest rate which is the return from lending money or the fee charged for borrowing money. The amount of money borrowed or invested is called the principal. The time period is the length of time, or number of periods during which interest is received or paid. For example, if an investor today places £100 (this is the principal) in a savings account paying a 10 per cent annual interest, then he or she will receive an interest of $10 at the end of year 1. If another investor borrows today £1,000 (this is the principal) from a building society for 1 year at an interest rate of 12 per cent, then he or she will pay an interest of £120 over the loan period. Why are interest payments made on loans? There are two basic reasons (these reasons exist even if inflation is not a consideration). First, most lenders prefer current consumption to future consumption; thus they are receiving a rate of interest as a compensation for delaying consumption until a given future period of time. Second, rational lenders prefer high liquid assets rather than assets with low liquidity. Therefore, interest is offered as compensation to the lender for the sacrifice of some liquidity. To understand the time value of money, you need an understanding of the future value and present value concepts.

Future value

A pound today is worth more than a pound to be received in the future, because a pound in hand today can be invested to yield a return in the future. For example, suppose that an investor is offered £30,000 today or £30,000 a year later; the investor will accept the £30,000 today because the money can immediately be invested (for example, in a deposit bank account) and earn a return one year later. This reward is required by the investor for allowing the borrower (for example, a bank) to use his or her money and for waiting for the repayment of the investment principal. If the interest is £3,000, then the rate of interest is 10 per cent (that is, £3,000/£30,000). The future value of the investment refers to the growth of £30,000 by moving it into the future; the future value is calculated by adding the interest of £3,000 to the principal of £30,000. Figure 3.2 illustrates the principal and the future value of the investment a year from now.

Figure 3.2. The future value of an investment

Present day	A year later
0	1
£30,000	£33,000 = £30,000 + £3,000

From Figure 3.2 it can be seen that the investor's future value can be expressed as:

Future value = Principal + (Interest rate)(Principal)

This can be written by using some mathematical notation:

$$FV_1 = PV + rPV$$
$$= PV(1 + r)$$

where

PV = principal = the original payment (or investment) at the beginning of the period under consideration.
r = interest rate per period.

Future value of a single payment over *N* years

Assume that a single sum of money, call it PV, is invested today for N periods at an interest rate of r per period. We assume that interest is paid on both the principal and the amount of interest previously earned and neither principal nor interest is withdrawn during earlier periods. We also assume that the interest payment occurs at the end of each period. Figure 3.3 shows the amount to which the principal will grow at the end of N periods when it is invested at r per cent per period.

Figure 3.4 summarizes the concept of the future value of a single payment.

Example 3.1 Calculating the future value of Mr Annis's account

Mr George Annis has £30,000, a gift from his father. After an investigation of his savings opportunities, he has found a deposit account that pays 10 per cent per annum. The future value of his account at the end of the first year is calculated as follows:

$$FV_1 = £30,000(1 + 0.10)$$
$$= £33,000$$

If Mr Annis makes no withdrawals from the account for another year, the

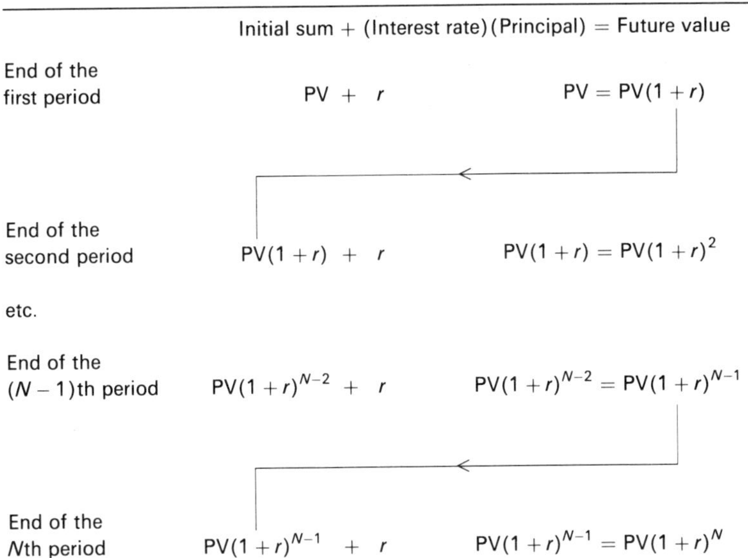

Figure 3.3. Deriving the future value formula for a single cash flow

Definition The future value is the amount to which a single payment (also called a lump sum) will grow by a specific date in the future when it is invested at a particular compound interest rate.
Calculation The future value of a single payment at the end of period N can be calculated by multiplying the single payment by the future value of £1, compounded annually at a specific interest rate for N periods. Mathematically, the future value of a single payment can be expressed as follows:

$$FV_N = PV(1 + r)^N$$

where

PV = the principal at the beginning of period 1.
r = the interest rate per period.
N = the number of periods the money will earn interest.

Interpretation The future value of a lump sum at the end of a specified number of periods can be viewed as the result of a process which takes the single lump sum and adds to it the compound interest (that is, the interest earned on both the lump sum and the amount of interest accumulated in prior periods).

Figure 3.4. The future value of a single payment concept

total amount of his investment at the end of the second year will be:

$$\begin{aligned} FV_2 &= £30{,}000(1 + 0.10)^2 \\ &= £30{,}000(1.2100) \\ &= £36{,}300 \end{aligned}$$

If Mr Annis leaves the £30,000 plus the accumulated interest in the account for another year, the total amount in his account at the end of the third year will be:

$$\begin{aligned} FV_3 &= £30{,}000(1 + 0.10)^3 \\ &= £30{,}000(1.3310) \\ &= £39{,}930 \end{aligned}$$

Continuing this way, we have

$$FV_4 = £30{,}000(1 + 0.10)^4$$
$$= £30{,}000(1.4641)$$
$$= 43{,}923$$

and finally

$$FV_5 = £30{,}000(1 + 0.10)^5$$
$$= £30{,}000(1.6105)$$
$$= £48{,}315$$

Therefore, the future value of his savings at the end of five years will be £48,315. The compound interest of Mr Annis's savings is £48,315 – £30,000 = £18,315. Stated differently, his future value is equal to the principal of £30,000 plus the compound interest of £18,315.

The future value can be also calculated by using 1-2-3. Figure 3.5 illustrates the calculation procedure. The future value in cell B8 is computed by employing the following formula: `+B4*(1+B5)^B6`.

```
           A              B              C                  D
1 CALCULATING THE FUTURE VALUE OF MR ANNIS' ACCOUNT
2 ================================================
3
4 Principal          £30,000
5 Interest Rate         10.0%
6 Term                      5
7                    ---------
8 Future Value -> £48,315
```

Figure 3.5. Calculating the future value of Mr Annis's savings

Problems

1 Create the worksheet shown in Figure 3.5 by storing the future value formula in cell C8.
2 Recalculate the future value by assuming that the discount rate is 11 per cent.
3 Recalculate the future value by assuming that the discount rate is 11 per cent and the period under consideration is eight years.
4 Discuss and compare your results in Problems 2 and 3 with that shown in Figure 3.5.
5 Discuss the benefits of using formulae to automate a worksheet.

Example 3.2 Compound value interest factors

The future value of a single sum of money can be calculated with the aid of a special table which provides the compound value interest factors for various interest rates and various periods. This table can easily be calculated by using the Lotus `/Data Table 2` command. This command provides a sensitivity analysis on two variables (a two-variable sensitivity analysis) and it can be applied with regard to one formula (a two-variable sensitivity analysis is a procedure by means of which the change in the output variable (for example, future value of £1) is calculated for a given change in two input variables (for example, interest rate and time periods)). The first step in building a table that computes the present value of £1 at different periods and different discount rates is to enter 12 periods (see range B9 ... B20 in Figure 3.6) and five interest rates (see range C7 ... G7 in Figure 3.6). The following formula stored in cell B5:

```
(1+B3)^B4
```

Note that the `/Range Format Text` command is used in cell B7 in order to display its contents in a text format. Next issue the `/Data Table 2` command, enter the table range B7 ... G20 and press the <Enter> key. The 'input cell 1' refers to cell B4 and the 'input cell 2' refers to cell B3. The result of the `/Data Table 2` is presented in Figure 3.6 (we display the results by using a fixed format with three decimal points). The result shows the future values of £1 pound at each combination of interest rates and time periods. For example, the number 1.518 is the future value of £1 at the end of four years and interest rate of 11 per cent.

Using 1-2-3's `/Data Table 2` command you can calculate compound value interest factors for any interest rate (remember that the tables included in the financial management textbooks display only compound factors for a limited number of interest rates).

	A	B	C	D	E	F	G
1			CALCULATING COMPOUND FACTORS				
2			============================				
3	Interest	10.0%					
4	Period	1					
5	Future Value	1.1					
6							
7	+B5		10.0%	11.0%	12.0%	13.0%	14.0%
8		0	1.000	1.000	1.000	1.000	1.000
9		1	1.100	1.110	1.120	1.130	1.140
10		2	1.210	1.232	1.254	1.277	1.300
11		3	1.331	1.368	1.405	1.443	1.482
12		4	1.464	1.518	1.574	1.630	1.689
13		5	1.611	1.685	1.762	1.842	1.925
14		6	1.772	1.870	1.974	2.082	2.195
15		7	1.949	2.076	2.211	2.353	2.502
16		8	2.144	2.305	2.476	2.658	2.853
17		9	2.358	2.558	2.773	3.004	3.252
18		10	2.594	[illegible]	[illegible]	[illegible]	3.707
19		11	2.853	3.152	3.479	3.836	4.226
20		12	3.138	3.498	3.896	4.335	4.818

Figure 3.6. Calculating compound value interest factors

Figure 3.6 can be utilized to calculate the future value of £30,000 compounded at 10 per cent for five years.

$$FV_5 = 30{,}000(1.611)$$

$$= £48{,}330$$

(The difference between this result and the result presented in Example 3.3 is due to rounding.)

Note that the compound factor of 1.611 can be found at the intersection of the interest rate column (that is 10 per cent) and the period row (that is 5). The relationship between the future value of £1, time and interest rates can be better illustrated with the aid of a 3-D graph. Figure 3.7 provides a graphical representation of a two-variable sensitivity analysis shown in Figure 3.6. From this graph it can be clearly seen that the future values of £1 increase both with time and with the compound rate. Figure 3.7 provides another powerful application of spreadsheets for financial management.

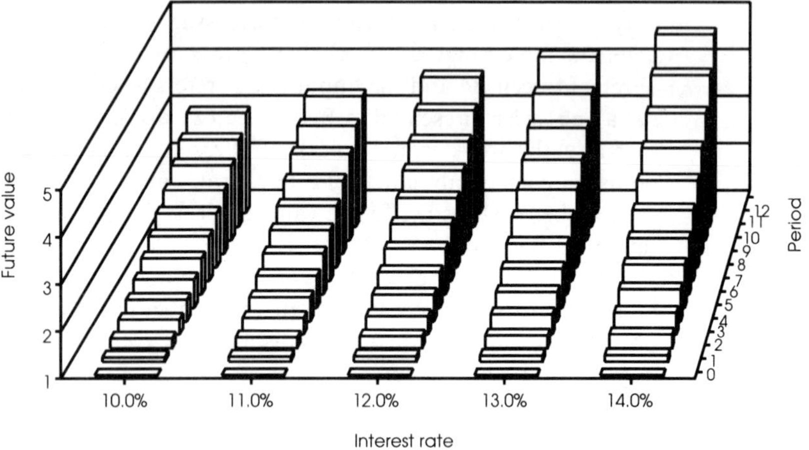

Figure 3.7. Relationship between the future value, time and compounding rate

Problems

1 Calculate the compound interest factors by using the following two ranges of values: period, 13 years to 26 years in steps of 1; discount rate, 15.5 per cent to 20.5 per cent in steps of 1 per cent. Discuss your results.

2 Graph your results in Problem 1 by using the graphic facilities of 1-2-3. Discuss the relationship between future value, time and interest rates.

Calculating the periodic interest rate using a single payment investment

We can use the future value of a single payment formula to calculate the periodic rate of interest required to compound a single payment to a target amount over a fixed number of periods. The interest rate per period is given by:

$$r = (FV_N/PV)^{1/N} - 1$$

Example 3.3 Calculating the periodic interest rate required to compound a single payment to a target amount over a fixed number of annual periods

Consider the information given in Example 3.1. Then

$$r = (£48{,}315/£30{,}000)^{1/5} - 1 = 10 \text{ per cent}$$

The annual interest rate can be also calculated by using the following financial function of 1-2-3:

`@RATE(48315, 30000, 5)` = 10 per cent

Problem

Use a procedure similar to that illustrated in Figure 3.5 and create a worksheet that recalculates the annual interest rate each time you change one of the following input variables: principal, future value and number of periods over which the amount invested will be compounded.

Calculating the number of periods

Once more, the future value of a single payment formula can be used to calculate the number of periods required for an initial payment to grow to a target value, given a fixed periodic interest rate. The number of periods for the conversion of future to present value (and vice versa) is expressed by:

$$N = \frac{\ln \mathrm{FV}_N - \ln \mathrm{PV}}{\ln(1+r)}$$

where

ln = the natural logarithm operator.

Example 3.4 Calculating the number of periods required for an initial payment to compound to a target amount, given a fixed periodic interest rate

Consider the information given in Example 3.1. Then

$$N = \frac{\ln(48{,}315) - \ln(30{,}000)}{\ln(1+0.10)} = 5 \text{ years}$$

The `@CTERM` financial function of 1-2-3 can also be used to calculate the number of periods of the investment.

`@CTERM(0.1, 48315, 30000)` = 5 years

Problem

Use a procedure similar to that illustrated in Figure 3.5 and create a worksheet that recalculates the number of periods each time you change one of the following input variables: principal, future value and annual interest rate.

Future value of an uneven stream of payments

In the previous section the ability to compound a single present value into a future value was explored. When a stream of uneven payments is to be compounded, a simple sum of all the individual future value payments will produce the total future value for the whole stream.

Future value of an uneven stream of payments	=	SUM OF	Payment/ investment at period t	×	Compound value interest factor
FV_N	=		$\sum_{t=1}^{N} C_t$	×	$(1+r)^{N-t}$

where

C_t = the payment/investment at the end of period t.

Example 3.5 Calculating the future value of an uneven stream of payments

Mr Annis can either receive immediately £30,000 from his father or receive the same amount of money over a five-year period. In the latter case, his annual payouts are given below:

End of year 1: £8,000
End of year 2: £7,000
End of year 3: £6,000
End of year 4: £5,000
End of year 5: £4,000

Mr Annis is considering placing his money in a savings account paying a 10 per cent annual interest rate. Assume that the interest payments will occur at the end of the year and Mr Annis will leave his deposit plus the accumulated interest until the end of year 5. The calculation of the future value of Mr Annis's investment is shown in Figure 3.8. Note that the last payment of £4,000 is expected to take place at the end of year 5, so its future value to that point in time 5 is £4,000. The future value is of the series of payments is £37,790. However, if he deposits immediately £30,000 in a savings account paying 10 per cent interest compounded annually, the future value of his account at the end of the fifth year will be £48,315 (see Example 3.1). Receiving an amount of £30,000 immediately is preferable to the other alternative, since money has a time value.

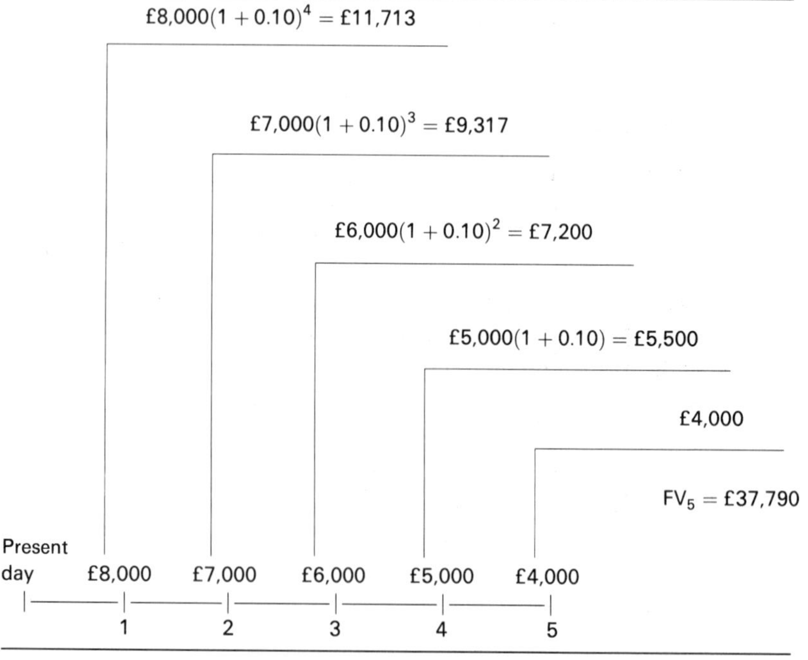

Figure 3.8. Calculating the future value of an uneven stream of payments

Example 3.6 Calculating the future value of an uneven stream of payments using 1-2-3.

1-2-3 does not offer a financial function which allows you to calculate directly the future value (FV) of an uneven stream of payments. However, this can be achieved by using the @NPV function of 1-2-3. The worksheet presented in Figure 3.9 stores the cash inflows of Mr Annis in the range B8 ... B12. The following formula calculates the future value of the given uneven stream of payments (see also Example 3.5):

```
@NPV(B4,B8...B12) * (1 + B4)^5
```

```
         A                 B               C           D          E          F
 1 CALCULATING THE FUTURE VALUE OF AN UNEVEN STREAM OF PAYMENTS
 2 ==============================================================
 3
 4 Interest                     10.0%
 5 ------------------------------------
 6            Year          Cash Flow
 7 ------------------------------------
 8               1            £8,000
 9               2             7,000
10               3             6,000
11               4             5,000
12               5             4,000
13                        --------------
14 FV ------>                £37,790
15 ------------------------------------
```

Figure 3.9. Using 1-2-3 to calculate the FV of an uneven stream of payments

Problem

Create the worksheet shown in Figure 3.9.

Future value of an annuity

An annuity is a series of payments or receipts of equal amounts of money per period for a specified number of periods. An ordinary annuity (or simply annuity) is one whose payments or receipts occur at the end of each period. The future value of an (ordinary) annuity is

Future value of an annuity	=	Constant amount	×	Future value factor of an annuity

$$\mathrm{FV}_N = \mathrm{CA} \times \frac{(1+r)^N - 1}{r}$$

where

CA = the amount invested at the end of each year.

N = the number of years for which the annuity will last.

Example 3.7 Calculating the future value of an annuity

Mr Annis plans to deposit £6,000 at the end of each of the five consecutive years in a bank deposit account paying 10 per cent interest compounded annually. The time line for our problem is presented as follows:

Present day	£6,000	£6,000	£6,000	£6,000	£6,000
	1	2	3	4	5

In this case, period 1 is the year that elapses from the end of the present day to the end of the first year, period 2 is the time that elapses from the end of the first year to the end of the second year, and so on.

The future value of his investment at the end of five years is:

$$£6,000 \frac{(1+0.10)^5 - 1}{0.10} = £36,631$$

The future value of the investment can also be calculated by using the following financial function of 1-2-3:

@FV(6000, 0.10, 5) = £36,631

Problem

Create a worksheet that can recalculate the future value of an annuity each time you change one of the following input variables: the annuity amount, the compound annual interest rate and the number of years for which the annuity will last.

Future value of an annuity due

An annuity whose payments or receipts occur at the beginning of each period is called an annuity due. The future value of an annuity due is expressed as follows:

$$\text{FVAD}_N = \text{FV}_N(1+r)$$

where

FV_N = the future value of an ordinary annuity.

Example 3.8 Calculating the future value of an annuity due

Consider the same data as in Example 3.7, but assume that the deposits are made at the beginning of each period. The following time line is used to depict the problem:

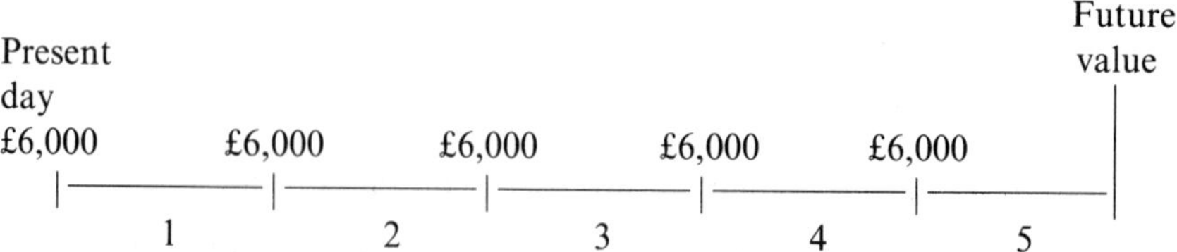

The future value of this annuity could easily be computed by using 1-2-3 as follows

FVAD_N = @FV(6000, 0.10, 5) * (1 + 0.10) = £40,294

Sinking fund problem

Often a firm or an individual may wish to determine the annuity amount that must be deposited every year to accumulate a certain lump sum in the future (see formula below). This type of arrangement is called a sinking fund.

$$\text{CA} = \frac{\text{FV}_N r}{(1+r)^N - 1}$$

Example 3.9 Calculating the sinking fund deposit

Suppose Mr Annis wishes to have £40,000 available in a bank account in five years to purchase a holiday flat. He wants to deposit a constant amount of money every year (at the end of the year) to help achieve his objective. If his money earns a compound annual interest rate of 10 per cent, then the sinking fund deposit is calculated as follows:

$$\text{CA} = \frac{(\pounds 40{,}000)(0.10)}{(1+0.10)^5 - 1} = \pounds 6{,}551.90$$

The sinking fund deposit can be calculated by using the following 1-2-3 formula:

CA = £40,000/`@FV(1,0.10,5)` = £6,551.90

where `@FV(1,0.10,5)` is the future value of investing £1 for five years at a compound annual rate of interest of 10 per cent.

Problem

Create a worksheet that can recalculate the annuity amount each time you change one of the following input variables: the lump sum to be received in the future, the compound annual interest rate and the number of years for which the annuity will last.

Figure 3.10 summarizes four issues relying on the future value of a single payment concept.

Figure 3.11 summarizes the topic of future value and in each case presents the 1-2-3

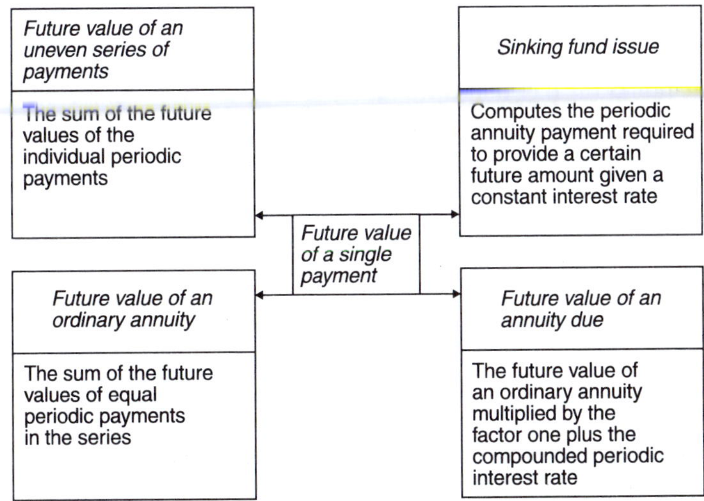

Figure 3.10. Four issues based on the future value of a single payment

Future value of a single payment
Description The amount to which a lump sum investment will grow over a period of time when compounded at a given rate of interest.
1-2-3 formula `@FV(lump_sum,interest_rate,term)*interest_rate+lump_sum`
Calculating the interest rate using a single payment investment
Description Calculates the periodic interest rate required to compound an initial investment to a specified future value over a given number of periods.
1-2-3 function `@RATE(future_value,present_value,term)`
Calculating the number of periods
Description Calculates the number of periods required for an initial investment earning a given interest rate to compound to a specified future value.
1-2-3 function `@CTERM(interest_rate,future_value,present_value)`
Future value of an uneven stream of payments
Description Calculates the sum of the individual future values of the individual payments of the stream.
1-2-3 formula `@NPV(discount_rate,range)*(1+discount rate)^term`
Future value of an ordinary annuity
Description Calculates the future value of a stream of equal payments assuming that these payments occur at the end of each period.
1-2-3 function `@FV(annuity_payment,interest_rate,term)`
Future value of an annuity due
Description Calculates the future value of a stream of equal payments assuming that these payments occur at the beginning of each period.
1-2-3 formula `@FV(annuity_payment,interest_rate,term)*(1+interest_rate)`
Sinking fund problem
Description Calculates the annuity amount that must be invested each year to accumulate a given lump sum in the future.
1-2-3 formula `Future value / @FV(£1,interest_rate,term)`

Figure 3.11. A summary of the topic of future value

formula or function that can be used to provide a solution to the future value problem under consideration.

Present value

Suppose an investor wishes to calculate the present value of £33,000 to be received one year from now (that is, bring the future amount of £33,000 back to the present). The present value of the investment would not include the reward associated with the future value. This loss is incorporated in the formulation of the present value which quantifies the fact that the pound in the future is worth less than the bound in hand today. If the reward associated with the future value is 10 per cent, then the calculation of the present value of the investor's future receipt of £33,000 is illustrated in Figure 3.12.

With the reward

$$\frac{£33{,}000}{(1+0.10)} = \frac{£30{,}000\,(1+0.10)}{(1+0.10)} = £30{,}000$$

Without the reward (the reward cancels out)

Figure 3.12. Calculating the present value of an investment

The reward associated with the present value is called the discount rate, the required rate of return, or the opportunity cost of capital. It is called the discount rate because it is used to reduce a future sum of money by moving it back to the present. It is called the required rate of return because it is the minimum acceptable rate demanded from an investor in order to make an investment. Finally, it is called the opportunity cost because it is the return forgone by investing funds in one investment rather than in alternative investments.

Present value of a single payment

As in the case of the future value, the present value concept is summarized in Figure 3.13.

Example 3.10 Calculating the present value of a single payment.

Mr George Annis wishes to buy a flat with the amount of £30,000 given by his father. Assume that he will let the flat and the rent will cover exactly the rates and maintenance costs. The price of the flat is £30,000 and he expects to be able to sell the flat five years from now for £60,000. The present value of his investment is given by

$$\text{PV} = \frac{£60{,}000}{(1 + 0.10)^5}$$

$$= £37{,}255.28$$

Figure 3.14 illustrates graphically the relationship between the present value of £1, time and discount rates. The present values, as presented in Figure 3.14, decline with both time and the discount rate used.

Problem

Calculate the present value of Mr Annis's property investment using 1-2-3.

Present value of an uneven stream of payments

When a stream of uneven payments is to be discounted, a simple sum of all the

---

Definition The present value is the current value of a future payment to be received at a specified date in the future when discounted at a given rate.

Calculation The present value of a single payment to be received at the end of period N can be calculated by multiplying the single payment by the present value of £1, discounted periodically at a specific discount rate for N periods. Mathematically, the present value of a single payment can be expressed as follows:

$$\text{PV} = \text{FV}_N/(1 + r)^N$$

where

FV_N = the payment to be received at the end of period N.
r = the periodic discount rate.
N = the number of periods until payment will be received.

Interpretation The present value of a lump sum to be received at the end of a specified number of periods can be viewed as the result of a process which takes the lump sum and reducing it by an amount reflecting the time value of money.

Figure 3.13. The present value of a single payment concept

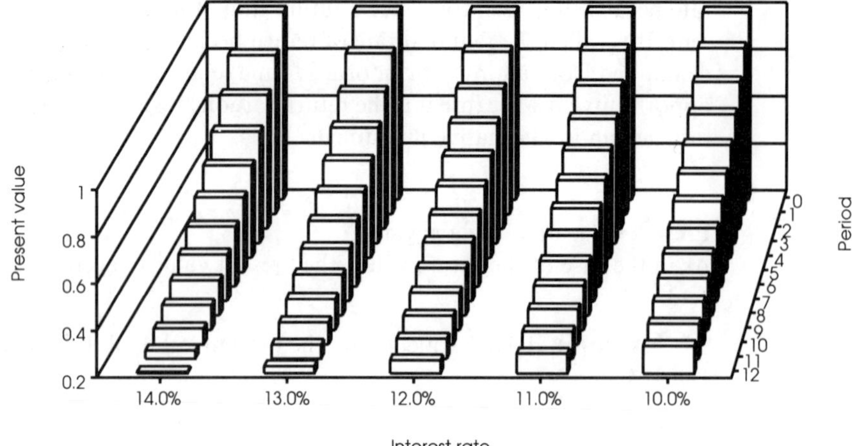

Figure 3.14. Relationship between present value and interest rate

individual present value payments will produce the total present value for the whole stream of payments (see formula below).

Future value of an uneven stream of payments	=	SUM OF	Future value at period t	$\times$	Discount value interest factor

$$PV = \sum_{t=1}^{N} AR_t \times \frac{1}{(1+r)^t}$$

where

AR_t = the amount received at the end of year t.

Example 3.11 Calculating the present value of an uneven stream of payments

Mr Ian Kitchen has asked Mr George Annis for a loan of £30,000 (Mr Annis has £30,000 given by his father as a gift). Mr Kitchen promises to pay the following payments:

Year 1: £10,000
Year 2: £9,000
Year 3: £8,000
Year 4: £7,000
Year 5: £6,000

Assume that each payment will occur at the end of the corresponding year and the annual discount rate is 10 per cent. The calculation of Mr Annis's present value is shown in Figure 3.15.

Problem

Calculate the present value of Mr Annis's uneven stream of payments using 1-2-3.

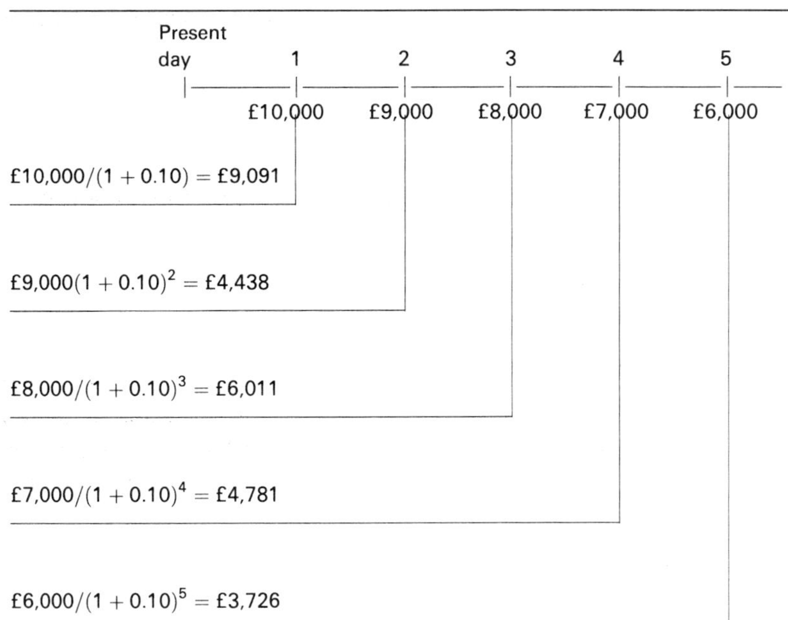

Figure 3.15. Calculating the present value of an uneven stream of payments at 10 per cent discount rate

Present value of an annuity

If we assume that the payments of an annuity occur at the end of each period, then its present value can be expressed as

Present value of an annuity	=	Constant amount	×	Present value factor of an annuity

$$PV = CA \times \frac{1-(1+r)^{-N}}{r}$$

Example 3.12 Calculating the present value of an annuity

Mr George Annis has been offered the opportunity to receive £7,913.93 at the year's end for the next five years. The time line for our problem is illustrated as follows:

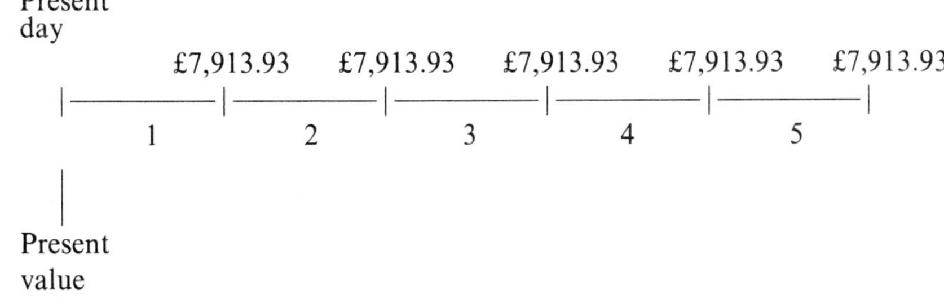

The present value of his annuity at 10 per cent discount rate is computed as follows:

$$£7{,}913.93\frac{1-(1+0.10)^{-5}}{0.10}=£30{,}000$$

The same results can be produced by using the following financial function of 1-2-3

`@PV(7913.93, 0.10, 5)` = £30,000

Problem

Create a worksheet that recalculates the present value of an annuity each time you change one of the following input variables: the annuity amount, the discount interest rate and the number of years for which the annuity will last.

Present value of an annuity due

An annuity whose payments or receipts occur at the beginning of each period is called an annuity due. To calculate the present value of an annuity due use the following formula:

$$\text{PVAD} = \text{PV}(1+r)$$

where

PV = the present value of an annuity whose payments are made at the end of each period

Example 3.13 Calculating the present value of an annuity due

Assume the same data given in Example 3.12, but in the present case the receipts occur at the beginning of each year. The following time line is used to illustrate the situation under consideration:

```
Present
day
£7,913.93   £7,913.93   £7,913.93   £7,913.93   £7,913.93
 |-----------|-----------|-----------|-----------|-----------|
       1           2           3           4           5
 |
 |
Present
value
```

The present value of the annuity can be calculated with the aid of the 1-2-3's financial function `@PV` as follows:

PVAD = `@PV(7913.93, 0.10, 5) * (1 + 0.10)` = £33,000

The periodic payment of a loan

The present value of an annuity's formula can be used to compute the periodic payment on a loan:

$$\mathrm{CA} = \mathrm{PV}\frac{r}{1-(1+r)^{-N}}$$

The term loan amortization refers to repayment of a loan by equal periodic payments.

Example 3.14 Calculating the periodic payment of a loan

Mr George Annis wishes to obtain a five-year loan of £10,000 at a 10 per cent annual interest rate to purchase a car. The annual payment of his loan is calculated as follows:

$$\mathrm{CA} = £10{,}000\frac{0.10}{1-(1+0.10)^{-5}} = £2{,}637.97$$

The annual payment of Mr Annis can also be calculated by using the following financial function of 1-2-3

`@PMT(10000, 0.10, 5)` = £2,637.97

Problem

Create a worksheet that can recalculate the periodic payment of a loan each time you change one of the following input variables: the amount borrowed, the discount interest rate and the number of years over which you will pay off the loan.

Present value of a perpetuity

A perpetuity is an annuity with an infinite life. The present value of a perpetuity is expressed as

$$\mathrm{PV} = \frac{\mathrm{CA}}{r}$$

Example 3.15 Calculating the present value of a perpetuity

Suppose CA = £100 and r = 10 per cent, then the present value of the perpetuity is

$$\mathrm{PV} = \frac{£100}{0.10} = £1{,}000$$

Non-annual compounding and discounting

In some cases, interest on an account is compounded more frequently than once a year. In practice semi-annual, quarterly, monthly, weekly, daily and even continuously compounded interest rates are used for different types of investments. If interest is compounded M times a year, then the following formula applies for the future value of a single payment:

$$\mathrm{FV}_N = \mathrm{PV}(1+r/M)^{MN}$$

Example 3.16 Calculating the future value of a single payment when interest is compounded more frequently than once a year.

Suppose we wish to calculate the future value of a current lump sum of £1,000 when the annual rate of interest is 10 per cent and compounding occurs annually, semi-annually, quarterly, monthly, weekly, daily and hourly. Figure 3.16 presents a number of future values for £1,000 at 10 per cent with various compounding periods. For example, for semi-annual compounding the future value can be calculated as follows

$$FV = £1{,}000(1 + 0.1/2)^2 = £1{,}102.500$$

The following formula is stored in cell C10

```
+$B$4*(1+$B$5/B10)^B10
```

To calculate the other future values copy the contents of cell C10 in the range C11 ... C16.

The results show that the shorter the compounding period is, the higher will be the future value of the investment, because by using more frequent compounding periods we are able to earn interest on interest more often.

Problem

Create the worksheet shown in Figure 3.16.

	A	B	C	D
1	THE FUTURE VALUE OF £1,000 UNDER DIFFERENT COMPOUNDING FREQUENCIES			
2	==========			
3				
4	Principal	£1,000		
5	Annual Interest Rate	10.0%		
6	----------			
7	COMPOUNDED PERIOD	TIMES INTEREST	FUTURE VALUE	
8		IS COMPOUNDED		
9	----------			
10	Annual	1	£1,100.000	
11	Semiannual	2	1,102.500	
12	Quarter	4	1,103.813	
13	Month	12	1,104.713	
14	Weekly	52	1,105.065	
15	Daily	365	1,105.156	
16	Hourly	8760	1,105.170	
17	----------			

Figure 3.16. The FV of £1,000 under different compounding frequencies

The present value of a single payment to be received at the end of year N, when discounting takes place more frequently than once a year, can be expressed as follows:

$$PV = FV_N/(1 + r/M)^{MN}$$

where M is the number of discounting periods per year.

Continuous compounding and discounting

As the number of compounding periods becomes infinite (and the compounding interval becomes infinitely small) the term $(1 + r/M)^{MN}$ approaches e^{rN}, where e is the base for natural logarithms (e is approximately 2.71828). Therefore, in terms of continuous compounding, the future value of a single payment is given by (for a proof see Appendix 3A)

$$FV_N = PV\,e^{rN}$$

Example 3.17 Calculating the future value of a single payment when interest is continuously compounded

Using the same data as in Example 3.16, we can calculate the future value of £1,000 under continuous compounding as follows

$$FV_1 = £1{,}000\,e^{0.10} = 1000 * \texttt{@EXP(0.10)} = £1{,}105.170$$

where `@EXP(0.10)` is the exponential function of 1-2-3 which raises e to the 0.10 power.

Problem

Create a worksheet that recalculates the future value of a single payment when interest is continuously compounded. Make sure to use the appropriate procedure so that the result can be automatically recalculated each time you change one of the input variables under consideration.

Similarly, for continuous discounting, we have the following formula:

$$PV = FV_N/e^{rN}$$

Example 3.18 Discount value interest factors under continuous discounting

Figure 3.17 provides a listing of discount value interest factors under continuous discounting for various time periods in the range 0 to 9 (in steps of 1) and various interest rates in the range 5 per cent to 10 per cent (in steps of 1 per cent). The values generated by using the `/Data Table 2` command (see also

```
--------------------------------------------------------------------------
              A                 B      C      D      E      F      G      H
 1 DISCOUNT VALUE INTEREST FACTORS UNDER CONTINUOUS COMPOUNDING
 2 ============================================================
 3 Principal                    1
 4 Annual Interest Rate     10.0%
 5 Year                         1
 6                        -------
 7 Present Value Factor 0.905
 8
 9                    +B7         5%     6%     7%     8%     9%    10%
10                          0  1.000  1.000  1.000  1.000  1.000  1.000
11                          1  0.951  0.942  0.932  0.923  0.914  0.905
12                          2  0.905  0.887  0.869  0.852  0.835  0.819
13                          3  0.861  0.835  0.811  0.787  0.763  0.741
14                          4  0.819  0.787  0.756  0.726  0.698  0.670
15                          5  0.779  0.741  0.705  0.670  0.638  0.607
16                          6  0.741  0.698  0.657  0.619  0.583  0.549
17                          7  0.705  0.657  0.613  0.571  0.533  0.497
18                          8  0.670  0.619  0.571  0.527  0.487  0.449
19                          9  0.638  0.583  0.533  0.487  0.445  0.407
--------------------------------------------------------------------------
```

Figure 3.17. Discount value factors for £1 at interest rate *r* for *N* years

Example 3.2). The following formula is stored in cell B7:

```
+B3/EXP(B4*B5)
```

This formula is then copied in cell B9 and the `/Range Format` command is used to display the contents of cell B9 in a text format. The range of the data table is B9 ... H19, the 'input cell 1' is B5 and the 'input cell 2' is B4.

Problems

1 Create the worksheet shown in Figure 3.17.

2 Plot a graph illustrating the relationship between present value of £1 under continuous compounding, time and interest rates. Discuss the results shown in the graph.

3 The following formula gives the future value of an annuity under continuous compounding:

$$FV_N = CA(e^{rN} - 1)/r$$

Create a worksheet that can be used to calculate the future value any time when you change an input variable. Discuss the relationship between future value of an annuity under continuous compounding and interest rates.

4 Likewise, the present value of an annuity under continuous discounting can be expressed as follows:

$$PV = CA(e^{rN} - 1)/(r\, e^{rN})$$

Set up a worksheet that can be used to update the result of the present value each time you change an input variable. Discuss the relationship between present value of an annuity under continuous compounding, interest rates and time.

Figure 3.18 presents a summary of four issues based on the present value of a single payment concept.

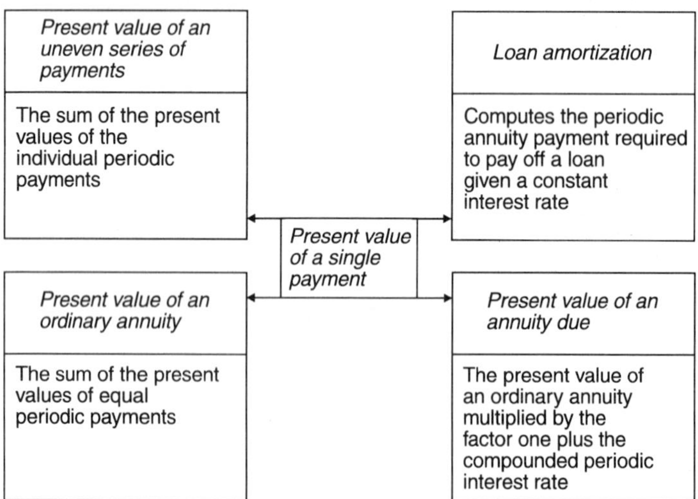

Figure 3.18. Four issues based on the present value of a single payment

Figure 3.19 provides a summary of the future value topic and in each case displays the 1-2-3 formula or function that can be utilized to provide a solution to a present value problem.

Present value of a single payment
Description The present value of a future lump sum of money discounted at a specified rate.
1-2-3 formula `Lump_sum-@PV(lump_sum,interest_rate,term)*interest_rate`
Present value of an uneven stream of payments
Description Calculates the sum of the individual present values of the separate payments of the stream.
1-2-3 formula `@NPV(discount_rate,range)`
Present value of an ordinary annuity
Description Calculates the present value of a stream of equal payments assuming that these payments occur at the end of each period.
1-2-3 function `@PV(annuity_payment,interest_rate,term)`
Present value of an annuity due
Description Calculates the present value of a stream of equal payments assuming that these payments occur at the beginning of each period.
1-2-3 formula `@PV(annuity_payment,interest_rate,term)*(1+interest_rate)`
Calculating the periodic amount of a loan
Description Calculates the periodic annuity payment required to pay off the entire principal and interest of a loan over a given period.
1-2-3 function `@PMT(present_value,interest_rate,term)`
Present value of a perpetuity
Description Calculates the present value of an annuity with infinite life.
1-2-3 formula `+Annuity / Rate`

Figure 3.19. Summary of the topic of present value

Using future and present values in practice

The future value and present value concepts have several practical uses, including:

- Calculating the monthly payment of a mortgage
- Investments in national savings certificates
- Investment in index-linked savings certificates
- Saving money in building societies
- Calculating the APR using a periodic interest rate
- Calculating the APR of a bank loan from the flat rate of the loan
- Calculating the compound annual rate of growth of the earnings per share
- Calculating the maturity value of an endowment assurance contract
- Calculating the yearly pension payment for an individual
- Calculating the number of periods related to an annuity investment
- Calculating an investment project's net present value (see Chapter 5)
- Calculating an investment project's profitability index (see Chapter 5)
- Calculating an investment project's internal rate of return (see Chapter 5)
- Calculating the market price of a debenture (see Chapter 11)
- Calculating the market price of a share (see Chapter 13)

Calculating the monthly payment of a mortgage

In the United Kingdom, a large number of domestic house purchases are financed by funds obtained from building societies. Home buyers are entitled to tax relief on the interest paid each year. When the mortgage amount exceeds £30,000, the tax relief will operate on the part of the loan that does not exceed £30,000 (this limitation was valid in the year ending 5 April 1992).

Example 3.19 Calculating the monthly payment of a mortgage

Assume that an investor has a £30,000 mortgage over 25 years at 14 per cent annual interest. The yearly repayment per £1,000 is calculated by using the periodic payment of a loan formula as follows:

`@PMT(1000, 0.14, 25)` = £145.50

The monthly payment per £1,000 equals the annual payment of £145.50 divided by 12, that is, £12.12. Finally, the (gross) monthly payment on the mortgage is calculated by multiplying £12.12 by 30 to produce £363.75. The tax relief on the interest paid each year is calculated by using the basic rate of tax and is limited to the first £30,000 of the loan. The basic rate of tax is presently (that is, 1990) 25 per cent, giving a net rate of 10.5 per cent (that is, 0.14 (1–0.25)). In this case, the net monthly payment of the mortgage is £286.07. Figure 3.20 summarizes the calculation of the monthly payments of the mortgage of the investor without and with the tax relief on the interest paid.

	A	B	C
1	CALCULATING THE MONTHLY PAYMENT OF A MORTGAGE		
2	===		
3			
4		WITHOUT TAX	WITH TAX
5		RELIEF	RELIEF
6			
7	Principal	£30,000	£30,000
8	Interest Rate	14.00%	10.50%
9	Term	25	25
10	Basic Unit	£1,000	£1,000
11			
12	Annual Payment per £1,000	£145.50	£114.43
13	Monthly Payment per £1,000	£12.12	£9.54
14	Monthly Payment	£363.75	£286.07
15		==============	==============

Figure 3.20. Calculating the monthly payment of a mortgage

The outstanding amount owed to the building society at the end of any year, say T, can be calculated by using the following formula:

$$\text{Principal}\,\frac{(1+r)^N-(1+r)^T}{(1+r)^N-1}$$

where

N = the number of periods over which you will pay off the mortgage.
T = the end of the year you need to calculate the outstanding amount owed.
r = the periodic interest rate.

For example, consider the mortgage information shown in Figure 3.20 and assume that you wish to calculate the outstanding amount owned at the end of year 10. In this case, we have

$$£30{,}000\,\frac{(1+0.14)^{25}-(1+0.14)^{10}}{(1+0.14)^{25}-1}=£26{,}810.3$$

Figure 3.21 presents graphically the profile of the mortgage used in this example in the case where a tax relief is applied.

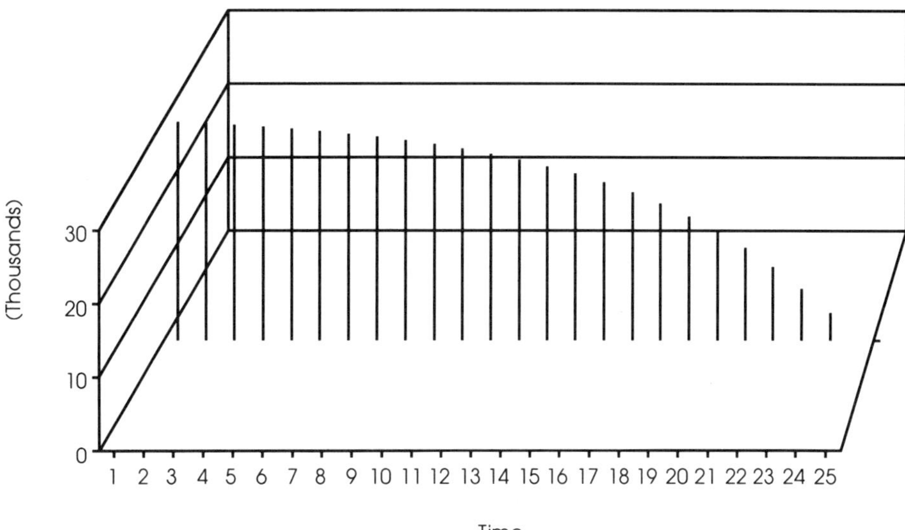

Figure 3.21. Profile of a mortgage

Problems

1 Use the data given in the above example and calculate the outstanding amount owed to the building society at the end of each of the 25 years. Illustrate your results graphically using 1-2-3.

2 Provide a sensitivity analysis of the outstanding amount owed to a building society with respect to changes in the periodic interest rate and year T (see formula above).

Investments in national savings certificates

Investments in national savings certificates are lump sum investments at a rate of return which is guaranteed for a full five-year period. The interest payments are free of income tax.

Example 3.20 Calculate the future value of an investment in the 30th issue of national savings certificates

Figure 3.22 shows the yearly interest rates offered by the 30th issue of national

```
     A          B              C          D          E          F
 1 INVESTING IN THE 30TH ISSUE OF NATIONAL SAVINGS CERTIFICATES
 2 ===========================================================
 3
 4          Principal----->     £1,000
 5          --------------------------
 6                      Year         Interest
 7          --------------------------
 8                         1       6.80%
 9                         2       7.50%
10                         3       8.60%
11                         4      10.00%
12                         5      11.40%
13                          ----------
14          AVERAGE                8.86%   <---- @AVG(C8..C12)
15          FUTURE VALUE     £1,528.77   <---- +C4*(1+B14)^5
```

Figure 3.22. The future value from investing in the 30th issue of national savings certificates

savings certificates (NSC). Assume that an investor purchased 40 units for £25 each (that is (40)(£25) = £1,000). If the investor held the certificates for the full five-year period, the average compound interest rate would be 8.86 per cent per annum. In this case, savings of £1,000 will grow to £1,528.77 over the period of five years (see Figure 3.22).

Investments in index-linked savings certificates

Investments in index-linked savings certificates are lump sum investments at a rate of return which is guaranteed to keep pace with inflation for a full five-year period. The interest payments are free of income tax.

Example 3.21 Calculating the future value of an investment in the 4th issue index-linked certificates

Figure 3.23 shows the yearly interest rates offered by the 4th issue index-linked certificates. Assume that an investor bought 40 units of £25 each (that is (40)(£25) = £1,000) and the five-year average rate of inflation (as measured by the Retail Prices Index) will be 5 per cent. If the certificates are held for the full five-year period, the average compound interest rate would be 4.05 per cent per annum and the total average rate would be 9.05 per cent. In this case, savings of £1,000 will grow to £1,542.16 (see Figure 3.23).

```
        A             B             C            E         F        G
 1 INVESTING IN THE 4TH ISSUE INDEX-LINKED CERTIFICATES
 2 ====================================================
 3
 4          Principal----->                     £1,000
 5          Average Inflation Rate ---->             5%
 6          ----------------------------
 7                     Year         Interest
 8          ----------------------------
 9                        1            3.00%
10                        2            3.25%
11                        3            3.50%
12                        4            4.50%
13                        5            6.00%
14                              ------------
15          AVERAGE                    4.05%
16          FUTURE VALUE       £1,542.16
17
```

Figure 3.23. The future value from investing in the 4th issue of index-linked certificates

The rate of return earned by an issue of index-linked certificates is not known in advance, because it is linked to uncertain inflation rates. Figure 3.24 calculates the future value of an investment of £1,000 at different five-year average inflation rates.

The results from the sensitivity are shown graphically in Figure 3.25.

Saving money in building societies

Building societies offer various investment opportunities and they have a number of advantages for investors. First, the societies provide a safe investment. A second advantage is that several schemes offered compare well with other forms of savings (for example, bank savings).

```
      A               B               C           E          F          G
21 SENSITIVITY ANALYSIS OF THE FV WITH RESPECT TO INFLATION RATE
22 ================================================================
23 Principal                        £1,000
24 Average Inflation Rate            5.00%
25 Interest rate                     4.05%
26 Total Rate                        9.05%
27                               £1,542.16
28
29
30                               +D28
31                       4.05%  £1,219.58
32                       5.05%  £1,279.32
33                       6.05%  £1,341.38
34                       7.05%  £1,405.83
35                       8.05%  £1,472.73
36                       9.05%  £1,542.16
37                      10.05%  £1,614.17
38                      11.05%  £1,688.86
39                      12.05%  £1,766.28
40                      13.05%  £1,846.51
```

Figure 3.24. Sensitivity analysis of the FV with respect to inflation rate

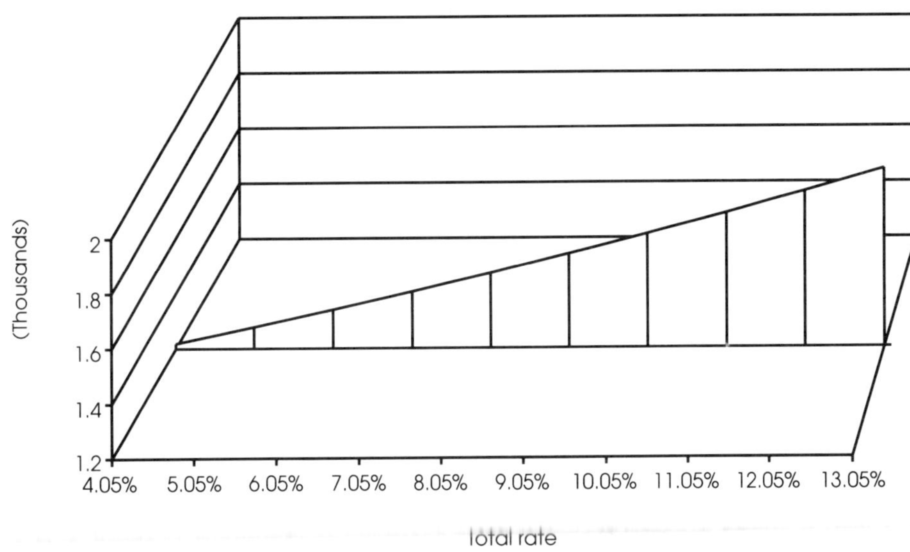

Figure 3.25. Index-linked certificates

Example 3.22 Calculating the future value of an investment in a building society

In February 1989 the Halifax Building Society offered a gross annual interest rate of 10.67 per cent for investments in the range of £500–£2,000. Assume that the gross interest rate offered will increase to 12.00 per cent in February 1992. Figure 3.26 calculates two net interest rates (assuming a basic tax rate of 25 per cent) and the future value of an investment comprised of two different annuities (the calculation uses net interest rates and assumes that the investor leaves the accumulated interest in the saving account for the whole period of five years). To calculate the future value of the investor store in cell C17 the

```
------------------------------------------------------------------------
                    A                    B             C          D
 1                               SAVING IN BUILDING SOCIETIES
 2                               ============================
 3
 4 First Annuity Amount --->               £500
 5 Second Annuity Amount -->               £800
 6
 7 ----------------------------------------------------------
 8                                     Interest rate:
 9                          Year          Gross          Net
10 ----------------------------------------------------------
11                             1         10.67%        8.00%
12                             2         10.67%        8.00%
13                             3         10.67%        8.00%
14                             4         12.00%        9.00%
15                             5         12.00%        9.00%
16                                                ------------
17                               FUTURE VALUE      £3,295.20
18
------------------------------------------------------------------------
```

Figure 3.26. Calculating the FV of an investment in a building society

following formula of 1-2-3:

```
@FV(B4,C11,3)+@FV(B5,C14,2)
```

Calculating the APR using a periodic interest rate

Consider the following two investments:

Investment A $\xrightarrow{\text{provides}}$ 3.1 per cent quarterly interest

Investment B $\xrightarrow{\text{provides}}$ 1.1 per cent monthly interest

When investors wish to compare these two investments, they need to put them on a common base. The annual percentage rate (APR), also called the effective interest rate, is used to express rates of interest charged on a periodic (for example, monthly) basis as a yearly compound rate.

A periodic interest rate can be employed to calculate the APR as follows:

Annual percentage rate	=	Future value of £1 at k% for N periods	−	Investment capital of £1
APR	=	$(1+k)^N$	−	1

where

k = the periodic rate of interest.

N = the number of periods (for example, months) over which the borrower will pay off the loan.

Example 3.23 Calculating the APR from the monthly interest rate

Figure 3.27 shows the monthly rates of interest charged by 14 UK firms (December 1989); we assume that it takes a year to repay the debt. The APR for Austin Reed is calculated by storing the following formula in cell D5:

```
(1+B5)^12-1
```

	A	B	C	D	E
1	CALCULATING THE APR FROM THE MONTHLY RATE				
2					
3	COMPANY	MONTHLY RATE (%)		APR	
4					
5	Austin Reed	2.01%		26.97%	
6	Burton	2.49%		34.33%	
7	C&A	2.40%		32.92%	
8	Currys	2.50%		34.49%	
9	Debenhams	2.49%		34.33%	
10	Halfords	1.80%		23.87%	
11	Harrods	2.20%		29.84%	
12	Littlewoods	2.20%		29.84%	
13	Marks and Spencer	2.50%		34.49%	
14	Mothercare	2.20%		29.84%	
15	Next	2.50%		34.49%	
16	Principles	2.49%		34.33%	
17	Queensway	2.40%		32.92%	
18	Sears	2.00%		26.82%	
19					

Figure 3.27. Calculating the APRs for 14 UK companies

where B5 stores the monthly interest rate charged by the firm. The contents of the cell D5 are copied in the range D6 ... D18.

Calculating the APR of a bank loan from the flat rate of the loan

The flat rate (also known as stated, or nominal, rate) is the interest rate that is charged on the amount borrowed. The flat rate can be employed to calculate the monthly interest rate, the latter is the rate that satisfies the following equation:

$$\text{PV} = \sum_{t=1}^{N} \frac{\text{AR}}{(1+k)^t}$$

where

AR = the amount of equal payments generated by the annuity, or AR = amount borrowed × flat rate/12.

N = the number of months for which payments will last.

The flat rate can be used to calculate the monthly interest compound rate which in turn can be employed to calculate the APR and vice-versa.

Example 3.24 Calculating a loan's APR from its flat rate

In 1986 National Westminster Bank plc offered a home improvement loan at a flat rate of 11 per cent. Figure 3.28 shows the calculation of the monthly interest rate and APR assuming a loan of £1,000. The monthly payment for the loan is stored in cell B6 and it is calculated by using the following formula:

`+B5*(1+B4)/12=£1000(1+0.11)/12` = £92.5

From the bank's point of view, the amount of the loan is a cash outflow and the monthly payments of £92.5 are cash inflows. The monthly rate of interest satisfies the following equation:

$$\pounds 1{,}000 = \sum_{t=1}^{12} \frac{\pounds 92.5}{(1+r)^t}$$

Figure 3.28. Calculating a loan's APR from its flat rate

	A	B	C	D	E	F
1	CALCULATING THE APR OFFERED BY A BANK FROM ITS FLAT RATE					
2	===					
3				FROM THE BANK'S POINT OF VIEW:		
4	Flat Rate	11.0%				
5	Principal	£1,000.0		Outflow	(£1,000)	
6	Monthly Payment	£92.5		1	£92.5	
7				2	92.5	
8				3	92.5	
9				4	92.5	
10				5	92.5	
11				6	92.5	
12				7	92.5	
13				8	92.5	
14				9	92.5	
15				10	92.5	
16				11	92.5	
17				12	92.5	
18					---------	
19			Monthly Interest Rate ---->		1.643%	
20			Annual Percentage Rate --->		21.602%	

This can be calculated by storing in cell E19 the following financial function of 1-2-3:

```
@IRR(0.01,E5...E17)
```

where 0.01 is a guessed value for the monthly interest rate. The APR is calculated as follows (see the contents of cell E20):

```
(1+E19)^12-1
```

If we know the APR, the amount borrowed and the life of the loan, then we can calculate the flat rate. The APR can be used to calculate the monthly interest rate (see the contents of cell B6 in Figure 3.29). The monthly payment is calculated by storing in cell B9 the following function:

```
+B5/@PV(1,B6,12)
```

Finally, the flat rate is calculated by storing in cell B10 the following function:

```
+B9*12/B5-1
```

Problem

Set up the worksheet shown in Figure 3.29 in such a way that can be used to update the annual percentage rate each time you change the flat rate or the principal.

Figure 3.29. Calculating a loan's flat rate from its APR

	A	B	C	D	E
1	CALCULATING THE FLAT RATE OFFERED BY A BANK FROM ITS APR				
2	===				
3					
4	Annual Percentage Rate	21.602%			
5	Principal	£1,000.0			
6	Monthly Interest Rate	1.643%			
7					
8					
9	Monthly Payment	£92.5			
10	Flat Rate	11.0%			
		=========			

Calculating the compound annual rate of growth of the earnings per share
The earnings per share of a firm indicate the profit after tax earned per share and they are calculated by dividing the earnings available to ordinary shareholders by the number of ordinary shares owned.

Example 3.25 Calculating the compound annual rate of growth of the earnings per share

Marks and Spencer plc had earnings of 2.10 pence per share in 1977. By 1988, a period of 12 years, they had grown to earnings of 12.07 pence per share. Figure 3.30 shows the calculation of the compound annual rate of growth of the firm's earnings per share (EPS).

Figure 3.30. Calculating the compound annual rate of growth in earnings per share

```
                   A                 B           C          D          E
1 M&S PLC:THE COMPOUND ANNUAL RATE OF GROWTH IN EPS
2 ==================================================
3
4 EPS-1977 (pence)                   2.10
5 EPS-1988 (pence)                  12.07
6                                ------------
7 COMPOUND ANNUAL GROWTH ->         15.69% <--- (B5/B4)^(1/12)-1
```

Calculating the maturity value of an endowment assurance contract
An endowment assurance policy is an annuity whose payments occur at the beginning of each period. Therefore, its maturity value can be calculated by using the future value formula of an annuity due described earlier in this chapter.

Example 3.26 Calculating the maturity value of an endowment assurance policy

Assume that a life assurance company has offered to Mr Annis a policy with monthly premiums each earning 1.3 per cent interest over a term of 10 years. If the monthly premium paid by Mr Annis is £10, then the maturity value of this policy is calculated as follows:

`@FV(10,0.013,120)*(1+0.013)` = £2,892

Calculating the yearly pension payment for an individual
The yearly pension payment of an individual involves finding the future value of his or her yearly contributions and then calculating the present value of an annuity.

Example 3.27 Calculating the yearly pension payment for an individual

An individual is 40 years old and plans to retire on his sixtieth birthday. He wants to establish a pension scheme that will require a series of equal, annual, beginning-of-year payments of £1000. If we assume an annual yield rate of 10 per cent, then the future value of the individual's yearly contributions would be

`@FV(1000,0.10,20)*(1+0.10)` = £63,002.5

In words, the individual will have £63,002.5 available at age 60.

Assume that he wishes to receive his money over a period of 15 years at the end of each year and the discount rate is also 10 per cent. Then the retirement plan will allow the individual to withdraw a yearly amount, call it CA, which satisfies the following equation:

`@PV(1,0.10,15)` CA = £63,002.5

Therefore we have:

CA = £63,002.5/`@PV(1,0.10,15)` = £8,283.2

Calculating the number of periods related to an annuity investment

We can use the future value of an annuity formula to calculate the number of periods required for a series of equal payments to compound to a specified future value. This can be achieved by using the following equation:

$$N = \frac{\ln(\mathrm{FV}_N r/\mathrm{CA} + 1)}{\ln(1 + r)}$$

or alternatively the 1-2-3 financial function `@TERM`.

Example 3.28 Calculating the number of periods required for a series of equal payments to compound to a specified future value

An individual wishes to determine how many years it would take for investment of £1,000 per year (for example, a pension scheme) to grow to £15,937.42, given a 10 per cent rate. The number of years is calculated by using 1-2-3 `@TERM` financial function as follows:

`@TERM(1000,0.10,15937.42)` = 10 years

Therefore, it will take 10 years for annual contributions of £1,000 to compound to a value of £15,937.42.

Figure 3.31 summarizes the procedures for solving ordinary annuity problems.

Summary

The basic idea of the concepts developed in the present chapter is that the value of a pound received today is more than the value of a pound received in the foreseen future. Stated differently, the pound received in the future is not as valuable as the pound received today.

1 *The future value topic* The future value is the amount at a specified future date of a single payment, or a series of equally spaced payments, calculated using a specified periodic compound interest rate. An annuity can be defined as a series of equally spaced payments for a specified number of periods; the future value of an annuity is simply the sum of individual future values of equal payments.

Interest can be compounded annually, semi-annually, quarterly, monthly, weekly, daily, or continuously. The future value increases with the frequency of the compounding period (other things being the same). The future value concept is used in several real applications, including the following: calculating the

Data for	Calculation of	Procedure
Annuity amount Interest rate Term	Future value	Multiply the annuity amount by the future value annuity factor of £1 per period at interest rate *r* for *N* periods.
Future value Interest rate Term	Annuity amount	Divide the future value by the future value annuity factor of £1 per period at interest rate *r* for *N* periods.
Annuity amount Future value Term	Interest rate	(a) Divide the future value by the annuity amount and then use the table giving the future value of an annuity of £1 per period at interest rate *r* for *N* periods. *Or* (b) Use the `@IRR` function of 1-2-3.
Annuity amount Interest rate Future value	Term	Use the `@TERM` function of 1-2-3.
Annuity amount Interest rate Term	Present value	Multiply the annuity amount by the present value annuity factor of £1 per period at interest rate *r* for *N* periods.
Present value Interest rate Term	Annuity amount	Divide the present value by the present value annuity factor of £1 per period at interest rate *r* for *N* periods.
Annuity amount Present value Term	Interest rate	(a) Divide the present value by the annuity amount and then use the table giving the present value of an annuity of £1 per period at interest rate *r* for *N* periods. *Or* (b) Use the `@IRR` function of 1-2-3.
Annuity amount Interest rate Present value	Term	Divide the present value by the annuity amount and then use the table giving the present value of an annuity of £1 per period at interest rate *r* for *N* periods.

Figure 3.31. Solving ordinary annuity problems

future value of bank deposits, calculating the maturity value of an endowment assurance contract, and so on.

2 *The present value topic* The present value is the current worth of a single payment, or a series of equally spaced payments, to be received in the future. The present value of an annuity is calculated as the sum of individual present values of equal payments. A perpetuity is an annuity having an infinite life. The present value of a perpetuity is calculated easily by dividing the annuity amount by the appropriate discount rate.

Interest can be discounted annually, semi-annually, quarterly, monthly, weekly, daily, or continuously. When the compounding period increases the present value decreases and vice versa (other things being the same). There exist many applications of the present value concept including the following: calculating the present value of government securities, calculating the periodic payments of a loan, and so on.

Questions for discussion

1 For each term shown below in the largest box provide a definition in your own words. Then check your responses against the definitions included in the chapter.

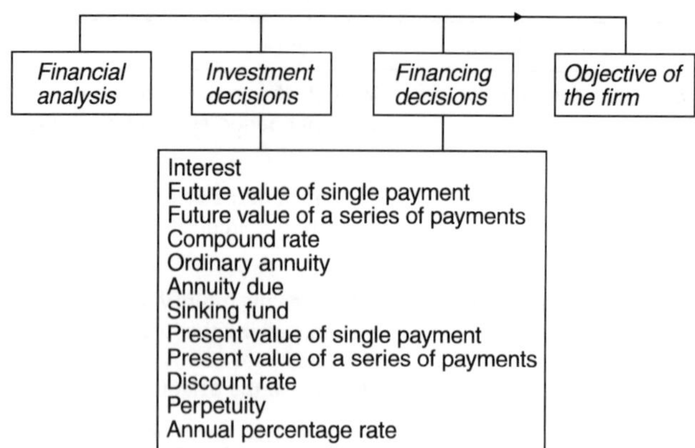

2 Discuss the following statements:
  (a) 'The pound in hand today is worth more than a pound to be received in a year from now.'
  (b) 'Do not count your future cash flows before discount.'
  (c) 'The time value of money plays an important role in several parts of the financial decision-making process.'

3 List examples where you can apply the future value concept.

4 From the 'Companies & Market' section of the *Financial Times* identify two cases where the time value of money can be used.

5 'Time value of money problems are frequently easier to understand with the help of a time line, which serves as a visual aid.' Do you agree? Provide an example illustrating a situation where a time line is used.

6 Comment on the following two typical pieces of advice:
  (a) 'Invest in a fixed-interest investment when the interest rates on offer are high, and are expected to fall in the foreseeable future.'
  (b) 'Invest in index-linked certificates during a time of inflation.'

7 In each of the following cases explain what effect the given factors would have on the future value of a single payment:
  (a) Increase in interest rate, or decrease in the number of years the money is left in the account.
  (b) Increase in interest rate, and decrease in the number of years the money is left in the account.
  (c) Increase in interest rate, and increase in the number of years the money is left in the account.
  (d) Increase in interest rate, increase in the number of years the money is left in the account and increase in the inflation during the period the principal is invested.

8 Explain the following:
  (a) 'The interest in a deposit account is compounded annually and paid quarterly.'
  (b) 'The interest in a deposit is compounded continuously and paid semi-annually.'
  (c) 'The interest in a deposit is compounded annually and paid net of tax monthly.'
  (d) 'The annual percentage rate is 26.82 per cent.'

9 List examples where you can apply the present value concept.

10 In each of the following cases explain what effect the given factors would have on the present value of a single future payment:
   (a) Decrease in discount date, or increase in the number of years until payment will be received.
   (b) Decrease in interest rate, and increase in the number of years until payment will be received.
   (c) Decrease in interest rate, and decrease in the number of years until payment will be received.
   (d) Decrease in interest rate, decrease in the number of years until payment will be received and increase in the inflation during the period involved.

11 You are given two investment projects, call them A and B. For each investment the cash flow stream provides an ordinary annuity. Consider the following possible situations:
   (a) Projects A and B are associated with the same discount rate (everything else stays the same).
   (b) Project A has a higher discount rate than B (other things being the same).
   (c) Project A has a longer useful life than project B (other things being equal).
   (d) Project A has a longer useful life than B and is associated with a higher discount rate (other things staying the same).

   Assuming that you prefer the investment with the higher present value (other things being the same) place your choices into the following diagram (for example project A):

		Discount rate:	
		Same	A greater than B
Life:	Same		
	A greater than B		

12 'If a fee is charged for the use of a credit card or if you pay a fixed fee when your monthly payment is late, the fee must be included in the APR calculation. If that fee is excluded, as in many quoted cases, the APR is misleading.' Do you agree? Substantiate your position by using a numerical example.

13 Prepare an analog model summarizing the main points discussed in the present chapter.

14 How can spreadsheets be used to facilitate the application of the concepts discussed in this chapter?

Appendix 3A The equation of the future value of a single payment under continuous compounding

Consider the following function:

$$f(k) = (1 + 1/k)^k$$

By definition we have the following:

$$\mathrm{e} = \lim_{k \to \infty} f(k) = \lim_{k \to \infty} (1 + 1/k)^k = 2.71828$$

Next the future value at the end of one year when compounding for M periods is given by

$$\mathrm{FV}_1 = \mathrm{PV}(1 + r/M)^M \tag{3A.1}$$

where r = the annual interest rate.

Let $k = M/r$. Then Equation (3A.1) can be expressed as

$$\mathrm{FV}_1 = \mathrm{PV}(1 + 1/k)^{kr} \tag{3A.2}$$

However, $\lim_{k\to\infty}(1 + 1/k)^{kr} = \mathrm{e}^r$. Therefore, substituting the last equation into Equation (3A.2), we take

$$\mathrm{FV}_1 = \mathrm{PV}\,\mathrm{e}^r$$

Finally, we have

$$\mathrm{FV}_N = \mathrm{PV}\,\mathrm{e}^{rN}$$

Appendix 3B Describing data using statistical measures

There are certain numerical measures that can be used to describe the important characteristics of a frequency distribution. These measures include those presented in Figure 3B.1.

Arithmetic mean Median Mode	Measures of central location of a distribution
Range Variance Standard deviation	Measures of variation of a distribution
Skewness Kurtosis	Measures of shape of a distribution

Figure 3B.1. Measures describing a frequency distribution

Marks and Spencer plc offers personal loans to households for home improvements. The minimum amount a household can borrow is £500 and the maximum amount is £7,500. Borrowers can also spread the cost over 12, 24, 36 and 60 months. Figure 3B.2 shows six total monthly funds borrowed together with the corresponding total monthly interest payments (we assume that each loan has a maturity of 12 months). This data will be used to calculate the eight statistical measures summarized in Figure 3B.1. The values in the data set are expressed in £000s, thus, the calculations provided in this appendix should be adjusted accordingly.

Measures of central location

In Appendix 2B, we discussed how to summarize numerical data into a frequency distribution and present such a distribution in graphical forms. A frequency distribution often shows a central tendency, that is, a tendency of higher frequencies around the value that lies centrally within the distribution and lower frequencies at its ends. Averages are measures used to represent the central value of a set of (numerical) data.

	A	B	C	D
1	FINANCIAL DATA TO BE USED FOR STATISTICAL ANALYSIS			
2	==			
3	Monthly Interest Rate ----->		1.86%	
4	--			
5	Month/Year	Amount Borrowed	Total Monthly Payments	
6		(£000s)	(£000s)	
7	--			
8	Jan-90	1,000	93.75	
9	Feb-90	970	90.94	
10	Mar-90	900	84.37	
11	Apr-90	1,100	103.12	
12	May-90	1,000	93.75	
13	Jun-90	1,030	96.56	

Figure 3B.2. Financial data to be used for calculating various statistics

Arithmetic mean

The arithmetic mean, or mean, is defined as the sum of a set of numerical values divided by the total number of values in the set. Mathematically, the mean of a set of values can be expressed as:

$$\mu = \frac{\sum_{i=1}^{N} x_i}{N}$$

where

x_i = the ith value in the data set.
N = the total number of values in the data set.

Example 3B.1 Calculating the mean of a data set.

Using the data shown in Figure 3B.2, the mean of the amounts borrowed can be calculated as follows:

$$\frac{1{,}000 + 970 + 900 + 1{,}100 + 1{,}000 + 1{,}030}{6} = £1{,}000$$

Thus, the mean value of our data set is £1,000. Stated differently the most 'representative' value in our data set is £1,000.

Some useful points

1 (Properties of the arithmetic mean) The arithmetic mean has the following properties:

(a) If a constant is added to (or subtracted from) each value of a data set, then the mean of the new set is equal to the mean of the original set plus (or minus) the constant under consideration. For example, the mean of the data set 2, 4, 6, is 4 and the mean of the data set 4, 6, 8 is 6.

(b) If each value of a data set is multiplied by a constant, then the mean of the new set is equal to the mean of the original set times the constant under consideration. For example, the mean of the data set 2, 4, 6, is 4, while the mean of the data set 4, 8, 12 is 8.

(c) The sum of the deviations of a set of values from their mean is zero. For example, consider the data set 2, 4, 6 whose mean is 4. Then the sum of $(2 - 4) + (4 - 4) + (6 - 4)$ is zero.

2 (A limitation of the mean) In some cases the mean may be 'unrealistic'. For example, assume that on 7 January 1990 an investor purchased 100 shares of Mepas Ltd, on 8 January 1990, he or she purchased 90 shares of the same firm and on 9 January 1990, the investor increased his or her existing number of shares by 60. It is unrealistic to say that the investor purchased on average 83.333 shares.

3 (Mean and extreme values) The mean is influenced by the value of each and every item in a data set. As a consequence, the mean of a data set is affected by extreme values in the set. In such a case you may be able to use the median or the mode. Alternatively, extreme values could be excluded when the mean is computed. However, note that such an alternative is clearly subjective and you should be very careful when you use it.

Median

When the values in a data set are ranked in increasing (or decreasing) order of magnitude, the median of the set divides the ranked values into two equal parts. Assume that a set of values has been arranged in order of magnitude. Then (a) the median of the set of values is the middle value if the total number of values in the set is odd, or (b) the median of the set of values is the arithmetic mean of the two middle values if the total number of values in the set is even.

Example 3B.2 Calculating the median of a data set

To calculate the median of the amounts borrowed (see Figure 3B.2), we have first to rank the numbers in column B in ascending order. The ranking can be performed by using 1-2-3's `/Data Sort` command, where the primary key in the command is column B (see Figure 3B.3).

```
        A                  B                       C                 D
 1 FINANCIAL DATA TO BE USED FOR STATISTICAL ANALYSIS
 2 ==================================================
 3 Monthly Interest Rate ----->                         1.86%
 4 ------------------------------------------------------------
 5 Month/Year       Amount Borrowed   Total Monthly Payments
 6                      (£000s)              (£000s)
 7 ------------------------------------------------------------
 8     Mar-90                 900                      84.37
 9     Feb-90                 970                      90.94
10     Jan-90               1,000                      93.75
11     May-90               1,000                      93.75
12     Jun-90               1,030                      96.56
13     Apr-90               1,100                     103.12
```

Figure 3B.3. Data after using the `/Data Sort` command

The median is £1,000 and it is calculated by just adding the two middle values and dividing the sum by 2.

Some useful points

1 (A property of median) The sum of deviations (signs are ignored) of a set of values from their median is always less than the sum of deviations from any other value in the data set.

The median does not have the algebraic properties of the mean.

2 (Median and extreme values) The median of a data set is affected by the position (determined by size) rather than by the magnitude of each number in the set. An extreme value in a data set does not easily affect the median. In cases where the set of data does contain extreme values, the median is preferred to the arithmetic mean. For example, consider an industry that is comprised of six firms. The debt to equity ratios of these firms are as follows: 10, 12, 12, 13, 13 and 65 per cent. The average value is 20.83 per cent, but it will be misleading to say that the debt to equity ratio of the average firm in the industry is 20.83 per cent. In this instance, the median should be used as a measure of the most representative value in the given set of data.

3 (Chance associated with a random selection of data) Since the median divides a set of data in half, a value selected randomly from the set is associated with a 50–50 chance of being equal to or less than the median.

4 (Locating the position of the median) If the total number of values, call it N, in a set of data is odd, the median is the value of $[(N+1)/2]$th larger number in the set. For example, the median of 41 numbers is the value of the 21st largest value in the set. If the total number of values in a set of data is even, the median is defined as the mean of the $[(N+1)/2]$th and $[(N+2)/2]$th largest values in the set. For example, the median of 42 numbers is the mean of the 21st and 22nd largest values in the set.

Mode

Assume that a set of numbers has been arranged in order of magnitude. Then the mode of the set of numbers is that value which occurs more frequently and exceeds a frequency of one.

Example 3B.3 Calculating the mode of a data set

From Figure 3B.3 it can be seen that the mode of the amounts borrowed is £1,000, since that value occurs two times and no other value occurs with that frequency.

Some useful points

1 (An advantage of the mode) The mode of a data set is unaffected by possible extreme values in the set. In addition it can be estimated even when the data is incomplete.

2 (Types of modes) A set of values may have a single mode, in which case it is called unimodal, it may have two modes and be called bimodal, or it may have several modes and be called multimodal. If a set of data has more than one mode, this probably indicates a lack of homogeneity in the data. The mode may not exist for some sets of numerical data.

Measures of dispersion

The measures of central location are used to represent the centre of a set of data. However, describing a set of data with a single measure is extremely misleading. For example, consider the following two data sets: 2, 4, 4, 6 and 1, 4, 4, 7. They both have 4 as a mean, mode and median. Thus, if one of these three measures is used to describe the two data sets under consideration, we would have to infer that they are identical. However, we can see that the spread of data in the second set is higher than that in the first one. Such sets of data can be better described if we use some measure of dispersion together with a measure of location.

Range
The range of a set of numbers is the difference between the largest and the lowest values in the set. For example, the range of the amounts borrowed, shown in Figure 3B.2, is £200.

Some useful points

1 (A disadvantage of the range) The range of a set of data can be a very poor measure of variation, since it depends only on two values in the set. Therefore, it tells us nothing about the spread of the data which falls between the two extreme values in the set. For example, consider the data sets, 0, 2, 3, 4, 100 and 0, 40, 50, 60, 100. They both have a range of 100, but the first one is the most variable.
2 (A possible alternative) If the range of your set of data provides an unreliable figure, sort the values in the set in increasing order of magnitude, disregard a few of the lowest and highest values and calculate the range of the remaining values.

Variance
The variance of a set of data is the average of the squared deviations of each value in the set about the mean. Mathematically, the variance of a set of numbers can be expressed as:

$$\sigma^2 = \frac{\sum_{i=1}^{N}(x - \mu)^2}{N}$$

where

μ = the mean of values in the data set.

Example 3B.4 Calculating the variance of a data set and interpreting the result

Below is shown the calculation of the variance of the data shown in column B in Figure 3B.2:

$$(1{,}000 - 1{,}000)^2 + (970 - 1{,}000)^2 + (900 - 1{,}000)^2 + (1{,}100 - 1{,}000)^2$$
$$+ (1{,}000 - 1{,}000)^2 + (1{,}030 - 1{,}000)^2 = 3{,}633.33$$

How can this value be interpreted? We know that it measures the dispersion of the values in a set of data around the mean, but it is very difficult to conclude whether it is large or not. In this case we could compare the variance of the data set with that of a comparable data set (see Figure 3B.4).

The mean of the data displayed in column B of Figure 3B.4 is £1,000. Its variance is 10,833.33. In this instance, we have two data sets having the same mean and values expressed in the same units. The variance of 10,833.33 is larger than that calculated earlier indicating that the values from the data set

	A	B	C	D
21				
22	Month/Year	Amount Borrowed	Total Monthly Payments	
23		(£000s)	(£000s)	
24				
25	Jul-90	1,000	93.75	
26	Aug-90	990	92.81	
27	Sep-90	820	76.87	
28	Oct-90	1,180	110.62	
29	Nov-90	1,000	93.75	
30	Dec-90	1,010	94.69	

Figure 3B.4. A set of comparable data

presented in Figure 3B.2 are more clustered around the mean than those from the data set shown in Figure 3B.4.

Some useful points

1 (Properties of the variance) The variance has the following properties:

(a) If a constant is added to (or subtracted from) each value of a data set, then the variance of the new set is equal to the variance of the original set. For example, the variance of the data set 3, 5, 6, 7 is 2.188 and the variance of the data set 5, 7, 8, 9 is also 2.188.

(b) If each value of a data set is multiplied by a constant, then the variance of the new set is equal to the variance of the original set times the constant squared. For example, the variance of the data set 5, 6, 8, 9 is 2.5 and the variance of the data set 10, 12, 16, 18 is 10.0.

(c) Consider two data sets having the same mean and the same number of observations. If the two data sets are combined, the variance of the combined data set is given by

$$\text{Combined variance} = (1/2)\,(\text{variance of the 1st data set}) + (1/2)\,(\text{variance of the 2nd data set})$$

For example, the two data sets 5, 6, 8, 9 and 1, 7, 9 and 11 have the same mean. The variance of the first data set is 2.50 and that of the second is 14.00. The variance of the combined data set (that is, 1, 5, 6, 7, 8, 9, 9, 11) is 8.25. This value can be also calculated as follows: $8.25 = (2.50 + 14.00)/2$.

2 (Characteristics of the variance) The variance has the following three characteristics: (a) it uses all the values in the data set; (b) it measures the dispersion (or spread) in the set of data; and (c) its magnitude is related to the deviation of every value in the data set from the mean.

3 (Interpretation of the variance) The variance measures variation in a set of data. A relatively small variance shows that the values in the data set tend to cluster close to the mean. A relatively high variance reveals that the values in the set are widely scattered from the mean. In the absence of any variation in the set of data, the variance is zero.

4 (A property for the sum of squared deviations) If the variance of a set of data is non-zero, the sum of the squared deviations of values in the set of data from any point other than the mean is always greater than the sum of the squared deviations of the values from their mean.

Standard deviation

The standard deviation of a set of data is the square root of the average squared deviations of the values in the set from their mean. Mathematically, the standard deviation of a data set can be expressed as the square root of variance:

$$\sigma = \sqrt{\sigma^2}$$

Example 3B.5 Calculating the standard deviation of a data set and interpreting the result

Consider Example 3B.4. The variance of the first data set is 3,633.33 and that of the second is 10,833.33. The standard deviation is defined as the square root of variance, thus the standard deviations of the two data sets are £60.28 and £104.28, respectively. The results indicate that the second data set is more variable than the first one.

Some useful points

1 (Properties of the standard deviation) The standard deviation has the following properties:

- **(a)** If a constant is added to (or subtracted from) each value of a data set, then the standard deviation of the new set is equal to the standard deviation of the original set. For example, the standard deviation of the data set 3, 5, 6, 7 is 1.48 and the standard deviation of the data set 5, 7, 8 9 is also 1.48.
- **(b)** If each value of a data set is multiplied by a constant, then the standard deviation of the new set is equal to the standard deviation of the original set times the constant. For example, the standard deviation of the data set 5, 6, 8, 9 is 1.58 and the standard deviation of the data set 10, 12, 16, 18 is 3.16.
- **(c)** Consider two data sets having the same mean and the same number of observations. If the two data sets are combined, the standard deviation of the combined data set is equal to the square root of the variance of the combined data set.

2 (Characteristics of the standard deviation) The standard deviation has the same characteristics as the variance (see useful point 2 associated with the variance).

3 (Interpretation of the standard deviation) The standard deviation can be interpreted in a similar fashion as the variance (see useful point 3 associated with the variance).

4 (Variance versus standard deviation) The standard deviation is expressed in the same units as is the mean. In practice, if the mean is expressed in pounds, the variance is expressed in 'squared pounds'. In this case, it is better to use the standard deviation which is also expressed in pounds.

Skewness and coefficient of skewness

Skewness is a measure indicating the degree to which a data set deviates from symmetry and the direction of the deviation. A set of data is positive skewed if the main concentration of the values in the data set occurs below the mean. Conversely, if the main concentration of the values in the set of data occurs above the mean, the data set is negative skewed. In mathematical terms, the skewness of a data set can be measured by using the skewness coefficient:

$$m^3 = \frac{\sum_{i=1}^{N}(x-\mu)^3}{\sigma^3}$$

Example 3B.6 Calculating the skewness coefficient of a data set

We refer to the data presented in Figure 3B.2 (see column B). The sum of the cubic deviations of the values in the set from the mean is calculated as follows:

$$(1{,}000 - 1{,}000)^3 + (970 - 1{,}000)^3 + (900 - 1{,}000)^3 + (1{,}100 - 1{,}000)^3$$
$$+ (1{,}000 - 1{,}000)^3 + (1{,}030 - 1{,}000)^3 = 0$$

Thus, the skewness coefficient is zero indicating that the values in the data set are symmetrically spread around the mean. Another indication for a perfectly symmetrical set of data is the case where the mean, median and mode are equal. From Examples 3B.1, 3B.2 and 3B.3 we see that the three measures of central tendency are equal.

Some useful points

1 (The mean, median and mode of skewed data sets) For positively skewed data sets the following is true: mean $>$ median $>$ mode. For negatively skewed sets of data the following is valid: mode $>$ median $>$ mean.

2 (Mean versus median) When we have a skewed data set, the median is a better measure of central tendency than the mean for the following reasons:
   - **(a)** the median moves in the direction of the skewness, but not as far as the mean;
   - **(b)** the median always has 50 per cent of the values in the data set above it and 50 per cent of the values below it, while such a distributional property is not generally valid for the mean.

Kurtosis and coefficient of kurtosis

Kurtosis is the degree of peakedness of a unimodal distribution. Usually the extent to which a frequency curve is peaked is measured relative to a symmetric frequency curve which is not very peaked or flat-topped. Such a curve is called mesokurtic. A frequency curve having the same mean with a mesokurtic curve but a higher peak than the mesokurtic curve is called leptokurtic. On the other hand, a frequency curve which has the same mean with a mesokurtic curve but is flatter than the mesokurtic curve is called platykurtic. Mathematically, the kurtosis of a set of numbers can be measured by using the following ratio which is known as kurtosis coefficient:

$$k_4 = \frac{\sum_{i=1}^{N}(x-\mu)^4}{\sigma^4}$$

Example 3B.7 Calculating the kurtosis coefficient of a data set

Consider the data presented back in Figure 3B.2 (see column B). The numerator of the kurtosis ratio is calculated as follows (figures are in £000s):

$$(1{,}000 - 1{,}000)^4 + (970 - 1{,}000)^4 + (900 - 1{,}000)^4 + (1{,}100 - 1{,}000)^4$$
$$+ (1{,}000 - 1{,}000)^4 + (1{,}030 - 1{,}000)^4 = 201{,}620{,}000$$

The standard deviation of the data is £60.28. Therefore, the kurtosis ratio would be

$$k_4 = \frac{201{,}620{,}000}{60.28^4} = 15.27$$

The kurtosis for a mesokurtic distribution is 3. Thus, it follows that our distribution curve is leptokurtic.

Some useful points

1 (Symmetric curves) For leptokurtic or platykurtic curves (with zero skewness) the mean, median and mode are equal because such curves are symmetric.

2 (A possible frequency curve shape) A frequency curve can be skewed and at the same time can have a kurtosis ratio either less than or greater than 3.

Example 3B.8 An easy way to calculate the variance, coefficient of skewness and coefficient of kurtosis of a data set

1-2-3 does not provide a function that can be used to calculate directly the skewness and kurtosis of a data set. However, we can use a simple procedure to do so. Figure 3B.5 shows the layout of the required worksheet. We assign a number to each measure of dispersion: number 2 for variance, number 3 for the coefficient of skewness and number 4 for the coefficient of kurtosis. Such a number is stored in cell D3. The following formula is stored in cell D8

```
(B8-$B$15)^$D$3
```

```
------------------------------------------------------------------------------
        A                 B                      C                   D       E
 1 CALCULATING THE VARIANCE,SKEWNESS AND KURTOSIS
 2 ================================================                Number ---|
 3 Monthly Interest Rate ----->                          1.86%      4.000 <|
 4 -------------------------------------------------------------------------
 5 Month/Year      Amount Borrowed   Total Monthly Payments   Procedure
 6                    (£000s)              (£000s)
 7 -------------------------------------------------------------------------
 8      Jan-90              1,000                    93.75              0
 9      Feb-90                970                    90.94        810,000
10      Mar-90                900                    84.37    100,000,000
11      Apr-90              1,100                   103.12    100,000,000
12      May-90              1,000                    93.75              0
13      Jun-90              1,030                    96.56        810,000
14              --------------------                          ------------
15                       1,000.00                             201,620,000
16                          60.28                                   15.27
------------------------------------------------------------------------------
```

Figure 3B.5. A worksheet calculating the measures of dispersion

Note that such a formula is dependent upon value stored in cell D3. Copy this formula in the range D9 ... D13.

Next we store in cell D15 the following formula

```
@IF(D3<>2,@SUM(D8 ... D13),@SUM(D8 ... D13)/6)
```

In words, if the number stored in D3 is not the representative of the variance, store in cell D15, the sum of the values in the range D8 ... D13, otherwise calculate the variance of the data set.

Lastly, the following formula is stored in cell D16

```
+D15/(B16)^D3
```

This formula calculates the skewness coefficient if D3 contains the value 3 or the kurtosis coefficient if the value 4 is stored in cell D3. This procedure recalculates the worksheet whenever you change the contents of cell D3.

This is not all. The same worksheet can also provide results when we store in cell D3 a number that is greater than 4. What do we get if we use numbers which are greater than 4? We get a series of indices that can also be used to describe several characteristics of the set of data. Such an analysis, however, is beyond the scope of this book.

Problems

1 Find the mean, median, mode, range, variance, standard deviation, skewness and kurtosis of the data given in column C of Figure 3B.5.

2 Compute the mean, median, mode, range, variance, standard deviation, skewness and kurtosis of the data given in column C of Figure 3B.4. Compare your results with those produced in Problem 1.

3 Discuss how 1-2-3 can help you with the solutions in Problems 1 and 2.

References and bibliography

Cissell, R., Cissell, H. and Flaspohler, D.C. (1982) *Mathematics of Finance*, 6th edn. Houghton Mifflin, Boston, MA.

Clayton, G.E. and Spivey, C.B. (1978) *The Time Value of Money*. Saunders, Philadelphia.

Shao, S.P. (1974) *Mathematics for Management and Finance*, 3rd edn. South-Western, Cincinnati.

Vichas, R.P. (1979) *Handbook of Financial Mathematics, Formulas, and Tables*. Prentice-Hall, New Jersey.

Wright, M.G. (1973) *Discounted Cash Flows*, 2nd edn. McGraw-Hill, London.

Zima, P. and Brown, R.L. (1984) *Theory and Problems of Contemporary Mathematics of Finance*, Schaum's Outline Series, McGraw-Hill, New York.

4 Financial analysis

This chapter includes:

- Profit and loss account and balance sheet statements
- Financial ratios
- Cash flow statement
- Forecasting sales

Financial analysis can assist creditors, investors and managers in evaluating the firm's past, current and projected performance. Financial statements are periodic summaries of detailed financial information of a firm. Therefore, the analysis of financial statements provides an important aid to financial analysis. Information from these statements is utilized to calculate financial ratios and to analyse the financial operations of the firm. Ratio analysis can assist to determine the efficiency with which a firm employs assets, the ability of the firm to earn profits and the risk associated with these profits.

This chapter presents the following financial statements, the balance sheet, the profit and loss account, the statement of retained earnings and the cash flow statement. The present chapter also discusses the use of financial ratios as a tool of analysis for financial management. Figure 4.1 illustrates how the concepts presented in the present chapter fit in the financial management framework introduced in Chapter 2.

Basic concepts, definitions and examples

Financial analysis can be defined as the utilization of analytical methods, including ratio analysis, in order to monitor and evaluate a firm's past, current and future financial position and performance. Financial analysis involves basically three major stages. The first stage deals with the selection of relevant information from the firm's financial statements and from other sources outside the firm (for example, financial information of similar firms or comparable industry financial data).

Once the financial data are collected, the second stage uses ratio analysis in order to monitor the firm's financial performance from period to period. The final stage is used to compare the firm's financial ratios with those of similar firms or with comparable industry ratios in order to draw conclusions and make recommendations. For example, the financial ratios of a firm can be compared with the ratios of similar firms in order to examine how well the firm performed in relation to its competitors.

A financial ratio is a relationship between two financial statement items at a specific point in time. A financial ratio makes related financial statement items comparable. A single financial statement item itself has no meaning but when expressed in terms of a

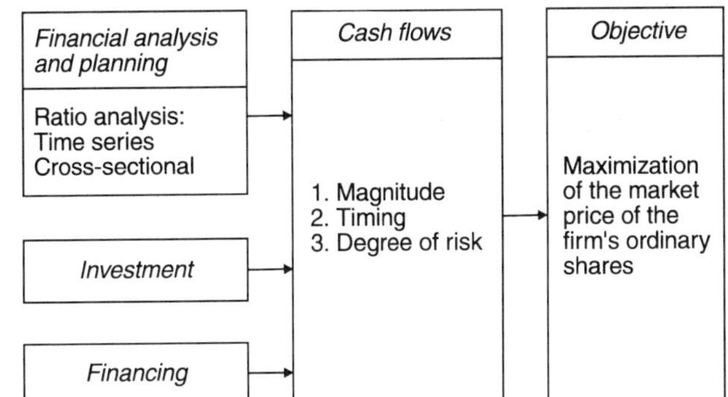

Figure 4.1. Relating financial analysis to the financial management framework developed in Chapter 2

related financial statement item it provides a meaningful figure. Pure ratios are obtained by extracting the financial items from the same financial statement (for example, balance sheet) and mixed ratios are calculated by using items from two different financial statements (for example, balance sheet and profit and loss account statement).

Example 4.1 Calculating the 1990 current ratio of GD Fashions plc

The current ratio of GD Fashions is calculated as follows (we are using GD Fashions' 1990 balance sheet):

$$\text{Current ratio} = \frac{\text{Current assets}}{\text{Current liabilities}}$$

$$= \frac{£3,798,000}{£1,520,000} = 2.50$$

The relationship between current assets and current liabilities can be stated as follows: current assets are 2.50 times the current liabilities.

Different interested parties in the firm (for example, creditors, shareholders, managers) are primarily concerned with different ratios. Short-term creditors may be most interested in examining the firm's balance sheet in order to judge its ability to meet current financial obligations as they become due. Long-term lenders, however, are primarily concerned with examining the firm's profit and loss account statement, since they are interested in the firm's past and future earnings and changes in its financial position. The current (and prospective) shareholders are interested in examining the firm's balance sheet and profit and loss account statement because they are concerned with the current and future level of risk and return of the firm. Therefore, the information provided by analysing the firm's financial position influences the shareholders' perceptions which in turn can significantly affect its share price.

The managers are responsible for the overall performance of the firm and they are using its financial statements for monitoring performance and identifying the major strengths and weaknesses of the firm. By analysing the firm's financial position, managers can discover specific problems before they become serious. For example, the analysis of financial statements may indicate that there is temporary lack of funds to meet obligations due and remedial action is required before the problem becomes serious. In this instance, managers probably arrange new short-term credit. The analysis of financial ratios assists managers in making decisions that are consistent with the objective of maximizing share price.

The accounting model

Companies communicate their package of financial information to interested parties (for example, creditors, shareholders, and so on) through financial statements. The basic financial statements of the firm are the profit and loss account, the balance sheet, and the statement of reserves.

The profit and loss account statement

The profit and loss account is a financial statement designed to illustrate a company's profitability (that is, the revenues earned and the expenses incurred) during a given period of time. The profit and loss account statement can be described by the relationship between revenues earned, expenses incurred and profit earned during a given period of time; such a relationship, called the profit and loss account equation, is given by:

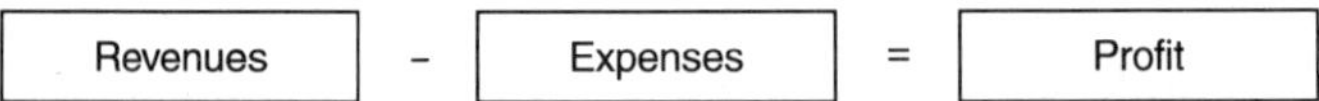

- Revenues are money earned by the firm during a specific period of time (for example, during the period 1 April 1988 to 31 March 1989). Revenues include the income from sales of goods or services, income from investments, and so on.
- Expenses are expenditures that are chargeable to the firm's trading activities during a specific period of time. Some expenses may involve the flow of cash (for example, wages, electricity) while others like depreciation do not involve the movement of cash.
- The profit in a given period is the difference between revenues and expenses of that period.

Figure 4.2 provides a general format of the profit and loss account statement.

	Turnover
minus	Cost of goods sold
equals	GROSS PROFIT
minus	Operating expenses
minus	Depreciation
equals	NET OPERATING PROFIT
minus/plus	Other expenses/revenues
equals	PROFIT BEFORE INTEREST AND TAX
minus	Interest
equals	PROFIT BEFORE TAX
minus	Tax
equals	PROFIT AFTER TAX

Figure 4.2. Calculating the accounting profit

Turnover

The turnover or sales of a firm during a specified period (usually called the accounting period) is the revenue earned from its trading activities during that same period. The profit and loss account statement includes only the revenues that were earned during the accounting period. The turnover during an accounting period can be calculated as follows:

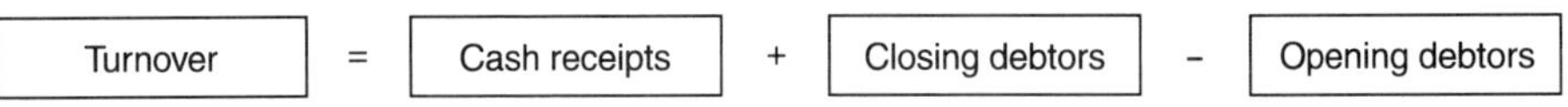

- Cash receipts during an accounting period occur when the firm's customers pay cash for its products or services during that same period.
- Debtors are parties who owe a firm money and come into existence when the firm's products or services are sold today with a promise to pay their price later. Closing debtors are those owing the firm money at the end of an accounting period. Opening debtors are those owing the firm money at the beginning of an accounting period.

Cost of goods sold

The cost of goods sold during an accounting period is the stock at cost used to earn the amount of sales for that period. The profit and loss account statement includes only the cost of those products that were sold during the accounting period. The cost of goods sold can be calculated as follows:

- The opening stock at the start of an accounting period is the closing stock of the last accounting period (that is, stock which was not sold during the last accounting period).
- Purchases refer to the cost of goods purchased during the accounting period for resale (for example, furniture in the case of a furniture retailer). The purchases can be calculated as follows:

- Cash payments during an accounting period occur when the firm pays cash to its suppliers for goods or services received.
- Creditors are parties to whom the firm owes money and come into existence when the firm receives goods or services today with a promise to pay their price later. Closing creditors are money owed by the firm at the end of an accounting period. Opening creditors are money owed by the firm at the beginning of an accounting period.

Gross profit/loss

The gross profit/loss in a given accounting period is the difference between turnover of this accounting period and the cost of goods sold incurred during that same period.

Gross profit/loss	=	Turnover	–	Cost of goods sold

Operating expenses

The operating expenses during an accounting period are expenses arising out of the operational activities of the firm during that same period. Typical operating expenses are salaries, rent, telephone, insurance, electric lighting, advertising expenses, and so on. The costs of goods sold and the operating expenses are called trading expenses.

Depreciation/amortization

Depreciation reflects the amount of value a given fixed asset loses over its useful life. There are several methods used to calculate depreciation (see Appendix 4B). Amortization reflects the amount of money an intangible fixed asset loses over its useful life (an intangible asset is an asset that lacks material form, for example, patents, copyrights, and so on). The amortization of an asset can be calculated in a similar fashion to the depreciation. The depreciation or amortization during an accounting period is a cost charged against the gross profit for that period.

Net operating (or trading) profit/loss

The net operating (or trading) profit/loss in a given accounting period is the difference between the gross profit/loss of this accounting period, the operating expenses and depreciation incurred during that same period.

Other revenues/expenses

These are revenues or expenses which do not form part of the firm's normal trading activities (these are also called non-trading revenues/expenses). For example, interest earned from an investment, profit earned from the sale of a fixed asset, money paid to employees for early retirement and so on.

Profit/loss before interest and tax

The profit/loss before interest and tax in a given accounting period is the profit achieved before the deduction of the period's financial costs such as interest and taxation. For example, the profit before interest and taxes of a firm that earns a short-term investment income (for example, interest received from an investment) can be calculated by adding the firm's short-term investment income to the net operating profit/loss.

Interest

Interest is the price paid by the firm to its creditors (for example, bank, long-term creditors, and so on) for the use of their money. The interest paid by the firm to its creditors is treated as a tax-deductible expense (that is, the interest cost is deducted from the firm's profit before interest and taxes for the accounting period before the firm's tax obligation is computed).

Profit/loss before tax

The profit/loss before tax in a given accounting period is the difference between the profit/loss before interest and tax for the accounting period and the interest expense incurred during that same period.

Tax

Corporate tax is money paid to central government out of the firm's profits. For example, if the profit before tax is £100,000 and the tax rate is 35 per cent, then the tax is £35,000 (that is, £100,000 × 0.35). The trading expenses and the other expenses (for example, interest) are treated as tax-deductible expenses. On the other hand, non-trading revenues (for example, interest received by an investment) are not tax deductible.

Profit after tax

The profit after tax in a given accounting period is the difference between the profit before tax of this accounting period and the corporate tax associated with the firm's profits during the same period.

Example 4.2. The profit and loss account statement of GD Fashions plc (1988–90)

Figure 4.3 shows the profit and loss account statment of GD Fashions plc for the years ended 31 March 1988, 1989 and 1990 (the `/Range Format` has been used to assign the format , to the range B9..D25).

```
-----------------------------------------------------------------------
               A                        B        C        D        E
 1
 2 GD Fashions plc:P&L statement for year ended 31 March:
 3 -----------------------------------------------------------
 4
 5
 6                                    1988     1989     1990
 7                                  (£000s)  (£000s)  (£000s)
 8 ----------------------------------------------------------
 9 Sales                             10,000   10,600   11,448
10 Cost of Goods Sold                 7,100    7,526    8,128
11                                  -------------------------
12 GROSS PROFIT                       2,900    3,074    3,320
13 Expenses                           2,000    2,120    2,290
14 Depreciation                          14       15       16
15                                  -------------------------
16 NET OPERATING PROFIT                 886      939    1,014
17 Short-term Investment Income          16       16       16
18                                  -------------------------
19 PROFIT BEFORE INTEREST & TAX         902      955    1,030
20 Interest                             255      259      260
21                                  -------------------------
22 PROFIT BEFORE TAX                    647      696      770
23 Taxation                             226      243      270
24                                  -------------------------
25 PROFIT AFTER TAX                     421      453      500
-----------------------------------------------------------------------
                   Assumptions for the firm's accounts:
 Interest on short-term investments:8% per year
 Interest on mortgage:11% per year
 Interest on short-term loans:10% per year
 Interest on other short-term liabilities:5% per year
 Interest on long-term loans:13% per year
 Corporate tax rate:35%
-----------------------------------------------------------------------
```

Figure 4.3. Profit and loss of GD Fashions, for years ending 31 March 1988–90

The interest on short-term income was 8 per cent per year and the amount invested in short-term securities in 1988 was £200,000, so the firm had an interest income of £16,000. The interest payable for 1988 is calculated as follows:

$$0.11 \times (500{,}000) + (0.13) \times (\pounds 1{,}000{,}000) + (0.1) \times (\pounds 250{,}000) + (0.05) \times (\pounds 900{,}000) = \pounds 255{,}000$$

where £500,000 is the firm's mortgage, £1,000,000 is the long-term debt, £250,000 is the short-term debt and £900,000 is short-term creditors. A similar calculation can be used for the interest payable during 1989 and 1990.

Figure 4.4 shows the 1-2-3 formulae used to produce the results shown in column B of Figure 4.3 (figures are in £000s). Similar formulae can also be used to produce the results sorted in columns C and D of Figure 4.4.

	Calculation	1-2-3 formula
Gross profit	10,000 − 7,100 = 2,900	+B9-B10
Net operating profit	2,900 − 2,000 − 14 = 886	+B12-B13-B14
Profit before interest and tax	886 + 16 = 902	+B16+B17
Profit before tax	902 − 255 = 647	+B19-B20
Profit after tax	647 − 226 = 421	+B22-B23

Figure 4.4. Calculating the items of the P & L statement (1988)

The balance sheet

The balance sheet is a financial statement designed to illustrate a company's financial position (that is, the assets owned, shareholders' funds and liabilities owed) at a specific point in time. The balance sheet can be described by the relationship between assets, shareholders' funds and liabilities; such a relationship, called the balance sheet equation, is expressed as:

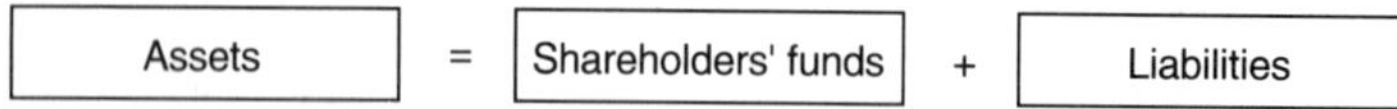

- Assets are resources of value that are owned by a firm and are expected to provide future benefits. For example, buildings, machinery, stocks, cash, and so on.
- Liabilities are debts owed by the firm to its creditors. For example, bank loans, purchases of materials on credit, and so on.
- Shareholders' funds is the amount of funds provided by its shareholders. Shareholders' funds is comprised of share capital and reserves or retained earnings. The former shows the amount of money invested in the firm by its shareholders, while the latter shows any trading profits that may have been reinvested in the business by its existing shareholders as a group.

Figure 4.5 presents a general format of the balance sheet (Appendix 4A introduces an alternative format of a balance sheet).

	Net fixed assets
plus	Current assets
equals	TOTAL ASSETS
	Total capital and reserves
plus	Long-term loans
plus	Current liabilities
equals	TOTAL CAPITAL AND LIABILITIES

where

TOTAL ASSETS = TOTAL CAPITAL AND LIABILITIES

Figure 4.5. The balance sheet

Net fixed assets

Fixed assets are assets which have a useful life of more than a year. Fixed assets include land and buildings, fittings and equipment. For example, the fixed assets of a supermarket can be shops and the land upon which they are built, cash tills, and so on. For accounting purposes, depreciation represents the annual reduction in the value of fixed assets as a result of their use. Net fixed assets show the (gross) value of the fixed assets, *minus* accumulated depreciation.

Current assets

Current assets are assets which will be converted into cash or consumed/sold usually within a year or less through the normal operations of the business. Current assets include stocks, debtors, short-term investments and cash. Short-term investments are generally investments in government securities which can be converted to cash quickly if additional funds are required.

Total capital and reserves

Total capital and reserves are made up of ordinary share capital, share premium account, preference share capital and reserves. The share premium account is opened when the firm issues ordinary shares priced in excess of their par value. For example, suppose 1,000 ordinary shares with a £1 par value are issued at £4 each, then the share premium account is £3,000.

Long-term loans

Long-term loans are money that has been loaned to the firm for a period greater than one year. They include debenture capital, long-term loans from banks, and so on. The capital employed is a sum made up of total capital and reserves and loan capital.

Current liabilities

Current liabilities are liabilities which are usually paid within a year. They include creditors, short-term loans from banks and accruals (or accrued expenses). Accruals are existing liabilities which are not yet paid. For example, taxes owed on past profits, rent owed, dividends owed, and so on.

Example 4.3. The balance sheet of GD Fashions plc (1988–90)

	1-2-3 Formula/Function
Net fixed assets 6,887 − 344 = 6,543	+B45-B46
Total current assets 1,750 + 1,160 + 200 + 452 = 3,562	@SUM(B52..B55)
Total assets 6,543 + 3,562 = 10,105	+B48+B57
Total shareholders' funds 3,000 + 1,500 + 100 + 233 + 2,442 = 7,275	@SUM(B63..B67)
Long-term debt 1,000 + 500 = 1,500	+B70+B71
Total capital employed 7,275 + 1,500 + 8,775	+B69+B73
Total current liabilities 900 + 250 + 180 = 1,330	@SUM(B79..B81)
Total capital and liabilities 8,775 + 1,330 = 10,105	+B75+B83

Figure 4.6. Calculating the items of the balance sheet (1988)

The balance sheet of GD Fashions plc at three particular points in time, 31 March, 1988, 31 March 1989 and 31 March 1990 are presented in Figure 4.7 (the `/Range Format` has been used to assign the format , to the range B45..D85). The 1-2-3 formulae or functions used to produce the results, shown in column B of Figure 4.7, are presented in Figure 4.6 (figures are in £000s). The 'ordinary shares issued' item of the balance sheet represents the number of shares owned times their par value. Figure 4.7 shows that GD Fashions had 3 million shares owned at £1 par value per share. Additionally, there was £1,500,000 of share

```
------------------------------------------------------------------------
                   A                      B        C        D         E
36 GD Fashions plc:Balance sheet as of 31 March:
37 ----------------------------------------------------
38
39
40                                      1988     1989     1990
41                                   (£000s) (£000s)  (£000s)
42 ----------------------------------------------------
43 FIXED ASSETS
44 ============================
45 Total Fixed Assets                  6,887    7,187    7,507
46 Accumulated Depreciation              344      359      375
47                                 -----------------------
48 NET FIXED ASSETS                    6,543    6,828    7,132
49
50 CURRENT ASSETS
51 ===========================
52 Stocks                              1,750    1,855    1,966
53 Debtors                             1,160    1,195    1,231
54 Short-Term Investments                200      200      200
55 Cash                                  452      488      401
56                                 -----------------------
57 TOTAL CURRENT ASSETS                3,562    3,738    3,798
58                                 -----------------------
59 TOTAL ASSETS                       10,105   10,566   10,930
60                                 =======================
61 CAPITAL EMPLOYED
62 ===========================
63 Ordinary Shares Issued              3,000    3,000    3,000
64 Preference Shares Issued              100      100      100
65 Share Premium Account               1,500    1,500    1,500
66 P&L Reserves c/f                      233      268      300
67 Other Reserves                      2,442    2,710    3,010
68                                 -----------------------
69 TOTAL SHAREHOLDERS FUNDS            7,275    7,578    7,910
70 Long Term Loan                      1,000    1,000    1,000
71 Mortgage                              500      500      500
72                                 -----------------------
73 LONG-TERM DEBT                      1,500    1,500    1,500
74                                 -----------------------
75 TOTAL CAPITAL EMPLOYED              8,775    9,078    9,410
76
77 CURRENT LIABILITIES
78 ===========================
79 Creditors                             900      988    1,000
80 Short-Term Loans                      250      250      250
81 Accruals                              180      250      270
82                                 -----------------------
83 TOTAL CURRENT LIABILITIES           1,330    1,488    1,520
84                                 -----------------------
85 TOTAL CAPITAL & LIABILITIES        10,105   10,566   10,930
86                                 =======================
```

Figure 4.7. Balance sheet of GD Fashions as at 31 March 1988–90

premium account, which means that the ordinary shares of the firm were sold in excess of their par value. The firm obtained a total of £1,500,000 over and above the par value of the ordinary shares, or equivalently £0.50 per ordinary share.

The other reserves of the firm at the end of 1988 were £2,442,000 representing the profits which were not distributed as dividends or as P&L reserves c/f (see also the next section). The other reserves of the firm at the end of 1989 were £2,710,000. If we compare these figures we find that £2,710,000 – £2,442,000 = £268,000. This figure is transferred from the retained earnings statement, slight deviation occurs due to rounding (see Figure 4.8). When trading profits are retained in the business after the payment of dividends and tax, they are generally used to expand the business.

The retained earnings statement

The retained earnings statement is designed to illustrate the changes in the amount of profits which have been retained in the business over a specified period of time. The statement of retained earnings can be described by the relationship between the current year's profit, the reserves brought forward (b/f) from the previous balance sheet, the profit available to the shareholders in the form of dividends, and the reserves carried forward (c/f) to the next balance sheet; such a relationship, called the equation of the retained earnings statement, is expressed as:

Profit + P&L reserves b/f = Dividends + Other reserves + P&L reserves c/f

- The P&L reserves b/f are part of the previous years' profits which are available for appropriation.
- Dividends represent the amount of profit recommended by the board of directors to be paid to shareholders.
- Other reserves are part of the (after-tax) profits kept by the firm rather than paid as dividends or classified as P&L reserves c/f.
- The P&L reserves c/f are part of the current year's (after-tax) profits which will be available in a subsequent year.

Example 4.4 The retained earnings statement for GD Fashions plc (1988–90)

The retained earnings statement of GD Fashions plc for the years ending

	A	B	C	D	E
25	PROFIT AFTER TAX	421	453	500	
26	P&L Reserve b/f	180	234	268	
27		-------	-------	-------	
28	AVAILABLE FOR APPROPRIATION	601	687	768	
29	Preference Dividends	14	14	14	
30	Ordinary Dividends	120	137	154	
31	Transfer to Other Reserves	234	268	300	
32		-------	-------	-------	
33	P&L RESERVES c/f	234	268	300	
34		=======	=======	=======	

Preference dividends:14%*(book value of preference shares)
Transfer to other reserves:
(available for appropriation funds-dividends)/2
Slight deviations occur due to rounding.

Figure 4.8. Retained earnings statements for GD Fashions plc for years ending 31 March 1988–90

31 March, 1988, 1989 and 1990 are shown in Figure 4.8. For example, GD Fashions had available for appropriation £601,000 during 1988, paid £14,000 in dividends to preference shareholders, £120,000 in dividends to ordinary shareholders and transferred to other reserves £234,000. Therefore, the P&L reserves c/f for 1988 simply equals the profit available for appropriation *less* the profit distributed as dividends *less* the profit transferred to other reserves. GD Fashions had a P&L reserves c/f of £234,000 in 1988 (slight deviations occur due to rounding).

Notice that the income and retained earnings statements cover a specified period of time (for example, a year) and the balance sheet shows the financial position of the firm at a specific point in time (for example, at the last day of the calendar year). Figure 4.9 illustrates the position of a firm's financial statements in time.

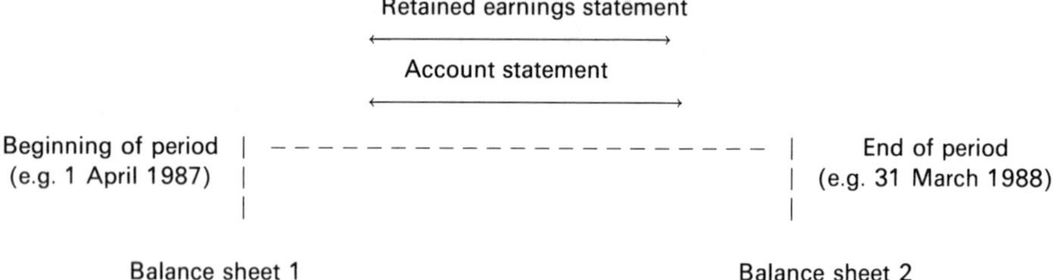

Figure 4.9. The position of a firm's financial statements in time

Figure 4.10 provides a summary of the information reflected by the firm's profit and loss account, retained earnings and balance sheet statements.

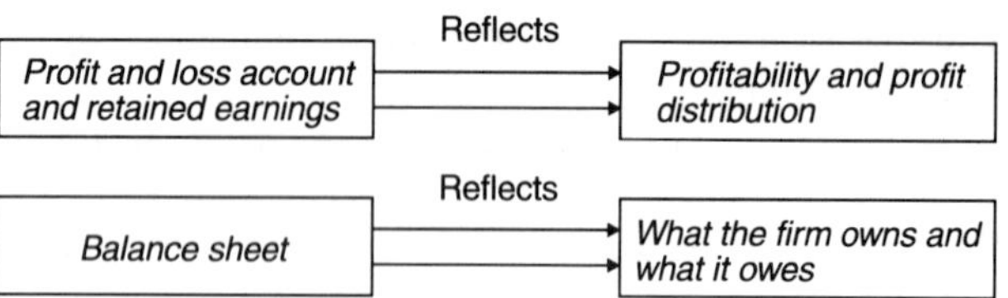

Figure 4.10. Information reflected by a firm's financial statements

Relationship of the financial statements

The statement of retained earnings designed for a period of time (for example, covering the period 1 April 1987 to 31 March 1988) is the connecting link between the profit and loss account statement for that same period and the balance sheet at the end of the period (for example, 31 March 1989). The reserves carried forward from the profit and loss account are shown in the balance sheet, together with the share capital. Figure 4.11 illustrates the relationship between three financial statements.

Financial ratio analysis

The balance sheet and the profit and loss account statement provide the input data for calculating financial ratios. There are two basic methods in which financial ratios are utilized: (a) in cross-sectional analysis; and (b) in time-series analysis.

Cross-sectional analysis

This method provides a comparison of the firm's position (at a fixed point in time) with other firms in the same industry (or firms in a similar position). In certain cases

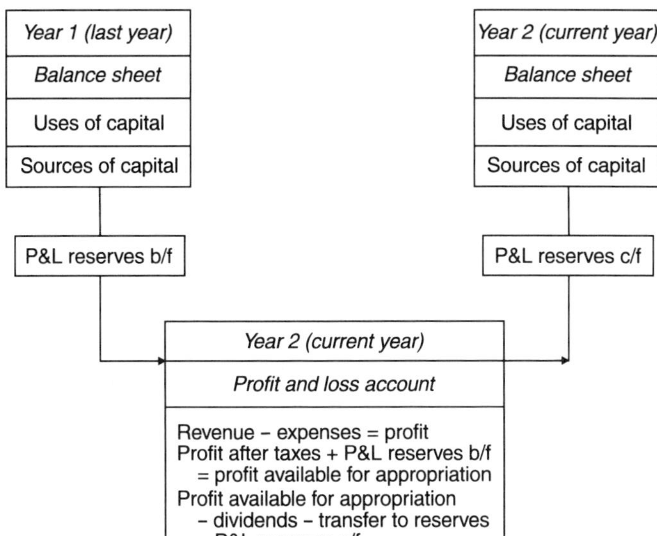

Figure 4.11. Relationship between the three financial statements

the industry average is used as a benchmark to produce meaningful comparisons. The ratios employed have been adapted through time leading to the following generally accepted five-group classification:

- Liquidity or solvency
- Activity
- Gearing
- Profitability
- Investment

The financial director of a firm should constantly monitor all these groups of ratios with the intention of satisfying the current (and future) shareholders. It is worth while noting that in addition to the financial ratios presented in this chapter, there may be other ratios which are better indicators in certain situations.

Solvency or liquidity ratios

These ratios indicate the ability of the firm to meet its maturing short-term financial obligations with cash flows generated from its current assets. Figure 4.12

Solvency ratios indicate the firm's business and financial risk

Ratio	Formula	Significance	Expressed in
Current or working capital	$\frac{\text{Current assets}}{\text{Current liabilities}}$	Ability of the firm to pay its short-term liabilities as they become due with cash flows generated from its current assets	Times
Quick or acid test	$\frac{\text{Current assets} - \text{stocks}}{\text{Current liabilities}}$	Ability of the firm to meet its short-term liabilities by generating cash flows from its most liquid assets	Times

Figure 4.12. The two most important liquidity ratios

gives information about the two most important liquidity ratios. Business risk is the risk that the firm might not be able to cover costs related to its cost of goods sold and its operating expenses. Financial risk is the risk that the firm might not be able to cover costs related to its long-term debt and its preference shares.

Example 4.5 Calculating two solvency ratios for GD Fashions plc for 1988, 1989 and 1990

The current and acid test ratios of GD Fashions and the companion industry averages are presented in Figure 4.13. The current ratio and acid ratio are decreasing and for 1989 and 1990 are relatively lower than the corresponding industry averages, but they are not low enough to cause concern. These results reveal that the firm for 1989 and 1990 had lower levels of current assets in relation to current liabilities than those of the average firm in the industry. They also reveal that GD Fashions is liquid and in a position to pay its short-term debt obligations as they come due. For example, with an acid test ratio of 1.21, GD Fashions could liquidate 82.64 per cent of its liquid assets (that is, 1/1.21) and still pay off all its current liabilities. In this case, we have the following: (liquid assets) × 82.64 per cent = current liabilities (that is, (£3,798 – £1,966) × 82.64 per cent = £1,514, the deviation is due to rounding).

Figure 4.13. Two solvency ratios for GD Fashions (1988–90) and the corresponding industry averages

	A	B	C	D	E
90					INDUSTRY
91					STANDARD
92	1> SOLVENCY	1988	1989	1990	1988-1990
93	============================				
94	Current	2.68	2.51	2.50	2.61
95	Acid Test	1.36	1.26	1.21	1.32

Activity ratios

These ratios indicate how efficiently a firm is utilizing its assets to generate sales. Some of the most important activity ratios are shown in Figure 4.14.

Example 4.6 Calculating five activity ratios for GD Fashions plc for 1988, 1989 and 1990

Fixed assets turnover, total assets turnover and working capital turnover are increasing and they are better than the corresponding industry averages (excluding the total asset turnover for 1988 and 1989) indicating that the firm is generating higher levels of sales from its assets relative to the average firm in the industry. Stock turnover is on the increase and it is better than the corresponding industry average. The firm may have a smaller investment of stocks relative to sales than the average firm in the industry.

The firm's average collection period decreases and is lower than the corresponding industry average. This may suggest that the firm's credit policy is more restrictive (that is, sales are restricted only to the very best customers) than the credit policy of the average firm in the industry. The activity ratios indicate that the firm is managing its resources effectively (see Figure 4.15).

Activity ratios indicate the firm's business risk

Ratio	Formula	Significance	Expressed in
Stocks turnover	$\frac{\text{Cost of goods sold}}{\text{Value of stocks}}$	Indicates how efficiently the firm is managing and selling its stocks	Times
Average collection period	$\frac{\text{Debtors}}{\text{Monthly sales}}$	Indicates the average number of months it takes for the firm to collect the money from its debtors	Periods
Net working capital turnover	$\frac{\text{Sales}}{\text{Net working capital}}$	Indicates how efficiently the firm uses its investments in net working capital in generating sales	Times
Fixed assets turnover	$\frac{\text{Sales}}{\text{Fixed assets}}$	Indicates how efficiently the firm utilizes its fixed assets in generating sales	Times
Total assets turnover	$\frac{\text{Sales}}{\text{Total assets}}$	Indicates how efficiently the firm utilizes its total assets in generating sales	Times

Figure 4.14. The most important activity ratios

	A	B	C	D	E
97					INDUSTRY
98					STANDARD
99	2> ACTIVITY	1988	1989	1990	1988-1990
100	============================				
101	Stock Turnover	4.06	4.06	4.13	3.82
102	Average Collection Period	1.39	1.35	1.29	1.50
103	Working Capital Turnover	4.48	4.71	5.03	4.01
104	Fixed Asset Turnover	1.53	1.55	1.61	1.40
105	Total Asset Turnover	0.99	1.00	1.05	1.00

Figure 4.15. Five activity ratios for GD Fashions (1988–90) and the corresponding industry averages

Gearing ratios

These ratios indicate the firm's extent of debt and its ability to meet its debt obligations as they come due. The liquidity ratios are mainly associated with the short-term obligations whereas the present ratios are related to the total liabilities (that is, long-term debt + current liabilities) or long-term debt. The five most important gearing ratios are presented in Figure 4.16.

Example 4.7 Calculating five gearing ratios for GD Fashions plc for 1988, 1989 and 1990

Figure 4.17 shows five gearing ratios calculated for GD Fashions for 1988 to 1990. The gearing ratios of the firm (except the times interest earned) are generally decreasing and they are lower than the companion industry averages. These results reveal that the gearing position of GD Fashions is less risky than its typical competitor and that the firm has used much less debt than the average firm in the industry. The times interest earned ratio is higher than the corresponding industry average revealing that the firm provides creditors with a larger margin of safety (that is, a lower level of risk) than the average competitor in the industry. The increase in the times interest earned is a positive indicator

Gearing ratios indicate the firm's financial risk

Ratio	Formula	Significance	Expressed in
Total debt to total assets	$\frac{\text{Total liabilities}}{\text{Total assets}}$	Indicates the proportion of total assets financed by total debt	%
Long-term debt to total assets	$\frac{\text{Long-term debt}}{\text{Total assets}}$	Indicates the proportion of total assets financed by the long-term debt	%
Long-term debt to fixed assets	$\frac{\text{Long-term debt}}{\text{Fixed assets}}$	Indicates the proportion of fixed assets financed by long-term debt	%
Total debt to equity	$\frac{\text{Total liabilities}}{\text{Shareholders' equity}}$	Indicates the amount of funds provided by total liabilities in relation to the amount of funds provided by the owners	%
Times interest earned	$\frac{\text{Profit before tax} + \text{interest}}{\text{interest}}$	Indicates the ability of the firm to meet its fixed interest charges after all expenses except interest and tax have been paid	Times

Figure 4.16. The most important gearing ratios

	A	B	C	D	E
107					INDUSTRY
108					STANDARD
109	3> GEARING	1988	1989	1990	1988-1990
110	============================				
111	Total Debt/Total Assets	28.00%	28.28%	27.63%	33.40%
112	Long Term Debt/Total Assets	14.84%	14.20%	13.72%	15.20%
113	Long Term Debt/Fixed Assets	22.93%	21.97%	21.03%	23.90%
114	Total Debt/Equity	39.44%	39.96%	38.67%	58.30%
115	Times Interest Earned	3.54	3.68	3.96	2.22

Figure 4.17. Five gearing ratios for GD Fashions (1988–90) and the corresponding industry averages

since more profits before tax are available to meet interest charges. Because the firm is able to cover its interest payments it may well have no difficulties in raising more funds through new debt. GD Fashions appears to be able to meet safely its long-term debt obligations as they come due.

Profitability ratios

These ratios indicate the ability of the firm to generate profits on sales, assets and owners' investments. The important profitability ratios are given in Figure 4.18.

Example 4.8 Calculating six profitability ratios for GD Fashions plc for 1988, 1989 and 1990

The gross profit margin is higher than the industry average suggesting that GD Fashions' pricing policies and the methods used to control production costs are more effective than those of the average firm in the industry. The firm's net profit margin is higher than the industry average revealing that GD

Profitability ratios indicate the firm's profitability

Ratio	Formula	Significance	Expressed in
Gross profit margin	$\frac{\text{Gross profit}}{\text{Sales}}$	Indicates the percentage of each sales pound left over after deducting the costs of goods sold	%
Net profit margin	$\frac{\text{Profit after tax}}{\text{Sales}}$	Indicates the percentage of each sales pound left over after deducting all expenses, including interest and tax	%
Return on current assets	$\frac{\text{Profit after tax}}{\text{Current assets}}$	Indicates the firm's ability in obtaining a satisfactory return on its current assets	%
Return on fixed assets	$\frac{\text{Profit after tax}}{\text{Fixed assets}}$	Indicates the firm's ability in obtaining a satisfactory return on its fixed assets	%
Return on investment	$\frac{\text{Profit after tax}}{\text{Total assets}}$	Indicates the firm's ability in obtaining a satisfactory return on its total assets	%
Return on ordinary shareholders' equity	$\frac{\text{Profit after tax}}{\text{Shareholders' equity}}$	Measures the rate of return gained on the book value of the ordinary shareholders' equity	%

Figure 4.18. The most important profitability ratios

Fashions may have lower expenses than the average firm in the industry. GD Fashions' high return on assets suggests that the firm is utilizing its assets better than its competitors. The return on equity ratio is higher than the industry average indicating that the firm has earned more return for its shareholders as compared with the return realized by the shareholders of the average firm in the industry. The profitability ratios indicate that GD Fashions enjoys a good financial health and its management team is able to generate satisfactory profits on sales, total assets and shareholders' funds (see Figure 4.19).

```
                  A                          B        C        D         E
117                                                                  INDUSTRY
118                                                                  AVERAGE
119 4> PROFITABILITY                       1988     1989     1990 1988-1990
120 ============================
121 Gross Profit Margin                  29.00%   29.00%   29.00%    23.20%
122 Net Profit Margin                     4.21%    4.27%    4.37%     2.50%
123 Return on Current Assets             11.82%   12.12%   13.16%     8.20%
124 Return on Fixed Assets                6.43%    6.63%    7.01%     4.00%
125 Return on Total Assets                4.17%    4.29%    4.57%     3.10%
126 Return on Equity                      5.87%    6.06%    6.40%     4.30%
```

Figure 4.19. Five profitability ratios for GD Fashions (1988–90) and the corresponding industry averages

Investment ratios

These ratios indicate the potential of a firm to be considered as an investment and they are thus useful to everybody who has funds to invest in the firm. Figure 4.20 shows five important investment ratios.

Investment ratios indicate the firm's performance (share prices and yields)

Ratio	Formula	Significance	Expressed in
Earnings per ordinary share	$\frac{\text{Profit after tax}}{\text{No. of ordinary shares}}$	Indicates the profit after tax earned per ordinary share	Pounds
Dividends per ordinary share	$\frac{\text{Ordinary dividends}}{\text{No. of ordinary shares}}$	Indicates the amount of dividends attributable to each ordinary share	Pounds
Ordinary dividend coverage	$\frac{\text{Profit after tax}}{\text{Total dividends}}$	Indicates the number of times dividends can be paid from the firm's profit after tax	Times
Total assets per ordinary share	$\frac{\text{Total assets}}{\text{No. of ordinary shares}}$	Indicates the value in total assets owned by each ordinary share	Pounds
Price to earnings	$\frac{\text{Share price (market)}}{\text{Earnings per share}}$	Indicates how much investors are willing to pay for the firm's reported earnings per share	Times

Figure 4.20. The most important investment ratios

Example 4.9 Calculating five investment ratios for GD Fashions plc for 1988, 1989 and 1990

The investment ratios of GD Fashions are presented in Figure 4.21. A comparison of the earnings per share ratio with the industry average is not meaningful since a firm's earnings per share ratio can be affected by internal activities (for example, stock dividends). In this case, a time-series analysis must be performed. The results show that the earnings per share of GD Fashions are on the increase, this is a very positive sign. The total assets per ordinary share are on the increase. The dividend cover ratio shows that the prospects of continuing to receive the expected dividends are good.

Finally, the price–earnings ratio is on the increase indicating that investors consider favourably the future prospects of the firm. For each year the price–earnings ratio is greater than the industry average suggesting that investors value GD Fashions more than the average firm in the industry, perhaps because its growth potential of earnings is perceived to be greater than that of the average firm in the industry. The investment ratios reveal that the overall performance of

	A	B	C	D	E
128					INDUSTRY
129					STANDARD
130					1988-1990
131	5> INVESTMENT	1988	1989	1990	
132	============================				
133	Earnings per Ordinary Share	0.14	0.15	0.17	
134	Dividend per Ordinary Share	0.04	0.05	0.05	
135	Ordinary Dividend Coverage	3.51	3.31	3.27	2.50
136	Total Assets/No of Shares	3.37	3.52	3.64	
137	Price/Earnings	14.25	15.89	16.20	12.34

Note: We assume that the market price per share of GD Fashions plc was £2.00 on 31 March 1988, £2.38 on 31 March 1989, and £2.75 on 31 March 1990.

Figure 4.21. Five investment ratios for GD Fashions (1988–90) and the corresponding industry averages

the firm is good and the market expects a good future earnings potential (slight deviations occur due to rounding).

Using the /Copy command of 1-2-3 in ratio calculations

When you calculate the ratios of a firm through time, the /Copy command of 1-2-3 will save you time by letting you duplicate formulae from one part of the worksheet to other parts. You can use formulae to calculate the financial ratios of a firm for the first year and then copy these formulae to other parts of the worksheet where they will calculate values using the financial data for other years (see example illustrated in Figure 4.22).

```
-------------------------------------------------------------------------
                A                  B        C       D         E
1                                  1988     1989      1990
2       P & L Statement
...
34
35
36      Balance Sheet
...
86
...
94                             Formulae      USE THE
95                             containing    /COPY
96      Ratios                 references    COMMAND
...                            to cells in   TO COPY
137                            colunm B      THE RANGE
                                             B94..B95
                                             TO THE
                                             RANGE
                                             C94..D95,
                                             THE RANGE
                                             B101..B105
                                             TO THE
                                             RANGE
                                             C101..D105
                                             ETC
-------------------------------------------------------------------------
```

Figure 4.22. Using the /Copy command in calculated ratios through time

Time series analysis

As the name suggests this method involves the analysis of the firm's financial ratios through time. Usually past ratios indicate the underlying trend of the firm's performance and, by using simple methods, future projections can be made. This method utilizes the same groups of ratios as the cross-sectional method.

The most useful and informative method of financial ratio analysis is one which combines both cross-sectional and time-series analyses. Such a combined analysis considers how a firm's ratios have changed over time relative to the changes over time of the corresponding industry ratios.

Example 4.10 Illustrating trend analysis: The case of Marks and Spencer plc

Figure 4.23 shows four financial ratios for Marks and Spencer over nine years (1980–88) and the companion industry standards over the same period. The comparison of Marks and Spencer trends with industry trends illustrates how

	A	B	C	D	E	F	G	H	I	K
1	FOUR FINANCIAL RATIOS OF MARKS AND SPENCER PLC (1980-88)									
2										
3										
4	RATIO	1980	1981	1982	1983	1984	1985	1986	1987	1988
5										
6	Return on FA	13.46	12.94	9.31	9.31	11.08	11.98	15.11	16.45	14.92
7	Industry	13.75	12.23	9.88	12.08	13.23	14.05	16.47	17.03	16.10
8										
9	Net Profit Margin	4.97	4.63	4.85	4.55	5.06	5.18	6.00	6.43	7.16
10	Industry	3.80	3.81	3.33	3.85	4.24	4.92	5.59	6.16	6.09
11										
12	Quick	0.34	0.51	0.46	0.52	0.35	0.44	0.48	0.38	0.66
13	Industry	0.86	0.85	0.83	0.86	0.81	0.74	0.73	0.73	0.80
14										
15	FA Turnover	2.73	2.83	1.94	2.07	2.22	2.34	2.54	2.56	2.09
16	Industry	3.66	3.22	2.97	3.08	3.14	2.87	2.93	2.73	2.65
17										
18										

Figure 4.23. Four financial ratios of Marks and Spencer and industry averages (1980–88)

well the firm has performed across time relative to its competitors. Such a trend analysis may help the firm's managers to provide an explanation related to the trends in the firm's financial ratios. For example, if the net profit margin ratio of Marks and Spencer rises, this may indicate rising industry profit margins or that the firm is performing better than its major competitors.

The quick ratio of Marks and Spencer appears to be considerably low. However, a cash retail firm such as Marks and Spencer realizes a rapid turnover of stocks enabling the firm to operate with low quick ratio.

The four financial ratios of Marks and Spencer, for the period of nine years, as well as the corresponding industry standards can be presented graphically as shown in Figure 4.24(a)–(d).

Figure 4.25 summarizes the financial ratio groups discussed in this chapter together with information related to each group.

Evaluation of ratio analysis

Ratio analysis has several advantages. First, ratios are easy to calculate. Second, properly used ratio analysis can help to evaluate a firm's financial position and performance. The financial position of the firm can be assessed when all ratios are compared with the firm's past ratio (time-series analysis) and the ratios of other firms in the industry at the same point in time (cross-sectional analysis). Third, financial ratios provide useful tools for implementing new policies. Finally, ratio analysis can be combined with statistical methods to produce useful tools for evaluating the financial performance of a firm.

We should also take into account the possible limitations of ratio analysis.

1 It is difficult to create industry average ratios for firms that operate in different industries. Comparing the ratios of a firm that engages in multiple lines of industry with single industry average ratios may not be meaningful.
2 The ratios of a firm can be compared with the industry average ratios to examine the performance of the firm in relation to the average firm in the industry. In some cases, industry average ratios are not available and thus the usefulness of ratio analysis becomes limited.
3 Different firms in the same industry may follow different accounting procedures

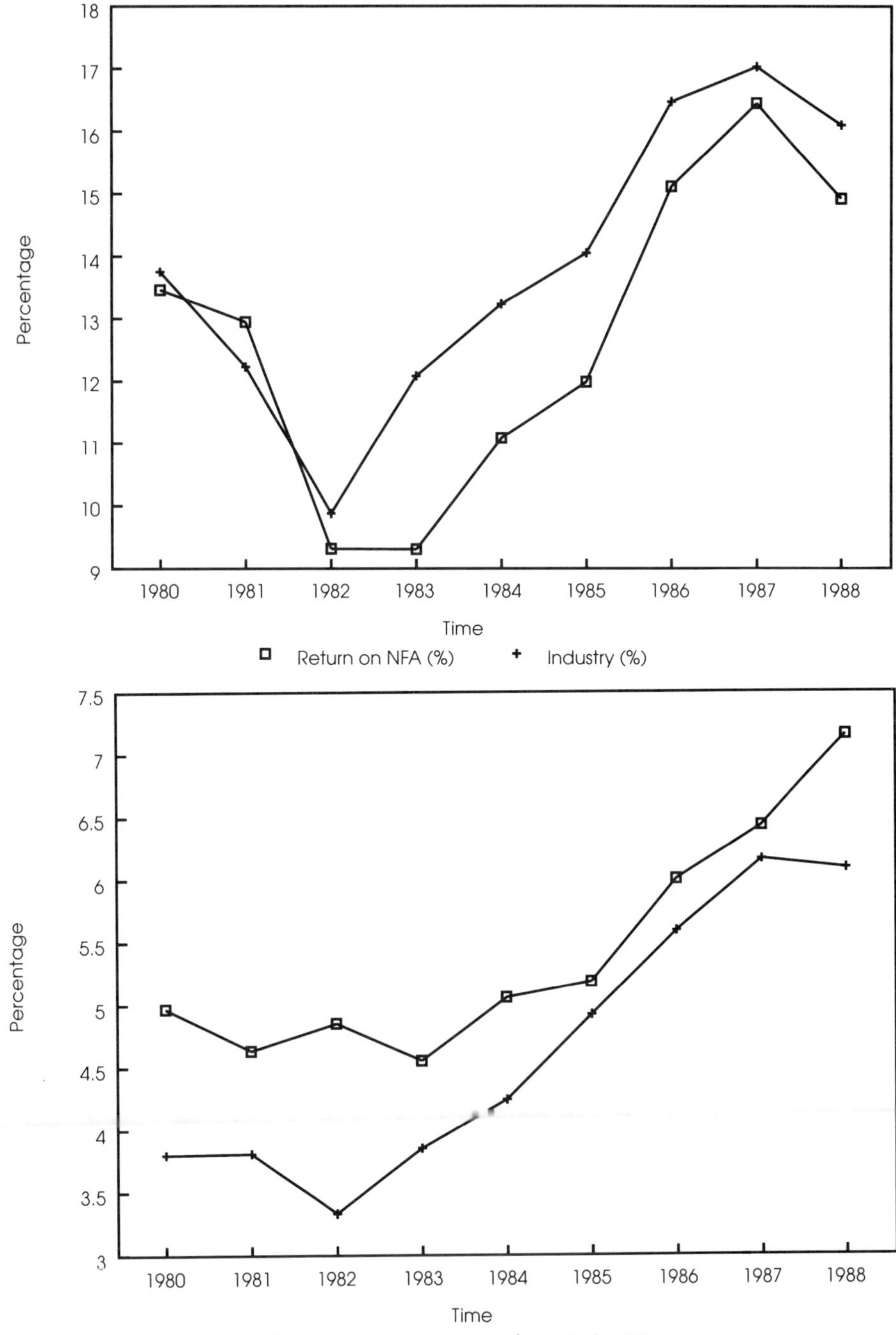

Figure 4.24a. Trend analysis of Marks and Spencer return on net fixed assets versus the industry average (1980–88)

Figure 4.24b. Trend analysis of Marks and Spencer net profit margin versus the industry average (1980–88)

for depreciation, leases, mergers and acquisitions, and so on. When a firm has different accounting methods from its competitors, comparing its ratios with those of its competitors can prove meaningless.

4 Ratio analysis is based upon historical data and does not take inflation into consideration. Comparing the firm's historical ratios over time, or

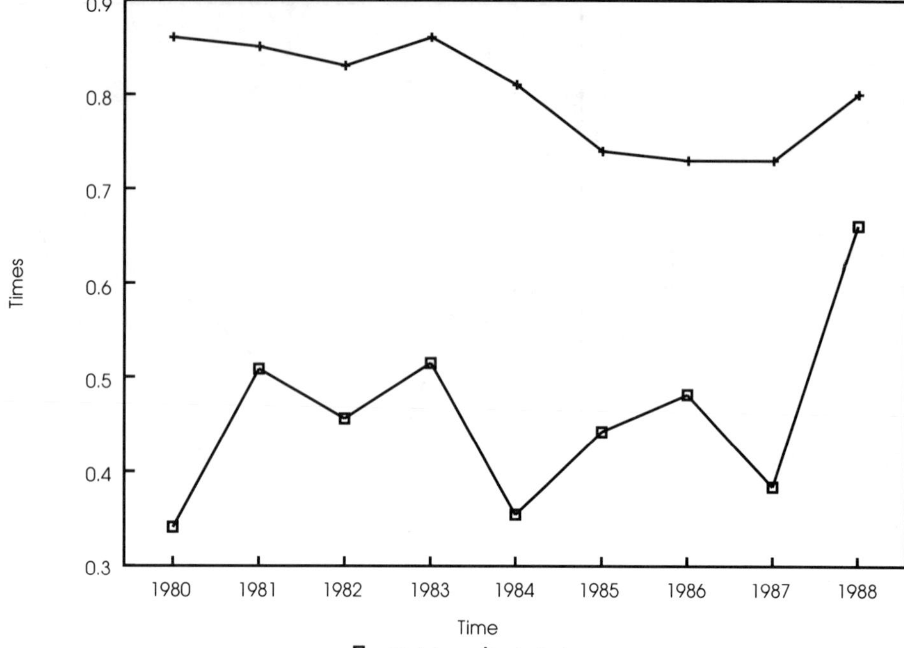

Figure 4.24c. Trend analysis of Marks and Spencer quick ratio versus the industry average (1980–88)

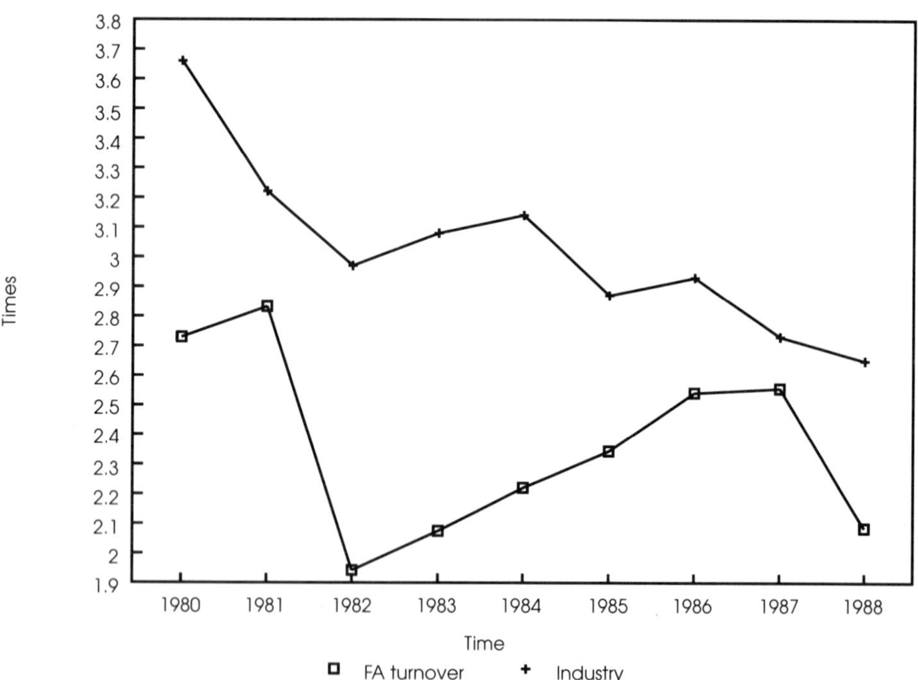

Figure 4.24d. Trend analysis of Marks and Spencer fixed asset turnover ratio versus the industry average (1980–88)

comparing financial ratios of firms of different ages may produce misleading conclusions.

5 Examining a ratio in isolation may create an unclear picture of the firm's financial situation. For example, examining the quick ratio in isolation may give a false

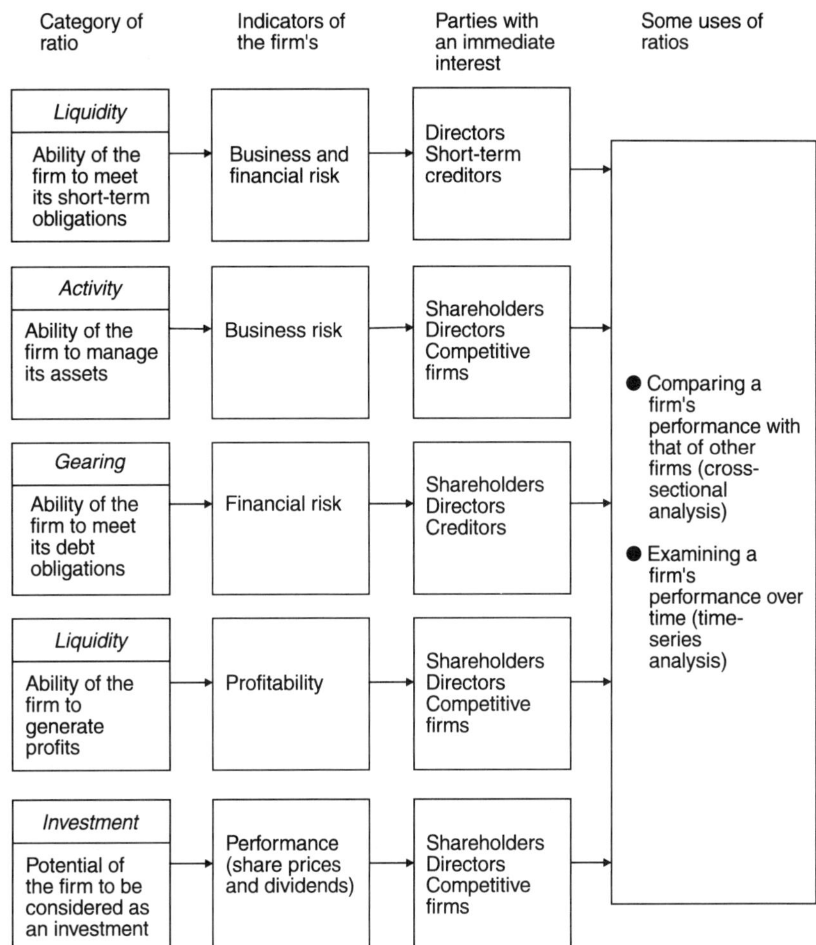

Figure 4.25. A summary of the ratio groups discussed in this chapter

description of the firm's liquidity; the true liquidity position of the firm emerges when the average collection period, quick and inventory ratios are examined simultaneously.

6 The management team may manipulate the firm's financial statements to reveal a better picture to external parties; therefore, certain ratios will not be accurate indicators of the firm's financial position.

7 Ratio analysis based upon interim financial statements can be misleading when the firm's sales are affected by seasonal factors.

8 Finally, ratios are based upon past data and attention is needed when they are used for predictive purposes. Management should not rely on predictions based upon single ratio trends. A simultaneous analysis of financial ratios can be conducted by utilizing both ratios and statistical methods.

Cash flow statement

In addition to the profit and loss account statement and the balance sheet there is another financial statement called the cash flow statement (or sources and uses of cash statement). The latter shows the cash receipts and cash payments for an accounting period and provides information about the impact of the firm's investing and financing activities on cash flows over the accounting period.

The information provided by the cash flow statement cannot be found in the other two statements, for example, the sources of cash used to finance the firm's new investments, the cash amount generated by the firm's operations, and so on. The cash flow statement is designed to classify the sources of cash (that is, the ways in which cash has been generated) for a specified period and the uses or applications of cash (that is, the ways in which the cash has been used) for the same period. Figure 4.26 provides some common sources and uses of cash.

The cash flow statement covers a specified period of time (for example, an accounting year) and uses all the items of the opening and ending balance sheets for the same period (the opening balance sheet for the current period is the closing balance sheet for the previous period). One way to construct the cash flow statement is to determine the changes in all items from the opening balance sheet to the closing one. Figure 4.27 summarizes the rules required to prepare a cash flow statement. For instance, a decrease in a firm's assets (for example, selling a fixed asset) is a source of cash and a decrease in its liabilities (for example, repayment of a loan) is a use of cash.

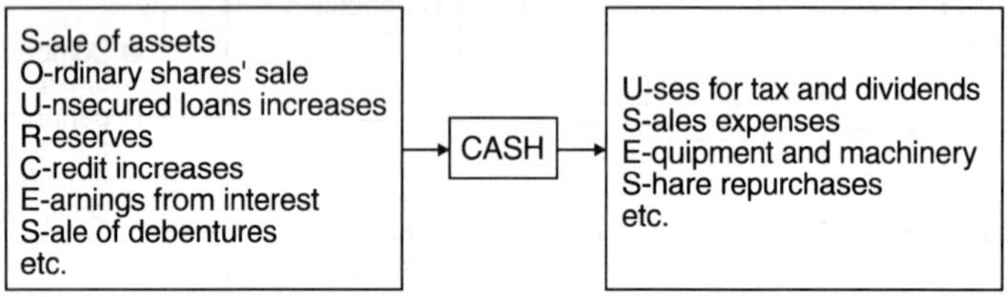

Sources		Uses
S-ale of assets O-rdinary shares' sale U-nsecured loans increases R-eserves C-redit increases E-arnings from interest S-ale of debentures etc.	→ CASH →	U-ses for tax and dividends S-ales expenses E-quipment and machinery S-hare repurchases etc.

Figure 4.26. Examples of sources and uses of cash

The cash flow equation is implied from the balance sheet equation and asserts that the total sources of cash are equal to the total uses of cash. The cash flow statement may be presented on a cash basis or on a net working capital basis. The former presents changes in current assets and current liabilities separately, while the latter incorporates these changes into a single item, the change in net working capital.

	Assets	= Liabilities	+ Issued shares	+ Reserves
Sources	Decrease	Increase	Increase	Increase
Uses	Increase	Decrease	Decrease	Decrease

Figure 4.27. Sources and uses of cash

Example 4.11 The cash flow statement for GD Fashions plc (1989)

The balance sheets of GD Fashions for the years 1988 and 1989, shown in Figure 4.7 (see Example 4.3), will be utilized to illustrate the preparation of the cash flow statement for the year ended 31 March 1989. The easiest way to prepare the cash flow statement is to include movements in reserves as a source or use of cash. In this case, the items of the cash flow statement are the changes in the firm's opening and closing balance sheets. The total sources and total uses of cash are equal because of the balance sheet equation (that is, for each balance sheet: Assets = Liabilities + Issued shares + Reserves).

Figure 4.28 shows a spreadsheet that calculates the changes in balance sheet items for GD Fashions and their classification as either 'sources' or 'uses' of cash. The value of each item for the year ended 31 March 1988 is compared with its corresponding value for the year ended 31 March 1989. The difference between the two is then considered to be either a source or use of cash. Remember from Figure 4.27 that an increase in assets is a use of cash, an increase in liabilities is a source of cash and an increase in reserves is a source of cash. Also note that an item of the balance sheet which shows no change provides neither a source nor a use of cash.

The net fixed assets were £6,543,000 at the year ended 31 March 1988 and £6,828,000 at the year ended 31 March 1989. The difference was £285,000, and it represents a use of cash. Similarly, the difference of £176,000 in current assets represents a use of cash. On the other hand, Figure 4.29 classifies the increase in reserves, and in current liabilities as sources of cash. The items 'Ordinary Shares Issued', 'Share Premium Account', 'Preference Shares Issued', 'Long-Term Loan', 'Mortgage' and 'Short-Term Loans' did not change and thus each of these

	A	B	C	D	E
1	GD Fashions plc:Changes in Balance Sheet Accounts (1989)				
2	--				
3		1988	1989	Change	
4		(£000s)	(£000s)	(£000s)	
5	--				
6	NET FIXED ASSETS	6,543	6,828	285	Use
7					
8	CURRENT ASSETS				
9	===========================				
10	Stocks	1,750	1,855	105	Use
11	Debtors	1,160	1,195	35	Use
12	Short-Term Investments	200	200	0	
13	Cash	452	489	37	
14		----------	----------	----------	
15	TOTAL CURRENT ASSETS	3,562	3,738	176	
16		----------	----------	----------	
17	TOTAL ASSETS	10,105	10,566	461	
18		==========	==========	==========	
19	CAPITAL EMPLOYED				
20	===========================				
21	Ordinary Shares Issued	3,000	3,000	0	
22	Share Premium Account	1,500	1,500	0	
23	Preference Shares Issued	100	100	0	
24	P&L Reserves c/f	233	268	35	Source
25	Other Reserves	2,442	2,710	268	Source
26		----------	----------	----------	
27	TOTAL SHAREHOLDERS FUNDS	7,275	7,578	303	
28	Long-Term Loan	1,000	1,000	0	
29	Mortgage	500	500	0	
30		----------	----------	----------	
31	LONG-TERM DEBT	1,500	1,500	0	
32		----------	----------	----------	
33	TOTAL CAPITAL EMPLOYED	8,775	9,078	303	
34					
35	CURRENT LIABILITIES				
36	===========================				
37	Creditors	900	988	88	Source
38	Short-Term Loans	250	250	0	
39	Accruals	180	250	70	Source
40		----------	----------	----------	
41	TOTAL CURRENT LIABILITIES	1,330	1,488	158	
42		----------	----------	----------	
43	TOTAL CAPITAL & LIABILITIES	10,105	10,566	461	
44		==========	==========	==========	

Figure 4.28. GD Fashions: changes in balance sheet accounts (1989)

items provides neither a source nor a use of cash. Finally, note that the total uses and total sources of cash are equal.

The changes in the balance sheet accounts shown in Figure 4.28 can be used to present the GD Fashions' cash flow statement for the year ended 31 March 1989 (see Figure 4.29). The cash flow statement is prepared by listing all sources of cash on the left and all uses of cash on the right (slight deviations occur due to rounding).

Figure 4.29. The cash flow statement for GD Fashions for year ended March 89

	A	B	C	D	E	F
47	GD Fashions plc:Changes in Balance Sheet Accounts (1989)					
48						
49	Sources (£000s)		Uses (£000s)			
50						
51	Increase in Reserves	303	Increase in Net Fixed Assets			285
52	Increase in Creditors	88	Increase in Stocks			105
53	Increase in Accruals	70	Increase in Debtors			35
54		--------	Increase in Cash			37
55		461				=====
56	Total Sources	========	Total Uses			461

Depreciation is neither a source nor a use of cash since depreciation is neither a way in which cash has been generated nor a way in which the cash has been used. The depreciation is included in the cash flow statement as a source of cash for the following reason. The profit before interest and tax for an accounting period is a source of cash, it is calculated by subtracting depreciation from the gross profit for that same period. In this case, depreciation is considered to be a use of cash. Including now in the cash flow statement the same amount of depreciation as a source of cash is a method of eliminating the depreciation from the statement. If depreciation is included as a source of cash, then the increase in gross assets (that is, before the increase of accumulated depreciation) is included as a use of cash.

Example 4.12 The cash flow statement for GD Fashions plc showing both changes in accumulated depreciation and changes in gross fixed assets (1989)

Figure 4.30 shows the increase in the accumulated depreciation as a source of cash and the increase in the fixed assets as a use of cash. The total sources of cash and total uses of cash differ from those presented in Figure 4.29, but this does not have any significance for decision making.

Figure 4.30. GD Fashions: an alternative format of the cash flow statement

	A	B	C	D	E	F
60	GD Fashions plc:Changes in Balance Sheet Accounts (1989)					
61						
62	Sources (£000s)		Uses (£000s)			
63						
64	Increase in Reserves	303	Increase in Fixed Assets			300
65	Increase in Creditors	88	Increase in Stocks			105
66	Increase in Accruals	70	Increase in Debtors			35
67	Increase in Depreciation	15	Increase in Cash			37
68		--------				-----
69		476	Total Uses			476
70	Total Sources	========				=====

Payment of cash dividends is a use of cash. However, if the cash flow statement includes the amount of increase in reserves, then the cash dividends should not be included in the statement as a use of cash. If the cash flow statement includes the net profit after tax then it should also include the payments of cash dividends as a use of cash. Likewise, if the cash flow statement includes the profit after tax, then the tax paid should not be included in the statement as a use of cash.

Finally, the cash flow statement can also be presented on a net working capital basis. In this instance, the changes in current assets and current liabilities are not presented separately. Instead, the statement includes a new entry related to the change in net working capital. A decrease in net working capital is a source of cash, while an increase in net working capital is a use of cash.

Example 4.13 The cash flow statement for GD Fashions plc showing the change in net working capital (1989)

Figure 4.31 shows the cash flow statement for GD Fashions for the year ended 31 March 1989, by replacing the current asset and current liability entries in Figure 4.30 with the change in net working capital (NWC) entry.

Figure 4.31. The cash flow statement for GD Fashions on a NWC basis

	A	B	C	D	E	F
71						
72	GD Fashions plc:Changes in Balance Sheet Accounts (1989)					
73	----------					
74	Sources (£000s)		Uses (£000s)			
75	----------					
76	Increase in Reserves	303	Increase in Net Fixed Assets			285
77		-----	Increase in NWC			18
78	Total Source	303				-----
79				Total Uses		303

Financial forecasting

Financial forecasting is the process of projecting or estimating a firm's future financial statements (see Figure 4.32). In this section we introduce the per-cent-of-sales forecast method, while in Appendix 4D we discuss two other sales forecasting methods: linear regression analysis and double exponential smoothing.

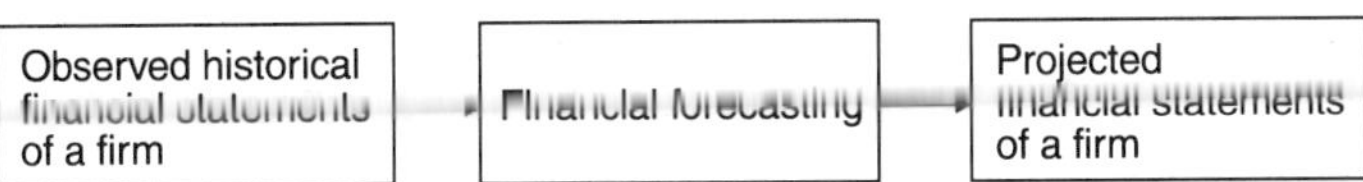

Figure 4.32. The financial forecasting process of a firm

For the sake of illustration, the forecasts presented in this section are for one year only.

Per-cent-of-sales method

This method projects the sales of a firm, estimates the future expenses, assets and liabilities of the firm as a percentage of the projected sales and uses these percentages to construct the firm's future financial statements. Assuming that you are given the financial statements of a firm for each of the three years (1988–90), the per-cent-of-sales method follows the steps below:

Step 1 Calculate the average percentage change in sales over the given time period.

Step 2 For each year express the balance sheet's and profit and loss account statement's items that vary directly with sales as a percentage of sales and then calculate for each item the average percentage. Where an item does not vary directly with sales (for example, preference shares) simply assume that the current year's amount of this item will remain the same for the future period(s).

Step 3 Multiply each percentage determined in the previous step by the sales projected to obtain the amount for the future period. Use these values to obtain the firm's financial statements for the future period(s). In the case of the balance sheet, since current liabilities plus total capital employed must balance the assets when totalled, any balance that remains will have to be obtained internally or externally.

Example 4.14 Projecting the profit and loss account and balance sheet statements for GD Fashions plc

Figures 4.33 and 4.34 show the use of the per-cent-of-sales method in the preparation of the 1991 profit and loss account and balance sheet statements, respectively, for GD Fashions. The sales increased from £10,000,000 in 1988 to £10,600,000 in 1989, that is an increase of 6 per cent. Similarly they increased by 8 per cent from 1989 to 1990. Thus, the average increase is 7 per cent which in turn

	A	B	C	D	E	F
1	Sales Growth ------------>	7.00%				
2						
3	GD Fashions plc:Projected Profit and Loss Account					
4						
5		HISTORICAL DATA			AVERAGE	PROJECTED
6					PERCENT	P&L FOR
7		1988	1989	1990	OF SALES	1991
8		(£000s)	(£000s)	(£000s)		(£000s)
9						
10	Sales	10,000	10,600	11,448	100.00%	12,249
11	Cost of Goods Sold	7,100	7,526	8,128	71.00%	8,697
12						
13	GROSS PROFIT	2,900	3,074	3,320	29.00%	3,552
14	Non-trading Expenses	2,000	2,120	2,290	20.00%	2,450
15	Depreciation	14	15	16	NA	17
16						
17	NET OPERATING PROFIT	886	939	1,014		1,085
18	Short-term Investment Income	16	16	16	NA	16
19						
20	PROFIT BEFORE INTEREST & TAX	902	955	1,030		1,101
21	Interest	255	259	260	NA	265
22						
23	PROFIT BEFORE TAXES	647	696	770		836
24	Taxation	226	243	270	NA	284
25						
26	PROFIT AFTER TAXES	421	453	500		552
27	P&L Reserve b/f	180	233	267		300
28						
29	AVAILABLE FOR APPROPRIATION	601	686	767		852
30	Preference Dividends	14	14	14	NA	14
31	Ordinary Dividends	120	137	153	NA	170
32	Transfer to Reserves	234	268	300	NA	334
33						
34	P&L RESERVES c/f	233	267	300		334
35						

Figure 4.33. GD Fashions: projected consolidated P&L account

	A	B	C	D	E	F
37	GD Fashions plc:Projected Balance Sheet		(£000s)			
38						
39		HISTORICAL DATA			AVERAGE	PROJECTED
40					PERCENT	BS FOR
41		1988	1989	1990	OF SALES	1991
42		(£000s)	(£000s)	(£000s)		(£000s)
43						
44	FIXED ASSETS					
45		0.05	0.05	0.05		
46	Total Fixed Assets	6,887	7,187	7,507		
47	Accumulated Depreciation	344	359	375		
48						
49	NET FIXED ASSETS	6,543	6,828	7,132	64.04%	7,845
50						
51	CURRENT ASSETS				1,373	
52						1,373
53	Stocks	1,750	1,855	1,966	17.39%	2,130
54	Debtors	1,160	1,195	1,231	11.21%	1,373
55	Short-Term Investments	200	200	200	NA	200
56	Cash	452	487	401	4.21%	515
57						
58	TOTAL CURRENT ASSETS	3,562	3,737	3,798	34.81%	4,219
59						
60	TOTAL ASSETS	10,105	10,565	10,930		12,064
61						
62	CAPITAL EMPLOYED					
63						
64	Ordinary Shares Issued	3,000	3,000	3,000	NA	3,000
65	Preference Shares Issued	100	100	100	NA	100
66	Share Premium Account	1,500	1,500	1,500	NA	1,500
67	P&L Reserves c/f	233	267	300	NA	334
68	Other Reserves	2,442	2,710	3,010	NA	3,344
69						
70	TOTAL SHAREHOLDERS FUNDS	7,275	7,577	7,910		8,278
71	Long Term Loan	1,000	1,000	1,000	NA	1,000
72	Mortgage	500	500	500	NA	500
73						
74	LONG-TERM DEBT	1,500	1,500	1,500		1,500
75						
76	TOTAL CAPITAL EMPLOYED	8,775	9,077	9,410		9,778
77						
78	CURRENT LIABILITIES					
79						
80	Creditors	900	988	1,000	9.02%	1,105
81	Short-Term Loans	250	250	250	NA	250
82	Accruals	180	250	270	2.17%	266
83						
84	TOTAL CURRENT LIABILITIES	1,330	1,488	1,520		1,621
85						
86	TOTAL CAPITAL & LIABILITIES	10,105	10,565	10,930		11,399
87						
88				FUNDS REQUIRED		665
89						

Figure 4.34 GD Fashions: projected balance sheet

provides a projected amount of sales of £12,249,000 (that is £11,448,000 $(1 + 0.07)$, the figure is rounded).

Sales percentages are calculated as historical averages of sales in 1988, 1989 and 1990. For example, debtors in 1988 were £1,160,000/£10,000,000 = 11.60 per cent, in 1989 they were £1,195,000/£10,600,000 = 11.27 per cent and in 1990 they were £1,231,000/£11,448,000 = 10.75 per cent (slight deviations occur due to rounding). Hence, the average per cent of sales is

$$(0.1160 + 0.1127 + 0.1075)/3 = 11.21 \text{ per cent}$$

The following assumptions are also made:

1 The interest on short-term investments is 8 per cent, the interest on the mortgage is 11 per cent. The interest on long-term loans is 13 per cent and on short-term loans is 10 per cent while the interest on creditors is 5 per cent.
2 The tax rate is 35 per cent. The preference dividends comprise 14 per cent of the book value of preference shares. The transfer to reserves is calculated as follows: (funds available for appropriation – dividends)/2.
3 The following items are assumed not to vary with sales: depreciation, interest, taxation, preference dividends, ordinary dividends, reserves, short-term investments, ordinary shares issued, share premium account, preference shares issued, long-term loan, mortgage and short-term loans. We use the abbreviation NA (that is, not applicable) to denote a figure that does not vary with the sales.

Next the calculated percentages are multiplied by the estimated sales in order to determine the projected items. For example, to get the projected debtors, we multiply, 0.1121 × £12,249,000 = £1,373,000 (note that a slight deviation occurs due to rounding).

Finally, Figure 4.34 shows that the firm has to raise £665,000 (figure is rounded) from external sources in order to finance the assets needed to generate £12,249,000 sales.

Summary

Financial statement analysis is the process of analysing and interpreting a firm's financial statements in order to monitor and evaluate the firm's financial situation. Ratio analysis provides a useful tool for financial statement analysis.

1 *Profit and loss account and balance sheet statements* The profit and loss account statement records in summary the revenues earned and the expenses incurred during a specific period of time, such as a year. The balance sheet shows in summary the assets, liabilities and capital of a firm as of a specific date, such as the last day of the firm's accounting year. The statement of retained earnings serves as a connecting link between the profit and loss account statement and the balance sheet.
2 *Financial ratios* Relationships between the items of the balance sheet and/or the items of the profit and loss account statement may be expressed in ratios. Ratios are usually grouped into five broad categories: (a) liquidity, (b) activity, (c) gearing, (d) profitability and (e) investment. Financial statement analysis often provides a clearer picture through studying financial ratios in a succession of financial statements (time-series analysis) and the comparisons of the firm's ratios with other firms at the same point in time (cross-sectional analysis). Ratio analysis is associated with several disadvantages. However, knowing such limitations can assist you to use it in a proper fashion.
3 *Cash flow statement* The cash flow statement shows in summary the changes in the firm's financial position during a specific period of time, such as a year. The information provided by the cash flow statement cannot be found in either the balance sheet or the profit and loss account statement.
4 *Forecasting sales* Forecasting sales provides the first step of most financial forecasts. In this chapter three methods for forecasting sales are discussed: the per-

cent-of-sales method, a method that uses the statistical approach of double exponential smoothing and a method that employs regression analysis.

Questions for discussion

1 For each term shown below in the largest box provide a definition in your own words. Then check your responses against the definitions included in the chapter.

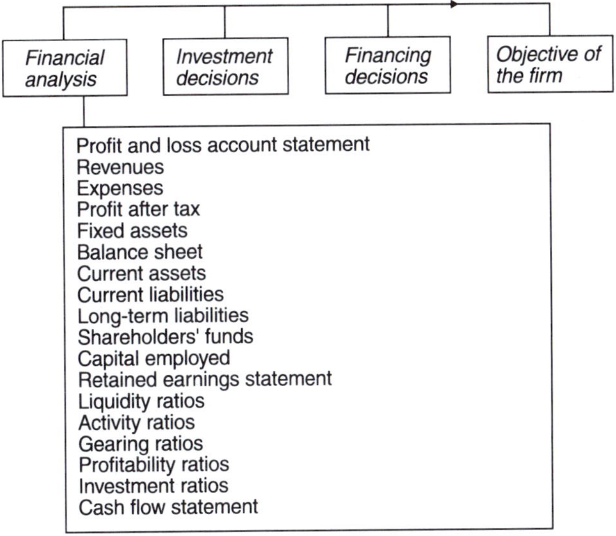

2 Discuss each of the following statements:
   (**a**) 'The purpose of the balance sheet and the profit and loss account statement is to inform interested parties about the operations and the financial situation of the firm.'
   (**b**) 'The balance sheet and the profit and loss account statement supplement and complement one another.'

3 Draw up a list of items that would be classified as fixed assets. Do the same with current assets, current liabilities, capital employed and operating expenses.

4 Classify the ratios presented in this chapter as follows: ratios using items only from the balance sheet, items only from the profit and loss account, or items from both financial statements.

5 Below are given the current ratios of three firms for the year 1986/87:

Marks and Spencer plc	0.8
Asda Group plc	0.6
Tesco plc	0.6

Do these companies have working capital problems? Discuss.

6 Miller plc's fixed assets and current liabilities are expected to be £6 million and £5 million, respectively, during the coming year. The firm's capital employed will be £11 million during the coming year. Calculate the current ratio of the firm.

7 'During a period of inflation, financial statements which are prepared in terms

of historical costs do not reflect the real profits of a firm.' Do you agree? Explain.

8 Consider the following two ratios which show interrelationships between ratios (the Du Pont Company was the first to utilize ratio interrelationships for financial analysis and developed the Du Pont system for ratio analysis):

$$\text{Return on investment} = (\text{Total asset turnover})\ (\text{Net profit margin})$$

$$\frac{\text{Profit after tax}}{\text{Total debt}} = \frac{(\text{Total asset turnover})\ (\text{Net profit margin})}{(\text{Total debt/Total assets})}$$

Show the validity of the above relationships. Explain how the method introduced by Du Pont can improve financial analysis. Illustrate each of these relationships by using an analog model.

9 The following relationship shows that the price of a firm's shares is related to five factors (*source*: Stewart (1973)).

$$\frac{\text{Price}}{\text{Shares}} = \frac{\text{Profits}}{\text{Sales}} \times \frac{\text{Sales}}{\text{Assets}} \times \frac{\text{Assets}}{\text{Equity}} \times \frac{\text{Equity}}{\text{Shares}} \times \frac{\text{Price}}{\text{Profits}}$$

$$\text{Share price} = \text{profitability} \times \text{Efficiency} \times \text{Gearing} \times \text{Book value} \times \text{P/E}$$

Discuss in detail such a relationship.

10 Discuss in detail the diagram shown below and explain its use.

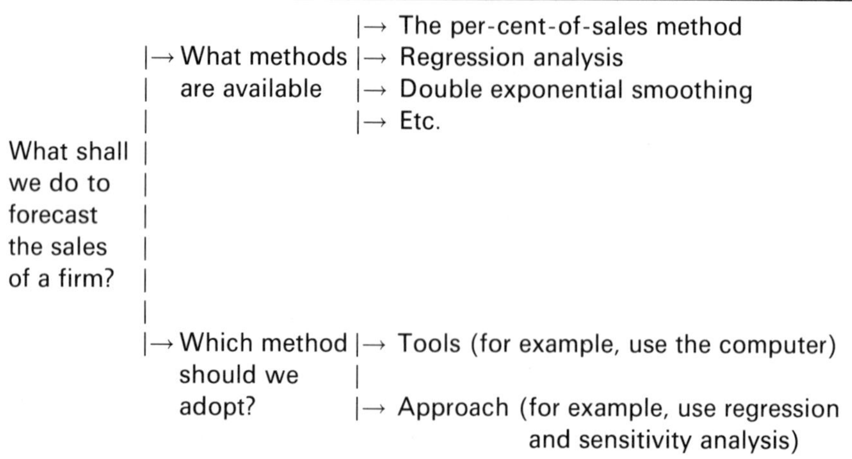

11 'Although each financial ratio is calculated and evaluated in a separate way from the other ratios, the financial position of the firm can properly be assessed when all ratios are analysed together.' Discuss. Substantiate your position by using an example.

12 'It is argued that the managers of a firm should make decisions that are consistent with the objective of maximizing the wealth of shareholders, rather than relying on financial ratio analysis to inform them of the correctness of the decisions made in the past.' Discuss this statement.

13 List the advantages of using comparative ratio analysis rather than ratios for a single data or period. List the advantages of employing trend analysis of a firm's financial ratios rather than ratios from a single period.

14 List as many advantages and disadvantages of using ratio analysis as a method for financial statement analysis.
15 Prepare an analog model summarizing the main points discussed in this chapter.
16 How can spreadsheets be used to facilitate the application of the concepts discussed in this chapter?

Appendix 4A An alternative format of balance sheet

Since the total assets are divided into fixed assets and current assets, the balance sheet can also be presented as shown in Figure 4A.1, where net current assets equal current assets minus current liabilities.

GDED Manufacturing plc
Balance sheet as at 31 December 19__

Fixed assets
+
Net current assets
=
Total capital and reserves
+
Long-term loans

Figure 4A.1. An alternative presentation of the balance sheet

Appendix 4B Depreciation methods

This appendix discusses three depreciation methods: straight-line, double-declining balance and sum-of-the-years' digits.

Straight-line depreciation method

The straight-line depreciation method computes an asset's depreciation by spreading evenly its original cost over its expected useful life. The annual depreciation expense is calculated by employing the following equation:

$$\text{SLN} = \frac{\text{Original cost} - \text{Salvage value}}{\text{Number of years of expected useful life}}$$

where salvage value is the market value at which the asset can be sold at the end of its usable life.

Example 4B.1 Calculating the depreciation of an asset using the straight-line depreciation method

A firm purchased a machine for £65,000. The estimated life of the machine is six years and its salvage value is £5,000. Then the annual depreciation using the straight-line depreciation method is calculated as follows:

$$\text{SLN} = \frac{£65{,}000 - £5{,}000}{6} = £10{,}000$$

The annual straight-line depreciation of the machine can be also calculated by using 1-2-3's financial function `@SLN` as follows:

`@SLN(65000,5000,6)` = £10,000

Double-declining balance depreciation method

The double-declining balance depreciation method sets a greater depreciation expense during the early years of an asset's life, and lower depreciation expense during its later years. Therefore, the double-declining balance depreciation method is called an accelerated depreciation method.

The equation used to calculate the double-declining depreciation for a period in the useful life of the asset is:

$$DDB_t = \frac{2 \times \text{Book value at period } t}{\text{Number of years of expected useful life}}$$

where the book value at period t equals the initial cost minus the total depreciation in all prior periods.

An argument used to justify the use of this method is that the maintenance expenses for an asset are likely to increase over its useful life. In this case, a higher charge for depreciation in the early years plus a lower charge for maintenance will tend to be approximately equal to a lower charge for depreciation in the later years plus a higher charge for maintenance.

Example 4B.2 Calculating the depreciation of an asset using the double-declining balance depreciation method

Consider the data given in Example 4B.1. The yearly depreciation of the machine by the double-declining balance depreciation method is presented in Figure 4B.1.

Figure 4B.1. Using the double-declining depreciation method

Year	Book value at the beginning of year (£)	Depreciation (£)	Year-end book value (£)
1	65,000	2 × 65,000/6 = 21,667	43,333
2	43,333	2 × 43,333/6 = 14,444	28,889
3	28,889	2 × 28,889/6 = 9,630	19,259
4	19,259	2 × 19,259/6 = 6,420	12,840
5	12,840	2 × 12,840/6 = 4,280	8,560
6	8,560	2 × 8,560/6 = 2,853	5,706

Figure 4B.2 shows how 1-2-3's financial function @BDB determines the annual depreciation with the double-declining balance depreciation method. The following function is stored in cell C5:

```
@DDB(65000,5000,5,B5)
```

Figure 4B.2. Using the financial function @DDB

```
        A            B                 C                 D         E         F
 1        USING THE DOUBLE-DECLINING BALANCE DEPRECIATION METHOD
 2       ----------------------------------------------------------
 3                 Year          Depreciation
 4       ----------------------------------------------------------
 5                   1              £21,667
 6                   2               14,444
 7                   3                9,630
 8                   4                6,420
 9                   5                4,280
10                   6                2,853
11       ----------------------------------------------------------
```

where B5 specifies the period for which the depreciation is calculated. To calculate the depreciation for the remaining periods just copy the contents of cell C5 into the range C6..C10.

The double-declining balance depreciation method ignores salvage value in the computation. However, the 1-2-3's function @DDB uses a salvage value figure only to ensure that the total depreciation does not exceed the initial cost of the asset less its salvage value. You will obtain the same results as those presented in Figure 4B.2 by assuming a salvage value of £4,500 rather than £5,000. Note also that when you use the @DDB function with a small salvage value, the asset will not fully depreciate in the final year of its life.

The sum-of-the-year's-digits depreciation method

The sum-of-the-years'-digits depreciation method calculates the yearly depreciation expense as a decreasing proportion of the asset's original cost less its salvage value. The following formula can be used to calculate the yearly depreciation with the sum-of-the-years'-digits depreciation method:

$$\text{SYD} = \frac{2(\text{Original cost} - \text{Salvage value}) \times (\text{Remaining life period} + 1)}{\text{Life} \times (\text{Life} + 1)}$$

Example 4B.3 Calculating the depreciation of an asset by using the sum-of-the-years'-digits depreciation method

Assume the same data given in Example 4B.1. Figure 4B.3 presents the yearly depreciation of the machine calculated utilizing the sum-of-the-years'-digits depreciation method.

Figure 4B.3. Using the sum-of-the-years'-digits depreciation method

Year	Remaining life	Depreciation (£)
1	5	2 × 60,000 × (5 + 1)/42 = 17,143
2	4	2 × 60,000 × (4 + 1)/42 = 14,286
3	3	2 × 60,000 × (3 + 1)/42 = 11,429
4	2	2 × 60,000 × (2 + 1)/42 = 8,571
5	1	2 × 60,000 × (1 + 1)/42 = 5,714
6	0	2 × 60,000 × 1/42 = 2,857

The yearly depreciation shown in Figure 4B.3 can be also calculated by utilizing the 1-2-3's financial function @SYD. The following function is stored in

Figure 4B.4. Using the financial function @SYD

```
       A            B              C                 D           E          F
1            USING THE SUM-OF-THE YEARS'-DIGITS DEPRECIATION METHOD
2           ---------------------------------------------------
3                  Year           Depreciation
4           ---------------------------------------------------
5                     1              £17,143
6                     2               14,286
7                     3               11,429
8                     4                8,571
9                     5                5,714
10                    6                2,857
11          ---------------------------------------------------
```

cell C5 (see Figure 4B.4):

```
@SYD(65000,5000,6,B5)
```

where B5 specifies the period for which the depreciation is computed. The depreciation for the remaining years is calculated by copying the contents of cell C5 into the range C6..C10. Comparing the results presented in Figures 4B.2 and 4B.4 we observe that the sum-of-the-years'-digits depreciation method does not accelerate depreciation quite as much as the double-declining balance depreciation method.

Figure 4B.5 shows graphically the results of the depreciation methods for the machine of the firm.

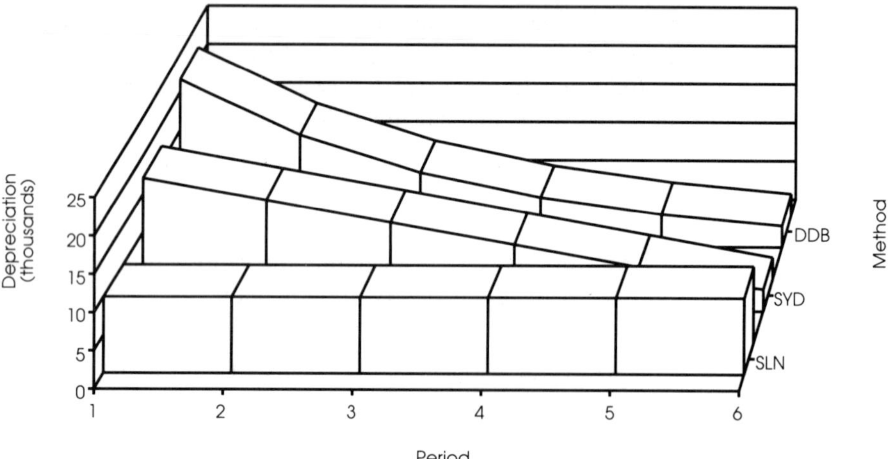

Figure 4B.5. Comparing three depreciating methods

Problems

1 On 1 March 1990, a machine was purchased for £126,000. The machine has an estimated life of six years and an estimated salvage value of £6,000. Calculate the annual depreciation of the machine using the following depreciation methods: straight-line, double-declining balance and sum-of-the-years'-digits.

2 Use the `/Data Table 1` command to conduct a sensitivity analysis of the depreciation using the straight-line depreciation method with respect to the salvage value of the machine (use a range of £3,000 to £9,000 in steps of £500).

3 Repeat Problem 2 using the sum-of-the-years'-digits depreciation method.

Appendix 4C Simple linear regression analysis using Lotus 1-2-3

If we want to explain the variation of a firm's trading expenses in period t, given its sales in period t, we have the following linear relationship:

$$Y_t = A + BX_t + U_t$$

where

Y_t = the value of the dependent variable (e.g. trading expenses) for period t
X_t = the value of the independent or explanatory variable (e.g. sales) for period t

A = the intercept of the linear relationship on the Y-axis (it is the value of the dependent variable when the value of the independent variable is zero)

B = the slope of the linear relationship between the dependent variable and independent variable (it represents the change in dependent variable for a given change in the independent variable)

U_t = a random disturbance term. It is assumed that the disturbance term has mean zero, constant variance and is independent of X_t. The random disturbance term has been included to indicate a less than perfect linear relationship between the dependent variable and independent variable

A simple linear regression is a statistical method that determines how one set of values (the dependent variable) is related to another set of values (the independent variable).

Having specified the linear relationship between two variables, the next step is to obtain estimators for its coefficients from the data available. The coefficients B and A can be estimated by using the ordinary least squares method. Such a method is a technique that determines the line that best fits the given pairs of observations on the dependent variable and independent variable. The ordinary least squares estimators of B and A can be expressed, respectively, as (estimators are methods for estimating B and A):

$$b = \frac{\text{Cov}(Y_t, X_t)}{\text{Var}(X_t)} = \frac{\sum_{t=1}^{T}(Y_t - \bar{Y})(X_t - \bar{X})}{\sum_{t=1}^{T}(X_t - \bar{X})^2}$$

$$a = \bar{Y}_t - b\bar{X}_t$$

where

T = the number of periods (for example, years) under consideration.

$\bar{Y}, \bar{X}$ = the means of the dependent variable and independent variable, respectively.

An estimator of the disturbance term, called residual, is the deviation of the fitted value from the actual value:

$$u_t = Y_t - a - bX_t$$

Example 4C.1 The relationship between the trading expenses and sales of Marks and Spencer plc (1976–87)

Figure 4C.1 shows the trading expenses and sales of Marks and Spencer for the period 1976–87 (figures are in £ million). The relationship between the trading expenses (dependent variable) and the sales (independent variable) can be determined by using the technique of regression analysis.

After using 1-2-3's `/Data Regression` command, the results shown in Figure 4C.2 are obtained.

The regression coefficients

The intercept on the Y-axis is 0.8093 and the slope of the regression line is 0.8916.

Year	Trading expenses	Sales
1976	804.9	900.9
1977	943.8	1065.0
1978	1117.7	1254.0
1979	1293.9	1473.0
1980	1487.3	1668.0
1981	1682.0	1873.0
1982	1964.7	2199.0
1983	2250.6	2506.0
1984	2551.6	2855.0
1985	2858.7	3194.0
1986	3318.6	3716.0
1987	3709.0	4184.0

Figure 4C.1. Trading expenses and sales of Marks and Spencer (1976–87)

```
-----------------------------------------------------------------------------
        A         B         C          D              E               F
29              Regression Output:
30 Constant                         0.8093   <----- a
31 Std Err of Y Est                12.1545   <----- SE(Yt)
32 R Squared                        0.9998
33 No. of Observations                  12
34 Degrees of Freedom                   10   <----- DF
35
36 X Coefficient(s)     0.8916    <-------------------------------- b
37 Std Err of Coef.     0.0034    <-------------------------------- SE(b)
-----------------------------------------------------------------------------
```

Figure 4C.2. The outcome after using the `/Data Regression` command

Degrees of freedom

The degrees of freedom are the number of sample observations that can be specified freely, once something is known about the sample. The degrees of freedom for our example are 10 (that is, 12 – 2), since 10 values of the residual can be specified freely once the values of the coefficients *a* and *b* are known (using these 10 values and the estimated equations for *a* and *b* the remaining two values of the residual can be obtained).

The standard error of the *Y*-estimate

The variance of the *Y*-estimate is the part of the total variation of the dependent variable which is not explained by the regression line and is attributed to the existence of the residuals. The standard error of the *Y*-estimate is equal to the square root of the variance of the *Y*-estimate and it shows how well the independent variable in the sample explains the dependent variable. In general, the larger the standard error of the *Y*-estimate is relative to the variability of the dependent variable's values the less the regression's explanation of the variation of the dependent variable.

The standard error of the *Y*-estimate can be calculated by using the following formula:

$$\mathrm{SE}(Y_t) = \mathrm{SQRT}\left[\frac{\sum_{t=1}^{T}(Y_t - a - bX_t)^2}{\mathrm{DF}}\right]$$

where

SQRT = the square root operator.

DF = degrees of freedom.

T = the number of observations in the sample.

Figure 4C.3 shows the calculation required to find the standard error of the Y-estimate.

THE RELATIONSHIP BETWEEN TRADING EXPENSES AND SALES

I	J	K	L	M	N
Year	Trading Expenses	Sales	$(Y_t - a - bX_t)^2$	X_t^2	$(X_t - \bar{X})^2$
1976	805.0	901.0	0.7	811,801.0	1,794,706.8
1977	943.8	1,065.0	43.0	1,134,225.0	1,382,192.1
1978	1,117.7	1,254.0	1.4	1,572,516.0	973,511.1
1979	1,293.9	1,473.0	409.2	2,169,729.0	589,312.1
1980	1,487.3	1,668.0	0.5	2,782,224.0	327,947.1
1981	1,682.0	1,873.0	126.2	3,508,129.0	135,178.8
1982	1,964.7	2,199.0	10.7	4,835,601.0	1,736.1
1983	2,250.6	2,506.0	238.9	6,280,036.0	70,401.8
1984	2,551.6	2,855.0	28.0	8,151,025.0	377,405.4
1985	2,858.7	3,194.0	102.8	10,201,636.0	908,844.4
1986	3,318.6	3,716.0	21.4	13,808,656.0	2,176,608.4
1987	3,709.0	4,184.0	494.5	17,505,856.0	3,776,544.4
		SUM	147.7	72,761,434.0	12,514,388.7
		SE(Yt) =	12.1545		
		SE(a) =	8.4603		
		SE(b) =	0.0034		

Figure 4C.3. Calculations of standard errors

The standard error of the Y-estimate shown above is 12.1545. It can be seen that the standard error of the Y-estimate is very small relative to the variability of the dependent variable's values (that is £910.58, the standard deviation of trading expenses) and thus it can be inferred that the changes in the sales account for a great deal of the variation in the trading expenses.

R-squared

The R-squared (R^2) indicates the proportion of the variability of the dependent variable which can be explained by the variability of the independent variable. The R-squared shown above is 0.9998, this means that the regression line explains 99.98 per cent of the total variation of the trading expenses.

The standard errors of the coefficients

In the regression outcome shown in Figure 4C.2, SE(b) is the standard error of the coefficient b. SE(b) estimates the standard deviation of the sampling distribution of the independent variable's coefficient. The larger the standard error of a coefficient in relation to the estimated coefficient, the less accurate you can be about the estimation of the coefficient and thus the prediction shown by the regression. The standard error of the slope coefficient shown above is 0.0034 and is very small in relation to the value of the coefficient.

1-2-3 does not provide a direct calculation of the standard error of the coefficient a. The following formula can be used to calculate the standard error of coefficient a:

$$\mathrm{SE}(a) = \mathrm{SE}(Y_t)\mathrm{SQRT}\left[\frac{\sum_{t=1}^{T} X_t^2}{T\sum_{t=1}^{T}(X-\bar{X})^2}\right]$$

The calculation of the standard error of a is presented in Figure 4C.3. The result of the following formula is stored in cell D25 (note that a slight deviation occurs due to rounding):

SE(a) = `+L24 * @SQRT(M22/(12 * N22))` = 8.4603

Statistical tests for the significance of the coefficient

Since the ordinary least squares regression coefficients are obtained from a sample of observations on trading expenses and sales, it is necessary to apply tests of significance in order to measure the size of the error in the validity of the estimates. The two most popular tests used are: the t-test and the F-test.

The t-test is applicable when testing whether the slope and the intercept are significantly different from zero. The t-test statistic of a coefficient is calculated by dividing the coefficient's regression value by its standard error. The t-test statistics for the significance of the coefficients a and b are:

$t(a) \rightarrow 0.0957$ $\qquad$ $t(b) \rightarrow 262.23$

The t-critical value using a two-tail test at a 5 per cent level of significance is 2.228. The first value is lower than 2.228 and the second is greater than 2.228. Thus, the coefficient a is not significantly different from zero, while the coefficient b is significantly different from zero.

The F-test can be applied to test the significance of the linear relationship as a whole. The F-statistic can be expressed as:

$$F(k-1, T-k) = \frac{R^2\mathrm{DF}}{(1-R^2)}$$

where

R^2 = the squared correlation coefficient (or coefficient of determination) given by Lotus.

DF = $T - k$, where T = the number of observations in the sample, and
k = the number of the regression coefficients.

$F(k-1, T-k)$ = F-statistic with $k-1$ and $T-k$ degrees of freedom.

Using the R-squared coefficient of 0.9998 the F-statistic is 49,990. The F-critical value for 1 and 10 degrees of freedom at a 5 per cent level of

Simple linear regression: $Y_t = a + bX_t + u_t$

Item	Mathematical expression	Interpretation
Slope	$b = \dfrac{\text{Cov}(Y_t, X_t)}{\text{Var}(X_t)} = \dfrac{\sum_{t=1}^{T}(Y_t - \bar{Y}_t)(X_t - \bar{X}_t)}{\sum_{t=1}^{T}(X_t - X_t)^2}$	The change in the dependent variable for a given change in the independent variable
Intercept	$a = \bar{Y}_t - b\bar{X}_t$	The value of Y_t when $X_t = 0$
Standard error of the Y-estimate	$\text{SE}(Y_t) = \text{SQRT}\left[\dfrac{\sum_{t=1}^{T}(Y_t - a - bX_t)^2}{\text{DF}}\right]$	A measure showing how well the independent variable explains the dependent variable
Standard error of the intercept	$\text{SE}(a) = \text{SE}(Y_t)\,\text{SQRT}\left[\dfrac{\sum_{t=1}^{T} X_t^2}{T\sum_{t=1}^{T}(X - \bar{X})^2}\right]$	A measure of the variation of the sampling distribution of the coefficient
Standard error of the slope	$\text{SE}(b) = \text{SE}(Y_t)\,\text{SQRT}\left[\dfrac{1}{\sum_{t=1}^{T}(X_t - \bar{X})^2}\right]$	A measure of the variation of the sampling distribution of the coefficient
R-squared	$R^2 = 1 - \dfrac{[\text{SE}(Y_t)]^2\text{DF}}{\sum_{t=1}^{T}(Y_t - \bar{Y})^2}$	The proportion of the variance of the dependent variable that can be attributed to the regression line
t-test statistic	$t_a = \dfrac{a}{\text{SE}(a)} \quad t_b = \dfrac{b}{\text{SE}(b)}$	A test for the significance of the coefficients a and b
F-test statistic	$F = \dfrac{R^2\text{DF}}{1 - R^2}$ degrees of freedom 1, $T - 2$	A test for the significance of the linear equation as a whole

Figure 4C.4. Summary of information related to a simple regression

significance is 4.96. Since the F-value is greater than the F-critical value it can be concluded that a linear relationship exists between the trading expenses and sales.

Figure 4C.4. summarizes information related to a simple linear regression.

Appendix 4D Forecasting sales

This appendix presents two methods that may be used to forecast sales: the use of linear regression analysis and double exponential smoothing.

Trend forecast method

This method forecasts sales by using the simple linear regression approach.

Example 4D.1 Forecasting sales by the trend forecast method

Let sales be the dependent variable and time be the independent variable (see

```
         A            B        C          D               E              F            G
   1 FORECASTING SALES USING THE TREND FORECAST METHOD
   2 ----------------------------------------------------
   3     YEAR         SALES
   4 --------------------  | ============================================
   5       1976          901 |
   6       1977        1,065 |                Regression Output:
   7       1978        1,254 |   Constant                                  (538,047)
   8       1979        1,473 |   Std Err of Y Est                            155.496
   9       1980        1,668 |   R Squared                                     0.974
  10       1981        1,873 |   No. of Observations                              11
  11       1982        2,199 |   Degrees of Freedom                                9
  12       1983        2,506 |
  13       1984        2,855 |   X Coefficient(s)              272.65
  14       1985        3,194 |   Std Err of Coef.               14.83
  15       1986        3,716 |
  16       1987        4,184 |  ============================================
  17 --------------------  |
```

Figure 4D.1. The results from a regression between sales and time

Figure 4D.1). Use 1-2-3 `/Data Regression` command with the independent variable range being A5..A15 and the dependent variable range being B5..B15. The forecasted sales for 1987 are (figure has been rounded):

$$-£538{,}047 + 272.65 \times 1987 = £3{,}708.55$$

Double exponential smoothing

This method forecasts sales using the local linear trend model whose coefficient are calculated with the aid of the moving average forecasting technique. The method of moving averages provides a series of arithmetic means computed from ranges of consecutive numerical observations by successively dropping one old observation and adding a new one for each arithmetic mean. The moving average technique is usually employed to smooth a time series in order to describe more clearly its underlying nature. The local linear trend model is used when the forecasting of data can be described by trend lines for each locality of time (see also Gilchrist, 1976, Chapter 5). Considering the sales of Marks and Spencer plc for each of the 12 years (1976–87), the double exponential smoothing method follows the steps below.

Step 1 Use the available data and calculate the first and second order moving averages (for example taking a period of, say, four years). The second order moving average is a moving average of the first order moving average.

Step 2 Use the following linear model to obtain forecasts k period ahead of t:

$$F_{t+k} = a_t + b_t k$$

where

t = the period in which the forecast is made.
k = the period ahead t for which I want to obtain a forecast for the variable under consideration (for example, if $t = 7$, and $k = 2$,
then I use the estimated coefficients for period 7
to forecast the variable under consideration for period 9).

a_t, b_t = the linear model's coefficients calculated using the following equations:

$$a_t = 2M_t(1) - M_t(2) \qquad b_t = 2(M_t(1) - M_t(2))/(N - 1)$$

$M_t(1)$ = the first order moving average at period t.
$M_t(2)$ = the second order moving average at period t.
N = number of observations used in each moving average.

Example 4D.2 Using the double exponential smoothing to forecast the sales of Marks and Spencer plc

Figure 4D.2 presents the yearly sales of Marks and Spencer for 12 years from 1976 to 1987 (figures are in £ million). We will use the double exponential method to forecast the sales for each year in the range 1983–88. Column C shows the four-year first order moving average. The value stored in cell C11 is calculated as follows:

$$\frac{£901 + £1{,}065 + £1{,}254 + £1{,}473}{4} = £1{,}173 = \text{@AVG(B8..B11)}$$

Copy the contents of cell C11 in the range C12..C19 to obtain the other first order moving averages. Note the power of 1-2-3 (and generally the power of a spreadsheet).

Next the value stored in cell D14 is calculated below

$$\frac{£1{,}173 + £1{,}365 + £1{,}567 + £1{,}803}{4} = £1{,}447 = \text{@AVG(C11..C14)}$$

Copy the contents of cell D14 in the range D15..D19 to calculate the second order moving averages.

	A	B	C	D	E	F	G
1	FORECASTING SALES USING THE DOUBLE EXPONENTIAL SMOOTHING METHOD						
2	------						
3	YEAR	SALES	FOUR-YEAR	FOUR-YEAR	VALUE OF	VALUE OF	FORECAST
4			MOVING	MOVING	a	b	k=1
5			AVERAGE	AVERAGE OF			
6			OF SALES	COLUNM C			
7	------						
8	1976	901					
9	1977	1,065					
10	1978	1,254					
11	1979	1,473	1,173				
12	1980	1,668	1,365				
13	1981	1,873	1,567				
14	1982	2,199	1,803	1,477	2,129	217	
15	1983	2,506	2,062	1,699	2,424	242	2,347
16	1984	2,855	2,358	1,948	2,769	274	2,665
17	1985	3,194	2,689	2,228	3,149	307	3,043
18	1986	3,716	3,068	2,544	3,592	349	3,456
19	1987	4,184	3,487	2,900	4,074	391	3,941
20							4,465

Figure 4D.2. Illustrating the double exponential smoothing

The value of the coefficient a for 1982 (see cell E14) is calculated by using a simple formula:

$$2(\text{C14}) - \text{D14} = (2)(£1{,}803) - £1{,}477 = £2{,}129$$

The value b for 1982 (see cell F14) is

2(C14 – D14)/3 = 2 (£1,803 – £1,477)/3 = £217

Therefore, if $t = 7$ and $k = 1$, the forecasted sales for 1983 are (the difference between the figure shown below and that shown in Figure 4D.2 is due to rounding):

£2,129 + £217(1) = £2,346

The value £4,465 is calculated as follows: £4,074 + £391(1) = £4,465. This is the forecasted sales figure for 1988. If $t = 12$ and $k = 2$, then the forecast of sales for 1989 is: £4,074 + £391(2) = £4,856. Additionally, the forecast of sales for 1990 is: £4,074 + £391(3) = £5,247.

References and bibliography

Brown, R.G. (1959) *Statistical Forecasting for Inventory Control.* McGraw-Hill, New York.

Brown, R.G. (1963) *Smoothing, Forecasting and Prediction of Discrete Time Series.* Prentice-Hall, New Jersey.

Chen, K.H. and Shimerda, T.A. (1981) An empirical analysis of the useful financial ratios, *Financial Management*, **10**, Spring, 51–60.

Foster, G. (1986) *Financial Statement Analysis*, 2nd edn. Prentice-Hall, New Jersey.

Gilchrist, W. (1976) *Statistical Forecasting.* John Wiley, Chichester.

Helfert, E.A. (1977) *Techniques of Financial Analysis*, 4th edn. Richard D. Irwin, Homewood, Illinois.

Horrigan, J.C. (1968) A short history of financial ratio analysis, *Accounting Review*, **43**, April, 284–94.

Koutsoyiannis, A. (1987) *Theory of Econometrics*, 2nd edn. Macmillan, Basingstoke.

Lev, B. (1974) *Financial Statement Analysis: A New Approach.* Prentice-Hall, New Jersey.

Makridakis, S., Wheelwright, S.C. and McGee, V.E. (1983) *Forecasting: Methods and Applications.* John Wiley, New York.

Murray, R. (1971) Lessons for financial analysis, *Journal of Finance*, **26**, May, 327–32.

O'Connor, M.C. (1973) On the usefulness of financial ratios to investors in common stock, *Accounting Review*, **48**, April, 339–52.

Stewart, S.S. Jr (1973) Share price maximisation: a tool for management decision-making, *California Management Review*, Winter, 54–8.

Tamari, M. (1978) *Financial Ratio Analysis and Prediction.* Paul Elek, London.

Westwick, C. (1973) *How to Use Management Ratios.* Gower Press, London.

5 Capital budgeting under conditions of certainty

This chapter includes:

- Capital budgeting process
- Accounting profit versus cash flow
- Capital budgeting methods
- Relating the NPV rule and the objective of the firm

The allocation of limited funds among alternative investment projects is one of the most crucial decisions within the firm, and it must be made carefully. Long-term investment opportunities frequently involve sizable expenditures which influence the future profitability of the firm. Poor capital budgeting decisions can lead to lower eanings and a lower share price. In contrast, sound capital budgeting decisions can increase the firm's earnings and share price.

This chapter views the capital budgeting decisions by viewing three tasks in evaluating projects: estimating cash outlays, estimating net cash flows and applying a decision rule for evaluating and selecting investment projects. Figure 5.1 shows how the capital budgeting evaluation methods fit into the financial management framework presented in Chapter 2.

Basic concepts, definitions and examples

A capital budgeting project (an investment project or simply a project) is a proposed investment in a long-term asset (that is, an asset which is intended to be used by the firm to yield a return over a period of time longer than a year). Examples of capital budgeting projects include the purchase of a building for new employees, the building of a warehouse for storing products, the purchase of new machinery and equipment for producing a new product, the purchase of new delivery vans, the replacement of existing equipment that has become obsolete over time, the installation of a new computer system, and so on.

Capital budgeting (or project analysis) is the process of searching for, identifying, analysing, selecting and following up capital budgeting investments. A capital expenditure is any outlay whose cash benefits are expected to last longer than one year. The cost of new buildings, land and equipment, the expenditure for research and development programmes, the expenditure for employee education and training are examples of capital expenditure. The capital budget of a firm is the amount of funds allocated for capital budgeting projects.

A capital budgeting decision is the allocation of limited funds among alternative

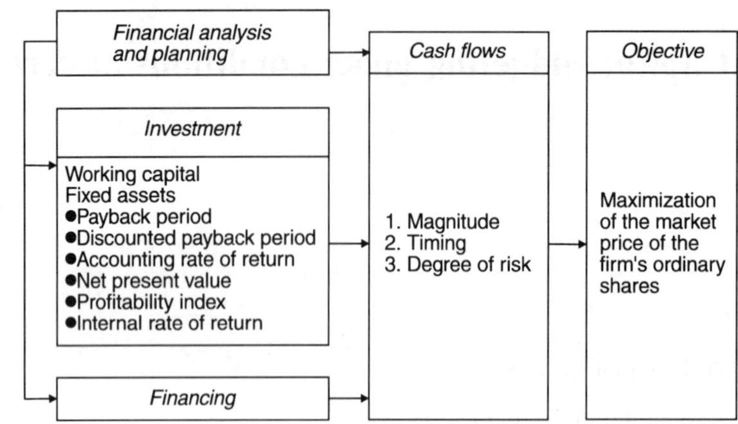

Figure 5.1. Relating the methods for evaluating investment projects with the framework of financial management introduced in Chapter 2

investment opportunities. For example, suppose a firm has four investment opportunities under consideration as follows: (a) purchasing new machinery for £1 million, (b) purchasing new cars for £0.5 million, (c) building new offices for £1 million and (d) purchasing a new computer system for £0.5 million. Assume that all four projects are profitable. If the firm has a maximum of £1.5 million to spend, then its capital budgeting decision involves the allocation of £1.5 million among two of the above projects.

Capital budgeting (or investment decision) techniques are utilized to evaluate capital budgeting projects. Capital budgeting methods include: payback period, discounted payback period, average rage of return, net present value, profitability index, internal rate of return and modified internal rate of return.

Capital budgeting projects can be broadly classified into three groups: expansion, replacement and regulatory. Expansion projects are those designed to increase existing capacity, or to produce new products or to enter new markets. If a textile firm decides to expand into the production and sale of a new commodity, installing new machinery to produce the new commodity is an expansion project. Replacement projects are those designed to replace old assets with new ones. An example of such a project is the replacement of a main computer with a new one which processes data faster. Regulatory projects are those undertaken by the firm in order to meet the requirements of external parties. For example, firms make capital expenditure in order to improve the safety of the working environment.

Capital budgeting projects can be also classified as follows: independent, mutually exclusive and contingent. When projects are independent, the acceptance or rejection of one does not directly eliminate the others from further consideration. For example, a firm may wish to purchase a new machine and a new computer at the same time. When projects are mutually exclusive, the acceptance of one eliminates the acceptance of all other projects. For example, purchasing a new machine for expanding production and leasing the machine for an extended period of time are mutually exclusive projects.

When projects are contingent, the acceptance (or rejection) of one is dependent upon the acceptance (or rejection) of the other. For example, consider the purchase of two new machines in order to develop a new product which is unrelated to the existing business and the purchase of new delivery vans required for the distribution of the product. If the firm decides not to develop the new product the need for the delivery vans goes. On the other hand, if the firm develops the new product, it needs the new delivery vans.

To simplify the analysis presented in this chapter we assume the following:

- a project's future cash flows are known with certainty;
- the cost of capital is given and is the same for all projects;
- the expected net cash flows of a project will be realized at the end of the time periods in which they are expected to occur.

Importance of making sound capital budgeting decisions

Making sound capital budgeting decisions is important for several reasons. First, investment decisions involve substantial capital expenditure which in the long run can affect the future cost structure of the firm. If an incorrect capital budgeting decision is made, large amount of funds may be tied up for several years. A poor investment decision can affect the future profitability of the firm as well as its competitive position. For example, consider an electronics firm which has rented a new building and equipment in order to expand into the production and sale of a new computer. The new project requires a substantial amount of fixed costs in terms of salaries, rent of the building and equipment, and so on. If the new investment turns out to be unprofitable, or does not generate the desired future cash flows, the firm will pay the fixed costs over extended periods of time unless it abandons the project.

Second, it is frequently difficult to reverse a capital budgeting decision without substantial loss to the firm. By way of illustration, consider a firm that has just purchased specialized machinery and equipment to start the production of precision tools in light engineering. If the new investment does not generate the desired future cash flows, it may be very difficult to liquidate it without costing the firm large sums of money.

Third, a decision to invest in a capital budgeting project involves, in effect, an implied sales forecast. For example, a decision to invest in an asset having a life of ten years, requires a ten-year sales forecast. If the management team of the firm fails to forecast correctly, the firm may face serious problems which can result in substantial expense. If the firm does not spend enough on long-term investments it may not be able to meet demand in the future. In order to improve its competitive position the firm must undertake considerable selling expenses, reduction of the prices of its products, and so on. If too much is invested in assets, the firm will suffer with unnecessary expense.

Finally, firms have a limited amount of funds that can be spent on capital budgeting projects. As a consequence, poor investment decisions will prevent the firm from realizing profits from other investments which could be accepted if the firm had not a limit on its capital budget.

The capital budgeting process

The capital budgeting process can be divided into the following five stages: search and identification, estimating cash flows, evaluating projects, selecting projects and post-acceptance analysis.

Search and identification

This stage involves the continuous and systematic search for new capital budgeting projects as well as the identification of such projects. The possibilities generated are subject to initial screening. Initial screening is necessary to keep the number of projects manageable and keep the costs down. Factors such as the amount and timing of capital expenditure, management competence in the area of interest, risk level, and strategic fit between the project and the firm should be used for initial screening. Projects that pass the initial screening are qualified for further analysis.

Estimating cash flows

Once an investment opportunity has been identified, the second stage in the capital budgeting process is to estimate the magnitude, timing and riskiness associated with the investment project's cash flows (in this case, cash flows are the actual pounds earned from an investment project or paid out to cover costs related to the project).

Evaluating projects

After the cash flows have been estimated, the third stage deals with the evaluation of the attractiveness of the new investment projects using one or more evaluation techniques (for example, net present value, internal rate of return, and so on).

Selecting projects

The fourth stage in the capital budgeting process is concerned with the selection of projects. During this stage a package of information is used, for example, the type of project, the evaluation method used, the level of risk associated with the project, the size of the firm's capital budget, and so on.

Post-acceptance analysis

The final stage reviews the performance of projects after they have been adopted for several reasons. First, the actual cash flows are compared to those forecasted in the estimation stage in order to detect possible errors. If this is the case, the information provided can be used to improve future estimates of cash flows. Second, this stage can detect inefficiencies in the current operation of the project which may be corrected before it is too late. Finally, this stage examines whether a project's costs are higher than planned and determines if it should be continued or abandoned by the firm. The capital budgeting process is summarized in Figure 5.2. In this chapter we deal with the estimation of cash flows, evaluation and selection stages.

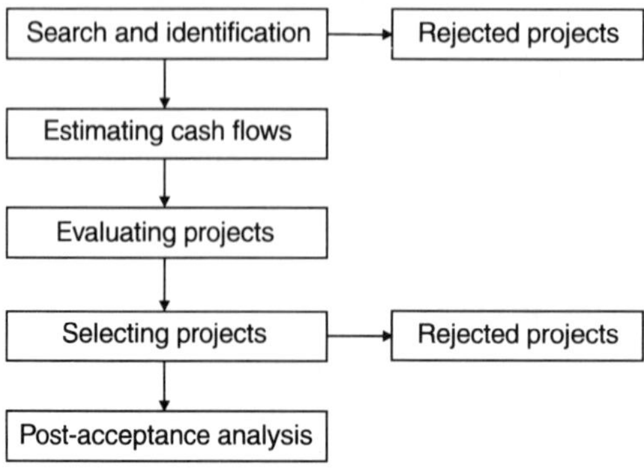

Figure 5.2. The capital budgeting process

Initial investment

Accountants recognize revenues at the point of sales, not when they are received and expenses related to the sales when they are incurred, not when they are paid. The financial director considers revenues and expenses only with respect to inflows and outflows of cash. For example, suppose that a computer firm, in the calendar year just ended, made a sale of a computer for £50,000. If the computer cost the firm £40,000 (paid in full during the last two months), then the net profit obtained in the calendar year just ended can be calculated as follows:

Revenues	-	Expenses	=	Net profit
£50,000	-	£40,000	=	£10,000

For determining the net cash flow we should consider revenues and expenses only with respect to inflows and outflows of cash. For example, if the revenue of £50,000 earned during the period has been received during that same period then:

Cash inflow	-	Cash outflow	=	Net cash flow
£50,000	-	£40,000	=	£10,000

But, if the computer sold to the customer on a year credit, then the firm's net cash flow associated with the computer can be calculated as follows:

Cash inflow	-	Cash outflow	=	Net cash flow
£0	-	£40,000	=	-£40,000

Comparing the profit and the net cash flow, it can be seen that the profit in a given accounting period is the difference between the revenues earned (but not necessarily received) during that period and the expenses related to those revenues (but not necessarily paid) during that same period. On the other hand, the (net) cash flow in a given accounting period is the difference between the cash inflow (that is, cash revenues) during that period and the cash outflow (that is, cash expenses) related to the cash inflow during that same period. Therefore, we can write:

Net cash flow	=	Cash revenues	-	Cash expenses

Once an investment project has been proposed, its initial cash outflow or initial investment and future net cash flows (NCF) must be estimated. The following time line shows the cash flows associated with an investment project:

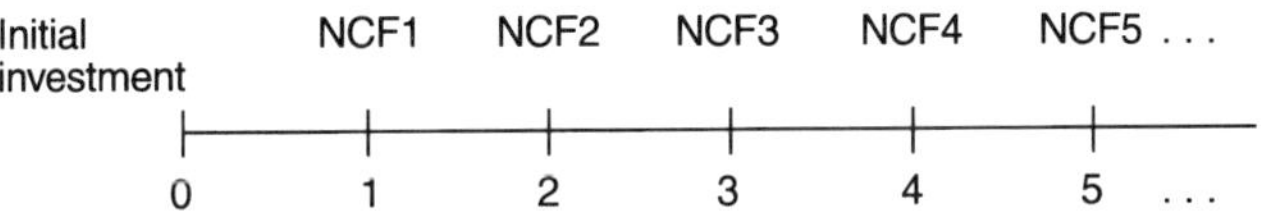

We assume that the initial outlay of an investment project occurs at time 0 and the subsequent cash flows are located at the last day of each year in the project's useful life. Thus, time 1 is the end of the first period, time 2 is the end of second period, time 3 is the end of the third period, and so on. For example, we can assume that the initial investment in a new project occurs on 31 March 1990 and the subsequent cash flows will occur on 31 March 1991, 1992, 1993, 1994 and 1995, respectively.

The initial investment is the initial cash outlay required for the acquisition of an investment project. The initial investment of any asset is comprised of several components that may need to be included in the analysis. These are:

1 The cost of acquiring the new asset
2 Installation and transportation costs
3 Additional working capital as a result of the new investment
4 Net proceeds from sale of the old asset
5 Taxes associated with the sale of the old asset and/or the purchase of the new one

Figure 5.3 shows a general format for calculating the initial investment of a capital project.

	Cost of asset
plus	Installation costs
plus	Additional working capital
minus	Proceeds from the sale of old asset
plus/minus	Taxes on sale of old asset
equals	Initial investment

Figure 5.3. Calculating the initial investment

Example 5.1 Calculating the initial investment for a capital budgeting project

Assume that AK Textiles plc is investigating the possibility of expanding its activities to the production of a new range of men's casual clothing. The machinery for the production of the new clothes requires an initial cost of £4,750,000 plus £500,000 shipping and installation costs. The machinery would be purchased and installed in March 1990, and it would also be paid for on 31 March 1990. The project requires £950,000 in additional working capital but it does not involve any gains or losses associated with the disposal of an old asset. The amount of initial investment can be calculated as follows:

£4,750,000 + £500,000 + £950,000 = £6,200,000

If the new investment project is accepted, then the firm has to obtain £6,200,000 to finance it. These funds can be obtained by issuing new ordinary shares and new debentures.

The following remarks are related to the initial investment:

1 Expansion projects usually create the need for additional investment in net working capital. The net working capital is the difference between current assets and current liabilities. For example, the expansion of a firm to a new market may require an initial increase in stocks (that is, more raw materials) and creditors (for example, purchasing raw material from other firms on credit). Replacement projects do not normally involve investments in net working capital.

   Some investment projects can also free working capital. For example, if a firm has obtained a new automated machinery system that can produce stocks of finished goods as needed, then the firm can reduce the amount of stocks of finished goods stored. Figure 5.4 shows how the initial cost of a project can be adjusted to reflect changes in net working capital (NWC).
2 A fixed asset can be depreciated reflecting the allocation of its initial cost, less

Figure 5.4. Initial investment and net working capital

Situation	Consequence
Increased investment in NWC at time zero	A cash outlay at time zero
Decreased investment in NWC at time zero	A cash inflow at time zero

salvage value, over its usable life. There are several methods used to calculate depreciation (see Appendix 4B). The acquisition, installation and transportation costs of a new investment project serve as the basis for calculating depreciation. For example, if an asset costs £5,250,000, has an estimated life of five years and no salvage value, then its depreciation using the straight-line method is £1,050,000 (that is, £5,250,000/5).

3 Under conditions where a new asset replaces an existing one, the initial cost of the new asset must be adjusted to reflect the tax consequences resulting from the sale of the existing asset. There are four possibilities summarized in Figure 5.5. For example, if an old machine is sold for more than its initial cost, then the total gains (that is, selling price – book value) can be divided into two types, the gain over the book value (that is, original cost – book value) and the capital gain (that is, selling price – original cost). Book value is the original cost of the asset less its accumulated depreciation.

Figure 5.5. Tax impact of selling an existing asset

Possibility	Consequence	Tax effect
Selling price = Book value	Neither a gain nor a loss on the sale	The proceeds of sale will not be taxed
Selling price < Book value	Operating loss which results in tax savings	(SP – BV) × Tax rate
Selling price > Book value *and* Selling price < Initial cost	Gain over the book value	(SP – BV) × Tax rate
Selling price > Initial cost	Gain over the book value *and* Gain over the capital	(IC – BV) × Tax rate *and* (SP – IC) × Capital gains rate

where SP = selling price, BV = book value, IC = initial cost

Estimating the profits associated with a new project

The accounting profit can be calculated as in Figure 5.6.

Figure 5.6. Calculating the accounting profit

	Turnover
minus	Cost of goods sold
equals	Gross profit
minus	Operating expenses
minus	Depreciation
equals	net operating profit
minus/plus	Other expenses/revenues
equals	Profit before interest and tax
minus	Interest
equals	Profit before tax
minus	Tax
equals	Profit after tax

Example 5.2 Estimating the profits expected from an investment project

The present example uses the project introduced in Example 5.1. We assume that the new project's expected life is five years. Its depreciation is calculated by using the straight-line method and its salvage value is zero. We also assume that the firm will finance the new project with funds obtained from a new ordinary share issue and a new debenture issue. The interest associated with the new funds will be £200,000 per year. The corporate tax rate is 34 per cent.

Each member of the firm's management team provides his or her contribution in the estimation process of the profits associated with a new project. The package of accounting information regarding the new project (that is, projected revenues and expenses) is used by the firm's chief accountant in order to estimate the annual profits after tax expected from the project (see Figure 5.7). The results indicate that the estimated profits for the project are expected to rise up to the end of the year 3 and then are expected to fall, reaching a level of £456,000 at the end of the year 5 (slight deviations exist due to rounding).

	A	B	C	D	E	F	G
1	ESTIMATING THE ANNUAL PROFITS AFTER TAX FOR THE NEW PROJECT (£000s)						
2	=====						
3							
4		1991	1992	1993	1994	1995	
5							
6	Turnover	6,500	6,825	7,166	6,808	6,468	
7	Trading Expenses	4,550	4,778	5,016	4,766	4,528	
8							
9	Trading Profit	1,950	2,048	2,150	2,042	1,940	
10	Depreciation	1,050	1,050	1,050	1,050	1,050	
11							
12	Operating Profit	900	998	1,100	992	890	
13	Interest	200	200	200	200	200	
14							
15	Profit Before Tax	700	798	900	792	690	
16	Tax (at 34%)	238	271	306	269	235	
17							
18	Profit After Tax	462	526	594	523	456	

Figure 5.7. Estimating the profits after tax expected from a new project

Problem

Set up the worksheet shown in Figure 5.7.

Estimating the future net cash flows of a project

In large firms, the accountant prepares forecasted income statements related to new investment projects (that is, he or she summarizes the future cash revenues, cash expenses and profit related to the new projects) and then the financial director uses these statements to evaluate the projects. The future net cash flows generated by a project are cash flows that result from undertaking the project and occur while the project is in operation. Net cash flows that occur as a direct result of a new project are calculated by taking the difference between the cash revenues and cash expenses attributable to the project. The cash revenues and cash expenses are comprised of several components and the net cash flows generated by an investment project can be determined by using the equations shown in Figure 5.8.

	Turnover
minus	Cost of goods sold
equals	Gross profit
minus	Operating expenses
minus	Depreciation
equals	Net operating profit
minus/plus	Other expenses/revenues
equals	Profit before tax
minus	Tax
equals	Profit after tax
plus	Depreciation
equals	Cash flow after tax
minus	Change in net working capital requirements
equals	Net cash flow

Figure 5.8. Calculating the net cash flow

Revenues and expenses may occur at different times during a given accounting year but for the sake of the theory we usually assume that they occur on the last day of the year.

Example 5.3 Estimating the net cash flows of an investment project

Once more, consider the data given in Example 5.1. We assume that the firm's project will require net working capital as shown in Figure 5.9. The results project the firm's net working capital requirements without and with the new project. Assuming that the project is undertaken, the net working capital increases up to the end of year 2. At the end of the project's life (that is, at the end of year 5), the investment in net working capital is recovered.

```
-------------------------------------------------------------------------------
              A                 B        C        D        E        F        G
21 ESTIMATING THE WORKING CAPITAL REQUIREMENTS (£000s)
22 ==================================================
23                                   ----------------------------------------
24                                    1991     1992     1993     1994     1995
25 WITHOUT THE PROJECT
26 Stocks                            4,650    5,420    6,190    6,950    7,720
27 Debtors                           2,790    3,260    3,720    4,180    4,640
28 Creditors                         2,290    2,670    3,040    3,430    3,800
29                                   ----------------------------------------
30                                   5,150    6,010    6,870    7,700    8,560
31 WITH THE PROJECT
32 Stocks                            5,800    6,380    6,770    7,110    7,000
33 Debtors                           3,200    3,520    3,740    3,930    3,800
34 Creditors                         2,500    2,750    2,920    3,070    2,240
35                                   ----------------------------------------
36                                   6,500    7,150    7,590    7,971    8,560
37
38 WORKING CAPITAL             950   1,350    1,140      720      271        0
-------------------------------------------------------------------------------
```

Figure 5.9. Net working capital required for the new project of AK Textiles

After estimating the net working capital requirements for the new project we can apply the formulae presented in Figure 5.8 for the estimation of the project's cash flows. The life of the project is five years and AK Textiles uses the straight-line depreciation method. Therefore, the annual depreciation is £1,050,000. To calculate the net cash flow generated by a project in a given period, you should first add the depreciation to the profit after tax of that period and then deduct from the result the changes in net working capital that occurred during that same period. For example, the first year's net cash flow of the project under consideration is calculated as follows (figures are rounded):

£594,000 + £1,050,000 – £400,000 = £1,244,000

Figure 5.10 estimates the net cash flows that result from investing in the project.

	A	B	C	D	E	F	G
41	ESTIMATING THE CASH FLOWS OF THE NEW PROJECT (£000s)						
42	==						
43			1991	1992	1993	1994	1995
44			----------	----------	----------	----------	----------
45	Turnover		6,500	6,825	7,166	6,808	6,468
46	Trading Expenses		4,550	4,778	5,016	4,766	4,528
47			----------	----------	----------	----------	----------
48	Trading Profit		1,950	2,048	2,150	2,042	1,940
49	Depreciation		1,050	1,050	1,050	1,050	1,050
50			----------	----------	----------	----------	----------
51	Profit Before Tax		900	998	1,100	992	890
52	Tax		306	339	374	337	303
53			----------	----------	----------	----------	----------
54	Profit After Tax		594	658	726	655	588
55	Depreciation		1,050	1,050	1,050	1,050	1,050
56			----------	----------	----------	----------	----------
57	Cash Flow After Tax		1,644	1,708	1,776	1,705	1,638
58	Changes in NWC		(400)	210	420	450	271
59			----------	----------	----------	----------	----------
60	Net Cash Flow		1,244	1,918	2,196	2,154	1,908

Figure 5.10. Estimating the net cash flows of AK Textiles' capital project

Problem

Set up the worksheets shown in Figures 5.9 and 5.10.

Accountants prepare their income statement using different principles from those used by a financial director for the estimation of a project's net cash flow, these differences being discussed below:

1 Accountants treat depreciation as an expense and for each period it is deducted from revenue in determining the period's operating profit. This treatment of depreciation is associated with the accounting convention of spreading capital expenditures over the life of the project. The deduction of depreciation from revenue permits the firm to reduce its tax payment, but depreciation does not represent an actual cash outlay. Thus, the cash flow after tax is computed by adding back the depreciation, which is deducted as an expense on the firm's income statement, to the profit after tax.

2 Interest expense is a real cash expense. Accountants calculate the profit before tax as the difference between profit before interest and tax and interest. Nevertheless, interest expense is not included in the net cash flow calculations because the dis-

counted process incorporates these costs into the determination of the discount rate. Including indirect expense in the cash flow analysis constitutes double counting. Likewise, any other kind of financing cost (for example, dividends) is not included in the cash flow estimation process.

3 When a firm expands its operations, there is usually an increase in the level of current assets and current liabilities. The former typically includes debtors (that is, sales that are not yet paid) and stocks and the latter usually includes creditors (that is, purchases that are not yet paid for). The difference between the increase in stocks, debtors and creditors is called the change in net working capital requirements.

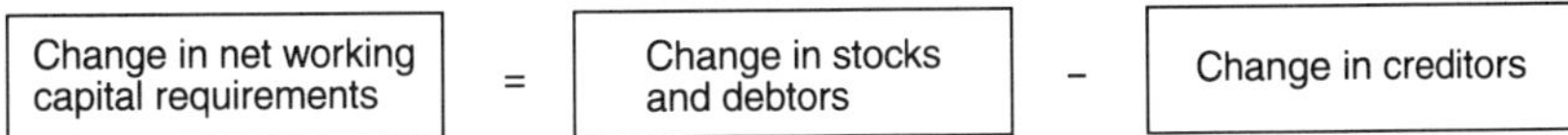

The accounting profit ignores the change in net working capital requirements. When cash flows are calculated, the change in net working capital requirements is added to the cash flow after tax to produce the net cash flow. The amount of the net working capital requirements is not depreciated and it is usually recovered at project termination. If the change in net working capital requirements is positive, this indicates that the increase in current liabilities is insufficient to finance the entire increase in current assets. In this case, the change in net working capital requirements is treated as an outflow. If the change in working capital requirements is negative, this indicates the existence of additional funds (for example, obtained when stocks are sold and not replaced, or obtained from a short-term loan, and so on). In this instance, the change in net working capital requirements is treated as an inflow. At the end of the project's life, we can assume that all stocks associated with the investment are sold off and not replaced and all debtors are collected.

4 At the termination of an investment project there may be a salvage value. The estimated salvage value (if any) constitutes a cash flow. In many cases, the salvage value is subject to some type of tax (for example, when the proceeds of sales exceed the initial cost of the assets). If a salvage value exists, then the terminal net cash flow of the project is equal to the cash flow after tax that occurs in the last year of the project's life plus the change in net working capital requirements for that same period plus the salvage value.

5 There are several overhead costs (for example, managerial salaries, rent, electricity, general administration expenses, and so on) that are indirectly related to a new investment. From the financial point of view, overhead costs that are indirectly related to the project should not be charged to the investment.

6 Frequently, there is an opportunity cost associated with an investment in a project, that is, the rate of return that a firm might have earned if it had invested its funds on an alternative investment project. If this is the case, opportunity costs should be included when deriving the net cash flows from an investment project.

7 Sunk costs are costs that have already occurred and cannot be recovered. They should not be included in the derivation of the net cash flows from an investment project. Sunk costs are irrelevant because they cannot be recaptured and remain unchanged with the acceptance or rejection of the project. For example, an oil company should ignore costs related to past research for finding oil when it evaluates a new drilling investment project.

Capital budgeting methods

Assume that time is divided into yearly intervals and consider a series of future cash flows occurring at the last day of each of a specified number of ensuing years. Figure 5.11 presents a classification of the methods that may be used to appraise investment projects.

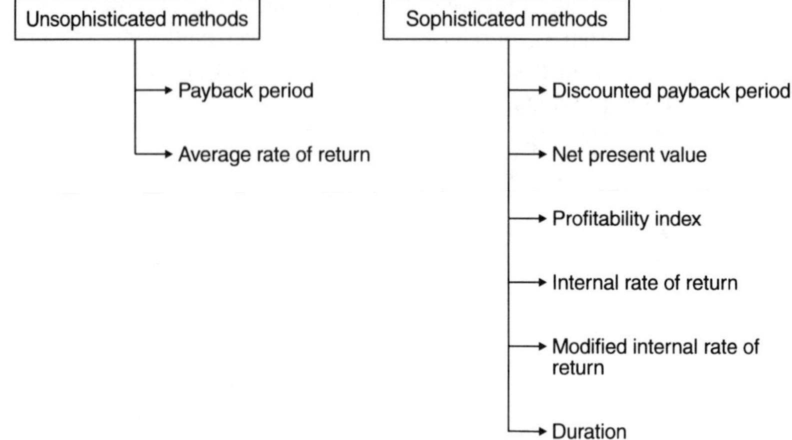

Figure 5.11. A classification of the capital budgeting techniques

Payback period

The payback period (PB) is commonly used to evaluate investment proposals. The concept of the payback period is summarized in Figure 5.12.

Definition The payback period of a project is the time required to recover its initial investment from the net cash flows generated by the project.

Calculation The payback period of a project is equal to the last full year, call it t, in which cumulative net cash flows are less than the initial investment plus the time required to recover the remainder of the initial investment from the cash flow in year $t+1$. If the future net cash flows are equal (an annuity situation), the payback period is computed by dividing the initial investment by the annuity's net cash flow:

$$\text{PB} = \frac{\text{Initial investment}}{\text{net cash flow}}$$

Interpretation The payback period of a project is the time lag in order to get the benefits from the project and provides some indication for the project's liquidity (that is, the speed with which the firm recovers the project's initial investment).

Figure 5.12. A summary of the payback period concept

Example 5.4 Calculating the payback period of a project

AK Textiles plc is considering a capital budgeting project that requires an initial investment of £6,200,000 and returns the following net cash flows: year 1: £1,244,000, year 2: £1,918,000, year 3: £2,196,000, year 4: £2,154,000 and year 5: £1,908,000. The payback period of this project can be calculated as follows:

$$\text{Payback period} = 3 + \frac{£6{,}200{,}000 - (£1{,}244{,}000 + £1{,}918{,}000 + £2{,}196{,}000)}{£2{,}154{,}000}$$

$$= 3.391 \text{ years}$$

Figure 5.13 shows a method of calculating the payback period of a project using 1-2-3. The following function is stored in cell D8:

```
@IF(@SUM($B$7..B8)>=0,@TRUE,@FALSE)
```

In other words, if the accumulated cash flows are greater than or equal to the initial investment store the value 1 (that is, true), otherwise store the value 0 (that is, false). Then the contents of cell D8 are copied in the range D9..D12.

Next, the following function is stored in cell E7:

```
@IF(#NOT#D7#AND#D8,A7-($B$7+C7)/B8," ")
```

In other words, if the contents of cell D7 are represented as 0 (that is, false) and the contents of cell D8 are represented by 1 (that is, true) then the payback period is A7 – ($B$7+C7)/B8, otherwise store the blank string "". Finally, copy the contents of cell E7 into the cell in the range E8..E12.

	A	B	C	D	E	F
1		CALCULATING THE PAYBACK PERIOD OF A PROJECT				
2						
3	Year	Cash flows	Accumulated	Money	Payback	
4			cash flows	recovered	period	
5		(£000s)	(£000s)			
6						
7	0	(6,200)				
8	1	1,244	1,244	0		
9	2	1,918	3,162	0		
10	3	2,196	5,358	0	3.391	
11	4	2,154	7,512	1		
12	5	1,908	9,420	1		
13						

Figure 5.13. Calculating the payback period of an investment project

The spreadsheet described above can calculate the payback of any project with a life up to five years. The method can be easily extended for projects with lives greater than five years.

Decision criterion for the payback period

When employing the payback period method, a firm must determine its maximum or target acceptable payback period for the project under consideration. The payback period's (PP) decision criterion (assuming independent projects) can be summarized as:

IF PAYBACK PERIOD ≤ TARGET PP THEN ACCEPT THE PROJECT

When mutually exclusive projects are being evaluated, only the best project (that is, the project with the smallest payback period) which meets the above decision criterion is selected.

Problem

Consider another investment project for AK Textiles plc (see Example 5.4) having the following estimated cash flows:

Year 0: £6,200,000
Year 1: £1,493,000
Year 2: £1,894,000

Year 3: £2,306,000
Year 4: £2,259,000
Year 5: £1,982,000

1 Calculate its payback period using the method shown in Figure 5.13.
2 Compare the cash flows of the second project with those given above in Example 5.4. Which project should be selected? (Assume that the two projects are mutually exclusive and the firm uses a target payback period of 3.1 years.)
3 Conduct a sensitivity analysis of the payback period with respect to changes in the initial investment (use the second project of AK Textiles and a range of initial investment of £6,000,000 to £6,700,000 in steps of £100,000). Graph the results from the sensitivity analysis and discuss the presented graph.

Evaluation of the payback period method

The payback period method is frequently utilized because it is simple to understand. It is argued that the payback period method is easy to apply. This argument, however, can be questioned today when the personal computer can easily compute the net present value and the internal rate of return of a project. Additionally, the payback period provides a crude measure of risk associated with the project and gives some indication of the project's liquidity. Projects with shorter payback periods are frequently viewed as having more liquidity and thus being less risky than those with longer payback periods. The payback period method also has some weaknesses.

Probably the most serious problem is that the method does not take fully into account the time value of money.

Example 5.5 Illustrating that the payback period method ignores the time value of money

The payback period method partially recognizes the time value of money, because in view of this method the shorter the payback period the better the investment project. Assume that AK Textiles plc is considering two projects A and B. The estimated cash flows are shown in Figure 5.14.

Year	Cash flows for project A (£000s)	Cash flows for project B (£000s)
0	(6,200)	(6,200)
1	1,244	100
2	1,918	200
3	2,196	5,060
4	2,154	2,149
5	1,908	1,880

Figure 5.14. The cash flows of two alternative investment projects A and B

The payback period of project A is 3.391 (see Example 5.4). The payback period of project B is calculated as follows:

$$\text{Payback period} = 3 + \frac{£6,200,000 - (£100,000 + £200,000 + £5,060,000)}{£2,149,000}$$

$$= 3.391 \text{ years}$$

According to the criterion of the payback period method, projects A and B would be equally desirable since they have the same payback period of 3.391 years. However, project A would be preferable because it realizes cash earlier than project B.

A second problem is that the method ignores net cash flows generated in periods after the initial investment has been recovered. The payback period, consequently, is not a measure of the project's profitability.

Example 5.6 Illustrating that the payback period method ignores the cash flows after the payback period

Assume that AK Textiles plc is evaluating two investment projects A and C. Estimated cash flow streams for A and C are given in Figure 5.15.

Year	Cash flows for project A (£000s)	Cash flows for project C (£000s)
0	(6,200)	(6,200)
1	1,244	1,200
2	1,918	1,900
3	2,196	2,200
4	2,154	2,302
5	1,908	10,000

Figure 5.15. The cash flows of two alternative investment projects A and C

Both the projects A and C have the same payback of 3.391 years, thus in view of the payback technique's criterion they are equally attractive. However, it can be seen from Figure 5.15 that project C returns larger net cash flows than project A after the expiry of the payback period. Therefore, project C is preferable to project A.

Discounted payback

The payback period method does not take into account the time value of money, this can be accomplished by using the discounted payback. The latter discounts the cash flows and then uses the discounted cash flows to calculate the payback in the usual way.

Example 5.7 Calculating the discounted payback period of a project

Consider the investment proposal of AK Textiles plc whose cash flows are given in Example 5.4 and assume a discount rate of 12 per cent. The worksheet in Figure 5.16 calculates the payback period in a similar fashion to that presented in Example 5.4, but it uses the discounted net cash flows shown in column C. The discounted net cash flow stored in cell C11 is calculated as follows:

```
+B11/(1+$C$4)^A11
```

To calculate the discounted net cash flows for years 2, 3, 4 and 5 copy the contents of cell C11 in the range C12..C15.

The payback period is 3.927 years. It is higher than the payback period of 3.391 (see Example 5.4) since it takes into account the time value of money.

	A	B	C	D	E	F
1		CALCULATING THE DISCOUNTED PAYBACK PERIOD OF A PROJECT				
2		==				
3						
4	Discount Rate ----->		12.0%			
5						
6	Year	Cash flows	Discounted	Accumulated	Money	Payback
7			cash flows	cash flows	recovered	period
8		(£000s)	(£000s)	(£000s)		
9						
10	0	(6,200)				
11	1	1,244	1,111	1,111	0	
12	2	1,918	1,529	2,640	0	
13	3	2,196	1,563	4,203	0	3.927
14	4	2,154	1,369	5,572	1	
15	5	1,908	1,083	6,654	1	
16						

Figure 5.16. Calculating the discounted payback period of a project

Problem

AK Textiles plc is considering another investment whose estimated cash flows are as follows:

Year 0: £6,200,000
Year 1: £1,493,000
Year 2: £1,894,000
Year 3: £2,306,000
Year 4: £2,259,000
Year 5: £1,982,000

1. Calculate the discounted payback period of this investment using the method shown in Figure 5.16.
2. Compare the cash flows of the second project with those given above in the example. Which project should be selected if they are mutually exclusive? (Assume that the firm uses a target payback period of 3.1 years.)

Like the payback period approach, the discounted payback period method does not take into consideration the net cash flows generated in periods after the recovery of the initial investment.

Average rate of return

There are a number of alternative definitions (and names) for the average rate of return and here we will base its definition upon cash flows rather than accounting information. Figure 5.17 presents a summary of the average rate of return concept.

Decision criterion for the average rate of return

The decision criterion for the average rate of return (ARR) can be summarized as follows:

IF AVERAGE RATE OF RETURN ≧ TARGET ARR THEN ACCEPT THE PROJECT

If mutually exclusive projects are being evaluated, only the best project (that is, the project with the largest average rate of return) which meets the above decision criterion is selected.

Definition One definition of the average rate of return of a project is: a measure of the profitability of an investment by relating the initial investment to the future annual average net cash flow.

Calculation The average rate of return of a project is equal to the average net cash flow over the life of the project divided by its initial investment:

$$\text{ARR} = \frac{\left(\sum_{t=1}^{N} \text{CF}_t\right)/N}{\text{Initial investment}}$$

N = the number of years over which cash flows occurred.

$\text{CF}_1, \ldots \text{CF}_N$ = the net cash flows in years $1, \ldots N$, respectively.

Interpretation The average rate of return of a project can be interpreted as the annual average rate of return expected from the project.

Figure 5.17. A summary of the average rate of return concept

Evaluation of the average rate of return method

The average rate of return is simple to understand and easy to apply. In addition, it takes into consideration the total benefits arising out of the investment project over its entire expected life, unlike the payback period method. Perhaps the major shortcoming of utilizing the average rate of return is that the method does not account for the timing of cash flows. As in the case of the payback period, one can use the discounted average rate of return. This approach discounts the cash flows and then uses the discounted cash flows to compute the average rate of return in the usual way.

Net present value

The present value method is one of the most commonly employed sophisticated capital budgeting approaches. The concept of the net present value can be presented in summary as shown in Figure 5.18.

Definition The net present value is a method of calculating the benefits from an investment project in terms of current money assuming that a required rate of return must be earned.

Calculation The net present value of an investment project is the present value of the expected future net cash flows from the project *minus* its initial investment. The formula for computing a project's net present value can be expressed as follows:

Net present value of an investment project	=	Present value of the project's expected future net cash flows	−	Project's initial investment

$$\text{NPV} = \sum_{t=1}^{N} \frac{\text{CF}_t}{(1+r)^t} - \text{INI}$$

where

r = the required rate of return (or discount rate) on the project.

N = the number of years over which cash flows have occurred.

$\text{CF}_1, \ldots \text{CF}_N$ = the net cash flows in years $1, \ldots N$, respectively.

Interpretation The net present value of a project measures its expected value in terms of current money after taking into account all its costs. Thus, it provides an absolute measure of the project's expected benefits in terms of current money assuming that a required rate of return must be earned.

Figure 5.18. A summary of the net present value concept

Example 5.8 Calculating the net present value of an investment project

The net present value method can be illustrated by using the project of AK Textiles plc presented in Example 5.3. The net present value (NPV) of the project is:

$$\text{NPV} = \frac{£1{,}244{,}000}{(1+0.12)} + \frac{£1{,}918{,}000}{(1+0.12)^2} + \frac{£2{,}196{,}000}{(1+0.12)^3} + \frac{£2{,}154{,}000}{(1+0.12)^4} + \frac{£1{,}908{,}000}{(1+0.12)^5}$$
$$- £6{,}200{,}000 = £454{,}000$$

Therefore, the expected worth from the project is £454,000. In other words, if the firm adopts the project, all the expected cash flows are realized and the discount rate is 12 per cent, then the firm's existing shareholders' current value of wealth increases by £454,000.

The net present value of the project can also be calculated by using 1-2-3. The worksheet in Figure 5.19 uses in cell B74 the following financial function of 1-2-3:

```
@NPV(B63,B68..B72)+B67
```

where B63 contains the discount rate of 12 per cent, B68..B72 is the range containing the net cash flows that occur at each year during the life of the investment and B67 contains the project's initial investment. Note that the initial investment is stored in cell B67 as a negative entry and so it has to be added to the present value of the net cash flows.

```
------------------------------------------------------------------------------
                A                 B          C         D         E        F        G
61 CALCULATING THE NPV OF A PROJECT OF AK TEXTILES
62 ===============================================
63 Discount Rate --->        12.0%
64 -------------------------------------------
65               YEAR    CASH FLOW (£000s)
66 -------------------------------------------
67                  0     (6,200)
68                  1      1,244
69                  2      1,918
70                  3      2,196
71                  4      2,154
72                  5      1,908
73                      ---------
74     NPV ------>           454
75
76
------------------------------------------------------------------------------
```

Figure 5.19. Calculating the NPV of a project using 1-2-3

Why do we use 1-2-3 to calculate the net present value when we can compute it using a calculator? The answer to this question can be stated simply as follows: 1-2-3 offers an edit facility for your entries which can save you time and it also provides a recalculation facility for enhancing your analysis. Suppose you are using your calculator to compute the net present value of an investment project with a useful life of 15 years. Assume that after entering in the calculator your 12th net cash flow you realize that your earlier entry of the 11th net cash flow was wrong. In this instance, you have to re-enter the net cash flows again. However, 1-2-3 makes it easy to edit entries if you make an error after typing in the entry.

On the other hand, you may wish to use the recalculation facility to examine what would happen to your result if one of the input variables changes. With 1-2-3, whenever you change a data value, the result of the net present value (and of any formula or function) that depends on that value can change automatically. For example, you can calculate the net present value of the AK Textiles' project for as many values of discount rate that you wish to use or save the results today until you need to use them again.

Decision criterion for the net present value

If the net present value of a project is greater than zero, the present value of the project's expected net cash flows is greater than its initial investment. Therefore, the current value of the firm's existing shareholders should rise as a result of accepting the project. The decision criterion for the net present value can be stated in summary as follows:

IF NET PRESENT VALUE $\geqq$ 0 THEN ACCEPT THE PROJECT

If mutually exclusive projects are being evaluated, the best project (that is, the project with the largest net present value) which meets the above decision criterion is selected.

Problem

Calculate the net present value of the AK Textiles' project, given the following estimated cash flows (use a worksheet similar to that shown in Figure 5.19; the discount rate is 12 per cent):

Year 0: £6,200,000
Year 1: £1,493,000
Year 2: £1,894,000
Year 3: £2,306,000
Year 4: £2,259,000
Year 5: £1,982,000

Consider also the project whose net present value was calculated in Example 5.8. Which project should AK Textiles select if the projects are mutually exclusive?

Evaluation of the net present value method

The first advantage of using the net present value is that it considers both the magnitude and the timing of a project's cash flows over its expected lifetime. The net present value approach is also consistent with the maximization of the ordinary shareholders' wealth (the objective assumed by the theory of financial management) and it provides a direct measure of a project's contribution to the ordinary shareholders' wealth.

There are also some disadvantages associated with the use of the net present value method. First, most business people find it difficult to interpret the net present value estimate because it is an absolute measure of return (unlike the internal rate of return which is stated in terms of a rate of return). Second, the net present value decision criterion may provide unsatisfactory results when mutually exclusive projects with different lives are being evaluated (see the method of the net present value with infinite replicated cash flows discussed later in this chapter).

Profitability index

The profitability index provides an alternative method of appraising investment projects and its concept is summarized in Figure 5.20.

Definition The profitability index is a method showing the number of times a project's total net cash flows (in today's values) cover its initial investment.

Calculation The profitability index (PI) of a project is the present value of the net cash flows divided by the initial investment. In general, the PI of a project can be calculated as follows

$$\text{PI} = \frac{\text{Net present value}}{\text{Initial investment}} + 1$$

Interpretation The profitability index of a project is a relative measure of the profitability associated with the project. It measures the present value return of the project for each pound of initial investment.

Figure 5.20. A summary of the profitability index concept

Example 5.9 Calculating the profitability index of an investment project.

The profitability index of AK Textiles plc's project can be easily calculated by using the net present value computed in Example 5.8. That is

$$\text{PI} = \frac{£454{,}000}{£6{,}200{,}000} + 1 = 1.073$$

Thus, for each pound of initial investment the project of AK Textiles returns £1.073.

Figure 5.21 provides a graph of the sensitivity of the profitability index with respect to changes in the initial investment.

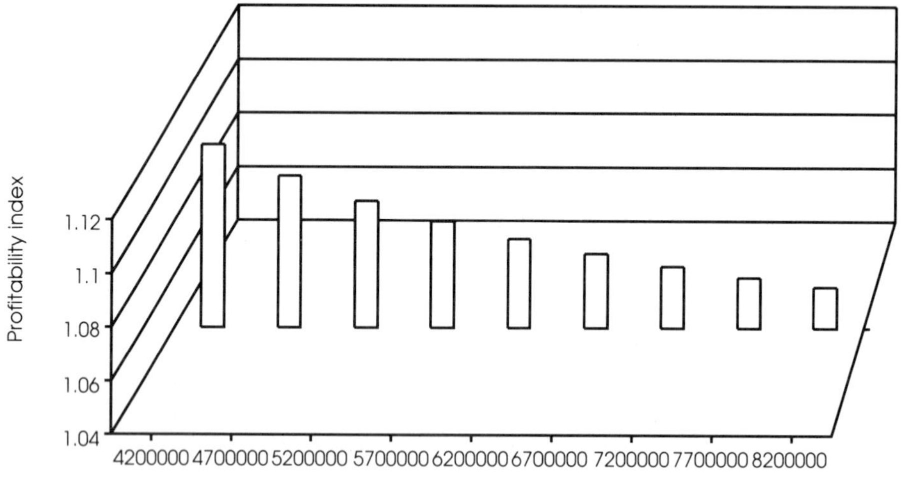

Figure 5.21. Graphing the results from a sensitivity of the PI to changes in initial cost

The NPV/cost ratio calculates the yield of an investment project in terms of current money assuming that a required rate of return must be earned. The NPV/cost ratio is just the net present value of the project divided by its initial investment. Therefore, the NPV/cost ratio of AK Textiles' project is 7.3 per cent. This can also be interpreted as a 7.3 per cent return on the £6,200,000 investment. Stated differently, the investment will return a net present value that is equal to 7.3 per cent of the initial investment.

The NPV/cost ratio is expressed as a percentage and thus is more intuitively understood as compared with the net present value method which expresses the benefits from a project in actual pounds.

Decision criterion for the profitability index

A project is accepted if the present value of the net cash flows is greater than or equal to its initial investment. The decision criterion for the profitability index is summarized below:

IF THE PROFITABILITY INDEX ≧ 1 THEN ACCEPT PROJECT

If mutually exclusive projects are being evaluated, only the best project (that is, the project with the largest profitability index) which meets the above decision criterion is selected.

Problem

AK Textiles plc is attempting to select the best of two mutually exclusive projects. The profitability index of the first project is calculated in Example 5.9. The initial investment and net cash flows of the second investment project are given below:

Year 0: £6,200,000
Year 1: £1,493,000
Year 2: £1,894,000
Year 3: £2,306,000
Year 4: £2,259,000
Year 5: £1,982,000

1 Calculate the profitability index of the second project of AK Textiles.
2 Conduct a sensitivity analysis of the second project's profitability index with respect to changes in the initial outflow (consider the range £4,200,000 to £8,200,000 in steps of £500,000). Discuss your results.
3 Which project should AK Textiles select?
4 Calculate the NPV/cost ratio for each project.
5 Which project has the largest NPV/cost ratio?

Evaluation of the profitability index method

The profitability index considers both the magnitude and the timing of a project's cash flows over its lifetime. The profitability index has the additional advantage that it provides a relative measure of the present value return for each pound of initial investment.

The profitability index has two disadvantages. First, most business people find it difficult to interpret the profitability index estimate because it does not have the same intuitive appeal of a rate of return. Second, the profitability index's criterion may provide unsatisfactory results when mutually exclusive projects with different sizes of investments are being evaluated.

Internal rate of return

The internal rate of return is probably the most popular method for evaluating investment projects. A summary of the internal rate of return concept is presented in Figure 5.22.

Figure 5.22. A summary of the internal rate of return concept

Definition The internal rate of return of an investment project is the break-even return level that equates the project's present value of net cash flows with its initial investment.
Calculation The internal rate of return of a project is the discount rate at which the project's net present value equals zero. The internal rate of return (IRR) can be calculated by solving the following equation:

$$\sum_{t=1}^{N} \frac{CF_t}{(1+IRR)^t} - INI = 0$$

Interpretation The internal rate of return of an investment project is expressed as a percentage and it can be interpreted as the rate of return a firm is expected to earn on the project.

The internal rate of return of a project can be approximated by using linear interpolation (that is, a mathematical method employed to find fractional values when the usual future value tables are used). This trial-and-error method involves utilizing various discount rates, calculating for each rate the net present value and looking for the change of the net present value's sign (that is, from positive to negative and vice versa). Then the interpolated internal rate of return can be computed by using the following equation:

$$IRR = r_1 + \frac{NPV_1}{NPV_1 - NPV_2}(r_2 - r_1)$$

where

$r_1 < r_2$.

NPV_1 = the net present value of the project (at discount rate r_1) before the change of the sign.

NPV_2 = the net present value of the project (at discount rate r_2) after the change of the sign.

Example 5.10 Calculating the internal rate of return of an investment project

Once again, consider the investment project of AK Textiles presented in Examples 5.1 and 5.3. We know from Example 5.8 that the net present value of the project at 12 per cent is £454,000. All the expected future net cash flows of the project are positive and the net present value is positive. Thus, the internal rate of return is greater than 12 per cent. The net present value of the project at 13 per cent is £282,000, at 14 per cent is £116,000 and at 15 per cent is –£44,000 (figures are rounded). Therefore, the internal rate of return of the project lies between 14 and 15 per cent. The internal rate of return is calculated as follows:

$$0.14 + \frac{£116{,}000}{(£116{,}000 + £44{,}000)}(0.15 - 0.14) = 14.72 \text{ per cent}$$

Therefore, the firm expects to earn 14.72 per cent from this investment project.

Example 5.11 Calculating the internal rate of return using 1-2-3

1-2-3's financial function `@IRR` calculates the internal rate of return of a project. The worksheet shown in Figure 5.23 stores the following function in cell B76:

```
@IRR(0.10,B67..B72)
```

where 0.10 is the initial guess for the internal rate of return and B67..B72 is the range of cash flows (that is, initial investment and net cash flows). 1-2-3 utilizes the guess of 10 per cent as the starting point of the iterative process of computing the internal rate of return.

The internal rate of return is displayed in Figure 5.23 with a two decimal points format (the actual figure is 14.72079 per cent, while the internal rate of return calculated in Example 5.10 is equal to 14.725 per cent).

```
               A                 B       C        D        E         F        G
61 CALCULATING THE IRR OF A PROJECT OF AK TEXTILES
62 ==============================================
63 Discount Rate --->        12.0%
64 --------------------------------------------
65              YEAR    CASH FLOW (£000)
66 --------------------------------------------
67                 0      (6,200)
68                 1       1,244
69                 2       1,918
70                 3       2,196
71                 4       2,154
72                 5       1,908
73                      ---------
74
75
76    IRR -------->       14.72%
```

Figure 5.23. Calculating the IRR of a project using 1-2-3

Decision criterion for the internal rate of return

The required rate of return (or discount rate) of a project is the return which will provide a standard for evaluating projects using the internal rate of return method. A good investment should have a required rate of return that is higher than the internal rate of return and therefore the following decision criterion can be applied:

IF IRR $\geq$ REQUIRED RATE OF RETURN THEN ACCEPT THE PROJECT

If mutually exclusive projects are being evaluated, only the best project (that is, the project with the highest internal rate of return) which meets the above decision criterion is selected.

Problem

AK Textiles plc is considering an investment project in addition to that presented in Example 5.11. The project's net cash flows are listed below:

Year 0: £6,200,000
Year 1: £1,493,000
Year 2: £1,894,000
Year 3: £2,306,000
Year 4: £2,259,000
Year 5: £1,982,000

1 Calculate the project's internal rate of return using the linear interpolation method. Compare this internal rate of return with that derived using 1-2-3's financial function @IRR.

2 Conduct a sensitivity analysis of the project's internal rate of return with respect to changes in the initial outflow (consider the range £4,200,000 to £8,200,000 in steps of £500,000). Discuss your results.

3 Consider also the project whose internal rate of return was calculated in Example 5.11; which project should AK Textiles prefer? (Assume these two projects are mutually exclusive.)

Evaluation of the internal rate of return method

Like the net present value method, the internal rate of return considers both the magnitude and the timing of a project's cash flows over the entire life of the project. Additionally, the internal rate of return is measured as a percentage, which is easy to understand.

The internal rate of return approach has some serious disadvantages. First, the decision criterion used may provide unsatisfactory results when mutually exclusive projects with different sizes of net investments are being evaluated. Second internal rates of return are not additive.

Example 5.12 Illustrating that internal rates of return do not obey the additivity principle

Consider two investment projects for AK Textiles plc whose cash flows are shown in Figure 5.24 (figures are in £000s). The net present value of project A + B is £768,000 and it equals the sum of the net present values of projects A and B. However, the internal rate of return of project A + B is not equal to 14.72 per cent + 14.91 per cent.

```
            A                B                  C                D
 1 THE ADDITIVITY PRINCIPLE WITH RESPECT TO THE NPV AND IRR
 2 =========================================================
 3 Discount Rate --->            12.0%
 4 ----------------------------------------------------------------
 5                YEAR   CASH FLOW        CASH FLOW      CASH FLOW
 6                       OF PROJECT A     OF PROJECT B   OF PROJECT A+B
 7 ----------------------------------------------------------------
 8                   0        (6,200)          (4,000)        (10,200)
 9                   1         1,244            1,000           2,244
10                   2         1,918            1,100           3,018
11                   3         2,196            1,200           3,396
12                   4         2,154            1,320           3,474
13                   5         1,908            1,500           3,408
14                       ------------------------------------------
15    NPV ------>                454              314             768
16    IRR -------->           14.72%           14.91%          14.79%
17 ----------------------------------------------------------------
```

Figure 5.24. The additivity principle with respect to the NPV and IRR

When the internal rate of return is calculated, one of the following problems may also occur:

- The project's internal rate of return may be undetermined.
- The project may have multiple internal rates of return.

The following rules may be helpful:

Rule 1 No positive internal rate of return exists if the cash flow sign never changes, or no positive internal rate of return exists if the initial investment is greater than the sum of the net cash flows.

Rule 2 If the internal rate of return is determined, the maximum number of (real) internal rates of return is equal to the number of the cash flow sign changes in the cash flow stream. For example, the stream of cash flows –£6,200,000 £1,244,000, £2,196,000, £2,154,000 and £1,908,000 has one internal rate of return because the cash flow sign changes once (that is, from a negative initial investment to a positive expected net cash flow of £1,244,000).

Rule 3 If a sign change occurs and the initial and final cash flows have the same sign, an even number of internal rates of return exists.

Rule 4 If a sign change occurs and the initial and final cash flows do not have the same sign, an odd number of internal rates of return exists.

Example 5.13 An example of undetermined internal rate of return

Consider an investment proposal with the following information: initial investment = £20,000, useful life = 2 years, net cash flow for year 1 = £56,000, and net cash flow for year 2 = –£42,000. The internal rate of return of this project is undetermined because the equation NPV = 0 does not have a real solution. When 1-2-3 cannot solve the equation NPV = 0, it displays an error message. However, note that if 1-2-3 displays an error message, it does not always mean that the internal rate of return is undetermined (for example, 1-2-3 displays an error message if you do not use properly its function `@IRR`).

Example 5.14 An example of multiple internal rates of return

The cash flows of an investment project are shown in Figure 5.25. We know that the maximum number of (real) internal rates of return equals the number of the cash flow sign changes in the cash flow stream. In our example there exist three sign changes and thus three internal rates of return. Each internal rate of return can be calculated by using the 1-2-3 financial function `@IRR`. For example, cell B15 contains the following function:

```
@IRR(B11,$B$6..$B$9)
```

where B11 contains the first guess for the internal rate of return. Similarly the second and the third guesses for the 1-2-3 function can be used to calculate the second and the third internal rates of the project, respectively. The three internal rates of return are 10, 20 and 30 per cent, respectively.

The second part of the worksheet presented in Figure 5.25 shows how changing the discount rate affects the net present value of the project. The results are derived with the aid of the `/Data Table 1` command (the input cell 1 is cell B15 which is referenced by the formula stored in cell B19).

Applying the internal rate of return criterion to this investment project can produce incorrect decisions. According to the internal rate of return decision rule you should accept a project whose internal rate of return is greater than the discount rate. Assume that the discount rate is 15 per cent. If, for example, you assume an internal rate of return of 20 per cent then you should accept the project. However, Figure 5.26 shows that at a discount rate of 15 per cent the net present value of the project is negative. Next, assume that you did not realize that the project has a multiple solution and your estimated internal rate of return is 20

```
                     A                   B              C              D
 1 INTERNAL RATE OF RETURN (MULTIPLE SOLUTIONS)
 2 ============================================
 3 ---------------------------------------
 4                     YEAR       CASH FLOW
 5 ---------------------------------------
 6                        0        (10,000)
 7                        1          38,000
 8                        2        (47,700)
 9                        3          19,800
10
11 First Guess of IRR ---->           8.00%
12 Second Guess of IRR --->          25.00%
13 Third Guess of IRR --->           70.00%
14
15 First IRR --------->              10.00%
16 Second IRR -------->              20.00%
17 Third IRR -------->               50.00%
18 ---------------------------------------
19 Net Present Value at 10%            0.00
20
21 A SENSITIVITY ANALYSIS OF THE NPV WITH RESPECT THE DISCOUNT RATE
22 ================================================================
23
24          ------------------------------
25                      +B19
26                   5.0%             29.15
27                  10.0%              0.00
28                  15.0%             -5.75
29                  20.0%              0.00
30                  25.0%              9.60
31                  30.0%             18.21
32                  35.0%             22.86
33                  40.0%             21.87
34                  45.0%             14.35
35                  50.0%              0.00
36          ------------------------------
```

Figure 5.25. An example of multiple internal rates of return

per cent. If your discount rate is 25 per cent, then according to the internal rate of return decision rule your project should be rejected. But at 25 per cent the project's net present value is positive.

The net present value profiles for four different projects are graphed in Figures 5.26(a)–(d).

What can you do in order to avoid the problem associated with multiple internal rates of return? First you can use the net present value which is safer. Second you can use the modified internal rate of return.

Modified internal rate of return method

Figure 5.27 summarizes the modified internal rate of return concept.

Example 5.15 Calculating the modified internal rate of a project

In the present example we refer to the information provided in Example 5.14. The present value of the cash outflows at 12 per cent is

$$£10{,}000 + £47{,}700/(1 + 0.12)\hat{\ }2 = £48{,}026$$

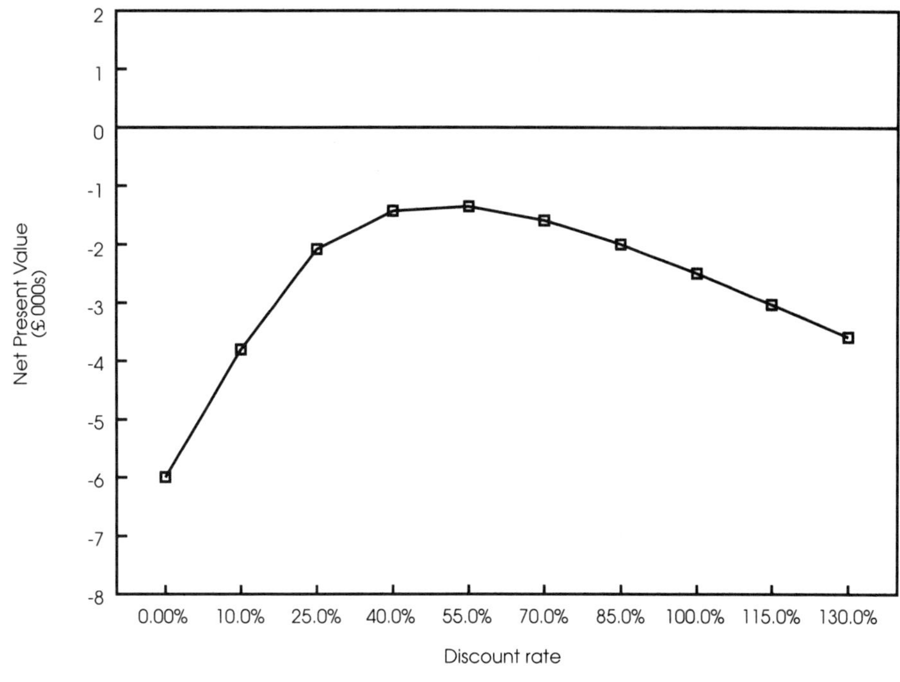

Figure 5.26a. Undetermined rate of return for project A

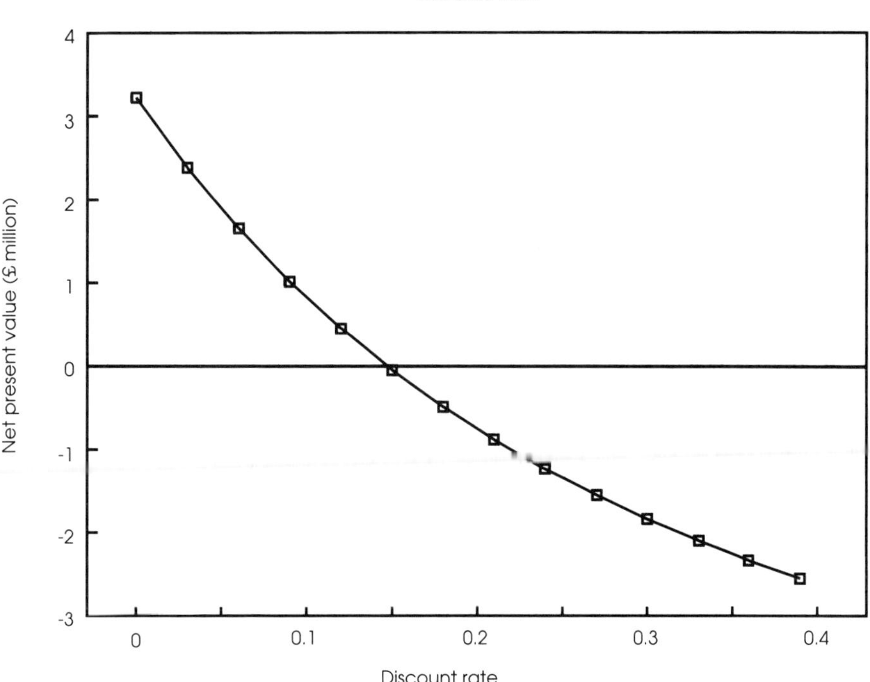

Figure 5.26b. Net present value for project B

The terminal value of the project is defined as the future value of the project's cash inflows compounded at the project's required rate of return. Therefore, the terminal value at 12 per cent is calculated as follows:

$$TV = £38{,}000 \times (1 + 0.12)\hat{}2 + £19{,}800 = £67{,}467$$

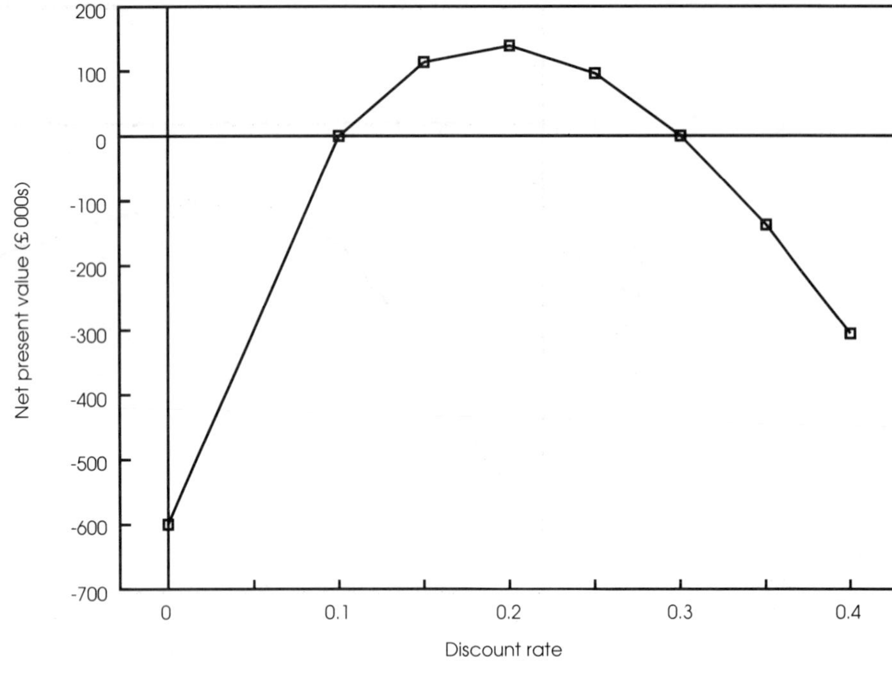

Figure 5.26c. Two internal rates of return for project C

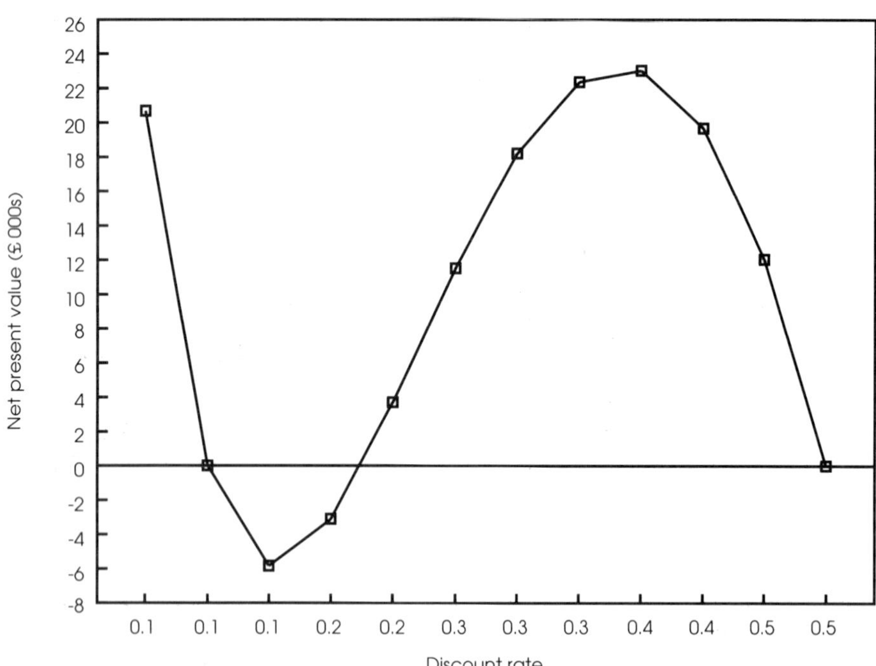

Figure 5.26d. Three internal rates of return for project D

Definition The modified internal rate of return of an investment project is the break-even return level that equates the project's present value of cash outflows with the present value of the project's terminal value.

Calculation The modified internal rate of return of a project is the rate MIRR which satisfies the following equation:

$$\sum_{t=0}^{N} \frac{CO_t}{(1+r)^t} = \frac{TV}{(1+MIRR)^N}$$

where

CO = the cash outflow in period t.

r = the required rate of return (or discount rate) on the project.

TV = the terminal or future value of project's cash flows.

Interpretation The modified internal rate of return of an investment project is expressed as a percentage and it can be interpreted as an indicator of the expected profitability of the project.

Figure 5.27. A summary of the modified internal rate of return concept

Therefore, the modified internal rate of return satisfies the following equation:

$$£48{,}026 = \frac{£67{,}467}{(1+\text{MIRR})^3}$$

or equivalently

$$\text{MIRR} = \left[\frac{£67{,}467}{£48{,}026}\right]^{1/3} - 1 = 11.997 \text{ per cent}$$

Since the modified internal rate of return is lower than the cost of capital, the project is unacceptable. The net present value of the project at 11.997 per cent is –£4.32 and thus the project will be rejected.

Duration

Duration accounts for both the amount of the project's net cash flows and the time period in which they are received. Figure 5.28 provides a summary of the duration concept.

Definition The duration of a project is a measure of the average maturity of a stream of net cash flows generated by an investment project.

Calculation The duration of a project represents a weighted average of maturity dates (that is, 1, 2, 3,...N), where the weight of a maturity date is equal to the ratio of the net cash flow to be received to the total present value of all net cash flows. In mathematical terms, the formula of the duration is:

$$D = \sum_{t=1}^{N} \frac{CF_t/(1+r)^t}{PV} t$$

N = the number of years over which cash flows occurred.

$CF_1, \ldots CF_N$ = the net cash flows in years $1, \ldots N$, respectively.

t = a given year number.

Interpretation The duration of a project is the average length of time before the benefits from the projects are received.

Figure 5.28. A summary of the duration concept

Example 5.16 Calculating the duration of an investment project

Consider the cash flow data given in Figure 5.29. Column C shows the discounted cash flows, and column D shows the duration's weights. For example, the first weight is 0.167 (that is, £1,111/(£454 + £6,200)). Column E shows the weighted discounted cash flows whose sum produces the duration of the project. Therefore, the average period of time before the benefits from the project occur is 2.97 years.

	A	B	C	D	E
1		CALCULATING THE DURATION OF A PROJECT			
2		====================================			
3	Discount Rate	12.0%			
4					
5	Year	Cash Flows	Discounted	Weight	Weighted
6		of Project A	Cash Flows		Discounted
7		(£000s)	(£000s)		Cash Flow
8					
9	0	(6,200)	(6,200)		
10	1	1,244	1,111	0.167	0.167
11	2	1,918	1,529	0.230	0.460
12	3	2,196	1,563	0.235	0.705
13	4	2,154	1,369	0.206	0.823
14	5	1,908	1,083	0.163	0.813
15			------		------
16		NPV ---------->	454	Duration -->	2.968
17			======		======

Figure 5.29. Calculating the duration of a project

The project's internal rate of return is 14.72 per cent (see Example 5.11). The net present value at 14.72 per cent is zero and the duration is 2.968 years. If the required rate of return is lower than 14.72 per cent, the net present value at that discount rate is positive and the duration longer than 2.968 years. On the other hand, if the required rate of return is higher than 14.72 per cent, we derive a negative net present value and a duration shorter than 2.968 years.

Earlier and/or larger net cash flows always shorten the duration of a project. For example, consider a project with the following net cash flows: year 1: 1,844, year 2: 2,318, year 3: 2,396, year 4: 2,354 and year 5: 2,108. Its duration is 2.841 years and as might be expected, the duration of this project is lower than that shown in Figure 5.29.

Ranking mutually exclusive projects

When two or more mutually exclusive projects are taken into consideration, the firm can select only one. The ranking of mutually exclusive projects may be different under the various accept–reject decision rules. For example, assume that the projects A and B in Example 5.5 are mutually exclusive. In view of the payback period method these projects are equally desirable, but A is preferable since it has a higher net present value. Likewise, if we assume that projects A and C in Example 5.6 are mutually exclusive, then conflict in ranking between the payback period method and the net present value method occurs. The net present value and the average rate of return are also given conflicting rankings when mutually exclusive projects are substantially different in the timing of cash flows. The net present value method and the profitability index method may rank mutually exclusive projects differently when the projects have substantially different cash flows.

Example 5.17 Differences between rankings by NPV and PI when two mutually exclusive projects are substantially different in the size of cash flows

Figure 5.30 shows two mutually exclusive investment projects A and D which have different sizes of cash flows. As can be seen, the net present value of project D exceeds that of project A, but the profitability index of project A is higher than that of project B (we assume a discount rate of 12 per cent). The net present value method is, theoretically, a better method than the profitability index approach, when conflicting rankings exist because it is consistent with the objective of maximizing the existing shareholders's wealth. When you choose the project with the higher net present value, among mutually exclusive alternatives, you increase the value of the firm by more than would competitive projects and thus maximize the existing shareholders' wealth. Therefore, project D will be accepted.

	A	B	C	D	E
1	CONFLICTING RANKINGS AMONG MUTUALLY EXCLUSIVE PROJECTS:NPV VERSUS PI				
2					
3	Year	Cash flows	Cash flows		
4		for Project A	for Project D		
5		(£000s)	(£000s)		
6					
7	0	(6,200)	(60,000)		
8	1	1,244	12,000		
9	2	1,918	16,400		
10	3	2,196	17,400		
11	4	2,154	20,100		
12	5	1,908	22,000		
13		--------	--------		
14	NPV ---->	454	1,431		
15	PI ----->	1.07	1.02		

Figure 5.30. Differences between rankings by NPV and PI

There are two basic conditions which cause the net present value and the internal rate of return methods to provide inconsistent rankings among mutually exclusive projects. These are: (a) projects that have differences in the size, or scale of cash flows; and (b) projects that have differences in the patterns of cash flows.

Example 5.18 Differences between rankings by NPV and IRR when two mutually exclusive projects are substantially different in the size of cash flows

Consider the two mutually exclusive projects A and D whose cash flows are presented in Example 5.17. The internal rates of return for projects A and D are 14.72 per cent and 12.87 per cent, respectively. Project A would be preferred because its internal rate of return is higher than that of project D. At a 12 per cent discount rate, project D has a higher net present value (see Example 5.17). In general, when the net present value and the internal rate of return methods provide conflicting rankings, the former method is preferable since the best project (that is, the project with the larger positive net present value) is the one which will have the most beneficial effect on the shareholders' wealth. Therefore, project D will be accepted.

Example 5.19 Differences between rankings by NPV and IRR when two mutually exclusive projects have different timings of cash flows

A firm is attempting to select the best of two mutually exclusive projects E and F. Figure 5.31 gives the relevant cash flows for each project. Looking at Figure 5.31, we observe that there exist significant differences in the timing of the projects' cash flows. The internal rate of return of project F is higher than that of project E, indicating that project F is the best project. However, the net present value of project E is greater than that of project F, implying that project E is preferable to F (we assume a discount rate of 12 per cent). In this case, we choose project E since it adds the most, among the two investment alternatives, to the shareholders' wealth.

	A	B	C	D	E
1	CONFLICTING RANKING BETWEEN MUTUALLY EXCLUSIVE PROJECTS:NPV VS IRR				
2	-------				
3					
4	Discount Rate	12.0%			
5	-------				
6	Year	Cash flows	Cash flows	Cash flows	
7		for Project E	for Project F	for E-F	
8		(£000s)	(£000s)	(£000s)	
9	-------				
10	0	(10,000)	(10,000)	0	
11	1	1,700	6,000	(4,300)	
12	2	2,500	4,200	(1,700)	
13	3	3,100	2,100	1,000	
14	4	4,300	1,300	3,000	
15	5	7,000	1,000	6,000	
16		-------	-------	-------	
17	NPV --->	2,422	1,594	828	
18	IRR --->	19.40%	21.03%	17.34%	

Figure 5.31. Conflicting rankings between mutually exclusive projects by NPV and IRR

Column E in Figure 5.31 shows the difference between the cash flows of the two projects. The rate of 17.34 per cent is called the crossover rate and it is the discount rate at which the projects' net present values are equal (see Figure 5.32). At a discount rate higher than the crossover rate of 17.34 per cent the net present value of project F is higher than that of project E. At a discount rate lower than 17.34 per cent the net present value of project F is lower than that of project E. The crossover discount rate is calculated by storing in cell D18 the function: `@IRR(0.10,D10..D15)`. Figure 5.32 presents the net present value profiles of projects E and F.

Figure 5.33 summarizes the cases where conflicting rankings can occur with mutually exclusive projects.

The use of the modified internal rate of return method avoids a significant problem associated with the internal rate of return approach, namely, the problem of multiple internal rates of return. In the case where we must choose between mutually exclusive projects that differ in size, the net present value and the modified internal rate of return methods may result in conflicting rankings.

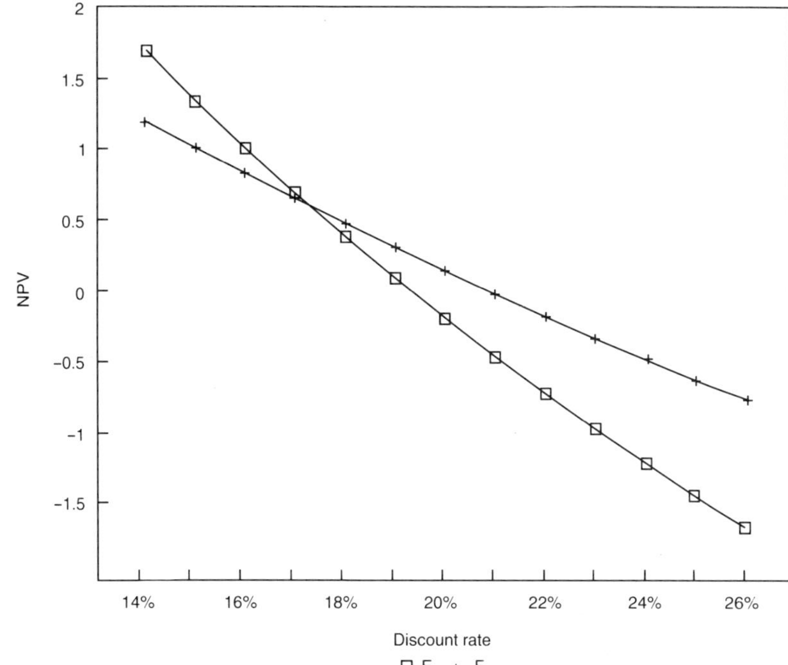

Figure 5.32. NPV profiles of mutually exclusive projects E and F

Net present value versus payback period

Cases where conflicting rankings can occur with mutually exclusive projects:

- Projects that have differences in the patterns of cash flows.
- Projects that have differences in the size of cash flows after the payback period.

Net present value versus discounted payback period

A case where conflicting rankings can occur with mutually exclusive projects:

- Projects that have differences in the size of cash flows after the payback period.

Net present value versus average rate of return

A case where conflicting rankings can occur with mutually exclusive projects:

- Projects that have differences in the patterns of cash flows.

Net present value versus profitability index

A case where conflicting rankings can occur with mutually exclusive projects:

- Projects that have differences in the size, or scale, of initial investment.

Net present value versus internal rate of return

Cases where conflicting rankings can occur with mutually exclusive projects:

- Projects that have differences in the size, or scale, of cash flows.
- Projects that have differences in the patterns of cash flows.

Figure 5.33. Conditions that can produce differences in ranking of mutually exclusive projects

Net present value with infinite replicated cash flows

The net present value method, introduced earlier in this chapter, should not be utilized to rank mutually exclusive projects with different lives because the project with the shorter life as compared with that of the longer life can be replicated more frequently in the long term. When we want to choose between mutually exclusive projects with different lives, we employ the technique of the net present value with infinite replicated cash flows. The concept of such a method is summarized in Figure 5.34.

Definition The net present value with infinite replicated cash flows is the net present value of a finite life project replicated infinitely at a constant scale.

Calculation A project's net present value with infinite replicated cash flows equals the net present value of the project at a given discount rate divided by the product of two terms: the present value of an ordinary annuity for £1 per year at the given rate for N years and the discount rate used to calculate the net present value. The following equation is the formula for computing the net present with replicated cash flows:

$$\text{NPV}(N, \infty) = \frac{\text{Traditional NPV}}{\text{PV}(1, r, N) * r}$$

where N is the finite life of the project, r is the discount rate and PV$(1,r,N)$ is the present value of an ordinary annuity.

Interpretation The net present value with infinite replicated cash flows adjusts the net present values of projects with different lives and makes the projects more comparable.

Figure 5.34. A summary of the NPV with infinite replicated cash flows concept

Example 5.20 Comparing projects with unequal lives

Figure 5.35 shows the cash flows of two mutually exclusive investment projects of AK Textiles plc with different useful lives. Assuming a discount rate of 12 per cent, the net present value of project G is higher than that of project A, indicating that project G is preferable to project A. The net present value with infinite replicated cash flows for project A is calculated as follows (figures are rounded):

$$\text{NPV}(N, \infty) = £454{,}000 \frac{(1+0.12)^5 0.12}{[(1+0.12)^5 - 1]0.12} = £1{,}050{,}000$$

	A	B	C	D
1	CALCULATING THE NPV WITH INFINITE REPLICATED CASH FLOWS			
2	------------------------------			
3	Discount Rate	12.0%		
4	------------------------------			
5	Year	Cash flows	Cash flows	
6		for Project A	for Project G	
7		(£000s)	(£000s)	
8	------------------------------			
9	0	(6,200)	(6,200)	
10	1	1,244	700	
11	2	1,918	1,000	
12	3	2,196	1,200	
13	4	2,154	1,400	
14	5	1,908	1,600	
15	6		1,800	
16	7		1,900	
17	8		2,500	
18		-------	------	
19	NPV -------->	454	585	
20	NPV(N,oo) --->	1,050	981	

Figure 5.35. The net present values with infinite replicated cash flows for projects A and G

After replicating infinitely the cash flows of project A at a constant scale, its net present value is £1,050,000. Similarly, the net present value with infinite replicated cash flows for project G is £981,000. In this case, both projects have the same (infinite) life and thus they are more comparable. Comparing these net present values we see that project A is more attractive than project G.

The net present value with infinite replicated cash flows can also be calculated by using the following 1-2-3 formula:

```
@NPV/(@PV(1,interest_rate,term)*interest_rate)
```

Problem

Create the worksheet shown in Figure 5.35.

Some useful points about the capital budgeting evaluation methods

1. (Using the payback period method as a screening device) The payback period method can be utilized as an initial screening device to eliminate unattractive investment projects and save further analysis and costs related with the evaluation of these projects. The payback period method can also be employed as a screening device for projects with small initial investments where the utilization of a discounted cash flow method may be unwanted.
2. (Using the payback period to reflect the risk of recovering invested funds) The payback period method can be used as a rough indicator of the riskiness of a project where you are unable to measure such risk using another method (for example, a project planned in a politically unstable country).
3. (Using an unsophisticated method as a supplement to sophisticated methods) The payback period method or the average rate of return method should be used along with discounted cash flow methods of appraising projects. For example, using the net present value method together with the payback period method for evaluating a project provides some indication of both the profitability and liquidity of the project.
4. (Payback period method and long-term projects) Since the payback period method ignores the cash flows that occur beyond the payback period it should not be used to evaluate long-term projects.
5. (Using the modified internal rate of return) If a project has more than one internal rate of return, the modified internal rate of return should be used for analysing the project.

The theory of Fisher

Throughout this work we assume that the objective of a firm is to maximize the wealth of its existing shareholders, while in the present chapter we show that firms should accept projects which provide positive net present values. In this section we will demonstrate the relationship between the firm's objective and the net present value approach. Specifically, we shall show the following result which provides an important implication of the results introduced by Fisher (1965).

In a perfect capital market managers will maximize the net present value of their firm by investing in those projects which have the most beneficial effect on the existing shareholders' wealth in the firm. The latter objective can be achieved if managers invest in projects with positive net present values where the total net present value of projects increases the existing shareholders' wealth in the firm as much as possible.

The production opportunity set

Assume that time is divided into only two periods: the current period (or period 0) and the next period (or period 1). Consider a shareholder with a current amount of cash PV which can be allocated as follows:

Period 0 (for example, current year) — Current consumption: C_0
→ Investment: $PV - C_0$

The shareholder faces several consumption opportunities and he or she can invest $PV - C_0$ on projects which will provide his or her consumption at period 1. The objective of the shareholder is to select, among all the attainable combinations of current and future consumption levels, the consumption combination that maximizes his or her expected utility (that is, the expected satisfaction or pleasure that will be received from a particular consumption combination).

The analysis requires the following assumptions:

1 Projects are infinitely divisible.
2 Accepting a project does not affect the returns on other projects.

The production opportunity set (efficient frontier or budget line) illustrates the best attainable combinations of current and future consumption levels which can be achieved with a given money income (by 'best' we mean combinations that are not wasting available consumption).

Example 5.21 The production opportunity set of an investor

Mr George Annis has a current amount of cash of £81,000 and he wishes to allocate it to current consumption and to an investment in real assets (for example, buying machinery and equipment). We assume that Mr Annis will consume all his cash during the next year.

It is also assumed that Mr Annis has four consumption patterns as shown in Figure 5.36. For example, he can choose to consume £40,000 this year and £68,000 next year. The consumption combinations on the production

```
      A   B           C          D          E          F          G          H
 1                                 THE CONSUMPTION COMBINATIONS OF MR ANNIS
 2                                 ========================================
 3
 4
 5  |-------------------|
 6  |CONSUMPTION:       |
 7  |YEAR 0    YEAR 1   |
 8  |-------------------|
 9  |        0   88,000 |
10  |   40,000   68,000 |
11  |   60,000   43,000 |
12  |   81,000        0 |
13  |-------------------|
```

Figure 5.36. Consumption possibilities of an investor

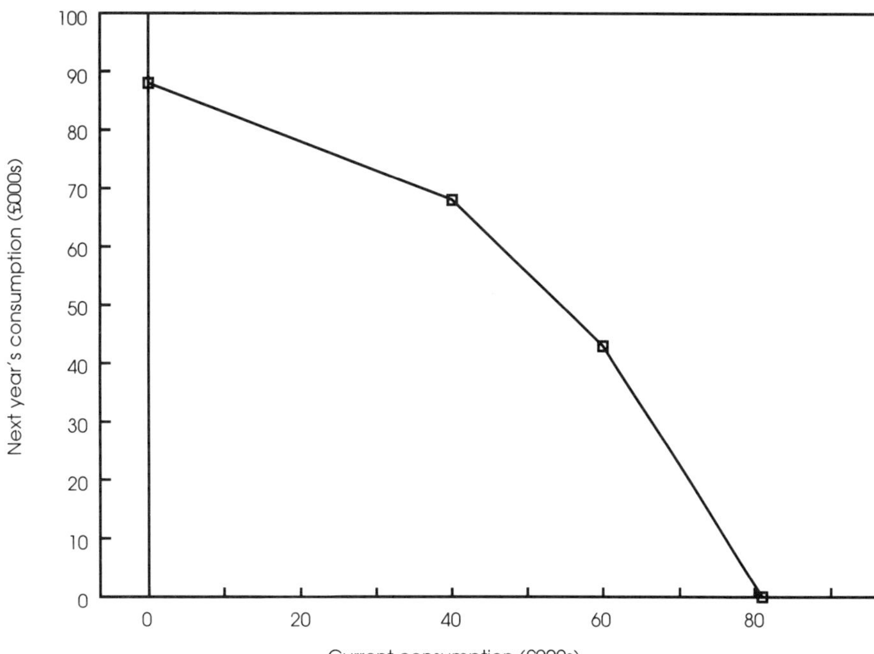

Figure 5.37a. The opportunity set of M. Annis

opportunity set of Mr Annis are not wasting available consumption. For example, if the investor was consuming £40,000 in the current year and £60,000 next year, he would waste a £8,000 available consumption. We also note that Mr Annis can consume all of £81,000 this year, but have nothing left for the next year, or he can consume nothing this year and obtain a maximum consumption of £88,000 next year.

Figure 5.37(a) shows Mr Annis's production opportunity set. Note that the slope of the production opportunity set at any point indicates the increase in the consumption at year 1 which is associated with the sacrifice of £1 of consumption at year 0. Figure 5.37(a) indicates that the marginal return on investment decreases as we move up the curve. The production opportunity set is concave to the origin (that is, bowed outward), reflecting the declining marginal return on investment. For example, if Mr Annis invests £21,000 of current consumption (that is, £81,000 – £60,000) he will realize next year a cash flow of £43,000. On the other hand, his next £20,000 of investment will provide a cash flow of only £25,000 (that is, £68,000 – £43,000).

All the combinations of current and future consumption levels that lie inside the production opportunity set are undesirable because they imply the waste of available consumption. Also all the consumption combinations outside the production opportunity set are unattainable with the investor's available resources.

The investor's preference

Among all the attainable combinations of current and future consumption levels shown by the production opportunity set an investor prefers the combination which maximizes his expected utility for consumption. Before proceeding to discuss the utility concept several assumptions are required.

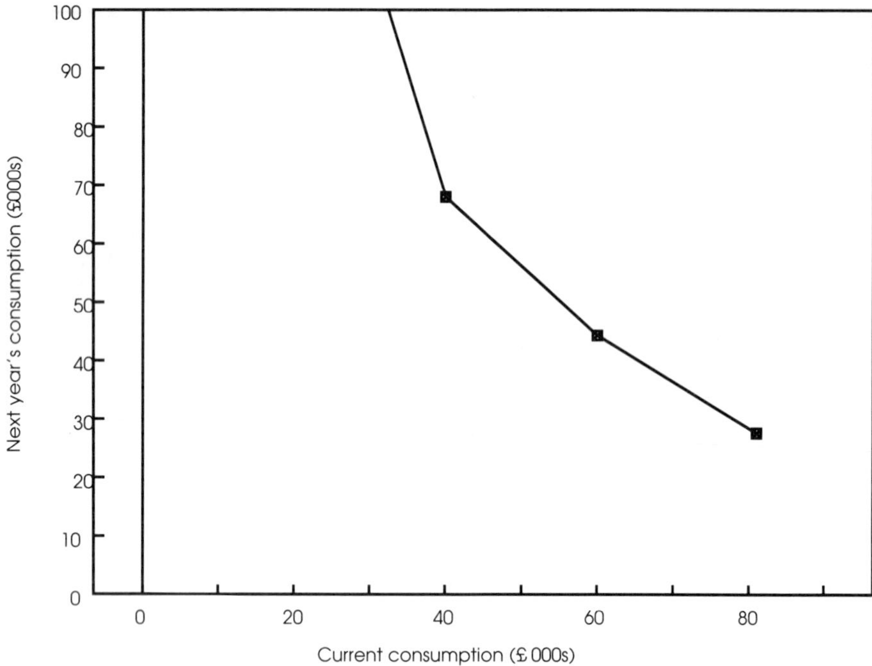

Figure 5.37b. An indifference curve

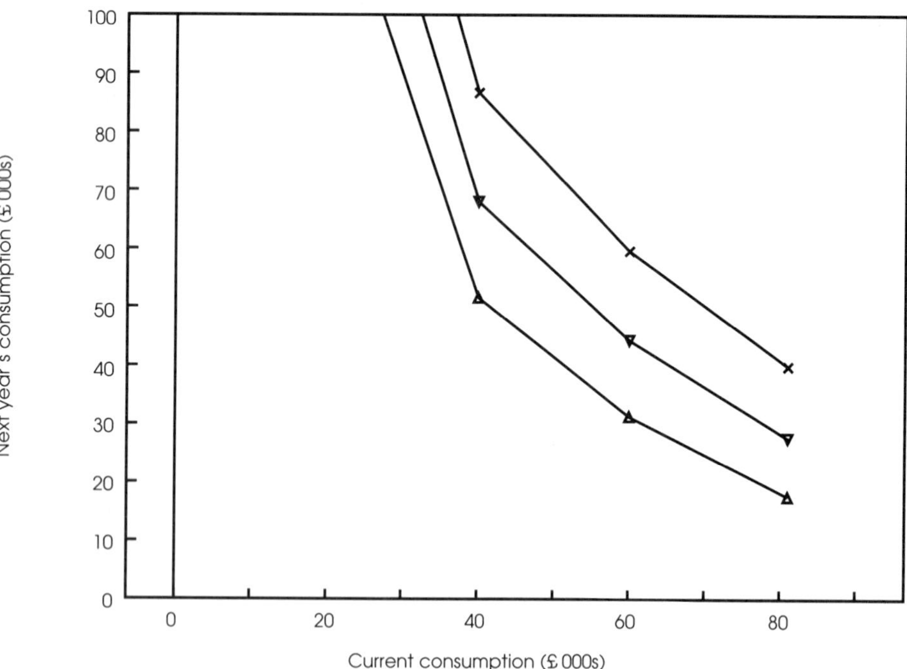

Figure 5.37c. An indifference map

1 For any two different consumption combinations an investor can tell us
(a) that he or she prefers the first to the second; or
(b) that he or she prefers the second to the first; or
(c) that he or she is indifferent to having the first or the second.

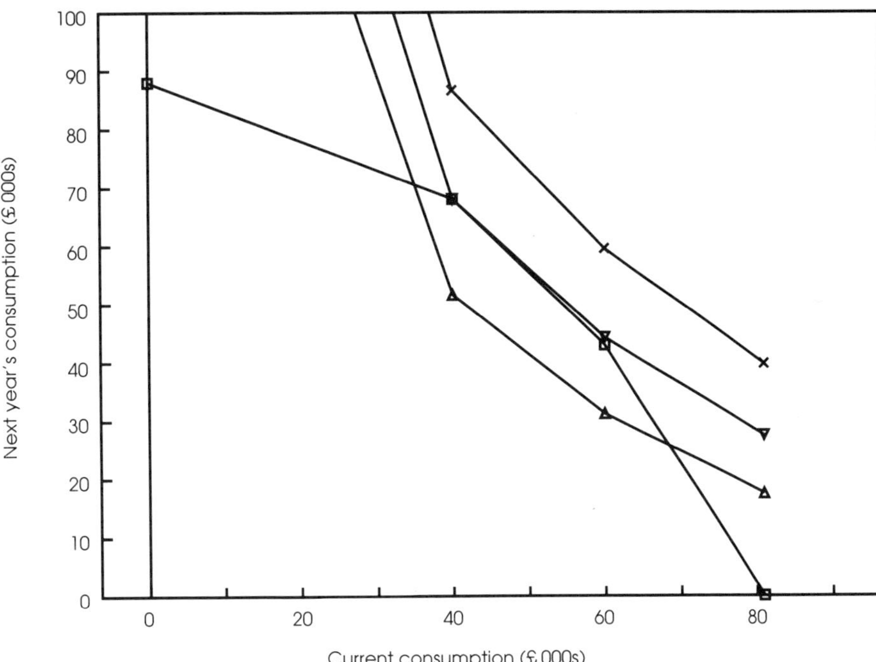

Figure 5.37d. M. Annis's preference

2 For any three consumption combinations, if the investor prefers the first to the second and the second to the third, he or she also prefers the first to the third.
3 An investor prefers (or at least would be indifferent) to achieve more consumption at period 1 if at the same time he or she did not have to take less consumption at period 0 and vice versa.
4 Among all the consumption combinations there exists a most preferred combination and a least preferred combination.
5 Consumption combinations are independent.
6 The indifference curves are convex to the origin (that is bowed inward). By definition, an indifference curve is a line graph showing all the consumption combinations which yield exactly the same utility to the investor concerned, so that he or she is indifferent to choice of consumption combinations.

These assumptions indicate that investors behave rationally and attempt to maximize expected utility for consumption. For example, an investor who prefers a consumption combination of (£20,000, £30,000) to (£10,000, £20,000), (£40,000, £50,000) to (£20,000, £30,000) and (£20,000, £30,000) to (£40,000, £50,000) has difficulty in making a rational choice between the three combinations of consumption (assuming, of course, that all the consumption combinations are attainable and are associated with the same amount of risk).

Example 5.22 The indifference curves representing Mr Annis's preference

Assume that Mr Annis has the following expected utility function:

$$U(C_0, C_1) = \sqrt{C_0} + \frac{1}{(1+k)}\sqrt{C_1}$$

where C_0 and C_1 are the current level of consumption and next year's level of

```
   A        B             C        D          E          F          G
1                   AN INDIFFERENCE SCHEDULE
2                   ========================
3  Utility k           12.0%
4  Utility Value     432.829
5
6
7
8  |-------------------------------------------------------------|
9  |CONSUMPTION:                       An Indifference Schedule for:|
10 |YEAR 0                                     E(U)=432.829        |
11 |-------------------------------------------------------------|
12 |                   0                       235,000             |
13 |              40,000                        68,000             |
14 |              60,000                        44,279             |
15 |              81,000                        27,559             |
16 |-------------------------------------------------------------|
```

Figure 5.38. Calculating an indifference schedule for Mr Annis

consumption, respectively, k is equal to: $-(1 + \text{slope})$ of the production opportunity set.

Assume that $U(C_0, C_1) = 432.829$, and $k = 0.12$. Figure 5.38 calculates the values of consumption C_1, using different values for consumption C_0. The formula stored in cell E12 is as follows:

```
((1+$C$3)*($C$4-@SQRT(B12)))^2
```

The contents of the cell E12 are copied in the range E13..E15. For example, the value stored in cell E12 is calculated as follows:

$$((1 + 0.12) \times (432.829 - 0))^2 = 235{,}000$$

The range of numbers (see column E of Figure 5.38) presents various combinations of C_0 and C_1 that will be equally satisfactory to the investor at a given time. Such a range is called an indifference schedule. An indifference curve is a graph of an indifference schedule (see Figure 5.37(b)).

The slope of the indifference curve measures the change in the consumption at period 1 obtained from an additional (marginal) pound of consumption at period 0 (this slope is called the marginal rate of substitution). The slope of an indifference curve decreases as we move down it indicating that the reduction of consumption in year 0 must be compensated by an addition to consumption in year 1 if total utility is to remain the same.

The marginal utility of an item (for example, money to spend on consumption) is the extra utility derived from an additional small increment of the item. Convex indifference curves reveal that the marginal utility of an item declines as more of it is consumed in a given period of time (the latter is called the law of diminishing marginal utility). For example, the first £1,000 you gain in a single time period may give you a lot of satisfaction. You might even receive more satisfaction from your second £1,000 gained during the same period. However, you must eventually reach a point where each successive gain of £1,000 gives you less satisfaction than the previous one.

An indifference map is a graph of a series of indifference schedules (see Figure 5.39). The higher the indifference curve (that is, the further it lies to the right) the greater the investor's satisfaction. There are no two indifference curves in

	A	B	C	D	E	F	G
1			MANY POSSIBLE INDIFFERENCE SCHEDULES				
2			====================================				
3	Utility k		12.0%				
4	Utility Value 1		402.829				
5	Utility Value 2		462.829				
6	Utility Value 3		432.829				
7							
8							
9	CONSUMPTION:			Indifference Schedules for:			
10	YEAR 0			UTILITY 1	UTILITY 2	UTILITY 3	
11							
12		0		203,553	268,705	235,000	
13		40,000		51,605	86,653	68,000	
14		60,000		31,267	59,548	44,279	
15		81,000		17,533	39,844	27,559	
16							

Figure 5.39. A series of indifference schedules for Mr Annis

the map shown back in Figure 5.37(c) that interact with each other, or cross. This is true because if Mr Annis is indifferent between all points along a curve, crossing curves would indicate that he would be indifferent between the two curves, which contradicts the utility concepts discussed earlier.

Consumption selection

Among the attainable combinations of current and future consumption levels shown by the production opportunity set, investors should select the consumption combination that maximizes their expected utility of consumption. Specifically, the consumption combination that maximizes investors' expected utility will be the one lying on the highest attainable indifference curve. A given point in the production opportunity set may intersect any number of indifference curves, but it can be tangent to only one indifference curve. Graphically, the utility-maximizing consumption combination will be at the point where the higher indifference curve (from the investor's indifference map) is tangential to the production opportunity set.

Example 5.23 The consumption combination that maximizes Mr Annis's expected utility

We can now determine from Examples 5.21 and 5.22 the consumption combination that Mr Annis will prefer. Mr Annis will select the consumption combination that provides the highest possible satisfaction level. Specifically, the investor's utility-maximizing consumption combination will be the one where his production opportunity set is tangent on the higher attainable indifference curve. From Figure 5.37(d) such a point corresponds to the consumption combination of £40,000 this year and £68,000 next year (see Figure 5.40). At this point of tangency the slope of the production opportunity set equals the slope of the highest attainable indifference curve.

Problems

1 If $k = 0.30$, calculate the investor's expected utility associated with the consumption combination of (£60,000, £43,000).

```
   A        B              C          D          E          F          G
 1  THE CONSUMPTION COMBINATION THAT MAXIMIZES EXPECTED UTILITY
 2  =============================================================
 3  Interest Rate        12.0%
 4  Utility Value 1: 402.829
 5  Utility Value 3: 432.829
 6  Utility Value 2: 462.829
 7
 8 |--------------------------------------------------------|
 9 |CONSUMPTION:                  Indifference Schedule for:
10 |YEAR 1            YEAR 2    UTILITY 1 UTILITY 2 UTILITY 3
11 |--------------------------------------------------------
12 |                0    88,000    203,553    235,000    268,705
13 |           40,000    68,000     51,605     68,000     86,653
14 |           60,000    43,000     31,267     44,279     59,548
15 |           81,000         0     17,533     27,559     39,844
16 |--------------------------------------------------------|
```

Figure 5.40. Determining the consumption combination that maximizes the investor's expected utility

2 Illustrate graphically the new choice of the investor by plotting the production opportunity set together with the investor's indifference map.

The production opportunity set under perfect capital markets

Let us consider a capital market where funds can be transferred between lenders and borrowers. The following assumptions are made:

1 Cash flows from investment are certain.
2 The capital market is perfect in the following senses:
  (**a**) no transaction costs or taxes exist;
  (**b**) information is freely available to investors;
  (**c**) all securities in the market are infinitely divisible;
  (**d**) no single buyer or seller of securities is large enough to affect their prices (a security is a general name given to anything that has a monetary value).
3 There exists a unique risk-free security where investors can borrow or lend money at the risk-free rate.

These assumptions can be used to derive the capital market opportunity line which shows the investor's new consumption combinations attainable by using the capital market's borrowing or lending facilities. If the cash amount $PV - C_0$ is invested at period 0, then the consumption next year will be:

$$C_1 = (PV - C_0)(1 + r)$$

where

PV = the investor's current amount of cash.
C_0 = the investor's current level of consumption.
r = is the unique riskless interest rate.

If the current amount of cash is given, the consumption level in year 1 is dependent upon the consumption level in year 0. The slope of the capital market opportunity line (that is, $-(1 + r)$) is negative indicating that the consumption level in year 1 increases (decreases) when the consumption level in year 0 decreases (increases).

Example 5.24 Calculating the new production opportunity set for Mr Annis

Suppose that there is access to the capital markets, where Mr Annis can invest a current amount of cash until next year or he can borrow against his next year's cash receipts in order to consume in the current year an amount greater than his current amount of cash. Assume that there are no limits to the amount that may be borrowed, provided that he can repay the debt and the interest in the second year. For illustration purposes the risk-free rate is assumed to be 12 per cent.

Figure 5.41 illustrates Mr Annis's consumption patterns without access to the capital market and with capital market opportunities. In the latter case his consumption patterns are calculated for three different current amounts of cash. For example, the value stored in cell G12 is calculated as follows:

($C$6-B12)*(1+$C3$) = £112,800

```
    A       B            C        D        E            F              G      H
1                    THE CAPITAL MARKET OPPORTUNITIES
2                    ================================
3   Interest Rate        12.0%
4   Present value 1    70,714
5   Present value 2    45,714
6   Present value 3   100,714
7
8   ------------------------------------------------------------------------
9   CONSUMPTION(NO CAPITAL MARKET)  CONSUMPTION (WITH CAPITAL MARKET)
10  YEAR 1            YEAR 2                PV 1         PV 2          PV 3
11  ------------------------------------------------------------------------
12                0    88,000             79,200       51,200       112,800
13           40,000    68,000             34,400        6,400        68,000
14           60,000    43,000             12,000     (16,000)        45,600
15           81,000         0           (11,520)     (39,520)        22,080
16          100,714                                                       0
17  ------------------------------------------------------------------------
```

Figure 5.41. The new production opportunity set

Then use the /Copy command to copy the contents of cell G12 in the range G13..G16.

If $C_0 = £40{,}000$, and $C_1 = £68{,}000$, then the following cases can be observed (see column G in Figure 5.41):

- **Case 1** The investor consumes nothing this year and invests £40,000 at 12 per cent interest to obtain £44,800 next year. Adding this to his next year's cash he can obtain a maximum consumption of £112,800 next year (that is, £44,800 + £68,000)
- **Case 2** The investor consumes £40,000 this year and £68,000 next year.
- **Case 3** The investor borrows £20,000 this year at 12 per cent rate of interest. Adding this to his current consumption of £40,000 yields a current consumption of £60,000. The future value of his debt is £22,400 (that is, £20,000 × (1 + 0.12)), leaving a consumption of £45,600 next year (that is, £68,000 – £22,400).
- **Case 4** The investor borrows £41,000 this year at 12 per cent rate of interest. This yields a current consumption of £81,000 and a future value of debt of £45,920 (that is, £41,000 × (1 + 0.12), leaving £22,080 available for consumption next year (that is, £68,000 – £45,920)).

Let us now compare the consumption patterns of Mr Annis with and without the capital market opportunities.

Without a capital market	With a capital market
No borrowing facilities The maximum amount that can be consumed in year 0 is £81,000	*Borrowing facilities* The maximum amount that can be consumed in year 0 is £100,714 [that is, £40,000 + £68,000/(1 + 0.12)]
No lending facilities The maximum amount that can be consumed in year 1 is £88,000	*Lending facilities* The maximum amount that can be consumed in year 1 is £112,800

Figure 5.42 illustrates graphically the three consumption lines together with the production opportunity set of Mr Annis (see Example 5.21). Note that the consumption line associated with a present value of £100,714 dominates the two consumption lines which are associated with present values of £70,714 and £45,714, respectively. This consumption line is exactly tangent to the production opportunity set at the point where $C_0 = £40{,}000$ and $C_1 = £68{,}000$ and it is called the capital market opportunity line. The slope of the capital market opportunity line is equal to $-(1 + 0.12)$ and this can be also calculated as $-112{,}800/100{,}724 = -1.12$ (figures are rounded). This indicates that when Mr Annis gives up a pound in year 0, he will receive in exchange £1.12 in year 1.

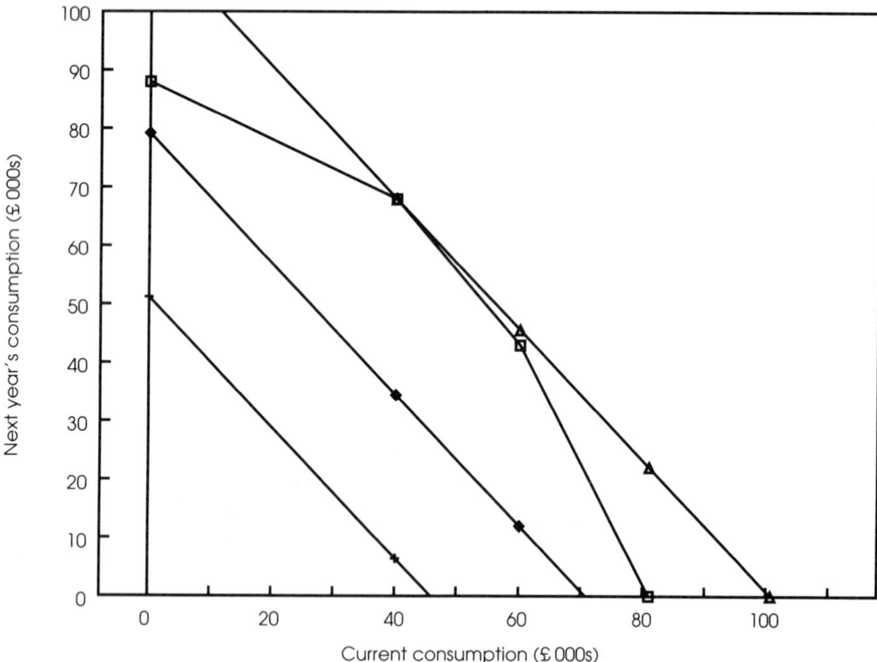

Figure 5.42. Many possible opportunity lines

With the introduction of a capital market the current and future consumption levels that lie to the left of the capital market opportunity line (including also those of the production opportunity set) are now undesirable, because they imply the waste of available consumption. For example, if Mr Annis has chosen from the production opportunity set the consumption combination (£60,000, £43,000), then he could obtain on the capital opportunity line a point offering higher current consumption and the same consumption £43,000 for year 1.

Mr Annis can now choose a consumption combination from the capital market opportunity line that maximizes his expected utility of consumption. The utility-maximizing consumption combination will be at the point where the capital market opportunity line is tangent to his highest attainable indifference curve.

Finally, note that the slope of the production opportunity set at the point of tangency with the capital market opportunity line is $-(1 + r)$ indicating that the rate of return associated with Mr Annis's dominance investment is equal to the (one-period) borrowing or lending risk-free rate.

Example 5.24 indicates the importance of capital markets. Capital markets facilitate the flow of funds between investors who are willing to lend their excess funds and investors who are willing to undertake investment opportunities but have insufficient funds. As an implication both parties of investors (that is, borrowers and lenders) can increase their wealth more than they could under the absence of capital markets.

Fisher separation theorem

The analysis presented in the few previous sections can also be extended to firms where there are many investors, with the financial management team acting in the shareholders' best interests (we assume that investors face the same production opportunity set). The whole analysis considers two types of decisions: investment and financing decisions.

- The investment decisions are made by the firm's management team and the best production decision is the one where the rate of return associated with the firm's investment is equal to the (one-period) borrowing or lending risk-free rate. Part of the outcome of the firm's investment may be payable to the shareholders in terms of dividends and the remainder will be retained for future investments.
- The financing decisions are made by the shareholders. A shareholder receives payment of dividends from the firm and then chooses his or her own combination of current and future consumption levels by borrowing or lending in the capital market.

This discussion leads to the Fisher separation theorem which can be stated as follows:

> *Given a perfect capital market, the investment decision (of choosing the consumption combination at the point of tangency between the production opportunity set and the capital market production line) is independent of the financing decision (of using the dividends payable by the firm and the borrowing or lending facilities in the capital market to construct a pattern of consumption the investor most desires).*

An important implication of the Fisher theorem is that investment decisions in real assets are made by managers. The task of managers is to maximize the net present value of the firm without paying any attention to the shareholders' personal preferences for current versus future consumption. As a consequence, in a perfect capital market managers will act in the best interest of the shareholders by investing in those projects which increase the existing shareholders' wealth in the firm by more than would competing projects. This implies that managers can adopt a simple rule: invest in projects with positive net present value because it will have the most beneficial effect on the wealth of the firm's shareholders. The implications of Fisher's analysis can be summarized as follows:

1 Managers should run the firm in the shareholders' best interests.
2 Each shareholder wishes to realize a current–future consumption level that maximizes his or her satisfaction.
3 Managers should accept all projects which increase the shareholders' wealth within the firm as much as possible.
4 Each shareholder receives cash flow from the firm and utilizes the capital market to get the mix of current and future consumption levels which increases as much as possible shareholder satisfaction.

Example 5.25 Illustrating that managers should invest in projects with positive net present values

Consider the data given in Example 5.24. We assume that capital market opportunities exist and the firm invests £41,000 in real assets. In this case, the amount of £40,000 (that is, £81,000 – £40,000) is available for consumption (that is, £41,000 is payable as dividends to its shareholders). This situation can be treated as an investment project with an initial cost of £41,000 and a future cash flow, next year, of £68,000. The net present value of this investment at 12 per cent discount rate is £19,714. Likewise, for the consumption pattern that has a current cash flow of £60,000 and a future cash flow, next year, of £43,000 the net present value at 12 per cent is calculated as follows:
$-£21{,}000 + 43{,}000/(1 + 0.12) = £17{,}393$, where $£81{,}000 - £60{,}000 = £21{,}000$ (note that the consumption pattern of (£60,000, £43,000) lies below the capital market opportunity line). Thus, managers would seek to invest in the project which increases the wealth of the existing shareholders within the firm as much as possible.

The theory of Fisher was extended by Hirshleifer (1958). He showed that in an imperfect capital market, where the borrowing and lending rates are different, Fisher's separation theorem is invalid because there exist two different capital market opportunity lines, one representing borrowing opportunities and the other representing lending opportunities. In this instance, lenders favour utilizing the net present value discounting at the lending rate and borrowers would prefer to use the net present value discounting at the borrowing rate (or the firm's cost of capital). However, there is no simple method that can be used to reconcile such cases. Although in an imperfect capital market the validity of Fisher's model is questionable, the net present value criterion can still be used for the following reasons:

1 It provides a logical rule for evaluating investment alternatives.
2 It is consistent with the objective of maximizing shareholders' wealth.
3 In many cases the net present value is superior to other existing capital investment rules (for example, internal rate of return).

Capital budgeting methods used in practice

The empirical literature relating to capital budgeting practices in business organizations is extensive. In this section we discuss the findings of four surveys concerning the capital budgeting methods used by business organizations (see Figure 5.43).

The results of Pike (1988) indicate that large UK firms are becoming increasingly more sophisticated in the use of discounted cash flow methods. There also appears to be a continuous trend towards usage of the payback period method, but mainly as a secondary investment appraisal technique.

Diacogiannis and Lai (1989) found that the payback period is popular among firms in the unlisted securities market but these firms prefer to utilize a combination of the payback period approach with one or more discounted cash flow methods. Their results reveal that the internal rate of return is preferred as the primary evaluation technique, despite the popularity of net present value among academics.

R.H. Pike
RESEARCH YEAR: Many
COUNTRY: UK
SIZE OF FIRMS: Large
POPULATION: Different populations
SAMPLE: 100

	1975 (%)	1981 (%)	1986 (%)
Payback	73	81	92
Average rate of return	51	49	56
Net present value	32	39	68
Internal rate of return	44	57	75

G.P. Diacogiannis and R. Lai
RESEARCH YEAR: 1988
COUNTRY: UK
SIZE OF FIRMS: Medium sized
POPULATION: 304
SAMPLE: 95

	% out of 95
Payback period	68
Discounted PP	23
Average rate of return	16
Net present value	29
Internal rate of return	52

L.J. Gitman and J.R. Forrester
RESEARCH YEAR: 1976
COUNTRY: USA
SIZE OF FIRMS: Large
POPULATION: 600
SAMPLE: 103

	Primary (%)	Secondary (%)
Payback period	8.9	44.0
Average rate of return	25.0	14.0
Net present value	9.8	25.0
Profitability index	2.7	2.2
Internal rate of return	53.6	14.0

A.V. Corr
YEAR: 1981
COUNTRY: CANADA
SIZE OF FIRMS: Various
POPULATION: Firms in eight manufacturing industries
SAMPE: 24

	Number of firms			
	Large	Medium	Small	Total
Payback	5	8	5	18
Average rate of return	2	6	3	11
Net present value	2	3	2	7
Profitability index	2	2	1	5
Internal rate of return	5	8	4	17
None provided	1	2	1	4

Figure 5.43. Capital budgeting methods in use: results from four surveys

Gitman and Forrester (1977) showed that more than one-half of the respondents to their questionnaires used discounted cash flow methods (that is, IRR, NPV and PI) as primary evaluation methods. The payback period approach is found to be the most popular secondary evaluation technique. Finally, Corr (1983) found that firms prefer among the discounted cash flow methods the internal rate of return and among the naive evaluation approaches the payback period. The findings of Corr also indicate that the size of the firm does not appear to affect significantly the choice of the evaluation method.

The results of these four empirical studies are not strictly comparable since these studies used samples drawn from different populations. However, for each individual study the following summary conclusions can be made:

1 There is a strong preference for using discounted cash flow techniques as primary evaluation techniques. The most popular discounted cash flow method used is the internal rate of return. This popularity may be due to the fact that managers prefer and understand more easily the concept of a rate of return than the concept of a pure pound return provided by the net present value. Stated differently, firms often prefer the internal rate of return rather than the net present value because the former provides a measure of the return of an investment relative to the initial amount invested, while the latter is only an absolute measure of the project's wealth.
2 The payback period method is widely used as a supplement to discounted cash flow approaches because:
   (**a**) it is simple to understand and calculate;
   (**b**) it reflects the liquidity of a project and so the risk of recovering the initial investment from cash flows generated by the project.
3 Firms are using more than one method for evaluating capital budgeting projects and they prefer to utilize a combination of discounted cash flow and naive evaluation techniques.

Summary

1 *Capital budgeting process* The capital budgeting process involves the following five phases:
   (**a**) search and identification;
   (**b**) estimating cash flows;
   (**c**) evaluating projects;
   (**d**) selecting projects;
   (**e**) post-acceptance analysis.
2 *Accounting profit versus cash flow* The net cash flow of a project for a given year is related to the project's cash revenues and the cash expenses which are expected to occur over that year. On the other hand, the accounting profit for a given year is related to revenues earned (but not necessarily received) during that year and the expenses associated with those revenues (but not necessarily paid) during that same period. The calculation of a project's net cash flows does not take into account sunk costs, the depreciation expense and interest expenses, but it con-siders opportunity costs, changes in net working captal and the value that can be realized at the termination of the project.
3 *Capital budgeting methods* The most widely used investment analysis is the cash

flow analysis. Such an analysis includes the following:

(a) calculating the initial investment;
(b) estimating the subsequent net cash flows;
(c) determining the appropriate discount rate;
(d) applying a method (or methods) for evaluating the project (or projects) under consideration. The following methods for evaluating and selecting investment projects were presented and discussed:

(i) payback period;
(ii) discounted payback period;
(iii) average rate of return;
(iv) net present value;
(v) profitability index;
(vi) regular internal rate of return; and
(vii) modified internal rate of return.

The decisions discussed can be grouped into two categories: the accept/reject decisions and the ranking of project decisions. Knowing the advantages and disadvantages of each capital budgeting method, you should be careful when you are using a method in isolation. Generally, do not rely on the use of a single capital budgeting technique, but instead use a combination of techniques.

4 *Relating the NPV rule and the objective of the firm* To act in the shareholders' best interest, the financial manager should attempt to undertake investment projects that increase the shareholders' wealth as much as possible. To do so the financial manager should attempt to invest in those acceptable projects which collectively provide the largest net present values.

5 *Capital budgeting methods used in practice* The empirical evidence discussed in this chapter reveals that the internal rate of return is used primarily by large or medium sized firms, while the payback period continues to be employed by those firms, mainly as a secondary evaluation approach.

Questions for discussion

1 For each term shown below in the largest box provide a definition in your own words. Then check your responses against the definitions included in the chapter.

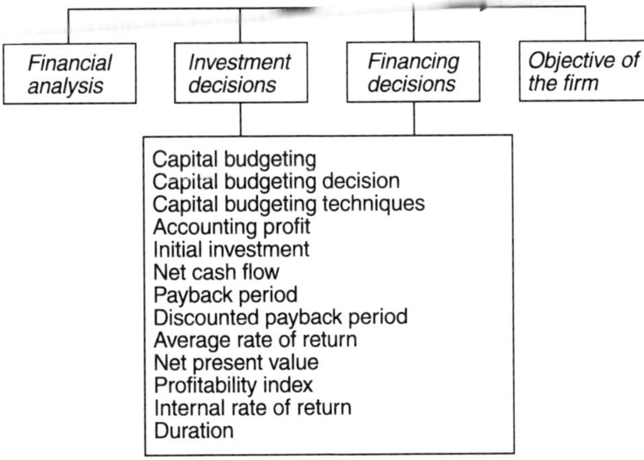

2 List examples for each of the following cases:
  (a) expansion projects;
  (b) replacement projects;
  (c) regulatory projects.

  Also provide a list of examples for each of the following categories of projects: independent; mutually exclusive; and contingent.

3 Discuss in detail the following statement: 'Capital investment projects are evaluated on the basis of their net cash flows rather than on the basis of their net accounting profits.'

4 Discuss how each of the following items should be treated in analysing an investment project:
  (a) sunk costs;
  (b) expenses associated with the project;
  (c) expenses associated with the existing facilities of the firm but with no association with the project;
  (d) revenues associated with the project;
  (e) depreciation associated with the project;
  (f) future depreciation on old assets;
  (g) interest expenses;
  (h) opportunity costs;
  (i) changes in net working capital requirements.

5 Comment in detail on each of the following two statements:
  (a) 'The firm should choose an investment project with a short payback rather than one with a larger net present value.'
  (b) 'The internal rate of return technique of investment evaluation is easier to use than the net present value since it avoids the necessity of calculating a discount rate.'

6 Evaluate each of the following two statements:
  (a) 'The net present value method provides correct recommendations in comparing mutually exclusive projects with substantially different lives.'
  (b) 'The modified internal rate of return is a better project evaluation method than the regular internal rate of return.'

7 Explain how each of the following will affect the net present value of an investment project:
  (a) an increase in the discount rate;
  (b) a decline on the initial investment;
  (c) an increase in useful life of the investment.

8 Consider two mutually exclusive investment projects, call them A and B. For each project the cash flow stream provides an ordinary annuity. Assume that the following possible situations exist:
  (a) projects A and B are associated with the same initial investment, other things are also the same;
  (b) project A has a higher initial outlay than B (other things stay the same);
  (c) project A has a higher annuity amount than project B (other things remain equal);
  (d) project A has higher initial investment than B and it also has a higher annuity amount than B (other things being the same).

Employ the internal rate of return decision rule and place your selection choices into the following diagram:

		Initial cash flow:	
		Same	A greater than B
Annuity amount:	Same		
	A greater than B		

Repeat this exercise by using the payback period decision rule. Compare and discuss your results with those based upon the internal rate of return decision rule.

9 Discuss the following statement: 'For most investment decisions that the firm faces, the net present value is usually a better evaluation method than other competing approaches. Despite this fact, do not rely on the utilization of a single capital budgeting technique, but instead use a combination of techniques.'

10 Discuss in detail some empirical evidence associated with the adoption of project evaluation methods. Why are some methods used more than others?

11 Identify and discuss the advantages and disadvantages of each of the following two naive methods as applied to investment decisions: payback period and average rate of return.

12 Identify and discuss the advantages and disadvantages of the internal rate of return method for capital budgeting decisions.

13 Identify and discuss the advantages and disadvantages of each of the following two discounted cash flow methods as applied to investment decisions: net present value and the profitability index.

14 Discuss and illustrate graphically the following statement: 'An investor would clearly like the consumption combination at the point of tangency of the capital market opportunity line with his or her highest attainable indifference curve.'

15 Discuss and evaluate the following statement: 'Managers act in the shareholders' best interest only by accepting projects which increase the shareholders' claims on the firm as much as possible.' Express this statement in terms of the internal rate of return decision rule.

16 Prepare an analog model summarizing the main points discussed in this chapter.

17 How can spreadsheets be used to facilitate the application of the concepts discussed in this chapter?

Appendix 5A The British corporation tax system

The imputation system

This system was established in 1973. Under the imputation system companies which have sufficient profits chargeable to tax normally pay this tax amount in two parts: (a) advanced corporation tax (ACT) which is payable only when the company pays a dividend to shareholders; and (b) mainstream corporation tax (MCT) which is equal to the total corporation tax for the accounting year *minus* the advanced corporation tax for that year. The advanced corporation tax is calculated by using the following equation:

ACT	=	Dividend amount	x	Tax credit coefficient

where the tax credit coefficient is based upon the basic rate of personal income tax, that is:

$$\text{Tax credit coefficient} = \frac{\text{Basic tax rate}}{1 - \text{Basic tax rate}}$$

Advanced corporation tax is paid under a quarterly accounting system. The four quarters are ending 31 March, 30 June, 30 September and 31 December, respectively. The advanced corporation tax of a firm is payable within 14 days after the end of the quarter during which the dividend is paid. For example, for the quarter ended 30 September the last day for payment of the tax is 14 October.

The mainstream corporation tax for companies which started trading after 6 April 1965 is payable nine months after the end of the chargeable accounting year. If the initial investment of a project occurs at the end of the first month of an accounting year, the mainstream corporation tax is not paid until 20 months after the occurrence of the initial investment.

Example 5A.1 Calculating the advanced corporation tax and the mainstream corporation tax of a firm

The 1989 accounting year of Gordon Electronics runs from 1 July 1989 to 30 June 1990. The taxable profit of the company for the year ended 30 June 1990 was £4,000,000. The shareholders of Gordon Electronics received on 1 May 1990 a total net dividend of £450,000. We assume for simplicity that during the 1989 accounting year the firm made only one dividend payment to its shareholders. Using a basic rate of personal income tax of 25 per cent, the advanced corporation tax of the firm would be:

$$£450{,}000\frac{0.25}{1-0.25} = £150{,}000$$

The total income of the shareholders for tax purposes is £600,000 (that is, £450,000 + £150,000). Assuming a corporate tax rate of 35 per cent, the amount of corporate tax is £1,400,000 (that is, £4,000,000×0.35). Therefore, the mainstream corporation tax on these profits will be £1,250,000 (that is, £1,400,000 – £150,000). This tax will be paid nine months after the end of the accounting year. Figure 5A.1 summarizes the results from this example.

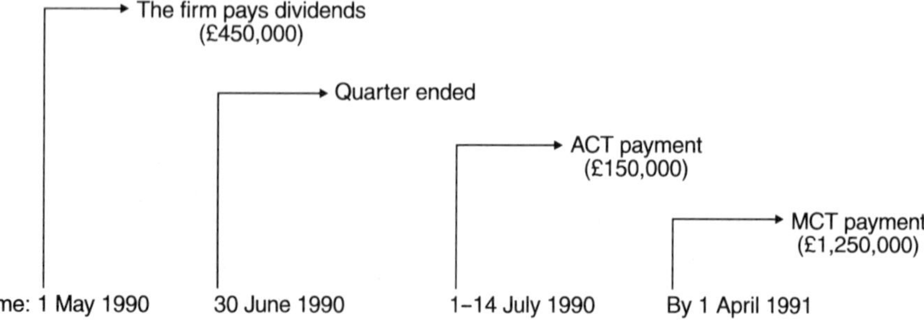

Figure 5A.1. Calculating the ACT and MCT of Gordon Electronics for the 1989 accounting year

If a firm pays an interim as well as a final dividend, then it must pay two instalments of advanced corporation tax.

The British depreciation system

Under the present UK corporation tax system, depreciation cannot be set against trading profits. Instead the tax system allows capital allowances (that is, standardized depreciation allowances) to be subtracted when calculating the firm's taxable profit. Capital allowances can be in the form of annual writing-down allowances which are expressed in percentages. From 1 April 1986 the following writing-down allowances are available:

Plant and machinery ⟶ 25 per cent a year on reducing balance basis.
Hotels ⟶ 4 per cent a year on a straight line basis.
Industrial buildings ⟶ 4 per cent a year on a straight line basis.

Example 5A.2 Calculating the writing-down allowances for a new machine

Taylor plc has the opportunity to invest in a new machine with an original cost of £10,000. The expected lifetime of the machine is five years and the firm estimates an expected salvage value of £1,000. The annual writing-down allowance for expenditures incurred when acquiring plant and machinery is 25 per cent a year on a reducing balance basis. Figure 5A.2 calculates the annual writing-down allowances associated with the firm's project. For example, the capital allowance for the first year is £2,500 (that is, 0.25 × £10,000). The difference between the initial investment and the corresponding capital allowance is carried forward and provides the initial amount to be used to calculate the capital allowance for the second year. Such an allowance is £1,875 (that is, £7,500 × 0.25), and so on.

Assuming that the machine's initial investment will occur at time zero, the tax relief of £875 (that is, £2,500 × 0.35) will be claimed at the end of the first period. The final capital allowance in year 5 is £1.373, that is, the balance that will occur at the end of year 4 *minus* the expected salvage value of the project.

```
            A             B          C          D          E          F          G          H
 1 CALCULATING THE ANNUAL WDA OF A MACHINE USING THE BRITISH SYSTEM
 2 ==================================================================
 3
 4 Initial cost -------------->  10,000
 5 WDA rate ------------------>      25%
 6 Salvage value  of machine >   1,000
 7 Corporation tax rate ----->       35%
 8
 9
10 -------------------------------------------------------------------------
11                       0          1          2          3          4          5          6
12 -------------------------------------------------------------------------
13 Balance b/f  10,000      7,500      5,625      4,219      3,164      1,373
14 25% WDA       2,500      1,875      1,406      1,055        791      1,373
15            ---------------------------------------------------------------
16 Balance       7,500      5,625      4,219      3,164      2,373          0
17
18 Tax on WDA                 875        656        492        369        277        481
```

Figure 5A.2. Calculating the annual WDA related to the investment of Taylor

Example 5A.3 Cash flow analysis using the British depreciation system

In addition to the data given in Example 5A.2, let us assume that the new machine of Taylor plc will require an increase in net working capital of £900 which will be recovered at project termination. It is estimated that the machine can generate profit before corporation tax of £4,000 per annum. The initial investment of the project is £10,900 (see Figure 5A.3).

The annual cash flow after tax, stored in cell C22 is calculated by using the following formula:

```
+C18+C19-C20
```

The net present value calculation assumes a discount rate of 12 per cent.

```
-------------------------------------------------------------------------
         A            B         C         D         E         F         G         H
 1 CALCULATING A PROJECT'S AFTER-TAX CASH FLOWS USING THE BRITISH SYSTEM
 2 =====================================================================
 3
 4 Initial cost ------------->  10,000
 5 WDA rate ----------------->      25%
 6 Salvage value  of machine >   1,000
 7 Corporation tax rate ----->      35%
 8 Cash Flow   -------------->   4,000
 9 Working Capital (WC) ----->     900
10 ---------------------------------------------------------------------
11                    0         1         2         3         4         5         6
12 ---------------------------------------------------------------------
13 Balance b/f   10,000     7,500     5,625     4,219     3,164     1,373
14 25% WDA        2,500     1,875     1,406     1,055       791     1,373
15              ---------------------------------------------------------
16 Balance        7,500     5,625     4,219     3,164     2,373         0
17
18 Tax on WDA                 875       656       492       369       277       481
19 Cash Flow                4,000     4,000     4,000     4,000     4,000
20 Tax (35%)                    0     1,400     1,400     1,400     1,400     1,400
21                        ===============================================
22 CF After Tax             4,875     3,256     3,092     2,969     2,877      (919)
23 WC             (900)                                               900
24              ---------------------------------------------------------
25 Cash Flows  (10,900)     4,875     3,256     3,092     2,969     4,777      (919)
26
27                                     Net Present Value --->             2,381
28                                                                     ========
-------------------------------------------------------------------------
```

Figure 5A.3. Cash flow analysis for the investment project of Taylor

Problems

1 Create the worksheet shown in Figure 5A.3.

2 Calculate the net present value of the Taylor project assuming a corporate tax rate of 34 per cent.

Appendix 5B The covariance between two variables

The covariance is a statistical measure indicating the direction of the relationship between the fluctuations of two variables. The following cases exist:

- If the covariance between two variables is positive, then the variables tend to move together. In other words, a positive covariance value indicates the tendency for one variable to increase as the other variable increases and vice versa.

- If the covariance between two variables is negative, then the variables move in opposite directions. In other words, a negative covariance value indicates the tendency for one variable to increase as the other variable decreases and vice versa.
- A covariance of zero indicates no relationship between the two variables.

Example 5B.1 Calculating the covariance between two variables

Figure 5B.1 shows the annual trading expenses and sales of Marks and Spencer plc for the period 1976–87, figures are in £million (see also Appendix 4C). The covariance between two variables can be calculated as an average of the products of two deviations, the deviation of the first variable from its mean and the deviation of the second variable from its mean. To calculate the covariance between two variables follow the steps:

Step 1 Calculate for each variable its mean.
Step 2 Calculate for each variable the deviations of the variable's value from its mean.
Step 3 Calculate the pairwise products of deviations.
Step 4 Calculate the average of the products of the two deviations derived in Step 3.

The average value of the trading expenses series shown in Figure 5B.1 is £1,998.6 million and the average value of the sales series is £2,240.7 million (figures are rounded to 1 decimal point). Column E shows the product deviations. For example,

$$(804.9 - 1{,}998.6)(900.9 - 2{,}240.7) = 1{,}559{,}319.9$$

Finally, the covariance is calculated as the average of the products of the two deviations. The covariance between the two variables is positive indicating the tendency of trading expenses to increase as the sales amount increases.

	A	B	C	D	E	F
1	THE COVARIANCE BETWEEN TRADING EXPENSES AND SALES OF M&S (1976-87)					
2						
3	Year	Trading	Sales	Product Deviation		
4		Expenses				
5						
6	1976	804.9	900.9	1,599,224.9		
7	1977	943.8	1,065.0	1,240,045.2		
8	1978	1,117.7	1,254.0	869,114.4		
9	1979	1,293.9	1,473.0	540,943.2		
10	1980	1,487.3	1,668.0	292,781.1		
11	1981	1,682.0	1,873.0	116,388.4		
12	1982	1,964.7	2,199.0	1,410.8		
13	1983	2,250.6	2,506.0	66,874.9		
14	1984	2,551.6	2,855.0	339,751.4		
15	1985	2,858.7	3,194.0	820,000.9		
16	1986	3,318.6	3,716.0	1,947,500.2		
17	1987	3,709.0	4,184.0	3,323,956.4		
18						
19	Average	1,998.6	2,240.7	929,832.7	<----- Covariance	

Figure 5B.1. Calculating the covariance between two variables

How can 1-2-3 help to calculate the covariance between these two variables? There is a simple and fast way to do so. Store in cell D6 the following formula calculating a product deviation:

```
(B6-$B$19)*(C6-$C$19)
```

Copy the formula stored in cell D6 in the range D7..D17. Finally, calculate the covariance by storing the following function in cell D19:

```
@AVG(D6..D17)
```

The covariance can be used to calculate the beta coefficient (or the slope) of the relationship between trading expenses and sales by using the following formula (see also Appendix 4C):

```
+D19/@VAR(C6..C17)
```

The last formula gives a beta of 0.892 which is exactly the same as that derived in Appendix 4C using the `/Data Regression` command of 1-2-3.
A quick way for determining whether there exists an apparent relationship between two variables is to graph the points corresponding to each pair of values. Such a graph is called a scatter diagram. 1-2-3 offers a command for creating scatter diagrams, this being `/Graph Options Format Graph Symbols` command. The results after issuing this command are displayed in Figure 5B.2.

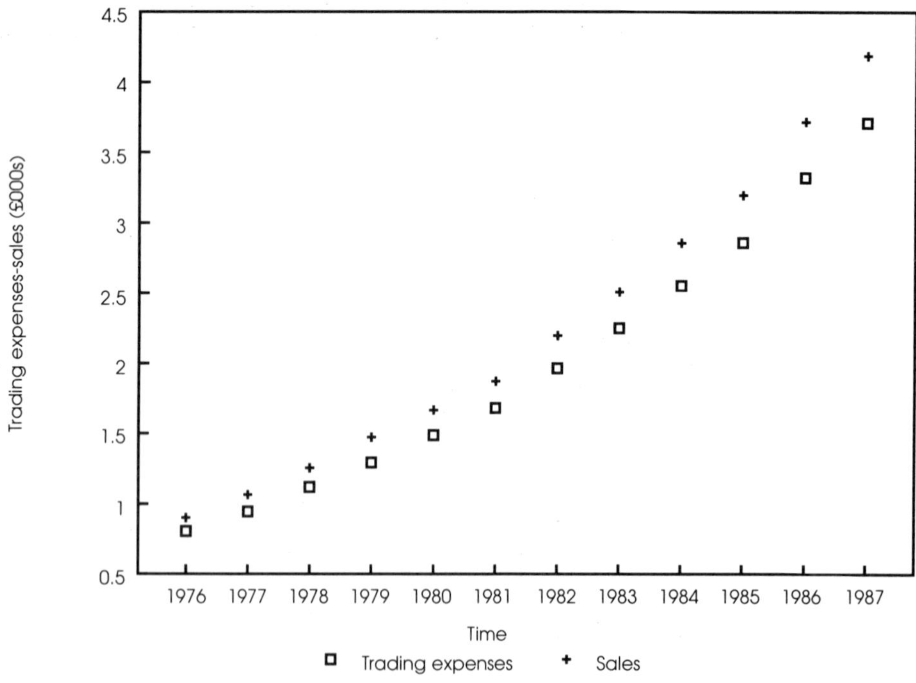

Figure 5B.2. Scatter diagram of sales versus trading expenses (1976–87)

Some useful points

1 (Calculating the covariance using the regression facilities of 1-2-3) There is another procedure that can be used to calculate the covariance between two

series of historical data. This relies on 1-2-3's regression facility. The slope of a regression line can be expressed as:

$$\text{Slope} = \frac{\text{Covariance between the dependent and independent variable}}{\text{Variance of the independent variable}}$$

Therefore, use 1-2-3 to calculate the slope of the regression between the two variables under consideration and then compute the covariance by multiplying the calculated slope by the variance of the independent variable.

2 (A general point) A positive (negative) covariance can emerge although some members in the pairs of the data change in opposite directions (the same direction). For example, the following two series of data have positive covariance: 1, 2, 4, 5, 6 and 1, 4, 2, 5, 4.

References and bibliography

Anderson, P.F. and Martin, J.D. (1977) Lease versus purchase decisions: a survey of current practice, *Financial Management*, **6**, Spring, 41–7.

Bacon, P.W. (1977) The evaluation of mutually exclusive investments, *Financial Management*, **6**, Summer, 55–8.

Bower, R.S. (1973) Issues in lease financing, *Financial Management*, **2**, Winter, 25–34.

Clark, J.J., Hindeland, T.J. and Pritchard, R.E. (1979) *Capital Budgeting: Planning and Control of Capital Expenditures*. Prentice-Hall, New Jersey.

Corr, A.V. (1983) *The Capital Expenditure Decision*, Ch. 3. National Association of Accountants and the Society of Management Accountants in Canada, Canada.

Diacogiannis, P.G. and Lai, R. (1989) Survey on the investment and financing decisions of the companies in the USM, Warwick Paper in Management, No. 33, April.

Dorfman, R. (1981) The meaning of internal rate of return, *Journal of Finance*, **36**, December, 1011–21.

Emery, G.W. (1982) Some guidelines for evaluating capital investment alternatives with unequal lives, *Financial Management*, **11**, Spring, 14–19.

Fama, E.F. and Miller, M.H. (1972) *The Theory of Finance*. Holt, Rinehart and Winston, New York.

Fawthrop, R.A. (1971) Underlying problems of discounted cash flow appraisal, *Accounting and Business Research*, Summer, 187–98.

Fisher, I. (1965) *The Theory of Interest*. Augustus M. Kelley, Publishers, New York. (Reprinted from 1930 edition.)

Gitman, L.J. and Forrester, J.R., Jr (1977) A survey of capital budgeting techniques used by major US firms, *Financial Management*, Autumn, 66–71.

Grinyer, J.R. (1974) Relevant criterion rates in capital budgeting, *Journal of Business Finance and Accounting*, **1**, Autumn, 357–74.

Hirshleifer, J. (1958) On the theory of optimal decisions, *Journal of Political Economy*, August, 329–52.

Hoskins, C.B. and Muney, G.A. (1979) Payback maligned method of asset ranking, *Engineering Economist*, **25**, Autumn, 53–65.

Isom, T.A. and S.P. Amembal (1982) *The Handbook of Leasing: Techniques and Analysis*. Petrocelli Books, New York.

Keane, S.M. (1974) Let's scrap IRR once for all, *Accountancy*, February.

Keane, S.M. (1979) The internal rate of return and the re-investment fallacy, *Abacus*, June, 48–55.

King, P. (1975) Is the emphasis of capital budgeting theory misplaced?, *Journal of Business Finance and Accounting*, **2**, Spring, 69–82.

Lewellen, W.G., Howard, P.L. and McConnell, J.J. (1973) Payback substitutes for discounted cash flow, *Financial Management*, **2**, Summer, 17–23.

Lorie, J.H. and Savage, L.J. (1955) Three problems in rationing capital, *Journal of Business*, October, 229–39.

Mao, J.C. (1966) The internal rate of return as a ranking criterion, *Engineering Economist*, **11**, Winter, 1–13.

Merrett, A.J. and Sykes, A. (1966) *Capital Budgeting and Company Finance*. Longmans, London.

Perty, G.H. (1975) Effective use of capital budgeting tools, *Business Horizons*, **19**, October, 57–65.

Pike, R.A. (1983) A review of recent trends in formal capital budgeting processes, *Accounting and Business Research*, Summer, 1–8.

Pike, R.A. (1988) An empirical study of the adoption of sophisticated capital budgeting practices and decision-making effectiveness. *Accounting and Business Research*, Autumn, 341–51.

Scholefield, H.H. (1972) Replacement of equipment, *Accounting and Business Research*, 316–24.

Solomon, E. (1956) The arithmetic of capital-budgeting decisions, *Journal of Business*, April, 124–9.

Statman, M. and Sepe, J.F. (1985) Managerial incentive plans and the use of the payback method, *Journal of Business Finance and Accounting*, Spring, 61–5.

Stephen, F.O. (1976) On deriving the internal rate of return from the accountant's rate of return, *Journal of Business Finance and Accounting*, **3**, Summer, 147–50.

Weingartner, H.M. (1966) Capital budgeting in interrelated projects—survey and synthesis, *Management Sciences*, March, 485–516.

Weingartner, H.M. (1969) Some new views on the payback period and capital budgeting decisions, *Management Science*, August, 594–607.

Wilkes, F.M. (1980) *On multiple rates of return, Journal of Business Finance and Accounting*, **7**, 569–83.

6 Advanced capital budgeting topics

This chapter includes:

- Capital budgeting and inflation
- The lease–buy decision
- Capital rationing and net present value

The preceding chapter showed how to estimate the cash flows associated with an investment project and introduced several evaluation methods that can be used to analyse potential investment projects. To keep the analysis simple, several implicit assumptions were taken into account including the assumption that expected cash flows are not affected by inflation and the case where there is no restriction on the size of the firm's capital budget.

The purpose of this chapter is to cover three advanced capital budgeting issues. The first issue introduces some methods that are used to incorporate the effects of inflation in the capital budgeting calculations. The second uses the net present value decision rule to analyse the desirability of leasing. The third and final issue deals with problems related to situations where there exist limitations on the availability of capital used to fund investment projects. Figure 6.1 shows how these three topics fit within the financial management framework introduced in Chapter 2.

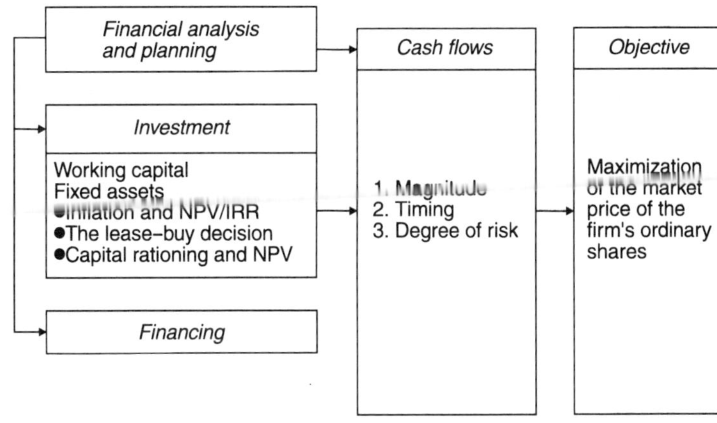

Figure 6.1. Relating three advanced capital budgeting topics to the financial management framework introduced in Chapter 2

Capital budgeting and inflation

The calculation of the net present value of a project requires the initial investment, the expected net cash flows and the discount rate. Because investment decisions on fixed assets involve long periods of time, both the expected net cash flows and the discount rate are affected by expected inflation (that is, the expected change in the price level over some future period of time).

Most of the future costs and revenues associated with an investment in fixed assets are affected during inflationary periods. For example, the labour and raw materials of a textile firm are usually affected when a rise in the general level of prices occurs. At the same time, the firm may pass on some or all of the increased costs to its customers. Two items that are generally unaffected by inflation are the firm's depreciation schedule on fixed assets and the part of fixed assets which is financed with fixed rate borrowed funds. This section discusses the effects of expected inflation on project evaluation.

Inflation and interest rates

If investors expect a rise in the level of prices, they will require a rate of return which provides a compensation for the expected inflation. The nominal discount rate (that is, a discount rate expressed in money terms) can be theoretically represented by the following equation:

1 + Nominal discount rate (DR)	=	1 + Real DR	×	1 + Expected inflation rate
$1 + r_N$	=	$(1 + r_R)$	×	$(1 + h)$

The nominal discount rate and the real discount rate (that is, the discount rate that could prevail in the market if the general price level remains constant) usually are not equal. Only if investors expect the general price level to remain constant will both rates be equal. However, investors are always expecting prices to change and so the nominal discount rate will deviate from the real discount rate. The latter can be calculated quite easily from the last equation by dividing the left-hand side of this equation by (1 + inflation rate) and subtracting from this ratio number one.

Example 6.1 Calculating the real discount rate

Tacca Clothes plc uses a nominal discount rate of 12 per cent to evaluate its investments in fixed assets (we assume that management is making decisions in a world of complete certainty). The financial director of the firm expects the inflation rate to be 5.5 per cent during the next year. Then the real discount rate for that period is 6.16 per cent:

$$r_R = \frac{1 + 0.120}{1 + 0.055} - 1 = 6.16 \text{ per cent}$$

Inflation and future cash flows

Inflation usually affects the revenues and expenses associated with a project and as a consequence it has an impact on the net cash flows expected by the project. Nominal net cash flows include the effects of future inflation, while real net cash flows exclude such effects. It is important to understand that during the evaluation phase of the capital budgeting process, nominal interest rates can only be used with nominal net cash flows and real interest rates can only be applied to real net cash flows.

When costs, revenues and the discount rate change at the same rate of inflation, the discounted cash flow calculations remain unaffected since the effects of inflation cancel each other out. In many instances, however, costs, revenues and discount rate do not change at the same rate of inflation. In such cases, inflation must be incorporated into the investment appraisal process.

Example 6.2 Investment appraisal and inflation

Tacca Clothes plc is considering the purchase of a new machine at a cost of £1,350,000. The machine has an expected life of five years and at the end of its useful life it is expected to be worthless. We assume a straight-line depreciation and a corporate tax rate of 34 per cent. Figure 6.2 presents a worksheet estimating the net cash flows of the project.

	A	B	C	D	E	F	G
1	ESTIMATING THE CASH FLOWS OF A PROJECT,NO INFLATION EFFECTS(£000s)						
2	========						
3			1	2	3	4	5
4			----	----	----	----	----
5	Annual Revenues		700	700	700	700	700
6	Salaries		130	130	130	130	130
7	Maintenance		85	85	85	85	85
8	Depreciation		270	270	270	270	270
9	Other Costs		40	40	40	40	40
10			----	----	----	----	----
11	Profit Before Tax		175	175	175	175	175
12	Tax		60	60	60	60	60
13			----	----	----	----	----
14	Profit After Tax		116	116	116	116	116
15	Depreciation		270	270	270	270	270
16			----	----	----	----	----
17	Net Cash Flow		386	386	386	386	386

Figure 6.2. Estimating the net cash flows of a project for Tacca Clothes plc

	A	B	C
21	CALCULATING THE NPV,PI,IRR OF THE PROJECT,NO INFLATION EFFECTS		
22	========		
23	Discount Rate --->	12.00%	
24			
25			
26	----		
27	Year	Cash Flow (£000s)	
28	----		
29	0	(1,350)	
30	1	386	
31	2	386	
32	3	386	
33	4	386	
34	5	386	
35		---------	
36	NPV ------->	40	
37	PI ------>	1.03	
38	IRR ------>	13.18%	
39		=========	

Figure 6.3. Discounted cash flow calculations for Tacca's project, no inflation effects

The firm uses a nominal discount rate of 12 per cent and Figure 6.3 shows the net present value, profitability index and internal rate of return for its new project. For example, if the cash flows and discount rate are unaffected by rising price levels in future periods, the net present value of the project is £40,000 (figures are rounded) and the project should be accepted.

Let us now consider the impact of inflation on the project's costs. We assume that the costs are expected to rise as follows: salaries by 5 per cent per year, maintenance by 8 per cent per year and other costs by 3 per cent per year. By adjusting at different rates, the net cash flows expected from the project decrease as shown in Figure 6.4.

Figure 6.4. Estimating the net cash flows of a project, with inflation effects

	A	B	C	D	E	F	G
41	ESTIMATING THE CASH FLOWS OF THE NEW PROJECT,WITH INFLATION EFFECTS						
42	================================						
43	Salaries	5.00%	Maintenance		8.00%	Other	3.00%
44							
45			1	2	3	4	5
46							
47	Annual Revenues		700	700	700	700	700
48	Salaries		130	137	143	150	158
49	Maintenance		85	92	99	107	116
50	Depreciation		270	270	270	270	270
51	Other Costs		40	41	42	44	45
52							
53	Profit Before Tax		175	161	145	129	111
54	Tax		60	55	49	44	38
55							
56	Profit After Tax		116	106	96	85	73
57	Depreciation		270	270	270	270	270
58							
59	Real Net Cash Flow		386	376	366	355	343
60							

Figure 6.5. Discounted cash flow calculations for Tacca's project, with inflation effects

	A	B	C	D	E	F	G
61	CALCULATING THE NPV,PI,IRR OF THE PROJECT,WITH INFLATION EFFECTS						
62	================================						
63							
64	Real Interest Rate	12.00%					
65							
66							
67	Year	Cash Flow (£000s)					
68							
69	0	(1,350)					
70	1	386					
71	2	376					
72	3	366					
73	4	355					
74	5	343					
75		---------					
76	NPV ------->	(25)					
77	PI ------>	0.98					
78	IRR ------>	11.23%					
79		=========					

Figure 6.5 shows the impact of inflation on the calculation of the net present value, profitability index and internal rate of return. The net present value changed from positive to negative indicating the fact that the annual expenses rise with inflation. In this case, the firm should reject the project.

A combination of the Figures 6.2, 6.3, 6.4 and 6.5, provides a model that shows the impact of inflation on the net cash flows associated with a project and incorporates inflation into a discounted cash flow analysis. If this model is created by using formulae, then you can predict a new situation based on the effects of changing one or more variables. For example, you can estimate the change in the net present value, profitability index and internal rate of return assuming that changes occur in the salaries, maintenance and other costs. Finally, Figure 6.6 compares graphically the net present value results with and without inflation adjustments.

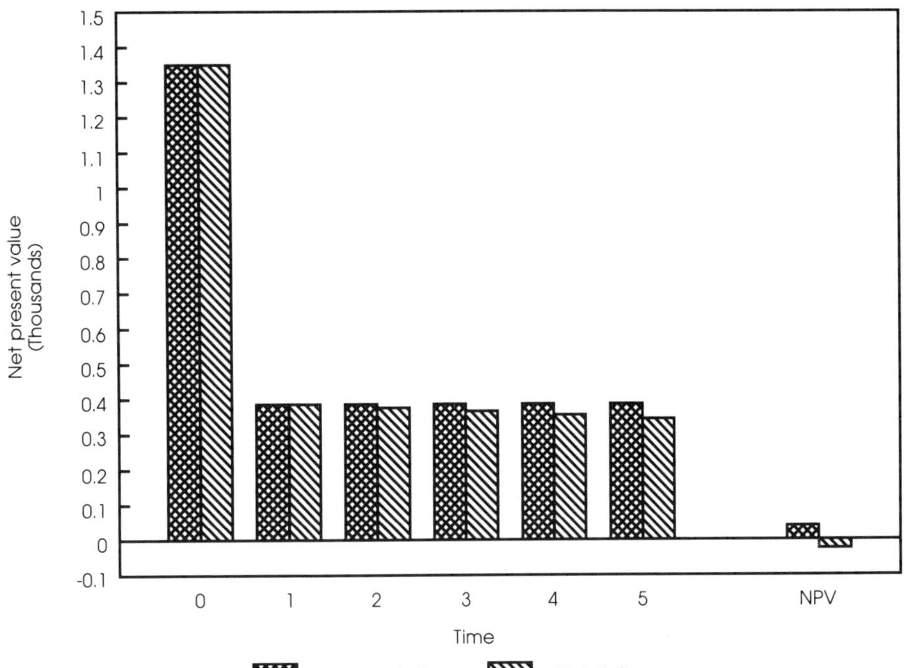

Figure 6.6. The NPV of a project with and without inflation adjustment

Problems

1 Set up a worksheet model like Figures 6.2, 6.3, 6.4 and 6.5, with labels and values as shown. Use the appropriate formulae in rows 11, 12, 14, 15, 17, 36, 37, 38, 48, 49, 50, 51, 53, 54, 56, 57, 59, 76, 77 and 78.

2 Discuss how changes in salaries, maintenance and other costs affect the net present value, the profitability index and the internal rate of return of Tacca's project.

3 Tacca Clothes plc is presently evaluating an investment project that has an economic life of five years and a cost of £1,280,000. The annual revenues associated with this project are expected to be £1,300,000 and the project is expected to have no salvage value. To earn these revenues, the firm will have for the first year the following expenses: salaries, £120,000, maintenance £70,000 and other costs £40,000. The new machine will be depreciated over its five-year life using the straight-line method.

Assume that the revenues are fixed and salaries, maintenance and other costs are expected to rise annually by 5 per cent, 8 per cent and 3 per cent, respectively. The corporate tax rate is 34 per cent. Assume a discount rate of 12 per cent. Calculate the net present value, profitability index and internal rate of return for the new project without considering the effects of inflation and then provide a discounted cash flow evaluation by taking into account the impact of inflation. Should Tacca Clothes undertake the investment?

4 Conduct a sensitivity analysis of the net present value of the project with respect to the nominal discount rate (other things remain the same).

5 Conduct a sensitivity analysis of the net present value of the project with respect to the nominal discount rate and the initial investment (other things remain the same).

6 Conduct a sensitivity analysis of the net present value of the project with respect to the nominal discount rate and the expected cost of salaries (other things remain constant).

Leasing

A firm may lease (rent) an asset in order to acquire its services rather than buying it. Lease is a contract between two parties by which one party agrees to let the other party use an asset for a stated period of time in return for specified periodic payments. The lessor is the individual or firm that owns the leased asset and receives lease payments. The lessee is an individual or firm that makes periodic payments to the lessor for the use of the asset. There are many kinds of leases but for our analysis it is convenient to divide leases into two broad categories: operating (or service) leases and financial (or capital) leases.

An operating lease is basically a short-term lease that can be cancelled by the lessee at short notice. Because the life of an operating lease contract is typically short, the sum of all the lease payments by the first lessee are insufficient to recover the full cost of the asset. As a result, the lessor expects to make subsequent leases for the remaining life of the asset. Operating leases are commonly used for leasing office and business equipment such as computer hardware, photocopiers, typewriters, motor vehicles, and so on. The lessor usually provides service, maintenance and insurance for the leased asset.

A financial lease is a long-term lease that obligates the lessee to make payments to the lessor throughout the lease period. The sum of the lease payments by the lessee over the lease period usually covers the cost of the asset. Examples of financial leases includes equipment, aircraft, ships, cars, warehouses and buildings. The lessor does not usually provide service, maintenance and insurance for the leased asset.

A sale and leaseback and a direct lease are two types of financial leases. A sale and leaseback is a financial lease arrangement in which a firm sells an asset it already owns to another party and then leases it back from the buyer. The proceeds from the sale of an asset provide funds for operations and the firm still uses the services of the asset. A direct lease occurs when a leasing company acquires an asset that it did not previously own and then leases it to a given lessee. The lessor may be the manufacturer of the asset or an independent party that purchases the asset from the manufacturer and then leases it to a lessee. Figure 6.7 compares operating and financial leases (operating leases can also be direct leases).

The lease–buy decision

When a firm has decided to acquire the services of an asset, it has the following choices: (a) to lease the asset, or (b) to purchase the asset. The lease–buy decision involves simultaneously an investment decision (that is, accept or reject the lease) and a financing decision (that is, lease the asset or purchase the asset and obtain

Characteristic	Operating lease	Financial lease
Duration	Short	Long
Party responsible for maintenance and insurance	Lessor	Lessee
Cancellation	Lessee can cancel lease at short notice	Cannot be cancelled or cancellation involves a large penalty

Figure 6.7. Comparing operating and financial leases

the funds needed via borrowing). The investment decision of whether to lease the asset is a capital budgeting problem, while the financing decision involves the comparison of the lease contract with other forms of debt in determining whether the former is more favourable than debt financing. Leasing and borrowing are compared because they impose the same financial commitment on the firm.

In order to evaluate whether leasing is preferred to buying the asset we need to conduct a discounted cash flow analysis. One way of performing the analysis is to calculate the net present value of the difference between the lease and buy alternatives; if the net present value is positive, leasing should be preferred to purchasing.

Example 6.3 Calculating the net present value of a lease from the lessee's viewpoint without considering corporation tax

Mindy plc wants to acquire a £10 million machine. The firm is considering whether to lease or purchase this machine. Cannon Leasing has offered to lease the machine to Mindy for a total of £12.34 million. The expected life of the machine is five years after which it is not expected to have any salvage value. The leasing arrangement requires annual payments that are made in advance. If the machine is purchased, the firm will finance it entirely with a five-year 12 per cent loan. To determine whether to lease or not to lease, a discounting cash flow analysis is required.

If Mindy decides to lease, the annual lease payment will be £2,468,000 payable at the beginning of each year. Figure 6.8 shows the lessee's net present value from the leasing alternative. The net present value is calculated by using 1-2-3 `@NPV` function with a discount rate of 12 per cent. The net present value is positive, indicating that the lease is preferable to the purchase of the machine.

The internal rate of return cannot be used to compare the leasing and buying alternatives of Mindy because it suffers from the following drawback: it does not take into account cases where the net present value increases as the discount rate increases. This drawback can be better understood by considering the two projects shown in Figure 6.9.

Viewed from the internal rate of return perspective, these two projects would appear to be equally desirable. Clearly, though, the first alternative is more attractive because it provides a positive net present value. The individual who discovers that the internal rate of return of the first alternative is lower than the cost of capital of 12 per cent may erroneously reject the proposal. Finally, another difference between the two projects is that the net present value of the first proposal increases as the discount rate increases, while for the second alternative, the net present value increases as the discount rate decreases.

Figure 6.8. Calculating the lessee's NPV without corporate tax (figures are in £000s)

```
            A                   B         C         D         E         F          G
                           LEASE-BUY DECISION WITHOUT TAX
 1                         ==============================
 2
 3 After tax discount rate --------->   12.0%   Term (years)              5
 4 Cost of the project ------------> 10,000   Cost of lease         12,340
 5
 6 -------------------------------------------------------------------------
 7 Year                          0         1         2         3         4         5
 8 -------------------------------------------------------------------------
 9 Purchase                 10,000
10
11 Lease payments           (2,468)   (2,468)   (2,468)   (2,468)   (2,468)
12                          -----------------------------------------------
13 Cash flow                  7,532   (2,468)   (2,468)   (2,468)   (2,468)
14
15                                       NPV ------->                36
16                                                               ========
```

Figure 6.9. The IRR and NPV on two projects (figures are in £000s)

Project	Cash flows (£) 0	1	2	3	4	IRR	NPV (at 12%)
A	7,532	–2,468	–2,468	–2,468	–2,468	11.77%	36
B	–7,532	2,468	2,468	2,468	2,468	11.77%	–36

Example 6.4 Calculating the net present value of a lease from the lessee's viewpoint when corporation tax is taken into account

Consider the case of the firm introduced in Example 6.3. Assume a corporate tax rate of 35 per cent and 25 per cent per annum writing-down allowances on reducing-balance basis. Assume that the corporate tax effect of the lease payments will be realized in years 1 to 5. Since lease is a form of debt finance, the discount rate to be used is the after-tax return obtained on a similar form of debt:

$0.12 \times (1 - 0.35) = 7.8$ per cent

The writing-down allowances shown in Figure 6.10 have been calculated using a 25 per cent reducing-balance method. The capital allowances assume a balancing allowance of £3,164 in the fifth year. For example, the writing-down allowance for the third year is calculated by multiplying the balance brought forward from the second year by the 25 per cent: £4,219 × 0.25 = £1,055. In this case, the balancing factor of £3,164 (that is, £4,219 – £1,055) is carried forward to the fourth year. The capital allowances for the fifth year are £1,107 (that is, £3,164 × 0.35). If the machine is leased, the lessee will loose the capital allowances, and thus we include these allowances in parentheses to indicate negative numbers.

The total capital allowances are £3,500. Such an amount can also be calculated by multiplying the corporate tax rate by the initial cost of the machine (that is, 0.35 × £10,000 = £3,500). The annual lease payment is £2,468 and the annual tax relief from the lease is £864 (that is, £2,468 × 0.35). The cash flows are shown in row 20 of Figure 6.10. For example, the cash flow for the second year is calculated as follows:

£864 – £875 – £2,468 = –£2,479

From the lessee's viewpoint, the net present value is negative and the decision is to purchase rather than lease the machine. On the other hand, the lessor pays £10,000 for the machine and receives an annual lease payment of £2,468 for five years. The lessor realizes a net present value which is the negative of the lessee's net present value. In this instance, the lessor will be willing to lease the machine, but the lessee should undertake the buying alternative.

Problems

1 Set up the worksheet shown in Figure 6.10 using the appropriate formulae.
2 Assume that the annual lease payment is £2,400,000. Do you recommend buying or leasing?

Figure 6.10. Calculating the lease's NPV when corporation tax is taken into consideration (figures are in £000s)

	A	B	C	D	E	F	G
1		LEASE -BUY DECISION WITH TAX					
2		============================					
3							
4	After tax discound rate ----->			7.8%	WDA ----------->		25%
5	Corporate tax rate ---------->			35%	Term (years) -->		5
6	Cost of the project --------->			10,000	Cost of lease ->		12,340
7							
8	==========	==========	==========	==========	==========	==========	==========
9	Year	0	1	2	3	4	5
10	----------	----------	----------	----------	----------	----------	----------
11	Balance b/f	10,000	7,500	5,625	4,219	3,164	
12	WDA	2,500	1,875	1,406	1,055	791	
13		----------	----------	----------	----------	----------	----------
14	Balance	7,500	5,625	4,219	3,164		
15	Capital allowances		(875)	(656)	(492)	(369)	(1,107)
16							
17	Lease payments	(2,468)	(2,468)	(2,468)	(2,468)	(2,468)	
18	Tax		864	864	864	864	864
19		----------	----------	----------	----------	----------	----------
20	Cash flow	7,532	(2,479)	(2,260)	(2,096)	(1,973)	(244)
21							
22					NPV --------->		(15)
23							=========

Advantages and disadvantages of leasing

Leasing offers a number of advantages. First, leasing may provide tax benefits to both the lessee and the lessor. From the viewpoint of the lessee, lease payments are tax-deductible expenses. On the other hand, leasing can be also beneficial to the lessor, who owns the leased asset. For example, if a firm has substantial losses, the lessor receives the tax benefits and passes some of those benefits to the lessee through lower lease payments.

Second, it is often argued that the utilization of leases increases the firm's debt capacity because the combination of leasing and borrowing provides more funds available than those obtained via long-term debt. Third, lease contracts usually pay fixed periodic payments which are not affected by changes in interest rates. This can be an advantage in periods of high interest rates. Fourth, from the lessee's point of view, operating leasing can be cancelled at short notice.

Leasing also has several potential disadvantages. First, in some instances the cost of leasing is higher than the cost of buying the asset by utilizing another source of capital (for example, debt). Second, the lessee may not be able to obtain any value from the asset after the termination of the lease. In leases involving assets such as land and buildings this loss can be substantial. Third, a firm may not be able to cancel a financial lease contract or cancellation may result in a large penalty.

Capital rationing

Capital rationing exists when a firm has only a fixed amount of capital to allocate to investment projects during a given time period. Capital rationing is concerned with the problem of selecting those projects that provide the highest overall net present value and cost no more than the limit placed on the size of the firm's capital budget.

Capital rationing is attributed to a variety of constraints which can be broadly classified as internal and external to the firm. For example, a conservatively managed firm may avoid obtaining new capital through additional debt because of the financial risk involved; it can also avoid the sale of new shares because it does not wish to increase the number of its existing shareholders. In such cases, the firm can use only internally generated funds and so it places a limit on the funds available for adopting investment projects. Furthermore, a small firm might have limited access to the capital market which in turn leads to capital constraints on the amount of capital available for investment.

The analysis of capital rationing assumes that the investment projects under consideration are independent. If the firm is also considering mutually exclusive projects, then the best should be selected and analysed with the firm's independent projects.

Example 6.5 A single period capital rationing problem

AK Textiles plc is considering six independent investment projects listed in Figure 6.11 along with their initial investments, net present values, profitability indices and internal rates of return. Assume that the firm sets a limit of £2.5 million on the amount of funds it is willing to invest in new projects and its discount rate (or cost of capital) is 12 per cent. The firm must select the optimal group of projects given its capital budget of £2.5 million. This capital rationing problem is for one period only. We also assume that the firm cannot adopt fractional projects (for example, the firm cannot build just 70 per cent of a factory).

Several combinations of projects are possible including:

Project combination	Total investment	Total NPV
D, E, F	£14,700,000	£2,450,000
C, D	£12,100,000	£1,850,000
C, F	£14,000,000	£1,800,000

Project	Initial investment	NPV	PI	IRR
A	6,200,000	454,000	1.07	14.72%
B	6,200,000	83,000	1.01	12.42%
C	8,000,000	950,000	1.30	19.41%
D	4,100,000	900,000	1.24	17.40%
E	4,600,000	700,000	1.17	16.30%
F	6,000,000	850,000	1.21	16.90%

Figure 6.11. An example of capital rationing (£2.5 million budget constraint)

The net present value method selects projects D, E and F, with a combined net present value of £2,450,000.

Alternatively, the profitability index decision rule selects projects C and D, with a combined net present value of £1,850,000. Thus, if we assume capital rationing conditions and that projects are not divisible, the profitability index decision rule does not necessarily select the combination of projects that is expected to provide the largest total net present value among competing combinations of projects. Finally, the internal rate of return method would result in the selection of projects C and D, which is not the best combination of projects.

What are the implications of accepting projects D, E and F in relation to the shareholders' wealth within the firm? Assume that the firm can only invest in the six projects presented in Figure 6.11. If it undertakes the projects D, E and F, then it increases the present value of its existing shareholders as much as possible under the capital rationing conditions. However, if the firm could invest in all six projects, the total increase of the present value of its existing shareholders' wealth would be £3,937,000. The difference between £3,937,000 and £2,450,000 is the opportunity cost of having a limit on the funds available for adopting projects. By limiting its capital budget to £2,500,000 it rejects three projects that could increase the present value of its existing shareholders' wealth by £1,487,000.

Example 6.5 assumes that the firm's capital is limited in only one period. But there are many other cases in which the budget limitation occurs in more than one period. In multi-period capital rationing the profitability index cannot be used. Multi-period capital rationing problems can be solved by using the technique of linear programming (see Appendix 6A).

Example 6.6 A two-period capital rationing problem

Atlas plc is considering two independent projects A and B each having a useful life of two years. We assume that both projects are divisible (that is, you can obtain a fraction of project A or project B). A decision to undertake a portion of a project may be achieved under a partnership arrangement. Figure 6.12 shows the cost commitments and net present values associated with the two projects (figures are in £million). Project A requires a cost of £2 million in period 1 and a cost of £3 million in period 2, whereas for project B the costs will be £3 million and £1 million in periods 1 and 2, respectively.

We assume that the firm has available in each of the two periods £10 million. Thus, we have a two-period capital rationing problem. Such a problem can be summarized as follows:

1 *Objective* Select the number of units of project A and/or project B which are undertaken so as to obtain a maximum total net present value.

Figure 6.12. Costs and NPVs of two investment projects A and B

Time	Project A	Project B
1	2	3
2	3	1
Net present value	7	9

2 *Constraints*

(a) For period 1 the total costs for new projects cannot be more than £10 million.

(b) For period 2 the total costs for new projects cannot be more than £10 million.

(c) We cannot invest negative amounts in projects (that is short-selling is forbidden).

If x and y represent the number of units of project A and project B, respectively, which are undertaken, the above linear programming problem can be stated mathematically as follows:

Maximize $\quad \text{NPV} = 7x + 9y$

Subject to: $\quad 2x + 3y \leqq 10$

$3x + y \leqq 10$

x and y are greater than or equal to zero.

The solution of this problem can be found by using a linear programming computer package (for example, What's Best!, a separate standalone package that works side by side with Lotus 1-2-3, produced by General Optimization Inc.). The best feasible solution to this problem is (for the derivation of this solution see Appendix 6A):

$x = 20/7 \quad \text{and} \quad y = 30/21$

In other words, the firm will undertake 20/7 (or 2.857) units of project A and 30/21 (or 1.428) of project B. In this case, the total net present value would be equal to

$(7)(20/7) + 9(30/21) = £32.85$ million

No other combination of x and y can have a greater net present value.

Figure 6.13 shows a graphical representation of the linear programming problem introduced above.

Example 6.7 A multi-period capital rationing problem

A firm is considering four independent investment projects. The firm's cost of capital is 12 per cent. Figure 6.14 shows the initial investment, the net cash flows and the net present value for each of the four projects. The net present values of the four projects are positive (figures are in £million).

The cost commitments associated with these four projects are presented in Figure 6.15 (figures are in £million).

Assume that the firm has £15 million to invest in the first year, £14 million in the second year, £16 million in the third year and £20 million in the fourth and final year. The firm cannot purchase a negative number of units of any project. In this case, we have the following linear programming problem:

Maximize: $\quad \text{NPV} = 22.44x + 11.10y + 16.45z + 24.39w$

Subject to: $\quad 22x + 17y + 8z + 3w \leqq 15$

$10x + 4y + 2z + 3w \leqq 14$

$10x + 7y + 3z + 5w \leqq 16$

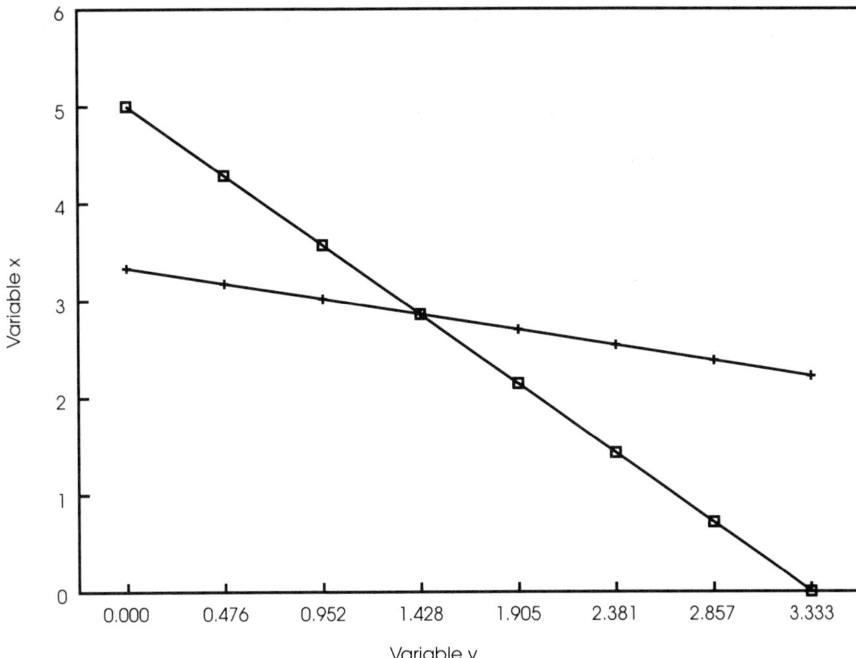

Figure 6.13. A graphic solution of a two-period capital rationing problem

```
     A          B          C          D          E          F          G
1 CALCULATING THE NET PRESENT VALUE FOR FOUR PROJECTS
2 -----------------------------------------------------------
3                              PROJECT
4     YEAR          A           B          C          D
5 -----------------------------------------------------------
6        0       -22        -17         -8         -3
7        1        20          8          5          8
8        2        22         12          9         12
9        3        24         16         18         15
10          ---------------------------------------
11 NPV         22.44      11.10      16.45      24.39
12          =======================================
```

Figure 6.14. Calculating the net present value for four investment projects

Time	Project A	Project B	Project C	Project D
0	22	17	8	3
1	10	4	2	3
2	10	7	3	5
3	12	7	8	6

Figure 6.15. Costs commitments of four investments projects

$$12x + \ 7y + 8z + 6w \leqq 20$$

x, y, z and w are greater than or equal to zero.

where $x,\ y,\ z,\ w =$ the number of units of project A, B, C and D, respectively, which are accepted.

The solution of the above problem is found to be:

$x = 0.0000, \quad y = 0.0000, \quad z = 0.1818 \quad$ and $\quad w = 3.0909$

This indicates that the firm will undertake 0 units of project A, 0 units of project B, 0.1818 of a unit of project C and 3.0909 units of project D. The total net present value that corresponds to this solution can be calculated as follows:

$$(16.45)(0.1818) + (24.39)(3.0909) = £78.37 \text{ million}$$

If we further impose the constraint that the firm cannot undertake a project more than once, the following linear programming problem emerges:

Maximize $\text{NPV} = 22.44x + 11.10y + 16.45z + 24.39w$

Subject to:

$$22x + 17y + 8z + 3w \leqq 15$$
$$10x + 4y + 2z + 3w \leqq 14$$
$$10x + 7y + 3z + 5w \leqq 16$$
$$12x + 7y + 8z + 6w \leqq 20$$
$$x \leqq 1$$
$$y \leqq 1$$
$$z \leqq 1$$
$$w \leqq 1$$

x, y, z and w are greater than or equal to zero.

In this case, the optimal solution is

$x = 0.0000$, $y = 0.0000$, $z = 0.1000$ and $w = 1.0000$

Figure 6.16 summarizes three uses of the net present value method.

Investment analysis under inflation
Calculate the net present value of a project based upon nominal cash flows and a nominal interest rate. If the net present value is positive, accept the project. Calculate the net present value of a project based upon real cash flows and a real interest rate. If the net present value is positive, accept the project.

Lease–buy decisions
Calculate the net present value of the difference between the lease and purchase alternatives. If the net present value is positive, leasing should be preferred to purchasing.

Constrained investment decisions
Calculate the net present values of the projects under consideration. Select those projects that collectively provide the highest net present value subject to a set of given constraints.

Figure 6.16. Uses of the net present value method

Summary

This chapter discussed three topics related to capital budgeting.

1 *Capital budgeting and inflation* Because investment decisions involve long time periods, it is necessary to incorporate the effects of inflation into the investment analysis. A failure to adjust for inflation in the evaluation process of a project may bias the calculated net present value and internal rate of return of the project.
2 *The lease–buy decision* Leasing takes two basic forms: operating and financial. An operating lease is characterized by two essential features: first, it is a short-term agreement between the lessee and the lessor; second, it can be cancelled at the option of the lessee at short notice. A financial lease is a longer-term lease as compared with the operating lease and it obligates the lessee to make a series of payments to the lessor during the life of the leased asset. Lease-or-purchase analysis uses the net present value of the difference between the lease and purchase payments and the following selection rule: if the net present value is positive, lease the asset; if the net present value is zero, do not lease the asset.
3 *Capital rationing and net present value* Capital rationing is the situation where a firm has a fixed capital budget to finance all its acceptable projects. Given a set of projects that are acceptable, the capital rationing problem is concerned with the selection of the mix of projects that increases the shareholders' wealth as much as possible. Linear programming provides a quantitative tool that can be utilized to solve capital rationing problems.

Questions for discussion

1 For each term shown below in the largest box provide a definition in your own words. Then check your responses against the definitions included in the chapter.

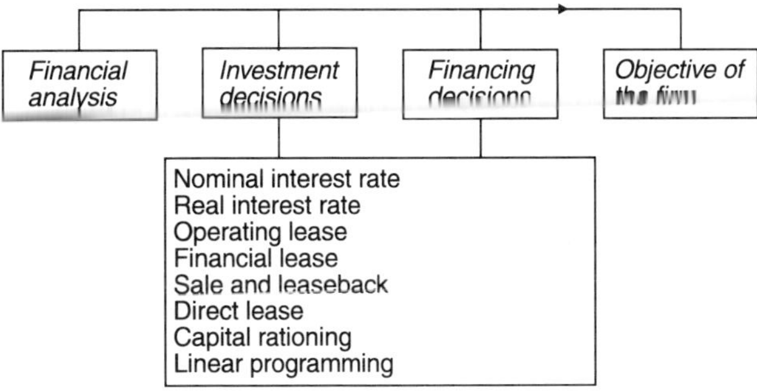

2 Discuss how inflation can be taken into consideration in estimating the net cash flows of an investment project. Also, discuss the alternative ways used to evaluate capital investment projects under conditions of inflation.

3 Discuss in detail the messages provided by the following diagram:

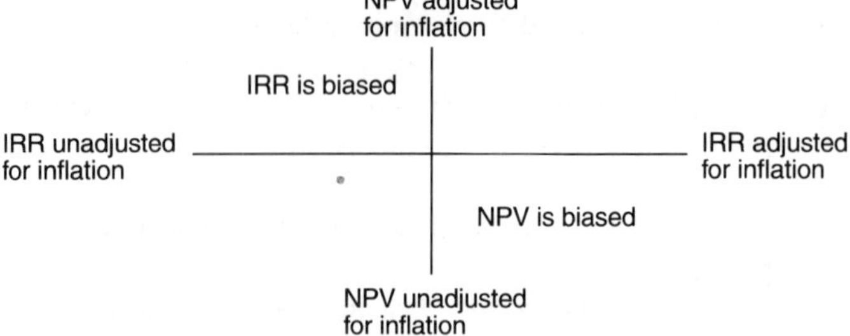

4 Provide a list with examples of assets that can be leased.

5 Discuss each of the following statements:

(**a**) 'Instead of raising new capital or using your own scarce capital to acquire a fixed asset, you can lease it and can thereby reduce possible initial costs, invest the working capital you save in other projects and enjoy the financial benefits from the utilization of the asset.'

(**b**) 'Leasing can help to minimize the effects of inflation.'

6 Provide a discussion for each of the following statements:

(**a**) 'As you are not the owner of a leased asset, leasing is not borrowing, so you have full utilization of the asset without decreasing your borrowing capacity.'

(**b**) 'The main advantage of leasing derives from the tax position of those parties who engage in leasing. Without the tax advantage leasing may be worthless.'

7 LD Photo is considering the acquisition of a new machine which allows faster development of photographs. The firm faces three possible alternatives: to lease the machine, to borrow money from the bank in order to buy the machine, to purchase the machine using internal funds.

	Lease	Purchase by borrowing from bank	Purchase by using internal generated funds
Case 1	Accept	Reject	Reject
Case 2	Reject	Reject	Accept
Case 3	Reject	Reject	Reject

Provide a reason (or reasons) behind each of the above nine possible decisions.

8 List and discuss possible reasons giving rise to capital rationing in firms.

9 Explain why capital rationing does not lead to the maximization of the wealth of the firm's shareholders. Substantiate your position by using a numerical example.

10 Describe how linear programming can be employed in the evaluation process of investment projects.

11 Use an analog model to illustrate the concepts discussed in the present chapter.

12 How can spreadsheets be used to facilitate the application of the concepts discussed in this chapter?

Appendix 6A Linear programming

Linear programming is a mathematical method employed to find the optimal solution to a problem that involves a number of constraints. Therefore, linear programming can be used to assist the firm in selecting investment projects under capital rationing conditions. The linear programming model involves the following two basic steps: first, identify the controllable variables of the problem and formulate the linear programming model; second, apply a technique with the aid of which you can solve the linear programming problem under consideration.

After identifying the controllable variables, the linear programming model is comprised of the objective function and a number of constraints. The objective function is a linear mathematical expression describing a specified objective. The constraints are conditions which place a limit on achieving the given objective. In general the linear programming model can be expressed as follows:

- *Maximize* (*minimize*) the objective function that is expressed as a linear function of the controllable variables.
- *Subject to* a number of constraints which are expressed as linear equalities or inequalities of the controllable variables. These constraints must be simultaneously satisfied.

Example 6A.1 An example of a linear programming model

Consider a firm that places constraints on the amount of funds that can be invested in long-term assets during a particular period of time, say three years. Given a group of independent projects and the budget constraint in each period, the firm wishes to select those projects that collectively provide the highest net present value.

Linear programming can be used to model such a situation. We assume that the firm is considering three positive valued investment proposals. Then, the controllable variables of the problem are the number of units of the three projects which are undertaken. The objective function is a linear function of the three controllable variables with coefficients the net present values of the projects calculated over the period of three years. The constraints are inequalities indicating the maximum capital available for each of the three periods and an inequality constraint ensuring that the three controllable variables are positive or zero.

A number of different procedures have been proposed to solve linear programming problems, but the approach introduced in this appendix is the Simplex method. Such a method involves the following steps:

Step 1 Convert the inequality constraints (except the ones indicating that the controllable variables are positive or zero) to linear equations by introducing a number of slack variables (that is, variables that can be used to transfer inequalities as equalities).

Step 2 Construct a matrix representing the objective function and the equality constraints.

Step 3 Perform the pivot operation, which involves interchanging rows and columns of the matrix representing the objective function and the constraints in Step 2, with the aim to discover an optimum solution.

Step 4 If all the elements of the objective function except that in the first column of the matrix derived in Step 3 are negative, then an optimal solution is found (this case is applicable when we wish to maximize the objective function). On the other hand, if one or more elements of the first row of the matrix formed in Step 3 are positive, repeat Step 3 and the present one.

Example 6A.2 Using the Simplex method for solving a linear programming problem

Consider the following linear programming model (figures are in £million):

Maximize NPV $= 7x + 9y$

Subject to: $2x + 3y \leqq 10$

$3x + \ \ y \leqq 10$

x and y are greater than or equal to zero.

The Simplex method involves the following four steps:

Step 1 After introducing two slack variables v and w, the inequality constraints of the problem can be written as:

$$2x + 3y + v = 10$$

$$3x + \ \ y + w = 10$$

where all variables are greater than or equal to zero.
Therefore, the linear programming model can take the following form:

Maximize NPV $= 7x + 9y$

Subject to $v = 10 - 2x - 3y$

$w = 10 - 3x - y$

Step 2 The linear programming problem can be expressed in a matrix notation as shown below:

$$\begin{array}{c} \\ \text{NPV} \\ v \\ w \end{array} \begin{array}{c} \begin{array}{ccc} 1 & x & y \end{array} \\ \begin{bmatrix} 0 & 7 & 9 \\ 10 & -2 & -3 \\ 10 & -3 & -1 \end{bmatrix} \end{array} \tag{6A.1}$$

Step 3 Since we try to maximize the objective function, we select from it the variable with the most positive coefficient. The largest net present value is associated with the variable y of the objective function. For $x = 0$, the two equalities presented previously can be written as:

$$3y + v = 10$$

$$y + w = 10$$

or equivalently

$$0v = 10 - 3y$$

$$w = 10 - y$$

For $v = w = 0$, the solutions for y are, respectively, $y = 10/3$ and $y = 10$. If $y = 10$, then $v = -20$ which contradicts our earlier assumption that v is greater than or equal to zero. Therefore, $y = 10/3$. This value of y is derived by using the equation between v and y. As a consequence, we will interchange the variables v and y. Looking at matrix (6A.1), -3 is at the intersection of the row of variable v and the column of variable y. This entry is the pivot element.

In order to perform the pivot operation on the matrix (6A.1) we must perform a number of special operations. After performing these operations matrix (6A.1) changes to the matrix which can be written in a general form as:

$$\begin{bmatrix} a^* & b^* & c \\ d & e & f \\ g^* & h^* & i \end{bmatrix} \qquad (6A.2)$$

where f is the pivot element, c, f, i are entries in the pivot column, d, e, f are entries in the pivot row and a^*, b^*, g^* and h^* are entries which will be calculated in the next phase.

To calculate the entries in the pivot column and pivot row we follow the following rule:

Rule 1 Replace the pivot element by 1, divide each entry in the pivot row and pivot column by -3 and multiply all entries in the pivot row (except the pivot element) by -1.

By using matrix (6A.1) we obtain:

c: $(9)/(-3) = -3$
f: $(1)/(-3) = -1/3$ (pivot element)
i: $(-1)/(-3) = 1/3$
d: $((10)/(-3))(-1) = 10/3$ (first entry of pivot row)
e: $((-2)/(-3))(-1) = -2/3$ (second entry of pivot row)

Therefore, matrix (6A.2) can be written as follows:

$$\begin{bmatrix} a^* & b^* & -3 \\ 10/3 & -2/3 & -1/3 \\ g^* & h^* & 1/3 \end{bmatrix} \qquad (6A.3)$$

Next we will calculate the entries a^*, b^*, g^* and h^* of matrix (6A.3). The rule here is summarized as follows:

Rule 2 Using matrix (6A.1), calculate the required entries of matrix (6A.3) using the following equation:

(Required entry) $\times$ (Pivot element) $- ij$

where

Required entry $=$ an entry that is not in the pivot row or pivot column.
$i =$ The entry of matrix (6A.1) that is in the pivot column and exactly opposite of the required entry.
$j =$ The entry of matrix (6A.1) that is in the required entry column and exactly opposite of the pivot element.

By using matrix (6A.1) we get

a^*: $((0)(-3) - (9)(10))/(-3) = 30$

b^*: $((7)(-3) - (9)(-2))/(-3) = 1$

g^*: $((10)(-3) - (10)(-1))/(-3) = 20/3$

h^*: $((-3)(-3) - (-2)(-1))/(-3) = -7/3$

Therefore, we can write the following matrix:

$$\begin{array}{c} \\ \text{NPV} \\ y \\ w \end{array} \begin{array}{c} \begin{array}{ccc} 1 & x & v \end{array} \\ \begin{bmatrix} 30 & 1 & -3 \\ 10/3 & -2/3 & -1/3 \\ 20/3 & -7/3 & 1/3 \end{bmatrix} \end{array} \tag{6A.4}$$

In matrix (6A.4), the NPV row has two positive entries indicating that the maximum of the objective function has not yet been achieved.

Step 4 The new objective function is

$$F = 30 + x - 3v$$

The coefficient of x is larger than that of v. Thus we set $v = 0$ and increase x. In this case, we have the following conditions:

$$y = 10/3 - 2/3x$$

$$w = 20/3 - 7/3x$$

For $y = w = 0$, the variable x takes the values $x = 5$ and $x = 20/7$, respectively. For $x = 5$, $w = -5$. This solution contradicts our earlier assumption that w is greater than or equal to zero. Consequently, $x = 20/7$ which is derived from the equation between w and x. In this instance, the pivot element is $-7/3$, the coefficient of x in the equation between w and x.

After performing the pivot operation we have the following general matrix:

$$\begin{bmatrix} a^* & b & c^* \\ d^* & e & f^* \\ g & h & i \end{bmatrix} \tag{6A.5}$$

where b, e, h are entries in the pivot column, g, h, i are entries in the pivot row and a^*, c^*, d^* and f^* are entries which will be calculated in the next phase.

The entries in the pivot column and pivot row are calculated in a fashion similar to this introduced earlier. By using matrix (6A.4) we have:

b: $1/(-7/3) = -3/7$

e: $(-2/3)/(-7/3) = 2/7$

i: $1/(-7/3) = -3/7$ (pivot element)

d: $((20/3)/(-7/3))(-1) = 20/7$ (first entry of pivot row)

e: $((1/3)/(-7/3))(-1) = 1/7$ (second entry of pivot row)

Thus, matrix (6A.5) can be expressed as

$$\begin{bmatrix} a^* & -3/7 & c^* \\ d^* & 2/7 & f^* \\ 20/7 & -3/7 & 1/7 \end{bmatrix} \tag{6A.6}$$

We next apply Rule 2 to obtain

a^*: $((30)(-7/3) - (20/3)(1))/(-7/3) = 230/7$

c^*: $((-3)(-7/3) - (1/3)(1))/(-7/3) = -20/7$

d^*: $((10/3)(-7/3) - (20/3)(-2/3))/(-7/3) = 30/21$

f^*: $((-1/3)(-7/3) - (-2/3)(1/3))/(-7/3) = -3/7$

Using these results we obtain the following matrix

$$\begin{array}{c} \\ \text{NPV} \\ y \\ x \end{array} \begin{array}{c} \begin{array}{ccc} 1 & w & v \end{array} \\ \begin{bmatrix} 230/7 & -3/7 & -20/7 \\ 30/21 & 2/7 & -3/7 \\ 20/7 & -3/7 & 1/7 \end{bmatrix} \end{array} \tag{6A.7}$$

In matrix (6A.7), only the first entry of the top row is positive indicating that we found the optimal solution. The maximum value for the net present value is 230/7 (or £32.85 million). Matrix (6A.7) also shows that the values of the controllable variables used to obtain the maximum net present value are 20/7 (or 2.857 units) and 30/21 (or 1.428 units).

Problem

1 A firm wishes to select the best combination between two independent investment projects A and B under capital rationing. Project A entails a cost of £2 million in the first year and £3 million in the second, while project B requires costs of £3 million and £1 million for the first and second year, respectively. The net present value of project A is £4 million and that of B is £8 million. The firm's fixed budget is £4 million for each of the two years. The firm can invest in more than one unit of project A or project B.

(a) Formulate a linear programming problem describing the firm's situation.

(b) Use the Simplex method to provide the optimal solution to the problem in part (a) and calculate the overall net present value of the optimal combination of projects A and B.

Appendix 6B The correlation coefficient

The (simple linear) correlation coefficient is a statistical measure indicating the direction and strength of the relationship between the fluctuations of two random variables. The value of the correlation coefficient ranges between −1 and 1 inclusive.

- If the correlation coefficient is +1.0, the two variables move in the same direction exactly in the same proportions. In this case the variables exhibit perfect positive correlation. When there is a positive perfect correlation, the observed values of the two variables all fall on a straight line having a positive slope.
- If the correlation coefficient is greater than zero but less than +1.0, then the relation between the two variables is positive. The values of the two variables usually move in the same direction. The closer the correlation coefficient is to +1.0, the more the values on the two variables tend to move in the same direction.
- If the correlation coefficient is zero, then there is no correlation between the two variables. In such a case, the variables are called uncorrelated. When there is no correlation, the two variables tend to change with no connection to each other.
- If the correlation coefficient is greater than −1.0 but less than zero, then the relation between the two variables is negative. The values of the two variables usually move in opposite directions. The closer the correlation coefficient is to −1.0, the more the values on the two variables tend to move in opposite directions.
- If the correlation coefficient between two variables is −1.0, the two variables move in opposite directions exactly in the same proportions. In this instance, we say that the variables are perfectly negatively correlated. When there is a negative perfect correlation, the observed values of the two variables all fall on a straight line having a negative slope.

In general, the sign of the correlation coefficient indicates the direction of the relationship between the fluctuations of two random variables and the size of the correlation coefficient indicates the strength of that relationship. The correlation coefficient is a relative statistical measure and it is independent of the units utilized in measuring the variables.

Example 6B.1 Calculating the correlation coefficient between two variables

The annual net funds and total fixed assets of Marks and Spencer plc for the period 1976–87 are presented in Figure 6B.1 (figures are in £million). The correlation coefficient (CC) is calculated by using the following formula:

$$\text{CC} = \frac{\text{Covariance between the two variables}}{(\text{Standard deviation of 1st variable})(\text{Standard deviation of 2nd variable})}$$

The correlation coefficient can be calculated by employing one of the following

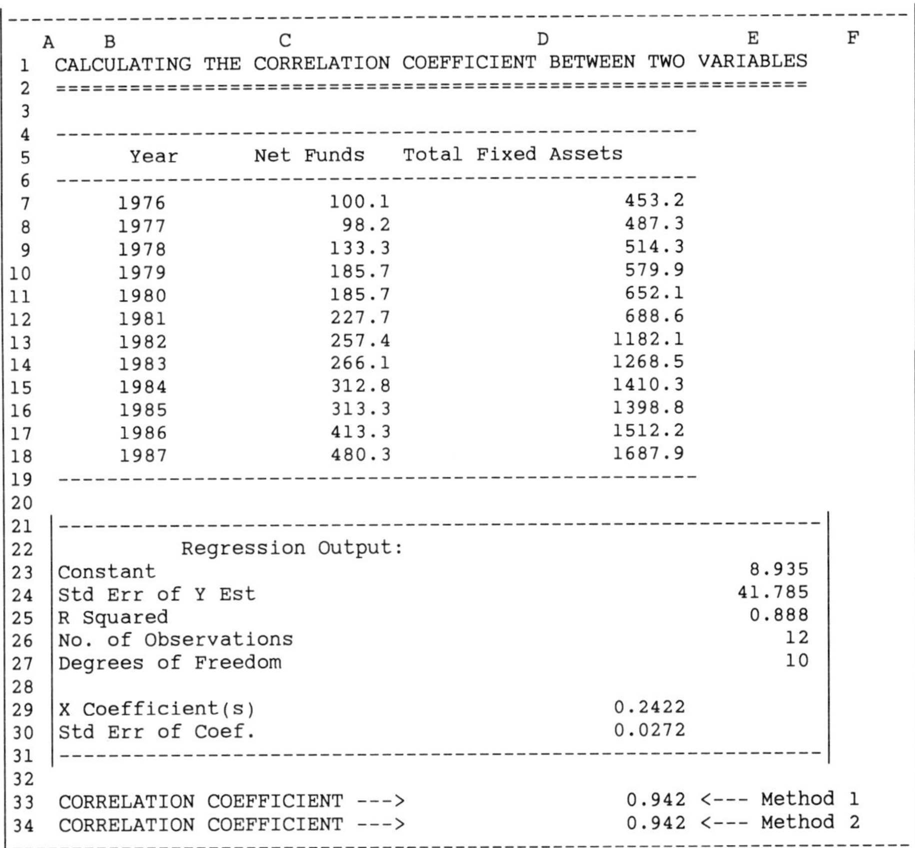

```
   A   B              C                    D                  E          F
 1  CALCULATING THE CORRELATION COEFFICIENT BETWEEN TWO VARIABLES
 2  ==============================================================
 3
 4  ----------------------------------------------------
 5       Year       Net Funds   Total Fixed Assets
 6  ----------------------------------------------------
 7      1976             100.1                  453.2
 8      1977              98.2                  487.3
 9      1978             133.3                  514.3
10      1979             185.7                  579.9
11      1980             185.7                  652.1
12      1981             227.7                  688.6
13      1982             257.4                 1182.1
14      1983             266.1                 1268.5
15      1984             312.8                 1410.3
16      1985             313.3                 1398.8
17      1986             413.3                 1512.2
18      1987             480.3                 1687.9
19  ----------------------------------------------------
20
21 |-------------------------------------------------------------|
22 |          Regression Output:                                 |
23 |Constant                                             8.935   |
24 |Std Err of Y Est                                    41.785   |
25 |R Squared                                            0.888   |
26 |No. of Observations                                     12   |
27 |Degrees of Freedom                                      10   |
28 |                                                             |
29 |X Coefficient(s)                        0.2422               |
30 |Std Err of Coef.                        0.0272               |
31 |-------------------------------------------------------------|
32
33  CORRELATION COEFFICIENT --->            0.942 <--- Method 1
34  CORRELATION COEFFICIENT --->            0.942 <--- Method 2
```

Figure 6B.1. Using two methods for calculating the correlation coefficient

procedures:

1 Calculate the covariance between the two variables and the standard deviation for each variable. Then the correlation coefficient is calculated by dividing the covariance by the product of the two standard deviations.
2 Calculate the coefficient of determination (or *r*-squared) of the regression line between the two variables, then the correlation coefficient equals the square root of the coefficient of determination. If the regression slope is positive (negative) then the correlation coefficient is positive (negative).
3 Calculate the slope of the regression line between the two variables and then use the following formula to calculate the correlation coefficient:

$$\text{CC} = \text{Slope of regression line} \frac{\text{Standard deviation of independent variable}}{\text{Standard deviation of dependent variable}}$$

In our example, the independent variable of the regression is 'total fixed assets' and the dependent variable is 'net funds generated'. Applying the second procedure discussed previously we have:

$$\text{CC} = \text{square root } (0.888) = 0.942 \text{ (since the slope is } > 0)$$

In addition, applying the third procedure outlined earlier yields:

$$CC = 0.2422 \frac{£443.30}{£113.95} = 0.942$$

where £443.30 is the standard deviation of the independent variable and £113.95 is the standard deviation of the dependent variable. The sign of the calculated correlation coefficient indicates that the relationship between 'net funds' and 'total fixed assets' for the period under consideration is positive and its size reveals a very strong relationship between the two variables.

Problems

1 Calculate the correlation coefficient between 'net funds' and 'total fixed assets' by using the covariance between the two variables and the standard deviation of each variable.

2 Plot a scatter diagram of the data shown in Figure 6B.1, taking 'total fixed assets' as the independent variable. Does the scatter diagram indicate that the variables 'net funds' and 'total fixed assets' are related?

Some useful points

1 (Correlation coefficient versus covariance) The correlation coefficient is a superior measure of the dependence between two variables than the covariance, because it also indicates the power of the relationship between those two variables. For example, the covariance between the two series of values 1.0, 2.0, 3.0, 4.0, 5.0, 6.0 and 2.5, 5.0, 7.5, 10.0, 12.5, 15.0 is 7.291 indicating only a positive relationship. However, the correlation coefficient is +1.0 indicating a perfect positive correlation.

2 (Test of significance) In several cases, the interpretation of a small (or large) value of the correlation coefficient as 'weak' (or 'strong') correlation between the variables must be made with caution. For example, you may find a large value of the coefficient that is not statistically significant, say at 5 per cent level. Therefore, when you deal with correlation analysis you should conduct a test examining the statistical significance of a correlation coefficient. Significance of the correlation coefficient means that the sample under consideration provides evidence about the existence of a relationship between the two variables.

3 (Correlation coefficient versus coefficient of determination) The meaning of the correlation coefficient is not as explicit as that of the coefficient of determination used in the regression analysis. The correlation coefficient tends to overstate the strength of the relationship between two variables. For example, if the coefficient of determination is 0.5, it indicates that only 50 per cent of the variation in the dependent variable is explained by the variation in the independent variable. However, the correlation coefficient of 0.707 indicates a relatively high correlation between the two variables. Thus, correlation analysis is inferior to regression analysis and it should not be used by itself.

4 (Correlation coefficient and outliers) We should be aware about the effect of outliers in correlation analysis because they can affect the correlation to such an extent that it may be better to substitute them with more meaningful numbers (an outlier is a number in a data set that differs markedly from most of the numbers in the set under consideration). For example, consider the following

two series of data, 1, 200, 3, 4, 5 and 2, 4, 6, 8, 10. We assume that the outlier of 200 is due to an error in calculation. The correlation coefficient between the two variables is only 0.334. However, the correlation coefficient between the two series 1, 2, 3, 4, 5 and 2, 4, 6, 8, 10 is 0.991.

5 (Indirect correlation) In some cases a correlation between two variables exists because each variable is strongly correlated to a third variable. For example, we would expect to find a positive correlation between the rates of return of a tobacco firm and an electronics firm over a period of, say, five years, because each rate of return is moving in the same direction as the rate of return of the *Financial Times* Actuaries 500-Share Index.

References and bibliography

Anderson, P.F. and Martin, J.D. (1977) Lease versus purchase decisions: a survey of current practice, *Financial Management*, **6**, Spring, 41–7.

Ang, J. and Peterson, P.P. (1984) The leasing puzzle, *Journal of Finance*, September, 1055–65.

Bernhard, R.H. (1969) Mathematical programming models for capital budgeting—a survey, generalisation and critique, *Journal of Financial and Quantitative Analysis*, June, 111–58.

Bhaskar, K.N. (1976) Linear programming and capital budgeting: the financing problem, *Journal of Business Finance and Accounting*, Summer, 159–94.

Bower, R.S. (1973) Issues in lease financing, *Financial Management*, **2**, Winter, 25–34.

Clark, T. (1978) *Leasing*. McGraw-Hill, Maidenhead.

Fawthrop, R.A. (1971) Underlying problems of discounted cash flow appraisal, *Accounting and Business Research*, Summer, 187–98.

Fawthrop, R.A. and Terry, B. (1976) The evaluation of an integrated investment and lease-finance decision, *Journal of Business Finance and Accounting*, Autumn, 79–111.

Franks, J.R. and Hodges, S.D. (1978) Valuation of financial lease contracts: a note, *Journal of Finance*, May, 657–69.

Hughes, J.S. and Lewellen, W.G. (1974) Programming solutions to capital rationing problems, *Journal of Business Finance and Accounting*, Spring, 55–74.

Isom, T.A. and Amembal, S.P. (1982) *The Handbook of Leasing: Techniques and Analysis*. Petrocelli Books, New York.

Lorie, J.H. and Savage, L.J. (1955) Three problems in rationing capital, *Journal of Business*, October, 229–39.

Ma, R. (1981) Comparative analysis of lease evaluation models: a review article, *Accounting and Business Research*, Spring, 153–62.

Myers, S., Dill, D.A. and Bautista, A.J. (1976) Valuation of financial lease contracts, *Journal of Finance*, June, 799–819.

Offer, A.R. (1976) The evaluation of the lease versus purchase alternatives, *Financial Management*, Summer, 67–74.

Weingartner, H.M. (1974) Mathematical programming and the analysis of capital budgeting problems. Kershaw, London.

Weingartner, H.M. (1977) Capital rationing: 'n' authors in search of a plot, *Journal of Finance*, December, 1403–32.

7 Incorporation of risk into capital budgeting decisions

This chapter includes:

- Risk-adjusted discount rate
- Certainty equivalent
- Probability analysis
- Sensitivity analysis
- Simulation analysis
- Decision trees
- The use of the risk-assessment methods in practice

In reality, there are few capital budgeting projects whose future cash flows are known with complete certainty. Since most capital investment projects have uncertain cash flows, it is important to learn how to measure risk and understand how to evaluate capital budgeting projects under conditions of risk.

There are a number of alternative approaches for dealing with investment project selection under conditions of risk including the following: subjective method, net present value/payback period method, risk-adjusted discount rate method, certainty equivalent method, probability distribution method, sensitivity analysis, simulation analysis and decision tree. The aim of this chapter is to present and evaluate these eight alternative risk-adjustment methods. Figure 7.1 presents the financial management framework presented in Chapter 2 in relation to the methods that can be used to incorporate risk into capital budgeting decisions.

Basic concepts, definitions and examples

When investment projects are evaluated, the future net cash flows and the discount rate used to discount those cash flows must be derived and utilized in the analysis. The information needed for capital budgeting decisions is not always known in advance with complete certainty. We can distinguish between four states in decision making: certainty, risk, uncertainty and complete ignorance.

1 *Certainty* This is a situation where the future net cash flows are known in advance with complete certainty and each future net cash flow is single-valued. For example, suppose that a firm purchases UK three-month Treasury securities, which are expected to yield 10 per cent. If we ignore the impact of inflation on the return from this investment, we can forecast its exact return with certainty since there is no chance that the UK government will not pay the interest and principal on schedule.

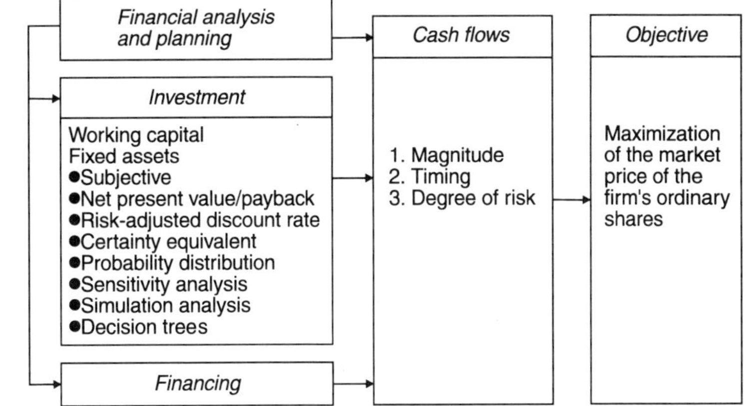

Figure 7.1. The methods for dealing with project selection under risk in relation to the financial management framework

2 *Risk* This is a situation where a probability distribution of the future net cash flows exists and the probabilities with their respective net cash flows are known. For example, assume that a firm is considering a new capital investment project with a useful life of one year. The future net cash flow associated with the firm's project is presently unknown, but instead we can form a probability distribution as follows: there is a chance of 40 per cent for a future net cash flow of £500,000 and a chance of 60 per cent for a future net cash flow of £800,000.

3 *Uncertainty* This is a situation where the decision maker can identify the possible future net cash flows but he or she has no knowledge about the probabilities associated with these cash flows. For example, suppose that a firm is considering an investment in a new product for which there is insufficient information to produce the probabilities associated with the future net cash flows from this project. An uncertain situation can be transformed into a risky situation if we assign to the former subjective probabilities (personal beliefs or judgements about the likelihood of a future event are known as subjective probabilities). The terms of risk and uncertainty will be used interchangeably in this book.

4 *Complete ignorance* This is a situation where the decision maker has neither knowledge of a project's future net cash flows nor knowledge of the probabilities associated with these cash flows. For example, a firm may be considering investment in a project so new that it has not enough information from which to produce future net cash flows and probabilities associated with these cash flows.

Figure 7.2 shows the four decision states discussed above.

There are many factors that give rise to risk and they can be divided into three major groups: general economic conditions, firm-related conditions and international conditions. General economic conditions usually affect the net cash flows of capital budgeting projects. For example, if a manufacturing firm make projections of the net cash flows related to a new project based on a normal price of oil and subsequently oil prices rise substantially, the net cash flows of the firm's project may be affected. Firm-related conditions may also influence the net cash flows of some investment projects. For example, the sales and marketing methods used by a firm affect the future net cash flows of its new projects. Additionally, the use of more borrowed funds also affects the risk associated with future net cash flows. Finally, direct investment in foreign countries is associated with different types of risk which do not occur

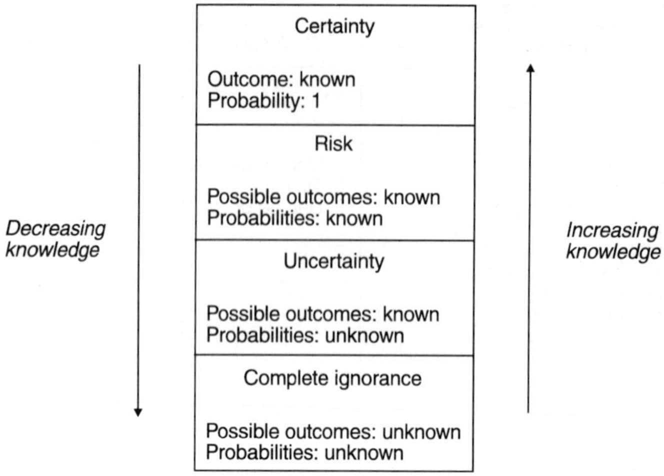

Certainty
Outcome: known Probability: 1
Risk
Possible outcomes: known Probabilities: known
Uncertainty
Possible outcomes: known Probabilities: unknown
Complete ignorance
Possible outcomes: unknown Probabilities: unknown

Decreasing knowledge (↓) — *Increasing knowledge* (↑)

Figure 7.2. States in decision making

in the case of domestic investment. For example, if a UK firm is considering investment in a politically unstable country, it should take into account political risks including currency control, taxation and government expropriation of assets.

Informal methods

There are two informal methods of dealing with risk when evaluating capital investment projects: the subjective method and the net present value/payback period method.

Subjective method

The subjective method of dealing with risk is based upon the decision maker's subjective judgement concerning the risk related to a project. For example, if the financial director of a firm is evaluating three mutually exclusive projects having similar net present values, he or she may select the one that has the lower degree of risk. If the three projects have significantly different net present values and also have differing levels of risk, the decision becomes more difficult. In this instance, the decision maker must evaluate the risk for each project subjectively and select the project having the preferred amount of risk and also a net present value offsetting the risk involved. The major advantage of using the subjective method is that it is simple to apply.

Net present value/payback period method

The net present value/payback period method combines the present value and the payback period when evaluating investment projects. Note that the net present value calculates the benefits from a project in terms of current money assuming that a required rate of return must be earned. On the other hand, the payback period provides a crude measure of risk because it evaluates how quickly the initial investment of a project is recovered from the net cash flows generated from the project. For example, a firm can adopt a decision criterion of accepting only projects that have a positive net present value as well as payback periods of less than four years.

As in the case of the subjective method, the net present value/payback period method is simple to apply. This method, however, has the same disadvantages as the payback period approach discussed in Chapter 5. First, it does not take into account the time value of money; second, it does not consider the cash flows in periods after the initial investment has been recovered; and, finally, the choice of a target payback period for decision purposes is largely a subjective one.

Indirect methods for incorporating risk into capital budgeting

The risk associated with an investment project can be incorporated in the evaluation stage of the capital budgeting process by adjusting properly the evaluation techniques used. For example, the net present value method can be adjusted for risk either via the cash flows or via the discount rate (see Figure 7.3).

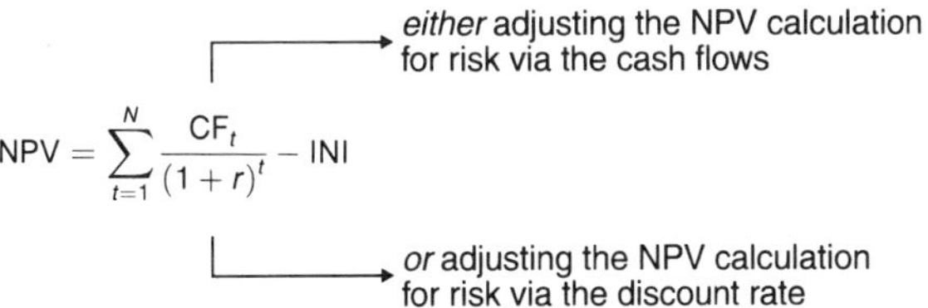

Figure 7.3. Incorporating risk into the net present value method

Risk-adjusted discount rate method

When investment projects are evaluated, we assume that investors (for example, financial directors) prefer the lowest level of available risk for any given level of expected return and the highest level of expected return for any given level of risk. This implies that investors accept additional risk only in exchange for a higher expected return. If the expected return on an investment is not sufficiently high to compensate for the risk involved, the investment is not undertaken. For example, if a firm can achieve an expected return of 10 per cent by investing funds in a riskless security (for example, Treasury bills), then it will probably require an expected return of 17 per cent from a risky investment. The additional 7 per cent is required as a compensation for the risk perceived in the investment. Figure 7.4 gives a summary of the risk-adjusted discount rate method.

Example 7.1 An application of the risk-adusted discount rate method

GD Fashions plc is considering an investment project with an expected life of five years. All the expected cash flow information to evaluate the project is given below

Year	Cash flow (£000s)
0	9,900
1	2,300
2	2,499
3	3,502
4	3,301
5	5,096

Definition The risk-adjusted discount rate method handles the riskiness of a project by adjusting the cost of capital (or discount rate) and then using such an adjusted discount rate in the evaluation phase of the project.

Calculation The risk-adjusted discount rate is calculated by adding an appropriate risk premium to the risk-free rate of return:

Risk-adjusted discount rate	=	Risk-free rate	+	Risk premium
RADR	=	r_f	+	p_r

where the risk premium is the additional return (to the risk-free rate) required to encourage the firm to invest in the asset as opposed to investing in the risk-free investment.

The risk-adjusted discount rate substitutes the discount rate in the net present value formula (see Figure 7.3). Likewise, the risk-adjusted discount rate becomes the required rate of return and this value is compared with the internal rates of return of projects to decide whether the projects should be accepted or rejected.

Interpretation Risk-adjusted discount rates represent the differential risk associated with the firm's investment projects. The firm increases the discount rate for more risky projects and decreases it for projects with less risk.

Figure 7.4. Summarizing the risk-adjustment discount rate method

The firm's financial director has estimated that the appropriate risk premium associated with this investment is 7 per cent. The risk-free rate of interest is 10 per cent. Therefore, the risk-adjusted discount rate is 17 per cent. Figure 7.5 shows the net present value of the firm's project using a discount rate is 17 per cent. The following 1-2-3 function is stored in cell B16:

```
@NPV(B4,B10..B14) + B9
```

```
            A                B        C        D          E          F    G
 1 INCORPORATING RISK INTO DCF ANALYSIS USING THE RADR METHOD
 2 =========================================================
 3
 4 Discount Rate          17.0%
 5
 6 -----------------------------------
 7                   YEAR CASH FLOW (£000s)
 8 -----------------------------------
 9                      0    (£9,900)
10                      1      2,300
11                      2      2,499
12                      3      3,502
13                      4      3,301
14                      5      5,096
15                          ---------
16   NPV ------>               £164
17   PI ------->               1.02
19   IRR ------>             17.63%
19 -----------------------------------
```

Figure 7.5. Using a risk-adjusted discount rate to compute the net present value and the profitability index of a project

If the discount rate equals the riskless rate of interest at 10 per cent, the net present value of the project is £2,306,000 (rounded) and the project would be accepted. However, when risk is taken into account, the appropriate discount rate for the project is 17 per cent, the project would be accepted, but its net present value is only £164,000 (rounded).

Problems

1 Set up the worksheet shown in Figure 7.5. Make sure that you store formulae for the calculation of the net present value, profitability index and internal rate of return and each formula is referred in cells into the worksheet.
2 Change the discount rate from 17 per cent to 16 per cent and discuss your results. Then change the discount rate from 16 per cent to 18 per cent and again provide a discussion of your results.
3 Assume that GD Fashions is considering another project with the following cash flows: year 0: £9,900,000, year 1: £1,500,000, year 2: £2,200,000, year 3: £4,000,000, year 4: £4,200,000 and year 5: £5,500,000. Evaluate such a project using a risk-adjusted discount rate of 17 per cent.
4 Assume that the new project of the firm and that evaluated earlier are mutually exclusive. Which project should be adopted? Why?

Evaluation of the risk-adjusted discount rate method
The risk-adjusted discount rate method has several advantages. First, it is simple to understand. Second, firms in actual practice can use the method by applying different risk-adjusted discount rates to different projects. Thus, the risk-adjusted discount rate method has the advantage of operational feasibility. Third, this method adjusts for the timing of (expected) net cash flows and simultaneously incorporates risk in the capital budgeting analysis.

Perhaps the biggest disadvantage of this method is the difficulty of determining the appropriate risk-adjusted discount rate for each project under consideration. Therefore, the assignment of the discount rates to the various projects under consideration is bound to be subjective. A second disadvantage is that the risk-adjusted discount rate approach implicitly assumes that the risk of receiving the net cash flows increases with time (note that the risk-adjusted discount rate is a function of both the risk-free rate and a risk premium). Many investment projects, however, do not exhibit increasing risk with time. In this instance, projects may be penalized by the risk-adjusted discount method.

Certainty equivalent method

Another method of considering risk in capital budgeting is the certainty equivalent approach. A summary of this approach is provided in Figure 7.6.

Definition The certainty equivalent method takes into account the riskiness of a project by adjusting its expected risky net cash flows and then using these cash flows in the evaluation phase of the project.
Calculation The certainty equivalent coefficient for time period t is a coefficient that converts the project's expected risky net cash flow for period t into an equivalent riskless net cash flow. By 'equivalent' we mean that investors are indifferent between the certain net cash flow and the expected risky net cash flow. To derive the certainty equivalent net cash flow (CENCF) for period t the following formula is used:

$$\text{CENCF}_t = \text{CEC}_t(\text{risky net cash flow in period } t)$$

where CEC_t is the certainty equivalent coefficient for period t.
In order to calculate the net present value of the project the riskless rate of interest is used, because the riskiness associated with the net cash flows has been effectively eliminated.
Interpretation Adjusts separately each period's net cash flows to account for the risk associated with those cash flows. The more risky the project's expected net cash flow, the lower the certainty equivalent coefficient.

Figure 7.6. Summarizing the certainty equivalent method

Example 7.2 An application of the certainty equivalent method

Consider the data given in Example 7.1. Let us further assume that the certainty equivalent coefficients for the future net cash flows are : 0.944, 0.892, 0.842, 0.795 and 0.750, respectively. In our example, the certainty equivalent coefficients decline with the length of time to reflect that the project is viewed as being less risky in the initial years of its life. The net present value of the project using the calculated certainty equivalent cash flows is shown in Figure 7.7 (figures are in £000s, slight deviations are due to rounding). The discount rate utilized in the calculation is 10 per cent. Since the net present value of the project is positive, the project should be accepted. If the internal rate of return method is employed, the certainty-equivalent internal rate of return would be compared with the riskless rate of interest of 10 per cent.

```
          A                  B          C          D          E           F        G
 1 INCORPORATING RISK INTO THE DCF ANALYSIS USING THE CE METHOD
 2 ===========================================================
 3
 4 Discount Rate            17.0%
 5 Risk Free Rate           10.0%
 6 ------------------------------------------------------------------------
 7                YEAR CASH FLOW               CEC    CE CASH FLOWS
 8 ------------------------------------------------------------------------
 9                   0    (9,900)                        (9,900)
10                   1     2,300              0.944       2,172
11                   2     2,499              0.892       2,228
12                   3     3,502              0.842       2,948
13                   4     3,301              0.795       2,624
14                   5     5,096              0.750       3,824
15                      ---------                    ----------
16   NPV ------>              164         NPV --->         297
17   PI ------->             1.02         PI ---->        1.03
18   IRR ------->          17.63%         IRR --->      11.07%
19 ------------------------------------------------------------------------
```

Figure 7.7. Using the certainty equivalent method in discounted cash flow analysis

In Appendix 7A we illustrate the calculation of the certainty equivalent coefficients by using the concept of utility theory. In Example 7.2, the risk-adjusted discount rate method and the certainty equivalent method did not provide identical results. The two methods are equivalent in the sense that they yield the same net present value only if the certainty equivalent coefficient for a period t can be expressed as (for a proof see Appendix 7A):

$$\text{CEC}_t = \frac{(1 + r_f)^t}{(1 + \text{RADR})^t}$$

where r_f = the risk-free rate and RADR = the risk-adjusted discount rate.

Evaluation of the certainty equivalent method

The certainty equivalent method adjusts simultaneously for the timing of (expected) net cash flows and the risk associated with those cash flows when determining a project's net present value. In addition, it adjusts for risk by modifying separately the net cash flow of each period. Next, the certainty equivalent approach allows you to specify directly the degree of risk associated with a particular future net cash flow and thus avoids the drawback of the risk-adjusted discount rate method that risk necessarily increases as you look further into the future. Lastly, the certainty equivalent method incorporates the decision maker's utility preference with respect to risk directly into the analysis and thus it is theoretically superior to the risk-adjusted discount rate method.

The certainty equivalent approach also has some disadvantages. First, the method is difficult to understand and explain. A second and probably more obvious weakness is the difficulty associated with the estimation of the certainty equivalent coefficients. The certainty equivalent coefficients depend upon the utility preferences of the decision maker (for example, the financial manager) and thus the method involves risk adjustments which are somewhat arbitrary.

The probability distribution method

Suppose a firm invests £100,000 in government securities (for example, Treasury bills), which are expected to yield 10 per cent over a year. The firm's return of £10,000 can be accurately forecasted, because a government failure to pay the interest is a rare situation (under the assumption that the government can always print money).

Making investment and financing decisions with a perfect knowledge of the future rarely exists in the real world. In reality, the outcomes from most investment and financing decisions made by the firm are not known in advance. For example, if a firm has presently invested £100,000 in a new investment project (expected to be operational for one year), its future net cash flow is presently unknown. Instead we can describe the situation with the aid of a probability distribution of expected cash flows (that is, a list of all possible cash flows each associated with a particular subjective probability (or chance) of occurrence). Figure 7.8 shows a probability distribution of net cash flows.

Figure 7.8. A probability distribution of net cash flows

Outcome	Probability	Interpretation
£80,000	0.20	20% change exists for a net cash flow of £80,000
£150,000	0.50	50% change exists for a net cash flow of £150,000
£200,000	0.30	30% change exists for a net cash flow of £200,000
	1.00	All possible outcomes are considered

The risk of an asset (for example, an investment project, a share, and so on) is defined as the variability associated with the asset's probable benefits (for example, probable cash flows, probable rates of return, and so on), where the probable benefits and the probability associated with each return are known.

The risk-adjusted discount rate and the certainty equivalent approaches discussed earlier in this chapter provide crude ways of incorporating risk into capital budgeting decisions as they do not make direct utilization of the information available from the probability distribution of expected net cash flows. As the name implies, the probability distribution method uses many probable net cash flows in each period for its analysis. The probability distribution approach makes the assumption that the risk premium associated with the project is included in the estimated probability distribution. Figure 7.9 summarizes the probability distribution approach.

Definition The probability distribution method is a statistical based approach for analysing project risk. This approach generates a probability distribution of net present values (or internal rates of return) from the yearly probability distributions of net cash flows.
Calculation The probability distribution of a project's net present value can be determined as follows:

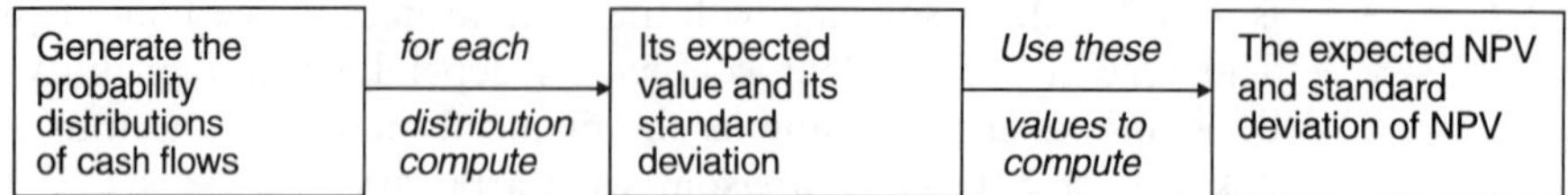

The method uses the risk-free rate to discount the characteristics of future net cash flows, because the riskiness of the cash flows has already been incorporated in the analysis.
Interpretation The probability distribution method describes the attractiveness of a project over its useful life by a probability distribution having two characteristics: an expected value and a standard deviation. The former shows the most likely estimate of the net present value from the project, while the latter measures the variability associated with the project's probable net present values. The more variable the net cash flows, the larger the standard deviation and thus the more risky the project is.

Figure 7.9. Summarizing the probability distribution method

The characteristics of the net present value distribution

We assume that a separate probability distribution is used to describe the probable net cash flows for each year in the useful life of a project. If such distributions are normal, then each is described by two statistics: the expected value and the standard deviation or variance of possible net cash flows (these statistics are discussed in Appendix 7B). Since each year's net cash flow is summarized by a (normal) probability distribution, the series of net cash flows over the life of the project will also be described by a (normal) probability distribution known as the net present value distribution. The evaluation process of a project uses the expected value and the standard deviation of the probability distribution of net present values.

Expected value of the net present value distribution

The expected value of the probability distribution of possible net present values uses as data inputs the expected values of the net cash flow distributions over the life of the project. Given a project with independent cash flows over time, the concept of the expected value of the net present value distribution is summarized in Figure 7.10.

Definition The expected value of the probability distribution of possible net present values is the present value of all the expected values of net cash flows discounted at the riskless interest rate.
Calculation The expected value of the net present value distribution is given by the expression:

$$\text{EV(NPV)} = \sum_{t=1}^{N} \frac{E(\text{CF})_t}{(1+r_f)^t} - \text{INI}$$

where

$E(\text{CF})_t$ = the expected value of the probability distribution of net cash flows in period t.
r_f = the risk-free rate of interest.
N = the number of years of the lifetime of the project.

Interpretation The expected value of the net present value distribution indicates the expected net pound return from the investment project.

Figure 7.10. Summarizing the concept of the expected value of the net present value distribution

The standard deviation of the net present value distribution

The standard deviation of the probability distribution of possible net present values depends upon the behaviour of the net cash flows from period to period. For example, a project's net cash flows of year 2 may be dependent on the net cash flows occurring in year 1. In this section we consider the following two cases: (a) independent net cash flows over time; (b) perfectly correlated net cash flows over time. In each of these two cases the data inputs used to calculate the standard deviation around the expected net present value are the standard deviations of the net cash flow distributions over the life of the project. Figure 7.11 summarizes the concept of the standard deviation of the net present value distribution on the assumption of independent cash flows over time.

Definition The standard deviation of the probability distribution of possible net present values is a statistical measure of the spread of the distribution from its expected value.

Calculation The formula for the standard deviation of the net present value distribution is:

$$\mathrm{SD(NPV)} = \left[\sum_{t=1}^{N} \frac{\mathrm{VAR(CF}_t)}{(1+r)^{2t}}\right]^{1/2}$$

where

$\mathrm{VAR(CF}_t)$ = the variance of the probability distribution of possible net cash flows in period t. The distributions of net cash flows for the various periods in the useful life of a project are assumed to be independent of one another.

r = the risk-free rate of interest.

N = the number of years of the lifetime of the project.

Interpretation The standard deviation of the net present value distribution measures the dispersion of the probability distribution of possible net present values around the expected net pound return from the project. The standard deviation of the net present value distribution is a measure of the project's risk. In general, the larger the standard deviation, the more risky the project.

Figure 7.11. The standard deviation of the net present value distribution (independent cash flows)

The formula for the standard deviation of the net present value distribution can be transferred into an equivalent relationship in order to derive an easier expression for calculation purposes. It can be proved that the standard deviation of the net present value distribution is the square root of the present value of all the variances of the probability distributions of net cash flows discounted at the interest rate of $(1+r)^2 - 1$, where r is the riskless rate of interest. Thus, the mathematical formula for the standard deviation presented in Figure 7.11 can be expressed as

$$\mathrm{SD(NPV)} = \left[\sum_{t=1}^{N} \frac{\mathrm{VAR(CF}_t)}{(1+k)^{t}}\right]^{1/2}$$

where $k = (1+r)^2 - 1$. This transformation allows the user to compute the standard deviation in a similar manner to an ordinary present value formula.

We assume that a project's net cash flows are perfectly correlated over time. In such a case, the deviation of a net cash flow for a period from the expected value of the probability distribution of possible net cash flows for that period implies that the net cash flows in all other periods deviate in exactly the same way. The concept of the standard deviation of the net present value distribution is summarized in Figure 7.12.

Definition The standard deviation of the probability distribution of possible net present values is a statistical measure of the spread of the distribution from its expected value.

Calculation The standard deviation of the probability distribution of possible net present values is the present value of all the standard deviations of the probability distributions of net cash flows discounted at the riskless interest rate. In this case, the following formula is used to calculate the standard deviation:

$$SD(NPV) = \sum_{t=1}^{N} \frac{SD(CF_t)}{(1+r)^t}$$

where

$SD(CF_t)$ = the standard deviation of the probability distribution of possible net cash flows in period t. The net cash flows are perfectly correlated over time.

r = the risk-free rate of interest.

N = the number of years of the lifetime of the project.

Interpretation The standard deviation of the net present value distribution measures the dispersion of the probability distribution of possible net present values around the expected net pound return from the project. The standard deviation of the net present value distribution can be utilized to measure the amount of risk associated with the project. In general, the larger the standard deviation, the larger the risk.

Figure 7.12. The standard deviation of the net present value distribution (perfect correlation)

The coefficient of variation takes into consideration the expected value and the standard deviation of the net present value distribution simultaneously. It is a relative risk measure since it monitors the variability of probable net present values with respect to their expected value. Such a risk measure is applicable when we compare two investment projects having different standard deviations of net present values as well as different expected net present values. The coefficient of variation of the net present value distribution is calculated by dividing the standard deviation of the net present value distribution by its expected value. In general, the higher the coefficient of variation, the greater the relative risk of a project.

Example 7.3 Ranking projects using the probability distribution method

Alpha Electronics plc is considering two investment projects A and B. Each project will require an initial investment of £19,000 and is expected to last three years. The annual risk-free rate is 10 per cent. The expected value and the standard deviation of the net present value distribution for project A are £2,138 and £3,732, respectively. The probability distributions used to summarize the annual net cash flows of project B are shown in Figure 7.13. Probabilities are assumed to be the same in each of the three periods. The expected value of the distribution of cash flows is found by multiplying each possible cash flow by its probability of occurrence and adding the resulting products. For example, using the first year's data we have: (0.10)(£4,000) + (0.20)(£6,000) + (0.40)(£8,000) + (0.20)(£10,000)+ (0.10)(£12,000) = £8,000.

The variance of the distribution of net cash flows for the first year is found by multiplying each possible squared deviation from the expected value of £8,000 by the corresponding probability of occurrence and adding the resulting products.

$$0.10 \times (4{,}000 - 8{,}000)^2 + 0.20 \times (6{,}000 - 8{,}000)^2 + 0.40 \times (8{,}000 - 8{,}000)^2$$
$$+ 0.20 \times (10{,}000 - 8{,}000)^2 + 0.10 \times (12{,}000 - 8{,}000)^2 = 4{,}800{,}000$$

Therefore, the standard deviation of cash flows for year 1 will be £2,191

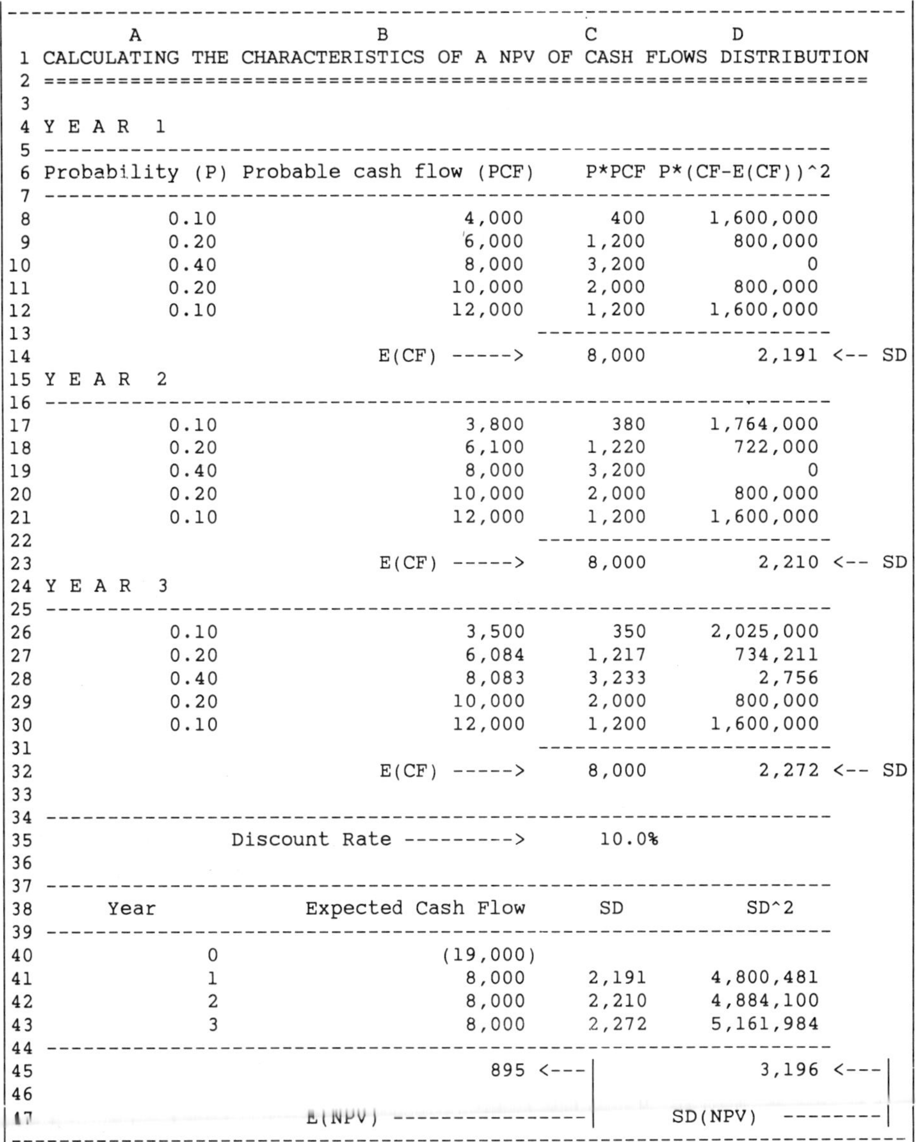

A	B	C	D	
CALCULATING THE CHARACTERISTICS OF A NPV OF CASH FLOWS DISTRIBUTION				
Y E A R 1				
Probability (P)	Probable cash flow (PCF)	P*PCF	P*(CF-E(CF))^2	
0.10	4,000	400	1,600,000	
0.20	6,000	1,200	800,000	
0.40	8,000	3,200	0	
0.20	10,000	2,000	800,000	
0.10	12,000	1,200	1,600,000	
	E(CF) ----->	8,000	2,191	<-- SD
Y E A R 2				
0.10	3,800	380	1,764,000	
0.20	6,100	1,220	722,000	
0.40	8,000	3,200	0	
0.20	10,000	2,000	800,000	
0.10	12,000	1,200	1,600,000	
	E(CF) ----->	8,000	2,210	<-- SD
Y E A R 3				
0.10	3,500	350	2,025,000	
0.20	6,084	1,217	734,211	
0.40	8,083	3,233	2,756	
0.20	10,000	2,000	800,000	
0.10	12,000	1,200	1,600,000	
	E(CF) ----->	8,000	2,272	<-- SD
	Discount Rate --------->	10.0%		
Year	Expected Cash Flow	SD	SD^2	
0	(19,000)			
1	8,000	2,191	4,800,481	
2	8,000	2,210	4,884,100	
3	8,000	2,272	5,161,984	
	895 <---		3,196 <---	
	E(NPV) ----------------		SD(NPV) --------	

Figure 7.13. The characteristics of the net present value distribution for a project

(rounded). The standard deviation for periods 2 and 3 can be calculated in a similar way, these are £2,210 and £2,272, respectively (figures are rounded). The expected value of the net present value distribution for project B is calculated as follows:

$$E(\text{NPV}_\text{B}) = \frac{£8{,}000}{(1+0.10)} + \frac{£8{,}000}{(1+0.10)^2} + \frac{£8{,}000}{(1+0.10)^3} - £19{,}000 = £895$$

Assuming mutual independence of cash flows over time, the variance of the net present value distribution for project B would be:

$$\mathrm{VAR}(\mathrm{NPV_B}) = \frac{2{,}191^2}{(1+0.21)} + \frac{2{,}210^2}{(1+0.21)^2} + \frac{2{,}272^2}{(1+0.21)^3} = 10{,}217{,}051$$

where $(1+0.10)^2 - 1 = 21$ per cent (note that the variance can be calculated by using the 1-2-3 financial function @NPV). Therefore, the standard deviation of the net present value distribution is £3,196.

The coefficients of variation of the net present value distributions for projects A and B are:

$$CV_A = \frac{£3{,}732}{£2{,}138} = 1.75$$

$$CV_B = \frac{£3{,}196}{£895} = 3.57$$

Therefore, project A would be preferred to project B because it is less risky.

Next, if we assume that the net cash flows are perfectly correlated over time, then the standard deviation of the net present value distribution is:

$$\mathrm{SD}(\mathrm{NPV_B}) = \frac{£2{,}191}{(1+0.10)} + \frac{£2{,}210}{(1+0.10)^2} + \frac{£2{,}272}{(1+0.10)^3} = £5{,}525$$

The standard deviation of the net present value distribution is larger than that of the same series of net cash flows under the assumption of mutual independence since correlated net cash flows tend to spread out the distribution.

In the case of a perfectly correlated series of net cash flows, the standard deviation of the net present value distribution for project A is £6,419. Once more, the coefficients of variation for projects A and B are 3.00 and 6.17, respectively. Given this information, project A would be preferred to project B because it is associated with less risk.

Should the firm accept project A? If we base our choice solely on the expected value of the net present value distribution, we would accept the project since it generates a positive expected net present value. However, if we also consider the risk involved, the decision becomes more difficult. In this instance, we have to take into account the risk preference of the members in the firm's management team. For example, if the members of the management team believe that the expected benefits of the project under consideration can be used to offset the risk involved, then project A should be accepted.

Problems

1 Create the spreadsheet shown in Figure 7.13 using the appropriate formulae or 1-2-3 functions (for example, use formulae to calculate the probable net cash flows in column C and the statistical function @SUM to calculate the expected values of the distributions of net cash flows).

2 Below is presented the probability distributions of net cash flows of project A introduced above in this Example. We assume that probabilities are the same in each of the three years. The project's initial investment is £19,000 and the risk-free rate of interest is 10 per cent.

Probability	Net cash flow		
	Year 1	Year 2	Year 3
0.10	4,000	3,220	4,220
0.20	6,000	6,490	6,090
0.40	8,400	8,600	8,500
0.20	10,700	10,600	11,000
0.10	14,000	13,200	12,600

(a) For each year, calculate the expected value of the probability distribution of net cash flows.

(b) For each year, calculate the standard deviation of the probability distribution of net cash flows.

(c) Assuming that the probability distributions of net cash flows are independent over time, calculate the expected value and standard deviation of the net present value distribution.

(d) Calculate the expected value and standard deviation of the net present value distribution given that the cash flows are perfectly correlated over time.

(e) Calculate the coefficient of variation of the net present value distribution from the information derived in part (d).

Probability of a project being a success

If the probability distribution of net present values is approximately normal, we can determine the probability of a project having a net present value above or below a specified level. In this case, we are using the following equation for standardizing a distribution:

$$Z = (\text{SNPV} - E(\text{NPV}))/\text{SD}(\text{NPV})$$

where SNPV = a specified level of the project's net present value.

Example 7.4 Calculating the probability that the net present value of a project is positive

Consider Example 7.3 and assume that we want to determine the probability that the expected net present value of project B will be less than or equal to zero. The standardized net present value in the case of the independent cash flows would be:

$$Z = (0 - £895)/£3,196 = -0.28$$

The value of −0.28 simply indicates that the net present value of zero lies 0.28 standard deviations below the expected value of the probability distribution of possible net present values. Using the table of areas for the standard normal probability distribution, we find that the probability value associated with 0.28 is 0.1103 (such a value can be found from the standard normal distribution table at the intersection of row 0.2 and column 0.08). Since the area of the left-hand side of the normal distribution's curve is 0.5, the probability of the net present value being less than or equal to zero is 0.3897 (that is, 0.5000 − 0.1103). Therefore, if we accept the project, then we accept a 38.97 per cent chance that project B will provide a net present value less than or equal to zero.

Stated differently, if we accept the project, then there exists a 61.03 per cent chance that the project will provide a positive net present value.

Problem Use project A given in Example 7.3 and determine the probability that its net present value will be less than or equal to zero (assume that the net cash flows of the projects are perfectly correlated over time and the probability distribution of net present values is normal).

Evaluation of the probability distribution method

The probability distribution approach has two certain advantages. First, it specifies the appropriate degree of risk associated with an investment project in a quantifiable fashion. It provides information about probability distributions of future net cash flows which can be utilized to calculate the expected value and the standard deviation of the net present value distribution. In addition, the probability of a project having a net present value less than or equal to zero can be calculated. This provides a valuable piece of information for the project's appraisal. Second, the probability distribution method can also use the coefficient of variation for selecting risky projects which in several instances is a better measure of risk than the standard deviation. This is because it takes into account the size of the net cash flows, whereas the standard deviation (or variance) does not. There are also some disadvantages associated with the use of the probability distribution method. First, it is not simple to understand. Second, it is very difficult to estimate probability distributions accurately. Different people are likely to provide different subjective probability distributions of future net cash flows. This in turn implies that the probability distribution of future net cash flows is biased towards the personal beliefs of the decision maker.

Sensitivity analysis

Sensitivity analysis is a procedure which measures the impact that a change in one or more input variables will have upon the output variable. Sensitivity analysis can be divided into a single variable sensitivity analysis and multiple variable sensitivity analysis.

Single variable sensitivity analysis

A single variable sensitivity analysis shows the sensitivity of the output variable (for example, the net present value of a project) to changes in any of the input variables (for example, the discount rate).

Example 7.5 The sensitivity of the net present value to changes in the discount rate

To examine the impact of changing the discount rate on the net present value follow the steps below.

Step 1 Calculate the net present value of the project using the most likely estimates for the initial investment, the net cash flows and the discount rate.

Step 2 Consider a range of values for the discount rate around its most likely estimate determined in Step 1. Then for each value in the range recalculate the net present value using the most likely estimates for the initial investment and the net cash flows.

Step 3 Use the information derived in Step 2 to determine how sensitive the project's net present value is to changes in the discount rate and make an accept/reject decision.

In Example 7.1, the investment project of GD Fashion has a net present value of £164,000 when a risk-adjusted discount rate of 17 per cent is used. However, the management team wants to calculate the project's net present value using different discount rates ranging from 13 per cent to 22 per cent in steps of 1 per cent. Figure 7.14 shows the effect of changes of the discount rate on the project's net present value (figures are in £000s). To derive the sensitivity results, the `/Data Table 1` command of 1-2-3 is used, the 'input cell 1' of the command is cell B4. The formula stored in cell B16 is copied in cell E8 (note that the formula in cell E8 is displayed in a text format since we used the `/Range Format Text` command of 1-2-3). The results reveal that the net present value of the project is sensitive to changes in the discount rate. For example, if the discount rate is 18 per cent the net present value is −£95,000 (rounded).

```
---------------------------------------------------------------------------
           A                 B        C         D           E          F    G
 1 SENSITIVITY OF THE NPV TO THE DISCOUNT RATE CHANGES
 2 ===================================================
 3
 4 Discount Rate            17.0%
 5
 6 ------------------------------ | ---------------------------------
 7              YEAR   CASH FLOW  |
 8 ----------------------------   |              +B16
 9                  0    (9,900)  |         13.0%          1310
10                  1     2,300   |         14.0%          1005
11                  2     2,499   |         16.0%           713
12                  3     3,502   |         16.0%           433
13                  4     3,301   |         17.0%           164
14                  5     5,096   |         18.0%           -95
15                      --------- |         19.0%          -343
16    NPV ------>          164    |         20.0%          -581
17                                |         21.0%          -811
18                                |         22.0%         -1032
19 ------------------------------ | ---------------------------------
---------------------------------------------------------------------------
```

Figure 7.14. Sensitivity of a project's net present value to changes in the discount rate

We could also examine the sensitivity of the net present value to changes in other input variables, for example, the initial investment, the sales related to the project, the expenses related to the project, and so on.

A two-variable sensitivity analysis

A two-variable sensitivity analysis shows the sensitivity of the output variable (for example, the net present value of a project) to changes in any two of the input variables (for example, the discount rate and the initial investment).

Example 7.6 Appraising the effect on a project's net present value of varying the values of the discount rate and the initial investment

Below are shown the steps required to perform a sensitivity analysis of the net present value with respect to changes in the discount rate (DR) and the initial investment.

Step 1 Calculate the net present value of the project using the most likely estimates for the initial investment, net cash flows and the discount rate.

Step 2 Consider a range of values for the discount rate around its most likely estimate determined in Step 1 and a range of values for the initial investment around its most likely value computed in Step 1. Then for each combination of values recalculate the net present value using the most likely estimates for the net cash flows.

Step 3 Use the information derived in Step 2 to determine how sensitive the project's net present value is to changes in both the initial investment and the discount rate and then make an accept/reject decision.

Consider the data given in Example 7.1. We use a range of discount rates from 13 per cent to 22 per cent in steps of 1 per cent and three different values of initial investment, £10,200, £9,900 and £9,600 (remember that the initial investment's figures are in £000s). 1-2-3 offers the `/Data Table 2` command which allows you to perform a two-variable sensitivity analysis. The results are presented in Figure 7.15 (the command's 'input cell '' is cell B4 and 'input cell 2' is cell B8. The formula stored in cell B15 is copied in cell D7.

	A	B	C	D	E	F	G
1	SENSITIVITY OF THE NPV TO CHANGES IN THE D.R. AND INITIAL INVESTMENT						
2	================						
3							
4	Discount Rate		17.0%				
5	------------						
6		YEAR	CASH FLOW				
7	------------			+B15	(10,200)	(9,900)	(9,600)
8		0	(9,900)	13.0%	1,010	1,310	1,610
9		1	2,300	14.0%	705	1,005	1,305
10		2	2,499	15.0%	413	713	1,013
11		3	3,502	16.0%	133	433	733
12		4	3,301	17.0%	(136)	164	464
13		5	5,096	18.0%	(395)	(95)	205
14			----------	19.0%	(643)	(343)	(43)
15	NPV ------>		164	20.0%	(881)	(581)	(281)
16				21.0%	(1,111)	(811)	(511)
17				22.0%	(1,332)	(1,032)	(732)
18	------------						

Figure 7.15. A two-variable sensitivity of a project's net present value

The results shown in Figure 7.15 indicate that the net present value is sensitive to changes in both the discount rate and initial investment. Figure 7.16 provides a graphical presentation of the results of the sensitivity analysis for discount rates in the range 13 per cent to 16 per cent in steps of 1 per cent.

1-2-3 allows you to enter formulae into a worksheet that refer to other cells in this worksheet. 1-2-3 remembers such formulae so when you change the values in the cells that are referred to by a formula (or formulae), it automatically recalculates your formula (formulae). This capability makes 1-2-3 a useful and powerful tool for deter-

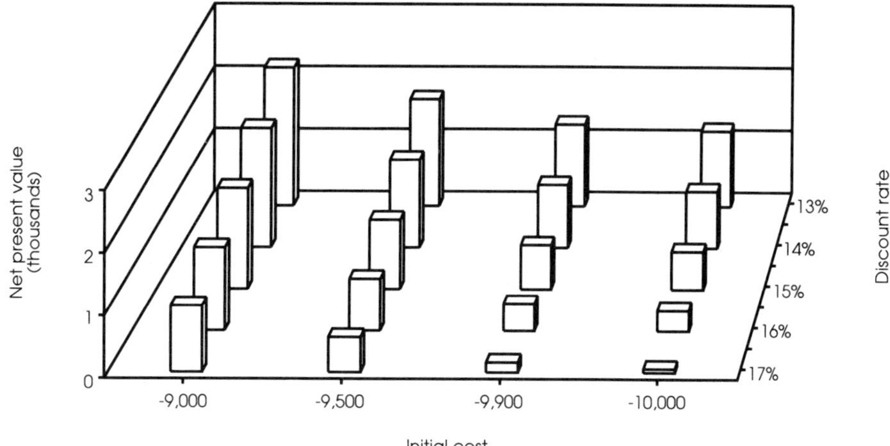

Figure 7.16. Graphing a two variable sensitivity: NPV vs discount rate and initial cost

mining the impact that a change in one or more of the input variables will have upon the output variable.

Example 7.7 A sensitivity analysis of the net present value and the internal rate of return with respect to one or more input variables

Referring to Example 7.1, the net cash flows of the new project of GD Fashions plc are estimated as shown in Figure 7.17 (figures are in £000s). In the same worksheet we can also see the net present value of the project using a risk-adjusted discount rate of 17 per cent and its internal rate of return.

A few assumptions concerning Figure 7.17 are in order:

- The 1988 turnover is £9,135,000.
- In each of the years 1991, 1992 and 1993, the turnover growth is 4 per cent. In 1994, the turnover is projected to be £9,120 (= £9,500(1 – 0.04)) and in 1995 the projection of the turnover is £9,485 (= £9,880(1 – 0.04)).
- Each year the trading expenses account for 60 per cent of the year's turnover.
- The corporate tax rate is 35 per cent.

If we use formulae between the cells of the worksheet shown in Figure 7.17, it can be automatically updated for any change of the input variables (for example, turnover per cent change, discount rate, and so on). Figure 7.18 shows the formulae used to calculate the net cash flows for 1991 and 1994.

To produce the results shown in Figure 7.17 follow the steps below.

1 Type in the values in cells E3 and E4.
2 Store in column C the formula shown in Figure 7.18.
3 Store in the worksheet the following formulae:

cell D8	`+C8*(1+$E$3)`
cell E9	`+D8* (1+$E$3)`
cell F8	`+C8*(1-E3)`
cell G8	`+D8*(1-E3)`

4 Copy the contents of the range C9. . C23 into the range D9. . G23.

```
--------------------------------------------------------------------------------------
              A                B          C         D        E          F        G
 1 ESTIMATING THE CASH FLOWS OF THE NEW PROJECT
 2 ============================================
 3        Turnover Percentage Change -->               4.00%
 4                Turnover for 1990 --->             9,135
 5
 6                                         1991      1992      1993       1994      1995
 7                                     -------------------------------------------------
 8 Turnover                               9,500     9,880    10,275      9,120     9,485
 9 Trading Expenses                       5,700     5,928     6,165      5,472     5,691
10                                     -------------------------------------------------
11 Trading Profit                         3,800     3,952     4,110      3,648     3,794
12 Depreciation                           1,800     1,800     1,800      1,800     1,800
13                                     -------------------------------------------------
14 Profit Before Tax                      2,000     2,152     2,310      1,848     1,994
15 Tax                                      700       753       809        647       698
16                                     -------------------------------------------------
17 Profit After Tax                       1,300     1,399     1,502      1,201     1,296
18 Depreciation                           1,800     1,800     1,800      1,800     1,800
19                                     -------------------------------------------------
20 Cash Flow After Tax                    3,100     3,199     3,302      3,001     3,096
21 Changes in NWC                          (800)     (700)      200        300     2,000
22                                     -------------------------------------------------
23 Net Cash Flow                          2,300     2,499     3,502      3,301     5,096
24
25 CALCULATING THE NPV AND THE IRR OF THE PROJECT
26 ==============================================
27 Discount Rate ---->     17.00%
28 --------------------------------------------
29             YEAR    CASH FLOW
30 --------------------------------------------
31                0     (9,900)
32                1      2,300
33                2      2,499
34                3      3,502
35                4      3,301
36                5      5,096
37                     ---------
38    NPV ------>          164
39    IRR -------->     17.63%
--------------------------------------------------------------------------------------
```

Figure 7.17. Calculating the net present value and internal rate of return of an investment project

```
--------------------------------------------------------------------------------------
          COLUMN C                          COLUMN F

 8     +E4*(1+$E$3)                        +C8*(1-E3)
 9     +C8*0.6                             +F8*0.6
10     --------------------                --------------------
11     +C8-C9                              +F8-F9
12                       1800                                1800
13     --------------------                --------------------
14     +C11-C12                            +F11-F12
15     +C14*0.35                           +F14*0.35
16     --------------------                --------------------
17     +C14-C15                            +F14-F15
18     +C12                                +F12
19     --------------------                --------------------
20     +C17+C18                            +F17+F18
21                       -800                                 300
22     --------------------                --------------------
23     +C20+C21                            +F20+F21
--------------------------------------------------------------------------------------
```

Figure 7.18. Formulae used to calculate the net cash flows for 1991 and 1994

5 Make sure that the method of 1-2-3 recalculation is set to automatic. After preparing the spreadsheet shown in Figure 7.17 where formulae are used, you can calculate the net cash flows for different values of the turnover percentage change. This application shows clearly the power of the spreadsheet since when you change the value in cell E3, 1-2-3 automatically updates the whole spreadsheet. You can change the value in cell E3 as many times as you wish, 1-2-3 each time will produce a new stream of net cash flows. Next, Figure 7.19 shows the formulae employed to calculate the net present value and the internal rate of return of the project.

Figure 7.19. Formulae used to calculate the net present value and the internal rate of return of the project

```
              COLUMN B
32                            -9,900
32    +C23
33    +D23
34    +E23
35    +F23
36    +G23
37    ------------------------
38    @NPV(B27,B32..B36)+B31
39    @IRR(0.1,B31..B36)
```

If we store the formulae shown in Figure 7.19 in the relevant cells, then 1-2-3 will automatically recalculate the net present value and the internal rate of return of the project every time we change the value in cell E3. Additionally, you can change the value of the risk-adjusted discount rate stored in cell B27. Each time you change the risk-adjusted discount rate, 1-2-3 will automatically update the net present value formula.

This type of analysis can also measure the impact that changes in more than two input variables (for example, turnover, trading expenses, and initial investment) will have upon the net present value or the internal rate of return of the project.

Problems

1 Set up the worksheet shown in Figure 7.17 by following the instructions given in the example above.

2 Calculate the net present value and the internal rate of return of the project by assuming a turnover percentage change of 5 per cent. Discuss your results.

3 Calculate the net present value and the internal rate of return of the project by changing the 1990 turnover amount from £9,135 to £8,800 and assuming a turnover percentage change of 6 per cent. Discuss the new results.

4 Calculate the net present value and the internal rate of return of the project by changing the 1990 turnover amount from £9,135 to £8,800, the tax rate from 35 per cent to 34 per cent and assuming a turnover percentage change of 7 per cent. Discuss the presented results.

Finally, note that a sensitivity analysis of the net present value with respect to one or more input variables should be conducted after deriving some reliable data related to the input variables. Remember that the results from a sensitivity analysis are reliable if the input data used and the assumptions made are reliable.

Evaluation of sensitivity analysis

Sensitivity analysis is useful in identifying variables whose changes are expected to have the greatest impact on the net present value or the internal rate of return of a project. It facilitates the identification of decision alternatives if the basic assumptions of the model have to be changed. Sensitivity analysis can also be used to monitor closely accepted investment projects in order to determine whether they should be continued, modified or terminated.

There are also some disadvantages associated with the use of sensitivity analysis. First, it is difficult to specify precisely the relationships between a particular variable and the net present value. Second, the final accept/reject decision is subjective, because sensitivity analysis does not provide a decision rule that can be utilized for accepting or rejecting investment projects.

Simulation analysis

Simulation analysis is a risk analysis method that involves utilizing predetermined probability distributions and random numbers to estimate, with the aid of a computer, a distribution of possible net present values (or internal rates of return). The net cash flows of a project can be calculated by using a mathematical model containing all the important factors that affect their values. The simulation approach requires the construction of a probability distribution for each factor affecting the net cash flows. Then, by using the computer, a random observation from each probability distribution can be selected. Each time putting together all the random selections into the mathematical model a random value of the net cash flow can be created. These random net cash flows are then used to estimate a distribution of possible net present values (or internal rates of return).

Below are summarized the steps required when using the simulation approach.

Step 1 Provide a mathematical model that truly reflects the relationship between a project's net cash flows and the factors affecting those cash flows.

Step 2 Create for each factor that affects the project's net cash flows a probability distribution and randomly select from each distribution a value.

Step 3 Use the values selected in Step 2 together with other information (for example, tax rate, depreciation method, and so on) and estimate the net cash flows of the project. Then estimate the project's net present value (or internal rate of return) by using the riskless rate of interest as the discount rate.

Step 4 Repeat Steps 2 and 3 many times (for example, 500 or more) and use the results to estimate the expected value and standard deviation of the distribution of possible net present values (or internal rates of return).

Example 7.8 Conducting a simulation analysis

In this example we use a three-factor simulation model: initial investment, amount of revenues, and expenses as a percentage of revenues (expenses include depreciation). Figure 7.20 shows the (subjective) probability distribution for each factor and additional information required for the evaluation of the project under consideration (we assume standard normal probability distributions for the variables used in the analysis).

```
---------------------------------------------------------------------------------
      A        B        C        D        E        F        G        H        I
 1                              SIMULATION ANALYSIS
 2                              ===================
 3
 4 ------------------------------------------------------------------------------
 5 Initial  Investment          Revenues                    Expenses
 6 Amount  Probability          Amount    Probability       as % of  Probability
 7 (£m)                         (£m)                        Revenue
 8 ------------------------------------------------------------------------------
 9      15     0.20                   16     0.30                 79.0%     0.04
10      18     0.60                   18     0.20                 80.0%     0.46
11      26     0.20                   20     0.20                 82.0%     0.46
12                                    22     0.30                 83.0%     0.04
13 ------------------------------------------------------------------------------
14
15                     Discount rate ------>           10%
16                     Expected life ------>            6 years
17                     Corporate tax rate ->           35%
---------------------------------------------------------------------------------
```

Figure 7.20. The data for the simulation problem

In order to estimate the probability distribution of the project's net present value follow the steps below:

Step 1 The mathematical model that can be used to calculate the net cash flows of the project can be expressed as:

Net cash flow = (Revenue − Expenses) × (1 − Tax rate) + Depreciation

where we assume that depreciation is calculated by using the straight-line depreciation method.

Step 2 We calculate the expected value and variance of each predetermined probability distribution (see Figure 7.21). For example, the expected value of the initial investment's probability distribution can be calculated as follows:

$$(0.20)(£15) + (0.60)(£18) + (0.20)(£26) = £19$$

On the other hand, the variance of the initial investment's probability distribution is

$$(0.20)(15 - 19)^2 + (0.60)(18 - 19)^2 + (0.20)(26 - 19)^2 = 13.60$$

Next we create a probability distribution for each of the three factors, by using the following formula:

$$x_i = E(x) + Z\sigma(x)$$

where

x_i = a value of the factor under consideration.
$E(x)$ = the expected value of the factor's probability distribution.
$\sigma(x)$ = the standard deviation of the factor's probability distribution.
Z = the distance between the expected value of the factor's probability distribution and the specified value of x_i measured in units of the standard deviation.

Columns B, E and H of Figure 7.22 present the Z values of a standard normal distribution. Columns C, F and I of Figure 7.22 show the values

```
--------------------------------------------------------------------------
       A       B        C        D        E        F        G        H        I
21 Calculating the means and the standard deviations of the distribution
22                   -------------------------------------------------------
23                   Amount    Probability  Pr*Amount     Pr*(Amount - Mean)^2
24                   -------------------------------------------------------
25                         15       0.20        3.00             3.20
26                         18       0.60       10.80             0.60
27                         26       0.20        5.20             9.80
28                                          ----------           -----
29                   Mean ------->             19.00            13.60 <- Var.
30
31
32                   -------------------------------------------------------
33                   Amount    Probability    Pr*Amount   Pr*(Amount - Mean)^2
34                   -------------------------------------------------------
35                         16       0.30         4.80             2.70
36                         18       0.20         3.60             0.20
37                         20       0.20         4.00             0.20
38                         22       0.30         6.60             2.70
39                                              --------         --------
40                   Mean ------->              19.00             5.80 <- Var.
41
42
43                   ------------------------------------------------
44                   Amount    Probability    Pr*Amount   Pr*(Amount - Mean)^2
45                   ------------------------------------------------
46                     79.00%       0.04         3.16%           0.04%
47                     80.00%       0.46        36.80%           0.01%
48                     82.00%       0.46        37.72%           0.01%
49                     83.00%       0.04         3.32%           0.04%
50                                             ---------        -------
51                   Mean ------->              81.00%           0.10% <- Var.
52
--------------------------------------------------------------------------
```

Figure 7.21. Calculating expected values and variances

of the initial investment, revenues and the percentage of expenses, respectively (all the factors' values presented have a format with two decimal points). For example:

19.00 – (3.00)SQRT(13.60) = 7.94

19.00 – (3.00)SQRT(5.80) = 11.78

81.00% – (3.00)SQRT(0.10%) = 71.51%

Based on the probability distribution of each of the factors that affect the net cash flows, one value for each factor will be randomly selected. This can be accomplished by using 1-2-3. Columns A, D and G of Figure 7.22 show several random numbers, between –3.00 and 3.00, created by using the 1-2-3's random number facility. The function `@RAND * (6) – 3` can be used to generate a random number between –3.00 and 3.00 and then the `/Copy` command can be employed to generate more random numbers between –3.00 and 3.00. Next a value of each factor is randomly selected from each probability distribution. For example, the random number –1.278 corresponds to the initial investment's value £8.86, the random number –2.814 corresponds to the revenue's value £11.78 and the random number 0.312 corresponds to the expense percentage's value 73.09 per cent. In this example correspondence of a

	A	B	C	D	E	F	G	H	I
61				Creating probability distributions					
62									
63	Initial Investment			Revenues			Expenses as % of Revenue		
64									
65	-2.611	-3.00	7.94	-2.814	-3.00	11.78	-2.401	-3.00	71.51%
66	-1.278	-2.75	8.86	-0.540	-2.75	12.38	0.940	-2.75	72.30%
67	-1.376	-2.50	9.78	-0.047	-2.50	12.98	0.312	-2.50	73.09%
68	-1.979	-2.25	10.70	0.002	-2.25	13.58	-0.866	-2.25	73.88%
69	-1.581	-2.00	11.62	1.871	-2.00	14.18	-1.014	-2.00	74.68%
70	1.423	-1.75	12.55	-1.791	-1.75	14.79	2.369	-1.75	75.47%
71	-1.747	-1.50	13.47	-2.734	-1.50	15.39	0.064	-1.50	76.26%
72	2.692	-1.25	14.39	1.724	-1.25	15.99	0.499	-1.25	77.05%
73	-1.917	-1.00	15.31	1.070	-1.00	16.59	-2.909	-1.00	77.84%
74	-0.409	-0.75	16.23	-0.613	-0.75	17.19	1.316	-0.75	78.63%
75	-0.401	-0.50	17.16	-0.306	-0.50	17.80	2.256	-0.50	79.42%
76	-0.444	-0.25	18.08	-0.897	-0.25	18.40	-1.345	-0.25	80.21%
77	-2.131	0.00	19.00	-1.944	0.00	19.00	1.938	0.00	81.00%
78	-0.365	0.25	19.92	1.933	0.25	19.60	2.555	0.25	81.79%
79	0.631	0.50	20.84	2.507	0.50	20.20	-2.014	0.50	82.58%
80	-2.987	0.75	21.77	-0.018	0.75	20.81	1.678	0.75	83.37%
81	-0.356	1.00	22.69	-0.826	1.00	21.41	1.556	1.00	84.16%
82	1.497	1.25	23.61	2.589	1.25	22.01	1.852	1.25	84.95%
83	0.107	1.50	24.53	1.900	1.50	22.61	0.561	1.50	85.74%
84	2.356	1.75	25.45	-1.037	1.75	23.21	-1.545	1.75	86.53%
85	1.156	2.00	26.38	-0.058	2.00	23.82	-1.075	2.00	87.32%
86	0.457	2.25	27.30	2.689	2.25	24.42	-1.286	2.25	88.12%
87	0.673	2.50	28.22	0.237	2.50	25.02	2.923	2.50	88.91%
88	0.876	2.75	29.14	2.254	2.75	25.62	2.326	2.75	89.70%
89	-2.068	3.00	30.06	0.735	3.00	26.22	-1.350	3.00	90.49%

Figure 7.22. Creating probability distributions

random number with the nearest value shown in Figure 7.22 is assumed. The selection of values can be performed with the aid of the `@VLOOKUP` function of 1-2-3. For example, the following function is stored in cell A107 (see Figure 7.23):

```
@VLOOKUP(A65, $B$65..$C$89, 1)
```

where A65 is the cell containing the random number (for example, −2.611) and B65..C89 is the range of the Z values and the factor values.

Step 3 Using the data derived in the previous step we calculate the project's net cash flow by employing the mathematical expression presented in Step 1. For example, we can calculate the following (figure is rounded to two decimal points):

$$\text{Net cash flow} = (11.78 - (11.78)(0.7309))(1 - 0.35) + 8.866 = £3.54$$

Next, assuming a discount riskless rate of 10 per cent, the net present value is equal to £6.54 (slight deviations occur due to rounding).

Step 4 Steps 2 and 3 are repeated many times and each time the net present value is estimated. Let us assume that 24 repetitions of Steps 2 and 3 are sufficient to develop a distribution of possible net present values (see Figure 7.23, slight deviations occur because of rounding). These values are used to calculate the expected value and the standard deviation of the distribution of possible net present values.

Figure 7.24(a)–(c) presents graphically the probability distributions of the initial

	A (Initial Investment)	D (Revenue)	G (Expenses as % of revenue)	H (Cash flow)	I (NPV)
101	Creating a probability of NPV				
102					
103	Initial Investment	Revenue	Expenses	Cash	NPV
104			as % of	flow	
105			revenue		
106					
107	8.86	11.78	0.73	3.54	6.55
108	13.47	17.19	0.83	4.10	4.40
109	13.47	18.40	0.82	4.42	5.79
110	11.62	19.00	0.78	4.67	8.73
111	12.55	23.21	0.77	5.55	11.64
112	23.61	14.18	0.88	5.03	-1.70
113	12.55	12.38	0.81	3.62	3.22
114	28.22	22.61	0.82	7.38	3.92
115	11.62	21.41	0.72	5.90	14.08
116	17.16	17.19	0.85	4.54	2.62
117	17.16	17.80	0.88	4.23	1.28
118	17.16	16.59	0.76	5.42	6.45
119	10.70	14.18	0.87	3.02	2.47
120	17.16	23.21	0.89	4.53	2.58
121	20.84	25.02	0.74	7.72	12.79
122	7.94	18.40	0.86	3.03	5.25
123	17.16	16.59	0.86	4.40	1.99
124	23.61	25.02	0.87	6.13	3.07
125	19.00	23.21	0.83	5.79	6.24
126	27.30	15.99	0.75	7.10	3.62
127	22.69	18.40	0.77	6.53	5.73
128	19.92	25.02	0.76	7.18	11.35
129	20.84	19.00	0.90	4.75	-0.17
130	21.77	24.42	0.88	5.51	2.25
131	10.70	20.20	0.76	4.90	10.64
132					
133		Expected NPV ------------------->			5.39
134		Standard deviation of NPV ------>			4.04

Figure 7.23. Creating a probability of net present value

investment, revenues and expenses as percentages of revenues. The distribution of possible net present values is shown graphically in Figure 7.24(d).

Evaluation of simulation analysis

Simulation analysis is a statistically based method for dealing with risk. It estimates the distribution of possible net present values that may be generated from a project and it uses the characteristics of such a distribution to determine whether the project should be accepted. Simulation analysis also provides other useful information regarding the return and risk of the project under consideration (for example, some extreme outcomes which result from an asymmetrical distribution of possible net present values).

An additional advantage is that a simulation analysis can be used to systematically evaluate investment projects under a variety of simulated conditions. It necessitates the decision maker to examine carefully the relationships between the factors influencing a project's net cash flows and helps improve the decision maker's perception of the project's return and risk characteristics.

A disadvantage is that simulation techniques do not specify the relationships between the factors influencing net cash flows. The simulation approach does not provide a decision rule that can be used for accepting or rejecting projects. For example, the analysis does not offer a decision rule to indicate whether a project's expected

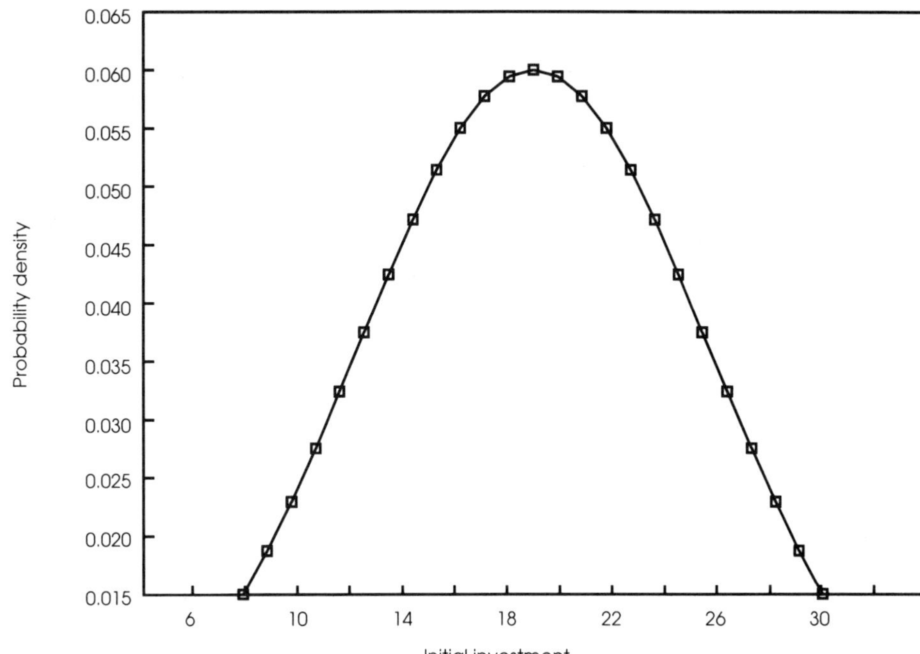

Figure 7.24a. The distribution of the initial investment for the firm's project

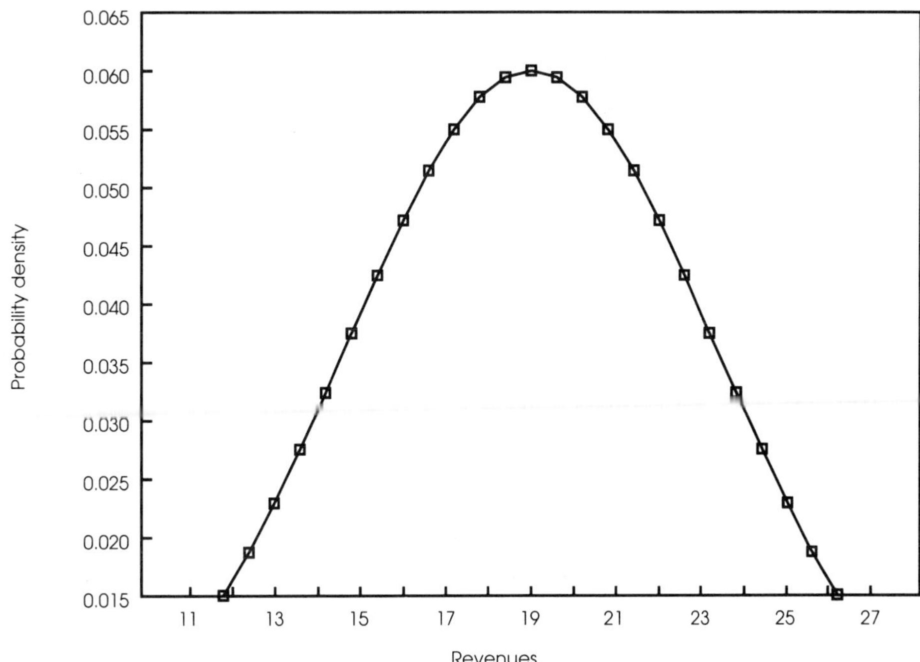

Figure 7.24b. The distribution of the revenues for the investment project

net present value is sufficient to compensate for its risk as measured by the standard deviation of the distribution of possible net present values. Thus the simulation analysis involves subjectivity in making decisions.

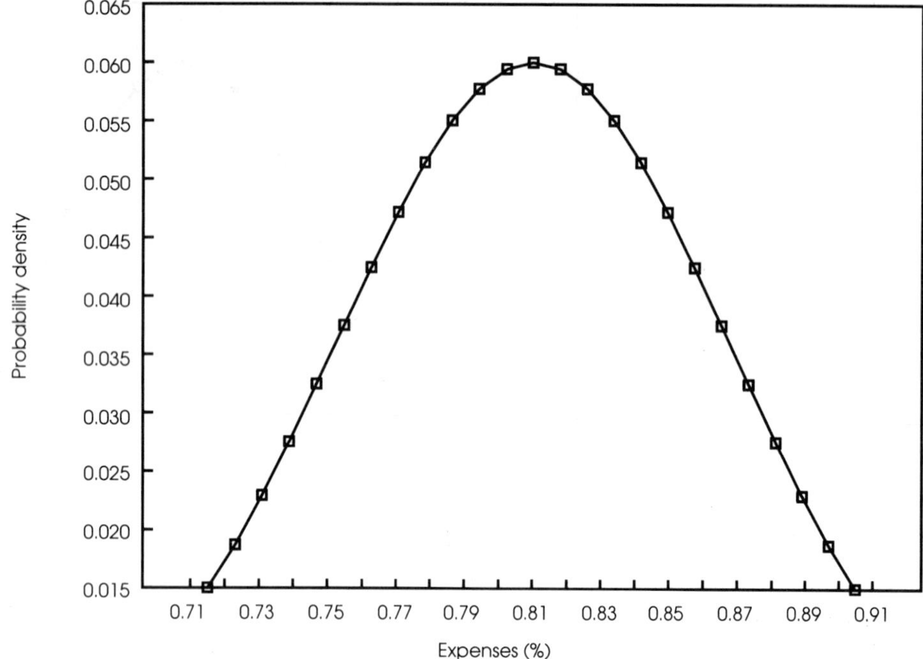

Figure 7.24c. The distribution of the expenses for the investment project

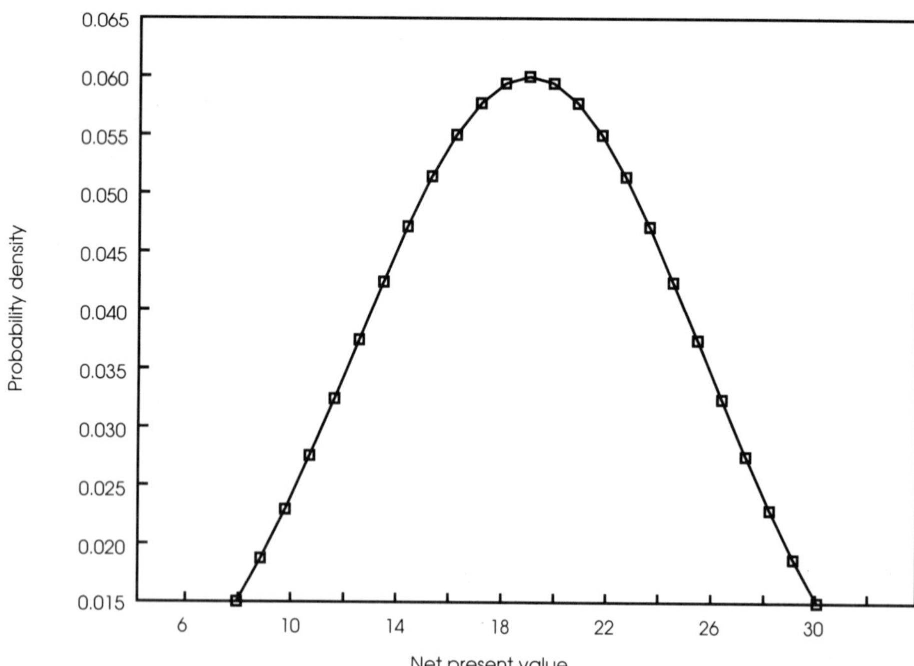

Figure 7.24d. The distribution of the projects net present value

Decision trees

A decision tree is a graphical method of showing in an organized manner all the possible outcomes that may result from a particular situation and their probabilities of occurrence. In capital budgeting a decision tree can be utilized to map out over time all the possible net cash flows of a project together with their respective probabilities and to facilitate the generation of a probability distribution of net present values. In order to construct a decision tree follow the steps below:

Step 1 Estimate the possible net cash flows of a project and assign probabilities to each net cash flow where the probabilities for any given period sum to 1.

Step 2 Calculate the net present values of all the possible combinations of net cash flows using the risk-free rate as the discount rate.

Step 3 Calculate the probability of each possible net present value and then determine the probability distribution of all possible net present values

Example 7.9 Using the decision tree approach in capital budgeting

Cannon plc plans to employ the decision tree approach to evaluate a proposed investment project, call it A. The risk-free rate is 10 per cent and the expected life of the project is two years. Project A will have no salvage value at the end of the second year. Cannon estimates that the project will cost £80,000.

The project's net cash flows are as follows: in year 1 there is a 20 per cent probability that it will generate a net cash flow of £40,000, a 60 per cent probability that it will generate £60,000 and a 20 per cent chance that it will generate £80,000. In year 2, the net cash flows of the project depend on the net cash flows that occur in year 1. Stated differently, the net cash flows in year 2 are conditional upon the net cash flows of year 1. Likewise, the probabilities assigned to the net cash flows in year 2 are conditional probabilities.

If the net cash flow of £40,000 is realized in year 1, then we have the following list: £40,000, £30,000, or £20,000 with probabilities of 30 per cent, 40 per cent, and 30 per cent, respectively. If the net cash flow in year 1 is £60,000, then the following three cash flows are possible in year 2: £100,000, £80,000, or £60,000 with probabilities of 20 per cent, 50 per cent, and 30 per cent, respectively. Finally, if the net cash flow is £80,000 in year 1, then we have the following pattern in year 2: £60,000, £65,000, or £80,000 with probabilities of 20 per cent, 60 per cent, and 20 per cent, respectively. Figure 7.25 shows the decision tree for Cannon's project. The initial investment is displayed in column A, with the possible cash flows in year 1 and their respective probabilities in columns C and B, respectively. The possible net cash flows in year 2 and their respective probabilities are presented in columns F and E, respectively. It may be noted that the decision tree displays nine distinct possibilities the project could take if the firm decides to accept the project. For example, one possibility is the combination of a net cash flow of £40,000 in year 1 and a net cash flow of £40,000 in year 2.

Column G in Figure 7.25 shows the possible net present values at a discount rate of 10 per cent. Each net present value is calculated by using the initial investment of £80,000 and the possible combination of the net cash flows in year 1 and 2. For example, consider the combination, year 1: £40,000 and year 2: £40,000, then the net present value can be calculated as follows (the figure is rounded):

$$\text{NPV}(A, 1) = \frac{\text{£}40{,}000}{(1 + 0.10)} + \frac{\text{£}40{,}000}{(1 + 0.10)^2} - \text{£}80{,}000 = -\text{£}10{,}579$$

where NPV(A, 1) denotes the net present value of project A for combination 1.

```
     A         B      C      D      E          F           G           H           I
1           USING THE DECISION TREE METHOD TO EVALUATE A PROJECT'S RISK
2           ===========================================================
3 Riskless rate of interest ---->           10%
4                                                               JOINT       WEIGHTED
5           PERIOD 1                  PERIOD 2          NPV     PROBAB.        NPV
6 ---------------------------------------------------------------------------------
7           0.20              |--     0.30     40,000   (10,579)     0.06       (635)
8           |--   40,000      --      0.40     30,000   (18,843)     0.08     (1,507)
9                             |--     0.30     20,000   (27,107)     0.06     (1,626)
10          |
11          0.60              |--     0.20    100,000    57,190      0.12      6,863
12 (80,000)|--    60,000      --      0.50     80,000    40,661      0.30     12,198
13                            |--     0.30     60,000    24,132      0.18      4,344
14          |
15          0.20              |--     0.20     60,000    42,314      0.04      1,693
16          |--   80,000      --      0.60     65,000    46,446      0.12      5,574
17                            |--     0.20     80,000    58,843      0.04      2,354
18
19 Expected value of the joint probability of the NPV ------>         29,258
20 Standard deviation of the joint probability of the NPV -->         4,275
```

Figure 7.25. An example of a decision tree

The other net present values are calculated in a similar fashion. The net present values range from –£10,579 (for combination 1) to £58,843 (for combination 9).

Each numerical value displayed in column H of Figure 7.25 represents a joint probability. In this instance, a joint probability is the percentage chance that a combination of net cash flows (and thus a possible net present value) will occur. For example, the joint probability that the net present value of –£10,579 will occur is 0.06 (that is, 0.20×0.30). Note that the sum of all the joint probabilities is 1 indicating that all possible combinations are considered. Therefore, we have generated a probability distribution of possible net present values for project A displayed in columns G and H. If such a probability distribution is normal, it can be fully described by its expected value and standard deviation of possible net present values. From this distribution, the expected net present value is £29,258 and the standard deviation is £4,275 giving a coefficient of variation of 0.146.

Finally, we can calculate the probability that the net present value of project A will be negative. By adding the three probabilities associated with negative net present values we arrive at a probability of 20 per cent (that is, $0.06 + 0.08 + 0.06$). Therefore, we find that there is a 20 per cent probability that the project's net present value will be less than zero. Stated differently, there is a probability of 80 per cent that the net present value of the project will be positive.

Should the firm accept the project? the answer is not straightforward. The project provides a positive expected net present value, but it also involves some risk. The final decision to accept or reject the project will be taken by the firm's management team. If the members of the team believe that the project will provide a sufficient return to compensate the firm for its riskiness, then they should accept the project.

Problems

1 Construct a decision tree for project A of Cannon plc displaying the internal rate of return of all possible outcomes and their respective probabilities. Calculate the

expected value and standard deviation of the probability distribution of possible internal rates of return.

2 Calculate the probability that the internal rate of return is lower than 10 per cent.

3 Create the spreadsheet shown in Figure 7.25 using the appropriate formulae or 1-2-3 functions (for example, use formulae to calculate the probable net present values in column G and the statistical functions `@SUM` and `@STD` to calculate the expected value and the standard deviation of the probability distribution of possible net present values).

4 Cannon is also evaluating another project, call it B, which has an expected useful life of two years. The initial investment of the project is £80,000 and the firm uses a 10 per cent discount rate. Three different cash flows are possible in the first year: £55,000 with an associated probability of 0.25; £60,000 with an associated probability of 0.50; and £75,000 with an associated probability of 0.25. The net cash flows in the second year and their associated probabilities are given below.

Year 1 CF: £55,000		Year 1 CF: £60,000		Year 1 CF: £75,000	
Probability	CF	Probability	CF	Probability	CF
0.30	45,000	0.15	100,000	0.20	145,000
0.40	25,000	0.70	90,000	0.60	120,000
0.30	20,000	0.15	70,000	0.20	110,000

For project B calculate the expected value and the standard deviation of the probability distribution of possible net present values by using the decision tree approach. If project B and project A (introduced in the example above) are mutually exclusive, which project should Cannon accept?

Evaluation of the decision tree method

Decision trees take into account the dependence of a project's net cash flows over time. Decision trees have the additional advantage of providing information about probability distributions of future net cash flows which can be utilized to calculate the expected value and the standard deviation of the probability distribution of possible net present values.

The decision tree method has several disadvantages including the following. First, it may become complex and difficult to understand when we deal with a long-life project. Second, the probabilities associated with the possible net cash flows are subjective and difficult to determine.

Figure 7.26 summarizes the input data used and the output data produces from six approaches dealing with the risk dimension in capital budgeting.

The use of risk assessment methods in practice

The theory of financial management emphasizes the importance of incorporating the riskiness of potential investment projects into capital budgeting decisions.

Figure 7.26. The input and output data associated with six approaches used to adjust for differential project risk in capital budgeting

Method	Input data	Output data
Risk-adjusted discount rate	Expected future net cash flows. A risk-adjusted discount rate	A single point estimate of net present value
Certainty equivalent	Certain future net cash flows. The risk-free rate of interest	A single point estimate of net present value
Probability distribution	Probability distributions for future net cash flows. The risk-free rate of interest	The expected value and the standard deviation of the probability distribution of net present values
Sensitivity analysis	Expected future net cash flows. Discount rate	A distribution of net present value
Simulation analysis	Probability distributions of factors which affect net cash flows. The risk-free rate of interest	A distribution of possible net present values
Decision tree	Conditional future cash flows and their associated conditional probabilities. The risk-free rate of interest	A probability distribution of possible net present values

Figure 7.27 presents some evidence on the risk assessment methods utilized in practice.

In view of the results of Pike (1988), three methods for making some allowance of risk are commonly used over time. These are sensitivity analysis, raising hurdle rates and shortening payback. Probability analysis was not used much in early years; however, since 1981 its popularity has increased dramatically.

Diacogiannis and Lai's (1989) findings show that sensitivity analysis, shortening payback, risk-adjusted discount rate and probability analysis represent the most widely used risk assessment by firms in the Unlisted Securities Market.

The results of Gitman and Forrester (1977) reveal the popularity of the risk-adjusted discount rate and the certainty equivalent methods. Finally, Corr (1983) concluded that sensitivity analysis is the most popular method used for assessing risk.

The results discussed in the present section are not strictly compatible since they are based on different samples. However, we can draw the following conclusions:

1 The most common method for dealing with risk in capital budgeting is sensitivity analysis. In recent years, the popularity of sensitivity analysis can be attributable to the increasing use of computer software (for example, spreadsheet packages) which has made the application of the method relatively simple.
2 From Pike's results we can conclude that there is a positive trend in the adoption of risk evaluation methods. The availability of various financial computer software packages for investment analysis provides a potential explanation for his findings.
3 Some firms are using more than one risk assessment method for evaluating risky investment projects.

R.H. Pike
RESEARCH YEAR: Many
COUNTRY: UK
SIZE OF FIRMS: Large
POPULATION: Different populations
SAMPLE: 100

	1975 (%)	1981 (%)	1986 (%)
Sensitivity analysis	28	42	71
Analysis under different assumptions	n/a	n/a	93
Reduced payback periods	25	30	61
Increased hurdle rates	37	41	61
Probability analysis	9	10	40
Beta analysis	0	0	16

G.P. Diacogiannis and Lai R.
RESEARCH YEAR: 1988
COUNTRY: UK
SIZE OF FIRMS: Medium Sized
POPULATION: 304
SAMPLE: 95

	% out of 85
Shortening payback period	42
Risk-adjusted DR	34
Probability analysis	31
Sensitivity analysis	56
Simulation	11
Beta analysis	3

Gitman L.J. and Forrester J.R.
RESEARCH YEAR: 1976
COUNTRY: USA
SIZE OF FIRMS: Large
POPULATION 600
SAMPLE: 103

	(%)
Increase the cost of capital	42.7
Certainty-equivalent	26.2
Subjective adjustment of cash flows	18.5
Decrease minimum payback period	12.6

A.V. Corr
YEAR: 1981
COUNTRY: CANADA
SIZE OF FIRMS: Various
POPULATION: Firms in eight manufacturing industries
SAMPLE: 24

	Regularly	Selected projects
Sensitivity analysis	10	4
Risk adjustment IRR	3	none
Simulation and probability analysis	none	3

Figure 7.27. Risk assessment methods used in practice

Summary

In the real world, firms do not operate in an environment of perfect certainty. Since the cash flows generated by most proposed projects are highly uncertain it is necessary to consider the risk dimension in capital budgeting analysis. There are a number of alternative approaches that may be used to incorporate risk in capital budgeting.

1 *Risk-adjusted discount rate* Under this approach the risk associated with an investment project is incorporated in the discount rate used in the calculation

of the net present value. The greater the risk, the higher should be the risk-adjusted discount rate.

2 *Certainty equivalent* This approach involves adjustments of the expected net cash flows rather than the discount rate. In view of the certainty equivalent method, we use for each period's net cash flow a certainty equivalent coefficient to convert it to a certain net cash flow. The greater the risk, the lower should be the certainty equivalent coefficient.

3 *Probability distribution* This is a statistical method calculating the return–risk characteristics associated with a project by using predetermined probability distributions of net cash flows. This approach defines risk as the dispersion of the probability distribution of possible net present values (or possible internal rates of return) and measures it by the standard deviation of such a distribution. The greater the standard deviation of the probability distribution of possible net present values, the greater should be the project's risk.

4 *Sensitivity analysis* This is an approach used in capital budgeting to investigate how sensitive is the decision variable (for example, net present value or internal rate of return) to changes in one or more key input variables. Sensitivity analysis identifies those input variables that have the greatest influences on the decision variable. The identification of such variables can lead to actions that may reduce the risk associated with the project under consideration.

5 *Simulation analysis* This is a risk analysis method that can be performed with the aid of a computer. We initially develop a net cash flow generating model which in turn is used to determine the distribution of a project's net present value (or internal rate of return). Risk is measured by the standard deviation of the probability distribution of possible net present values. The greater the standard deviation of the probability distribution, the greater should be the project's risk.

6 *Decision trees* In capital budgeting the decision tree approach is used to provide a graphic display over time of all the possible net cash flows associated with a proposed investment project together with their respective probabilities. The decision tree approach facilitates the generation of a probability distribution of possible net present values. The risk is measured by the standard deviation of the probability distribution of possible net present values.

7 *The use of risk assessment methods in practice* The empirical evidence presented in this chapter indicates that sensitivity analysis is the most popular risk assessment method used in practice. Other popular methods utilized to incorporate consideration of risk in capital budgeting analysis are shortening payback period and risk-adjusted discount rate.

Questions for discussion

1 For each term shown below in the largest box provide a definition in your own words. Then check your responses against the definitions included in the chapter.

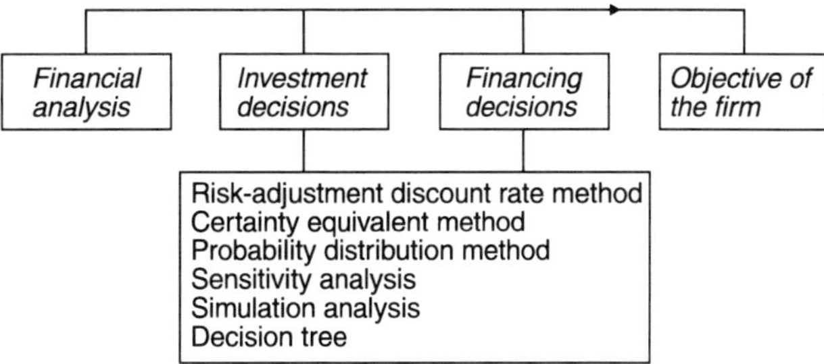

2 Discuss in detail the diagram shown below and explain its use.

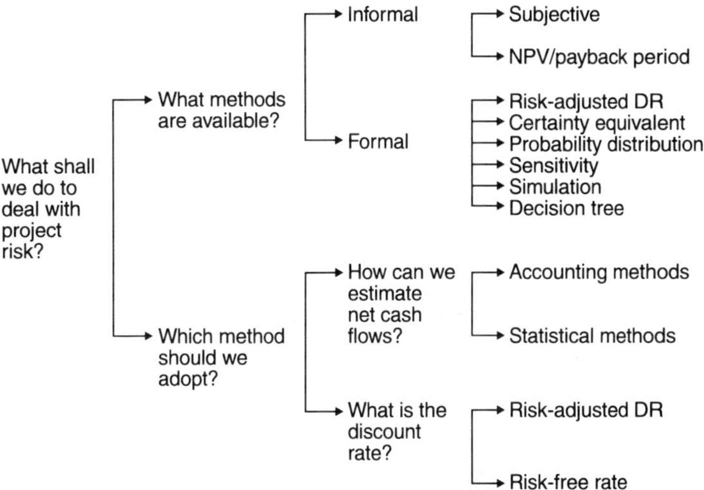

3 Discuss and illustrate with an example how a firm can select the risk-adjusted discount rate by using the payback period method.

4 'The discount rate used in net present value calculations must increase in order to account for the greater risk associated with the more distant cash flows.' Do you agree with this statement? Fully discuss your answer.

5 Discuss the following statement: 'When the risk of an individual project is different from the risk of the average project undertaken by the firm, then the appropriate discount rate to be used in the evaluation process can be found by adjusting the firm's average cost of capital for the riskiness of the project.'

6 'The utilization of the standard deviation as a measure of risk may lead to a wrong decision.' Discuss. Substantiate your position by using a numerical example. Present and discuss an alternative measure for risk that can be used to improve the standard deviation. Once more, use an example to illustrate your case.

7 Wilson Publishers uses the probability distribution approach to evaluate risky capital budgeting projects. Past experience has been used to estimate the risk–return characteristics associated with 'average' risk projects. We also assume that the firm's managers prefer more return to less and they are risk averse. Fill the blank areas in the following diagram.

		Standard deviation of the probability distribution of net present values		
		High	Medium	Low
Expected value of the probability distribution of net present values	High			
	Medium	Reject		
	Low			

8 Identify and discuss the advantages and disadvantages of each of the following two risk-adjustment methods: the risk-adjusted discount rate and the certainty equivalent approach. When do these two methods provide the same net present value?

9 Identify and discuss the advantages and disadvantages of the probability distribution approach of handling risk in capital budgeting.

10 Identify and discuss the advantages and disadvantages of each of the following methods for dealing with risk in capital budgeting: sensitivity analysis and simulation analysis.

11 Identify and discuss the advantages and disadvantages of the decision tree approach for evaluating risky investment alternatives.

12 Present an analog model summarizing the main points discussed in the present chapter.

13 Discuss the alternative routes for performing sensitivity analysis using the spreadsheet.

14 How can spreadsheets be used to facilitate the application of the concepts discussed in this chapter?

Appendix 7A Calculating the certainty equivalent coefficients

In this appendix we consider two issues related to the certainty equivalent method. First, we present a hypothetical example illustrating how we can calculate the certainty equivalent coefficients by using the economic concept of utility theory. Second, we provide a mathematical expression for calculating the certainty equivalent coefficients which is based on the following assumption: the certainty equivalent method and the risk-adjustment method produce the same adjusted net present values for a given series of cash flows.

Example 7A.1 Calculating the certainty equivalent coefficients applicable to a project's net cash flows by employing the concept of utility theory

Assume that the utility function of a risk-averse investor is represented as follows:

$$U(Y) = (Y - 0.6)^{1/2}$$

where Y denotes a project's expected net cash flow in a given period.

The investor is considering an investment project with the following information. It will generate a net cash flow of £9 with a 0.5 probability and a net cash flow of £13 with a 0.5 probability (cash flow figures are in £000s). The expected (risky) net cash flow is calculated by summing the products of the probable net cash flows and their respective probabilities:

$$E(\text{CF}) = (0.5)\,(£9) + (0.5)\,(£13) = £11.50$$

Next, we can convert the risky net cash flow of £11.50 to a certain equivalent net cash flow by using the utility function of the investor. The expected utility of the project can be calculated as follows:

$$E(U) = 0.5U(9) + 0.5U(13) = 0.5(9 - 0.6)^{1/2} + 0.5(13 - 0.6)^{1/2}$$
$$= 3.21$$

Since the investor would be indifferent between the risky net cash flow and the certainty equivalent net cash flow, then the latter satisfies the following equation:

$$U(Y^*) = 3.21$$

where Y^* is the certainty equivalent net cash flow. The last equation can be written equivalently as

$$(Y^*) - (0.6)^{1/2} = 3.21$$

Thus, the certainty equivalent net cash flow is £10.90 indicating that the investor would accept a certain amount of £10.90 in exchange for the expected net cash flow of £11.50. In this case, the certainty equivalent coefficient is 0.948 (that is, £10.90/£11.50). With the aid of the previous discussion, the certainty equivalent coefficient of our example can be mathematically expressed as follows:

$$\frac{(E(U))^2 + 0.6}{E(\text{CF})}$$

Risk-adjustment discount rate method versus certainty equivalent method

The risk-adjustment discount rate method and the certainty equivalent method produce the same adjusted net present values if the following condition holds:

Present value of expected net cash flows discounted at the risk-adjusted discount rate	=	Present value of certainty equivalent net cash flows discounted at the riskless rate

$$\sum_{t=1}^{N} \frac{\text{CF}_t}{(1 + \text{RADR})^t} = \sum_{t=1}^{N} \frac{(\text{CEC}_t)(\text{CF}_t)}{(1 + r_\text{f})^t}$$

From the last equation it can be seen that the two methods produce the same adjusted net present values if:

$$\text{CEC}_t = \frac{(1 + r_\text{f})^t}{(1 + \text{RADR})^t} \quad \text{for each } t$$

Cash flow	Probability
£400,000	0.10
£760,000	0.80
£440,000	0.10

Figure 7B.1. A probability distribution of cash flows

Appendix 7B The normal distribution

Probability is the percentage chance of occurrence of an uncertain event. For example, assume that there exists a 0.80 probability that a new investment project of Marks and Spencer plc will be successful. This means that there is an 80 per cent chance of a successful investment and a 20 per cent chance that the firm's investment will be unsuccessful. A probability distribution of cash flows is a list of all possible cash flows each associated with a particular subjective probability (or chance) of occurrence. Figure 7B.1 presents a probability distribution of cash flows.

A variable that can be described by a probability distribution is called a random or stochastic variable. For example, the cash flow variable described by the probability distribution shown in Figure 7B.1 is a random variable. If a random variable is limited to certain disconnected values in some range of values, then it is called discrete. For example, the cash flow variable presented in Figure 7B.1 is discrete. If a random variable assumes any value in some range of values, then it is called continuous. For example, assume that we wish to determine the number of times investors purchase shares of Marks and Spencer during a particular day. We find that at 10.00 a.m. investors purchased 2 million shares, at 10.30 a.m. another group of investors purchased 1 million shares and finally, at 11.00 a.m. only 0.1 million shares were purchased. The number of shares purchased is a discrete variable but the elapsed time between the first purchase of 2 million and the second purchase of 1 million shares is a continuous variable.

There are certain numerical measures that can be used to summarize the important characteristics of a probability distribution. We assume that a probability distribution can be characterized by two statistics: the expected value or mean and the standard deviation. The definitions for these statistics are provided below and for an application see Example 7.3.

- *Expected value or mean* The expected value of a random variable, say x, is equal to the sum of the products obtained by multiplying each probable value of x by the corresponding probability. The expected value of a probability distribution shows the most probable outcome of the distribution.

  Mathematically, the expected value of a random variable x can be expressed as:

  $$E(x) = \sum_{i=1}^{N} p_i x_i$$

  where x_i is a probable value of the random variable x and p_i is the probability of value x_i to occur.

- *Variance* The variance of a random variable, say x, is equal to the weighted average of the squared deviations of the various values of x from their expected value, with weights being the respective probabilities associated with the different values of x. The variance of a probability distribution measures the variation of the random variable's values around their expected value.

Mathematically, the variance of a random variable x can be expressed as:

$$\sigma^2(x) = \sum_{i=1}^{N} p_i(x_i - E(x))^2$$

where $E(x)$ is the expected value of x.

- *Standard deviation* The standard deviation of a random variable, say x, is equal to the square root of the variance of x. The standard deviation of a probability distribution measures the variation of the random variable's values around their expected value.

The normal distribution

The normal distribution is a bell-shaped continuous distribution with the following probability density function (such a function gives the probability that the random variable x takes a value in the interval $(-\infty, +\infty)$):

$$f(x) = \frac{1}{\sigma(x)\text{SQRT}(2\pi)} \mathrm{e}^{-Z^2/2}$$

where

SQRT	= the square root operator.
π	= the constant 3.142.
e	= the constant 2.718.
Z	$= \dfrac{x_i - E(x)}{\sigma(x)}$.
x_i	= a value of the random variable x.
$E(x)$	= the expected value of the random variable x.
$\sigma(x)$	= the standard deviation of the random variable x.

A normal distribution is completely determined by its expected value and its standard deviation. The graph of a normal distribution is a bell-shaped curve with the following characteristics:

1. It extends indefinitely in both directions.
2. It is symmetrical about its expected value.
3. The total area under the bell-shaped curve is equal to 1.

The expected value and the standard deviation of a normal distribution can be used to describe the area under the normal curve (see Figure 7B.2). Knowing this, we can conclude that about 68 per cent of the values in the distribution are between one standard deviation below the mean and one standard deviation above the mean; about 95 per cent of the values in the distribution are between two standard deviations below the mean and two standard deviations above the mean; and about 99 per cent of the values in the distribution are between three standard deviations below the mean and three standard deviations above the mean.

When a normal distribution has a mean of zero and a standard deviation of one, it is called a standard normal distribution. A normal distribution can be changed to a

Interval	% of total area under the normal curve
One standard deviation above and below the expected value	68.27
Two standard deviations above and below the mean expected value	95.45
Three standard deviations above and below the expected value	99.73

Figure 7B.2. Areas under a normal curve

standard form by using the Z-score transformation:

$$Z = \frac{x_i - E(x)}{\sigma(x)}$$

The table of areas for the standard normal probability distribution (SNPD) can be used to find an area below the curve (see Figure 7B.2).

Example 7B.1 Using the table of areas for the standard normal probability distribution

Consider the investment project B presented in Example 7.3. Suppose we wish to determine the probability that the project's expected net present value will be greater than £1,503.

Then we have (figure is rounded to two decimal points):

$$Z = \frac{\text{£}1{,}503 - \text{£}895}{\text{£}3{,}196} = 0.19$$

Using the table of areas for the standard normal probability distribution (see Appendix D at the end of the book), we see that the value of 0.19 is associated with a probability occurrence of 0.0753 (such a value can be found from the table at the intersection of row 0.1 and column 0.09). This indicates that the area between the expected net present value of £895 and a net present value of £1,503 is 7.53 per cent (note that if NPV = £895, then $Z = 0$ and if NPV = £1,503, then $Z = 0.19$). Since the entire area to the right of the mean is equal to 0.5, that part of the area to the right of $Z = 0.19$ is 0.4247 (that is, 0.5000 – 0.0753). Therefore, if we accept the project, there is a 42.47 per cent chance that it will provide an expected net present value that exceeds £1,503.

Problem Determine the probability that the expected value of the net present value of project B will be: (a) lower than £1,400 and (b) in the range £200 to £2,000.

References and bibliography

Ang, J.S. and Lewellen, W.C. (1981) Risk adjusted in capital investment projects evaluations, *Financial Management*, **11** Summer, 5–14.

Bar-Yosef, S. and Mesnick, R. (1977) On some definitional problems with the method of certainty equivalents, *Journal of Finance*, **32**, December, 1729–37.

Corr, A.V. (1983) *The Capital Expenditure Decision*. National Association of Accountants and the Society of Management Accountants of Canada, Canada.

Diacogiannis, P.G. and Lai, R. (1989) Survey on the investment and financing decisions of the companies in the USM, Warwick Paper in Management, No. 33, April.

Fairley, W.B. and Jacoby, H.D. (1975) Investment analysis using the probability distribution of the internal rate of return, *Management Science*, **21**, August, 1428–37.

Gitman, L.J. and Forrester, J.R., Jr. (1977) A survey of capital budgeting techniques used by major US firms, *Financial Management*, Autumn, 66–71.

Greer, W.R. (1974) Theory versus practice in risk analysis: an empirical study, *Accounting Review*, **49**, July, 496–505.

Hayes, R.H. (1975) Incorporating risk version into risk analysis, *Engineering Economist*, **20**, Winter, 99–121.

Hertz, D.P. (1964) Risk analysis in capital investment, *Harvard Business Review*, **42**, January–February, 95–106.

Hillier, F.S. (1963) The derivation of probabilistic information for the evaluation of risky investments, *Management Sciences*, **9**, April, 443–57.

Hodder, J.E. and Riggs, H.E. (1985) Pitfalls in evaluating risky projects, *Harvard Business Review*, **63**, January–February, 128–35.

Hoskins, C.J. (1993) Distinctions between risk and uncertainty, *Journal of Business Finance*, **5**, Spring, 10–12.

Keane S. (1976) The investment discount rate—in defense of the market rate of interest, *Accounting and Business Research*, **23**, Summer, 228–36.

Keeley, R. and Westerfield, R. (1972) A problem in probability distribution techniques for capital budgeting, *Journal of Finance*, **27**, June, 703–9.

Lizenberger, R.H. and Budd, A. (1970) Corporate investment criteria and the evaluation of risk assets, *Journal of Finance and Quantitative Analysis*, **5**, December, 395–420.

Mao, J. (1970) Survey of capital budgeting: theory and practice, *Journal of Finance*, **25**, May, 349–60.

Miller, E.M. (1978) Uncertainty-induced bias in capital budgeting, *Financial Management*, **7**, Autumn, 12–18.

Osteryoung, J.S., Scott, E. and Roberts, G.S. (1977) Selecting projects with the coefficients of valuation, *Financial Management*, **6**, Summer, 65–70.

Paine, N.R. (1964) Uncertainty and capital budgeting, *Accounting Review*, **39**, April, 330–2.

Pike, R.H. (1988) An empirical study of the adoption of sophisticated capital budgeting practices and decision making effectiveness, *Accounting and Business Research*, 341–52.

Robichek, A.A. (1975) Interpreting the results of risk analysis, *Journal of Finance*, **30**, December, 1384–6.

Robichek, A.A. and Myers, S.W. (1973) Conceptual problems in the use of risk-adjusted discount rates, *Journal of Finance*, **21**, December, 727–30.

Schall, L.D. and Geijsbeek, W.R., Jr. (1978) Survey and analysis of capital budgeting methods, *Journal of Finance*, **33**, March, 281–7.

Schall, L.D. and Sundem, G.L. (1980) Capital budgeting methods and risk: a further analysis, *Financial Management*, **9**, Spring, 7–11.

Schwendiman, C.J. and Pinches, G.E. (1975) An analysis of alternative measures of investment risk, *Journal of Finance*, **30**, March, 193–200.

8 Portfolio theory

This chapter includes:

- Security analysis
- Portfolio analysis
- Portfolio selection
- Modified investment analysis

The modern portfolio theory was developed by Harry Markowitz, presenting it in 1952 in an article entitled 'Portfolio Selection'. Markowitz was the first to show the important benefits from diversification that arise from combining individual securities into portfolios and to demonstrate that the portfolio decision problem of an investor is equivalent to the maximization of his or her expected utility. Markowitz's analysis includes three basic stages: security analysis, portfolio analysis and portfolio selection.

The objective of this chapter is twofold. First, it introduces the analysis related to the model of Markowitz. Second, it presents a modification of the portfolio selection model of Markowitz and explains how 1-2-3 can help in the analysis. Figure 8.1 shows the relation between the discipline of financial management and portfolio theory.

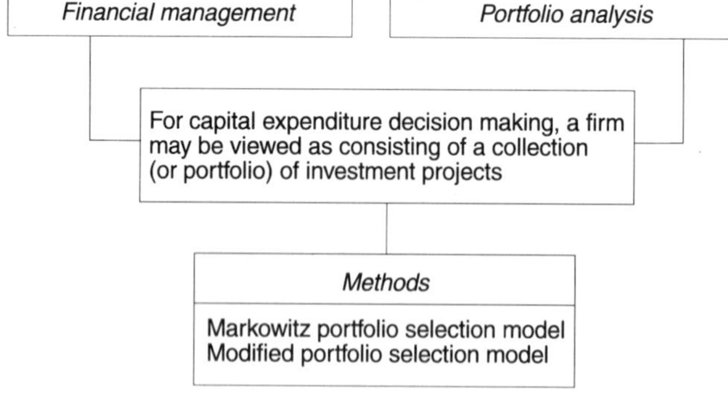

Figure 8.1. Relating financial management and portfolio theory

Basic concepts, definitions and examples

From the viewpoint of portfolio theory, a security is a general term for anything that has a monetary value. The following are examples of securities:

1. The ordinary shares, preference shares and debentures of Marks and Spencer plc.
2. The gilts issued by the UK Government.
3. Property such as land and buildings.

4 Antiques, coins and art objects.
5 Commodities such as silver and gold.

Different securities offer different risk–return characteristics as listed below.

High risk: options, Gold
Medium risk: ordinary shares, unit trusts
Low risk: government securities, property, e.g. land
Secure investments: banks and building society deposits, annuities

The analysis in this chapter will be limited to the consideration of ordinary shares, though the theory which will be presented would still apply to other types of securities (for example, property, commodities, and so on). Investors can combine two or more individual securities to form portfolios. One of the main incentives for forming portfolios is diversification, that is, a strategy of allocating funds in more than one security with the objective of reducing the risk of the investment.

Example 8.1 A portfolio of five individual securities

Figure 8.2 shows the securities of a portfolio.

Security	Stock Exchange industry classification
Allied Lyons	Brewery
Boots	Stores
GKN	Motor components
Marks and Spencer	Stores
National Westminster	Banks

Figure 8.2. A portfolio of ordinary shares

Portfolio theory, as developed by Markowitz (1952, 1959), is based on four assumptions:

1 Investors have a single investment horizon.
2 Investors view each individual security as being represented by a probability distribution of expected rates of return. The expected value of this distribution is a measure of the security's expected return and the variance (or standard deviation) of return provides a measure of its risk. Investors can also estimate the covariance between expected security rates of return.
3 A portfolio of individual securities is completely described by the expected portfolio return and variance of portfolio return.
4 Investors are single-period expected utility maximizers. The expected utility function of an investor is dependent upon the expected value and variance of his or her portfolio's expected rate of return. From this is follows that, for any given level of risk, investors prefer more return to less and, conversely, for any given level of return, investors prefer less risk to more.

With the aid of these assumptions, portfolio theory attempts to model portfolio selection under conditions of risk. More specifically, portfolio theory deals with the combination of individual securities into portfolios with quantitatively prescribed risk and return characteristics and the selection of a portfolio that maximizes the investor's single-period expected utility. There are three phases involved in formulating the model of Markowitz. The phases are:

- *Security analysis* This focuses on the estimation of the risk/return characteristics of individual securities as well as on the estimation of the covariability of all the securities under consideration (the estimation of the covariability can also constitute a major part of the portfolio analysis phase).
- *Portfolio analysis* This uses the estimated data from the previous phase and identifies the best combinations of individual securities that can be achieved through diversification.
- *Portfolio selection* This considers the best portfolio possibilities traced out by means of the portfolio analysis phase and selects the portfolio that maximizes the investor's expected utility.

Security analysis

Security analysis deals with the concepts of risk and return associated with individual securities and presents methods of quantifying them. The rest of the present section presents the following concepts:

- The single-period rate of return of a security.
- The expected return and the variance of rate of return.
- The covariance and correlation coefficient between rates of return.

The single-period rate of return of a security

The single-period rate of return of a security (in our case an ordinary share) may come from two sources: (a) capital gains (or losses), that is, profits (or losses) caused by a change in the price of the security from one period to the next; and (b) income from dividends received during the specified period. Figure 8.3 summarizes the concept of the rate of return of an ordinary share (or simply share).

Definition The single-period rate of return of a share is the rate of profit (or loss) realized by holding the share over the specified period.

Calculation The single-period rate of return of a share is calculated by summing the percentage price appreciation/depreciation and the percentage cash return (or dividend yield) on the share during the specified period. Mathematically, the single-period rate of return is given by:

Single-period rate of return on a share	=	Percentage price appreciation/ depreciation	+	Percentage cash return (or dividend yield) on the share

$$R_{it} = \frac{P_{it} - P_{it-1}}{P_{it-1}} + \frac{D_{it}}{P_{it-1}}$$

where

P_{it-1} = the price of share i at the end of the period $t-1$.

P_{it} = the price of share i at the end of period t.

D_{it} = the dividends per share (if any) of firm i from the end of period $t-1$ to the end of period t.

Interpretation The rate of return of a share shows the percentage increase (or decrease) in its owner's wealth associated with holding the share over a specified period of time.

Figure 8.3. A summary of the rate of return's concept

The mathematical representation of the single-period rate of return shown in Figure 8.3 can be used to measure both historical and future expected rates of return. When we consider future expected rates of return, we use the expected price of the share at the end of the given single period (for example, a month) and the dividends expected over that given single period. The equation presented in Figure 8.3 measures security return over any single time period, such as a year, a month, or a week.

In the case where there is no divided payment, the dividend yield equals zero. If the sum of the security's price at the end of a period plus the dividend payment received during that period is greater (less) than the security's value at the beginning of the period, then it results in a positive (negative) rate of return. If the sum of the security's price at the end of a period plus the dividend payment received during that period equals the security's value at the beginning of the period, then it results in a zero rate of return.

Example 8.2 Calculating the expected rate of return associated with a share

Suppose that each share of GD Stores plc is currently selling at £2.50 and the firm expects to pay cash dividends of £0.12 per share during the next month. If the expected price at the end of the next month is £2.70, the rate of return is calculated, by using the equation presented in Figure 8.3, as follows:

$$R_{it} = \frac{£2.70 - £2.50}{£2.50} + \frac{£0.12}{£2.50} = 12.80 \text{ per cent}$$

Therefore, the rate of return that investors anticipate to receive is 12.80 per cent.

The rate of return of this share is uncertain, since the expected sale price and the expected dividends per share are uncertain. Figure 8.4 shows a two-variable sensitivity analysis of the rate of return with respect to changes in sale price and expected dividends per share. The 'input cell 1' is cell C5 and the 'input cell 2' is cell C6. The results reveal that the rate of return increases as both sale price and dividends per share increase.

	A	B	C	D	E	F	G
1	SENSITIVITY OF RATE OF RETURN TO CHANGES IN SALE PRICE & DIVIDENDS						
2	==						
3							
4	Current Price		£2.50				
5	Expected Price		£2.70				
6	Expected Dividend		£0.12				
7			---------				
8	Rate of Return		12.8%				
9							
10		+C8	0.11	0.12	0.13	0.14	0.15
11		2.55	6.4%	6.8%	7.2%	7.6%	8.0%
12		2.60	8.4%	8.8%	9.2%	9.6%	10.0%
13		2.65	10.4%	10.8%	11.2%	11.6%	12.0%
14		2.70	12.4%	12.8%	13.2%	13.6%	14.0%
15		2.75	14.4%	14.8%	15.2%	15.6%	16.0%
16		2.80	16.4%	16.8%	17.2%	17.6%	18.0%
17		2.85	18.4%	18.8%	19.2%	19.6%	20.0%

Figure 8.4. Examining the effect of changes in sale price and expected dividends per share on the rate of return

The sensitivity table's results are depicted in Figure 8.5.

Problem Create the worksheet shown in Figure 8.4.

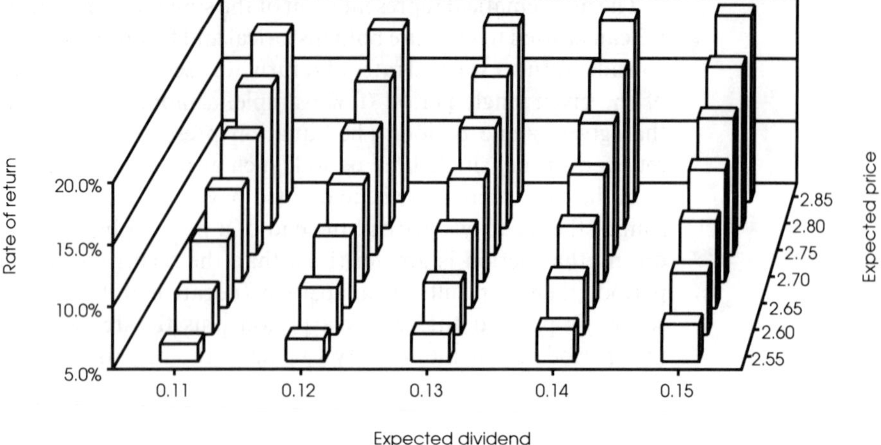

Figure 8.5. Graphing the results of the sensitivity of rate of return to changes in sale price and expected dividend

Example 8.3 Calculating the historical rate of return of Marks and Spencer plc for May 1987

Assume that at the end of April 1987 an investor purchased a share of Marks and Spencer for 215 pence. The share price of Marks and Spencer at the end of May 1987 was 233 pence. The dividend per share of the firm during May 1987 was 3.10 pence. Then the total return from holding the share of Marks and Spencer during May 1987 was equal to the percentage change in share price plus any dividends received, expressed as a proportion of the initial price:

$$R_{it} = \frac{233 - 215}{215} + \frac{3.10}{215}$$

$$= 8.37 \text{ per cent} + 1.44 \text{ per cent} = 9.81 \text{ per cent}$$

This indicates that our investor earned a 9.81 pence for every pound invested in this one-month investment. Stated differently, his or her wealth would increase by 9.81 per cent or 21.1 pence per share purchased (ignoring transaction costs).

If the investor did not sell the share of Marks and Spencer at the end of May 1987, then what would be the rate of return during that month? It would again by 9.81 per cent (Appendix 8A calculates the Marks and Spencer's share rate of return over the period January 1985 to December 1988).

Problem Create a worksheet which calculates the rate of return from holding a share of Marks and Spencer during May 1987.

The price of the share at the end of a specified period and the cash dividends per share received during that period must be adjusted for cases such as stock splits and stock dividends.

Example 8.4 Calculating the rate of return of a share after adjusting for a stock split (or scrip issue) and a stock dividend

Figure 8.6 presents monthly prices and dividends on a share of LA Supermarket plc (each price occurred approximately at the end of the month). On 30 June 1988, the shareholders of the firm received three shares for each share held. In

November 1988, the firm declared a 4 per cent stock dividend (that is, for every 25 shares owned, a shareholder would receive an additional share). In this case, the following adjustments are made:

Prices and dividends per share before the stock split should be reduced by one-third.
Prices after the stock split but before the stock dividend should be reduced by 1/(1 + 0.04).
Dividends per share before the stock split should be reduced by 1/(1 + 0.04) in addition to the previous reduction of one-third.
Dividends per share after the stock split but before the stock dividend should be reduced by 1/(1 + 0.04).

On 31 May 1988, the share price was £17.50. Therefore, the adjusted share price would be

$$\frac{£17.50}{3}\frac{1}{(1+0.04)} = £5.609$$

The adjusted dividend per share, for June 1988, is calculated as follows:

$$\frac{£0.015}{3}\frac{1}{(1+0.04)} = £0.0048$$

The adjusted share price, for 31 July 1988, is computed as follows:

$$\frac{£6.80}{(1+0.04)} = £6.538$$

Lastly, the adjusted dividend per share, for November 1988 is £0.0173 (that is, £0.018/(1 + 0.04)).

	A	B	C	D	E	F	G
1	RATE OF RETURN WHEN A STOCK-SPLIT AND A STOCK DIVIDEND OCCURRED						
2							
3				Stock Split &	Adjusted	Adjusted	Rate of
4	Month	Price	Dividend	Stock Dividend	Price	Dividends	Return
5		(£)	(£)		(£)	(£)	
6							
7	May	17.50	0.000		5.609	0.0000	
8	Jun	19.50	0.015	3.00	6.250	0.0048	11.51%
9	Jul	6.80	0.000		6.538	0.0000	4.62%
10	Aug	7.10	0.000		6.827	0.0000	4.41%
11	Sep	7.50	0.000		7.212	0.0000	5.63%
12	Oct	7.80	0.000		7.500	0.0000	4.00%
13	Nov	7.88	0.018	4.00%	7.577	0.0173	1.26%
14	Dec	7.85	0.000		7.850	0.0000	3.60%
15							

Figure 8.6. Calculating the rate of return after adjusting for stock split and stock dividend

Problems

1 Create the worksheet shown in Figure 8.6 using the appropriate formulae.

2 If the stock slip was 4 to 1 and the stock dividend was 5 per cent, calculate the monthly rates of return for LA Supermarket plc.

Measurement of expected return and risk of an individual security

In reality, the rate of return from an ordinary share is not known in advance, because at the beginning of the investment period neither the end-of-period share price nor the amount of dividend payment per share is known with certainty. Instead we can describe it with the help of a probability distribution, that is, a list of probabilistic rates of return and the (subjective) probability associated with each rate of return (the probability associated with a possible rate of return is the chance that such a rate of return will occur).

Example 8.5 A probability distribution for rates of return

The rate of return next month on a share of KL Supermarket plc is unknown now and it can only be described by a probability distribution of possible values. Assume that there is a 0.30 probability for a future possible return of 10 per cent, a 0.40 probability for a future possible return of 12 per cent and a 0.30 probability for a future possible return of 18 per cent. Figure 8.7 presents the probability distribution of rates of return for KL Supermarket.

Figure 8.7. A probability distribution of rates of return

Probabilistic rate of return (%)	Probability	Interpretation
10	0.30	30% chance exists for a future return of 10%
12	0.40	40% chance exists for a future return of 12%
18	0.30	30% chance exists for a future return of 18%
	1.00	All probabilistic outcomes are considered

We assume that the expected rate of return and the standard deviation of rate of return are the only two parameters used to distinguish one probability distribution of rates of return from another. These two parameters are used to summarize information contained in probability distributions. Figure 8.8 summarizes the concept of the expected rate of return.

Figure 8.8. A summary of the expected rate of return's concept

Definition The expected rate of return (or expected return) of a security is the weighted average of all possible rates of return, with each rate of return weighted by its respective probability.

Calculation The expected rate of return of a security is calculated by multiplying each possible rate of return by its respective probability and then summing up all the products. Mathematically, the expected rate of return of a security can be expressed as follows:

$$E(R_i) = \sum_{k=1}^{N} p_k R_{ik}$$

where R_{ik} is the kth possible outcome for the rate of return on security i, p_k is the probability of getting the rate of return R_{ik} and N is the total number of possible rates of return.

Interpretation The expected rate of return measures an expected outcome and it describes the most probable outcome from the distribution of rates of return.

Example 8.6 Calculating the expected (or *ex-ante*) returns on two shares

Using the data given in Example 8.5, we can calculate the expected return of all the probable rates of return as follows (we label a share of KL Supermarket as security 1):

$$E(R_1) = (0.30) \times (0.10) + (0.40) \times (0.12) + (0.30) \times (0.18)$$
$$= 13.20 \text{ per cent}$$

Therefore, on average, the share is expected to yield a return of 13.20 per cent. Investors purchasing that share now will not actually earn 13.20 per cent on the share next month. They would expect to earn only an average return of 13.20 per cent if they invested repeatedly in the share. Thus, the expected return of 13.20 per cent represents our best statistical guess of the expected return which can be used to summarize one part of information about the distribution of rates of return.

For the sake of comparison, we consider another security (call it security 2) whose next month rate of return is described now in terms of the following probability distribution. There is a 0.30 probability for a future possible return of 11 per cent, a 0.40 probability for a future possible return of 5 per cent and a 0.30 probability for a future possible return of 13 per cent. Following a similar procedure, we can find the expected return of security 2 to be 9.20 per cent. By comparing the two expected returns we can expect, on average, a higher return from security 1 than from security 2.

Problem Create a worksheet illustrating the calculation of the expected returns on security 1 and security 2.

Example 8.7 Calculating the historical (or *ex-post*) mean returns on two shares

The equation presented in Figure 8.8 can be adapted to calculate the mean return (or average return) of a series of historical rates of return. The monthly rates of return of Marks and Spencer, covering a period of six months starting from May 1987, are shown in Figure 8.9.

Month	Rate of return (%)	
	Marks & Spencer	National Westminster
May	9.81	6.30
June	8.58	9.13
July	−4.74	6.72
Aug.	7.05	−0.14
Sept.	−8.91	3.14
Oct.	1.70	1.33

Figure 8.9. Rates of return of Marks and Spencer and National Westminster Bank (May–October 1987)

The calculation of the mean return assumes equal probability for each rate of return and that the distribution of rates of return does not change over time. In this instance, the probability is equal to one-sixth, and the mean return of Marks and Spencer's share is computed as the average value of the monthly rates of return:

$$r_i = \tfrac{1}{6}(0.0981 + 0.0858 - 0.0474 + 0.0705 - 0.0891 + 0.0170)$$
$$= 2.25 \text{ per cent}$$

Similarly, the mean return of the share of National Westminster is 4.41 per cent.

Problem Create a worksheet illustrating the calculation of the mean returns on the shares of Marks and Spencer and National Westminster Bank over the period May 1987 to October 1987.

It should be noted that the expected return summarizes only one of the characteristics of the probability distribution of rates of return—the central location. It does not, however, provide any information about the spread of the distribution. Figure 8.10 summarizes the concept of the variance of rate of return.

Definition The variance of rate of return on a security is defined as the weighted average squared deviations of possible rates of return from their expected rate of return, with the probabilities of the distribution of rates of return being used as weights.

Calculation The variance of rate of return on a security is calculated by multiplying the squared deviations of each possible rate of return from the expected rate of return by the probability associated with that rate of return and then summing up all the products. The formula for the variance of the rate of return on a security is

$$\sigma^2(R_i) = \sigma_i^2 = \sum_{k=1}^{N} p_k(R_{ik} - E(R_i))^2$$

where R_{ik} is the kth possible outcome for the rate of return on security i, p_k is the probability of getting the rate of return R_{ik} and N is the total number of possible rates of return.

Interpretation The variance of a security's rates of return represents one measure of the spread of the distribution of rates of return relative to their expected return. In other words, it measures the average variability in the possible rates of return around their expected return. The greater the variance of return, the larger the chance that the actual return will be substantially different from the expected return and, as a consequence, the greater the risk of the security (other things remain unchanged).

Figure 8.10. A summary of the variance of rate of return's concept

Example 8.8 Calculating the variance of rate of return on a security

Based on the data in Example 8.5 and using the equation shown in Figure 8.10, the variance of rate of return turns out to be 0.00106

$$\sigma^2(R_1) = 0.3(0.10 - 0.132)^2 + 0.4(0.12 - 0.132)^2 + 0.3(0.18 - 0.132)^2$$

$$= 0.00106$$

Next, for the second probability distribution introduced in Example 8.6, with an expected value of 9.20 per cent, the variance of rates of return is 0.00124. These results show that the rates of return of security 2 are more variable than the rates of return of security 1.

We may expect to earn from security 1 a 13.20 per cent return. However, we may earn a 14 per cent return or a 12.60 per cent return. Since security 1 has lower risk than security 2, we will be closer to our estimate of 13.20 per cent than we will be in the higher risk security 2.

Knowing that the variance of security 1 (see above) is 0.00106 , its standard deviation of rate of return is equal to the square root of the variance, that is 3.256 per cent. Similarly, the standard deviation of rates of return of security 2 is 3.521 per cent.

Problem Create a worksheet illustrating the calculation of the variances and standard deviations of rates of return on security 1 and security 2.

The standard deviation of rate of return is measured in the same units as the returns themselves; thus, it is more intuitively appealing than the variance. For example, if the rates of return are measured in per cent, the variance is measured in per cent squared, which has no meaning.

Example 8.9 Calculating the historical variance of rates of return on two shares

Here we use the data presented in Example 8.7. The calculation of the (sample) variance of rates of return is shown below:

$$\begin{aligned} s^2(R_i) &= \tfrac{1}{5}(0.0981 - 0.0225)^2 + \tfrac{1}{5}(0.0858 - 0.0225)^2 \\ &\quad + \tfrac{1}{5}(-0.0474 - 0.0225)^2 + \tfrac{1}{5}(0.0705 - 0.0225)^2 \\ &\quad + \tfrac{1}{5}(-0.0891 - 0.0225)^2 + \tfrac{1}{5}(0.0170 - 0.0225)^2 \\ &= 0.0064 \end{aligned}$$

Dividing by 5 gives an unbiased estimate for the variance. We are loosing one degree of freedom since the sum of squared deviations is taken around the sample mean and not around the unknown population parameter.

Similarly, the (sample) variance of rate of return on the share of National Westminster is 0.0013. Consequently, the rate of return provided by the share of Marks and Spencer over the period May 1987 to October 1987 was more risky than that provided by the share of National Westminster over the same period.

Problem Create a worksheet illustrating the calculation of the variances of rates of return on the share of Marks and Spencer and share of National Westminster (use monthly observations over the period May 1987 to October 1987).

Example 8.10 Calculating the coefficient of variation

The coefficient of variation of a probability distribution of rates of return takes into account both security risk and return and can also be used to compare the risk/return characteristics of securities. Note that the coefficient of variation is useful when it provides more information than the standard deviation. This is not the case for securities 1 and 2 (see Examples 8.6 and 8.9), since security 2 provides a lower expected return than security 1 and it is also more risky than security 1.

However, if we consider another security, call it 4, with an expected return of 15.80 per cent and a standard deviation of rate of return of 5.618 per cent, then we have:

$$CV_1 = \frac{3.256\%}{13.20\%} = 0.247 \qquad CV_4 = \frac{5.618\%}{15.80\%} = 0.356$$

Therefore, security 4 is more risky than security 1.

Covariance of rates of return

The expected return and the variance of rate of return summarize information about the probability distribution associated with a single security. However, these statistics do not provide any information about the interrelationships between the rates of return on securities. In order to discover the existence of a relationship between the fluctuations of rates of return on two securities, we use the statistical measure of covariance (see Figure 8.11).

Definition The covariance between the rates of return on any two securities is defined as the weighted average of the products of two different deviations: the deviations of the rates of return on the first security from its expected return and the deviation of the rates of return of the second security from its expected return. The weights are being determined by the joint probability of observing the rates of return on the two securities.

Calculation The covariance between the rates of return on any two securities is calculated by multiplying each product of pair deviations by the joint probability associated with each pair of rates of return and then summing up all the triple products. Algebraically, the covariance between the rates of return on two securities may be defined as follows:

$$\textbf{Cov}\,(R_i, R_j) = \sigma_{ij} = \sum_{k=1}^{N} p_k(R_{ik} - E(R_i))(R_{jk} - E(R_j))$$

where p_k is the joint probability of observing the rates of return R_{ik} and R_{jk} and N is the total number of possible rates of return.

Interpretation The covariance between the rates of return on any two securities is an absolute statistical measure of the degree of association between the rates of return and reflects the dispersion of the rates of return about their respective expected values.

- A positive value for covariance indicates that the securities' rates of return tend to move together; when one security produces a rate of return above its expected return, the other security is likely to do so as well.
- A negative value for covariance indicates that the securities' rates of return tend to move in opposite directions; when one security produces a rate of return above its expected return, the other security is likely to produce a rate of return below its expected return.
- A zero value for covariance indicates that there is no relationship between the rates of return for the two securities

The covariance measures the extent to which the security rates of return are jointly responsive to the same underlying events (for example, two firms in the electronics industry can respond similarly to an increase in consumer spending on colour televisions).

Figure 8.11. A summary of the covariance concept

The scale of measurement for the covariance is exactly the same as that of the variance. If the rates of return on two securities are measured in per cents then the covariance is expressed in per cents squared, which is meaningless.

Example 8.11 Calculating the covariance between the rates of return on two shares

Assume the data given in Examples 8.5 and 8.6. Invoking the equation presented in Figure 8.11, the covariance of rates of return is shown below:

$$\begin{aligned}\text{Cov}\,(R_1, R_2) &= 0.3(0.10 - 0.132)(0.11 - 0.092) + 0.4(0.12 - 0.132)\\ &\quad (0.05 - 0.092) + 0.3(0.18 - 0.132)(0.13 - 0.092)\\ &= 0.00058\end{aligned}$$

This positive covariance indicates that the rates of return tend to move in the same direction.

Even if some of the probable rates of return on one security are above (below) its expected return and the corresponding probable rates of return on the other security are below (above) its expected return, it is still possible to observe a positive covariance. This would occur if the positive products exceeded the negative products.

Problem Create a worksheet illustrating the calculation of the covariance between the rates of return of securities 1 and 2.

Example 8.12 Calculating an historical covariance of rates of return

The covariance between the rates of return on the shares of Marks and Spencer and National Westminster is calculated as follows (mean returns are given in Example 8.7):

$$
\begin{aligned}
s(R_i, R_j) &= \tfrac{1}{5}(0.0981 - 0.0225)(0.0630 - 0.0441) \\
&\quad + \tfrac{1}{5}(0.0858 - 0.0225)(0.0913 - 0.0441) \\
&\quad + \tfrac{1}{5}(-0.0474 - 0.0225)(0.0672 - 0.0441) \\
&\quad + \tfrac{1}{5}(0.0705 - 0.0225)(0.00140 - 0.0441) \\
&\quad + \tfrac{1}{5}(-0.0891 - 0.0225)(0.0314 - 0.0441) \\
&\quad + \tfrac{1}{5}(0.0170 - 0.0225)(0.0133 - 0.0441) \\
&= 0.0004
\end{aligned}
$$

When the covariance of historical returns is positive it does not necessarily mean that all pairs of rates of return contain rates with the same sign. For example, in August 1987, the rate of return of Marks and Spencer was 0.0705, whereas National Westminster's rate of return was −0.0014. The positive covariance indicates that, on average, the rates of return on Marks and Spencer and National Westminster move together.

Problem Create a worksheet illustrating the calculation of the covariance of rates of return associated with the shares of Marks and Spencer and National Westminster over the period May 1987 to October 1987

The correlation coefficient

The covariance of rates of return shows only the direction of the association between the two variables. It does not provide any information about the power of the relationship between the two variables. The correlation coefficient is a better descriptor than covariance of the relationship between the rates of return on securities (see Figure 8.12).

A correlation coefficient falls within the range −1 to +1. The closer we approach the value of +1 (or −1), the stronger is the positive (or negative) relationship between the security rates of return. The covariance of rates of return on any two securities and the product of standard deviations of the security rates of return are measured in the

Definition The correlation coefficient between the rates of return on two securities is simply the covariance between the rates of return divided by the product of the two standard deviations of rates of return.

Calculation The correlation coefficient between the rates of return on security i and the rates of return on security j is calculated with the aid of the following formula:

$$\mathrm{CC}(R_i, R_j) = \frac{\mathrm{Cov}\,(R_i, R_j)}{\sigma(R_i)\sigma(R_j)}$$

Interpretation The correlation coefficient between the rates of return on any two securities is a relative statistical measure of the direction and power of the relationship between their rates of return. The sign of the correlation coefficient indicates the direction of the relationship between the rates of return and the size of the coefficient indicates the strength of the relationship between the rates of return.

Figure 8.12. A summary of the correlation coefficient's concept

same units. Therefore, the correlation coefficient becomes a pure number, independent of any change in the units of measurement for the covariance and the product of standard deviations.

Example 8.13 Calculating the correlation coefficient of rates of return

In this example we use the data given in Examples 8.11 and 8.8. The standard deviation of rate of return for security 1 is 3.256 per cent and the standard deviation of rate of return for security 2 is 3.521 per cent. Therefore, the correlation coefficient is

$$\mathrm{CC}(R_1, R_2) = \frac{0.00058}{(0.03256)(0.03521)} = 0.506$$

A correlation coefficient of 0.506 means that the rates of return on these two shares vary in a moderate fashion with each other.

Problem Create a worksheet illustrating the calculation of the correlation coefficient between the rates of return of securities 1 and 2.

Example 8.14 Calculating a historical correlation coefficient of rates of return

The correlation coefficient between the rates of return on the shares of Marks and Spencer and National Westminster is calculated as follows:

$$\mathrm{CC}(R_i R_j) = \frac{0.0004}{(0.08)(0.0361)} = 0.139$$

This value indicates that the rates of return do not vary closely with each other.

Problem Create a worksheet illustrating the calculation of the correlation coefficient between the rates of return shown in this example.

Examples 8.7, 8.9, 8.12 and 8.14 calculate mean values, variances, covariance and correlation coefficient from historical data. Historical data may be helpful in making future projections, but remember that there is no evidence revealing that historical rates of return are repeated. Figure 8.13 summarizes the risk and return characteristics for individual securities as well as two concepts which serve as quantitative measures of the association between the rates of return on two securities.

Expected return Measures the most probable outcome from the distribution of rates of return. The scale of measurement of the expected return is the same as the original data of rates of return.
Variance of rate of return Measures the variability of a probability distribution of rates of return around its expected return. The scale of measurement of the variance is the square of the scale of measurement of the original data.
Standard deviation of rate of return Measures the variability of a probability distribution of rates of return around its expected return. The standard deviation is expressed in the same units as the rates of return themselves.
Coefficient of variation Measures relative variation in rates of return. The coefficient of variation is independent of the units used in measuring rates of return.
Covariance between rates of return Measures the direction of the dependence between rates of return. The scale of measurement of the covariance is the square of the scale of measurement of the original data.
Correlation coefficient Measures the direction and the strength of the association between rates of return. The correlation coefficient is independent of the units used in measuring rates of return.

Figure 8.13. Summarizing various concepts used in security analysis

Portfolio analysis

Allocating funds to a single security can be an extremely risky investment. For example, consider an investor who purchased, during 1979, a large number of shares in Airfix Industries Ltd. During 1980, the price of the firm's shares dramatically declined and in January 1981 the firm was liquidated (despite the existence of a 'healthy' overall market). Investors can largely eliminate these unhappy results by investing in portfolios. The primary reason for investing in portfolios is diversification, that is, the allocation of funds to a variety of securities in order to reduce risk. Having discussed the characteristics of individual securities we can now begin to analyse investments in portfolios. Specifically, the following concepts are introduced:

- Portfolio rate of return.
- Calculating the risk/return characteristics of portfolios.
- Efficient frontier.

These concepts are initially discussed by considering a portfolio of two securities, and then the results are extended to portfolios of many securities.

Portfolio rate of return

Consider a portfolio of two securities, labelled 1 and 2. We assume that we wish to invest £2,000, and we place £1,000 of it in security 1 and £1,000 in security 2. In this case, we can calculate the proportion of the money that is invested in each of the securities. For example, the investment proportion (or the portfolio weight) related to security 1 is one-half (0.5 or 50 per cent) and it can be calculated by dividing £1,000 by the total amount we have invested in both securities.

The rate of return on a two-security portfolio is a weighted average of the rates of return on the two individual securities in the portfolio, where the weight associated to a security is the proportion of portfolio funds invested in the security.

Example 8.15 Calculating the rate of return on a two-security portfolio

Consider a portfolio consisting of security 1 and security 2. We expect that these securities will produce rates of return of 12.4 per cent and 10 per cent, respectively, at the end of one period. If an investor allocates 50 per cent of his or her investable funds to the first security (and 50 per cent to the second), the portfolio's (expected) rate of return over the specified period is:

$$(0.5)(12.4\%) + (0.5)(10.0\%) = 0.1120 \text{ or } 11.20 \text{ per cent}$$

Assume now that 60 per cent of the funds are committed to security 1 and 40 per cent are committed to security 2. In this case, the (expected) rate of return is calculated as follows:

$$(0.6)(12.40\%) + (0.4)(10.0\%) = 11.44 \text{ per cent}$$

How can we define a portfolio? If we simply say a portfolio is a collection of securities, then we cannot distinguish between two portfolios created by combining the same securities. A portfolio can be defined by the proportions invested in its securities. For example, the first portfolio introduced in the present example is defined by the proportions 0.5 and 0.5, whereas the second one is defined by the proportions 0.6 and 0.4.

The investment proportions defining our portfolios must sum to unity. Why? This happens because all the funds under consideration (that is, £2,000) are invested in the first security or the second one to form portfolios. If we assume that the investment proportions can be positive or zero, then they can take values in the range zero to unity, provided that the sum of the proportions equals unity.

We can express the proportion invested in security 2 in terms of the proportion invested in security 1, since the sum of the two investment proportions equals one. Thus, Figure 8.14 shows a sensitivity analysis of the rate of return with respect to the proportion invested in security 1. Cell E6 contains the result of the formula 1 – E5, while cell E8 contains the result of the formula `+E5*E3+E6*E4`. The 'input cell 1' is cell E5. Note that the sensitivity results show the rate of return of 11 different investments.

Problem Create the results presented in Figure 8.14.

```
---------------------------------------------------------------------
        A          B          C          D          E          F          G
 1 SENSITIVITY OF PORTFOLIO RETURNS TO CHANGES IN INVESTMENT PROPORTIONS
 2 ==================================================================
 3 Rate of Return for Security 1                  12.4%
 4 Rate of Return for Security 2                  10.0%
 5 Proportion Invested in Security 1               0.6
 6 Proportion Invested in Security 2               0.4
 7                                             ---------
 8                                                11.44%
 9
10                              +E8
11                         0          10.0%
12                       0.1          10.2%
13                       0.2          10.5%
14                       0.3          10.7%
15                       0.4          11.0%
16                       0.5          11.2%
17                       0.6          11.4%
18                       0.7          11.7%
19                       0.8          11.9%
20                       0.9          12.2%
21                         1          12.4%
---------------------------------------------------------------------
```

Figure 8.14 Examining the effect of changes in investment proportions on the rate of return of a two-security portfolio

Calculating the risk return characteristics of a two-security portfolio

The rate of return of a portfolio can be described by a probability distribution. We assume that such a probability distribution can only be characterized by its expected return and the variance of rates of return. The expected return of a two-security portfolio is simply a weighted average of the expected rates of return of the securities which are included in the portfolio, where we are weighting by the proportions of portfolio funds invested in the securities.

Example 8.16 Calculating the expected return of a two-security portfolio

Consider an investor who allocates 60 per cent of his money to security 1 and 40 per cent to security 2. Security 1 is expected to earn a return of 13.20 per cent and security 2 is expected to produce a return of 9.20 per cent. Overall, the investor anticipates earning an expected return on his or her portfolio of 11.60 per cent:

$$E(R_p) = (0.60)(13.20\%) + (0.40)(9.20\%)$$
$$= 11.60 \text{ per cent}$$

Problem Create a worksheet presenting the calculation of the expected return of the two-security portfolio discussed in Example 8.16.

Example 8.17 Calculating the historical mean return of a two-security portfolio

A share in Marks and Spencer produced a mean return of 2.25 per cent over the period May 1987 to October 1987. Over the same period, the mean return of National Westminster was 4.41 per cent. In this instance, the mean return on a portfolio of 50 percent Marks and Spencer and 50 per cent National Westminster was

$$E(R_p) = (0.50)(2.25\%) + (0.50)(4.41\%)$$
$$= 3.33 \text{ per cent}$$

The contribution of each security to the portfolio's expected return is:

Security 1 $\rightarrow$ (0.50)(2.25%) = the mean return on Marks and Spencer weighted by the proportion of the portfolio's total value invested in Marks and Spencer

Security 2 $\rightarrow$ (0.50)(4.41%) = the mean return on National Westminster weighted by the proportion of the portfolio's total value invested in National Westminster.

Consequently, the mean returns of individual securities should be analysed in relation to how they influence the mean return of the portfolio created by combining them.

Problem Create a worksheet presenting the calculation of the mean return of the two-security portfolio discussed in Example 8.17.

The risk of a portfolio is defined as the variability associated with the portfolio's probable rates of return. The risk of a portfolio can be measured by the variance (or the standard deviation) of its rate of return.

Example 8.18 Calculating the variance of rate of return on a two-security portfolio

The standard deviation of rate of return on security 1 is 0.03256 and the standard deviation of the rate of return on security 2 is 0.03521. The covariance between the security rates of return is 0.00058. Suppose that 60 percent of portfolio funds are invested in security 1 and 40 per cent in security 2. The variance of rate of return on the 60 : 40 portfolio is (figures are rounded):

$$\sigma^2(R_p) = (0.60)^2(0.03256)^2 + (0.40)^2(0.03521)^2 + 2(0.60)(0.40)(0.00058)$$
$$= 0.00086$$

From the equation presented in Figure 8.12 we see that the covariance between the rates of return of two securities can be expressed as a product of the correlation coefficient and the standard deviations of the two securities. The correlation coefficient between the rates of return is 0.506 (see Example 8.13). Thus, the variance of rate of return for the portfolio under consideration can also be calculated as follows:

$$\sigma^2(R_p) = (0.60)^2(0.03256)^2 + (0.40)^2(0.03521)^2$$
$$+ 2(0.60)(0.40)(0.03256)(0.03521)(0.506)$$
$$= 0.00086$$

The portfolio standard deviation of rate of return is 0.02930. The standard deviation of the portfolio made up of securities 1 and 2 is lower than the standard deviation of each individual security contained in the portfolio. This reveals the reduction of risk through the effects of diversification. Moreover, the portfolio risk is lower than 0.03389, the average of the risks of the individual securities included in the portfolio.

Problem Use the data provided in this example, and create a worksheet calculating the variance of rate of return on a two-security portfolio defined by the proportions 0.6 and 0.4.

The risk of a two-security portfolio depends upon the correlation coefficient between the security rates of return. According to Markowitz, the benefits from diversification can be achieved by combining securities with less than perfectly positively correlated rates of return so that the portfolio risk becomes significantly lower than the risks of the securities that are included in the portfolio. The important point to note is that the lower the correlation between the security rates of return, the lower will be the risk of the portfolio containing them. A numerical example may help better understanding of this point.

Example 8.19 The benefits from Markowitz diversification

This example demonstrates the benefits of combining securities with low correlation. From Figure 8.15 we see that the rates of return on securities 1 and 3 are perfectly positively correlated. In this case, the portfolio risk is not reduced through diversification, since the rates of return on one security are not offset by the rates of return on the other security. Note that the portfolio risk of 0.03256 is exactly the same as the risk of each of the securities contained in the portfolio. With perfectly positively correlated rates of return the risk of the portfolio is simply equal to the average of the risks of the individual securities making up the portfolio. The results presented in Figure 8.16 indicate that the securities 1 and 4 are negatively correlated with respect to their probable rates of return. The risk of the portfolio combining securities 1 and 4 is 0.00015 which is lower than the risk of either security 1 or security 4 separately. In this instance, the portfolio risk (that is, 0.00015) is less than the average risks on the component securities (that is $(0.03256 + 0.05621)/2 = 0.04439$).

The situation presented in Figure 8.17 reveals that the rates of return on securities 1 and 5 are perfectly negatively correlated. The risk of the portfolio

```
-----------------------------------------------------------------------------
        A          B          C          D          E          F          G
 1 --------------------------------------------------------------------------
 2                               Rate of Return for:
 3             Probability Security 1 Security 3
 4 --------------------------------------------------------------------------
 5                     0.3       0.10       0.09
 6                     0.4       0.12       0.11
 7                     0.3       0.18       0.17
 8 --------------------------------------------------------------------------
 9 Probable Returns for:  Probable Square Deviations Covar. Correlation
10 Security 1 Security 3 Security 1  Security 3              Coefficient
11 --------------------------------------------------------------------------
12  0.03000       0.02700  0.00031    0.00031          0.00031
13  0.04800       0.04400  0.00006    0.00006          0.00006
14  0.05400       0.05100  0.00069    0.00069          0.00069
15  ----------------------------------------          ---------
16  0.13200       0.12200  0.03256    0.03256          0.00106      1.000
17
18  Variance               0.00106
19  Standard Deviation     0.03256
-----------------------------------------------------------------------------
```

Figure 8.15. Portfolio variance when $CC(R_1,R_3) = 1.00$

```
-----------------------------------------------------------------------------
        A          B          C          D          E          F          G
41 --------------------------------------------------------------------------
42                               Rate of Return for:
43             Probability Security 1 Security 4
44 --------------------------------------------------------------------------
45                     0.3       0.10       0.24
46                     0.4       0.12       0.14
47                     0.3       0.18       0.10
48 --------------------------------------------------------------------------
49 Probable Returns for:  Probable Square Deviations Covar. Correlation
50 Security 1 Security 4 Security 1  Security 4              Coefficient
51 --------------------------------------------------------------------------
52  0.03000       0.07200  0.00031    0.00202         -0.00079
53  0.04800       0.05600  0.00006    0.00013          0.00009
54  0.05400       0.03000  0.00069    0.00101         -0.00084
55  ----------------------------------------          ---------
56  0.13200       0.15800  0.03256    0.05621         -0.00154     -0.841
57
58  Variance               0.00015
59  Standard Deviation     0.01217
-----------------------------------------------------------------------------
```

Figure 8.16. Portfolio variance when $CC(R_1,R_4) = -0.841$

```
-------------------------------------------------------------------------------
        A             B              C              D              E          F          G
61 ----------------------------------------------------------------------------
62                               Rate of Return for:
63              Probability Security 1 Security 5
64 ----------------------------------------------------------------------------
65                       0.3      0.100      0.180
66                       0.4      0.120      0.160
67                       0.3      0.180      0.100
68 ----------------------------------------------------------------------------
69 Probable Returns for:  Probable Square Deviations Covar. Correlation
70 Security 1 Security 5 Security 1  Security 5              Coefficient
71 ----------------------------------------------------------------------------
72  0.03000          0.05400  0.00031    0.00031          -0.00031
73  0.04800          0.06400  0.00006    0.00006          -0.00006
74  0.05400          0.03000  0.00069    0.00069          -0.00069
75  ------------------------------------------          ---------
76  0.13200          0.14800  0.03256    0.03256          -0.00106    -1.000
77
78  Variance                  0.00004
79  Standard Deviation        0.00651
-------------------------------------------------------------------------------
```

Figure 8.17. Portfolio variance when $CC(R_1, R_5) = -1.00$

constituting of securities 1 and 5 is just 0.00004. In this instance, the risk of 0.00004 is lower than 0.03256, the average of the risks of the individual securities comprising the portfolio. Note that, in practice, the rates of return are not perfectly correlated. Most shares in the market will tend to be positively correlated. On average, they tend to fall or rise together because they are affected to some extent by general economic and political factors. Consequently, diversification can help to reduce risk but it cannot completely eliminate it.

Example 8.20 Calculating the historical variance of rate of return on a two-security portfolio

Over the period May 1987 to October 1987, the variance of rate of return on a share of Marks and Spencer was 0.0064. Over the same period, the variance of rate of return on a share of National Westminster was 0.0013. The corresponding covariance between the rates of return was 0.0004. The variance of rate of return for a portfolio containing equal proportions of the two securities can be calculated as follows:

$$s^2(R_p) = (0.5)(0.5)(0.0064 + 0.0013) + 2(0.5)(0.5)(0.0004)$$
$$= 0.00213$$

What is the relationship between the risk of a portfolio and the risks of the securities composing that portfolio? Unlike portfolio expected returns, the risk of a portfolio (as measured by the variance or standard deviation) is not generally a weighted average of the variances (or standard deviations) of the individual securities in the portfolio. To understand why, let us express the variance of the two-security portfolio under consideration as follows:

$$s^2(R_p) = (0.50)[(0.50)(0.0064) + (0.50)(0.0004)]$$
$$+ (0.50)[(0.50)(0.0013) + (0.50)(0.0004)]$$
$$= 0.00213$$

Both terms in the previous expression are dependent on the covariance between the security rates of return. The contribution of each security to the portfolio risk is:

Security 1 $\rightarrow (0.50)[(0.50)(0.0064) + (0.50)(0.0004)] =$ The covariance between the rate of return on Marks and Spencer and the rate of return on the portfolio, weighted by the fraction of the portfolio's total value invested in Marks and Spencer.

Security 2 $\rightarrow (0.50)[(0.50)(0.0013) + (0.50)(0.0004)] =$ The covariance between the rate of return on National Westminster and the rate of return on the portfolio, weighted by the fraction of the portfolio's total value invested in National Westminster.

Therefore, investors holding portfolios should be concerned about the risk of each individual security in a portfolio rather than the risk of each individual security as measured by the standard deviation of rate of return.

Problem Use the data provided in this example, and create a worksheet calculating the variance of rate of return on a two-security portfolio defined by the proportions 0.5 and 0.5.

Efficient frontier

Portfolio analysis deals with the calculation of the efficient frontier. Under the mean/standard deviation framework, a portfolio is efficient if:

1. no other portfolio with the same expected return can have a lower standard deviation; and
2. no other portfolio with the same or lower standard deviation can have a higher expected return.

A portfolio that satisfies condition (1) is called a minimum standard deviation portfolio and the locus of these portfolios is called the minimum standard deviation portfolio set. The locus containing the set of efficient portfolios (conditions (1) and (2) above) is known as the efficient frontier. Portfolios lying along the efficient frontier dominate all other risk/return combinations lying to the right or below the efficient frontier.

Example 8.21 Calculating the mean/standard deviation efficient frontier using two individual securities

The expected return and the standard deviation of rate of return on a portfolio vary with the composition of the portfolio. Thus, the two-security efficient frontier can be calculated by using a series of different investment proportions of portfolio funds invested in securities 1 and 2 (see Examples 8.16 and 8.18).

Figure 8.18 computes the efficient frontier employing the 1-2-3's `/Data Table 1` command. Note that each of cells F9, F11, F12 and F13 contains the results of a formula. The 'input cell 1' is cell F8. The results are depicted in Figure 8.19 (portfolio standard deviation is shown on the horizontal axis and portfolio expected return is shown on the vertical axis). The efficient frontier is the positively sloped segment of the curve shown in Figure 8.19.

```
       A          B          C           D          E          F         G
 1 CALCULATING THE EFFICIENT FRONTIER
 2 ===================================
 3 Rate of Return for Security 1                           0.13200
 4 Rate of Return for Security 2                           0.09200
 5 Standard Deviation for Security 1                       0.03256
 6 Standard Deviation for Security 2                       0.03521
 7 Correlation Coefficient                                 0.50600
 8 Proportion Invested in Security 1                           0.6
 9 Proportion Invested in Security 2                           0.4
10                                                       ---------
11 Portfolio Expected Return                               0.11600
12 Portfolio Variance of Rate of Return                    0.00086
13 Portfolio Standard Deviation of Rate of Return          0.02930
14
15
16
17
18                     +F9       +F11       +F12       +F13
19               0     1.0    0.09200    0.00124    0.03521
20             0.1     0.9    0.09600    0.00112    0.03345
21             0.2     0.8    0.10000    0.00102    0.03196
22             0.3     0.7    0.10400    0.00095    0.03077
23             0.4     0.6    0.10800    0.00089    0.02991
24             0.5     0.5    0.11200    0.00087    0.02941
25             0.6     0.4    0.11600    0.00086    0.02930
26             0.7     0.3    0.12000    0.00087    0.02958
27             0.8     0.2    0.12400    0.00091    0.03023
28             0.9     0.1    0.12800    0.00098    0.03123
29               1     0.0    0.13200    0.00106    0.03256
```

Figure 8.18. Calculating the efficient frontier

Problems

1 Create the worksheet shown in Figure 8.18 using the appropriate formulae.

2 Assume a correlation coefficient of 1.0 (other things remain the same) and graph the minimum variance portfolio set. (*Hint*: just type 1 in cell F7 and press function key [F8].) What do you observe?

3 Assume a correlation coefficient of 0 (other things being equal) and graph the minimum variance portfolio set. (*Hint*: just type 0 in cell F7 and press function key [F8].) What do you observe?

4 Assume a correlation coefficient of −1 (other things remain unchanged) and

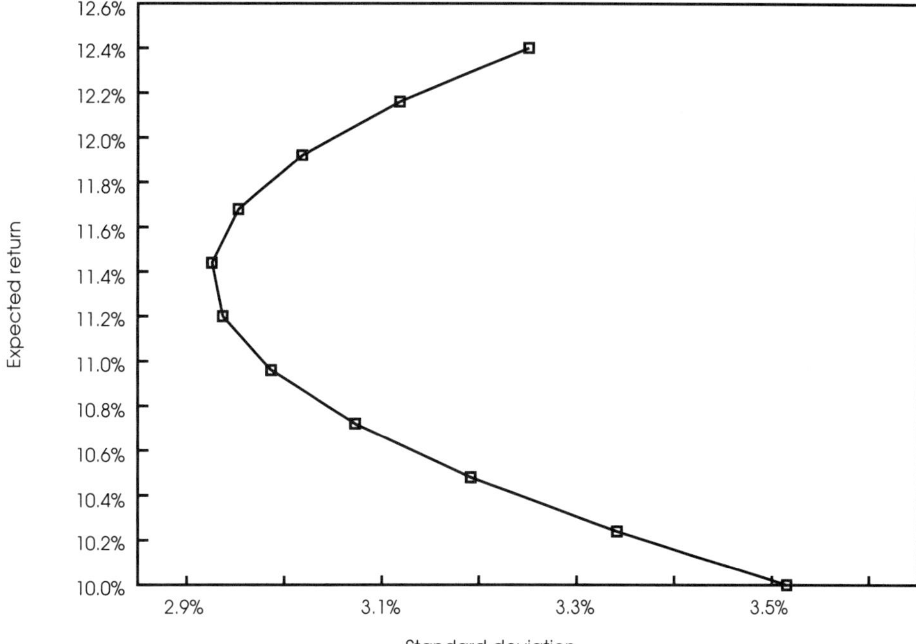

Figure 8.19. Minimum variance portfolio set with two securities

graph the minimum variance portfolio set. (*Hint*: just type −1.0 in cell F7 and press function key [F8].) What do you observe?

5 How can you graph the results obtained in Questions 2, 3 and 4 in a single graph?

Portfolio selection

An investor will prefer one of the portfolios on the efficient frontier (see Figure 8.19) and his or her selection is dependent upon personal preferences for a low portfolio expected return versus a larger and more risky portfolio expected return. For example, a very aggressive (risk-averting) investor might seek an increase in portfolio expected return and be willing to undertake considerable risk to get it; such an investor might select the portfolio defined by the investment proportions 0.9 and 0.1. Another timid (risk-averting) investor might be willing to avoid risk by sacrificing additional portfolio expected return; such an investor might select the portfolio defined by the investment proportions 0.7 and 0.3.

Generalizing the results

All the basic concepts introduced earlier in this chapter can be generalized by constructing portfolios containing more than two securities. The formulae for the expected return and risk of a portfolio of many securities are essentially the same as those in the case of a two-security portfolio, only they become more lengthy. Figure 8.20 contains a summary of two general formulae used to calculate portfolio expected return and risk, respectively.

Expected return	Variance of rate of return
The expected return of a portfolio made up of N securities is a weighted average of the expected returns of the component securities, the weights being the proportions of total funds invested in each security:	Consider a portfolio composed of N securities. The variance of the portfolio's rate of return is comprised of two parts: the first part shows the sum of security variances times the square of the proportion invested in each security; the second part shows the sum of the covariances between security pairs, where each covariance term is multiplied by two times the proportions invested in each security:
$E(R_p) = \sum_{i=1}^{N} x_i E(R_i)$	$\sigma^2(R_p) = \sum_{i=1}^{N} x_i^2 \sigma_i^2 + \sum_{\substack{i=1 \\ i \neq j}}^{N} \sum_{j=1}^{N} x_i x_j \text{Cov}(R_i, R_j)$

where

N = number of securities in the portfolio.
x_i = investment proportion associated with security i. The sum of these proportions equals one.
$E(R_i)$ = the expected return on security i.
σ_{ij} = the covariance between the rates of return on securities i and j.

Figure 8.20. The expected return and variance of rate of return for a portfolio comprised of N securities

Example 8.22 Calculating the expected return and variance of rate of return for a portfolio containing three securities

Figure 8.21 shows the expected returns, standard deviations and pairwise covariances of three securities.

Security	Expected return (%)	Standard deviation (%)	Covariances (%)
1	13.20	0.03256	1 & 2: 0.00058
2	9.20	0.03521	1 & 3: 0.00005
3	14.60	0.03040	2 & 3: 0.00095

Figure 8.21. The statistical characteristics of three securities

Using the first equation presented in Figure 8.20, the expected return of the portfolio containing equal investment in each of the three securities is:

$$E(R_p) = (1/3)(0.1320) + (1/3)(0.0920) + (1/3)(0.1460)$$
$$= 0.1233$$

Calculation of the portfolio variance is more difficult. The first component of the expression of variance (see Figure 8.20) can be calculated as follows:

$$\sum_{i=1}^{3} x_i^2 \sigma_i^2 = (1/3)^2(0.03256)^2 + (1/3)^2(0.03521)^2 + (1/3)^2(0.03040)^2$$
$$= 0.00036$$

The second component of the equation of variance (see Figure 8.20) is obtained as follows:

$$\sum_{i=1}^{3}\sum_{\substack{j=1\\ \neq i}}^{3} x_i x_j \sigma_{ij} = (1/3)(1/3)(0.00058) + (1/3)(1/3)(0.00005) + (1/3)(1/3)(0.00058) + (1/3)(1/3)(0.00095) + (1/3)(1/3)(0.00005) + (1/3)(1/3)(0.00095)$$

$$= 2(1/3)(1/3)(0.00058) + 2(1/3)(1/3)(0.00005) + 2(1/3)(1/3)(0.00095)$$

$$= 0.00035$$

Therefore, the portfolio's variance of rate of return is

$$\sigma^2(R_p) = 0.00036 + 0.00035 = 0.00071$$

The standard deviation of rate of return is 0.02665 indicating that the risk of our portfolio is less than the risk of each of the securities included in the portfolio.

Note that a two-security portfolio requires for the calculation of its variance only one covariance value, a three-security portfolio requires three covariance values and an N-security portfolio requires $(N^2 - N)/2$ covariance values. For example, if $n = 30$, the portfolio variance requires 435 covariance values.

Systematic and unsystematic risk

The total risk of a portfolio, as shown in Figure 8.20, is composed of two parts. The first part is called unsystematic risk or diversifiable risk, while the second part is called systematic risk or undiversifiable risk. The unsystematic risk is the variability of a security's rate of return caused by factors unique to the firm. For example, a good management team, a strike of the firm's employees, the development of a new product, the level of operating and financial gearing used by the firm, and so on. The unsystematic risk can be reduced or eliminated by diversification, since bad returns caused by factors unique to some securities in the portfolio are offset by good returns related to other securities in the portfolio.

The systematic risk is the variability of a security's rate of return resulting from factors that affect all shares in the market to a greater or lesser extent. Examples of such factors include changes in price levels, changes in interest rates, a new political event, an increase in international oil prices. The systematic risk cannot be eliminated through diversification because it is common to all securities (see Example 8.23).

Efficient frontier and portfolio selection

We may now extend the concept of the efficient frontier in the case of considering portfolios containing many securities. The individual securities can be combined into portfolios. All the possible combinations represent the set of available investment opportunities. Among these opportunities we prefer the portfolios with the higher expected returns and lower standard deviations.

In general, the minimum variance portfolio set can be determined by solving the following quadratic programming problem. Choose the proportions invested in N securities that minimize the portfolio risk subject to three constraints: (a) the portfolio has a particular level of expected return; (b) the sum of the proportions of portfolio funds invested in the individual securities equals 1; and (c) each investment proportion is either positive or zero. The top half of the minimum variance portfolio set is the efficient frontier.

Once the efficient frontier is identified, the investor's risk/return preferences are taken into consideration. Investors are generally risk averse if they dislike risk and like larger expected returns. In other words:

- For any level of expected return they prefer the lowest level of risk.
- For any level of risk they prefer the highest level of expected return.

The final choice of an individual investor is dependent upon the following two factors: (a) his or her preferences regarding a particular risk/return combination; and (b) relevant investment opportunities on the efficient frontier. The first factor shows what investors *wish* to do, whereas the second one reveals what investors *can* do. A combination of these two factors gives the investor's optimal portfolio, that is, the efficient portfolio that maximizes his or her expected utility with reference to the risk/return trade off (an example of portfolio selection is provided later in this chapter). Conservative investors would select efficient portfolios with low risk in exchange for a low expected return. More aggressive investors should choose efficient portfolios with higher risk in exchange for a higher expected return.

The portfolio selection problem was described by Fama and Miller (1972) as follows: 'Efficient set theorem: The optimal portfolio of a risk-averse investor, who behaves as if he was an expected utility maximizer, is efficient.'

Naive diversification and diversification across industries

Naive diversification involves investing in a number of randomly selected securities. Naive diversification is expected to reduce the unsystematic risk of a portfolio, but it is not expected to reduce its systematic risk. As you might imagine, the unsystematic portion of the rates of return of the securities contained in a portfolio are unrelated to each other. On the other hand, the systematic portion of the rates of return of the securities included in the portfolio move together, since the basic political and economic factors influence the values of all securities. (Appendix 8B shows mathematically the effect of diversification on portfolio risk.)

Diversification across industries deals with investing in a number of randomly selected securities from different industries. Evidence indicates that diversification across industries is not much better than naive diversification, because the rates of returns on securities from different industries are often highly correlated.

We should point out that naive (or industry) diversification and Markowitz diversification are two different methods for reducing portfolio risk. The former does not guarantee a minimum level of risk at a specific level of expected return.

Example 8.23 The benefits from diversification across industries

This example illustrates how diversification works to reduce portfolio risk as measured by the variance of portfolio rate of return. Consider the following five securities: Allied Lyons (AL), Boots, GKN, Marks and Spencer (M&S) and

National Westminster (NW). The variances of these securities and the pairwise covariances are shown in Figure 8.22 (the results are estimated by using monthly rates of return over the period January 1985 to December 1988).

Figure 8.22. The variances and pairwise covariances for five securities

Variance	Covariances
AL 0.00625	AL–GKN: 0.00193 AL–Boots: 0.00362 AL–M&S: 0.00390 AL–MW: 0.00293
GKN 0.00905	GKN–Boots: 0.00499 GKN–M&S: 0.00355 GKN–NW: 0.00302
Boots 0.01004	Boots–M&S: 0.00348 Boots–NW: 0.00431
M&S 0.00598	M&S–NW: 0.00394
NW 0.00707	

We form the following four portfolios:

Portfolio 1: Boots, GKN.
Portfolio 2: Boots, GKN, Allied Lyons.
Portfolio 3: Boots, GKN, Allied Lyons, Marks and Spencer.
Portfolio 4: Boots, GKN, Allied Lyons, Marks and Spencer, National Westminster.

Figure 8.23. Diversification across industries

Number of securities	Unsystematic risk	Systematic risk	Total risk
1	0.00905		0.00905
2	0.00477	0.00250	0.00727
3	0.00282	0.00234	0.00516
4	0.00196	0.00268	0.00464
5	0.00154	0.00285	0.00439

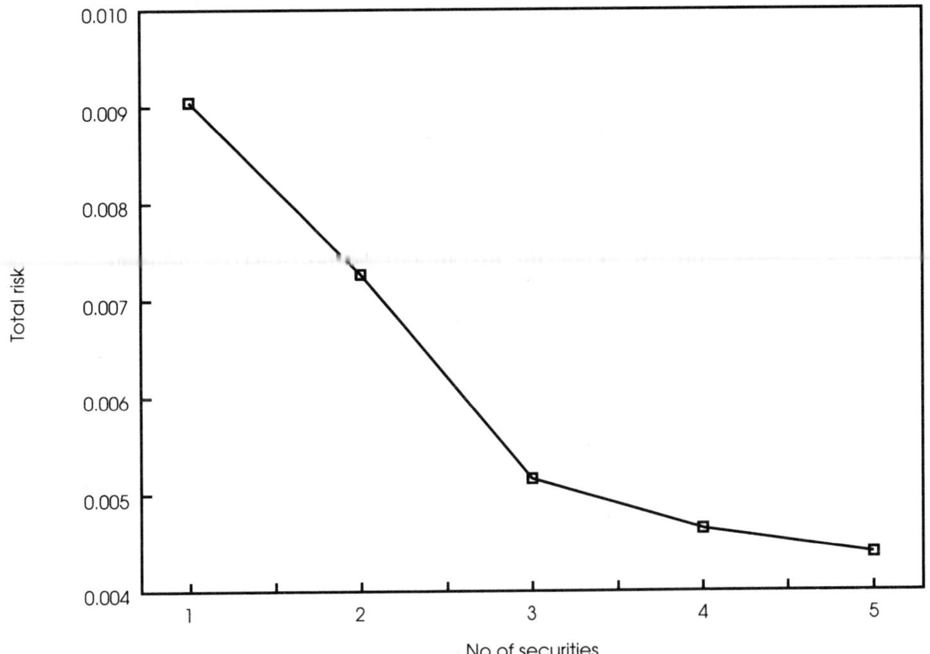

Figure 8.24. Impact of the number of securities held on total portfolio risk

For each portfolio we calculate the systematic and unsystematic portion of total risk (see Figure 8.20). As we can see from Figure 8.23, the unsystematic risk decreases fast as more securities are added to the portfolio, but at a decreasing rate. Moreover, the total portfolio risk, as measured by the variance, declines as the number of securities held increases. Note that the portfolio risk is reduced, but it is not eliminated through diversification. The total portfolio risk and portfolio size are portrayed graphically in Figure 8.24.

Problem You are given the following combinations of securities: (a) Allied Lyons and GKN; (b) Allied Lyons, GKN and Boots; (c) Allied Lyons, GKN, Boots and Marks and Spencer; and (d) Allied Lyons, GKN, Boots, Marks and Spencer and National Westminster. Examine the benefits from the diversification (assume equally weighted portfolios). Provide a graph illustrating such benefits.

The crucial question is how many securities should be included in a portfolio in order to achieve the benefits from diversification? Empirical studies indicate that risk is reduced substantially in portfolios containing ten to fifteen shares as compared with the risk of holding one share (see Evans and Archer, 1968; Solnik, 1974; Fama, 1976, pp. 245–54). Many empirical studies on portfolio diversification use portfolios consisting of equal investment in each security. However, when we employ market value weights, a greater number of securities held in portfolios is required to reduce the risk by a comparable amount.

The impact of diversification upon portfolio risk has two important implications. Firstly, small investors can substantially reduce portfolio risks by holding portfolios made up of 10 to 15 securities only. Secondly, institutional investors cannot achieve a substantial additional reduction in overall risk by investing in a large number of securities (for example, 200 securities) rather than in a considerably smaller number of securities (for example, 50 securities). Furthermore, the costs of holding a large number of securities are much higher than those related to the maintenance of a portfolio comprised of a relatively small number of securities.

The modified efficient frontier

The portfolio analysis, as developed by Markowitz, assumes that the proportions of portfolio funds invested in the securities contained in the portfolio are between 0.0 and 1.0. When the investment proportions are non-negative, we say that investors are unable to sell securities short. However, such an assumption was later relaxed by Black (1972). Short-selling occurs when an investor sells shares that he or she does not own, anticipating that their price is going to decline in the near future, at which time he or she buys back at a lower price and returns them to the lender. Figure 8.25 provides an example of short-selling (we assume no dividend payments and zero transaction costs).

In 1977 Roll modified Markowitz's model by allowing the possibility of short-selling of securities.

Portfolio analysis

Roll (1977) calculated the minimum variance portfolio set by solving the mathematical optimization problem presented in Figure 8.26. Roll assumed that

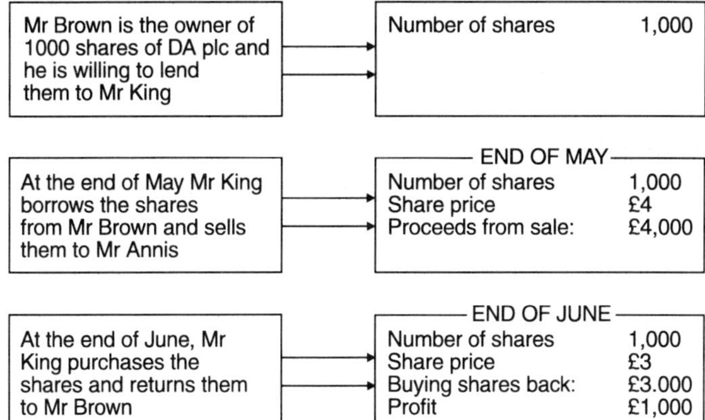

Figure 8.25. An example involving short-selling of shares

Figure 8.26. Calculating the minimum variance portfolio set

Problem Given a number of individual securities, choose the proportions invested in these securities that minimize the variance of portfolio rate of return subject to two constraints: (a) the portfolio has a particular level of expected return; and (b) the sum of the proportional allocations of the portfolio wealth invested in securities contained in the portfolio equals unity.

Mathematical formulation The minimum variance portfolio set is calculated by solving the following optimization problem:

$\underset{X_p}{\text{Minimize}}\, \sigma^2(R_p)$ Subject to the constraints (a) $X_p'R = E(R_p)$

(b) $X_p'u = 1$

where X_p, V and R are defined in Appendix 8D.
$u =$ the $(N \times 1)$ unit vector.
$'$ denotes the transposed vector.

the covariance matrix V (of all risky security returns under consideration) is non-singular and that the return vector R contains at least two different entries. The solution of this optimization problem gives the investment portfolio vector of a minimum variance portfolio as follows:

$$X_p = V^{-1}(Ru)A^{-1}\begin{bmatrix} E(R_p) \\ 1 \end{bmatrix}$$

where V^{-1} is the inverse of the covariance matrix, (Ru) is a matrix having in its first column the return vector R and in its second column the unit vector, A is the efficient set's information matrix and Er_p is the mean return of the minimum variance portfolio p (Appendix 8C surveys briefly a branch of mathematics called matrices).

The information matrix is always a (2×2) square matrix containing the following information:

$$A = \begin{bmatrix} a & b \\ b & c \end{bmatrix}$$

where

$$a = R'V^{-1}R \qquad b = R'V^{-1}u \qquad c = u'V^{-1}u$$

The variance of a minimum variance portfolio can be expressed as (for a proof see

Appendix 8D):

$$\sigma^2(R_p) = \frac{a - 2bE(R_p) + c[E(R_p)]^2}{ac - b^2}$$

Example 8.24 Calculating the proportions of funds invested in individual securities which define a minimum variance portfolio

Consider the following five individual securities: Allied Lyons, Boots, GKN, Marks and Spencer and National Westminster. Figure 8.27 presents the return vector, the covariance matrix and the corresponding unit vector (figures are rounded to three decimal points). The security characteristics were calculated by using monthly rates of return over a period of four years.

Figure 8.27. Data required to calculate the minimum variance portfolio set

Return vector			Covariance matrix			Unit vector
0.02615	0.00625	0.00193	0.00362	0.00390	0.00293	1
0.00180	0.00193	0.00905	0.00499	0.00355	0.00302	1
0.01469	0.00362	0.00499	0.01004	0.00348	0.00431	1
0.00926	0.00390	0.00355	0.00348	0.00598	0.00394	1
0.01248	0.00293	0.00302	0.00431	0.00394	0.00707	1

For example, the mean return of Allied Lyons over the period of four years was 0.02615, while the mean return of Marks and Spencer over the same period was 0.00926. The Allied Lyons' sample variance of rate of return over the period of four years was 0.00625, whereas the Marks and Spencer's sample variance of rate of return over the same period was 0.00598. The sample covariance between the rates of return of Allied Lyons and Marks and Spencer was 0.00390.

In order to calculate the investment proportion vector defining a minimum variance portfolio follow a four-step procedure:

1 Compute the inverse of the covariance matrix. This task can be performed with the aid of 1-2-3's `/Data Matrix Invert` command. Type in a worksheet the covariance matrix (see Figure 8.28). Then issue the command `/Data Matrix Invert` and use as a 'range to invert' the range A3..E7. Finally, use cell A10 as the top cell of the range you wish to store the inverse matrix.

2 Calculate the information matrix A and its inverse.

(a) Form the (5 × 2) return-unit matrix. In this case, we have the following matrix:

$$(Ru) = \begin{bmatrix} 0.02615 & 1 \\ 0.00180 & 1 \\ 0.01469 & 1 \\ 0.00926 & 1 \\ 0.01248 & 1 \end{bmatrix}$$

(b) Find the product of the matrices $(Ru)'$ and the inverse of the covariance matrix. This can be achieved by utilizing the 1-2-3's `/Data Matrix`

```
       A          B          C          D          E          F        G
 1 ---------------------------------------------------------------------------
 2 COVARIANCE MATRIX
 3     0.00625    0.00193    0.00362    0.00390    0.00293
 4     0.00193    0.00905    0.00499    0.00355    0.00302
 5     0.00362    0.00499    0.01004    0.00348    0.00431
 6     0.00390    0.00355    0.00348    0.00598    0.00394
 7     0.00293    0.00302    0.00431    0.00394    0.00707
 8 ---------------------------------------------------------------------------
 9 INVERSE OF THE COVARIANCE MATRIX
10     298.706     44.622    -66.375   -182.058     -0.931
11      44.622    176.879    -72.608    -93.311      2.217
12     -66.375    -72.608    178.578     24.712    -64.113
13    -182.058    -93.311     24.712    412.315   -129.533
14      -0.931      2.217    -64.113   -129.533    252.153
```

Figure 8.28. Computing the inverse of the covariance matrix

`Multiply` command. For this purpose the following information is required: 'First range to multiply': C18..G19, 'second range to multiply': A10..E14 and 'top cell of output range': A25. The results are shown in Figure 8.29.

```
       A          B          C          D          E          F          G
15 ---------------------------------------------------------------------------
16    MATRIX (R u)                                MATRIX (R u)'
17  0.02615          1
18  0.00180          1      0.02615    0.00180    0.01469    0.00926    0.01248
19  0.01469          1            1          1          1          1          1
20  0.00926          1
21  0.01248          1
22 ---------------------------------------------------------------------------
23                                 -1
24                    MATRIX (R u)'V
25    5.219    -0.418      0.186    -2.364     0.985
26   93.964    57.798      0.193    32.124    59.793
```

Figure 8.29. Calculating the product of two matrices

(c) Find the product of the matrices $(Ru)'V^{-1}$ and (Ru). This product can be found by using again the `/Data Matrix Multiply` command. Figure 8.30 presents the results (the entries of matrix A is formatted by using the `/Range Format Fixed` command with one decimal point).

```
       A          B          C          D          E          F        G
27 ---------------------------------------------------------------------------
28                      -1                                       -1
29 MATRIX A = (R u )'V  (R u)                        MATRIX A
30     0.129      3.608                            13.248    -0.196
31     3.608    243.872                            -0.196     0.007
```

Figure 8.30. Computing the information matrix A and its inverse

(d) The inverse of the information matrix A is shown in Figure 8.30 (its entries are formatted by using the `/Range Format Fixed` command with one decimal point).

3 Compute two different products between matrices:

(a) The product between V^{-1} and (Ru). The results are shown in Figure 8.31.

```
          A            B            C            D            E            F           G
32 ------------------------------------------------------------------------------------------
33                     -1                                    -1      -1
34    MATRIX V    (R u)                    MATRIX V    (R u)A
35     5.219     93.964                     50.726     -0.365
36    -0.418     57.798                    -16.862      0.486
37     0.186      0.193                      2.421     -0.035
38    -2.364     32.124                    -37.619      0.688
39     0.985     59.793                      1.334      0.225
```

Figure 8.31. Multiplying matrices

(b) The product between $V^{-1}(Ru)$ and A^{-1}. The results are presented in Figure 8.31.

4 Assume a value for the mean return $E(R_p)$ and calculate the corresponding investment proportion vector. Figure 8.32 shows the results for three different values of $E(R_p)$.

```
          A            B            C            D            E            F           G
40 ------------------------------------------------------------------------------------------
41      MEAN                      0.010        MEAN                      0.020       MEAN
42                                    1                                      1
43
44 Investment proportions |Investment proportions |Investment Proportions
45 for mean return of 1.0%|for mean return of 2.0%|for mean return of
46
47                   0.1421                           0.6494                      1.5675
48                   0.3178                           0.1492                     -0.1560
49                  -0.0108                           0.0134                      0.0572
50                   0.3121                          -0.0641                     -0.7450
51                   0.2388                           0.2521                      0.2763
```

Figure 8.32. Calculating the investment proportions of two minimum variance portfolios

The positive investment proportions mean that you are buying the shares. The negative investment proportions mean that you sell the shares short. For example, suppose we have £10,000 of your own money to invest in these five securities. We sell short £108 of GKN (security 3), and utilize the proceeds, in addition to £10,000, to invest £10,108 to the other four shares.

Consider the minimum standard deviation portfolios shown in Figure 8.32. Then, there exists a scalar, call it a, such that:

$$a\begin{bmatrix}0.1421\\0.3178\\-0.0108\\0.3121\\0.2388\end{bmatrix} + (1-a)\begin{bmatrix}0.6494\\0.1492\\0.0134\\0.0641\\0.2521\end{bmatrix} = \begin{bmatrix}1.5675\\-0.1560\\0.0572\\-0.7450\\0.2763\end{bmatrix}$$

The scalar can be computed as follows:

$$a = \frac{1.5675 - 0.1421}{0.6494 - 0.1421} = 2.810$$

The latter is based on the argument of Roll (1977) that a (convex) linear combination of two minimum variance portfolios is a minimum variance portfolio. This important property implies that we can use the investment proportions of only two minimum variance portfolios and generate an infinite number of other minimum variance portfolios.

Portfolio selection

Diacogiannis (1987) proved that the investor's portfolio problem, as described by Roll (1977), is equivalent to maximizing the investor's expected utility of portfolio rate of return. He proved the following revised version of the efficient set theorem for risky securities: 'The optimal portfolio of a risk-averse investor, who behaves as if he or she was an expected utility maximizer, is mean–standard deviation efficient and different from the global boundary portfolio.' (Diacogiannis, 1987, p. 218).

Additionally, Diacogiannis (1981) provided expressions for the indifference curves of a risk-averse investor whose utility function can be approximated by a quadratic utility function of portfolio rate of return. He proved that the highest indifference curve of a risk-averse investor can be expressed in the space of mean return and standard deviation as follows (for a proof see Appendix 8E):

$$E(R_p) = -\sqrt{\sigma^2(R_o) + k^2 - \sigma^2(R_p)} + E(R_o) + k$$

where

$$k = (cE(R_o) - b)/(ac - b^2)$$

$$E(R_o) + k - \sqrt{\sigma^2(R_o) + k^2} < E(R_p) < E(R_o) + k$$

with $E(R_o)$ and $\sigma(R_o)$ being the mean return and the standard deviation of the portfolio where the indifference curve touches the efficient frontier. The constants a, b and c are the entries of the information matrix of the efficient set.

Example 8.25 Computing the mean–standard deviation efficient frontier and the indifference curve of a risk-averse investor

The important information for the selection of an optimal portfolio can be classified as follows:

- A relevant opportunity set containing efficient portfolios.
- The preference of the investor in terms of risk and return.

Figure 8.33 shows the constants of the efficient frontier calculated in Example 8.24. Column B shows the mean returns of different minimum variance portfolios, while column C presents the variance of these portfolios. The variance, stored in cell C11, is calculated by using the minimum variance portfolio formula as follows (note that all numerical figures presented are displayed using a pre-defined format):

```
($E$3-2*$E$4*B11+$E$5*B11^2)/($E$3*$E$5-$E$4^2)= 0.00517
```

Given the preceding expression, we can now produce a schedule of values for portfolio risk given different values for mean return. The contents of cell C11 are copied in the range C12..C22. Each cell in the range D11..D22 presents the standard deviation of a minimum variance portfolio which is calculated by just taking the square root of variance.

If we plot the contents of columns B and D, we obtain Figure 8.34. The vertical axis shows the mean return and the horizontal axis refers to the standard deviation of rate of return. This graph represents the minimum standard deviation portfolio set for our sample of securities. All the portfolios lying on the minimum standard deviation portfolio set dominate all the risk/return combinations lying to the right of the set. Each point on the minimum standard deviation portfolio set represents a portfolio, where the proportion vector defining that portfolio is calculated as in Example 8.24. The minimum standard deviation portfolio set contains a portfolio with the lowest possible level of standard deviation, called the global minimum standard deviation portfolio. The mean return of this portfolio equals b/c, where b and c are two entries of the information matrix A (see Example 8.24). In our case, the mean return of the global minimum standard deviation portfolio is 0.01479 (that is, 3.608/243.872).

The efficient frontier is simply the positively sloped segment of the minimum standard deviation portfolio set. Each portfolio lying on the efficient frontier dominates all the minimum standard deviation portfolios lying on the negatively sloped segment of the standard deviation portfolio set and all the portfolios lying to the right of this set. The efficient frontier is available to the investor who must now decide which portfolio to choose.

The efficient portfolio that would be selected by an investor depends on his or her preferences in relation to risk and return. The investor's tastes for risk and return are summarized in a family of indifference curves. An indifference curve is a graph in the risk and return space constructed so that the investor is indifferent with regard to the opportunities that lie on it. An indifference curve indicates a particular level of utility. Assume that the personal preference of an investor is the efficient portfolio with risk 0.73011 and mean return of 0.21479. In order to calculate the investor's indifference curve which is tangent to the efficient frontier, we need to compute the following (see cell E8):

k value = `(E5*E6 – E4)/(E3*E5 – E4^2)` = 2.6448

Next, we translate the equation of the target indifference curve into a 1-2-3 formula as follows (this formula is stored in cell E11):

```
-@SQRT($E$7^2+$E$8^2-C11)+$E$6+$E$8
```

The contents of cell E11 are copied in the range E12..E22. Note that the rate of return stored in cell E18 (that is, 0.21479) equals the rate of return stored in cell B18, indicating that the indifference curve is tangent to the efficient frontier at the point with coordinates 0.73011 and 0.21479.

Figure 8.35 describes graphically the efficient frontier and the preference structure of the investor. The investor is indifferent among risk and return combinations lying on the indifference curve $U1$. Note that the investor's indifference curve is upward sloping, revealing the preference for a higher mean return and aversion to risk. For any two different points on an indifference curve, the point that is associated with the higher mean return must also be associated with higher risk. We see that the investor chose to hold the portfolio that is just tangent to an indifference curve. At this point the investor maximizes his or her expected utility, obtaining the highest mean return for the least risk.

	A	B	C	D	E	F	G
1	THE EFFICIENT FRONTIER & INDIFFERENCE CURVES OF AN INVESTOR						
2	==						
3	Constant a				0.129		
4	Constant b				3.608		
5	Constant c				243.872		
6	Mean Return of the Optimal Portfolio				0.2148		
7	Stand. Dev. of the Optimal Portfolio				0.7301		
8	k Value				2.6448		
9							
10		MEAN	VAR	SD	U1	U2	U3
11		0.00579	0.00517	0.07191	0.11681	0.05693	0.16315
12		0.00879	0.00458	0.06765	0.11670	0.05683	0.16304
13		0.01179	0.00422	0.06496	0.11664	0.05677	0.16297
14		0.01479	0.00410	0.06404	0.11662	0.05674	0.16295
15		0.06479	0.03716	0.19277	0.12265	0.06265	0.16909
16		0.11479	0.13634	0.36924	0.14083	0.08043	0.18758
17		0.16479	0.30164	0.54922	0.17140	0.11033	0.21870
18		0.21479	0.53305	0.73011	0.21479	0.15275	0.26288
19		0.26479	0.83059	0.91137	0.27166	0.20828	0.32082
20		0.31479	1.19425	1.09282	0.34290	0.27777	0.39348
21		0.36479	1.62402	1.27437	0.42978	0.36239	0.48221
22		0.41479	2.11992	1.45599	0.53407	0.46374	0.58890

Figure 8.33. Calculating the efficient frontier and the indifference curves of a risk-averse investor

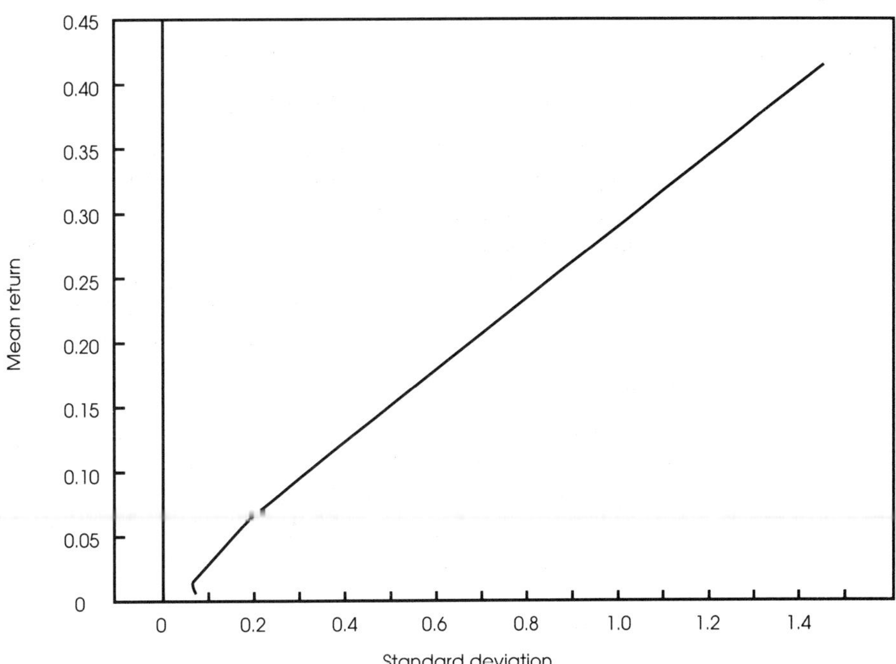

Figure 8.34. The efficient frontier

Columns F and G of Figure 8.33 compute two other indifference curves of the same investor. The first of these curves is calculated by assuming a risk level higher than 0.73011, while the second one is computed by assuming a risk level lower than 0.73011. That is, the following formulae are stored in cells F11 and G11, respectively:

```
-@SQRT(($E$7+0.2)^2+$E$8^2-C11)+$E$6+$E$8
```

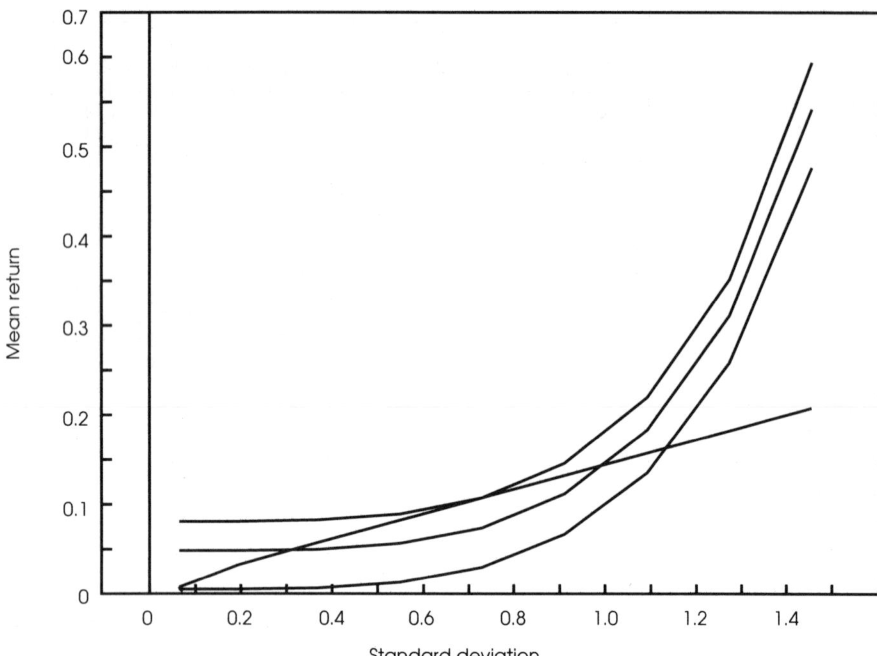

Figure 8.35. The optimal portfolio of an investor

```
-@SQRT(($E$7-0.2)^2+$E$8^2-C11)+$E$6+$E$8
```

The investor is indifferent among the risk and mean return combinations lying on the indifference curve U2. However, he or she would prefer any combination lying on curve U1 to any combination lying on curve U2. In general, the highest attainable indifference curve represents the highest level of satisfaction. In other words, the investor's portfolio lying at the point of tangency between the efficient frontier and the highest attainable indifference curve provides the greatest satisfaction over all the available efficient portfolios.

Problems

1 Create the worksheet shown in Figure 8.33 using the appropriate formulae.
2 Consider another risk-averse investor who prefers the efficient portfolio with mean return of 0.26479 and standard deviation of 0.91137. Graph the investor's risk–mean return preferences. Also graph the investor's risk–mean return preferences, efficient frontier and optimal portfolio.

Summary

There are three main steps involved in selecting portfolios: security analysis, portfolio analysis and portfolio selection.

1 *Security analysis* Security analysis deals with the estimation of the risk and return characteristics of individual securities. The analysis assumes that investors base their decisions solely in terms of risk and expected return; they always prefer more return to less and they are averse to greater exposure to risk. Then return and risk are measured by the expected return and standard deviation of the probability distribution of rates of return, respectively. The

greater the standard deviation of rate of return, the greater is the risk associated with an individual security.

2 *Portfolio analysis* Portfolio analysis is concentrated around the theory of Markowitz which provides a framework of risk reduction through diversification. Markowitz showed that if risk is measured by the standard deviation of rate of return and securities are not perfectly positively correlated, investors can always enjoy the benefits from diversification. The model of Markowitz uses certain data estimated during the process of security analysis and calculates a set of portfolios each of which is associated with minimum risk at a given level of expected return. When dealing with a portfolio, the risk and expected return of an individual security should be analysed in terms of their contribution to the risk and expected return on the portfolio. Empirical evidence reveals that diversification can result in a reduction of portfolio risk and such a reduction can be achieved by holding a relatively small number of securities.

3 *Portfolio selection* This final stage is concerned with the combination between the opportunities available to an investor and his or her personal tastes in terms of risk and return. The efficient frontier represents the relevant opportunity set available to the investor. The final decision is to select an efficient portfolio that maximizes the investor's expected utility.

Modified investment analysis The original Markowitz analysis can be modified in order to provide algebraic solutions to the efficient set and the portfolio selection problem. These algebraic solutions can be used within a worksheet to portray graphically the risk/return preferences, efficient frontier and optimal portfolio of an investor.

Questions for discussion

1 For each term shown below in the largest box provide a definition in your own words. Then check your responses against the definitions included in the chapter.

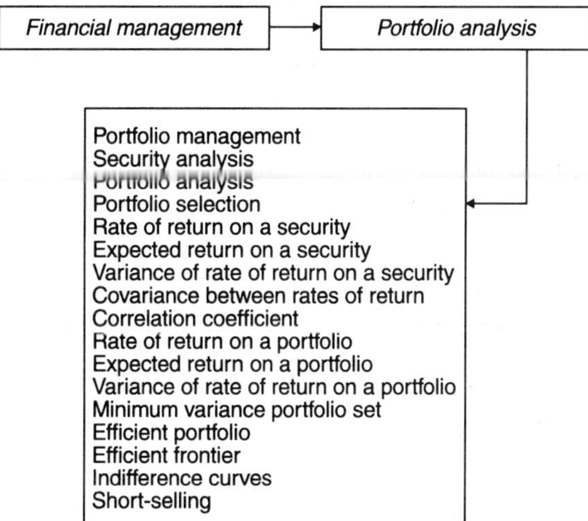

2 (a) Discuss how we can calculate the single-period rate of return on a given individual security.

(b) Discuss how we can calculate a portfolio's single-period rate of return.
(c) What is the difference between a security's (or portfolio's) expected rate of return and realized rate of return?

3 Compare and contrast the following risk measures for an individual security: (a) variance of the return on the security; (b) standard deviation of the return on the security; and (c) the risk of an individual security within a portfolio as measured by the covariance between the return on the security and the return on the portfolio.

4 (a) Discuss the following two sets of investment proportions defining two different portfolios:

0.25	0.25	0.25	0.25	Portfolio 1
0.25	0.10	0.30	0.35	Portfolio 2

(b) Assume that an investor wishes to invest £1,000 in portfolio 1. How much of his or her money would be invested in each security? If the investor decides to hold portfolio 2, how much money must be invested in each of the four securities?
(c) Can an investment proportion be negative? Explain. Provide an example where a portfolio contains a security with a negative investment proportion.

5 An investor is considering the following two investment opportunities:
(a) Purchase 3,000 shares of Marks and Spencer plc.
(b) Purchase 500 shares of Marks and Spencer, 500 shares of Argos, 500 shares of Sainsbury, 500 shares of Jarvis, 500 shares of United Biscuits and 500 shares of Siebe.

Assume that the investor can afford either alternative, which investment should he or she choose? Fully discuss your answer.

6 Discuss verbally and graphically each of the following two statements:
(a) 'For a given set of individual securities, the objective of portfolio analysis is to form portfolios of securities which are not dominated by other portfolios under consideration.'
(b) 'In view of portfolio selection, the objective of an investor is to select the best portfolio from those that lie on the mean–standard deviation efficient frontier.'

7 Do you agree with each of the following three statements? Fill in the appropriate boxes by using either the word 'agree' or the word 'disagree'. In each case, explain your answer.

Portfolio risk is defined as the danger of losing the capital invested in the portfolio.		
A larger expected return can be obtained by accepting a larger amount of risk.		
Risk averse investors always prefer to invest their money in government securities (for example, Treasury bills) rather than ordinary shares.		

8 Do you agree with each of the following four statements? Fill in the appropriate boxes by using either the word 'agree' or the word 'disagree'. In each case, provide an explanation for your answer.

As long as security returns are not perfectly positively correlated, the benefits of diversification within a portfolio can be obtained.

Since investors prefer greater expected returns and wish to avoid risk they should always invest in securities whose returns are negatively correlated.

The risk (standard deviation) of a portfolio comprised of two securities with perfectly positive returns is a weighted average of the risks (standard deviations) of the two securities in the portfolio.

The risk (variance) of a portfolio composed of N securities with no perfectly correlated returns is a weighted average of the risks (variances) of these N securities.

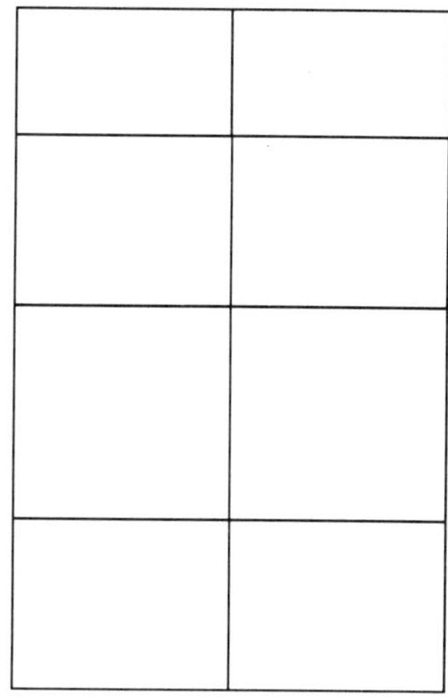

9 An investor is considering four portfolios of ordinary shares, call them A, B, C and D. The expected return (ER) and the standard deviation of return (SD) for each of these portfolios are given in the diagram below. Fill in the blank boxes in the diagram below and explain in detail each of your answers.

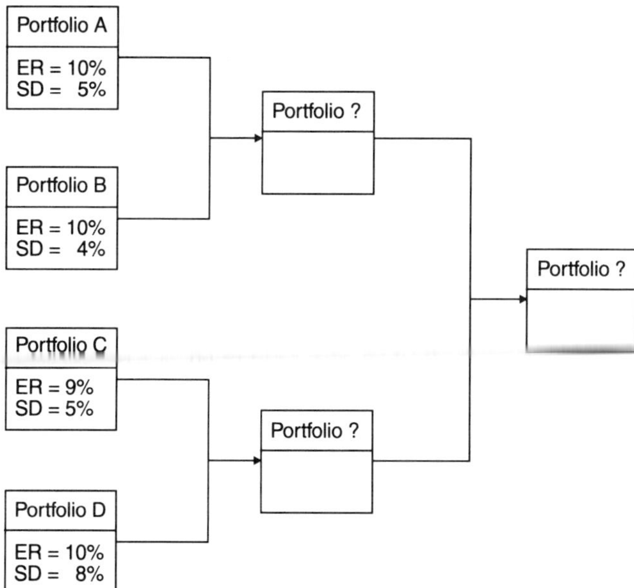

10 Compare and contrast the portfolio analysis model developed by Markowitz and the modified portfolio analysis model proposed by Ross.

11 Assume that short sales of risky securities are allowed. Discuss verbally and graphically the locus of minimum variance portfolios in expected return–variance space as well as in expected return–standard deviation space.

12 Discuss in detail the following statement: 'The Markowitz model is cast in terms of expectations for the future which are usually unobservable. As a result, historical data is often utilized in the analysis.'

13 Prepare an analog model summarizing the main points discussed in the present chapter.

14 How can spreadsheets be used to facilitate the application of the concepts discussed in this chapter?

Appendix 8A Calculating historical rates of return for Marks and Spencer plc

In the present appendix we calculate the simple rate of return and the continuously compounded rate of return of Marks and Spencer plc by using monthly share price data. The continuously compounded rate of return is calculated as follows:

$$\dot{R}_{it} = \ln(1 + R_{it}) = \ln\left(\frac{P_{it} + D_{it}}{P_{it-1}}\right)$$

where ln is the natural logarithm operator. The other terms are defined in Figure 8.3.

The continuously compounded rate of return is justified on two grounds:

- It approximates changes under continuous compounding.
- It can improve the symmetry in the distribution of returns by reducing the skewness of the distribution.

Example 8A.1 Calculating the monthly rates of return for Marks and Spencer plc (January 1985 to December 1988)

Figure 8A.1 shows the monthly historical prices and cash dividend payments of Marks and Spencer for the period December 1984 to December 1988. The rate of return of the Marks and Spencer's share for January 1985 is calculated as follows:

$$\begin{aligned} R_{\text{January}} &= \frac{(P_{\text{January}} - P_{\text{December}})}{P_{\text{December}}} + \frac{D_{\text{January}}}{P_{\text{December}}} \\ &= \frac{£120.00 - £117.00}{£117.00} + \frac{£0.00}{£117.00} \\ &= 2.56 \text{ per cent} \end{aligned}$$

Cell D7 contains the result of the following formula (the results are presented by using the `/Range Format Percent` command with two decimal points):

```
(B7-B6+C7)/B6
```

The contents of cell D7 are copied in the range D8..D30. Similarly, the contents of cell I8 are copied in the range I9..I30.

Figure 8A.2 presents the continuously compounded rates of return for Marks and Spencer for the 48-month period of January 1985 to December 1988. The rate of return stored in cell D42 is computed by using the following formula (the results are presented by using the `/Range Format Percent` command with two

	A	B	C	D	E	F	G	H	I
1	A> THE SIMPLE MONTHLY RATES OF RETURN ON MARKS AND SPENCER								
2									
3		SHARE	DIVIDEND	SHARE			SHARE	DIVIDEND	SHARE
4	PERIOD	PRICE		RETURN		PERIOD	PRICE		RETURN
5									
6	Dec-84	117.00							
7	Jan-85	120.00		2.56%		Jan-87	181.00		-1.63%
8	Feb-85	124.00		3.33%		Feb-87	190.00		4.97%
9	Mar-85	136.00		9.68%		Mar-87	212.00		11.58%
10	Apr-85	144.00		5.88%		Apr-87	215.00		1.42%
11	May-85	137.00	2.32	-3.25%		May-87	233.00	3.10	9.81%
12	Jun-85	138.00		0.73%		Jun-87	253.00		8.58%
13	Jul-85	134.00		-2.90%		Jul-87	241.00		-4.74%
14	Aug-85	150.00		11.94%		Aug-87	258.00		7.05%
15	Sep-85	154.00		2.67%		Sep-87	235.00		-8.91%
16	Oct-85	167.00		8.44%		Oct-87	239.00		1.70%
17	Nov-85	184.00	1.25	10.93%		Nov-87	200.00	1.55	-15.67%
18	Dec-85	180.00		-2.17%		Dec-87	171.00		-14.50%
19	Jan-86	176.00		-2.22%		Jan-88	183.00		7.02%
20	Feb-86	171.00		-2.84%		Feb-88	180.00		-1.64%
21	Mar-86	187.00		9.36%		Mar-88	176.00		-2.22%
22	Apr-86	218.00		16.58%		Apr-88	174.00		-1.14%
23	May-86	211.00	2.65	-2.00%		May-88	179.00	3.55	4.91%
24	Jun-86	197.00		-6.64%		Jun-88	177.00		-1.12%
25	Jul-86	207.00		5.08%		Jul-88	174.00		-1.69%
26	Aug-86	196.00		-5.31%		Aug-88	173.00		-0.57%
27	Sep-86	218.00		11.22%		Sep-88	150.50		-13.01%
28	Oct-86	197.00		-9.63%		Oct-88	163.00		8.31%
29	Nov-86	197.00	1.40	0.71%		Nov-88	173.00	1.70	7.18%
30	Dec-86	184.00		-6.60%		Dec-88	144.00		-16.76%

Figure 8A.1. Calculating the simple rates of return for Marks and Spencer (Jan. 1985 to Dec. 1988)

decimal points):

```
@LN((B42+C42)/B41)
```

The contents of cell D42 are copied in the range B43..B65. Likewise, the contents of cell I43 are copied in the range I44..I66. From the results we see that the continuously compounded rates of return provide close estimates for the simple rates of return.

Another method to calculate the continuous compounded rates of return is to use the 1-2-3's financial function @LN together with the simple rates of return. For example,

`@LN(1+D7)` = 2.53 per cent

Given the monthly returns in Figure 8A.2, the mean return is 0.66 per cent and the standard deviation of rate of return is 7.93 per cent. Therefore we have:

- There is a 68 per cent probability that the population mean return will be between −7.27 per cent (that is, 0.66% − 7.93%) and 8.59 per cent (that is, 0.66% + 7.93%).
- There is a 95 per cent probability that the population mean return will be between −15.20 per cent (that is, 0.66% − 2(7.93%)) and 16.52 per cent (that is, 0.66% + 2(7.93%)).
- There is a 99 per cent probability that the population mean return will be

Figure 8A.2. Calculating the continuously compounded rates of return for Marks and Spencer (Jan. 85 to Dec. 88)

	A	B	C	D	E	F	G	H	I
36	B> THE CONTINUOUS COMPOUNDED RATES OF RETURN ON MARKS AND SPENCER								
38		SHARE	DIVIDEND	SHARE			SHARE	DIVIDEND	SHARE
39	PERIOD	PRICE		RETURN		PERIOD	PRICE		RETURN
41	Dec-84	117.00							
42	Jan-85	120.00		2.53%		Jan-87	181.00		-1.64%
43	Feb-85	124.00		3.28%		Feb-87	190.00		4.85%
44	Mar-85	136.00		9.24%		Mar-87	212.00		10.96%
45	Apr-85	144.00		5.72%		Apr-87	215.00		1.41%
46	May-85	137.00	2.32	-3.30%		May-87	233.00	3.10	9.36%
47	Jun-85	138.00		0.73%		Jun-87	253.00		8.24%
48	Jul-85	134.00		-2.94%		Jul-87	241.00		-4.86%
49	Aug-85	150.00		11.28%		Aug-87	258.00		6.82%
50	Sep-85	154.00		2.63%		Sep-87	235.00		-9.34%
51	Oct-85	167.00		8.10%		Oct-87	239.00		1.69%
52	Nov-85	184.00	1.25	10.37%		Nov-87	200.00	1.55	-17.04%
53	Dec-85	180.00		-2.20%		Dec-87	171.00		-15.67%
54	Jan-86	176.00		-2.25%		Jan-88	183.00		6.78%
55	Feb-86	171.00		-2.88%		Feb-88	180.00		-1.65%
56	Mar-86	187.00		10.35%		Mar-88	176.00		-2.25%
57	Apr-86	218.00		15.34%		Apr-88	174.00		-1.14%
58	May-86	211.00	2.65	-2.02%		May-88	179.00	3.55	4.80%
59	Jun-86	197.00		-6.87%		Jun-88	177.00		-1.12%
60	Jul-86	207.00		4.95%		Jul-88	174.00		-1.71%
61	Aug-86	196.00		-5.46%		Aug-88	173.00		-0.58%
62	Sep-86	218.00		10.64%		Sep-88	150.50		-13.93%
63	Oct-86	197.00		-10.13%		Oct-88	163.00		7.98%
64	Nov-86	197.00	1.40	0.71%		Nov-88	173.00	1.70	6.93%
65	Dec-86	184.00		-6.83%		Dec-88	144.00		-18.35%

between −23.13 per cent (that is, 0.66% − 3(7.93%)) and 24.45 per cent (that is, 0.66% + 3(7.93%)).

Problems

1 Create the worksheet shown in Figure 8A.1.

2 Create the worksheet shown in Figure 8A.2 (use the formula `@LN(1+simple return)` in order to calculate the compounded rates of return).

Appendix 8B Portfolio risk and the effects of diversification

Deriving the equations for portfolio expected return and portfolio risk

Consider a portfolio, call it *p*, which is comprised of *N* risky securities. The rate of return of portfolio *p* at period *t* can be expressed as follows:

$$R_{pt} = \sum_{i=1}^{N} x_i R_{it} \qquad (8B.1)$$

where R_{it} = the rate of return of security *i* at period *t*.

The expected value operator has the following property: the expected value of a constant times a random variable is equal to the constant multiplied by the expected value of the random variable. Therefore, we can write:

$$E(R_p) = E\left(\sum_{i=1}^{N} x_i R_i\right) = \sum_{i=1}^{N} x_i E(R_i) \tag{8B.2}$$

where we have dropped the time subscript.

The variance of the portfolio p is given by

$$\begin{aligned}\text{Var}(R_p) &= E[R_p - E(R_p)]^2 \\ &= E\left[\sum_{i=1}^{N} x_i R_i - \sum_{i=1}^{N} x_i E(R_i)\right]^2\end{aligned} \tag{8B.3}$$

Rearranging terms into Equation (8B.3) we get

$$\text{Var}(R_p) = E[x_1(R_1 - E(R_1)) + \ldots + x_N(R_N - E(R_N))]^2 \tag{8B.4}$$

By squaring the term in brackets Equation (8B.4) provides:

$$\begin{aligned}\text{Var}(R_p) = {} & E[x_1^2(R_1 - E(R_1))^2 + \ldots + x_N^2(R_N - E(R_N))^2 \\ & + 2x_1x_2(R_1 - E(R_1))(R_2 - E(R_2)) \\ & + \ldots + 2x_{N-1}x_N(R_{N-1} - E(R_{N-1}))(R_N - E(R_N))]\end{aligned}$$

Separating terms yields

$$\begin{aligned}\text{Var}(R_p) = {} & x_1^2E(R_1 - E(R_1))^2 + \ldots + x_N^2E(R_N - E(R_N))^2 \\ & + 2x_1x_2E[(R_1 - E(R_1))(R_2 - E(R_2))] \\ & + \ldots + 2x_{N-1}x_NE[(R_{N-1} - E(R_{N-1}))(R_N - E(R_N))]\end{aligned}$$

or equivalently

$$\text{Var}(R_p) = \sum_{i=1}^{N} x_i^2 \text{Var}(R_i) + \sum_{\substack{i=1 \\ i\neq j}}^{N} \sum_{j=1}^{N} x_i x_j \text{Cov}(R_i, R_j) \tag{8B.5}$$

Portfolio risk and the effects of diversification

The variance of an equally weighted portfolio (call it p) is given by (see Appendix 8D):

$$\text{Var}(R_p) = \sigma_p^2 = X_p' V X_p$$

If N is the number of securities in the portfolio, then

$$X_p' = [1/N, 1/N, \ldots, 1/N]$$

Number of security variances $= N$
Number of different pairwise covariances $= N(N-1)/2$
With equal investment, the variance of p can be written as:

$$\sigma_p^2 = \frac{\sigma_1^2 + \sigma_2^2 + \ldots + \sigma_N^2}{N^2} + \frac{2[\sigma_{12} + \sigma_{13} + \ldots + \sigma_{NN-1}]}{N^2} \tag{8B.6}$$

where

$\sigma_i^2 =$ the variance of the rate of return on security i, $i = 1, 2, \ldots, N$.
$\sigma_{ij} =$ the covariance between the rates of return on securities i and j, $i, j = 1, 2, \ldots, N$ and i is different from j.

From equation (8B.6), the total portfolio risk, can be expressed as:

$$\sigma_p^2 = \frac{1}{N}\frac{\sigma_1^2 + \sigma_2^2 + \ldots + \sigma_N^2}{N} + \frac{N-1}{N}\frac{2[\sigma_{12} + \sigma_{13} + \ldots + \sigma_{NN-1}]}{N(N-1)}$$

The last equation reveals that the total risk of an equally weighted portfolio can be expressed as a weighted average of two components, the first component is the average of the individual security variances and the second is the average of the security covariances. Thus:

Total portfolio risk	=	Weighted component of total risk due to the average of the individual security variances	+	Weighted component of total risk due to the average of pairwise covariances
σ_p^2	=	$\frac{1}{N}\overline{\text{VAR}}_i$	+	$\frac{N-1}{N}\overline{\text{COV}}_{ij}$

where

$$\overline{\text{VAR}}_i = \frac{\sigma_1^2 + \sigma_2^2 + \ldots + \sigma_N^2}{N}$$

$$\overline{\text{COV}}_{ij} = \frac{2[\sigma_{12} + \sigma_{13} + \ldots + \sigma_{NN-1}]}{N(N-1)}$$

As the portfolio becomes more diversified, N becomes very large and the total portfolio risk tends to approach the average covariance term. Thus, diversification can be used to eliminate the individual security risk, but the part of the total risk caused by the covariation between the securities cannot be eliminated by diversification.

Appendix 8C Matrices

A matrix is a rectangular array of numbers arranged in rows and columns.

$$A = \begin{bmatrix} a_{11} & a_{12} & \cdots & a_{1j} & \cdots & a_{1M} \\ a_{21} & a_{22} & \cdots & a_{2j} & \cdots & a_{2M} \\ \vdots & \vdots & & \vdots & \vdots & \vdots \\ a_{i1} & a_{i2} & \cdots & a_{ij} & \cdots & a_{iM} \\ \vdots & \vdots & & \vdots & \vdots & \vdots \\ a_{N1} & a_{N2} & \cdots & a_{Nj} & \cdots & a_{NM} \end{bmatrix} \begin{matrix} \\ \\ \\ \rightarrow i\text{th row} \\ \\ \\ \end{matrix}$$

$\uparrow$ jth column

where :

$a_{ij} \rightarrow$ they are (real) numbers; $i = 1, 2, \ldots, N$; and $j = 1, 2, \ldots, M$.

$a_{ij} \rightarrow$ they are called the entries of the matrix

$a_{11}, a_{22}, \ldots, a_{NM} \rightarrow$ they are called the entries of the diagonal

The dimension of a matrix indicates the number of rows and the number of columns describing the matrix. In the example above, A has dimension N by M (that is, N rows and M columns) or simply $(N \times M)$. A matrix with the same number of rows and columns is called a square matrix. For convenience, matrices will be denoted by capital letters and their entries will be denoted by lower case letters.

Example 8C.1 Dimension of matrices

The following are two examples of matrices:

$$A = \begin{bmatrix} 6 & 7 & 9 \\ 3 & 5 & 6 \end{bmatrix} \qquad B = \begin{bmatrix} 2 & 3 & 4 \\ 4 & 5 & 7 \\ 4 & 8 & 9 \end{bmatrix}$$

The dimension of the matrix A is (2×3). The matrix B is a square matrix with dimension (3×3).

Special matrices

The identity matrix

The identity matrix is a square matrix having 'ones' in the diagonal from upper left to lower right and zeros elsewhere.

Example 8C.2 The (3×3) identity matrix

The following is a (3×3) identity matrix

$$\begin{bmatrix} 1 & 0 & 0 \\ 0 & 1 & 0 \\ 0 & 0 & 1 \end{bmatrix}$$

Symmetric matrix

A square matrix is called symmetric if all its entries above the diagonal are the same with those below it.

Example 8C.3 A (3 × 3) square matrix

The following is a (3 × 3) square matrix

$$\begin{bmatrix} 3 & 5 & 4 \\ 5 & 2 & 8 \\ 4 & 8 & 6 \end{bmatrix}$$

Addition of matrices

If $A = (a_{ij})$ and $B = (b_{ij})$ are two $(N \times M)$ matrices, then the sum $A + B$ is defined as the $(N \times M)$ matrix $(a_{ij} + b_{ij})$.

Example 8C.4 Adding two matrices

If A and B are two matrices given by:

$$A = \begin{bmatrix} 6 & 7 & 9 \\ 3 & 5 & 6 \end{bmatrix} \qquad B = \begin{bmatrix} 2 & 5 & 6 \\ 3 & 8 & 4 \end{bmatrix}$$

Then

$$A + B = \begin{bmatrix} 6+2 & 7+5 & 9+6 \\ 3+3 & 5+8 & 6+4 \end{bmatrix} = \begin{bmatrix} 8 & 12 & 15 \\ 6 & 13 & 10 \end{bmatrix}$$

Multiplication of a matrix by a real number

If $A = (a_{ij})$ is an $(N \times M)$ matrix and h a real number, then the product of A and the real number h is the $(N \times M)$ matrix (ha_{ij}).

Example 8C.5 Multiplying a matrix by a real number

If A is the matrix given by:

$$A = \begin{bmatrix} 6 & 7 & 9 \\ 3 & 5 & 6 \end{bmatrix}$$

Then

$$3A = \begin{bmatrix} 3 \times 6 & 3 \times 7 & 3 \times 9 \\ 3 \times 3 & 3 \times 5 & 3 \times 6 \end{bmatrix} = \begin{bmatrix} 18 & 21 & 27 \\ 9 & 15 & 18 \end{bmatrix}$$

Matrix multiplication

In order to multiply two matrices the number of columns in the first matrix must be equal to the number of rows in the second matrix, that is:

$$\text{Dimension: } \underset{(N \times M)}{A} \quad \underset{(M \times S)}{B}$$

must be the same

If $A = (a_{ij})$ is a matrix of dimension $(N \times M)$ and $B = (b_{jk})$ a matrix of dimension $(M \times S)$, then the product $A \times B$ is the matrix $C = (c_{ik})$ of dimension $(N \times S)$.

Example 8C.6 Multiplying two matrices.

Let A and B equal the following two matrices:

$$A = \begin{bmatrix} 6 & 7 & 9 \\ 3 & 5 & 6 \end{bmatrix} \qquad B = \begin{bmatrix} 2 & 3 & 4 \\ 4 & 5 & 7 \\ 4 & 8 & 9 \end{bmatrix}$$

In order to multiply two matrices the number of columns in the first matrix must be equal to the number of rows in the second matrix. Therefore it is possible to multiply matrix A (2×3) with matrix B (3×3) (but we cannot multiply matrix B (3×3) with matrix A (2×3)).

First row × *First column* × *Second column* × *Third column*

$$[6 \quad 7 \quad 9] \times \begin{bmatrix} 2 \\ 4 \\ 4 \end{bmatrix} = \begin{matrix} 6 \times 2 \\ + \\ 7 \times 4 \\ + \\ 9 \times 4 \\ \hline 76 \end{matrix} \times \begin{bmatrix} 3 \\ 5 \\ 8 \end{bmatrix} = \begin{matrix} 6 \times 3 \\ + \\ 7 \times 5 \\ + \\ 9 \times 8 \\ \hline 125 \end{matrix} \times \begin{bmatrix} 4 \\ 7 \\ 9 \end{bmatrix} = \begin{matrix} 6 \times 4 \\ + \\ 7 \times 7 \\ + \\ 9 \times 9 \\ \hline 154 \end{matrix}$$

Second row × *First column* × *Second column* × *Third column*

$$[3 \quad 5 \quad 6] \times \begin{bmatrix} 2 \\ 4 \\ 4 \end{bmatrix} = \begin{matrix} 3 \times 2 \\ + \\ 5 \times 4 \\ + \\ 6 \times 4 \\ \hline 50 \end{matrix} \times \begin{bmatrix} 3 \\ 5 \\ 8 \end{bmatrix} = \begin{matrix} 3 \times 3 \\ + \\ 5 \times 5 \\ + \\ 6 \times 8 \\ \hline 82 \end{matrix} \times \begin{bmatrix} 4 \\ 7 \\ 9 \end{bmatrix} = \begin{matrix} 3 \times 4 \\ + \\ 5 \times 7 \\ + \\ 6 \times 9 \\ \hline 101 \end{matrix}$$

The result matrix is:

$$\underset{(2 \times 3)}{C} = \underset{(2 \times 3)}{A} \times \underset{(3 \times 3)}{B} = \begin{bmatrix} 76 & 125 & 154 \\ 50 & 82 & 101 \end{bmatrix}$$

It must be noted that the resulting matrix always inherits the number of rows of the first matrix and the number of columns of the second matrix.

Matrix inversion

If $A = (a_{ij})$ is a matrix of dimension $(N \times N)$, the matrix $B = (b_{ij})$ of dimension $(N \times N)$ is called the inverse of A if and only if $AB = I_N$, where I_N is the $(N \times N)$ identity matrix. Not all square matrices have inverses, the inverse of a square matrix exists if the matrix's determinant is non-zero (see Example 8C.7).

Example 8C.7 Calculating the inverse of a square matrix

Consider the square matrix B given in Example 8C.6. We wish to calculate the inverse of matrix B. Such an inverse exists only if the determinant of B is non-zero. The determinant of B can be obtained by use of either the elements in the ith row or those of the jth column $(i = j = 1, 2, 3)$. We decide to select the first row.

In this case, we can write

	First entry (+)	*Second entry* (−)	*Third entry* (+)
First row	2 y y	y −3 y	y y 4
	y 5 7	4 y 7	4 5 y
	y 8 9	4 y 9	4 8 y

where we ignore the entries containing the letter ‘y’. Then the determinant can be calculated as follows:

First cell (+) *Second cell* (−) *Third cell* (+)

$$\textit{Determinant} = 2 \times (5 \times 9 - 8 \times 7) - 3 \times (4 \times 9 - 4 \times 7) + 4 \times (4 \times 8 - 4 \times 5) = 2$$

Note that each quantity in parentheses is the determinant of a (2×2) matrix.

The matrix B's determinant is non-zero, thus, matrix B can be inverted. To calculate the entries of the inverse of matrix B we must first assign to each entry either a positive or a negative sign starting with a positive one, that is:

$$\begin{matrix} + & - & + \\ - & + & - \\ + & - & + \end{matrix}$$

Next the entries of the inverse matrix are calculated as follows:

First cell

First column	$+(5 \times 9 - 8 \times 7)/2 = -5.5$
Second column	$-(3 \times 9 - 8 \times 4)/2 = 2.5$
Third column	$+(3 \times 7 - 5 \times 4)/2 = 0.5$

Second cell

First column	$-(4 \times 9 - 4 \times 7)/2 = -4$
Second column	$+(2 \times 9 - 4 \times 4)/2 = 1$
Third column	$-(2 \times 7 - 4 \times 4)/2 = 1$

Third cell

First column	$+(4 \times 8 - 4 \times 5)/2 = 6$
Second column	$-(2 \times 8 - 4 \times 3)/2 = -2$
Third column	$+(2 \times 5 - 4 \times 3)/2 = -1$

The inverse matrix of B is:

$$B^{-1} = \begin{bmatrix} -5.5 & 2.5 & 0.5 \\ -4.0 & 1.0 & 1.0 \\ 6.0 & -2.0 & -1.0 \end{bmatrix}$$

Note that $BB^{-1} = I3$, where $I3$ is the (3×3) identity matrix.

Transpose matrix

If $A = (a_{ij})$ is a matrix of dimension $(N \times M)$, then the transpose of A is the $(M \times N)$ matrix (a_{ji}). To generate the transpose of a given matrix, we simply interchange its rows with its columns. Thus, the first row of the matrix becomes the transpose's first column, the second row becomes the transpose's second column, and so on. The transpose of the matrix A is denoted A'.

Example 8C.8 The transpose of a matrix

Consider the following matrix:

$$A = \begin{bmatrix} 6 & 7 & 9 \\ 3 & 5 & 6 \end{bmatrix} \longrightarrow \text{dimension} : (2 \times 3)$$

Then

$$A' = \begin{bmatrix} 6 & 3 \\ 7 & 5 \\ 9 & 6 \end{bmatrix} \longrightarrow \text{dimension} : (3 \times 2)$$

Vectors

A column vector (or a column matrix) of dimension $(N \times 1)$ is a matrix having N rows and one column. A row vector (or a row matrix) of dimension $(1 \times N)$ is a matrix having one row and N columns (a row vector is the tranpose of a column vector and vice versa).

The unit vector

The unit vector is a column vector consisting of 'ones'. For example, the (3×1) vector is given as follows:

$$\begin{bmatrix} 1 \\ 1 \\ 1 \end{bmatrix}$$

Figure 8C.1 summarizes some general remarks on operation of matrices.

Name	Remarks
Addition	The dimension of the matrices must be the same.
Multiplication	Two matrices can be multiplied only if the number of columns in the first matrix equals the number of rows in the second matrix.
Inverse	A square matrix has a unique inverse if it exists. The inverse of a square matrix exists if its determinant is non-zero.

Figure 8C.1. Remarks on operation of matrices

Appendix 8D Expressing portfolio return and risk using a matrix notation

Return vector

The return vector of security returns is a rectangular array of numbers arranged in only one column. For example, consider the following data:

Mean return on Allied Lyons (AL): 0.02615
Mean return on Boots: 0.00180
Mean return on GKN: 0.01469

Mean return on Marks and Spencer (MS): 0.00926
Mean return on National Westminster (NW): 0.01248

The (5 × 1) return vector is given as follows:

$$R = \begin{bmatrix} 0.02615 \\ 0.00180 \\ 0.01469 \\ 0.00926 \\ 0.01248 \end{bmatrix}$$

Covariance matrix

The covariance matrix of security returns is a rectangular array of numbers arranged in columns and rows. The covariance matrix is square (that is, the number of rows equals the number of columns) and symmetric (that is, all its entries above the diagonal are the same as those below it). The covariance matrix consists of the security variances in the diagonal from upper left to lower right and the pairwise covariances in all other positions. For example, suppose you are given the following data:

Variances

AL	0.00625
GKN	0.00905
Boots	0.01004
M&S	0.00598
NW	0.00707

Covariances:
AL-GKN: 0.00193 AL-Boots: 0.00362 AL-M&S: 0.00390 AL-MW: 0.00293
GKN-Boots: 0.00499 GKN-M&S: 0.00355 GKN-NW: 0.00302
Boots-M&S: 0.00348 Boots-NW: 0.00431
M&S-NW: 0.00394

The (5 × 5) covariance matrix is given below:

$$V = \begin{bmatrix} 0.00625 & 0.00193 & 0.00362 & 0.00390 & 0.00293 \\ 0.00193 & 0.00905 & 0.00499 & 0.00355 & 0.00302 \\ 0.00362 & 0.00499 & 0.01004 & 0.00348 & 0.00431 \\ 0.00390 & 0.00355 & 0.00348 & 0.00598 & 0.00394 \\ 0.00293 & 0.00302 & 0.00431 & 0.00394 & 0.00707 \end{bmatrix}$$

Expected return of portfolio

The expected return (or mean) of a portfolio is the average reward that would most likely be gained from investing in the portfolio over a period of time. It can be expressed as:

$$E(R_p) = r_p = X_p'R$$

where

X_p = A ($N \times 1$) column vector containing the proportions invested in the securities included in portfolio p.

R = A ($N \times 1$) column vector of security expected returns.

It is assumed that the entries in the investment proportion vector sum to 1.

Variance and standard deviation of rates of return on a portfolio

The variance of a portfolio's rate of return is the average variability of the possible returns around its expected return. The variance is given by:

$$\sigma^2(R_p) = X_p' V X_p$$

where

$V =$ the $(N \times N)$ covariance of returns of N risky securities.

The standard deviation of portfolio returns is the square root of variance.

Covariance vector

The vector of covariances can be expressed as follows:

$$V_c = VX_p$$

The ith entry of the covariance vector is simply the contribution of the individual security i to the variance of a portfolio's rate of return. Such a contribution is referred as the covariance between the rate of return on security i and the rate of return on portfolio p. The ith entry of the covariance vector measures the risk of security i in portfolio p.

The variance of a minimum variance portfolio is calculated as follows:

$$\sigma^2(R_p) = [E(R_p)\ 1]A^{-1}(R\,u)'V^{-1}VV^{-1}(R\,u)A^{-1}\begin{bmatrix} E(R_p) \\ 1 \end{bmatrix}$$

$$= [E(R_p)\ 1]A^{-1}(R\,u)'V^{-1}(R\,u)A^{-1}\begin{bmatrix} E(R_p) \\ 1 \end{bmatrix} \quad \text{(since } VV^{-1} = I,\ I = (N \times N) \text{ identity matrix)}$$

$$= [E(R_p)\ 1]A^{-1}AA^{-1}\begin{bmatrix} E(R_p) \\ 1 \end{bmatrix} \quad \text{(since } A = (R\,u)'A^{-1}(R\,u))$$

$$= [E(R_p)\ 1]A^{-1}\begin{bmatrix} E(R_p) \\ 1 \end{bmatrix} \quad \text{(since } AA^{-1} = I,\ I = (2 \times 2) \text{ identity matrix)}$$

The inverse of matrix A is

$$A^{-1} = \begin{bmatrix} c/(ac - b^2) & -b/(ac - b^2) \\ -b/(ac - b^2) & a/(ac - b^2) \end{bmatrix}$$

Therefore, substituting the inverse of A into the last equation and manipulating yields:

$$\sigma^2(R_p) = \frac{a - 2bE(R_p) + c[E(R_p)]^2}{ac - b^2}$$

Appendix 8E Mean–standard deviation indifference curves

In this appendix the following procedure is followed:

Step 1 Formulate the equation of the indifference curve of a risk averse investor whose utility function can be approximated by a quadratic polynomial of portfolio rate of return.

Step 2 Express the utility curve of the investor in terms of the following:
(a) The expected return of the investor's optimal portfolio.
(b) The variance of rate of return of the investor's optimal portfolio.
(c) The constants a, b, c of the efficient frontier.

Formulating the equation of the indifference curve

Assume that the utility function of a risk averse investor can be expressed as:

$$U(R_p) = R_p + gR_p^2$$

where R_p is the rate of return on portfolio p and $g < 0$.

Since $\sigma^2(R_p) = E(R_p^2) - [E(R_p)]^2$, the expected utility of the investor is a function of expected return and variance of rate of return on portfolio p

$$E(U(R_p)) = E(R_p) + g[E(R_p)]^2 + g\sigma^2(R_p) \tag{8E.1}$$

By dividing both members of Equation (8E.1) by g, it follows that

$$\frac{1}{g} E(R_p) + [E(R_p)]^2 + \sigma^2(R_p) = \frac{E(U(R_p))}{g}$$

The last equation is equivalent to

$$\frac{1}{g} E(R_p) + [E(R_p)]^2 + \sigma^2(R_p) + \frac{1}{4g^2} = \frac{E(U(R_p))}{g} + \frac{1}{4g^2} \tag{8E.2}$$

By rearranging terms in Equation (8E.2) we take

$$\left([E(R_p)]^2 + \frac{1}{g} E(R_p) + \frac{1}{4g^2}\right) + \sigma^2(R_p) = \frac{E(U(R_p))}{g} + \frac{1}{4g^2} \tag{8E.3}$$

The first term in parentheses of the left-hand side of Equation (8E.3) is a perfect square, thus we can write

$$\left([E(R_p)] + \frac{1}{2g}\right)^2 + \sigma^2(R_p) = \frac{E(U(R_p))}{g} + \frac{1}{4g^2} \tag{8E.4}$$

Re-expressing Equation (8E.4) in terms of the characteristics of the investor's optimal portfolio

Equation (8E.1) can be expressed in matrix notation as follows:

$$E(U(R_o)) = X_o'R + g[X_o'R]^2 + gX_o'VX_o \tag{8E.5}$$

where

X_o = a $(N \times 1)$ decision column vector of investment proportions defining the optimal portfolio o. '$'$' denotes the transpose of the vector X_o.
R = the $(N \times 1)$ vector of expected returns.
V = the $(N \times N)$ covariance matrix of returns on N risky securities.

Assuming that short-selling of risky securities is available, the objective of a risk-averse investor who tries to maximize his or her expected utility can be stated as follows:

Maximize $E(U(R_o))$

Subject to $X_o'u = 1$

where $u =$ the $(N \times 1)$ unit vector.
Consider the following Lagrangian

$$L(X_o, l) = X_o'R + g[X_o'R]^2 + gX_o'VX_o + l(1 - X_o u)$$

where l is a Lagrangian multiplier.
The first order conditions for maximum value give

$$R + 2g[X_o'R]R + 2gVX_o - lu = 0 \tag{8E.6}$$

From Equation (8E.6) it immediately follows that

$$(1 + 2gE(R_o))R + 2gVX_o = lu \tag{8E.7}$$

Dividing both sides of Equation (8E.7) by $(1 + 2gE(R_o))/2$ and rearranging terms we obtain

$$-\frac{g}{1 + 2gE(R_o)} VX_o = (Ru)' \begin{bmatrix} 1/2 \\ -l/2(1 + 2gE(R_o)) \end{bmatrix} \tag{8E.8}$$

Pre-multiplying both sides of Equation (8E.8) by $(Ru)'V^{-1}$ the following expression is derived:

$$-\frac{g}{1 + 2gE(R_o)} \begin{bmatrix} E(R_o) \\ 1 \end{bmatrix} = A \begin{bmatrix} 1/2 \\ -l/2(1 + 2gE(R_o)) \end{bmatrix} \tag{8E.9}$$

where the (2×2) matrix A is defined as follows:

$$A = \begin{bmatrix} a & b \\ b & c \end{bmatrix} = \begin{bmatrix} R'V^{-1}R & R'V^{-1}u \\ R'V^{-1}i & u'V^{-1}u \end{bmatrix} \tag{8E.10}$$

We assume that the covariance matrix V is non-singular and that the return vector R contains at least two different entries. If we pre-multiply Equation (8E.9) by A^{-1} we get

$$\begin{bmatrix} 1/2 \\ -l/2(1 + 2gE(R_o)) \end{bmatrix} = -\frac{g}{1 + 2gE(R_o)} A^{-1} \begin{bmatrix} E(R_o) \\ 1 \end{bmatrix} \tag{8E.11}$$

Equation (8E.11) gives

$$\frac{-g}{1 + 2gE(R_o)} = \frac{ac - b^2}{2[(cE(R_o) - b]} \tag{8E.12}$$

Solving Equation (8E.11) for g we take

$$g = \frac{-(ac - b^2)}{2[E(R_o)(ac - b^2) + cE(R_o) - b]} \tag{8E.13}$$

Since the optimal portfolio of the investor is efficient, its variance can be expressed as

$$\sigma^2(R_o) = \frac{a - 2bE(R_o) + c[E(R_o)]^2}{ac - b^2} \tag{8E.14}$$

Substituting Equations (8E.13) and (8E.14) into Equation (8E.1) and simplifying, yields

$$E(U(R_o)) = \frac{cE(R_o) - a + [E(R_o)]^2(ac - b^2)}{2[cE(R_o) - b + E(R_o)(ac - b^2)]} \tag{8E.15}$$

Next we combine Equations (8E.13) and (8E.15) to get

$$\frac{E(U(R_o))}{g} = -\frac{cE(R_o) - a}{ac - b^2} - [E(R_o)]^2 \tag{8E.16}$$

Equation (8E.13) gives

$$\frac{1}{2g} = -E(R_o) - k \tag{8E.17}$$

where

$$k = (cE(R_o) - b)/(ac - b^2)$$

Equation (8E.16) can be rewritten as

$$\frac{E(U(R_o))}{g} + \frac{1}{4g^2} = -\frac{cE(R_o) - a}{ac - b^2} - [E(R_o)]^2 + \frac{1}{4g^2} \tag{8E.18}$$

Therefore, in view of Equation (8E.18), (8E.17) and (8E.14), we take

$$\frac{E(U(R_o))}{g} + \frac{1}{4g^2} = \sigma^2(R_o) + k^2 \tag{8E.19}$$

Finally, substituting Equation (8E.19) and (8E.17) into Equation (8E.4) we get

$$[-E(R_p) + E(R_o) + k]^2 + \sigma^2(R_p) = \sigma^2(R_o) + k^2 \tag{8E.20}$$

Equation (8E.20) gives

$$E(R_p) = -\sqrt{\sigma^2(R_o) + k^2 - \sigma_p^2(R)} + E(R_o) + k \tag{8E.21}$$

Equation (8E.21) expresses $E(R_p)$ in terms of the risk–return characteristics of the investor's optimal portfolio and the constants a, b, and c defined in Equation (8E.10).

The target indifference curve to the efficient frontier is given by Equation (8E.21) where

$$E(R_o) + k - \sqrt{\sigma^2(R_o) + k^2} < E(R_p) < E(R_o) + k$$

Appendix 8F The studentized range test for normality

The studentized range test examines a sample of observations in order to determine whether they drew from a normal population (for a detailed description of the test see David *et al.*, 1954). The studentized range test can be applied in a sample of monthly rates of return. In this case, the test statistic is given by

$$\text{SR} = \frac{\text{Max}\,(R_i) - \text{Min}\,(R_i)}{s(R_i)}$$

where

Max (R_i) = the maximum value of the security i's monthly rate of return over the sampling period.

Min (R_i) = the minimum value of the security i's monthly rate of return over the sampling period.

$s(R_i)$ = the sample standard deviation of rates of return.

We can infer that the security rates of return are drawn from a normal distribution if the following inequality holds:

$$\text{SR} < \text{SR}(f, T)$$

where

$\text{SR}(f, T) =$ the fractile of the distribution of the studentized range in samples of size T, with T denoting the total number of rates of return in the sample. (By definition a fractile is a value below which a specified fraction of the data must lie.)

Example 8F.1 Calculating the studentized range for Marks and Spencer's rates of return (period January 1985 to December 1988)

Figure 8F.1 shows the monthly compounded rates of return of a share of Marks and Spencer for a four-year period from January 1985 to December 1988. The minimum and the maximum returns in the sample are −16.76 per cent and 16.58 per cent, respectively. The sample standard deviation (see cell I34) is calculated by

	A	B	C	D	E	F	G	H	I
1	CALCULATING THE STUDENTIZED RANGE (MONTHLY DATA)								
2									
3		SHARE	DIVIDEND	SHARE			SHARE	DIVIDEND	SHARE
4	PERIOD	PRICE	PAID	RETURN		PERIOD	PRICE	PAID	RETURN
5									
6	Dec-84	117.00							
7	Jan-85	120.00		2.56%		Jan-87	181.00		-1.63%
8	Feb-85	124.00		3.33%		Feb-87	190.00		4.97%
9	Mar-85	136.00		9.68%		Mar-87	212.00		11.58%
10	Apr-85	144.00		5.88%		Apr-87	215.00		1.42%
11	May-85	137.00	2.32	-3.25%		May-87	233.00	3.10	9.81%
12	Jun-85	138.00		0.73%		Jun-87	253.00		8.58%
13	Jul-85	134.00		-2.90%		Jul-87	241.00		-4.74%
14	Aug-85	150.00		11.94%		Aug-87	258.00		7.05%
15	Sep-85	154.00		2.67%		Sep-87	235.00		-8.91%
16	Oct-85	167.00		8.44%		Oct-87	239.00		1.70%
17	Nov-85	184.00	1.25	10.93%		Nov-87	200.00	1.55	-15.67%
18	Dec-85	180.00		-2.17%		Dec-87	171.00		-14.50%
19	Jan-86	176.00		-2.22%		Jan-88	183.00		7.02%
20	Feb-86	171.00		-2.84%		Feb-88	180.00		-1.64%
21	Mar-86	187.00		9.36%		Mar-88	176.00		-2.22%
22	Apr-86	218.00		16.58%		Apr-88	174.00		-1.14%
23	May-86	211.00	2.65	-2.00%		May-88	179.00	3.55	4.91%
24	Jun-86	197.00		-6.64%		Jun-88	177.00		-1.12%
25	Jul-86	207.00		5.08%		Jul-88	174.00		-1.69%
26	Aug-86	196.00		-5.31%		Aug-88	173.00		-0.57%
27	Sep-86	218.00		11.22%		Sep-88	150.50		-13.01%
28	Oct-86	197.00		-9.63%		Oct-88	163.00		8.31%
29	Nov-86	197.00	1.40	0.71%		Nov-88	173.00	1.70	7.18%
30	Dec-86	184.00		-6.60%		Dec-88	144.00		-16.76%
31									
32		Minimum Rate of Return -------->							-16.76%
33		Maximum Rate of Return -------->							16.58%
34		Sample Standard Deviation of Rate of Return -->							7.73%
35						Studentized Range ----->			4.313
36									

Figure 8F.1. Studentized range test for Marks and Spencer's monthly returns (period: 1985–88)

using the following 1-2-3 formula:

```
@SQRT(@VAR(RAN1,RAN2)*@COUNT(RAN1,RAN2)/(@COUNT(RAN1,RAN2)-1))
```

where RAN1 = D7..D30 and RAN2 = I7..I30.

The studentized range is found as follows:

$$SR = \frac{16.58\% + 16.76\%}{7.73\%} = 4.313$$

Using the sample size of 48 and a significant level of 5 per cent, the critical value is approximately 5.35 (see statistical table in David *et al.*, 1954). The computed studentized statistic is less than 5.35. This suggests that the sample under consideration provides convincing evidence that the security returns obey a normal population.

References and bibliography

Ambachtsheer, K. (1974) Profit potential in an 'almost efficient' market, *Journal of Portfolio Management*, Autumn.

Ball, R. and Brown, P. (1968) 'An empirical evaluation of accounting income numbers', *Journal of Accounting Research*, Autumn, 159–78.

Black, F. (1972) Capital market equilibrium with restricted borrowing, *Journal of Business*, July, 444–455.

David, H.A., Hartley, H.O. and Pearson, E.S. (1954) The distribution of the ratio, in a single normal sample, of range to standard deviation, *Biometrica*, 482–93.

Davies, P. and Canes, M. (1978) 'Stock prices and the publication of second-hand information', *Journal of Business*, **51**, January, 43–56.

Diacogiannis, P.G. (1981) Portfolio selection in mean–standard deviation space, *Spoudes*, 496–515.

Diacogiannis, P.G. (1986) Some empirical evidence on the intertemporal stationary of the security returns distributions for the London Stock Exchange, *Journal of Accounting and Business Research*, **17**, 43–8.

Diacogiannis, P.G. (1987) The mean–standard deviation efficient set theorem: a note, *Managerial and Decision Economics*, **8**, Winter, 217–19.

Dryden, M.M. (1970) Filter tests of UK share prices, *Applied Economics*, **1**, 261–75.

Evans, J. and Archer, S.H. (1968) Diversification and the reduction of dispersion: an empirical analysis, *Journal of Finance*, December, 761–7.

Fama, E.F. (1965) The behaviour of stock market prices, *Journal of Business*, **38**, 34–105.

Fama, E.F. (1976) *Foundation of finance*. Blackwell, Oxford.

Fama, E.F. and Miller, M. (1972) *The Theory of Finance*, Dryden Press, Hinsdale, Illinois.

Fama, E., Fisher, L., Jensen, M. and Roll, R. (1969) The adjustment of stock prices to new information, *International Economic Review*, February, 1–21.

Firth, M. (1975) The information content of large investment holdings, *Journal of Finance*, December, 1265–81.

Firth, M. (1978) *Unit Trusts: Performance and Prospects*. MCB Publications, Bradford.

Hawanini, G. and Michel, P. (1982) Market efficiency of the Brussels Stock Exchange, in: Stoneham, P. (ed.) *Major Stock Markets in Europe*. Gower, Aldershot.

Jaffe, J. (1974) Special information and insider trading, *Journal of Business*, July, 410–28.

Jennergren, P. (1975) Filter tests of Swedish share prices, in: Elton, E.J. and Gruber, M.J.G. (eds), *International Capital Markets*. North Holland, Amsterdam.

Jennergren, P. and Korsvold, P. (1975) The non-random character of Norwegian and Swedish stock market prices, in: Elton, E.J. and Gruber, M.J.G., *International Capital Markets*. North Holland, Amsterdam.

Jensen, M. (1968) The performance of mutual funds in the period 1954–1964, *Journal of Finance*, May, 389–416.

Johnston, J., Price, G. and VanVleck, F. (1966) *Linear Equations and Matrices*. Addison-Wesley, Reading, Mass.

Juttner, D. and McHugh, N. (1976) Is the Australian stock market really efficient in the weak sense? *The Investment Analyst*, April.

Kaplan, R. and Roll, R. (1972) Investor evaluation of accounting information: some empirical evidence, *Journal of Business*, April, 225–57.

King, B.F. (1966) Market and industry factors in stock price behaviour, *Journal of Business Studies*, **39**, 139–90.

Koo, L. (1980) *The Stock Exchange in Singapore in the Context of the Efficient Market Hypothesis*. Singapore Stock Exchanges Publications, Singapore.

Kraus, A. and Stoll, H. (1972) Price impacts of block trading on the New York Stock Exchange, *Journal of Finance*, June, 569–88.

Lintner, J. (1965) Evaluation of risk assets and the selection of risky investments in stock portfolios and capital budget, *Review of Economic and Statistics*, **47**, 13–37.

Markowitz, H. (1952) Portfolio selection, *Journal of Finance*, **VVI,** 77–91.

Markowitz, H. (1959). *Selection: Efficient Diversification of Investments*, John Wiley, New York.

Merton, R.C. (1972) An analytic derivation of the efficient portfolio frontier, *Journal of Finance and Quantitative Analysis* **7**, 1851–72.

Niarchos, N. (1972) The stock market in Greece, in: Szego, G.P. and Shell, K. (eds), *Mathematical Methods in Investment and Finance*.

Niederhoffer, V. and Osborn, M. (1966) Market making and reversal on the Stock Exchange, *Journal of American Statistical Association*, **61** December, 897–916.

Pettit, R. (1972) Dividend announcements, security performances, and capital market efficiency, *Journal of Finance*, December, 993–1007.

Roll, R. (1977) A critique of the asset pricing theory's tests—Part I: On past and potential testability of the theory, *Journal of Financial Economics*, **4**, March, 129–76.

Sharpe, W. (1964) Capital asset prices: a theory of market equilibrium under conditions of risk, *Journal of Finance*, **19**, September, 425–42.

Sharpe, W. (1966) Mutual funds performance, *Journal of Business*, January, 119–38.

Siong, S. (1982) *The Behaviour of Malaysian Stock Market Prices 1973–1981: A Statistical Study*. Malaysian Stock Exchange Publication.

Solnik, B.H. (1974) Why not diversify internationally rather than domestically? *Financial Analyst's Journal*, July August, 40 54.

Wong, C. (1981) Comparative study of capital market efficiency for three Pacific Basin stock markets: Hong Kong, Kuala Lumpur, Singapore, Far East Stock Exchange Papers.

9 Asset pricing models

This chapter includes:

- Capital market line
- Capital asset pricing model
- Arbitrage pricing theory
- Efficient markets

Chapter 8 discussed a method for selecting an investor's optimal portfolio from the efficient frontier of risky securities. According to this method, an investor can identify his or her optimal portfolio by noting the point of tangency between his or her higher attainable indifference curve and the mean/standard deviation efficient frontier. We shall now discuss relevant risk measures for individual securities or portfolios and introduce models regarding the way capital assets are priced in relation to their risks.

More specifically, this chapter develops the capital market line and the capital asset pricing model (CAPM) and then summarizes the empirical tests related to the capital asset pricing model. The present chapter also explores an alternative approach to the capital asset pricing model: the arbitrage pricing theory proposed by Ross (1976, 1977). Finally, it deals with the concept of market efficiency and reviews several efficient market tests. Figure 9.1 presents the relation between the discipline of financial management and portfolio theory.

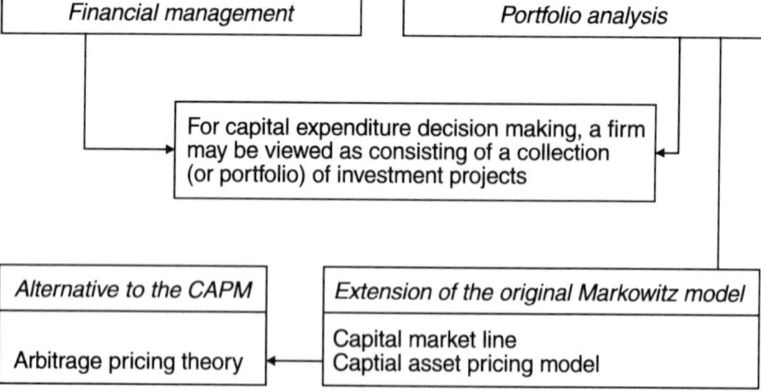

Figure 9.1. Relating financial management aspects and portfolio theory

Basic concepts, definitions and examples

In this chapter we discuss models concerning the way portfolios and individual securities are priced in the capital market. We begin by developing two equilibrium risk/return relationships: the capital market line; and the capital asset pricing model (or security market line). These two models rest upon the following assumptions:

1. Investors are risk averse and prefer more expected returns on their portfolios to fewer returns.
2. All investors have a common investment horizon and identical expectations about the distributions of the security rates of return at the end of this horizon.
3. There exists a riskless security where investors can borrow or lend any amount at the risk-free rate. No inflation and no change in the level of the risk-free rate exists.
4. There is no default risk for both individual investors and firms.
5. The capital market is perfect in the sense that: (a) there are no transaction costs; (b) there are no taxes; (c) securities are infinitely divisible; (d) information is costless and available to every investor; and (e) no single buyer or seller of securities is large enough to affect their prices.
6. All the risky securities are marketable.

Before we review the limitations of these assumptions, a brief discussion of the assumptions will be presented. Investors evaluate portfolios on the basis of expected returns and standard deviations of portfolio rates of return. They view the portfolio rates of return in a probabilistic fashion and base their decisions on only two parameters of the probability distribution of portfolio rates of return, namely, its expected return and its standard deviation. We also assume risk-avoiding investors who prefer more expected return on their portfolios to less. As a consequence, investors prefer to invest in expected return/standard deviation efficient portfolios.

According to the second assumption, investors perceive the same efficient frontier derived using the Markowitz model. This assumption does not mean that all investors have complete agreement about the future prices of the securities; it simply means that all investors agree about the expected security returns, security standard deviations and security covariances at the end of some period of time which is the same for all investors. To some extent, this assumption is consistent with assumption 5(d) above, if investors have the same information at the same time, then every investor can have the same view of the efficient frontier.

Without default risk, transaction costs and taxes, there can only be one riskless rate in the market. Suppose there are two riskless rates of interest, then investors can always borrow at the lower rate as many funds as possible and invest in the security offering the higher rate. This will give to investors high returns at zero risk which is clearly unacceptable. Supply and demand will simply force the two rates to be equal. Corporate failure is usually related to events which are unique to a firm, for example, managerial incompetence. Assumption 4 is needed since the risk measures used in portfolio analysis (for example, the covariance between the rate of return of a security and the rate of return on the market) do not capture default risk.

The assumption of the perfect capital market implies that at any moment there is a single security price and the market is in equilibrium (that is, the total quantity of risky securities that investors want to buy is equal to the total quantity that other investors want to sell). Whenever a disequilibrium occurs, the forces of supply and demand will simply restore the equilibrium.

Finally, the assumption that all risky securities are marketable simplifies the analysis, in the presence of non-marketable assets (for example, human capital) the analysis becomes more complicated.

Let us now provide a brief evaluation of the assumptions discussed above. In reality, a large number of investors choose to invest in portfolios rather than in single securities. For example, many investors prefer to invest their funds in unit trusts as opposed to an investment in the ordinary shares of a firm. Therefore, the assumption that investors are risk averse does seem to hold. The second assumption of common investment horizon and identical expectations is violated in the real world. For example, the investment horizon of a young executive may be 25 years, while the investment horizon of another individual who requires to accumulate funds to finance his or her studies may be five years.

The assumption that the borrowing rate equals the lending rate is also invalid in the real world. For example, if the borrowing and lending rates were equal, then banks and building societies would not be able to make any money. The assumption of the perfect capital market is clearly unrealistic. In the real world, investors pay taxes and transaction costs when they purchase or sell securities. Information is not usually costless, you pay a fee to buy the *Financial Times* or the *Investor's Chronicle*. Additionally, information is not available to every investor, for example, the share price database of the London Business School is not used by all investors in the country.

Finally, the assumption that all securities in the market are marketable is clearly invalid. For example, selling yourself or buying another human being is illegal, selling an historical object is not permitted by law, and so on.

Most of these assumptions can be seen to be not representative of the real world. However, the final test of a theoretical model is not how realistically its assumptions reflect the real world but how well the model fits real data.

The capital market line and the capital asset pricing model are summarized in Figure 9.2.

Figure 9.2. Summarizing the capital market line and the capital asset pricing model

Capital market line	Capital asset pricing model
A single period equilibrium relationship between expected return and risk. It holds for efficient portfolios only	A single period equilibrium relationship between expected return and risk. It holds for individual securities or portfolios (efficient or not)
where portfolio risk is measured by the standard deviation of rate of return.	*where* risk is measured by beta (the risk of the security in the market portfolio relative to the risk of the market portfolio).

The capital market line

According to the capital market line, all investors have identical expectations. Thus, they will all observe the same efficient frontier of Markowitz in the expected return–standard deviation space. Investors can combine the riskless security with different efficient portfolios. The best combinations (that is, efficient portfolios) are lying on the straight line drawn from the riskless security tangent to the efficient frontier of Markowitz. The portfolio at the point of tangency is called the market portfolio and the existence of an equilibrium implies that every risky security is included in the market portfolio. If any security were not included in the market portfolio, it would not be held at all (remember that investors are holding only combinations of the riskless security and the market portfolio). This would mean that the market was not in equilibrium, because the total quantity of risky securities that investors want to buy would not be equal to the total quantity that other investors want to sell. The proportion of the market portfolio's fund invested in security i can be determined as follows:

$$x_i = \frac{\text{market value of security } i}{\text{sum of all market values of all the risky securities in the market}}$$

These proportions are positive implying that short-selling of risky securities does not occur at equilibrium.

The market portfolio is an expected return–standard deviation efficient portfolio. The efficiency of the market portfolio is a necessary condition for the validity of the exact linear relationship between risk (measured by the standard deviation) and expected return for every efficient portfolio at equilibrium. (Roll, 1977, proved that the efficiency of the market portfolio is also a sufficient condition for the capital market line.) The new linear efficient frontier is the same for all investors and is composed of different linear combinations of only two funds: the riskless security and the market portfolio. Different investors who choose to hold risky portfolios will choose to invest in the same optimal combination of risky securities (that is, in the market portfolio). Individual preference will determine only the amount of borrowing or lending. That is, the financing decision to borrow or lend is independent of (or separated from) the choice to invest in the market portfolio. This implication of the theory is called the separation theorem.

The capital market line can be expressed mathematically as follows (Appendix 9A presents a proof of the capital market line):

$$E(R_q) = R_f + \frac{E(R_m) - R_f}{\sigma_m}\sigma_q$$

where

$E(R_q)$ = the expected return on portfolio q.
R_f = the return on the riskless security.
$E(R_m)$ = the expected return on the market portfolio.
σ_m = the standard deviation of rate of return on the market portfolio.
σ_q = the standard deviation of rate of return on portfolio q.

In words, the capital market line asserts the equilibrium expected return on any efficient portfolio is equal to the sum of the risk-free rate and a risk premium measured by the product of the market price of risk and the portfolio's risk. The risk premium associated with a security represents the additional return to the risk-free rate return providing some compensation for risk bearing. The risk-free rate is frequently referred to as the reward for waiting, whereas the risk premium is often referred to as the reward for taking on risk. The higher the standard deviation of rate of return on an efficient portfolio, the higher is its expected return.

An investor might choose to hold a lending portfolio by investing his own money in a combination between a riskless security (for example, investing in a government security) and the market portfolio. Another investor might choose to hold a borrowing portfolio which would be constructed by borrowing funds at the risk-free rate and use these funds, plus her own funds, to invest in some risky portfolio.

In general, the capital market line is the efficient frontier for portfolios composed of the riskless security and the market portfolio.

Example 9.1 Calculating the expected returns on portfolios using the capital market line

Assume that the market portfolio has an expected return of 18 per cent, and a standard deviation of rate of return of 15 per cent. The risk-free rate is 10 per cent. The standard deviation of a portfolio, call it q, lying on the capital market line is 12 per cent. The expected return of portfolio q is 16.4 per cent:

$$E(R_q) = 0.10 + \frac{0.18 - 0.10}{0.15} 0.12$$

$$= 0.10 + 0.064 = 16.4 \text{ per cent}$$

Therefore, if an investor is willing to accept a change in risk from 0 to 12 per cent, he or she demands an increase in expected return from 10 per cent to 16.4 per cent. The expected return of portfolio q is lower than that of the market portfolio, since portfolio q has lower risk than the market portfolio.

To generate the expected returns on more portfolios lying on the capital market line, the `/Data Table 1` command of 1-2-3 can be used. Column C of Figure 9.3 shows the standard deviations of 12 different combinations between the riskless security and the market portfolio. Cell F8 contains the result of the formula `+F3+((F4-F3)/F5)*F6`. The 'input cell 1' is cell F6. Column D contains the expected return of portfolios on the capital market line. Columns E and F show the proportions of funds invested in the riskless security and market portfolio, respectively.

The capital market line includes only one portfolio comprised of only risky securities. All other points along the capital market line represent combinations

```
----------------------------------------------------------------------------
          A          B           C            D          E            F          G
 1 THE CAPITAL MARKET LINE
 2 =======================
 3 Riskless Rate of Interest                                       10.0%
 4 Expected Return on the Market Portfolio                         18.0%
 5 Standard Deviation on the Market Portfolio                      15.0%
 6 Standard Deviation on Portfolio q                               12.0%
 7                                                             ---------
 8                                                                 16.4%
 9
10                              +F8        +F6/F5              (1-E10)
11                     0.0%       10.0%         0.00                1
12                     3.0%       11.6%         0.20              0.8
13                     6.0%       13.2%         0.40              0.6
14                     9.0%       14.8%         0.60              0.4
15                    12.0%       16.4%         0.80              0.2
16                    15.0%       18.0%         1.00                0
17                    18.0%       19.6%         1.20             -0.2
18                    21.0%       21.2%         1.40             -0.4
19                    24.0%       22.8%         1.60             -0.6
20                    27.0%       24.4%         1.80             -0.8
21                    30.0%       26.0%         2.00               -1
22                    33.0%       27.6%         2.20             -1.2
----------------------------------------------------------------------------
```

Figure 9.3. Calculating the expected return of efficient portfolios

of the market portfolio and the riskless security. The proportions defining an efficient portfolio are calculated by using the method discussed below. The proportion invested in the market portfolio is equal to the standard deviation of rate of return on the efficient portfolio under consideration divided by the standard deviation of rate of return on the market portfolio. The proportion invested in the riskless security equals one minus the proportion invested in the market portfolio. The portfolios of the capital market line are obtained by comparing the market portfolio with the risk-free borrowing or lending. For example, the efficient portfolio with expected return of 12.0 per cent and standard deviation of 16.4 per cent is generated by combining the market portfolio with risk-free borrowing. On the other hand, the efficient portfolio with risk and return characteristics of 18.0 per cent and 19.6 per cent, respectively, is obtained by combining the market portfolio with risk-free lending.

Graphically, the capital market line runs from the riskless rate of interest on the vertical axis through the market portfolio (see Figure 9.4). The slope of the line is equal to the difference between the return on the riskless security and the expected return on the market portfolio divided by the risk of the market portfolio: (18 per cent – 10 per cent)/15 per cent = 0.5333. This slope represents the additional expected return for each additional unit of risk accepted.

Problems

1 Create the results shown in Figure 9.3.
2 Present graphically the capital market line calculated in Problem 1.

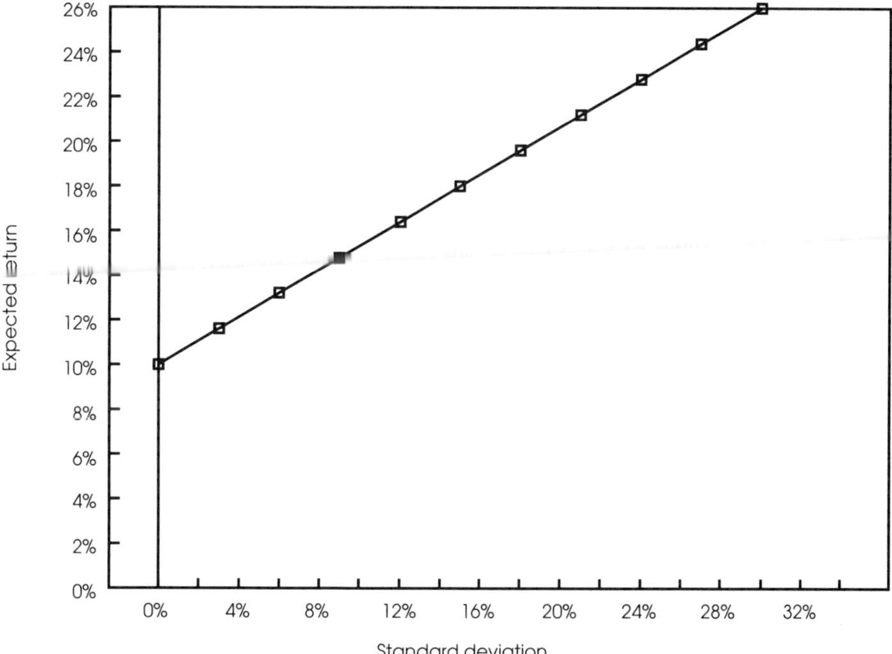

Figure 9.4. The resulting capital market line

The capital asset pricing model

In the previous section the existence of an equilibrium linear relationship between expected rate of return and standard deviation of rate of return for efficient portfolios was determined. The analysis can be extended to a different equilibrium relationship which indicates the expected return/risk trade-offs for individual securities or inefficient portfolios. The assumptions discussed earlier guarantee the efficiency of the market portfolio. Such a condition is necessary for the validity of an exact linear relationship between expected return and risk for individual securities or portfolios at equilibrium (Roll, 1977, proved that the efficiency of the market portfolio is also a sufficient condition for an exact relationship between expected return and risk):

$$E(R_i) = R_f + (E(R_m) - R_f)b_i$$

where

$E(R_i)$ = the expected return on security or portfolio i.
R_f = the return on the riskless security.
$E(R_m)$ = the expected return on the market portfolio.
b_i = the beta coefficient of security or portfolio i.

This equilibrium relationship is called the capital asset pricing model or the security market line, the version of the capital asset pricing model above is called the r_f-version (for a proof of the capital assets pricing model see Appendix 9A). The capital asset pricing model indicates that an investor can obtain above the riskless return only by taking on additional risk.

The beta coefficient (or simply beta) for security i can be expressed as:

$$b_i = \sigma_{im}/\sigma_m^2$$

where σ_{im} = the covariance between the rate of return on the market portfolio and the rate of return on security i, σ_m^2 = the variance of rate of return on portfolio m (Appendix 9B calculates the beta of Marks and Spencer plc using historical data).

The covariance between the rate of return on security i and the rate of return on the market portfolio measures the risk of security i in the market portfolio. Thus, the beta coefficient can be defined as the risk of security i in m relative to the total risk of the market portfolio. Figure 9.5 compares the risk of i in the market portfolio with the beta of the market portfolio with respect to itself (the beta of the market portfolio must be +1, by definition).

Condition	Consequence	Remark
$b_i = 1$	The security has the same risk with the market portfolio	Security i is expected, in equilibrium to earn the same return as does the market portfolio
$b_i > 1$	The security i is more risky than the market portfolio	The security i is called 'aggressive'. It will have an expected return which exceeds that of the market portfolio
$b_i < 1$	The security i is less risky than the market portfolio	The security i is called 'defensive'. It will have an expected return which is lower than that of the market portfolio

Figure 9.5. Measuring a security's beta versus the market portfolio's beta

According to the discussion provided earlier in this chapter, investors are willing to hold only the market portfolio as their portfolio of risky securities. In terms of individual securities, investors are concerned with the contribution of each security to the risk of the market portfolio.

Appendix 9B shows that the unsystematic risk of a security can be eliminated via the process of diversification. Therefore, in the capital asset pricing model, the relevant risk of a security (or portfolio) is its covariance within the market portfolio (that portion of the total risk which cannot be eliminated by diversification). Since unsystematic risk can disappear via the process of diversification, investors should be rewarded only for taking on systematic risk. The higher the beta of a security (or portfolio), the higher its expected return. As in the case of the capital market line, the capital asset pricing model shows that the expected return provides compensation for waiting and compensation for bearing risk.

Example 9.2 Calculating the expected returns on securities using the capital asset pricing model.

In Example 9.1, the market portfolio was assumed to have an expected return of 18 per cent and a standard deviation of 15 per cent. The risk-free rate was assumed to be 10 per cent. The covariance between the rate of return on a security *i* and the rate of return on the market is 0.02. Substituting the data in the capital asset pricing model yields:

$$E(R_i) = 0.10 + (0.18 - 0.10)0.02/(0.15\hat{\ }2)$$

$$= 0.10 + 0.071 = 17.1 \text{ per cent}$$

In this case, if an investor is willing to accept a change in security risk from 0 to 0.02 he or she demands an increase in expected return from 10 per cent to 17.1 per cent. The beta of the security *i* is 0.89 (that is, 0.02/(0.15^2)). The expected return of security *i* is lower than that of the market portfolio because security *i* has a beta lower than 1.

The `/Data Table 1` command can be utilized to generate the expected returns on more securities or portfolios lying on the security market line. Figure 9.6 presents the results. Cell F9 stores the results of the formula `+F3+(F4-F3)*F7`. The 'input cell 1' is represented by cell F7. Column C shows the betas of different securities or portfolios lying on the capital market line. Column D presents the corresponding risk premiums and column F includes the corresponding expected returns. Figure 9.6 shows both defensive and aggressive securities (or portfolios). For example, the security (or portfolio) with beta of 0.8 is defensive, while the security (or portfolio) with beta of 1.2 is aggressive.

The capital asset pricing model is portrayed graphically in Figure 9.7 (note that only two points are required to plot a straight line). The vertical axis refers to expected return, whereas beta appears on the horizontal axis. The vertical intercept of the capital asset pricing model is equal to 10 per cent. The security market line begins at 10 per cent and slopes upwards to the right. The slope of the line is equal to the difference between the expected return on the market portfolio and the return on the riskless security: 18 per cent – 10 per cent = 8 per cent. The slope of the line shown in Figure 9.7 represents the additional expected return for each additional unit of risk accepted.

```
       A          B          C            D              E          F
 1 THE CAPITAL ASSET PRICING MODEL
 2 ===============================
 3 Riskless Rate of Interest                                      10.0%
 4 Expected Return on the Market Portfolio                        18.0%
 5 Standard Deviation on the Market Portfolio                     15.0%
 6 Covariance between M and Security i                             0.02%
 7 Beta for Security i                                             0.89
 8                                                             ---------
 9                                                                17.1%
10
11                          (F4-F3)*F7       +F9
12                   0.0                0.0%         10.0%
13                   0.2                1.6%         11.6%
14                   0.4                3.2%         13.2%
15                   0.6                4.8%         14.8%
16                   0.8                6.4%         16.4%
17                   1.0                8.0%         18.0%
18                   1.2        16.0    9.6%         19.6%
19                   1.4               11.2%         21.2%
20                   1.6               12.8%         22.8%
21                   1.8               14.4%         24.4%
22                   2.0               16.0%         26.0%
23                   2.2               17.6%         27.6%
```

Figure 9.6. Calculating the expected return of securities

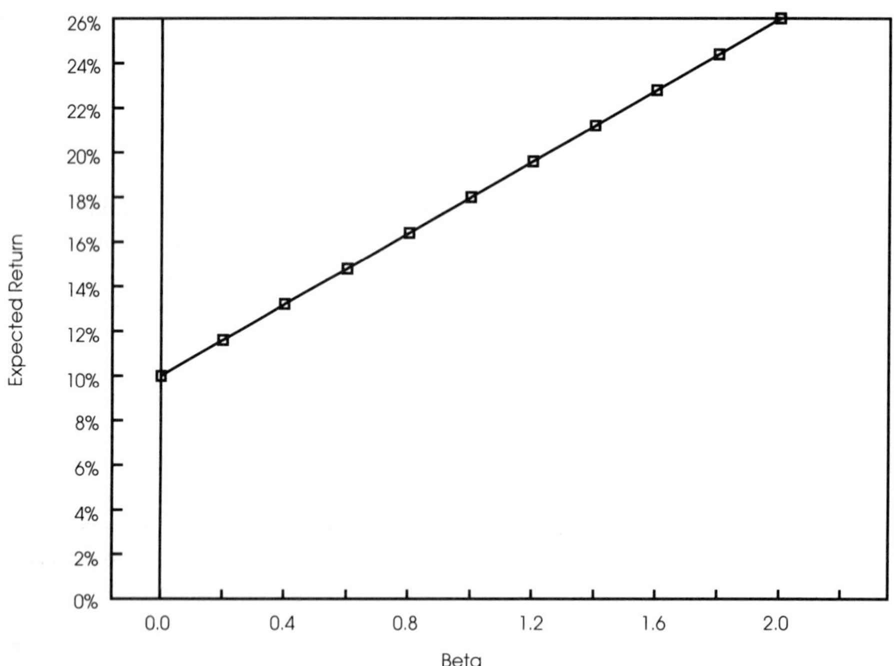

Figure 9.7. The resulting capital asset pricing model

Problems

1 Create the results shown in Figure 9.6.
2 Present graphically the security market line calculated in Problem 1.

The beta of a portfolio is simply a weighted average of the betas of the securities making up the portfolio, where the weights are equal to the proportions of the respective securities in the portfolio. The beta coefficient can be estimated from historical data via the statistical technique of regression analysis (see Appendix 9B).

The capital market line versus the security market line

The capital market line or the security market line is a linear equilibrium relationship between expected return and risk. For efficient portfolios, the appropriate risk measure is the standard deviation of rate of return. On the other hand, the risk for individual securities or inefficient portfolios is measured by beta, a measure for systematic risk. Only efficient portfolios are lying on the capital market line, while all individual securities and portfolios are positioned on the security market line. Each line intercepts the expected return axis at the riskless rate of interest. The slope

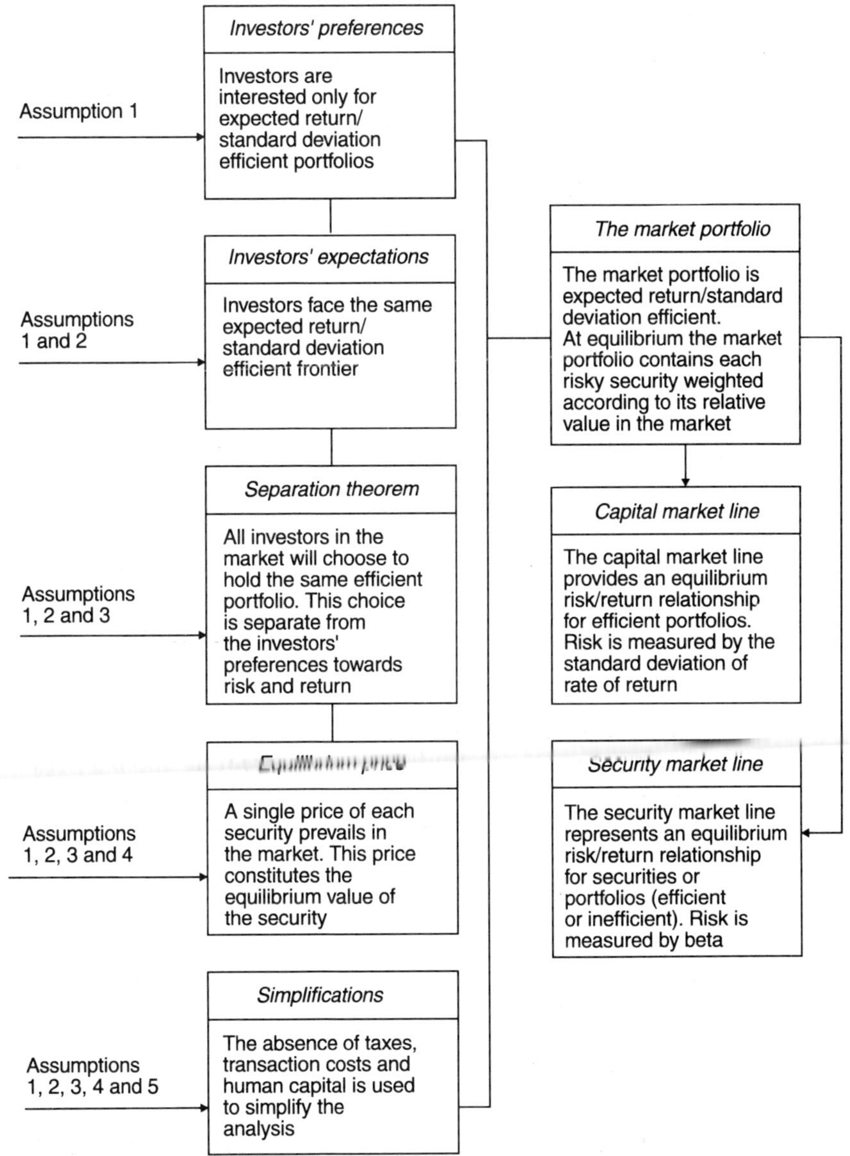

Figure 9.8. A summary of the capital market line and security market line

of each line is positive indicating that investors expect a higher return as risk increases. Figure 9.8 summarizes the capital market line and security market line.

The two-factor capital asset pricing model

The r_f-version of the capital asset pricing model assumes that a riskless security exists, where investors can borrow (or lend) at the same rate. Such an assumption is very unrealistic and Black (1972) developed a risk/return exact linear relationship by considering the case where investors can neither borrow nor lend at the riskless rate of interest. Black's model assumes that short-selling of risky securities is permitted and uses two (minimum standard deviation) portfolios: the market portfolio and another portfolio whose rate of return has no correlation with the rate of return of the market portfolio. The rate of return of the market portfolio is uncorrelated with the rates of return of an infinite number of portfolios that have the same expected return, but only one of them lies on the minimum standard deviation (variance) portfolio set. This is called the minimum standard deviation zero-beta portfolio. Its beta is zero of course, since it is uncorrelated with the market portfolio. The capital asset pricing model of Black can be expressed as:

$$E(R_i) = E(R_z) + (E(R_m) - E(R_z))b_i$$

where

$E(R_i)$ = the expected return on security or portfolio i.
$E(R_z)$ = the expected return on the minimum standard-deviation zero-beta portfolio.
b_i = the beta coefficient of security or portfolio i.

Black's model is called the two-factor capital asset pricing model or the r_z-version of the capital asset pricing model.

The two-factor capital asset pricing model has the following two implications: Firstly, at equilibrium investors hold portfolios consisting of combinations of the market portfolio and its corresponding minimum standard deviation zero-beta portfolio. Secondly, the market portfolio is expected return/standard deviation efficient because: (a) all investors choose expected return/standard deviation efficient portfolios from the same efficient frontier; and (b) the market portfolio is a linear combination of efficient portfolios.

Roll (1977) proved that Black's relationship held for every efficient portfolio (even if only a sample of securities is considered) as opposed to Black's original model which held only for the market portfolio. The expected return of a portfolio whose rate of return is uncorrelated with the rate of return of an efficient portfolio can be expressed as (see Roll, 1977):

$$E(R_z) = \frac{a - bE(R_m)}{b - cE(R_m)}$$

where a, b, c are the entries of the minimum variance set's information matrix which were defined in Chapter 8.

Example 9.3 Calculating the efficient frontier (or sample capital market line)

In Chapter 8 (see Example 8.24), we estimated the minimum variance boundary portfolio set using the rates of return on five securities. We found the following entries for the set's information matrix: constant a: 0.130, constant b: 3.600, and constant c: 243.870. Consider an efficient portfolio, call it p, with mean and standard deviation of 3.81 per cent and 10.57 per cent, respectively. Then, the minimum standard deviation portfolio whose rate of return is uncorrelated with the rate of return of this efficient portfolio has a mean return of 0.13 per cent:

$$E(R_z) = \frac{0.130 - (3.600)(0.0381)}{3.600 - (243.870)(0.0381)} = 0.13 \text{ per cent}$$

Column B of Figure 9.9 shows the mean returns of various minimum standard deviation portfolios. Cell C13 contains a formula that is used to calculate the minimum standard deviation of the portfolio with mean return of 0.181 per cent:

```
@SQRT((($E$3-2*$E$4*B13+$E$5&B13^2)/($E$3*$E$5-$E$4^2)))
```

The contents of cell C13 are copied in the range C14..C30.

The sample capital market line has a structure similar to the capital market line developed earlier in this chapter, but it uses the mean return of the zero-beta portfolio rather than the riskless rate of interest. Cell D13 stores the results of a formula that calculates the mean return of an efficient portfolio on the sample capital market line

```
+$E$8+($E$6-$E$8)*(C13/$E$7)
```

	A	B	C	D	E	F
1	CALCULATING A SAMPLE CAPITAL MARKET LINE					
2	==					
3	Constant a					0.130%
4	Constant b					3.600%
5	Constant c					243.870%
6	Mean Return of the Optimal Portfolio					3.810%
7	Stand. Dev. of the Optimal Portfolio					10.57%
8	Return on the Orthogonal Portfolio					0.13%
9						
10						
11		MEAN	SD	SAMPLE CML		
12		0.181%	0	0.13%		
13		0.181%	7.93%	2.89%		
14		0.440%	7.41%	[illegible]		
15		0.699%	6.99%	2.56%		
16		0.958%	6.67%	2.45%		
17		1.217%	6.47%	2.38%		
18		1.476%	6.40%	2.36%		
19		1.865%	6.56%	2.41%		
20		2.253%	6.99%	2.56%		
21		2.642%	7.66%	2.80%		
22		3.031%	8.51%	3.09%		
23		3.419%	9.49%	3.44%		
24		3.808%	10.57%	3.81%		
25		4.197%	11.72%	4.21%		
26		4.585%	12.91%	4.63%		
27		4.974%	14.15%	5.06%		
28		5.363%	15.41%	5.50%		
29		5.751%	16.70%	5.95%		
30		6.140%	18.00%	6.40%		

Figure 9.9. Calculating a sample capital market line (original data: monthly rates of returns over four years)

We use the standard deviation stored in cell C13, since there exists a portfolio lying on the sample capital market line that corresponds to a standard deviation of 7.93 per cent. The contents of cell D13 are copied in the range D14..D30.

These results can be presented graphically as illustrated in Figure 9.10. Note that Figure 9.9 contains in row 12 some additional entries. These entries are used in the graph to show the minimum standard deviation zero-beta portfolio. The type of 1-2-3 graph used in *XY*. The sample capital market line is represented graphically by a target line to the efficient frontier at the point with coordinates of 3.81 per cent and 10.57 per cent (slight deviations occur due to rounding). Such a line intercepts the mean return axis at 0.13 per cent.

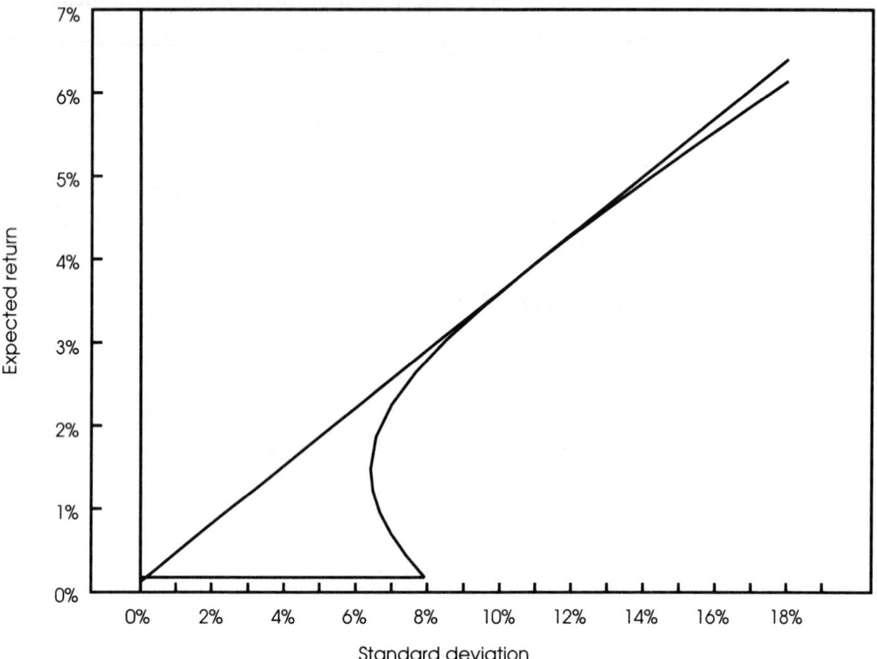

Figure 9.10. A sample capital market line

Problems

1 Create the results shown in Figure 9.9.
2 Present graphically the capital market line calculated in Problem 1.

Capital asset pricing model: the empirical evidence

There have been several attempts to test the implications of the capital asset pricing model (that is, the r_f-version), using (historical) rates of return of securities and (historical) rates of return on a market index (for example, an equity market index is a portfolio used to represent the whole market of equities). These studies include: Lintner (his study reproduced in Douglas, 1968), Jacob (1971), Miller and Scholes (1972), Black *et al.* (1972), Blume and Friend (1973) and Fama and MacBeth (1973). The testable implications of the capital asset pricing model are summarized as follows:

1 The relationship between average (historical) return and beta is linear.
2 Beta is the only risk that is related to the average (historical) return.
3 The (market index's) risk premium (that is, the average market *minus* the risk-free rate of return) is positive.

The implications of the capital asset pricing model were empirically examined by using two testing methodologies, a two-stage cross-sectional methodology and a time-series methodology.

The two-stage cross-sectional methodology used to test the first implication is summarized as follows:

Procedure Compute the beta coefficients by regressing each security's rates of return and the market index's rates of return. Such regressions are called first-pass regressions. Then, regress the average holding period returns of the securities (or portfolios) on the estimated betas and compare the regression coefficients with the risk-free rate and the market index's risk premium, respectively. The cross-sectional regression is called second-pass regression.

Decision If the first coefficient of the second-pass regression is equal to the risk-free rate and the second coefficient is equal to the market index's risk premium, then accept the first implication of the capital asset pricing model (see Figure 9.11).

There are several econometric problems associated with this methodology including the following:

1 If the risk-free rate is not stationary over time, and if it is uncorrelated with the rate of return on the market proxy used, then there exists the case of a missing variable. If an important independent variable is left out of the regression equation, the procedure utilized to estimate security betas will produce biased coefficients. If the beta coefficients are biased, then the intercept and the slope of the cross-sectional regression line will be biased.
2 If there is no linearity between the expected returns and beta, then the second-pass regression is misspecified. In this case, the estimated linear regression coefficients will be biased.
3 If the variance of the error terms changes through time (that is, the error term is heteroscedastic), then the coefficients of the first-pass regression will be inefficient and hence less accurate. In this case, standard statistical tests for the significance of the coefficients are less valid.
4 If there are measurement errors in variables, then the coefficient betas of the first-pass regression will be biased. As a consequence, the coefficients of the second-pass regression will also be biased. One way to reduce the errors in variables is to work with portfolios rather than individual securities. The portfolio error term is just the weighted average of security error terms. Therefore, the errors of the individual securities tend to cancel out each other. This means that errors in measuring the variables are likely to be less serious in portfolios than they would be if individual securities were used.

The time series methodology used to test the first implication is summarized below:

Procedure Regress the (historical) excess returns of the portfolios on the (historical) excess returns of the market index and examine whether the intercept of the regression is significantly different from zero (Excess portfolio return = Portfolio rate of return minus Risk-free rate and Excess market index return = rate of return of the market index minus Risk-free rate).

Decision If the first coefficient of the time-series regression is significantly different from zero, then accept the first implication of the capital asset pricing model.

The time-series methodology may produce the following econometric problem: if successive error terms are not independent, the estimates of the regression coefficients will be inefficient and hence less accurate. In this instance, standard statistical tests for the significance of the coefficients are less valid.

A summary of the two-stage cross-sectional methodology used to test the second implication is given below:

Procedure Compute the beta and the unsystematic risk for each portfolio in the sample. Then, regress the average holding period returns of the portfolios on the estimated betas and unsystematic risk; compare the regression coefficients with the risk-free rate of return, the market risk premium and the number zero, respectively.

Decision If the first coefficient of the second-pass regression is equal to the risk-free rate, the second coefficient is equal to the market index's

Author/date/ duration	Tests based on individual securities			
	First implication	Second implication	Third implication	Capital asset pricing model
Lintner (1968) Annual returns	Accepted	Rejected	Accepted	Rejected
Jacob (1971) Monthly returns	Accepted	—	Accepted	Rejected
Miller and Scholes (1972) Annual returns	Accepted	Rejected	Accepted	Rejected
Author/date duration	**Tests based on portfolios**			
	First implication	Second implication	Third implication	Capital asset pricing model
Black *et al.* (1972) Monthly returns	Accepted	—	Accepted	Rejected
Blume and Friend (1973) Monthly returns	Accepted	Accepted	Accepted	Rejected
Fama and Macbeth (1973) Monthly returns	Accepted	Accepted	Accepted	Rejected

Figure 9.11. Summary results of the capital asset pricing model's tests

risk premium and the third coefficient is equal to zero, then accept the second implication of the capital asset pricing model.

Finally, the third implication of the capital asset pricing model can be tested during the previous tests by examining the sign of the second-pass regression coefficient.

Figure 9.11 summarizes several tests of the r_f-version of the capital asset pricing model. The conclusions about the validity of the capital asset pricing model have been questioned by Roll (1977). The next section provides a discussion of the Roll critique.

The problem of testing the CAPM: Roll's critique

Roll's (1977) main result can be summarized as follows:

If the covariance matrix of security returns is non-singular and the mean return security vector contains at least two distinct entries, then the following is true: a portfolio is mean/standard deviation efficient if, and only if, there exists an exact linear risk/return relationship, where risk is measured by beta.

Roll's conclusion holds for the whole population of risky securities in the market, as well as for any sample of securities drawn from this population. The consequences of Roll's results are very important. In fact, it can be concluded that the mean/standard deviation efficiency of the market portfolio and the validity of the capital asset pricing model are joint hypotheses. Consequently, the only way to test the capital asset pricing model directly is to test the following implication: the market portfolio is mean/standard deviation efficient.

However, the true market portfolio contains all the risky securities (for example, shares, coins, art objects, land, and so on) in proportion to their relative value in the market. This implies that one can test the capital asset pricing model directly if given all the securities that comprise the market portfolio and the equilibrium proportions of each security in the market portfolio. Since it is not possible to identify all the risky securities and their weights in the market portfolio, it is impossible to identify the market portfolio itself. This argument led Roll to conclude that it is impossible to test the capital asset pricing model.

Roll also relies on his main result and points out that earlier tests of the capital asset pricing model (see Figure 9.11) provide nothing more but tests of the mean/standard deviation efficiency of the market proxy used.

Example 9.4 Calculating a sample beta/return relationship

Consider the sample of the securities given in Example 8.24 (see Chapter 8). Choose an efficient portfolio, call it p, with mean 3.81 per cent and standard deviation of 10.57 per cent (these values are calculated in Example 9.3). The covariance vector and the beta vector related to portfolio p are given below (the variance of portfolio p is 0.01117):

$$VX = (Ru)'A^{-1}(r_p\ 1) = \begin{bmatrix} 0.0076 \\ 0.0001 \\ 0.0041 \\ 0.0024 \\ 0.0034 \end{bmatrix} \qquad B = VX/0.01117 = \begin{bmatrix} 0.6809 \\ 0.0079 \\ 0.3642 \\ 0.2141 \\ 0.3031 \end{bmatrix}$$

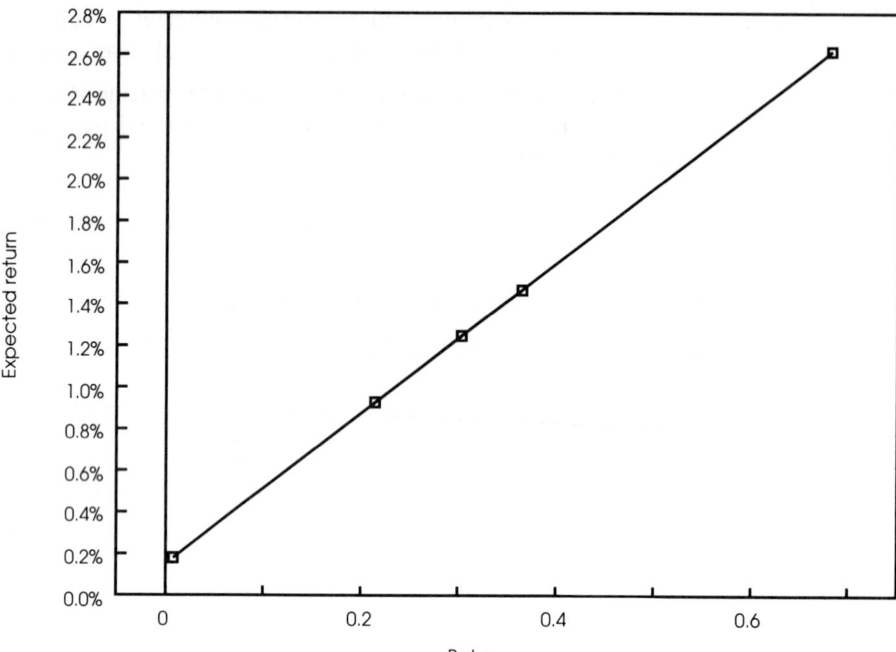

Figure 9.12. A sample risk/return relationship

The risk/return relationship can be examined by plotting the mean returns on the securities and their corresponding betas. The mean returns are as follows: Allied Lyons, 2.615 per cent; Boots, 0.180 per cent; GKN, 1.469 per cent; Marks and Spencer, 0.926 per cent; and National Westminster, 1.248 per cent. The risk/return relationship is depicted in Figure 9.12 (slight deviations occur due to rounding). This example shows that the mean/standard deviation efficiency of portfolio p implies the existence of an exact linear relationship between mean returns and betas. This relationship has the same form with the capital asset pricing model, but the former is valid in a sample of securities.

The risk/return relationship shown in Figure 9.12 can be also represented by the following equation:

$$r_i = 0.13 \text{ per cent} + (3.81 \text{ per cent} - 0.13 \text{ per cent})b_i$$

Consider a minimum variance portfolio, call it s, defined by the following proportions: Allied Lyons, 0.6494; Boots, 0.1492; GKN, 0.0134; Marks and Spencer, −0.0641; and National Westminster, 0.2521. The mean return of portfolio s can be computed as follows (small deviations are due to rounding):

$$\begin{aligned} r_s &= (0.6494)(2.615 \text{ per cent}) + (0.1492)(0.180 \text{ per cent}) \\ &\quad + (0.0134)(1.469 \text{ per cent}) + (-0.0641)(0.926 \text{ per cent}) \\ &\quad + (0.2521)(1.248 \text{ per cent}) \\ &= 2.0 \text{ per cent} \end{aligned}$$

The beta of portfolio s would be

$$b_s = (0.6494)(0.6809) + (0.1492)(0.0079) + (0.0134)(0.3642) + (-0.0641)(0.2141) + (0.2521)(0.3031) = 0.511$$

In view of the sample risk/return relationship, the mean return of portfolio s is

$$r_s = 0.13 \text{ per cent} + (3.81 \text{ per cent} - 0.13 \text{ per cent})0.511 = 2.0 \text{ per cent}$$

This part of the example reveals the following conclusion (see Roll, 1978): if the selected index is mean/standard deviation efficient, all individual securities and portfolios (efficient or not) would lie on the straight line derived from the efficiency of the index. In this case, it will be impossible to find a security or portfolio which outperforms (or underperforms) the index used.

There exist further tests of the capital asset pricing model carried out after Roll's critique. Gibbons (1982) adopted a multivariate statistical methodology which: (a) avoids the measurement errors in variables, and (b) increases the precision of the parameters. His results rejected both the original capital asset pricing model and the zero-beta capital asset pricing model. Gibbons recognized Roll's criticism and he claimed that his conclusions are based upon a robust methodology.

The method of Shanken (1987) utilizes beliefs about the correlation between the rates of return on a market proxy and the rates of return on the true market portfolio. He introduced a joint test examining the validity of the following joint hypotheses: the correlation between the rates of return of the proxy used and the rates of return of the unobservable market portfolio is in excess of 0.7, and the capital asset pricing model is valid. His results rejected the capital asset pricing model. The work of Shanken is important, because he demonstrated that tests on the capital asset pricing model do not rely only upon the identification of the true market portfolio, but they can also be based upon a prior belief about the correlation of a proxy and the true market portfolio. On the critical side, it is difficult to justify the prior belief on correlation, since the market portfolio is unobservable.

The arbitrage pricing model

An alternative approach to characterization of expected returns on risky securities is the arbitrage pricing model proposed by Ross (1976, 1977). Proponents of the arbitrage pricing theory argue that it has the following two advantages over the capital asset pricing model:

1. It is based upon less restrictive assumptions with respect investors' preference towards risk and return.
2. The market portfolio plays no special role.

A two-factor arbitrage pricing model

We assume that the rate of return on security i, during a given period of time, is expressed as follows:

$$R_{it} = a_i + b_{i1}F_{1t} + b_{i2}F_{2t} + e_{it} \tag{9.1}$$

where

$i = 1, 2, \ldots, N$.

F_{kt} = the unknown common factor k that affects the security rates of return during the period $t, k = 1, 2$.

b_{ik} = the sensitivity of the ith security's rate of return to the fluctuations in the common factor F_{kt} (it is also called the k-factor sensitivity coefficient of security i), $k = 1, 2$.

e_{it} = the security i's disturbance term. A security's e's are independent with any other security's e's and each disturbance term has a finite variance. The expected value of the disturbance term equals zero.

Taking the expected value of Equation (9.1) we produce:

$$E(R_i) = a_i + b_{i1}E(F_1) + b_{i2}E(F_2) \tag{9.2}$$

Subtracting Equation (9.2) from Equation (9.1) and rearranging terms yields:

$$R_{it} = E(R_i) + b_{i1}[F_{1t} - E(F_1)] + b_{i2}[F_{2t} - E(F_2)] + e_{it} \tag{9.3}$$

Equation (9.3) is called a security return generating model, because it is used to describe security rates of return.

Consider a diversified portfolio, call it p, that uses no wealth and has zero-systematic risk. In this instance, we can write

$$X'_p u = 0 \tag{9.4}$$

$$X'_p B_1 = 0 \tag{9.5}$$

$$X'_p B_2 = 0 \tag{9.6}$$

$$X'_p e \approx 0$$

where X_p = the $(N \times 1)$ investment proportion vector defining portfolio p, u = the $(N \times 1)$ unit vector, B_1 = the $(N \times 1)$ vector of betas related to factor F_1, B_2 = the $(N \times 1)$ vector of betas related to factor F_2 and e = the $(N \times 1)$ vector of disturbance terms.

The arbitrage pricing theory also assumes that all portfolios which use no wealth and have zero risk earn a zero expected return. Therefore, we have

$$X'_p R = 0 \tag{9.7}$$

From Equations (9.4), (9.5), (9.6), and (9.7) we see that the investment proportion vector X_p is orthogonal to the vectors u, B_1, B_2 and R. As a consequence, we can express the vector R as a linear combination of vectors u and B_1 and B_2:

$$R = h_1 u + h_2 B_1 + h_3 B_2 \tag{9.8}$$

Therefore,

$$E(R_i) = h_1 + h_2 b_{i1} + h_3 b_{i2} \tag{9.9}$$

Consider a portfolio, call it z, that is riskless. Then Equation (9.8) gives:

$$E(R_z) = h_1 \tag{9.10}$$

Now consider two portfolios, call them $p1$ and $p2$. The first portfolio has a unit sensitivity to the first factor and a zero sensitivity to the second factor, while portfolio $p2$ has a a zero sensitivity to the first factor and a unit sensitivity to the second factor.

In this case,

$$h_2 = E(R_{p1}) - E(R_z) \tag{9.11}$$

and

$$h_3 = E(R_{p2}) - E(R_z) \tag{9.12}$$

Substituting Equations (9.10), (9.11) and (9.12) into Equation (9.9) we observe

$$E(R_i) = E(R_z) + [E(R_{p1}) - E(R_z)]b_{i1} + [E(R_{p2}) - E(R_z)]b_{i2} \tag{9.13}$$

Note that the term $[E(R_{p1}) - E(R_z)]b_{i1}$ represents the risk premium that is associated with the first factor and $[E(R_{p2}) - E(R_z)]b_{i2}$ is the risk premium associated with the second factor.

Example 9.5 A two-factor arbitrage pricing model

Consider five diversified portfolios whose expected return can be described by a two-factor arbitrage pricing model. If an investor holds a combination of the five portfolios, assume that he or she holds a well diversified portfolio (that is a portfolio with no unsystematic risk). Figure 9.13 shows the changes in the two (orthogonal) factors and the sensitivity coefficients of each security in relation to factors 1 and 2.

	A	B	C	D	E	F
1						
2		% CHANGES ON:			SENSITIVITY COEFFICIENTS:	
3		FACTOR 1:	FACTOR 2:		FACTOR 1:	FACTOR 2:
4						
5		-8.00%	-3.00%		0.530	1.969
6		-4.00%	50.00%		0.400	0.420
7		25.00%	30.00%		1.110	0.610
8		45.00%	-15.00%		0.504	1.300
9		50.00%	2.02%		0.765	0.860
10						
11	MEAN	21.60%	12.80%			

Figure 9.13. Data for the arbitrage pricing model example

The arbitrage pricing theory asserts the following: 'If a portfolio requires zero net cash outlay, has no risk, then it must produce an expected return of zero.'

Consider Mr Annis who believes that portfolios 1, 2, 3 and 4 are undervalued and portfolio 5 is overvalued. Then he wants to take advantage of this situation by short selling £x worth of portfolio 5 and uses the proceeds to buy £x worth in portfolios 1, 2, 3 and 4. Mr Annis evaluates the situation and decides to hold a portfolio (call it p) which is comprised of portfolios 1, 2, 3, 4 and 5 as follows:

Portfolio 1:	0.110
Portfolio 2:	0.200
Portfolio 3:	0.400
Portfolio 4:	0.150
Portfolio 5:	−0.860
	0.000

Portfolio p is an arbitrage portfolio because it involves no net cash payment by Mr Annis. The sensitivity coefficients of portfolio p can be calculated as shown in

	A	B	C	D	E	F
12						
13		INVESTMENT	SENSITIVITY	WEIGHTED	SENSITIVITY	WEIGHTED
14		PROPORTIONS	COEFFICIENTS	COEFFICIENT	COEFFICIENTS	COEFFICIENT
15			FOR FACTOR 1		FOR FACTOR 2	
16		(1)	(2)	(1)x(2)	(4)	(1)x(4)
17						
18		0.110	0.530	0.058	1.969	0.217
19		0.200	0.400	0.080	0.420	0.084
20		0.400	1.110	0.444	0.610	0.244
21		0.150	0.504	0.076	1.300	0.195
22		-0.860	0.765	-0.658	0.860	-0.740
23		------------		-------------		-------------
24		0.0000		0.0000		0.0000
25						

Figure 9.14. Calculating the systematic risk of an arbitrage portfolio

Figure 9.14. Portfolio p is a zero-systematic risk portfolio because it involves zero systematic risk.

Using the two-factor arbitrage model, the expected returns of portfolio 1 can be calculated as follows (we assume a risk-free rate of 10 per cent):

$$0.1000 + (0.216 - 0.100) \times 0.530 + (0.128 - 0.100) \times 1.969 = 21.669 \text{ per cent}$$

Similarly:

Expected return $E(R2) \rightarrow$ 15.818 per cent
Expected return $E(R3) \rightarrow$ 24.586 per cent
Expected return $E(R4) \rightarrow$ 19.492 per cent
Expected return $E(R5) \rightarrow$ 21.285 per cent

As a result, the expected return of Mr Annis's portfolio will be (approximately) zero (see Figure 9.15).

	A	B	C	D	E	F
26	Risk-Free Rate ->		10.0%			
27						
28		INVESTMENT	EXPECTED	WEIGHTED		
29		PROPORTIONS	PORTFOLIO	EXPECTED		
30			RETURN	RETURNS		
31						
32		0.1100	21.669%	2.384%		
33		0.2000	15.818%	3.164%		
34		0.4000	24.586%	9.835%		
35		0.1500	19.472%	2.924%		
36		-0.8600	21.285%	-18.305%		
37				-------------		
38				0.000%		
39						

Figure 9.15. Calculating the expected return of an arbitrage riskless portfolio

The analysis presented above can be generalized by assuming a k factor security return generating model. The k factor arbitrage pricing model can be proved in a similar fashion to the two-factor arbitrage pricing model:

$$E(R_i) = E(R_z) + [E(R_{p1}) - E(R_z)]b_{i1} + \ldots + [E(R_{pk}) - E(R_z)]b_{ik}$$

The arbitrage pricing theory: the empirical evidence

Several empirical tests of the arbitrage pricing model have been presented in the literature, these include, Gehr (1978), Roll and Ross (1980), Reinganum (1981), Johnson (1981) and Hughes (1982). Empirical examination of the arbitrage pricing model has relied on the following methodology. Estimate the sensitivity coefficients employing the multivariate technique of factor analysis (that is, a technique which attempts to explain the correlations between a large set of security (or portfolio) returns in terms of a small number of factors). Then examine the (cross-sectional) relationship between the security (or portfolio) average returns and the sensitivity coefficients.

Figure 9.16 summarizes five studies of the arbitrage pricing model.

Figure 9.16. Summary results of the arbitrage pricing model's empirical tests

Author	Country	Type of data	Conclusion
Gehr (1978)	USA	Monthly returns for 24 indices and 41 equities	• Accept the model • One factor is priced
Roll and Ross (1980)	USA	Daily returns for 1260 equities	• Accept the model • 3–4 factors are priced
Reinganum (1981)	USA	Daily returns	• Reject the model
Johnson (1981)	UK	Monthly returns 35 indices and 1308 equities	• Accept the model
Hughes (1982)	Canada	Monthly returns for 20 equities	• Accept the model • 3–4 factors are priced

The arbitrage pricing model's tests have been criticized by Diacogiannis (1986b) on the ground that they have left untested several assumptions related to the multivariate statistical method used. The empirical tests of the arbitrage pricing model (see Figure 9.16) assume that the rates of return of securities in the market are affected by a small number of unobservable factors. These factors remain the same across different security groups and are stable throughout the time.

To test these hypotheses, Diacogiannis employed monthly data from November 1956 to December 1981 for 200 British securities. The main selection criterion for these securities was that they must be continuously listed on the London Stock Exchange for the entire sample period. The sample of 200 securities was used to create randomly five master groups of 40 securities each. Then from each master group seven sub-groups of securities were formed. Additionally, for each security, the monthly observations were divided into five sub-periods, three with 100 observations each and two with 150 observations each.

The results, shown in Figures 9.17 and 9.18, reveal the following:

- It is very difficult to assess which is the appropriate group size that has to be used in order to investigate the empirical validity of the arbitrage pricing model.
- The security return generating model is not observable and changes with the group size. Consequently, the model cannot be tested unambiguously using time series from the London Stock Exchange.

Diacogiannis (1986b) also tested the number of factors across five sub-periods and his results revealed that the number of factors changes throughout the time. As a consequence, the arbitrage pricing model cannot be utilized for forecasting purposes.

Figure 9.17. The number of factors versus group size (November 1956 to December 1981)

Group size	Average number of factors	Average of cumulative percentage of total variance accounted for by the common factors
5	1	52.5
10	2	56.5
15	3	60.1
20	4	57.9
25	5	59.1
30	6	61.6
35	7	62.4
40	9	62.8

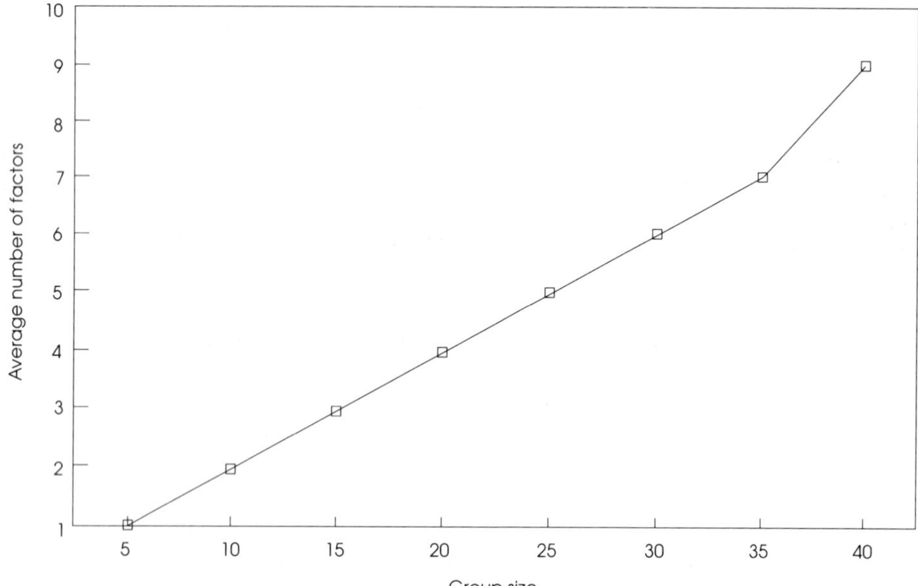

Figure 9.18. Average number of factors versus group size

Figure 9.19 summarizes the models of capital asset discussed in this chapter. Strictly speaking the capital asset pricing model cannot be considered as a special case of the arbitrage pricing theory, since some of the assumptions of the latter are different from the assumptions of the former.

Forms of the efficient market hypothesis

Consider a market meeting the following conditions:

- It is a well-established market with a large number of competing buyers and sellers (for example, the London Stock Exchange).
- Its participants share the same information.
- Its participants prefer a high expected return to a low one and low risk to high risk.

In such a competitive market share prices adjust almost immediately to information

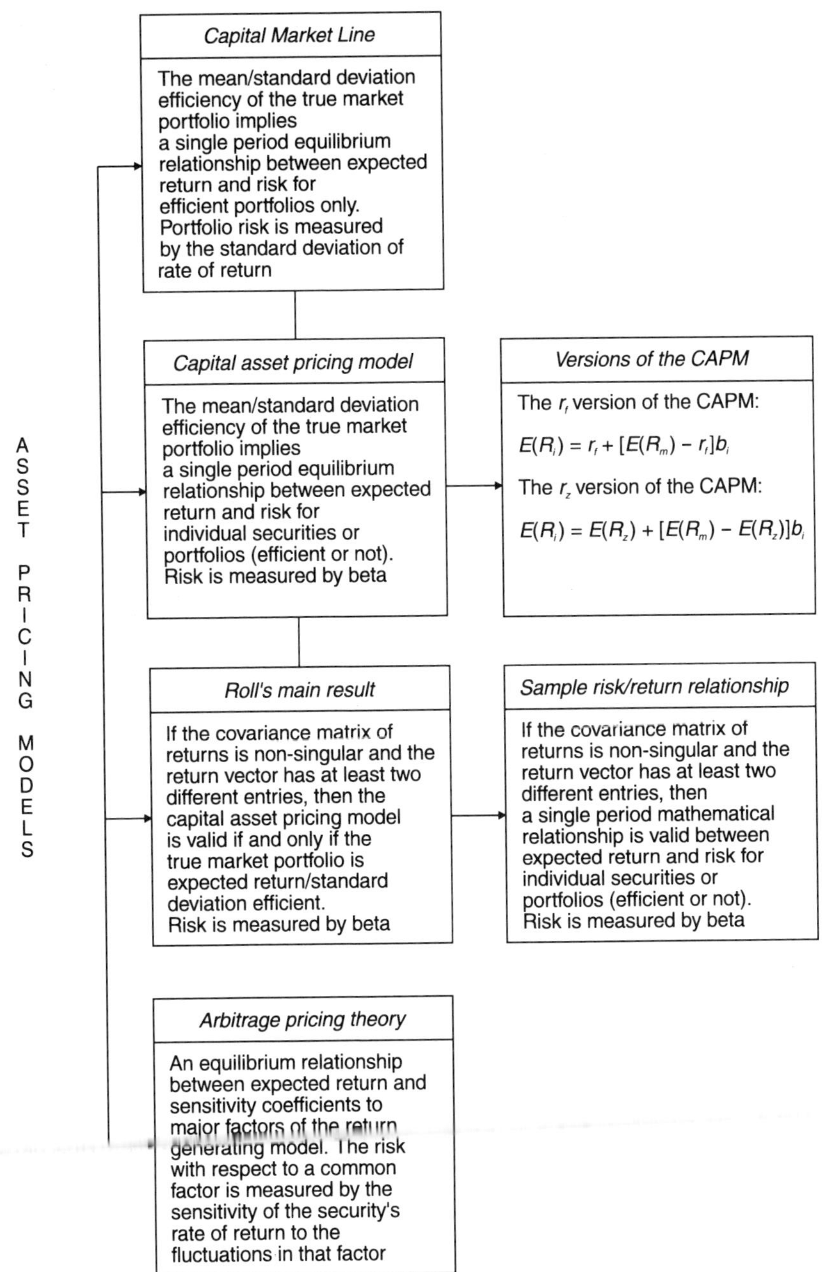

Figure 0.10. A summary of the asset pricing models discussed in this chapter

and trading strategies cannot be used to obtain, on average, abnormal returns on security investments of a given level of risk. The basis for distinguishing normal from abnormal returns is the concept of the intrinsic value. The intrinsic value (or fair value) of a security (for example, an ordinary share) is the present value of the security's expected cash flows discounted using the investors' required rate of return on that security. Any substantial difference between price and intrinsic value indicates abnormal returns.

A competitive market, composed of a large number of investors, is said to be efficient with respect to a set of information, if prices in the market, at all times, respond fully and quickly to all information in the given information set (see Figure 9.20). The body of theory around the efficient market concept is called the efficient market hypothesis (EMH).

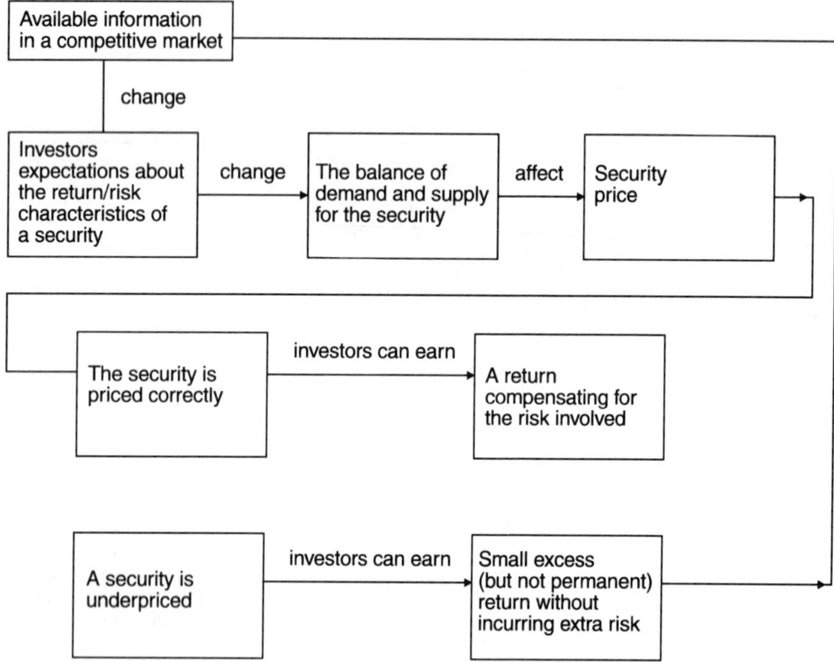

Figure 9.20. The concept of market efficiency

Fama (1970) considers three forms of the efficient market hypothesis: weak, semi-strong and strong.

Weak form efficiency

The capital market is said to be efficient in the weak form if past prices cannot be used to earn consistently abnormal profits.

Example 9.6 Return from investment and weak market efficiency

Suppose that the price of a firm's share follows a recurring pattern such that the price rises on the first trading day of the summer. If the market is efficient in the weak form, then this systematic pattern in the movements of the share price cannot be utilized to consistently earn a return above normal. Investors who recognize it will attempt to buy the shares of the firm on the last trading day of the spring in order to take advantage of the phenomenon. The competition between a large number of investors will drive up the firm's share price, thus, only a normal return can be expected—commensurate with the risk associated with the share.

Semi-strong form efficiency

The capital market is said to be efficient in the semi-strong form if publicly available information (for example, historical share prices, stock splits, dividend announcements, and so on) cannot be used to earn consistently abnormal profits.

Example 9.7 Share price and semi-strong market efficiency

Suppose that the profits of a firm will be announced in five days and a very large number of investors expects the profits to be high. Recently, a number of stockbrokers were recommending the shares of the firm, because they believe that the new management team's philosophy is very effective in generating profits. Investors are always looking forward trying to anticipate events. In our case, the investors' increased demand to buy the shares of the firm will cause an increase in the share price (see Figure 9.21). In an efficient market, the expected good news is quickly and properly assessed by a large number of investors and is incorporated into the price of shares. For example, the increase in the firm's share price from 97 pence to 105 pence indicates that a large number of investors have been changing their minds about the share and these expectations have already been built into the share price of 105 pence.

Assume that the profits of the firm were up by 25 per cent, but its share price has fallen after the announcement of the profits. Why? The increase in the profits was good, but investors had expected even better. The investors' expectations changed, the supply for the firm's shares increased, resulting in an immediate decrease in price. For example, the information related to the announcement made the investors anticipate a price fall and their expectations were incorporated in the share price that occurred after the announcement.

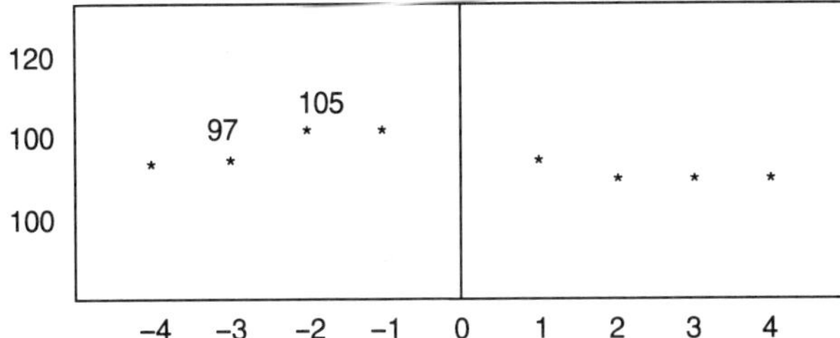

Figure 9.21. Price before and after the announcement of earnings

Strong form efficiency

The capital market is said to be efficient in the strong form if all information (that is, public or private) cannot be used to earn consistently abnormal profits.

Under the strong form, it is argued that investors with information that has not yet been made public cannot generate abnormal returns consistently (examples of insiders include directors, major shareholders, and so on). The theory argues that there are several reasons which prevent or discourage insiders to use private information for profit generation, including: (a) in most countries inside trade is against the law, and (b) competitive activity among insiders will quickly prevent abnormal returns.

Example 9.8 An example indicating the argument of the strong form of the efficient market hypothesis

Assume that a pharmaceutical firm discovers a new drug, but it wishes to wait for a few weeks before announcing the discovery. There is a number of employees having access to that inside information, for example, the directors of the firm, major shareholders, laboratory technicians, and so on. According to the strong form they could not use the information to generate profits until the firm announces the discovery of the drug to the public officially. This is a surprising event, because evidence indicates that investors utilize inside information to earn profits.

Fair game

It is difficult (if not impossible) to provide a direct test for the efficient market hypothesis. The empirical investigations related to the efficient market hypothesis rely on the implications of the hypothesis and the conditions required for its validity. Among these conditions is the following: a fair game states that a set of information on securities, available at period *t*, cannot be utilized to earn a return above the actual return at period $t+1$. The set of information could include one or more of the following:

Week form of EMH ⟶ Historical prices of securities.
Semi-strong form of EMH ⟶ Publicly available information, including historical prices of securities.
Strong form of EMH ⟶ All information (public or private).

The notion of a fair game can be explained further in Figure 9.22.

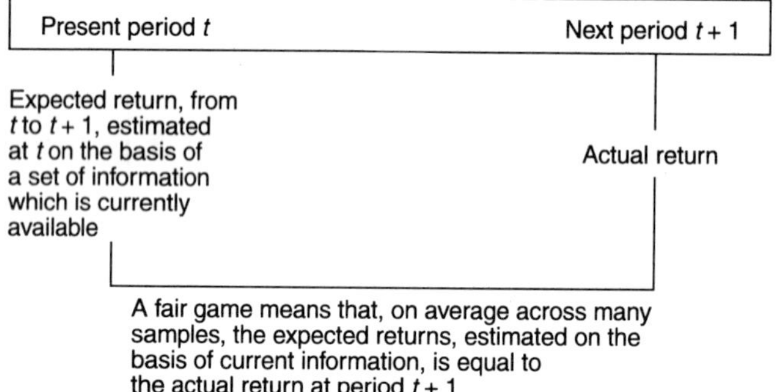

Figure 9.22. The concept of the fair game model

Random walk

The random walk hypothesis suggests that security returns (or successive price changes) from one period to the next are independently and identically distributed. The former implies that the occurrence of the next period's share return will not be connected in any way with the occurrence of any other historical returns; the latter implies that all the parameters of the distribution (for example, mean, standard deviation, and so on) will be the same with or without the available information. The random walk hypothesis is a statistical hypothesis that might be applied to any time series data.

Example 9.9 Explaining the concept of random walk using Lotus 1-2-3

The concept of the random walk can be understood by using the 1-2-3's mathematical function `@RAND` (that is, a function that generates random numbers). Figure 9.23, illustrates the generation of 15 random numbers in the range 0–20 per cent (type in cell D5 the function `@RAND*0.20` and copy the contents of cell D5 to the range D6..D19). Each random number stored in the worksheet represents the periodic return of a security. Since these returns are random, they are unrelated.

The function @RAND can also be used to generate the returns for another security, making the returns to be identically distributed (in order to generate another random series of returns, while you are working with the worksheet shown in Figure 9.23, press the function key [F9]).

	A	B	C	D	E	F	G	H	I
1									
2				RANDOM					
3				NUMBER					
4									
5			1	8.61%	<--------@RAND*0.2				
6			2	14.66%					
7			3	10.02%					
8			4	17.86%					
9			5	0.73%					
10			6	9.35%					
11			7	12.68%					
12			8	8.76%					
13			9	4.69%					
14			10	5.44%					
15			11	1.02%					
16			12	0.70%					
17			13	5.50%					
18			14	18.02%					
19			15	18.19%					
20									

Figure 9.23. Generating a series of random numbers using 1-2-3

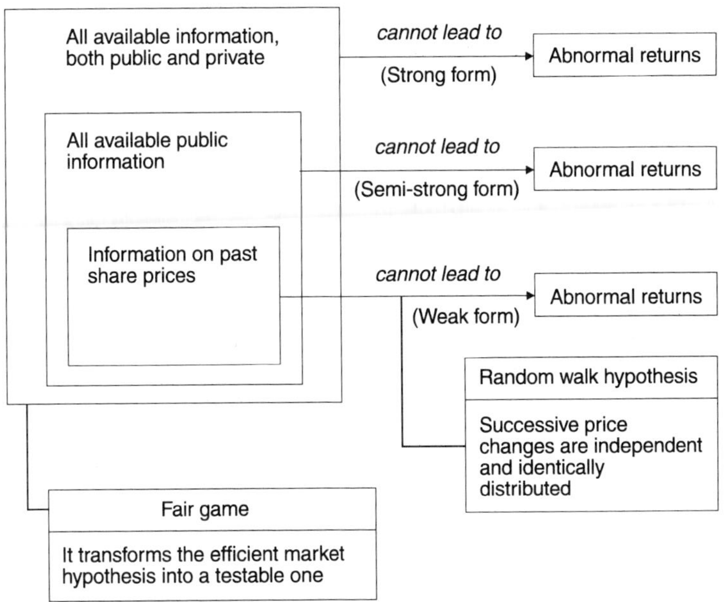

Figure 9.24. Forms of the efficient market hypothesis

The random walk model constitutes a stronger condition than the fair game model on the ground that the latter does not require independently and identically distributed returns. If the random walk hypothesis is valid, then the market is efficient in a weak form, but the validity of the weak form does not imply the validity of the random walk hypothesis. Figure 9.24 summarizes the forms of the efficient market hypothesis.

Empirical tests of the efficient market hypothesis

There exist various studies testing empirically each of the forms of the efficient market hypothesis.

Empirical tests of the weak form of the efficient market hypothesis

The tests of the weak form of the efficient market hypothesis investigate whether past share prices can be used to predict future share prices. This section describes four different tests that have been utilized to test the weak form of the efficient market hypothesis: serial correlation tests, filter tests, moving average tests and runs tests.

Serial correlation tests

A serial correlation test is a statistical method examining whether the numerical observations in a time-series data are linearly related over time. If the market is efficient in a weak form, then the future price changes of a security cannot be predicted from its historical price changes. In this case, the degree of association between the historical and future price changes is zero. Serial correlation can also be measured in lags, for example, we can examine the relationship between the next price change and the price change three periods previously. The serial correlation between the price change in period t and the price change three periods previously is called third-order serial correlation. We can test the statistical significance of the serial correlation by using the following regression line:

$$P_t - P_{t-1} = a + b(P_{t-1-T} - P_{t-2-T}) + e_t$$

where

$P_t, P_{t-1-T}, P_{t-2-T}$ = prices for periods $t, t-1-T$ and $t-2-T$, respectively, $T = 0, 1, 2, \ldots$

Example 9.10 FTA All Share Index: a serial correlation test.

Figure 9.25 shows the monthly changes for the FTA All Shares Index (January 1985–December 1988; *source*: Datastream) and calculates the following changes: $(P_t - P_{t-1}), (P_{t-1} - P_{t-2})$ and $(P_{t-2} - P_{t-3})$. For example, cell C7 contains the results of the formula `+B7-B6`, the contents of cell C7 are copied in the range C8..C53. To examine the statistical significance of the correlation coefficient between $(P_t - P_{t-1})$ and $(P_{t-1} - P_{t-2})$ the `/Data Regression` command of 1-2-3 is used. The range of the independent variable is D8..D53 and the range of the dependent variable is C8..C53.

The R-squared coefficient indicates the variation of the dependent variable explained by changes in the independent variable. If changes in the independent

	A	B	C	D	E
1	FT-ALL SHARES INDEX:SERIAL CORRELATION TEST				
3	PERIOD	PRICE	$P_t - P_{t-1}$	$P_{t-1} - P_{t-2}$	$P_{t-2} - P_{t-3}$
6	Jan-85	592.94			
7	Feb-85	612.82	19.88		
8	Mar-85	605.82	-7.00	19.88	
9	Apr-85	616.59	10.77	-7.00	19.88
10	May-85	626.60	10.01	10.77	-7.00
11	Jun-85	638.90	12.30	10.01	10.77
12	Jul-85	600.52	-38.38	12.30	10.01
13	Aug-85	616.98	16.46	-38.38	12.30
14	Sep-85	646.82	29.84	16.46	-38.38
15	Oct-85	629.29	-17.53	29.84	16.46
16	Nov-85	672.15	42.86	-17.53	29.84
17	Dec-85	688.02	15.87	42.86	-17.53
18	Jan-86	682.94	-5.08	15.87	42.86
19	Feb-86	692.74	9.80	-5.08	15.87
20	Mar-86	747.39	54.65	9.80	-5.08
21	Apr-86	818.22	70.83	54.65	9.80
22	May-86	807.46	-10.76	70.83	54.65
23	Jun-86	787.18	-20.28	-10.76	70.83
24	Jul-86	820.28	33.10	-20.28	-10.76
25	Aug-86	773.01	-47.27	33.10	-20.28
26	Sep-86	822.97	49.96	-47.27	33.10
27	Oct-86	771.10	-51.87	49.96	-47.27
28	Nov-86	811.26	40.16	-51.87	49.96
29	Dec-86	807.41	-3.85	40.16	-51.87
30	Jan-87	835.48	28.07	-3.85	40.16
31	Feb-87	913.67	78.19	28.07	-3.85
32	Mar-87	986.25	72.58	78.19	28.07
33	Apr-87	988.79	2.54	72.58	78.19
34	May-87	1032.40	43.61	2.54	72.58
35	Jun-87	1108.80	76.40	43.61	2.54
36	Jul-87	1149.10	40.30	76.40	43.61
37	Aug-87	1188.40	39.30	40.30	76.40
38	Sep-87	1155.72	-32.68	39.30	40.30
39	Oct-87	1214.90	59.18	-32.68	39.30
40	Nov-87	876.00	-338.90	59.18	-32.68
41	Dec-87	795.51	-80.49	-338.90	59.18
42	Jan-88	870.22	74.71	-80.49	-338.90
43	Feb-88	910.31	40.09	74.71	-80.49
44	Mar-88	914.24	3.93	40.09	74.71
45	Apr-88	896.75	-17.49	3.93	40.09
46	May-88	928.19	31.44	-17.49	3.93
47	Jun-88	932.77	4.58	31.44	-17.49
48	Jul-88	963.88	31.11	4.58	31.44
49	Aug-88	969.89	6.01	31.11	4.58
50	Sep-88	898.42	-71.47	6.01	31.11
51	Oct-88	935.09	36.67	-71.47	6.01
52	Nov-88	968.72	33.63	36.67	-71.47
53	Dec-88	925.65	-43.07	33.63	36.67

1ST ORDER SERIAL CORRELATION

Regression Output:	
Constant	6.61
Std Err of Y Est	65.71
R Squared	0.00
No. of Observations	46.00
Degrees of Freedom	44.00
X Coefficient(s)	0.02
Std Err of Coef.	0.15
F-STATISTIC	0.02

2ND ORDER SERIAL CORRELATION

Regression Output:	
Constant	7.63
Std Err of Y Est	66.29
R Squared	0.00
No. of Observations	45
Degrees of Freedom	43
X Coefficient(s)	-0.07
Std Err of Coef.	0.15
F-STATISTIC	0.20

Figure 9.25. The relationship between past and future changes for the FTA All Share Index

variable do not affect the dependent variable, we would expect the *R*-squared not to be significantly different from zero. In this instance, the past changes for the FTA All-Share Index cannot be used to predict its future changes. The existence of the relationship between past changes and future changes can be examined by testing the statistical significance of the *R*-squared using an *F*-test.

The R-squared is 0.0005 and the following F-statistic is required to test the significance of R-squared (the R-squared shown in Figure 9.25 is 0.00, since we use the `/Range Format` command with two decimal points):

$$F = \frac{0.0005(46 - 2)}{(1 - 0.0005)} = 0.02$$

The F-critical value for 1 and 44 degrees of freedom at a 5 per cent level of significance is between 4.00 and 4.08. Since the F-value is lower than the F-critical value, it can be concluded that the changes $(P_t - P_{t-1})$ and $(P_{t-1} - P_{t-2})$ are not related linearly over time.

These results reveal that the linear regression model between $(P_t - P_{t-1})$ and $(P_{t-1} - P_{t-2})$ cannot be used to predict the next period's change for the FTA All Share Index.

Similarly, the results of the second regression shown in Figure 9.25 suggest no relationship between the next change for the index and the price change two periods previously.

Filter rules

These are mechanical trading rules providing signals for buying and selling shares. A filter rule is a technique that can be used to examine whether a price trend has been established and whether it is likely to continue. In this instance, we investigate whether a mechanical trading rule can generate a greater expected return than a simple buy-and-sell strategy. If the return (after transaction costs) obtained by using the former strategy is greater than the return obtained by using the latter, then the market is not efficient.

Example 9.11 A filter rule

Suppose the filter is 3 per cent and assume that the share of ABC has been falling in price. When the share price stops declining and moves up by 3 per cent above its low point, then buy. If the share prices rises and then begins to fall, once the price has fallen 3 per cent from its previous high, then sell. Moves of less than 3 per cent are ignored.

Moving average rules

These are mechanical trading rules that can be applied to produce signals for buying and selling shares. As in a filter rule, a moving average rule can be used to investigate whether a price trend has been established and whether it is likely to continue. In this case, we also examine whether a mechanical trading rule can generate greater expected return than a simple strategy of buy-and-sell. If the return (after transaction costs) obtained by utilizing the trading rule is greater than the return obtained by employing the buy-and-sell strategy, then the market is inefficient.

Example 9.12 A moving average rule

Suppose that the latest moving average of the ABC's share prices is 100 pence. The following decision criterion is considered: if the share price moves above 100 pence by 10 per cent, then buy. Hold the shares until the price moves 10 per cent below 100 pence.

Runs tests

These are methods of testing for randomness in price changes by examining whether prices tend to have 'runs' of price increases or price decreases, rather than having mixed increases or decreases.

A run is a sequence of changes in security prices, all having the same sign. The number of runs in a sequence of price changes equals the number of reversals in sign plus one. A price gain is represented by +, a price drop is represented by − and no change in price is represented by 0.

Example 9.13 Calculating the number of runs related to a sequence of prices

Consider the following sequence of prices: 5,6,7,8,−1,5,6,7,8,−2,6,7,8,9,−2. In this case, we have the following sequence of runs: + + + + − + + + + − + + + + −. This sequence includes six runs and shows a systematic pattern.

If there exists a systematic pattern in the sequence of runs, then the market is not efficient. For example, if the number of +'s or −'s in a series of +'s or −'s is greater than the number of reversals (that is, +−, or −+), then price changes are positively correlated. In this instance, the number of runs is small. On the other hand, if the number of +'s or −'s in a series of +'s or −'s is large or the number of runs is large, then the price changes are negatively correlated.

Figure 9.26 summarizes a number of tests of the weak form for different stock exchanges.

Author(s)	Country	Type of data series	Type of test	Weak form of EMH
Fama (1965)	USA	Weekly Daily Monthly	Serial correlation runs	Accepted
King (1966)	USA	Monthly	Serial correlation	Accepted
Dryden (1970)	UK	Daily	Serial correlation	Accepted
Niarchos (1972)	Greece	Monthly	Serial correlation	Accepted
Conard and Juttner (1973)	Germany	Daily	Serial correlation runs	Rejected
Jennergren (1975)	Norway	Daily	Filter	Accepted
Juttner and McHugh (1976)	Australia	Daily	Serial correlation runs	Rejected
Wong (1981)	Hong Kong	Monthly	Serial correlation runs	Accepted
Hawanini and Michel (1982)	Belgium	Weekly	Serial correlation	Rejected
Koo (1982)	Singapore	Monthly	Serial correlation runs	Accepted
Siong (1982)	Malaysia	Daily Monthly	Serial correlation runs	Accepted
Diacogiannis (1986a)	UK	Monthly	Intertemporal stationarity of security return distribution	The distributions change over time

Figure 9.26. Tests of the weak form of the efficient market hypothesis

Empirical tests of the semi-strong form of the efficient market hypothesis

The tests of the semi-strong form of the efficient market hypothesis attempt to establish how quickly and precisely share prices respond to new publicly available information. If the new information were not incorporated quickly into the share prices, then abnormal returns could be earned and the market would not be efficient. Also, if the new information were not incorporated precisely, then investors should be able to earn abnormal returns and the market would be inefficient.

Empirical tests of the semi-strong form of the efficient market hypothesis usually consider a certain type of public information (for example, earnings announcements, announcements on accounting changes, stock dividends and splits, and so on) and attempt to investigate its impact on share prices. The method of computing abnormal returns based on a security return generating model was frequently utilized in the empirical tests (this method is discussed in Chapter 17). Figure 9.27 presents a summary of several empirical investigations on the semi-strong form of the efficient market hypothesis.

Author(s)	Type of information	Semi-strong form of EMH
Ball and Brown (1968)	They examined the effect of annual earnings announcements on share prices	Accepted
Fama *et al.* (1969)	They examined the effect of stock splits on share prices	Accepted
Kaplan and Roll (1972)	They examined the impact of changes in depreciation policy on share prices	Accepted
Pettitt (1972)	He examined the impact of dividend announcements on share prices	Accepted
Kraus and Stoll (1972)	They examined the impact of all block trades of 10,000 or more on share prices	Accepted
Firth (1975)	He examined the impact of an acquisition announcement on share prices	Accepted
Davies and Canes (1978)	They examined whether analysts' information could be used to earn abnormal returns	If transaction costs are more than 2 per cent the market is efficient in the semi-strong form

Figure 9.27. Tests of the semi-strong form of the efficient market hypothesis

Empirical tests of the strong form of the efficient market hypothesis

The tests of the strong form of the efficient market hypothesis attempt to investigate whether investors can earn abnormal returns using inside or private information (the latter refers to specified information, for example, the ability of an investor to forecast price changes, the advance knowledge of an analyst to evaluate the impact of different economic factors on share prices, and so on). Empirical investigations in this area are limited by the difficulty in obtaining non-public information. As a consequence, several tests examine the performance of professionally managed funds, since they presumably rely on non-public information. Figure 9.28 summarizes several studies on the strong form of the efficient market hypothesis.

Market anomalies

As noted earlier, many empirical investigations provided evidence which was consistent with the existence of the semi-strong form of the efficient market hypothesis. In recent years, however, several types of anomalies have been found in the capital markets. In this section we present evidence with respect to the following two types

Author(s)	Type of information	Strong form of EMH
Niederhoffer and Osborn (1966)	Monopolistic information (for example, a specialist having specific information on oil prices)	Rejected
Sharpe (1966)	Non-public information known by professional managers of mutual funds (unit trusts)	Accepted
Jensen (1968)	Non-public information known by professional managers of mutual funds (unit trust)	His findings are consistent with the strong form of EMH
Jaffe (1974)	Inside information	Rejected
Ambachtsheer (1974)	Forecasting ability of investors	Rejected
Firth (1978)	Private information known by professional managers of unit trusts	Accepted

Figure 9.28. Tests of the strong form of the efficient market hypothesis

of anomalies:

1 *The size effect* Share investments in small-sized firms earn significantly higher rates of return as compared with similar investments in large-sized firms.
2 *The January effect* Shares seems to provide an excess return in January as compared with any other month in the year.

Figure 9.29 summarizes the results of four studies dealing with market anomalies.

Author(s)	Country/interval of rates of return	Conclusion
Banz (1981)	USA/monthly rates of return	On average, small firms of the New York Stock Exchange have had significantly higher risk-adjusted returns than large firms
Barry and Brown (1984)	USA/monthly rates of return	Size effect is detected in the data used even after adjustment for risk
Reinganum (1983)	USA/monthly rates of return	There is significant positive return in January and exceptionally larger return during the first few trading days of January
Kato and Schallheim (1985)	Japan/monthly rates of return	Average returns for small firms are higher than those of large firms in January

Figure 9.29. A summary of four studies regarding market anomalies

Implications of efficient capital markets

The efficiency of the capital market has the following implications:

1 In an efficient market, a security's market price, at all times, should be equal to its intrinsic value. The efficient market hypothesis may not be valid for a security at a particular time. A security with an intrinsic value greater than its market price is known as an under-priced security, while a security with an intrinsic value lower than its market price is referred to as an over-priced security. In an efficient market, the forces of supply and demand will quickly drive an under-priced (over-priced) security towards its new intrinsic value.

2 The market efficiency does not imply that investors will not earn high returns, it simply states that in a highly competitive market investors cannot expect to earn consistently high returns beyond the fair market return for the level of risk involved. If the return of an investor becomes abnormally large, then other investors would attempt to enter the business and the abnormal return would be quickly eliminated.
3 The efficient market theory neither implies that the price of a security will remain unchanged, nor that the prices are random. When new information is released, security prices adjust quickly and correctly towards their intrinsic value. In an efficient market, the only factor which can change a security's price is new information; predicted events cannot change the security price, because they are already incorporated in the price. New information is unpredictable (if it were predictable it would not be new) and thus the price changes will also be unpredictable (that is, random).
4 The market efficiency does not imply that the managers and analysts are incompetents. In highly competitive markets with many participants and with access to public information, it is difficult for any group to earn abnormal returns. The operations of professional investment analysts make the market efficient and their action is very valuable to society because market efficiency offers a healthy pricing mechanism necessary for the growth of the nation's wealth.
5 The market efficiency does not imply that security or portfolio analysis is not useful. On the contrary, if the market is efficient, then security or portfolio analysis offers several useful methods of application.
6 For practical purposes, the capital market efficiency does not necessarily imply that literally all investors have all relevant information, but it simply shows that share prices behave as if there is a universal knowledge of that information.
7 If an efficient capital market security prices are guiding scarce capital resources to their best use. For example, if investors expect high profits from the firms in a particular industry, their actions to purchase the shares of the firms in that industry will increase the share prices. This in turn will encourage further capital investments. The new capital investments are supported by the investors who anticipate further increase in prices and as a consequence they provide the needed capital.
8 In an efficient market, a long-term investment has a zero net present value. This is particularly true in an efficient market for shares, but the markets for real assets (for example, plant and equipment) do not have the same degree of efficiency as the share markets. It is the lack of competition which results in projects with positive net present value. For example, suppose a company produces a new personal computer and it expects a positive net present value from its investment. The net present value is positive since there are not many competitors in the market, as more and more companies produce the same product the competition will result in lower cash flows.
9 The dividend-irrelevance theory asserts that in perfect capital markets the total market value of a firm is independent of its dividend policy (see also Chapter 16). Investors are indifferent between receiving dividends or capital gains (ignoring taxation and transaction costs), indicating that it is impossible to generate abnormal returns by either policy. Therefore, the efficient market hypothesis supports the dividend irrelevance theory (ignoring taxation and transaction costs).

10 In an efficient market the competition between investors results in correctly priced securities, thus a firm can obtain external funds at a cost which is fairly and correctly set by the market.

11 In an efficient market, the share price of a company reflects the decisions made by the company's financial management team. Good decisions will drive up the share price and bad decisions will result in a lower share price.

12 Since the market is not efficient in the strong form, it may be possible to make abnormal returns consistently by using inside information or other private information (for example, forecasting ability). In an efficient market the only way to generate abnormal profits consistently is by luck.

Efficient capital market versus perfect capital market

The capital market theory is based upon the perfect market assumption. The perfect capital market constitutes a more general notion than that of the efficient market. A market can be efficient even when there are transaction costs and taxes. If capital markets were perfect, then it would follow that all available information, at all times, would be reflected in security prices.

Summary

1 *Capital market line* The capital market line expresses a linear equilibrium relationship between expected return and risk for efficient portfolios. The capital market line states that the expected return of an efficient portfolio is equal to the risk-free rate plus an additional compensation for taking on risk. Portfolio risk is measured by the standard deviation of rate of return.

2 *Capital asset pricing model* The total risk of a security (or portfolio) is separated into two components: systematic risk is the market related component of the total security risk; unsystematic risk represents the second component of risk resulting from any volatility independent of market fluctuations.

The capital asset pricing model specifies that in equilibrium there exists an exact linear relationship between expected return and risk that applies to all individual securities and efficient or inefficient portfolios in the market. The capital asset pricing model reveals that the expected return on any security or portfolio (efficient or not) is equal to the riskless rate of interest plus a risk premium compensating the investors for bearing the systematic risk associated with the security or portfolio. The relevant measure of risk here is the beta of the security or portfolio: this is the risk of the security or portfolio in the market portfolio relative to the risk of the market portfolio.

Roll criticized several tests related to the capital asset pricing model and forcefully argued that the capital asset pricing model cannot be tested because the true market portfolio is unobservable. Attempting to test the capital asset pricing model by using a market proxy is nothing more than testing the mean/standard deviation efficiency of that market proxy.

3 *Arbitrage pricing theory* The arbitrage pricing theory is an equilibrium risk/return relationship. It assumes the returns on securities (or portfolios) are generated by a factor model and that investors cannot earn in the market a positive return with no risk and without using their own wealth. The arbitrage pricing model asserts that there is a linear relationship between expected return for each

security (or portfolio) under consideration and its various sensitivities to major factors of the return generating process.

The arbitrage pricing theory of Ross does not specify the nature of each factor in the return generating model or how many factors there are in the model. Tests revealing the acceptance or rejection of the arbitrage pricing theory of Ross should be interpreted with caution because they left untested several empirical assumptions regarding the structure of data whose validity cannot always be guaranteed.

3 *Efficient market hypothesis* A competitive market is said to be efficient with respect to a set of information if prices in the market fully and quickly reflect all information in that information set. If this is true, available information cannot help investors to select shares that will do any better than average. In an efficient market investors can earn a return commensurate with the risk involved. The efficient market hypothesis can be divided into three categories: weak form, semi-strong form and strong form. The weak form asserts that past share prices are useless for predicting future price changes. The semi-strong form states that publicly available information cannot be utilized to consistently make above-average returns. Lastly, according to the strong form, private and public information cannot help to consistently generate above-average return.

The results of the tests discussed in the present chapter support the weak form and the semi-strong form of the efficient market hypothesis. The results related to the strong form of the capital market efficiency are mixed. It seems that individuals who manage unit trusts cannot use information to consistently realize above-average returns. However, the results indicate that sometimes inside information can produce above-average returns.

Questions for discussion

1 For each term shown below in the largest box provide a definition in your own words. Then check your responses against the definitions included in the chapter.

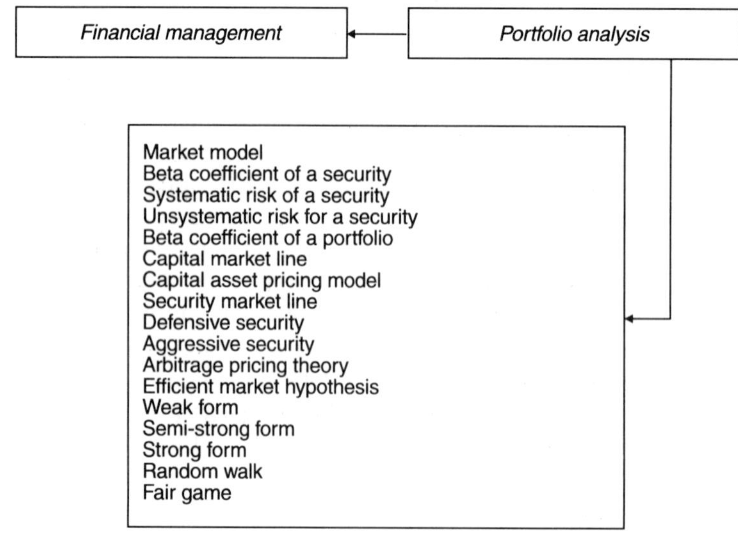

2 Compare and contrast the Markowitz model and the capital market line.
3 State the assumptions of the capital asset pricing model. Indicate why each assumption is necessary for the derivation of the model.
4 'Many of the assumptions of the capital asset pricing model do not hold in the real world.' Discuss. Can we conclude that the capital asset pricing model is invalid because it is based upon unrealistic assumptions? Discuss.
5 Give a reason or reasons for each of the following cases:
   (a) The beta coefficient of Marks and Spencer plc was 0.88 (*source*: Risk Measurement Service, April 1990).
   (b) The beta coefficient of BOC Group was 1.25 (*source*: Risk Measurement Service, April 1990).
   (c) The beta coefficient of Bellway plc was 1.00 (*source*: Risk Measurement Service, April 1990).
   (d) The beta coefficient of Bellway plc changed from 1.00 (*source*: Risk Measurement Service, April 1990) to 1.09 (*source*: Risk Measurement Service, January 1991).
6 Other things being equal, indicate what would be the effect on the beta of a firm of such event shown below (use either the word 'increase' or the word 'decrease' to indicate a choice). Discuss in detail each of your answers

The variance of the market index decreases		
The correlation between the returns of the security and the market index decreases		
The firm's debt to equity ratio increases from 20 per cent to 60 per cent		
The covariance between the returns of the security and the market index increases		

7 (a) You are given the following information.

Firm	Expected return using the CAPM
United Friendly Ins. plc	13.51
Regalian Properties plc	25.39
General Electric	19.45
BTR plc	20.88

If the market index's mean return is 20 per cent and the risk-free rate is 11 per cent, classify each of the above shares as defensive or aggressive.
   (b) Do you agree with the following diagram? If not prepare a diagram similar to the one below displaying correctly the four firms.

	Aggressive security		
Low beta	*United Friendly Ins plc	*BTR plc	High beta
	*General Electric plc	*Regalian Properties plc	
	Defensive security		

8 Other things being equal, indicate what would be the effect on the expected return of a defensive firm and an aggressive firm of each event shown below (use either the word 'increase' or the word 'decrease' to indicate a choice). Discuss in detail each of your answers.

	Defensive	Aggressive
Beta coefficient increases		
Risk-free rate increases		
The market index's expected return decreases		

9 Compare and contrast the one-factor market model with the capital asset pricing model.

10 You are given the following information (*source*: Risk Measurement Service, April 1990)

Firm	Market capitalization (£ million)	Variability (standard deviation %)	Beta
Oakwood Group plc	3	75	0.95
Pavion Int. plc	2	72	1.16
Glaxo Holdings plc	11,511	31	1.21
Hanson plc	10,889	27	0.98

What implications do you observe? Discuss.

11 Compare and contrast the capital market line with the capital asset pricing model.

12 You are given four portfolios on the capital market line, call them 1, 2, 3 and 4. The following diagram shows the risk-free rate, the market index's expected return and the expected return on each portfolio.

Risk-free rate	Market expected return	Portfolio expected return	
9%	20%	15%	Portfolio 1
9%	20%	22%	Portfolio 2
9%	20%	10%	Portfolio 3
9%	20%	25%	Portfolio 4

(a) Calculate the investment proportions defining each of the four portfolios (consider each portfolio's rate of return as a combination of the risk-free rate and the rate of return of the market index).
(b) Rank the portfolios from most risky to least risky using the standard deviation as a risk measure.
(c) Rank the portfolios from most risky to least risky using beta coefficient as a risk measure.

13 Identify and discuss two possible applications of the capital asset pricing model.

14 Consider two portfolios p and q lying on the capital market line. Portfolio p's beta is greater than that of the market, while portfolio q's beta is 0.8. Illustrate graphically the capital market line and identify the position of portfolios p and q on that line.

15 'Tests of the capital asset pricing model performed using a portfolio other than the true market portfolio are not tests of the model.' Discuss this statement.

16 'The capital asset pricing model has been the premier model of capital markets for many years. As an alternative to the capital asset pricing model, Ross presented the arbitrage pricing theory. UK evidence indicates that the Ross theory may be true, but the existing statistical methodology provides an ambiguous test of the theory for the London Stock Exchange.' Fully discuss this statement.

17 Compare and contrast the capital asset pricing model with the arbitrage pricing theory.

18 Compare and contrast the following:
(a) weak form with semi-strong form market efficiency;
(b) weak form with strong market efficiency;
(c) semi-strong with strong market efficiency;
(d) efficient market hypothesis and random walk hypothesis.

19 Discuss the implications of the empirical results for market efficiency presented in this chapter.

20 Prepare an analog model summarizing the main points discussed in this chapter.

21 How can spreadsheets be used to facilitate the application of the concepts discussed in this chapter?

Appendix 9A Proving of the capital market line and capital asset pricing model

Recalling that the capital market line is the straight line from the risk-free tangent to the expected return–standard deviation efficient frontier. The tangent of the angle w at point m is given by:

$$\text{tangent}(w) = \frac{r_m - r_f}{\sigma_m}$$

If q is a portfolio lying on the capital market line, then the tangent of the angle w at point q can also be expressed as

$$\text{tangent}(w) = \frac{r_q - r_f}{\sigma_q}$$

Therefore, it can be written

$$\frac{r_m - r_f}{\sigma_m} = \frac{r_q - r_f}{\sigma_q}$$

Rearranging terms in the last equation we observe the equation of the capital market line

$$r_q = r_f + \frac{r_m - r_f}{\sigma_m}\sigma_q \tag{9A.1}$$

A proof of the capital asset pricing model

Assume N risky securities under consideration. The capital market line can be used to express the expected return on the market portfolio as follows:

$$r_m = r_f + \frac{r_q - r_f}{\sigma_q}\sigma_m \tag{9A.2}$$

We use matrix notation to rewrite Equation (9A.2) as shown below

$$X'_m R = r_f X'_m u + h\sqrt{X'_m V X_m} \tag{9A.3}$$

where

$X_m =$ the $(N \times 1)$ vector defining the market portfolio.
$R =$ the $(N \times 1)$ vector of expected returns.
$u =$ the $(N \times 1)$ unit vector.
$V =$ the $(N \times N)$ covariance matrix.

Differentiating Equation (9A.3) with respect to X'_m we observe

$$R = r_f u + h\frac{2VX_m}{2\sigma_m}$$

or equivalently

$$R = r_f u + \frac{r_q - r_f}{\sigma_q}\frac{VX_m}{\sigma_m} \tag{9A.4}$$

However, from the capital market line the following equality is valid:

$$\frac{r_m - r_f}{\sigma_m} = \frac{r_q - r_f}{\sigma_q} \tag{9A.5}$$

Combining Equations (9A.4) and (9A.5) yields:

$$R = r_f u + \frac{r_m - r_f}{\sigma_m}\frac{VX_m}{\sigma_m} \tag{9A.6}$$

A cross-section of Equation (9A.6) is written as follows:

$$r_m = r_f + (r_m + r_f)\frac{\sigma_{im}}{\sigma_m}$$

where σ_{im} is the covariance between the rate of return on security i and the rate of return on the market portfolio m.

Appendix 9B The single index model

The single index model describes a (linear) relationship between the rates of return on individual securities (or portfolios) and the rates of return on a market index. It is based upon the assumption that security (or portfolio) rates of return have the tendency to fluctuate with the rates of return on a common factor (that is, the market index). According to the single index model, the rate of return of a security can be divided into two components:

Security rate of return	=	Component of return that is related to market index's rate of return (systematic)	+	Component of return that is independent of the market index's rate of return (unsystematic)
R_{it}	=	$b_i R_{mt}$	+	$a_i + e_{it}$

where

$i = 1, 2, \ldots, N.$

R_{it} = the (random) rate of return on the security i at period t.

R_{mt} = the (random) rate of return on the market index at period t.

a_i = the component of security i's rate of return that is not related to the fluctuations of the market index's rates of return. When the index's expected return is equal to zero the security i's return is equal to a_i and thus a_i is also known as the intercept coefficient related to security i.

b_i = the sensitivity of security i's rates of return to the fluctuations in the market index's rates of return. The beta is known as the slope coefficient related to security i.

e_{it} = a random zero mean noise term for security i with zero expected value and constant variance. It is also assumed that e_{it} and R_{mt} are independent and that e_{it} is independent of e_{jt} (that is, the noise term for another security j).

The market is represented by widely available stock market indices (for example, the FT Actuaries All-Shares Index). The unsystematic components reflects the combined effect of factors which are unique to each firm, but which are assumed to have no effect on the market index's rate of return (for example, the discovery of an important new product, a local labour strike, the size of the firm, and so on).

Using the single index model, the expected return of a security can be expressed as follows:

Security expected return	=	Component of expected return that is related to the market index's expected return (systematic)	+	Component of expected return that is unrelated to the market index's expected return (unsystematic)
$E(R_i)$	=	$b_i E(R_m)$	+	a_i

where

$i = 1, 2, \ldots, N.$

$E(R_i)$ = the expected return of security i.

$E(R_m)$ = the expected return of the market index.

Using the market model, the variance of return on a security can be separated as follows:

Variance of return on a security	=	Component of variance that is related to the market index (systematic)	+	Component of variance that is unrelated to the market index (unsystematic)

$$\sigma_i^2 = b_i^2\sigma_m^2 + \sigma_{ei}^2$$

where

σ_m^2 = the variance of the rate of return on the market index m.
σ_{ei}^2 = the variance of e_{it} $(i = 1, 2, \ldots, N)$.

The first component of security i's total risk (that is, the systematic risk) is the product of two terms. The first term shows how sensitive is security i's rate of return to movements in the market index rates of return. For example, a security's beta of 0.8 indicates that the security's systematic return is expected to increase by 0.8 per cent after the return on the market increases by 1 per cent. The second term is the market variance which measures the variability associated with the market index's rates of return. Clearly, investors would prefer to invest in aggressive securities when the market is rising and in defensive securities when the market is falling. Since the variance of the market index is constant with respect to all securities in the index, the beta coefficient provides a measure of the security's systematic risk. Systematic risk is also called non-diversifiable risk.

The second component of security i's total risk (that is, the unsystematic risk) measures that part of security i's variability that is independent of the overall state of the market. This part of risk arises from events that are specific to the firm. Unsystematic risk is also known as diversifiable risk or specific risk.

Uses of the single index model
The single index model provides several uses, including the following: estimating the systematic risk of a security or portfolio; simplifying Markowitz portfolio analysis; and examining the effects of diversification on portfolio risk.

Estimating beta
The single index model can be used to estimate the beta of securities or portfolios.

Example 9B.1 Estimating the beta for Marks and Spencer (January 1985 to December 1988)

Figure 9B.1 shows 48 monthly log-rates of return on Marks and Spencer plc and 48 monthly log-rates of return on the FT-Actuaries All-Share Index. The beta can be estimated with the aid of 1-2-3's command `/Data Regression`. The range for the independent variable is C5..C52, while the range for the dependent variable is B5..B52. The regression results reveal that the beta of Marks and Spencer is 0.857. Thus, over the period January 1985 to December 1988, Marks and Spencer's shares were defensive. The t-statistics of 7.209 indicate that the beta coefficient is significantly different from zero at 99 per cent level of confidence. (Figure 9B.2 plots the estimated regression equation.)

	A	B	C	E–H	I	K
1	MONTHLY LOG RETURNS ON M&S AND CHANGES ON THE FTA SHARE INDEX					
3	PERIOD	M&S	INDEX			ERROR
5	Jan-85	2.53%	3.61%			2.86%
6	Feb-85	3.28%	3.30%			2.60%
7	Mar-85	9.24%	-1.15%	Regression Output:		-1.21%
8	Apr-85	5.72%	1.76%	Constant	-0.002	1.28%
9	May-85	-3.30%	1.61%	Std Err of Y Est	0.054	1.15%
10	Jun-85	0.73%	1.94%	R Squared	0.530	1.44%
11	Jul-85	-2.94%	-6.20%	No. of Observations	48	-5.54%
12	Aug-85	11.28%	2.70%	Degrees of Freedom	46.000	2.09%
13	Sep-85	2.63%	4.72%			3.82%
14	Oct-85	8.10%	-2.75%	X Coefficient(s)	0.857	-2.58%
15	Nov-85	10.37%	6.59%	Std Err of Coef.	0.119	5.42%
16	Dec-85	-2.20%	2.33%			1.77%
17	Jan-86	-2.25%	-0.74%	T-STATISTIC	7.209	-0.86%
18	Feb-86	-2.88%	1.42%			0.99%
19	Mar-86	10.35%	7.59%			6.28%
20	Apr-86	15.34%	9.06%			7.53%
21	May-86	-3.26%	-1.32%			-1.36%
22	Jun-86	-6.87%	-2.54%			-2.41%
23	Jul-86	4.95%	4.12%			3.30%
24	Aug-86	-5.46%	-5.94%			-5.32%
25	Sep-86	10.64%	6.26%			5.14%
26	Oct-86	-10.13%	-6.51%			-5.81%
27	Nov-86	0.71%	5.08%			4.12%
28	Dec-86	-6.83%	-0.48%			-0.64%
29	Jan-87	-1.64%	3.42%			2.70%
30	Feb-87	4.85%	8.95%			7.44%
31	Mar-87	10.96%	7.64%			6.32%
32	Apr-87	1.41%	0.26%			-0.01%
33	May-87	9.36%	4.32%			3.47%
34	Jun-87	8.24%	7.14%			5.89%
35	Jul-87	-4.86%	3.57%			2.83%
36	Aug-87	6.82%	3.36%			2.65%
37	Sep-87	-9.34%	-2.79%			-2.62%
38	Oct-87	1.69%	4.99%			4.05%
39	Nov-87	-17.04%	-32.71%			-28.27%
40	Dec-87	-15.67%	-9.64%			-8.49%
41	Jan-88	6.78%	8.95%			7.44%
42	Feb-88	-1.65%	4.53%			3.65%
43	Mar-88	-2.25%	0.43%			0.14%
44	Apr-88	-1.14%	-1.93%			-1.89%
45	May-88	4.80%	3.45%			2.73%
46	Jun-88	-1.12%	0.49%			0.19%
47	Jul-88	-1.71%	3.28%			2.58%
48	Aug-88	-0.58%	0.62%			0.30%
49	Sep-88	-13.93%	-7.65%			-6.79%
50	Oct-88	7.98%	4.00%			3.20%
51	Nov-88	6.93%	3.53%			2.80%
52	Dec-88	-18.35%	-4.55%			-4.13%

Figure 9B.1. Estimating the beta for Marks and Spencer (January 1985–December 1988)

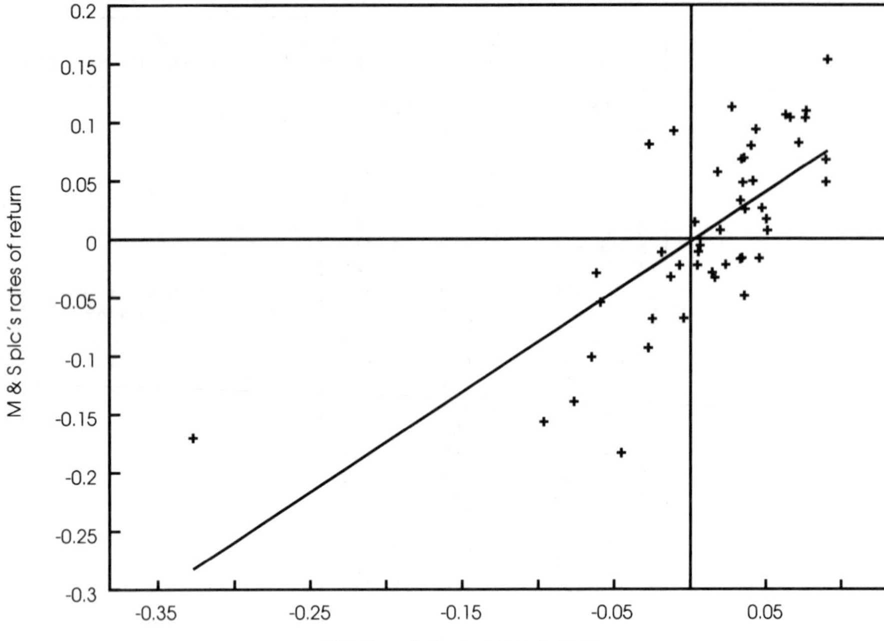

Figure 9B.2. Plotting the sample points and estimated regression equation for Marks and Spencer (January 1985–December 1988)

The *R*-squared indicates the proportion of total risk which can be explained by the systematic risk. Thus, the following is true:

1	=	Proportion of total risk explained by the systematic risk (that is, *R*-squared)	+	Proportion of total risk explained by the unsystematic risk (that is, 1 minus *R*-squared)

The results presented in Figure 9B.1 reveal that 53.0 per cent of the total variability in the rates of return of Marks and Spencer can be explained by the variability in the rates of return of the FT-Actuaries All-Shares Index.

Simplifying Markowitz's analysis

The single index model can be also utilized as a simplified approximation to the original Markowitz approach. Figure 9B.3 shows the calculations required for portfolio analysis using the original Markowitz specification and the single index model. The number of covariances is calculated as follows: the covariance matrix has N rows and N columns, meaning that there are N^2 entries. The number of variances is N, thus, the covariance matrix contains $N^2 - N = N(N-1)$ covariances. Since the covariance matrix is symmetric, we have to estimate only those covariances above its diagonal, that is, a total of $N(N-1)/2$ covariances.

For example, assume that 100 securities are taken into consideration, then the original approach of Markowitz requires 100 expected returns, 100 standard deviations and 4,950 pairwise covariances, a total of 5,150 parameters. However, the pairwise covariances can be calculated by using only 201 input variables from the single index model.

Figure 9B.3. Number of inputs required for Markowitz analysis using the original Markowitz approach and the single index model

Markowitz model		Single index model	
Expected returns	N	Betas	N
Standard deviations	N	Standard deviations	N
Pairwise covariances	$N(N-1)/2$	Market standard deviation	1
TOTAL	$N(N+3)/2$		$2N+1$

Portfolio diversification using the single index model

Consider a portfolio p comprised of N risky securities. Using the single index model, the variance of the portfolio p can be expressed as:

$$\sigma_p^2 = b_p^2\sigma_m^2 + \sigma_{ep}^2$$

where

b_p = a weighted average of the betas of the individual securities in p.
σ_{ep}^2 = a weighted average of the unsystematic risks of the individual securities in p.

Assume equal investment in pounds sterling in each security in p, then the total portfolio risk is given by:

$$\sigma_p^2 = b_p^2\sigma_m^2 + \frac{1}{N}\frac{\sigma_{e1}^2 + \sigma_{e2}^2 + \ldots + \sigma_{eN}^2}{N}$$

where

σ_{ei}^2 = the unsystematic risk of the individual security i (where, $i = 1, 2, \ldots, N$).

The first component on the expression of portfolio variance shows the product of the square of the portfolio beta and the variance of the market. The second component is represented by the product of $1/N$ and the unsystematic risk of the portfolio. As the portfolio becomes more diversified, the number N gets larger. As a consequence, $1/N$ becomes smaller, resulting in a portfolio having low unsystematic risk. As the number of securities in the portfolio becomes larger, the portfolio risk approaches the systematic risk. The systematic risk cannot be eliminated by diversification. The only way to avoid systematic risk is never to invest in risky securities.

Example 9B.2 An example revealing the benefits from diversification

The amount of diversification is greatly affected by the number of securities making up a portfolio. The important question is how many securities can be considered by an investor in order to achieve the benefits from diversification? This question can be answered after examining the effects of diversification on the variance of the portfolio rate of return. Figure 9B.4 calculates the total portfolio risk as portfolio size increases. It is assumed that the securities are combined into

	A	B	C	D	E	F
1						
2	Name	Weight	Systematic	Unsystematic		
3						
4	Glaxo Holdings LTD	1	1.24	0.0324		
5						
6			0.0678	0.0324		
7						
8						
9	Glaxo Holdings LTD	0.200	1.24	0.0324		
10	Lucas Industries	0.200	1.23	0.0676		
11	Guinness Plc	0.200	1.20	0.0484		
12	Blue Circle Industries	0.200	0.96	0.0441		
13	Boots Co Ltd	0.200	0.82	0.0625		
14						
15			0.0524	0.0102		
16						
17	Glaxo Holdings LTD	0.100	1.24	0.0324		
18	Lucas Industries	0.100	1.23	0.0676		
19	Guinness Plc	0.100	1.20	0.0484		
20	Blue Circle Industries	0.100	0.96	0.0441		
21	Boots Co Ltd	0.100	0.82	0.0625		
22	BOC Group	0.100	1.27	0.0400		
23	B.I.C.C.	0.100	1.09	0.0400		
24	BTR Limited	0.100	1.07	0.0256		
25	Allied Lyons Plc	0.100	0.84	0.0484		
26	Asda Group Plc	0.100	0.74	0.0441		
27						
28			0.0483	0.0045		
29						
30	Glaxo Holdings LTD	0.067	1.24	0.0324		
31	Lucas Industries	0.067	1.23	0.0676		
32	Guinness Plc	0.067	1.20	0.0484		
33	Blue Circle Industries	0.067	0.96	0.0441		
34	Boots Co Ltd	0.067	0.82	0.0625		
35	BOC Group	0.067	1.27	0.0400		
36	B.I.C.C.	0.067	1.09	0.0400		
37	BTR Limited	0.067	1.07	0.0256		
38	Allied Lyons Plc	0.067	0.84	0.0484		
39	Asda Group Plc	0.067	0.74	0.0441		
40	Beecham Group Plc	0.067	0.74	0.0256		
41	GKN	0.067	1.10	0.0484		
42	General Electric	0.067	0.94	0.0529		
43	British Telecom	0.067	0.70	0.0361		
44	Cadbury Schweppes	0.067	0.86	0.0676		
45						
46			0.0429	0.0030		

Figure 9B.4. The effects of diversification using the single index model (*Source*: Betas and unsystematic figures for securities are from Risk Measurement Service, January 1989)

portfolios with equal investment proportions and the market variance is 0.0441. We start with the risk of an individual security (that is, Glaxo Holdings Ltd). Then, this security is combined with four other randomly selected securities to form a portfolio containing five securities. Next, these five securities are combined with five other randomly selected securities to construct a portfolio comprising ten securities, and so on until all 30 securities are considered. For each of the six portfolios we calculate the systematic and unsystematic risk. For example, the systematic risk of the portfolio consisting of five securities can be calculated as follows:

$$(0.2)^2[1.24 + 1.23 + 1.20 + 0.96 + 0.82]^2(0.0441) = 0.0524$$

	A	B	C	D	E	F
47						
48						
49	Name	Weight	Systematic	Unsystematic		
50						
51	Glaxo Holdings LTD	0.050	1.24	0.0324		
52	Lucas Industries	0.050	1.23	0.0676		
53	Guinness Plc	0.050	1.20	0.0484		
54	Blue Circle Industr	0.050	0.96	0.0441		
55	Boots Co Ltd	0.050	0.82	0.0625		
56	BOC Group	0.050	1.27	0.0400		
57	B.I.C.C.	0.050	1.09	0.0400		
58	BTR Limited	0.050	1.07	0.0256		
59	Allied Lyons Plc	0.050	0.84	0.0484		
60	Asda Group Plc	0.050	0.74	0.0441		
61	Beecham Group Plc	0.050	0.74	0.0256		
62	GKN	0.050	1.10	0.0484		
63	General Electric	0.050	0.94	0.0529		
64	British Telecom	0.050	0.70	0.0361		
65	Cadbury-Schweppes	0.050	0.86	0.0676		
66	Courtaulds Limited	0.050	1.27	0.0729		
67	British Gas Plc	0.050	0.68	0.0400		
68	British Petroleoum	0.050	0.92	0.0289		
69	Grand Metropolitan	0.050	1.02	0.0324		
70	Hansons Plc	0.050	0.99	0.0400		
71						
72			0.0427	0.0022		
73						
74	Glaxo Holdings LTD	0.040	1.24	0.0324		
75	Lucas Industries	0.040	1.23	0.0676		
76	Guinness Plc	0.040	1.20	0.0484		
77	Blue Circle Industr	0.040	0.96	0.0441		
78	Boots Co Ltd	0.040	0.82	0.0625		
79	BOC Group	0.040	1.27	0.0400		
80	B.I.C.C.	0.040	1.09	0.0400		
81	BTR Limited	0.040	1.07	0.0256		
82	Allied Lyons Plc	0.040	0.84	0.0484		
83	Asda Group Plc	0.040	0.74	0.0441		
84	Beecham Group Plc	0.040	0.74	0.0256		
85	GKN	0.040	1.10	0.0484		
86	General Electric	0.040	0.94	0.0529		
87	British Telecom	0.040	0.70	0.0361		
88	Cadbury Schweppes	0.040	0.86	0.0676		
89	Courtaulds Limited	0.040	1.27	0.0729		
90	British Gas Plc	0.040	0.68	0.0400		
91	British Petroleum	0.040	0.92	0.0289		
92	Grand Metropolitan	0.040	1.02	0.0324		
93	Hanson Plc	0.040	0.99	0.0400		
94	Natl Westminster	0.040	0.97	0.0400		
95	P&O Steam Nav Co	0.040	0.98	0.0361		
96	Plessey Co Plc	0.040	1.05	0.1024		
97	Trusthouse Forte	0.040	1.07	0.0324		
98	Hawker Siddeley GRP	0.040	0.99	0.0289		
99						
100			0.0432	0.0018		

Figure 9B.4. *(Continued)*

The unsystematic risk of the portfolio comprising five securities can be calculated as shown below:

$$(0.2)^2[0.0324 + 0.0676 + 0.0484 + 0.0441 + 0.0625] = 0.0102$$

Therefore, the total risk of this portfolio is 0.0626 (that is, 0.0102 + 0.0524).

For a single security there is a considerable level of risk. However, as the

	A	B	C	D	E	F
101						
102						
103	Name	Weight	Systematic	Unsystematic		
104						
105	Glaxo Holdings LTD	0.033	1.24	0.0324		
106	Lucas Industries	0.033	1.23	0.0676		
107	Guinness Plc	0.033	1.20	0.0484		
108	Blue Circle Industr	0.033	0.96	0.0441		
109	Boots Co Ltd	0.033	0.82	0.0625		
110	BOC Group	0.033	1.27	0.0400		
111	B.I.C.C.	0.033	1.09	0.0400		
112	BTR Limited	0.033	1.07	0.0256		
113	Allied Lyons Plc	0.033	0.84	0.0484		
114	Asda Group Plc	0.033	0.74	0.0441		
115	Beecham Group Plc	0.033	0.74	0.0256		
116	GKN	0.033	1.10	0.0484		
117	General Electric	0.033	0.94	0.0529		
118	British Telecom	0.033	0.70	0.0361		
119	Cadbury Schweppes	0.033	0.86	0.0676		
120	Courtaulds Limited	0.033	1.27	0.0729		
121	British Gas Plc	0.033	0.68	0.0400		
122	British Petroleum	0.033	0.92	0.0289		
123	Grand Metropolitan	0.033	1.02	0.0324		
124	Hanson Plc	0.033	0.99	0.0400		
125	Natl Westminister	0.033	0.97	0.0400		
126	P&O Steam Nav Co	0.033	0.98	0.0361		
127	Plessey Co Plc	0.033	1.05	0.1024		
128	Trusthouse Forte	0.033	1.07	0.0324		
129	Hawker Siddeley GRP	0.033	0.99	0.0289		
130	Imperial Chemical Ind	0.033	1.10	0.0289		
131	Marks & Spencer	0.033	0.81	0.0324		
132	Royal Insurance	0.033	1.01	0.0361		
133	Tate & Lyle Ltd	0.033	1.07	0.0324		
134	Thorn EMI Plc	0.033	1.16	0.0784		
135						
136			0.0438	0.0015		
137						
138	No of Securities	Systematic	Unsystematic	Total	SR/TR	UR/TR
139	1	0.0678	0.0324	0.1002	67.67%	32.33%
140	5	0.0524	0.0102	0.0626	83.70%	16.30%
141	10	0.0483	0.0045	0.0528	91.42%	8.58%
142	15	0.0429	0.0030	0.0460	93.39%	6.61%
143	20	0.0427	0.0022	0.0449	95.01%	4.99%
144	25	0.0432	0.0018	0.0450	95.96%	4.04%
145	30	0.0438	0.0015	0.0453	96.70%	3.30%

Figure 9B.4. *(Continued)*

portfolio size becomes larger, the unsystematic risk becomes smaller. For example, for the portfolio of 25 securities only 4.04 per cent of its total risk can be explained by the unsystematic risk. Note that the risk of a portfolio cannot go below the market risk. It can only approach the market risk as the number of securities in the portfolio increases.

Figure 9B.5 presents a graph of portfolio variance against the number of securities contained in the portfolio. As Figure 9B.5 reveals, the major benefits provided by diversification occur with the first 15 securities. Increasing the portfolio size continuous to reduce unsystematic risk, but the benefits are diminishing.

Finally, Figure 9B.6 provides a summary of the concept of total risk.

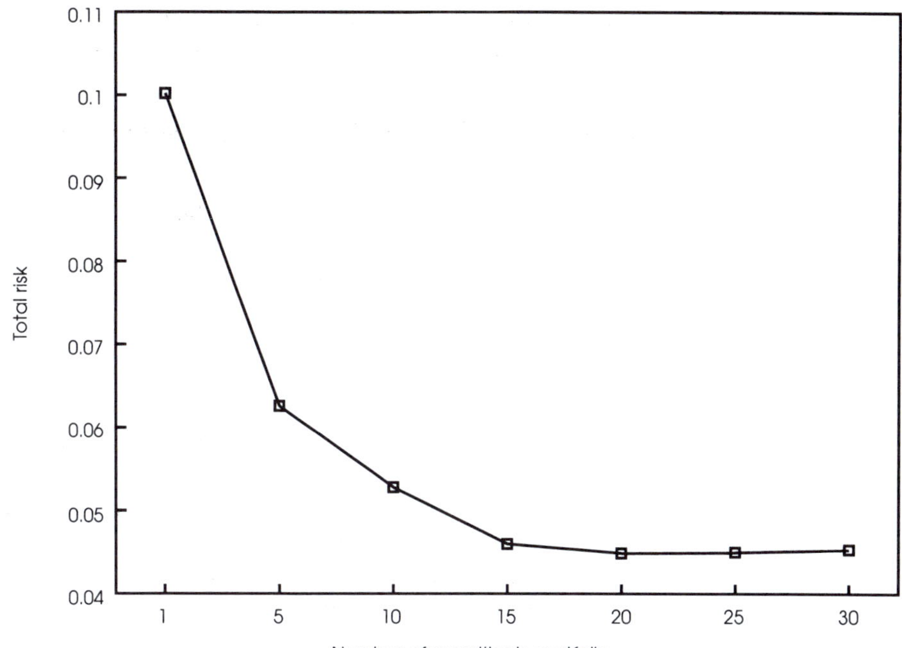

Figure 9B.5. The effects of diversification on portfolio risk

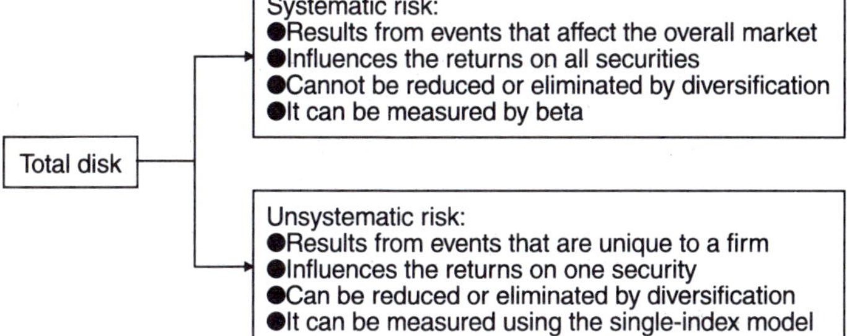

Figure 9B.6. Summarizing the concept of total risk

Capital asset pricing model versus single index model

By comparing the capital asset pricing model and a single index model we observe the following:

1 The capital asset pricing model is an equilibrium model which highlights a cross-sectional linear relationship between expected return and beta. A single index model is a linear model which describes the return generating process for securities, it relates the rate of return on a security and the rate of return on the market.
2 The slope of the line represented by the capital asset pricing model is equal to the difference between the expected return on the market portfolio and the return on the riskless security. The slope of the characteristic line represented by the market model equals the beta coefficient.
3 In theory both models assume a single period horizon. For empirical purposes,

however, each model assumes that the joint distribution of security returns is multivariate normal and stationary throughout the sample period used.

Appendix 9C Multiple linear regression analysis

A multiple linear regression is a statistical method for determining how one variable (usually called the dependent variable) is related to two or more variables (usually called the independent variables). The form of a multiple regression with n independent variables for a time-series data is as follows:

Dependent variable = constant + independent variables' part + error term

$$Y_{it} = a_i + b_1X_{1t} + b_2X_{2t} + \ldots + b_nX_{nt} + e_{it}$$

where

Y_{it} = the variable being affected by the independent variables.

$X_{1t} \ldots X_{nt}$ = the variables that influence the value of the dependent variable.

$b_1 \ldots b_n$ = the multiple regression coefficients corresponding to the independent variables $X_{1t}, \ldots, X_{nt}$, respectively. Each coefficient represents how much the dependent variable will change given a change of one unit in the corresponding independent variable.

a_i = the intercept on the Y-axis (that is, the value of the dependent variable when $X_{1t} = X_{2t} = \ldots = X_{nt} = 0$). This intercept represents the value of the dependent variable regardless of the effect of the independent variables.

e_{it} = the error term, each error term is the difference between an actual value of the dependent variable and the corresponding predicted value of the dependent variable from the regression line. The error term is assumed to have zero mean and constant variance. It is also assumed that the error term is independent of $X_{1t}, X_{2t}, \ldots, X_{nt}$ and that e_{it} is independent of e_{jt} (that is, the error term for another security).

Example 9C.1 A multiple linear regression with three independent variables

Figure 9C.1 shows the monthly rates of return on Marks and Spencer plc and the FT-Actuaries All-Share Index for the four-year period from January 1985 to December 1988. Figure 9C.1 also includes 48 expected inflation rates and 48 unexpected inflation rates. The inflation rate for month t is measured by using the following formula:

$$\text{IR}_t = \ln(\text{RPI}_t/\text{RPI}_{t-1})$$

where

RPI_t, RPI_{t-1} = the retail price index for month t and $t-1$, respectively.

The expected inflation rate for month t is measured by the actual inflation rate of month $t-2$. For example, the expected inflation for January 1985 is the inflation rate observed in November 1984. The unexpected rate of inflation for month t is measured as follows:

$$\text{UIR}_t = \text{IR}_t - \text{EIR}_t$$

	A	B	C	D	E	F
1	MONTHLY RETURNS ON M&S, CHANGES ON FTA SHARE INDEX AND INFLATION RATE					
2						
3			FTA SHARE	EXPECTED	UNEXPECTED	
4	PERIOD	RATE OF RETURN	INDEX	INFLATION RATE	INFLATION RATE	
5						
6	Jan-85	2.53%	3.61%	0.23%	1.88%	
7	Feb-85	3.28%	3.30%	-2.21%	3.09%	
8	Mar-85	9.24%	-1.15%	2.11%	-1.13%	
9	Apr-85	5.72%	1.76%	0.87%	1.26%	
10	May-85	-3.30%	1.61%	0.97%	-0.55%	
11	Jun-85	0.73%	1.94%	2.13%	-1.92%	
12	Jul-85	-2.94%	-6.20%	0.42%	-0.63%	
13	Aug-85	11.28%	2.70%	0.21%	0.10%	
14	Sep-85	2.63%	4.72%	-0.21%	0.31%	
15	Oct-85	8.10%	-2.75%	0.31%	0.00%	
16	Nov-85	10.37%	6.59%	0.10%	0.00%	
17	Dec-85	-2.20%	2.33%	0.31%	-1.78%	
18	Jan-86	-2.25%	-0.74%	0.10%	1.57%	
19	Feb-86	-2.88%	1.42%	-1.47%	1.99%	
20	Mar-86	10.35%	7.59%	1.68%	-0.65%	
21	Apr-86	15.34%	9.06%	0.52%	-0.42%	
22	May-86	-3.26%	-1.32%	1.03%	-1.03%	
23	Jun-86	-6.87%	-2.54%	0.10%	-0.41%	
24	Jul-86	4.95%	4.12%	0.00%	0.31%	
25	Aug-86	-5.46%	-5.94%	-0.31%	0.82%	
26	Sep-86	10.64%	6.26%	0.31%	-0.10%	
27	Oct-86	-10.13%	-6.51%	0.51%	0.30%	
28	Nov-86	0.71%	5.08%	0.20%	0.10%	
29	Dec-86	-6.83%	-0.48%	0.81%	-2.63%	
30	Jan-87	-1.64%	3.42%	0.30%	1.92%	
31	Feb-87	4.85%	8.95%	-1.82%	2.22%	
32	Mar-87	10.96%	7.64%	2.22%	-2.03%	
33	Apr-87	1.41%	0.26%	0.40%	0.79%	
34	May-87	9.36%	4.32%	0.20%	-0.10%	
35	Jun-87	8.24%	7.14%	1.19%	-1.19%	
36	Jul-87	-4.86%	3.57%	0.10%	-0.20%	
37	Aug-87	6.82%	3.36%	0.00%	0.29%	
38	Sep-87	-9.34%	-2.79%	-0.10%	0.39%	
39	Oct-87	1.69%	4.99%	0.29%	0.19%	
40	Nov-87	-17.04%	-32.71%	0.29%	0.19%	
41	Dec-87	-15.67%	-9.64%	0.49%	-0.58%	
42	Jan-88	6.78%	8.95%	0.48%	-1.85%	
43	Feb-88	-1.65%	4.53%	-0.10%	1.46%	
44	Mar-88	-2.25%	0.43%	-1.36%	1.75%	
45	Apr-88	-1.14%	-1.93%	1.36%	-0.98%	
46	May-88	4.80%	3.45%	0.39%	1.23%	
47	Jun-88	-1.12%	0.49%	0.38%	-0.01%	
48	Jul-88	-1.71%	3.28%	1.62%	-1.24%	
49	Aug-88	-0.58%	0.62%	0.38%	-0.28%	
50	Sep-88	-13.93%	-7.65%	0.38%	0.74%	
51	Oct-88	7.98%	4.00%	0.09%	0.37%	
52	Nov-88	6.93%	3.53%	1.12%	-0.11%	
53	Dec-88	-18.35%	-4.55%	0.46%	-0.01%	
54						

Figure 9C.1. Data on monthly rates of return for M&S, monthly rates of changes of the FT-Actuaries All-Share Index and monthly inflation rates (*source*: Datastream)

where

EIR_t = the expected inflation rate for month t.

The regression equation can now be expressed as follows:

$$R_{it} = a_i + b_1 R_{mt} + b_2 \mathrm{EIR}_t + b_3 \mathrm{UIR}_t + e_{it}$$

where

R_{it} = the rate of return of Marks and Spencer for month t.
R_{mt} = the rate of return of the FT-Actuaries All-Share Index for month t.

Figure 9C.2 shows the regression results (note that the independent variables' range is C6..E53 and the dependent variable's range is B6..B53).

	A	B	C	D	E	F
60						
61		Regression Output:				
62	Constant			-0.010		
63	Std Err of Y Est			0.054		
64	R Squared			0.555		
65	No. of Observations			48		
66	Degrees of Freedom			44		
67						
68	X Coefficient(s)		0.860	2.038	0.832	
69	Std Err of Coef.		0.118	1.365	0.994	
70	T-STATISTIC		7.264	1.493	0.837	
71						

Figure 9C.2. A multiple regression

The standard error of the Y estimate is 1.24, calculated by using the following formula:

$$\mathrm{STD}(Y) = \sqrt{\frac{\sum_{t=1}^{N} (e_{it})^2}{\mathrm{DF}}}$$

where

DF = the degrees of freedom (sample size minus number of coefficients).

The R-squared ($R\hat{}2$) indicates the proportion of the variability of the dependent variable which can be explained by the variability of the independent variables. In our case, 55.5 per cent of the variation in the dependent variable is explained by the variation in the independent variables.

The t-statistics for the significance of the coefficients b_1, b_2 and b_3 are given by:

$t(b_1) = 7.264$, $t(b_2) = 1.493$ and $t(b_3) = 0.837$

The t-critical value for a two-tailed test at a 5 per cent level of significance with 44 degrees of freedom is approximately 2.021. Since $7.264 > 2.021$, the sample provides convincing evidence that the rate of return on Marks and Spencer is related to the rate of return of the FT-Actuaries All-Share Index. However, since $1.493 < 2.021$ and $0.837 < 2.021$, the conclusion is that the rate of return is unrelated to both the expected inflation rate and the unexpected inflation rate.

References and bibliography

Ambachtsheer, K. (1974) Profit potential in an 'almost efficient' market, *Journal of Portfolio Management*, Autumn.

Ball, R. and Brown, P. (1968) An empirical evaluation of accounting income numbers, *Journal of Accounting Research*, Autumn, 159–78.

Banz, R.W. (1981) The relationship between return and market value of common stock, *Journal of Financial Economics*, 3–18.

Barry, C.B. and Brown, S.J. (1984) Anomalies in security returns and the specification of the market model, *Journal of Finance*, July, 807–18.

Black, F. (1972) Capital market equilibrium with restricted borrowing, *Journal of Business*, July, 444–5.

Black, F., Jensen, M.C. and Scholes, M. (1972) The capital asset pricing model: some empirical tests, in: Jensen, M.C. (ed.), *Studies in the Theory of Capital Markets*. Praeger, New York.

Blume, M.E. and Friend, I. (1973) A new look at the capital asset pricing model, *Journal of Finance*, **viii,** 1, 19–34.

Conard, K. and Juttner, D. (1973) Recent behaviour of stock market prices in Germany and the random walk hypothesis, *Kyklos*.

Davies, P. and Canes, M. (1978) Stock prices and the publication of second-hand information, *Journal of Business*, **51,** January, 43–56.

Diacogiannis, P.G. (1986a) Some empirical evidence on the intertemporal stationarity of security return distributions, *Accounting and Business Research*, **17,** Winter, 43–8.

Diacogiannis, P.G. (1986b) Arbitrage pricing model: a critical examination of its empirical applicability for the London Stock Exchange, *Journal of Business Finance and Accounting*, **13,** Winter, 489–504.

Douglas, G. (1968) *Risk in the Equity Markets: An Empirical Appraisal of Market Efficiency*. University Microfilms, Ann Arbor, Mich.

Dryden, M.M. (1970) Filter tests of UK sharc prices, *Applied Economics*, **1,** 261–75.

Elton, E. and Gruber, M.J. (1981) *Modern Portfolio Theory and Investment Analysis*. John Wiley, New York.

Evans, J. and Archer, S.H. (1968) Diversification and the reduction of dispersion: an empirical analysis, *Journal of Finance*, December, 761.

Fama, E.F. (1965) The behavior of stock market prices, *Journal of Business*, **38,** 34–105.

Fama, E.F. (1970) Efficient capital markets: A review of the theory and empirical work, *Journal of Finance*, May, 383–417.

Fama, E.F. (1976) *Foundation of Finance*. Blackwell, Oxford.

Fama, E.F. and MacBeth, J.D. (1973) Risk, return and equilibrium: empirical tests, *Journal of Political Economy*, 607–36.

Fama, E.F. and Miller, M. (1972) *The Theory of Finance*. Dryden Press, Hinsdale, Ill.

Fama, E., Fisher, L., Jensen, M. and Roll, R. (1969) The adjustment of stock prices to new information, *International Economic Review*, February, 1–21.

Firth, M. (1975) The information content of large investment holdings, *Journal of Finance*, December, 1265–81.

Firth, M. (1978) *Unit Trusts: Performance and Prospects*. MCB Publications, Bradford.

Gehr, A. (1978) Some tests of the arbitrage pricing theory, *Journal of Midwest Finance Association*, **7,** 91–105.

Gibbons, M.R. (1982) Multivariate tests of financial models: a new approach, *Journal of Financial Economics*, March, 3–28.

Hawanini, G. and Michel, P. (1982) Market efficiency of the Brussels Stock Exchange, in: Stoneham, P. (ed.). *Major Stock Markets in Europe*. Gower, Aldershot.

Hughes, P. (1982) A test of the arbitrage pricing theory, Working Paper, University of British Columbia.

Jacob, N.L. (1971) The measurement of systematic risk for securities and portfolios: some empirical results, *Journal of Financial and Quantitative Analysis*, **6,** 815–33.

Jaffe, J. (1974) Special information and insider trading, *Journal of Business*, July, 410–28.

Jennergren, P. (1975) Filter tests of Swedish share prices', in: Elton, E.J. and Gruber, M.J.G. (eds), *International Capital Markets*. North Holland, Amsterdam.

Jennergren, P. and Korsvold, P. (1975) The non-random character of Norwegian and Swedish stock market prices, in: Elton, E.J. and Gruber, M.J.G., *International Capital Markets*. North Holland, Amsterdam.

Jensen, M. (1968) The performance of mutual funds in the period 1954–1964, *Journal of Finance*, May, 389–416.

Johnson, K.J. (1981) An orthogonal factor model for pricing capital assets, Working Paper, Department of Management Sciences, University of Manchester Institute of Science and Technology.

Johnston, J., Price, G. and VanVleck, F. (1966) *Linear Equations and Matrices*. Addison-Wesley, Reading, Mass.

Juttner, D. and McHugh, N. (1976) Is the Australian stock market really efficient in the weak sense?, *The Investment Analyst*, April.

Kaplan, R. and Roll, R. (1972) Investor evaluation of accounting information: some empirical evidence, *Journal of Business*, April, 225–57.

Kato, K. and Schallheim, J.S. (1985) Seasonal and size anomalies in the Japanese stock market, *Journal of Finance and Quantitative Analysis*, February, 243–60.

King, B.F. (1966) Market and industry factors in stock price behaviour, *Journal of Business Studies*, **39,** 139–90.

Koo, L. (1982) *The Stock Exchange in Singapore in the Context of the Efficient Market Hypothesis*, Singapore Stock Exchanges Publications.

Kraus, A. and Stoll, H. (1972) Price impacts of block trading on the New York Stock Exchange, *Journal of Finance*, June, 569–88.

Lintner, J. (1965) Evaluation of risk assets and the selection of risky investments in stock portfolios and capital budget, *Review of Economic and Statistics*, **47,** 13–37.

Lintner, J. (1968) In Douglas, G.W. (ed.), *Risk in the Equity Markets: An Empirical Appraisal of Market Efficiency*. University Microfilms, Ann Arbor, Mich.

Markowitz, H. (1959) *Portfolio Selection: Efficient Diversification of Investments*. John Wiley, New York.

Merton, R.C. (1972) An analytic derivation of the efficient portfolio frontier, *Journal of Finance and Quantitative Analysis*, **7,** 1851–72.

Miller, M. and Scholes, M. (1972) Rates of return in relation to risk: a reexamination of some empirical findings, in: Jensen, M.C. (ed.), *Studies in the Theory of Capital Markets*. Praeger Publishers, New York.

Niarchos, N. (1972) The stock market in Greece, in: Szego, G.P. and Shell, K. *Mathematical Methods in Investment and Finance*.

Niederhoffer, V. and Osborn, M. (1966) Market making and reversal on the Stock Exchange, *Journal of American Statistical Association*, **61**, December, 897–916.

Pettit, R. (1972) Dividend announcements, security performances, and capital market efficiency, *Journal of Finance*, December, 993–1007.

Reinganum, M.R. (1981) The arbitrage pricing theory: some empirical results, *Journal of Finance*, **36,** May, 337–49.

Reinganum, M.R. (1983) The anomalous stock market behaviour of small firms in January: empirical tests for tax-loss selling effect, *Journal of Financial Economics*, June, 89–104.

Roll, R. (1977) A critique of the asset pricing theory's tests—Part I: On past and potential testability of the theory, *Journal of Financial Economics*, **4,** March, 129–76.

Roll, R. (1978) Ambiguity when performance is measured by the securities market line, *Journal of Finance*, September, 1051, 1069.

Roll, R. and Ross, S.A. (1980) An empirical investigation of the arbitrage pricing theory, *Journal of Finance*, **35,** December, 1073–103.

Ross, S.A. (1976) The arbitrage theory of capital asset pricing, *Journal of Economic Theory*, December, 341–60.

Ross, S.A. (1977) Return risk and arbitrage, in: Friend, I. and Bickskler, J. (eds), *Studies in Risk and Return*. Ballinger, Cambridge, Mass.

Shanken, J. (1982) The arbitrage pricing theory: is it testable?, *Journal of Finance*, **37,** December, 1129–40.

Shanken, J. (1987) Multivariate proxies and asset pricing relations: living with roll critique, *Journal of Financial Economics*, 91–110.

Sharpe, W. (1964) Capital asset prices: a theory of market equilibrium under conditions of risk, *Journal of Finance*, **19,** September, 425–42.

Sharpe, W. (1966) Mutual funds performance, *Journal of Business*, January, 119–38.

Siong, S. (1982) *The Behaviour of Malaysian Stock Market Prices 1973–1981: A Statistical Study*. Malaysian Stock Exchange Publication.

Solnik, B.H. (1974) Why not diversify internationally rather than domestically? *Financial Analyst's Journal*, July–August, 48–54.

Weston, J.F. (1973) Investment decisions using the capital asset pricing model, *Financial Management*, **2,** Spring, 25–33.

Wong, C. (1981) Comparative study of capital market efficiency for three Pacific Basin stock markets: Hong Kong, Kuala Lumpur, Singapore, Far East Stock Exchange Papers.

10 Management of working capital

This chapter includes:

- Working capital definitions
- The trade-off between risk and return
- Models for balancing cash and marketable securities
- Managing debtors
- Managing stocks
- Managing creditors
- Managing accruals
- Managing short-term borrowing

Decisions concerning a firm's current assets and current liabilities are important because they influence the expected return and risk characteristics of the firm. The latter affect investors' perceptions and result in a change in the market value of the firm's ordinary shares.

In this chapter we concentrate on the management of current assets and current liabilities. We introduce several models with the aid of which we can determine the optimal quantities of assets (for example, stocks) that firms should hold. Figure 10.1 presents the relationship between the concepts discussed in this chapter and the objective of the firm discussed in Chapter 2.

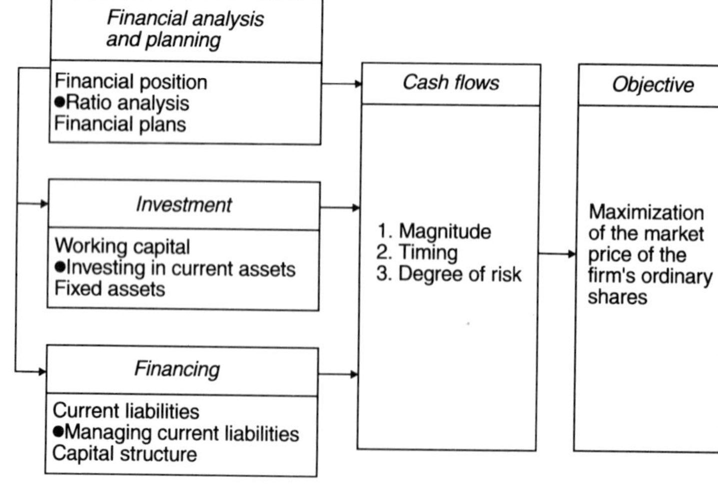

Figure 10.1. The relationship between the concept of working capital management and the objective of the firm introduced in Chapter 2

Basic concepts, definitions and examples

Working capital (or gross working capital) includes, stocks, debtors, short-term investments and cash. Working capital is defined as the sum in pounds sterling of a firm's current assets. The net working capital is defined as the difference between a firm's total current assets and its total current liabilities (the latter includes creditors, accruals and short-term borrowing).

Example 10.1 The net working capital of Marks and Spencer plc (1986–88)

From Figure 10.2, we see that Marks and Spencer plc had at the end of 1988 an amount of £700 million in working capital. The net working capital of Marks and Spencer at the end of 1988 is calculated as follows:

	Total current assets	→ £700,000,000
less	Total current liabilities	→ £623,500,000
	Net working capital	→ £ 76,500,000

The net working capital was negative for 1986 and 1987, but the firm had no real difficulties:

- Stock turnover was very high as compared with that of the industry.
- The firm had 'net assets of financial activities' of £18.3 million in 1986 and £51.3 million in 1987 (the 'net assets of financial activities' are equal to the assets *minus* the liabilities of the firm's financial service activities, for example chargecard).
- The firm could easily get short-term finance against its land and buildings (land and buildings in 1986: £1,244 million; in 1987: £1,322.6 million).

Problem Create the worksheet shown in Figure 10.2.

	A	B	C	D
1	MARKS AND SPENCER PLC:CALCULATING THE NET WORKING CAPITAL (1986-88)			
2	================================	=========	=========	=========
3		1986	1987	1988
4	Current Assets	(£000s)	(£000s)	(£000s)
5	Stocks	235,300	255,400	287,900
6	Debtors	91,600	106,500	120,500
7	Total Cash & Equivalent	140,300	96,800	291,600
8		--------	--------	--------
9	Total Current Assets	467,200	458,700	700,000
10				
11	Current Liabilities			
12	Current Taxation	139,100	161,800	194,900
13	Dividends Payable	70,100	82,300	94,400
14	Creditors	236,900	255,300	308,500
15	Borrowing Payable < 1 Year	35,600	30,500	25,700
16		--------	--------	--------
17	Total Current Liabilities	481,700	529,900	623,500
18				
19	Net Working Capital	(14,500)	(71,200)	76,500
20		=========	=========	=========

Figure 10.2. The current assets and liabilities of Marks and Spencer (1986–88)

Figure 10.3 depicts the operating cycle of a manufacturing firm. We assume that the firm offers credit terms on its sales; purchases of raw materials are paid for in cash or they are made on credit terms through the establishment of creditors or accruals. The raw materials are converted into finished goods which are then sold to the customers of the firm. Cash payments from sales provide an immediate source of cash to the firm. When a sale of finished goods is made on credit, a current asset, debtors, is created. Finally, when the debtors are collected, cash flows back into the firm and the operating cycle is completed (note that firms that offer no credit hold no debtors).

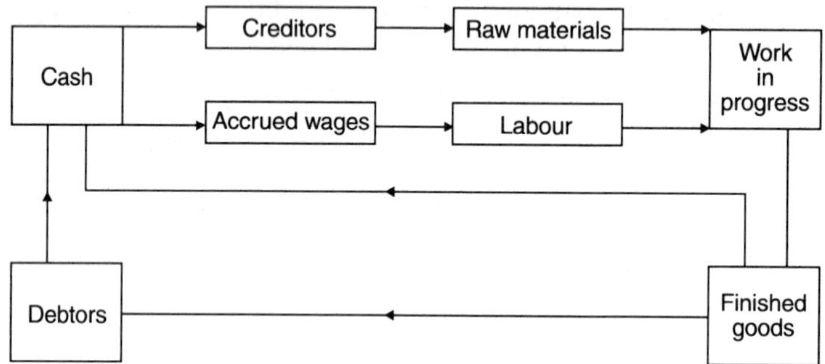

Figure 10.3. A simplified view of the cash flow cycle of a manufacturing firm

The working capital policy of a firm deals with the decisions concerning investments in current assets and also concerning how these investments will be financed. Since the management of current assets and current liabilities is closely related, the term working capital management is usually used in reference to the management of current assets, the management of current liabilities, and the management of all relationships between current assets and current liabilities. Therefore, the objective of working capital management is to maintain the level of net working capital that maximizes the wealth of the firm's ordinary shareholders.

There are several reasons revealing the importance of working capital management, these include the following:

1 Working capital represents that portion of total assets that is most manageable. The financial director of a firm has considerable control in managing its current assets and current liabilities.
2 There exists a direct relationship between sales growth and net working capital. Higher stocks and creditors are needed to support sales increases. On the other hand, increased sales result in a higher level of debtors.
3 There exists a direct relationship between working capital management and the firm's liquidity. Effective working capital management provides the firm with adequate liquidity both to pay its maturing short-term obligations as they come due and to conduct the firm's normal day-to-day operations. There are cases where firms fail because they do not maintain sufficient liquidity, even though they have growing sales.
4 There exists a direct relationship between profitability and working capital management. The level of a firm's working capital influences its profitability because of the cost in financing the firm's current assets.

Working capital ratios

In this section we present several ratios related to the current assets and current liabilities of a firm (note that some of these ratios have also been introduced in Chapter 4).

Current assets

By using an effective current asset policy the firm can increase its return and at the same time decrease the associated risk. This implies that the management of current assets plays a major role in creating a successful firm and the current assets of the firm should, therefore, be studied in greater detail. Listed below are four current assets together with their corresponding measures:

• Stocks	Stock turnover ratio
• Debtors	Average collection period
• Short-term investments	Rate of return
• Cash	Magnitude of cash available

The management of the (total) current assets of a firm can be measured with the following three ratios:

1 *Return on current assets* Indicates how effectively the firm is using its current assets to generate profits.
2 *Current assets to total assets* Indicates the proportion of total asset invested in current assets.
3 *Current assets turnover* Indicates how efficiently the firm is using the current assets to generate sales.

The current assets ratios of a firm are normally compared with industry standards or with historical standards within the same firm.

Current liabilities

Likewise, the management of the current liabilities is also important and its main components are:

• Creditors	Average payment period
• Short-term loan	Rate of interest charged
• Accruals	Magnitude of payments outstanding

Since the short-term credit is a source of finance, it determines the cash available to the firm (which is vital to its short-term operations). The management of the total current liabilities can be measured by using the following ratios:

1 *Current liabilities to total liabilities* Indicates the proportion of short-term debt in relation to the total debt.
2 *Short-term interest earned* Indicates the ability of the firm to meet its short-term interest payments from profits before interest and tax.
3 *Current liabilities turnover* Indicates how efficiently the firm is using the current liabilities to generate sales.

The analysis of the ratios related to current liabilities usually involves their comparison with industry standards or with historical standards within the same firm.

Net working capital

The net working capital is the appropriate measure of the firm's funds available and its magnitude is of great importance. The following ratios indicate additional information on how well the firm uses its net working capital:

1 *Current* Ability to meet short-term obligations from current assets.
2 *Acid test* Ability to meet short-term obligations from quick assets.
3 *Net working capital turnover* Indicates how efficiently management is using the net working capital to generate sales.
4 *Return on net working capital* Indicates how effectively management is using the net working capital to generate profits (that is, Return on net working capital = Profit after tax/net working capital).

The risk–return trade-off

The management of working capital usually implies a risk–return trade-off. The term risk, in this context, is defined as the probability that the firm will not be able to meet its financial obligations as they come due with cash flows generated from its current assets. The risk–return trade-off will be discussed in terms of using either of the two policies: a conservative policy or an aggressive policy.

Conservative policy

Maintaining a high level of net working capital means that the firm chooses to keep relatively high levels of current assets or/and low levels of current liabilities. This situation allows the firm to appear to be less risky as it can easily meet its short-term obligations from its current assets. However, excessive funds may be idle which implies that the firm does not achieve its maximum return potential. As this policy results in a lower expected profitability and a lower risk that the firm will run into financial difficulties, it is known as a conservative policy.

Aggressive policy

Maintaining a low level of net working capital means that the firm has decided to hold relatively low levels of current assets and/or high levels of current liabilities. In this case, the firm appears to be more risky as it cannot immediately meet its short-term obligations from its current assets. As the firm keeps low levels of assets, the surplus funds can be used to generate additional profits and the return is usually high. As this policy results in a higher expected profitability and a higher risk that the firm will run into financial difficulties, it is known as an aggressive policy.

Conservative policy versus aggressive policy

Under a conservative policy the firm maintains a high level of net working capital, whereas under an aggressive policy it holds a low level of net working capital. A conservative policy provides a low risk and a low profit, whereas an aggressive policy provides a high risk and high profits.

Example 10.2 Risk–return trade-off for three alternative working capital policies

In this example we examine how different working capital policies influence the profitability and the risk of a firm. Figure 10.4 shows the balance sheet and the profit and loss account statements of Kapas plc for three different working capital policies: a conservative, an average (which is the current working capital of the firm) and an aggressive. We assume that all policies have the same level of fixed assets.

```
     A        B        C        D            E              F            G            H
 1 A. KAPAS PLC:BALANCE SHEET
 2 -------------------------------------------------------------------------------------
 3                                     CONSERVATIVE   AVERAGE       AGGRESSIVE
 4                                       (£000s)      (£000s)        (£000s)
 5 -------------------------------------------------------------------------------------
 6
 7 Fixed Assets                           6,000        6,000        6,000
 8 Current Assets                         5,450        5,100        4,500
 9                                     ------------------------------------
10 TOTAL ASSETS                          11,450       11,100       10,500
11
12 Capital Employed                       5,400        5,000        4,300
13 Long-Term Debt                         4,250        4,300        4,400
14 Current Liabilities                    1,800        1,800        1,800
15                                     ------------------------------------
16 TOTAL CAPITAL & LIABILITIES           11,450       11,100       10,500
17
18 B. KAPAS PLC:P & L ACCOUNT STATEMENT
19 Sales                                 25,000       25,000       25,000
20 Costs of Goods Sold                   16,250       16,250       16,250
21 Operating Expenses                     8,000        8,000        8,000
22                                     ------------------------------------
23 PBIT                                     750          750          750
24 Interest                                 587          592          602
25                                     ------------------------------------
26 Profit Before Tax                        163          158          148
27 Tax (at 35%)                            57.1         55.3         51.8
28                                     ------------------------------------
29 Profit After Tax                       106.0        102.7         96.2
30
31 C. KAPAS PLC:THE PROFITABILITY-RISK TRADE-OFF
32 -------------------------------------------------------------------------------------
33                                     CONSERVATIVE   AVERAGE       AGGRESSIVE
34 -------------------------------------------------------------------------------------
35 Current Ratio                           3.03         2.83         2.50
36 Current Assets/Total Assets            47.60%       45.95%       42.86%
37
38 Total Assets Turnover                   2.18         2.25         2.38
39 Net Working Capital Turnover            6.85         7.58         9.26
40
41 Times Interest-Earned                   1.24         1.27         1.25
42
43 Return on Current Assets                1.94%        2.01%        2.14%
44 Return on Net Working Capital           2.90%        3.11%        3.56%
45 -------------------------------------------------------------------------------------
```

Figure 10.4. Kapas plc: profitability and risk for three alternative working capital policies

Under the conservative policy the firm would maintain the higher level of current assets, while under the aggressive policy it would maintain the lower level. We assume that the current liabilities would be the same under each policy. Consequently, the conservative policy would operate with a high level of working capital, whereas the aggressive policy would operate with a lower level.

Additionally, we make the assumption that the firm's profit before interest and taxes (PBIT) would remain the same under each of the three policies. Interest rates are forecasted to be 9 per cent on current liabilities and 10 per cent on long-term debt. Lastly, the firm's tax rate is 35 per cent.

Note that higher levels of current assets are associated with lower financing costs. Under the conservative policy the firm would pay £587,000 in interest, while under the aggressive one it would pay £602,000.

The profitability of the firm is measured here by the following ratios:

- Return on current assets
- Return on net working capital

The conservative policy produces a lower return on current assets and the aggressive policy a higher return than that produced by the average policy. Likewise, the conservative policy yields the lower return on net working capital, whereas the aggressive policy yields the higher one.

The risk of the firm is measured here by the following ratios:

- Current
- Current assets/total assets

Note that the higher the current assets/total assets ratio, the larger the amount of the current assets of the firm. Utilizing the current ratio as a risk measure, the conservative policy is associated with the lower risk, while the aggressive policy is most risky. Likewise, the current assets/total assets ratio is highest under the conservative policy and lowest under the aggressive policy.

The profitability and the risk of the firm are expected to be higher under the aggressive policy and lower under the conservative policy (see Figure 10.4). The trade-off between profitability and risk is clear, the firm is expected to increase its potential profits by increasing its risk.

Choosing the aggressive or conservative policy does not lead directly to the maximization of the shareholders' wealth. To achieve the desired objective, the firm should also consider additional factors, for example, cash flows and the degree of operating and financial gearing.

Problems

1 Use the data presented in Example 10.2 and create a worksheet calculating the seven ratios shown in Figure 10.4.

2 Assume that the current liabilities are expected to be as follows (other things remain constant, the long-term debt is equal to: total assets – capital employed – current liabilities):
Conservative policy: £1,700,000
Average policy: £1,800,000
Aggressive policy: £1,900,000
Calculate the ratios shown in Figure 10.4. Compare your results with those derived in Problem 1. What do you observe?

Example 10.3 Risk–return trade-off: a sensitivity analysis

Six out of the seven ratios calculated in Example 10.2 are directly dependent on the amount of current assets. Figure 10.5 provides a sensitivity analysis of the ratios calculated in Example 10.2 with respect to changes in current assets (these ratios are related to the aggressive policy). The current assets are taking values in the range £4,100 to £4,800 in steps of £50 (remember figures are in £000s). This range corresponds to several aggressive policies. Note that Figure 10.5 is a continuation of Figure 10.4. The range B49 ... G49 contains the results of the formulae calculating the ratios under consideration (the `/Range Format Text` command is used in the range B49 ... G49 in order to display the appropriate formulae). The 'input cell 1' is cell G8. The results of the sensitivity analysis indicate that the potential return of the firm increases as the working capital policy becomes more risky.

	A	B	C	D	E	F	G	H
47	D. SENSITIVITY TABLE							
48								
49		+G35	+G36	+G38	+G39	+G43	+G44	
50	4,800	2.67	44.44%	2.31	8.33	1.60%	2.56%	
51	4,750	2.64	44.19%	2.33	8.47	1.68%	2.71%	
52	4,700	2.61	43.93%	2.34	8.62	1.77%	2.87%	
53	4,650	2.58	43.66%	2.35	8.77	1.86%	3.03%	
54	4,600	2.56	43.40%	2.36	8.93	1.95%	3.20%	
55	4,550	2.53	43.13%	2.37	9.09	2.04%	3.38%	
56	4,500	2.50	42.86%	2.38	9.26	2.14%	3.56%	
57	4,450	2.47	42.58%	2.39	9.43	2.23%	3.75%	
58	4,400	2.44	42.31%	2.40	9.62	2.33%	3.95%	
59	4,350	2.42	42.03%	2.42	9.80	2.44%	4.15%	
60	4,300	2.39	41.75%	2.43	10.00	2.54%	4.37%	
61	4,250	2.36	41.46%	2.44	10.20	0.03	4.59%	
62	4,200	2.33	41.18%	2.45	10.42	0.03	4.82%	
63	4,150	2.31	40.89%	2.46	10.64	0.03	5.06%	
64	4,100	2.28	40.59%	2.48	10.87	0.03	5.31%	

Figure 10.5. A sensitivity analysis of ratios with respect to changes in current assets

Problem

Create the worksheet shown in Figure 10.5. Note that column G of the worksheet shown in Figure 10.4 contains the results of the following forumulae:

cell G10: `+G7+G8`
cell G13: `+G16-G12-G14`
cell G16: `+G10`
cell G23: `+G19-G20-G21`
cell G24: `+G14*0.09+G13*0.1`
cell G26: `+G23-G24`
cell G27: `0.35*G26`
cell G29: `+G26-G27`

cell G35: `+G8/G14`
cell G36: `+G8/G10`
cell G38: `+G19/G10`
cell G39: `+G19/(G8-G14)`
cell G43: `+G29/G8`
cell G44: `+G29/(G8-G14)`

A risk–return relationship in the net working capital context

The current assets/total assets (CA/TA) ratio can be expressed as:

$$CA/TA = \frac{\text{Return on fixed assets}}{\text{Return on fixed assets} + \text{Return on current assets}}$$

If the amount of fixed assets remains constant, this relationship indicates that the risk associated with holding current assets increases as the profitability associated with holding current assets increases and vice versa (note that an increase/decrease in the return on fixed assets ratio increases/decreases both the numerator and denominator by the same amount).

Example 10.4 A risk–return relationship in the context of net working capital

Figure 10.6 provides the data for the graphical representation of a risk–return relationship associated with holding current assets. Column A contains the profit after tax (PAT) for various levels of current assets (we consider the same assumptions as Examples 10.2 and 10.3). The return on fixed assets (ROFA) ratio is calculated by dividing the amount of PAT by the amount of fixed assets. For example in cell B7 we store the result of the following formula:

```
+A7/$C$3
```

```
      A                 B                C               D           E          F
1              A RISK-RETURN RELATIONSHIP
2              ===========================
3 Fixed Assets ------->          6,000
4 ---------------------------------------------------------
5     PAT             ROFA             ROCA           CA/TA
6 ---------------------------------------------------------
7     76.70           1.28%            1.60%          44.44%
8     86.45           1.44%            1.86%          43.66%
9     96.20           1.60%            2.14%          42.86%
10   105.95           1.77%            2.44%          42.03%
11   115.70           1.93%            2.75%          41.18%
12   125.45           2.09%            3.10%          40.30%
13   135.20           2.25%            3.47%          39.39%
14   144.95           2.42%            3.87%          38.46%
15   154.70           2.58%            4.30%          37.50%
16   164.45           2.74%            4.77%          36.51%
17   174.20           2.90%            5.28%          35.48%
18   183.95           3.07%            5.84%          34.43%
19   193.70           3.23%            6.46%          33.33%
20 ---------------------------------------------------------
```

Figure 10.6. Net working capital: a risk–return relationship

The contents of cell B7 are copied in the range B8 . . . B19. The return on current assets (ROCA) ratio is calculated in example 10.3 (see Figure 10.5). Next the CA/TA ratio, stored in cell D7, is calculated as follows:

```
+B7/(B7 + C7)
```

Finally, the contents of cell D7 are copied in the range D8 . . . D19. The results reveal that as the CA/TA ratio decreases, the profitability associated with the current assets increases (other things being the same).

The relationship between risk and return is depicted in Figure 10.7.

Problems

1 Create the worksheet shown in Figure 10.6.
2 Create the graph illustrated in Figure 10.7.

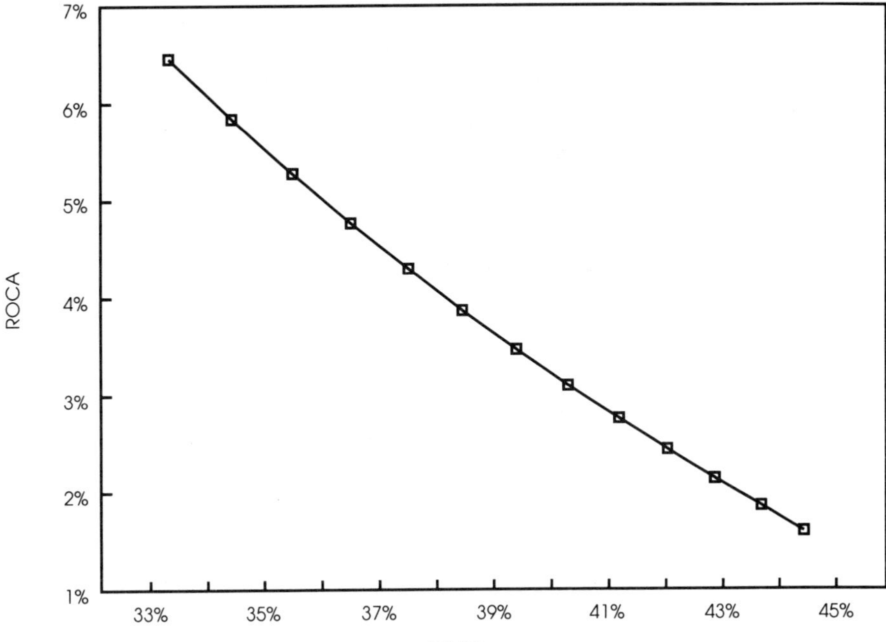

Figure 10.7. The relationship between the risk and return associated with current assets

Managing cash

Cash is ready money owned by the firm, including, coins, paper money, cheques and money on deposit with banks. Cash is the most liquid of all assets. There are several motives for holding cash, including the following:

1. *Transaction motives* Cash is necessary to allow a firm to continue operating from day to day, for example, cash is needed to purchase parts and materials, to pay labour services, and so on.
2. *Precautionary motives* Since future cash flows are uncertain, the firm must have additional cash available to meet uncertain future events. For example, suppose a firm expects during a particular month to receive a £25,000 payment from a customer and utilize these funds to purchase material costing also £25,000. Assume that the customer's payment arrives later than expected. For such cases, the firm needs to hold a certain amount of cash in reserves. Another example would be to keep precautionary balances in order to meet an unexpected breakdown of plant and machinery.
3. *Speculative motives* In this case, the firm chooses to have additional cash balances in the anticipation of future profitable opportunities. For example, a firm may plan to hold additional cash for purchasing materials at a special discount. Another example would be that a firm may choose to accumulate additional cash for a possible future acquisition of another firm.

Either excessive cash or inadequate cash can be costly to a firm. A cash surplus results in unnecessary costs (for example, the return the firm could earn if that excess cash were invested in government securities) which in turn reduce the profitability of the firm.

Inadequate cash balances expose the firm to many unnecessary costs (for example, forgone cash discounts, difficulties in meeting its financial obligations, and so on). Therefore, we can specify an appropriate goal of cash management as follows:

> *The goal of cash management is to determine the optimal cash balance which minimizes the total costs related to the investment in cash, but without exposing the firm to undue risk in meeting its financial needs.*

Cost-balancing models for managing cash

Below are discussed two major cash management models: the Baumol model and the Miller–Orr model.

Baumol's EQQ model

The Baumol model is based upon the following assumptions:

1. The cash balance over time is known with certainty.
2. Cash outflows occur at a constant rate.
3. Cash inflows occur periodically when securities are liquidated.
4. The costs for each transaction (for example, administrative costs) are fixed, regardless of the transaction's size.
5. The selling of short-term investments and the transformation of the proceeds into the cash account occur instantaneously.

The Baumol model can be used to determine the distributions of current assets between cash and short-term investments. The model of Baumol recognizes the following two types of costs: holding costs and transaction costs. Holding costs are opportunity costs occurring when holding surplus cash instead of earning a return by investing the excess cash (for example, in government securities). Transaction costs occur when a firm keeps inadequate cash balances. In this case, it needs additional costs to raise more cash, for example, costs associated with selling marketable securities (that is, brokerage fees), if it had any, or costs associated with borrowing money (that is, interest expenses). In view of the model of Baumol, total costs equal holding costs plus transaction costs. Total costs can be expressed mathematically as follows:

$$\text{Total costs} = \frac{Ck}{2} + \frac{TF}{C} \tag{10.1}$$

where

C = amount of cash reinvested by borrowing or selling short-term investments (for example, government securities). The firm begins with £C and ends with zero, thus, the average amount it holds over a given period is £$C/2$.

k = the opportunity cost of holding cash (it is equal to the forgone rate of return on short-term investments or the cost of borrowing).

T = total amount of net new cash needed for transactions over a given time period (usually a year).

F = Fixed costs per transaction of selling securities or borrowing money.

To summarize, total costs equal the costs associated with the forgone interest on the average balance $C/2$ plus the costs of making T/C transactions per period when selling securities. The larger the average cash balance, the higher the total costs (other things remain the same. Also, the larger the number of transactions, the higher the total costs (other things remain constant).

Example 10.5 Calculating the holding, transaction and total costs for different cash balances

In 1988, GD Clothing Ltd invested £580,000 in government securities yielding an annual return of 14 per cent. The firm predicted that it had to use £245,000 of these invested funds to cover net cash outflows expected to occur during 1989. These cash outflows are expected to occur at a constant rate throughout the year. The transaction costs associated with each liquidation of government securities is £87,500. Figure 10.8 calculates the holding costs, transaction costs and total costs for different cash balances in the range £11,500–£32,500 using steps of £3,000. The total costs represent the sum of the holding and transaction costs for each cash balance. For example, the total costs for $C = £11,500$ are calculated as follows:

$$\text{Total costs} = \frac{(£11{,}500)(0.14)}{2} + \frac{(£245{,}000)(£87{,}500)}{£11{,}500}$$

$$= £805 + £1{,}864 = £2{,}669$$

```
---------------------------------------------------------------------
       A            B               C             D              E
 1                          COSTS FOR DIFFERENT CASH BALANCES
 2                          =================================
 3 Total Cash Required                         £245,000
 4 Fixed Costs per Transaction                  £87.500
 5 Interest Rate Earned on Securities               14%
 6
 7 ------------------------------------------------------------------
 8            Cash          Holding       Transaction   Total
 9            Balance (£)   Costs (£)     Costs (£)     Costs (£)
10 ------------------------------------------------------------------
11                   11,500          805         1,864          2,669
12                   14,500        1,015         1,478          2,493
13                   17,500        1,225         1,225          2,450
14                   20,500        1,435         1,046          2,481
15                   23,500        1,645           912          2,557
16                   26,500        1,855           809          2,664
17                   29,500        2,065           727          2,792
18                   32,500        2,275           660          2,935
19 ------------------------------------------------------------------
---------------------------------------------------------------------
```

Figure 10.8. Holding, transaction and total costs for different cash balances

Figure 10.9 illustrates graphically the relationships among holding costs, transaction costs and total costs. It can be seen that holding costs increase as cash balances increase, while transaction costs decrease as cash balances increase. Total costs first decrease, reaching the value of £2,450 and then increase as cash balances increase.

Problems

1. Create the spreadsheet shown in Figure 10.8.
2. Create the graph illustrated in Figure 10.9.

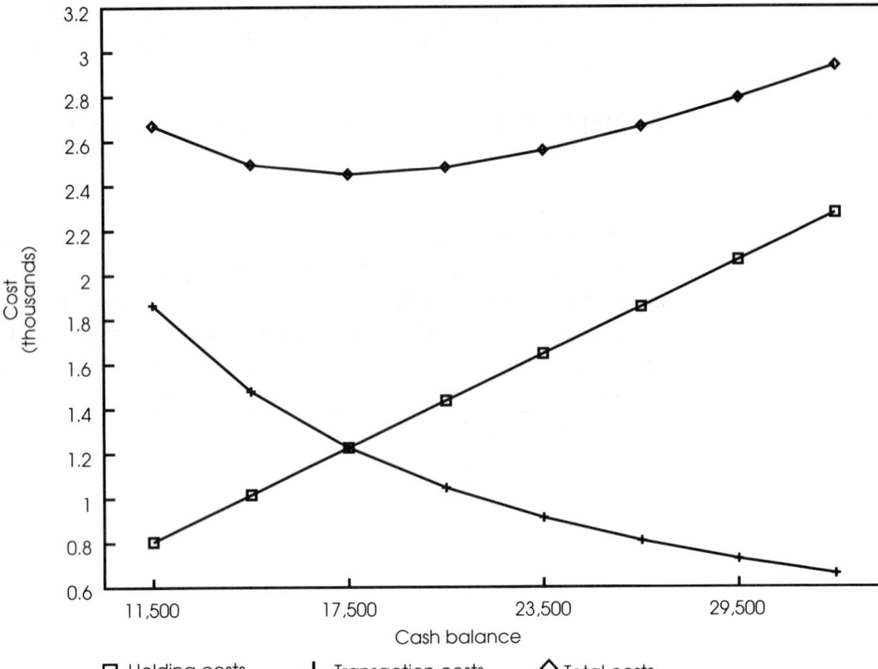

Figure 10.9. A graphic presentation of Baumol model for GD Clothing Ltd

In Figure 10.9 the total cost function is represented by a U-shaped curve, indicating the existence of a minimum value. A mathematical formula can be developed for determining the optimal amount of funds to be transferred to the firm's cash account from short-term investment. Such an optimal amount of cash occurs at the point where total costs (that is, holding costs and transaction costs) are minimized. Figure 10.10 provides a summary of the Baumol model.

Definition A mathematical model which determines, under conditions of certainty, the level for the cash balance, so that the holding costs of cash plus the transaction costs of converting marketable securities into cash are minimized.

Calculation Based on the model's assumptions, the equation for determining the optimal cash balance is:

$$C^* = \sqrt{\frac{2FT}{k}}$$

where F, T and k are as defined in Equation (10.1).

Interpretation It computes the optimum amount of funds needed to transfer to the firm's cash account in order to minimize the relative costs of having excess cash versus running out of cash. If $2FT/k$ were to increase, for example, nine times, the optimal cash balance would increase three times. Thus, there exist some economies of scale in cash management which should be given considerable attention.

Figure 10.10. Baumol model for determining the optimal cash balance

Example 10.6 Calculating the optimal cash balance to be transferred from short-term investment using the Baumol model

Assume the data used in Example 10.5. Using these values we can calculate the optimal transaction size as follows:

$$C^* = \sqrt{\frac{(2)(£87{,}500)(£245{,}000)}{0.14}} = £17{,}500$$

With $C^* = £17{,}500$, total costs are minimized at £2,450 (that is $(£17{,}500)(0.14)/2 + (£245{,}000)(£87{,}500)/£17{,}500 = £2{,}450$). Therefore, as the cash balance of GD Clothing approaches zero (or some minimum acceptable level), the firm should sell £17,500 worth of government securities to replenish its cash account.

The number of transactions occurring during the year can be calculated by dividing the total cash required by the optimal cash balance:

$$\frac{£245{,}000}{£17{,}500} = 14$$

Each transaction should be made every 26 days (that is 365/14). Any value different from 14 can prove costly to the firm. Indeed, if the firm makes 13 transactions, it will run out of cash at the end of the year. On the other hand, if the firm makes 15 transactions, it will have a cash surplus at the end of the year.

Finally, the firm begins each 26-day transaction with £17,500 and ends with zero. Consequently, the optimal average amount it should hold is £8,750.

Example 10.7 Sensitivity of the optimal cash balance to changes in the interest rate earned on short-term investments and in the fixed costs associated with a transaction

Consider the data given in Example 10.6. Figure 10.11 shows the sensitivity of the optimal cash balances to changes in two variables: the interest rate earned on short-term investments and the fixed costs per transaction associated with selling securities. We assume that the interest rate earned on securities takes values in the range 8–16 per cent in steps of 1 per cent, while the fixed costs take values in the range £81.5–£89.5 in steps of £2. The 'input cell 1' is cell D5, whereas the 'input cell 2' is cell D4.

```
     A           B              C              D              E              F
 1 SENSITIVITY OF OPTIMAL TRANSACTION SIZE TO CHANGES IN k AND F
 2 ============================================================
 3 Total Amount of New Cash (T)              £245,000
 4 Fixed Costs per Transaction (F)             £87.50
 5 Rate of Return on Securities (k)               14%
 6                                        ------------
 7 Optimal Transaction Size ----->            17500.0
 8
 9
10 +D7               81.5           83.5           85.5           87.5           89.5
11          8%    22342.5        22615.0        22884.2        23150.3        23413.4
12          9%    21064.7        21321.6        21575.4        21826.3        22074.4
13         10%    19983.7        20227.5        20468.3        20706.3        20941.6
14         11%    19053.8        19286.1        19515.7        19742.7        19967.0
15         12%    18242.6        18465.1        18684.9        18902.2        19117.0
16         13%    17526.9        17740.7        17951.9        18160.6        18367.0
17         14%    16889.3        17095.3        17298.8        17500.0        17698.9
18         15%    16316.7        16515.6        16712.3        16906.6        17098.7
19         16%    15798.5        15991.2        16181.6        16369.8        16555.8
20 ------------------------------------------------------------------------------
```

Figure 10.11. A two-variable sensitivity table of the optimal cash balance

The results reveal that the optimal cash balance decreases as the rate of return on short-term investments increases. In other words, less cash should be held as the rate of return on short-term investments increases. On the other hand, the optimal cash balance increases as the fixed costs associated with a transaction increase. In other words, more cash should be held as the fixed costs per transaction increase.

Figure 10.12 illustrates the results of the sensitivity analysis included in Figure 10.11.

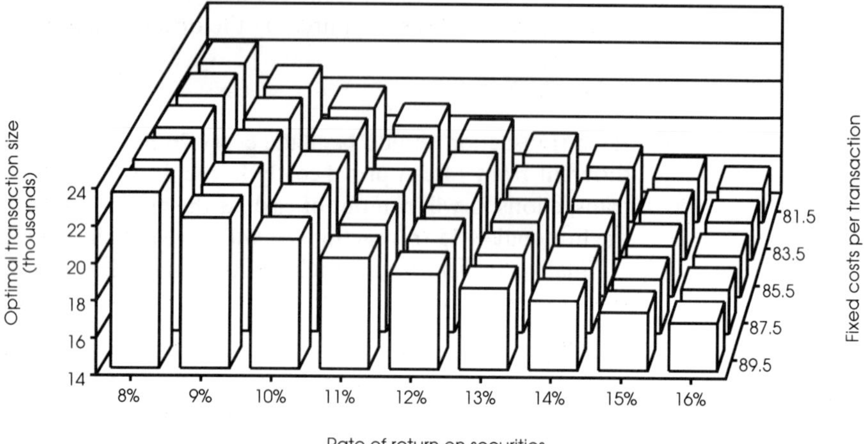

Figure 10.12. Sensitivity of the optimal cash balance with respect to changes in the interest rate and transaction costs

Problem

Create the worksheet presented in Figure 10.11.

The Miller–Orr model

The Miller–Orr model for cash management is based upon less restrictive assumptions as compared with that of Baumol:

1 There exists random changes in cash inflows and cash outflows and, thus, in call balances.
2 The distributions of cash flows are approximately normal.
3 Cash balances can move in either positive or negative directions.

The Miller–Orr model is summarized in Figure 10.13.

If the standard deviation or the transaction costs for buying or selling securities increase, the optimal return point increases. However, taking the cube root diminishes the effect of increased standard deviation and transaction costs. Therefore, there exist some economies of scale in cash management which should be taken into consideration.

The optimal return point and the optimal upper limit are dependent on the transaction costs of selling and buying securities, the standard deviation of daily cash balances and the interest rate on short-term investments. These optimal values increase with both the standard deviation and transaction costs (other things remain the same) and decrease with the interest rate (other things remain constant).

Definition A mathematical model which computes, under conditions of uncertainty, an optimal cash balance range.

Calculation Based on the model's assumption, the equation for determining the optimal cash balance (or optimal return point) and the optimal value of the upper limit are, respectively:

$$Z = \sqrt[3]{\frac{3B\sigma^2}{4i}} + L$$

$$\text{Upper limit} = 3Z - 2L$$

where

- B = Fixed costs per transaction of converting marketable securities (or short-term investments) into cash and vice versa.
- σ^2 = the variance of daily cash balances.
- i = the daily interest rate on marketable securities.
- L = the lower cash limit (this limit is set subjectively).

Interpretation The model computes the optimal return point and the optimal value of the upper limit that minimizes total costs associated with cash (where total costs = holding costs + transaction costs). The following cases exist:

- If and when the cash balance reaches the upper limit, then transfer to short-term investment the following amount of cash: upper limit $- Z$. Then cash balance is reduced to the return point Z.
- If and when the cash balance reaches the lower limit, then transfer from short-term investment to cash the following amount: $Z -$ lower limit. Then cash balance increases to the return point Z.
- If the cash balance states between the upper and lower limit no transfer takes place.

Figure 10.13. The Miller–Orr model for determining the optimal cash balance

Example 10.8. Applying the Miller–Orr model

The financial director of Blue Ltd has established in view of his experience a lower cash limit of £1,360. He has recorded for each of the preceding 100 working days net cash inflows and cash outflows and he has prepared a series of 100 net cash flows. These daily net cash flows fluctuate randomly and have a standard deviation of £480. The annual rate of return on short-term investment is 14 per cent and the fixed costs for converting short-term investment into cash are £87.50.

The optimal return point would be:

$$Z = \left[\frac{3(\pounds 87.50)(\pounds 480)^2}{4(0.14/365)}\right]^{1/3} + \pounds 1{,}360$$

$$= \pounds 3{,}404 + \pounds 1{,}360 = \pounds 4{,}763$$

The upper limit can be found as follows:

$$\text{Upper limit} = 3(\pounds 4{,}763) - 2(\pounds 1{,}360)$$

$$= \pounds 11{,}569$$

The firm should not hold more than £11,569 during the specified period. If the cash balance reaches £11,569, the firm should invest £6,806 (that is, £11,569 – £4,763) in short-term investments. If the cash balance falls to £1,360, sell £3,403 (that is £4,763 – £1,360) of short-term investments and transfer the proceeds into the cash account. In either case, the cash balance will return to £4,763.

The spread between the lower and upper limit can be found as follows:

$$3Z - 3L = 3(£4{,}763) - 3(£1{,}360)$$
$$= £10{,}209$$

Note that the optimal return point (in our case, £4,763) is not midway between the upper limit (that is, £11,569) and lower limit (that is, £1,360). The optimal return point is above the lower point one-third of the distance between upper and lower limits (that is, $£1{,}360 + (£11{,}569 - £1{,}360)/3 = £4{,}763$). This also means that the cash balance reaches the lower limit more often than it reaches the upper limit.

The average cash balance is calculated as follows:

$$\text{Average cash balance} = \frac{4(£4{,}763) - £1{,}360}{3} = £5{,}897$$

The daily cash balance is random. However, we know that, on average, the cash balance will be £5,897.

Problems

1 Provide a sensitivity analysis of the optimal return point with respect to changes in the daily interest rate on short-term investments (other things remain the same).
2 Provide a sensitivity analysis of the optimal return point with respect to changes in the standard deviation and transaction costs (other things remain unchanged).
3 Provide a graphical illustration of the results produced in Problem 2.

In many cases, the assumption of the Miller–Orr model that the cash flows are random is not completely valid. If the cash flows do not fluctuate in a random fashion, some other method of cash management may provide better results.

Managing marketable securities

Short-term investments refer to investments in securities that have short maturity (that is, a maturity up to one year). Therefore, short-term investments include long-term debentures that are maturing within one year and also securities that are originally issued with maturity up to one year (for example, short-term government securities, deposit accounts, term deposits with banks, and so on). The basic motives for investing in short maturity securities (also called marketable securities) include the following:

1 *Substitute for cash motive* Marketable securities can be viewed as a short-term use of cash. They provide the liquidity needed to conduct predictable or unpredictable transactions (for example, an unpredictable financing need).
2 *Investments motive* Firms hold marketable securities as short-term investment of residual cash. Excess cash can be temporarily placed in marketable securities and, conversely, when the firm needs more cash, marketable securities can be converted quickly into cash.

We can now specify the appropriate goal for marketable securities management.

The goal of marketable securities management is to invest the temporary excess cash of a firm in order to reduce unnecessary costs related to these excessive cash balances.

This goal does not consider the liquidity position of a firm which can be explored via careful cash budgeting.

Characteristics of marketable securities

In addition to the return associated with marketable securities, the following characteristics should be considered when selecting marketable securities.

- *Marketability* This is the ability of the investor to sell a short-term security quickly and with little or no loss of the amount of money paid when the security was initially purchased. Firms tend to invest in securities that offer high marketability since it may be necessary to convert marketable securities into cash before their maturity date. Firms which purchase less marketable securities can earn higher returns, but in such cases they may have problems to sell the securities quickly and at a reasonable price.
- *Maturity* This is the length of time remaining before the principal amount of the marketable security is paid to the investor. The shorter the maturity of a security, the least likely are price fluctuations before the maturity date.
- *Default risk* This is the risk associated with the failure to pay the interest or principal. The lower the default risk, the lower will be the likely return on the investment.

Yield on a marketable security

The concept of a yield on a marketable security is summarized in Figure 10.14.

Definition The yield on a marketable security (for example, a government security) is the rate of return earned by the investment in the security.

Calculation The yield of a marketable security is calculated as follows:

$$\text{Yield} = \frac{P_2 - P_1 + I}{P_1} \frac{365}{N}$$

where

P_1 = the purchase price of the security.
P_2 = the sale price of the security.
I = the interest paid on the security over the period is held.
N = the number of days the security is held.

Interpretation The yield of a marketable security shows the percentage increase (or decrease) in the firm's wealth associated with holding the security over a given period of time.

Figure 10.14. A summary of the yield on a marketable security

Example 10.9 Calculating the yield of a marketable security

Tate Systems plc purchases £10,000 worth of a marketable security that pays £420 interest until maturity. The purchase price is £10,000 and the security matures in 202 days. Then the yield on this security would be:

$$\text{Yield} = \frac{\pounds 10{,}000 - \pounds 10{,}000 + \pounds 420}{\pounds 10{,}000} \frac{365}{202} = 7.59 \text{ per cent}$$

Problems

1 Create a spreadsheet showing the sensitivity of a marketable security's yield with respect to changes in the number of days the security is held and the interest paid (use the data related to the marketable security available to Tate Systems plc).

2 Present graphically the results of Problem 1.

The portfolio of marketable securities

Figure 10.15 shows the factors which influence the composition of a firm's portfolio of marketable securities. The worth of a marketable security is based upon its risk and expected return (that is, its yield). External factors influence the risk and expected return of marketable securities. The firm considers the risk levels and expected returns of many marketable securities and in view of its preference in terms of risk and expected return chooses the composition of its portfolio of marketable securities (for example, a very conservative management team may decide to invest a given amount of money in domestic Treasury bills).

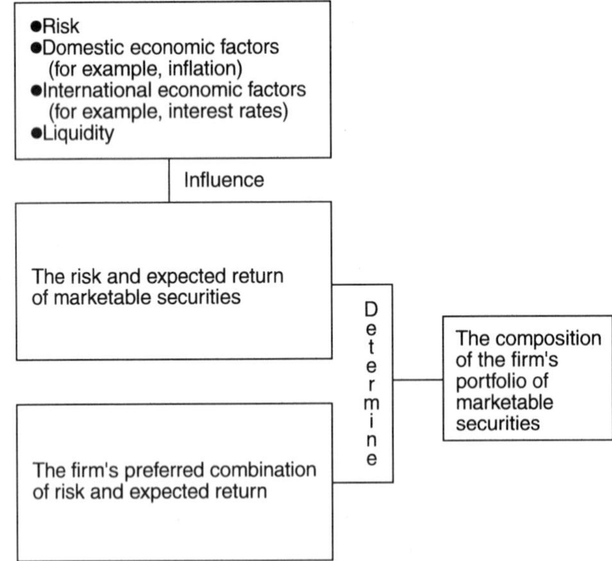

Figure 10.15. Factors influencing the composition of a firm's portfolio of marketable securites

Models of marketable securities management

Marketable securities management is concerned with the firm's decision as to how much cash to invest in marketable securities in order to maintain its necessary liquidity while minimizing total costs related to its cash investment. Earlier we discussed the Baumol and Miller–Orr models which deal with the balancing of the various costs associated with the firm's cash balance and its portfolio of marketable securities.

Managing debtors

Debtors consists of money which a firm expects to collect from its customers for goods and services sold to them on credit. Two basic motives for holding debtors are as follows:

1 *Facilitating trade motive* When a firm decides to extend credit to current and new customers (that is, other firms or individuals), it essentially offers a means of facilitating trade.
2 *Competitive motive* One policy by which a firm can increase its market share, and thus increase its profitability, is to win customers from its competitors by offering better credit terms. This policy could be especially sound in firms belonging to different industries.

The higher the level of debtors, the greater the cost of financing those debtors. On the other hand, if the firm attempts to reduce debtors, it may realize lower sales. Thus, the goal of the debtors' management can be stated as follows:

> *The goal of debtors management is to set credit terms, monitor payment patterns and apply necessary collection procedures so as to realize high earnings, low risk and a higher share price.*

Credit policy

Credit policies are management guidelines regarding the extension of credit to customers and how much credit to extend. The important components of a firm's credit policy are the following:

- *Credit standards* They are criteria used by a firm to determine which customers must receive credit trade.
- *Cash discounts* These allow the customers of a firm to pay less than the sale price of goods if payment is made within the discount period (that is, the length of time the discount is offered).
- *Credit period* It measures the length of time for which credit is extended.
- *Collection policies* These are the procedures used to collect overdue debts.

Credit standards

In evaluating proposed changes in credit standards the firm must recognize three major variables: sales volume, the cost of financing debtors and bad debt expenses.

Sales volume

Relaxing credit standards may result in an increrase in the firm's sales and net profits. On the other hand, a tightening of standards may decrease the firm's sales and net profits.

Cost of financing debtors

A relaxation of credit standards may increase the costs associated with carrying debtors (for example, clerical and collection costs). Tightening credit standards can be expected to have the opposite effect.

Bad debt expenses

Easing credit standards may increase bad debts, while bad debts may increase as the firm raises its credit standards.

Example 10.10 Marginal cost/benefit analysis of AK Manufacturing plc's proposal to relax credit standards

Case 1 After collecting and evaluating credit information on applicants, AK Manufacturing plc has placed all applicants into six different risk classes, A to F. Under its current credit policy, the firm extends trade credit only to customers in risk classes A and B. The price of the firm's product is £6, variable costs are £4 per unit and total fixed costs are £40,000. The firm's current average collection period is 55 days, sales are 500,000 units and bad debt expense is 2 per cent of sales. The firm does not currently offer any cash discount.

AK Manufacturing is attempting to evaluate whether to relax its credit policy by extending trade credit to customers in risk class C. In this case, it considers the following changes:

- The credit term change will result in a 10 per cent increase in sales and an increase in average collection period to 65 days.
- Bad debts are expected to increase from 2 per cent of sales to 2.5 per cent.

The required before tax rate of return (that is, the opportunity cost) of the additional investment on debtors is 14 per cent.

Figure 10.16 calculates the expected net benefits associated with the proposed case:

Change in gross profit:

(10 per cent)(500,000 units)(£6 – £4) = £100,000

Cost of financing debtors before the change:

$$\frac{(500{,}000 \text{ units})(£4) + (£40{,}000)}{365}(55 \text{ days})(0.14) = £43{,}036$$

Cost of financing after the change:

$$\frac{(550{,}000 \text{ units})(£4) + (£40{,}000)}{365}(65 \text{ days})(0.14) = £55{,}847$$

Change in cost of financing debtors:

£55,847 – £43,036 = £12,811

Bad debt expense before the change:

(0.02)(500,000 units)(£6) = £60,000

Bad debt expense after the change:

(0.025)(550,000 units)(£6) = £82,500

Change in bad debt expense:

£82,500 – £60,000 = £22,500

```
                        A                          B         C         D
 1 AK MANUFACTURING:AN ANALYSIS TO RELAX ITS CREDIT STANDARDS
 2 ============================================================
 3
 4 A> CALCULATING THE EXPECTED NET BENEFITS
 5
 6 Increase in Sales                            10.0%
 7 Sales Volume                               500,000
 8 Sales Price Per Unit                          £6.0
 9 Variable Costs per Unit                       £4.0
10                                          ----------
11 Change In Gross Profit                    £100,000
12
13 Fixed Costs                                £40,000
14 Opportunity Cost                             14.0%
15 Average Collection Period                      55
16
17 New Sales                                  550,000
18 New Average Collection Period                  65
19                                          ----------
20 Cost of Financing Debtors Before Change    £43,036
21 Cost of Financing Debtors After Change     £55,847
22                                          ----------
23 Change in Cost of Financing Debtors        £12,811
24
25 Existing Bad Debt Expense                     2.0%
26 New Bad Debt Expense                          2.5%
27 Bad Debt Expense Before the Change         £60,000
28 Bad Debt Expense After the Change          £82,500
29                                          ----------
30 Change in Bad Debt Expense                 £22,500
31
32 Net Benefit/Cost                           £64,689
33                                          ==========
34
35
36 B> SENSITIVITY ANALYSIS:BENEFITS VERSUS CHANGES IN SALES AND BAD DEBTS
37
38
39 +B32                                          2.5%      3.0%      3.5%
40                                    7.0%     38,435    22,385     6,335
41                                    7.5%     42,811    26,686    10,561
42                                    8.0%     47,186    30,986    14,786
43                                    8.5%     51,562    35,287    19,012
44                                    9.0%     55,938    39,588    23,238
45                                    9.5%     60,313    43,888    27,463
46                                   10.0%     64,689    48,189    31,689
47                             [illegible] [illegible] [illegible] [illegible]
48                                   11.0%     73,440    56,790    40,140
49                                   11.5%     77,816    61,091    44,366
50                                   12.0%     82,192    65,392    48,592
```

Figure 10.16. An analysis for relaxing the credit standards for AK Manufacturing plc

Therefore, the net benefit from the change of the firm's credit policy would be:

£100,000 – £12,811 – £22,500 = £64,689

The firm expects to obtain net benefits of £64,689 from the proposed relaxation of credit standards. This result indicates that the firm should adopt the change in its credit standards.

The firm assumes that the estimates of the percentage increase in sales and the percentage of bad debts expected are correct and it wishes to examine the sensitivity of the marginal benefit/cost with respect to changes in these two variables. Figure 10.16 presents the results after using the `/Data Table 2` command. The 'input cell 1' is cell B6 and the 'input cell 2' is cell B26. The analysis presented indicates that the new credit policy should be adopted.

Finally, the results of the sensitivity analysis in Figure 10.16 are illustrated graphically in Figure 10.17.

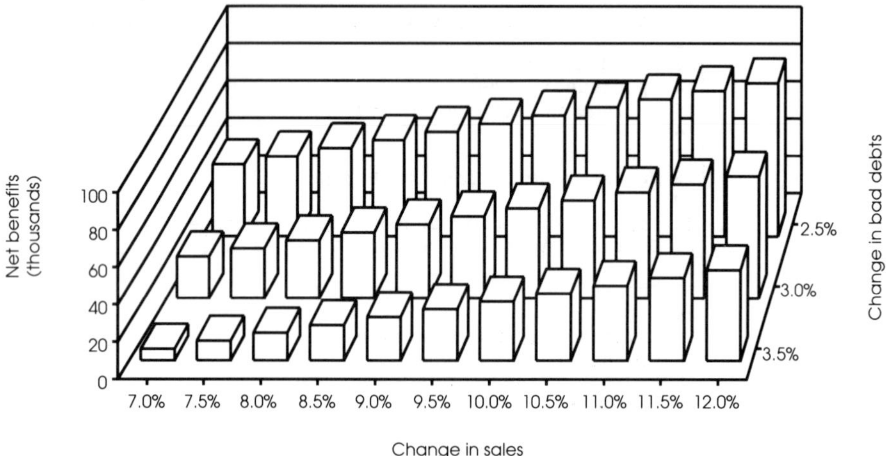

Figure 10.17. Sensitivity of net benefits to changes in sales and bad debts

Problems

1 Create the worksheet shown in Figure 10.16 (use in each of the cells B11, B17, B20, B21, B23, B27, B28, B30 and B32 a formula).

2 Conduct a sensitivity analysis of the net benefit/cost with respect to the percentage increase in sales (use the range of 7–12 per cent in steps of 0.5 per cent) and the increase in the average collection period (use the range of 56–71 days in steps of 5 days). Discuss your results. Present graphically the results of your sensitivity table.

3 Conduct a sensitivity analysis of the net benefit/cost with respect to the percentage increase in bad debts (use the range of 2–5.5 per cent in steps of 0.5 per cent) and the increase in the average collection period (use the range of 56–71 days in steps of 5 days). Discuss your results. Produce a graph illustrating the results of your sensitivity table.

Credit terms

Credit terms include the credit period, any cash discount offered for an early payment and the cash discount period.

Credit period

Increasing the credit period should increase sales as customers would be attracted by the longer time over which credit is granted. At the same time, the average collection period and bad debt expenses are also expected to increase. An increase in sales results in an increase in the cost of financing debtors. Shortening the credit period is likely to have the opposite effects.

Cash discounts

Increasing the size of a cash discount usually has the following consequences: sales increase as a result of the price decrease. An increase in sales would result in an increase in the firm's debtors and thus the firm would have higher costs of financing debtors. On the other hand, the average collection period would decrease and thus the firm's cost of financing debtors is expected to decrease. The net effect of these two conflicting forces on the cost of debtors depends on the existing individual circumstances around the change. In addition, decreases in the average collection period would reduce bad debts. Decreasing or eliminating a cash discount would tend to have the opposite effects.

The cash discount period

Increasing the cash discount period should increase sales and reduce bad debts. When the cash discount period is increased, the average collection period tends to increase, because some customers who did not take the cash discount in the past would do so now. As a consequence, the cost of financing debtors also decreases. On the other hand, customers who already were taking the cash discount could now pay later. This would increase the average collection period and as a result the cost of financing debtors would tend to increase. Additionally, as sales increase, debtors are expected to increase and this is expected to result in a higher cost of financing debtors. The net effect of these two forces depends on the existing individual circumstances around the change.

The effect of a change in the cash discount period on the average collection period is uncertain and the average collection period affects the level of bad debt expense. Therefore, the effect of a change in the cash discount period on bad debt expense is uncertain. Shortening the cash discount period should have the opposite effects from those discussed above.

Example 10.11 Marginal cost/benefit analysis of AK Manufacturing plc's proposal to relax credit terms

We assume the data given in Example 10.10. In addition, we consider the following two cases:

Case 2 The change in credit terms is expected to increase sales by 12 per cent and decrease the average collection period from 55 days to 50 days. Bad debts are expected to decrease from 2 per cent to 1.8 per cent. Finally, AK Manufacturing expects that 40 per cent of its customers will take the cash discount of 2 per cent.

Case 3 Sales will increase by 15 per cent and the average collection period will decrease from 55 to 45 days. The firm expects 1.5 per cent of sales in bad debts. Variable costs per unit are expected to increase from £4 to £4.4. Finally, the percentage of the customers who will take advantage of the cash discount of 2 per cent is expected to be 60 per cent.

The expected net benefit/cost associated with each of the proposed cases is

	A		B	C	D
1	AK MANUFACTURING:AN ANALYSIS TO RELAX ITS CREDIT STANDARDS				
2	==				
3			CASE 1	CASE 2	CASE 3
4			----------	----------	----------
5	Increase in Sales		10.0%	12.0%	15.0%
6	Sales Volume		500,000	500,000	500,000
7	Sales Price Per Unit		£6.0	£6.0	£6.0
8	Variable Costs per Unit		£4.0	£4.0	£4.4
9			----------	----------	----------
10	Change In Gross Profit		£100,000	£120,000	£120,000
11					
12	Fixed Costs		£40,000	£40,000	£40,000
13	Opportunity Cost		14.0%	14.0%	14.0%
14	Average Collection Period		55	55	55
15					
16	New Sales		550,000	560,000	575,000
17	New Average Collection Period		65	50	45
18			----------	----------	----------
19	Cost of Financing Debtors Before Change		£43,036	£43,036	£47,255
20	Cost of Financing Debtors After Change		£55,847	£43,726	£44,359
21			----------	----------	----------
22	Change in Cost of Financing Debtors		£12,811	£690	(£2,896)
23					
24	Existing Bad Debt Expense		2.0%	2.0%	2.0%
25	New Bad Debt Expense		2.5%	1.8%	1.5%
26	Bad Debt Expense Before the Change		£60,000	£60,000	£60,000
27	Bad Debt Expense After the Change		£82,500	£60,480	£51,750
28			----------	----------	----------
29	Change in Bad Debt Expense		£22,500	£480	(£8,250)
30					
31	% Discount Cost Before the Change		0.0%	0.0%	0.0%
32	% of Customers Before the Change		0.0%	0.0%	0.0%
33	% of Customers After the Change		0.0%	40.0%	60.0%
34	% Discount Cost After the Change		0.0%	2.0%	2.0%
35			----------	----------	----------
36	Discount Costs Before the Change		£0	£0	£0
37	Discount Costs After the Change		£0	£26,880	£41,400
38			----------	----------	----------
39	Change in Discount Costs		£0	£26,880	£41,400
40					
41	Net Benefit/Cost --------------->		£64,689	£91,950	£89,746
42					
43	+C41		55	50	45
44		2.2%	84,889	89,262	93,634
45		2.1%	86,233	90,606	94,978
46		2.0%	87,577	91,950	96,322
47		1.9%	88,921	93,294	97,666
48		1.8%	90,265	94,638	99,010
49		1.7%	91,609	95,982	100,354
50		1.6%	92,953	97,326	101,698

Figure 10.18. An analysis for changing the credit terms for AK Manufacturing

calculated as shown in Figure 10.18. AK Manufacturing estimates the net effect on its profits in a similar fashion as that used when it evaluated changes in credit standards (see Example 10.10). The change in discount costs for Case 2 is calculated as follows:

Discount costs after the change:

$$(560{,}000)(£6)(0.40)(0.02) = £26{,}880$$

Change in discount costs:

£26,880 – £0 = £26,880

For each of the three cases (shown in Figure 10.18) the firm expects a net benefit (that is, a positive net change in the profit before tax). Case 2 produces the higher net benefit.

Figure 10.18 also presents the sensitivity of the net benefit related to Case 2 with respect to changes in the percentage discount cost after the change and in the average collection period. The percentage discount cost after the change takes values in the range of 2.2–1.6 per cent in steps of 0.1 per cent, while the average collection period takes values in the range 55–45 days in steps of 5 days. The results were produced with the aid of the `/Data Table 2` command (note that 'input cell 1' is C34 and 'input cell 2' is C17). Given these results, AK Manufacturing should choose the terms offered by Case 2.

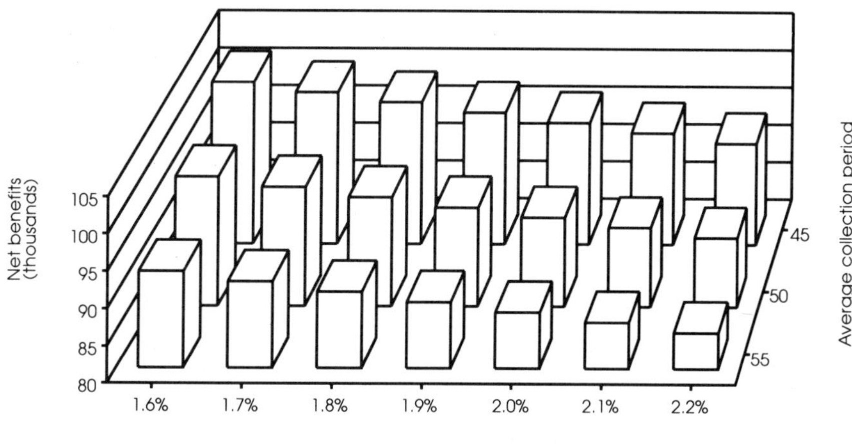

Figure 10.19. Sensitivity of net benefits to changes in bad debts and average collection period

Finally, the results of the sensitivity analysis are presented graphically in Figure 10.19.

Problems

1 Create the worksheet shown in Figure 10.18.
2 Assume also the following case: sales will increase by 17 per cent. Bad debts are expected to decrease from 2 per cent of sales to 1.7 per cent. The firm expects that 65 per cent of its customers will take the cash discount of 2 per cent and its average collection period will decrease from 55 days to 44 days. All other variables will remain the same as in Example 10.10. Do you recommend this change in policy? Explain.

Collection policies

Collection policy decisions involve three steps: monitoring debtor accounts, choosing one or more collection procedures and evaluating the trade-offs involved in changing collection policy.

Monitoring debtor accounts
There are several methods that can be used to monitor the debtor accounts of a firm. For example, the firm can compare its average collection period ratio with the industry average in order to examine whether its collection policy is effective.

Choosing one or more collection procedures
Among the most commonly utilized collection procedures are the following: (a) sending letters reminding the customer that accounts are overdue and requesting payment; (b) telephoning the customer and requesting immediate payment; (c) visiting the customer and attempting to collect the payment; (d) taking legal action against the customer.

Evaluating the trade-offs involved in changing collection policy
Changing collection policy involves several trade-offs between profits and costs. If a firm adopts an aggressive collection policy, sales, costs of financing debtors and bad debts should be decreased, while collection expenditure should be increased. The benefits of a less aggressive policy may include more sales and lower collection expenditure. On the other hand, the costs of financing debtors and bad debts are increased. Figure 10.20 summarizes the trade-offs related to changes in collection policy.

Figure 10.20. Trade-offs expected to result from two collection policies

Collection policy:	More aggressive	Less aggressive
Sales	Decrease	Increase
Financing debtors	Decreases	Increases
Bad debt	Decreases	Increases
Collection expenditure	Increases	Decreases

If a firm can evaluate the effect of a new collection policy on the variables summarized in Figure 10.20, then it can provide an analysis for the new collection period with the aid of which it should decide whether or not to adopt that new policy. Such an analysis is very similar to that discussed in Example 10.10.

Example 10.12. Evaluating whether or not a firm should change its current collection policy

AK Manufacturing plc wishes to compare its current collection policy with a new proposed collection policy. We consider the following data:

Proposed policy B The average collection period is 52 days. Under this policy, the sales will remain at £3,000,000 and bad debts at 1.8 per cent of sales. The outflows related to the firm's collection policy are £16,000. Figure 10.21 initially calculates the net present value of the proposed change. The investment in debtors, stored in cell E8, is calculated as follows:

$$+\text{E4} * \text{E5} * \text{E6}/365 = \frac{(0.75)(55\text{ days})(\pounds 3{,}000{,}000)}{365} = \pounds 339{,}041$$

The cash outflow related to credit, stored in cell E13, is computed as follows (we

```
     A         B         C         D          E            F            G
1 ANALYSING CHANGES IN THE COLLECTION POLICY
2 ===========================================
3                                        Policy A     Policy B    CHANGE
4 Variable Cash Outflows (% of sales)     75.0%        75.0%
5 Average Collection Period                  55           52
6 Sales (£)                            3,000,000   3,000,000
7                                      ----------------------
8 Investment in Debtors                  339,041      320,548     (18,493)
9
10 Cash Outflows Related to Collections    8,000       16,000
11 Bad Debts (% of sales)                   2.0%         1.8%
12                                     ----------------------
13 Cash Outflows Related to Credit       443,300      442,000      (1,300)
14
15                          Required Rate of Return                 14.0%
16
17                                     Years -------->                 5
18                                                            -----------
19                                     Net Present Value --->    14,030
20                                                            ===========
21 A> THE SENSITIVITY OF NPV TO CHANGES IN COLLECTION POLICY & BAD DEBTS
22
23          +G19        2.00%     1.90%      1.80%       1.70%       1.60%
24          8,000     18,493    25,188     31,882      38,577      45,271
25         10,000     14,030    20,725     27,419      34,114      40,808
26         12,000      9,567    16,262     22,956      29,651      36,345
27         14,000      5,104    11,799     18,493      25,188      31,882
28         16,000        641     7,336     14,030      20,725      27,419
29         18,000    (3,822)     2,873      9,567      16,262      22,956
30         20,000    (8,285)   (1,590)      5,104      11,799      18,493
31         22,000   (12,748)   (6,053)        641       7,336      14,030
32
33 B> THE SENSITIVITY OF NPV TO CHANGES IN COLL. POLICY AND TIME PERIOD
34
35          +G19           5         7          9          11          13
36          8,000     31,882    35,218     37,784      39,759      41,278
37         10,000     27,419    29,643     31,354      32,670      33,683
38         12,000     22,956    24,068     24,923      25,582      26,088
39         14,000     18,493    18,493     18,493      18,493      18,493
40         16,000     14,030    12,918     12,063      11,405      10,898
41         18,000      9,567     7,344      5,633       4,316       3,303
42         20,000      5,104     1,769      (798)     (2,773)     (4,292)
43         22,000        641   (3,806)    (7,228)     (9,861)    (11,887)
```

Figure 10.21. AK Manufacturing plc: analysing changes in the collection policy

assume a tax rate of 35 per cent):

$$(E6 * (1 - E4) - E6 * E11 - E10) * (1 - 0.35)$$
$$= ((£3{,}000{,}000)(1 - 0.75) - ((£3{,}000{,}000)(0.02) - £8{,}000)(1 - 0.35)$$
$$= £443{,}300$$

The contents of cell E8 and E13 are copied in cells F8 and F13, respectively. The incremental value of investment is simply –£18,493. The incremental net cash flow is –£1,300 revealing that each period the proposed credit policy decreases cash flows by £1,300. The following formula is used to calculate the net present value, stored in cell, G19:

```
-@PV(-G13,G15,G17) - G8
```

The net present value is positive, indicating that the firm should accept the proposed policy.

Figure 10.21 also shows the following two sensitivity tables:

- Sensitivity of the net present value with respect to changes in the collection policy and bad debt.
- Sensitivity of the net present value with respect to changes in the collection policy and time period over which the net present value is calculated.

The results indicate that the firm should change its current collection period.

Problems

1 Create the worksheet shown in Figure 10.21.
2 Create a graph illustrating the results from the sensitivity of the net present value with respect to changes in the collection policy and bad debts.
3 Create a graph illustrating the results from the sensitivity of the net present value with respect to changes in the collection policy and time period over which the net present value is calculated.

Credit analysis

Credit analysis is the process of investigating the creditworthiness of potential customers. The following steps are used in credit analysis:

1 Gathering information about the potential customer who applies for credit. Such information can be provided by the applicant (that is, individual customer or firm) or external sources (for example, financial statements in the case of a business applying for credit).
2 Providing an analysis of the credit information. Credit analysis involves examining the financial statements of the applicant and previous payment records. For example, the firm can use ratio analysis in order to evaluate the applicant's creditworthiness.
3 Making the credit decision. Taking into account the results provided in the previous step and his or her own judgements, the person who deals with the credit decision decides whether or not to grant credit to the applicant. If the decision is made to grant credit, then the firm must decide how much credit has to be granted.

Managing stocks

Stocks consist of all goods which are held for sale, or are for conversion into finished saleable goods, during the regular course of business. Stocks include the following: raw materials, work-in-process and finished goods. Raw materials contain items purchased by the firm and used to manufacture a product. Work-in-process stock consist of materials which are in the various stages of production but not yet ready for sale to customers. Finished goods are items which have been produced and are ready to be sold to customers. Clearly, not all firms hold all three types of stocks. A retail firm typically has only finished goods stocks. Nearly all firms hold stocks but the level of stocks varies from firm to firm. Below are listed some motives for holding a particular level of stocks:

1 *Meet customer demand motive* Most firms invest substantial amounts of money in stocks and it is common practice to hold sufficient stocks in order to meet an expected increase in demand for their products in the immediate future. On the other hand, holding higher levels of finished goods also enables the firm to meet quickly unexpected orders for its products.
2 *Marketing motive* Frequently firms realize higher sales because of the reputation of having a complete line of products and being able to meet orders quickly.
3 *Cost reduction motive* A firm can realize significant cost savings by purchasing larger quantities of stocks than required for a particular level of sales. For example, purchasing a large quantity of stocks reduces the delivery costs. In addition, a firm can benefit by purchasing raw material before a price increase. Finally, holding insufficient raw material often results in unnecessary costs.

From the financial manager's point of view, the appropriate goal of stock management can be states as follows:

The goal of stock management is to determine the stock balance which minimizes the total costs related to the investment in stocks in order to increase the ordinary share value.

Frequently such a goal conflicts with the interests of other managers within the firm. The production manager normally would like to have a large amount of stocks to avoid production delays. The marketing manager wants a large amount of finished goods in order to satisfy customer demands. Finally, the purchasing agents may wish to have large amounts of raw materials because they are concerned about possible storage and price increases. The firm must determine the optimal level of stocks that reconciles these conflicting objectives.

The size of the investment in stocks is determined by the following three factors:

1 *Demand for sales* There is a direct relationship between sales and the level of stocks. In general, increasing (decreasing) sales results in increasing (decreasing) amounts of raw materials, work-in-process and finished goods.
2 *Production cycle's length* Generally, the level of a firm's stocks is dependent on the length of the production cycle. The shorter the production cycle, the lower the level of the firm's stocks.
3 *Durability and style of finished goods* The durability and style of finished goods affects the levels of stock. For example, a firm that produces a popular product holds a large amount of stock.

The economic order quantity model

Stock management involves a trade-off between the costs and benefits associated with holding a certain stock level. The economic order quantity model is a technique available to help stock management.

Economic order quantity model

The economic order quantity (EOQ) stock management model is similar to the Baumol economic quantity model for cash management. The EOQ model relies on the following simplifying assumptions:

1 The demand for a particular stock item is known with certainty.
2 The rate at which the firm uses stocks is steady throughout the year. That is, the firm has even distribution of sales over the planning period (for example, if annual demand is 12,000 items for a period of a year, 1,000 items should be used each month).
3 The carrying costs are constant per unit of stock, per unit of time (that is, there are no quantity discounts).
4 The costs of ordering stocks are fixed regardless of the size of the order. Orders of new stocks are delivered instantly.

Costs of holding stocks can be classified either as carrying costs or ordering costs.

Carrying costs are the costs for holding stocks for a given period of time. Carrying costs include storing and insuring costs, handling costs, spoilage and obsolescence costs and the cost of funds invested in stocks. The assumptions of certainty, constant demand and instantaneous delivery ensure that there are no stockout costs and the reorder point of stocks is zero (stockout costs refer to lost sales or production down time caused by low investment in stocks). Thus, with an order size of Q, the average holding of stocks is $Q/2$. If C is the carrying costs per unit, then the total carrying costs are equal to $CQ/2$. In this instance, the total carrying costs increase when the average level of stock rises.

Ordering costs are the costs related to placing, processing, receiving and checking an order. These costs are normally expressed as pounds sterling per order. If a firm sells S units per period (for example, a year), the number of orders placed per year is equal to S/Q, where Q is the size of an order. Consequently, the total ordering costs would be: SO/Q, where O is the fixed ordering costs per order.

The total costs per period associated with an order size Q are equal to the sum of carrying costs and ordering costs. After discussing the various costs associated with economic order quantity model, we summarize the model as shown in Figure 10.22.

Definition A mathematical model which computes the stock level that minimizes total stock costs.
Calculation Based on the model's assumptions, the equation for determining the optimal stock level is:

$$Q^* = \sqrt{\frac{2SO}{C}}$$

where

S = total sales demand for an item of stock during the planning period.
O = fixed ordering cost in pounds sterling per order placed.
C = carrying cost per unit for the planning period.

Interpretation It determines how often and in what quantity to order stocks, and the average amount of holding stocks. If $2SO/C$ were to increase, for example, 16 times, the economic order quantity would increase 4 times. Thus, there exist some economies of scale in stock management which should be taken into consideration.

Figure 10.22. Economic order quantity model for stocks

Example 10.13 Calculating the optimal level of stocks for Doco Televisions Ltd

Doco Televisions Ltd sells television sets to various retailers located in the northern region of the country. The estimated demand over a 12-month period is 150 sets per month (or 1,800 per year). The cost involved in placing and taking delivery of an order is £100 and carrying costs are £36 per set.

Then the economic order quantity equals:

$$Q^* = \sqrt{\frac{2(1{,}800)(£100)}{£36}} = 100 \text{ sets}$$

If each time the firm orders 100 television sets from the manufacturer, it will minimize total stock costs. The firm should place 18 orders (that is, 1,800/100) during the period of 12 months (or one order every 20 days, that is, 365/18) to satisfy the demand. Summarizing we can state the following: at time 0, 100 sets are received and sold over a time period of 20 days. At the beginning of time 1, another 100 sets are received and sold over the next period of 20 days, and so on.

In each period of 20 days, the stock of the firm can vary from a high of 100 units to a low of zero. Thus, the average amount of holding stock during a period of 20 days will be 50 (that is, 100/2).

Finally, the total cost of following such a policy would be:

$$\text{Minimum total stock costs} = \frac{(£36)(100)}{2} + \frac{(1{,}800)(£100)}{100}$$

$$= £1{,}800 + £1{,}800 = £3{,}600$$

The economic order quantity can also be located with the aid of a sensitivity table. Figure 10.23 shows a sensitivity table using three formulae. The sensitivity variable is the monthly demand (in units). We examine how changes in this variable affect the carrying costs, ordering costs and total costs (note that cells D8, D9 and D10 contain the results of the following three formulae, respectively:

	A	B	C	D	E
1			COSTS FOR DIFFERENT ORDER SIZES		
2			================================		
3	Total Sales Demand			1,800	
4	Demand per Month			150	
5	Carrying Costs Per Unit			£36	
6	Ordering Costs Per Unit			£100	
7				--------------	
8		Carrying Costs		£2,700	
9		Ordering Costs		£1,200	
10		Total Cost		£3,900	
11				==============	
12					
13					
14			+D8	+D9	+D10
15		50	900	3,600	4,500
16		75	1,350	2,400	3,750
17		100	1,800	1,800	3,600
18		125	2,250	1,440	3,690
19		150	2,700	1,200	3,900
20		175	3,150	1,029	4,179
21		200	3,600	900	4,500
22					

Figure 10.23. Sensitivity of carrying, ordering and total costs to changes in the ordering size expressed in units

+D4 * D5/2, +D3 * D6/D4 and +D8 + D9). The /Data Table 1 command of 1-2-3 is used with 'input cell 1' being cell D4.

The larger the ordering size, the larger the average stock level and thus the higher the carrying costs of the firm. On the other hand, the larger the ordering size, the fewer orders and so the lower the ordering costs (other things remain the same). The total costs are calculated by combining carrying costs and ordering costs. As the ordering size starts to increase, total costs decrease, reach a minimum, and then start to increase again. Total costs are minimized at the economic order quantity of 100 sets.

The results of the sensitivity table are depicted in Figure 10.24. The economic order quantity occurs at the point where the carrying cost line intersects the ordering cost line. Note that within the range of 75–125 units, the graph of the total costs is quite flat, revealing that total costs are relatively insensitive for small deviations from the economic order quantity of 100 sets.

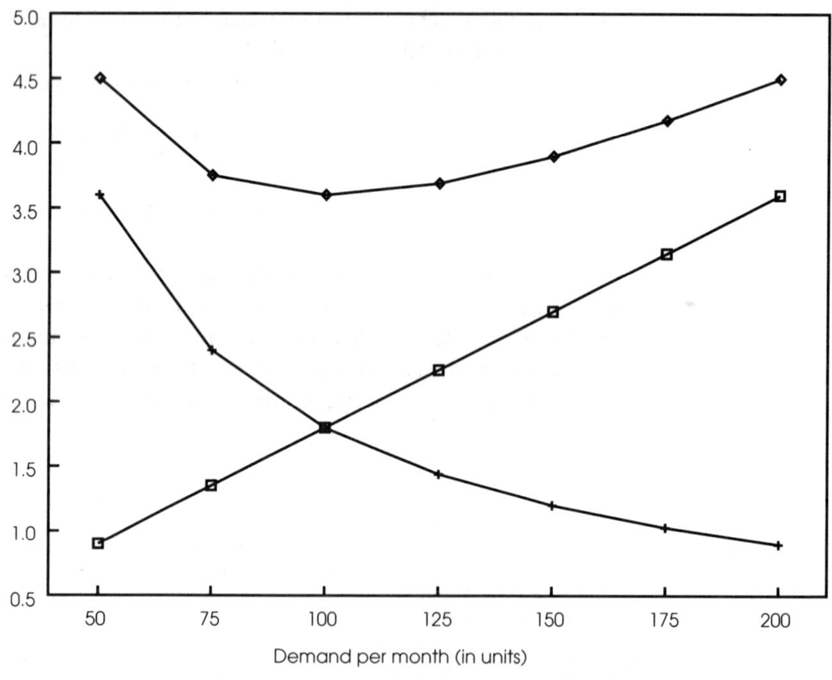

Figure 10.24. A graphical representation of the economic order quantity model

Problems

1 Create a worksheet that calculates the number of televisions Doco Televisions Ltd should order at a time in order to minimize the total stock costs.
2 Create the worksheet presented in Figure 10.23.
3 Create the graph illustrated in Figure 10.24.

Extensions of the basic EOQ model

The basic EOQ model just introduced relies on several assumptions which do not always conform to reality. They are simplifications that permit the development of the basic EOQ model. In the present section we discuss how the analysis is affected by removing some if these unrealistic assumptions.

Non-zero lead time

The basic EOQ model assumes that stock orders are delivered instantly when the previous balance of stock is depleted. In other words, it assumes that the lead time is zero (lead time refers to the time between the date of placing an order and the date of the stock delivery). This assumption is clearly unrealistic, because, in reality, some time usually elapses between order payment and receipt. To avoid running out of stock, the firm should reorder new stock before its present stock holdings drop to zero. Figure 10.25 summarizes the calculation of the reorder point assuming a non-zero lead time.

Definition The reorder point of stock is the point at which the new stock order is placed.

Calculation Based on the assumptions that the demand for a particular stock item is constant during the planning period and the lead time is constant and known with certainty, the reorder point of stocks can be expressed as follows:

$$Q_r = \frac{S}{365} \times n$$

where

S = total sales demand for a stock item during the planning period.
n = lead time, measured in days.

Interpretation Whenever the stock level drops to the reorder point, order an amount equal to the economic order quantity. The reorder point analysis is helpful in ensuring that the firm avoids costs of running out-of-stock.

Figure 10.25. Summarizing the concept of the reorder point with non-zero lead time

Example 10.14 Calculating the reorder point with non-zero lead time

Assume that Doco Televisions Ltd (see Example 10.13) needs five days to place and receive an order of televisions. Then the reorder point would be approximately:

$$Q_r = \frac{1{,}800}{365} \times 5 = 25$$

If the lead time is constant and known with perfect certainty, then the optimal economic order quantity remains unaffected. The firm starts with 100 sets and 15 days later its stock has fallen to 25 sets. At that time, the firm places an order for 100 additional sets which will be received five days later, just as its existing stock balance falls to zero. This analysis is based upon the assumption that the lead time and the daily sales are known in advance with complete certainty. If, however, the lead time or the daily sales change, there is a possibility of running out of stock. For example, if the firm's sales increase to six sets a day, a firm would run out of television sets before the arrival of its new order.

Problem

Create a worksheet which calculates the reorder point for Doco Televisions Ltd (assume that there are 300 working days per year).

Safety stocks

The basic EOQ model assumes a perfect certainty with respect to the demand in units.

One method of incorporating uncertainty into the stock policy is to maintain a safety stock. Such a stock represents the additional stock quantity needed to meet unexpected demands or delays in shipping beyond the expected lead time. In general, the greater the uncertainty regarding either the demand for the firm's product or the delays in shipping, the larger the safety stock that should be maintained. The larger the safety stock carried, the greater the stock-holding cost but the lower the cost of running out of stock. Therefore, the firm should add the safety stock up to a point where the additional stock-holding cost equals the stockout cost. Figure 10.26 provides a summary of the concept of reorder point with a safety stock and lead time.

Figure 10.26. Summarizing the concept of the reorder point with a safety stock and lead time

Definition The reorder point of stock is the point at which the new stock order is placed.

Calculation If a firm maintains a safety stock and it faces a constant level of demand during the planning period, the reorder point of stock can be calculated by adding the safety stock to the reorder point of stock computed under certainty:

$$Q_r = SS + \frac{S}{365} \times n$$

where

SS = the safety stock.
S = total sales demand for an item of stock during the planning period.
n = lead time, measured in days.

Interpretation Whenever inventory drops to the reorder point, order an amount equal to the economic order quantity. The reorder point analysis is helpful in ensuring that the firm reduces the possibility of a stockout.

Example 10.15 Calculating the reorder point with a safety stock

We consider once more Doco Televisions Ltd (see also Examples 10.13 and 10.14). Figure 10.27 presents the expected stockout costs, carrying costs and total costs at different safety stock levels in the range 0–20. The extent of the stockout at different levels of safety stock and the probability that the firm will run out of stock are determined as follows:

1 When the safety stock is 20, the firm will never run out of stock. In this case, the size of the stockout will be zero and the probability of stockout will also be zero.
2 If the firm maintains a safety stock of 15 sets, it would be short of 5 sets assuming that the actual demand for the televisions turns out to be 20 sets greater than anticipated. In this case, the chance that the firm will run out of stock is 3 per cent.
3 If the firm has a safety stock of 10 sets then:
   (a) the firm would be short of 10 sets assuming that the actual demand for the televisions turns out to be 20 sets greater than anticipated. In this case, the probability that the firm will run out of stock is 3 per cent;
   (b) the firm would be short of 5 sets assuming that the actual demand for the televisions turns out to be 15 sets greater than anticipated. In this case, the probability that the firm will run out of stock is 7 per cent.

The extent of the stockout and the probability of stockout for the remaining two cases can be determined in a similar fashion.

	A	B	C	D	E	F	G
1	DOCO TELEVISIONS LTD:CALCULATING THE SAFETY STOCK LEVEL						
2	==						
3	Carrying Costs per Unit			£36			
4	Stockout Cost per Unit			£140			
5	--						
6	Safety	Extend	Stockout	Probability	Expected	Carrying	Total
7	Stock	of	Cost	of running	Stockout	Cost	Costs
8		Stockout		out of stock	Cost		
9	--						
10	20	0	0	0	0	720	720
11							
12	15	5	700	0.03	21	540	561
13							
14	10	10	1400	0.03	42		
15		5	700	0.07	49		
16					----------		
17					91	360	451
18							
19	5	15	2100	0.03	63		
20		10	1400	0.07	98		
21		5	700	0.25	175		
22					----------		
23					336	180	516
24							
25	0	20	2800	0.03	84		
26		15	2100	0.07	147		
27		10	1400	0.25	350		
28		5	700	0.3	210		
29					----------		
30					791	0	791
31	--						

Figure 10.27. Calculating the safety stock level for Doco Televisions Ltd

The expected stockout cost is a weighted average cost, where the weights are the probabilities of stockout. For example, if the safety stock is 10 sets, the expected stockout cost would be:

$$(0.03)(\pounds1{,}400) + (0.07)(\pounds700) = \pounds91$$

For each level of safety stock the total costs are simply equal to the stockout cost plus any carrying cost. When the safety stock is 10 sets, the total costs are lowest.

The recorder point is calculated below:

$$Q_r = 10 + \frac{1{,}800}{365} \times 5 = 35$$

Therefore, the optimal ordering policy of the firm is to place a new order whenever the number of television sets falls to 35. Doco Televisions Ltd expects to have in stock 10 television sets when the new order of 100 sets is received.

The average stock amount is equal to half the EOQ plus the safety stock:

$$\text{Average stock amount} = \frac{100}{2} + 10 = 60 \text{ sets}$$

Problem

Create the worksheet shown in Figure 10.27.

Quantity discounts

In many cases discounts for quantity are offered to customers who purchase large quantities. Thus, the firm has to determine if it will order the economic order quantity or some larger amount and realize the savings offered by the discount on the purchase. This determination can be accomplished by comparing the additional stock-holding costs with the saving costs offered by the discount. If the latter are greater than the former, the firm should take the advantage of the quantity discount.

Example 10.16 Doco Televisions Ltd: determining whether or not a quantity discount is worth while

Suppose that Doco Televisions Ltd is offered a £1 quantity discount per television set on orders of 200 or more television sets. In this case, the total stock costs can be calculated as follows:

$$\text{Total stock costs} = \frac{(£36)(200)}{2} + \frac{(1{,}800)(£100)}{200} = £4{,}500$$

Therefore, the total stock costs will increase from £3,600 to £4,500, where the former figure represents the total stock costs for ordering an economic quantity of 100 sets (see Example 10.13). With the aid of these two cost values, the (annual) change in the total stock costs would be:

$$\text{Change in total stock costs} = £4{,}500 - £3{,}600 = £900$$

On the other hand, the discount saving on the annual demand is calculated as follows:

$$\text{Discount saving} = (£1)(1{,}800) = £1{,}800$$

Since the discount saving exceeds the change in total stock costs, Doco Televisions Ltd should take advantage of the discount.

Note that we can consider in the analysis quantity discounts and the addition of safety stock simultaneously. In this case, remember that when a large stock quantity is purchased, the firm requires a smaller safety stock.

Figure 10.28 summarizes the current assets concepts discussed in the present chapter.

Managing creditors

Creditors consist of money which a firm owes to its suppliers for goods or services sold to it on credit. There are two basic motives given as to why a firm uses creditors:

1 Desirability motive. The credit provided by the firm's suppliers (usually called trade credit) is desirable since it can be manipulated. A firm can affect the size and cost of its creditors by arranging to pay earlier or delay payments.
2 Convenience motive. A firm that establishes and maintains creditworthiness with a supplier can normally use that source of credit for a long time.

Trade credit constitutes a primary source of short-term funds. An appropriate goal of creditors' management can be stated as follows:

Working capital item	Cash	Short-term investments	Debtors	Stocks
Motives	• Transaction • Precautionary • Speculation	• Substitute for cash • Investment	• Facilitating trade • Competitive	• Meet customer demand • Marketing • Cost reduction
Objective	• Minimize total costs related to the cash investment while maintaining the firm's liquidity	• Invest temporary excess cash while maintaining the firm's liquidity	• Set credit terms, monitor payment patterns and apply collection procedures so as to realize high profits and relatively low risk	• Minimize total costs related to stock investment and thereby increase the firm's ordinary share value
Problems if item is too small	• Liquidity problems	• Insufficient safety margin to protect against unanticipated needs for cash	• Credit policy may be too restrictive • Lost sales	• Slowing or stoppage of of production • Lost sales
Problems if item is too small	• Holding costs	• Loss of earning a possible higher return in fixed assets	• Credit policy may be too loose • Collection problems	• High carrying costs
Models used in the management process of the asset	• Baumol's economic order quantity (EOQ) • Miller–Orr	• The same as those of cash	• Models comparing marginal revenues and marginal costs	• Basic EOQ • EOQ with non-zero time lead • EOQ with non-zero time lead and safety stock • EOQ when quantity discounts exist

Figure 10.28. A summary of the current assets concepts discussed in the present chapter

The goal of creditors' management is to provide short term funds at the lowest possible cost to the firm.

Cost of credit

We are starting with a few definitions. Credit period is the number of days for which credit is granded. The discount period specifies the maximum number of days after the beginning of the credit period that the firm can take advantage of the cash discount. Trade credit involves two types of costs: visible and hidden. When a firm elects to pay off the trade credit exactly on time there are no visible costs. In this case, however, the suppliers of trade credit pass costs on to the buying firm in the price of the product or service (for example, credit checking costs, bad debt losses, and so on). If payment is made after the discount period, both visible and hidden costs exist. The former are related to a forgone cash discount offer and the latter occur because of the possible deterioration of the firm's credit rating (for example, the supplier may insist on imposing a more expensive trade credit). Figure 10.29 shows in summary the four cases discussed above.

	On time payment	Delayed payment
Visible	There is no cost	Cost of a missed cash discount
Hidden	Suppliers of trade credit pass costs on to buyers	Costs related to a possible deterioration of credit rating

Figure 10.29. Costs of trade credit

The cost of not taking a cash discount can be expressed in quantitative terms, but it is difficult to provide a quantitative measurement for hidden costs. In general, the cost of trade credit incurred by not taking a cash discount can be summarized as shown in Figure 10.30.

Figure 10.30. A summary of the percentage cost of not taking a cash discount

Definition A mathematical equation that computes the annual percentage cost of not taking the cash discount under some common credit terms.

Calculation The annual percentage cost of not taking the cash discount and paying at the end of the credit period is given by the following equation:

$$\text{Percentage cost of not taking a cash discount} = \frac{\text{Discount per cent}}{100 \text{ per cent} - \text{Discount per cent}} \times \frac{365}{\text{Credit period} - \text{Discount period}}$$

where the discount per cent is the stated cash discount expressed in percentage terms and the credit and discount periods are expressed in days.

Interpretation The first component of the above equation (that is, (Discount per cent/(100 per cent − Discount per cent))) converts the discount from purchase price into an equivalent of interest rate paid to the supplier of goods or services. Multiplying the first component of the above equation by the second one results in an annualized interest rate the firm must pay to borrow money using trade credit after the discount period has ended.

Example 10.17 Calculating the percentage cost of not taking a cash discount for AG Toys Ltd

AG Toys Ltd purchases £30,000 worth of goods per day from AC Ltd. Suppose that AC Ltd is the only supplier of the firm. AG Toys Ltd has been given by its supplier the following credit terms: if payment is made within 10 days, starting on 1 July, AC Ltd offers a 1.5 per cent discount, otherwise full payment is required within 30 days. The diagram below shows the payment periods of AG Toys Ltd. In this case, the credit period is equal to 30 days, while the discount period equals 10 days.

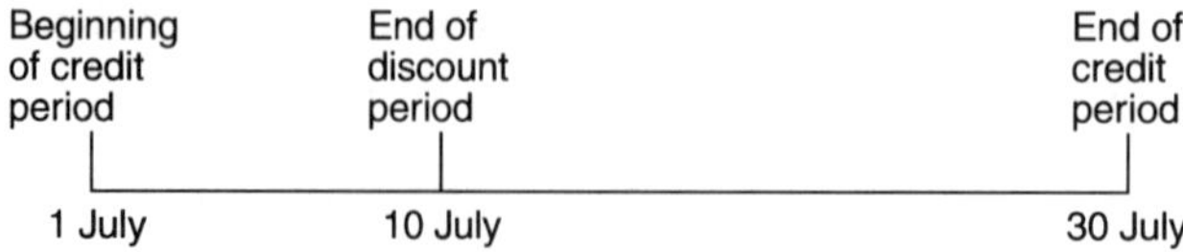

If the firm decides to take advantage of the cash discount, the payment should be made on 10 July. On the other hand, if the firm does not take advantage of the cash discount, the payment should be made on 30 July, as there is no extra cost for delaying the payment until the end of the credit period.

Under the credit terms offered, the firm should pay £29,550 on the 10 July or pay £30,000 on 30 July. If the firm fails to pay within the discount period, then it will keep £29,550 for another 20 days which will cost the firm £450 in terms of the forgone discount. Therefore, the annual percentage cost of forgoing the discount can be calculated as follows (a slight deviation occurs due to rounding):

$$\text{Percentage cost of not taking a cash discount} = \frac{1.5 \text{ per cent}}{100 \text{ per cent} - 1.5 \text{ per cent}} \times \frac{365}{30 - 10} = (0.0152)(18.25)$$

$$= 27.79 \text{ per cent}$$

The first component of the above equation (that is, 0.0152 per cent) can be considered as an interest rate for a 20-day period paid to the lender (that is, the supplier of the goods). Note that the same result would be produced if we use £450 instead of 1.5 per cent and £30,000 instead of 100 per cent. Such an interest is annualized by multiplying it by 18.25. Thus, the payment for the purchases on 30 July results in an annualized cost of 27.79 per cent which is a high cost indeed.

The annual percentage cost of not taking the cash discount is equivalent to paying an annual interest rate of 27.76 per cent on a bank loan. This argument can be discussed with the aid of the results in Figure 10.31.

The second part of Figure 10.31 shows the balance sheet of AG Toys Ltd. In each of the two cases presented, the amount of total assets equals the amount of total equity and liabilities. If the firm does not take advantage of the cash discount, every purchase is paid on the 30th day, thus, the amount of purchases in the last of the 30 days can be calculated as follows:

(£1,000)(30) = £30,000

On the other hand, if the firm decides to take the discount, every purchase is paid on the 10th day and the amount of purchases equal to the discount price multiplied by 10:

(£1,000 – (£1,000)(1.5)/100)(10) = £9,850

We assume that the amount of £20,150 (that is, £30,000 – £9,850) can be obtained from a bank loan.

Next consider the profit and loss account statement of AG Toys Ltd. The earnings before tax for the two alternatives are equal only when the cash discount on purchases equals the bank loan interest. The cash discount on purchases is £5,600 (that is (£373,338)(1.5)/100) which equals the interest on the bank loan (that is (£20,150)(27.79)/100). If the bank offers to the firm a loan at any annual interest rate lower than 27.79 per cent and the discount is taken, then the profit after tax should be higher than £69,331. Therefore, forgoing the discount is equivalent to borrowing at an annual interest rate of 27.79 per cent.

Example 10.18 Providing a sensitivity of the percentage cost of not taking a cash discount with respect to changes in the discount and the difference (credit period – discount period)

In the present example we are using the data provided in Example 10.17. The

```
            A                   B                          C              D
 1              THE COST OF TRADE CREDIT
 2              ========================
 3
 4 1> Calculating the Cost of not Taking the Cash Discount
 5
 6              Discount                                    1.5
 7
 8              Cost of not Taking Cash Discount         27.79%
 9                                                 ============
10
11 2> AG Toys Ltd:Balance Sheet
12
13              Fixed Assets                            200,000
14              Current Assets                           90,000
15                                                 ------------
16              Total Assets                            290,000
17                                                 ============
18
19                                                 Without the  With the
20                                                 discount(£)  discount(£)
21              Creditors                                30,000        9,850
22              Bank Loan                                     0       20,150
23
24              Equity & Other Liabilities              260,000      260,000
25                                                 -------------------------
26              Total Equity and Liabilities            290,000      290,000
27                                                 =========================
28
29 3> AG Toys Ltd:Profit and Loss Account
30
31              Tax Rate ------------------------>        35.0%
32
33                                                 Without the  With the
34                                                 discount(£)  discount(£)
35              Sales                                   550,000      550,000
36              Net Purchases                           373,338      367,738
37
38              Other Expenses                           70,000       70,000
39                                                 -------------------------
40              PBIT                                    106,662      112,263
41              Interest on Loan                              0        5,600
42                                                 -------------------------
43              Profits Before Tax                      106,662      106,662
44              Tax (35%)                                37,332       37,332
45                                                 -------------------------
46              Profit After Tax                         69,331       69,331
                                                   =========================
```

Figure 10.31. Two financial statements for AG Toys Ltd

percentage cost of not taking the cash discount is affected by the discount and the difference (credit period – discount period). Figure 10.32 shows a sensitivity of the percentage cost with respect to changes in these two variables. We assume that the discount takes place in the range 1–2.5 in steps of 0.5 and the difference (credit period – discount period) takes values in the range 20–50 in steps of 5. The `/Data Table 2` command of 1-2-3 uses as 'input cell 1' cell B6 and as 'input cell 2' cell B5.

The percentage cost decreases as the difference (credit period – discount period) increases (where we assume that the discount period remains constant). From the results we observe that such a decrease becomes higher as the discount increases. For example, if the discount is 1 per cent, the percentage cost decreases

```
---------------------------------------------------------------------
                     A                        B       C       D       E
 1 A TWO VARIABLE SENSITIVITY OF THE COST OF NOT TAKING THE DISCOUNT
 2 ==================================================================
 3
 4
 5 Discount (%)                            1.5
 6 Credit Period - Discount Period          20
 7                                     --------
 8 Cost of not Taking Cash Discount    27.79%
 9                                     ========
10
11
12 +B8                                     1.0     1.5     2.0     2.5
13                                  20  18.43%  27.79%  37.24%  46.79%
14                                  25  14.75%  22.23%  29.80%  37.44%
15                                  30  12.29%  18.53%  24.83%  31.20%
16                                  35  10.53%  15.88%  21.28%  26.74%
17                                  40   9.22%  13.90%  18.62%  23.40%
18                                  45   8.19%  12.35%  16.55%  20.80%
19                                  50   7.37%  11.12%  14.90%  18.72%
---------------------------------------------------------------------
```

Figure 10.32. A two-variable sensitivity of the cost of not taking discount

from 18.43 per cent to 7.37 per cent, while if the discount is 2.5 per cent, the percentage decreases from 46.79 per cent to 18.72 per cent.

The results of the sensitivity are shown graphically in Figure 10.33.

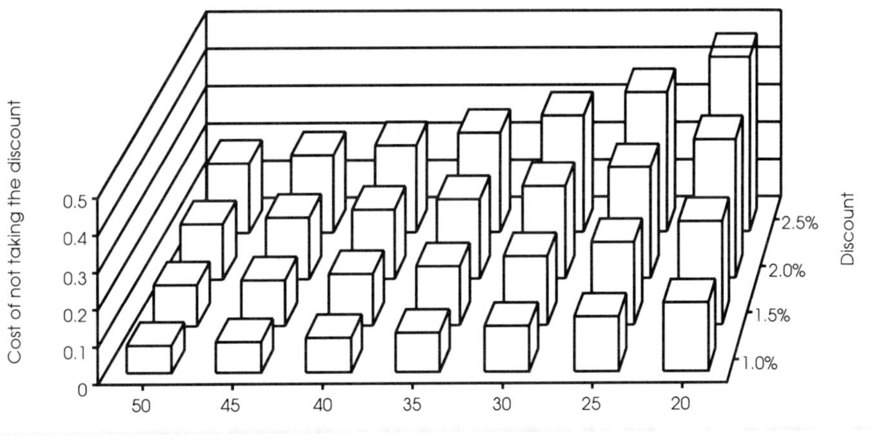

Figure 10.33. A graphical representation of the results shown in Figure 10.32

Problems

1 Create the worksheet shown in Figure 10.31 using the appropriate formula in cell B8.
2 Calculate the profit after tax of AG Toys plc when the discount is 2 per cent.
3 Create the worksheet presented in Figure 10.32.

Managing accruals

Accruals are current liabilities for certain services provided to the firm for which payment is not made until the end of pre-specified periodic time intervals. Accruals include wages, rent and taxes. For example, the salary of a firm's executives accrues hour by hour and day by day, but payment is made only weekly, biweekly or in relation to any other pre-specified periodic time interval. Accruals represents trade credit from suppliers (for example, employees, Government, and so on) without charging interest. The main motive for accruals is that they provide a source of short-term financing. When managing accruals we have to examine how the timing of payments to the firm's employees, Government, and others influences the cost of that source of financing. Therefore, we can state the following:

The goal of accruals management is to provide as much as possible short-term financing at zero cost to the firm.

From the viewpoint of management of accruals, however, there are some limitations. For example, there are laws that state how frequently employees must be paid. Such a situation creates an upper limit to the amount of funds that can be obtained from accruals.

Example 10.19 Calculating the annual savings from changing the salary payment interval

Doco Televisions Ltd currently pays its employees a total amount of £240,000 at the end of a two-week period. These wages accumulate between the paydays and return to zero at the last date of a two-week period, when the employees receive their payments. The average level of accrued wages is the average between £240,000 and 0, or £120,000. Suppose that the firm wishes to change its pay period from two weeks to four weeks. If it does so, the average level of accrued wages would be £240,000 (that is, £480,000/2). The new plan would increase the amount of accruals by £120,000 (that is, £240,000 – £120,000). This amount of accruals provides a short-term source of funds. If the opportunity cost of the firm is 14 per cent, then the annual savings obtained from changing the pay period is calculated as follows:

$$(0.14)(£120,000) = £16,800$$

Therefore, the firm saves £16,800, since accruals provide a costless source of financing.

Problem

If Doco Televisions Ltd has a weekly payroll of £120,000, prepare a worksheet calculating the annual savings obtained from changing the pay period from one week to (a) two weeks, (b) three weeks, and (c) four weeks. What do you observe?

Managing short-term borrowing

Short-term borrowing represents a short-term credit to firms and includes loans made available by other firms and financial institutions. The most important motive for short-term borrowing is to provide the firm with financing to meet temporary increases in working capital (for example, to cover seasonal increases in stocks). Short-term borrowing differs from creditors and accruals in certain points. First, the firm receives cash rather than materials on credit from its suppliers or time and services from its employees. Second, the cost of short-term borrowing is never zero, while the cost of creditors or accruals can be zero in certain circumstances. Third, short-term borrowing is not affected by the level of sales, while creditors and accruals tend to vary with the firm's sales.

The goal of short-term borrowing management can be stated as follows:

The goal of short-term borrowing management is to provide short-term financing at the lowest possible cost to the firm.

Cost of short-term borrowing

There are several methods for calculating the amount of interest in pounds sterling charged by banks. Each method gives a different interest rate, even if the stated interest rate is the same. The comparison between the different types of bank loans can be easier if we calculate for each type the effective rate of interest (see Figure 10.34).

Definition The effective rate of interest is the true percentage interest paid by the borrower for a bank loan.

Calculation The before-tax effective rate of interest (ERI) can be calculated by using the following equation:

$$\text{ERI} = \frac{\text{Interest amount} - \text{Fees}}{\text{Available funds}} \; \frac{365}{\text{Loan maturity}} \qquad (10.2)$$

where

Interest amount = (Stated interest rate)(Principal)(Loan maturity)/365

Available funds = the net amount of funds that the firm can utilize after considering the amount borrowed and other factors (for example, interest paid in advance).

The after-tax effective interest rate is computed as follows:

After-tax ERI = ERI(1 − Tax rate)

Interpretation The before-tax effective rate of interest is the before-tax cost of the short-term loan to the borrowing firm. It takes into consideration the loan's stated interest rate and other factors (for example, loan service fees) that influence the total cost of the loan. The after-tax effective rate of interest is the after-tax cost of the short-term loan to the borrowing firm. Such a rate takes into account the before-tax effective interest rate and the fact that the interest payments are tax reductible.

Figure 10.34. Summarizing the concept of the effective rate of interest

Equation (10.2) can be used to compute the effective interest rate of different types of bank loans.

Simple interest policy

Under the simple interest policy, the borrower receives the face value of the loan and repays the principal plus the interest at the end of the loan period.

Example 10.20 Calculating the after-tax effective rate of interest

Doco Television Ltd receives from a bank a 40 days, £100,000 loan at 12 per cent annual stated interest rate. The principal plus the interest will be paid at maturity.

The corporate tax rate is 35 per cent. The interest amount would be:

$$\text{Interest amount} = (0.12)(£100{,}000)\frac{40}{365} = £1{,}315.07$$

The before-tax effective tax rate can be calculated with the aid of Equation (10.2):

$$\text{ERI} = \frac{£1{,}315.07 - 0}{£100{,}000}\;\frac{365}{40} = 12 \text{ per cent}$$

In this case, the effective rate of interest equals the stated interest rate, because the loan principal equals the available funds from the loan. The compound annual effective rate is calculated as follows:

$$\left(1 + \frac{£1{,}315.07}{£100{,}000}\right)^{\frac{365}{40}} - 1 = 12.64 \text{ per cent}$$

Finally, the after-tax effective interest rate is

$$\text{After-tax ERI} = 0.12(1 - 0.35) = 7.80 \text{ per cent}$$

Problems

1 Create for Doco Television Ltd a two-variable sensitivity of the after-tax ERI with respect to changes in the loan amount and annual stated interest rate (other things remain the same).

2 Graph the results of the sensitivity table produced in Problem 1.

Variable interest policy

Under the variable interest policy, the interest rate changes over the life of the loan as interest rates change.

Example 10.21 Calculating the before-tax effective interest rate when the stated annual interest rate varies

Assume that Doco Televisions plc borrows £100,000 for 40 days. The annual interest rate is 11.5 per cent for the first 15 days, 12.0 per cent for the next 14 days, and 13.0 per cent for the remaining 11 days. The interest will be paid when the loan is repaid. The interest amount is calculated as follows:

$(£100{,}000)(0.115)(15)/365 =$	£472.60
$(£100{,}000)(0.120)(14)/365 =$	£460.27
$(£100{,}000)(0.130)(11)/365 =$	£391.78
Total interest amount	£1,324.66

The before-tax effective interest rate will therefore be

$$\text{ERI} = \frac{£1{,}324.66}{£100{,}000}\;\frac{365}{40} = 12.09 \text{ per cent}$$

Discount interest policy

Under the discount interest policy, the borrower receives the face value of the loan net of the interest and repays the loan's principal at maturity.

Example 10.22 Calculating the before-tax discount interest rate under a discount interest policy

Consider the data provided in Example 10.20 and assume that the interest amount is paid in advance. The before-tax effective rate of interest can be determined as follows:

$$\text{ERI} = \frac{£1{,}324.66 - 0}{£100{,}000 - £1{,}324.66}\,\frac{365}{40} = 12.25 \text{ per cent}$$

Since the firm receives £98,675.34 and must pay back £100,000, the effective rate of interest of the discounted loan is higher than the effective rate of interest calculated in Example 10.20.

Problems

1 Create for Doco Televisions Ltd a two-variable sensitivity table of the before-tax ERI with respect to changes in the loan amount and annual stated interest rate (other things remain constant).
2 Graph the results of the sensitivity table produced in Problem 1.

Compensating balance

A compensating balance is an amount that the borrower maintains in either a checking account or a time deposit account at the lending bank.

Example 10.23 Calculating the before-tax discount interest rate when the borrower maintains a compensating balance

Assume the discounted loan for Doco Televisions Ltd given in Example 10.20. It is further assumed that the firm must maintain a compensating balance of 12 per cent of the amount borrowed in a checking account. The firm currently keeps in the lending bank a checking account balance of zero. Using Equation (10.2), the effective rate of interest with the compensating balance is given by

$$\text{ERI} = \frac{£1{,}324.66 - 0}{£100{,}000 - (£100{,}000)(0.12)}\,\frac{365}{40} = 13.73 \text{ per cent}$$

The effective rate of interest with a compensating balance is higher than the effective rate of interest calculated in Example 10.20, since the compensating balance requirements increase the effective rate of interest. Suppose that the checking account pays an interest of 7 per cent per year. Then the £12,000 maintained in the bank will generate £92.055 in interest income over the period of 40 days (that is, £12,000)(0.07)(40/365) = £92.055). In this case, the effective rate of interest would be

$$\text{ERI} = \frac{£1{,}324.66 - £92.055}{£100{,}000 - (£100{,}000)(0.12)}\,\frac{365}{40} = 12.78 \text{ per cent}$$

Problems

1 Create for Doco Televisions Ltd a two-variable sensitivity table of the before-tax ERI with respect to changes in the loan amount and the percentage of the compensating balance (other things remain constant).

2 Graph the results of the sensitivity table produced in Problem 1.
3 Create for Doco Televisions Ltd a sensitivity table of the before-tax ERI with respect to interest rate paid on the checking account (other things remain the same).
4 Graph the results of the sensitivity table produced in Problem 3.

Figure 10.35 provides a summary of the current liabilities concepts discussed in the present chapter.

Working capital item	Creditors	Accruals	Short-term borrowing
Motives	• Desirability • Convenience	• Financing	• Financing
Objective	• Provide short-term financing at the lowest possible cost to the firm	• Provide as much as possible short-term financing at zero cost to the firm	• Provides short-term financing at the lowest possible cost to the firms
Problems if item is too small	• Unable to hold sufficient current assets to meet demand or conditions necessary for production	• The firm does not obtain the full benefits from using a free source of short-term financing	• Unable to hold sufficient current assets to meet demand or conditions necessary for production
Problems if item is too large	• High costs	• Not applicable because their size is affected greatly by factors external to the firm (for example, Government laws)	• High costs

Figure 10.35. Summarizing the current liabilities concepts introduced in the present chapter

Summary

1 *Working capital definitions* Working capital includes a firm's current assets and net working capital is defined as the difference between the firm's current assets and current liabilities. A working capital policy is concerned with two types of decisions: (a) What current assets should a firm own and how much should be invested in current assets? (b) How should these assets be financed? Working capital management refers to the management of all current assets and current liabilities and the management of all relationships between current assets and current liabilities.

2 *The trade-off between risk and return* In the working capital context there exists a trade-off between risk and return. The risk is measured by the probability that the firm may experience difficulties in meeting its financial obligations as they come due (for example, in this context, the current assets/total assets ratio can be considered as a risk indicator). Return is measured by a profitability financial ratio associated with holding current assets (for example, the return on current assets ratio). A conservative working capital policy uses high levels of working capital and offers low risk and low return. Alternatively, an aggressive policy

utilizes low levels of working capital and provides high risk and high return. In order to maximize shareholders' wealth, the financial director should combine his or her working capital policy with additional factors, for example, cash flows, operating and financial gearing used, and so on.

3 *Models for balancing cash and marketable securities* Cash management models are mathematical models used to determine optimal cash balances. In this chapter two cash management models are discussed: the Baumol model and the Miller–Orr model. The former assumes that the firm knows with certainty the cash balances over time and that the cash flows occur at a steady rate. Its objective is to determine the optimal cash balance so that the holding costs (for example, the forgone return the firm could earn by investing its excess cash) plus transaction costs (for example, costs of selling securities) are minimized. The Miller–Orr model assumes random cash balances which can move in both positive and negative directions. The objective of the Miller–Orr model is to determine the optimal cash balance range so as to minimize the sum of holding costs and transaction costs.

4 *Managing debtors* The investment of a firm in debtors is affected by its credit policy which can be defined as having the following three components: credit standards, credit terms and collection policies. Credit standards are the criteria utilized by a firm to determine to which customers it will provide trade credit. Credit terms are the terms offered to potential customers who wish to purchase the products of the firm on credit. Collection policies are procedures used to collect accounts that have not been paid within the specified time. In order to determine optimal credit policies, the firm should make a direct comparison of the sales gains and the costs resulting from changes in its credit policy (such costs may involve costs of financing debtors, bad debts, and so on).

5 *Managing stocks* The financial objective of keeping a low stock level often conflicts with the objective of maintaining a large stock level in order to avoid production delays and stockouts. This conflict can be resolved by the economic ordering quantity (EOQ) model. The EOQ model can be utilized to determine the firm's optimal level of stock to be ordered and how often stock quantities should be ordered. The optimal level of stock minimizes the total stock costs. The basic EOQ model is based on a number of simplifying assumptions some of which can be revised to allow more realistic conditions. The model can be modified in the event of non-zero lead time, quantity discounts, or fluctuating demand for a stock item over time.

6 *Managing creditors* The firm should compare the cost of not taking a cash discount with the costs of alternative short-term sources of financing its purchases when making short-term financing decisions. If such a cost is higher than the costs of alternative sources of short-term funds and if excess cash is not available, then the firm should borrow money from other sources and pay for its purchases within the discount period. If no discount is offered for early payments, or if the discount is forgone, the firm should delay payments until the end of the credit period.

7 *Managing accruals* Accruals, for example wages and taxes, represent a source of short-term funds. The goal of accruals management is to provide as much financing as possible at a zero cost. Note, however, that firms have little control over some accrued items (for example, wages and government taxes).

8 *Managing short-term borrowing* Short-term borrowing constitutes a primary source of short-term financing. The goal of short-term borrowing is to provide short-term funds at the lowest possible cost to the firm. In order to compare the different types of bank loans, it is convenient to calculate for each type of loan the effective rate of interest. Four types of loans were discussed: a simple interest loan, a variable interest loan, a discounted loan and a loan with a compensating balance.

Questions for discussion

1 For each term shown below in the largest box provide a definition in your own words. Then check your responses against the definitions included in the chapter.

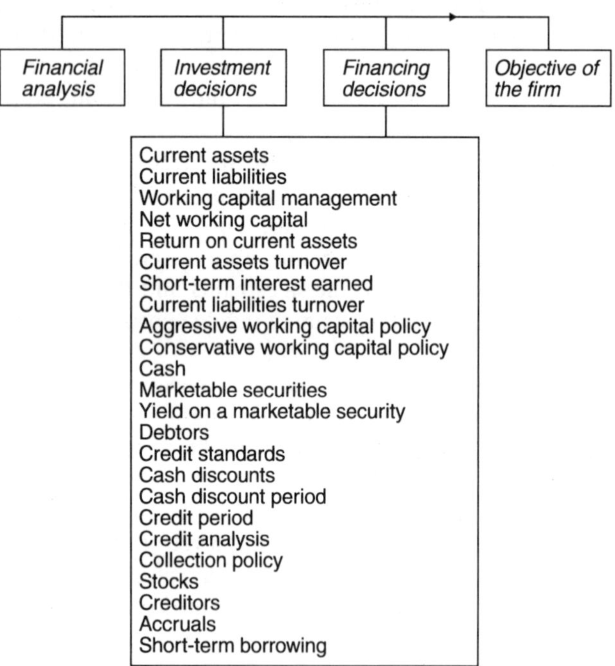

2 (a) List examples of current assets and examples of current liabilities.
(b) Identify two financial ratios that can be used to relate the current assets and current liabilities presented in part (a).
(c) Discuss how the ratios identified in part (b) can be used to analyse the working capital of a firm.
(d) List examples of external environment factors that influence the level of net working capital maintained by a firm.

3 (a) The diagram below can be used to indicate the effect each of the situations displayed on the left-hand side will have on a firm's current assets, current liabilities, current assets to total assets (CA/TA) ratio and current liabilities to total liabilities (CL/TL) ratio. Fill in the blank boxes.

	Current assets	Current liabilities	CA/TA	CL/TL
Increase in stocks	Increases			
Increase in creditors				
Decrease in debtors				
Decrease in short-term loans				

(b) Discuss the sensitivity of the CA/TA ratio to changes in the firm's current assets.

4 Marks and Spencer's 1989 balance sheet shows total current assets of £659.1 million and current liabilities of £743.1 million. Such a situation appears to indicate working capital problems for Marks and Spencer. Do you agree? Discuss.

5 (a) Below you are given three statements related to the working capital management. Fill in the blank boxes by using either the word 'Agree' or the word 'Disagree'.

	Agree	Disagree
The objective of the working capital management is to determine and maintain the composition of current assets and current liabilities that maximizes shareholders' wealth.		
Working capital management influences the liquidity and profitability of the firm.		
Working capital decisions affect only the expected profitability but not the risk that the firm may be unable to meet its financial obligations as they come due.		

(b) Discuss in detail each reply provided in part (a).

6 At the end of its financial year, AK Rotta is considering three alternative working capital investment policies A, B and C. Under policy A the firm's current assets will be 1.5 times its fixed assets. Policy B requires the firm to have £6 million current liabilities and a net working capital of £1 million. Under policy C, the firm's current liabilities and current ratio will be £12.5 million and £2 million, respectively. We assume that the fixed assets are to remain the same throughout the next year and the firm's profit after tax for the next year is 22 per cent of its projected sales. Which policy is riskier? Which policy is least risky? Give reasons for your answers (use the current assets to total assets ratio as a risk indicator).

7 Motor Spares is considering the opportunity to acquire another firm in the same industry. The new financial director has to find the best way of obtain-

ing additional funds for the acquisition. She has assessed the market conditions and concluded that demand for a new issue of preference shares or a new issue of ordinary shares does not exist. Moreover, the firm does not have any internal available funds. Taking into account all these facts she has identified the following possible policy mainly concerned with the area of the working capital. 'Reduce the current assets from £10 million to £5 million and increase the current liabilities from £2 million to £4 million.' What is the likely impact of such a policy on total assets, the current assets to total assets ratio, the current ratio, the current liabilities to total liabilities ratio, the firm's net working capital and finally the return on current assets ratio?

8 Below are given four combinations between current assets and current liabilities. Each combination provides a strategy for managing working capital. Discuss fully the risk and return consequences of each of the four cases.

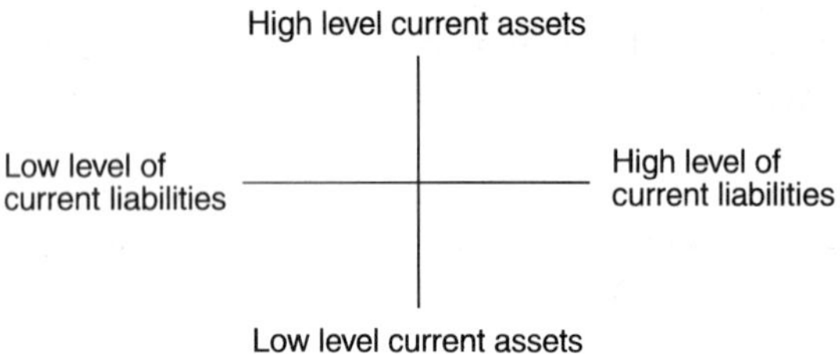

9 (a) Prove the following relationship:

$$\frac{\text{Current assets}}{\text{Total assets}} = \frac{\text{Return on fixed assets}}{\text{Return on fixed assets} + \text{Return on current assets}}$$

Discuss this relationship. What does it represent?

(b) Examine the sensitivity of the current assets to total assets ratio to changes in the return on current assets (other things being the same).

(c) Graph the relationship identified in part (b).

10 (a) Prove the following relationship:

$$\text{Current ratio} = \frac{\text{Current liabilities turnover}}{\text{Current assets turnover}}$$

Discuss this relationship.

(b) Examine the sensitivity of the current ratio to changes in the current liability turnover and current assets turnover ratios (other things being the same).

(c) Graph the relationship identified in part (b).

11 Choose one of the following two firms and discuss its working capital policy or policies over a period of five years:

- Marks and Spencer plc
- Asda Group plc

12 (**a**) Fill in the following black boxes:

Motive	Current asset
Substitute for cash	
Facilitating trade	
Meet customer demand	
Precautionary	Cash
Competitive	
Investment	
Speculation	

(**b**) Discuss in detail each reply given in part (a).

13 The quick assets of a firm are cash, short-term investments and debtors. Discuss the results of a two-variable sensitivity analysis of cash with respect to changes in short-term investments and debtors (other things remain constant).

14 Compare and contrast the following two cash management models:

(**a**) Baumol's economic order quantity model;

(**b**) Miller–Orr model.

15 (**a**) Below are summarized the trade-offs related to changes in the collection policy of debtors. Fill in the empty boxes.

Collection policy:

	More aggressive	Less aggressive
Sales		
Financing debtors		
Bad Debt		Increase
Collection expenditures	Increase	

(**b**) Discuss in detail each reply provided in part (a).

16 Do you agree with the following statements? Discuss in detail each of your answers.

(**a**) 'The main goal of cash management is to maximize the firm's return from investments in marketable securities.'

(**b**) 'The primary goal of debtor's management is to set credit terms, monitor payment patterns and apply necessary collection procedures so as to realize high earnings.'

(**c**) 'The benefits of good stock management contribute to high earnings, low risk and a higher value of the firm's ordinary shares.'

(**d**) 'The primary goal of short-term borrowing is to provide financing at zero cost to the firm.'

(e) 'The goal of creditors' management is to provide short-term funds at the lowest possible cost to the firm.'

17 The lecturer of financial management asks in the examination of the subject the following question: 'What are the shortcomings of the basic economic order quantity model for stock?' Fully discuss your answer.

18 Discuss briefly three extensions of the basic economic order quantity model for stocks.

19 Discuss the results of a two-variable sensitivity analysis of the cost of not taking a cash discount with respect to changes in the discount and the credit period (other things remain the same).

20 'A firm can realize some savings by making less frequent payments to its employees (for example, paying employees monthly as opposed to weekly).' Do you agree with this statement? Provide a numerical example which justifies your answer.

21 Compare and contrast each of the following four types of loans: a simple interest loan, a variable interest loan, a discounted loan and a loan with compensating balance.

22 Prepare an analog model summarizing the main points discussed in the present chapter.

23 How can spreadsheets be used to facilitate the application of the concepts discussed in this chapter?

Appendix 10A Sampling methods

The entire set of possible observations of a certain phenomenon is called a statistical population or simply a population. For example, all the limited liability companies in the United Kingdom make up a population of limited liability companies. Each individual item in a population is called an element of the population. For example, Marks and Spencer plc is an element of the population of limited liability companies. A portion of a population is called a sample of the population. For example, the UK firms whose shares are traded in the London Stock Exchange constitute a sample of the population of UK limited liability companies.

Analysing an entire population may be impossible, it may be too time-consuming or it may be impractical. As a consequence, a representative sample from the population should be used to provide information about the population. A parameter (for example, mean, standard deviation, or variance) is a descriptive characteristic of a population. A statistic (for example, mean, standard deviation, or variance) calculated using a sample drawn from the population is a characteristic of that sample.

When a sample is used to provide information about the population from which it is drawn it must be a representative sample. If the sample is not representative, the conclusions about the population may be incorrect. One method that can be used to select a representative sample is a process known as random sampling. A random sample can be defined as the sample selected in a way such that each element in the population has a known, non-zero chance of being included in the sample. There are several methods that could be used for selecting a random sample from the population of interest. In this appendix two methods are discussed: simple random sampling and systematic sampling.

Simple random sampling

A simple random sample is a sample chosen in such a way that each element in the population under investigation is equally likely to be included in the sample. In view of this method, you assign a number to each observation of the population and then you perform a random selection from these numbers.

Example 10A.1 Selecting a simple random sample from a population of companies

Figure 10A.1 shows the current assets, current liabilities, net working capital and current ratio for each of 45 supermarkets for the year 1987/88 (*source*: Business

	A	B	C	E	F	G
1	SUPERMARKETS:Working Capital and Current Ratio (1987-88)					
2	No	Company	CA	CL	NWC	CA/CL
3	01	Lennons Group plc	7,748	637	7,111	12.16
4	02	Laws Stores plc	3,129	476	2,653	6.57
5	03	Nevins Ltd	1,151	693	458	1.66
6	04	Taskers (Blackpool) Ltd	1,027	623	404	1.65
7	05	King Bros. Ltd	411	291	120	1.41
8	65	Goodfellows ltd	776	568	208	1.37
9	07	Morris & Co. Ltd	6,384	4,818	1,566	1.33
10	08	Walter Willson Ltd	4,529	3,567	962	1.27
11	09	J.B. Walker Ltd	160	126	34	1.27
12	10	Marks & Spencer plc	685,000	623,500	61,500	1.10
13	11	Brookton ltd	5,262	5,124	138	1.03
14	12	S.L. Shaw Ltd	539	568	(29)	0.95
15	13	Gateway Foodmarkets Ltd	686,301	740,555	(54,254)	0.93
16	14	Normans Group plc	23,958	26,114	(2,156)	0.92
17	15	Milbank Foods Ltd	805	883	(78)	0.91
18	16	Landmark Superstore Ltd	198	223	(25)	0.89
19	17	Asda Group ltd	332,400	391,400	(59,000)	0.85
20	18	G.W. Proudfood Ltd	812	973	(161)	0.83
21	19	Oshwal Distributors Ltd	83	105	(22)	0.79
22	20	Gateway Corporation plc	664,100	884,000	(219,900)	0.75
23	21	Stewarts Supermarket plc	18,611	25,030	(6,419)	0.74
24	22	Kwik Save Group plc	76,017	91,214	(15,197)	0.83
25	23	L.C. Seward & Sons Ltd	308	449	(141)	0.69
26	24	Michael Supermkt Ltd	170	266	(96)	0.64
27	25	Jacques & Son Ltd	150	236	(86)	0.64
28	26	Bretzel Foods Ltd	746	1,222	(476)	0.61
29	27	Tates Ltd	1,650	2,777	(1,127)	0.59
30	28	WM Morrison Supermarkets Plc	49,408	83,492	(34,084)	0.59
31	29	Chateautree Ltd	63	112	(49)	0.56
32	30	Simco Supermarkets Ltd	1,749	3,117	(1,368)	0.56
33	31	Thomas Foodmarket Ltd	91	163	(72)	0.56
34	32	R.& N. Food Supplies Ltd	44	87	(43)	0.51
35	33	Tesco plc	253,800	508,700	(254,900)	0.50
36	34	Bejam group plc	46,980	95,795	(48,815)	0.49
37	35	Waitrose Ltd	35,535	72,890	(37,355)	0.49
38	36	R.T. Willis Ltd	897	1,895	(998)	0.47
39	37	Savacentre Plc	39,797	84,280	(44,483)	0.47
40	38	WM Low plc	16,214	34,729	(18,515)	0.47
41	39	International Stores Ltd	55,541	121,034	(65,493)	0.46
42	40	Superfood & Wine Co. Ltd	321	759	(438)	0.42
43	41	J. Sainsbury Plc	354,200	913,000	(558,800)	0.39
44	42	Fine Fare Ltd	103,653	342,447	(238,794)	0.30
45	43	Carrefour Ltd	29,176	109,536	(80,360)	0.27
46	44	Melias Ltd	3,351	13,523	(10,172)	0.25
47	45	City Grocers Ltd	292	1,429	(1,137)	0.20

Figure 10A.1. A population of 45 supermarkets

Ratio Analysis, 1989, published by ICC Business Ratios, Field House, 72 Oldfield Road, Hampton, Middlesex). Assume that these 45 firms make up a population of firms from which we wish to draw a random sample of 30 firms. Each firm is assigned a two-digit number starting with 01 and finishing at 45. The mathematical function `@RAND` of 1-2-3 can be used to generate random numbers. The following formula generates random numbers between 10 and 460.

```
@INT(@RAND * 450) + 10
```

The `@INT` function is used to transform the corresponding random number into an integer. To generate more random numbers, copy the last formula as many times as required. Figure 10A.2 shows the results after copying the last written formula 29 times.

Figure 10A.2. Generating randomly 30 numbers between 1 and 460

	A	B	C	D	E	F
50		326	52	237		
51		280	232	318		
52		180	251	422		
53		211	337	128		
54		275	449	199		
55		25	126	316		
56		257	381	333		
57		159	107	357		
58		311	381	35		
59		80	161	454		

Suppose we decide to start at cell B50 in Figure 10A.2. The company numbers in our example have only two digits. The first two digit number is 32. Thus, the first company in the sample is R. & N. Food Supplies Ltd. The second two digit number is 28 and the corresponding element of the population (WM Morrison Supermarkets plc) provides the second member of the sample. The sixth two digit number is 02 (where we add the zero digit in every two digit random number of Figure 10A.2). In this case, company number 02 (that is, Laws Stores plc) is in the sample, and so on.

Systematic sampling

A systematic random sample is a sample which contains every kth element of a population that is organized in an orderly way.

Example 10A.2 Selecting a systematic random sample from a population of companies

Consider the population presented in Example 10A.1. We wish to draw a random sample comprised of 15 companies. First we sort the company names into an alphabetical order. This can be achieved by using 1-2-3's `/Data Sort` command. The Data-Range for the command is A3..A47 (see Figure 10A.1), the Primary-Key is cell B3 and the order of sorting is A (Ascending). After using properly this command, 1-2-3 will sort the records in alphabetical order so that your data looks like Figure 10A.3. Also note that we re-number the sorted companies starting from number 1 and finishing at number 45.

	A	B	C	E	F	G
1	SUPERMARKETS:Working capital and current ratio (1987-88)					
2	No	Company	CA	CL	WC	CA/CL
3	1	Asda Group ltd	332,400	391,400	(59,000)	0.85
4	2	Bejam group plc	46,980	95,795	(48,815)	0.49
5	3	Bretzel Foods Ltd	746	1,222	(476)	0.61
6	4	Brookton ltd	5,262	5,124	138	1.03
7	5	Carrefour Ltd	29,176	109,536	(80,360)	0.27
8	6	Chateautree Ltd	63	112	(49)	0.56
9	7	City Grocers Ltd	292	1,429	(1,137)	0.20
10	8	Fine Fare Ltd	103,653	342,447	(238,794)	0.30
11	9	G.W. Proudfood Ltd	812	973	(161)	0.83
12	10	Gateway Corporation plc	664,100	884,000	(219,900)	0.75
13	11	Gateway Foodmarkets Ltd	686,301	740,555	(54,254)	0.93
14	12	Goodfellows ltd	776	568	208	1.37
15	13	International Stores Ltd	55,541	121,034	(65,493)	0.46
16	14	J. Sainsbury Plc,	354,200	913,000	(558,800)	0.39
17	15	J.B. Walker Ltd	160	126	34	1.27
18	16	Jacques & Son Ltd	150	236	(86)	0.64
19	17	King Bros. Ltd	411	291	120	1.41
20	18	Kwik Save Group plc	76,017	91,214	(15,197)	0.83
21	19	L.C. Seward & Sons Ltd	308	449	(141)	0.69
22	20	Landmark Superstore Ltd	198	223	(25)	0.89
23	21	Laws Stores plc	3,129	476	2,653	6.57
24	22	Lennons Group plc	7,748	637	7,111	12.16
25	23	Marks & Spencer plc	685,000	623,500	61,500	1.10
26	24	Melias Ltd	3,351	13,523	(10,172)	0.25
27	25	Michael Supermkt Ltd	170	266	(96)	0.64
28	26	Milbank Foods Ltd	805	883	(78)	0.91
29	27	Morris & Co. Ltd	6,384	4,818	1,566	1.33
30	28	Nevins Ltd	1,151	693	458	1.66
31	29	Normans Group plc	23,958	26,114	(2,156)	0.92
32	30	Oshwal Distributors Ltd	83	105	(22)	0.79
33	31	R.& N. Food Supplies Ltd	44	87	(43)	0.51
34	32	R.T. Willis Ltd	897	1,895	(998)	0.47
35	33	S.L. Shaw Ltd	539	568	(29)	0.95
36	34	Savacentre Plc	39,797	84,280	(44,483)	0.47
37	35	Simco Supermarkets Ltd	1,749	3,117	(1,368)	0.56
38	36	Stewarts Supermarket plc	18,611	25,030	(6,419)	0.74
39	37	Taskers (Blackpool) Ltd	1,027	623	404	1.65
40	38	Tates Ltd	1,650	2,777	(1,127)	0.59
41	39	Tesco plc	253,800	508,700	(254,900)	0.50
42	40	The Superfood & Wine Co. Ltd	321	759	(438)	0.42
43	41	Thomas Foodmarket Ltd	91	163	(72)	0.56
44	42	WM Low plc	16,214	34,729	(18,515)	0.47
45	43	WM Morrison Supermarkets Plc	49,408	83,492	(34,084)	0.59
46	44	Waitrose Ltd	35,535	72,890	(37,355)	0.49
47	45	Walter Willson Ltd	4,529	3,567	962	1.27

Figure 10A.3. An ascending sort on company name field

After sorting the data, we wish to select every third element to be in the sample. A random starting point for the sample is determined by selecting a number between 1 and 3. In our case, we randomly choose number 1 as a starting point. Beginning with number 1, every third element is chosen until the sample of 15 companies is completed.

The selection of our sample will be conducted with the aid of 1-2-3's `/Data Query` command. Figure 10A.4 shows a criterion for selecting the appropriate

	A	B	C	E	F	G
50	No	Company	CA	CL	WC	CA/CL
51	0					
52						

Figure 10A.4. A database criterion

elements from the population of supermarkets. Cell B51 contains the following formula:

`@IF(@MOD(A3,3) = 0,1,0)`

In words, if the firm's number is divided exactly by 3, then return number 1, otherwise return 0. Since the first company's number is not divided exactly by 3, the `@IF` function returns 0.

Our criterion instructs 1-2-3 to choose a firm whose corresponding number is divided exactly by 3. After creating the criterion, use the `/Data Query` command with the following ranges

Input range: A2..F47; Criterion range: A50..F51; and
Output range: A54..F69.

When you choose the Extract option of the `/Data Query` command, 1-2-3 will copy the records that match the criterion from the database into the Output range. The results are presented in Figure 10A.5.

	A	B	C	E	F	G
53						
54	No	Company	CA	CL	WC	CA/CL
55	3	Bretzel Foods Ltd	746	1,222	(476)	0.61
56	6	Chateautree Ltd	63	112	(49)	0.56
57	9	G.W. Proudfood Ltd	812	973	(161)	0.83
58	12	Goodfellows ltd	776	568	208	1.37
59	15	J.B. Walker Ltd	160	126	34	1.27
60	18	Kwik Save Group plc	76,017	91,214	(15,197)	0.83
61	21	Laws Stores plc	3,129	476	2,653	6.57
62	24	Melias Ltd	3,351	13,523	(10,172)	0.25
63	27	Morris & Co. Ltd	6,384	4,818	1,566	1.33
64	30	Oshwal Distributors Ltd	83	105	(22)	0.79
65	33	S.L. Shaw Ltd	539	568	(29)	0.95
66	36	Stewarts Supermarket plc	18,611	25,030	(6,419)	0.74
67	39	Tesco plc	253,800	508,700	(254,900)	0.50
68	42	WM Low plc	16,214	34,729	(18,515)	0.47
69	45	Walter Willson Ltd	4,529	3,567	962	1.27

Figure 10A.5. A systematic sample

Some useful points

1 (Systematic sample versus simple random sample) If there exists a predetermined pattern to the population, a systematic selection may result in a non-representative sample. For example, consider a population of quoted companies where the shares of every tenth company in the population are not traded very often on the London Stock Exchange. Then a sample containing every tenth element of the population is not a representative one. However, this problem does not occur in simple random sampling.

2 (The `@RAND` function) The outcome of the `@RAND` function changes each time you recalculate the worksheet. If you want to store the permanent value of the `@RAND` function, use the `/Range Value` command.

References and bibliography

Acher, S.H. (1966) A model for the determination of firm cash balance, *Journal of Finance and Quantitative Analysis*, **1**, March, 1–11.

Bean, V.L. and Griffith, R. (1966) Risk and return in working capital management, *Mississippi Valley Journal of Business and Economics*, **1**, Autumn, 28–48.

Beranek, W. (1967) Financial implications of lot-size inventory models, *Management Science*, **2**, April, 401–8.

Beranek, W. (1968) *Working Capital Management*. Wadsworth, Belmont, Calif.

Bonocore, J.J. (1980) Getting a picture of cash management, *Financial Executive*, **48**, May, 30–3.

Brew, J.M. (1966) Gilt-edged curves, *Investment Analyst*, December, 3–23.

Crum, R.L., Klingman, D.D. and Tavis, L.A. (1983) An operational approach to integrated working capital planning, *Journal of Economics and Business*, **35**, August, 343–78.

Daellenbach, H.G. (1974) Are cash management optimisation models worthwhile?, *Journal of Financial and Quantitative Analysis*, **9**, September, 607–26.

Giltman, L.J. and Sachdeva, K.J. (1982) A framework for estimating the required working capital investment, *Review of Business Economic Research*, **17**, Spring, 36–44.

Glautier, M.W.E. (1971) Towards a reformulation of the theory of working capital, *Journal of Business Finance*, **3**, Spring, 37–42.

Knight, W.D. (1972) Working capital management—Satisfying versus optimization, *Financial Management*, **1**, Spring, 33–40.

Lambrix, R.J. and Singvi, S.S. (1979) Managing the working capital cycle, *Financial Executive*, **47**, June, 32–41.

Lawson, G.H. and Pike, R.H. (1984) *Key Issues in Working Capital Management*. MCB University Press, Bradford.

Magge, J.F. (1956a) Guides to inventory policy, I, *Harvard Business Review*, January–February, 49–60.

Magge, J.F. (1956b) Guides to inventory policy, II, *Harvard Business Review*, March–April, 49–60.

Magge, J.F. (1956c) Guides to inventory policy, III, *Harvard Business Review*, May–June, 103–16 and 57–70.

Mehta, D.R. (1974) *Working Capital Management*. Prentice Hall, Englewood Cliffs, NJ.

Merville, L.J. and Tavis, L.A. (1973) Optimal working capital policies: a chance-constrained programming approach, *Journal of Financial and Quantitative Analysis*, **8**, January, 47–60.

Miller, M.H. and Orr, D. (1968) A model of the demand for money by firms, *Quarterly Journal of Economics*, August, 413–35.

Orgler, Y.E. (1970) *Cash Management*. Wadsworth, Belmont, Calif.

Schiff, M. (1972) Credit and inventory management: separate or together?, *Financial Executive*, **40**, November, 28–33.

Smith, K.V. (1973) State of the art or working capital management, *Financial Management*, **2**, Autumn, 50–5.

Smith, K.V. (1974) *Management of Working Capital: A Reader*. West, New York.

Smith, K.V. (1979) *Guide to Working Capital Management*. McGraw-Hill, New York.

Smith, K.V. (1980) On working capital as an investment by the firm, in: Smith, K.V. (ed.), *Readings on the Management on Working Capital*. West Publishing Co., St. Paul.

Snyder, A. (1964) Principles of inventory management, *Financial Executive*, **32**, April.

Stancill, J.McN. (1971) *The Management of Working Capital.* Intext Educational, Scranton, PA.

Vander, W.J. and Maier, S.F. (1985) *Managing Corporate Liquidity: An Introduction to Working Capital Management.* John Wiley, New York.

Van Horne, J.C. (1969) A risk–return analysis of a firm's working-capital position, *Engineering Economist*, **14**, 71–89.

Vienott, A.F., Jr. (1966) The status of mathematical inventory theory, *Management Science*, **12**, July, 745–77.

Walker, E.W. (1964) Toward a theory of working capital, *Engineering Economist*, **9**, 21–35.

Weston, J.F. and Tuan, P.D. (1980) Comment on analysis of credit policy changes, *Financial Management*, **9**, Winter, 59–63.

11 Valuation of debentures and preference shares

This chapter includes:

- Valuation of debentures
- Returns on investments in debentures
- Sensitivity of debenture prices
- Interest rates and inflation
- Valuation of preference shares

The valuation of debt securities (for example, debentures) is essential for the financial director of a firm who makes decisions involving the financing of the firm's operations with funds provided by long-term creditors. To understand how debt securities are valued, one must understand the factors that affect the value of a debt security and the sensitivity of the latter to changes in those factors.

The primary objective of this chapter is to discuss the valuation of debt securities and the sensitivity of a debt security's prices to changes in various factors such as interest rates, term to maturity, and so on. Figure 11.1 shows how the concepts discussed in this chapter are related to the framework introduced in Chapter 2.

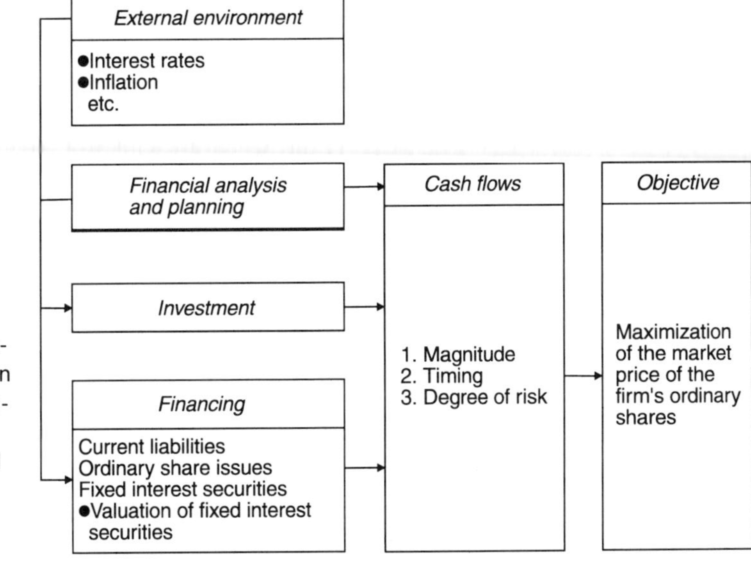

Figure 11.1. Relating the concepts described in the present chapter to the framework of financial management introduced in Chapter 2

Basic concepts, definitions and examples

A debenture is a long-term debt security representing a contractual agreement between the issuer (that is, a firm) and the holder by which the issuer promises to pay the principal to the holder by a specified future date and a series of periodic interest payments up to the repayment date. Each new debenture holder receives a printed debenture certificate as evidence of lending his or her money to the firm. Such a certificate represents the firm's promise to pay a specified periodic fixed income and eventually repay the money borrowed.

The par value (face value, or maturity value) of a debenture is the price printed on the face of the debenture certificate. In general, it is the price that the issuer promises to pay the holder when the debenture is retired. Usually, the corporate debentures sold in the United Kingdom have a face value of £100. The coupon interest rate of a debenture determines the annual amount of interest to be paid and is expressed as a percentage of the debenture's par value. The annual interest on a debenture equals the coupon rate times its par value. The maturity of a debenture is the length of time remaining before the debenture is retired. The maturity (or redemption) date of a debenture issue is the date when the issuing firm repays the amount owed to the debenture holders and retires the debenture issue.

Example 11.1 The debentures of Marks and Spencer plc

Marks and Spencer plc obtains part of its external funds by selling debentures to the public. For example, the following information was extracted from the firm's 1987 annual report:

Debenture loans—secured	1987 (£million)	1986 (£million)
7 1/4—1993/1998	15.0	15.0

The coupon interest rate of 7 1/4 per cent indicates that each debenture pays an annual interest of £7.25 (that is (£100) (0.0725)). Many debentures pay interest semi-annually, where a payment is equal to one-half of the annual interest amount. The redemption date is 1993/1998, in this case, the company is entitled to repay the whole or any part of the face value of the amount borrowed at any time between 1993 and 1998. To illustrate these points imagine that it is the end of March 1988 and interest is paid semi-annually. If the debenture will mature at the end of March 1996, the debenture's interest payments form an annuity of £3.625 per period for 16 periods (that is 7 1/4 per cent for eight years).

In many cases, lenders require a protection against situations where the firm is unable to pay either the interest or the maturity value of its debentures. Mortgage debentures are debentures secured by the firm's real property, for example, land and buildings. Mortgage debentures can be generally classified as first-mortgage debentures and second-mortgage debentures. The former have the first claim on specified secured assets in the event of default, while the latter have a secondary claim on assets already secured by the first mortgage. The Marks and Spencer's debentures are first-mortgage debentures being secured on certain freehold and leasehold properties of the firm.

The market value of a debenture is the price that can be obtained from the sale of the debenture in the marketplace. If the market price of a debenture is above the par value, the debenture is said to sell at a premium. A debenture with a market price below the par value sells at a discount.

Valuation of debentures

Debenture valuation refers to the process used to determine the value of a debenture. The valuation process is based upon the utilization of the time value of money concept (discussed in Chapter 3) in conjunction with the risk–return concepts (discussed in Chapter 8). A valuation model for debentures identifies the factors influencing the debenture's value and is represented by a mathematical equation showing the relationship between the value and these factors. Theoretically, the value of a debenture is determined by the following three factors: (a) the magnitude of the future cash flows to be received (that is, the annual interest payments and the par value to be paid at the end of the debenture's life); (b) the timing of these cash flows; and (c) the risk associated with these cash flows. Figure 11.2 presents a summary of the intrinsic value concept.

Definition The intrinsic value of a debenture is the present value of a series of expected cash flows to be received over its life span, all discounted at a discount rate which is commensurate with the risk associated with the debenture.

Calculation. The intrinsic value of a debenture is calculated by using the following formula:

Intrinsic value of a debenture	=	Present value of the series of the interest payments	+	Present value of the par value payable at maturity

$$V_d = \sum_{t=1}^{T} \frac{I}{(1+r_d)^t} + \frac{B_T}{(1+r_d)^T}$$

where

r_d = investors' required rate of return on the firm's debentures.

Interpretation The intrinsic value of a debenture can be viewed as the result of a process which takes the future cash flows of the debenture and discounts them back to the present at a required rate of return reflecting the riskiness associated with these cash flows.

Figure 11.2. The intrinsic value concept for a debenture

Note that in an efficient market, the current market price of a debenture is the best estimate of its intrinsic value. In cases where there exist market inefficiencies, the debenture's market price deviates from its intrinsic value.

Example 11.2 Calculating the present value of a debenture when interest is paid annually

The debentures of a firm have eight years remaining to maturity. Each debenture has a par value of £100 and the annual coupon rate is 7.25 per cent (we assume that the coupon rate is constant over the life of the debenture). Interest is paid at the end of each year and the investors' annual required rate of return on the firm's debentures is 10 per cent. The expected cash flows of the debenture are shown in Figure 11.3 with the aid of a time line.

The present value of the debenture is £85.33. This present value is calculated by

Actual year	88	89	90	91	92	93	94	95	96
Time	0	1	2	3	4	5	6	7	8
Cash flow		£7.25	£7.25	£7.25	£7.25	£7.25	£7.25	£7.25	£7.25 + £100

Figure 11.3. The cash flows of a debenture

using the following equation:

$$V_d = \sum_{t=1}^{8} \frac{£7.25}{(1+0.10)^t} + \frac{£100}{(1+0.10)^8}$$

The first term of the right-hand side in the last equation represents the present value of an annuity of £7.25 per year for eight years. The second term of the right-hand side in the valuation equation represents the present value of a lump sum to be received at the end of year 8. The current market price of the debenture is £85.33, thus an investor requiring a 10 per cent return on the firm's debentures would be willing to pay today £85.33. The present value of the debenture can be calculated with the aid of 1-2-3's financial function `@NPV`. Figure 11.4 shows the worksheet outlay where the following function is stored in cell B20:

```
@NPV(C5, B11..B18)
```

```
       A             B              C            D          E            F
 1 CALCULATING A DEBENTURE'S PRESENT VALUE (ANNUAL INTEREST PAYMENTS)
 2 =================================================================
 3 Coupon Rate                     7.25%
 4 Par Value                       £100
 5 Required Rate of Return        10.00%
 6
 7
 8 -----------------------
 9 Year    Cash Flow
10 -----------------------
11        1          £7.25
12        2          £7.25
13        3          £7.25
14        4          £7.25
15        5          £7.25
16        6          £7.25
17        7          £7.25
18        8        £107.25
19           -------------
20 Value            £85.33
```

Figure 11.4. Using the `@NPV` to calculate the present value of a debenture

Problems

1. Set up the worksheet shown in Figure 11.4 storing the `@NPV` function in cell B20.
2. Calculate the present value of a debenture having a required rate of return of 7.2 per cent and eight years to maturity. What do you observe? Discuss.
3. Calculate the present value of a debenture having a required rate of return of 7.2 per cent, a coupon rate of 6 per cent and eight years to maturity. What do you observe? Discuss.

In Example 11.2 the present value of the debenture is below the par value of £100. As long as the investors' required rate of return exceeds the coupon rate, the debenture's present value would be below the par value. If the required rate of return was lower than the coupon rate, the debenture's present value would be higher than the par value (for example, if the required rate of return was 7 per cent, the present value of the 7.25 coupon rate debenture would be £101.49). If the coupon rate and the required rate of return are equal, the debenture would sell exactly for its par value.

Example 11.3 Calculating the present value of a debenture when interest is paid semi-annually and examining the relationship between the present value of a debenture and the frequency of its coupon payments

Referring to the data in Example 11.2, assume that the firm pays interest semi-annually. The calculation of the debenture's present value is shown in Figure 11.5. The present value stored in cell C12 is calculated as follows:

```
@PV(C8,C9,C10)+C4/(1+C9)^C10
```

That is, the present value of the debenture equals the present value of an annuity of £3.625 per period for 16 periods plus the present value of the par value at the end of the sixteenth semi-annual period.

```
-----------------------------------------------------------------------------
      A          B               C              D        E           F
 1 CALCULATING A DEBENTURE'S PRESENT VALUE (SEMIANNUAL INTEREST PAYMENTS)
 2 ==========================================================================
 3 Coupon Rate                      7.25%
 4 Par Value                        £100
 5 Required Rate of Return         10.00%
 6
 7 Semiannual Rate                  3.625%
 8 Semiannual Interest             £3.625
 9 Semiannual RRR                   5.000%
10 Semiannual Periods                  16
11                              --------------
12 Value                           £85.10
-----------------------------------------------------------------------------
```

Figure 11.5. A debenture's market price with semi-annual interest payments

The calculations shown in Figure 11.5 assume that the debenture's semi-annual required rate of return is one-half of the annual required rate of return. Note, however, that the utilization of a semi-annual discount rate of 3.625 per cent will result in a slightly greater than 10 per cent annual required rate of return (that is $(1 + 0.05)^2 - 1 = 10.25$ per cent). The required rate of return, which will yield an annual required rate of return of 10 per cent if compounding occurs twice a year, can be calculated as shown below:

$$(1 + 0.10)^{1/2} - 1 = 4.881 \text{ per cent}$$

Using 4.881 per cent in the valuation process we find the debenture's present value to be £86.27. This price is slightly higher than the price of the debenture calculated in Example 11.2. In general, we can state the following: a debenture's price is an increasing function of the frequency of coupon payments (other things being equal). Figure 11.6 plots the relationship between the present value of the debenture under consideration and the frequency of its coupon payments (we assume only 12 frequencies, the first one assumes that interest is paid annually and the last one assumes that interest is paid monthly). The curve indicates that as the frequency of the debenture's coupon payments increases, its value decreases.

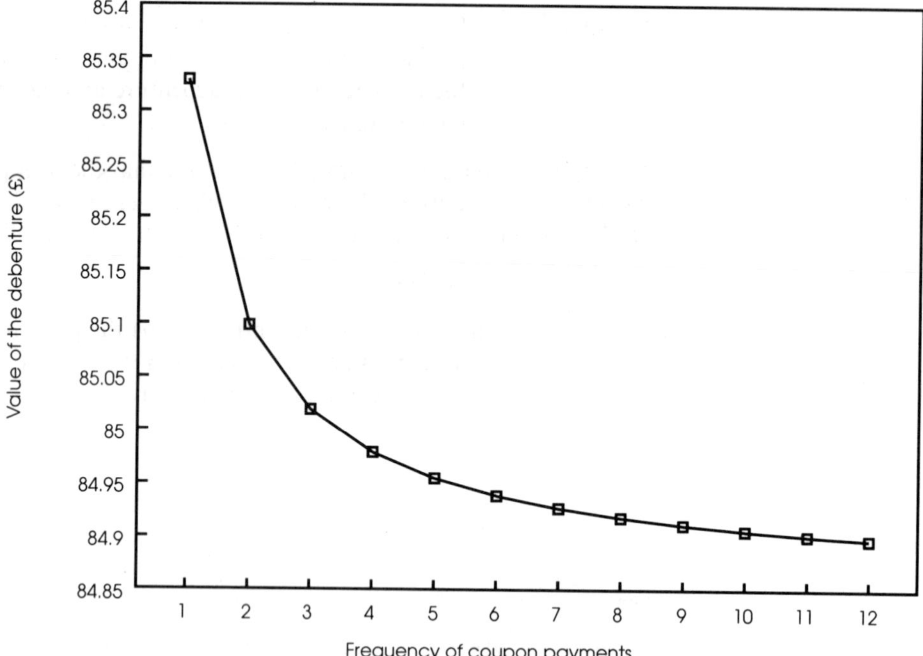

Figure 11.6. The relationship between the present value of a debenture and the coupon payments

A special case

A perpetual debenture pays constant interest payments and has no maturity date. In other words, the cash flow payable in a perpetual debenture is an annuity whose payments continue indefinitely. The present value of a perpetual debenture is calculated as follows:

$$V_d = \frac{I}{r_d}$$

Example 11.4 Calculating the present value of a perpetual debenture

If a debenture pays £4 each year, forever, and investors in this debenture require a return of 10 per cent, then the present value of the debenture is £40 (that is £4/0.10).

Returns on investments in debentures

At any time, an investor can do one of the following things:

- Purchase a debenture, hold for a given period and then sell before the maturity date.
- Purchase a debenture and hold to the maturity date.

In the former case, the single period rate of return on the debenture can be divided into two parts, interest income received during the period held and capital gain (or loss) caused by a change in its price over the holding period. Suppose an investor bought a firm's debenture for a price of V_d pounds and expects to sell it a year later at V_{d1} pounds. Assume that the investor will receive an interest of I pounds at the end of his or her holding period. The equation for calculating the investor's expected one-period rate of return is as follows:

Expected one-period rate of return on a debenture	=	Interest yield	+	Capital gain/loss expressed as a percentage of the buying price

$$R_d = \frac{1}{V_d} + \frac{V_{d1} - V_d}{V_d}$$

Example 11.5 Calculating the expected one-period rate of return on a debenture

Mr Annis bought a 7 1/4 coupon rate debenture at the end of March 1988 for a price of £85.33. Mr Annis purchased such a debenture on the expectation that he would receive £86.33 from selling the debenture a year later. The rate of return on the debenture for the period March 1988 to March 1989 is

$$R_d = \frac{7.25}{85.33} + \frac{(86.33 - 85.33)}{85.33} = 0.085 + 0.0117 = 9.67 \text{ per cent}$$

That is, if the future price of the 7 1/4 coupon debenture is expected to be £86.33, the debenture's rate of return will be 9.67 per cent.

Consider an investor who purchases a debenture and decides to hold it until its maturity, N years from now. This investment has an initial cost equal to the purchase price of the debenture. The investor expects to realize from his or her investment the following future cash flows:

- A stream of equal sums of money, where each sum of money equals the annual interest payment of the debenture.
- A single payment at the maturity date which is equal to the debenture's par value.

The return of the investor can be defined as the internal rate of return of his or her investment. This return is also known as the required rate of return on the investment, yield to maturity, or redemption yield of the debenture. In other words, the redemption yield is the compound return earned on a debenture if it is purchased at a specific price and held until its maturity date.

Example 11.6 Calculating the redemption yield of a debenture

Recall the 7 1/4 coupon rate debenture in Example 11.2. Assume that the present value of the debenture is £85.33 and its holder plans to keep it until maturity in eight years from now. We also assume that the payments of the interest and the par value will be realized at the end of each year within the holding period. The redemption yield of the debenture is the rate of return that satisfies the following valuation equation:

$$£85.33 = \sum_{t=1}^{8} \frac{£7.25}{(1+r_d)^t} + \frac{£100}{(1+r_d)^8}$$

In this instance, we can calculate the redemption yield in the same fashion as we compute the internal rate of return of an investment project (see Chapter 5). The result of the following function is stored in cell B20:

```
@IRR(0.08,B10..B18)
```

where 0.08 is a guess for the internal rate of return (see Figure 11.7). Thus, the rate of return the investor will earn, if the 7 1/4 coupon rate debenture is held until maturity, is 10 per cent.

Note that both the interest payments and the par value of £100 will be paid in the future. Therefore, if the interest payments of the 7 1/4 coupon rate debenture are not reinvested at the redemption yield of 10 per cent, then the actual yield eventually realized will be different from 10 per cent.

```
--------------------------------------------------------------------------------
        A            B             C             D          E          F
 1 CALCULATING A DEBENTURE'S REDEMPTION YIELD (ANNUAL INTEREST PAYMENTS)
 2 ===============================================================================
 3 Coupon Rate                           7.25%
 4 Par Value                             £100
 5 Value                                £85.33
 6
 7 ----------------------
 8 Year    Cash Flow (£)
 9 ----------------------
10        0          -85.33
11        1            7.25
12        2            7.25
13        3            7.25
14        4            7.25
15        5            7.25
16        6            7.25
17        7            7.25
18        8          107.25
19          ---------------
20 Yield             10.00%
--------------------------------------------------------------------------------
```

Figure 11.7. Calculating the redemption yield of a debenture

Problems

1 Set up the worksheet shown in Figure 11.7 storing the @IRR function in cell B20.
2 Calculate the redemption yield of a debenture having a present value of £90, an annual coupon rate of 7.25 per cent and eight years to maturity. What do you observe? Discuss.
3 Calculate the present value of a debenture having a present value of £110, an annual coupon rate of 6 per cent and eight years to maturity. What do you observe? Discuss.

In Example 11.6 the present value of the debenture is lower than the par value of £100. As long as the present value is below the par value, the redemption yield will be above the coupon rate of the debenture. If the present value of the debenture is higher than

£100, then the debenture's redemption yield will be lower than its coupon rate (for example, if the present value of a debenture is £103, its coupon rate is 7.25 per cent and it matures in eight years, then its redemption yield will be 6.75 per cent). If the present value of a debenture equals £100, then its redemption yield is equal to the coupon rate carried by the debenture.

If the redemption yield of a debenture remains constant, then we have:

1 When a debenture is purchased today for a price lower than £100 and held until its maturity date, its value rises gradually towards £100 as the years to maturity diminish, resulting in a capital gain.
2 When a debenture is purchased today for a price higher than £100 and held until its maturity date, its value gradually decreases towards £100 as the years to maturity diminish, providing a capital loss.
3 When a debenture is purchased today for £100 and held until its maturity date, no capital gain or loss results.

Example 11.7 Sensitivity of the redemption yield to changes in the number of years to maturity.

1-2-3 does not provide a function that can be used to examine how sensitive a debenture's redemption yield is to changes in the number of years to maturity. Below we provide a formula that can be used to conduct a sensitivity analysis of the redemption yield with respect to changes in the number of years to maturity. Several financial management books are using the following equation for estimating the redemption yield (RY):

$$\mathrm{RY} = \frac{I + (100 - V_d)/N}{(100 + V_d)/2} \tag{11.1}$$

where N = number of years to maturity

I = annual interest in pounds.

V_d = the present value of the debenture.

Note that Equation (11.1) provides only an approximation to the redemption yield (we call this approximation 1) calculated using the method described in Example 11.6 (we call the latter a regular redemption yield). The accuracy of the approximation can be examined by comparing the redemption yields calculated using Equation (11.1) with the regular redemption yields.

Equation (11.1) can be slightly modified to produce more accurate results. The yield to maturity of the debenture considered in Example 11.6 is 10 per cent. Thus, we wish to compute a number k such that:

$$0.10 = \frac{I + (100 - V_d)/N}{(100 + V_d)/k} \tag{11.2}$$

The value of k that satisfies Equation (11.2) is 2.040 (the value of k is rounded to three decimal point). Substituting the value of k back to the last equation we have:

$$RY = \frac{I + (100 - V_d)/N}{(100 + V_d)/2.040} \tag{11.3}$$

To examine the accuracy of the approximation given by Equation 11.3 (we call this approximation 2), consider the results presented in Figure 11.8. Column B shows the redemption yields of the debenture under consideration for different maturities. The results were produced with the aid of 1-2-3's `/Data Table 1` command. Column D contains the regular redemption yields and column E shows the results derived by using Equation (11.1). It is clear that the results derived using Equation (11.3) can better approximate the redemption yields as compared with the results produced using Equation (11.1).

```
     A          B          C             D                  E                 F
 1 EXAMINING THE ACCURACY OF TWO APPROACHES USED TO ESTIMATE THE RY
 2 ================================================================
 3
 4 Annual Coupon Rate                       7.25%
 5 Annual Interest Amount                   7.25
 6 Present Value                           85.33
 7 Par Value                                 100
 8 Years to maturity                           8
 9                                 --------------
10 Yield to maturity                       10.00%
11
12
13            +D10                 Regular RY        Existing Approximation
14      8        10.00%  |                 10.00%                9.80%
15     10         9.60%  |                  9.60%                9.41%
16     14         9.13%  |                  9.15%                8.95%
17     18         8.88%  |                  8.92%                8.70%
18     22         8.71%  |                  8.78%                8.54%
19     25         8.63%  |                  8.71%                8.46%
20     29         8.54%  |                  8.64%                8.37%
21     33         8.47%  |                  8.60%                8.30%
22     37         8.42%  |                  8.56%                8.25%
23     41         8.37%  |                  8.55%                8.21%
24     45         8.34%  |                  8.53%                8.18%
```

Figure 11.8. Comparing the accuracy of two methods used to estimate the redemption yield

Obviously, Equation (11.3) cannot be used to calculate a single redemption yield since it is based upon the value of that redemption yield. However, this method is useful in conducting a sensitivity analysis of the redemption yield with respect to changes in the expected life of the debenture. The sensitivity results are shown graphically in Figure 11.9, while Figure 11.10 provides a graphical comparison of all the results presented in Figure 11.8.

The redemption yield approximation formula

In Example 11.7 we presented an approximation for the redemption yield of a debenture that can be used to examine the sensitivity of the redemption yield to changes in the expected life of the debenture. However, it was pointed out that such an approximation can only be used for sensitivity analysis. In this section we present another method for calculating the redemption yield which in many cases provides a better approximation than that given by Equation (11.1). This approximated method follows two steps:

Step 1 Calculate an approximate redemption yield by using Equation (11.1).

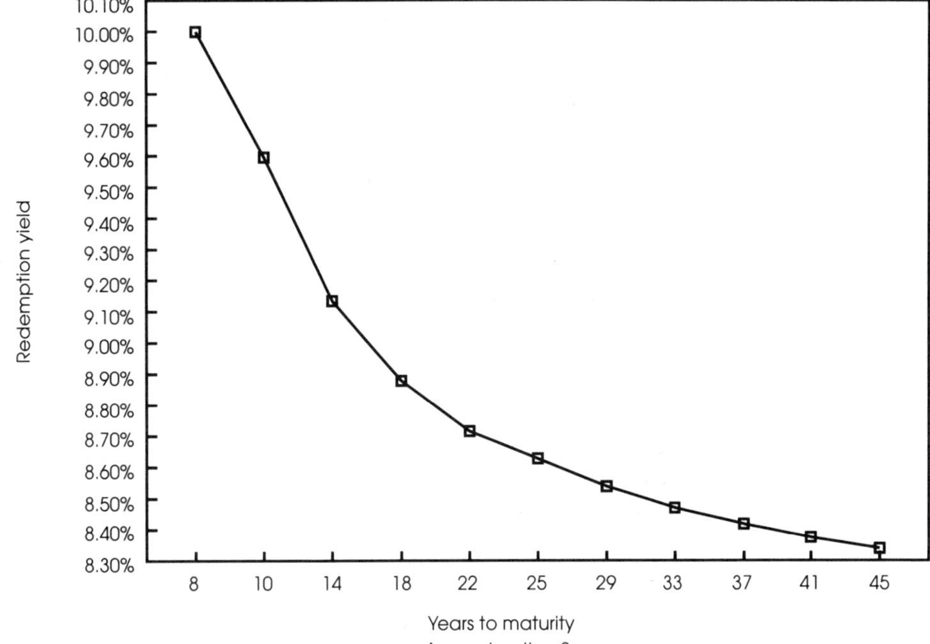

Figure 11.9. Sensitivity of the redemption yield to changes in the number of years to maturity

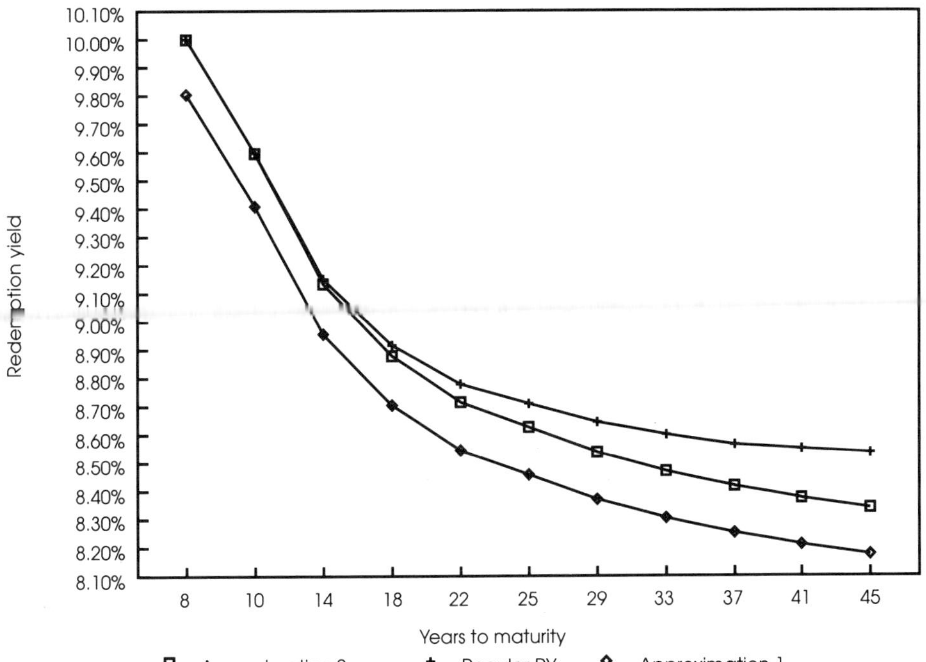

Figure 11.10. Comparison of regular redemption yield with results derived from using short-cut methods

Step 2. Calculate a new approximate redemption yield by using the following equation:

$$RY^* = \frac{I - I/(1 + RY)^T}{V}$$

where

RY = a redemption yield calculated with the aid of Equation (11.1).

V = the present value of the debenture *minus* the present value of £100 discounted at RY.

We call the last equation redemption yield approximation formula (RYAF).

Example 11.8 Calculating the redemption yield of a debenture using the redemption yield approximation formula

Consider the data given in Figure 11.11. The actual redemption yield is calculated with the aid of the @IRR function of 1-2-3 (see cell E15). The result stored in cell B11 is found by using Equation (11.1). Cell B13 shows the redemption yield calculated by utilizing the RYAF (percentage figures are presented with two decimal points):

$$RY^* = \frac{7.25 - 7.25/(1 + 0.098)^8}{38.005} = 10.05 \text{ per cent}$$

It is evident that the redemption yield computed by employing the RYAF provides a better approximation for the actual redemption yield than the approximation stored in cell B11.

The accuracy of the figure stored in cell B13 can be examined with the aid of a sensitivity analysis (see range B19..G33). This is a sensitivity of one variable with five equations:

Cell C19 refers to the equation stored in cell B11
Cell D19 refers to the equation stored in cell B13
Cell E19 refers to the equation stored in cell E15
Cell F19 stores the difference referring to the equations stored in cells B13 and E15, respectively.
Cell G19 stores the difference referring to the equations stored in cells E15 and B11, respectively.

The results reveal that the RYAF offers a better approximation for the actual redemption yield as compared with the approximation provided by Equation (11.1).

The approximation derived by employing the RYAF becomes more accurate as the present value of the debenture approaches its par value. For example, if the present value of the debenture in Figure 11.11 was £95, then the difference between the approximated redemption yield and the actual redemption yield would be 0.0040 per cent.

Problems

1 Set up the worksheet shown in Figure 11.11.
2 Use the RYAF to calculate the redemption yield for each of the following two cases:

Debenture A Interest rate: 8 per cent
Par value: £100

```
----------------------------------------------------------------------------
          A                B          C         D          E          F          G
 1 CALCULATING A DEBENTURE'S REDEMPTION YIELD USING THE RYAF
 2 ----------------------------|----------------------
 3                             |         Year Cash Flow
 4                             |----------------------
 5 Interest Rate       7.25%   |            0  -85.33
 6 Par value             100   |            1    7.25
 7 Annual Interest     £7.25   |            2    7.25
 8 Maturity (years)        8   |            3    7.25
 9 Present Value      £85.33   |            4    7.25
10                  ---------  |            5    7.25
11 RY (Equ. (11.1))    9.80%   |            6    7.25
12 Value             £38.005   |            7    7.25
13 RY Using RYAF      10.05%   |            8  107.25
14                             |               --------
15 ----------------------------|                10.00%  <- Actual RY
16
17
18
19                                +B11     +B13     +E15     +B13-E15  +E15-B11
20                       7.00%    9.53%    9.77%    9.72%      0.05%     0.19%
21                       8.00%   10.61%   10.88%   10.83%      0.05%     0.22%
22                       9.00%   11.69%   12.00%   11.95%      0.05%     0.26%
23                      10.00%   12.77%   13.11%   13.06%      0.05%     0.29%
24                      11.00%   13.85%   14.23%   14.18%      0.05%     0.33%
25                      12.00%   14.93%   15.35%   15.30%      0.05%     0.37%
26                      13.00%   16.01%   16.48%   16.42%      0.05%     0.42%
27                      14.00%   17.09%   17.60%   17.55%      0.05%     0.46%
28                      15.00%   18.17%   18.73%   18.67%      0.06%     0.51%
29                      16.00%   19.25%   19.86%   19.80%      0.06%     0.56%
30                      17.00%   20.32%   20.99%   20.93%      0.06%     0.60%
31                      18.00%   21.40%   22.12%   22.06%      0.06%     0.66%
32                      19.00%   22.48%   23.25%   23.19%      0.06%     0.71%
33                      20.00%   23.56%   24.38%   24.33%      0.06%     0.76%
----------------------------------------------------------------------------
```

Figure 11.11. Applying the redemption yield approximation formula

Maturity: 8 years
Present value £92

Debenture B Interest rate: 9 per cent
Par value: £100
Maturity: 8 years
Present value £105

3 Plot a graph that compares the regular redemption yield for debenture A (or debenture B) with the redemption yield found using the RYAF (use the relationship between coupon rate and redemption yield, other things remain the same). Discuss the resulting graph.
4 Plot a graph that compares the regular redemption yield for debenture A (or debenture B) with the redemption yield found using the RYAF (use the relationship between present value and redemption yield, other things remain constant). Discuss the resulting graph.

Gilt-edged securities

A gilt-edged security (a government security, or a gilt) is a fixed interest security issued by the Government, which promises to pay the holders a series of specified interest payments and to repay the principal of the loan at a specified maturity date (most government securities have a maturity date). Interest is normally paid every six

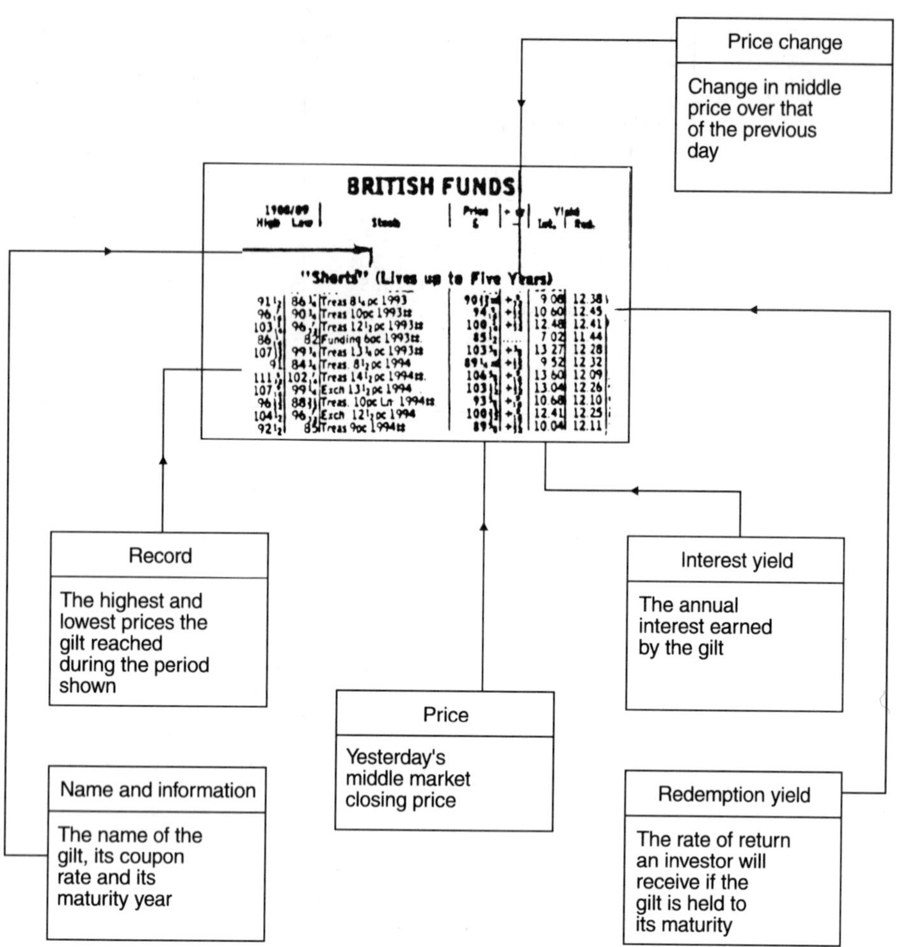

Figure 11.12. A summary of the quoted information on gilt-edged securities

months. In Figure 11.12 we show an example of a list of gilts taken from the *Financial Times* (14 July 1990).

Gilts are issued at a nominal value of £100. Theoretically, gilts provide a secure investment because they are guaranteed by the British Government. Gilts can be classified as follows:

Short-dated These have a life up to five years.
Medium-dated These have a life of between five and fifteen years.
Long-dated These have a life of more than fifteen years.
Undated These are government securities with no maturity date and they may never be paid.

Example 11.9 Reading the quoted information on a gilt

Imagine that it is 14 July 1990 and you see in the *Financial Times* the following short-dated gilt:

Treasury 12 1/2 pc 1993 100 3/16 +13/32 12.48 12.41

Treasury is the name of the gilt. The coupon rate of this gilt is 12 1/2 indicating the fixed rate of interest associated with the security. The coupon rate of a gilt is expressed as a percentage of its par value of £100. The redemption date for this gilt will be 14 July 1993, so the holder will receive £12.5 per annum for every £100 of the gilt held until July 1993. At the maturity date the Government will also pay to the investor the amount of gilt held (for example, if the investor holds 10 gilts, then the government will pay £1,000). Interest payments are usually made every six months. The Treasury 12 1/2 pc 1993 pays interest on 14 January and 14 July each year until 14 July 1993 (every Monday the *Financial Times* replaces the high/low column with a column displaying details about coupon payment dates).

The price shown is the previous day's middle price, thus, sellers will get slightly less than the quoted price and buyers will pay slightly more. The column next to that of price shows how much the price of a gilt has risen or fallen as compared with the previous day's closing price. The interest yield indicates how much a gilt is actually yielding in income terms. The interest yield (running yield, or flat yield) for the Treasury 12 1/2 pc 1993 is 12.48 per cent and it is calculated by dividing the annual interest by the current price:

$$\text{Interest yield} = \left(\frac{12.5000}{100.1875}\right) \times 100 = 12.48 \text{ per cent}$$

The yields to maturity or redemption yields published by the *Financial Times* are calculated using semi-annual compounding. The Treasury 12 1/2 pc 1993 has six semi-annual periods before its maturity. The cash flows of this yield are shown in Figure 11.13. The semi-annual redemption yield can be calculated by using the following financial function of 1-2-3:

```
@IRR(0.1,E7..E13)
```

where 0.1 is a guess for the semi-annual redemption yield.

The *Financial Times* obtains the annual redemption yield by multiplying the semi-annual yield by 2. Thus, the redemption annual yield is 12.42 per cent. The redemption yield of 12.42 per cent is lower than the interest yield of 12.48 per

```
                 A                      B    C       D                E         F
 1               CALCULATING THE REDEMPTION YIELD OF A GILT
 2               ==========================================
 3
 4  -------------------------------- | ----------------------------
 5                 D A T A           |           PERIOD  CASH FLOW
 6 Par Value                    100  | ----------------------------
 7 Interest Rate             12.50%  |                0   -100.1870
 8 Price                    100.187  |                1      6.2500
 9 Semiannual Interest Rate   6.25%  |                2      6.2500
10 Semiannual Interest        6.25   |                3      6.2500
11 Semiannual Periods            6   |                4      6.2500
12 --------------------------------  |                5      6.2500
13                                                    6    106.2500
14                                                       ------------
15                            SEMIANNUAL YIELD ------>          6.21%
16                            YIELD TO MATURITY ----->         12.42%
17 ------------------------------------------------------------------
```

Figure 11.13. Calculating the redemption yield of a gilt

cent, because the latter does not take into consideration the capital loss of £0.1875 (that is, £100.1875 – £100.0000) which will be realized on redemption of the gilt.

An investor who buys a gilt 'cum div' will be eligible to receive the imminent six-monthly interest payment even if he or she has not held the gilt for six months. A few weeks before the dividend is due, a gilt goes 'ex div' meaning that an investor who purchases the gilt on or after it has gone 'ex div' is not entitled to receive the upcoming interest payment.

Interest on gilts is paid out every six months, but in the meantime interest is accruing. The prices on short-dated gilts are quoted 'clean', that is, they do not include accrued interest while accrued interest is included in the quoted prices of other gilts (for example, long-term dated) until they go 'ex div'. If an investor buys a gilt 'cum div', he or she will actually pay slightly more that its price quoted in the *Financial Times* in order to take into consideration the accrued interest that will be received. On the other hand, if an investor purchases a gilt 'ex-div', he or she will pay a little less than the price quoted in the *Financial Times* in order to take into account the interest forgone.

Example 11.10 Calculating the accrued interest for a short-dated gilt

Assume that Treasury 12 1/2 pc 1993 is going to be purchased 89 days after the last coupon payment date. In Figure 11.12 the gilt's quoted price is 100 3/16 and its accrued interest is £3.0821 (that is (90)(£12.5)/365). (We used 90 days instead of 89 because the gilt will be paid for on the date after the purchase has taken place.) The total price of the gilt would be £103.2696 (that is, £100.1875 + £3.0821). Note that this price excludes transaction costs.

Example 11.11 Calculating the interest forgone for a short-dated gilt

In Figure 11.12 the Treasury 8 1/2 per cent 1994 has 'xd' after its price, standing for 'ex-div'. Suppose an investor buys this gilt 'ex-div' 20 days before the interest payment. The quoted price of £89.2500 should be adjusted for the 20 days' interest forgone. The forgone interest is £0.4658 (that is (20)(£8.5)/365). Thus, the total price would be £88.7842 (that is £89.2500 – £0.4658). Note that this price excludes transaction costs.

Figure 11.14 provides an example of how we can present graphically gilt data by using a three-dimensional diagram. We use the redemption yields of low-coupon, five-year government securities over the period 1981–90 (the data was obtained from the Datastream). We can see that the shape of the redemption yield curve changes every year. The largest fluctuations in the low-coupon, five-year government securities occurred in 1982 and the smallest took place in 1989. Additionally, the higher redemption yields were offered in 1981 and the lower redemption yields were observed in 1987.

Comparing gilt-edged securities

Some investors find gilts attractive because they are looking for a fixed income and others invest in gilts in the hope of making capital gains. The coupon of a gilt tells the investor whether he or she will realize a return in the form of income or capital

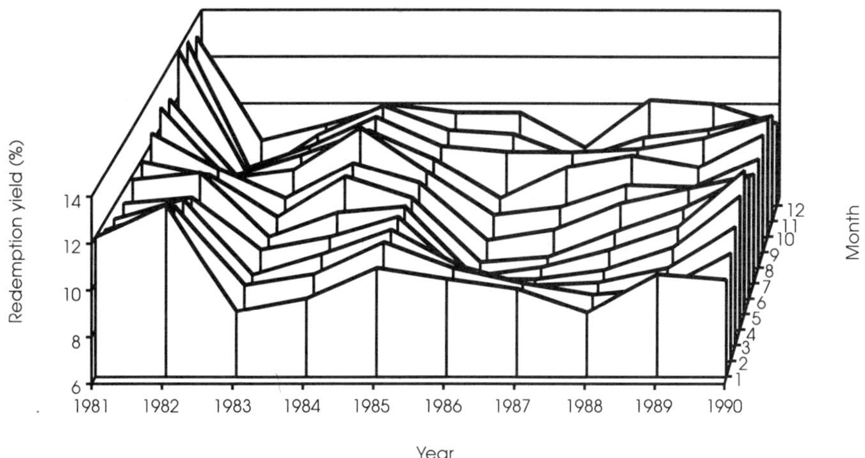

Figure 11.14. British Government securities presented using a three-dimensional diagram

gains. For example, consider the following two gilts taken from Figure 11.12:

	Price		Yield	
			Int.	Red.
Funding 6 pc 1993	85 1/2	...	7.02	11.44
Treasury 12 1/2 pc 1993	100 3/16	...	12.48	12.41

Funding 6 per cent pays lower interest than Treasury 12 1/2 per cent, but the former provides investors with capital gains. If an investor purchases Funding 6 per cent at 85 1/2, then at the maturity date he or she will have a capital gain of £14.5. On the other hand if an investor buys Treasury 12 1/2 per cent at 100 3/16, then he or she will realize a higher income as compared with that of Funding 6 per cent and a small capital loss at redemption. The choice is dependent on the tax position of the investor.

The interest yield gives misleading information for the return on a low coupon gilt, because it does not take into consideration the capital gains or losses on either the sale or redemption of the gilt. For example, the interest yield of Funding 6 per cent is 7.02 per cent while its redemption yield is 11.44 per cent, a difference of 4.42 per cent. For high coupon gilts, the interest yield can be taken as an approximation of the redemption yield, since we show earlier that the majority of the return on a high coupon yield is in the form of income rather than capital gain. For example, the interest yield of Treasury 12 1/2 per cent is close to its redemption yield, the difference between the two yields is only 0.07 per cent.

The redemption yield alone cannot be utilized for comparing gilts. If the redemption yield was the only method for choosing among gilts, then the demand for the lower redemption yield gilts would drop until the yields of all gilts became equal. In order to be able to compare gilts (or other fixed interest securities) we need to understand the sensitivity of gilt prices to interest rate changes and the factors that affect such sensitivity. For example, one could compare the sensitivity of gilt prices to interest rate changes or the sensitivity of gilt prices to both interest rate and term to maturity changes (these issues are discussed later in the chapter).

Spot rates

A spot rate is defined as the rate of return of a bond that promises to make only one payment to its owner (such a bond is called a zero coupon or a pure discount bond). In the United Kingdom, 'bond' is utilized to describe a debt security when is issued by the Government, while a debt security which is issued by a private business organization is called a 'debenture'. For simplicity, we will use below annual spot rates.

Example 11.12 Estimating the spot rates for three debt securities

Consider three debt securities A, B and C of identical risk with the following data:

Debt security A	It has a zero coupon rate, one year remaining until maturity and sells for £95.
Debt security B	It sells for £91, has an annual coupon rate of 4 per cent and matures in two years.
Debt security C	It has an annual coupon rate of 8 per cent, two years remaining to maturity and a market price of £98.154.

Since the three debt securities are of identical risk, their cash flows arising in the same year should be discounted at the same rate. This implies that funds invested in any of these three debt securities for one year will produce the same rate of return, r_1. Also funds invested in debt security B or debt security C for one year at r_1 will produce the same rate of return r_2. The rates r_1 and r_2 are not necessarily equal.

The spot rates are estimated as follows:

For debt security A: $£95 = \dfrac{£100}{(1+r_1)}$, thus $r_1 = 5.26$ per cent.

The rate of 5.26 per cent is the discount rate applicable to the cash flow of £100 to be received in one year.

For debt security B: $£91 = \dfrac{£4}{(1+r_1)} + \dfrac{£104}{(1+r_2)^2}$

where $r_1 = 5.26$ per cent, hence, $r_2 = 9.21$ per cent.

The rate of 9.21 per cent represents today's estimate of next year's one-year spot rate.

For debt security C: $98.154 = \dfrac{£8}{(1+r_1)} + \dfrac{£108}{(1+r_2)^2}$

where $r_1 = 5.26$ per cent, therefore, $r_2 = 9.21$ per cent.

Example 11.13 Duplicating the cash flows of a debt security using the cash flows of two other debt securities of identical risk

In this example we use the same data as in Example 11.12. Assume that debt security C is more expensive than a combination of debt security A and debt security B. Then we can duplicate the cash flows of debt security C by using a combination of debt security A and debt security B. In this case, instead of buying debt security C we can but the appropriate combination of the other two securities.

In other words, we want to calculate two numbers (or weights) such that each cash flow of debt security C is a weighed average of the corresponding cash flows of debt security A and debt security B. Mathematically, using matrix notation, we try to estimate w_1 and w_2 such that:

$$\begin{bmatrix} 100 & 4 \\ 0 & 104 \end{bmatrix} \begin{bmatrix} w_1 \\ w_2 \end{bmatrix} = \begin{bmatrix} 8 \\ 108 \end{bmatrix}$$

The solution of this system of linear equations is (figures have be rounded to three decimal points):

$w_1 = 0.0385$ and $w_2 = 1.0385$

If an investor purchases 1 debt security A and 27 debt securities B, then he or she has duplicated the cash flows of 26 debt securities C since the following equalities approximately hold (note that $1/26 = 0.0385$ and $27/26 = 1.0385$):

$(£100 + (27)(£4))/26 = £8$

and

$(£0 + (27)(£104))/26 = £108$

Finally, note that the price of debt security C is a weighted average of the prices of debt security A and debt security B, that is (a slight deviation occurs due to rounding):

$(£95)(0.0385) + (£91)(1.0385) = £98.154$

Sensitivity of debenture prices

From the valuation equation for debentures (see Figure 11.2) it can be seen that the market price of a debenture is affected by the following factors (the analysis that follows is also applicable to other fixed interest securities, for example gilts):

- The coupon rate
- The interest period (see Example 11.3)
- The number of years to maturity

At any point in time the structure of debenture prices can be examined with respect to each of these three variables. The examination of the relationship between the redemption yields and the term to maturity of debentures that are similar in all other respects is known as a term structure analysis.

Sensitivity of price to changes in the coupon rate

From the valuation model for debentures (see Figure 11.2), we can observe the following:

- If the coupon rate increases, the price of the debenture rises (other things being equal).
- If the coupon rate decreases, the price of the debenture declines (other factors remain the same).

Example 11.14 The sensitivity of the debenture price to changes in the coupon rate

Consider the data displayed in Figure 11.15. The market price of the debenture (see cell C8) is calculated by using the following formula:

```
@PV(C3*C4,C6,C5)+C4/(1+C6)^C5
```

This formula consists of two parts, the present value of the interest payments (that is, the present value of an annuity) and the present value of the par value paid at the end of the eighth year.

The sensitivity of the debenture price to changes in the coupon rate is conducted with the aid of the Lotus `/Data Table 1` command (cell C10 contains the formula stored in cell C8 and the `/Range Format Text` command is used to display the contents of cell C10 as text). The results show that debenture price increases (decreases) as the coupon rate increases (decreases), other things remain the same.

For example, if coupon rate increases from 7.25 per cent to 11.25 per cent, then the debenture price increases by 25.01 per cent (that is, £106.67/£85.33 – 1); if, on the other hand, the yield to maturity decreases from 7.25 per cent to 3.25 per cent, the debenture price decreases by 25.01 per cent (that is, 1 – £63.99/£85.33).

	A	B	C	D	E	F	G
1	SENSITIVITY OF PRICES TO CHANGES IN THE COUPON RATE						
2	==						
3	Coupon Rate		7.25%				
4	Par Value		100				
5	Years to Maturity		8				
6	Yield to Maturity		10.00%				
7			-------				
8	Market Price		85.33				
9	--						
10			+C8				
11		3.25%	63.99				
12		4.25%	69.32				
13		5.25%	74.66				
14	COUPON	6.25%	79.99				
15		7.25%	85.33				
16		8.25%	90.66				
17		9.25%	96.00				
18		10.25%	101.33				
19		11.25%	106.67				
20	--						

Figure 11.15. The effects of changes in the coupon rate on debenture price

Sensitivity of price to changes in the term to maturity

As a debenture approaches its maturity date, the difference between its market price and its face value decreases. For a constant redemption yield, the price of a debenture approaches its par value as the debenture approaches its maturity date.

Example 11.15 Sensitivity of price to changes in the term to maturity

Assume the same data given in Example 11.14. We also assume that the redemption yield does not change over the life of the debenture. Figure 11.16

provides the following sensitivities:

- Price with respect to the term to maturity
- Capital gain from the debenture with respect to the term to maturity
- Percentage change in capital gains with respect to the term to maturity

The `/Data Table 1` command of 1-2-3 is used and the results are presented in Figure 11.16. The results reveal the following:

1. If the redemption yield of a debenture does not change over its life, then the market price of the debenture approaches £100 as the debenture approaches its maturity date (see column C). If the purchase price of the debenture is below the par value, a capital gain will be realized in a future sale (or at the redemption date). If the purchase price of a debenture is greater than the par value, a capital loss will result in a future sale (or at the redemption date).
2. If the maturity yield remains constant, then the capital gain of the debenture holder decreases as the debenture approaches its maturity date. The percentage change in capital gains decreases at an increasing rate as the debenture approaches its maturity date.

	A	B	C	D	E	F	G
1	SENSITIVITY OF PRICES TO CHANGES IN THE TERM TO MATURITY						
2	===						
3	Coupon Rate		7.25%				
4	Par Value		100				
5	Years to Maturity		8				
6	Yield to Maturity		10.00%				
7			-------				
8	Market Price		85.33				
9	--						
10		+C8		+C4-D8		(C4-C8)/C8	
11		8	85.33	14.67	17.19%		
12		7	86.61	13.39	15.46%		
13		6	88.02	11.98	13.61%		
14		5	89.58	10.42	11.64%		
15	YEAR	4	91.28	8.72	9.55%		
16		3	93.16	6.84	7.34%		
17		2	95.23	4.77	5.01%		
18		1	97.50	2.50	2.56%		
19		0	100.00	0.00	0.00%		
20	--						

Figure 11.16. Sensitivity of price to changes in the term to maturity

Assume that the redemption yield remains constant and consider an investor who purchases a debenture at £85.33. After a year the investor decides to sell the debenture at £86.61. Then his or her single period rate of return is calculated as follows:

$$\frac{7.25 + 86.61 - 85.33}{85.33} = 10 \text{ per cent}$$

In words, if the redemption yield remains unchanged, the one-year rate of return of a debenture is equal to its redemption yield.

Sensitivity of prices with respect to changes in the redemption yield and the coupon rate
For a given change in yield, the higher the coupon of the debenture is, the smaller the price fluctuation will be. This provides an important consideration when investing in debentures (and other debt securities paying fixed interest). For example, if an investor expects interest rates to decline, then debentures with low-coupon interest payments will be preferable to high-coupon debentures.

Example 11.16 The sensitivity of the debenture price with respect to changes in the redemption yield and the coupon rate

Using the data provided in Example 11.14, Figure 11.17 shows the effects of changes in the redemption yield and the coupon rate on the debenture price. The `/Data Table 2` command of 1-2-3 is used, where the cells in the range B11..B19 store the sensitivity values for the redemption yield and the cells in the range C10..G10 store the sensitivity values for the coupon rate (the 'input cell 1' is cell C6 and the 'input cell 2' is cell C3).

The results reveal that for a given change in yield, the prices of low-coupon debentures are more sensitive to changes in redemption yield than those of high-coupon debentures (other things being the same). For example, consider two debentures having the same redemption yield of 10 per cent and coupon rates of 5.25 per cent and 7.25 per cent, respectively. Next assume that the yield increases to 15.50 per cent. Then the following changes are calculated:

For coupon rate of 5.25 per cent: $(74.66 - 54.75)/54.36 = 36.63$ per cent.

For coupon rate of 7.25 per cent: $(85.33 - 63.58)/63.58 = 34.20$ per cent.

The results shown in Figure 11.17 are graphically illustrated in Figure 11.18.

	A	B	C	D	E	F	G
1	SENSITIVITY OF PRICES TO CHANGES IN REDEMPTION YIELD & COUPON RATE						
2	==						
3	Coupon Rate		7.25%				
4	Par Value		£100				
5	Years to Maturity		8				
6	Redemption Yield		10.00%				
7			-------				
8	Market Price		£85.33				
9	----------------	----------------	----------	----------	COUPON RATE		---------
10		+C8	5.25%	6.25%	7.25%	8.25%	9.25%
11		1.75%	125.92	133.32	140.73	148.13	155.54
12		4.50%	104.95	111.54	118.14	124.73	131.33
13		7.25%	88.17	94.09	100.00	105.91	111.83
14	YIELD	10.00%	74.66	79.99	85.33	90.66	96.00
15		12.75%	63.70	68.54	73.38	78.22	83.06
16		15.50%	54.75	59.17	63.58	67.99	72.41
17		18.25%	47.40	51.45	55.49	59.54	63.58
18		21.00%	41.32	45.05	48.77	52.50	56.22
19		23.75%	36.27	39.71	43.16	46.60	50.05

Figure 11.17. Assessing the effect of changes in the redemption yield and the coupon rate on price

Sensitivity of prices with respect to changes in coupon rate and term to maturity
The prices of low-coupon debentures are more sensitive to changes in the term to maturity than the prices of high-coupon debentures (other things remain the same).

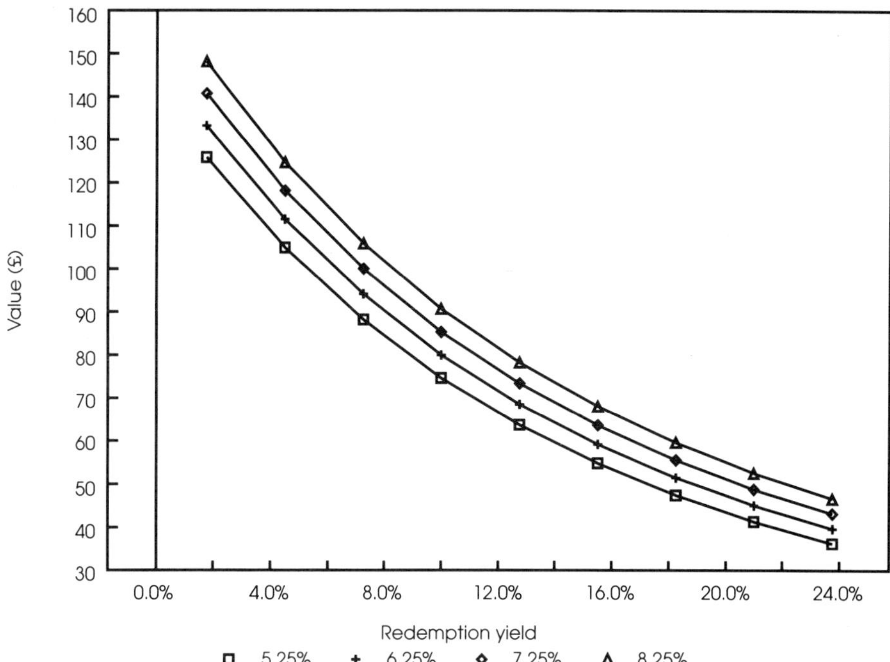

Figure 11.18. Sensitivity of prices to yield and coupon rate changes

Example 11.17 The sensitivity of the debenture price with respect to changes in the term to maturity and the coupon rate

Figure 11.19 determines the impact of changes in the term to maturity and the coupon rate on the debenture price (the 'input cell 1' for the `/Data Table 2` command is cell C5 and the 'input cell 2' is cell C3). The results reveal that a given change in the term to maturity will cause the price of the low-coupon debenture

	A	B	C	D	E	F	G
1	SENSITIVITY OF PRICES TO CHANGES IN TERM TO MATURITY & COUPON RATE						
2	===						
3	Coupon Rate		7.25%				
4	Par Value		£100				
5	Years to Maturity		8				
6	Redemption Yield		10.00%				
7			-------				
8	Value		£85.33				
9	--				COUPON RATE		---------
10		+C8	5.25%	6.25%	7.25%	8.25%	9.25%
11		0	100.00	100.00	100.00	100.00	100.00
12		2	91.76	93.49	95.23	96.96	98.70
13		4	84.94	88.11	91.28	94.45	97.62
14	YEARS	6	79.31	83.67	88.02	92.38	96.73
15		8	74.66	79.99	85.33	90.66	96.00
16		10	70.81	76.96	83.10	89.25	95.39
17		12	67.63	74.45	81.26	88.08	94.89
18		14	65.01	72.37	79.74	87.11	94.47
19		16	62.84	70.66	78.48	86.31	94.13
20	--						

Figure 11.19. Sensitivity of price to changes in the term to maturity and the coupon rate

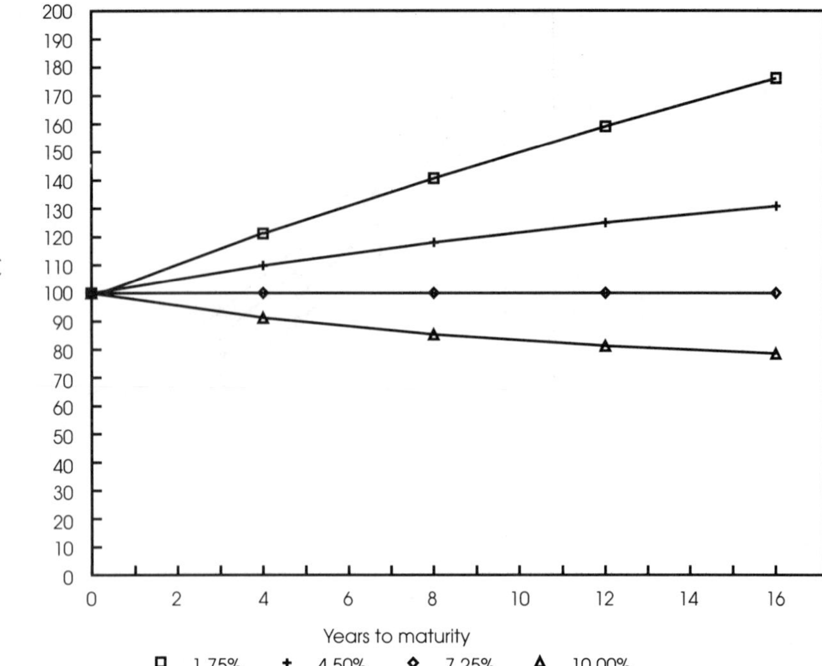

Figure 11.20. Relationships between a debenture's value, redemption yield and debenture maturity

to change more in percentage terms than the price of the high-coupon debenture. For example, consider two debentures having the same redemption yield of 10 per cent and coupon rates of 5.25 per cent and 7.25 per cent, respectively. Then we can calculate the following changes:

For coupon rate of 5.25 per cent: $(91.76 - 62.84)/62.84 = 46.02$ per cent.

For coupon rate of 7.25 per cent: $(95.23 - 78.48)/78.48 = 21.34$ per cent.

The results of the sensitivity table are presented graphically in Figure 11.20.

Figure 11.21. summarizes some results related to pricing of debentures.

Inflation and interest rates

Much of the original economic research on measuring the purchasing power of a currency and examining the effect of inflation on the rate of interest was conducted by the American economist Irving Fisher (1930). The theory of Fisher shows that lenders should demand a rate of interest that provides a compensation for both the rate they would have been willing to accept (when inflation is zero) plus the expected rate of inflation.

Measuring inflation

Inflation is a substained upwards movement in the general level of prices. Inflation can be measured by the Consumer Price Index (CPI). This index is a ratio showing the price of a 'basket' of goods and services in various equally spaced time intervals (for example, months) in relation to the price of the 'basket' in a base period. The index is 100 in the base period and correspondingly higher in later periods if items

Theorem	Implication(s)
Debenture prices move inversely to changes in redemption yields.	An increase in interest rates will cause the price of a debenture to fall. In this case, investors can minimize losses if they keep the debentures as long as possible. Conversely, a fall in the interest rates creates an increase in the price of a debenture. In this case, investors might prefer to sell the debentures quickly before a fall in the price occurs.
If a debenture's yield remains constant over its life, then the difference between its market price and its par value will decrease at an increasing rate as its maturity date approaches.	If the purchase price of a debenture is lower than the par value, a capital gain will be realized at the maturity date. If the purchase price of a debenture is greater than the par value, a capital loss will result at the maturity date.
For a given change in yield, the higher the coupon rate is, the smaller the percentage of price change will be.	If an investor expects interest rates to fall, then debentures with low-coupon interest payments will be preferable to high-coupon debentures. Investors should pruchase high-coupon debentures if they expect an increase in the interest rates.

Figure 11.21. A summary of three principles on debentures

in the 'basket' have risen. The rate of inflation measures the rate of change in the amount of goods and services the pound can buy from one period to the next. If inflation is measured by the consumer price index, the rate of inflation between two periods is calculated as follows:

Inflation rate	=	Change in the consumer price index (CPI)	÷	Value of the CPI at the end of the first period

$$IR_t = (CPI_t - CPI_{t-1}) \div CPI_{t-1}$$

where

CPI_{t-1} = the consumer price index at the end of period $t-1$.

CPI_t = the consumer price index at the end of period t.

Example 11.18 Calculating the yearly rate of inflation using the consumer price index (1974–88)

Column B of Figure 11.22 shows the yearly values of the consumer price index (*source*: Financial Statistics). The following formula is stored in cell C7:

(B7 − B6)/B6 = (29.1–25.1)/25.1 = 15.94 per cent

The contents of the cell C7 are copied in the range C8..C21.

The most serious factor for the high inflation during 1973–74 was the huge rise in oil and other import prices. The high rate of inflation observed in 1980 was attributed by many economists to cost–push pressures arising mainly from the

	A	B	C	D	E	E	G	H
1	CALCULATING THE RATE OF INFLATION (1974-1988)							
2								
3								
4	YEAR	CPI	INFLATION RATE					
5								
6	1973	25.1						
7	1974	29.1	15.94%					
8	1975	36.1	24.05%					
9	1976	42.1	16.62%					
10	1977	48.8	15.91%					
11	1978	52.8	8.20%					
12	1979	59.9	13.45%					
13	1980	70.7	18.03%					
14	1981	79.1	11.88%					
15	1982	85.9	8.60%					
16	1983	89.8	4.54%					
17	1984	94.3	5.01%					
18	1985	100	6.04%					
19	1986	103.4	3.40%					
20	1987	107.7	4.16%					
21	1988	113	4.92%					

Figure 11.22. Calculating the rate of inflation (1974–88)

increase of wages above what is justified by increased output per worker. The decline of the inflation rate between 1980 and 1985 may be attributable to the massive increase in unemployment or the reduction in real earnings.

Real and nominal interest rates

The nominal interest rate is simply the quoted rate used for borrowing or lending money in financial markets. For example, the interest rates you read about in the newspapers or business magazines are nominal interest rates. Inflation should not be ignored when measuring the return on lending or borrowing transactions and this argument is illustrated as follows.

A bank pays 6 per cent annually on deposits. If a householder deposits £1,000 today, he or she will have in his or her account £1,060 a year later. Now suppose that the inflation rate will be 8 per cent during the year, then the interest on the loan will not be enough to compensate the householder for the inflation incurred. Stated differently, the householder will purchase fewer goods and services with £1,060 than the £1,000 could buy a year ago.

The real interest rate corrects the nominal rate for expected inflation. Specifically, the real interest rate can be expressed as:

$$k = \frac{1 + r}{1 + \text{IR}} - 1 \tag{11.4}$$

where

r = the nominal interest rate.
IR = the rate of expected inflation.

Example 11.19 Calculating the real interest rate required on an investment

Imagine that it is 1987 and you expect the inflation rate during 1988 to be 3.40 per cent (that is, the inflation rate of 1986, see Figure 11.22). If you purchase a three-month Treasury bill having a nominal annualized yield of 9.31 per cent, your real rate of interest would be:

$$\frac{1+0.0931}{1+0.0304} - 1 = 5.72\,\text{per cent}$$

Actual inflation rates might vary from expectations, thus, there is no guarantee that the required real rate of interest will be earned.

Example 11.20 The sensitivity of real interest rate with respect to changes in the rate of expected inflation

Figure 11.23 shows the extent to which the real interest rate changes in response to changes in the rate of expected inflation. For example, if investors expect the inflation rate to be 3.78 per cent, they will have a real interest rate of 5.33 per cent. If the actual rate of inflation turns out to be higher, for example equal to 6.44 per cent, they would realize an actual real return of only 2.70 per cent.

```
        A          B          C          D          E          F
 1 SENSITIVITY OF THE REAL RATE TO CHANGES IN THE EXPECTED INFLATION RATE
 2 ======================================================================
 3
 4 Treasury Bill Rate             9.31%
 5 Expected Inflation             3.40%
 6                                ------
 7 Real Interest Rate             5.72%
 8
 9 -----------------------------------------
10                  +C7
11              3.40%             5.72%
12              3.78%             5.33%
13              4.16%             4.94%
14              4.54%             4.56%
15              4.92%             4.18%
16              5.30%             3.81%
17              5.68%             3.43%
18              6.06%             3.06%
19              6.44%             2.70%
20 -----------------------------------------
```

Figure 11.23. Assessing the effect of changes in the expected rate of inflation on the real rate

Rearranging Equation (11.4) yields:

$$r = k + \text{IR}(1 + k) \tag{11.5}$$

This equation says that the nominal interest rate is equal to the real interest rate plus a premium (that is, an additional rate of interest). The former compensates investors for delaying present consumption and the latter compensates investors (that is, lenders) for expected inflation. For example, if $k = 5.72$ per cent and $\text{IR} = 3.40$ per cent, then $r = 5.72$ per cent $+ 3.60$ per cent $= 9.32$ per cent. Note that 3.60 per cent is the additional rate of interest that compensates the lender for inflation.

If the nominal interest rate can be expressed as in Equation (11.5), then inflation is incorporated into the cost of borrowing. Thus, borrowers will be better off only if inflation is higher than expected. They will be worst off if inflation is lower than expected.

Example 11.21 The relationship between annual inflation rates and three-month UK rates on Treasury bills (1975–88)

Figure 11.24 plots the relationship between inflation rates and three-month UK rates on Treasury bills for the period 1975–88. Notice that the real interest rates were actually negative during two periods, 1975 to 1977 and 1980. During these periods investors in three-months Treasury bills were earning high interest rates but inflation was higher than these rates. Inflationary pressures eased in 1978 and also later from 1983 to 1988. During these two periods the nominal interest rates on three-months Treasury bills exceeded the inflation rate and as a result investors realized positive real rates.

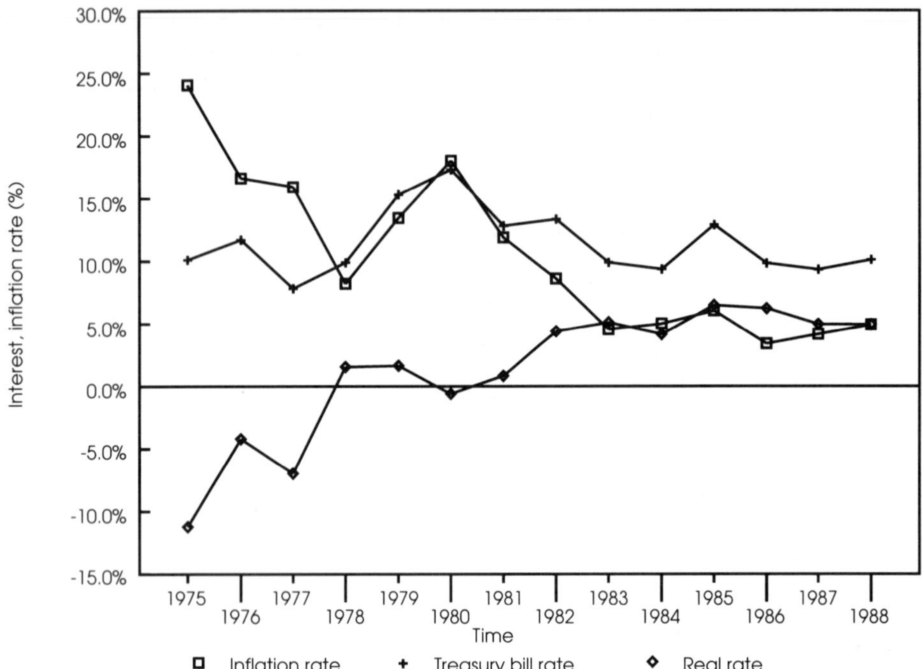

Figure 11.24. Annual inflation rates versus three-month Treasury bill rates

Valuation of preference shares

A preference share is a security that pays usually a fixed periodic dividend and has priority over ordinary shares with regard to dividends and assets. Many preference shares have a par value of £100. Dividends are expressed as a percentage of the par value. Preference shares are similar to debentures in that they typically pay the holder fixed payments. Usually preference shares have no maturity date. The required rate of return for preference shares is less than that of ordinary shares, because preference shares are associated with less risk. Figure 11.25 summarizes the valuation concept for preference shares with no maturity date.

Example 11.22 Calculating the intrinsic value of a preference share

Each of the preference shares of AD Stores plc pays an annual dividend per share of £11.4. The investors' required rate of return on the firm's preference shares is 12 per cent per annum. We assume that the series of dividends per share is an

Definition The intrinsic value of a preference share with no maturity date is the present value of a series of dividends, all discounted at a discount rate which is commensurate with the risk associated with the preference share.
Calculation We assume that the preference share has no maturity date, future dividends are expected to be constant and each dividend payment is made annually. Then the intrinsic value of a preference share can be calculated by dividing the constant annual preference dividends per share by the investors' required rate of return on the preference share:

$$V_p = \frac{D_p}{r_p}$$

Interpretation The intrinsic value of a debenture can be viewed as the result of a process which takes the future cash flows of the preference share and discounts them back to the present at a required rate of return reflecting the riskiness associated with these cash flows.

Figure 11.25. The intrinsic value of a preference share with no maturity date

annuity with infinite life span. Then the intrinsic value of the preference share would be

$$V_p = \frac{£11.4}{0.12} = £95$$

Problems

1 Conduct a sensitivity analysis of the AD Stores' preference share price with respect to changes in the investors' required rate of return.
2 Graph the results produced in Problem 1. Discuss the resulting graph.

Summary

1 *Valuation of debentures* The inrinsic value of a debenture using the *N*-periods valuation model involves estimating the present value of the future benefits it is expected to provide (that is, future interest payments and principal repayment), all discounted at the investors' required rate of return. The required rate of return depends on the risk associated with the return from the debenture. The value of a perpetual debenture is equal to the constant annual interest payment divided by the investors' required rate of return on that debenture.
2 *Returns on investments in debentures* There are three alternative rates of return associated with debentures. The current yield equals the annual interest payment of the debenture divided by the debenture's current price. The single period rate of return equals the current yield on the debenture plus the percentage price appreciation (depreciation) realized over the period the debenture was held. The redemption yield of a debenture is the rate of return investors realize if they purchase the debenture at a specific price and hold it until its maturity date.
3 *Sensitivity of debenture prices* The following results are valid:

(a) The higher the coupon rate, the higher the debenture price (other things remain the same).
(b) The price of a debenture approaches its par value as its maturity date approaches (provided that the firm does not go into liquidation).
(c) Other things being the same, low-coupon debentures are more price sensitive

to yield changes than are high-coupon debentures (this property is not valid for perpetuities).

(d) Low-coupon debentures are more price sensitive to changes in the term to maturity than are high-coupon debentures (other things remain equal).

4 *Interest rates and inflation* Since the price of a debenture depends on the level of interest rates, and interest rates are affected by inflation, it is very important to understand the relationship between inflation and interest rates. In the view of the theory of interest developed by Fisher, nominal rates of interest depend on expected real interest rates and expected rates of inflation over some future period.

5 *Valuation of preference shares* The intrinsic value of a preference share that has no maturity and pays a fixed periodic dividend equals the annual constant preference dividends per share divided by the investors' required rate of return on the preference share.

Questions for discussion

1 For each term shown below in the largest box provide a definition in your own words. Then check your responses against the definitions included in the chapter.

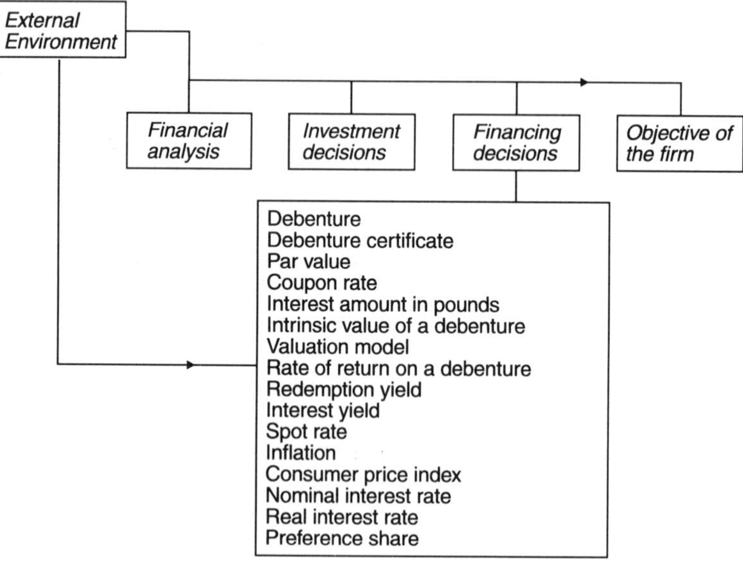

2 'In an efficient capital market, the market price of a debenture should be equal to the present value of all the cash flows associated with the debenture discounted at an appropriate discount rate, over its expected life span.' Explain the justification for this statement.

3 Consider an investor facing the following two equally risky alternatives:

(a) Purchase a debenture that offers a coupon rate of 12 per cent and has two years to maturity.

(b) Purchase a debenture that offers a coupon rate of 6 per cent. This debenture will also mature in two years.

We assume that the required rate of return applicable to both debentures is 10 per cent and it will remain unchanged over the next two years. Identify the best investment.

4 **(a)** The figure below shows two variables that are used in the valuation model for debentures. It also indicates that as the coupon rate increases, the value of the debenture increases (other things being the same). Fill in the three blank spaces. Each time discuss how an increase or decrease in a value of a variable influences the value of the debenture (assume that other things remain the same).

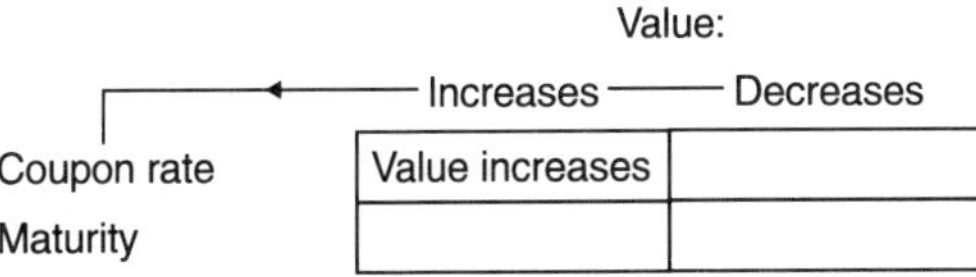

(b) Choose two of your answers given in part (a) and illustrate each case by using a numerical example.

5 Compare and contrast the following: (a) expected rate of return on a debenture; (b) interest yield; (c) redemption yield; and (d) spot rate.

6 Carefully discuss each of the following two statements:

(a) 'Debenture prices move inversely with interest rates.'
(b) 'Purchase a debenture with a high coupon rate if the market interest rate is expected to rise.'

7 Discuss the following information (*source*: *Financial Times*, 14 July 1990):

1988/89			Price	+ or	Yield	
High	Low	Stock		–	Int.	Red.
103 3/16	96 7/32	Treasury 12 1/2 pc 1993	100 3/16	+13/32	12.48	12.41

8 Mr George Annis prefers to invest in gilts offering low-coupon rates, while Miss Ruth Kitchin invests in high-coupon gilts. Give reasons for each investment strategy.

9 **(a)** Below, you are given three statements related to the concept of inflation. Fill in an appropriate reply by using either the word 'Agree' or the word 'Disagree'.

	Agree	Disagree
During periods of inflation it is better to lend money than to borrow money.		
If inflation expectations increase, the debenture prices tend to decrease.		
The relationship between real and nominal interest rate is positive and linear.		

(b) Discuss in details each reply given in part (a).

10 Prepare an analog model summarizing the main points discussed in this chapter.

11 How can spreadsheets be used to facilitate the application of the concept discussed in this chapter?

Appendix 11A Statistical inference: estimation

Statistical inference is a process by which conclusions about the characteristics of a population are made based on samples drawn from the population. One of the most important procedures utilized for statistical inference is estimation. Estimation is concerned with estimating the parameters of a population from the corresponding statistics of a sample drawn from the population. For example, consider the population of all possible monthly rates of change of the FT-A price index for debentures. A random sample of 36 monthly observations can be obtained and the mean of such a sample can be used to estimate the mean of the population. Figure 11A.1 provides a diagram summarizing the concept of statistical estimation.

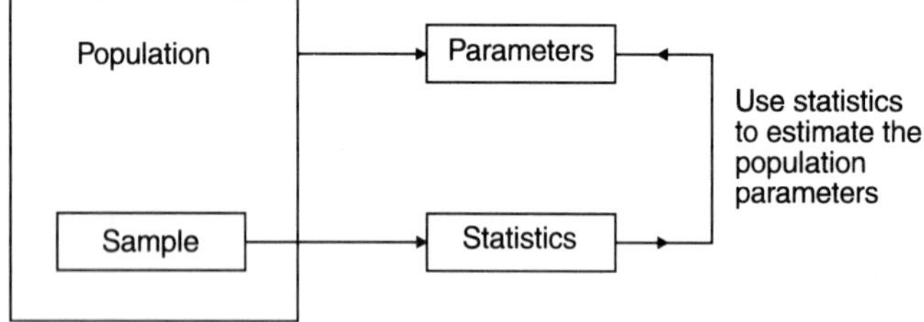

Figure 11A.1. A summary of the statistical estimation concept

An estimator is a sample statistic that is employed to estimate the value of a population parameter. A point estimate is simply the numerical value of an estimator. For example, the mean of a sample of 36 monthly rates of change of the FT-A price index for debentures is an estimator of the mean of the population of all possible monthly observations for the index. If the sample mean is –0.047 per cent, then this value is a point estimate of the population mean.

To ensure that estimators are satisfactory the following properties are required:

- Unbiasedness An estimator of a population parameter is called unbiased if the mean of its sampling distribution is equal to the true population parameter (the sampling distribution is obtained by using repeated random samples from the population).
- Efficiency An estimator of a population parameter is called efficient if it has the smallest variance as compared with any other unbiased estimator of the parameter (an efficient estimator is also called best unbiased).
- Consistency An estimator of a population parameter is called consistent if, as the size of sample increases, it becomes almost certain that its value is very near to the parameter value.

As the sample gets larger the likelihood of the validity of these properties increases, in this case, they are called asymptotic properties. Consider a sample of observations from a total population of observations. The mean of the sampling distribution of means equals the population mean, thus, the sample mean is an unbiased estimator

	A	B	C	D	E
1	THE RATES OF CHANGE FOR TWO INDICES (1987-89)				
2					
3	Month/Year	FTA debenture	Rate of	FTA pref. shares	Rate of
4		price index	change	price index	change
5					
6	Dec-86	108.90		78.63	
7	Jan-87	113.05	3.81%	79.01	0.48%
8	Feb-87	117.19	3.66%	82.12	3.94%
9	Mar-87	121.39	3.58%	83.88	2.14%
10	Apr-87	124.60	2.64%	86.41	3.02%
11	May-87	125.63	0.83%	87.40	1.15%
12	Jun-87	124.81	-0.65%	89.10	1.95%
13	Jul-87	123.11	-1.36%	88.37	-0.82%
14	Aug-87	119.40	-3.01%	87.56	-0.92%
15	Sep-87	113.73	-4.75%	84.51	-3.48%
16	Oct-87	113.75	0.02%	82.75	-2.08%
17	Nov-87	117.82	3.58%	84.17	1.72%
18	Dec-87	118.99	0.99%	86.01	2.19%
19	Jan-88	116.01	-2.50%	83.95	-2.40%
20	Feb-88	119.08	2.65%	86.85	3.45%
21	Mar-88	119.92	0.71%	88.36	1.74%
22	Apr-88	119.82	-0.08%	88.46	0.11%
23	May-88	119.65	-0.14%	91.76	3.73%
24	Jun-88	119.15	-0.42%	92.61	0.93%
25	Jul-88	118.03	-0.94%	93.43	0.89%
26	Aug-88	117.59	-0.37%	92.78	-0.70%
27	Sep-88	115.85	-1.48%	90.06	-2.93%
28	Oct-88	116.61	0.66%	87.71	-2.61%
29	Nov-88	118.27	1.42%	90.62	3.32%
30	Dec-88	117.61	-0.56%	86.63	-4.40%
31	Jan-89	116.12	-1.27%	85.95	-0.78%
32	Feb-89	118.11	1.71%	89.30	3.90%
33	Mar-89	118.07	-0.03%	89.95	0.73%
34	Apr-89	116.82	-1.06%	89.11	-0.93%
35	May-89	115.11	-1.46%	88.68	-0.48%
36	Jun-89	113.32	-1.56%	88.08	-0.68%
37	Jul-89	112.88	-0.39%	87.75	-0.37%
38	Aug-89	113.42	0.48%	88.43	0.77%
39	Sep-89	114.91	1.31%	89.49	1.20%
40	Oct-89	110.40	-3.92%	88.69	-0.89%
41	Nov-89	108.25	-1.95%	86.43	-2.55%
42	Dec-89	106.25	-1.85%	85.40	-1.19%
43			---------		
44	Mean ------>		-0.00047		
45	Variance ----->		0.00042		
46	Sample Variance ->		0.00043		

Figure 11A.2. Calculating the sample variance using 1-2-3 (Release 2.2)

of the population mean. The sample variance is a biased estimator of the population variance. However, the following modified formula for the variance provides an unbiased estimator of the population variance:

$$\text{Sample variance} = n\,\frac{(\text{variance})}{n-1}$$

where n = the total number of observations in the sample.

Example 11A.1 Calculating the sample variance using 1-2-3 (Release 2.2)

Figure 11A.2 shows a sample of 36 monthly rates of change of the FT-A price index for debentures (*source*: Datastream). The variance of the rates of change is calculated by using all 36 observations. The sample variance (cell C46) is calculated as follows:

`@VAR(C7..C42)*@COUNT(C7..C42)/(@COUNT(C7..C42)-1)` = 0.00043

The statistical function `@COUNT` counts the number of observations in the sample. The product `@VAR(C..C41)*@COUNT(C6..C41)` gives the sum of the squared deviations from the mean. This sum is then divided by `(@COUNT(C6..C41)-1)`, or 35, to produce the unbiased estimator of the population variance. The sample standard deviation is simply the square root of the sample variance.

Problem

Calculate the mean, variance and sample variance for the sample of the rates of change of the FTA price index for preference shares (see Fig. 11A.2).

Some useful points

1 (Using lotus' Release 3) Lotus Release 3 offers two statistical functions, `@STDS` and `@VARS`, that can be used to calculate directly the sample standard deviation and the sample variance, respectively.

2 (Mean distribution versus median distribution) The sampling distribution of the mean has the same mean with that of the sampling distribution of the median (in each case, the mean is equal to the population mean). However, the variance of the sampling distribution of the median is larger than the variance of the sampling distribution of the mean. Consequently, only the sample mean gives an efficient estimate of the population mean.

References and bibliography

Bauman, W.S. (1969) Investment returns and present value, *Financial Analyst Journal*, **27**, November–December, 107–20.

Bower, R.S., Johnson, K.B., Lutz, W.J., and Topley, T.C. (1977) Investment opportunities and stock valuation, *Journal of Business Research*, **5**, March, 36–61.

Gordon, M. (1963) *The Investment, Financing and Valuation of Corporation*. Richard D. Irwin, Homewood, Ill.

Granger, C.W.J. (1975), Some consequences of the valuation model when expectations are taken to be optimum forecasts, *Journal of Finance*, **31**, March, 135–145.

Hubbard, C.L. and Hawkins, C.A. *Theory of Valuation*. International Textbooks, Scranton, Pa.

Malkier, B.C. (1963) Equity yields and structure of share prices, *The American Economic Review*, **53**, December, 1004–31.

Mao, J.C.T. (1966) 'The valuation of growth stocks: the investment opportunity approach', *Journal of Finance*, **21**, March, 95–102.

Stone, B.K. (1975) The conformity of stock values based on discounted dividends to a fair return process, *Bell Journal of Economics*, **6**, Autumn, 698–702.

Wendt, P.F. (1965) Current growth stock evaluation methods, *Financial Analyst Journal*, **21** March–April, 91–201.

Williams, J.B. (1938) *The Theory of Investment Value*. Harvard University Press, Cambridge, Mass.

12 The determinants of redemption yields

This chapter includes:

- Risk on investment in debentures
- Term structure of interest rates
- Duration

Chapter 11 developed a model for estimating the intrinsic value of a debenture. In view of this model, the intrinsic value of a debenture is based on the expected future cash flows that the debenture holder will receive during the holding period and the rate of return investors would require as compensation for lending their money to the firm. The investors' required rate of return is affected directly by several types of risk (for example, inflation, risk, interest rate risk, and so on).

The term to maturity of a debenture may affect its redemption yield (other things being the same). The relationship between redemption yield and number of years to maturity is important to the firm, which has to decide whether to obtain funds by issuing short- or long-term public debt. Additionally, such a relationship is important to the investors, who have to decide whether to supply the firm with short- or long-term funds.

The objective of this chapter is to discuss the various types of risk which affect a debenture's required rate of return as well as to introduce three theories involving the relationship between the redemption yield and term to maturity. Figure 12.1 relates the primary topic discussed in this chapter with the financial management framework introduced in Chapter 2.

Risks on investments in debentures

The rate of return necessary to attract investors to purchase the debentures of a firm can be divided into two parts as follows:

The risk-free real rate is determined by the interaction of the supply and demand for borrowed funds in a world with no inflation or risk. The risk premium is the extra return required from the investors to offset the risks arising from investing in debentures. The risk premium is a sum of six types of risk associated with investments in debentures. These are inflation risk, interest rate risk, maturity risk, default risk, liquidity risk and reinvestment risk.

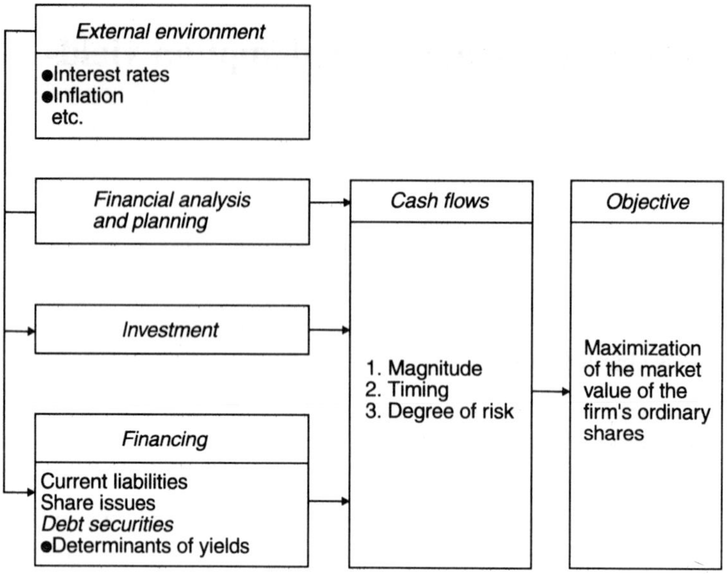

External environment
- Interest rates
- Inflation
etc.

Financial analysis and planning

Investment

Financing
Current liabilities
Share issues
Debt securities
- Determinants of yields

Cash flows
1. Magnitude
2. Timing
3. Degree of risk

Objective
Maximization of the market value of the firm's ordinary shares

Figure 12.1. Relating the concepts discussed in the present chapter to the financial management framework introduced in Chapter 2

Inflation risk

Inflation risk arises from the uncertainty associated with future rates of inflation. According to Fisher's theory, the nominal interest rate is equal to the real interest rate plus a premium for expected inflation. However, there is no guarantee that actual inflation will be equal to expected inflation. The divergence between actual and expected inflation gives rise to an inflation premium to compensate for inflation risk. In this case, the nominal interest rate may be thought of as consisting of the real interest rate plus a premium for expected inflation plus a premium which reflects inflation risk. When the actual rate of inflation is less than predicted, lenders gain and borrowers lose. Conversely, when the actual rate of inflation is higher than expected, borrowers will profit at the expense of lenders.

Interest rate risk

Interest rate risk (or price risk) arises from unpredictable movements in the market price of a debenture due to changes in interest rates. Debenture prices are inversely related to market interest rates. If market interest rates rise, debenture prices fall and vice versa. For example, consider a debenture with £100 face value and a 7.25 per cent coupon rate. The debenture pays interest annually and it matures in eight years. If the required rate of return is 7.25 per cent, then its market price would be £100 (remember that when a debenture's coupon rate equals the investors' required rate of return, the debenture's price will be equal to its par value). Assume that the yield on comparable debentures (that is, debentures with comparable quality and maturity) rises to 10 per cent. Then the demand for the 7.25 coupon debenture will decline and as a consequence its price will drop until it becomes £85.33 (that is, the price of the debenture for a 10 per cent required rate of return). Duration can be considered as a measure of interest rate risk (duration is discussed later in the chapter).

Maturity risk

Maturity risk arises from investing in long-term debentures because long-term debenture are more price sensitive to a given interest rate rise than are short-term debentures. This situation results in a maturity premium risk to compensate for the additional risk involved. To illustrate, assume that a debenture bears a 7.25 per cent coupon rate, pays annual interest, has 15 years remaining to maturity and a face value of £100. If the investors' required rate of return on this debenture is 7.25 per cent, then the market price of the debenture would be £100. Consider an investor who buys the debenture for £100. Assume that the required rate of return will remain the same over the next year. In this case, selling the debenture for £100 will result in a zero return from capital. If the market interest rate rises to 10 per cent over the next year, the market price of the debenture will be £79.74 (note that we have 14 years to maturity). Thus, the investor will realize a capital loss of £20.26 from selling the debenture.

On the other hand, assume that the debenture is purchased again at £100, and it has only three years to maturity. If the market interest rate increases to 10 per cent over the next year, then the market price of the debenture will be £95.23 (note that we have two years to maturity) and the capital loss from selling the debenture will be £4.77.

Default risk

This arises when the borrower is unable to pay the periodic interest payments or repay the par value of the debenture on schedule. The default risk premium of a debenture can be calculated as the difference between promised yield and expected yield (the promised yield is another name for the redemption yield which is calculated by using the (promised) payments of the debenture). The debenture's expected yield is equal to the yield of a default-free debt security (having similar maturity and coupon rate as the debenture) plus a risk premium. The latter reflects risks, such as liquidity risk, over and above the yield of the default-free debt security. For example, assume that a debenture promises a yield of 10 per cent, but there is some probability that the borrower will be unable to make all coupon payments as promised. We also assume that the debenture's expected yield is 8.5 per cent and the yield on a default-free debt security with similar maturity to that of the debenture is 7.5 per cent. The difference between the expected yield and the yield on the default-free debt security is 1 per cent. The default premium is 1.5 per cent (that is, 10.0 per cent −8.5 per cent). The larger the uncertainty about default, the higher the interest rate lenders require.

Liquidity risk

Liquid assets are those assets that can be quickly converted into cash (for example, the shares and debentures of large companies). Liquidity risk arises from investing in less liquid debentures. For example, assume you own a debenture which cannot be sold quickly. If you decide to sell your debenture, you may receive less than you expected due to the lack of liquidity.

Reinvestment rate risk

It arises from the uncertainty about the return investors will be able to obtain when their debentures mature and funds are reinvested. For example, assume that an investor with a ten-year holding period purchases a debenture maturing in four years from today. In this case, the investor does not know what interest rates will be in four years from now and thus there is an uncertainty associated with the return he or she will be able to realize upon reinvestment. The greater the investors' uncertainty, the higher will be the premium.

The term structure of interest rates

The relationship at any point in time between the redemption yields and the term to maturity of debt securities (for example, debentures, government securities, and so on), that are alike with respect to other attributes, is called the term structure of interest rates. A graphical representation of the term structure of interest rates is called a yield curve. Yield curves are depicted for debt securities of similar risk of default (for example, government securities). The yield curve changes daily with the redemption yields and for a given day it provides an estimate of that day's term structure of interest rates. The term structure of interest rates can be used by a firm's financial director who has to decide whether to finance the firm's operations by employing short-term or long-term debt. The yield curve could follow several patterns including the following:

- Upward sloping yield curve It shows that yields right now on short-term securities are lower than yields right now on long-term securities.
- Downward sloping yield curve It shows that yields right now on short-term securities are higher than yields right now on long-term securities.
- Flat yield curve It shows that yields right now on short-term securities are equal to yields right now on long-term securities.

The yield curve is very useful for market analysis. First, it indicates the current conditions in financial markets. Second, it reveals the beliefs of market participants about future interest rates. For example, an upward sloping yield curve indicates that investors in aggregate currently believe that interest rates will rise in the future. As a consequence, use long-term financing now to avoid higher costs later. On the other hand, a downward sloping curve reveals that investors in aggregate currently feel that interest rates will fall in the future. Therefore, you can borrow short-term in anticipation of refinancing at lower costs when interest rates fall.

Example 12.1 Yield curves for government securities

Figures 12.2 and 12.3 present yield curves for UK Government securities on two different dates (*source: Financial Times*, 1 February 1983 and 17 November 1989). The yield curve shown in Figure 12.2 is upward sloping, whereas the yield curve in Figure 12.3 is downward sloping.

Example 12.2 History of term structure: government securities, January 1981 to December 1990

This example uses the following monthly data (*source: Financial Statistics*, various issues):

1 120 gross redemption yields for short-dated (5 years) British Government securities.

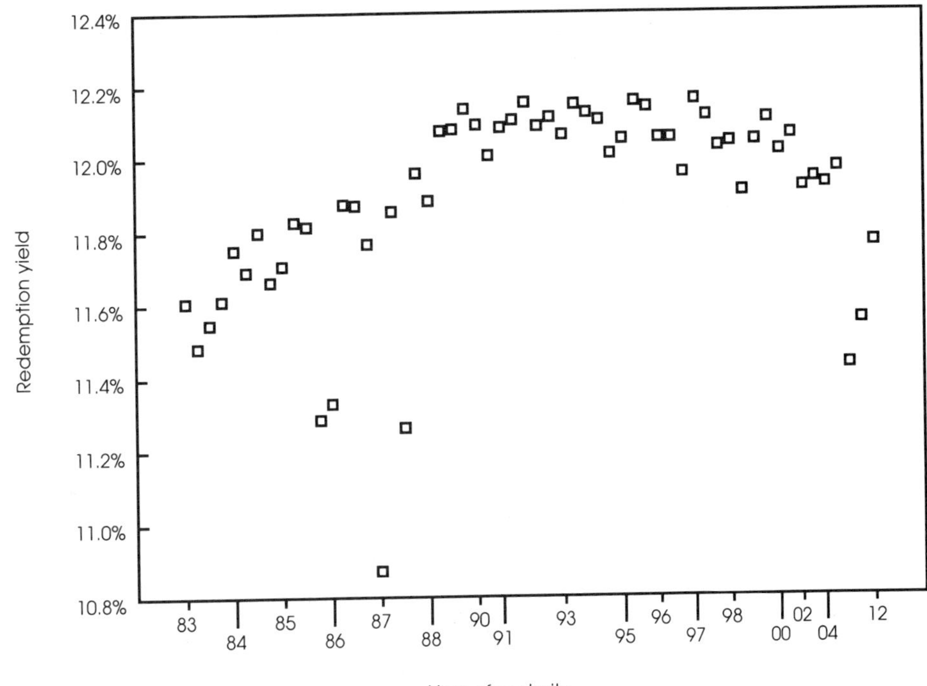

Figure 12.2. Yield curve as of 31 January 1983

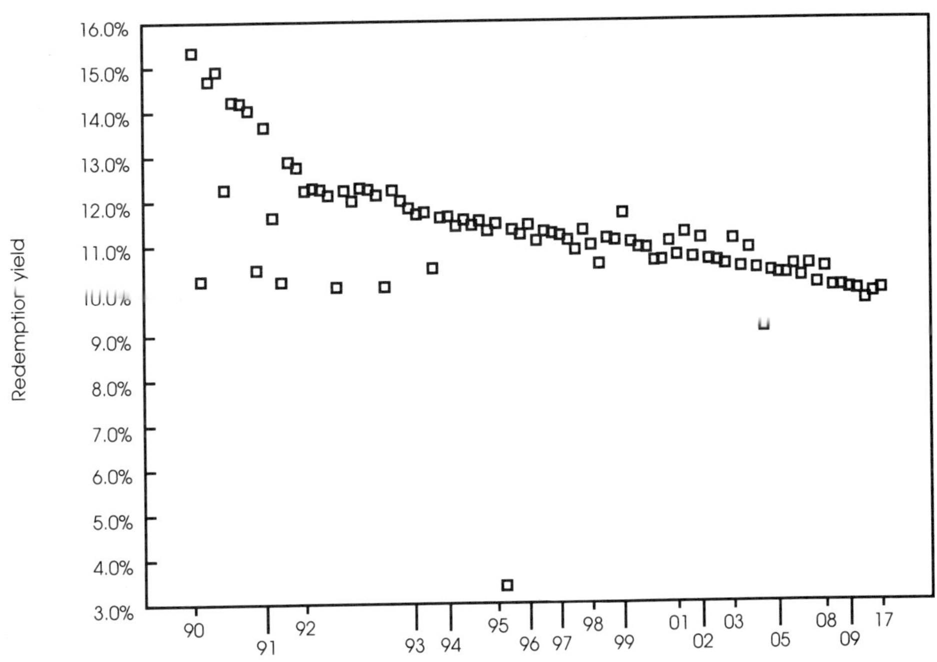

Figure 12.3. Yield curve as of 16 November 1989

2 120 gross redemption yields for medium-dated (10 years) British Government securities.

3 120 gross redemption yields for long-dated (20 years) British Government securities.

Figure 12.4 presents a three-dimensional diagram which plots each of the three times series of yields. In this diagram we are plotting redemption yields vertically and time horizontally.

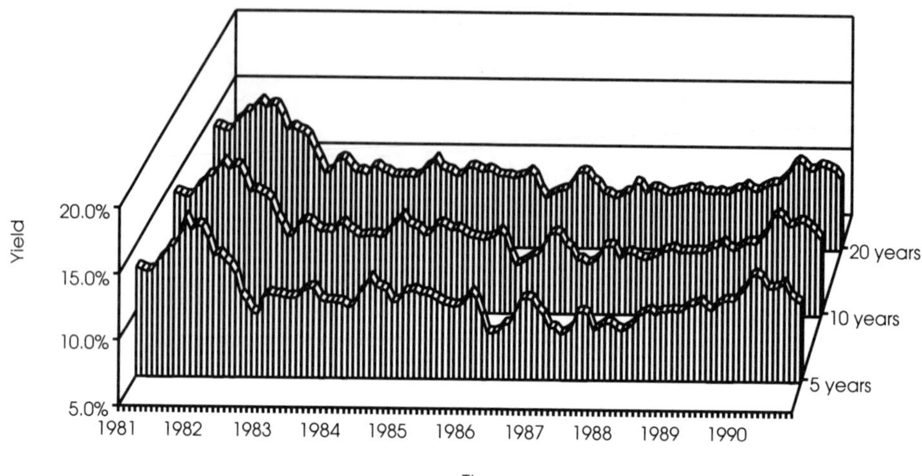

Figure 12.4. British Government securities gross redemption yields

Next we examine our data of yields in order to identify downward sloping or upward sloping yield curves. A comparison of the yields between the short-dated and medium-dated securities reveals that in 58 months out of 120, the yields of the medium-dated securities were higher than the yields of the short-dated securities. Likewise, there were 58 cases in which the yields of the long-dated securities were higher than the yields of the short-dated securities.

Figure 12.4 indicates a close relationship between the yields of short-dated and medium-dated securities as well as a close relationship between the yield of medium-dated and long-dated securities. To examine these relationships we use the `/Data Regression` command of 1-2-3. The results are presented below:

Regression line between short-dated and medium-dated	$-0.0317 + 1.0035\ RY_M$ (49.5)	R-squared $= 0.95$
Regression line between medium-dated and long-dated	$0.5284 + 0.9863\ RY_L$ (74.6)	R-squared $= 0.98$

where

RY_M = the redemption yield on medium-dated securities.

RY_L = the redemption yield on long-dated securities.

t-statistics are included in parentheses.

The regression results indicate strong relationships between the yields of short-dated and medium-dated securities and between medium-dated and long-dated securities.

Hypotheses of the term structure of interest rates

Three main hypotheses have been developed about the determinants of the shape of the yield curve: the unbiased expectations hypothesis, and liquidity preference hypothesis and the market segmentation hypothesis.

The unbiased expectations hypothesis

This hypothesis was first expressed by Fisher (1896) and further developed by Lutz (1940). The unbiased expectations hypothesis or simply the expectations hypothesis assumes that markets for debt securities have no default risks, no taxes, no transaction costs and operate as though investors were risk neutral. The unbiased expectations hypothesis states:

> *The expected redemption yield of a long-term debt security (for example, a debenture or a government security) is a geometric average of the current short-term yield and future short-term yields expected to prevail over the life of the long-term debt security.*

An illustration of this argument now follows. Consider an investor who wishes to invest the same amount of money in one of the following two investments:

Investment 1 Purchase a three-year debt security (for example, a government security) and hold it to maturity.

Investment 2 Purchase a series of three one-year debt securities (for example, government securities).

The second investment involves the following: purchase currently a one-year debt security and hold it to maturity. When it matures, invest the proceeds in a second one-year debt security and hold it to maturity. When the second one-year debt security matures, invest the proceeds in a third one-year debt security.

Assume that the yield to maturity of the three-year debt security is known with certainty. The yield of the first one-year debt security is presently known, but the yields of the second and third one-year debt securities cannot be presently known with certainty. Assume, however, that the investor can form expectations about these two future yields. Figure 12.5 shows the expected returns related to the investor's existing investment opportunities.

In equilibrium the expected return from the first investment equals that of the second. Therefore, we can write:

Expected return per pound invested in a 3-year debt security	=	Expected return per pound invested in a series of 1-year debt securities over a period of 3 years

$$(1 + R_3)^3 = (1 + R_1)(1 + r_{12})(1 + r_{23})$$

The analysis discussed above can be generalized to a T-year holding period. The general form for the long-term rate can now be stated as follows:

Expected return per pound invested in a T-year debt security	=	Expected return per pound invested in a series of 1-year debt securities over a period of T years

$$(1 + R_T)^T = (1 + R_1)(1 + r_{12})(1 + r_{23}) \ldots (1 + r_{(T-1)T}) \qquad (12.1)$$

Investment 1:		R_3 = the actual yield (or spot rate) of the debt security. This is known at present.		
End of period:	0	1	2	3
Investment 2:	R_1 = the actual yield (or spot rate) from the end of year 0 to the end of year 1. This is known at present.	r_{12} = the expected yield for a one-period load beginning at the end of year 1.	r_{23} = the expected yield for a one period load beginning at the end of year 2.	
Return:		Expected return per pound initially invested:		
		Investment 1: $(1 + R_3)^3$		
		Investment 2: $(1 + R_1)(1 + r_{12})(1 + r_{23})$		

Figure 12.5. The expected returns from two investments in debt securities

Implications of the unbiased expectations theory

Under the expectations hypothesis, securities of different maturity can be considered perfect expected substitutes for one another. An investor is able to realize the same yield for a given holding period, regardless of whether he or she invests in a (long-term) debt security having a life equal to the holding period, or in series of one-year debt securities over the holding period. As a consequence, expectations about future short-term interest rates are utilized to predict long-term redemption yields:

$$R_T = [(1 + R_1)(1 + r_{12})(1 + r_{23}) \ldots (1 + r_{(T-1)T})]^{1/T} - 1$$

In words, the last equation states that the yield to maturity of a long-term debt security is a geometric average of the current short-term yield and the expected yields on a series of short-term debt securities with equal maturity.

Example 12.3 Calculating the three-year yield of a debt security as a geometric average of the yields of three one-year debt securities

Consider an investor who faces the following investment opportunities:

Investment 1 Purchase a three-year debt security and hold it to maturity.
Investment 2 Purchase a series of three one-year debt securities.

The amount the investor wishes to invest is £10,000. Assume that the current rate of the first one-year debt security is 7.50 per cent (this is known at the present time). Additionally, we assume that the expected rate next year of the second one-year debt security is 10 per cent and the expected rate the year after the next year of the third one-year debt security is 11 per cent. That is:

Investment 1:			R_3	
End of period	0	1	2	3
Investment 2:	7.50%	10%	11%	

According to the expectation theory, the market will be in equilibrium if the first investment provides a yield of 9.49 per cent. This yield is calculated as follows:

$$R_3 = [(1 + 0.075)(1 + 0.10)(1 + 0.11)]^{1/3} - 1$$
$$= 9.49 \text{ per cent}$$

In practice, the redemption yield of a long-term debt security cannot be calculated by averaging the current one-year yield and a stream of expected future one-year yields, because the latter cannot be observed in advance. However, there is another use of the expectation hypothesis, namely, the expectations hypothesis' geometric average equation can be employed to provide an estimate of the expected yield of a debt security for one year beginning at the end of year $T - 1$ ($T = 2, 3, 4, \ldots$). Such an estimate can be expressed as:

The expected yield of a debt security for one year beginning at the end of year $T-1$	=	The future value at the end of period T per pound invested in a T-year debt security	÷	The future value at the end of period $T-1$ per pound invested in a $(T-1)$-year debt security	−1

$$r_{(T-1)T} = (1 + R_T)^T \div (1 + R_{T-1})^{T-1} - 1$$

where

R_T = the redemption yield of a T-year debt security
R_{T-1} = the redemption yield of a $(T - 1)$-years debt security.

Thus, the expected yield of a debt security for one year beginning at the end of the year $T - 1$ is related to the currently observed yields on two debt securities having maturities of T and $T - 1$ years, respectively.

Under the unbiased expectation hypothesis, $r_{(T-1)T}$ is the rate investors expect to earn from holding a debt security for one year beginning at the end of year $T - 1$. It is also the implicit forward interest rate (or yield) for one year beginning at the end of year $T - 1$ and is denoted by $f_{(T-1)T}$.

Therefore, if the unbiased expectation theory is correct, forward interest rates must be equal to expected future interest rates, that is:

$$f_{(T-1)T} = r_{(T-1)T}$$

This indicates that forward rates can be used to provide unbiased estimates of expected future redemption yields.

In general, a forward rate is the rate agreed now for lending money for a certain period of time starting at a future date. For example, if an investor makes a commitment now to lend \$90 for one year starting in 12 months and £100 to be repaid at the end of the loan, the forward rate for a one-year loan starting at the end of year 1 is:

$$f_{12} = \frac{£100}{£90} - 1 = 11.11 \text{ per cent}$$

The rate of 11.11 per cent can be thought of as today's estimate of the spot rate for next year. Forward rates are frequently estimated by using the current spot rate over a given maturity and the current spot rate over a longer maturity.

Example 12.4 Calculating one-year forward rates from spot rates

Figure 12.6 shows the redemption yields of 10 debt securities. The first security has term to maturity of 10 years, the second has 9 years, and so on. The one-year forward rate expected to prevail at the beginning of the ninth year is 14.6 per cent. This is calculated as follows:

$$\frac{(1+10.0\%)^\wedge 10}{(1+9.50\%)^\wedge 9} - 1 = (1+\text{B7})^\wedge\text{A7}/(1+\text{B8})^\wedge\text{A8} - 1 = 14.6$$

where ^ stands for 'power of'.

Then the formula stored in cell C7 is copied in the range C8 .. C15 to calculate the remaining one-year forward rates.

	A	B	C	D	E
1		CALCULATING ONE-YEAR FORWARD YIELDS			
2		====================================			
3					
4					
5	YEAR	REDEMPTION YIELD	ONE-YEAR FORWARD YIELD		
6					
7	10	10.0%	14.6%		
8	9	9.5%	11.1%		
9	8	9.3%	10.7%		
10	7	9.1%	10.3%		
11	6	8.9%	10.9%		
12	5	8.5%	9.3%		
13	4	8.3%	9.2%		
14	3	8.0%	8.4%		
15	2	7.8%	8.1%		
16	1	7.5%			
17					

Figure 12.6. Calculating one-year forward rates

Forward rates can also be computed for periods longer than one year. Consider the following two investments:

Investment 1 Purchase a T-year debt security and hold it to maturity.

Investment 2 Hold a $(T-K)$ debt security until it matures, and invest the proceeds at the end of period $T-K$ in a K-year debt security (where K is a positive integer with $K < T$).

The forward rate for K years beginning at the end of year $T-K$ can be calculated by using the following equation:

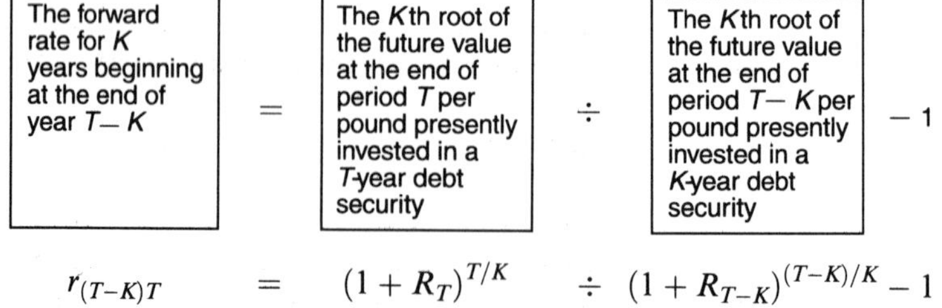

$$r_{(T-K)T} = (1+R_T)^{T/K} \div (1+R_{T-K})^{(T-K)/K} - 1$$

where

R_T = the redemption yield of a T-year debt security.

R_{T-K} = the redemption yield of a $(T-K)$-year debt security.

Example 12.5 Calculating the forward rate for a term longer than one year

Consider an investor who faces the following two investment opportunities:

Investment 1 Purchase a six-year debt security yielding 8.90 per cent and hold it to maturity.

Investment 2 Purchase a four-year debt security yielding 7.80 per cent and hold it to maturity. At the end of year 4 invest the proceeds from the investment in a two-year debt security.

Since $T = 6$ years and $K = 2$ years, $T/K = 3$ and $(T-K)/K = 2$. The Kth root of the future value at the end of year 6 per pound presently invested in the six-year debt security is calculated as follows:

$(1 + 0.089)\hat{}3 = £1.291$

The Kth root of the future value at the end of year 4 per pound presently invested in the two-year debt security is calculated as follows:

$(1 + 0.078)\hat{}2 = £1.162$

Therefore, the two-year forward rate beginning at the end of the fourth year would be

$T_{46} = £1.291/£1.162 - 1 = 11.1$ per cent

Example 12.6 Term structure of interest rates under the unbiased expectations hypothesis

Figure 12.7 shows two series of the expected one-period yields over a period of 10 years. The value stored in cell D10 is calculated as follows:

$(C9 * C10)\hat{}(1/A10) - 1 = ((1.030)(1.060))\hat{}(1/2) - 1 = 4.49$ per cent

We calculate the value stored in cell D11 as shown below

$((1 + D10)\hat{}\$A\$10 * C11)\hat{}(1/\$A\$11) - 1$

$= (((1 + 4.49\%)\hat{}2)(1.065))\hat{}(1/3) - 1 = 5.16$ per cent

The contents of the cell D11 are copied in the range D12..D18. Likewise, the value stored in cells G10 and G11 are calculated as follows:

$(F9 * F10)\hat{}(1/A10) - 1 = (1.120 * 1.107)\hat{}(1/2) - 1 = 11.35$ per cent

$((1 + G10)\hat{}A10 * F11)\hat{}(1/A11) - 1 = (((1 + 11.35\%)\hat{}2)(1.094))\hat{}(1/3) - 1$

$= 10.69$ per cent

The two yield curves under the unbiased expectations hypothesis are shown in Figure 12.8.

	A	B	C	D	E	F	G
1	CALCULATING THE YIELD CURVE USING THE UNBIASED EXPECTATION HYPOTHESIS						
2	=======						
3							
4	-------						
5	PERIOD	EXPECTED	(1+RATE)	REDEMPTION	EXPECTED	(1+RATE)	REDEMPTION
6		ONE-PERIOD		YIELD	ONE-PERIOD		YIELD
7		YIELDS			YIELDS		
8	-------						
9	1	3.00%	1.030	3.00%	12.00%	1.120	12.00%
10	2	6.00%	1.060	4.49%	10.70%	1.107	11.35%
11	3	6.50%	1.065	5.16%	9.40%	1.094	10.69%
12	4	7.10%	1.071	5.64%	8.10%	1.081	10.04%
13	5	7.90%	1.079	6.09%	6.80%	1.068	9.38%
14	6	8.50%	1.085	6.49%	5.50%	1.055	8.73%
15	7	9.00%	1.090	6.84%	4.20%	1.042	8.07%
16	8	9.60%	1.096	7.18%	2.90%	1.029	7.41%
17	9	9.60%	1.096	7.45%	1.60%	1.016	6.75%
18	10	9.60%	1.096	7.66%	0.30%	1.003	6.08%
19	-------						

Figure 12.7. Redemption yields under the unbiased expectations hypothesis

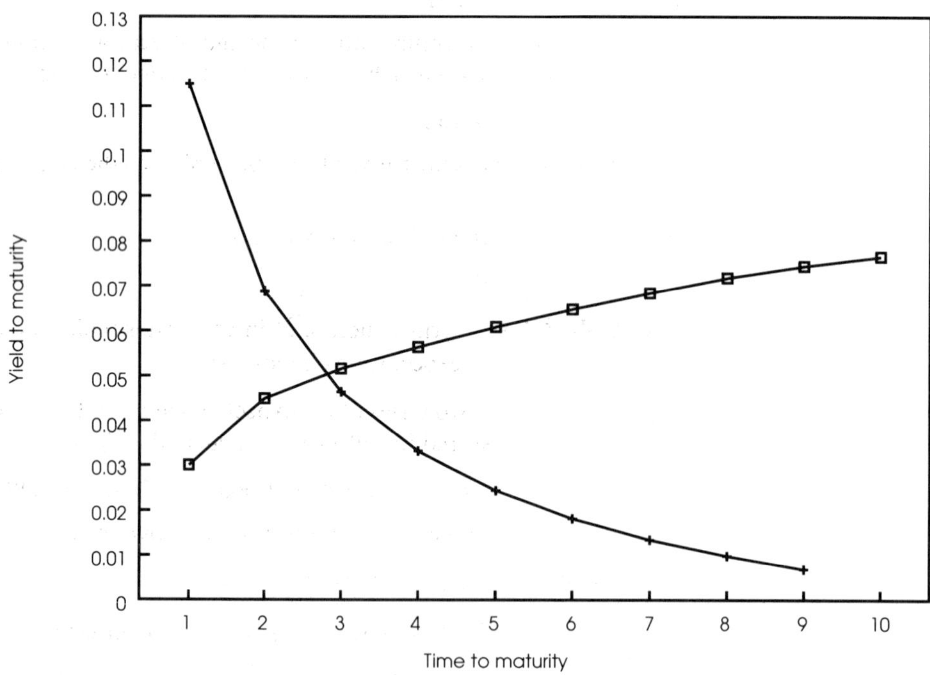

Figure 12.8. Yield curves under the unbiased expectations hypothesis

A strict version of the unbiased expectations hypothesis asserts that current and expected future yields are dependent on expectations about future rates of inflation. Therefore, lenders require an inflation premium sufficient to offset the uncertainty about future inflation.

The liquidity preference hypothesis

The liquidity preference hypothesis (or the liquidity premium hypothesis) modifies the unbiased expectation hypothesis by introducing risk aversion towards longer lengths of lending time. The liquidity expectation hypothesis was developed by Hicks (1946) and it asserts:

> *Risk-averse lenders prefer to make short-term loans and risk-averse borrowers prefer to obtain long-term debts. Lenders would lend for longer periods of time only if they receive a liquidity premium as a compensation for the risk of lending long.*

From the lender's viewpoint, long-term debt securities are more risky than short-term debt securities since it is more difficult to predict the more distant future. Thus, lenders prefer short-term over long-term debt and are willing to accept lower yields (other things being equal) on short-term debt securities as compared with those of long-term debt securities. On the other hand, borrowers (mainly firms) are said to prefer long-term debt securities to short-term in order to reduce the risk of inability to pay their financial obligations as they come due. As a result, borrowers are willing to pay higher interest rates (other things being equal) for long-term funds as compared with short-term funds. Therefore, the liquidity preference hypothesis asserts that lenders demand an extra return as compensation for bearing the risk of lengthening the maturity of their investment.

According to the liquidity preference theory, the long-term interest rates incorporate both expectations about future short-term interest rates and liquidity premiums. The forward rates can be expressed as:

$$f_{(T-1)T} = r_{(T-1)T} + L_{(T-1)T} \tag{12.2}$$

where

$T = 2, 3, \ldots$

$r_{(T-1)T}$ = the expected yield for one year beginning at the end of year $T - 1$.

$L_{(T-1)T}$ = the liquidity premium for the period from the end of year $T - 1$ to the end of year T

Using Equations (12.1) and (12.2) we calculate the T-year rate as follows:

$$R_T = [(1 + R_1)(1 + r_{12} + L_{12})(1 + r_{23} + L_{23}) \ldots (1 + r_{(T-1)T} + L_{(T-1)T})]^{1/T} - 1$$

Under the liquidity preference hypothesis, investors form expectations of future rates but they are uncertain about what rates they will actually realize; as a result, they believe that forward future rates may be above their current expectations of future interest rates. Thus in view of the liquidity preference hypothesis, forward rates overestimate the (expected) spot rates.

Assume that investors in aggregate expect future short-term interest rates to be equal to the current short-term interest rate. Then the yield curve would be upward sloping due to the presence of liquidity premiums. When investors in aggregate expect increases in interest rates, liquidity premiums will accentuate the upward slope of the yield curve.

Example 12.7 Term structure of interest rates under the liquidity preference hypothesis

Under the liquidity preference hypothesis, the actual yield is calculated by adding the liquidity premium to the expected yield (see Figure 12.7). Figure 12.9

	A	B	C	D	E	F	G
1	CALCULATING THE YIELD CURVE USING THE LIQUIDITY PREFERENCE HYPOTHESIS						
2							
3							
4							
5	PERIOD	EXPECTED	(1+RATE)	REDEMPTION	LIQUIDITY	(1+RATE	REDEMPTION
6		ONE-PERIOD		YIELD	PREMIUM	+PREMIUM)	YIELD
7		RATE					
8							
9	1	3.00%	1.030	3.00%	0.00%	1.030	3.00%
10	2	6.00%	1.060	4.49%	0.30%	1.063	4.64%
11	3	6.50%	1.065	5.16%	0.45%	1.070	5.40%
12	4	7.10%	1.071	5.64%	0.60%	1.077	5.97%
13	5	7.90%	1.079	6.09%	0.75%	1.087	6.50%
14	6	8.50%	1.085	6.49%	0.90%	1.094	6.98%
15	7	9.00%	1.090	6.84%	1.05%	1.101	7.41%
16	8	9.60%	1.096	7.18%	1.20%	1.108	7.83%
17	9	9.60%	1.096	7.45%	1.35%	1.110	8.17%
18	10	9.60%	1.096	7.66%	1.50%	1.111	8.46%
19							

Figure 12.9. Redemption yields under the liquidity preference hypothesis

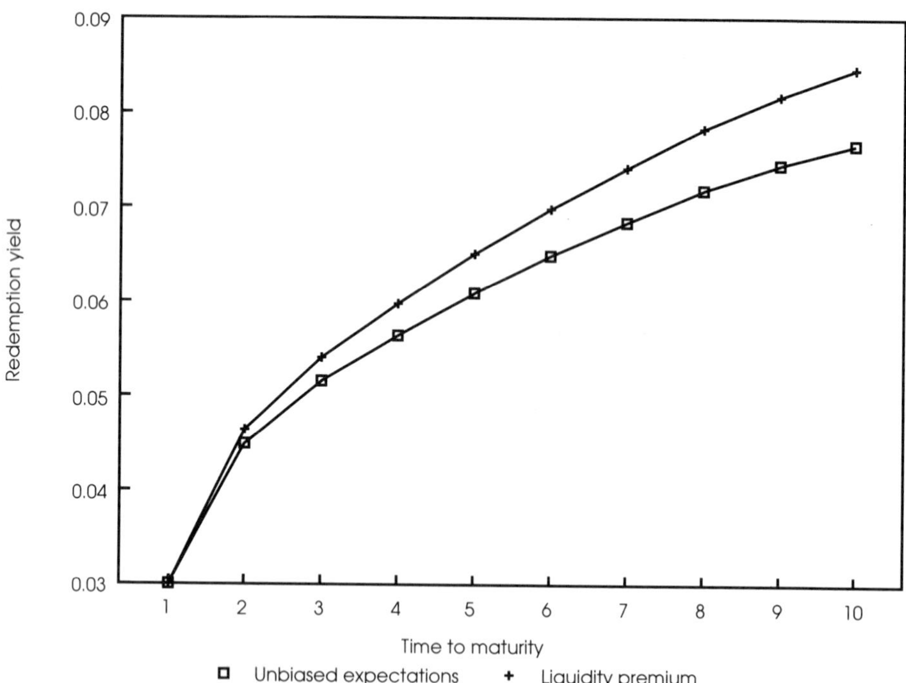

Figure 12.10. Yield curves without and with liquidity

presents the results. From Figure 12.10 we see that the yield curve with liquidity premiums is above the yield curve implied by the unbiased expectations hypothesis.

The market segmentation hypothesis

This hypothesis was introduced by Culbertson (1957) and Walker (1954) and emphasizes that investors are risk averse and operate only in their preferred ranges of maturities; for example, some lenders prefer to lend their funds on a short-term basis, while others prefer to invest their funds on a long-term basis. The market segmentation hypothesis asserts:

> *Lenders strongly prefer to invest in assets with maturities matching to some extent their liabilities and borrowers strongly prefer to issue liabilities with maturities matching to some extent their assets.*

The market segmentation hypothesis suggests that each maturity constitutes a separate market (that is, a segment) for debt securities, because of either individual preferences or institutional pressures. For example, an investor with an amount of £20,000 which is not required for five years would invest in debt securities maturing in five years. Commercial banks demand debt securities with short to medium maturities, because their liabilities are mostly short- to medium-term deposits. Other institutions such as insurance companies with long-term liabilities (that is, their life insurance policies) will prefer to buy long-term debt securities to ensure that they have sufficient funds to meet their insurance payments in the distant future. A firm should also prefer to match its liabilities with the maturities of its investments. If the firm's investments are long term, then it should be expected to finance them using long-term debt securities (for example, debentures).

By matching the maturity of assets with that of liabilities you avoid some risk. For example, assume that a firm must make an investment with a useful life of 25 years. If this investment is financed with debt securities which mature in 15 years, the firm is presently uncertain about the rate of interest it will pay to refinance its investment opportunities after the maturity of its debt securities. On the other hand, if the firm's investment is financed with debt securities which mature beyond 25 years, the firm is presently uncertain about the market price of the debt securities at the end of year 25 (assume that the firm will try to repurchase the debt securities at the end of year 25). In this case, the firm incurs a risk of paying a high price for the principal amount borrowed. The market segmentation hypothesis argues that both of these types of risk should be taken into account and it suggests that investors should match a liability with an asset of equal life span, and vice versa.

With the market segmentation theory, investors do not deviate from their preferences for particular ranges of maturities irrespective how attractive are the yields offered on other maturities. Therefore, yields would be determined solely by the interaction of supply and demand within each of the segmented markets. As a result, there is relatively little substitution between debt securities of different maturities.

Depending on the demand and supply conditions for debt securities in each segmented market, the yields of short-term debt securities may be lower or higher than those of long-term debt securities. If the yield at the interaction between the supply and demand curves for the short-term funds is lower than the yield at the interaction between the supply and demand curves for the long-term funds, then the yield curve is upward sloping. On the other hand, if the yield at the interaction between the supply and demand curves for the short term-funds is higher than the yield at the interaction between the supply and demand curves for the long-term funds, then the result is a downward sloping curve.

Example 12.8 The yield curve under the market segmentation hypothesis

Figure 12.11 presents the yield curve according to the market segmentation hypothesis. The yield curve is divided into two segments: a segment

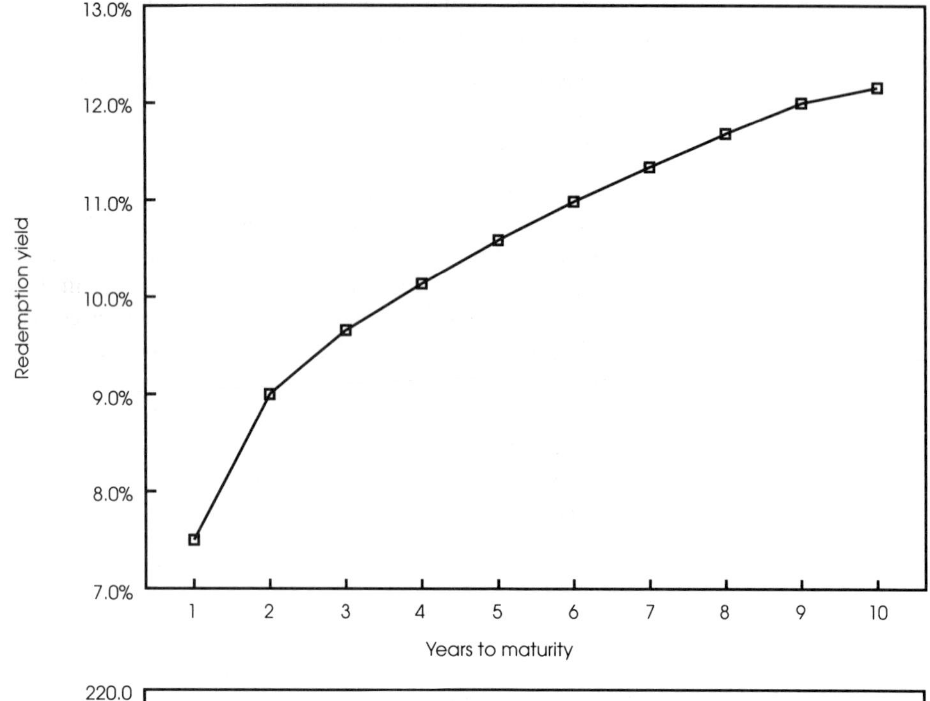

Figure 12.11. (a) Yield curve showing years to maturity

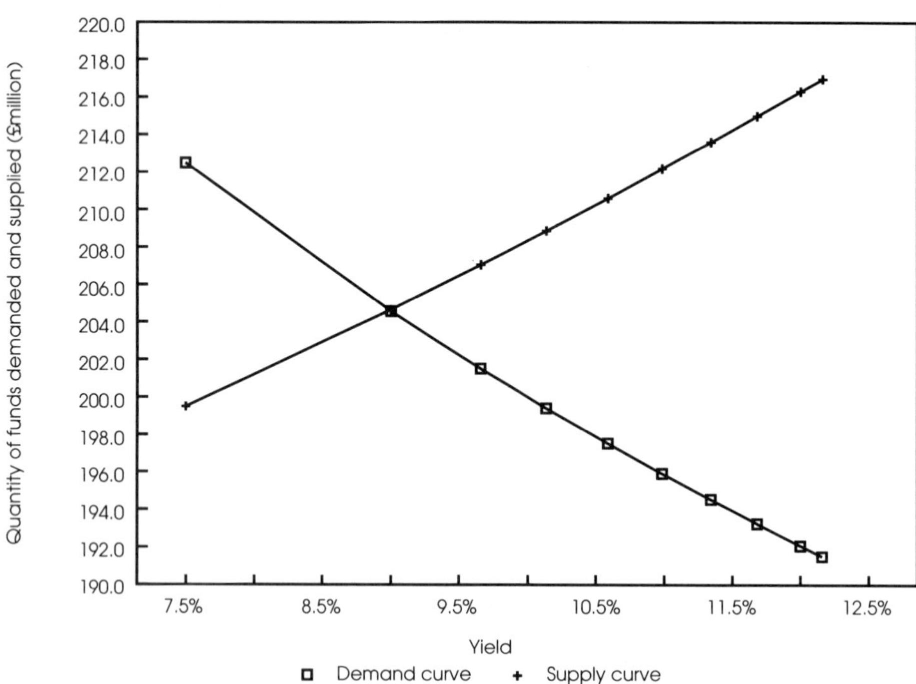

Figure 12.11. (b) Demand and supply for short-term funds

corresponding to short-term funds available for loans and a segment corresponding to long-term funds. Each segment is associated with a schedule of supply and demand for funds. The suppliers of these funds are those parties who invest in securities (for example, debenture holders), whereas the demanders

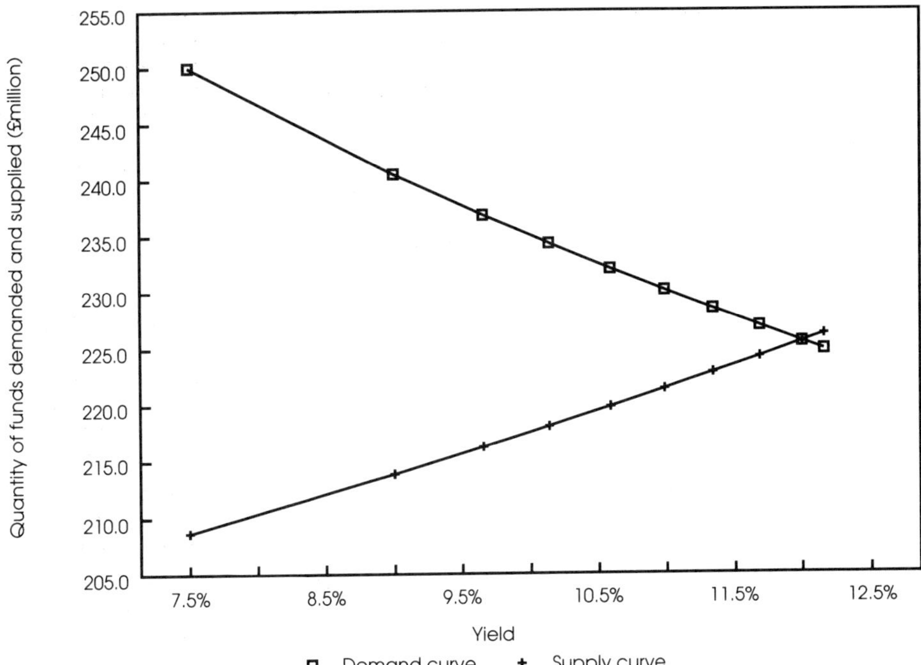

Figure 12.11. (c) Demand and supply for long-term funds

of these funds are those who issue the securities (for example, firms). For each segment, the yield is determined by the intersection of supply and demand.

In addition to the investors' preference, the market segmentation theory also considers other factors which may affect the shape of the yield curve including institutional pressures and government policies. For example, if insurance companies deposit a large quantity of funds into commercial banks, then it will be an upward pressure on the long-term interest rates and downward pressure on the short-term interest rates. In addition, an increase in the borrowing requirements of the public sector can result in an increase in the long-term interest rates.

The preferred habitat hypothesis was introduced by Modigliani and Sutch (1966) and provides a more moderate version of the market segmentation hypothesis. According to the preferred habitat hypothesis, investors adjust their preference maturity ranges only if significant premiums are offered from securities of other maturities. Such premiums derive from maturity ranges where there is insufficient demand. For example, if the supply of long-term debt securities is much higher than the demand for these securities, a premium will exist on long-term debt securities. In general, the premium can be positive or negative and this is illustrated in the discussion that follows. Consider an investor who faces two investment opportunities:

Investment 1 Purchase a two-year debt security and hold it to maturity.
Investment 2 Purchase two one-year debt securities.

The second investment is concerned with the following procedure: purchase currently a one-year debt security and hold it to maturity, then reinvest the proceeds in a second one-year debt security and hold it to maturity. The unbiased expectations hypothesis

	Unbiased expectations hypothesis	Liquidity preference hypothesis	Market segmentation hypothesis
Argument	Any long-term expected yield is a geometric average of the relevant future short-term yields	Risk averse lenders prefer to make short-term investments. Consequently, lenders can be induced to lend for longer periods only by receiving a compensation for the extra risk involved in long-term lending	Lenders strongly prefer to invest in assets with maturities matching their liabilities and borrowers prefer strongly to issue liabilities with maturities matching their assets
Risk	Does not consider a liquidity premium	Considers a liquidity premium which is positive	Premiums can be positive or negative
Maturity	It assumes that investors are indifferent to maturity	The risk premium on short-term debt securities is dependent of the maturity length; the longer the maturity, the higher the premium	It asserts that investors have maturity preferences
Substitutability	Securities of different maturity are perfect expected substitutes for one another (ignoring transaction costs)	Short- and long-term debt securities are imperfect substitutes	There is relatively little substitution between debt securities of different maturities
Determinants of interest rates	The investors' expectations of short-term interest rates	Interest rates expectations and liquidity risk premiums	The supply and demand conditions within a segmented market

Figure 12.12. Comparing three hypotheses attempting to explain the term structure of interest rates

uses the following relationship:

$$(1 + R_2)^2 = (1 + R_1)(1 + r_{12})$$

The preferred habitat hypothesis suggests that investors will shift from one maturity to another in their borrowing or lending activities only if significant premiums are offered. Suppose that the market is dominated by investors who prefer a one-year time horizon. In order to entice investors to purchase the two-year debt security, a positive premium must be offered. This results in the following relationship:

$$(1 + R_2)^2 = (1 + R_1)(1 + r_{12} + L_{12}) \quad \text{where} \quad L_{12} > 0$$

The last equation can also result from the liquidity preference hypothesis. Suppose that the market is dominated by investors who prefer a two-year time horizon. The investors will be willing to purchase one-year debt securities if these are offered at a (negative) premium. As a consequence, the following relationship exists:

$$(1 + R_2)^2 = (1 + R_1)(1 + r_{12} + L_{12}) \quad \text{where} \quad L_{12} < 0$$

Figure 12.12 compares the three hypotheses proposed to explain the shape of the yield curve.

Duration

Duration accounts for both the size of a debenture's cash flows and the time period they are paid. Figure 12.13 summarizes the concept of the duration of a debenture.

Definition Duration is a measure of the average length of time of the stream of payments generated by a debenture.

Calculation One method of calculating duration is as follows: a debenture's duration is a weighted average of the time periods to maturity, where the weights for each period are equal to the present values of the cash flows from the debenture in each time period divided by the current price of the debenture. The present value of the debenture's time-weighted cash flow is given by:

Present value of a debenture's time-weighted cash flows	=	Present value of the time-weighted interest payments	+	Present value of the time-weighted principal payable at maturity

$$\text{PV}(T) = \sum_{t=1}^{T} \frac{t, I}{(1 + r_d)^t} + \frac{TB_T}{(1 + r_d)^T}$$

where

r_d = the investors' required rate of return on the debenture.

The duration is defined as follows:

$$D = \frac{\text{PV}(T)}{V_d}$$

where

PV_d = the current market price of the debenture (that is, the present value of the series of the debenture's interest and principal payments)

Interpretation The duration of a debenture measures the average length of time until all interest payments and principal are recovered. The longer the duration of a debenture, the longer average time is taken to receive the cash flows from the debenture.

Figure 12.13. Summarizing the concept of a debenture's duration

Example 12.9 Calculating the durations of two debentures

Consider two debentures, one with a coupon rate of 7.25 per cent and one with a coupon rate of 10 per cent. Each debenture will mature in eight years. The investors' required rate of return applicable to the first debenture is 10 per cent and the investors' required rate of return for the second debenture is 12 per cent. Figure 12.14 calculates the duration for each debenture. The time-weighted cash flows are generated by multiplying the (ordinary) cash flows by their corresponding time. The latter is measured in years. The duration is calculated by dividing the present value of a debenture's time-weighted cash flows by its current market price (that is, the present value of the series of the debenture's interest and principal payments). For example, the duration for the first debenture is calculated as follows (see displayed number in cell C20):

```
@NPV(C5,C11..C18)/B20
```

where B20 contains the present value of the debenture at 10 per cent.

	A	B	C	D	E	F	G
1		CALCULATING THE DURATIONS OF TWO DEBENTURES					
2		==					
3	Coupon Rate		7.25%	Coupon Rate			10.00%
4	Par Value		£100	Par Value			£100
5	Required Rate of Return		10.00%	Required Rate of Return			12%
6							
7							
8		Cash Flows:			Cash Flows:		
9	Year	Ordinary	Time-Weighted	Ordinary		Time-Weighted	
10							
11	1	£7.25	£7.25		£10.00	£10.00	
12	2	7.25	14.50		10.00	20.00	
13	3	7.25	21.75		10.00	30.00	
14	4	7.25	29.00		10.00	40.00	
15	5	7.25	36.25		10.00	50.00	
16	6	7.25	43.50		10.00	60.00	
17	7	7.25	50.75		10.00	70.00	
18	8	107.25	858.00		110.00	880.00	
19							
20		85.33	6.19		90.06	5.75	

Figure 12.14. Illustrating the calculation of the durations of two debentures

The duration for the 7.25 per cent coupon debenture is 6.19 years indicating that the average time taken to receive the cash flows on this debenture is 6.19 years. Similarly, the average time required to receive the cash flows on the 10 per cent coupon debenture is 5.75 years. For the smaller coupon debenture, the present value of its first year's payment represents 7.72 per cent of the total present value of £85.33 (that is, the one-year present value of £7.25 is £6.59, thus £6.59/£85.33 = 7.72 per cent). On the other hand, the corresponding proportion for the 10 per cent coupon debenture is 9.91 per cent. Thus, the duration of the 7.25 per cent coupon debenture is longer than that of the 10 per cent coupon debenture.

Problems

1. Set up the worksheet shown in Figure 12.14.
2. Consider a third debenture with the following information:
   Coupon rate: 11 per cent
   Required rate of return: 13 per cent
   Years to maturity: 8
   Par value: £100
   Calculate its duration. Compare its duration with those shown in Figure 12.14. What do you observe?

Properties of duration

Duration has several properties including the following:

- The duration of a zero coupon debenture (or bond) is equal to the original life of the debenture expressed in years, because for $I = 0$ there is only one cash flow which occurs at the maturity of the debenture. The duration of a debenture is always less than (or equal to) the term to maturity (expressed in years), because of the low contribution of the early cash flows to duration.

Sensitivity of duration to changes in redemption yield and coupon rate

Duration is affected by changes in the required rate of return (or redemption yield), the coupon rate and the number of years to maturity. Specifically, duration decreases as the redemption yield and coupon rate increase (other things remain the same).

Example 12.10 Analysing the impact of changes in the redemption yield and the coupon rate on duration

Consider the 7.25 per cent coupon rate debenture presented in Example 12.9. In the present example we perform a sensitivity analysis of duration with respect to changes in the redemption yield and the coupon rate (other things remain constant). We assume that the redemption yield receives values in the range 6–14 per cent (in steps of 1 per cent) and the coupon rate takes values in the range 7.25–12.25 per cent (in steps of 1 per cent).

The `/Data Table 2` command of 1-2-3 is used to calculate the duration for different values of the redemption yield and the coupon rate (note 'input cell 1' is cell C5 and 'input cell 2' is cell C3). The results show that duration decreases as the yield and the coupon rate increase (Figure 12.15). In general, debentures with smaller coupon rates have longer durations than debentures with higher coupon rates. The results of the sensitivity analysis are illustrated graphically in Figure 12.16.

Sensitivity of duration to changes in term to maturity and coupon rate

If the debenture is selling below par value duration increases at a decreasing rate with the number of years to maturity and then declines at an increasing rate (other things being the same). On the other hand, if the debenture is selling at its par value or above, duration increases at a decreasing rate with the number of years to maturity (other things being constant). In all cases the decline of duration occurs for very large maturities.

Example 12.11 Sensitivity of duration with respect to changes in the number of years to maturity and the coupon rate

Lotus does not provide a direct method for conducting a sensitivity analysis of the net present value of an unequal series of cash flows with respect to the number of years to maturity, because the `@NPV` function does not include the number of years to maturity. Figure 12.17 shows the effect of changes in the number of years to maturity and the coupon rate to duration (the way of conducting such an analysis is discussed in Appendix 12A). From these results it can be seen that long-term debentures have longer durations than short-term debentures (other things remain the same). Note that the slight deviation that occurred between the value stored in cell D15 and the value stored in cell C27 is due to formatting.

	A	B	C	D	E	F	G	H
1		A. CALCULATING THE DURATION FOR A DEBENTURE						
2		==						
3	Coupon Rate		7.25%					
4	Par Value		£100					
5	Required Rate of Ret		10.00%					
6								
7	--							
8		Cash Flows:						
9	Year	Ordinary	Time-Weighted					
10	--							
11	1	7.25	7.25					
12	2	7.25	14.50					
13	3	7.25	21.75					
14	4	7.25	29.00					
15	5	7.25	36.25					
16	6	7.25	43.50					
17	7	7.25	50.75					
18	8	107.25	858.00					
19		----------------------						
20		85.329	6.19					
21								
22								
23		B. YIELD,COUPON RATE AND DURATION SENSITIVITY						
24		==						
25								
26	--							
27					COUPON RATE			
28								
29		+C20	7.25%	8.25%	9.25%	10.25%	11.25%	12.25%
30		6%	6.41	6.29	6.18	6.08	6.00	5.91
31		7%	6.36	6.23	6.12	6.02	5.94	5.85
32		8%	6.30	6.18	6.07	5.97	5.87	5.79
33	REDEMPTION	9%	6.25	6.12	6.01	5.90	5.81	5.73
34	YIELD	10%	6.19	6.06	5.95	5.84	5.75	5.67
35		11%	6.13	6.00	5.89	5.78	5.69	5.61
36		12%	6.07	5.94	5.82	5.72	5.63	5.54
37		13%	6.01	5.88	5.76	5.66	5.57	5.48
38		14%	5.96	5.82	5.70	5.60	5.50	5.42
39	--							

Figure 12.15. Assessing the effect of changes in the redemption yield and coupon rate on duration

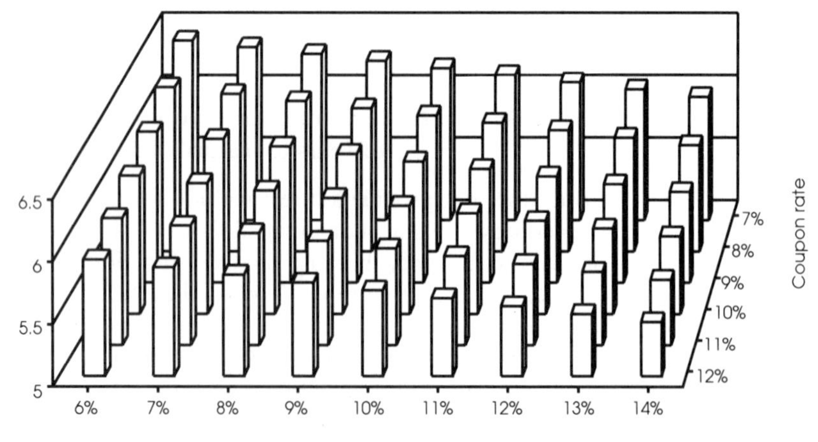

Figure 12.16. Sensitivity of duration with respect to redemption yield and coupon rate (eights years to maturity)

```
       A         B          C          D          E          F          G
 1 A. CALCULATING THE DURATION FOR A DEBENTURE
 2 ===========================================
 3 Coupon Rate                     7.25%
 4 Par Value                        £100
 5 Required Rate of Return        10.00%
 6 Years to Maturity                   8
 7
 8 Current Market Price           £85.33
 9 1st Term                         5.87
10 2nd Term                        -3.73
11 3rd Term                        56.62
12 4th Term                       -51.48
13 Time-Weighted Present Value    528.09
14                             ---------
15 Duration                         6.19
16                             =========
17
18
19
20
21 B. SENSITIVITY BETWEEN DURATION,MATURITY AND COUPON RATE
22 ========================================================
23
24 ---------------------------------------------------------------------
25                                        COUPON RATE
26           +D15           7.25%      8.25%      9.25%     10.25%     11.25%
27                   8     6.1889     6.0604     5.9461     5.8439     5.7519
28                  18     9.5950     9.3515     9.1506     8.9820     8.8385
29                  28    10.6925    10.4947    10.3365    10.2071    10.0993
30 YEARS TO         38    10.9799    10.8598    10.7650    10.6881    10.6246
31 MATURITY         48    11.0312    10.9676    10.9176    10.8773    10.8441
32                  58    11.0271    10.9959    10.9714    10.9517    10.9355
33                  68    11.0163    11.0017    10.9902    10.9810    10.9734
34                  78    11.0085    11.0019    10.9967    10.9925    10.9891
35                  88    11.0041    11.0012    10.9989    10.9971    10.9955
36                  98    11.0019    11.0007    10.9997    10.9988    10.9982
37                 108    11.0009    11.0003    10.9999    10.9995    10.9993
38                 118    11.0004    11.0002    11.0000    10.9998    10.9997
39                 128    11.0002    11.0001    11.0000    10.9999    10.9999
40                 138    11.0001    11.0000    11.0000    11.0000    11.0000
41                 148    11.0000    11.0000    11.0000    11.0000    11.0000
42                 158    11.0000    11.0000    11.0000    11.0000    11.0000
43                 168    11.0000    11.0000    11.0000    11.0000    11.0000
44 ---------------------------------------------------------------------
```

Figure 12.17. Sensitivity of duration to changes in maturity and coupon rate

The sensitivity results which are illustrated graphically in Figure 12.18 reveal that the duration increases at a decreasing rate with the time to maturity and in some cases it declines with maturity (other things being the same). The latter, however, occurs when maturity is many years ahead.

Debenture volatility and duration

Debenture volatility is defined as the absolute value of the proportional change in the price of a debenture in response to a given change in the redemption yield. Debenture volatility can be expressed as:

$$\text{Vol}(CR\%, R\%, T) = \left[\frac{\Delta V_d / V_d}{\Delta r_d}\right]$$

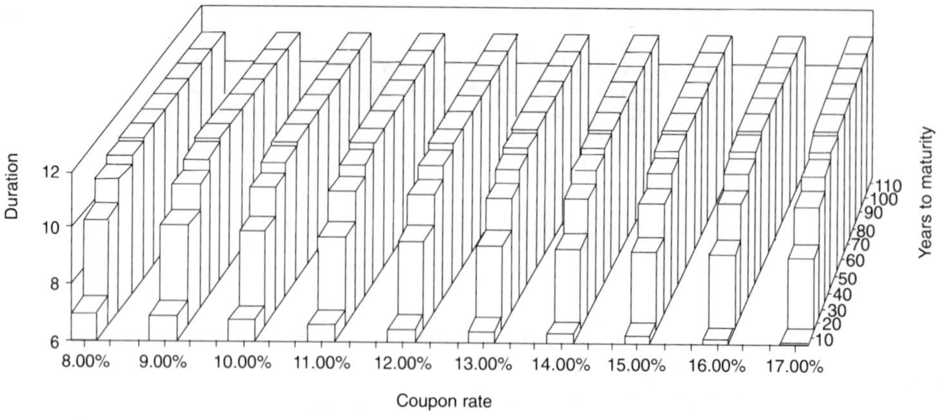

Figure 12.18. Sensitivity of duration to coupon rate and years to maturity changes

where

$\text{Vol}(CR\%, R\%, T) =$ the volatility of a debenture having a coupon rate of CR per cent, a redemption yield of R per cent, and T years to maturity.

$\Delta V_p / V_p =$ percentage change in price.

$\Delta r_d =$ the change in redemption yield.

$\Delta =$ means 'a change in'

Duration is a measure of the sensitivity of the price of the debt security to changes in the redemption yield used to discount the cash flows of the debt security. Therefore, duration can be used to assess the debenture's interest rate risk. The longer the duration of a debenture, the more sensitive its price to changes in yields (other things being the same). The duration can be expressed as:

Duration	= −	The percentage change in the price of the debenture	÷	The percentage change in 1 plus the redemption yield

$$D = -\frac{\Delta V_d}{V_d} \div \frac{\Delta(1 + r_d)}{(1 + r_d)}$$

By combining the price volatility equation discussed earlier and the last equation, we can express the price volatility as follows:

$$\text{Vol}(CR\%, R\%, T) \approx \frac{D}{1 + r_d}$$

In words, the price volatility of a debenture is approximately equal to the duration divided by 1 plus the redemption yield.

Example 12.12 Calculating a debenture's volatility

Consider the two debentures given in Example 12.9 and assume a 1 per cent change in interest rates. The price volatility of the 7.25 per cent coupon debenture is calculated as follows:

$$\text{Vol}(7.25\%,\ 10\%,\ 8) \approx \frac{6.19}{1+0.10} = 5.63$$

Thus, if the yield increases by 1 per cent, we would expect a 5.63 per cent decrease in the debenture price.

Similarly, the price volatility of the 12 per cent coupon rate debenture is given by:

$$\text{Vol}(10\%,\ 12\%,\ 8) \approx \frac{5.75}{1+0.12} = 5.13$$

These results indicate that the 7.25 per cent coupon debenture is more price sensitive than the 10 per cent coupon debenture to a given change in the redemption yield.

Figure 12.19 plots the sensitivity of volatility with respect to changes in the number of years to maturity and redemption yield.

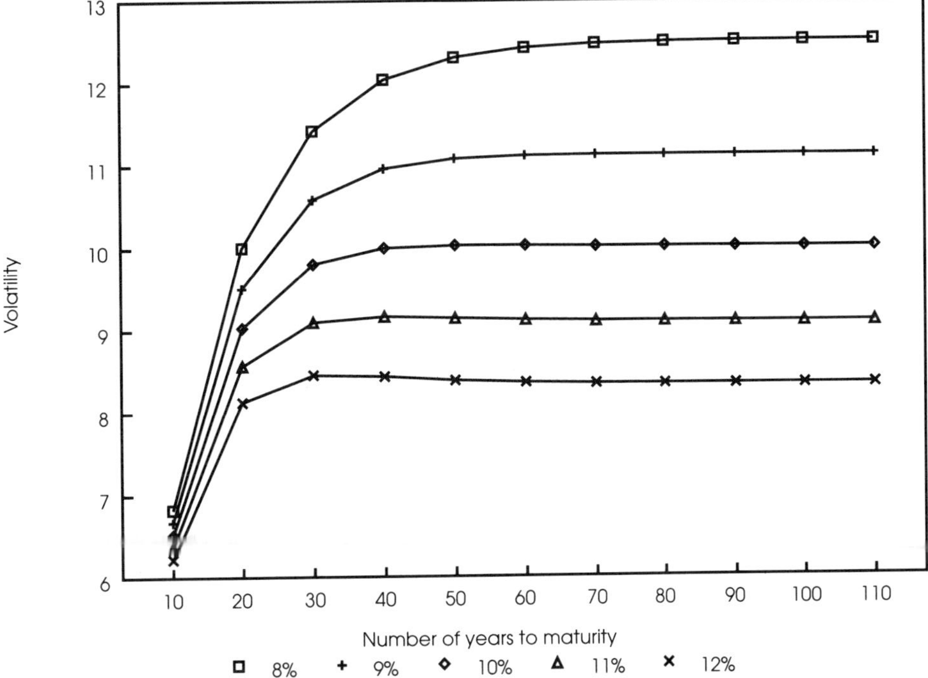

Figure 12.19. Sensitivity of volatility to maturity and redemption yield changes

Summary

1 *Risk of investment in debentures* The investors' required rate of return on a firm's debenture is composed of a riskless return plus a risk premium. The latter reflects the return demanded by investors as compensation for the risk they undertake. The risk premium is a sum of six types of risk: inflation risk, interest rate risk, maturity risk, default risk, liquidity risk and reinvestment risk. Since

each of these types of risk contributes to the total debenture risk, it influences directly the debenture value.

2 *Term structure of interest rates* The term structure of interest rates is the relationship at a point in time between the redemption yields and the time left until maturity for debentures that are alike with respect to all attributes expect that they differ in maturity. Yield curves provide graphical representations of term structure of interest rates. There are several theories attempting to explain the shape of yield curves: (a) the unbiased expectations hypothesis; (b) the liquidity preference hypothesis; and (c) the market segmentation hypothesis.

3 *Duration* Duration is a measure of the sensitivity of a debenture's price to redemption yield changes. Duration can be utilized to assess a debenture's interest rate risk. Debentures with lower coupon rates have more interest rate risk than debentures with higher coupon rates because the former will have longer durations (other things remain the same).

Questions for discussion

1 For each term shown below in the largest box provide a definition is your own words. Then check your responses against the definitions included in the chapter.

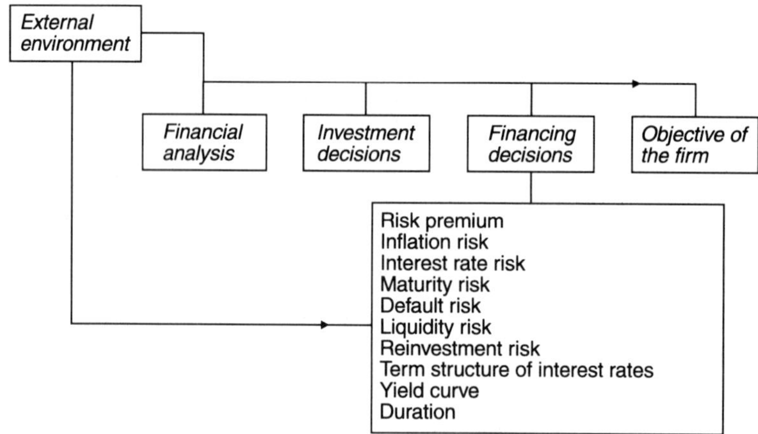

2 Discuss fully each of the following two statements:
(a) 'When investigating the yield curve of gilts, one should utilize in the analysis debt securities associated with similar levels of risk and yield quotations all taken as of the same date.'
(b) 'The yield curve is a valuable tool of market analysis.'

3 The *Financial Times* publishes daily information related to gilts (including redemption periods, prices, redemption yields, and so on) under the heading 'British Funds'. Choose a particular day of the week and plot the redemption yields against time to maturity of all 'Shorts', 'Five to Fifteen Years' and 'Over Fifteen Years' gilts quoted in the *Financial Times* that day. Discuss the resulting yield curve.

4 Consider the following two cases: (a) On 31 January 1984, the quoted redemption yields of short-term gilts were lower than those of long-term yields; (b) On 10 November 1989, the quoted redemption yields of

short-term gilts were higher than those of long-term yields. In view of the theories presented in the current chapter, identify and discuss the determinants of the yield curve associated with each of the above cases.

5 Compare and contrast the following three theories on the term structure of debenture yields discussed in this chapter: (a) unbiased expectations hypothesis; (b) liquidity premium hypothesis; and (c) market segmentation hypothesis.

6 Provide a discussion related to the preferred habitat hypotheses introduced by Modigliani and Sutch (1966). How can such a hypothesis compare to the liquidity premium hypothesis?

7 (a) Below you are given four statements related to the yield curve concept. Fill in an appropriate reply by using either the word 'Agree' or the word 'Disagree'.

	Agree	Disagree
The upward sloping yield curve usually occurs in periods of economic prosperity.		
Short-term borrowing costs are usually higher than long-term borrowing costs.		
The unbiased expectation hypothesis is not consistent with the efficient market hypothesis.		
The upward sloping yield curve occurs in periods where there exists reduced economic activity.		

(b) Discuss in detail each reply given in part (a).

8 'Duration is a measure of a debenture's sensitivity to a change in interest rates.' Fully discuss this statement. Provide a numerical example of how to compute the duration of a debenture.

9 Discuss fully each of the following three relationships between duration and the indicated variable (in each case consider the given variable and assume other things remain the same):

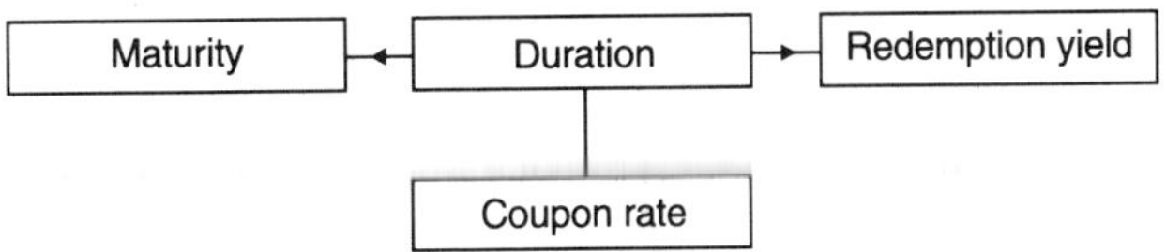

10 Discuss the following: 'If the redemption yield of a debenture rise by 1 per cent from a 10 per cent rate, the price of the debenture with a duration of 5.8 years will fall by 5.27 per cent.'

11 Prepare an analog model summarizing the main points discussed in the present chapter.

12 How can spreadsheets be used to facilitate the application of the concepts discussed in this chapter?

Appendix 12A Sensitivity of duration to changes in term to maturity and coupon rate with 1-2-3

The present value of the debenture's time-weighted cash flows is given by the following equation (we assume a constant coupon rate):

$$\mathrm{PV}(T) = \frac{I}{(1+r_d)} + \frac{2I}{(1+r_d)^2} + \frac{3I}{(1+r_d)^3} + \cdots + \frac{TI}{(1+r_d)^T} + \frac{100T}{(1+r_d)^T} \qquad (12A.1)$$

Multiply both sides of Equation (12A.1) by $(1+r_d)/I$ to obtain:

$$\mathrm{PV}(T)(1+r_d)/I = 1 + \frac{2}{(1+r_d)} + \frac{3}{(1+r_d)^2} + \cdots + \frac{T}{(1+r_d)^{T-1}} + \frac{100T/I}{(1+r_d)^{T-1}} \qquad (12A.2)$$

By dividing Equation (12A.1) by I yields:

$$\mathrm{PV}(T)/I = \frac{1}{(1+r_d)} + \frac{2}{(1+r_d)^2} + \frac{3}{(1+r_d)^3} + \cdots + \frac{T}{(1+r_d)^T} + \frac{100T/I}{(1+r_d)^T} \qquad (12A.3)$$

Subtract Equation (12A.3) from Equation (12A.2) to get

$$\mathrm{PV}(T)r_d/I = 1 + \frac{1}{(1+r_d)} + \frac{1}{(1+r_d)^2} + \cdots + \frac{1}{(1+r_d)^{T-1}} + \frac{T}{(1+r_d)^T} + \frac{100T/I}{(1+r_d)^{T-1}} - \frac{100T/I}{(1+r_d)^T}$$

or equivalently

$$\mathrm{PV}(T)r_d/I = [1 + \mathrm{PV}(1)] - \frac{T}{(1+r_d)^T} + \frac{100T/I}{(1+r_d)^{T-1}} - \frac{100T/I}{(1+r_d)^T} \qquad (12A.4)$$

where $\mathrm{PV}(1)$ = the present value for one pound at r_d for $(T-1)$ periods.

Every term on the right-hand side of Equation (12A.4) is a function of the term to maturity; thus, the last equation can be used in 1-2-3 for the sensitivity analysis. We employ the following notation:

Term 1: $[1 + \mathrm{PV}(1)]$ Term 2: $\dfrac{T}{(1+r_d)^T}$

Term 3: $\dfrac{100T/I}{(1+r_d)^{T-1}}$ Term 4: $\dfrac{100T/I}{(1+r_d)^T}$

We can now use 1-2-3's functions to calculate the duration (see Figure 12.17).

Cell D8:	`@PV(D3*D4,D5,D6)+D4/(1+D5)^D6`	Current market price
Cell D9:	`1+@PV(1,D5,D6-1)`	Term 1
Cell D10:	`-D6/(1+D5)^D6`	Term 2
Cell D11:	`(D6/D3)/(1+D5)^(D6-1)`	Term 3
Cell D12:	`-(D6/D3)/(1+D5)^D6`	Term 4
Cell D13:	`@SUM(D9..D12)*D3*D4/D5`	Time-weighted present value
Cell D14:	`----------`	
Cell D15:	`+D13/D8`	Duration

Note that each of the above formulae is dependent upon the value stored in cell D6 (the number of years to maturity). Therefore, the duration formula stored in cell D15 (see Figure 12.17) can be used as the formula in the `/Data Table 2` command of 1-2-3.

Appendix 12B Confidence intervals

Recall from Appendix 11A that statistical inference is concerned with making conclusions about a population parameter based on information provided by a random sample drawn from that population. It is unlikely to provide a statistic that is exactly equal to the corresponding population parameter. If we take repeated random samples of the same size from a population and compute the value of an estimator (for example, the mean), we find that the estimators' value will vary from sample to sample. In each of those cases, it is preferable to use an interval describing the range in which the population parameter falls. In statistics these intervals are known as confidence intervals. A better definition of a confidence interval is as follows: it is a range of values within which a population parameter lies with a stated probability.

Confidence interval estimates for means

Consider a population from which we take repeated random samples of a given size and compute the mean for each sample. The probability distribution of these sample means is known as sampling distribution of the mean. The confidence limits for estimation of the population mean are given in summary in Figure 12.B.1 (we assume samples of large sizes).

Lower limit ⟶ Mean $- z$ SD

Upper limit ⟶ Mean $+ z$ SD

where

Mean = the mean of the sample under consideration.
z = the number of standard deviations associated with the desired level of confidence.
SD = the standard deviation of the sampling distribution of the mean.

If sampling is from an infinite population or if sampling is with replacement from a finite population, SD is computed as follows:

$$\frac{s}{\sqrt{n}}$$

where

s = the standard deviation of the sample under consideration.
n = the sample size.

If sampling is without replacement from a finite population, SD is found as follows:

$$\frac{s}{\sqrt{n}}\sqrt{\frac{N-n}{N-1}}$$

where

N = the population size.

Figure 12B.1. A summary of the confidence interval for means

Example 12B.1 Calculating a confidence interval for the mean of a population of monthly rates of change of the FT-A price index for debentures

Consider a population of 300 monthly rates of change of the FT-A price index for debentures. A random sample of 36 monthly observations with a mean of –0.047 per cent and standard deviation of 2.077 per cent is taken from this population (note that the sample standard deviation provides an unbiased estimator for the population standard deviation if the sum of the squared deviations from the mean is divided by $n - 1$). The standard error of the sampling distribution of the mean is estimated as follows:

$$\frac{0.02077}{\sqrt{36}}\sqrt{\frac{300-36}{300-1}} = 0.325 \text{ per cent}$$

The confidence interval for the mean can be found by using the t distribution because the sample size is smaller than 30. The lower limit of 95 per cent confidence interval for the population mean is

$$-0.00047 - (1.96000)(0.00325) = -0.684 \text{ per cent}$$

The upper limit of the 95 per cent confidence interval for the population mean would be

$$-0.00047 + (1.96000)(0.00325) = 0.590 \text{ per cent}$$

Hence, the population mean is between −0.684 per cent and 0.590 per cent with a 95 per cent level of confidence.

Problem

Compute the 99 per cent confidence interval for the population mean of monthly rates of return of the FT-A price index for debentures (assume a sample mean of −0.047 per cent and a sample standard deviation of 2.077 per cent).

Some useful points

1 (Calculating the limits using 1-2-3 Release 3) The limits presented in Figure 12B.1 can be calculated by using the following formulae of 1-2-3, respectively (we assume a 95 per cent level of confidence and the sampling is with replacement):

```
@AVG(ran)-1.96*@STDS(ran)/@SQRT(@COUNT(ran))

@AVG(ran)+1.96*@STDS(ran)/@SQRT(@COUNT(ran))
```

where ran is the range containing the sample observations.

2 (Confidence intervals for small samples) The confidence limits defined in Figure 12B.1 assume that the sample size is greater than or equal to 30. For a sample size smaller than 30, the confidence interval for the mean can be found by using the t-distribution. In such a case the lower and upper limits are given by the following two equations, respectively:

Lower limit⟶Mean $- ts/\sqrt{n}$

Upper limit⟶Mean $+ ts/\sqrt{n}$

where

t = the t distribution table's value corresponding to a given level of significance and n degrees of freedom, where n is the sample size. Note that this is a two-test value.

s = the sample standard deviation.

References and bibliography

Bauman, W.S. (1969) Investment returns and present value, *Financial Analyst Journal*, **27**, November–December, 107–20.

Bower, R.S., Johnson, K.B., Lutz, W.J. and Topley, T.C. (1977) Investment opportunities and stock valuation, *Journal of Business Research*, **5**, March, 36–61.

Culbertson, J.M. (1957) The term structure of interest rates, *Quarterly Journal of Economics*, November, 489–504.

Fisher, I. (1896) Appreciation and interest, Publications of the American Economic Association, **XI**, August.

Gordon, M. (1963) *The Investment, Financing and Valuation of Corporations*. Richard D. Irwin, Homewood, Ill.

Granger, C.W.J. (1975) Some consequences of the valuation model when expectations are taken to be optimum forecasts, *Journal of Finance*, **31**, March, 135–45.

Hicks, J.R. (1946) *Value and Capital*, 2nd edn. Oxford University Press, London.

Hubbard, C.L. and Hawkins, C.A. (1969) *Theory Of Valuation*. International Textbooks, Scranton, Pa.

Lutz, F.A. (1940) The Structure of interest rates, *Quarterly Journal of Economics*, November, 36–63.

Macaulay, F.R. (1938) *Some Theoretical Problems Suggested by the Movements of Interest Rates, Bond Yields and Stock Prices in the United States since 1956*. National Bureau of Economic Research, New York.

Malkier, B.G. (1963) Equity yields and structure of share prices, *The American Economic Review*, **53**, December, 1004–31.

Mao, J.C.T. (1966) The valuation of growth stocks: the investment opportunity approach, *Journal of Finance*, **21**, March, 95–102.

Modigliani, F. and Sutch, R. (1966) Innovation and interest rate policy, *American Economic Review*, May, 178–197.

Stone, B.K. (1975) The conformity of stock values based on discounted dividends to a fair return process, *Bell Journal of Economics*, **6**, Autumn, 698–702.

Walker, C.E. (1954) Federal Reserve policy and the structure of interest rates on government securities, *Quarterly Journal of Economics*, February, 22–3.

Weil, R.L. (1973) Macaulay's duration: an appreciation, *Journal of Business*, October, 589–92.

Wendt, P.F. (1965) Current growth stock evaluation methods, *Financial Analyst Journal*, **21**, March–April, 91–201.

Williams, J.B. (1938) *The Theory of Investment Value*. Harvard University Press, Cambridge, Mass.

13 Valuation of ordinary shares

This chapter includes:

- Methods for evaluating the ordinary shares of a firm
- The dividend valuation method
- Valuing unquoted firms

The theory of financial management assumes that the primary objective of the firm is to maximize the market price of its ordinary shares. In order to maximize the market share price the firm must first understand its determinants. The expectations of investors about future events related to a firm (for example, expected dividend payments, risk associated with the expected dividends, and so on) determine the market price of its ordinary shares. In order to maximize the market share price of a firm, the investment and financing decisions must be made in a way that enhances the attractiveness of the firm's ordinary shares to investors.

The objective of this chapter is to discuss five valuation methods for ordinary shares. Figure 13.1 shows how the methods discussed in this chapter fit in the financial management framework introduced in Chapter 2.

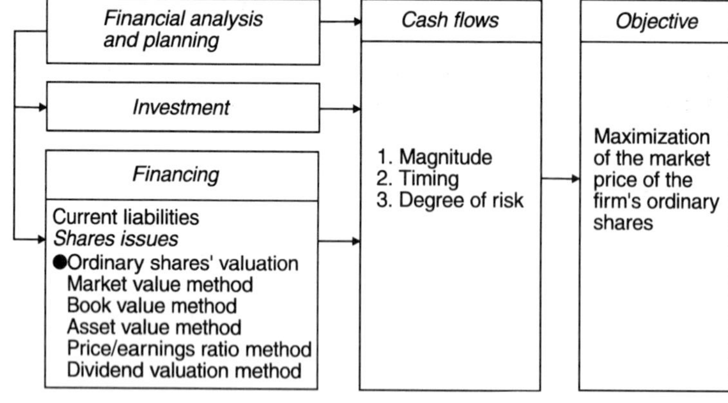

Figure 13.1. The ordinary shares valuation methods in relation to the financial management framework introduced in Chapter 2

Basic concepts, definitions and examples

An ordinary share is a security which represents ownership in the firm and confers certain rights on the holder (for example, voting rights). A share certificate is a document issued by a firm to one of its shareholders providing evidence that he or she is the owner of a specified number of shares. The par value (or face value) is the price printed on the face of the share certificate. Equity is another name for the ordinary shares of a firm.

The cash income an investor will receive from buying an ordinary share takes the form of dividends (if any) paid during the holding period and a sale price at the end of the holding period. Ordinary dividends represent that portion of a firm's profits which are distributed to the ordinary shareholders. Capital gains refer to the amount by which the proceeds from the sales of an ordinary share exceed its purchase price. If the purchase price of an ordinary share is greater than its selling price a capital loss occurs.

Example 13.1 Investing in Marks and Spencer plc

An investment of £1,000 in Marks and Spencer's shares in 1977 would have grown to £6,600 over a ten-year period, producing a capital gain (before tax) of £5,600. Over the same ten-year period the investor would also have been paid around £740 in dividends. What factors affected the share price of the company? Over the period 1977–86 Marks and Spencer's earnings per share (EPS) have risen from 2.10 pence to 8.35 pence, an increase of 298 per cent. The steady rise in profits has meant that each year the firm has been able to pay out a slightly higher dividend on each ordinary share. Over the period 1977–86 the company's dividends per share (DPS) have risen from 0.95 pence to 3.90 pence, an increase of 311 per cent (see Figures 13.2 and 13.3).

Dividend income is only part of the investors' total income. The stockmarket price of Marks and Spencer has risen over the period 1977–86; it has actually increased around five and a half times, faster than earnings per share and dividends per share. At the end of September 1987, the shares reached a high of 236 pence, but in the October 1987 share crash, the shares fell to 160 pence. They recovered by the end of December 1987 to 182 pence, but they fell to below 160 in December 1988 mainly because the company was criticized for selling high price merchandise.

Year	EPS	DPS
1977	2.10	0.95
1978	2.64	1.24
1979	3.47	1.45
1980	3.62	1.95
1981	3.79	2.20
1982	4.61	2.63
1983	5.07	3.02
1984	[illegible]	[illegible]
1985	6.84	3.76
1986	8.35	3.90

Figure 13.2. The earnings per share and dividends per share of Marks and Spencer plc (1977–86)

Problem

Create the graph shown in Figure 13.3.

Valuation of ordinary shares

This section discusses the following five methods for evaluating the ordinary share value of a firm:

- Market value method
- Book value method

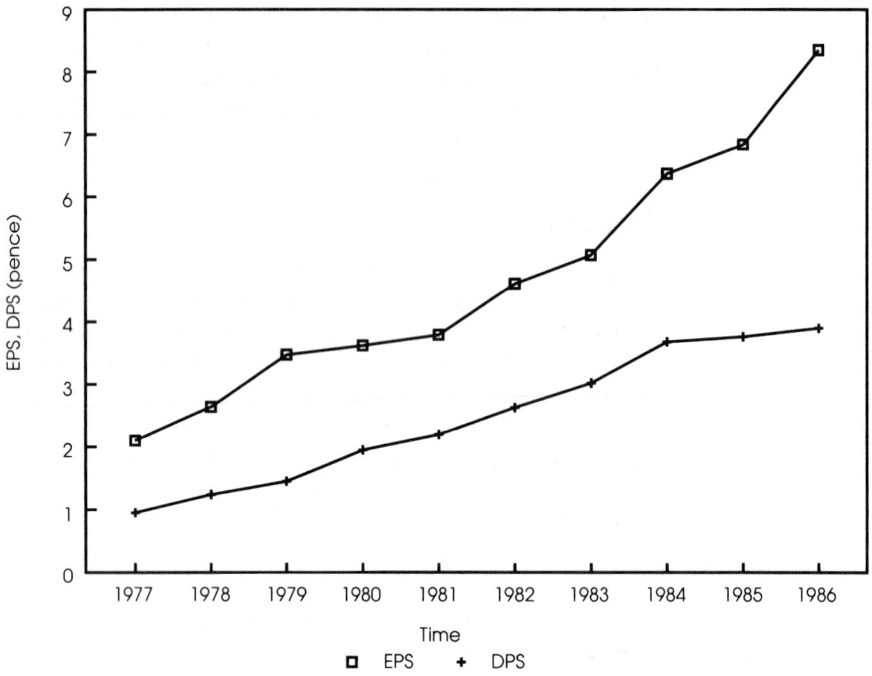

Figure 13.3. The EPS and DPS of Marks and Spencer (1977–86)

- Asset value method
- Price/earnings ratio method
- Dividend valuation method

Market value method

This is an obvious approach for quoted companies. The market value per share is simply the price for which the share can be sold on the market. The total market value of the shares of a firm (or a firm's market capitalization) is equal to the number of outstanding shares times the price per share (outstanding shares are those held at any point in time by investors).

Book value method

This valuation method relies on accounting data included in the firm's balance sheet. The book value per share at any point in time is equal to the total ordinary shareholders' equity, after subtracting claims of preference shareholders, divided by the number of shares outstanding. That is:

$$\text{Book value per share} = \frac{\text{Total shareholders' equity} - \text{Preference shares}}{\text{Ordinary shares outstanding}}$$

As this method uses historical data it does not necessarily reflect the current market price of the firm. A major disadvantage of the book value method is the lack of considering of the firm's expected earnings potential.

Example 13.2 Estimating the book value per share of a firm

AG Textiles has currently (that is 31 March 1989) a goodwill of £2,000,000 which will last for four years (the value of the goodwill is the value of the firm over and above the normal value of its net assets). The present value of the goodwill at a discount rate of 10 per cent is £1,584,933 (see Figure 13.4). The present value is calculated as follows:

PV = `@PV(500000,0.10,4)` = `@PV(B5,B6,B4)` = £1,584,933

We assume that the firm has no preference shares. The total value of the firm is £3,084,933. The book value per share can be found by dividing the total value by the number of outstanding ordinary shares:

$$\text{Book value per share} = \frac{£3,084,933}{2,000,000} = £1.54$$

Problems

1 Set up the worksheet shown in Figure 13.4.
2 If the annual amount of goodwill is £600,000 instead of £500,000, calculate the book value of an ordinary share for AG Textiles.
3 Conduct a sensitivity analysis of the book value of an ordinary share of AG Textiles with respect to the annual amount of goodwill (consider the following values for the annual amount of goodwill: £300,000–£700,000 in steps of £50,000).
4 Plot a graph illustrating the results derived in Problem 3.

	A	B	C	D
1	AG TEXTILES:ESTIMATING THE VALUE PER ORDINARY SHARE			
2	==			
3	Goodwill	£2,000,000		
4	Life of Goodwill	4		
5	Annual Amount of Goodwill	£500,000		
6	Discount Rate	10.00%		
7		--------------		
8	Present Value of Goodwill	£1,584,933		
9				
10	Book Value of the Firm's Tangible Assets	£4,000,000		
11	Total Debt Obligation of the Firm	£2,500,000		
12	Goodwill	£1,584,933		
13		--------------		
14	Total Value	£3,084,933		
15				
16	Number of Ordinary Shares	2,000,000		
17		--------------		
18	Book Value Per Share	£1.54		
19		==============		

Figure 13.4. Estimating the book value per share for AG Textiles

Asset value method

The asset value method uses the actual market value of a firm's assets rather than their historical value. This method considers an actual market value that could be obtained if the firm's assets are sold and then calculates the residual value after creditors and preference shareholders are paid. The residual value is available for distribution to ordinary shareholders and the value of a share is calculated by dividing the residual value by the number of outstanding ordinary shares. As in the case of the book value method, the asset value method does not take into account the expected earnings potential of a firm.

Example 13.3 Estimating the asset value per share of a firm

The financial director of AG Textiles found, after conducting an investigation, that the current market value of the firm's assets would be £3,500,000 (see also the data given in Example 13.2). Thus, the firm's asset value per share is calculated to be

$$\frac{£3{,}500{,}000 + £1{,}584{,}933 - £2{,}500{,}000}{2{,}000{,}000} = £1.29$$

The price earnings ratio method

This method assumes that a firm's earnings after tax are valued in the same way as those of the industry to which the firm belongs. If the industry price/earnings ratio is obtained (for example, from published sources), the market value per ordinary shares can be expressed as follows:

Market value per share = Industry price/earnings ratio × Expected earnings per share of the firm

The price/earnings ratio method is believed to provide a better valuation approach than the book value and asset value methods because it implicitly takes into account expected earnings.

Example 13.4 Estimating the value of an ordinary share using the price/earnings method

The next year's earnings per share of AG Textiles are expected to be £0.27. We assume that the average price/earnings ratio for the industry is 10. Then we can estimate the value per ordinary share as shown below:

$$V_o = (£0.27)(10) = £2.70$$

This can be also expressed as follows:

$$V_o = \frac{£0.27}{1/10} = £2.70$$

Thus, under the price/earnings ratio approach, the market value per share is the present value of a perpetuity of expected earnings per share at a rate equal to the inverse of the price/earnings ratio.

The dividend valuation method

The value of an ordinary share is based on the expected cash flows its owner will realize over the period he or she held the share. The expected cash flows received from holding an ordinary share may take the following two forms: cash dividend payments made during the holding period and/or capital gains or losses realized at the time of the sale of the share. The basic dividend valuation model is based upon the following two assumptions:

1 Time is divided into yearly intervals. All the expected cash flows associated with an ordinary share are paid annually at the end of each year.
2 The risks that accompany the firm's shares (for example, financial and business risks) are incorporated in the investors' required rate of return.

The analysis that follows begins by introducing a one-year dividend valuation model, and then moves on to introduce dividend valuation models which assume holding periods greater than one year.

One-year dividend valuation model

The one-year valuation model assumes that shares are purchased at the beginning of a specified period and held for one year. The holding period rate of return that investors expect from an ordinary share is divided into the following two parts: the first part is equal to the capital appreciation or depreciation relative to the size of the investment (that is, the purchasing price of the share) and the second part equals the dividend income received during the holding period divided by the size of the investment. Mathematically, the rate of return can be represented as follows:

$$r_o = \frac{P_1 - P_0}{P_0} + \frac{D_1}{P_0}$$

After rearranging the last equation yields:

$$P_0 = \frac{D_1}{(1 + r_o)} + \frac{P_1}{(1 + r_o)}$$

In words, the current intrinsic value of the ordinary share equals the present value of the expected dividends per share for year one plus the present value of the share's selling price expected at the end of year one.

Example 13.5 Calculating the current intrinsic value of an ordinary share (one-year valuation model)

To illustrate the use of the one-year model in determining the intrinsic value of a share, consider the case of GD Fashions plc. Assume that investors expect a 10 pence dividend per share over the next year and the firm's share to sell for 218 pence one year from today. If the required rate of return of the investors is 14 per cent, the current intrinsic value of the firm's share would be:

$$P_o = \frac{10}{(1 + 0.14)} + \frac{218}{(1 + 0.14)} = 200 \text{ pence}$$

If the share value was below 200 pence, say at 196.55 pence, the expected rate of return from investing in the firm's shares would be 16 per cent. As a consequence, the ordinary shares of the firm would become more desirable to investors and the demand for purchasing the shares would force their price up to 200 pence. If the current share price was above 200 pence, say at 203.57 pence, then the investment in the firm's shares would have an expected rate of return of 12 per cent. In this case, investors would prefer to invest their money in other competitive investments which offer similar risk to that of GD Fashions and higher expected return as compared with the expected return of GD Fashions. As a result, the share price of the firm would decrease until it became 200 pence.

Two-year dividend valuation model

The two-year valuation model assumes that share are purchased at the beginning of a specified period and held for two years. Since the intrinsic value of an ordinary share equals the present value of all the expected cash flows the owner will realize over the holding period, we have the following equation:

$$P_o = \frac{D_1}{(1 + r_o)} + \frac{D_2}{(1 + r_o)^2} + \frac{P_2}{(1 + r_o)^2}$$

where

D_2 = the (expected) dividends per share to be received at the end of year two.

P_2 = the (expected) intrinsic value of the ordinary share at the end of year two.

Example 13.6 Calculating the current intrinsic value of an ordinary share (two-year valuation model)

Consider again GD Fashions plc (see Example 13.5). Assume that investors in aggregate expect the firm's dividends per share and share price to rise by the end of the second year. The dividends per share and share price expected two years from now are 10.900 pence and 237.620 pence, respectively. The intrinsic value shown in Figure 13.5 is calculated by using the following financial function of 1-2-3:

```
@NPV(C4,D8..D9)
```

Therefore, if the investors' required rate of return is 14 per cent, the intrinsic value of the firm's ordinary shares is 200 pence.

Problem

Set up the worksheet shown in Figure 13.5.

```
     A                B                  C                  E                 F
1 CALCULATING THE INTRINSIC VALUE OF A SHARE(TWO-PERIOD VALUATION MODEL)
2 ========================================================================
3
4 Required Rate of Return -->                  14.0%
5 ------------------------------------------------------------------------
6 YEAR      EXPECTED DIVIDENDS  EXPECTED PRICE  TOTAL CASH FLOWS
7 ------------------------------------------------------------------------
8         1             10.000                              10.000
9         2             10.900         237.620             248.520
10                                              --------------------
11          Intrinsic Value ---------------->               200.000
12 -------------------------------------------------------------------
```

Figure 13.5. Applying the two-year valuation model for ordinary shares

T-year dividend valuation model

The analysis discussed previously can be generalized for T years. Assume that shares are purchased at the beginning of a specified period and held for T years. Figure 13.6 summarizes the concept of the T-year dividend valuation model.

Example 13.7 Calculating the current intrinsic value of an ordinary share (eight-year valuation model)

Figure 13.7 presents a spreadsheet calculating the current intrinsic value of an ordinary share assuming an eight-period valuation model (figures are in pence). The following financial function of 1-2-3 is stored in cell D17:

```
@NPV(C4,D8..D15)
```

Problem

Set up the worksheet shown in Figure 13.7.

Definition The intrinsic value of an ordinary share is the present value of a series of expected cash flows to be received over a period of T years in the future, all discounted at a discount rate which is commensurate with the risk associated with the share.

Calculation The intrinsic value of an ordinary share, using the T-year dividend valuation model, is calculated as follows:

Intrinsic value of an ordinary share	=	Present value of the series of expected dividend payments	+	Present value of the intrinsic value of the share at the end of the holding period

$$P_o = \sum_{t=1}^{T} \frac{D_t}{(1+r_o)^t} + \frac{P_T}{(1+r_o)^T}$$

where

$D_1, D_2, \ldots, D_T$ = the (expected) dividend per share to be received at the end of years 1, 2, and T, respectively.

P_T = the (expected) intrinsic value of the ordinary share at the end of period T.

r_o = investors' required rate of return on the firm's ordinary shares.

Interpretation The intrinsic value of an ordinary share can be viewed as the result of a process which takes the future cash flows associated with the ordinary share and discounts them back to the present at a required rate of return reflecting the riskiness associated with these cash flows.

Figure 13.6. The concept of the intrinsic value of an ordinary share

```
      A              B                  C                 E              F
 1 CALCULATING THE INTRINSIC VALUE OF A SHARE(EIGHT-PERIOD VAL. MODEL)
 2 ==================================================================
 3
 4 Required Rate of Return -->               14.0%
 5 ------------------------------------------------------------------
 6 YEAR      EXPECTED DIVIDENDS   EXPECTED PRICE   TOTAL CASH FLOWS
 7 ------------------------------------------------------------------
 8         1             10.000                              10.000
 9         2             10.900                              10.900
10         3             11.620                              11.620
11         4             12.500                              12.500
12         5             13.600                              13.600
13         6             14.690                              14.690
14         7             15.820                              15.820
15         8             17.120          403.689             420.120
16                                                   --------------
17          Intrinsic Value --------------->                200.000
```

Figure 13.7. A spreadsheet calculating the intrinsic value of an ordinary share of GD Fashions (eight-period valuation model)

In a competitive capital market, where investors are assumed to share the same accurate information, the intrinsic value of a share is equal to its market price. In such a market, the investors' expectations about the risk and return associated with the future cash flows from a share determine the current price of the share. Therefore, if the market is efficient, investors can only expect to earn a return commensurate with the risk associated with the future cash flows from the share.

Some useful points about the T-*year dividend valuation model*

1 (A firm's value when it does not pay current dividends) If a firm pays no current dividends, its share price is not zero because investors believe that either the firm

will pay dividends at some future point in time or they expect to realize something which is as good as dividend payments. For example, the investors may expect to realize capital gains, or the firm can repurchase its own shares on the open market, an action which can be seen as a form of dividend payout for the continuing shareholders.

2 (Valuation model and dividends) Since the T-year valuation model calculates the current intrinsic value of existing ordinary shares, the future dividend inputs of the model are related to the existing shares only. For example, suppose we are at the beginning of the year and GD Fashions plc has 1,000,000 shares owned. The dividends at the end of the year are expected to be £100,000 and the market price per share at the same time is expected to be 218 pence. If the firm issues some additional shares near the end of the year which are entitled to a dividend payment, then the current intrinsic value calculation should not include the dividends paid to a new share. If the investors' required rate of return is 14 per cent, the current intrinsic value of the firm's ordinary share would be 200 pence.

3 (Data and dividend valuation models) Remember that the garbage-in–garbage-out rule is applicable to the T-year dividend valuation model (and many other mathematical models). The T-year dividend valuation model produces an answer for any type of numerical data you use. However, it provides a reliable answer only if the input data used is reliable. The more reliable the data you use, the more confident you can be to rely on your results.

Figure 13.8 summarizes the T-year dividend valuation model.

Figure 13.8. A summary of the T-year dividend valuation model

T-year dividend valuation model

The intrinsic value of an ordinary share is the present value of the future dividend payments per share expected during the holding period plus the present value of the future sale price expected to be received at the end of the holding period

Factors affecting the value of an ordinary share:

- Dividends per share expected at the end of years 1 to T.
- Share price expected at the end of year T.
- Investors' required rate of return on the firm's shares.

Special cases of the T-period valuation model

In this section we consider three special cases of the general valuation model:

- Zero growth dividend valuation model.
- Constant growth dividend valuation model.
- A supernormal growth dividend valuation model.

Zero growth dividend valuation model

The zero growth dividend valuation model assumes that the most recent dividend per share (which has already been paid) will remain fixed over time and the firm will continue operating forever. Under these assumptions, the T-year valuation model can be reduced to the following simpler equation:

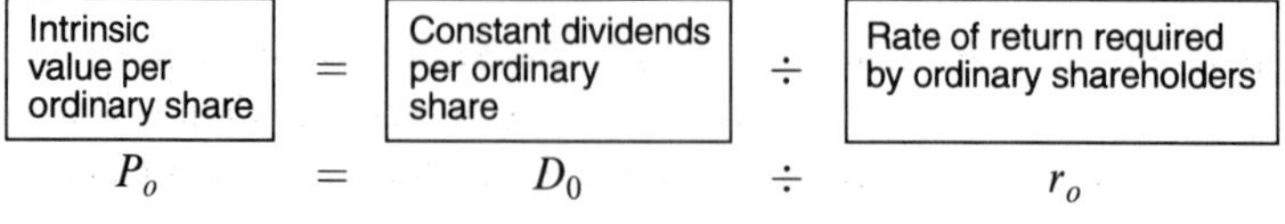

$$P_o = D_0 \div r_o$$

where

D_o = the constant ordinary dividends per share payable forever.
r_o = the rate of return required on the firm's ordinary shares.

Example 13.8 Calculating the intrinsic value of an ordinary share using the zero growth dividend valuation model

Assume that investors expect AD Computers plc to pay a dividend of 10 pence per year on each ordinary share forever. If the required rate of return of the investors in this share is 0.11 per cent, then the intrinsic value of the share is

$$P_o = \frac{10}{0.11} = 90.91 \text{ pence}$$

Constant growth dividend valuation model

The constant growth dividend valuation model assumes that dividends per share grow forever at an annual (compound) rate, where the expected dividend growth is less than the investors' required rate of return. In view of this model, the (expected) dividend payable for year t can be represented by:

$$D_t = D_o(1+g)^t$$

where

D_o = current year's dividends per ordinary share, which have already been paid.

g = the constant annual ordinary dividend growth rate.

t = time period in years.

In this case, the general dividend valuation model can be used to derive the following equation:

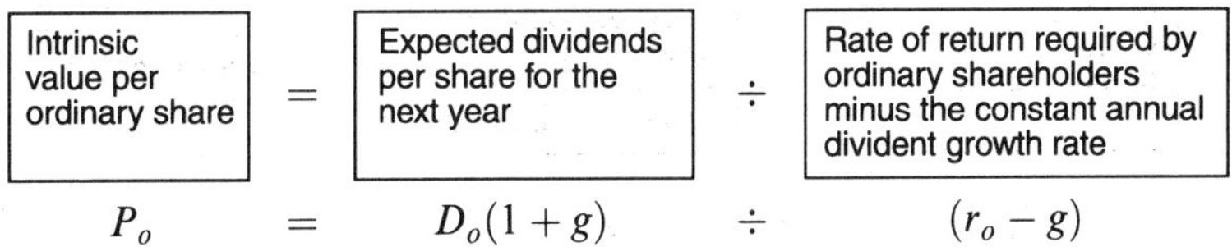

$$P_o = D_o(1+g) \div (r_o - g)$$

Example 13.9 Calculating the intrinsic value of an ordinary share using the constant growth dividend valuation model

The most recent dividend per share of RD Stores plc was 12 pence. Assume that the firm's dividends per share are expected to grow at 9 per cent a year forever. If the investors' required rate of return in this share is 14 per cent, then the intrinsic value of the share can be calculated as follows:

$$P = \frac{12}{0.14 - 0.09} = 240 \text{ pence}$$

Figure 13.9 shows graphically the dividends per share of the firm over a period of 50 years. The actual annual dividend per share increases with time (other things remain the same).

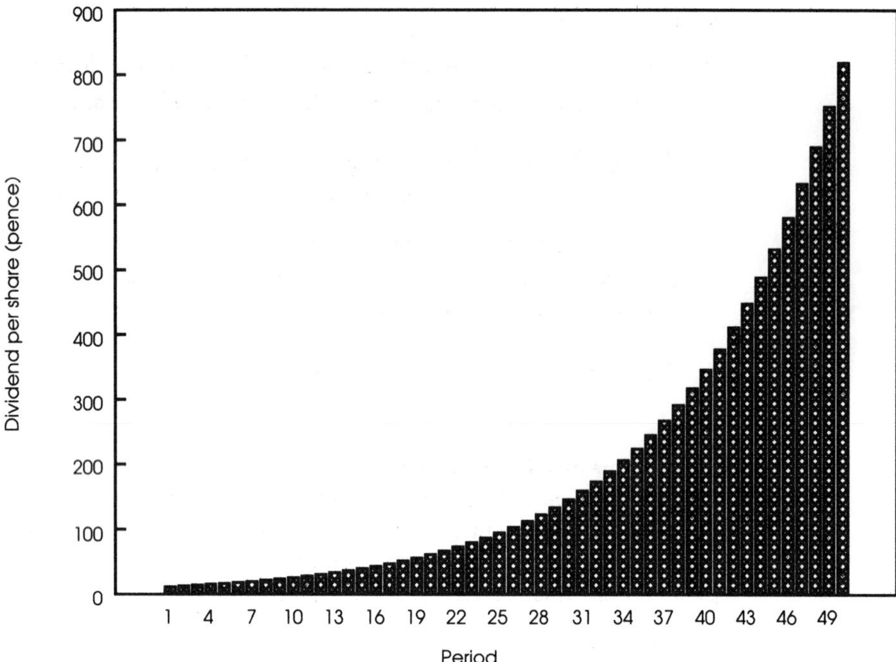

Figure 13.9. RD Stores plc: dividend per share

A one-stage supernormal growth dividend valuation model

A one-stage supernormal growth dividend valuation model assumes that the annual dividends per share of a firm will initially grow at a supernormal constant rate for H years (for example, five years) and then will grow at a normal constant rate forever. Each growth rate is assumed to be less than the investors' required rate of return. The following equation represents a supernormal growth dividend valuation model.

Intrinsic value per ordinary share	=	Present value of expected future dividends per share during the supernormal period	+	Expected future intrinsic value of the ordinary share at the end of the supernormal period

$$P_o = PV_D + \frac{D_{H+1}}{(r_o - g_1)(1 + r_o)^H}$$

where

H = years of supernormal growth.

PV_D = the present value of the expected dividends per share during the period of supernormal growth

D_{H+1} = dividends per share expected at the end of year $H + 1$

g_1 = a constant dividend growth rate, after the period of supernormal growth, that continues forever.

Example 13.10 Calculating the intrinsic value of an ordinary share using a one-stage supernormal growth dividend valuation model

PD Electronics plc is experiencing a period of rapid growth in earnings per share and dividends per share. Investors expect the dividends per share to grow at a supernormal rate of 11 per cent per annum for the following five years and at 5 per cent a year thereafter. The required rate of return on the share is 14 per cent and the share currently pays a 50 pence dividend. The spreadsheet in Figure 13.10 calculates the intrinsic value of the share. The present value of the dividends during the period of supernormal growth is calculated by using the following financial function of 1-2-3 (see cell B16):

```
@NPV(B3,B10..B14)
```

Next, the share value at the end of year 5 is calculated with the help of the following formula (see cell B17):

```
+B14*(1+B5)/(B3-B5)
```

The following formula is utilized to calculate the present value of the share price at the end of year 5 (see cell B18):

```
+B17/(1+B3)^A14
```

Lastly, the intrinsic value is calculated by adding the contents of cell B16 and B18 (figures are in pence, slight deviations due to rounding).

```
----------------------------------------------------------------------------
                      A                                      B
 1 COMPUTING THE INTRINSIC VALUE OF A SHARE (SUPERNORMAL VALUATION MODEL)
 2 =========================================================================
 3 Required Rate of Return  -------------->                       14.0%
 4 Supernormal Growth Rate ---------------->                      11.0%
 5 Normal Growth Rate -------------------->                        5.0%
 6 Current Dividends --------------------->                         50
 7 -------------------------------------------------------------------
 8                                      YEAR     EXPECTED DIVIDENDS
 9 -------------------------------------------------------------------
10                                         1                      55.50
11                                         2                      61.61
12                                         3                      68.38
13                                         4                      75.90
14                                         5                      84.25
15
16 Present Value of Dividends (years 1-5)                        230.94
17 Share Value at the End of Year 5                              982.95
18 Present Value of Share Price                                  510.51
19                                                ---------------------
20 Intrinsic Value                                               741.46
----------------------------------------------------------------------------
```

Figure 13.10. Computing the intrinsic value using a supernormal growth model

Problems

1 Set up the worksheet shown in Figure 13.10.
2 Provide a sensitivity analysis of the intrinsic value shown in Figure 13.10 with respect to changes in the supernormal growth rate and in the constant dividend growth rate after the period of supernormal growth.

Example 13.11 The sensitivity of PD Electronics plc's current intrinsic value per share to changes in the period of supernormal growth and the expected future intrinsic value of the share at the end of the period of supernormal growth

Consider the data given in Example 13.10. In the present example we perform a sensitivity analysis of the current intrinsic value per share of GD Electronics with respect to the number of years in the period of supernormal growth and the expected future intrinsic value of the share at the end of the period of supernormal growth. The sensitivity values of the period of supernormal growth are 4, 5, 6, 7, 8, 9, 10, 11 and 12. On the other hand, the sensitivity values for the expected future intrinsic value of the share are £880.00, £982.95, £1,030.00, £1090.35, £1,160.00 and £1,200.43.

The financial function @NPV of 1-2-3 does not express directly the number of years used in the calculation of the net present value. We can prove, however, that the present value of a series of dividends per share that grow at a constant rate can be expressed as (see Appendix 13A):

$$\text{PV} = D_1 \frac{1 - a^T}{r_o - g}$$

where

D_1 = the expected dividends per share in year 1.

$a = (1 + g)/(1 + r_o)$

g = the supernormal dividend growth rate.

H = years of supernormal growth.

The last equation contains the number of years in the period of supernormal growth and it can be used in the sensitivity analysis (see Figure 13.11, figures are in pence). The present value of dividends per share during the supernormal growth period, shown in cell F10, is calculated as follows (the deviation is due to rounding):

$$50(1 + 0.11) \frac{1 - 0.974^5}{0.14 - 0.11} = 230.942 \text{ pence}$$

Cell F14 shows the present value of the share. The 'Input cell 1' of 1-2-3's sensitivity table is cell F7 and the 'Input cell 2' is cell F11.

The results of the sensitivity analysis shown in Figure 13.11 are presented graphically in Figure 13.12. From the graph it can be seen that the present value increases as the expected future intrinsic value increases. However, it increases less as we move from 4 years to 12 years.

Problem

Create the worksheet shown in Figure 13.11.

Example 13.12 Calculating the intrinsic value of an ordinary share using a two-stage supernormal growth dividend valuation model

AK Manufacturing plc expects the dividends per share to grow at a rate of 11 per cent per annum for the next 5 years, 9 per cent a year for years 6 to 11 and finally 5 per cent a year thereafter. The present value shown in cell B25 (see Figure 13.13) is calculated as follows:

+B24 – B23 = PV of dividends (year 1–11) – PV of dividends (years 1–5)

= 456.009 – 230.942 = 225.067 pence

```
      A            B            C            D            E            F            G
 1 A SENSITIVITY ANALYSIS USING A SUPERNORMAL VALUATION MODEL
 2 ==========================================================
 3 Required Rate of Return    --------------->            14.0%
 4 Supernormal Growth Rate ---------------->              11.0%
 5 Normal Growth Rate --------------------->               5.0%
 6 Current Dividends ---------------------->               50
 7 Number of Years for Supernormal Period ->               5
 8 Constant a ----------------------------->            0.974
 9                                                    ---------
10 Present Value of Dividends                         230.942
11 Expected Future Intrinsic Value                    982.951
12 Present Value of Intrinsic Value                   510.514
13                                                    ---------
14 Present Value of the Share                         741.456
15
16
17 +F14            880.00     982.95    1030.00    1090.35    1160.00    1200.43
18           4     751.97     812.93     840.78     876.31     917.76     941.44
19           5     687.99     741.46     765.89     797.05     833.41     854.18
20           6     631.86     678.76     700.20     727.53     759.42     777.65
21           7     582.62     623.77     642.57     666.55     694.52     710.51
22           8     539.43     575.52     592.02     613.05     637.59     651.61
23           9     501.55     533.21     547.68     566.13     587.65     599.95
24          10     468.32     496.09     508.78     524.96     543.84     554.63
25          11     439.17     463.53     474.66     488.86     505.42     514.88
26          12     413.59     434.96     444.73     457.18     471.71     480.01
27 --------------------------------------------------------------------------------
```

Figure 13.11. A two-variable sensitivity analysis of the current intrinsic value of a share

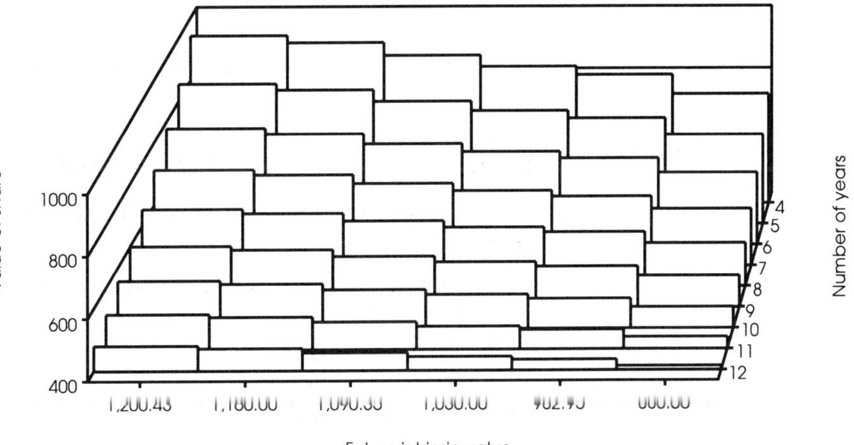

Figure 13.12. Sensitivity of current intrinsic value to number of years in a supernormal period and the expected intrinsic value of the share

Therefore, the intrinsic value of the share would be (see cell B29 of Figure 13.13)

$$+B23 + B25 + B27 = 230.942 + 225.067 + 390.065 = 846.074 \text{ pence}$$

Problems

1 Set up the worksheet shown in Figure 13.13.

2 Provide a sensitivity analysis of the intrinsic value shown in Figure 13.13 with respect to changes in the first supernormal growth rate and in the constant dividend growth rate after the period of the second supernormal growth.

```
                          A                                B
 1 CALCULATING THE INTRINSIC VALUE OF A SHARE(SUPERNORMAL VALUATION)
 2 ==============================================================
 3 Required Rate of Return    --------------->             14.0%
 4 1st Supernormal Growth Rate ----------->                11.0%
 5 2nd Supernormal Growth Rate ----------->                 9.0%
 6 Normal Growth Rate --------------------->                5.0%
 7 Current Dividends ---------------------->                 50
 8 --------------------------------------------------------------
 9                                       YEAR    EXPECTED DIVIDENDS
10 --------------------------------------------------------------
11 First Supernormal Period                 1              55.50
12                                          2              61.61
13                                          3              68.38
14                                          4              75.90
15                                          5              84.25
16 Second Supernormal Period                6              91.84
17                                          7             100.10
18                                          8             109.11
19                                          9             118.93
20                                         10             129.63
21                                         11             141.30
22
23 Present Value of Dividends (years 1-5)                 230.942
24 Present Value of Dividends (years 1-11)                456.009
25 Present Value of Dividends (years 6-11)                225.067
26 Expected Future Intrinsic Value                       1648.507
27 Present Value of the Intrinsic Value                   390.065
28                                            ---------------------
29 Intrinsic Value of Share                               846.074
```

Figure 13.13. A two-stage supernormal model

Figure 13.14 summarizes the *T*-year dividend valuation model with its special cases.

Estimating the growth rate in dividends per share

Historical data can be used in many ways to provide a forecast for the annual growth rate in expected dividends per share including:

- A method based on dividend payout ratio and retention rate.
- A naive forecasting method.
- The method of simple averages.
- Single moving average method.
- A simple linear regression trend method.

A method based on dividend payout ratio and retention rate

A firm can finance new investments by using either the proceeds obtained from the sale of new ordinary shares or part of the firm's current reserves. Assume that a firm plans to retain some of the present year's earnings and use them next year to make investments. In this case, the firm's earnings for next year can be expressed as follows:

Earnings for next year	=	Present year's earnings	+	Present year's reserves	×	Return on reserves

$$E_t(1+g) \quad = \quad E_t \quad + \quad \text{RES}_t \quad \times \quad R \tag{13.1}$$

where R is assumed to be constant over time.

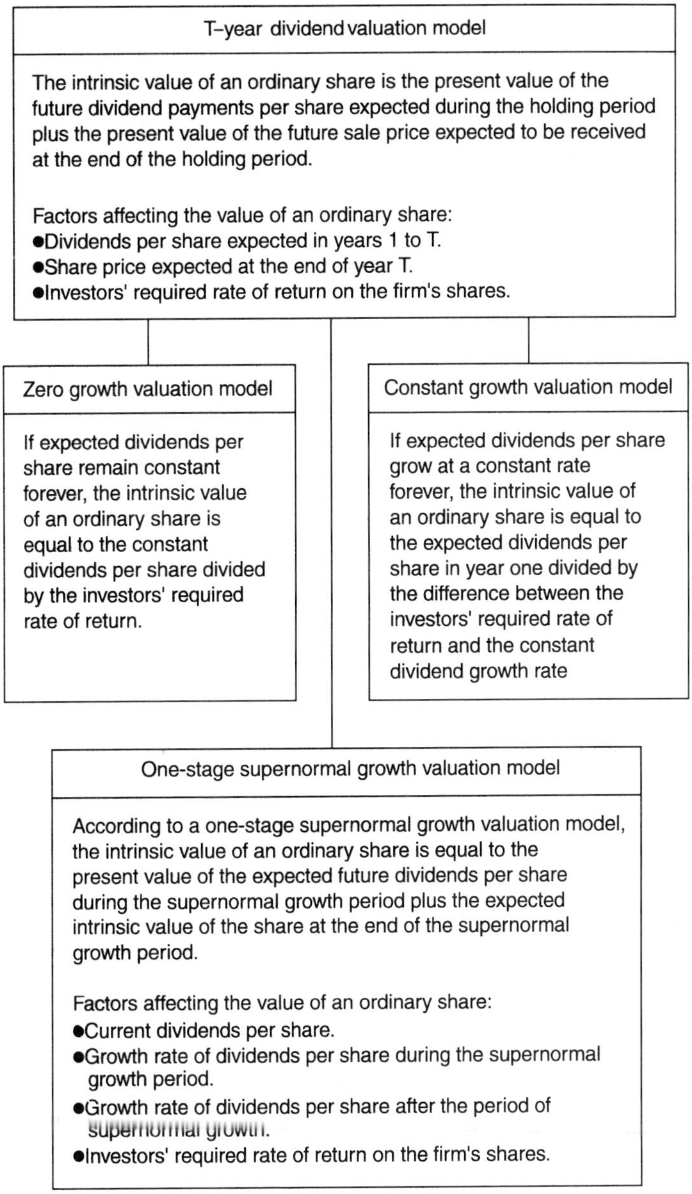

T–year dividend valuation model

The intrinsic value of an ordinary share is the present value of the future dividend payments per share expected during the holding period plus the present value of the future sale price expected to be received at the end of the holding period.

Factors affecting the value of an ordinary share:
- Dividends per share expected in years 1 to T.
- Share price expected at the end of year T.
- Investors' required rate of return on the firm's shares.

Zero growth valuation model

If expected dividends per share remain constant forever, the intrinsic value of an ordinary share is equal to the constant dividends per share divided by the investors' required rate of return.

Constant growth valuation model

If expected dividends per share grow at a constant rate forever, the intrinsic value of an ordinary share is equal to the expected dividends per share in year one divided by the difference between the investors' required rate of return and the constant dividend growth rate

One-stage supernormal growth valuation model

According to a one-stage supernormal growth valuation model, the intrinsic value of an ordinary share is equal to the present value of the expected future dividends per share during the supernormal growth period plus the expected intrinsic value of the share at the end of the supernormal growth period.

Factors affecting the value of an ordinary share:
- Current dividends per share.
- Growth rate of dividends per share during the supernormal growth period.
- Growth rate of dividends per share after the period of supernormal growth.
- Investors' required rate of return on the firm's shares.

Figure 13.14. *T*-year dividend valuation model with three special cases

Assume that the growth rate in earnings is constant over time and dividends are a constant fraction of earnings. As a consequence, earnings and dividends will grow at the same rate. Using Equation (13.1) we can write:

$$(E_t)(g) = (\text{RES}_t)(R) \qquad (13.2)$$

Dividing both sides of Equation (13.2) by E_t and noting that $\text{RES}_t/E_t = 1 -$ dividend payout ratio, gives

$$g = (1 - \text{dividend payout ratio})(R)$$

where the dividend payout ratio is constant over time. In view of the last equation, the dividend growth rate depends on the dividend payout ratio and the rate of return on reserves.

Assume that the investment projects selected in the present year have an expected return equal to the returns from investment projects in future years. In this instance, the expected return on reserves can be approximated by the historical return on equity. Therefore, the dividend growth rate is given by:

$$g = (1 - \text{dividend payout ratio})(\text{ROE}) \qquad (13.3)$$

where ROE is the ratio of earnings per share to book value of equity per share.

Example 13.13 Estimating the growth rate in dividends per share by using the dividend payout ratio and the return on equity ratio

RD Stores plc has a dividend payout ratio of 0.60. The historical ROE of the firm is 0.225 and we assume that it provides a good estimate for future returns on reserves. Then the constant growth rate would be

$g = (1\text{–}0.60)(0.225) = 9$ per cent

A naive forecasting method

This method uses the actual growth rate of the most recent period as a forecast for the next period. The dividend growth rate over a year t can be calculated as follows:

$$g_t = \frac{\text{DPS}_t - \text{DPS}_{t-1}}{\text{DPS}_{t-1}}$$

where

DPS_t = dividends per share for year t.

DPS_{t-1} = dividends per share for year $t - 1$.

Example 13.14 Forecasting dividend growth rates by using a naive forecasting method

Figure 13.15 contains the annual dividends per share (DPS) of Marks and Spencer for each of 12 years in the period 1977–88. The growth rate stored in cell C8 is calculated below:

`(B8 – B7)/B7` = (1.24 – 0.95)/0.95 = 30.53 per cent

The remaining growth rates are calculated by simply copying the contents of cell C8 in the range C9..C18. The 1978 forecast is 1977's actual growth rate, the 1979 forecast is 1978's actual growth rate, and so on.

One measure that can be used to test the accuracy of a forecasting method is the mean absolute deviation. The mean absolute deviation indicates how much, on average, the forecasted values vary from the actual values. The value of 13.59 per cent, stored in cell E9, is calculated, by using the `@ABS` mathematical function of 1-2-3, as follows:

`@ABS(30.53% – 16.94%)` = 13.59 per cent

Finally, the mean absolute deviation, stored in cell E20, is a simple average of the absolute deviations stored in the range E9..E18. In general, the larger the mean absolute deviation, the smaller the accuracy of the forecasting method.

```
       A         B           C             D             E            F
 1 FORECASTING GROWTH RATES BY USING A NAIVE FORECASTING METHOD
 2 ============================================================
 3
 4 --------------------------------------------------------------
 5     YEAR      DPS    GROWTH RATE    FORECAST     ABSULUTE DEVIATION
 6 --------------------------------------------------------------
 7     1977      0.95
 8     1978      1.24         30.53%
 9     1979      1.45         16.94%        30.53%     13.59%
10     1980      1.95         34.48%        16.94%     17.55%
11     1981      2.20         12.82%        34.48%     21.66%
12     1982      2.63         19.55%        12.82%      6.72%
13     1983      3.02         14.83%        19.55%      4.72%
14     1984      3.68         21.85%        14.83%      7.03%
15     1985      3.76          2.17%        21.85%     19.68%
16     1986      3.90          3.72%         2.17%      1.55%
17     1987      4.50         15.38%         3.72%     11.66%
18     1988      5.10         13.33%        15.38%      2.05%
19                                                   ---------
20          Mean Absolute Deviation ---->            10.62%
```

Figure 13.15. Forecasting growth rates by using a naive forecasting method

The method of simple averages

According to this method, the average of all the historical growth rates in a given data set is used as a forecast for the next period. When we calculate the average of all historical growth rates, the high growth rates observed in several years will tend to be offset by the low growth rates in other years. Therefore, this method reduces the chances of being misled by an extreme value of the dividend growth rate.

The method of simple averages calculates averages over time in the following manner: each time a new observation becomes available, the new average is calculated by including the latest observation in the set of the existing observations.

Example 13.15 Forecasting dividend growth rates by using the method of simple averages

The spreadsheet displayed in Figure 13.16 uses the method of simple averages to forecast growth rates. Cell D10 stores the following formula:

```
@AVG($C$8..C9)
```

Cell C8 in the average formula must be absolute since the present forecasting method uses an average of all past data. To obtain all the average values, copy the contents of cell D10 in the range D11..D18.

The mean absolute deviation is 9.21 per cent. However, a single value as 9.21 per cent provides no information about the accuracy of the forecasting method used. The accuracy of the present forecasting method can be examined by comparing its mean absolute deviation with that of the naive forecasting method (see Example 13.14). The comparison indicates that the method of simple averages improved the forecast provided by the naive forecasting method.

	A	B	C	D	E	F
1	APPLYING THE METHOD OF SIMPLE AVERAGES					
2	=====================================					
3						
4						
5	YEAR	DPS	GROWTH RATE	FORECAST	ABSOLUTE DEVIATION	
6						
7	1977	0.95				
8	1978	1.24	30.53%			
9	1979	1.45	16.94%	30.53%	13.59%	
10	1980	1.95	34.48%	23.73%	10.75%	
11	1981	2.20	12.82%	27.31%	14.49%	
12	1982	2.63	19.55%	23.69%	4.15%	
13	1983	3.02	14.83%	22.86%	8.03%	
14	1984	3.68	21.85%	21.52%	0.33%	
15	1985	3.76	2.17%	21.57%	19.40%	
16	1986	3.90	3.72%	19.15%	15.42%	
17	1987	4.50	15.38%	17.43%	2.05%	
18	1988	5.10	13.33%	17.23%	3.89%	
19					---------	
20		Mean Absolute Deviation ---->			9.21%	

Figure 13.16. Forecasting growth rates by using the method of simple averages

Problems

1 Set up the worksheet shown in Figure 13.16.

2 In addition to the mean absolute deviation, the mean squared error is frequently used to test the accuracy of a forecasting method. An error is defined as the difference between the actual value and the forecasted value. The mean squared error is an average of all the squared errors calculated from the data under consideration. Compute the mean squared error of the naive forecasting method illustrated in Figure 13.15.

3 Compute the mean squared error using the data presented in Figure 13.16. Compare your results with these obtained in Problem 2.

Single moving average method

The essence of this method is to generate the next period's forecast by averaging the most recent observations in the data set. The single moving average method calculates averages over time as follows: each time a new observation becomes available, the new average is calculated after deleting the oldest observation and adding the latest one. The method initially requires the selection of the number of historical observations to be included in the average. Once the number of observations to be utilized for the calculation of the averages has been selected, it is held constant.

Example 13.16 Forecasting dividend growth rates by using the single moving average method

Given the annual dividends per share of Marks and Spencer for 1977 to 1988, we utilize three observations for each average. Cell D11 (see Figure 13.17) stores the formula `@AVG(C8..C10)` which calculates an average using the following three observations: 30.53 per cent, 16.94 per cent, and 34.48 per cent. This figure is our forecast for 1981. The other moving averages are obtained by copying the contents of cell D11 into the range D12..D18.

```
        A          B            C                D              E              F
 1 APPLYING THE SINGLE MOVING AVERAGE METHOD
 2 ========================================
 3
 4 ---------------------------------------------------------------------------
 5      YEAR      DPS    GROWTH RATE    FORECAST     ABSOLUTE DEVIATION
 6 ---------------------------------------------------------------------------
 7      1977      0.95
 8      1978      1.24             30.53%
 9      1979      1.45             16.94%
10      1980      1.95             34.48%
11      1981      2.20             12.82%       27.31%     14.49%
12      1982      2.63             19.55%       21.41%      1.87%
13      1983      3.02             14.83%       22.28%      7.45%
14      1984      3.68             21.85%       15.73%      6.12%
15      1985      3.76              2.17%       18.74%     16.57%
16      1986      3.90              3.72%       12.95%      9.23%
17      1987      4.50             15.38%        9.25%      6.13%
18      1988      5.10             13.33%        7.09%      6.24%
19                                                        ---------
20            Mean Absolute Deviation ---->               8.514%
```

Figure 13.17. Forecasting growth rates by using the single moving average method

The single moving average method provides a better forecast than the naive forecasting method.

Problems

1 Set up the worksheet shown in Figure 13.17.

2 Compare the mean squared error computed from the data shown in Figure 13.17 with that computed from the data presented in Figure 13.15.

A simple linear regression trend method

This approach forecast growth rates by using a straight trend line fitted to the data under consideration. Assuming a constant dividend growth and continuous compounding, the dividends per share for year t can be expressed as:

$$D_t = D_o e^{gt} \tag{13.4}$$

where

g = the compounded annual growth rate in dividends per share.

t = the year indicator, $t = 1, 2, 3, \ldots, T$.

Taking the natural logarithm of both sides of Equation (13.4) yields

$$\ln D_t = \ln D_o + gt \tag{13.5}$$

In view of Equation (13.5), g can be obtained by regressing the natural logarithm of D_t against time.

Example 13.17 Using the relationship between dividends per share and time to forecast dividend growth rates of Marks and Spencer

Column C of the spreadsheet shown in Figure 13.18 calculates the natural logarithm for each annual dividend per share of Marks and Spencer in the period 1977–86. The mathematical function `@LN(B7)` is stored in cell C7, then the contents of cell C7 are copied into the range C8..C16. The regression has as dependent variable the natural logarithm of dividends per share and as independent variable the time in years. The regression results are obtained by employing the `/Data Regression` command of 1-2-3.

	A	B	C	D E F	G	H
1	FORECASTING GROWTH RATES USING A SINGLE REGRESSION ANALYSIS					
2	============					
3						
4	------------					
5	YEAR	DPS	Ln(DPS)			
6	------------			------------		
7	1	0.95	-0.051	Regression Output:		
8	2	1.24	0.215	Constant		-0.082
9	3	1.45	0.372	Std Err of Y Est		0.102
10	4	1.95	0.668	R Squared		0.963
11	5	2.20	0.788	No. of Observations		10
12	6	2.63	0.967	Degrees of Freedom		8
13	7	3.02	1.105			
14	8	3.68	1.303	X Coefficient(s)	0.161	
15	9	3.76	1.324	Std Err of Coef.	0.011	
16	10	3.90	1.361			
17	11	4.50		T-STATISTIC	14.343	
18	12	5.10		------------		

Figure 13.18. Estimating the growth rate using a linear regression trend method

The *R*-squared shows that the variation of the independent variable explains 96.3 per cent of the variation in the dependent variable. This value indicates a highly significant time trend. On the other hand, the *t*-statistic is much higher than the critical value at the 1 per cent level of significance which in turn confirms our conclusion about the strong relationship between the logarithm form of the annual dividends per share and time. If the dividend growth is 16.1 per cent, then we have

$$\text{Dividends per share for year } 11 = 3.90e^{(0.161)(1)} = 4.58 \text{ pence}$$

$$\text{Dividends per share for year } 12 = 3.90e^{(0.161)(2)} = 5.38 \text{ pence}$$

Each forecasted dividend payment per share provides a good approximation of the actual dividends per share. However, note that this method may be less suitable for another public limited company.

Some useful points about dividend valuation models

1 (Constant growth dividend valuation model and dividend pattern) The constant growth dividend valuation model is more suitable for relatively large firms which pay moderate dividend payments. However, it is unlikely to be useful for firms having an unstable dividend pattern. In such cases, it would probably be better to use the supernormal growth dividend valuation model which allows the valuation of a share over time as the dividend rates of growth change.

2 (Cases where the constant growth dividend valuation model is inappropriate) If a firm pays no dividends and it is expected never to pay dividends, then the general dividend valuation model and the constant growth valuation model are inappropriate. If a firm pays no current dividends and after, say, a year decides

to pay dividends, the dividend growth rate is infinite and the constant growth valuation model is inappropriate.

3 (The constant growth dividend valuation model when dividends are paid semi-annually) The constant growth dividend valuation model, introduced earlier in this chapter, assumes annual dividend payments. In the United Kingdon, firms usually pay dividends on a semi-annual basis, thus, for practical purposes the annual data should be adjusted before the valuation model is used.

Example 13.18 Using the constant growth valuation model with semi-annual data

The most recent semi-annual dividend per share of GA Manufacturing plc is 5 pence. Investors expect the firm's dividends to grow at an annual rate of 8 per cent and they require a 15 per cent annual rate of return on the firm's ordinary shares. To calculate the intrinsic value of GA Manufacturing's share by using the constant growth valuation model with semi-annual data follow the steps:

Step 1 Calculate the semi-annual growth rate and the semi-annual required rate of return.

Semi-annual growth rate: $(1 + 0.08)\,\hat{}\,(1/2) - 1 = 3.92$ per cent

Semi-annual required rate of return:

$$(1 + 0.15)\,\hat{}\,(1/2) - 1 = 7.24 \text{ per cent}$$

Step 2 Calculate the semi-annual expected dividends per share for the next period.

Expected dividends per share for period 1:

$$5 \times (1 + 0.0392) = 5.196 \text{ pence}$$

Step 3 Calculate the intrinsic value of the share using semi-annual data.

Intrinsic value: $5.196/(0.0724 - 0.0392) = 156.50$ pence

The expected dividends per share for period 2 would be $5.196\times (1 + 0.0392) = 5.400$ pence. Therefore, the total expected dividends per share for the next year are 10.596 pence. The intrinsic value using yearly data is calculated as follows:

$10.596/(0.15 - 0.08) = 151.37$ pence

The last result is different from that derived utilizing semi-annual data. Therefore, if a firm's dividends are paid every six months, the correct procedure would be to use semi-annual data in calculating its intrinsic value per share.

4 (Ex-dividend and the constant dividend valuation model) Investors who own ordinary shares before they go ex-dividend are entitled to receive the most recent declared dividend. Investors who buy ordinary shares on or after they have gone ex-dividend are not entitled to receive the latest declared dividend payment. Share

prices are usually expected to drop by the full amount of the dividend on the ex-dividend date (other things being the same) since potential buyers are no longer entitled to that dividend. The constant dividend valuation model calculates the share price by assuming implicitly that the first dividend payment per share would be received during the coming year. If we wish to value a share by assuming that investors are eligible to receive also the latest declared dividend, the intrinsic value of the share is calculated as follows:

$$P_o = \frac{D_1}{r_o - g} + D_0$$

where D_0 is the most recently declared dividend per share.

For example, suppose that the expected dividend per share during the coming year is 4.2 pence and the investors' required rate of return is 15 per cent. If the annual expected rate of increase in future dividends is 5 per cent, the intrinsic value of the ordinary share is

$$P_o = 4.2/(0.15 - 0.05) + 4 = 46 \text{ pence}$$

where the most recent declared dividend on the firm's share was 4 pence.

The price/earnings ratio and the constant growth valuation model

We assume that the rate of growth in earnings per share and the rate of increase in the dividend payout ratio are constant. The constant dividend valuation model can be also expressed as

$$P_o = \frac{cE_1}{r_o - g}$$

where

c = the dividend payout ratio.

E_1 = the expected earnings per share for year 1.

Thus, the price/earnings ratio, the ratio of the price today to anticipated earnings per share for the next year, is given by

$$P_o/E_1 = \frac{c}{r_o - g} \qquad (13.6)$$

Equation (13.6) reveals that the price/earnings ratio depends on the dividend payout ratio, the investors' required rate of return on the firm's shares and the expected growth in dividends per share.

Example 13.19 Calculating the price/earnings ratio of a firm using the constant growth dividend valuation model

RD Stores plc retains 40 per cent of its earnings for future investments. The firm's earnings per share for the next year are forecasted at 20 pence and are expected to grow at a rate of 9 per cent annually. The investors' required rate of return in this share is 14 per cent. The intrinsic value per share is

$$P_o = (1 - 0.40) \times 20/(0.14 - 0.09) = 240 \text{ pence}$$

Therefore, the price/earnings ratio is given by

$$240/20 = 0.60/(0.14 - 0.09) = 12$$

Problem

Examine the sensitivity of the price/earnings ratio to changes in the dividend payout ratio and the investors' required rate of return.

Growth opportunities

Consider a firm that has no growth opportunities and assume that its earnings per share stream is an annuity with infinite life. If the firm pays all of its earnings out to shareholders as dividends, the intrinsic value per share would be equal to the present value of a perpetuity paying an annual amount equal to the constant earnings per share. That is

$$P_o = E_1/r_o$$

Suppose that the firm has growth opportunities (that is, opportunities to invest funds in profitable investments), then the firm's intrinsic value per share is given by

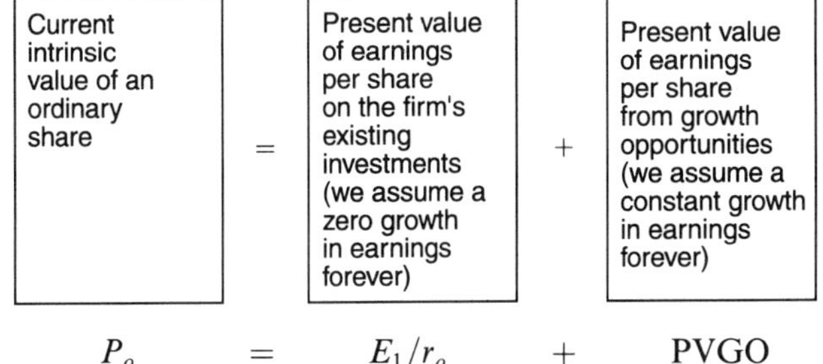

$$P_o \quad = \quad E_1/r_o \quad + \quad \text{PVGO}$$

where PVGO can be calculated by using the constant growth dividend valuation model.

Example 13.20 Calculating the intrinsic value per share as a sum of the present value of the earnings per share on the firm's existing investments and the present value of the earnings per share from growth opportunities

The intrinsic value of a share of RD Stores plc is 240.00 pence (see Example 13.19). The firm's constant dividend payout ratio is 60 per cent and its most recent dividend per share is 12.00 pence. The firm's intrinsic value per share can be calculated by following the steps below.

Step 1 Calculate the current earnings per share and reinvested earnings per share.
The current earnings per share will be equal to: $12/0.60 = 20.00$ pence.
The reinvested earnings per share will be equal to:

$$20.00 - 12.00 = 8.00 \text{ pence.}$$

Step 2 If the earnings per share are expected to remain constant forever, the present value of the earnings per share on the firm's existing investments can be calculated as follows:

$20.00/0.14 = 142.86$ pence

Step 3 Calculate the value of the firm's investments at the end of year 1. RD Stores' return on equity equals the constant dividend growth rate divided by the retention ratio (see Equation 13.3). That is:

$$\text{ROE} = \frac{0.09}{1 - 0.60} = 22.50 \text{ per cent}$$

The reinvested earnings per share for the first year are 8.00 pence. Thus, the firm's investment opportunities generate the following annual cash flow per share, starting at the end of year 2:

$0.225 \times 8.00 = 1.80$ pence

Since we assume a perpetuity, the value of 1.80 pence at the end of year 1 will be

$1.80/0.14 = 12.86$ pence

The firm has to reinvest 8.00 pence per share in order to realize 12.86 pence per share, the value per share of the investments at the end of year 1 would be

$12.86 - 8.00 = 4.86$ pence

Step 4 Calculate the present value of the earnings per share from the growth opportunities available to the firm.

The growth opportunities of the firm are expected to produce a value per share of 4.86 pence which is forecasted to grow at an annual rate of 9 per cent forever. Using the constant growth dividend valuation model, we can calculate the present value of earnings per share from growth opportunities as follows:

$4.86/(0.14 - 0.09) = 97.20$ pence

Step 5 Calculate the firm's current intrinsic value per share.

The current intrinsic value of a share is equal to the sum of the values calculated in Steps 2 and 4 (a slight difference occurs due to rounding):

$142.87 + 97.20 = 240$ pence

The calculations performed in this example are summarized in Figure 13.19.

Problem

Set up the worksheet shown in Figure 13.19.

Estimating the value of a firm in practice

There are two general approaches used for valuing the shares of an unquoted company: use information from comparable companies to help in the valuation pro-

```
                A                       B        C         D         E
 1 CALCULATING THE INTRINSIC VALUE OF A SHARE
 2 ==========================================
 3 Constant Growth Rate               9.0%
 4 Dividend                          12.00
 5 Required Rate of Return            14.0%
 6                                ---------
 7 Price                            240.00
 8 Payout Ratio                       60.0%
 9 Current EPS                       20.00
10                                ---------
11 Constant growth                  142.86
12
13 Retained earnings                  8.00
14 Return on Equity                  0.225
15 Generated Funds Per Share          1.80
16                                ---------
17 Present Value of EPS              12.86
18
19 Net Present Value                  4.86
20 PVGO                              97.14
21 Intrinsic Value                  240.00
```

Figure 13.19. Calculating the intrinsic value of a share as a sum of two present values

cess; and forecast the inputs of a dividend valuation model directly. Each of these methods produces reliable results only if we use valid assumptions and reliable data. Below we shall employ the former method for valuing an ordinary share.

Example 13.21 Valuing a share in Super Store Ltd

Super Store Ltd is a company selling mostly clothes, food and household products. Aston plc, B&C plc and Mepas Stores plc are three comparable quoted firms having the following characteristics:

1. They are in the same line of business as Super Store.
2. They have similar beta coefficients.
3. They pay dividends on a regular basis and have similar dividend growth rates as that of Super Store.
4. They are larger and more diversified than Super Store. Aston and B&C are about twice the size of Super Store and Mepas Stores is six times larger than Super Store.

The appropriate financial information for the three comparable firms is presented in Figure 13.20. For each firm, the market price per share (see row 13 of Figure 13.20) is the latest quoted price (that is, the last price in the financial year ended March 1990). The dividends per share and the earnings per share for the financial year ended March 1989 were calculated from the profit and loss account statements of the firms. The growth rates in dividends were calculated by using historical data over the last five years.

Using the market values of the three comparable firms, the average market value per share is 131.00 pence (see Figure 13.20, cell E22). The price/earnings ratios of the three firms are displayed in row 24. With respect to Aston's price/earnings ratio, Super Store should have a value of $12 \times 10 = 120.00$ pence. Likewise, with respect to the B&C's and Mepas Store's price/earnings ratios, Super Store should have values of 118.18 pence and 114.40 pence, respectively.

CALCULATING THE INTRINSIC VALUE OF A SHARE IN SUPER STORE LTD

D A T A

	Super Store Ltd
Earnings per Share	12
Dividends per Share	6
Growth Rate in Dividends	5.80%

	Aston	B&C	Mepas Stores
Market Price Per Share	120	130	143
Dividends Per Share	5	7	9.00
Earnings Per Share	12	13	15
Annual Dividend Growth	6.40%	5.50%	6.00%

METHOD	Aston	B&C	Mepas Stores	AVERAGE
Market Valuation	120	130	143	131.00
Price Earnings Ratio (P/E)	10.000	9.848	9.533	
PRICE FOR SUPER STORE	120.00	118.18	114.40	117.53
Dividends Valuation Model	10.83%	11.18%	12.67%	11.56%
VALUE FOR SUPER STORE				110.17
Required Rate of Return	10.50%	11.00%	11.30%	10.93%
VALUE FOR SUPER STORE				123.66

Figure 13.20. Calculating the intrinsic value of a share using four valuation methods

With respect to the average ratio, Super Store should have a per share value of 117.53 pence.

We can use the constant growth dividend valuation model to calculate the investors' required rate of return for each of the comparable firms. For example, the investors' required rate of return on the ordinary shares of Aston is:

$$k_o = 5 \times (1 + 0.0640)/120 + 0.0640 = 10.83 \text{ per cent}$$

Similarly, the investors' required rates of return on the B&C and Mepas Store shares are 11.18 per cent and 12.67 per cent, respectively. The average required rate of return is 11.56 per cent. The value of Super Store based on this average required rate of return is 110.17 pence. For each of the comparable firms the required rate of return is also calculated by using the capital asset pricing model (see Chapter 9). In this case, the average value of the required rate of return is 10.93 per cent. The value of Super Stores based on a required rate of return of 10.93 per cent is 123.66 pence. The four valuation methods discussed above indicate that the share value of Super Store is in the range 110.17–131.00 pence. Note, however, that the risk associated with the shares of Super Store is higher than that associated with the shares of each comparable firm, because Super Store's shares are less marketable than the shares of the other three firms. This probably suggests that the value of a share in Super Store should approximate the lower prices shown in Figure 13.20. If the required rate of return for the ordinary shares of Super Store is in the range 10.93–11.93 per cent, then Figure 13.21 calculates the average intrinsic value by using the constant growth dividend valuation model. The results are in line with our earlier suggestion that the intrinsic value of the share should be around the lower estimated prices.

	A	B	C	D	E
38					
39		Rate of	Value		
40		Return			
41					
42		10.93%	123.74		
43		11.03%	121.38		
44		11.13%	119.10		
45		11.23%	116.91		
46		11.33%	114.79		
47		11.43%	112.75		
48		11.53%	110.79		
49		11.63%	108.89		
50		11.73%	107.05		
51		11.83%	105.27		
52		11.93%	103.56		
53			---------		
54	Average Intrinsic Value ->		113.11		

Figure 13.21. Calculating the average intrinsic value of a share in Super Store

Some useful points

1 (The importance of comparability of variables used in the analysis) If you are attempting to value the shares of a firm by using the average price/earnings ratio of a number of comparable firms, remember to provide comparability between the variables employed in your calculations. For example, if the earnings per share of the subject firm were estimated by utilizing accounting data for the latest five years, then you should also be using the latest five year average earnings in computing the price/earnings ratio of each comparable firm.

2 (Estimating a range of values for the subject firm) In most cases, the subject firm's value lies within a range of values estimated by using the appropriate financial characteristics of the compatible firms. Obviously, the selection of the most appropriate value within this range is based upon the subjective judgement of the analyst.

3 (Marketability) The risk associated with the shares of a subject firm is usually higher than that associated with the shares of each of the comparable firms because the subject firm's shares are less marketable than the shares of the comparable firms. This is a difference that must be taken into account when valuing a subject firm by reference to the share prices of comparable quoted firms.

4 (Valuation of firms in unrelated industries) If the subject firm has operations in two or more unrelated industries, then you should value each division within them separately. In this case, you probably have to use a number of comparable firms for each different division within the subject firm.

Share price information

Most share prices of those firms whose shares are traded on the London Stock

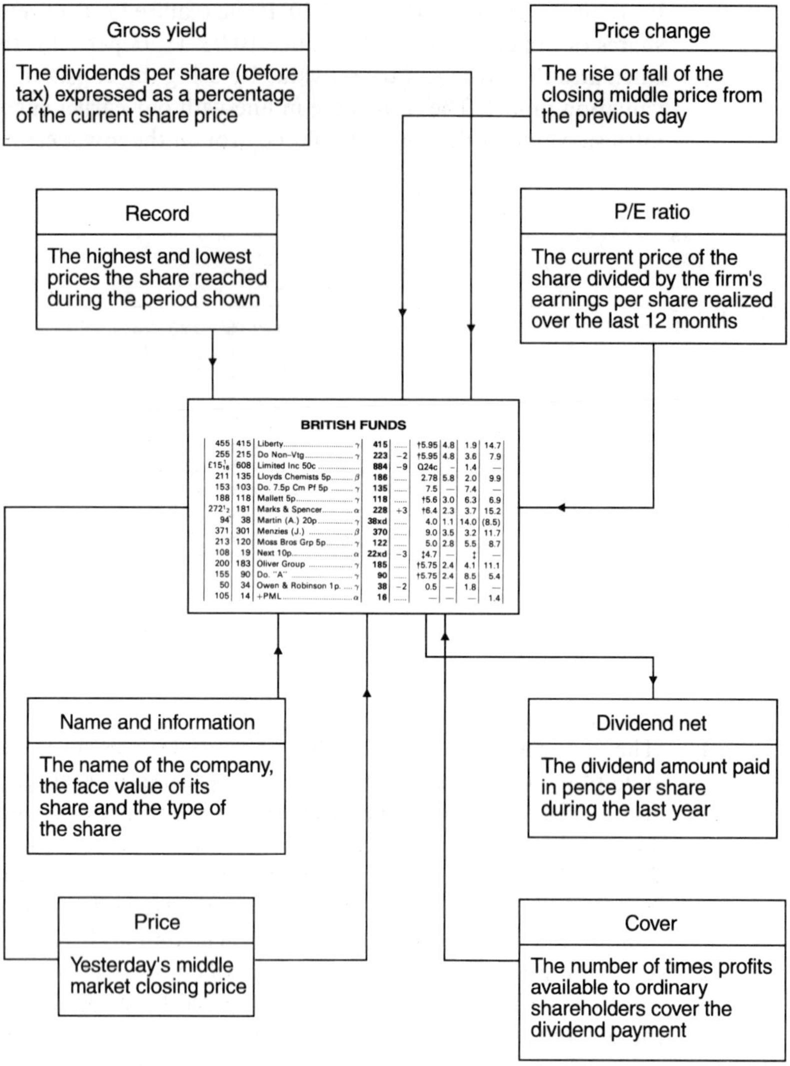

Gross yield

The dividends per share (before tax) expressed as a percentage of the current share price

Price change

The rise or fall of the closing middle price from the previous day

Record

The highest and lowest prices the share reached during the period shown

P/E ratio

The current price of the share divided by the firm's earnings per share realized over the last 12 months

BRITISH FUNDS

455	415	Liberty.......γ	415	......	†5.95	4.8	1.9	14.7
255	215	Do Non-Vtg.......γ	223	−2	†5.95	4.8	3.6	7.9
£15$\frac{1}{16}$	608	Limited Inc 50c	884	−9	Q24c	–	1.4	—
211	135	Lloyds Chemists 5p.......β	186	......	2.78	5.8	2.0	9.9
153	103	Do. 7.5p Cm Pf 5p ....γ	135	......	7.5	—	7.4	—
188	118	Mallett 5p.......γ	118	......	†5.6	3.0	6.3	6.9
272½	181	Marks & Spencer.......α	228	+3	†6.4	2.3	3.7	15.2
94	38	Martin (A.) 20p.......γ	38xd	......	4.0	1.1	14.0	(8.5)
371	301	Menzies (J.) ....β	370	......	9.0	3.5	3.2	11.7
213	120	Moss Bros Grp 5p.......γ	122	......	5.0	2.8	5.5	8.7
108	19	Next 10p.......α	22xd	−3	‡4.7	—	‡	—
200	183	Oliver Group ....γ	185	......	†5.75	2.4	4.1	11.1
155	90	Do. "A" ....γ	90	......	†5.75	2.4	8.5	5.4
50	34	Owen & Robinson 1p. ....γ	38	−2	0.5	—	1.8	—
105	14	+PML.......α	16	......	—	—	—	1.4

Name and information

The name of the company, the face value of its share and the type of the share

Dividend net

The dividend amount paid in pence per share during the last year

Price

Yesterday's middle market closing price

Cover

The number of times profits available to ordinary shareholders cover the dividend payment

Figure 13.22. A summary of the quoted information on share prices (*Source*: *Financial Times*, 6 December 1990)

Exchange are quoted daily in the *Financial Times*. Figure 13.22 presents a sample of share quotations together with a brief explanation for each quoted piece of information.

Consider the following quote from Figure 13.22:

1990					Div		Y'ld	
High	Low	Stock	Price	+/−	Net	C'vr	Gr's	P/E
272 1/2	181	Marks & Spencer..a	228	−3	6.4	2.3	3.7	15.2

We may now discuss the information shown in more detail.

- *High–Low* The period of 1990 indicates that the recorded values cover the period January 1990–December 1990. The highest price recorded for Marks and Spencer's shares during this period was 272 1/2 pence and the lowest was 181 pence. For any firm, during the early part of the calendar year the period covered is longer than 12 months. For example, in March 1990 the recorded information would cover a period of 15 months (that is, January 1989–March 1990).

- *Stock* This column gives the name and type of share. Frequently a price appears immediately after the name of the share, for example, Next 10p. This indicates the face (or nominal) value of the share which has only legal and accounting significance. The *Financial Times* shows the face value of a share if it is different from 25 pence.

  At the end of the Stock column, the *Financial Times* displays one of the three Greek letters; alpha, beta, gamma. The Greek letter alpha indicates that the shares are the most heavily traded issues, the Greek letter beta indicates that the shares are not traded as actively as those of the alpha group and the Greek letter gamma indicates that the shares are the least traded of the three.
- *Price* This is the middle price of the share at close of the business on the previous working day. Unless otherwise indicated, the price is expressed in pence. For example, Marks and Spencer's shares middle price at 16:30 hours on 5 December 1990 was 228 pence.
- *+/−* The change in the closing middle price from the previous date is expressed in the same units of currency as the middle price displayed in the price column. For example, the middle price of Marks and Spencer's shares rose by 3 pence on 5 December 1990.
- *Div Net* Companies in the United Kingdom pay dividends to shareholders net of basic income tax. Marks and Spencer's 'Div Net' is equal to 6.4 meaning that the firm paid total dividends per share of 6.4 pence (after basic income tax of 25 per cent) in its last financial year.
- *C'ver* The dividend cover tells the number of times profits available to ordinary shareholders cover the dividend payment. For example, Figure 13.22 shows a dividend cover for Marks and Spencer of 2.3 meaning that the firm's dividend was covered 2.3 times by its net earnings. The dividend cover ratio is calculated by dividing the firm's net earnings per share by the net dividends per share.
- *Y'ld Grs* The gross yield is the amount of dividend payment per share (before income tax) expressed as a percentage of the current market price of the share. The gross dividend per share of Marks and Spencer can be calculated as follows:

  $$\frac{6.4}{1 - 0.25} = 8.534 \text{ pence}$$

  Then, the gross dividend yield of Marks and Spencer (at 5 December 1990) would be

  $$\frac{8.534}{228} \times 100 = 3.742 \text{ per cent}$$

- *P/E* The price/earnings ratio is calculated by dividing the market share price by the firm's earnings per share over the last 12 months. The price/earnings ratio indicates how high the firm's share is in relation to its earnings per share. For example, the Marks and Spencer price/earnings ratio is 15.2 (see Figure 13.22), meaning that the current share price (that is, the share price on 5 December 1990) is 15.2 times the net earnings per share of last year.

Summary

1 *Methods for evaluating the ordinary shares of a firm* This chapter discussed five methods that can be used to evaluate an ordinary share in a firm: (a) market value method; (b) book value method; (c) asset value method; (d) price/earnings ratio method; and (e) dividend valuation method. The better method is the dividend valuation method.

2 *The dividend valuation method* The value of an ordinary share using the T-year dividend valuation method involves estimating the present value of all future cash flows it is expected to provide. The cash flows associated with the valuation of ordinary shares are generally more uncertain than those associated with the valuation of debentures or preference shares. Investors normally require a higher rate of return on ordinary shares than on debentures or preference shares because ordinary shares are considered to be more risky than fixed cost sources of financing.

The Gordon (or constant growth dividend valuation) model provides a special case of the general dividend valuation model. In view of the Gordon's model, the present value of an ordinary share is determined by the following three variables: (a) the firm's current dividends per share; (b) the annual constant dividend growth rate; and (c) the investors' required rate of return for the firm's ordinary shares. The one-stage supernormal growth dividend valuation model assumes that dividends on ordinary shares grow at an above-normal rate over a specified number of years and then grow at a constant normal rate forever. According to the one-stage supernormal growth valuation model, the present value of an ordinary share is dependent on the following variables: (a) current dividends per share; (b) growth rate of dividends per share during the supernormal growth period; (c) growth rate of dividends per share after the period of supernormal growth; and (d) investors' required rate of return on the firm's ordinary shares.

3 *Valuing unquoted firms* There are two general approaches used to value the shares of an unquoted company: determine the intrinsic value of the unquoted firm by employing information on comparable firms; and utilize forecasting analysis to estimate the inputs of a dividend valuation model. Note that the reliability of the results provided by each method is dependent upon the validity of the assumptions and the reliability of the data used.

Questions for discussion

1 For each term shown below in the largest box provide a definition in your own words. Then check your response against the definitions included in the chapter.

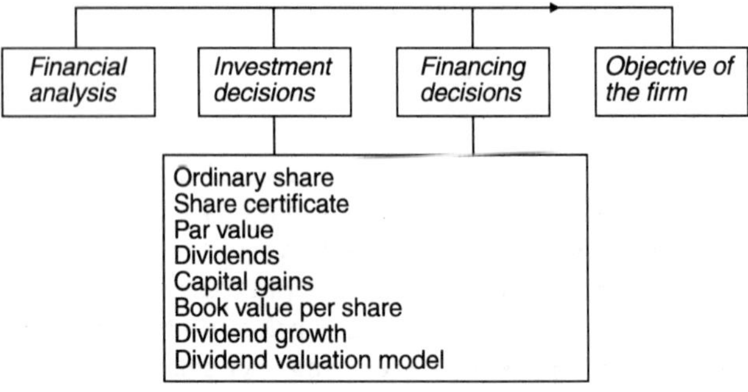

2 Compare and contrast the following valuation methods for ordinary shares:
   (a) market value method;
   (b) book value method;
   (c) asset value method;
   (d) price earnings ratio method;
   (e) dividend valuation method.

3 Compare and contrast the following four valuation models:
   (a) T-period valuation model;
   (b) zero growth valuation model;
   (c) constant growth valuation model;
   (d) supergrowth valuation model.

4 Discuss in detail the diagram shown below and explain its use.

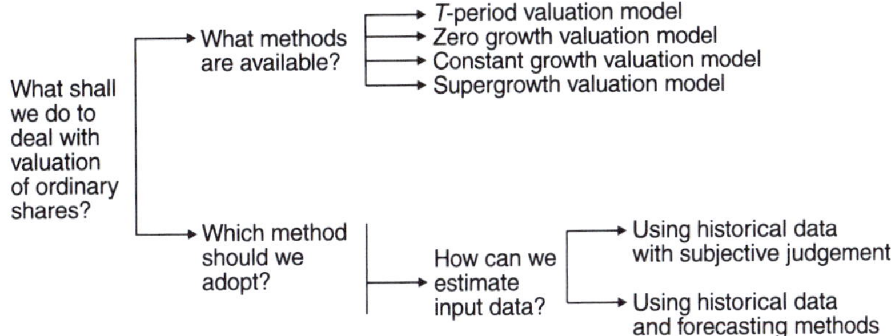

5 (a) The input variables required for the constant growth dividend valuation model are shown below. This figure also indicates that as the current dividends per share (DPS) ratio increases, the present value of the ordinary share increases (other things being the same). Fill in the five blank spaces. Each time discuss how an increase or decrease in the value of a variable affects the value of the ordinary share, assuming all other things equal.

	Increases	Decreases
Current DPS	Share value increases	
Dividend growth		
Cost of equity		

   (b) Choose three of your answers in part (a) and illustrate each case by employing a numerical example.

6 Compare and contrast debenture price valuation, preference share price valuation and ordinary share price valuation.

7 Discuss how each of the following situations might affect the share value of a firm, other things being equal (use the constant growth valuation model):
   (a) The firm's sales are expected to rise at a faster rate.
   (b) The firm's expenses rise more slowly than its sales.
   (c) The covariance between the rates of return of the firm's shares and those of the market index increase.
   (d) The Bank of England takes action to lower the interest rates.
   (e) Inflation is expected to increase over the next three years.
   (f) A fall in the rate of interest and a decline in investors' aversion to risk.

8 Discuss carefully each of the following statements:
 (a) 'If a firm does not pay current dividends, the market value of its ordinary shares is not zero.'
 (b) 'The valuation models for a perpetual debenture, preference shares, and zero ordinary share dividend valuation model are identical.'
 (c) 'The constant growth dividend valuation model is not suitable for firms that have unstable dividend patterns.'

9 Discuss fully the four relationships indicated in the following diagram:

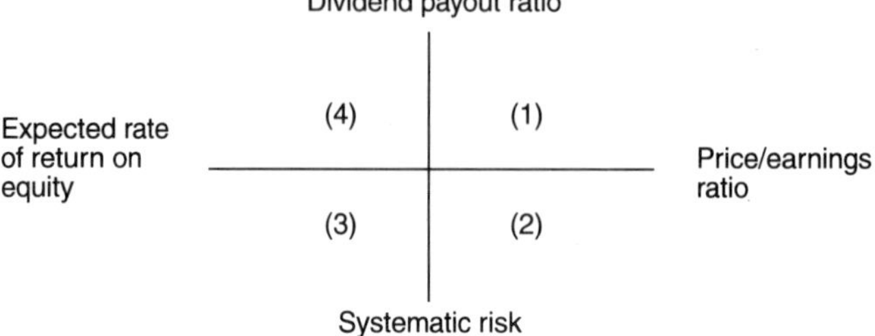

10 Explain how we can value an unquoted firm.

11 Discuss the following information (*source: Financial Times*, 6 December 1990):

1990					Div		Y'ld	
High	Low	Stock	Price	+/−	Net	C'vr	Gr's	P/E
226	55	Burton Group 50p	88	+1	6.0	2.8	9.4	4.9

12 Prepare an analog model summarizing the main points discussed in this chapter.

13 How can spreadsheets be used to facilitate the application of the concepts discussed in this chapter?

Appendix 13A Proof of the equation: $\mathbf{PV} = D_1 \dfrac{1 - a^T}{r_o - g}$

The present value of a series of dividends per share that are expected to increase at a constant rate each year can be written as follows:

$$\text{PV} = \frac{D_0(1+g)}{(1+r_o)} + \frac{D_0(1+g)^2}{(1+r_o^2)} + \frac{D_0(1+g)^3}{(1+r_o)^3} + \cdots + \frac{D_0(1+g)^T}{(1+r_o)^T}$$

The last equation is equivalent to

$$\text{PV} = D_0[a + a^2 + a^3 + \cdots + a^T] \quad (13\text{A}.1)$$

where

$$a = (1+g)/(1+r_o)$$

Equation (13A.1) gives

$$\text{PV}/a = D_0[1 + a + a^2 + \cdots + a^{T-1}] \quad (13.\text{A}.2)$$

Subtracting Equation (13A.1) from Equation (13A.2) we take:

$$\mathrm{PV}/a - \mathrm{PV} = D_0[1 - a^T]$$

Therefore,

$$\mathrm{PV} = \frac{D_0[1 - a^T]a}{1 - a}$$

$$= \frac{D_0(1+g)[1 - a^T]}{r_o - g}$$

$$= D_1 \frac{1 - a^T}{r_o - g}$$

Appendix 13B Confidence intervals for standard deviations

Consider a population from which we draw repeated random samples of a given size and compute the standard deviation for each sample. The probability distribution of these sample standard deviations is called sampling distribution of the standard deviation. The lower and upper limits for the standard deviation of a normally distributed population as estimated with the aid of a sample are presented in Figure 13B.1.

Lower limit $\longrightarrow$ SD $- z$ SD/SQRT($2n$)

Upper limit $\longrightarrow$ SD $+ z$ SD/SQRT($2n$)

where

SD = the standard deviation of the sample under consideration.

z = the number of standard deviations associated with the desired level of confidence.

SQRT = the square root operator.

n = the sample size.

Figure 13B.1. Summary of the confidence interval for standard deviation

Example 13B.1 Calculating a confidence interval for a population's standard deviation

Consider the population of 300 monthly rates of change for the FTA price index for debentures. The standard deviation of a random sample of 36 monthly observations was computed to be 2.077 per cent (note that the sample standard deviation provides an unbiased estimator for the population standard deviation if the sum of the squared deviations from the mean is divided by $n - 1$). We assume that the population is approximately normally distributed.

The lower limit of the 95 per cent confidence interval for the population standard deviation would be

$$0.02077 - (1.9600)(0.02077)/\mathrm{SQRT}(72) = 1.597 \text{ per cent}$$

The upper limit of the 95 per cent confidence interval for the population standard deviation is calculated as follows:

$$0.02077 + (1.9600)(0.02077)/\mathrm{SQRT}(72) = 2.557 \text{ per cent}$$

Therefore, we can be 95 per cent confident that the standard deviation of the population is between 1.597 per cent and 2.557 per cent.

Problem

Compute the 99 per cent confidence interval for the standard deviation of 2.077 per cent given in Example 13B.1.

Some useful points

1 (Calculating the confidence limits using 1-2-3 Release 3) The lower limit shown in Figure 13B.1 can be calculated by using the following formula of 1-2-3 (we assume 95 per cent level of confidence and a normally distributed population):

```
@STDS(ran)-1.96*@STDS(ran)/@SQRT(2*@COUNT(ran))
```

where ran is the range containing the sample observations. Similarly, the upper limit for the confidence interval of standard deviation is calculated by using the formula below (we assume 95 per cent level of confidence and a normally distribution population):

```
@STDS(ran)+1.96*@STDS(ran)/@SQRT(2*@COUNT(ran))
```

2 (The sampling distribution of the standard deviation) For a sample size greater than 100, the sampling distribution of the standard deviation is very close to normal.

References and bibliography

Bauman, W.S. (1969) Investment returns and present value, *Financial Analyst Journal*, **27**, November–December, 107–20.

Bower, R.S., Johnson, K.B., Lutz, W.J. and Topley, T.C. (1977) Investment opportunities and stock valuation, *Journal of Business Research*, **5**, March, 36–61.

Gordon, M. (1963) *The Investment, Financing and Valuation of Corporations*. Richard D. Irwin, Homewood, Ill.

Granger, C.W.J. (1975) Some consequences of the valuation model when expectations are taken to be optimum forecasts, *Journal of Finance*, **31**, March, 135–45.

Hubbard, C.L. and Hawkins, C.A. (1969) *Theory of Valuation*. International Textbooks, Scranton, Pa.

Malkier, B.G. (1963) Equity yields and structure of share prices, *The American Economic Review*, **53**, December, 1004–31.

Mao, J.C.T. (1966) The valuation of growth stocks: the investment opportunity approach, *Journal of Finance*, **21**, March, 95–102.

Myers, S. (1977) Determinants of corporate borrowing, *Journal of Financial Economics*, 147–75.

Stone, B.K. (1975) The conformity of stock values based on discounted dividends to a fair return process, *Bell Journal of Economics*, **6**, Autumn, 698–702.

Wendt, P.F. (1965) Current growth stock evaluation methods, *Financial Analyst Journal*, **21**, March–April, 91–201.

Williams, J.B. (1938) *The Theory of Investment Value*. Harvard University Press, Cambridge, Mass.

14 The cost of capital

This chapter includes:

- The weighted average cost of capital
- The weighted marginal cost of capital
- Calculating the cost of capital in practice
- Empirical evidence on the cost of capital methods

The cost of capital is used extensively in financial management. First, the cost of capital provides a basic input of data in capital budgeting analysis. With the net present value or profitability index the firm's cost of capital is used to discount the future cash flows of an investment project. It is also utilized as a basic piece of information in the internal rate of return decision rule, the internal rate of return is compared with the cost of capital to determine the acceptability of a project. Second, knowledge of a firm's cost of capital and how it is affected by the firm's financial decisions helps the financial director to determine the firm's optimal capital structure. Third, the cost of capital constitutes a basic input of data in other financial management decisions, for example leasing. The present chapter focuses on the measurement of the cost of capital. Figure 14.1 shows how the cost of capital concept is related to the financial management framework introduced in Chapter 2.

Basic concepts, definitions and examples

Simply stated, the cost of capital is the cost to the firm of raising long-term funds to finance investment projects. The principal forms of long-term financing are reserves, ordinary shares, long-term debt and preference shares. These sources of finance can be classified as shown in Figure 14.2.

Each individual source of finance has its own cost which can be simply defined as the current cost to the firm of obtaining funds from that particular source. For example, if the cost of new preference shares is 10.3 per cent, the firm pays £0.103 to acquire £1 of preference share capital. The explicit cost of a source of capital is called the specific cost of capital of that source.

Capital structure refers to the composition of long-term financing used by a firm. For example, the capital structure of a firm may consist of 40 per cent long-term debt, 50 per cent equity and 10 per cent preference shares. The weighted average cost of capital or simply the cost of capital is expressed as a percentage and it is calculated as a weighted average of the costs of the various sources, where each source is weighted by its relative proportion in the firm's long-run capital structure.

Each specific cost of capital is based on the return required by the investors of that

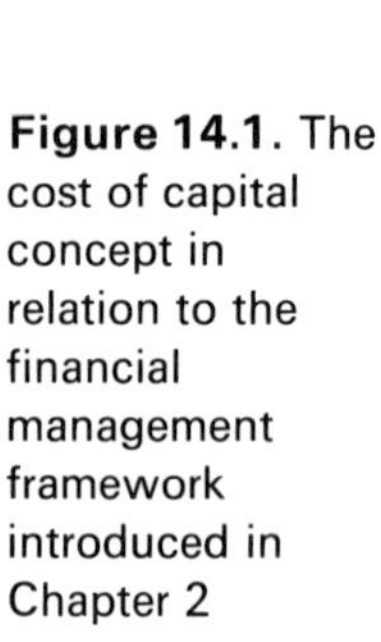

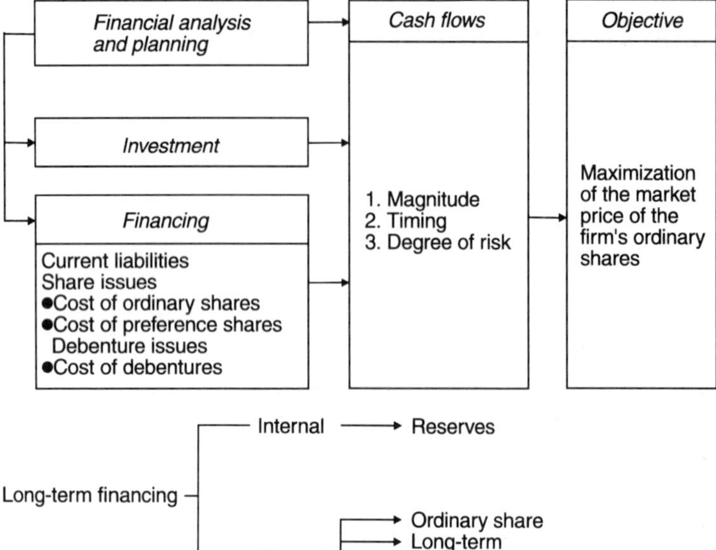

Figure 14.1. The cost of capital concept in relation to the financial management framework introduced in Chapter 2

Figure 14.2. Principal sources of long-term finance

particular source. However, it is not exactly the same as the investors' required rate of return because of income tax considerations in the case of debentures and flotation costs in the case of issuing new debentures and shares. Flotation costs are any costs involved in selling new securities; these costs include legal fees, printing and advertising expenses and sales commissions. By way of illustration, assume that a firm issues £10 million of new ordinary shares; if flotation costs are 3.5 per cent, the firm would receive only £9.65 million after paying flotation costs.

Next we consider an example illustrating the difference between the required rate of return in a firm's debentures and the cost the firm pays to acquire funds by issuing debentures. Assume that the rate of return required in a firm's debentures is 6.83 per cent. The cost of debentures after flotation expenses is higher than the required rate of return of 6.83 per cent because flotation costs reduce the cash proceeds from the sale of the debentures. If flotation costs are taken into account, the firm's (before-tax) cost of debt is 7.36 per cent. The before-tax cost of debentures must be adjusted to reflect that interest expenses are deductible from corporation tax, thus the after-tax cost of debentures is 4.78 per cent (we assume a corporate tax rate of 35 per cent). In view of our example, we can present the following diagram:

Required rate of return	Cost of debt capital after flotation costs	Cost of debt capital after flotation costs and tax
→	→	
6.83 per cent	7.36 per cent	4.78 per cent

To this end, the cost of capital is a weighted average of the rates of return required by investors (that is, debenture holders and shareholders) adjusted (if necessary) for flotation costs and tax requirements, where each specific cost is weighted by its relative proportion in the firm's capital structure. This definition can also be expressed as shown in Figure 14.3.

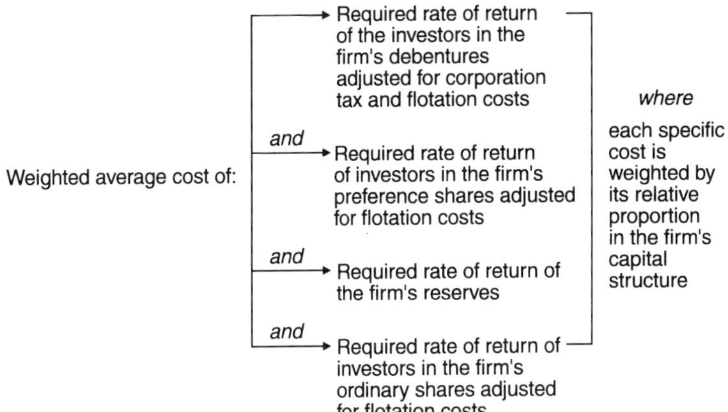

Figure 14.3. Defining the weighted average cost of capital

The cost of capital can alternatively be defined as the minimum rate of return a firm must earn on its investment if the market value of the firm is to remain unchanged. In view of this definition, the cost of capital is treated as a 'break-even' point. If the firm earns a lower return than its cost of capital, the firm's market value will fall. Conversely, if the rate of return of the firm is greater than its cost of capital, the firm's market value will rise.

The cost of capital is also referrred to as a hurdle rate because it serves as a cut-off rate for evaluating investment projects. If the internal rate of return of a project is higher than the firm's cost of capital and the new project has the same level of risk as the firm's existing investments, it should be accepted because the firm will realize a return greater than its cost of capital. Conversely, the firm should reject an investment project having the same risk as the firm's existing investments and internal rate of return less than its cost of capital.

Example 14.1 A decision rule using the cost of capital

Consider a firm that faces the following investment opportunities each of which has the same level of risk as the firm's existing investments.

Project	Cost (£)	Internal rate of return (%)
A	400,000	12.85
B	500,000	6.92
C	1,000,000	13.46
D	600,000	16.92
E	400,000	6.43
F	1,000,000	9.46

Assume that the existing capital structure of the firm consists of ordinary share capital, preference share capital and debenture capital. The investments will be financed with the proceeds from an issue of ordinary shares, an issue of preference shares and an issue of debentures. If the cost of capital is 11.17 per cent, we accept all the investments whose internal rate of return is above 11.17 per cent. Figure 14.4 illustrates graphically the decision rule for accepting investment projects with internal rates of return greater than the cost of capital of 11.17 per cent. The internal rates of return of projects D, C and A are greater than or equal

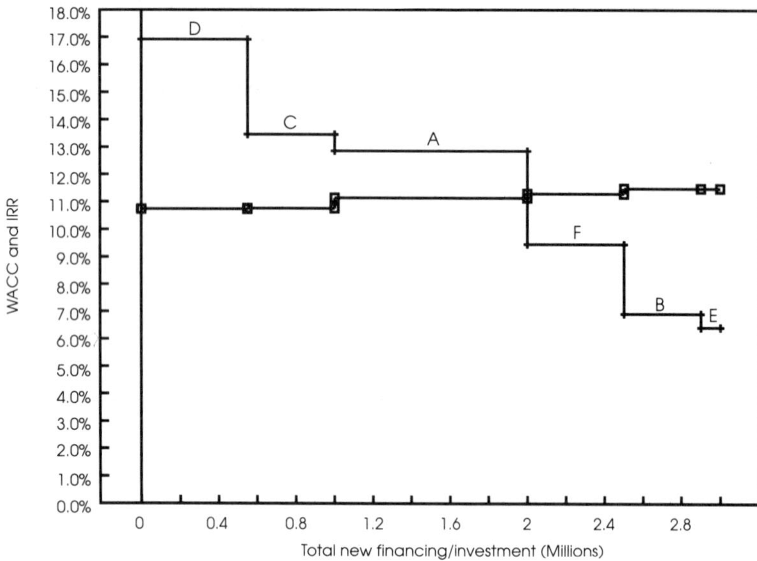

Figure 14.4. Illustrating a decision graphically

to the firm's cost of capital. Figure 14.4 shows that projects B, E and F should be rejected because the cost of capital of 11.17 per cent is greater than their internal rates of return.

Problem

Plot the graph shown in Figure 14.4 by using the graphing facilities of 1-2-3.

The present chapter uses the following assumptions:

1. The firm pays cash benefits (for example, ordinary dividends, interest, and so on) to investors annually at the end of each year.
2. The new investment projects of a firm have the same level of risk as its existing investments.
3. The firm's business and financial risk remains unaffected by investment and financing decisions (this assumption is relaxed later). This assumption implies that the changing cost of a source of capital over time should be influenced only by changes in the supply and demand for that source.
4. The new investment projects of a firm are financed with the same proportions of capital sources (for example, ordinary shares, debentures, and so on) as the firm employs to finance its existing projects.

Specific costs of capital

This section is concerned with measuring the cost of capital for debentures, preference shares, ordinary shares and reserves. The specific costs of capital are calculated with the aid of the valuation models presented in Chapters 11 and 13. The general procedure utilized in calculating the cost of a source of capital is summarized in Figure 14.5.

Determining the cost of new debentures

By following the general procedure illustrated in Figure 14.5, the required rate of

---

The required rate of return of a source of capital is the discount rate that satisfies the following valuation equation:

$$V = \sum_{t=1}^{T} \frac{CF_t}{(1+r)^t}$$

where

V = the purcharse price of a financial asset (for example, a debenture).

CF_t = the expected cash flow from a financial asset in year t.

T = the expected life of a financial asset.

Then

Cost of capital = required rate of return adjusted for tax considerations in the case of debentures and flotation costs in the case of new debentures and shares.

Figure 14.5. The determination of specific costs of capital

return on a particular debenture issue satisfies the following valuation equation:

$$V_d = \sum_{t=1}^{T} \frac{I}{(1+r_d)^t} + \frac{B_T}{(1+r_d)^T}$$

where

V_d = the current market price of the debenture.

I = the annual amount of interest paid on the debenture (in pounds sterling).

B_T = the principal payment in year N.

r_d = the investors' required rate of return on this particular debenture issue.

T = the number of years required for the debenture to mature.

In words, the investors' required rate of return on a debenture is the rate of return that equates the present value of the future annual interest payments and principal repayment to the current market price of the debenture.

Example 14.2 Calculating the investors' required rate of return on a particular debenture issue

```
        A          B          C          D          E         F        G
 1 INVESTORS' RRR ON A DEBENTURE ISSUE (N-PERIOD VALUATION MODEL)
 2 ==============================================================
 3 Current market value of debentures (£)---------------------->     96
 4 Coupon rate ------------------------------------------->     6%
 5
 6
 7 --------------------------------------------------------------
 8 Period    Interest (£)          Par value          Cash flows
 9 --------------------------------------------------------------
10        0                                            (£96)
11        1     £6.00                                   6.00
12        2      6.00                                   6.00
13        3      6.00                                   6.00
14        4      6.00                                   6.00
15        5      6.00                                   6.00
16        6      6.00              £100               106.00
17                                                 ----------
18         Investors' required rate of return -->      6.83%
19 --------------------------------------------------------------
```

Figure 14.6. Calculating the investors' required rate of return on a debenture issue

GD Fashions plc plans to issue six-year debentures each having a par value of £100 and carrying a coupon rate of 6 per cent. Each debenture is expected to sell at £96. The investors' required rate of return (RRR) can be calculated by using the 1-2-3's `@IRR` financial function (see Figure 14.6).

The following function is stored in cell F18:

```
@IRR(G4,F10..F16)
```

where the coupon rate is used as a guess for the internal rate of return.

Problem

Set up the worksheet shown in Figure 14.6.

In order to calculate the cost of a debenture, flotation costs and tax consequences on the debenture interest must be taken into account. The cost of a debenture after flotation costs can be calculated by following the method discussed in Example 14.2. However, in the calculation process the current market price of the debenture must be substituted by the net proceeds from the sale of the debenture. The latter can be calculated by subtracting flotation costs from the current market price of the debenture.

Example 14.3 Calculating the cost of a debenture before tax and after flotation costs

Consider the data given in Example 14.2 and assume that the flotation costs are 2.5 per cent of the current market price of the debenture. In Figure 14.7, the current cash flow is –£93.6 (that is $-93 \times (1 - 0.025)$) and the cost of debentures is calculated by using the following function stored in cell F18:

```
@IRR(G4,F10..F16)
```

where the coupon rate is used as a guess for the internal rate of return.

Note that the firm's cost of debentures is higher than the investors' required rate of return due to the existence of the flotation costs.

```
        A          B            C              D            E           F         G
 1 CALCULATING THE COST OF A DEBENTURE AFTER FLOTATION COSTS
 2 =========================================================
 3 Current market value of debentures (£)----------------->   96
 4 Coupon rate ------------------------------------------->  6.00%
 5 Flotation costs --------------------------------------->  2.50%
 6
 7 ------------------------------------------------------------
 8 Period   Interest (£)        Par value          Cash flows
 9 ------------------------------------------------------------
10       0                                            (£93.6)
11       1    £6.00                                     6.00
12       2     6.00                                     6.00
13       3     6.00                                     6.00
14       4     6.00                                     6.00
15       5     6.00                                     6.00
16       6     6.00               £100                106.00
17
18          Investors' required rate of return -->      7.36%
19 ------------------------------------------------------------
```

Figure 14.7. Calculating the cost of a debenture when flotation costs are considered

Problem

Set up the worksheet shown in Figure 14.7.

The interest payments by the firm to the debenture holders are deductible by the firm as expenses in the computation of its taxable profits (provided that the firm is profitable). Thus, the after-tax cost of debentures is equal to the cost of debentures adjusted for flotation costs times (1 – tax rate). Mathematically, the after-tax cost of debentures to the firm can be expressed as:

$$r_{dt} = (1 - \text{Tax})\, r_d$$

where

Tax = the corporate tax rate.

Example 14.4 Calculating the after-tax cost of debentures

Consider the data given in Example 14.3 and assume that the corporate tax rate is 35 per cent. Figure 14.8 shows that the after-tax cost of debentures to the firm is 4.78 per cent.

```
      A          B          C          D          E          F       G
 1 CALCULATING THE COST OF DEBENTURES (N-PERIOD VALUATION MODEL)
 2 =================================================================
 3 Current market value of debentures (£)----------------->   96
 4 Coupon rate ------------------------------------------->    6%
 5 Flotation costs --------------------------------------->    3%
 6 Corporate tax rate ------------------------------------>   35%
 7 -----------------------------------------------------------------
 8 Period   Interest (£)        Par value         Total flows
 9 -----------------------------------------------------------------
10 Current                                          (£93.6)
11         1     £6.00                                6.00
12         2      6.00                                6.00
13         3      6.00                                6.00
14         4      6.00                                6.00
15         5      6.00                                6.00
16         6      6.00            £100              106.00
17
18              Before-tax cost of debentures ------>    7.36%
19              After-tax cost of debentures ------->    4.78%
20 -----------------------------------------------------------------
```

Figure 14.8. Calculating the after-tax cost of debentures of GD Fashions

Problems

1 Set up the worksheet shown in Figure 14.8.
2 Calculate the after-tax cost of a debenture that has six years to maturity, and a 9 per cent coupon (paid annually). Assume that the present value of a debenture is £93, flotation costs are 2.5 per cent of the sale price and the corporate tax rate is 35 per cent.

The cost of preference shares

Most preference shares pay annual cash dividends and have no stated maturity dates. If the preference shares pay fixed annual dividends and have no maturity date, the required rate of return for preference shareholders is computed by dividing the annual preference dividends per share by the current market price of the preference share. The preference share dividends are paid out of the firm's after-tax profits and as a consequence no tax adjustment is needed. However, the firm pays flotation costs for new issues of preference shares. Hence, the cost of preference shares can be expressed as follows:

$$r_p = \frac{D_p}{V_p(1 - f_p)}$$

where

f_p = flotation costs expressed as a percentage of V_p.

Example 14.5 Calculating the cost of new preference shares

GD Fashions plc plans to sell preference shares for £20 per share. The issue is expected to pay an annual dividend of £2 per share and to have no maturity date. The flotation costs are 3 per cent of the offering price per share. The cost of preference shares is 10.3 per cent (the figure has been rounded; see Figure 14.9). The cost of preference shares is higher than the firm's cost of debt (see Example 14.4) for the following two reasons: (a) the interest payments on debt are tax deductible, while the dividends on preference shares are not; and (b) and investment in preference shares is riskier than an investment in debentures because dividend payments on preference shares are made after interest payments on debentures. Additionally, the debentures have a prior claim on the firm's assets over the preference shares in the event of the firm being liquidated.

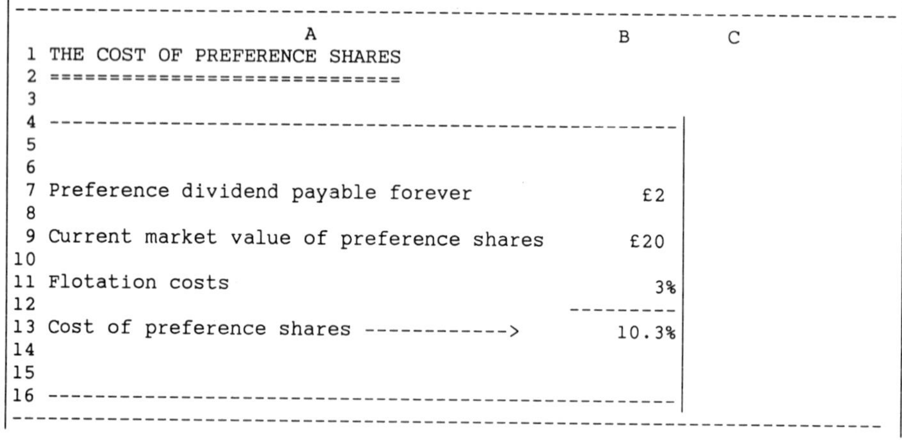

	A	B	C
1	THE COST OF PREFERENCE SHARES		
2	==============================		
3			
4			
5			
6			
7	Preference dividend payable forever	£2	
8			
9	Current market value of preference shares	£20	
10			
11	Flotation costs	3%	
12		---------	
13	Cost of preference shares ------------>	10.3%	
14			
15			
16			

Figure 14.9. Calculating the cost of a preference share

Problem

Set up the worksheet shown in Figure 14.9.

The cost of ordinary shares

Once more following the general procedure presented in Figure 14.5, the investors' required rate of return on an ordinary share is the rate of return that equates the current market value of the ordinary share to the present value of its future expected cash flows—that is, the expected annual dividend cash payments and expected price of the ordinary share at the end of the holding period. The rate of return required by the buyers of a firm's ordinary shares satisfies the following equation:

$$P_o = \sum_{t=1}^{T} \frac{D_t}{(1+r_0)^t} + \frac{P_T}{(1+r_0)^T}$$

where

P_0 = the current market price of the ordinary share.

$D_1, D_2, \ldots, D_T$ = the expected ordinary dividends per share in years $1, 2, 3, \ldots, T$, respectively.

P_T = the expected market price of the ordinary share in year T.

Example 14.6 Calculating the investors' required rate of return on an ordinary share issue and the cost of ordinary shares

GD Fashions plc's ordinary shares are currently selling for £4 per share. The firm's expected dividends per share for the next eight years are £0.30, £0.32, £0.34, £0.38, £0.44, £0.46, £0.48 and £0.50, respectively, and the investors are expected to sell the share for £7 at the end of the eighth year. The investors' required rate of return (RRR) is calculated by using the 1-2-3's @IRR financial function (see Figure 14.10).

	A	B	C	D	E	F	G	I
1	INVESTORS' RRR ON ORDINARY SHARES (N-PERIOD DIVIDEND VAL. MODEL)							
2	====================							
3	Current market value of ordinary shares (£) ----------->						4	
4	----------							
5	Period	Expected ordinary		Market value of		Total flows		
6		dividends per share (£)		ordinary share (£)		(£)		
7	----------							
8	0					-4.00		
9	1	0.30				0.30		
10	2	0.32				0.32		
11	3	0.34				0.34		
12	4	0.38				0.38		
13	5	0.44				0.44		
14	6	0.46				0.46		
15	7	0.48				0.48		
16	8	0.50		7		7.50		
17	----------							
18		Investors' required rate of return --->				14.97%		

Figure 14.10. Calculating the investors' required rate of return on an ordinary share issue

The following function is stored in cell F18:

```
@IRR(0.1,F8..F16)
```

where 0.1 is a guess for the internal rate of return.

In order to calculate the cost of an ordinary share after flotation costs, substitute the price of the share contained in cell F8 by the net proceeds from the sale of the share. For example, if the firm incurs flotation costs of 3.5 per cent of the offering share price, the cost of its ordinary shares is 15.62 per cent.

Problem

Calculate the cost of ordinary shares after flotation costs using a worksheet layout similar to that shown in Figure 14.10.

If dividends grow over time at a constant rate g and the time horizon N becomes infinitely large, we saw in Chapter 13 that the current market price of the firm's ordinary shares can be expressed as:

$$P_o = \frac{D_1}{r_0 - g}$$

where

D_1 = next year's expected dividends per ordinary share ($D_1 = D_0(1+g)$).

D_0 = the current ordinary dividends per share.

g = the annual constant growth rate of dividends (where $r_o > g$).

Using the constant growth dividend valuation model with flotation costs, one can produce the cost of ordinary shares after flotation costs:

$$r_o = \frac{D_1}{P_o(1 - f_o)} + g$$

where

f_o = flotation costs expressed as a percentage of P_o.

Example 14.7 Calculating the cost of ordinary shares using the constant growth dividend valuation model

GD Fashions plc's ordinary shares have a current market price of £4. The firm has a current dividend payment per share of £0.28 and its expected annual dividend growth rate is 8 per cent. The sale of ordinary shares involves flotation costs of 3.5 per cent. The cost of the firm's ordinary shares is calculated as follows:

$$r_o = \frac{£0.28(1+0.08)}{£4(1-0.035)} + 0.08 = 15.83 \text{ per cent}$$

The cost of ordinary shares is higher than the cost of debentures (see Example 14.3) and the cost of preference shares (see Example 14.5) because an investment in ordinary shares is riskier than an investment in preference shares or an investment in debentures.

Problems

1 Set up a worksheet calculating the cost of the ordinary shares for GD Fashions plc (use the constant dividend growth model).

2 Use the constant dividend growth model to calculate the cost of ordinary shares for the following case:
Current market price of ordinary share = £3.8, current dividends per share = 0.24, annual dividend growth rate = 10 per cent and flotation costs = 3.5 per cent of the share's current market price.

The cost of ordinary shares can be also determined by using the capital assets pricing model (discussed in Chapter 9). An example is provided later in the chapter.

The cost of reserves

The portion of the firm's income not paid to ordinary shareholders as dividends is called reserves. The decision to retain funds instead of distributing them involves an opportunity cost, namely, the minimum rate of return that the firm's ordinary shareholders could earn in alternative investments of similar levels of risk.

When the firm retains part of its profits, it assumes that its ordinary shareholders cannot earn on alternative investments as much as the firm can via its reinvested profits. In this case, the shareholders require that the reinvested profits should produce a return which is at least equal to their required rate of return. Thus, it can be assumed (from the firm's point of view) that the cost of reserves is equal to the rate of return required by the firm's ordinary shareholders. However, in practice, expenses are incurred (that is, flotation costs) in issuing ordinary shares (or any other type of security), so the cost of reserves is lower than that of ordinary shares.

Example 14.8 Calculating the cost of reserves for GD Fashions plc

When GD Fashions utilizes its reserves for financing part of all of its investment opportunities, there are no flotation costs involved. Thus:

$$r_r = \frac{0.28(1 + 0.08)}{4} + 0.08$$

$= 15.60$ per cent (the figure has been rounded).

Weighted average cost of capital

The specific cost of each source of capital the firm is employing, along with the proportions of its total capital structure accounted for by each source of capital, are utilized to compute the firm's weighted average cost of capital. The weighted average cost of capital represents the weighted cost of all long-term capital sources, where we are weighting the specific cost of each source of capital by the proportion of that source of capital in the firm's capital structure. That is:

$$\text{WACC} = w_o r_o + w_r r_r + w_p r_p + w_d r_{dt}$$

where

w_j = the percentage of the total long-term capital supplied by capital source j and $w_0 + w_r + w_p + w_d = 1$.

The weights used in the weighted average cost of capital can be historical or target.

Historical weights

Historical weights use the firm's existing capital structure. They rely on the assumption that such a structure is optimal and thus should be maintained in the future. Historical weights can be book value weights or market value weights. According to the historical weighting scheme, the book value weight of a long-term source of capital (for example, ordinary shares) is calculated by dividing the book value of that source of capital by the total book value of all long-term sources of capital used by the firm. Similarly, the market value weight of a long-term source of capital (for example, ordinary shares) is calculated by dividing the market value of that source of capital by the total market value of all long-term sources of capital employed by the firm.

Example 14.9 Calculating the cost of capital for GD Fashions plc using market value weights

Figure 14.11 shows the market value of each long-term source of capital of GD

Fashions plc. For example, the market value of ordinary shares is computed by multiplying the number of ordinary shares owned by the current market price per share. GD Fashions has currently 3,625,000 shares outstanding and each share costs £4, thus the market value of the firm's ordinary shares is £14,500,000 (that is (£4)(3,625,000)). A similar method can be used to calculate the market value of debentures and preference shares.

Figure 14.11. Calculating capital cost weights based on market values

	A	B	C	D	E	F	G	H
1	THE MARKET VALUE PROPORTIONS OF A FIRM'S SOURCES OF CAPITAL							
6	SOURCE OF CAPITAL		MARKET VALUE (£)		MARKET VALUE PROPORTION			
8	Ordinary shares		14,500,000			48.33%		
9	Reserves		500,000			1.67%		
10	Preference shares		3,000,000			10.00%		
11	Debentures		12,000,000			40.00%		
13	Total market value		30,000,000			100%		

The total market value of all the sources is £30,000,000. The weights are computed by dividing the market value of each capital source by £30,000,000. For example, the capital cost weight for preference shares is calculated as follows:

$$\frac{£3{,}000{,}000}{£30{,}000{,}000} = 10 \text{ per cent}$$

The market value weights and the specific costs of capital determined earlier (see Examples 14.4, 14.5, 14.7 and 14.8) are used to compute the firm's weighted average cost of capital (see Figure 14.12).

Figure 14.12. Calculating GD Fashions' weighted average cost of capital

	A	B	C	D	E	F	G	H
21		CALCULATING THE WEIGHTED AVERAGE COST OF CAPITAL						
26–27	SOURCE OF CAPITAL		MARKET VALUE PROPORTION		SPECIFIC COST		WEIGHTED COST	
29	Ordinary shares		48.33%		15.83%		7.65%	
30	Reserves		1.67%		15.60%		0.26%	
31	Preference shares		10.00%		10.30%		1.03%	
32	Debentures		40.00%		4.78%		1.91%	
34	Total market value		100%					
36	Weighted average cost of capital --------------------->						10.85%	

Problem

Set up the worksheets shown in Figures 14.11 and 14.12.

Market value weights versus book value weights

The use of market value weights for computing a firm's weighted average cost of capital is preferred to the use of book value weights for the following two reasons: (a) the book value weights ignore the changes in the market values of securities; and (b) the cost of capital for the ordinary shares, preference shares and debentures is calculated by using market values.

However, there are also two disadvantages associated with market value weights: (a) the market value weights fluctuate more than the book value weights because the market values of the securities fluctuate more than the book values; and (b) it is frequently difficult to calculate the market value weights for some types of securities, while the book value weights can be calculated easily by using data from the firm's balance sheet.

Target weights

Target weights reflect the firm's desired capital structure proportions. These proportions should be selected so as to maximize the market value of the firm's share price. Target weights rely on the assumption that the target capital structure of a firm is optimal and consequently should be maintained in the future. Historical weights are not necessarily the same as target weights because the former do not always reflect the current target capital structure of the firm. As a consequence, different weighting schemes may produce different weighted average costs of capital. As in the case of historical weights, target weights can be book value or market value weights. From the theory viewpoint, it is preferable to utilize target weights based on market values.

Advantages and disadvantages of the weighted average cost of capital method

The weighted average cost of capital method has a number of advantages. The weighted average cost of capital is calculated by weighting the cost of each specific source of capital by its proportion in the firm's capital structure, where the specific costs of capital are calculated separately. As a consequence, the method can reflect changes related to any of the components used in the calculation. For example, changes in the firm's capital structure or changes in the cost of debentures will be reflected by changes in the weighted average cost of capital.

A second advantage is that the weighted average cost of capital can be adjusted to take account of the risks associated with investment projects. Risk-adjusted discount rates lower than the weighted average cost of capital should be used with projects with less than average risk, and rates higher than the weighted average cost of capital should be employed with projects having more than average risk. A third advantage is that the method can be appropriate in estimating divisional costs of capital which reflect both differential levels of risk and differential debt capacity between divisions.

A main disadvantage of the weighted average cost of capital method is that it loses its simplicity when it is used to assign the various degrees of riskiness associated with the investment projects of a firm. Additionally, the weighted average cost of capital method becomes more complicated when it is utilized to calculate separate divisional costs of capital.

Risk and the weighted average cost of capital

The investment projects accepted by a firm can influence its business risk. If this is the case, then the investors (that is, debenture holders, preference shareholders and ordinary shareholders) will probably require higher returns as compensation for the extra risk, and vice versa. Alternatively, financial risk is affected by the firm's capital structure. For example, if a firm increases its borrowed funds (everything else being the same), then it increases the risk associated with its ordinary shares. This is true because additional borrowed funds increase the variability of earnings available to the firm's ordinary shareholders as well as the risk of being unable to cover fixed financial costs. The weighted average cost of capital of a firm provides a way of linking the firm's business risk and financial risk as shown in Figure 4.13.

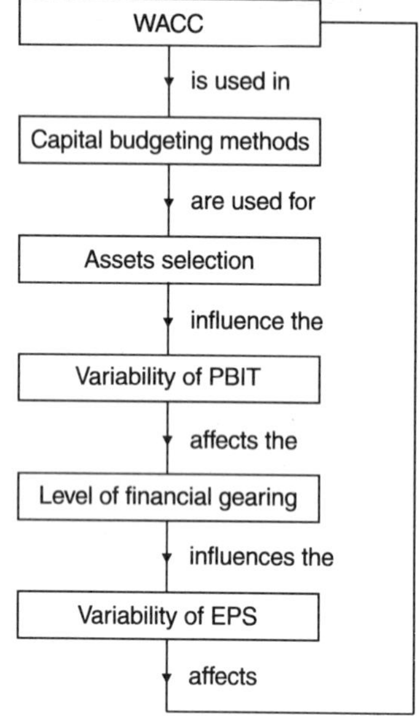

Figure 14.13. The weighted average cost of capital as a connection between business risk and financial risk

At any given point in time, the weighted average cost of capital of one firm can differ from that of another firm because of the differences in the level of business risk and financial risk associated with each firm.

Marginal cost of capital

The specific costs are likely to increase gradually as more new financing is required because the suppliers of capital perceive the firm as a more risky entity. This is not the only cause of changes in the weighted average cost of capital. The cost of raising equity funds externally is higher than the cost of retained earnings. Once the retained earnings have been used up, the weighted average cost of capital will increase with the addition of more equity through the sale of expensive new ordinary shares.

The marginal cost of capital for a particular source of capital is the cost of obtaining an additional pound of new funds from that source. If additional financing employs more than one source of capital, the marginal cost of capital is a weighted average of the various costs of new capital. The weight for each source of capital is the ratio of the future market value of that source to the future market value of all the sources. Thus, the weights are marginal weights reflecting the target capital structure the firm is considering to use in the future.

The marginal cost of capital and the weighted average cost of capital are producing identical results if both of the following conditions are satisfied: (a) the specific costs of capital used to calculate the marginal cost of capital are equal to the firm's current specific costs of capital; and (b) the methods of financing the firm's new projects do not affect its existing capital structure weights.

Example 14.10 Calculating the marginal cost of capital for GD Fashions plc

GD Fashions plc has compiled the following financial data:

Type of financing	Proportion in capital structure	Cost
Ordinary share	50%	15.60%
Preference shares	10%	10.30%
Debentures	40%	4.78%

The firm's target capital structure of 50 per cent ordinary shares, 10 per cent preference shares and 40 per cent debentures is measured on the basis of the current market values of the three sources of funds. Assume that GD Fashions needs to use all three sources of funds to finance new investments (if a firm can finance itself completely with its reserves, then the firm's marginal cost of capital is equal to the cost of its reserves). The marginal cost of capital of the firm is

$$\text{WACC} = (0.50)(0.1560) + (0.10)(0.1030) + (0.40)(0.0478)$$

$$= 0.0780 + 0.0103 + 0.0191 = 10.74 \text{ per cent}$$

GD Fashions can utilize 10.74 per cent as the discount rate for the net present value method or as the hurdle rate when using the internal rate of return approach.

Break points in marginal cost of capital

A firm cannot raise any amount of new funds needed at the same marginal cost of capital. For example, as a firm issues large quantities of ordinary shares, the cost of ordinary shares will rise. Similarly, if a firm attempts to raise its long-term debt (or preference shares) beyond its capacity, it will have to pay a higher cost to compensate investors for the higher risk involved. As we consider three external sources of capital in determining the marginal cost of capital, an increase in any one of them will lead to changes in the firm's marginal cost of capital. The value in pounds sterling of new funds that can be raised before the firm's marginal cost of capital rises is defined as a break point. A break point attributable to the change in the cost of ordinary shares (and similarly for all the other sources) can be represented as follows:

Break point created by a change in the cost of ordinary shares	=	Funds available from ordinary shares before their cost changes	÷	Target capital structure proportion for ordinary shares

$$BP_0 = F_0 \div W_0$$

Example 14.11 Calculating a break point for ordinary shares

Assume the same data as in Example 14.10. Figure 14.14 shows the break point for ordinary shares.

```
 ---------------------------------------------------------------------------
        A           B          C          D          E          F          G
 1          CALCULATING A BREAK POINT FOR ORDINARY SHARES
 2          ===========================================
 3 --------------------------------------------------------------------------
 4 Cost of reserves -------------------------------->                15.60%
 5
 6 Market value proportion for ordinary shares ----->                50.00%
 7
 8 Reserves ---------------------------------------->              £500,000
 9
10                   Break Point for Ordinary Shares -->         £1,000,000
11 --------------------------------------------------------------------------
 ---------------------------------------------------------------------------
```

Figure 14.14. GD Fashions plc: calculating a break point for ordinary share

The break for the firm's ordinary shares will be:

$$BP_o = \frac{£500{,}000}{0.50} = £1{,}000{,}000$$

Reserves are £500,000. In order to keep the firm's target capital structure unchanged, reserves must be 50 per cent of the total additional new funds. Reserves must be exhausted before the firm obtains extra funds through a new issue of ordinary shares. Thus, £1,000,000 of additional funds can be obtained before the cost of ordinary shares increases above 15.60 per cent. The additional £1,000,000 will consist of £500,000 reserves, £100,000 of new preference shares and £400,000 of new debentures.

Problem

Set up the worksheet shown in Figure 14.14.

The weighted marginal cost of capital schedule

Since each source of funds could have several increases, the combined number of changes (that is, the break points) is magnified. A graph relating the weighted average cost of capital of the firm to different amounts of new financing is called the weighted marginal cost of capital (WMCC) schedule. This schedule can be used to determine the discount rate required in the process of capital budgeting.

Example 14.12 Calculating the weighted marginal cost of capital schedule for GD Fashions plc

Assume that the management of GD Fashions plc is considering further expansion. For simplicity we assume that break points increase in a stepwise manner. The firm can obtain additional funds according to the following schedule:

- Cost of equity The cost of equity will be 15.60 per cent for the first £500,000. It will increase to 15.83 per cent for additional funds in the range £500,000 to £1,000,000 and, finally, above £1,000,000 the cost of equity will increase to 16.10 per cent.

- Cost of preference shares The cost of preference shares will be 10.30 per cent for the first £55,000. The cost of any additional funds raised through an issue of preference shares will be 10.50 per cent.
- Cost of debentures The (after-tax) cost of debentures will be 4.78 per cent for the first £400,000. Above £400,000 the (after-tax) cost of debentures will rise to 5.50 per cent.

To calculate the weighted marginal cost of capital schedule follow the steps below:

Step 1 Calculate the break points in the weighted marginal cost of capital schedule. The break points for equity and the corresponding costs are shown in Figure 14.15.

Break point	Cost
Equity	
$\frac{500,000}{0.50} = £1,000,000$	Up to £1,000,000 the cost is 15.60 per cent
$\frac{£1,000,000}{0.50} = £2,000,000$	Between £1,000,000 and £2,000,000 the cost is 15.83 per cent Above £2,000,000 the cost is 16.10 per cent
Preference shares	
$\frac{£55,000}{0.10} = £550,000$	Up to £550,000 the cost is 10.30 per cent Above £550,000 the cost is 10.50 per cent
Debentures	
$\frac{£400,000}{0.40} = £1,000,000$	Up to £1,000,000 the (after-tax) cost is 4.78 per cent
$\frac{£1,000,000}{0.40} = £2,500,000$	Between £1,000,000 and £2,500,000 the (after-tax) cost of debentures is 5.50 per cent

Figure 14.15. Calculating the break points

Step 2 Calculate the cost of capital in each of the intervals between the break points. The weighted average cost of capital in each of the four intervals between the break points is shown in Figure 14.16. For example, the weighted average cost of capital in the second interval is calculated as follows:

$$\text{WACC}_2 = (0.50)(0.1560) + (0.10)(0.1050) + (0.40)(0.0478)$$

$$= 0.0780 + 0.0105 + 0.0191 = 10.76 \text{ per cent}$$

The weighted average cost of capital for GD Fashions plc can be presented graphically using the 1-2-3 graphic facilities. Figure 14.17 shows the data for the weighted marginal cost of capital schedule. For the graph purpose we assume that the weighted average cost of capital after £2,500,000 of new capital will be 11.50 per cent. Figure 14.18 plots the weighted marginal cost of capital schedule for GD Fashions. The `/Graph Option Scale Y-Scale Manual` command of 1-2-3 is used in order to specify a range for the vertical axis. In our example, we use the range from 10.4 per cent to 12.0 per cent. It is evident

```
          A                B              C          D           E           G           H
41 CALCULATING THE VARIOUS WEIGHTED AVERAGE COSTS OF CAPITAL
42 ===============================================================
43
44 ---------------------------------------------------------------
45 Upper range    Source of    Desired market      Specific Weighted
46 of total new   capital      value proportion    cost     cost
47 financing                   (wj, j=1,2,3)       SPj      wj*SPj
48 ---------------------------------------------------------------
49      £550,000       OE           50.00%           15.60%   7.80%
50                     PS           10.00%           10.30%   1.03%
51                     DE           40.00%            4.78%   1.91%
52
53             Weighted average cost of capital ---->    10.74%
54 ===============================================================
55    £1,000,000       OE           50.00%           15.60%   7.80%
56                     PS           10.00%           10.50%   1.05%
57                     DE           40.00%            4.78%   1.91%
58
59             Weighted average cost of capital ---->    10.76%
60 ---------------------------------------------------------------
61 ---------------------------------------------------------------
62 Upper range    Source of    Desired market      Specific Weighted
63 of total new   capital      value proportion    cost     cost
64 financing                   (wj, j=1,2,3)       SPj      wj*SPj
65 ---------------------------------------------------------------
66    £2,000,000       OE           50.00%           15.83%   7.92%
67                     PS           10.00%           10.50%   1.05%
68                     DE           40.00%            5.50%   2.20%
69
70             Weighted average cost of capital ---->    11.17%
71 ===============================================================
72    £2,500,000       OE           50.00%           16.10%   8.05%
73                     PS           10.00%           10.50%   1.05%
74                     DE           40.00%            5.50%   2.20%
75
76             Weighted average cost of capital ---->    11.30%
77 ---------------------------------------------------------------
```

Figure 14.16. Calculating the weighted average cost of capital in each interval between the break points

```
                 A                  B          C            D
 1 THE MARGINAL COST OF CAPITAL SCHEDULE
 2 ======================================
 3
 4 -----------------------------------------------
 5 Total New Financing Points    WACC
 6 -----------------------------------------------
 7                       £0      10.74%
 8                  550,000      10.74%
 9                  550,000      10.76%
10                1,000,000      10.76%
11                1,000,000      11.17%
12                2,000,000      11.17%
13                2,000,000      11.30%
14                2,500,000      11.30%
15                2,500,000      11.50%
16                2,900,000      11.50%
17 -----------------------------------------------
```

Figure 14.17. The data for the weighted marginal cost of capital schedule for GD Fashions plc

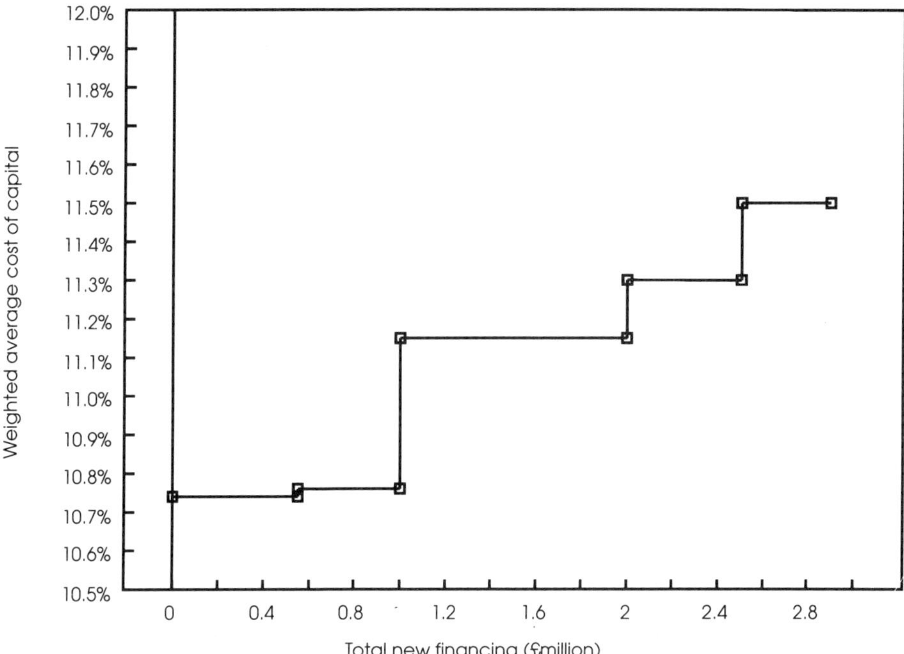

Figure 14.18. Weighted marginal cost of capital

from Figure 14.18 that the weighted marginal cost of capital is an increasing function of the level of total new capital raised.

Problems

1 Set up the worksheets shown in Figures 14.16 and 14.17.
2 Create the graph shown in Figure 14.18.

Deriving the optimal capital budget

The weighted marginal cost of capital schedule can be used to develop a rule for capital budgeting decisions. Assume that a firm is considering a number of possible investments and it has ranked them in order by their internal rates of return. A graph relating the internal rates of return from these projects to the cumulative funds invested is called the investment opportunities schedule (IOS). The optimal capital budget can be derived by combining the firm's weighted marginal cost of capital schedule and its investment opportunities schedule. The point of intersection of the two schedules is called the hurdle rate and any investment project with an internal rate of return greater than (or equal to) the hurdle rate should be accepted.

Example 14.13 Combining the weighted marginal cost of capital schedule and investment opportunities schedule

Figure 14.19 shows the cash flows of six projects available to GD Fashions plc.

We assume that all projects have the same level of risk so that the same marginal cost of capital schedule is relevant for all six projects (this assumption can be relaxed by using a risk-adjustment method in order to incorporate risk into the analysis; see Chapter 7). We also assume that the weighted marginal cost of capital schedule and the investment opportunities schedule are derived

	A	B	C	D	E	F
1	CALCULATING THE IRRS AND NPVS FOR SIX INVESTMENT PROJECTS					
2	==					
3						
4	Hurdle Rate --------------->				11.17%	
5	--					
6	PROJECT D	PROJECT C	PROJECT A	PROJECT B	PROJECT E	PROJECT F
7	--					
8	(600,000)	(1,000,000)	(400,000)	(300,000)	(400,000)	(1,000,000)
9	160,000	250,000	100,000	60,000	80,000	220,000
10	170,000	260,000	110,000	70,000	90,000	240,000
11	185,000	290,000	115,000	75,000	100,000	270,000
12	220,000	320,000	120,000	80,000	105,000	290,000
13	230,000	350,000	130,000	84,000	110,000	300,000
14	--					
15	16.92%	13.46%	12.85%	6.92%	6.43%	9.46%
16						
17	95,618	61,964	17,786	(32,954)	(48,904)	(44,849)
18	--					

Figure 14.19. Calculating the internal rates of return and net present values for six projects for GD Fashions plc

correctly. Figure 14.20 presents the data for the two schedules. By combining graphically the investment opportunities schedule and the weighted marginal cost of capital schedule we can obtain Figure 14.21. The `/Graph Option Scale Y-Scale Manual` command of 1-2-3 is used to set upper and lower limits for the graph's y-axis. The lower limit is set to be 0 and the upper limit is selected to be 0.18. In Figure 14.21, the weighted marginal cost of capital is an increasing function of the level of total new capital raised and the investment opportunities schedule is a decreasing function of the amount of money required to adopt potential investment projects.

It can be seen that GD Fashions should accept projects A, C and D which require a total outlay of £2,000,000. Acceptance of the projects A, C and D will result in a rise in the firm's value. Projects B, E and F are rejected because their internal rates of return are expected to be below the hurdle rate of 11.17 per cent. If this hurdle rate is utilized to calculate the net present values of the projects,

	A	B	C	D	E	F
20	THE MCC SCHEDULE AND THE IOS					
21						
22	------------------------------------					
23	Total New Fund	WACC	IOS			
24	------------------------------------					
25	0	10.74%	16.92%			
26	550,000	10.74%	16.92%			
27	550,000	10.76%	13.46%			
28	1,000,000	10.76%	13.46%			
29	1,000,000	11.15%	12.85%			
30	2,000,000	11.15%	12.85%			
31	2,000,000	11.30%	9.46%			
32	2,500,000	11.30%	9.46%			
33	2,500,000	11.50%	6.92%			
34	2,900,000	11.50%	6.92%			
35	2,900,000	11.50%	6.43%			
36	3,000,000	11.50%	6.43%			
37	------------------------------------					

Figure 14.20. The data for the weighted marginal cost of capital schedule and the investment opportunities schedule for GD Fashions plc

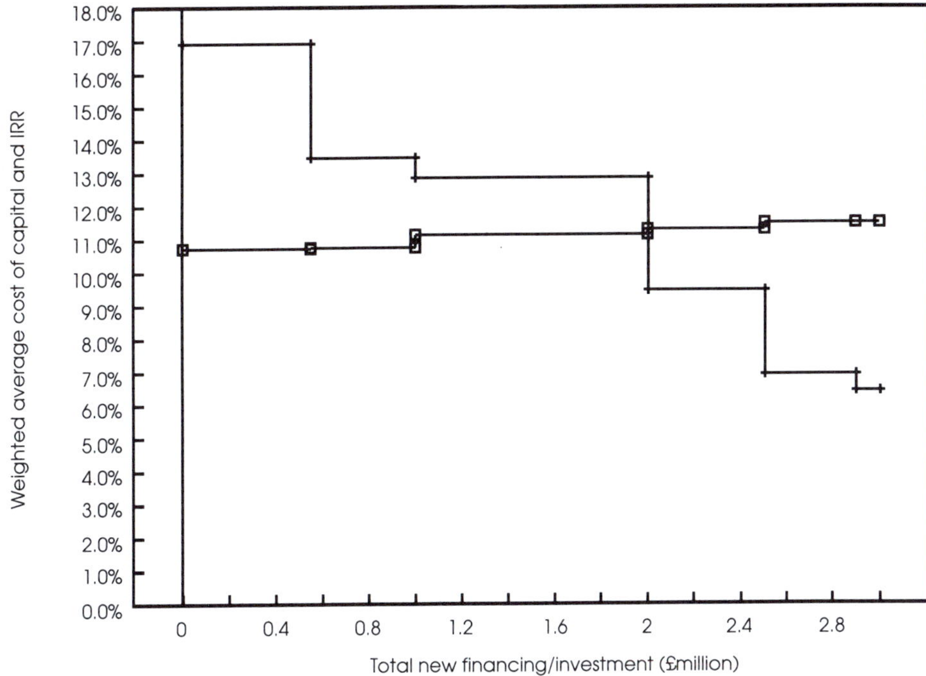

Figure 14.21. Using the MCC schedule and IOS to select projects for GD Fashions plc

then projects A, C and D will have positive net present values, while projects B, E and F will have net present values lower than zero.

Problem

Set up the worksheet shown in Figure 14.19.

Calculating the cost of capital in the real world

In this section we utilize the methods described earlier for the estimation of the cost of capital of Marks and Spencer plc. In general, note that the cost of capital estimate is reliable if it is based upon valid assumptions and reliable data. The following implicit assumptions are made:

1 The new project has the same risk as the firm and it will be financed with the same proportions of capital sources as the firm utilizes to finance existing projects.
2 The firm's debt is risk free.
3 The expected return on an ordinary share in the firm can be estimated by using the following risk–return relationship:

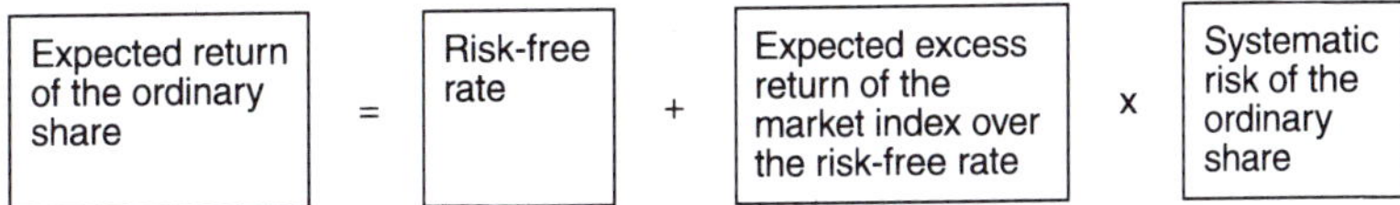

The calculation of the cost of capital will be based on data available on the period March 1987, therefore, the results are valid around this period. The sources of information are the London Business School Risk Measurement Service (LBSRMS) and Datastream. The following data is collected (note that data such as the rates on Treasury bills is also quoted in the *Financial Times*):

3 months Treasury bill rate → 10.38 per cent
Marks and Spencer's beta → 0.91

The three-month Treasury bill rate is considered to be a proxy for the risk-free rate. The quoted rate should be annualized before it is used in the calculation process of the weighted average cost of capital. This can be achieved by following a three-step procedure.

Step 1 Calculate the cost of the Treasury bill that has a par value of £100:

$$£100 - (£10.38)(91)/365 = £97.41$$

Step 2 Calculate the quarterly compounded rate:

$$\frac{(£100 - £97.41)}{£97.41}\frac{365}{91} = 10.66 \text{ per cent}$$

Step 3 Calculate the annual rate of return corresponding to the quarterly compounded rate in Step 2.

$$(1 + 0.1066/4)^4 - 1 = 11.09 \text{ per cent}$$

Therefore, the risk-free rate to be used is approximately 11.09 per cent. According to the LBSRMS, over the last 60 months the annual return on ordinary shares has averaged 9 per cent more than the Treasury bill rate (this return is not adjusted for personal taxes). Thus, the mean return on the market index is 20.09 per cent (that is, 11.09 per cent + 9 per cent). The beta has been estimated using historical monthly rates of return for five years and over that period its standard error is 0.16. Note that the standard error provides a measure of the precision of the estimate and the lower this figure, the larger the precision of the estimate.

Cost of debt
Assume that the debt of Marks and Spencer is risk free. Since interest payments are tax deductible, the after-corporate-tax cost of debt is

$$0.1109(1 - 0.35) = 7.21 \text{ per cent}$$

where the corporate tax rate is 35 per cent.

Cost of equity
When evaluating a project, the firm estimates the after-corporate-tax cash flows of the project. It should therefore use an after-corporate-tax but before personal tax discount rate. Observable market rates will provide these numbers and will give investors the return on which they can pay personal tax. The shareholders' required rate of return in Marks and Spencer's ordinary shares is calculated as follows:

$$0.1109 + (0.2009 - 0.1109)0.91 = 19.28 \text{ per cent}$$

Weighted average cost of capital
Preference shares are omitted because the preference share capital is very small as compared with the debt capital or the ordinary share capital of the firm. We assume

that the market value of debt is equal to its book value. The market value of equity is estimated as an average of the market capitalization of Marks and Spencer over five years (the market capitalization of a firm at a particular point in time is equal to the number of ordinary shares owned times the price per share at that time). The average market value equity proportion over the period March 1983 to March 1987 was approximately 98 per cent. Using the data derived above, the weighted average cost of capital is calculated as follows:

$$(0.0721)(0.02) + (0.1928)(0.98) = 19.04 \text{ per cent}$$

Example 14.14 A sensitivity of the weighted average cost of capital with respect to changes in the cost of debt and the relative proportion of total capital supplied by debt

Let us examine the sensitivity of the weighted average cost of capital with respect to changes in two variables: the cost of long-term debt and the proportion of debt capital in the firm's capital structure. The sensitivity can be performed by using 1-2-3's `/Data Table 2` command. We assume that the before-tax cost of long-term debt is in the range 11.09–12.49 per cent and the debt proportion takes values in the range 5–1 per cent (that is, the ordinary shares' proportion lies in the range 95–99 per cent). The average value of the weighted average cost of capital is 19.83 per cent (see Figure 14.22). If the use of the book value of debt is not a good approximation of the market value of debt, then sensitivity analysis can be used to calculate the weighted average cost of capital for other debt proportions.

	A		B	C	D	E	F
1	A TWO-VARIABLE SENSITIVITY ANALYSIS OF THE WACC OF M&S						
2	===						
3							
4	Risk Free Rate		11.09%				
5	Corporation Tax Rate		35.0%				
6	Risk Premium		9.0%				
7	Systematic Risk		0.91				
8	Debt Proportion		2.0%				
9			--------				
10	WACC After Basic Tax Rate		19.04%				
11	------------------------------						
12	+B10		5.0%	4.0%	3.0%	2.0%	1.0%
13		11.09%	18.46%	18.65%	[illegible]	19.04%	19.23%
14		12.09%	19.42%	19.63%	19.83%	20.03%	20.23%
15		12.19%	19.52%	19.72%	19.93%	20.13%	20.33%
16		12.29%	19.62%	19.82%	20.03%	20.23%	20.43%
17		12.39%	19.71%	19.92%	20.12%	20.33%	20.54%
18		12.49%	19.81%	20.02%	20.22%	20.43%	20.64%
19	------------------------------						
20				AVERAGE VALUE ----->			19.83%

Figure 14.22. A two-variable sensitivity analysis of the weighted average cost of capital

The results of the sensitivity analysis are shown graphically in Figure 14.23.

Problem

Create the worksheet shown in Figure 14.22.

The after-corporate-tax weighted average cost of capital, as calculated in Example

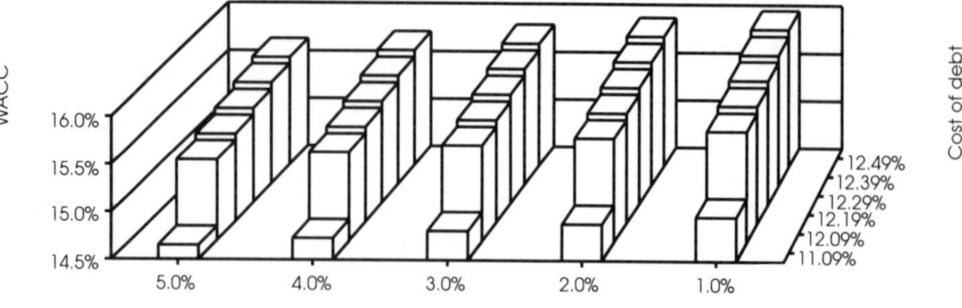

Figure 14.23. Sensitivity of Marks and Spencer's WACC to changes in cost of debt and debt–equity mix

14.14, is not a reasonable cost for all the potential projects of the firm because different investment projects have different risk levels. For a specified new investment project, the final adjustment to be made is concerned with the risk associated with the type of the new project. It is reasonable to assume that capital investment projects are considered to span three categories of risk: low, medium and high. For example, cost reduction projects may fall in the low risk category, while expansion projects may fall in either of the other two categories. Target adjustment factors can be established for these three risk categories based on past experience, subjective judgement, or beta estimates of other firms in a similar business and with similar financial characteristics (for example, similar capital structures).

Example 14.15 Adjusting the after-corporate-tax weighted average cost of capital for the risk associated with different types of investment projects

Assume that Marks and Spencer uses different after-corporate-tax weighted average costs of capital for different projects and it presently has the following three risk/return bands:

WACC	Risk	Adjusted factor
12–18.9%	Low	59.39–156.10%
19–23.9%	Medium	157.50–226.19%
24%>	High	227.59%

Risk bands should be based upon the past experience and subjective judgement of the firm's finance management team. For example, a project with medium risk has adjustment factors in the range 157.50–226.19 per cent (157.50 per cent corresponds to 19 per cent and 226.19 per cent corresponds to 23.9 per cent). The finance management team may make any choice (within the range 157.50–226.19 per cent) based upon their risk experience; in this case, several factors can be taken into account, for example, a new product that will be sold to its current customers probably will be assigned a factor of 157.50 per cent, but a new product that will be sold to new customers probably will be assigned a factor greater than 157.50 per cent. We assume an adjustment factor of 191.85 per cent (that is, the average between 157.50 per cent and 226.19 per cent). Then the after-corporate-tax weighted average cost of capital is computed as follows:

$$\text{WACC} = (0.0721)(0.02) + (0.2680)(0.98) = 26.41 \text{ per cent}$$

where $0.1109 + 0.09 \times 0.91 \times 1.9185 = 26.80$ per cent.

Using the CAPM to calculate a firm's cost of capital

Consider a firm that is financed wholly by equity. In this case, the firm's beta on its ordinary shares (called equity beta) equals the beta of the firm's existing assets (called asset beta). Under the capital asset pricing model, this implies that the cost of equity capital is identical to the firm's cost of capital.

Many firms, however, finance investment projects from funds generated through equity and debt. The shareholders of a geared firm bear both business risk of the firm's assets and financial risk associated with the use of gearing. The greater the gearing of a firm, the riskier are its ordinary shares. Therefore, the firm's equity beta will be greater than its assets beta. In the present section we will use a method that calculates the asset beta using the equity beta and debt beta. Assuming the presence of corporation tax, the beta of the geared firm's assets can be expressed as a weighted average of the equity beta and debt beta (for a proof see Appendix 14.A):

$$b_a = \frac{1}{1 + (1 - T_c)D/E_G} b_o + \frac{(1 - T_c)D/E_G}{1 + (1 - T_c)D/E_G} b_d$$

where

T_c = corporate tax rate.

D = the market value of the geared firm's debt.

E_G = the value of equity of the geared firm.

b_o = the beta of the geared firm's equity.

b_d = the beta of the geared firm's debt.

Example 14.16 Calculating the asset beta of a firm and its cost of capital

Victoria Textiles plc has 200,000 ordinary shares currently selling at £1.5 per share. The firm currently has outstanding debt of £80,000. The equity beta of the firm is 1.2 and its debt beta is 0.03. Assuming a corporate tax rate of 35 per cent, the asset beta would be

$$b_a = \frac{1}{1 + (1 - 0.350)0.267} 1.20 + \frac{(1 - 0.350)0.267}{1 + (1 - 0.35)0.267} 0.03 = 1.027$$

where 0.267 is the debt/equity ratio of the firm.

Figure 14.24 presents the results of the sensitivity of the asset beta to changes in the amount of long-term debt used. The results reveal that the asset beta of the firm falls with increasing gearing because increased gearing adds back an extra, lower risk, cash flows, the tax savings on debt.

The firm's cost of capital is calculated by using the capital asset pricing model with a beta equal to the asset beta. That is:

$$r = 0.09 + (0.18 - 0.09)(1.027) = 18.24 \text{ per cent}$$

```
                A              B            C           D             E           F
 1 CALCULATING THE COST OF CAPITAL OF A FIRM
 2 =========================================
 3 Corporate Tax Rate                               35.00%
 4 Market Value of Debt                             £80,000
 5 Market Value of Equity                          £300,000
 6 Equity Beta                                         1.2
 7 Debt Beta                                          0.03
 8                                               ----------
 9 Asset Beta                                        1.027
10
11                                  +D9          +D4/D5
12                       80,000       1.027       0.267
13                       85,000       1.018       0.283
14                       90,000       1.009       0.300
15                       95,000       1.000       0.317
16                      100,000       0.992       0.333
17                      105,000       0.983       0.350
18                      110,000       0.975       0.367
19                      115,000       0.967       0.383
20                      120,000       0.959       0.400
21
22
23 Riskless Rate of Interest                         9.00%
24 Market Expected Rate of Return                   18.00%
25                                               ----------
26 Cost of Capital Using CAPM                       18.24%
27
28 Cost of Equity                                   19.80%
29 Cost of Debt                                      9.27%
30 Proportion of Equity                             0.852
31 Proportion of Debt                               0.148
32                                               ----------
33 Weighted Average Cost of Capital                 18.24%
```

Figure 14.24. Computing the cost of capital of Victoria Textiles

Using the equation of the weighted average cost of capital gives

$$\text{WACC} = (0.0927)(0.148) + (0.1980)(0.852) = 18.24 \text{ per cent}$$

Given the asset beta, the equity beta can be calculated as follows:

$$b_o = [1 + (1 - 0.35)(0.267)]1.027 - (1 - 0.35)(0.267)(0.03)$$
$$= 1.20$$

Problems

1 Prove by using a numerical example that the higher the gearing, the higher the beta of the geared firm's equity.

2 Present the results of Problem 1 graphically.

In practice, it is difficult to determine the beta for the firm's debt. A special case occurs when we assume that the firm's debt is riskless. For a riskless debt, the beta of the debt is zero and the firm's cost of debt can be approximated by the risk-free rate. If the beta of the debt is approximately zero, then the asset beta is given by

$$b_a = \frac{1}{1 + (1 - T_c)D/E_G} b_o$$

Other methods of determining the cost of equity

The literature offers several other methods for calculating the cost of equity including the following: (a) return on capital employed; (b) the cost of debentures plus an expected risk premium; (c) earnings per share to market price per share; (d) dividend yield; (e) interest rate on borrowed funds; and (f) historical dividend yield plus an estimate of dividend growth.

Return on capital employed

From the point of view of the financial director, the return on capital employed measures the rate of return earned on the book value of the firm's equity (that is, ordinary share capital plus reserves). The return on capital employed is defined as the ratio of profit after tax to the firm's book value of equity. This ratio relies upon historical data rather than focusing on the actual rate of return/loss (that is, dividend yield plus price appreciation/depreciation) earned by the firm's shareholders.

Debenture yield plus an expected risk premium

In view of the second approach, the cost of equity is equal to the cost of debentures plus an expected premium for risk of shares over debentures. This method is useful when neither the constant growth dividend valuation model nor the capital asset pricing model approaches can be utilized in the analysis.

Earnings per share to market price per share

This method defines the cost of equity of a firm as the ratio of the firm's expected earnings per share to price per share. This method, however, fails to consider the growth in the firm's earnings per share.

Dividend yield

The cost of equity is calculated by dividing the dividends per share by the firm's price per share. This method, however, ignores capital gains or losses realized from the share during the period it was held.

Interest rate on borrowed funds

This is a simple method, but it ignores the risk associated with the firm's ordinary shares.

Historical dividend yield plus an estimate of dividend growth

This method is similar to the constant dividend valuation model. The present method, however, uses an historical dividend yield rather than the firm's current yield. As a consequence, it may produce a poor measure for the cost of new ordinary shares.

Figure 14.25 summarizes the disadvantages of nine methods used to calculate the cost of equity.

Some useful points about the weighted average cost of capital calculation

1 (Avoid making unreliable assumptions) You cannot avoid making assumptions when you estimate the cost of capital of a firm, but make sure that your assumptions will produce a reliable estimate of the firm's cost of capital. For example,

Method	Disadvantages
Return on capital employed	It relies upon book values
EPS/market price per share	It does not take into account how the firm's earnings are growing
Cost of debentures plus a risk premium	It is difficult to estimate the risk premium
Interest rate on borrowed funds	It ignores the risk associated with the firm's ordinary shares
N-period dividend valuation model	It is very difficult to obtain good input data for the expected dividends and expected share price
Dividend yield	It ignores capital gains/losses of ordinary shares
Constant growth dividend valuation model	It does not consider risk directly
Historical dividend yield plus an estimate of dividend growth	It may be a poor measure of new cost of equity
Capital asset pricing model	Difficult to measure its inputs (for example, beta). Applicable only to publicly traded corporations. It underestimates the cost of equity if the index used to calculate the beta is not mean–standard deviation efficient

Figure 14.25. Disadvantages of the methods used to compute the cost of equity

avoid using book value weights if they are not good approximations of the market value weights.

2 (Avoid using unreliable data) Remember that the equation used to calculate the weighted average cost of capital is only as reliable as the input data. The estimation of the cost of capital is usually based upon historical data. Avoid utilizing data which precludes estimating a reliable figure. For example, when the shares are very thinly traded the beta estimates are biased. With daily data, this bias can be severe (see Scholes and Williams, 1977; Dimson, 1979).

3 (Remember that the systematic risk and market return are changing with time) Use historical estimates for the beta coefficients (for example, those published in the London Business School Risk Measurements Service), but remember that history does not always provide an unbiased estimate of the beta coefficient. For example, consider a firm whose beta coefficient is estimated using 60 monthly observations. Assume that the estimated beta coefficient is 0.80. Avoid using this estimate for calculating the firm's cost of equity if the firm has recently been involved in an activity that produces a substantial change in its historical beta (for example, if the firm has acquired another firm with a beta of 1.2 or if the firm has obtained a substantial amount of new debt).

The average excess return of the market index over the risk-free rate is 9 per cent (see London Business School Risk Measurement Service). However, this figure is an average over a long period of time, thus, its use may produce a bias in the cost of equity figure.

In general, improperly estimated cost of capital may result in a decision to accept a project that looks profitable but turns out to be unprofitable.

4 (The problems with the misspecification of the underlying models) The capital asset pricing model is valid if the market portfolio is mean–standard deviation efficient.

Roll (1977) proved that the relationship between the expected return of securities in the index and their systematic risk is valid if and only if the index is mean–standard deviation efficient. If the index is not efficient, then we have a misspecification of the risk–return relationship which in turn may introduce a bias in the cost of ordinary shares (see Appendix 14A). Also, the market model used to estimate the beta coefficient may be misspecified if an important variable that influences the security returns is left out of the regression equation. In this case, the beta estimate is biased.

5 (Conducting a sensitivity analysis) After you have derived a reliable estimate of the cost of capital, conduct a sensitivity analysis to examine the effect on the cost of capital of variations in the key assumptions used. With the aid of electronic spreadsheets the effect on the cost of capital of changes in the key variables can be automatically produced. Sensitivity analysis can be performed with respect to one or more variables simultaneously. It can also be conducted by using each variable separately and then combining the results graphically in order to identify the most critical variables which influence the firm's cost of capital.

6 (Projects with different risk characteristics) Estimate the firm's cost of capital and then provide a revision of this estimate in light of your risk experience. The cost of capital estimated by using the weighted cost of capital method is not the reasonable cost for all the potential projects of the firm. One way to deal with the problem is to establish target rates for different risk categories of projects according to past experience and subjective judgement. Then choose the rate that will be utilized for a particular project based upon your understanding of the risk involved. Note that real analysis is concerned with whether an estimate of the cost of capital is good enough for a specific project rather than an attempt to provide an exact figure for the cost of capital.

7 (Divisional cost of capital) Firms with many divisions frequently use separate divisional costs of capital in order to reflect the different levels of risk and debt capacity of each division. One of the methods often used to deal with this situation is explained as follows.

(a) For each division within the firm identify several publicly traded companies which have similar product lines and capital structure as that division.
(b) Calculate for each division a range of values for the cost of equity by using the beta coefficients of similar publicly traded firms.
(c) Determine the cost of equity for a particular division using your understanding of the risk involved (for example, the financial director could choose the average value in the range of values estimated in the previous step).
(d) Calculate for each division other possible specific costs of capital (for example, cost of debentures).
(e) Consider each division as a separate firm and estimate its target capital structure.
(f) Use your estimates to calculate the cost of capital for each division.

8 (How often should the cost of capital be calculated?) There is no rule indicating the frequency of the cost of capital revision. However, it is important to revise the cost of capital frequently, especially when the economic conditions have changed. By way of illustration, suppose a firm uses a cost of capital estimated when economic conditions were favourable and assume that presently these conditions start to deteriorate. Then the cost of capital should be re-estimated to account for the risk involved with the changing economic conditions. The cost of capital of a firm could also be reviewed when the business environment is perceived to have changed.

Empirical results indicate that many (large or medium sized) firms recalculate their cost of capital each time a major project is evaluated. In this case, it is easy to see that the internal situations of a firm (for example, capital structure) may be altered as a result of undertaking a large project.

Empirical evidence on the cost of capital

A relatively small number of surveys have been conducted in the area of the cost of capital. Figure 14.26 summarizes seven of these studies.

Author(s)/ method of study	Country/population studied	Sample size	Response rate (%)	Cost of capital	Risk assessment
Brigham (1975) Interviews & questionnaire	UK/ Companies with average assets value of £2.8 million	33	100	Yes	Yes
Petty *et al.* (1975) Mail questionnaire	USA/ 1971 Fortune '500' Listing	500	22	Yes	Yes
Schall *et al.* (1978) Mail questionnaire	USA/ COMPUSTAT Annual Industry File with firms exceeding a certain size and capital expenditure level	407	46	Yes	
Gitman and Mercurio (1982) Mail questionnaire	USA/ 1980 Fortune '1000' Listing	1,000	17.7	Yes	Yes
Pike (1982) Interviews questionnaire	UK/ Largest 300 UK quoted firms measured by market capitalization in November 1979	208	72.1	Yes	Yes
Scott and Johnson (1982) Mail questionnaire	USA/ 1979 Fortune '1000' Listing	1,000	21.1	Yes	Yes
Corr (1983) Interviews	USA and Canada/16 USA firms and 8 firms in Canada	24	100	Yes	Yes

Figure 14.26. Summarizing seven studies in the area of the cost of capital

Some of the findings of the studies shown in Figure 14.26 are summarized as follows:

1 The most popular approach to estimate the firm's overall cost of capital is the weighted average cost of capital method (Schall *et al.*, 1978; Gitman and Mercurio, 1982; Corr, 1983). Gitman and Mercurio (1982) found that the majority of the firms surveyed are using target weights or market value weights. However, Brigham (1975) and Corr (1983) found that historical weights are more commonly used.

2 The preferred approach to estimate the cost of equity is the constant growth dividend valuation model (Petty *et al.*, 1975; Gitman and Mercurio, 1982).
3 The cost of capital is often revised in the light of the changing market conditions (Gitman and Mercurio, 1982; Pike, 1982; Corr, 1983).
4 The future trend in the area of the cost of capital is also anticipated by the various studies presented in Figure 14.26. Greater use of multiple hurdle rates for different projects or divisions within firms is anticipated. As a consequence, more frequent revisions of hurdle rates are also expected (Brigham, 1975; Pike, 1982).

Summary

1 *The weighted average cost of capital* The cost of capital of a firm is a weighted average of the various long-term capital sources used by the firm, where the weights are the proportions of each type of capital in the firm's capital structure. The cost of each capital source is closely related to the investors' required rates of return on the securities of the firm. However, the specific costs of capital are different from the corresponding required rates of return because of tax considerations in the case of debentures (interest expenses are tax deductible) and flotation costs (for example, administration costs) associated with issuing debentures and shares. In general, market value weights are preferable to book value weights.
2 *The weighted marginal cost of capital* The marginal cost of capital of a long-term source of capital is the cost of obtaining an additional pound of new funds from that source. If additional new financing employs more than one source of capital, the weighted marginal cost of capital is determined by multiplying each specific cost of capital by its corresponding marginal weight and summing up the weighted values.

The weighted marginal cost of capital schedule is a graph relating the firm's weighted average cost of capital to various levels of new financing. The investment opportunities schedule is a graph that shows the internal rates of return of the investment projects available to the firm in a given time. This graph lists the project's internal rates of return in ascending order. The intersection between the weighted marginal cost of capital schedule and the investment opportunities schedule determines the discount rate to be used for evaluating the firm's capital budgeting projects.
3 *Calculating the cost of equity in practice* The required rate of return on a firm's equity can also be calculated by using the capital asset pricing model. In the United Kingdom, the London Business School Risk Measurement Service computes and provides betas for the firms quoted on the London Stock Exchange.
4 *Empirical evidence on the cost of capital methods* The empirical findings on the area of the cost of capital presented in this chapter reveal that firms are using the weighted average cost of capital method to measure their overall cost of capital. Additionally, it was found that the dominance approach used to estimate the cost of equity was the constant growth dividend valuation model.

Questions for discussion

1 For each term shown below in the largest box provide a definition in your own words. Then check your responses against the definitions included

in the chapter.

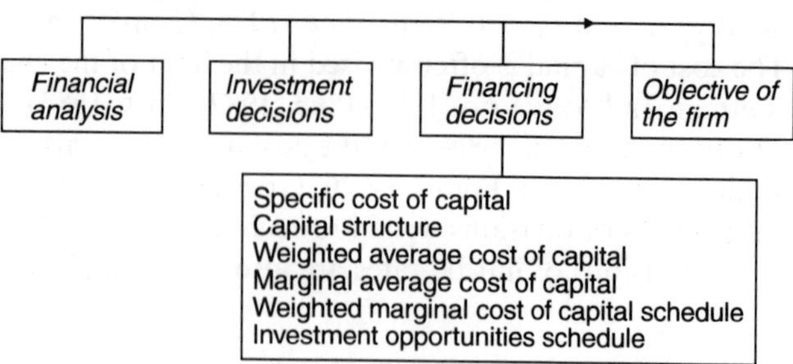

2 Discuss this statement carefully: 'The cost of capital is one of the most important and useful concepts in financial management.'

3 Fill in the blank boxes shown in the diagram below. Provide a brief justification for each of your answers.

	Cost of new debentures	Cost of new preference shares	Cost of new ordinary shares	Cost of reserves
Corporate tax adjustment	Yes			
Flotation cost adjustment				
Based upon fixed future cash flows				

4 Evaluate critically and explain:

(a) 'From the viewpoint of the firm, the cost of new debentures is equal to the rate of return required by investors.'

(b) 'The reserves of a firm are earnings that have been retained for reinvestment and they belong to ordinary shareholders. Therefore, they are a free form of financing.'

(c) 'The cost of new preference shares is just the investors' required rate of return adjusted for corporation tax and flotation costs.'

5 Explain each of the four statements given below:

Cost of new debentures

(a) The explicit cost of new preference shares is less than the cost of new ordinary shares

(d) The cost of new ordinary shares is greater than the cost of reserves

Cost of new preference shares

Cost of reserves

(b) The explicit cost of new debentures is less than the cost of new preference shares

(c) The explicit cost of reserves is greater than the cost of new debentures

Cost of new ordinary shares

6 'In practice firms may finance an investment by using the proceeds from a debenture issue and then finance subsequent investments with a mix of long-term debt and equity. In the first case, the after-tax cost of debentures should be used to evaluate the investment, while in the second the firm should employ in the evaluation process the weighted average cost of capital.' Do you agree?

7 The Gordon model (constant dividend growth valuation model) and the capital asset pricing model are often utilized to estimate the implicit cost of reserves. Compare and contrast these two models. Under which circumstances do the Gordon model and the capital asset pricing model give the same results? Demonstrate your answer by using a numerical example.

8 List a number of events that could affect a textile firm's (for example, Marks and Spencer's) average cost of capital. Other things being the same, explain how each of your factors would affect (that is, increase, decrease or no change) the firm's average cost of capital.

9 Identify the strength and weakness of the weighted average cost of capital approach.

10 A manufacturing firm wishes to select the best among the following two risky projects: the first project involves replacing five machines with new ones and the second project is concerned with the expansion into the production and sale of a new product in a new market. The firm's weighted average cost of capital is 14 per cent. The first project has an internal rate of return of 13 per cent while the internal rate of return of the second is 14.5 per cent. The financial director of the firm is considering going ahead with the second project. Do you agree? Fully discuss your answer.

11 Discuss fully the following statement: 'The weighted marginal cost of capital schedule and the investment opportunities schedule are utilized to find the appropriate discount rate for use in decision making purposes.'

12 Prepare an analog model summarizing the main points discussed in the present chapter.

13 How can spreadsheets be used to facilitate the application of the concepts discussed in this chapter?

Appendix 14A Inefficient market proxy and the cost of equity

Suppose that the market proxy under consideration, call it m, is mean–standard deviation inefficient. Then, there exists a mean–standard deviation efficient proxy, for which we can write:

$$r_i = r_f + (r_{m'} - r_f)b_{im'} \tag{14A.1}$$

where m' is a mean–standard deviation proxy whose mean equals the mean of proxy m. Equation (14A.1) can be written as:

$$r_i = r_f + (r_{m'} - r_f)b_{im'} + (r_m - r_f)b_{im} - (r_m - r_f)b_{im} \tag{14A.2}$$

Equation (14A.2) is equivalent to

$$r_i = r_f + (r_m - r_f)b_{im} + (r_m - r_f)(b_{im'} - b_{im}) \tag{14A.3}$$

In words, the cost of equity for a mean–standard deviation proxy equals the sum of three terms: the first term is the risk-free rate of interest; the second is the risk premium associated with the firm's shares; and the last term is an error associated with the use of the inefficient market proxy. The error term is different from zero because the systematic risk of security i in portfolio m is different from that of security i in portfolio m'. The greater the difference between b_{im} and $b_{im'}$, the greater the bias in the cost of equity figure estimated using the capital asset pricing model.

Deriving the equation of asset beta

We assume the existence of corporation tax. The following relationship equates the cost of equity calculated using the capital asset pricing model and the cost of equity computed using the Modigliani and Miller approach (see Chapter 15):

$$r_f + (r_m - r_f)b_o = r_U + (1 - T_c)(r_U - r_d)\frac{D}{E_G} \tag{14A.4}$$

where r_U = the cost of equity of the all equity firm with

$$r_U = r_f + (r_m - r_f)b_a \tag{14A.5}$$

The cost of debt can be expressed as

$$r_d = r_f + (r_m - r_f)b_d \tag{14A.6}$$

Substituting Equations (14A.5) and (14A.6) into Equation (14A.4) yields

$$r_f + (r_m - r_f)b_o = r_f + (r_m - r_f)b_a + (1 - T_c)[r_f + (r_m - r_f)b_a - r_f - (r_m - r_f)b_d]\frac{D}{E_G} \tag{14A.7}$$

Simplifying Equation (14A.5) gives

$$b_o = b_a + (1 - T_c)[b_a - b_d]\frac{D}{E_G} \tag{14A.8}$$

Rearranging terms in Equation (14A.8), we obtain

$$b_a = \frac{1}{1 + (1 - T_c)D/E_G}b_o + \frac{(1 - T_c)D/E_G}{1 + (1 - T_c)D/E_G}b_d$$

QED

Appendix 14B Statistical inference: hypothesis testing

The concepts of hypothesis testing can be introduced by considering the following example. Suppose an individual confirms during a job interview that he or she is not married, has two university degrees and can drive a car. After the interview, the firm's managing director discusses with his colleagues that the applicant should be employed if his or her statements abount being unmarried and having two university degrees are true. In this case, we have to test the hypothesis 'the appliant should be employed' versus the hypothesis 'the applicant should not be employed'. Let us call the first of these hypotheses the null hypothesis and the second one alternative hypothesis.

If the null hypothesis is accepted, the applicant will be employed by the firm. On the other hand, if the null hypothesis is rejected, the alternative hypothesis should be accepted. In order to make the final decision, the firm checks the validity of the applicant's claims. If the applicant is married, has no university degree or one university degree, the null hypothesis is rejected and the alternative hypothesis is accepted (that is, the firm should not employ the applicant).

In a similar fashion statistical hypothesis testing examines the validity of quantitative statements with the aid of statistical tests. For example, we can examine with the aid of a statistical test whether the monthly rates of change of the FT-A price index for preference shares influence the monthly rates of change of the FT-A price index for debentures. The statistical hypothesis testing is one of the most important methods in statistical inference. In testing a hypothesis, we begin by making a statement concerning a parameter of a population. Then we consider a random sample drawn from the population, and estimate the corresponding sample statistic. Finally, by using the estimated statistic and a decision rule, we conclude whether the hypothesis is true or false. In general, the statistical testing of hypotheses involves the following five steps:

Step 1 Formulate the null and alternative hypotheses.
Step 2 Decide on the statistical test to be employed for testing whether the null hypothesis is true or false.
Step 3 Decide on the level of significance and identify the critical value for the test.
Step 4 Calculate the test statistic.
Step 5 Compare the test statistic calculated in Step 4 with the critical value and make a decision whether to accept or reject the null hypothesis.

Example 14B.1 Testing the existence of a relationship between two variables

Suppose we wish to examine whether the monthly rate of change of the FT-A price index for debentures are affected by the monthly rates of change of the FT-A price index for preference shares (a sample of 36 observations for each variable is provided in Appendix 11A). Then follow the procedure outlined below:

Step 1 The null and alternative hypotheses are written, respectively as:
Null hypothesis There is not a relationship between the monthly rates of change of the FT-A price index for debentures and the monthly rates of change of the FT-A price index for preference shares.
Alternative hypothesis There is a relationship between the monthly rates of change of the FT-A price index for debentures and the monthly rates of change of the FT-A price index for preference shares.

Step 2 One way to test the null hypothesis established in Step 1 is to run a simple regression between the monthly rates of change of the FT-A price index for debentures (dependent variable) and the monthly rates of change of the FT-A price index for preference shares (independent variable) and examine the statistical significance of the regression line's slope. The latter can be achieved by employing the t-statistic (see also Chapter 4). A statistic utilized to test a hypothesis about a population parameter is known as a test statistic.

Since the existence of a relationship between two variables can be examined by simply testing the statistical significance of the slope of the regression line between the variables, the null and alternative hypotheses formulated in Step 1 are stated, respectively, as

H_0: Regression line's slope $= 0$

H_1: Regression line's slope $\neq 0$

where the null hypothesis is designated as H_0, while the alternative hypothesis is designated by H_1.

Step 3 We wish to test the null hypothesis at the 5 per cent level of significance. The significance level represents the probability of being wrong in rejecting a true null hypothesis or accepting a false null hypothesis. The critical value of the test corresponds to a specified significance level as determined from the sampling distribution under consideration. In our example, the critical value can be found from the table giving the critical values of the t-distribution. For 34 degrees of freedom, the critical value using a two-tail test is approximately equal to 2.042 (note that this is a two-tailed test value, that is, we are looking for the t-value for a tail area of $0.025 = 0.05/2$).

Step 4 The t-statistic is calculated by dividing the estimated slope of the regression line by the estimated standard error of the slope (see Chapter 4 for the formula of the slope's standard error). The results from the regression between the two variables under consideration are presented in Figure 14B.1.

	A	B	C	D	E
50		Regression Output:			
51	Constant			-0.002	
52	Std Err of Y Est			0.015	
53	R Squared			0.461	
54	No. of Observations			36	
55	Degrees of Freedom			34	
56					
57	X Coefficient(s)		0.641		
58	Std Err of Coef.		0.119		

Figure 14B.1. The outcome of the `/Data Regression` command

The t-statistic is simply 5.387 (that is 0.641/0.119).

Step 5 Since the sample t, 5.387, is greater than the critical value 2.042 we reject the null hypothesis at 5 per cent level of significance (or 95 per cent level of confidence). In this case, rejecting the null hypothesis means that our sample shows convincing evidence, at the 5 per cent level of significance, that the population slope coefficient is not equal to zero. Therefore, there exists a relationship between the two variables.

Some useful points

1 (Acceptance and rejecting regions) The critical value of a test statistic separates the area under the curve of the sampling distribution of the test statistic into two regions. The first is called acceptance region and the second is known as rejection region. If the value of the test statistic falls in the acceptance region, the null hypothesis is accepted. On the other hand, the null hypothesis is rejected for a test statistic's values falling in the rejection region.

2 (One-tailed test versus two-tailed test) One-tailed test is applicable when the alternative hypothesis specifies a direction. In this case, the alternative hypothesis is

expressed as an inequality. For example, consider the following null and alternative hypotheses, respectively:

H_0: Regression line's slope > 1

H_1: Regression line's slope < 1

The null hypothesis will be rejected only when there exists a significant deviation from 1 in one direction only. Thus, we have a one-tailed test. On the other hand, if the alternative hypothesis specifies no direction a two-tailed test is applied. In this instance, the alternative hypothesis is expressed as an equality or it uses the 'not equal' sign. For example, we can set up the following null and alternative hypotheses, respectively:

H_0: Regression line's slope $= 0$

H_1: Regression line's slope $\neq 0$

The null hypothesis will be rejected when the test statistic deviates from zero in either direction. Hence, such a hypothesis results in a two-tailed test.

3 (Errors in hypothesis testing) When testing hypotheses two potential errors may occur: (a) the null hypothesis is rejected when it is actually true (such an error is called a Type I error); and (b) the null hypothesis is accepted when it is actually false (such an error is called a Type II error). Figure 14B.2 summarizes the four possible results that can occur when testing hypotheses.

Figure 14B.2. Summarizing the results that can occur from hypothesis testing

	The null hypothesis is true	The null hypothesis is false
Accept the null hypothesis	The decision is correct	Type II error occurs
Reject the null hypothesis	Type I error occurs	The decision is correct

References and bibliography

Ang, J.S. (1973) Weighted average versus true cost of equity, *Financial Management*, **2**, Autumn, 56–60.

Arditti, F.D. (1973) The weighted average cost of capital: some questions on its definition, interpretation and use, *Journal of Finance*, **28**, September, 1001–7.

Arditti, F.D. and Levy, H. (1977) The weighted average cost of capital as a cutoff rate: a critical analysis of the classical textbook weighted average, *Financial Management*, **6**, Autumn, 24–34.

Baranek, W. (1977) The weighted cost of capital and shareholders wealth maximisation, *Journal of Financial and Quantitative Analysis*, **12**, March, 17–31.

Barges, A. (1963) *The Effect of Capital Structure on the Cost of Capital*. Prentice-Hall, Englewood Cliffs, NJ.

Baumol, W. and Malkiel, B.G. (1967) The firm's optimal debt–equity combination and the cost of capital, *Quarterly Journal of Economics*, **81**, November, 547–78.

Ben-Horim, M. (1979) Comment on the weighted average cost of capital as a cut-off rate, *Financial Management*, **8**, Summer, 18–21.

Boudreaux, K.J. and Long, H.W. (1979) The weighted average cost of capital as a cutoff rate: a further analysis, *Financial Management*, **8** Summer, pp. 7–14.

Brennan, M.J. (1973) A new look at the weighted-average cost of capital, *Journal of Business Finance*, **5**, 24–30.

Brigham, E.F. (1975) Hurdle rates for screening capital expenditure proposals, *Financial Management*, Autumn, 17–26.

Chen, A. (1978) Recent developments in the cost of debt capital, *Journal of Finance*, **33**, June, 863–83.

Corr, A.V. (1983) *The Capital Expenditure Decision*. National Association of Accountants and the Society of Management Accountants of Canada, Canada.

Dimson, E. (1979) Risk measurement when shares are subject to infrequent trading, *Journal of Financial Economics*, June, 197–226.

Dimson, E. and Marsh, P. (1982) Calculating the cost of capital, *Long Range Planning*, 112–20.

Durand, D. (1959) Cost of debt and equity funds for business: trends and problems of measurement, in: Solomon, E. (ed.), *The Management of Corporate Capital*, Free Press, New York.

Ezzell, J.R. and Porter, R.B. (1976) Flotation costs and the weighted average cost of capital, *Journal of Financial and Quantitative Analysis*, **11**, September, 403–14.

Ezzell, J.R. and Porter, R.B. (1979) Correct specification of the cost of capital and net present value, *Financial Management*, **8**, Summer, 15–17.

Fox, A.F. (1977) The cost of retained earnings—a comment, *Journal of Business Finance and Accounting*, **4**, Winter, 463–8.

Gitman, L.J. and Mercurio, V.A. (1982) A survey of capital budgeting techniques used by major US firms, *Financial Management*, Autumn, 66–71.

Grinyer, J.M. (1976) The cost of equity, the capital asset pricing model and management objectives under uncertainty, *Journal of Business Finance and Accounting*, **3**, Winter, 101–21.

Haley, C.W. and Schall, L.D. (1978) Problems with concepts of the cost of capital, *Financial and Quantitative Analysis*, **13**, December, 847–70.

Keane, S.M. (1975) Some aspects of the cost of debt, *Accounting and Business Research*, Autumn, 298–304.

Lewelly, W.C. (1976) *The Cost of Capital*. Kental/Hunt, Dubuque, Iowa.

Modigliani, F. and Miller, M.H. (1958) The cost of capital, corporation finance and the theory of investments, *American Economic Review*, **48**, June, 261–97.

Modigliani, F. and Miller, M.H. (1959) The cost of capital, corporation finance and the theory of investments: reply, *American Economic Review*, **49**, September, 655–69.

Nantell, T.J. and Carlson, C.R. (1975) The cost of capital as a weighted average, *Journal of Finance*, **30**, December, 1343–55.

Nantell, T.J. and Carlson, C.R. (1976) The cost of retained earnings, in: Brigham, E.F. and Johnson, R.E. (eds), *Issues in Managerial Finance*. Dryden Press, Hinsdale, Ill.

Petry, G.H. (1975) Empirical evidence of the cost of capital weights, *Financial Management*, **4**, Winter, 58–65.

Petty, J., Scott, D.F. and Bird, M.M. (1975) The capital expenditure decision-making process of large corporations, *Engineering Economist*, Spring, 159–71.

Pike, R.H. (1982) *Capital Budgeting in the 1980s*. ICMA, UK.

Robichek, A.A. and McDonald, J.G. (1965) The cost of capital concept: potential use and misuse, *Financial Executive*, **33**, June, 20–49.

Roll, R. (1977) A critique of the asset pricing theory tests, *Journal of Financial Economics*, March, 129–76.

Schall, L.D., Sundem, G.L. and Geijsbeek, W.R. (1978) Survey and analysis of capital budgeting methods, *Journal of Finance*, March, 281–8.

Scholes, M. and Williams, J. (1977) Estimating betas from non-synchronous data, *Journal of Financial Economics*, December, 309–27.

Scott, D.F. and Johnson, D.J. (1982) Financing policies and practices in large corporations, *Financial Management*, Summer, 51–9.

15 Gearing and capital structure

This chapter includes:

- Operating gearing and business risk
- Financial gearing and financial risk
- Combined gearing and combined risk
- Theories on capital structure

In financial management, operating gearing results from the use of assets having fixed costs, while financial gearing results from the use of sources of capital having fixed costs. A firm employs operating and financial gearing in an effort to magnify the potential gains for its ordinary shareholders. However, gearing also involves potential risks. For example, increasing financial gearing results in increasing the firm's risk of being unable to pay its fixed financing costs. The amount of gearing in the firm's asset structure or capital structure can influence its market value by affecting its total risk and return. Several theoretical approaches have been developed attempting to explain how changes in a firm's financial gearing affect its total market value and the firm's weighted average cost of capital. Some of these theories are based on assumptions whose validity cannot be guaranteed in the real world.

The objective of this chapter is to develop the concepts of operating, financial and combined gearing. Additionally, it discusses several theories related to the capital structure of a firm. Figure 15.1 presents the concepts discussed in this chapter in relation to the general financial management framework introduced in Chapter 2.

The utilization of gearing in financial management is analogous to the use of physical gearing. The latter permits the magnification of force when a lever is applied to a fulcrum. The objective of gearing in finance may be defined as the use of fixed-cost assets or fixed-cost funds in order to magnify profits. There are two types of gearing in finance: operating gearing and financial gearing.

Operating gearing

Operating gearing refers to the magnifying effect that changes in sales can have on the firm's profit before interest and tax (PBIT) as a result of the utilization of certain fixed operating costs. In the short run, the operating costs of the firm can be categorized as variable, fixed and semi-variable costs. Variable costs may be defined as those which change directly and proportionally with changes in the level of sales, for example, direct labour costs, costs of materials, fuel costs, and so on. Fixed costs may be defined as those which remain unchanged despite changes in the level of sales, for example, directors' salaries, depreciation, insurance expenses, and so on.

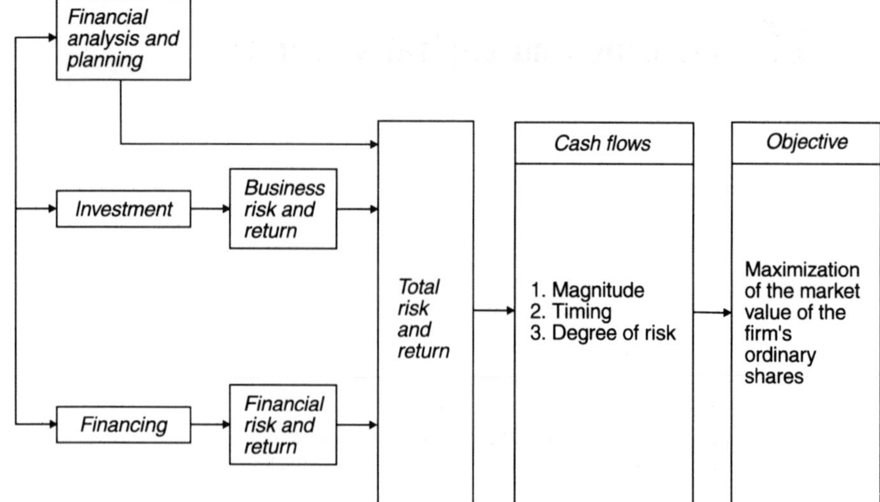

Figure 15.1. Relating the concepts of business risk and financial risk to the framework introduced in Chapter 2

Semi-variable costs may be defined as those which are partly fixed and partly variable, for example overtime rates. Sales commissions may be fixed for a certain level of sales and then increased for higher levels of sales, and so on. Obviously, in the long run all costs are variable. Operating gearing can be described in quantitative terms by the degree of operating gearing (see Figure 15.2 and Appendix 15A).

Definition The degree of operating gearing is a measure of a firm's operating gearing.
Calculation The degree of operating gearing can be calculated as follows:

$$\text{DOG} = \frac{\text{Percentage change in PBIT}}{\text{Percentage change in units sold}} = \frac{U(\text{SP} - \text{VC})}{\text{PBIT}}$$

where

U = number of units sold.
SP = sale price per unit.
VC = variable cost per unit.
PBIT = profit before interest and tax.

Interpretation The degree of operating gearing measures the extent to which changes in sales affect profit before interest and tax. The greater the degree of operating gearing, the higher the operating gearing.

Figure 15.2. Summarizing the degree of operating gearing concept

Example 15.1 Calculating the degree of operating concept

GPD Manufacturing plc manufactures one product that sells for £2 per unit. The firm's fixed operating costs are £10,000 and the variable operating cost per unit is £1. The current level of sales of the firm is 20,000 units. We consider the following two cases: (a) a decrease from 20,000 to 10,000 units; and (b) an increase from 20,000 to 30,000 units. Figure 15.3 calculates the profit before interest and tax for various sales levels. For example, if the level of the firm's sales is 20,000 units (see column C labelled as basic case), the profit before interest and tax would be:

$$\text{PBIT} = 20{,}000 \times (£2 - £1) - £10{,}000 = £10{,}000$$

The degree of operating gearing can be computed by using two methods. The first one involves calculating the percentage change in profits before interest and tax resulting from a percentage change in sales. From Figure 15.3 we have:

Percentage change in profit before interest and tax = 100 per cent
Percentage change in sales = 50 per cent

Therefore we can write

$$\text{DOG} = \frac{100\%}{50\%} = 2$$

The degree of operating gearing can also be calculated as follows (see Figure 15.2):

$$\text{DOG} = \frac{20{,}000(£2 - £1)}{£10{,}000} = 2$$

Since the degree of operating gearing is greater than 1, operating gearing exists. A degree of operating gearing of 2 suggests that for every 1 per cent change in sales, there will be a 2 per cent change in profit before interest and tax. The relationship between sales and profit before interest and tax is positive indicating that both variables move in the same direction. For example, a 2 per cent decrease in sales would result in a 4 per cent decrease in profit before interest and tax.

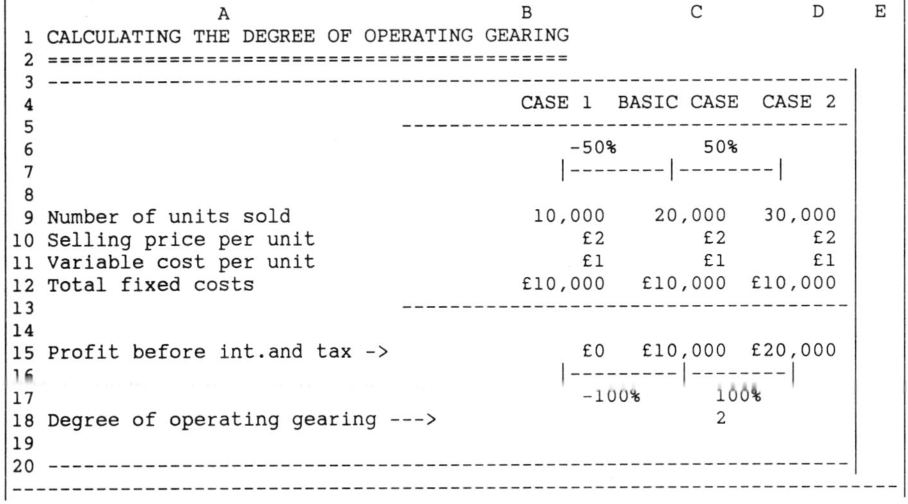

	A	B	C	D	E
1	CALCULATING THE DEGREE OF OPERATING GEARING				
2	==				
3					
4		CASE 1	BASIC CASE	CASE 2	
5					
6		-50%	50%		
7					
8					
9	Number of units sold	10,000	20,000	30,000	
10	Selling price per unit	£2	£2	£2	
11	Variable cost per unit	£1	£1	£1	
12	Total fixed costs	£10,000	£10,000	£10,000	
13					
14					
15	Profit before int.and tax ->	£0	£10,000	£20,000	
16					
17		-100%	100%		
18	Degree of operating gearing --->		2		
19					
20					

Figure 15.3. Calculating the degree of operating gearing for GPD Manufacturing

Operating break-even point for units sold and sales amount

Operating break-even analysis examines the interrelationship between sales, operating costs and profit before interest and tax at various levels of output. The operating break-even point in units of output occurs when the profit before interest and tax is equal to zero. The results from a break-even analysis can be presented graphically by using a line chart.

Example 15.2 Operating break-even analysis

Consider the data given in Example 15.1. The top part of Figure 15.4 calculates

```
      A         B         C         D         E         F         G         H
 1 GPD MANUFACTURING:OPERATING BREAK-EVEN ANALYSIS
 2 ===============================================
 3
 4
 5 -------------------------------------------------------------------
 6 Selling price per unit                                  £2.0
 7 Variable cost per unit                                  £1.0
 8 Total fixed costs                                    £10,000
 9                                                     ---------
10
11 Operating break-even point in units ---->            10,000
12
13
14 Operating break-even point in £ sales  ---->  £20,000
15
16 -------------------------------------------------------------------
17
18 -------------------------------------------------------------------
19          Number    Total     Total     Fixed     Total     PBIT
20          of units  sales     variable  costs     costs
21          sold                costs
22 -------------------------------------------------------------------
23             2,000   £4,000    £2,000  £10,000   £12,000  (£8,000)
24             4,000    8,000     4,000   10,000    14,000   (6,000)
25             6,000   12,000     6,000   10,000    16,000   (4,000)
26             8,000   16,000     8,000   10,000    18,000   (2,000)
27            10,000   20,000    10,000   10,000    20,000         0
28            12,000   24,000    12,000   10,000    22,000     2,000
29            14,000   28,000    14,000   10,000    24,000     4,000
30            16,000   32,000    16,000   10,000    26,000     6,000
31            18,000   36,000    18,000   10,000    28,000     8,000
32 -------------------------------------------------------------------
```

Figure 15.4. Linear operating break-even analysis

the operating break-even point in terms of units of output as well as in terms of pounds sterling of sales. The latter is defined as the total revenue from sales available at the break-even quantity of sales. The second part of Figure 15.4 calculates the profit before interest and tax at various units of sales.

$$\text{Break-even point in units} = \frac{£10{,}000}{£2 - £1} = 10{,}000 \text{ units}$$

The operating break-even point in terms of pounds sterling of sales is calculated as follows:

$$\text{Break-even point in terms of pounds sterling of sales} = \frac{£10{,}000}{1 - £1/£2} = £20{,}000$$

We assume that the fixed costs remain constant within the sales range of 2,000 to 18,000 units. We also assume a constant sale price per unit and a constant variable cost per unit. Such assumptions imply a linear relationship between the number of units sold and total revenue from sales as well as a linear relationship between the number of units sold and total costs. These two relationships are presented graphically in Figure 15.5. The break-even point occurs at the intersection of the two lines. If the number of units sold is lower than 10,000, the firm realizes operating losses. On the other hand, if the number of units sold is above 10,000, the firm realizes operating profits.

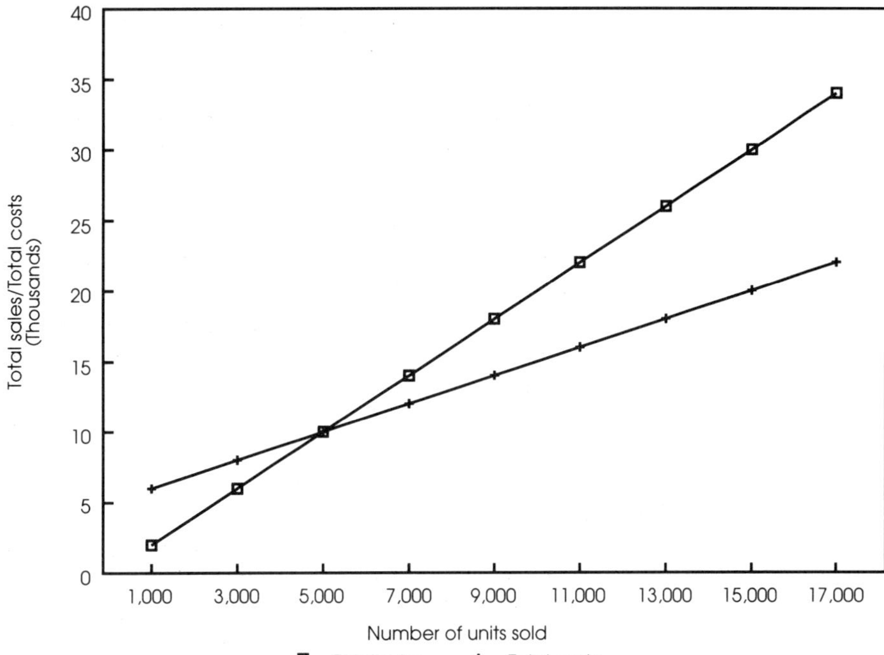

Figure 15.5. Operating break-even analysis chart for GPD Manufacturing plc

Problems

1 Set up the worksheet shown in Figure 15.4.
2 Produce the graph shown in Figure 15.5.

Properties of the degree of operating gearing

The equation of the degree of operating gearing (see Figure 15.2) can be written as follows:

$$\mathrm{DOG} = \frac{U(\mathrm{SP} - \mathrm{VC})}{\mathrm{PBIT}} = 1 + \frac{\mathrm{FC}}{\mathrm{PBIT}}$$

where FC = fixed operating costs. With the aid of this equation we can prove the following properties:

1 If the profit before interest and tax is positive and fixed costs exist, the degree of operating gearing is greater than 1.
2 The degree of operating gearing is undefined at the operating break-even point.
3 The degree of operating gearing is negative below the operating break-even point. Thus, a negative degree of operating gearing reveals that gearing is being calculated at a level of sales lower than the operating break-even quantity of sales. The degree of operating gearing is positive above the operating break-even point revealing that gearing is being calculated at a level of sales greater than the operating break-even quantity of sales.
4 The degree of operating grearing is large around the operating break-even point.

5 A positive degree of operating gearing approaching 1 indicates a relatively large amount of profit before interest and tax.

Example 15.3 The relationship between the degree of operating gearing and the number of units sold

Recall the information given in Example 15.1. Figure 15.6 shows the relationship between the degree of operating gearing and number of units sold for GPD Manufacturing. Column B calculates the profit before interest and tax for different levels of sales. Columns C and D show the degrees of operating gearing at different levels of sales. The degree of operating gearing is negative below and positive above the break-even point of 10,000 units. Additionally, the degree of operating gearing cannot be determined at the break-even point. In absolute terms the degree of operating gearing increases as we approach the operating break-even point. Also for positive values of profit before interest and tax, the degree of operating gearing decreases as the number of units sold increases (other things remain the same).

The relationship between the degree of operating gearing and profit before interest and tax is illustrated graphically in Figure 15.7. The horizontal line plotted at 1 reveals the limited value of operating gearing (this line is plotted by using column E of Figure 15.6). The degree of operating gearing is greater than 1.00 for sales levels that are greater than the operating break-even quantity of sales.

	A	B	C	D	E	F
1	THE RELATIONSHIP BETWEEN DOG AND NUMBER OF UNITS SOLD					
2						
3	Selling price per unit		£2.0			
4	Variable cost per unit		£1.0			
5	Total fixed costs		£10,000			
6						
7	Number of	PBIT	Negative	Positive		
8	units sold	(£)	DOG	DOG		
9						
10	0	(10,000)	0.00		1	
11	3,000	(7,000)	-0.43		1	
12	5,000	(5,000)	-1.00		1	
13	7,000	(3,000)	-2.33		1	
14	9,000	(1,000)	-9.00		1	
15	11,000	1,000		11.00	1	
16	13,000	3,000		4.33	1	
17	15,000	5,000		3.00	1	
18	17,000	7,000		2.43	1	
19	19,000	9,000		2.11	1	
20	21,000	11,000		1.91	1	

Figure 15.6. The relationship between the degree of operating gearing and number of units sold

Problems

1 Set up the worksheet shown in Figure 15.6.

2 Use the data shown in Figure 15.6 and graph the relationship between the degree of operating gearing and profit before interest and tax. Discuss the resulting graph.

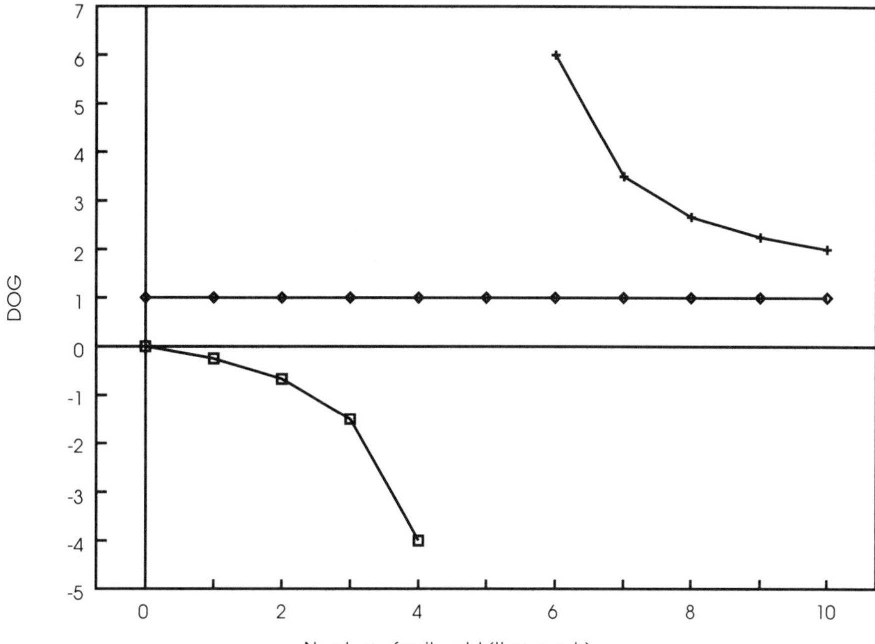

Figure 15.7. Relationship between DOG and number of units sold for GPD Manufacturing plc

Evaluation of the operating break-even analysis

Break-even analysis has several advantages including the following. First, it can be utilized to assess the profitability and risk of a firm or the profitability and risk associated with the production and sale of a new product. Second, it can be used to determine how sensitive alternative production methods are to changes in costs and sale price. Finally, break-even analysis can be employed to determine the number of units required to be produced in order to achieve a target level of operating profit.

Five of the disadvantages of break-even analysis are discussed below. First, the basic break-even model assumes that the firm's sale price per unit and its variable cost per unit remain unchanged over all levels of sales (that is, the assumption of linearity). Selling price and cost per unit, however, can vary with the level of sales, resulting in a non-linear revenue function. In this case, the results produced using the basic linear break-even model may be invalid. Second, some costs are partly fixed and partly variable and it may be difficult (or even impossible) to classify them into fixed and variable components for the analysis.

Third, when many products are involved, it may be difficult to apply break-even analysis. If each product is analysed separately, problems can arise in allocating the fixed costs between the different products. Fourth, the break-even model assumes that fixed costs remain unchanged only over a relevant range of output. Therefore, a break-even analysis may be reliable only over that range. Finally, break-even analysis does not take into account the time value of money and treats costs and revenues as they all occur at the same time. When the analysis is applied to long time periods, costs and revenues must be adjusted to reflect the time value of money.

Business risk

Business risk (or operating risk) is defined as the inherent variability of the firm's profit before interest and tax. A means of measuring the firm's business risk is the coefficient of variation of probable values of profit before interest and tax. The coefficient of variation is determined by dividing the standard deviation of the probability distribution of profit before interest and tax by its expected value:

$$CV(PBIT) = \frac{\sigma(PBIT)}{E(PBIT)}$$

where σ(PBIT) is the standard deviation of the probability distribution of probable values of profit before interest and tax and *E*(PBIT) is the expected value of the probability distribution of probable values of profit before interest and tax.

In general, the higher the coefficient of variation, the greater the degree of business risk (other things being the same).

Example 15.4 Calculating the business risk of a firm

Figure 15.8 shows a probability distribution of possible values of profit before interest and tax for GPD Manufacturing plc. This distribution offers a 25 per cent chance of a value of profit before interest and tax of £2,000, a 50 per cent chance of a value of profit before interest and tax of £10,000 and, finally, a 25 per cent chance of a value of profit before interest and tax of £22,000. The expected value of the profit before interest and tax's distribution is calculated as follows:

$$(0.25)(£2{,}000) + (0.50)(£10{,}000) + (0.25)(£22{,}000) = £11{,}000$$

Next we calculate the variance of the distribution of profit before interest and tax as follows:

$$(0.25)(2{,}000 - 11{,}000)^2 + (0.50)(10{,}000 - 11{,}000)^2 + (0.25)(22{,}000 - 11{,}000)^2 = 53{,}125{,}000$$

The square root of variance is £7,289. Finally, the coefficient of variation is equal to

$$CV = \frac{£7{,}289}{£11{,}000} = 0.663$$

	A	B	C	D	E
1	CALCULATING THE BUSINESS RISK FOR A FIRM				
2	==				
3					
4	Probability	25%	50%	25%	
5	Number of units sold	12,000	20,000	32,000	
6	Selling price per unit	£2.0	£2.0	£2.0	
7	Variable cost per unit	£1.0	£1.0	£1.0	
8	Total fixed costs	£10,000	£10,000	£10,000	
9					
10	PBIT ----->	£2,000	£10,000	£22,000	
11					
12	Weighted PBIT --------------->	£500	£5,000	£5,500	
13	Expected PBIT ------------------->		£11,000		
14					
15	Deviations of PBIT ------>	27,562,500	18,000,000	7,562,500	
16	Standard deviation of PBIT -->		£7,289		
17					
18	Coefficient of variation of PBIT ----->		0.663		
19					

Figure 15.8. The coefficient of variation of probable values of profit before interest and tax

Problem

Set up the worksheet shown in Figure 15.8.

Factors influencing business risk
Business risk is affected by a number of factors, including the following:

1 Demand variability The more unstable the demand for a firm's products, the more business risk (others factors remain the same).
2 Sales price variability The more certain the selling prices for the firm's products, the lower the firm's business risk (other things being the same).
3 Operating gearing The higher the proportion of fixed costs in the firm's cost structure, the more business risk (other things being equal).
4 General economic conditions Firms whose sales are less sensitive to changes in general economic conditions have less business risk.

Financial gearing

Financial gearing is the second form of gearing. Financial gearing refers to the magnifying effect that changes in profit before interest and tax can have on the firm's earnings per share (EPS) as a result of the utilization of certain sources of capital obtained at fixed costs (for example, preference shares, debentures, and so on). The degree of financial gearing is used to describe financial gearing in quantitative terms. Figure 15.9 summarizes the degree of financial gearing concept (see also Appendix 15A).

Definition The degree of financial gearing is a measure of a firm's financial gearing.
Calculation The degree of financial gearing can be calculated as follows:

$$\text{DFG} = \frac{\text{Percentage change in EPS}}{\text{Percentage change in PBIT}} = \frac{\text{PBIT}(1 - T)}{(\text{PBIT} - IN)(1 - T) - PD}$$

where

IN = the amount of annual interest (in pounds sterling) paid by the firm.
I = the corporate tax rate.
PD = the annual dividends paid on preference shares.
PBIT = profit before interest and tax.

Interpretation The degree of operating gearing measures the extent to which changes in profits before interest and tax affect the firm's earnings per share. The greater the degree of financial gearing, the higher the financial gearing.

Figure 15.9. Summarizing the degree of financial gearing concept

Example 15.5 Calculating the degree of financial gearing

GPD Manufacturing plc expects its profit before interest and tax for the current year to be £10,000. The firm pays £2,920 annual interest for its debentures and £2,000 per year preference dividends. The corporate tax rate is assumed to be 35 per cent. Figure 15.10 calculates the earnings per share for three different levels of profit before interest and tax as £0, £10,000 and £20,000. For example, if the profit before interest and tax is equal to £10,000 (see column D in Figure 15.10 labelled as basic case), the earnings per share are calculated

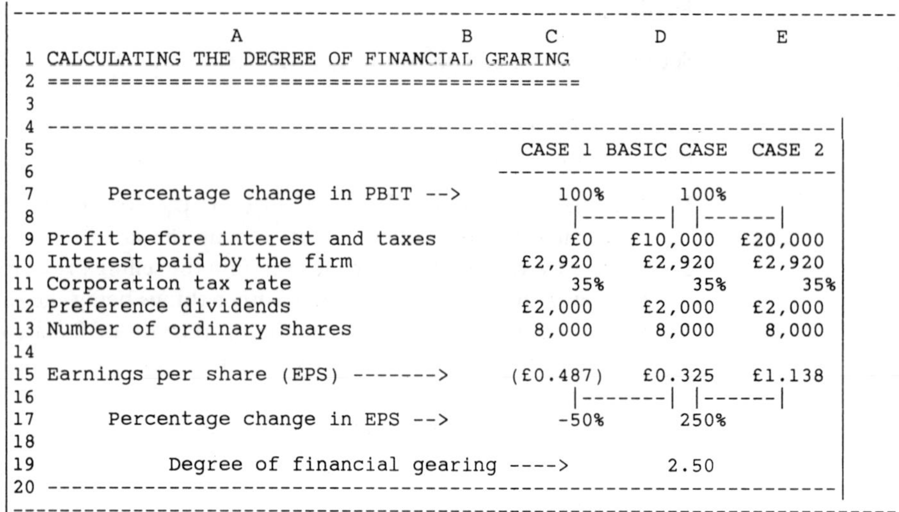

	A	B	C	D	E
1	CALCULATING THE DEGREE OF FINANCIAL GEARING				
2	==				
3					
4					
5			CASE 1	BASIC CASE	CASE 2
6					
7	Percentage change in PBIT -->		100%		100%
8					
9	Profit before interest and taxes		£0	£10,000	£20,000
10	Interest paid by the firm		£2,920	£2,920	£2,920
11	Corporation tax rate		35%	35%	35%
12	Preference dividends		£2,000	£2,000	£2,000
13	Number of ordinary shares		8,000	8,000	8,000
14					
15	Earnings per share (EPS) ------->		(£0.487)	£0.325	£1.138
16					
17	Percentage change in EPS -->		-50%		250%
18					
19	Degree of financial gearing ---->			2.50	
20					

Figure 15.10. Calculating the degree of financial gearing for GPD Manufacturing plc

as follows:

$$\text{EPS} = \frac{(£10{,}000 - £2{,}920)(1 - 0.35) - £2{,}000}{8{,}000} = 0.325 \text{ pence}$$

There are two methods used for calculating the degree of financial gearing. The first one calculates the degree of financial gearing by dividing the percentage change in earnings per share by the percentage change in profit before interest and tax.

$$\text{DFG} = \frac{250 \text{ per cent}}{100 \text{ per cent}} = 2.5$$

The second approach for calculating the degree of financial gearing is presented below:

$$\text{DFG} = \frac{£10{,}000(1 - 0.35)}{(£10{,}000 - £2{,}920)(1 - 0.35) - £2{,}000} = 2.5$$

In our example, the degree of financial gearing is greater than 1, thus, financial gearing exists. A degree of operating gearing of 2.5 indicates that for every 1 per cent change in profit before interest and tax there will be a 2.5 per cent change in earnings per share. Additionally, we observe that both variables move in the same direction since their relationship is positive. For example, a 2 per cent increase in profit before interest and tax would result in a 5 per cent increase in earnings per share.

Financial break-even point for profit before interest and tax

Financial break-even analysis examines the interrelationship between profit before interest and tax and earnings per share. The financial break-even point is defined as the value of profit before interest and tax that makes earnings per share equal to zero. The results from a break-even analysis can be presented graphically by using a line chart.

Example 15.6 Plotting the relationship between profit before interest and tax and earnings per share for GPD Manufacturing plc

Consider the case discussed in Example 15.5. The relationship between profit before interest and tax and earnings per share is shown graphically in Figure 15.11. The value of profit before interest and tax that satisfies the equation EPS = 0, is calculated as follows:

$$\text{Financial break-even point} = \frac{£2{,}000}{1 - 0.35} + £2{,}920 = £5{,}997$$

If the profit before interest and tax is lower than £5,997, the firm realizes negative earnings per share. On the other hand, if the profit before interest and tax is positive, the firm's earnings per share are positive.

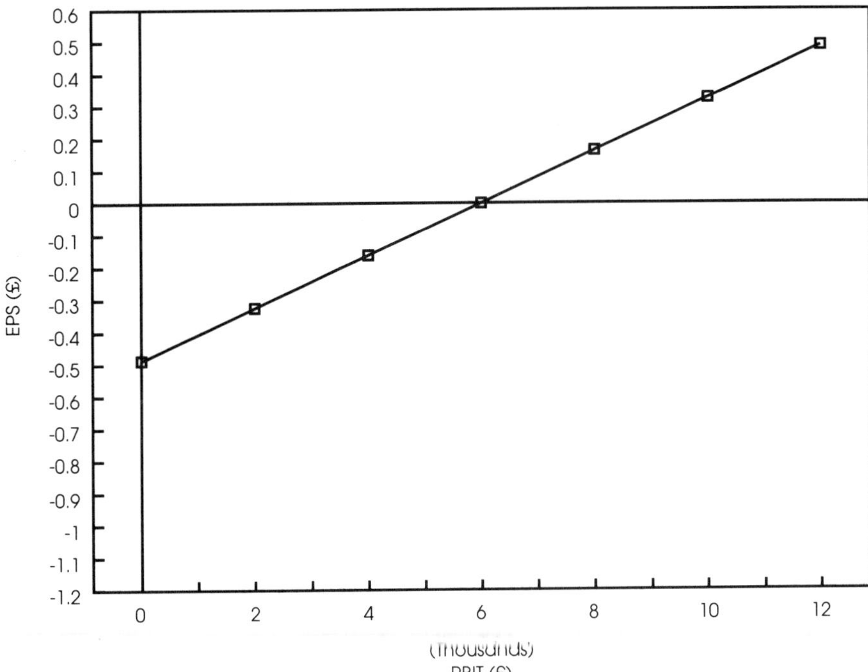

Figure 15.11. The relationship between profit before interest and tax and earning per share for GPD Manufacturing plc

Properties of the degree of financial gearing

The degree of financial gearing (see Figure 15.9) can be expressed as follows:

$$\text{DFG} = \frac{\text{PBIT}(1 - T)}{(\text{PBIT} - IN)(1 - T) - PD} = 1 + \frac{IN(1 - T) + PD}{(\text{EPS})(NS_0)}$$

where NS = the number of the firm's ordinary shares.

With the aid of this equation we can prove the following properties:

1 If earnings per share are positive and fixed financial costs exist, the degree of financial gearing is greater than 1.

2 The degree of financial gearing is undefined at the financial break-even point.
3 The degree of financial gearing is negative below the financial break-even point. Thus, a negative degree of financial gearing indicates that gearing is being calculated at a level of profit before interest and tax lower than the financial break-even point. The degree of financial gearing is positive above the financial break-even point revealing that gearing is being calculated at a level of profit before interest and tax greater than the financial break-even point.
4 The degree of financial gearing is large around the financial break-even point.
5 A positive degree of financial gearing approaching 1 indicates a relatively large amount of earnings per share.

Example 15.7 The relationship between the degree of financial gearing and profit before interest and tax

This example demonstrates the relationship between the degree of financial gearing and profit before interest and tax for GPD Manufacturing plc. The results are presented in Figure 15.12 and shown graphically in Figure 15.13. For values of profit before interest and tax greater than the financial break-even point of £5,997, the degree of financial gearing is greater than 1. In addition, the degree of financial gearing cannot be determined at the financial break-even point. In absolute terms the degree of financial gearing increases as we approach the financial break-even point. For positive values of earnings per share, the degree of financial gearing decreases as profit before interest and tax increases (other things remain constant).

Problem

Produce the results shown in Figure 15.12 by using 1-2-3's `/Data Table 1` command.

	A	B	C	D	E	F
1	RELATIONSHIP BETWEEN THE DOG AND PBIT					
2	----------					
3	Interest paid by the firm			£2,920		
4	Corporation tax rate			35%		
5	Preference dividends			£2,000		
6	Number of ordinary shares issued			8,000		
7	----------					
8	PBIT	EPS	Negative DFG	Positive EPS		
9	(£)	(£)				
10	----------					
11	997	-0.406	-0.20		1	
12	1,997	-0.325	-0.50		1	
13	2,997	-0.244	-1.00		1	
14	3,997	-0.162	-2.00		1	
15	4,997	-0.081	-5.00		1	
16	5,997	0.000	NA		1	
17	6,997	0.081		7.00	1	
18	7,997	0.163		4.00	1	
19	8,997	0.244		3.00	1	
20	9,997	0.325		2.50	1	
21	----------					

Figure 15.12. The relationship between the degree of financial gearing and profit before interest and tax

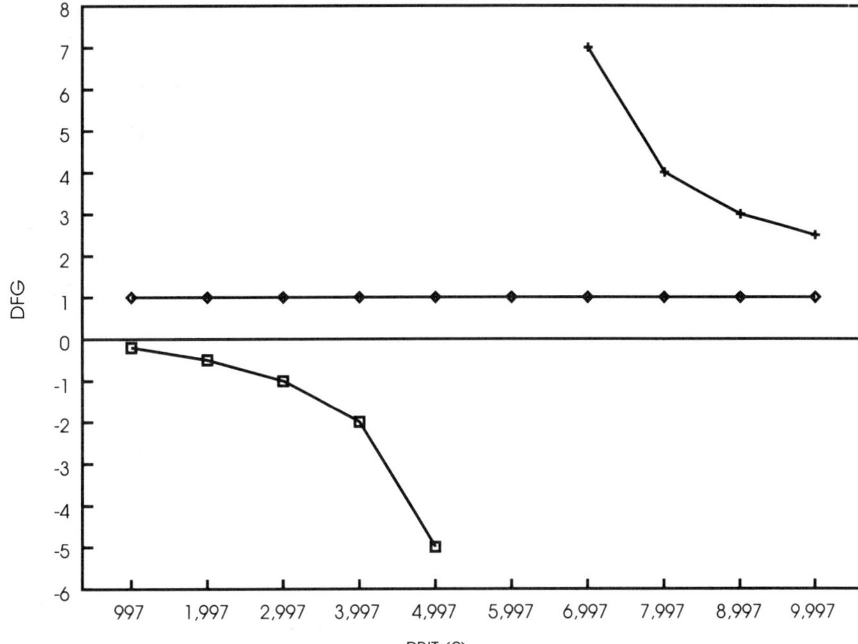

Figure 15.13. Relationship between DFG and PBIT for GPD Manufacturing plc

Combined gearing

Recall that operating gearing deals with the relationship between sales and profit before interest and tax, whereas financial gearing is concerned with the relationship between profit before interest and tax and earnings per share. Combined gearing is a combination of operating and financial gearing. Combined gearing measures the relationship between sales and earnings per share. The degree of combined gearing provides a quantitative description of combined gearing. Figure 15.14 presents a summary of the combined gearing concept (see also Appendix 15A).

Definition The degree of combined gearing is a measure of a firm's combined gearing.
Calculation The degree of combined gearing can be calculated as follows:

$$\text{DCG} = \frac{\text{Percentage change in EPS}}{\text{Percentage change in units sold}} = (\text{DOG})(\text{DFG})$$

where

DOG = degree of operating gearing
DFG = degree of financial gearing

Interpretation The degree of combined gearing measures the extent to which changes in units sold affect the firm's earnings per share. The greater the degree of combined gearing, the higher the combined gearing.

Figure 15.14. Summarizing the degree of combined gearing concept

Example 15.8 Calculating the degree of combined gearing

Putting together the results presented in Figures 15.3 and 15.10, we have Figure 15.15. The degree of combined gearing can be calculated by using one

```
                   A                              B          C          D    E
 1 CALCULATING THE DEGREE OF COMBINED GEARING
 2 =========================================
 3                                             CASE 1                CASE 2
 4  Percentage change in units --->              50%        50%
 5                                                |---------|---------|
 6 Number of units sold                       10,000     20,000     30,000
 7 Selling price per unit                         £2         £2         £2
 8 Variable cost per unit                         £1         £1         £1
 9 Total fixed cost                          £10,000    £10,000    £10,000
10 Profit before inter. and tax                   £0    £10,000    £20,000
11 Interest paid by the firm                  £2,920     £2,920     £2,920
12 Corporation tax rate                          35%        35%        35%
13 Preference dividends                       £2,000     £2,000     £2,000
14 Number of ord. shares issued                8,000      8,000      8,000
15
16 Earnings per share ----->               (£0.487)     £0.325     £1.138
17                                                |---------|---------|
18    Percentage change in EPS ->               250%       250%
19 Degree of combined gearing ------>                       5.00
20 ---------------------------------------------------------------------
```

Figure 15.15. Calculating the degree of combined gearing

of the following two methods. First, it can be computed by dividing the percentage change of earnings per share by the percentage change in sales. Namely:

$$\text{DCG} = \frac{250 \text{ per cent}}{50 \text{ per cent}} = 5$$

The second approach for computing the degree of combined gearing simply multiplies the degree of operating gearing by the degree of financial gearing. The degree of operating gearing for GPD Manufacturing is 2 (see Example 15.1) and the degree of financial gearing is 2.5 (see Example 15.5). Consequently, we have DCG = 5.

An interpretation of the degree of combined gearing of 5 goes as follows: a 1 per cent change in sales from a level of 20,000 units produces a 5 per cent change in earnings per share.

Figure 15.16 presents graphically two relationships for GPD Manufacturing plc. First, the relationship between sales revenue and profit before interest and tax and, second, the relationship betwen sales revenue and earnings available to ordinary shareholders (EAS). We assume that within the sale range of £36,000–£47,000 (or in terms of units 18,000–23,500) the fixed costs remain the same and there occurs no change in the selling price per unit and variable cost per unit. Both profit before interest and tax and earnings available to ordinary shareholders are increasing functions of sales.

Figure 15.17 plots the degree of operating gearing, degree of financial gearing and degree of combined gearing for the data of sales revenue used in Figure 15.16. It is evident that each degree of gearing decreases as the sales revenue increases.

Problem

Create the worksheet shown in Figure 15.15.

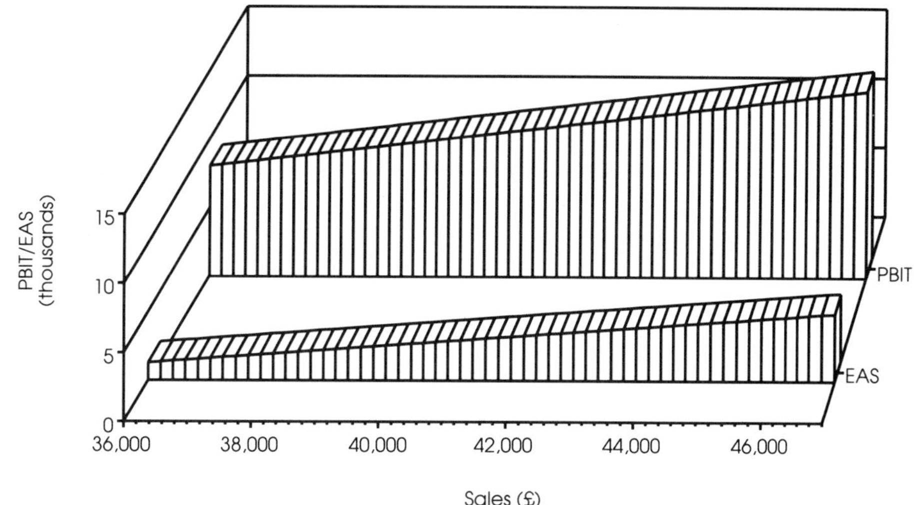

Figure 15.16. GPD Manufacturing: relationship among sales and PBIT and among sales and EAS

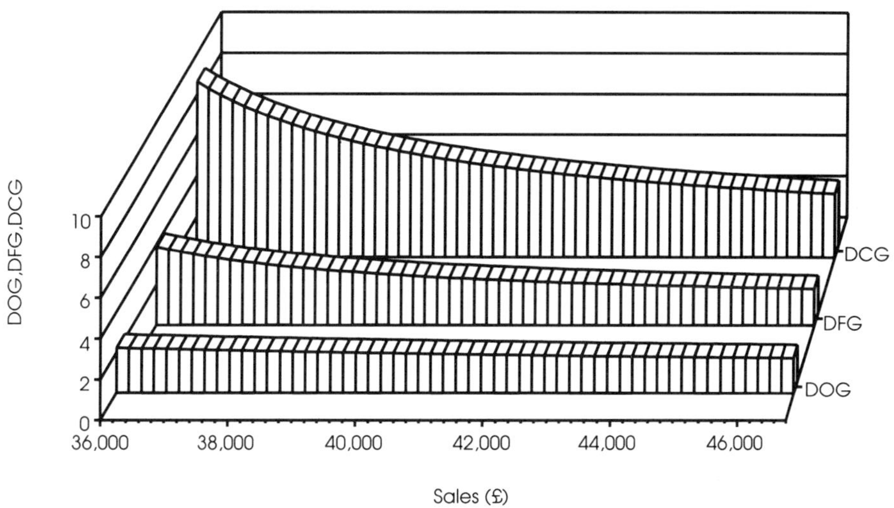

Figure 15.17. GPD Manufacturing: DOG, DFG and DCG for different levels of sales

Total (combined) risk

A change in the firm's asset structure or a change in its capital structure affects its overall risk-return characteristics. Total risk is defined as the inherent variability the firm's earnings per share. This risk can be measured by the coefficient of variation of the earnings per share's probability distribution:

$$\text{CV(EPS)} = \frac{\sigma(\text{EPS})}{E(\text{EPS})}$$

where σ(EPS) and E(EPS) are the standard deviation and the expected value, respectively, of the probability distribution of probable values of earnings per share. The larger the coefficient of variation, the larger the total risk faced by the firm.

Example 15.9 Calculating the total risk of a firm

The probabilities associated with three possible levels of profit before interest and tax and three possible levels of earnings per share are shown in Figure 15.18. The expected value of the probability distribution of earnings per share is a weighted average of the three probable values of earnings per share stored in cells B14, C14 and D14, respectively. On the other hand, the standard deviation of the probability distribution of earnings per share is equal to the square root of the average squared deviations of the individual earnings per share from their expected value. The coefficient of variation is 1.356 (that is, £0.5513/£0.4065).

	A	B	C	D	E
1	CALCULATING THE TOTAL RISK FOR GPD MANUFACTURING				
2	==				
3	Probabilities ------>	25%	50%	25%	
4	Number of units sold	12,000	20,000	32,000	
5	Selling price per unit	£2	£2	£2	
6	Variable cost per unit	£1	£1	£1	
7	Total fixed cost	£10,000	£10,000	£10,000	
8	Profit before inter. and tax	£2,000	£10,000	£22,000	
9	Interest paid by the firm	£2,920	£2,920	£2,920	
10	Corporation tax rate	35%	35%	35%	
11	Preference dividends	£2,000	£2,000	£2,000	
12	Number of ord. shares issued	8,000	8,000	8,000	
13					
14	Earnings per share ----->	-0.3248	0.3253	1.3003	
15	Weighted EPS ------------->	-0.0812	0.1626	0.3251	
16	Expected EPS ------------------>		£0.4065		
17					
18	Deviations of EPS ----->	0.2378	0.0595	0.0066	
19	Standard deviation of EPS -->		£0.5513		
20	Coefficient of variation of EPS ----->		1.356		

Figure 15.18. Coefficient of variation of probable values of earnings per share

Problem

Set up the worksheet shown in Figure 15.18.

Financial risk

The variability of earnings per share (not due to operating gearing) can be described as the firm's financial risk. This risk can be expressed as follows:

Financial risk = CV(EPS) – CV(PBIT)

where CV(EPS) is the coefficient of variation of the probability distribution of earnings per share and CV(PBIT) is the coefficient of variation of the probability distribution of profit before interest and tax.

Factors influencing financial risk

Financial risk depends on a number of factors, including the following:

1. *Increasing/decreasing costs for new debentures and preference shares* High costs for obtaining funds via a new issue of debentures or a new issue of preference shares decrease both the firm's earnings per share and its degree of financial gearing, whereas low fixed financial costs have the opposite effect.

2 *Changes in corporate tax rates* When the corporate tax rate changes, the firm's earnings per share may be affected and this in turn may have an influence on its financial risk.

3 *Financial gearing* The higher the proportion of fixed financial costs in the firm's capital structure, the higher its financial risk (other things being equal).

Figure 15.19 provides a summary of operating gearing, financial gearing and combined gearing.

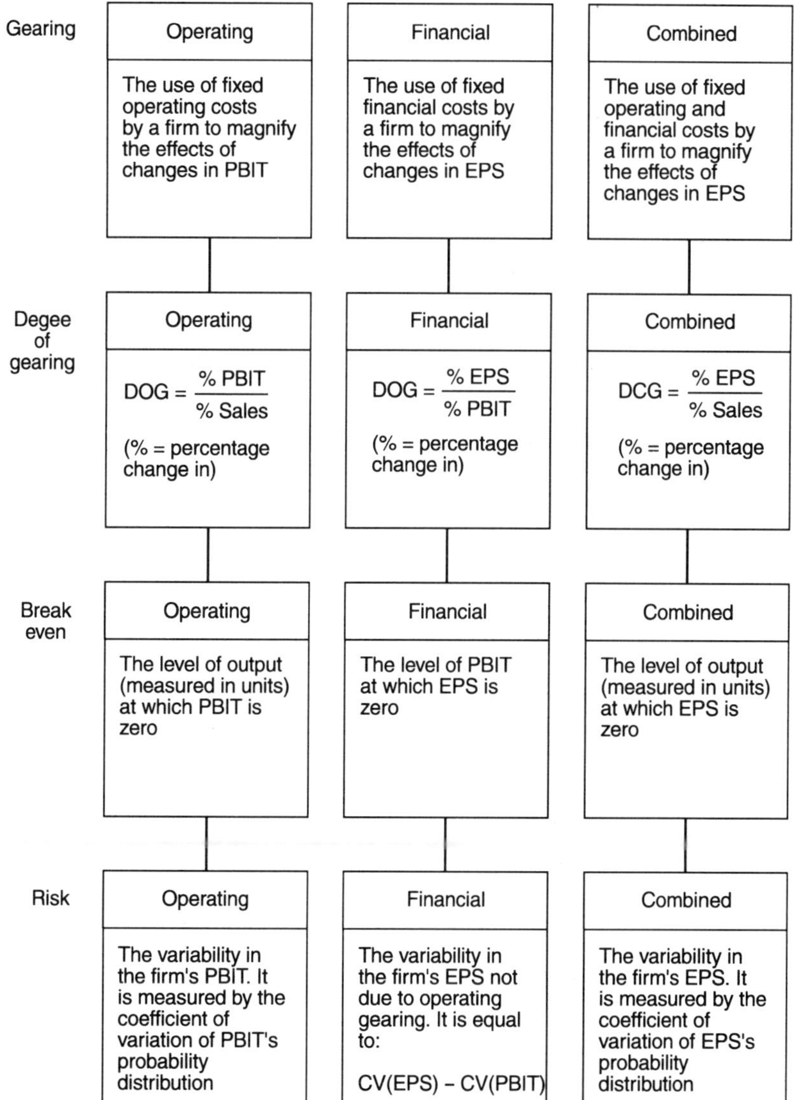

Figure 15.19. A summary of operating gearing, financial gearing and combined gearing

Capital structure theories

There are seven approaches that attempt to explain the relationship between a firm's capital structure, cost of capital and market value: these are summarized in Figure 15.20.

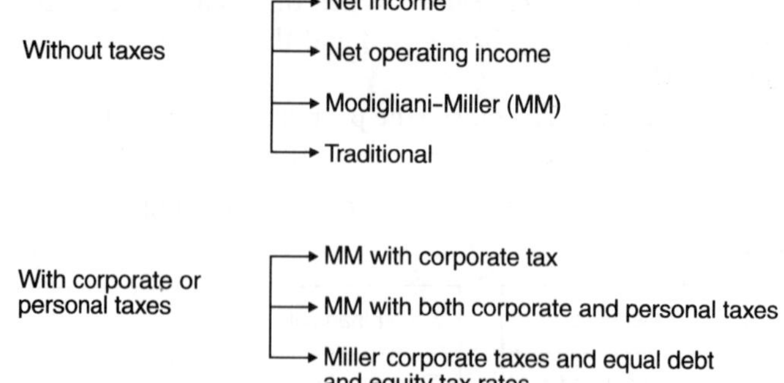

Figure 15.20. Approaches related to the effect of gearing on a firm's value

In a world without corporate taxes or other restrictive assumptions (for example, all borrowed funds are risky) the four approaches shown in Figure 15.20 provide some conflicting implications. As we shall discuss below, the net income approach and the traditional approach show that the total market value of a firm is affected by its capital structure, in contrast to the net operating income and the proposition of Modigliani–Miller asserting that the total market value of a firm is independent of its capital structure. When corporate tax or personal taxes are taken into account, the argument of Modigliani–Miller generally breaks down.

Capital structure theories with no taxes

Each of the four approaches to be discussed in this section assume a world with no taxes.

Net income approach

This approach is based upon the following assumptions:

1. There are no corporate or personal taxes.
2. There are only two sources of funds used by a firm: perpetual debt and ordinary share capital.
3. The firm's total assets are constant (this enables us to discuss capital structure without regard to investment decisions).
4. The firm's profit before interest, also known as net operating income, is expected to remain constant through time.
5. The firm pays all earnings out as dividends (this allows us to discuss capital structure without considering the issue or how a firm's dividend policy influences its value).
6. The firm is expected to continue its operations forever.
7. An increase in the firm's gearing does not affect the cost of equity or the cost of debt.

The net income approach asserts:

> *The total market value and the weighted average cost of capital of a firm are dependent on its capital structure.*

If we assume that the firm pays out all its earnings as dividends, there is no growth in earnings and the firm has an infinite life span, then the stream of dividend payments can be considered as a perpertuity. In this case, the market value of equity is NP/r_o, where NP = the constant earnings available to shareholders and r_o = the cost of equity. The total value of the firm can be expressed as follows:

$$V = NP/r_o + I/r_d \qquad (15.1)$$

where I = the amount in pounds sterling of annual interest and r_d = the cost of debt.

The weighted average cost of capital of a firm is equal to the weighted costs of equity and long-term debt where the weight of each specific cost of capital is the ratio of the market value of that source of capital to the total market value of the firm. That is

$$\text{WACC} = r_o E/(E + D) + r_d D/(E + D) \qquad (15.2)$$

where E = the market value of equity and D = the market value of debt.

In view of the net income approach, the firm prefers to increase the amount of debt in its capital structure since debt is a cheaper source of capital than equity. As a consequence, the firm's weighted average cost of capital (see Equation 15.2) tends to decrease. More debt increases the total value of the firm as well because in Equation (15.1) the interest increases by an amount equal to the amount that dividends decrease and the cost of debt is less than the cost of equity.

Under the net income approach the optimal capital structure is achieved when the firm uses the highest possible degree of gearing.

Example 15.10 Illustrating the net income approach

Assume that AD Computers plc has no long-term debt outstanding and its current earnings before interest are £700,000. The firm pays out all its earnings as dividends. AD Computers needs to raise external funds to finance a number of new capital budgeting projects and we assume that the introduction of debt will not change either its cost of debt or its cost of equity. The firm is considering the following two alternatives:

Plan I   Sell £1,000,000 in 8 per cent debentures.
Plan II   Sell £1,500,000 in 8 per cent debentures.

The expected value of the earnings before interest are £700,000 under each plan. Figure 15.21 calculates the market value of AD Computers and its cost of capital under each plan.

Assuming a perpetual life for the firm, its market value of shares under Plan I is calculated as follows:

£600,000/0.14 = £4,285,714

Next, the firm's total market value under Plan I is equal to:

£4,285,714 + £1,000,000 = £5,285,714

The firm's weighted average cost of capital under Plan I would be

$$0.14\frac{£4,285,714}{£5,285,714} + 0.10\frac{£1,000,000}{£5,285,714} = 13.24 \text{ per cent}$$

The total market value and the cost of capital for Plan II are calculated in a similar fashion. From the results it can be seen that the total market value of the firm increases and the weighted average cost of capital decreases as additional debt is used.

```
                    A                                  B                C
 1              THE NET INCOME APPROACH
 2              =======================
 3 Cost of Ordinary Shares --------->                14.0%
 4 Cost of Debentures ------------>                  10.0%
 5 ------------------------------------------------------------------------
 6                                                 PLAN I          PLAN II
 7 ------------------------------------------------------------------------
 8 Market Value of Debentures                  £1,000,000       £1,500,000
 9 Net Operating Income                           700,000          700,000
10 Total Debenture Interest                       100,000          150,000
11                                             ----------------------------
12 Earnings Available to Shareholders            £600,000         £550,000
13
14 Total Market Value of Shares                £4,285,714       £3,928,571
15
16 Total Market Value                          £5,285,714       £5,428,571
17                                             ----------------------------
18 Weighted Average Cost of Capital                13.24%           12.89%
19                                             ============================
```

Figure 15.21. Illustrating the net income approach

The power of 1-2-3 is its ability to utilize formulae to make calculations based upon numeric entries in the worksheet. Suppose you enter formulae into the above worksheet that refer to other cells in that worksheet. Then when you change the values in the cells that are referred to by a formula, 1-2-3 automatically recalculates the results. Such a worksheet can calculate the firm's total market value and its weighted average cost of capital as many times as you wish to consider. For example, you can examine the sensitivity of the firm's total market value to changes in the weighted average cost of capital and in debt funds used.

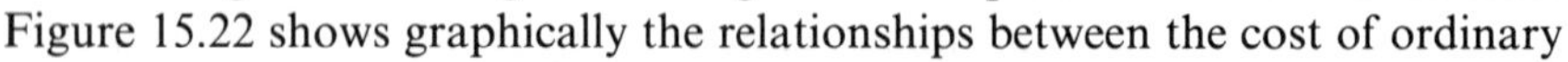

Figure 15.22 shows graphically the relationships between the cost of ordinary

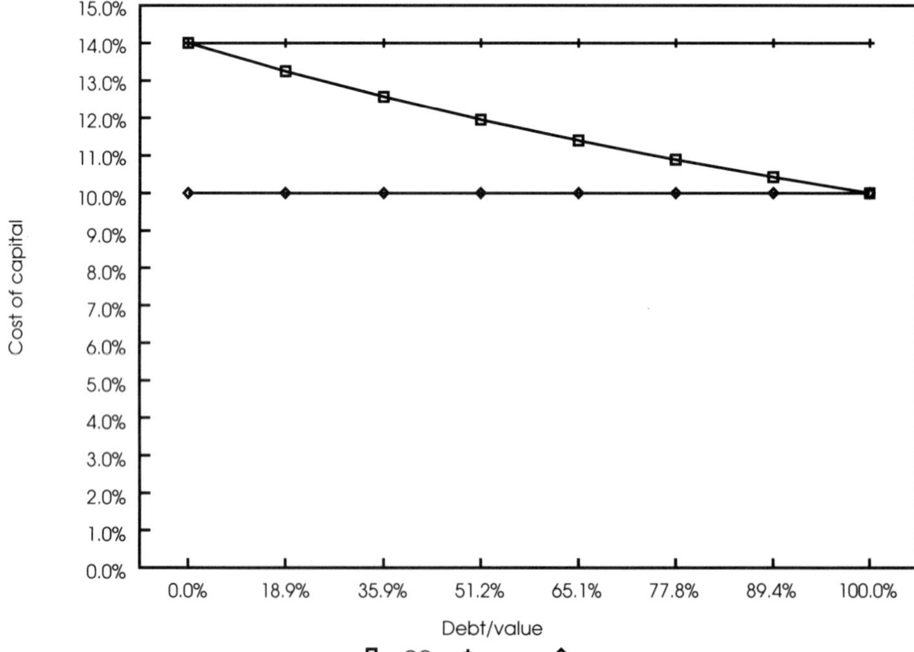

Figure 15.22. AD Computers plc: cost of capital and financial gearing—the net income approach

shares, the cost of debt and the weighted average cost of capital, and financial gearing (that is, the ratio of long-term debt to total market value). Since the cost of ordinary shares and the cost of debt remain the same as the firm's gearing increases, both curves are parallel to the *X*-axis. The weighted average cost of capital decreases as the firm's gearing increases and approaches the cost of debt when the debt to total market value ratio approaches 100 per cent. At the point where the weighted cost of capital is equal to the cost of debt, the cost of capital is minimized, the firm's market value is maximized and the firm achieves its optimal capital structure.

Problem

Create the worksheet shown in Figure 15.21.

The major disadvantage of the net income approach is that it fails to consider the financial risk introduced as a result of increasing debt. In practice, the greater the level of debt relative to equity, the greater is the risk that the interest payments and principal payments on the borrowed funds may not be met. In view of the net income approach, the optimal capital structure of a firm will be 100 per cent debt financing. However, this is unrealistic since it does not take into account the effects of extreme gearing on the value of ordinary shares. If a firm uses a very high proportion of debt in its capital structure, the investors will sell their shares, thereby causing a decrease in the market price of the firm's shares. The net income approach does not recognize such a case and is therefore inadequate as a theory of capital structure.

Net operating income approach

This approach employs the following assumptions:

1 The firm uses only two types of capital: ordinary share capital and long-term debt capital. Preference shares are omitted in order to simplify the analysis.
2 There are no transaction costs and corporate taxes.
3 The firm pays out all its earnings as dividends to its shareholders.
4 The firm's profit is constant.
5 The firm has fixed total assets, but its capital structure can be changed by selling ordinary shares and using the proceeds to retire long-term debt and vice-versa.
6 The firm's business risk is constant.
7 The cost equity changes as the firm utilizes more debt.
8 The firm is expected to continue operating forever and its debentures never mature.
9 The value of the equity is found by subtracting the value of the debt from the firm's total value.

The net operating income approach suggests:

> *The total market value and the weighted average cost of capital of a firm are independent from its capital structure.*

Under the net income approach the total market value of the firm is equal to the market value of equity plus the market value of debt. Under the net operating income approach the total market value of the firm can be expressed as follows:

$$V = \frac{\text{NOI}}{\text{WACC}}$$

where NOI = net operating income.

Since the net operating income is expected to be constant through time and the weighted average cost of capital is constant, the total market value of the firm remains unchanged by increases in gearing. The market value of equity is calculated by subtracting the market value of debt from the firm's total market value. With the aid of the assumptions of the net operating income approach, the cost of equity is NP/E, where NP = the constant earnings available to ordinary shareholders (NP = NOI – interest on debt) and E = the market value of equity.

Under the net operating income there is no optimal capital structure.

Example 15.11 Illustrating the net operating income approach

Assume that AD Computers plc exists in a hypothetical world where the assumptions of the net operating income are valid. We assume that the overall cost of capital of the firm is 14 per cent and remains constant. In this world the total market value of the firm under plan I (see Example 15.10) will be calculated as follows (see cell B10 in Figure 15.23 and please remember our earlier assumptions associated with the NOI approach).

$$\frac{£700{,}000}{0.14} = £5{,}000{,}000$$

The weighted average cost of capital is

$$\frac{£700{,}000}{£5{,}000{,}000} = 14 \text{ per cent}$$

Note, that the calculation of the weighted average cost of capital constitutes a circular mathematical problem. We started by assuming that the weighted average cost of capital is 14 per cent and we ended by deriving that the weighted average cost of capital is 14 per cent. In this case, the net operating income approach recognizes that both the firm's weighted average cost of capital and its

	A	B	C
1	THE NET OPERATING INCOME APPROACH		
2	================================		
3	Cost of Ordinary Shares ---------->	14.0%	
4	Cost of Debentures ------------>	10.0%	
5			
6		PLAN I	PLAN II
7			
8	Net Operating Income	£700,000	£700,000
9			
10	Total Market Value	5,000,000	5,000,000
11			
12	Market Value of Debentures	1,000,000	1,500,000
13			
14	Market Value of Ordinary Shares	£4,000,000	£3,500,000
15			
16	Cost of Ordinary Shares	15.00%	15.71%
17			
18	Weighted Average Cost of Capital	14.00%	14.00%
19			

Figure 15.23. Illustrating the net operating income approach

total market value cannot be used independently. That is, if the overall cost of capital is known, then we can calculate the overall value of the firm and vice versa. This theory also proves that if the overall cost of capital of the firm remains constant, its total market value is also constant and vice versa.

The market value of the firm's ordinary shares under Plan I can be computed as follows:

£5,000,000 – £1,000,000 = £4,000,000

Given the market value of the firm, the cost of ordinary shares would be

$$\frac{£700{,}000 - 0.10(£1{,}000{,}000)}{£4{,}000{,}000} = 15 \text{ per cent}$$

We can proceed similarly for Plan II. Thus, the weighted average cost of capital of 10 per cent remains unaffected by the firm's capital structure. 1-2-3 formulae can be used in the worksheet shown in Figure 15.23 in order to recalculate automatically the firm's weighted average cost of capital when you change the values in the cells that are referred to by the weighted average cost of capital formula (this is a similar case as that discussed in Example 15.10).

Figure 15.24 provides a graphical representation of the relationships between the cost of ordinary shares (r_o), the cost of debentures (r_d) and the weighted average cost of capital with the level of gearing (that is the ratio of long-term debt to total market value). Since the cost of debentures and the weighted average cost of capital are unaffected by the firm's gearing, both the curves are parallel to the *X*-axis. The cost of ordinary shares increases as the firm's gearing increases.

In view of the net operating income approach, the weighted average cost of capital is unaffected by the firm's capital structure which in turn implies that there is no one optimal capital structure.

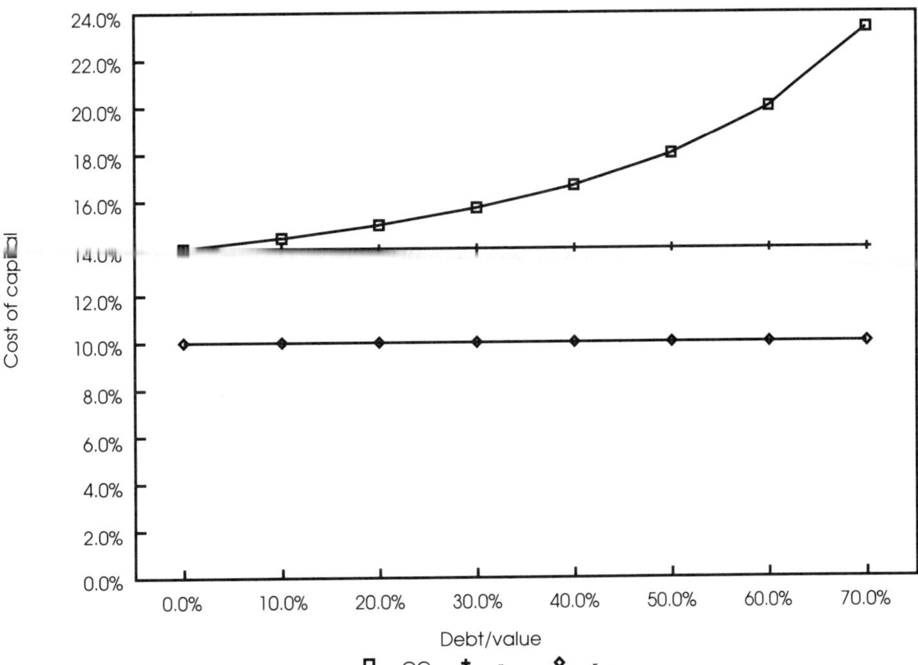

Figure 15.24. AD Computers plc: cost of capital and financial gearing—the net operating income approach

Problem

Create the worksheet shown in Figure 15.23.

In view of the net operating income approach, the firm's weighted average cost of capital does not change the different degrees of financial gearing. This encourages the firm to ignore important issues such as avoiding a very high proportion of debt in its capital structure.

Modigliani–Miller approach

This approach assumes the following:

1 The capital market is perfect, that is, there are no transaction costs; there are no taxes; securities are infinitely divisible; information is costless and available to every investor; and no single buyer or seller of securities is large enough to affect their prices.
2 There are no flotation costs for issuing new securities.
3 There are no costs associated with the liquidation of the firm.
4 Business risk is the same among all firms with similar operating environments.
5 The value of the equity is found by subtracting the value of the debt from the firm's total value.
6 Firms and individuals can borrow or lend at the same interest rate.
7 The firm pays all its earnings as dividends.

The net operating income approach does not provide operational justification for the proposition that the value of a firm is independent of its capital structure. The Modigliani–Miller argument is used as a support to the net operating income approach. Their works provides a behavioural justification for having a constant weighted average cost of capital and, thus, a constant market value of the firm. The Modigliani–Miller approach asserts:

> *The total market value and the weighted average cost of capital of a firm are independent of its capital structure.*

The original work of Modigliani and Miller includes a difficult mathematical analysis and it was decided to illustrate their argument by using a hypothetical example.

Example 15.12 Illustrating the Modigliani–Miller approach

Basically, the present example uses the mathematical analysis of Modigliani and Miller and shows that the total market value of a firm is independent of its capital structure. Their argument results from a process known as 'arbitrage' which precludes making profits from perfect substitutes.

Suppose U Computers plc is an all-equity firm (no long-term debt) and G Electronics is a firm that uses long-term debt in its capital structure. Figure 15.25 provides a package of information on the two firms. It is also assumed that both firms carry the same business risk and the capital market is perfect.

In Figure 15.26 the market value of a share in U Computers is calculated as follows:

$$\frac{£5,833,333}{350,000} = 16.67 \text{ pence}$$

	A	B	C
1	PART A:THE DATA		
2	--	----------	----------
3		FIRM U	FIRM G
4	--	----------	----------
5	Net Operating Income	£700,000	£700,000
6			
7	Number of Ordinary Shares Outstanding	350,000	200,000
8			
9	Market Value of Long-term Debt	0	1,000,000
10			
11	Interest Rate	0.00%	10.00%
12			
13	Cost of Ordinary Shares	12.00%	13.00%

Figure 15.25. Financial data of two firms U Computers and G Electronics

U Computers' total market value is equal to the market value of its ordinary shares plus the market value of its debt. The firm's weighted average cost of capital can be calculated by dividing the net operating income by its total market value:

$$\frac{£700{,}000}{£5{,}833{,}333} = 12 \text{ per cent}$$

The total market value of U Computers is higher than the total market value of G Electronics (see Figure 15.26). Next it will be shown that the total market value of the two firms has to be the same. In Figure 15.26, the market value per share is calculated by dividing the market value of ordinary shares by the number of ordinary shares. Also, the debt to equity ratio is computed by dividing the market value of debt by the market value of ordinary shares.

Suppose a rational investor owns 500 shares of ordinary stock of firm G Electronics. According to Modigliani and Miller the shares of G Electronics are overvalued. Their argument can proceed as shown in Figure 15.27.

Assume that the investor sells 500 shares in G Electronics at £23.08 per share. Using the sale proceeds (that is, £11,538) he or she purchases 692.31 shares of U

21	PART B:CALCULATING THE D/E RATIO		
22	--	----------	----------
23		FIRM U	FIRM G
24	--	----------	----------
25	Net Operating Profit	£700,000	£700,000
26	Interest	0	100,000
27		----------	----------
28	Earnings Available to Ord. Shareholders	£700,000	£600,000
29			
30	Market Value of Ordinary Shares	5,833,333	4,615,385
31		----------	----------
32	Total Market Value	£5,833,333	£5,615,385
33			
34	Weighted Average Cost of Capital	12.00%	12.47%
35			
36	Market Value Per Share	16.67	23.08
37			
38	Dividend per Share	2.00	2.30
39			
40	Debt/Equity Ratio	0.00%	21.67%

Figure 15.26. Calculating the market value per share and debt/equity ratio for each of the two firms

Figure 15.27. The Modigliani–Miller argument related to the firm's financial policy

A	B	C
PART C:THE TOTAL NUMBER OF SHARES		
No of shares of firm G owned by an investor		500.00
STEP 1:Sell the shares at 23.08 per share		£11,538
STEP 2:Purchase ordinary shares of firm U		692.31
STEP 3:Obtain the same debt/equity ratio		£2,500
STEP 4:Purchase additional ordinary shares of firm U		150.00
Total number of shares purchased		842.31

Computers. Also, the investor can reach the level of financial risk of G Electronics by borrowing additional funds. His or her personal debt is equal to the debt/equity ratio of G Electronics multiplied by £11,538:

$$0.2167 \times 11{,}538 = £2{,}500$$

In this instance, the investor substitutes personal or home-made gearing for corporate gearing. With the additional funds obtained he or she purchases 150 shares of U Computers. Therefore, the investor owns 842.31 shares of U Computers.

By following this action the investor can also increase total dividend payments (see Figure 15.28). Thus, for the same amount of risk the investor can earn an additional £285 by selling the overvalued share of G Electronics and using the proceeds from the sale to purchase shares in U Computers. The gain of £285 is called a gain from arbitrage.

Figure 15.28. Calculating the gains from arbitrage

A	B	C
PART D:GAINS FROM ARBITRAGE		
	Holding shares from firm U only	Holding shares from firm G only
Number of Shares	842.31	500.00
Total Dividends	£1,685	£1,150
Interest on Borrowing	£250	0
Net Return	£1,435	£1,150
Gains from Arbitrage ------>	£285	

Arbitrage profits will increase the demand for the shares in U Computers and will decrease the demand for G Electronics' shares. As a result, the share price of U Computers will be driven up and the cost of ordinary shares will be reduced, while the price of a share of firm G will be driven down and the cost of ordinary shares to the company will be increased. The arbitrage procedure will continue until the total value of the two firms and their weighted average costs of capital will be equal. Assuming that the market value of both firms will be £7,000,000, Figure 15.29 calculates the weighted average cost of capital of G Electronics. The cost of equity is that cost in the weighted average cost of capital that equates the weighted average cost of capital to 12 per cent. That is:

$$\text{Cost of equity} = \frac{£7{,}000{,}000}{£6{,}000{,}000}0.12 - \frac{1{,}000{,}000}{£6{,}000{,}000}0.10 = 12.33 \text{ per cent}$$

If the cost of equity for G Electronics is 12.33 per cent, its weighted average cost of capital will be 12 per cent. This is equal to the weighted average cost of capital of U Computers. Additionally, the total value of G Electronics is computed as follows: £700,000/0.12 = £5,833,333.

```
                          A                                    B            C
81 PART E:CALCULATING THE FIRM G'S WACC
82 ------------------------------------------------------------
83 Total Market Value of Firm G                          £7,000,000
84
85 Market Value of Long-term Debt of Firm G              £1,000,000
86
87 Value of Ordinary Shares (Firm G)                     £6,000,000
88
89 Cost of Ordinary Shares (Firm G)                          12.33%
90                                                     ------------
91 WACC (Firm G)                                             12.00%
92 ------------------------------------------------------------
```

Figure 15.29. Calculating firm G's cost of capital

The Modigliani–Miller theory has been criticized on a number of grounds. First, the opponents are concerned with the assumption of a perfect capital market. It is true that capital markets have periods of inequilibrium. However, Modigliani and Miller think that capital markets are sufficiently perfect to ensure adequate arbitrage opportunities.

Second, the arbitrage process is based on the assumption that personal gearing is a perfect substitute for corporate gearing. In practice, however, the risk of an individual shareholder is limited to his or her relative holdings in the firm, while with personal borrowing the individual carries full personal liability. Additionally, firms can usually borrow at lower rates than individuals, as they have a better credit standing than individuals.

If individuals can borrow at higher rates than firms, they would be willing to pay extra for the shares of geared firms. In this case, the Modigliani–Miller approach could still be valid as the demand for investors for geared firms will wipe out any premium they will be willing to pay for geared shares.

Third, the Modigliani–Miller argument assumes the absence of bankruptcy costs. In a perfect capital market, such an assumption means that the assets of a failed firm can be sold at their market values. In the real world, however, we can identify several costs to bankruptcy which may reduce the claims of the ordinary shareholders if the firm is liquidated.

Traditional approach

The traditional approach constitutes a moderate view with regard to the relationship between gearing and valuation. This approach assumes the following:

1 There are no taxes.
2 There are no transaction costs.
3 The cost of equity and debt remain constant up to a point and the former is greater than the latter.

This approach asserts:

The total market value and the weighted average cost of capital of a firm are usually dependent on its capital structure.

The traditional approach is similar to the net income approach in arguing that the total market value and the weighted average cost of capital of a firm are dependent on its capital structure. But it also has the following differences from the net income approach:

- The total market value of a firm does not necessarily increase for all degrees of gearing.
- The weighted average cost of capital of a firm does not necessarily decrease for all degrees of gearing.

In one respect the traditional approach produces results which are consistent with the net operating income approach. Suppose a firm increases its debt by the following amount:

$$\text{DA} = \frac{r_o V - \text{NOI}}{r_o - r_d}$$

where

V = the firm's total market value.
r_o = the firm's cost of ordinary shares.
r_d = the firm's cost of new long-term debt.

In this case, the total market value and the weighted average cost of capital remain constant.

Under this approach there exists an optimal capital structure which can also be achieved before the firm uses its highest possible degree of gearing.

Example 15.13 Illustrating the traditional approach

Figure 15.30 shows an example illustrating the traditional approach. In Case 2, the earnings available to ordinary shareholders are calculated by subtracting the debt interest payment from the net operating income. Also in Case 3, the total market value of the firm is simply the sum of the market value of its ordinary shares and the market value of its debt. In each case, the weighted average cost of capital is calculated by dividing the net operating profit by the total market value.

This example illustrates that the total market value and the weighted average cost of capital of the firm are usually affected by its capital structure. More specifically, in the top part of Figure 15.30, the total market value increases and the weighted average cost of capital decreases with gearing. In view of the traditional approach, this result occurred because cheaper debt is substituted for more expensive equity. However, as gearing increases, the ordinary shareholders begin requiring a higher rate of return from the firm until a point

	A	B	C	D
1	THE TRADITIONAL APPROACH:THE TMV INCREASES WITH ADDITIONAL DEBT			
2	==			
3				
4		CASE 2	CASE 3	
5				
6	Cost of ordinary shares	11.0%	12.0%	
7	Coupon rate (=cost of debentures)	0.0%	4.0%	
8				
9	Net Operating Income	£700,000	£700,000	
10	Market value of debentures	£0	£3,000,000	
11	Total debenture interest	£0	£120,000	
12				
13	Earnings available to ordinary shareholders	£700,000	£580,000	
14				
15	Total market value of ordinary shares	£6,363,636	£4,833,333	
16				
17	Total market value	£6,363,636	£7,833,333	
18				
19	Weighted average cost of capital	11.00%	8.94%	
20				
21	THE TRADITIONAL APPROACH:THE TMV DECREASES WITH ADDITIONAL DEBT			
22	==			
23				
24		CASE 3	CASE 4	
25				
26	Cost of ordinary shares	12.0%	13.0%	
27	Coupon rate (=cost of debentures)	4.0%	4.5%	
28				
29	Net Operating Income	£700,000	£700,000	
30	Market value of debentures	£3,000,000	£3,500,000	
31	Total debenture interest	£120,000	£157,500	
32				
33	Earnings available to ordinary shareholders	£580,000	£542,500	
34				
35	Total market value of ordinary shares	£4,833,333	£4,173,077	
36				
37	Total market value	£7,833,333	£7,673,077	
38				
39	Weighted average cost of capital	8.94%	9.12%	
40				

Figure 15.30. The traditional approach

is reached at which the advantage of cheaper debt cannot be observed. Thus according to the traditional approach, the market value of the firm first rises, and then declines as gearing increases. In effect, investors are willing to pay less for the higher risk when gearing rises. Additionally, the weighted average cost of capital decreases at first and then rises.

Next we assume that the firm's cost of long-term debt will be 4.5 per cent and the cost of equity will be 13 per cent for any amount of debt funds equal to or greater than £3,500,000 and lower than £4,000,000. Then:

$$DA = \frac{0.13(£7,833,333) - £700,000}{0.13 - 0.045} = £3,745,098$$

If the firm's long-term debt will be £3,745,098, then Cases 2 and 4 (see Figure 15.30) will provide the same total market value and weighted average cost of capital, an instance where the net operating income approach is valid. Figure 15.31 provides a graphical illustration of the traditional approach used in the

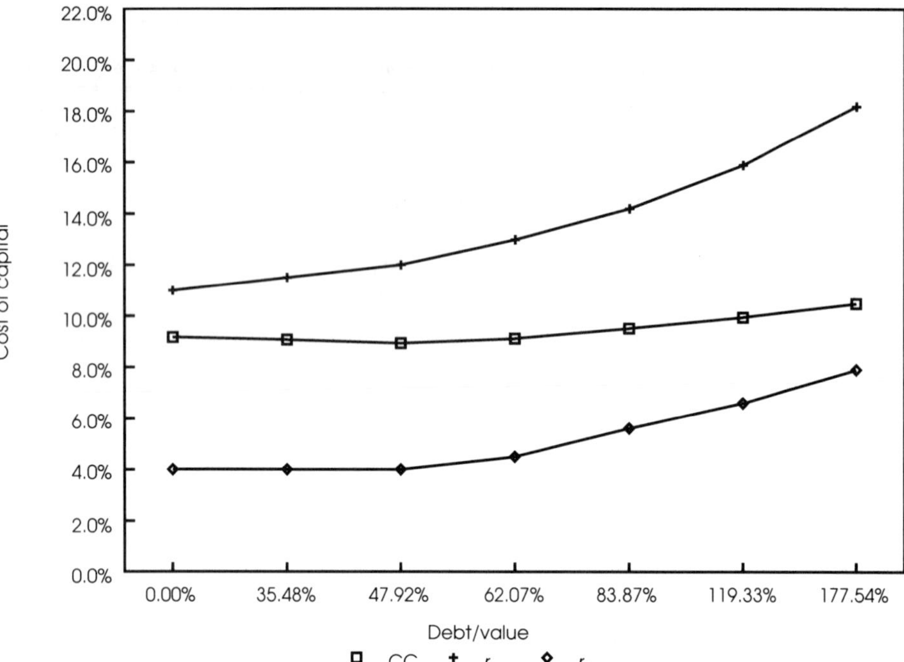

Figure 15.31. AD Computers plc: cost of capital and financial gearing—the traditional approach

present example. As we can see, the weighted average cost of capital rises and then declines as the gearing rises. In our example, the lower weighted average cost of capital occurs when the debt equity ratio of the firm is between 62.07 per cent (that is, debt £3,000,000 and equity £4,833,333) and 83.87 per cent (that is debt £3,500,000 and equity £4,173,077).

The traditional approach is unable to refute the Modigliani and Miller approach. The latter is now accepted as the only logically correct theory in the absence of taxes, transaction costs and other market imperfections.

Capital structure theories with taxes

The Modigliani–Miller argument presented earlier in this chapter breaks down when corporation tax is taken into consideration. This section is divided into two parts. The first part discusses the relationship between a firm's value and its financial gearing when corporation tax is introduced. The second part assumes the existence of corporation tax and discusses the relationship between the cost of capital and financial gearing.

Value of the firm with corporation tax

The proposition of Modigliani and Miller that the value of a firm is unaffected by its capital structure relies upon a set of assumptions, including the absence of corporation tax. Their proposition can be modified as follows:

> MM PROPOSITION I WITH CORPORATE TAX *In the presence of corporate tax, the total market value of a firm is positively related to the amount of long-term debt used in its capital structure.*

It would be easier to illustrate the first part of the above proposition by considering an example.

Example 15.14 Calculating the cash flows from the two financing plans when the corporation tax is taken into account

GD Computers plc has expected profits before interest and tax of £700,000 and its tax rate is 35 per cent. We assume that the firm distributes all its earnings as dividends. The firm is evaluating the following two financing plans (ignoring flotation costs):

Plan 1 Use only equity in its capital structure.
Plan 2 Use £1 million in 10 per cent debentures in addition to its existing equity.

Assume that both plans are identical in all respects except that one uses only equity and the other utilizes a mix of debt and equity. Figure 15.32 calculates the profit before interest and tax under each of the financing plans.

In the case of Plan U, taxable income is £700,000 and the net earnings available to shareholders (EAS) are calculated as follows:

$$\begin{aligned} EAS_U &= £700{,}000(1 - 0.35) \\ &= £700{,}000 - £245{,}000 \\ &= £455{,}000 \end{aligned}$$

For the other plan, the net earnings available to shareholders will be

$$\begin{aligned} EAS_G &= (£700{,}000 - 0.10(£1{,}000{,}000))(1 - 0.35) \\ &= £700{,}000(1 - 0.35) - £100{,}000 + (0.10)(£1{,}000{,}000)(0.35) \\ &= £390{,}000 \end{aligned}$$

Under Plan G, the earnings available to ordinary shareholders will be less than those if the other alternative is adopted. However, under Plan U the firm will have more ordinary shares as compared with the ordinary shares if the other alternative is undertaken. The tax payment of the geared firm will be lower than that of the full equity financed firm as the payment of interest is deductible for tax purposes.

In the case of Plan U, the cash flow available to shareholders will be £455,000, while in the case of Plan G the cash flow available to shareholders will be £390,000 + £100,000 = £490,000. The latter can also be calculated as the amount available to shareholders under Plan U plus the interest payable to the firm's debenture holders. Namely, this cash flow will be

$$\begin{aligned} CF_G &= (£700{,}000 - (0.10)(1{,}000{,}000))(1 - 0.35) + (0.1)(£1{,}000{,}000) \\ &= (£700{,}000)(1 - 0.35) + (0.35)(0.10)(£1{,}000{,}000) \\ &= £455{,}000 + £35{,}000 = £490{,}000 \end{aligned}$$

Figure 15.32 summarizes the calculations of cash flows.

	A	B	C	D
1	CASH FLOWS TO INVESTORS UNDER TWO FINANCING PLANS			
2	==			
3	Interest Rate on Debt	10.00%		
4	Corporate Tax Rate	35.00%		
5				
6		PLAN U	PLAN G	
7				
8	Debt	£0	£1,000,000	
9	Profit Before Interest and Tax	700,000	700,000	
10	Interest	0	100,000	
11		------------	------------	
12	Profit Before Tax	700,000	600,000	
13	Tax	245,000	210,000	
14		------------	------------	
15	Earnings Available to Shareholders	£455,000	£390,000	
16	Cash Flow to Investors	£455,000	£490,000	
17		============	============	

Figure 15.32. Calculating the cash flows to investors under two financing plans

Problem

Create the worksheet shown in Figure 15.32.

From the calculations performed in Example 15.14 the following relationship emerges:

$$\mathrm{CF_G} = \mathrm{EAS_U} + T_c r_d D$$

In words, the annual cash flow available to investors under a debt–equity financing plan is equal to the annual cash flow under a full equity financing plan plus the annual value of the tax savings on debt. The latter, also known as tax shelter, is equal to the corporate tax rate times the expected annual interest payment. The debt–equity financed firm saves money on taxes and this money can be utilized to pay debt or to provide a return to ordinary shareholders.

We can now provide an expression for the present value of the debt–equity financed firm. We assume that the cash flows and the tax savings in debt are received in perpetuity. Then the present value of the debt–equity financed firm is equal to the present value of the full equity financed firm plus the present value of a stream of tax savings on debt. The present value of a full equity financed firm is found by discounting its annual after tax cash flow, $\mathrm{EAS_U}$, at the appropriate after tax discount rate:

$$V_{\mathrm{U}} = \frac{\mathrm{EAS_U}}{r_{\mathrm{U}}}$$

The tax shelter is realized when the firm uses long-term debt. Therefore, the risk associated with the tax shelter is exactly the same as that of the debt used. As a consequence, the stream of tax shelters should be discounted using the (before-tax) cost of debt. The present value of the tax shelter perpetuity is:

$$\frac{T_c r_d D}{r_d} = T_c D$$

Therefore, the present value of the geared firm would be

$$V_{\mathrm{G}} = V_{\mathrm{U}} + T_c D$$

The last equation reveals that under corporation tax, the value of the debt–equity financed firm increases by an amount equal to the present value of tax savings on debt caused by the tax deductibility of interest. The tax savings on debt increase with the amount of debt indicating that the firm can increase its value by substituting debt for equity (other things remain the same). As a consequence, in a world of corporation tax the firm's value is affected by its capital structure.

Example 15.15 Calculating the present value of a geared firm with corporation tax

In addition to the situation presented in Example 15.14, we assume that the appropriate after corporation tax discount rate for the firm under the all equity financing plan is 12.5 per cent. The market value of the firm with £1,000,000 in debt will be

$$V_G = £455{,}000/0.125 + (0.35)(£1{,}000{,}000) = £3{,}990{,}000$$

Note that the increased value of the geared firm is based on the debt amount, not the rate of interest paid on debt.

The cost of capital with corporation tax

So far we have seen that under a situation of corporation tax, the firm is able to increase its total value as it increases the proportion of debt in its capital structure. In this section, we present the following proposition:

MM PROPOSITION II WITH CORPORATION TAX *In the presence of corporation tax, the weighted average cost of capital decreases as the firm increases the amount of long-term debt in its capital structure.*

To calculate the weighted average cost of capital we need the following inputs:

- Market value of equity.
- Cost of equity.
- Market value of debt.
- Cost of debt.

The market value of equity of the geared firm can be expressed as follows (for a proof see Appendix 15B):

$$E_G = V_U - (1 - T_c)D$$

The cost of equity of the geared firm is given by (for a proof see Appendix 15B):

$$r_{Go} = r_U + (1 - T_c)(r_U - r_d)\frac{D}{E_G}$$

Finally, the weighted average cost of capital is a weighted average of the cost of equity and cost of debt where the weight for each source of capital is the ratio of the market value of that source to the total market value of the firm.

Example 15.16 Calculating the weighted average cost of capital of a geared firm with corporation tax

In order to calculate the weighted average cost of capital for GD Computers plc under the debt–equity financing plan (see Examples 15.14 and 15.15), we need the following inputs:

- Market value of equity.
- Cost of equity.
- Market value of debt.
- Cost of debt.

The market value of equity of the geared firm is calculated as follows:

$$\frac{455{,}000}{0.125} - (1 - 0.35)(£1{,}000{,}000) = £2{,}990{,}000$$

Therefore, the cost of equity of the geared firm will be:

$$r_{Go} = 0.125 + (1 - 0.35)(0.125 - 0.10)\frac{£1{,}000{,}000}{£2{,}990{,}000} = 13.04 \text{ per cent}$$

The market value of debt and the cost of debt are £1,000,000 and 10 per cent, respectively. The firm's weighted average cost of capital may be found as follows:

$$\begin{aligned} \text{WACC} &= 0.1304\frac{£2{,}990{,}000}{£3{,}990{,}000} + (1 - 0.3500)0.1000\frac{£1{,}000{,}000}{£3{,}990{,}000} \\ &= 11.40 \text{ per cent} \end{aligned}$$

The weighted average cost of capital's calculations are summarized in Figure 15.33.

The weighted average cost of capital can alternatively be calculated by utilizing the following method (for a proof see Appendix 15B):

$$\text{WACC} = 0.125 \times \left(1 - \frac{£1{,}000{,}000}{£3{,}990{,}000}0.35\right) = 11.40 \text{ per cent}$$

	A	B	C	D
1	CALCULATING THE WACC OF THE GEARED FIRM			
2	==			
3	Interest Rate on Debt	10.00%		
4	Corporate Tax Rate	35.00%		
5	Cost of Equity of Ungeared Firm	12.50%		
6				
7		PLAN U	PLAN G	
8				
9	Debt	£0	£1,000,000	
10	PBIT	700,000	700,000	
11	Interest	0	100,000	
12				
13	Profit Before Tax	700,000	600,000	
14	Tax	245,000	210,000	
15				
16	Earnings Available to Shareholders	455,000	390,000	
17	Cash Flow to Investors	455,000	490,000	
18				
19	Value of Ungeared Firm		3,640,000	
20	After Tax Value of Debt		650,000	
21				
22	Value of Equity of Geared Firm		£2,990,000	
23	Cost of Equity of Geared Firm		13.04%	
24				
25	Weighted Average Cost of Capital		11.40%	
26				

Figure 15.33. Calculating the weighted average cost of capital under corporation tax

Problem

Create the worksheet shown in Figure 15.33. If the debt amount of the firm rises from £1,000,000 to £1,200,000, calculate the weighted average cost of capital (assume that the annual interest rate is 10 per cent).

The value of the firm with corporation and personal taxes

In general, when corporation and personal taxes are introduced into the analysis, the original proposition of Modigliani and Miller is invalid. The present section is divided into two parts. In the first part we discuss the relationship between a firm's value and its financial gearing when corporation and personal taxes are introduced, while in the second we discuss the relationship between the cost of capital and financial gearing under the existence of corporation and personal taxes.

Value of the firm with corporation and personal taxes
Here the following proposition holds:

> *If there is a gain (loss) from utilizing long-term debt, then in the presence of corporation and personal taxes the total market value of the firm is positively (negatively) related to the amount of long-term debt used. Alternatively, if there is neither a gain nor a loss from using long-term debt, then the total market value of the firm remains constant.*

In order to find the market value of the firm, we need to find first its future annual cash flows. By way of illustration, we use Example 15.17.

Example 15.17 Calculating the cash flows from two financing plans when the income from debt is taxed at the same personal tax rate as equity income

Consider the data given in Example 15.16. Additionally, we assume that the personal tax rate on equity income and the personal tax rate on interest income are equal.

Under Plan U, the after personal tax earnings (APTE) available to the ordinary shareholders (see Figure 15.34) will be equal to

$$\begin{aligned}\text{APTE}_\text{U} &= (1 - 0.25)(£455{,}000)\\ &= £341{,}250\end{aligned}$$

where we assume that the personal tax rate that applies to equity income is 25 per cent.

Next, let us calculate the after personal tax earnings available to the ordinary shareholders under plan G.

$$\begin{aligned}\text{APTE}_\text{G} &= (1 - 0.25)(£390{,}000)\\ &= £292{,}500\end{aligned}$$

In the case of the full equity financing plan, the cash flow available to the firm's shareholders will be £341,250, while under the debt–equity financing plan the cash flow available to investors of the geared firm will be equal to

$$\begin{aligned}CF_G &= £341{,}250 + (1 - 0.35)(0.35)(0.10)(£1{,}000{,}000)\\ &= £341{,}250 + £26{,}250 = £367{,}500\end{aligned}$$

This indicates that the cash flow available to ordinary shareholders of the geared firm is £26,250 greater than that under the full equity plan. The amount of £26,250 is called a tax shelter.

The calculations are summarized in Figure 15.34.

	A	B	C
1	AFTER TAX CASH FLOWS WITH EQUAL PERSONAL TAXES ON EQUITY AND DEBT		
2	==		
3	Interest Rate on Debt	10.00%	
4	Personal Tax Rate	25.00%	
5	Corporate Tax Rate	35.00%	
6	--		
7		PLAN U	PLAN G
8	--		
9	Amount Borrowed	£0	£1,000,000
10	Interest	0	100,000
11	Personal Tax to Debenture Holders	0	25,000
12		------------	------------
13	After-Tax Earnings to Debenture Holders	0	75,000
14	Earnings Available to Shareholders	455,000	390,000
15	Personal Tax to Shareholders	113,750	97,500
16		------------	------------
17	After-Tax Earnings to Shareholders	£341,250	£292,500
18			
19	Cash Flow to Investors	£341,250	£367,500
20		============	============

Figure 15.34. After-tax cash flows with equal taxes on equity and debt

Problem

Create the worksheet presented in Figure 15.34. If the debt amount of the firm rises from £1,000,000 to £1,200,000, calculate the cash flow to investors under plan G (assume that the annual interest rate is 10 per cent).

From the calculations generated in Example 15.17, we see that the annual cash flow available to the geared firm's shareholders is given by

$$CF_G = CF_U + (1 - T_{pd})T_c r_d D$$

where T_{pd} = the personal tax rate on interest.

In other words, the annual cash flow available to investors under the debt–equity financing plan is equal to the annual cash flow under the full equity financing plan plus a tax shelter. The latter is equal to $(1 - T_{pd})$ times the value of the tax reduction on the debentures' interest. The tax shelter constitutes the tax savings on debt after personal tax is taken into account.

We assume that the yearly interest amount on debentures will be paid forever. Under the debt–equity financing plan, the present value of the firm is equal to the present value of the firm under the full equity financing plan plus the present value of the tax shelter on the geared firm's debt. Stated otherwise, the present value of the tax shelter constitutes the gain attributable to debt. Therefore, the present value of the geared firm is

$$V_G = V_U + T_c D$$

Example 15.18 Calculating the market value of a geared firm when equity income and debt investors are taxed at the same personal tax rate

In the present example we use the same data as in Example 15.17. We assume that the interest payments on debentures and the dividend payments on the ordinary shares will continue forever. If the appropriate after corporation and personal taxes discount rate for the full equity firm is 11 per cent, then its present value would be:

$$V_U = \frac{£341,250}{0.11} = £3,102,273$$

The present value of the tax shelter is calculated as follows:

$$T_c D = 0.35 * £1,000,000 = £350,000$$

Therefore, the market value of the geared firm is

$$V_G = £3,102,273 + £350,000 = £3,452,273$$

The income from an equity investment is not always taxed at the same rate as an interest income. For example, an investor can defer his or her tax on capital gains until a future period in which his or her other income is low. Let us now discuss the effect of financial gearing on the firm's value when the personal tax rate applicable to income from investments in shares is different from that applicable to income from investments in debentures. To simplify the analysis we assume that a firm's profit before interest and tax is £1. We denote by T_{pd} the personal tax rate on debenture income and by T_{po} the personal tax rate on equity income.

From the viewpoint of the firm, the interest payable to the debenture holders is tax deductible, thus a pound paid to a debenture holder as interest is free of corporate tax. In this instance, the debenture holder needs to pay personal tax and his or her earnings after paying the tax on interest are £$(1 - T_{pd})$. On the other hand, a pound of equity earnings is initially taxed at the corporate tax rate, therefore, an ordinary shareholder receives from the firm only £$(1 - T_c)$ which is also subject to the personal tax rate on equity income. In this situation, the earnings of an ordinary shareholder after both corporation and personal taxes will be

$$£(1 - T_c) - £T_{po}(1 - T_c) = £(1 - T_c)(1 - T_{po})$$

Figure 15.35 shows the calculations of net income after corporation and personal tax from paying £1 to debenture holders and £1 to shareholders.

Figure 15.35. Income after corporation and personal tax from a £1 distribution of profit before interest and tax

	Net income paid out as interest	Net income paid out as ordinary dividends
Profit before interest and tax	£1	£1
Corporation tax	0	T_c
Earnings after corporation tax	£1	£$(1 - T_c)$
Personal tax	£T_{pd}	£$T_{po}(1 - T_c)$
Net income after corporate and personal taxes	£$(1 - T_{pd})$	£$(1 - T_c)(1 - T_{po})$

As in previous cases, we can prove that the cash flow available to investors under the debt–equity financing plan is equal to the cash flow under the full equity financing plan plus a net tax shelter. Namely,

$$\mathrm{CF_G} = \mathrm{CF_U} + Sr_dD$$

where $S = [(1 - T_{pd}) - (1 - T_c)(1 - T_{po})]$.

Example 15.19 Calculating the value of a geared firm when the income to debenture holders and the income to shareholders are taxed at different personal tax rates

Once again, we use the data of Example 15.17. In addition we assume that the personal tax rate on debt income is different from the personal tax rate on equity income. Then

$$S = (1 - 0.40) - (1 - 0.35)(1 - 0.25) = 0.1125$$

and

$$SD/(1 - T_{pd}) = (0.1125)(£1{,}000{,}000)/(1 - 0.40) = £187{,}500$$

Thus, the market value of the firm under the debt–equity plan, assuming that the life of the firm and debt are infinite, will be (see Figure 15.36):

$$\mathrm{CF_G} = \frac{£341{,}250}{0.11} + £187{,}500 = £3{,}289{,}773$$

	A	B	C
1	AFTER TAX CASH FLOWS WITH DIFFERENT PERSONAL TAXES ON EQUITY & DEDT		
2	==========		
3	Interest Rate on Debt	10.00%	
4	After Taxes Cost of Equity	11.00%	
5	Personal Tax Rate on Equity Income	25.00%	
6	Personal Tax Rate on Debenture Income	40.00%	
7	Corporate Tax Rate	35.00%	
8	----------		
9		PLAN U	PLAN G
10	----------		
11	Amount Borrowed	£0	£1,000,000
12	Interest	0	100,000
13	Personal Tax to Debenture Holders	0	40,000
14		----------	----------
15	After-Tax Earnings to Debenture Holders	0	60,000
16	Earnings Available to Shareholders	455,000	390,000
17	Personal Tax to Shareholders	113,750	97,500
18		----------	----------
19	After-Tax Earnings to Shareholders	£341,250	£292,500
20	Cash Flow to Investors	£341,250	£352,500
21		==========	==========
22	Present Value of the Ungeared Firm		£3,102,273
23	Tax Shelter from each £1 of Interest Payment		0.1125
24	Value of the Geared Firm		£3,289,773
25			==========

Figure 15.36. Value of the geared firm with different personal taxes on equity and debt

Problem

Set up the worksheet presented in Figure 15.36. If the debt amount of the firm rises from £1,000,000 to £1,200,000, calculate the value of the firm under plan G (assume that the annual interest rate is 10 per cent).

Let us now discuss the effect of financial gearing on the firm's value when corporation tax is taken into consideration along with personal income tax. Once again, under the debt–equity financing plan, the present value of the firm is equal to the present value of the full equity financed firm plus the present value of the tax shelter (for a proof see Appendix 15C)

$$V_G = V_U + KD$$

where

$K = [1 - (1 - T_c)(1 - T_{po})/(1 - T_{pd})]$ = the tax advantage to gearing.

Appendix 15C provides a formula for the cost of equity under corporation and personal equity.

The value of a geared firm under the UK tax system

In the United Kingdom, the Revenue deems the advanced corporation tax to cover the shareholders' basic income tax rate. Shareholders are receiving dividend income net of basic rate income tax. Therefore, the tax saving on corporate interest payments can be expressed as

$$T = T_c - T_{pd}$$

In this case, the annual cash flow available to the investors of the geared firm is given by

$$CF_G = CF_U + (T_c - T_{pd})r_d D$$

The present value of the tax savings on debt, assuming that the tax savings on debt are received in perpetuity, is (for a proof of this see Appendix 15C):

$$\frac{T_c - T_{pd}}{1 - T_{pd}} D$$

As a consequence, the value of the geared firm would be

$$V_G = V_U + \frac{T_c - T_{pd}}{1 - T_{pd}} D$$

Miller's argument

The assumptions of Miller's (1977) model are:

1 The personal tax rate that applies to equity income is zero.
2 Income is certain.
3 The pre-tax rate for borrowing and lending is the same for firms and individuals.

Miller's work asserts the following:

> *In a world with perfect certainty and zero personal tax rate on equity income, the value of the firm is independent of its capital structure.*

Miller argues that as long as the value of the firm increases with gearing, firms will prefer more debt in their capital structure. The demand for more debt will increase the interest rates paid on debentures up to a point at which the advantage of issuing additional debt disappears.

Suppose that firms have no long-term debt outstanding and investors pay no taxes on the income from ordinary shares. In view of Miller's model, firms can increase their value by T_c for each pound of long-term debt they include in their capital structure.

However, as firms borrow more, they need to persuade taxpaying investors to switch from shares (whose income is tax free) to debentures (whose interest payments are taxable). Thus, they have to offer a higher interest on their debentures to compensate investors for the personal tax on interest received. Consider an investor who can purchase either debentures or ordinary shares. If he or she invests £1 in debentures, then the net return after personal tax on interest income is £$(1 - T_{pd})$. Alternatively, if the investor invests £1 in ordinary shares, the equity income will be £$(1 - T_c)$. The investment in debentures would be more profitable if T_{pd} is less than T_c. If $T_{pd} = T_c$, then the investor will be indifferent between purchasing debentures or ordinary shares. Therefore, according to Miller, firms will continue to attract more debt by offering to investors a higher interest rate as long as the corporate tax savings on the new debt are greater than the personal tax cost. At the point at which $T_{pd} = T_c$, the advantage of debt financing disappears.

Let us now examine the position of a single firm. Miller proposed the following model:

$$V_G = V_U + [1 - (1 - T_c)(1 - T_{po})/(1 - T_{pd})]D$$

If the personal tax rate on equity income is zero and the market is in equilibrium, then the personal tax rate on interest income is equal to the corporate tax rate. In this case, his model reduces to $V_G = V_U$.

If the personal tax rate on interest income is equal to the personal tax rate on equity income, then Miller's model implies $V_G = V_U + T_c D$, Modigliani and Miller's conclusion in a world of corporate taxes.

Example 15.20 Computing the tax advance of gearing

Figure 15.37 calculates the tax advantage of gearing for the following four cases:

1 If $T_{po} = T_{pd}$, the tax advance of gearing is £14,000.
2 If the personal tax rate on equity income is zero and $T_c > T_{pd}$, the tax advance of gearing is £5,333.
3 If the corporation tax rate is zero and $T_{po} = T_{pd}$, the tax advance of gearing is zero. In this case, the market value of the firm is unaffected by its capital structure.
4 If the personal tax rate on equity income is zero and $T_c = T_{pd}$, the tax

	A	B	C	D	E
1	CALCULATING THE TAX ADVANTAGE OF GEARING				
2	==				
3					
4	Debt Amount	£40,000			
5					
6	Corporation Tax Rate	35%	35%	0%	35%
7	Personal Tax Rate on Equity Income	25%	0%	25%	0%
8	Personal Tax Rate on Interest	25%	25%	25%	35%
9					
10	Factor K	0.35	0.13	0.00	0.00
11	Tax Advantage of Gearing	£14,000	£5,333	£0	£0

Figure 15.37. Computing the tax advantage of gearing using Miller's model

Approach	Proposition	Remarks
Net income	The total market value and the overall cost of capital of a firm are dependent on its capital structure	• The cost of debt and cost of equity remain constant as the level of financial gearing changes • The firm has an optimal capital structure • Unrealistic as it ignores the risk from excessive debt
Modigliani–Miller	The total market value and the overall cost of capital of a firm are independent of its capital structure	• The cost of equity increases as the relative debt level increases • There is no one optimal capital structure • Unrealistic since it ignores bankruptcy costs
Traditional	The total market value and the overall cost of capital of a firm are usually dependent on its capital structure	• The cost of equity rises with financial gearing • The cost of debt rises after a certain financial gearing has occurred • The optimal capital structure is treated as a range rather than as an individual point
Modigliani–Miller approach with corporation tax	The total market value and the overall cost of capital of a firm are usually dependent on its capital structure	• The cost of equity rises with financial gearing • An optimal capital structure contains a very high proportion of debt
The effect of financial gearing on the firm's value in a world of corporation and personal taxes	The total market value of a firm is usually dependent on its capital structure	• The cost of equity depends on the level of the firm's financial gearing

Figure 15.38. A summary of five alternative theories of capital structure

advance of gearing is zero. In this case, the market value of the firm is independent of its capital structure.

Figure 15.38 summarizes five alternative theories each of which attempts to determine the effect of financial gearing on the firm's value.

Summary

1 *Operating gearing and business risk* Operating gearing results from the utilization of fixed costs in an effort to magnify profit before interest and tax from a given increase in sales. The degree of operating gearing is used to measure the relationship between sales and profit before interest and tax. Other things being equal, the higher a firm's percentage of fixed costs, the higher the degree of operating gearing.

Business risk refers to the risk that the firm will be unable to cover operating costs. The business risk of a firm is measured by the variability of its profit before interest and taxes. Other things being the same, the higher a firm's operating gearing, the higher its business risk.

2 *Financial gearing and financial risk* Financial gearing involves the use of fixed costs as sources of long-term financing (for example, debentures, preference shares, and so on) in an effort to magnify the effects of changes in profit before interest and taxes one earnings per share. The relationship between earnings per share and profit before interest and taxes is measured by the degree of financial gearing. The greater a firm's fixed financing costs, the higher its degree of financial gearing (other things considered equal).

Financial risk is that part of total risk that arises from using financial gearing. It refers to the risk that the firm will be unable to pay its fixed financing costs. The financial risk of a firm is measured by the variability of the firm's earnings per share (not due to operating gearing). The higher a firm's degree of financial gearing, the greater its financial risk (other factors remain the same).

3 *Combined gearing* Combined gearing measures total gearing attributable to both fixed operating costs and fixed financing costs. More specifically, it refers to the use of operating costs and fixed financing costs in an attempt to magnify the effects of changes in sales on earnings per share. The degree of combined gearing relates a firm's earnings per share with its sales and it provides a measure of combined gearing.

Combined (or total) risk results from both business and financial risk. It refers to the risk that the firm will be unable to cover total costs. The combined risk is measured by the variability of the earnings per share. The greater a firm's use of fixed operating costs and fixed financing costs, the greater the combined gearing and combined risk.

4 *Theories on capital structure* Capital structure refers to the composition of various types of long-term capital used by a firm. An optimal capital structure may be defined as the capital structure that maximizes the market value of the firm. The theory of financial management offers several arguments concerning the relationship between a firm's capital structure and its value. In a world without taxes and other market imperfections, Modigliani and Miller argue that both the total market value and the firm's cost of capital are independent of its capital structure. On the other hand, other arguments (for example, net income approach) assert that the capital structure of a firm affects both the firm's cost of capital and its total market value.

When taxes are taken into account, it can be shown that a firm's market value is affected by its capital structure. As a consequence, we can identify an optimal capital structure. In practice, it is difficult to determine the optimal capital structure for a firm. However, we can treat that structure as a range of values (for example, a debt to total value ratio of 45 to 55 per cent) rather than a single value.

Questions for discussion

1 Describe how each of the following situations could affect the operating gearing of a manufacturing firm:

(a) The inflation rate is expected to increase in the near future.
(b) The electricity board announced an increase in the price of the electricity.
(c) The firm's monthly insurance payment decreases by 5 per cent.
(d) The Bank of England lowers interest rates.

2 For each term shown below provide a definition in your own words. Then check your responses against the definitions included in the chapter.

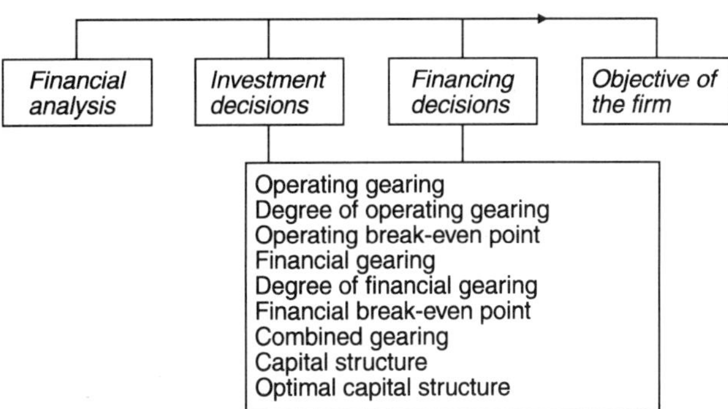

3 Describe how each of the following situations could affect the financial gearing of a manufacturing firm:
(a) A new issue of preference shares is sold.
(b) A new issue of ordinary shares is sold.
(c) The proceeds from a new issue of ordinary shares are used to retire part of long-term debt.
(d) A new issue of debentures is sold.
(e) The firm decides to retain 85 per cent of its profits.

4 The financial analyst of a consultancy firm is comparing the combined risks of three similar firms A, B and C. Consider the following cases:
(a) Firm A has higher fixed costs than firm B as well as greater interest charges (other things being the same).
(b) Firm C has a higher degree of operating gearing than B and also pays greater preference dividends (other things being constant).
(c) Firm A has the same fixed costs as firm C and a greater degree of financial gearing as compared with firm C (other things remain constant).
Which of these three firms has the lowest combined risk? Which firm has the greatest combined risk?

5 Consider a manufacturing firm that produces only one product. The diagram below is designed to show how an output variable (PBIT, DOG, EPS, or DFG) is affected by a change in an input variable (other things being constant). Fill the blank spaces (NA means not applicable).

	PBIT	DOG	EPS	DFG
Increase in number of units sold	increase			
Increase in unit price				
Increase in variable cost per unit				
Decrease in fixed costs				
Increase in long-term debt	NA	NA		
Increase in preference dividends				

Provide a short discussion of the answers you have given.

6 Discuss fully each of the four statements given below.

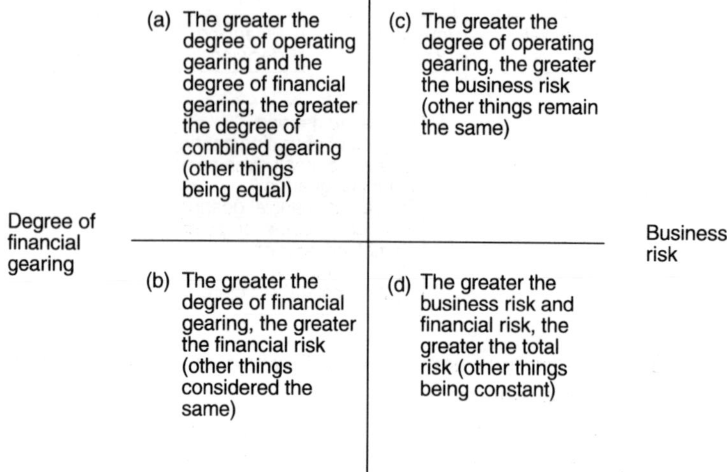

7 Consider the following diagram

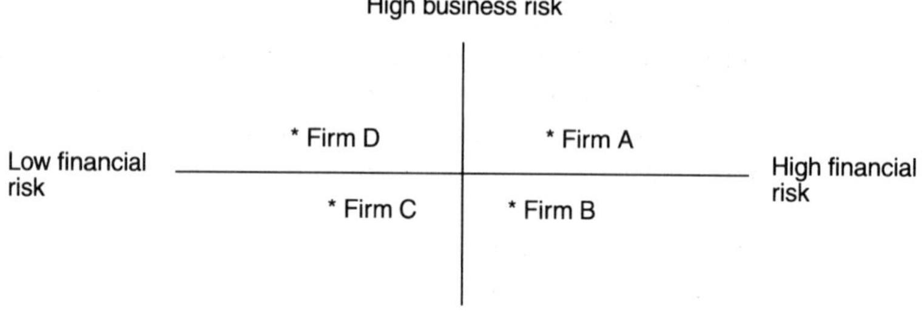

(a) Explain why firm A has high business risk and high financial risk.
(b) Explain why firm B has low business risk and high financial risk.
(c) Explain why firm C has low business risk and low financial risk.
(d) Explain why firm D has high business risk and low financial risk.

8 Discuss the advantages and disadvantages of linear operating break-even analysis.

9 State the assumptions used by the net income approach in support of the following proposition:
'The total market value and the weighted average cost of capital of a firm are dependent on its capital structure.'
Is this proposition realistic? If not what is its main weaknesses?

10 Discuss carefully each of the following propositions:
(a) 'In a simplified world without transaction costs, taxes, or other market imperfections, the total market value of a firm remains unaffected regardless of the firm's degree of financial gearing.'
(b) 'In the absence of transaction costs, taxes and other market imperfections,

the overall cost of capital of a firm remains unchanged regardless of the amount of debt employed.'

Are these propositions realistic? If not what are their main weaknesses?

11 Discuss carefully and evaluate the following proposition: 'Financial gearing is irrelevant in a world with both corporate and personal taxes.'

12 At the end of a teaching session, the lecturer in financial management provides in summary the following conclusion related to the traditional approach to capital structure:

'The total market value of a firm does not necessarily increase for all degrees of gearing. The weighted average cost of capital of a firm does not necessarily decrease for all degrees of gearing.'

State the assumptions used by the traditional approach. Discuss fully the above view of traditionalists.

13 Prepare an analog model summarizing the main points discussed in this chapter.

14 How can spreadsheets be used to facilitate the application of the concepts discussed in this chapter?

Appendix 15A Deriving the measurement equations for DOG, DFG and DCG

Deriving the measurement equation for the degree of operating gearing

From the main text, the degree of operating gearing and the profit before interest and tax were, respectively, defined as:

$$\text{DOG} = \frac{\text{dPBIT}}{\text{PBIT}} \div \frac{\text{d}U}{U} \qquad (15\text{A}.1)$$

$$\text{PBIT} = U(\text{SP} - \text{VC}) - \text{FC} \qquad (15\text{A}.2)$$

We assume that the sale price per unit, the variable cost per unit and the operating fixed costs are constant. In this case, the change in profit before interest and tax is given by the equation below:

$$\text{dPBIT} = \text{dU}(\text{SP} - \text{VC}) \qquad (15\text{A}.3)$$

On merging Equation (15A.3) into Equation (15A.1) the following equation is obtained:

$$\text{DOG} = \frac{\text{d}U(\text{SP} - \text{VC})}{\text{PBIT}} \div \frac{\text{d}U}{U} \qquad (15\text{A}.4)$$

Simplifying Equation (15A.4) yields:

$$\boxed{\text{DOG} = \frac{U(\text{SP}-\text{VC})}{\text{PBIT}}}$$

Deriving the measurement equation for the degree of financial gearing

From the main text, the degree of financial gearing and the earnings per share were, respectively, defined as:

$$\mathrm{DFG} = \frac{\mathrm{dEPS}}{\mathrm{EPS}} \div \frac{\mathrm{dPBIT}}{\mathrm{PBIT}} \tag{15A.5}$$

$$\mathrm{EPS} = \frac{(\mathrm{PBIT} - \mathrm{IN})(1 - T) - \mathrm{PD}}{\mathrm{NS}_o} \tag{15A.6}$$

We assume that the annual interest paid, the annual dividends on preference shares, the corporate tax rate and the number of the firm's ordinary shares are constant. Under such an assumption, the change in earnings per share is represented by the following equation:

$$\mathrm{dEPS} = \frac{\mathrm{dPBIT}(1 - T)}{\mathrm{NS}_o} \tag{15A.7}$$

Substituting Equations (15A.7) and (15A.6) into Equation (15A.5) we derive:

$$\mathrm{DFG} = \frac{\mathrm{dPBIT}(1 - T)}{(\mathrm{PBIT} - \mathrm{IN})(1 - T) - \mathrm{PD}} \div \frac{\mathrm{dPBIT}}{\mathrm{PBIT}} \tag{15A.8}$$

Simplifying Equation (15A.8) gives:

$$\boxed{\mathrm{DFG} = \frac{\mathrm{PBIT}(1-T)}{(\mathrm{PBIT}-\mathrm{IN})\,(1-T)-\mathrm{PD}}}$$

Deriving the measurement equation for the degree of combined gearing

The degree of combined gearing, the degree of financial gearing and the degree of operating gearing can be expressed, respectively, as:

$$\mathrm{DCG} = \frac{\mathrm{dEPS}}{\mathrm{EPS}} \div \frac{\mathrm{d}U}{U} \tag{15A.9}$$

$$\mathrm{DFG} = \frac{\mathrm{dEPS}}{\mathrm{EPS}} \div \frac{\mathrm{dPBIT}}{\mathrm{PBIT}} \tag{15A.10}$$

$$\mathrm{DOG} = \frac{\mathrm{dPBIT}}{\mathrm{PBIT}} \div \frac{\mathrm{d}U}{U} \tag{15A.11}$$

Combining Equations (15A.9), (15A.10) and (15A.11) yields:

$$\boxed{\mathrm{DCG} = (\mathrm{DOG})\,(\mathrm{DFG})}$$

Appendix 15B Proofs for various equations

Proof of the equation: $E_G = V_U - (1 - T_c)D$

The value of a geared firm is expressed as a sum of the value of its ordinary shares and its debt (we assume that the firm does not use preference share capital):

$$V_G = E_G + D$$

Therefore, by comparing the last equation with the equation $V_G = V_U + T_c D$ we have

$$E_G + D = V_U + T_c D \tag{15B.1}$$

Equation (15B.1) gives

$$E_G = V_U - (1 - T_c)D \qquad \text{QED}$$

Proof of the equation: $r_{Go} = r_U + (1 - T_c)(r_U - r_d)\dfrac{D}{E_G}$

The expected annual cash flow to the shareholders and debenture holders of the geared firm can be expressed as

$$CF_G = V_U r_U + T_c r_d D$$

On the other hand, the shares of the geared firm earn an expected annual return, call it r_{Go}, and the debentures of the firm earn an annual interest rate, call it r_d. Therefore, the expected annual cash flow of the geared firm may be also expressed as

$$CF_G = E_G r_{Go} + D r_d \tag{15B.2}$$

Since all earnings are paid out as dividends, the following equality holds:

$$V_U r_U + T_c r_d D = E_G r_{Go} + D r_d$$

or by rearranging terms we can write

$$r_{Go} = \frac{V_U}{E_G} r_U - (1 - T_c)\frac{D}{E_G} r_d$$

Substituting the equation $V_U = E_G + (1 - T_c)D$ into the last equation and simplifying yields

$$r_{Go} = r_U + (1 - T_c)(r_U - r_d)\frac{D}{E_G} \qquad \text{QED}$$

Proof of the equation: $\text{WACC} = r_U\left(1 - \dfrac{D}{(E_G + D)} T_c\right)$

The weighted average cost of capital under corporation tax is expressed as follows:

$$\text{WACC} = \frac{E_G}{(E_G + D)} r_{Go} + (1 - T_c) r_d \frac{D}{(E_G + D)}$$

Substituting the cost of equity into the last equation implies:

$$\frac{E_G}{(E_G+D)}\left[r_U+(1-T_c)(r_U-r_d)\frac{D}{E_G}\right]+(1-T_c)r_d\frac{D}{(E_G+D)}$$

$$=\frac{E_G}{(E_G+D)}r_U+(1-T_c)(r_U-r_d)\frac{D}{(E_G+D)}+(1-T_c)r_d\frac{D}{(E_G+D)}$$

$$=r_U\left(1-\frac{D}{(E_G+D)}T_c\right)$$

QED

Appendix 15C The cost of equity under corporation and personal taxes

Proof of the equation: $V_G = V_U + KD$

$K = [1 - (1 - T_c)(1 - T_{po})/(1 - T_{pd})]$

Under corporation and personal taxes the geared firm's annual cash flow to investors can be expressed as

$$CF_G = CF_U + Sr_dD \tag{15C.1}$$

$$\text{where } S = [(1 - T_{pd}) - (1 - T_c)(1 - T_{po})] \tag{15C.2}$$

Since the tax shelter is a perpetuity, its present value can be found by dividing the annual tax shelter by the appropriate after personal tax rate. If we assume that the debenture holders' future income is certain, the interest tax shelter can be discounted at the after personal tax riskless interest rate on debentures $(1 - T_{pd})r_d$.

Therefore, dividing Equation (15C.1) by $(1 - T_{pd})r_d$, we take

$V_G = V_U + KD$

where $K = [1 - (1 - T_c)(1 - T_{po})/(1 - T_{pd})]$ QED

The cost of equity under corporation and personal taxes

Since cash flows are perpetual and all earnings are paid out as dividends, the ungeared firm's cash flow to investors may be expressed as

$$CF_U = V_Ur_U \tag{15C.3}$$

Substituting Equation (15C.3) into Equation (15C.1) yields

$$CF_G = V_Ur_U + Sr_dD \tag{15C.4}$$

The shares of the geared firm earn an expected annual return, call it r_{Go}, and the debentures of the firm earn an annual interest rate, call it r_d. Therefore, the expected annual cash flow of the geared firm may be written as

$$CF_G = E_Gr_{Go} + Dr_d \tag{15C.5}$$

Since all earnings are paid out as dividends, the annual cash flows of the firm equal those of the shareholders, thus the following equality is valid:

$$V_Ur_U + Sr_dD = E_Gr_{Go} + Dr_d$$

After solving the last equation for the cost of equity we get

$$r_{Go} = \frac{V_U}{E_G} r_U - \frac{D}{E_G} r_d[1 - S] \tag{15C.6}$$

However, S can be expressed as

$$S = K(1 - T_{pd}) \tag{15C.7}$$

where

$$K = [1 - (1 - T_c)(1 - T_{po})/(1 - T_{pd})] \tag{15C.8}$$

Substituting Equation (15C.7) into Equation (15C.6), we find

$$r_{Go} = \frac{V_U}{E_G} r_U - \frac{D}{E_G} r_d[1 - K(1 - T_{pd})] \tag{15C.9}$$

Next, the market value of the ungeared firm is given by

$$V_U = E_G + D - KD = E_G + D(1 - K) \tag{15C.10}$$

Substituting V_U in Equation (15C.9) we obtain

$$r_{Go} = \frac{E_G + D(1 - K)}{E_G} r_U - \frac{D}{E_G} r_d[1 - K(1 - T_{pd})] \tag{15C.11}$$

or equivalently

$$r_{Go} = r_U + \frac{D}{E_G}(1 - K)r_U - \frac{D}{E_G} r_d[1 - K(1 - T_{pd})] \tag{15C.12}$$

After rearranging terms Equation (15C.12) gives

$$r_{Go} = r_U + \frac{D}{E_G}[r_U - Kr_U - r_d + r_d K - r_d KT_{pd}] \tag{15C.13}$$

Finally, Equation (15C.13) can be rewritten as follows:

$$r_{Go} = r_U + \frac{D}{E_G}[(r_U - r_d)(1 - K) - r_d KT_{pd}]$$

Proof of the equation: present value of tax shelter $= \frac{T_c - T_{pd}}{1 - T_{pd}} D$

Recalling that the tax shelter is a perpetuity, its present value can be found by dividing the net annual tax shelter by the $r_d(1 - T_{pd})$:

$$\text{Present value of tax shelter} = \frac{T_c - T_{pd}}{r_d[1 - T_{pd}]} r_d D = \frac{T_c - T_{pd}}{1 - T_{pd}} D \qquad \text{QED}$$

Appendix 15D Confidence intervals for a population's simple regression coefficients

Since a simple regression line is estimated using a sample data, different samples might provide different regression coefficients. Consequently, regression analysis should also include the construction of confidence intervals for the population's regression coefficients. Recall that a confidence interval for a parameter is a range of values, together with a statement indicating how confident we are that the parameter is lying within that interval.

Confidence interval for the intercept of a population regression line

The confidence interval limits for the intercept of a population regression line are summarized in Figure 15D.1.

Lower limit ⟶ Alpha − t SE(D) k

Lower limit ⟶ Alpha + t SE(D) k

where

Alpha = the intercept coefficient of the regression between two variables calculated using a sample of observations.

t = the t-distribution table's value corresponding to a given level of significance and $n-2$ degrees of freedom, where n is the number of sample pairs of the data. Note that this is a two-test value.

SE(D) = the sample standard error (or standard deviation) of the dependent variable estimate.

$$k = \text{SQRT}\left[\frac{1}{n} + \frac{(\text{Mean of the independent variable})^2}{(\text{Variance of the independent variable})n}\right].$$

SQRT = the square root operator.

Figure 15D.1. The confidence interval limits for the intercept of a population regression line

Example 15D.1 Calculating the lower and upper confidence limits on the intercept of a population regression line

Consider the regression results presented in Appendix 14B. The intercept is found to be −0.0020 and the standard error of the dependent variable is 0.0155. We use 1-2-3 for the following calculations:

(Mean of the independent variable)^2 = $(0.00253)^2 = 0.000006$
(Variance of the independent variable) n = $(0.0000047)(36) = 0.000169$
k = SQRT[1/36 + 0.000006/0.000169] = 0.2515

The critical value of t using a two-tailed test with 34 degrees of freedom and a 5 per cent level of significance is approximately 2.0420. Therefore, the 95 per cent confidence limits would be found by (we use a format of four decimal points):

Lower limit: $-0.0020 - (2.0420)(0.0155)(0.2515) = -0.0100$
Upper limit: $-0.0020 + (2.0420)(0.0155)(0.2515) = 0.0060$

Thus, from all possible samples that could be drawn from the population of returns, 95 per cent will give a regression intercept between −0.0100 and 0.0060. Stated differently, we can be 95 per cent confident that the interval between −0.0100 and 0.0060 covers the intercept of the population regression line.

Lower limit $\longrightarrow$ Slope $- t$ SE(S)
Lower limit $\longrightarrow$ Slope $+ t$ SE(S)

where

Slope = the slope of the regression between the two variables using a sample of observations.

t = the t-distribution table's value corresponding to a given level of significance and $n-2$ degrees of freedom, where n is the number of sample pairs of data. Note that this is a two-test value.

SE(S) = the sample standard error of the slope.

Figure 15D.2. A summary of the confidence interval for the slope of a population regression line

Confidence interval about the slope of a population regression line

Figure 15D.2 provides a summary of the confidence interval limits for the slope of a population regression line.

Example 15D.2 Calculating the lower and upper confidence limits on the slope of a population regression line

Consider the regression results presented in Appendix 14B. In this appendix we found (slight deviations occur due to rounding):

Slope = 0.6413

SE(S) = 0.1189

The critical value of t with 34 degrees of freedom and a 5 per cent level of significance is approximately 2.0420.

Hence, the confidence internal's lower and upper limits would be

$$0.6413 - (2.0420)(0.1189) = 0.3985$$

and

$$0.6413 + (2.0420)(0.1189) = 0.8841$$

Therefore, from all possible samples that could be drawn from the population of returns 95 per cent will give a slope coefficient between 0.3985 and 0.8841.

Some useful points

1 (Calculating k using 1-2-3) The number k shown in Figure 15D.1 can be calculated by using the following function of 1-2-3:

```
@SQRT(1/@COUNT(ran)+@AVG(ran)^2/(@VAR(ran)*@COUNT(ran)))
```

where ran is the range containing the observations of the independent variable.

2 (The standard error of the slope) The standard error of the slope given by 1-2-3 can be calculated by using the following formula:

$$\text{SE(S)} = \frac{\text{Standard error of the dependent variable estimate}}{\text{SQRT[(variance of the independent variable) } n]}$$

In the case of Example 15D.2 we have (a slight deviation occurs due to rounding):

$$\text{SE(S)} = \frac{0.0155}{\texttt{@SQRT(0.00047 * 36)}} = 0.119$$

References and bibliography

Baruch, L. (1974) On the association between operating leverage and risk, *Journal of Financial and Quantitative Analysis*, **9**, September, 627–42.

Bird, P.W. (1973) What is capital gearing?, *Accounting and Business Research*, Spring, 92–7.

Cahlon, J.M. and Gentry, J.A. (1982) On the relationship between systematic risk and the degree of operating and financial leverage, *Financial Management*, **11**, Summer, 15–23.

Coates, J.H. and Wooley, R.C. (1975) Corporate gearing in the ECC, *Journal of Business Finance and Accounting*, Spring, 1–8.

Fox, R.B. (1976) Leverage in UK companies 1967–1973, *Managerial Finance*, **2**, 229–55.

Ghandi, J.K.S. (1966) On the measurement of leverage, *Journal of Finance*, **21**, December, 715–26.

Gritta, R.D. (1979) The effect of financial leverage on air carrier earnings: a break-even analysis, *Financial Management*, **8**, Summer, 53–60.

Haugen, R.A. and Wichern, D.W. (1975) The intricate relationship between financial leverage and the stability of stock prices, *Journal of Finance*, **30**, December, 1283–92.

Helfert, E.A. (1977) *Techniques of Financial Analysis*, 4th edn. Richard D. Irwin, Homewood, Ill.

Lister, R.J. (1976) Corporate gearing-capacity and valuation, *Investment Analyst*, April, 31–4.

Mandelker, G.N. and Rhec, S.G. (1984) The impact of the degree of operating and financial leverage on systematic risk of common stock, *Journal of Financial and Quantitative Analysis*, **19**, March, 45–57.

Miller, M.H. (1977) Debt and taxes, *Journal of Finance*, May, 261–75.

Percival, J.R. (1974) Operating leverage and risk, *Journal of Business Research*, **2**, April, 223–7.

Raun, D.L. (1964) The limitations of profit graphs, break-even analysis, and budgets, *Accounting Review*, **39**, October, 927–45.

Reinhardt, U.E. (1973) Break-even analysis for Lockheed's Tri Star: an application of financial theory, *Journal of Finance*, **28**, September, 821–38.

Shalit, S.S. (1975) On the mathematics of financial leverage, *Financial Management*, **4**, Spring, 57–66.

Stowe, J.D. and Ingere, C.A. (1984) Microeconomic influences in operating leverage, *Journal of Economics and Business*, **36**, May, 233–41.

Wippern, R.F. (1966) Financial structure and the value of the firm, *Journal of Finance*, **21**, December, 615–34.

16 Dividend policy

This chapter includes:

- Dividend policy theories
- Factors influencing dividend policy
- Dividend policy: empirical evidence
- Final remarks on dividend policy

The important question in this chapter is: to pay dividends or not to pay dividends. The literature offers several arguments each of which provides an explanation for observed dividend payments. However, none of these reasons adequately explains the firm's complex rationale for paying dividends. Among the theoretical arguments suggested are the following:

- To maintain or increase the firm's share price.
- To provide a signal to investors about the future prospects of the firm.
- To satisfy the investors' preference with respect to the dividend payments.

Much of the debate about dividend policy has focused around the first of these three reasons. Three theories have been advanced in this debate: the dividend-irrelevance theory, the dividend-relevance theory and the tax-differential theory.

In this chapter we will view various theories and empirical evidence on dividend policy. Figure 16.1 shows the relationship between the concepts discussed in this chapter and the objective of the firm present in Chapter 2.

Basic concepts, definitions and examples

When an investor buys an ordinary share in a firm he or she becomes one of the owners of the firm (also called an ordinary shareholder). Dividends represent a portion of a firm's distributable profits which are paid out to its ordinary shareholders (when the term dividend is utilized without qualification, it refers to a cash dividend). In the United Kingdom, public limited companies pay a dividend twice a year: (a) an interim dividend can be paid out to the shareholders during the firm's financial year, such a dividend is declared before the full profits of the firm are known; and (b) a final dividend after the year-end (see also Appendix 16A).

The board of directors of a firm is usually empowered to declare and pay interim dividends. Final dividends, however, must have the approval of the shareholders, which is why payment of final dividends is delayed until after the annual general meeting.

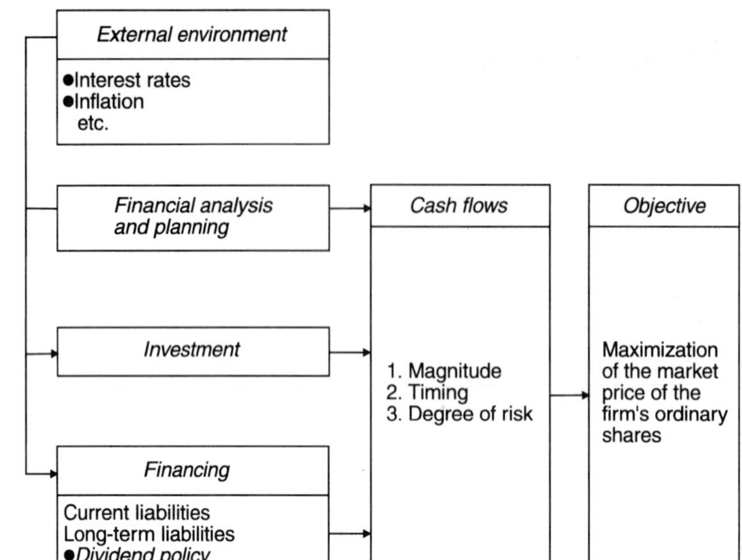

Figure 16.1. The relationship between the concepts described in the present chapter and the framework of financial management presented in Chapter 2

The dividend payout ratio can be calculated by using the following formula:

$$\text{Dividend payout ratio} = \frac{\text{Dividends per share}}{\text{Earnings per share}}$$

where the dividends per share are calculated by adding to the final dividend per share the interim dividend per share. In words, the dividend payout ratio is the proportion of distributable profits actually paid out in dividends. The dividends paid to the shareholders represent partial compensation for the use of their investment funds. Retained earnings refers to the portion of distributable profits that is left in the firm after the dividend payment is made. These retained earnings can be used as a regular source to finance investment opportunities or to retire debt. The retention ratio of a firm is simply equal to:

$$\text{Retention ratio} = 1 - \text{Dividend payout ratio}$$

Ex means without. Investors who own a share before it is quoted 'ex-dividend' are entitled to receive the most recently declared dividends. Investors who buy the share on or after it has gone ex-dividend are not entitled to its most recently declared dividend. Ex-dividend date is the date on which the right to the most recently declared dividends no longer accompanies the share when it is sold.

A firm's dividend policy determines the amount of profits to be paid out or retained in the firm for investment purposes. According to the theory of financial management, a firm should adopt a dividend policy that maximizes the shareholders' wealth.

Example 16.1 The dividend payout ratio of Marks and Spencer plc (1985–89)

Figure 16.2 presents the following financial information for Marks and Spencer plc for a period of five years: profits available to ordinary shareholders, number of ordinary shares and dividends paid to ordinary shareholders.

Figure 16.2. Calculating the dividend payout ratio of Marks and Spencer (1985–89) (*source*: Extel Financial UK Listed Companies Service)

	A	B	C	D	E	F	G
1	MARKS & SPENCER PLC:THE DIVIDEND PAYOUT RATIO 1985-1989						
2	==						
3							
4							
5	YEAR	DISTRIBUTABLE	NUMBER	DIVIDENDS	EARNINGS	DIVIDENDS	DIVIDEND
6		PROFITS	OF	PAID	PER	PER	PAYOUT
7			SHARES	TO ORDINARY	SHARE	SHARE	
8				SHAREHOLDERS	(pence)	(pence)	
9		(£m)	(m)	(£m)			
10							
11	1985	183.70	2,640	89.76	6.96	3.40	48.86%
12	1986	221.50	2,646	103.19	8.37	3.90	46.59%
13	1987	269.10	2,654	119.43	10.14	4.50	44.38%
14	1988	323.40	2,660	135.66	12.16	5.10	41.95%
15	1989	349.40	2,673	149.69	13.07	5.60	42.84%
16							

The annual earnings per share are calculated by dividing the distributable profits by the corresponding number of shares. For example, for 1985, we have (100 converts £ to pence)

$$\text{Earnings per share} = \frac{£183.70}{2{,}640} \times 100 = 6.96 \text{ pence}$$

The annual dividends per share are computed by dividing the dividends paid to shareholders by the corresponding number of shares. For example, for 1985, we take (100 converts £ to pence):

$$\text{Dividends per share} = \frac{£89.76}{2{,}640} \times 100 = 3.40 \text{ pence}$$

For each year shown in Figure 16.2, Marks and Spencer paid an interim dividend and a final dividend. For example, in 1985 its interim dividend per share was 1.08 pence, while its final dividend per share was 2.32 pence, a total of 3.40 pence. The interim dividend was announced on 23 October 1984 and was paid on 18 January 1985, whereas the final dividend was announced on 7 May 1985 and was paid on 12 July 1985. The interim dividend's ex-dividend date for 1985 was 29 October 1985. That is, if an investor purchased Marks and Spencer's shares on 29 October 1985 or after that date, he or she would not have received the interim dividend of 1.08 per share. The final dividend's ex-dividend date for 1985 was 13 May 1985. This discussion can be summarized in Figure 16.3.

Figure 16.3. The dates related to the dividends of Marks and Spencer plc (1985)

Financial year ended 31.3.85

Declaration date of interim dividends	Ex-dividend date for interim dividends	Date of payment of interim dividends	Declaration date of final dividends	Ex-dividend date for final dividends	Date of payment of final dividends
23.10.84	29.10.84	18.1.85	7.5.85	13.5.85	12.7.85

By examining the dividends per share of Marks and Spencer we observe that the firm has a non-decreasing pattern of dividends per share over the period 1985–89. Comparing the earnings per share and the dividends per share we see that the firm increases the latter as the former increases over time, but it does not pay out a fixed portion of each year's earnings per share. For example, in 1985 the difference between the earnings per share and the dividends per share was 3.56 pence, while for 1989 this difference increased to 7.47 pence.

Dividends can also be announced in percentages with respect to the nominal value of a single ordinary share. The nominal value of a share in Marks and Spencer is 25 pence. Thus, the 1985 dividends per share can be announced as 13.60 per cent (that is, $3.40 \times 100/25$).

Using the earnings per share and the dividends per share we can calculate the dividend payout ratio. For example, for 1985, the dividend payout ratio is calculated as follows:

$$\text{Dividend payout ratio} = \frac{3.40}{6.96} = 48.86 \text{ per cent}$$

The dividend payout ratio of Marks and Spencer decreases over time. This, however, does not imply that the dividends per share decrease over time. It simply shows that the firm's earnings per share increase over time and the firm's dividend policy is to maintain modestly growing dividends. For example, the earnings per share increased by 21.14 per cent between 1986 and 1987 from 8.37 pence to 10.14 pence, but the dividend payment increased over the same period by 15.38 per cent from 3.90 pence to 4.50 pence.

Next, we can use the information given in Figure 16.2 to calculate the retained earnings of the firm. For example, for 1985, the firm's retained earnings were £93.94 million. The retained earnings of the firm increase with time. The retention ratio for 1984 is calculated as follows:

$$\text{Retention ratio} = 1 - 48.86 \text{ per cent} = 51.14 \text{ per cent}$$

Figure 16.4 presents a two-variable sensitivity table of the projected dividend payout ratio with respect to changes in the firm's earnings per share and dividends per share. The range of the earnings per share is 13.07 to 14.67 pence in steps of 0.4 pence and the range of the dividends per share is 5.60 to 8.30 pence in steps of 1 pence. The 'input cell 1' of the data table is cell D24 and the 'input cell 2' is cell D25. The results indicate that the dividend payout ratio increases as the dividends per share increase, but decreases as the earnings per share increase.

The results of the sensitivity analysis are shown graphically in Figure 16.5.

```
     A        B            C              D             E            F              G
21 B> MARKS & SPENCER PLC:THE SENSITIVITY OF THE DIVIDEND PAYOUT RATIO
22 =================================================================
23
24 Earnings per Share                   13.07
25 Dividends per Share                   5.60
26                                 ------------
27 Dividend Payout Ratio --->           42.84%
28
29
30                      +E27             5.60         6.60         7.60          8.60
31                          13.07       42.84%       50.49%       58.14%        65.79%
32                          13.47       41.57%       48.99%       56.42%        63.84%
33                          13.87       40.37%       47.58%       54.79%        62.00%
34                          14.27       39.24%       46.25%       53.25%        60.26%
35                          14.67       38.17%       44.99%       51.80%        58.62%
```

Figure 16.4. A two-variable sensitivity analysis of the dividend payout ratio

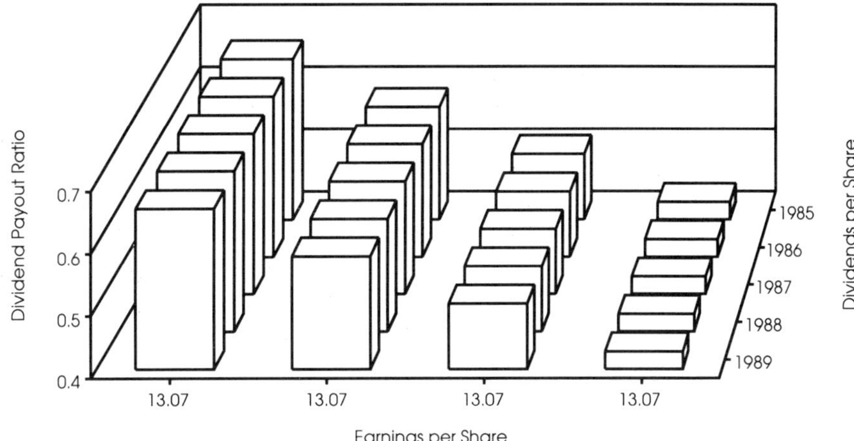

Figure 16.5. Graphing the two-variable sensitivity of dividend payout ratio

Problems

1 Create the worksheet shown in Figure 16.2 using formulae for the calculation of the earnings per share, dividends per share and dividend payout ratio.
2 Create the worksheet presented in Figure 16.4.

Dividend policy theories

From the theory point of view, the primary objective of financial management is to maximize the firm's current ordinary share price. An important question is whether the firm's dividend policy affects the price of its shares. The answer to this question is a controversial one and the present section discusses existing claims concerning the relevance of dividend policy.

The dividend-irrelevance theory

This theory is based upon the following assumptions:

1 The capital market is perfect (that is, there are no taxes; no transaction costs exist, information is freely available to investors, securities are infinitely divisible; and no single buyer or seller of securities is large enough to affect their prices). The absence of flotation costs implies that the cost of acquiring equity capital is the same, regardless of whether the firm retains its profits or pays them as dividends and then raises external funds via an issue of ordinary shares.
2 Investors have complete certainty about the future investments and profits of the firm. Namely, investors can forecast future prices and dividends with perfect certainty.
3 The firm has a fixed investment policy which is not affected by its dividend policy.

Under the assumptions just listed, Miller and Modigliani (1961) presented the following argument (Appendix 16B presents a mathematical proof of the Miller and Modigliani argument):

The total market value of the firm is independent of its dividend policy.

According to this theory, shareholders should be indifferent between retaining their profits in the firm or receiving cash dividends because they can create their own dividends, or they can reinvest the dividend receipts themselves (assuming, of course, the absence of taxes and transaction costs). If some of the shareholders prefer a higher dividend payment as compared with that offered by the firm, they can sell a part of their shares in order to increase their current income. Alternatively, if some of the shareholders prefer a lower dividend payment as compared with that paid by the firm, they can reinvest a portion of their dividend income by purchasing more shares. Since shareholders do not need dividends in order to realize a desired income, the price they will pay for the shares of a firm will be independent of the size of the firm's dividend payout ratio.

Example 16.2 An example illustrating that in a perfect capital market shareholders can adjust their own level of dividends by selling or buying shares

Consider an investor who owns 5,000 shares of GA Manufacturing. The firm's current price per share is £2.00. Recently the firm paid £0.10 per share in cash dividends. In this case, the investor received a dividend payment of £500. If, however, the investor would have preferred to receive a £1,000 income from the firm, then he or she could sell 250 shares and obtain an additional income of £500 (assuming, of course, the absence of taxes and transaction costs).

Now suppose another investor also owns 5,000 shares of the same firm and he or she would prefer a dividend payment of only £300. Then he or she could use the cash of £200 to purchase 100 additional shares of GA Manufacturing (here we also assume the absence of taxes and transaction costs).

As we see from this example, the dividend-irrelevant theory argues that investors are indifferent regarding the payment of dividends because they can arrange their own dividends by selling or buying ordinary shares.

Figure 16.6 shows a single-variable sensitivity which is applied on three

```
      A           B          C          D          E          F          G
 1 A SENSITIVITY ANALYSIS USING ONE VARIABLE AND MANY FORMULAE
 2 ============================================================
 3 Number of Shares Owed                 5,000
 4 Dividends per Share                    £0.1
 5 Current Share Price                      £2
 6 Dividend Payment                       £500
 7 Preferable Dividend Income            £1000
 8                                    ---------
 9 Number of Shares to Sell/Buy           -250
10 --------------------------------------------
11               +D9        +D3+B11   -B11*D5
12        1000       -250     4,750      £500
13         900       -200     4,800      £400
14         800       -150     4,850      £300
15         700       -100     4,900      £200
16         600        -50     4,950      £100
17         500          0     5,000        £0
18         400         50     5,050    (£100)
19         300        100     5,100    (£200)
20         200        150     5,150    (£300)
```

Figure 16.6. A single-variable sensitivity applied to many formulae

formulae. The sensitivity is conducted with respect to the preferable dividend income and the three formulae are as follows (we assume the absence of taxes and transaction costs):

`+D9` The number of shares to sell or buy in order to realize a desired income (a negative amount of shares indicates the sale of shares, while a positive amount indicates the purchase of shares).

`+D3+B11` The total number of shares after selling or buying shares.

`-B11*D5` The amount of money realized from the sale of shares or the amount of money paid for purchasing new shares.

The preferable income takes values in the range £1,000–£200 in steps of £100. The numerical value stored in cell D9 is calculated by using the following formula:

```
(D6-D7)/D5
```

Finally, note that the `/Data Table 1` refers to cell D7, the 'input cell 1'.

Problem

Create the worksheet presented in Figure 16.6.

The dividend-relevance theory

The dividend-relevance theory makes the following assumptions:

1 The firm finances investment projects exclusively from its retained earnings. That is, a decision by the firm to increase/decrease its investment projects implies a change in its dividend policy and vice versa.
2 The firm's cost of capital remains constant.
3 The firm's ordinary shares have an infinite life.
4 The dividend growth is constant.

The dividend-relevance theory maintains:

The total market value of the firm is dependent on its dividend policy. Specifically, relatively high payout ratios result in higher share prices and relatively low payout ratios imply lower share prices.

The basic argument of this theory is as follows: since investors are risk averse, they prefer dividend payments in the near future as opposed to retention of funds and promise of dividend payments in the more distant future. Therefore, investors are not indifferent between current dividends and the retention of earnings and they are prepared to purchase shares from firms with high payout ratios. This, in turn, results in higher share prices. Let us now discuss further the dividend relevance theory by using the constant growth dividend valuation model. The current market price of an ordinary share can be expressed as follows (for a proof see Appendix 16B):

$$P_0 = \frac{(1-b)E}{r_0 - bR}$$

where

b = the fraction of earnings per share retained in the firm,
$(1-b)$ = the dividend payout ratio.

E = the current earnings per share of the firm.
r_0 = the required rate of return on equity capital.
R = the rate of return on the firm's reinvested earnings.

In this case, we can see that the current market price of the ordinary share is expressed as a function of four variables: the dividend payout ratio; the earnings per share; the required rate of return on equity capital; and the rate of return on reinvested earnings. Based on the valuation equation, the higher the dividend payout ratio, the higher the current share value (other things remain the same).

Figure 16.7 shows the implications of the relationship between the required rate of return on equity capital and the rate of return on reinvested earnings.

Condition	Implication
$r_0 > R$	An increase (decrease) in b (that is, a decrease (increase) in the dividend payout ratio) implies a decrease (increase) in the price of the firm's shares.
$r_0 < R$	A decrease (increase) in b (that is, an increase (decrease) in the dividend payout ratio) implies an increase (decrease) in the price of the firm's shares.
$r_0 = R$	$MV_0 = E/r_0$, that is the market value of the firm is independent of its dividend policy.

Figure 16.7. The implications of the relationship between r_0 and R

If there are no transaction costs and taxes and the required rate of return on equity capital equals the rate of return on the reinvested earnings, then the investors are indifferent as to how the earnings stream is divided between dividends and retained earnings. This special case provides a reconciliation between the dividend-irrelevant and dividend-relevant theories and its asserts that the total market value of the firm is independent of its dividend policy.

Example 16.3 Examining the sensitivity of the share price with respect to changes in the retention ratio and in the rate of return on reinvestment earnings

The current earnings per share of Allis plc are £2. The required rate of return on equity capital is 20 per cent. Figure 16.8 shows the sensitivity of the firm's share price with respect to changes in two variables: the retention ratio and the rate of return on reinvested earnings. We assume that the rate of return on reinvested earnings takes six values, two being less than 20 per cent, one equal to 20 per cent and three being greater than 20 per cent. The `/Data Table 2` command of 1-2-3 is employed with cells E4 and E5 used as 'input cell 1' and 'input cell 2', respectively.

If the rate of return on reinvestment is equal to the required rate of return on equity capital, the share price is £10 (that is, 2/0.20). If the rate of return on reinvestment is lower than the required rate of return of 20 per cent, then we see that the share price decreases as the retention ratio increases (other things remain the same). On the other hand, if the rate of return on reinvestment is higher than 20 per cent, the share price increases as the retention ratio increases (other things being equal).

The results of the sensitivity analysis just discussed are presented in Figure 16.9.

	A	B	C	D	E	F	G
1	THE SENSITIVITY OF PRICE TO CHANGES IN b and R						
2	===						
3	Current Earnings per Share				£2		
4	Fraction of Earnings Retained (b)				0.6		
5	Rate of Return on Reinvested Earnings (R)				16%		
6	Required Rate of Return				20%		
7					---------		
8			Share Price --->		£7.69		
9							
10	+E8	16%	18%	20%	22%	24%	26%
11	0.30	9.21	9.59	10.00	10.45	10.94	11.48
12	0.35	9.03	9.49	10.00	10.57	11.21	11.93
13	0.40	8.82	9.37	10.00	10.71	11.54	12.50
14	0.45	8.59	9.24	10.00	10.89	11.96	13.25
15	0.50	8.33	9.09	10.00	11.11	12.50	14.29
16	0.55	8.04	8.91	10.00	11.39	13.24	15.79
17	0.60	7.69	8.70	10.00	11.76	14.29	18.18
18	0.65	7.29	8.43	10.00	12.28	15.91	22.58
19	0.70	6.82	8.11	10.00	13.04	18.75	33.33

Figure 16.8. Allis plc: a two-variable sensitivity of the share price

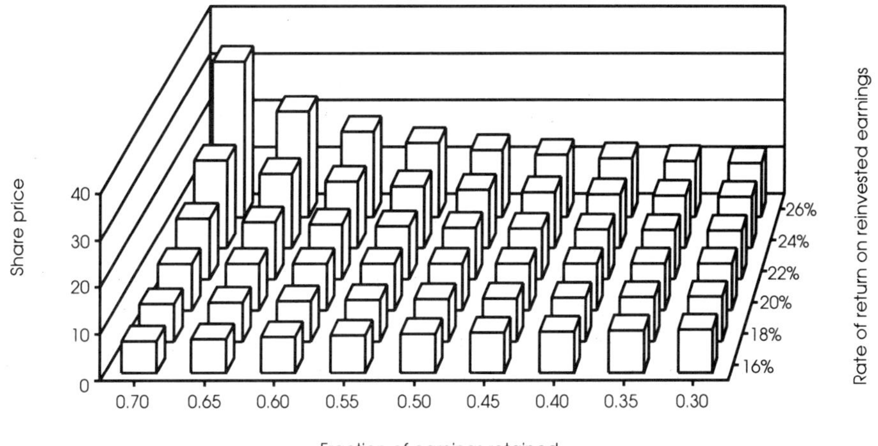

Figure 16.9. Allis plc: a graph of two-variable sensitivity of the share price

Problem

Create the worksheet shown in Figure 16.8.

Tax-differential theory

The tax-differential theory holds:

> *The total market value of the firm is dependent on its dividend policy. Specifically, firms should have low dividend payout ratios.*

In view of the tax-differential theory, investors prefer to receive capital gains instead of dividend income for the following reason: capital gains can be deferred until a period in which they can be taxed at a more favourable capital gain tax rate. Therefore, although capital gains are theoretically taxed at the same rate as dividends, the effective tax rate that applies to capital gains is lower than that on dividends. Since investors would prefer to receive their return in share price appreciation, firms should retain more earnings. As a consequence they should maintain low dividend payout ratios. This theory also supports the existence of a negative relationship between the sizes of dividend payments and share prices. For example, maintaining a low dividend payout ratio will actually result in higher share prices.

Example 16.4 Illustrating the main point of the tax-differential theory

Consider an investor who wishes to purchase either 1,000 shares in firm A or 1,000 shares in firm B. We assume the following:

1 Both shares have the same level of risk.
2 Each share has a market price of £2.
3 Each share earns a return of £0.20 (that is, percentage price appreciation + dividend yield). A share in firm B pays less dividend than a share in firm A.
4 The objective of the investor is to maximize his or her after-tax return.

We also consider the following two cases:

Case 1 Both dividends and capital gains are taxed at the same rate of 40 per cent.

Case 2 The dividends are taxed at 40 per cent and the capital gains are taxed at 25 per cent.

If the tax rates on dividends and capital gains are equal, the investor's after-tax return would be £120 (see Figure 16.10). In this case, shares in firms A and B have the same risk and the same after-tax return. As a consequence, investors should be indifferent between the two shares.

In contrast, if the dividends are taxed at a higher rate than the capital gains, we see that a share in firm B earns a higher after-tax return than a share in firm A. Thus, the investor will choose to invest in firm B. The resulting demand for the shares in firm B will make their price higher than that of the shares in firm A.

The second part of Figure 16.10 presents a sensitivity table of the after-tax return with respect to changes in the tax rate that applies to dividend income (DI). Here we use the `/Data Table 1` command where cell G4 is considered to be the 'input cell 1' required by 1-2-3. In both cases, the after-tax return increases as the tax rate that applies to dividend income decreases. Figure 16.11 provides a graphical presentation of the results of the sensitivity table shown in Figure 16.10.

Problems

1 Create the worksheet shown in Figure 16.10 using the appropriate formulae.
2 Create the graph shown in Figure 16.11.

Under the imputation system the shareholders of a firm receive their return in dividend income net of basic rate income tax. This creates a bias towards high dividend payout ratios. On the other hand, advanced corporation tax becomes due whenever dividends are paid during the accounting year of the firm. Paying tax earlier rather than later has a cost. This induces a bias towards low dividend payout ratios. Since we have to take into consideration the tax position of the firm and the tax positions of its shareholders it is difficult to provide a general rule describing the influence of the imputation system on dividend policy.

```
        A            B           C          D         E          F         G
 1 TOTAL AFTER TAX RETURN ON TWO SHARES IN FIRMS A AND B
 2 ====================================================
 3 Dividend Income Tax Rate       40%  Dividend Payment Tax Rate       40%
 4 Capital Gain Tax Rate          40%  Capital Gain Tax Rate           25%
 5 ----------------------------------------------------------------------
 6                            FIRM A     FIRM B          FIRM A     FIRM B
 7 ----------------------------------------------------------------------
 8 Number of Shares            1,000      1,000           1,000      1,000
 9 Share Price                 £2.00      £2.00           £2.00      £2.00
10 Dividend                    £0.15      £0.10           £0.15      £0.10
11 Capital Gain                £0.05      £0.10           £0.05      £0.10
12 Total Dividends            £90.00     £60.00          £90.00     £60.00
13 Total Capital Gains        £30.00     £60.00          £37.50     £75.00
14                        ------------------      ------------------
15 After Tax Return          £120.00    £120.00         £127.50    £135.00
16                        ==================      ==================
17
18
19
20
21 B> THE SENSITIVITY OF THE AFTER-TAX RETURN TO CHANGES IN DI TAX RATE
22 ====================================================================
23
24                 |          +F15       +G15           |
25                        49%  115.50     111.00
26                 |      46%  117.00     114.00          |
27                        43%  118.50     117.00
28                 |      40%  120.00     120.00          |
29                        37%  121.50     123.00
30                 |      34%  123.00     126.00          |
31                        31%  124.50     129.00
32                 |      28%  126.00     132.00          |
33                        25%  127.50     135.00
34                 |      22%  129.00     138.00          |
35                        19%  130.50     141.00
36                 |--------------------------------------|
```

Figure 16.10. Calculating the after-tax return of two shares

If a firm has tax losses (for example, when it has an accounting loss) and decides to pay dividends, then it cannot obtain a relief for the advanced corporation tax until it resumes paying mainstream corporation tax. Charitable and pension fund institutions would prefer to receive high dividend payments, because they do not pay tax on their income. Finally, high-income investors may have a preference for retaining their earnings within the firm with the expectation of capital gains.

Comparing three theories on dividends

The dividend-irrelevance theory is based on a set of simplified assumptions and it is theoretically correct under these assumptions. A number of arguments have been advanced against the dividend-irrelevance theory which are mostly centred around the realism of the theory's assumptions. The supporters of the dividend-relevance theory argue that dividends are relevant under conditions of uncertainty and when investors pay transaction costs.

- *Dividends under uncertainty* Investors prefer to receive current dividends rather than the firm retaining its earnings because there is uncertainty about when and if these retained earnings will produce higher future dividend payments. As a con-

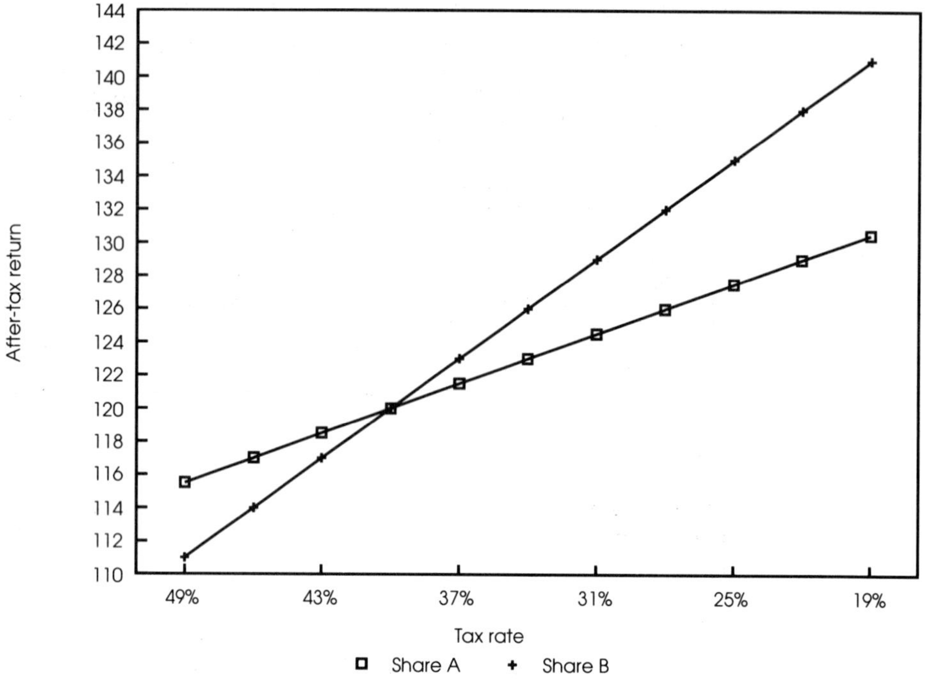

Figure 16.11. Graphical presentation of the sensitivity of the after-tax return

sequence, investors are not indifferent as to how the earnings are divided between dividends and retained earnings.

- *Existence of transaction costs* Attacks upon the dividend-irrelevance theory can also be made with respect to the assumption that there are no transaction costs in the capital market. In the real world, investing excess dividends or selling shares to obtain additional income could involve high transaction costs. Thus, an investor who wishes to increase his or her income would prefer to receive higher dividends than pay transaction costs for selling off a portion of his or her shares. Likewise, an investor who wishes to reduce his or her income would prefer to receive lower dividend payments than pay transaction costs for purchasing additional shares.

The tax-differential theorists provide two main arguments for low dividend payout: the existence of different tax rates on dividend income and capital gains; and the existence of flotation costs when raising external equity capital.

- *Existence of different tax rates* The dividend-irrelevance theory argues that investors are indifferent as to whether they receive cash dividends or capital gains. This argument seems reasonable in a world without personal taxes. However, once differential personal tax rates are taken into account, the supporters of the tax-differential theory disagree with the argument of Miller and Modigliani. Since capital gains tax can be deferred, the effective tax rate that applies to such gains is lower than that of dividends. Therefore, shareholders should prefer to receive low dividend payments.
- *Existence of flotation costs* The dividend-irrelevance theory assumes that additional funds can be acquired through external financing. In reality, raising new equity capital could involve substantial flotation costs to the firm, making the

cost of internal funds cheaper than the cost of external equity. Therefore, shareholders should prefer to receive low dividend payout allowing the firm to retain the additional earnings.

The dividend-relevance theory can also be compared with the tax-differential theory. The former asserts that firms should maintain high dividend payout ratios. If this is the case, then an investor who prefers a low dividend payout should use a portion of his or her dividend income to purchase new shares, an action that involves unwanted transaction costs. However, a similar argument can be made against the tax-differential theory. Specifically, if a firm adopts a low dividend payout policy, then shareholders who prefer high dividends will sell part of their holdings, and in doing so they pay undesirable transaction costs.

From the theoretical viewpoint there is no clear answer as to whether investors are in favour of receiving dividend income or capital gains. Among the dividend-irrelevance, dividend-relevance and tax-differential theories, the first one relies on the most unrealistic assumptions, while the third dividend policy seems to avoid several of the restrictive assumptions of the dividend-irrelevant theory (for example, the assumption of a tax-less world). Note, however, that the validity of a theory cannot be tested by the realism of its assumptions: it can be tested by examining how the theory fits real data. Later in the chapter we will discuss several empirical studies on the determinants of the dividend policy.

Figure 16.12 summarizes the dividend-irrelevant, dividend-relevant and tax-differential theories.

Dividend signalling approach

The dividend signalling approach states:

Dividends have an impact on a firm's share price because they convey information to investors about the firm's profitability.

This approach argues that dividends serve as a signal to inform the investors about the current and future profitability of the firm. For example, if a firm has a target dividend payout ratio which is stable over time, an increase (decrease) of the ratio will be interpreted by investors as a message that the firm's management team expects higher (lower) levels of future cash flows. Accordingly, the price of the firm's shares may increase (decrease) following the announcement of a higher (lower) dividend payout.

In some instances the dividend announcement has an impact on the share price because managers do not communicate effectively with the investors. For example, if a firm decreases its dividend payment and uses the available funds to finance a profitable investment, it is likely to increase its future prospects (note that issuing new ordinary shares involves flotation costs). If the managers effectively communicate this message to investors, the share price might remain unaffected by the dividend reduction. Therefore, the announcement of the size of the next dividend payment can affect the share price of the firm only to the extent that managers announce unexpected information.

Miller and Modigliani claim that the dividend declaration does not itself determine the firm's share price. They assert that a dividend announcement provides only a way

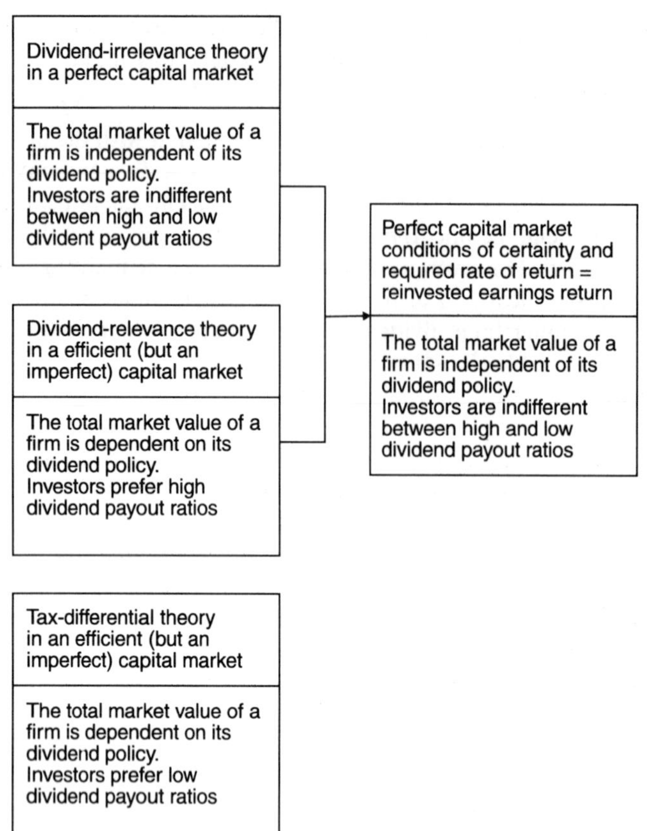

Figure 16.12. A summary of three theories on dividend policy

of informing the owners and prospective investors about the future profitability of the firm. Thus, share prices are affected directly by the investors' expectations about the firm's future performance and not by its dividend policy. Such an argument is consistent with the dividend-irrelevance theory.

Clientele effect

The clientele effect was originally suggested by Miller and Modigliani (1961) and asserts:

> *Each firm tends to attract a group of investors whose preferences with respect to the payment and stability of dividends are consistent with its dividend policy.*

There is a wide selection of firms with different dividend policies. Some have low dividend payout ratios and others have high dividend payout ratios. Similarly, investors have particular requirements for dividends. Some prefer to receive low dividend payments and others favour high dividend payments. Here are some examples:

- Investors with low incomes and high current needs would prefer high dividend payout ratios.
- Investors in high-tax brackets would prefer low dividend payout ratios.

Clientele effect advocates argue that if investors have preferences for different dividend policies, they will seek out firms whose dividend policies are in line with their objectives.

The clientele theory assumes the existence of imperfect capital markets. In such markets shareholders incur transaction costs when they shift their investments among other firms which are more attractive to them. A reduction in dividends or a failure to maintain a desired dividend payout ratio can produce unwanted transaction costs which in turn force the firm's share price to a lower level. If a firm's dividend payout ratio follows a stable pattern, which is approved by its shareholders, then the dividend policy of the firm would not affect its share price. The firm's dividend policy can influence its share price only when the investors in aggregate are not attracted by its dividend policy. Therefore, the clientele theory is in line with the dividend-irrelevance theory.

Dividend policies

There are several dividend policies including the following:

- Constant dividend payout ratio.
- Stable per-share dividends.
- Residual dividend.

Constant dividend payout ratio policy

This policy claims the following:

> *Establish a dividend policy that pays a constant percentage of earnings per share as dividends to the shareholders.*

Under the constant dividend payout ratio policy, the level of dividends paid will fluctuate from period to period with variations in earnings. This probably provides an explanation of why this kind of policy is very rarely adopted.

Stable per-share dividends policy

This policy can be summarized as follows:

> *Establish a dividend policy that maintains a modestly growing pattern of dividend payments over time.*

The stable per-share dividends suggest that a firm should increase its dividend payments as earnings per share increase over time, but it should avoid increasing its dividend payout ratio above a level that cannot be maintained in the future.

Next, we discuss two reasons indicating why investors prefer stable dividend payments to unstable ones. First, investors in lower tax brackets tend to choose firms that follow a stable per-share dividends policy because they prefer specific periodic dividend payments. Unfortunately, in the real world, the suggestion of Miller and Modigliani to sell a number of shares for income when dividends are not sufficient involves transaction costs. Second, a cut in dividends may be interpreted by investors as a negative signal about the future expected earnings of the firm and may result in a share price decline.

Example 16.5 The dividend policy of Marks and Spencer plc

Figure 16.13 shows the earnings per share and dividends per share of Marks and

Spencer plc from 1977 to 1988. It can be seen that the tendency of Marks and Spencer is to pay stable, but increasing, dividends per share. In 1980 the earnings per share of the firm were 3.62 pence and in 1981 the earnings per share increased to just 3.79 pence (an increase of 4.70 per cent). But the firm maintained steady dividends per share and even increased its dividends per share from 1.95 pence in 1980 to 2.20 pence in 1981 (an increase of 12.82 per cent). In 1987, earnings per share improved 21.56 per cent from 8.35 pence in 1986 to 10.15 pence. In 1987, however, the firm's dividend payment was 4.50 pence per share. This provided an improvement in dividends of only 15.38 per cent from 3.90 pence in 1986 to 4.50 pence in 1987.

	A	B	C	E	F
1	M & S:THE EARNINGS PER SHARE AND DIVIDENDS PER SHARE,1977-88				
2					
3	Year	Earnings Per	Dividends Per		
4		Share	Share		
5					
6	1977	2.10	0.95		
7	1978	2.64	1.24		
8	1979	3.47	1.45		
9	1980	3.62	1.95		
10	1981	3.79	2.20		
11	1982	4.61	2.63		
12	1983	5.07	3.02		
13	1984	6.37	3.12		
14	1985	6.84	3.40		
15	1986	8.35	3.90		
16	1987	10.15	4.50		
17	1988	12.07	5.10		
18					

Figure 16.13. Marks and Spencer plc: dividend policy (1977–88)

Figure 16.14 shows a graphical presentation of the earnings per share and the dividends per share of Marks and Spencer for the period 1977–88.

Lintner's model on dividend policy

Lintner (1956) examined the dividend policies of 28 firms by analysing the results produced from interviewing their managers. His findings are summarized as follows:

1 Firms establish long-term target dividend payout ratios.
2 In general, management try to avoid increases in their dividend rates if they do not expect to maintain the increase in the future. Most firms seem to adopt a fairly stable dividend policy.
3 Current earnings constitute a major factor affecting the firm's dividend decision.
4 In general, investment requirements do not influence the dividend policy of the firm.

Lintner introduced a model that was consistent with his findings. Lintner's model is explained below.

The target dividend payment per share of a firm for period t (DPS_t) can be represented as a product of its target dividend payout ratio (DPR) and the earnings per

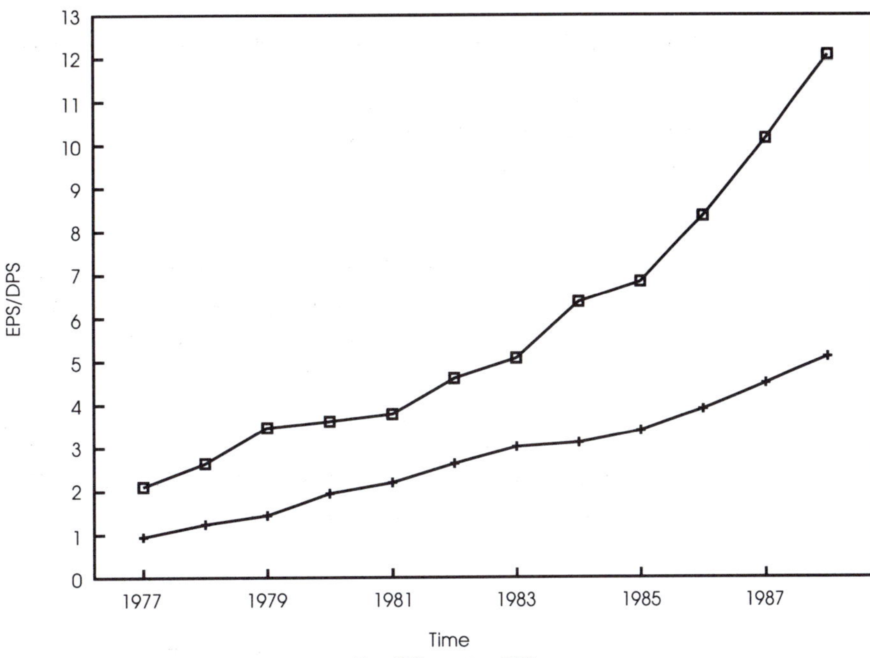

Figure 16.14. Marks and Spencer plc: earnings per share and dividends per share (1977–88)

share for period t (EPS_t):

$$DPS_t = \text{Target DPR} \times EPS_t$$

The last equation can also be expressed as follows:

$$DPS_t - DPS_{t-1} = \text{Target DPR} \times EPS_t - DPS_{t-1}$$

In words, the difference Target DPR $\times$ $EPS_t - DPS_{t-1}$ shows the deviation between period t's target dividend payment per share and the previous period's dividend payment per share. We call such a difference the target change in dividend payment per share.

Suppose that the dividend payment per share of a firm is dependent simply on its fixed dividend payout ratio. This policy, however, can make managers increase their dividends to levels that cannot be maintained. To avoid the consequences of reducing dividend payments, managers should increase dividends steadily even if they realize a large increase in earnings per share. To achieve such a policy, they should take only a fraction of the difference between the target dividend payment per share and the last period's actual dividend payment per share. Stated differently, the deviation Target DPS $\times$ $EPS_t - DPS_{t-1}$ should be adjusted accordingly in order to move only partially towards the target dividend payout ratio. Consequently, we should introduce an adjustment coefficient (AC) such that:

$$DPS_t - DPS_{t-1} = AC\ (\text{Target DPR} \times EPS_t - DPS_{t-1})$$

Given this discussion, the dividend payment per share for period t can be represented by using the following equation:

$$DPS_t = DPS_{t-1} + AC\ (\text{Target DPR} \times EPS_t - DPS_{t-1})$$

In words, the dividend payment per share for period t is equal to the previous period's dividend payment per share plus a fraction of the target change in dividend payment per share.

The adjustment coefficient and the target dividend payout ratio can be estimated with the aid of the following regression model:

$$\text{DPS}_t = a + b_1\text{EPS}_t + b_2\text{DPS}_{t-1} + e_t$$

where

b_1 = describes the relationship between the dividend payment per share for period t and the earnings per share for period t. We expect b to be positive. This means that for each unit increase in earnings per share there will be an increase equal to $b_1\text{EPS}_t$ in dividend payment per share.

b_2 = describes the relationship between the dividend payment per share for period t and the dividend payment per share for period $t - 1$. We expect b to be positive. This means that for each unit increase in DPS_{t-1} there will be an increase equal to $b_2\text{DPS}_{t-1}$ in dividend payment per share.

$$\text{AC} = 1 - b_2$$

$$\text{Target DPR} = b_1/\text{AC}.$$

The findings of Lintner indicated that the variability of the independent variables in the model explained 85 per cent of the variability in dividends for his sample of firms.

Example 16.6 Estimating the parameters in Lintner's model

Figure 16.15 presents the historical earnings per share and dividends per share for Miles plc for the period 1971–90. The regression model introduced by Lintner includes not only the current dividends per share (or the current payment per share) but also the one year lagged (past) values of the dividends per share. Column C shows the firm's dividends per share lagged one year. The regression results are derived with the aid of the `/Data Regression` command of 1-2-3. The independent variables' range is B9 ... C27 and the dependent variable's range is D9 ... D27. The t-statistics are calculated as follows (slight deviations are due to rounding):

$$t(b_1) = \frac{0.0838}{0.0158} = 5.31 \qquad t(b_2) = \frac{0.8642}{0.0457} = 18.91$$

With 16 degrees of freedom, both coefficients are significantly different from 0 at the 95 per cent significance level, indicating a significant relationship between the current year's dividends per share and the current year's earnings per share and past dividends per share.

The adjustment coefficient would be

$$\text{AC} = 1 - 0.8642 = 0.1358$$

The target dividend payout ratio is estimated below:

$$\text{Target DPR} = 0.0838/0.1358 = 61.71 \text{ per cent}$$

The results indicate that for every period the firm will adjust its previous period's dividends per share by 13.58 of the target change in dividends per share.

	A	B	C	D
1	MILES PLC:DETERMINING THE FACTORS INFLUENCING DIVIDEND POLICY			
2				
3	Year	Earnings Per	Dividends Per	Dividends Per
4		Share	Share Lagged	Share
5		(pence)	1 Year	(pence)
6			(pence)	
7				
8	1971	4.90		2.91
9	1972	4.92	2.91	2.95
10	1973	5.03	2.95	2.95
11	1974	5.07	2.95	3.05
12	1975	5.20	3.05	3.06
13	1976	5.31	3.06	3.06
14	1977	5.39	3.06	3.07
15	1978	5.61	3.07	3.12
16	1979	5.88	3.12	3.21
17	1980	6.19	3.21	3.23
18	1981	6.41	3.23	3.30
19	1982	6.72	3.30	3.35
20	1983	7.42	3.35	3.51
21	1984	8.20	3.51	3.76
22	1985	8.36	3.76	3.91
23	1986	7.00	3.91	4.00
24	1987	7.03	4.00	4.02
25	1988	6.18	4.02	4.02
26	1989	4.30	4.02	4.02
27	1990	4.00	4.02	3.60
28				
29				
30				
31				
32	Regression Output:			
33	Constant			-0.0062
34	Std Err of Y Est			0.0795
35	R Squared			0.9658
36	No. of Observations			19
37	Degrees of Freedom			16
38				
39	X Coefficient(s)		0.0838	0.8642
40	Std Err of Coef.		0.0158	0.0457
41			--------	--------
42	t-statistics ----->		5.3132	18.8915
43				
44	Adjustment Coefficient ------>		0.1358	
45	Target Payout Ratio --------->		61.71%	

Figure 16.15. Using Lintner's model

Problem

Create the worksheet shown in Figure 16.15.

Residual dividend policy

This policy asserts the following:

> *A firm would pay dividends after all its investment projects have been financed. The residual dividend policy leads to the maximization of the firm's share price.*

According to the residual dividend policy, a firm pays dividends after it has utilized its net earnings to adopt all profitable investment projects. If the firm needs all its earnings for financing its investment opportunities, then it would pay no dividends to its shareholders. Under this policy, the dividend decision of a firm can be treated as follows:

Step 1 Determine the firm's optimal amount for investment.
Step 2 Determine the target debt/equity ratio.
Step 3 Determine the amount of equity required to finance the investment projects of the firm so as to maintain the target debt/equity ratio.
Step 4 Use the reserves to supply part or all the equity required. Pay dividends only if there exist more earnings than those required for financing the investment projects.

Example 16.7 The residual dividend policy of Power Manufacturing

Power Manufacturing follows a residual dividend policy. The firm has decided to invest in three projects requiring initial amounts of £250,000, £350,000 and £400,000, respectively. The target debt/equity ratio of the firm is 60 per cent. The firm has 800,000 ordinary shares. In this case, we follow the steps below:

Step 1 The optimal amount for investment is £1,000,000.
Step 2 We use a target debt/equity ratio of 60 per cent.
Step 3 The amount of equity needed to finance the new investments is £600,000 (that is (0.60)(£1,000,000)).
Step 4 The firm can pay out £1,000,000 in dividends. Thus, the firm will pay £1.25 per share in annual dividends.

The above-mentioned calculations are summarized in Figure 16.16. In addition, we calculate the amount of equity needed to finance the projects, the amount of available dividends and the dividends per share for different investment requirements. We use the `/Data Table 1` command of 1-2-3 with 'input cell 1' being cell C5. Note the cells C8, C10 and C11 contain formulae. The function `@IF(C10<0,0,+C10)` states the following: if cell C10 contains a negative number, return zero, otherwise return the amount available for dividends. Likewise, the function `@IF(C10<0,0,+C11)` can be interpreted as: if cell C10 contains a negative number, return zero, otherwise return the dividends per share.

Problem

Create the worksheet displayed in Figure 16.16.

Foregoing profitable investment opportunities has a negative impact on the firm's value. Thus, the residual dividend policy is consistent with the shareholders' wealth maximization objective. However, it has a major disadvantage when adopted in the short run, namely, the dividend payout ratio of the firm will vary as its earnings and investment opportunities vary.

Factors influencing dividend policy

A firm's dividend policy is affected by various factors which may be divided into five groups: profitability and stability factors; liquidity, investment and financing factors; economic factors; factors related to shareholders' requirements; and legal constraints.

```
           A                   B                   C                  D
 1 POWER MANUFACTURING:AN APPLICATION OF THE RESIDUAL POLICY
 2 ==========================================================
 3 Debt/Equity Ratio                             60.0%
 4 Number of Shares                            800,000
 5 New Financing/Investment (£)              1,000,000
 6 Retained Earnings (£)                     1,600,000
 7                                   -----------------
 8 Equity Needed (£)                           600,000
 9                                   -----------------
10 Available Dividends (£)                   1,000,000
11 Dividend Per Share (£)                         1.25
12
13                   +C8             @IF(C10<0,0,+C10) @IF(C10<0,0,+C11)
14      1,000,000        600,000         1,000,000              1.25
15      1,500,000        900,000           700,000              0.88
16      2,000,000      1,200,000           400,000              0.50
17      2,500,000      1,500,000           100,000              0.13
18      3,000,000      1,800,000                 0              0.00
19      3,500,000      2,100,000                 0              0.00
20      4,000,000      2,400,000                 0              0.00
```

Figure 16.16. The dividend policy of Power Manufacturing

Profitability and stability factors

Here we will discuss two factors:

1 *Growth of earnings* In general, if earnings are growing over time, then the firm can retain higher proportions of its earnings and also pay higher dividends.

2 *Stability of earnings* If a firm's earnings are unstable over time, then the firm may avoid an increase in its dividend payout ratio because of the risk of being unable to maintain the increase in the future. Conversely, a firm with relatively stable earnings has a greater ability to maintain a relatively high dividend payout ratio in the future. A firm in this position is, thus, most likely to pay a higher dividend than a firm with unstable earnings.

Liquidity, investment and financing factors

In this case six factors are discussed.

1 *Liquidity position* As cash dividends are paid with cash, firms with low amounts of liquid assets (that is, cash and short-term investments) may be unable to pay large dividends. In many cases the firm can borrow money to pay dividends. However, this may limit the firm's borrowing capacity and thus restrict it to support profitable investment projects.

2 *Availability of investment opportunities* Firms that face many profitable investment opportunities frequently choose to utilize internally generated funds to finance part of their investments. This may result in relatively low dividend payout ratios. Similarly, the fewer the investment opportunities available to the firm, the less the need of funds and probably the higher the dividend payout ratios.

3 *The expected rates of return on investments* The price of a firm's shares is affected by the expected rates of return on its investments. Thus, if the shareholders expect high return on investments, they are more likely to accept a lower dividend payment because they also expect to receive future capital gains.

4 *Ability of raising external finance* If a firm has difficulties in obtaining external funds (for example, this could be the case with a new firm), then it prefers to

finance its investments by using internally generated funds. This causes the dividend payout to be either very low or zero. Conversely, the greater the ability of the firm to obtain external funds (for example, a large established firm), the greater its ability to pay relatively high dividends.

5 *Cost of raising external finance* In the present of flotation costs, the specific cost of retained earnings is lower than the specific cost of new ordinary shares. Therefore, retained earnings become a more attractive source of funds and this may result in a relatively low dividend payout ratio.
6 *Level of debt/equity ratio* A firm with a high debt/equity ratio may prefer to retain a large proportion of its earnings. This results in a low or zero dividend payout. Conversely, a firm with a small debt/equity ratio may be willing to pay a relatively high dividend and finance some of its new investments by using new debt.

Economic factors

In this case we will discuss two factors.

1 *Level of inflation* With rising prices, firms find it more expensive to purchase new fixed assets because, in many cases, depreciation allowances fail to cover the costs of the new assets. In these circumstances, firms prefer to retain a large fraction of their earnings (pay lower dividends). Furthermore, in periods of high inflation there exist high interest rates, making debt financing more expensive. Therefore, firms tend to pay lower dividends and obtain new equity financing from retained earnings.
2 *Corporation tax* The higher the corporate tax rate, the lower the firm's earnings per ordinary share (all other things being equal). If the corporate tax rate is high, the firm may pay out a low proportion of its net profit in dividends.

Factors related to shareholders' requirements

In the present case three factors are discussed.

1 *Control* If the majority of the shareholders do not wish new shares to be sold, the firm's only source of new equity capital will be retained earnings. Under these circumstances, the firm may be required to maintain a low dividend payout ratio. In some cases, a firm with low dividend payments is in danger of being acquired by another firm which promises higher dividends after the acquisition has occurred.
2 *Tax position of the shareholders* Shareholders in high tax brackets would have a preference for retained earnings rather than dividend income because they must pay tax on dividends in the year received. On the other hand, if a firm has shareholders in a lower tax bracket, it may establish a relatively high payout ratio in order to supplement their current income with dividend income.
3 *Separation of ownership management* In view of this argument, dividends are paid because of the separation of the ownership and management. A firm's dividend policy and changes in that policy are interpreted by investors as signals for the firm's future profitability.

Legal constraints

Two cases are discussed.

1 *Law requirements* If a firm cannot pay its financial obligations as they come due, then dividends cannot be paid. This is designed to protect the claims of creditors. On the other hand, the firm cannot pay dividends if such payments would cause insolvency. Moreover, a firm can pay dividends if there is a current operating profit, even if it realizes current losses on fixed assets.
2 *Income policy* When the Government sets up an income policy, it is asking industry and labour to stay within limits in their price and wage policies in an attempt to control rising prices. In the United Kingdom from 1973 to 1979 firms were only permitted to increase their dividends by a percentage of the previous year's dividends as part of the Government's income policy. Such a percentage was in the range 5–12.5 per cent.

Dividend policy: empirical evidence

In this section we divide the empirical evidence on dividend policy into two categories: the first one is concerned with the studies providing evidence on the reasons for paying dividends and the second one discusses the empirical evidence on the factors influencing dividend policy.

Reasons for paying dividends

The empirical studies investigating the reasons for paying dividends can be broadly classified as follows:

1 Those focusing on the relationship between the market value of equity and dividend payout.
2 Those testing the signalling effect of dividend announcements on the firm's value.
3 Those examining the possibility of clientele effects.
4 A study attempting to discover corporate dividend payment practices of UK firms.

Figures 16.17, 16.18 and 16.19 summarize various studies dealing with the reasons for paying dividends.

Finally, Diacogiannis and But (1991) examined, with the aid of a questionnaire design, the dividend policy practices of UK firms. Using a population of 600

Author(s)	Country/time period/interval	Conclusions
Black and Scholes (1974)	USA/1936–66/ annual	There is no significant relationship between portfolio returns and dividend payout
Litzenberger and Ramaswamy (1979)	USA/1936–77/ monthly	There is a strong positive relationship between the expected security returns and dividend yield
Miller and Scholes (1982)	USA/1940–78/ monthly	There is a statistically insignificant relationship between share returns and dividend yields (that is, dividend policy is irrelevant)

Figure 16.17. A summary of studies testing the relationship between dividends and value

Author(s)	Country/data/ interval	Conclusions
Pettit (1972)	USA/135 firms/ monthly, daily	Announcement of dividend changes provide important messages to investors for assessing the prices of shares
Watts (1973)	USA/310 firms/ monthly	On average, there exists a positive relationship between future earnings changes and current dividend changes. This is consistent with the signalling approach. However, this relationship is not economically significant, as it cannot be used to earn abnormal returns after transaction costs are taken into account
Kwan (1981)	USA/183 firms/ quarterly	After improving the methodology of Pettit (1972), it can be concluded that the market reacts to dividend change announcements. Specifically, when firms announce unexpectedly large changes in dividends, then statistically abnormal returns are observed. These abnormal returns follow, on average, the direction of the change in dividends
Woolridge (1983)	USA/411 firms/—	Firms that announce an increase (decrease) in dividends generally produce positive (negative) abnormal share returns
Divecha and Morse (1983)	USA/668 firms/ daily	• Dividend announcements signal the management beliefs about the future profitability of the firm. Specifically, the results reinforce previous studies that positive dividend change announcements produce positive share returns • Firms with positive dividend changes and increased dividend payout ratios seem to have lower abnormal returns than those with positive dividend changes and decreased payout ratios
Kane *et al.* (1986)	USA/—/quarterly	• Unexpected earnings and dividend announcements produce abnormal share return • Investors evaluate earnings and dividend announcements in relation to each other

Figure 16.18. A summary of studies testing the dividend signalling approach

companies whose shares are trading on the London Stock Exchange, they received a number of 176 usable replies. They reported the following results:

- Most of the participants disagree with the irrelevance proposition of Modigliani and Miller.
- The signalling effect is highly recognized by UK finance practitioners.
- The dividend clientele effect is highly ignored by UK finance practitioners.

Author(s)	Country/data	Conclusions
Elton and Gruber (1970)	USA/all shares listed on the NYSE that paid dividends during 1 April 1966–31 March 1967	The clientele theory is supported
Pettit (1977)	USA/914 accounts of individual investors handled by a large retail brokerage house	The results are consistent with the clientele theory

Figure 16.19. A summary of studies testing the clientele theory

Factors affecting dividend policy

The empirical studies on the factors influencing dividend policy can be broadly divided into two groups:

1. Those which investigated the significance of various factors with the aid of regression analysis.
2. Those which examined the factors affecting dividend policies with the help of questionnaire designs.

Figures 16.20 and 16.21 summarize several studies.

Author(s)	Country/number observations/ type of analysis	Factors tested	Conclusions
Lintner (1956)	USA/28 firms/time series regression analysis	Assuming that t is the current year, then: • Earnings per share in period t • Dividends per share in period $t-1$	Each of the two factors affects significantly the firm's changes in dividend level between periods
Pettit (1977)	USA/914 accounts of individual investors handled by a large retail brokerage house/cross-sectional regression analysis	• The systematic risk of the investor's portfolio. The age of the investor is a factor: • The age of the investor • The gross family income averaged over the last three years • The difference between the income and capital gains tax rates for the investor	There is a significant relationship between dividend yield and each of the following three factors: systematic risk, age and gross average family income
Lee *et al.* (1987)	USA/—/time-series regression analysis	Assuming that t is the current year, then: • Earnings per share in year t • Dividends per share in year $t-1$ • Dividends per share in year $t-2$	• Each of the three factors is statistically significant at the 95 per cent level of significance • The addition of the third factor (that is, dividends per share lagged for two years) improves the forecasting ability of the model that uses only the first two factors

Figure 16.20. A summary of studies on the factors influencing dividend policy (technique used: regression analysis)

Figure 16.21. A summary of studies on the factors influencing dividend policy (research data was obtained with the aid of questionnaire designs)

Author(s)	Country/number of firms	Conclusions
Baker *et al.* (1985)	USA/562 firms	The following ranking of factors affecting the divided policy was observed: • Anticipated level of future earnings • Pattern of past dividends • Availability of cash • The concern about maintaining or increasing share price etc.
Partington (1988)	Australia/93 firms	He ranked the factors influencing the dividend policy as follows: • Increase profits • Stability of earnings • Share price etc.
Diacogiannis and But (1991)	UK/176 firms	The following ranking of factors involved in formulating dividend policy was observed: • Share price • Earnings stability • Increase profits • Company growth etc.

Summary

1 *Dividend policy theories* The theory of finance offers several controversial arguments related to the importance of paying dividends. The dividend-irrelevance theory argues that in perfect capital markets investors are indifferent between dividend income and capital gains (assuming that the investment decision of the firm is made before to the dividend decision). According to this theory, investors do not have a preference for either high or low payout ratios, thus, there is no optimal payout ratio that maximizes the firm's share price.

In view of the dividend-relevance theory, investors have a preference for current dividends rather than future capital gains, because the latter are associated with a higher level of uncertainty than the former. This theory suggests that the higher dividend payout ratios result in higher share prices.

The tax-differential theory argues that investors prefer a low dividend payout because the effective tax rate that applies to capital gains is lower than that of dividend income. According to this theory, shares paying low dividends would sell at higher price than comparable shares which pay higher dividends.

The supporters of a high dividend payout policy also argue that in the real world dividends affect the share price because they communicate information about the prospects of the firm. Modigliani and Miller, however, insist that the basic factor influencing the firm's value is the investors' expectations about its future performance rather than its dividend payments.

Lastly, the clientele theory asserts that the firm should choose any dividend policy it wishes, and then attract those investors who prefer its dividend policy. Additionally, once a particular dividend policy has been established, the firm should avoid changing it. A change in dividend policy may cause the firm's shareholders to pay unwanted transaction costs if they try to move to another firm whose dividend policy is consistent with their objectives. The clientele theory is in line with the dividend-irrelevance theory.

From the theoretical viewpoint, it is very difficult to infer whether investors prefer to receive low dividends, high dividends or no dividends. In terms of the underlying assumptions, we see that the dividend-irrelevance theory uses the most unrealistic assumptions.

2 *Factors influencing dividend policy* There exist numerous factors affecting the dividend policy of a firm. These factors can be classified into five groups: profitability and stability factors; liquidity, investment and financing factors; economic factors; factors related to shareholders' requirements; and legal constraints.

3 *Dividend policy: empirical evidence* Studies in the United States tend to support the theory that dividends provide useful messages to investors for assessing share prices. However, these results cannot be generalized. US studies related to the clientele theory are mixed but the majority support the clientele theory. Although there is a little research in the United Kingdom about dividend policy, the existing findings support the dividend signalling approach and reject the clientele theory.

In summary, there appears to be no general and consistent answer on whether the dividend is relevant or irrelevant. The best that can probably be said is that the dividend policy of a firm, in practice, must reflect various important factors such as the reserves as a source of funds, the firm's capital structure requirements, investors' preferences and legal constraints.

4 *Final remarks on dividend policy* Although the theory suggests various dividend policies, most firms in practice seem to adopt a policy that maintains a stable or modestly increased dividend pattern over time. As a final point let us give some general views with respect to the dividend policy.

(a) Establish a constant or modestly increased dividend pattern over time. Raise the dividend per share as earnings per share increase over time, but avoid increasing dividend payments to levels that cannot be safely maintained. As Lintner's (1956) evidence suggests, establish a target payout ratio and each time adjust the dividend payout towards this target ratio.

(b) Avoid large changes in dividend payout. If substantial changes in dividend payout are to occur, the firm's management should probably communicate the reasons for the dividend changes to investors.

(c) It is cheaper to finance new investment opportunities with internally generated funds rather than with the proceeds obtained from selling new ordinary shares.

Questions for discussion

1 For each term shown below in the largest box provide a definition in your own words. Then check your responses against the definitions included in the chapter.

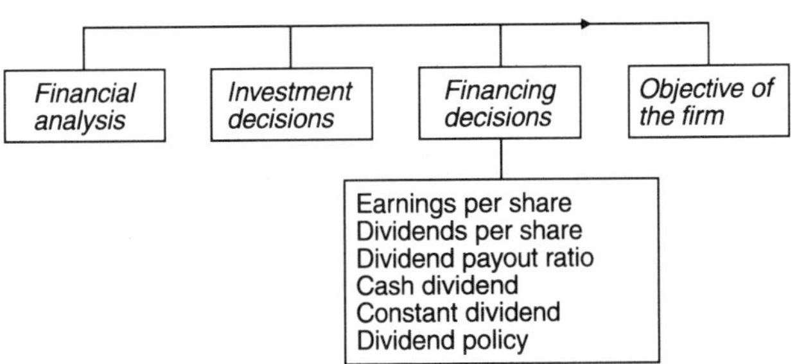

2 Discuss carefully each of the following two propositions:
   (a) 'The total market value of the firm is affected by its dividend policy.'
   (b) 'Each firm tends to attract a group of investors whose preferences are consistent with its dividend policy.'

   Are these two propositions consistent? Discuss.

3 State the assumptions used by Miller and Modigliani in support of the following proposition:

   'Dividend policy cannot affect the total market value of the firm.'

   Is this proposition realistic? If not identify and discuss its main weaknesses.

4 The following five theories are concerned with the payment of dividends: (a) the dividend-irrelevance; (b) dividend-relevance; (c) tax-differential; (d) dividend signalling; and (e) clientele effect.

   Discuss what optimal dividend policy is implied by each of these theories.

5 Discuss and evaluate each of the following four statements:
   (a) 'A firm should maintain a constant dividend payout ratio.'
   (b) 'The cash dividends per ordinary share should be constant or steadily increased from period to period.'
   (c) 'A firm should maintain a low regular dividend plus an extra dividend, if warranted by its profitability.'
   (d) 'Dividends should be paid after the firm's investment needs are fulfilled.'

6 (a) Indicate (on a three equal interval scale) the importance of each of the following factors that might affect a firm's actual dividend policy (a choice should be indicated by placing 'y' in the appropriate box):

	Not important	Important	Very important
Tax status of the shareholders			
Shareholders' risk preference			
Share price of the firm			
Earnings stability			
Debt repayment			
Ability to raise external funds			
Investment needs			
Profits fall			

   (b) Discuss in detail each choice made in part (a).
   (c) In addition to the factors given in part (a), list five factors that might affect the dividend policy of a firm.

7 (a) Indicate (on a three equal interval scale) the importance you attach to each of the following reasons for paying dividends (a choice should be indicated by placing 'y' in the appropriate box):

	Not important	Important	Very important
To meet shareholders' preference for income			
To reduce surplus of cash			
To indicate the management's anticipation of future profits			
To maintain or increase the firm's share price			
To follow past habits of dividend payments			

(**b**) Discuss in detail each choice made in part (a).

8 Other things being the same, in which of the four firms would you prefer to invest your money? Fully discuss your answer.

Dividends per share of firm 4   Dividends per share of firm 1

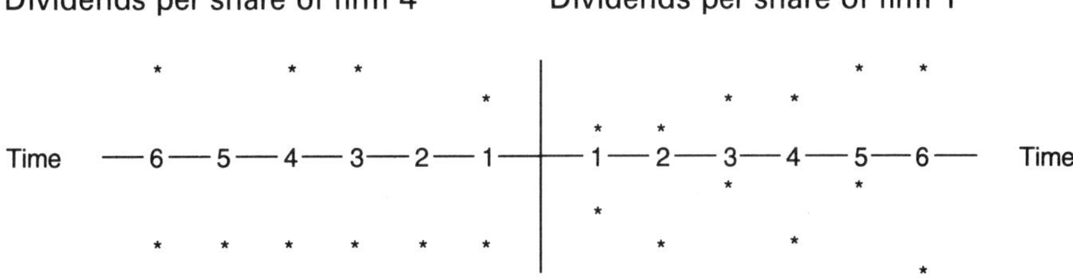

Dividends per share of firm 3   Dividends per share of firm 2

9 Discuss the conclusions related to the empirical evidence presented in this chapter. Are dividends relevant or irrelevant? Discuss.

10 Prepare an analog model summarizing the main points discussed in the present chapter.

11 How can spreadsheets be used to facilitate the application of the concepts discussed in this chapter?

Appendix 16A Scrip dividends and stock splits

A scrip dividend is a dividend in the form of new ordinary shares rather than cash. From the company point of view, scrip dividends have the following two advantages:

1. The cash that would be distributed to ordinary shareholders is retained within the firm for future investments.
2. Under the UK tax system, when the firm does not pay cash dividends, it can defer the payment of corporation tax. By doing so the firm improves its cash flow.

A share split is a distribution of new shares to the firm's current ordinary shareholders, where the number of the new shares is proportional to the number of shares already owned. In fact, the reason for a stock split is simple. A stock split reduces the market price per ordinary share which, in turn, will make the firm's ordinary shares more attractive to small investors.

Appendix 16B Dividend policy theories

The dividend-irrelevance theory

Assuming a perfect capital market and certainty, the price of a share *i* must be such that the rate of return to investors on share *i* will be the same over any given interval of time. This rate of return can be expressed as:

$$R_{it} = \frac{P_{it+1} - P_{it}}{P_{it}} + \frac{D_{it}}{P_{it}} \tag{16B.1}$$

where

P_{it} = the price of share *i* at the start of period *t*.
D_{it} = the dividends per share *i* paid on the last day of period *t*.

Equation (16B.1) can be used to express P_{it} as follows:

$$P_{it} = \frac{P_{it+1} + D_{it}}{1 + R_{it}} \tag{16B.2}$$

We assume no external financing. Then multiplying Equation (16B.2) by the number of ordinary shares at the start of period *t* yields

$$NS_tP_{it} = \frac{NS_tP_{it+1} + NS_tD_{it}}{1 + R_{it}} \tag{16B.3}$$

Equation (16B.3) is equivalent to

$$NS_tP_{it} = \frac{NS_tD_{it} + (NS_t + \mathrm{d}NS)P_{it+1} - \mathrm{d}NSP_{it+1}}{1 + R_{it}} \tag{16B.4}$$

where

$\mathrm{d}NS$ = the number of new shares sold during *t*.

Suppose that the firm uses its net profits for the period *t* and new ordinary shares to finance its investment. Then

$$\mathrm{d}NSP_{it+1} = I_t - (X_t - NS_tD_{it}) \tag{16B.5}$$

where

I_t = the amount invested in year *t*.
X_t = the net profits for the period *t*.

Substituting Equation (16B.5) into Equation (16B.4) and simplifying gives:

$$NS_tP_{it} = \frac{X_t - I_t + (NS_t + \mathrm{d}NS)P_{it+1}}{1 + R_{it}} \tag{16B.6}$$

Therefore the share price of a firm is independent of its dividend policy.

The dividend-relevance theory

The constant growth dividend valuation model for ordinary shares is given by:

$$P_0 = \sum_{t=1}^{\infty} \frac{D_t}{(1 + r_0)^t}$$

where

P_0 = the current market value of an ordinary share.

D_t = the ordinary dividends per share at the end of period t.
r_0 = the required rate of return of the ordinary shareholders.

If b is the fraction of retained earnings which is reinvested, then $1 - b$ is the dividend payout. The dividends per share at the end of period 1, 2, 3, ... can be, respectively, expressed as:

$$D_1 = (1 - b)E$$

$$D_2 = (1 - b)E(1 + bR)$$

$$D_3 = (1 - b)E(1 + bR)^2$$

etc.

where

E = the current earnings per share.
R = the rate of return on reinvested earnings.

Then the current market value of an ordinary share can be expressed as

$$P_0 = \sum_{t=1}^{\infty} \frac{(1 - b)E(1 + bR)^t}{(1 + r_0)^{t+1}}$$

The last equation can be rewritten as follows:

$$P_0 = (1 - b)E\frac{1}{1 + r_0}[1 + F + F^2 + \cdots +] \tag{16B.7}$$

where

$$F = \frac{1 + bR}{1 + r_0}$$

The term included in the brackets (see Equation (16B.7)) is an infinite geometric progression, thus,

$$[1 + F + F^2 + \ldots] = \frac{1 + r_0}{r_0 - bR} \tag{16B.8}$$

Substituting Equation (16B.8) into Equation (16B.7) and simplifying gives

$$P_0 = \frac{(1 - b)E}{r_0 - bR} \tag{16B.9}$$

Appendix 16C A statistical analysis of the dividends per share of Marks and Spencer

Testing the significance of the correlation coefficient

The sample correlation coefficient can be used to make inference about the unknown correlation coefficient of the population from which the sample was drawn. If we want to test for a non-zero correlation coefficient we have the following two hypotheses:

H_0: The coefficient correlation in the population is not significantly different from zero, that is, there is no relationship between the two variables.

H_1: The coefficient correlation in the population is significantly different from zero, that is, there is a relationship between the two variables.

If the number of pairs of observations is less than 50 and the dependent and independent variables of a simple linear regression are normally distributed, the following statistic has a t-distribution with $n - 2$ degrees of freedom:

$$ST = \frac{\sqrt{r^2(n-2)}}{\sqrt{1-r^2}}$$

where

n = the sample size
r = the sample correlation coefficient.

If ST is lower than the critical value of t for the specified significance level, then the null hypothesis is accepted.

Example 16C.1 Marks and Spencer: comparing the dividends per share in one year with the previous year's dividends per share

Column B of Figure 16C.1 contains the annual dividends per share of Marks and Spencer for the 14-year period from 1977 to 1990 (dividends are in pence). We want to examine how successive values of dividends per share (DPS) are related to each other.

This can be achieved by comparing the observed values of dividends per share for the 13 years 1978–90 with the same data but referring to 1977–89. For a single time series, when we compare the observation at one time period with the previous time period's observation, we say that we compare the time series with itself, lagged by one period. Column C in Figure 16C.1 stores the firm's dividends per share lagged by one year.

The statistic for the correlation coefficient's significance test is estimated as follows (a slight deviation occurs due to rounding):

$$ST = \frac{\sqrt{0.9378(13-2)}}{\sqrt{1-0.9378}} = 12.8819$$

The critical value of t for 11 degrees of freedom at the 5 per cent level of significance is 2.201 (the test is two-tailed). Since the computed value of 12.8819 is greater than 2.201, the null hypothesis of no relationship is rejected. Therefore, we can conclude that there exists a relationship between successive values of dividends per share.

Problem

Create the worksheet shown in Figure 16C.1.

A single linear dividend growth model
In view of the preceding analysis, we see that the dividends per share of Marks and Spencer are related linearly to the dividends per share of the previous year which in turn are related linearly to the dividend per share in the year before (with R-squared of 94.79 per cent, there exists a good approximation for a linear relationship). In this

```
-------------------------------------------------------------------------
     A      B           C          D     E         F         G         H    I
 1 M & S PLC:THE RELATIONSHIP BETWEEN t YEAR'S DPS AND t-1 YEAR'S DPS
 2 ------------------------------ |-----------------------------------
 3 YEAR     DPS 1-YEAR LAGGED DPS |
 4 ------------------------------ |
 5  1977  0.95                    |
 6  1978  1.24              0.95  |        Regression Output:
 7  1979  1.45              1.24  |Constant                       -0.1120
 8  1980  1.95              1.45  |Std Err of Y Est                0.4862
 9  1981  2.20              1.95  |R Squared                       0.9378
10  1982  2.63              2.20  |No. of Observations                 13
11  1983  3.02              2.63  |Degrees of Freedom                  11
12  1984  3.68              3.02  |
13  1985  3.76              3.68  |X Coefficient(s)    1.2102
14  1986  3.90              3.76  |Std Err of Coef.    0.0939
15  1987  4.50              3.90  |
16  1988  5.10              4.50  |T-STATISTIC        12.8819
17  1989  5.60              5.10  |T-STATISTIC        12.8819
18  1990  7.90              5.60  |
19                                |
20 ------------------------------ |-----------------------------------
-------------------------------------------------------------------------
```

Figure 16C.1. Calculating the statistic required to test the relationship between successive values of dividends per share

case, we can write:

$$D_1 = a + bD_0 \tag{16C.1}$$

where

D_1 = the dividends per share for year 1.
D_0 = the dividends per share for year 0.
a, b = the regression constant coefficients.

However, we can also write:

$$D_2 = a + bD_1 \tag{16C.2}$$

where

D_2 = the dividends per share for year 2.

Substituting Equation (16C.1) into Equation (16C.2) and manipulating we get:

$$D_2 = a + b(a + bD_0) = a(1 + b) + b^2 D_0$$

Using a similar method, we can prove the following expression:

$$D_t = a(1 + b + b^2 + \cdots + b^{t-2} + b^{t-1}) + b^t D_0 \tag{16C.3}$$

The use of Equation (16C.3) in 1-2-3 will make the analysis difficult. If, however, we follow the method below, the analysis can become less complicated. We can express the dividends for year $t - 1$ as follows:

$$D_{t-1} = a(1 + b + b^2 + \cdots + b^{t-2}) + b^{t-1} D_0 \tag{16C.4}$$

Subtracting Equation (16C.4) from Equation (16C.3) and simplifying yields:

$$D_t - D_{t-1} = ab^{t-1} + b^t D_0 - b^{t-1} D_0$$

or equivalently

$$D_t = D_{t-1} + g_{t-1} \tag{16C.5}$$

where

$$g_{t-1} = b^{t-1}[a + D_0(b - 1)] \quad (16C.6)$$

Equation (16C.5) states that the dividends per share for year t equal the dividends per share for year $t - 1$ plus a growth factor which does not remain constant over time. If $a = 0$, then Equation (16C.6) gives $g_t - 1 = b^{t-1}D_0(1 - b)$.

Example 16C.2 Calculating the dividends per share of Marks and Spencer plc using a single linear dividend growth model

In Example 16C.1 we estimated the coefficients of the regression between dividends per share and dividends per share lagged by one year (where for each variable the same number of observations are available). If the current dividends per share are 7.90 pence (see Figure 16C.2), then the value of the growth factor, stored in cell C12, is calculated as follows (here we use Equation (16C.6)):

```
+$C$5^(B12-1)*($C$4+$C$6*($C$5-1))
```

where cell C5 contains the value of the coefficient b, cell C4 contains the value of the coefficient a and cell C6 contains the current dividends per share. The contents of cell C12 are copied in the range C13 ... C18.

Next the dividends per share, stored in cell D12, are calculated by using the following formula (that is, the dividends per share at year $t - 1$ plus the corresponding dividend growth):

```
+D11+C12
```

Finally, the contents of cell D12 are copied in the range D13 ... D18.

Problem

Create the worksheet shown in Figure 16C.2 by using the `/Data Table 1` command.

```
      A          B           C               D              E
 1 CALCULATING THE DIVIDENDS USING A LINEAR DIVIDEND GROWTH MODEL
 2 ================================================================
 3
 4 Coefficient a           -0.1120
 5 Coefficient b            1.2102
 6 Current Dividends          7.90
 7
 8 ----------------------------------------------------------------
 9                Year Growth Factor  Dividends Per Share (p)
10 ----------------------------------------------------------------
11                   0        0.00              7.90
12                   1        1.55              9.45
13                   2        1.87             11.32
14                   3        2.27             13.59
15                   4        2.74             16.34
16                   5        3.32             19.66
17                   6        4.02             23.68
18                   7        4.86             28.54
19
20 ----------------------------------------------------------------
```

Figure 16C.2. Calculating the dividends per share with the aid of a linear growth model

Marks and Spencer: the statistical analysis of Lintner's study

Let us next investigate whether or not the statistical analysis of Lintner's study can be applied to the dividend policy of Marks and Spencer.

Example 16C.3 Marks and Spencer: applying the statistical model of Lintner

Figure 16C.3 shows the results from the regression between the dividends per share variable and two independent variables, which are earnings per share and dividends per share lagged by one year. For each variable 12 observations are available.

M & S:THE EARNINGS PER SHARE AND DIVIDENDS PER SHARE,1977-89

Year	Earnings Per Share (pence)	Dividends Per Share Lagged 1 Year (pence)	Dividends Per Share (pence)
1977	2.10		0.95
1978	2.64	0.95	1.24
1979	3.47	1.24	1.45
1980	3.62	1.45	1.95
1981	3.79	1.95	2.20
1982	4.61	2.20	2.63
1983	5.07	2.63	3.02
1984	6.37	3.02	3.68
1985	6.84	3.68	3.76
1986	8.35	3.76	3.90
1987	10.15	3.90	4.50
1988	12.07	4.50	5.10
1989	13.01	5.10	5.60

Regression Output:

Constant		0.3194
Std Err of Y Est		0.1784
R Squared		0.9869
No. of Observations		12
Degrees of Freedom		9
X Coefficient(s)	0.0922	0.8093
Std Err of Coef.	0.0552	0.1440
t-statistics --->	1.6706	5.6205

Figure 16C.3. Regression output (dependent variable: dividends per share; independent variables: earnings per share and dividends per share lagged by one year)

Note that the coefficient of the earnings per share variable is statistically insignificant on the basis of the *t*-test at the 95 per cent level of confidence. However, the *R*-squared of 98.69 per cent accepts the hypothesis that all the coefficients are statistically significant. These results provide a signal of multicollinearity (that is, there exists an exact or almost exact linear relationship between the independent variables). Indeed, if we regress the dividends per share variable on the earnings per share variable (where for each variable 12 observations are available) we get the results shown in Figure 16C.4. These results indicate a very high collinearity between the independent variables. One

```
-------------------------------------------------------------------------
        A              B                    C                    D
37            Regression Output:
38 Constant                                                   0.4108
39 Std Err of Y Est                                           0.3917
40 R Squared                                                  0.9228
41 No. of Observations                                            12
42 Degrees of Freedom                                             10
43
44 X Coefficient(s)                     0.3682
45 Std Err of Coef.                     0.0337
46                                     --------
47            t-statistics --->        10.9327
48 ---------------------------------------------------------------------
-------------------------------------------------------------------------
```

Figure 16C.4. The relationship between the variable of dividends per share lagged by one year and the earnings per share variable

way out of the extreme collinearity is to drop the earnings per share variable from the regression.

References and bibliography

Baker, H.K. *et al.* (1985) A survey of management views on dividend policy, *Financial Management*, Autumn, 78–83.

Black, F. and Scholes, M. (1974) The effects of dividend yield and dividend policy on common stock prices and returns, *Journal of Financial Economics*, **1**, May, 1–22.

Brennam, M. (1971) A note on dividend irrelevance and the Gordon valuation model, *Journal of Finance*, **26**, December, 1115–23.

Brittain, J.A. (1966) *Corporate Dividends Policy*. The Brookings Institution, Washington, DC.

Diacogiannis, G. and But, H.W. (1991) A survey of the dividend policy of London Stock Exchange companies, Warwick Paper in Management.

Divecha, A. and Morse, D. (1983) Market responses to dividend increase and changes in payout ratios, *Journal of Financial and Quantitative Analysis*, June, 163–73.

Donelly, B. (1985) The dividends discount model comes into its own, *Institutional Investor*, 157–62.

Elton, E.J. and Gruber, M.J. (1970) Marginal Stockholders' tax rates and the clientele effect, *Review of Economics and Statistics*, February, 68–74.

Gordon, M.J. (1959) Dividends, earnings and stock prices, *Review of Economics and Statistics*, **41**, May, 99–105.

Gordon, M.J. (1962) *The Investment, Financing and Valuation of a Corporation*. Irwin, Homewood, Ill.

Gordon, M.J. (1963) Optimal investment and financing policy, *Journal of Finance*, May, 264–72.

Kane, A., Lee, Y.K. and Marcus, A. (1986) Signalling, information content, and the reluctance to cut dividends, *Journal of Financial and Quantitative Analysis*, November, 855–70.

Kwan, C. (1981) Efficient market tests of the informational contents of dividend announcements: critique and extension, *Journal of Financial and Quantitative Analysis*, June, 193–206.

Lee, C.F., Wu, C.C. and Djarraya, M. (1987) A further empirical investigation of the dividend adjustment process, *Journal of Econometrics*, July, 267–85.

Lintner, J. (1956) Distribution of income of corporations among dividends, retained earnings and taxes, *American Economic Review*, **46**, May, 97–113.

Litzenberger, R. and Ramaswamy, K. (1979) The effect of personal taxes and dividends on capital asset prices: theory and empirical evidence, *Journal of Financial Economics*, June, 163–96.

Miller, M.H. and Modigliani, F. (1961) Dividend policy growth and the valuation of shares, *Journal of Business*, **34**, October, 411–33.

Miller, M.H. and Scholes, M. (1982) Dividends, taxes: some empirical evidence, *Journal of Political Economy*, December, 1118–41.

Partington, G.H. (1988) The determinants of dividend policy, Working Paper.

Pettit, R.R. (1972) Dividend announcements, security performance and capital market efficiency, *Journal of Finance*, December, 993–1007.

Pettit, R.R. (1977) Taxes, transactions costs and clientele effects of dividends, *Journal of Financial Economics*, December, 419–36.

Richards, P.H. (1976) Dividends controls—fact or fancy? *Investment Analyst*, April, 24–30.

Schnabel, J.A. (1981) The table dividend hypothesis, *Journal of Business Research*, **9**, March, 13–27.

Soter, D.S. (1979) Dividend controversy—what it means for corporate policy, *Financial Executive*, May, 38–43.

Walter, J.E. (1956) Dividend policies and common stock prices, *Journal of Finance*, **11**, March, 29–41.

Walter, J.E. (1967) *Dividend policy and Enterprise Valuation*. Wadsworth, Belmont, Calif.

Watts, R. (1973) The information content of dividends, *Journal of Business*, **46**, April, 191–211.

Whittington, G. (1972) The profitability of retained earnings, *Review of Economics and Statistics*, **54**, May, 152–60.

Wittebort, S. (1981) Do investors really care about dividends? *Institutional Investor*, March, 213–19.

Woolridge, J. (1983) Dividend changes and security prices, *Journal of Finance*, December, 1607–15.

17 Mergers

This chapter includes:

- Types of mergers
- Motives for mergers
- Evaluation of mergers
- Empirical studies on mergers

A firm can pursue internal expansion by investing in projects it developed itself (for example, building a new plant) or external expansion through a merger with another existing firm. Mergers are designed by some firms for rapid expansion and by others for survival. This chapter discusses the motives for mergers and presents the possible benefits and costs of a merger. It also reviews several empirical studies regarding the profitability of mergers.

Figure 17.1 shows how the concepts presented in this chapter are related to the financial management framework introduced in Chapter 2.

Basic concepts, definitions and examples

A merger takes place when the managers and shareholders of two or more previously existing companies agree to combine their companies into one new company. A takeover occurs when the management of a company (the buyer, acquirer, bidder or offeror) makes a unilateral offer to the shareholders of another company (the target, victim, acquiree, or offeree) to purchase their shares so as to gain control of the target company. Usually a takeover take place against the will of the managers of the target firm and it can be considered as a hostile merger. The offer to buy an interest in a company is often called a bid. In practice, the distinction between mergers and takeovers is not always easy. For this reason, we will use the two words interchangeably, however, we will distinguish between the company that initiates the merger and the target company.

Example 17.1 Three cases of merger offers

Thorn–EMI

On 16 October 1979 Thorn Electronics Industries (an engineering, electrical and TV rental company) made a bid for EMI (a music, electronics and leisure company). Below is presented the timetable of events:

16 October 1979: Thorn launched a bid of (approximately) £160 million for EMI.

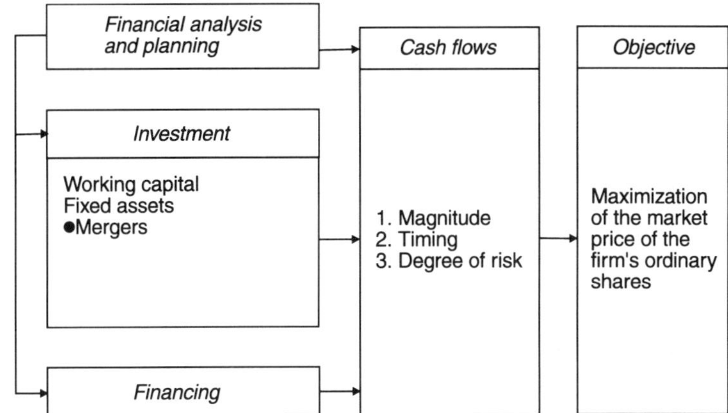

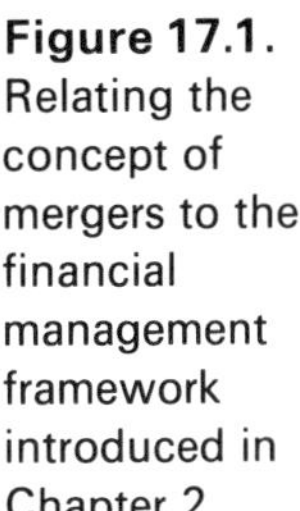
Figure 17.1. Relating the concept of mergers to the financial management framework introduced in Chapter 2

17 October 1979:	EMI rejected the Thorn bid.
6 November 1979:	Thorn revised the original offer.
13 November 1979:	Thorn issued an offer document.
5 December 1979:	Thorn's bid for EMI was successful.

Tesco–Hillards

In 1987 Tesco (a food retailer) made a takeover bid for Hillards (also a food retailer). The takeover timetable was as follows:

16 March 1987:	Tesco posted its offer to Hillards' shareholders.
27 March 1987:	Hillards' shareholders were advised not to accept.
7 April 1987:	Tesco extended its original offer until 1 May.
23 April 1987:	Hillards rejected Tesco and predicted an increase in profits of 45 per cent.
27 April 1987:	Tesco raised its offer.
15 May 1987:	56.5 per cent of Hillards' shareholders accepted the offer.
18 May 1987:	The board of Hillards accepted defeat.

GEC–Plessey

On 9 December 1985 GEC (an electrical, telecommunications and business systems company) announced a bid for Plessey (an electronics and telecommunications company). GEC was much larger than Plessey, GEC sales were £5,222 million in 1984/85, while Plessey's sales were £1,416 million during the same period. The timetable of events related to the bid is presented below:

3 December 1985:	GEC made a proposal of a £1.2 billion merger with Plessey. The offer was rejected by Plessey.
9 December 1985:	GEC announced its bid for Plessey.
23 December 1985:	Offer document was issued by GEC.
20 January 1986:	Bid was referred to the Monopolies and Mergers Commission.
6 August 1986:	The Monopolies and Mergers Commission decided to block the bid because it was against public interest.

Mergers generally are classified as follows:

- Horizontal This is a merger involving the combination of two or more firms that have similar business lines. For example, a horizontal merger occurred in 1985 when British Home Stores (a retailing firm) was combined with Habitat Mothercare (also a retailing firm).
- Vertical merger This is a merger between a firm and one of its suppliers or customers. For example, the combination in 1982 of the British Oxygen Company with Mountain Medical (a US company manufacturing mobile oxygen concentrators for home care) was a vertical merger.
- Conglomerate merger This is a merger involving two or more firms in unrelated business lines. The merger in 1986 between Hanson Trust (an industrial conglomerate) and Imperial Group (a tobacco manufacturer which also comprised two other divisions: brewing and leisure, and foods) provides an example of a conglomerate merger.

Motives for mergers

There are many motives for mergers of firms including synergy, undervalued assets, desire to grow, agency problems, securing a good management team and diversification.

Synergy

Synergy is often regarded as the primary motivation for many mergers. If synergy occurs, the market value of the combined firms is greater than the sum of the pre-merger values of the two individual firms. This (also known as the '2 + 2 = 5 effect') can be expressed algebrically as follows:

$$PV_C > PV_A + PV_B$$

where PV_C = the post-merger market value of the combined firms, PV_A = the pre-merger market value of firm A, and PV_B = the pre-merger market value of firm B. The above inequality will hold only if the merger provides an increase in revenues or a reduction in costs.

Synergistic effects can arise from operating economies, or increased market power, or through financial economies.

Synergistic operating economies

When the operating costs of a firm are reduced through a business combination, we say that the firm is experiencing synergistic operating economies. Such economies can result in a higher operating profit after tax and may be achieved by either horizontal, vertical, or even conglomerate mergers.

A horizontal merger may enable the combined firms to reduce fixed costs by eliminating duplicate plans (such economies are called plant economies), or unnecessary managerial positions and other personnel. A horizontal merger can also eliminate or reduce duplicate facilities such as research and development programmes. A vertical merger can drive down costs by reducing stocks levels, improving the distribution of products or combining separate research and sales departments. A conglomerate merger may also offer benefits such as improving computer services, consolidating the accounting departments or offering improved marketing programmes. Note that conglomerate mergers offer fewer opportunities to achieve operating economies than horizontal or vertical mergers.

Market power

Via a merger a firm may be able to increase monopolistic power, thereby achieving an increase in long-term profitability. For example, a horizontal merger may offer the potential to reduce the price of the combined firms' products, or it may allow a reduction in the price paid to a supplier by buying larger quantities. A vertical combination between a firm and either a supplier or a customer may also result in lower prices for the products of the combined firms.

Increasing market power may be necessary if one of the following situations occurs:

1 A decrease in demand of a firm's products or services. In this instance, a merger may take place in order to reduce the possibility of financial distress. For example, when the demand for houses decreases dramatically many building societies consider a merger as the only route to their survival.
2 An increase in sales of foreign goods and services in the domestic market. In this case, firms may be willing to merge in order to reduce such international competition. For example, business combinations between firms in the electronics and electrical industries are common in recent years.

Merger activity can be blocked by the Secretary of State if the Monopolies and Mergers Commission (MMC) decides that a proposed merger is against the interest of the public. For example, the MMC can decide that a merger is detrimental to the public interest on the grounds that it does not increase competition or it increases costs because of reduced competition.

Synergistic financial economies

When the financial costs of a firm are reduced through a business combination, we say that the firm is experiencing synergistic financial economies. A merger may offer the following benefits:

1 It can reduce the cost of capital by reducing the costs of issuing new securities. This can happen because the combined firms have larger requirements for external funds and the costs of issuing new securities are lower for larger quantities than smaller quantities.
2 A merger can reduce the risk of financial distress and thus improve the combined firms' ability to obtain additional debt. If borrowing is increased, the tax-deductible interest will also rise and an additional value attributable to the merger will be realized. As a result, the market value of the combined firms would be greater than the sum of the market values of the separate firms.
3 A merger may reduce the cost of debt because the earnings of the merged firms are likely to have more stability than the earnings of each of the firms separately. In such a situation, the combined firms can obtain a lower cost of capital since they offer extra protection to creditors. However, after the merger firm A must protect the debt of firm B and vice versa. The shareholders realize a gain from the lower cost of debt but they also pay a price by providing a guarantee to each other's borrowed funds. In an efficient market, the return will be zero because shareholders' costs equal their benefits.

4 A merger can reduce the taxes of the combined firms. If a profitable firm merges with a firm that has been operating at a net loss, then tax benefits are received which would otherwise be impossible to realize.

Undervalued assets

If the shares of the selling firm are undervalued, then from the viewpoint of the buying firm a merger may be considered cheap relative to an internal expansion. The ratio of the market value of a firm to its book value is called the valuation ratio:

$$VR = \frac{NS_B \times PV_B}{\text{Book value}}$$

where

NS_B = the number of ordinary shares of the selling firm.

PV_B = the selling firm's current market price per ordinary share.

The market value of a firm falls below the book value of its assets only if the firm operates at a very low profit or a loss. A valuation ratio below unity indicates an undervalued firm. The lower the valuation ratio, the greater the buying firm's return from a merger.

Growth

A firm can grow internally by investing in projects it develops itself (for example, purchasing and installing new fixed assets, developing new products, and so on) or externally via a merger. The latter method is frequently faster than the firm's growth through internal development. For example, suppose that a firm requires three years to expand its productive capacity in order to satisfy fully the demand for its products. In this case, the merger is the only way of achieving a fast growth. Furthermore, a merger enables the buying firm to acquire new products and facilities (for example, research and development facilities) quickly, avoiding the delays associated with an internal expansion.

Agency problem

The agency problem can arise when the managers of a firm make decisions which directly conflict with the objective of maximizing shareholders' wealth. Key directors with a little ownership interest may not provide support for a merger because they believe that it will affect significantly the security of their job or at least their autonomy. Alternatively, if there is no potential conflict between the shareholders and the key directors of a firm, then the latter group could be in favour of a merger. Agency problems may influence merger activity and thus the objective of maximizing shareholders' wealth.

Securing a good management team

A firm may desire to merge with another firm in order to secure a better management team. For example, a firm may decide to go the merger path because: (a) It is not well managed and it cannot hire a good management team without a merger, or (b) It wishes to obtain a key director or directors who can adequately manage opportunities in new fields and the merger is the only way to do so.

Diversification

It is frequently claimed that one of the important reasons for mergers is the reduction of risk achieved through diversification. Consider a portfolio comprised of the selling firm and the buying firm where the two firms are in unrelated industries. The rate of earnings on this portfolio is dependent on the rate of earnings of the two firms and the proportion of funds invested in each firm. Thus, we can apply the diversification principle used in portfolio theory as follows. If the earnings of the buying firm and the selling firm are not positively perfectly correlated, the merger will reduce the variability of the combined earnings series of the two firms. In view of the diversification motive for mergers, a reduction in the risk will result in a lower required rate of return on equity and this would have a favourable impact upon the firm's share price.

An argument against the diversification motive for mergers is that investors are able to diversify risk on their own (homemade diversification) and do not need the firm to diversify for them. In general, a merger cannot be considered as favourable if its motive is solely to increase the value of the firm's shares through the reduction of earnings variability.

On the other hand, it can be also argued that corporate diversification can provide the benefit of reducing the risk of financial distress. For example, a firm that faces liquidity problems may decide to go the merger avenue in order to solve its existing liquidity problems.

Figure 17.2 summarizes several motives for mergers.

Synergy

Synergistic operating economies
- Reduction of operating costs
- Acquisition of new facilities and programmes
- Improvement of product distributions

Market power

Synergistic financial economies
- Reduction of financing costs
- Provision of extra borrowing capacity
- Provision of greater tax benefits

Undervalued assets

Growth
- Faster expansion than internal growth permits
- Acquisition of new products and facilities

Agency problem

Securing a good management team
- Replacing inefficient management
- Gaining new management skills

Figure 17.2. Motives for mergers

Evaluating mergers

Assume that firm A (the buyer) wishes to analyse the possible purchase of firm B (the seller). The present value of the incremental cash flows created by the merger can be expressed as follows:

Present value of the incremental cash flows created by the merger	=	Post-merger maket value of the combined firms	−	Pre-merger market value of the buying firm	−	Pre-merger maket value of the selling firm

$$PV_{AB} = PV_C - PV_A - PV_B$$

The net present value to firm A from the merger with firm B is equal to the present value of the future benefits from the merger minus the merger's initial cost. The former equals the present value of firm B plus the present value of the incremental cash flows attributable to the merger. Therefore, the net present value of the merger to firm A would be:

Net present value of the merger to firm A	=	Pre-merger market value of the selling firm	+	Present value of the incremental cash flows created by the merger	−	The cost of the merger paid for the selling firm

$$NPV_A = PV_B + PV_{AB} - \text{Cost} \tag{17.1}$$

Appraising a merger deal: paying with cash

Suppose that the buying firm A offers to pay cash for the selling firm B. The analysis starts by establishing the range of the cash payment that firm A would be willing to pay for firm B. The minimum amount of cash payment acceptable to firm B for the merger is equal to its pre-merger market value. In this instance, we can write the following:

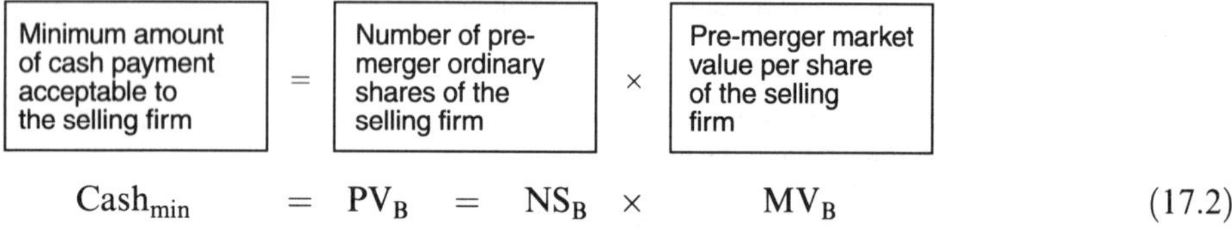

$$Cash_{min} = PV_B = NS_B \times MV_B \tag{17.2}$$

Example 17.2 Calculating the minimum amount of cash payment acceptable to EMI for the merger with Thorn

On 16 October 1979, Thorn launched a bid for EMI. Thorn offered to pay for EMI with its shares, but in this section we assume that the offered price was paid in cash. Before the bid, EMI had approximately 111.200 million shares outstanding (the actual number of shares was 111,165,302, the calculations below round this figure). Each share of EMI was selling at 95 pence. The minimum price acceptable to EMI can be calculated by applying Equation (17.2):

(111.200 million)(£0.950) = £105.640 million

The maximum amount of cash payment acceptable to firm A for the merger should be equal to the benefits created by the merger (in present value terms). Such an amount is calculated as follows:

Maximum amount of cash payment acceptable to the buying firm	=	Pre-merger market value of the selling firm	+	Present value of the incremental cash flows created by the merger

$$Cash_{max} = PV_B + PV_{AB} \quad (17.3)$$

Example 17.3 Calculating the maximum amount of cash payment acceptable to Thorn for the merger with EMI

Assume that the present value of the incremental cash flows created by the merger between Thorn and EMI is £53.932 million. Then the maximum amount acceptable to Thorn is calculated below.

$CASH_{MAX}$ = £105.640 million + £53.932 million = £159.572 million

The actual amount of cash payment (or the bid price) offered by the buying firm to the selling firm can be expressed as follows:

Amount of cash payment offered by the buying firm	=	Minimum price acceptable to the selling firm	+	Bid premium for the selling firm

$$Cash = PV_B + Premium \quad (17.4)$$

The bid premium is defined as the difference between the amount of cash offered to the selling firm and the minimum price acceptable by the selling firm.

Example 17.4 Calculating the bid premium offered by Thorn to EMI

Using the results from Examples 17.2 and 17.3 we can calculate the bid premium for EMI as follows:

£159.572 million – £105.640 million = £53.932 million

Thus, Thorn offered £53.932 million above the minimum price of £105.640 million.

A combination of Equations (17.1) and (17.4) gives:

Net present value of the merger to firm A	=	Present value of the incremental cash flows created by the merger	–	Bid premium for the selling firm

$$NPV_A = PV_{AB} - Premium \quad (17.5)$$

The last equation reveals that the net present value to firm A from the merger with firm B is dependent only on the present value of the incremental cash flows created by the merger and the bid premium paid to the selling firm. Thus, it is not necessary to perform a full capital budgeting analysis when we appraise mergers. Instead, a merger can be evaluated by estimating the present value of the incremental cash flows created by the merger and comparing it with the bid premium. If the latter is lower than the former, then the net present value to A of the merger with B is positive.

The selling firm's net present value of the merger with firm A equals the bid premium as shown below.

$$NPV_B = (PV_B + \text{Premium}) - PV_B$$
$$= \text{Premium} \quad (17.6)$$

Example 17.5 Sensitivity of the net present value of the merger to each merged firm with respect to changes in the bid premium

Imagine that it is 16 October 1979. The bid premium for EMI offered by Thorn is £53.932 million (see Example 17.4). Assume that the present value of the incremental cash flows created by the merger is estimated to be £53.932 million. Figure 17.3 provides a sensitivity analysis of the net present value of the merger with Thorn and the net present value of the merger with EMI with respect to changes in the bid premium. The `/DataTable 1` command of 1-2-3 is used with 'input cell 1', the sensitivity value stored in cell B4. (Note that the `/Range Format Text` command of 1-2-3 is employed.)

```
                  A                       B              C           D
 1 SENSITIVITY OF THE NPVs OF THE MERGER TO BID PREMIUM CHANGES
 2 ==============================================================
 3 Value Created by Merger               53.932
 4 Bid Premium                           53.932
 5 ----------------------------------------------------------------
 6                                              +B3-B4      +B4
 7                                        0.000     53.932       0.000
 8                                        6.742     47.191       6.742
 9                                       13.483     40.449      13.483
10                                       20.225     33.708      20.225
11 PREMIUM VALUES                        26.966     26.966      26.966
12                                       33.708     20.225      33.708
13                                       40.449     13.483      40.449
14                                       47.191      6.741      47.191
15                                       53.932      0.000      53.932
16 ----------------------------------------------------------------
```

Figure 17.3. Sensitivity of net present value of the merger to each merged firm with respect to changes in the bid premium

From these results it can be seen that the net present value to Thorn of the merger with EMI decreases as the premium increases, whereas the net present value to EMI of the merger with Thorn increases as the premium increases. The net present values are equal when the premium is equal to £26.966 million. The results of the sensitivity analysis are illustrated graphically in Figure 17.4.

Problems

1 Create the worksheet shown in Figure 17.3.
2 Create the graph shown in Figure 17.4.

Appraising a merger deal: paying with shares

When firm A (the buyer) offers to pay for firm B (the seller) with its shares, an exchange ratio must be established. The exchange ratio is defined as the number of

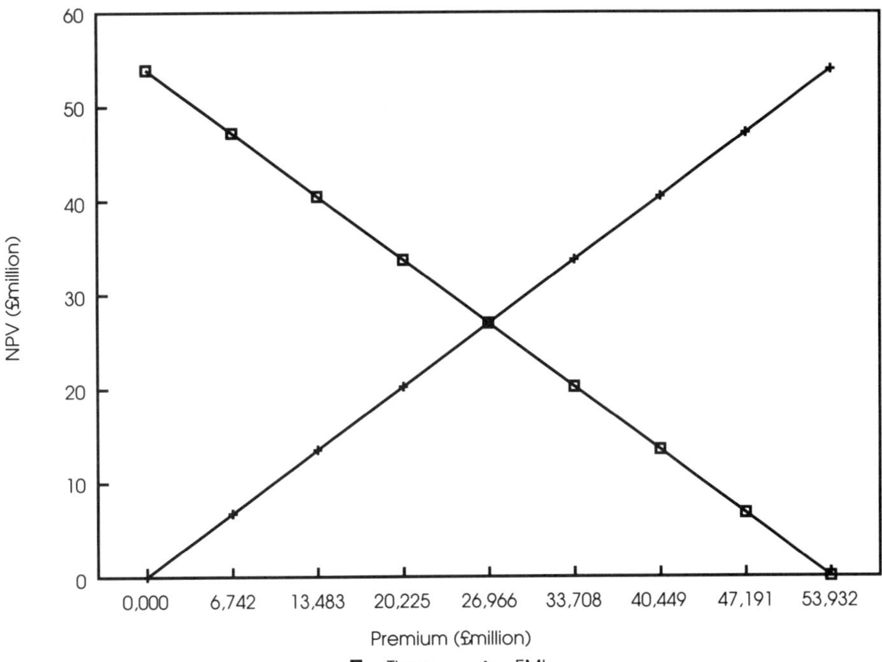

Figure 17.4. Sensitivity of the NPVs to bid premium changes

new shares of the buying firm that are exchanged for every outstanding share of the selling firm. The number of shares the buying firm issues to the selling firm equals the exchange ratio times the number of outstanding shares of the selling firm.

Example 17.6 Calculating the number of Thorn shares required to purchase EMI

On 16 October 1979, Thorn launched a bid for EMI offering 7 of its shares for every 20 shares of EMI. Thorn's bid provided an exchange ratio of 7/20. Before the bid, EMI had 111.200 million outstanding shares. Based on this data, the shareholders of EMI should have received 38.920 million (that is (7)(111.200 million)/20) of Thorn's shares in the event of a merger.

The post-merger share price of the combined firms is calculated as follows:

Post-merger share price of the combined firms	=	Post-merger maket value of the combined firms	÷	Post-merger number of shares of the combined firms

$$P_C = PV_C \div (NS_A + E \times NS_B)$$

where

NS_A = the number of pre-merger shares of firm A.

NS_B = the number of pre-merger shares of firm B.

E = the exchange ratio.

Example 17.7 Calculating the post-merger share price of the combined firms

Before the bid Thorn had 142.400 million shares (the actual number of shares was 142,138,930, the calculations below round this figure). Assuming the post-merger market value of the Thorn–EMI combination is estimated to be £743.412 million, the estimated post-merger share price of the combined firms would be:

$$P_C = \frac{£743.412 \text{ million}}{142.400 \text{ million} + (7)(111.200 \text{ million})/20} = £4.100$$

The total price that the buying firm pays to the selling firm can be found as follows:

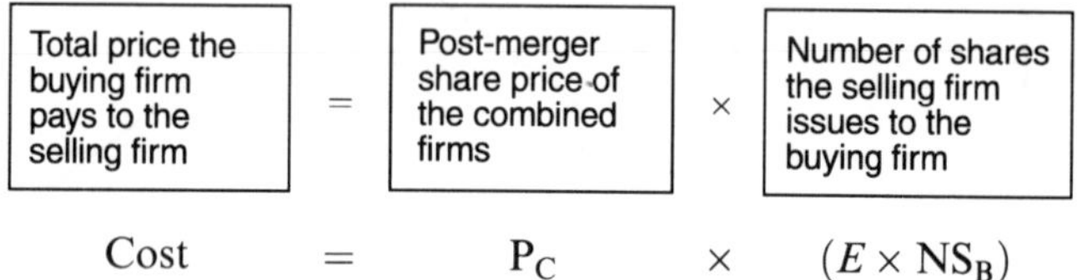

$$\text{Cost} = P_C \times (E \times NS_B)$$

Example 17.8 Calculating the total cost of a merger

Using the same data as in Examples 17.6 and 17.7, the total cost would be:

$$\text{Cost} = (£4.100)(7/20)(111.200) = £159.572 \text{ million}$$

Equation (17.1) can be used to calculate the net present value of the merger to firm A.

Example 17.9 Calculating the net present value of a merger

Using the data presented in Examples 17.6, 17.7 and 17.8, the present value of the incremental cash flows created by the merger would be equal to the post-merger market value of the combined firms minus the sum of the pre-merger present values of Thorn and EMI:

$$PV_{AB} = £743.412 \text{ million} - (111.200 \text{ million})(£0.950)$$
$$-(142.400 \text{ million})(£4.100) = £53.932 \text{ million}$$

where £4.100 is the pre-merger market price per share of Thorn.

The net present value of the merger to Thorn can be calculated by using Equation (17.1):

$$NPV_A = (111.200)(0.950) + 53.932 - 159.572 = 0$$

Therefore, if the additional present value created by the merger is £53.932, then the merger proposal is marginally acceptable to Thorn's shareholders.

The net present value of the merger for EMI would be

$$NPV_B = £159.572 - (111.200 \text{ million})(£0.950) = £53.932 \text{ million}$$

Shares are worth what investors are prepared to pay for them. Investors' expectations about the magnitude, timing and riskiness of a firm's expected cash flows influence its share price. If investors in aggregate expect bad news after a firm has announced the merger terms or if they think that the firm is paying too much for the merger, then the firm's share price will fall. Changes in the firm's share price affect the net present value of the merger to the firm. The net present value to a firm of a merger with another firm is also sensitive to changes in the exchange ratio and in the incremental cash flows created by the merger.

Example 17.10 The sensitivity of the net present value of a merger to each firm with respect to changes in the exchange ratio

Figure 17.5 calculates the net present value of the merger for Thorn and the net present value of the merger from EMI's viewpoint for different values of the exchange ratio (other things remain the same). The following calculations are recorded (see column E of Figure 17.5):

Item	Calculation/value	1-2-3 Formula
Bid price per share	0.350 × 4.100 = £1.435	+E4*E5
Total bid price	1.435 × 111.200 = £159.572 million	+E10*E8
Present value for Thorn	4.100 × 142.400 = £583.840 million	+E5*E6
Present value for EMI	0.950 × 111.200 = £105.640 million	+E7*E8
Incremental value	53.932	
Post-merger value	Sum of the values in C10..C14	
Post-merger share price	4.100	+E16/(E6+E4*E8)
Total cost	4.100 × 0.350 × 111.200 = £159.572 million	+E18*E4*E8
Premium	159.572 − 0.950 × 111.200 = £53.932 million	+E19-E7*E8
Net present value (Thorn)	53.932 − 53.932 = 0.0000 million	+E14-E20
Net present value (EMI)	£53.932 million	+E20
Thorn's share price gain	4.100–4.100 = £0.000	+E18-E5
EMI's share price gain	0.350 × 4.100 − 0.950 = £0.485	+E4*E18-E7

If the present value of the incremental cash flows is £53.932 and the exchange ratio is 7/20 (that is 0.350), the shareholders of the buying firm would realize a zero gain per share as the result of the merger. On the other hand, the shareholders of the selling firm would realize a gain of £0.485 per share.

The net present value of the merger to Thorn can be calculated by using two different procedures which provide identical results. For example, if the exchange ratio is 0.350 and the present value of the incremental cash flows is £58.932 million, then the net present value of the merger from Thorn's point of view is calculated as follows:

$$NPV_A = £105.640 + £53.932 - £159.572 = 0$$

or equivalently

$$NPV_A = £53.932 - £53.932 = 0$$

The second method just reveals that all we require to calculate the net present value of the merger to the selling firm is the present value of the incremental cash flows created by the merger and the bid premium.

	A	B	C	D	E
1	A TRADEOFF BETWEEN THE EXCHANGE RATIO AND THE NPV OF THE MERGER				
2	==				
3					
4	Exchange Ratio	0.220	0.250	0.300	0.350
5	Thorn's Share Price (£)	4.100	4.100	4.100	4.100
6	Thorn's Number of Shares (m)	142.400	142.400	142.400	142.400
7	EMI's Share Price (£)	0.950	0.950	0.950	0.950
8	EMI's Number of Shares (m)	111.200	111.200	111.200	111.200
9					
10	Bid Price Per Share	0.902	1.025	1.230	1.435
11	Total Bid Price	100.302	113.980	136.776	159.572
12	Present Value for Thorn	583.840	583.840	583.840	583.840
13	Present Value for EMI	105.640	105.640	105.640	105.640
14	Incremental Value	53.932	53.932	53.932	53.932
15					
16	Post-Merger Value (Thorn-EMI)	743.412	743.412	743.412	743.412
17					
18	Post-Merger Share Price	4.455	4.368	4.230	4.100
19	Total Cost	108.992	121.427	141.103	159.572
20	Premium	3.352	15.787	35.463	53.932
21	Net present value (Thorn)	50.580	38.145	18.469	0.000
22	Net Present Value (EMI)	3.352	15.787	35.463	53.932
23					
24	Thorn's Share Price Gain/Loss	0.355	0.268	0.130	0.000
25	EMI's Share Price Gain/Loss	0.030	0.142	0.319	0.485
26					

Figure 17.5. Examining the effect of changes in the values of the exchange ratio on the net present value to each firm

Note that the copy command is used to copy the contents of the range E10..E25 into the range B10..D25; see Figure 17.5.

Problem

Create the spreadsheet shown in Figure 17.5.

Example 17.11 The sensitivity of the net present value of a merger to each firm with respect to changes in the exchange ratio, share prices and incremental cash flows

Figure 17.6 shows the calculations of the net present value of the merger from Thorn's viewpoint and the net present value of the merger to EMI when changes of the following variables occur:

- Exchange ratio
- Share price of Thorn
- Share price of EMI
- Incremental value created by the merger

The formulae stored in column C are identical with those discussed in Example 17.10 (only the column location changes from E in Figure 17.5 to C in Figure 17.6).

The results assume that the price of Thorn's share decreases, this can be interpreted in several ways:

1. Investors in aggregate were expecting better news than a merger with EMI.
2. Investors had not much information to assess properly the benefits from the merger.

3 Investors believed that Thorn's investment might not be profitable because its initial cost (that is, the bid price) was too high.

It is also assumed that the price of EMI's share increases. The main reason for this probably is that investors in aggregate had anticipated an improvement in EMI from the merger with Thorn.

If the present value of the incremental cash flows created by the merger is greater than the bid premium, then the net present value of the merger to the buying firm is positive. For example, if the exchange ratio is 0.400 (or 8/20), the price of Thorn's shares is 380 pence, the price of EMI's shares is 110 pence and the present value of the incremental cash flows is £43.932 million, then the net present value of the merger to Thorn is –£2.112 million. For the same data, the net present value of the merger for EMI is £46.044 million.

Problem

Create the spreadsheet shown in Figure 17.6.

	A	B	C	E	F
1	SENSITIVITY OF THE NET PRESENT VALUE OF A MERGER TO FOUR VARIABLES				
2	===				
3					
4	Exchange Ratio	0.280	0.350	0.400	0.450
5	Thorn's Share Price (£)	4.400	4.100	3.800	3.500
6	Thorn's Number of Shares (m)	142.400	142.400	142.400	142.400
7	EMI's Share Price (£)	0.800	0.950	1.100	1.250
8	EMI's Number of Shares (m)	111.200	111.200	111.200	111.200
9					
10	Bid Price Per Share	1.232	1.435	1.520	1.575
11	Total Bid Price	136.998	159.572	169.024	175.140
12	Present Value of Thorn	626.560	583.840	541.120	498.400
13	Present Value of EMI	88.960	105.640	122.320	139.000
14	Incremental Value	63.932	53.932	43.932	31.932
15					
16	Post-Merger Value (Thorn-EMI)	779.452	743.412	707.372	669.332
17					
18	Post-Merger Share Price	4.492	4.100	3.785	3.478
19	Total Cost	139.850	159.572	168.364	174.046
20	Premium	50.890	53.932	46.044	35.046
21	Net Present Value (Thorn)	13.042	0.000	-2.112	-3.114
22	Net Present Value (EMI)	50.890	53.932	46.044	35.046
23					
24	Thorn's Share Price Gain/Loss	0.392	0.000	-0.315	-0.622
25	EMI's Share Price Gain/Loss	0.308	0.485	0.564	0.615
26					

Figure 17.6. Examining the effect of changes in the values of the exchange ratio, share prices and incremental cash flows on the net present value to each firm

The difficulty in evaluating pre-merger and post-merger values

The post-merger present value of the combined firms is dependent upon the pre-merger present value of each combined firm and the present value of the incremental cash flows created by the merger. If the market anticipates the possible event of a merger before its negotiations, the observed pre-merger share prices would reflect the perception of the investors about the merger offer. In this instance, the observed pre-merger present values would be biased. For example, if investors anticipate good news from the merger and this is reflected in share prices, then the pre-merger present values would be overestimated.

A method that deals with this problem, is to estimate the pre-merger values before the market anticipates the merger and then provide an adjustment to these values to reflect movements in the general share price index (see Lewellen and Ferri, 1983).

The estimation of the present value of the incremental cash flows created by the merger is difficult. For example, it is difficult to estimate the benefits derived from operating economies or know in advance the full impact of the elimination of bad management. It is probably better to estimate a range of values rather than attempting to estimate a single value.

One possible way to proceed with the estimation procedure is as follows: identify a possible motive for a forthcoming merger, then estimate the incremental cash flows created by this motive and discount the estimated cash flows at the appropriate required rate of return. Remember that the required rate of return should be associated only with the incremental cash flows from the merger and it would be a mistake to employ the selling (or buying) firm's cost of capital. If you feel that your estimation is good enough, then conduct a sensitivity analysis of the present value with respect to changes in the incremental cash flows and the required rate of return.

Cash versus shares in financing a merger

There are several factors which can influence the decision to finance a merger by cash or by ordinary shares, including the following:

1 A cash payment made to the ordinary shareholders of the selling firm is taxable if they realize capital gains from the transaction. On the other hand, if the shareholders of the selling firm exchange their shares in return for ordinary shares in the buying firm, then such a transaction is tax free. However, offering new shares to the shareholders of the target firm can dilute the earnings per share of the buying firm.
2 If the share price of the buying firm is overvalued, then offering shares to the selling firm can be less costly than paying the merger by cash.
3 If the buying firm offers cash and the merger is very profitable, then its shareholders will share all the future profits from the merger. A reverse situation could also occur. In that case, the shareholders of the buying firm will share all the future losses attributable to the merger.

The problem with the earnings per share in valuation of mergers

The initial effect of a merger on the buying firm's earnings per share (EPS) could provide misleading messages about the desirability of the merger, because it does not take into consideration the possibility of a future growth in earnings attributable to the merger.

Example 17.12 Future EPS with and without the merger when the initial dilution in the EPS is wiped out in the long run

Assume that firm A is considering the possibility of merging with firm B. Firm A has 140 million outstanding shares and firm B has 110 million outstanding shares. The exchange ratio is 6 shares of firm A for every 20 shares of firm B. Currently, firm A has £80 million of earnings after tax and firm B's earnings after tax amount to £4 million. Firm A estimates that, without the merger, its earnings will

	A	B	C	D	E	F	G
1			CASE 1:EARNINGS PER SHARE AND GROWTH				
2			===================================				
3	Exchange Ratio			0.300	Growth rate for Firm B		6.00%
4	Growth Rate for Firm A			14.00%	No of Shares for B (m)		110.000
5	No of Shares of Firm A(m)			140.000	Earnings of Firm B (m)		£4.000
6	Earnings of Firm A (m)			£80.000			
7							
8		BUYING:		SELLING:		COMBINED FIRMS:	
9	YEAR	EARNINGS	EPS	EARNINGS	EPS	EARNINGS	EPS
10							
11	1979	£91.200	£0.651	£4.240	£0.039	£106.640	£0.616
12	1980	103.97	0.743	4.494	0.041	127.222	0.735
13	1981	118.52	0.847	4.764	0.043	149.986	0.867
14	1982	135.12	0.965	5.050	0.046	175.200	1.013
15	1983	154.03	1.100	5.353	0.049	203.171	1.174
16	1984	175.60	1.254	5.674	0.052	234.246	1.354
17	1985	200.18	1.430	6.015	0.055	268.818	1.554
18	1986	228.21	1.630	6.375	0.058	307.336	1.777
19	1987	260.16	1.858	6.758	0.061	350.305	2.025
20							

Figure 17.7. Future EPS with and without the merger between firms A and B

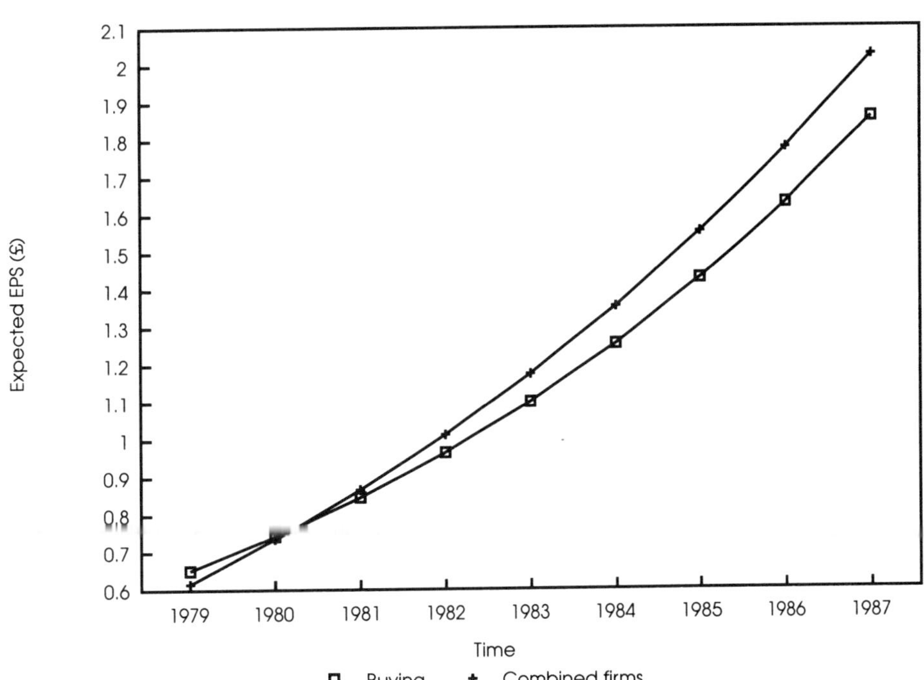

Figure 17.8. Effect of merger on EPS: an initial EPS gain from the merger

be expected to increase by 14 per cent each year for the next nine years. With the merger, however, firm A expects to realize higher earnings after tax and column F of Figure 17.7 shows those estimated earnings.

Figure 17.7 reveals that the EPS without the merger will be greater than the EPS with the merger for the years 1979 and 1980. After 1980, the combined firms will realize a higher EPS relative to the EPS of firm A without the merger (the post-merger number of shares is: (140 million)(110 million)0.3 = 173 million).

Although there is an initial dilution in EPS, it can be seen that over the years firm A will realize some benefits from merging with firm B. It is apparent that the initial EPS dilution can provide a misleading signal about the desirability of a merger. Thus, decisions about mergers should not be based solely upon the initial trend of the EPS. Such decisions require a long-run analysis and it could be better to rely upon a present value investment analysis.

The EPS with and without the merger are graphed in Figure 17.8.

Problem

Create the worksheet shown in Figure 17.7.

Example 17.13 Future EPS with and without the merger when the initial gain in the EPS is wiped out in the long run

This example presents a reserve situation to that discussed in Example 17.12. In the present case, firm A is considering a merger opportunity with firm D. The relevant data is given in Figure 17.9 (number of shares and earnings are in millions). It is assumed that the merger of firm A with firm D will produce a favourable effect upon future earnings and the earnings after tax for the combined firms are expected to grow by £20 million each year for the next nine years. It can be seen that the EPS of the combined firms rise initially as the result of the merger but over the years the combined EPS is lower than the EPS of firm A without the merger (note that the post-merger number of shares is 152.75 million).

As in the case of Example 17.12, the results shown in Figure 17.9 should reveal the mistake that can be made by focusing on EPS analysis rather than a present value investment analysis.

Figure 17.10 illustrates graphically the EPS of firm A without and with the merger.

Problem

Create the worksheet shown in Figure 17.9.

	A	B	C	D	E	F	G
1			CASE 2:EARNINGS PER SHARE AND GROWTH				
2			====================================				
3	Exchange Ratio (7/20)			0.350	Growth rate for Firm D		5.00%
4	Growth Rate for Firm A			14.00%	No of Shares for D (m)		65.000
5	No of Shares of Firm A(m)			130.000	Earnings of Firm D (m)		£6.000
6	Earnings of Firm A (m)			£80.000			
7	-------						
8		BUYING:		SELLING:		COMBINED FIRMS:	
9	YEAR	EARNINGS	EPS	EARNINGS	EPS	EARNINGS	EPS
10	-------						
11	1979	£91.200	£0.702	£6.300	£0.097	£117.500	£0.769
12	1980	103.97	0.800	6.615	0.102	130.583	0.855
13	1981	118.52	0.912	6.946	0.107	145.469	0.952
14	1982	135.12	1.039	7.293	0.112	162.410	1.063
15	1983	154.03	1.185	7.658	0.118	181.691	1.189
16	1984	175.60	1.351	8.041	0.124	203.638	1.333
17	1985	200.18	1.540	8.443	0.130	228.624	1.497
18	1986	228.21	1.755	8.865	0.136	257.072	1.683
19	1987	260.16	2.001	9.308	0.143	289.464	1.895
20	-------						

Figure 17.9. Future EPS with and without the merger between firms A and D

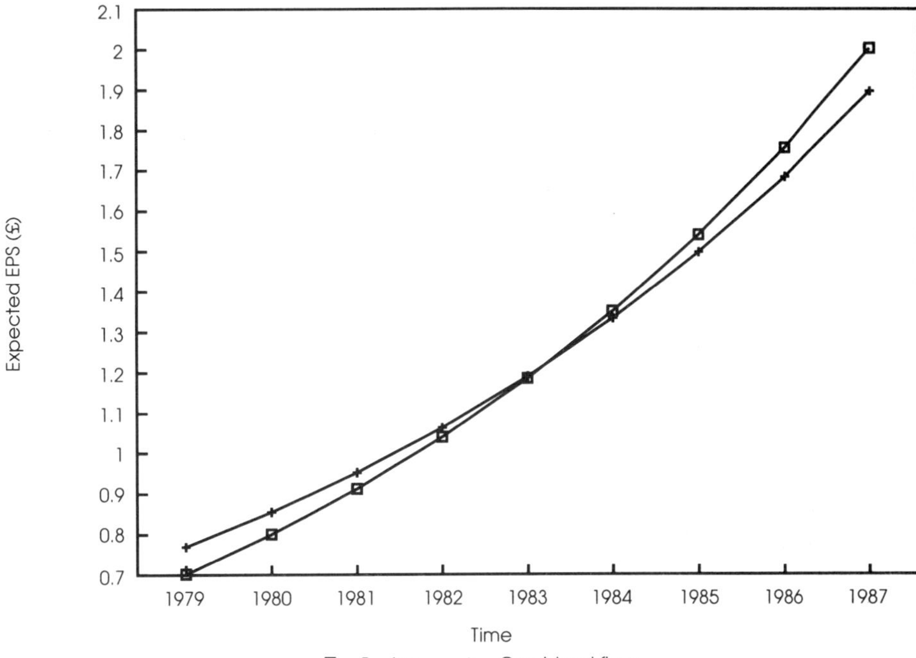

Figure 17.10. Effect of merger on EPS: an initial EPS dilution from the merger

Price/earnings (P/E) ratios are frequently utilized in appraising the possibility of a merger. The P/E exchange ratio can be defined as follows:

$$\text{P/E exchange ratio} = \frac{\text{Pre-merger P/E ratio of the buying firm}}{\text{Pre-merger P/E ratio of the selling firm}}$$

Example 17.14 shows the following: If the P/E exchange ratio is lower (higher) than 1.0, then the earnings per share of the combined firms will be lower (greater) than the pre-merger earnings per share of the buying firm.

Example 17.14 Comparing the EPS of the combined firms with those of the buying firm

Assume that firm A is considering two mergers: with firm B and firm D. The EPS of each of the three firms are shown in Figure 17.11. The P/E exchange ratio stored in cell C14 is calculated as follows:

$7.700/59.427 = 0.130$

The P/E exchange ratio is lower than 1 and thus we should expect the earnings per share of the combined firms to be lower than the earnings per share of the buying firm. We assume that the cost of merger of firm A with firm B is £257.400 million and the post-merger price per share for firm A is the same as that before the merger (the assumption is made for simplicity). Using this data we calculate the earnings per share of the combined firms as follows (a slight deviation occurs due to rounding):

$£84.000/(140.340 + 58.104) = £0.424$

	A	B	C	D	E
1		EARNINGS PER SHARE AND P/E EXCHANGE RATIO			
2					
3					
4	BEFORE THE MERGER	FIRM A	FIRM B	FIRM D	
5					
6	Earnings After Tax	£80.740	£4.340	£40.320	
7	No of Shares	140.340	110.220	104.345	
8					
9	EPS	£0.575	£0.039	£0.386	
10	Share Price	£4.430	£2.340	£2.500	
11					
12	P/E Ratio	7.700	59.427	6.470	
13					
14	P/E Exchange Ratio		0.130	1.190	
15					
16					
17	AFTER THE MERGER		FIRM AB	FIRM AD	
18					
19	Cost of Merger		£257.400	£260.000	
20	No of Shares		58.104	58.691	
21	Earnings After Tax		£84.000	£120.320	
22					
23	EPS		£0.424	£0.606	
24					

Figure 17.11. The initial impact of P/E ratio on EPS of the combined firms

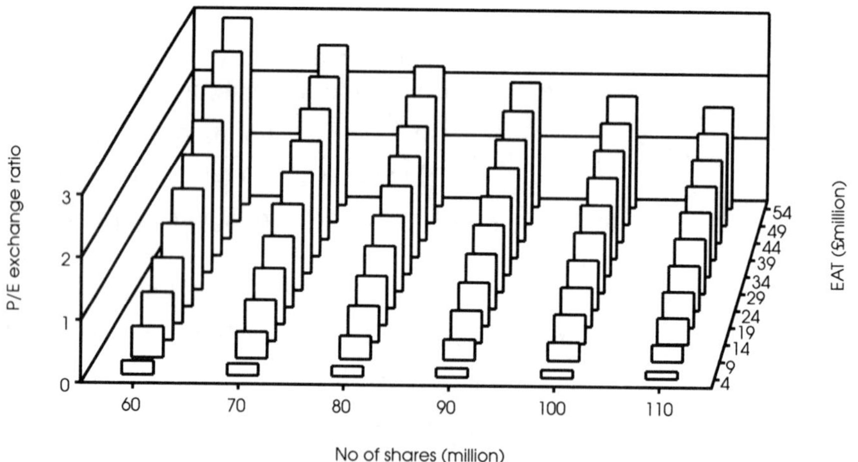

Figure 17.12. Sensitivity of P/E exchange ratio to changes in earnings after tax and number of shares

This value is lower than the pre-merger earnings per share of the buying firm of £0.575. A similar analysis shows that if the P/E exchange ratio is greater than 1.0, then the earnings per share of the combined firms will be greater than the pre-merger earnings per share of the buying firm (see column D in Figure 17.11).

Figure 17.12 shows the sensitivity of the P/E exchange ratio to changes in earnings after tax and number of shares. Both the earnings after tax and number of shares are referred to the selling firm. The range for earnings after tax is £4 million to £54 million in steps of £5 million, while the range for the number of shares is 60 million to 110 million in steps of 10 million. The P/E exchange ratio increases with the earnings after tax, while it decreases as the number of shares increases.

Problem

1 Create the worksheet shown in Figure 17.11.
2 Use 1-2-3's `/Data Table 2` command to conduct a sensitivity analysis of the P/E exchange ratio with respect to earnings after tax and number of shares of the selling firm (employ for earnings after tax the sensitivity range of £10 million to £90 million in steps of £10 million and for the number of shares the range of 50 million to 130 million in steps of 10 million).

The rule to accept a merger whenever the P/E exchange ratio is greater than 1.0 seems to be simple, but the use of this approach can lead to a wrong decision. The analysis using the P/E exchange ratio is based solely on the initial impact of the EPS and not on the EPS in the long run. However, we showed earlier the problems associated with an EPS criterion in mergers evaluation.

Methodological issues

There have been numerous studies attempting to evaluate the performance of mergers. These studies can be broadly classified into those using accounting data and those employing share returns.

Studies using accounting data

Early empirical studies on the area of merger performance used accounting data to examine the financial characteristics of the firms involved in business combinations. Some studies are based on univariate analysis and other on multivariate analysis. The studies in the former group have considered a number of accounting variables from a sample of firms engaged in business combinations (for example, rate of return on net assets, price earnings ratio, earnings per share, sales per share, and so on). These variables were compared with some control variables (for example, industry average ratios, average ratios derived from a control group, and so on).

A multivariate analysis study combines a number of financial variables together into one measurement which can be used for judging merger benefits. The most common multivariate analysis models employed have been regression analysis (for example, Shick and Jen, 1974) and discriminant analysis (for example, Tzoannos and Samuels, 1972). Figure 17.13 summarizes the results of several studies using accounting data.

All of the studies presented in Figure 17.13 reached the same conclusion: mergers seem to be unprofitable from the acquiring firm's viewpoint. In terms of the common financial characteristics of the acquired firms, the results seem to be less consistent. Generally, the acquired firms had low profitability and low P/E ratio before the acquisition; other financial characteristics do not seem to play an important role in the acquisition decision. However, these studies have been criticized on several grounds, for example, sample size used, reliability and homogeneity of data employed, control devices utilized to screen out other events, problems of capturing the performance of share prices over short-term periods (for example, using daily data), methodologies employed, and so on.

Studies using share returns

A number of studies attempted to examine the average behaviour of abnormal share

Author(s)	Country/sample period	Measure(s)	Conclusion
Kelly (1967)	USA/1946–60	• Percentage changes in share price • P/E ratio • EPS • Sales per share • Profit margin	There were no substantial benefits for the acquiring firms' shareholders
Hogarty (1970)	USA/1953–64	• Indices of investment performance based on changes in share prices	Investment performance of acquiring firms was worse than that of their respective industries
Singh (1971)	UK/1955–60	• Rate of return on net assets	• Mergers did not increase the profitability of acquiring firms • The acquired firms in the sample tended to have low valuation ratios and low profitability when they were compared against the companies of a control group
Tzoannos and Samuels (1972)	UK/1967–68	Their discriminant model included: • Trend in gearing • Volatility in gearing • Level of gearing • Trend in the ratio of profit to capital employed • Volatility of profit to capital • The acid test to liquidity • P/E ratio; • Cash flow ratio • Trend in dividends per share; • Volatility of dividends per share	The acquiring firms had the following characteristics as compared with the acquired firms: • Above average downward trend in capital gearing • A lower absolute level of capital gearing • A higher than average increase in profits to capital employed • A higher than average increase in the trend of dividends The acquired firms had the following characteristics as compared with the acquiring firms: • A higher rate of increase in capital gearing • A higher absolute level of capital gearing • A slower increase in profits • A slower rate of increase in dividends • A lower P/E ratio
Utton (1974)	UK/1961–70	• Rate of return on net assets	Mergers did not provide substantial profits for the shareholders of the acquiring firm
Shick and Jen (1974)	USA/1958–66	Their regression model included: • Share dividends; • Short- and long-term dividend growth rates • A gearing measure • A measure of earnings variability • A size variable • A firm-specific variable	There were significant merger benefits to the shareholders of the acquiring firms during the first year after the merger, but insignificant benefits for the next two years

Figure 17.13. A summary of studies on mergers using accounting data

returns of firms preceding and following their announcement of business combinations. The methodology used is similar to that introduced by Fama *et al.* (1969). Namely, it employs a security return generating model in which the rate of return of a security during a period t is divided into two parts: (a) that part of the return on the security which captures the common factor (or factors) adjustment to any new information generated during period t; and (b) that part which captures the effect of new information arriving at period t and regarding events specific to the firm (for example, the announcement of a merger). In evaluating abnormal returns the following security return generating models can be used:

- A single index model or a multi-index model.
- A model proposed by Fama and MacBeth (1973).
- The ex-post form of the capital asset pricing model.

A time-series methodology using a single or multi-index model

A single index model describes security returns as follows:

$$R_{it} = a_i + b_i R_{mt} + e_{it}$$

where

R_{it} = the rate of return for security i over period t.

R_{mt} = the rate of return on a market index over period t.

a_i = the return on security i when the return in the market is zero.

b_i = the sensitivity of security i's rates of return to the fluctuations in the market index' rates of return. The beta coefficient is a measure of systematic risk.

e_{it} = a stochastic disturbance term in the return on security i at period t assumed to have zero mean and constant variance. It is also assumed that the disturbance term is independent of the market index's rates of return and uncorrelated across i. This term can be interpreted as a measure of abnormal returns of security i in period t.

Abnormal returns can be estimated by employing the following methodology:

Step 1 Estimate the coefficient a_i and b_i for each security in the sample by regressing the rates of return of each security against the rates of return of the market index.

Step 2 Use the estimates from Step 1 and compute the residual or abnormal return of security i at period t as follows:

$$\hat{e}_{it} = R_{it} - \hat{a}_i - \hat{b}_i R_{mt}$$

where

$\hat{a}_i, \hat{b}_i$ = the ordinary least squares estimates of the single index parameters.

Step 3 Compute for each time period prior to and subsequent to the announcement period the average residual across firms.

Step 4 Compute the cumulative average residuals for any time period desired.

Step 5 Examine the statistical significance of the cumulative average residuals.

According to this methodology the acquiring firm's return is related in each period to the return of the market index which is common to all firms. Thus, this methodology utilizes the market portfolio as the control group. If all events other than the business combination that influence the return of a firm have the same impact on the firm's control group, then we can use the market model to isolate the effect of any non-market event (for example, the announcement of a merger) on shareholders' returns. Consequently, the abnormal return in a particular period can be calculated as the difference between actual returns and predicted returns.

A similar procedure can be followed in the case when security returns can be described with the aid of a multi-index model.

The Fama–MacBeth Methodology

The capital asset pricing model is expressed as follows:

$$E(R_i) = E(R_z) + b_i[E(R_m) - E(R_z)]$$

where

$i = 1, 2, \ldots, N.$

$N =$ the number of securities in the market portfolio.

$E(R_i) =$ the expected rate of return on security i over period t.

$E(R_m) =$ the expected rate of return of the market portfolio over period t.

$E(R_z) =$ the expected rate of return in period t on the minimum variance portfolio whose rate of return is uncorrelated with that of the market portfolio. Portfolio z is riskless with respect to the market portfolio.

$b_i =$ the risk of security i in the market portfolio relative to the total risk of the market portfolio.

The capital asset pricing model is cast in terms of expectations. Since data on expectations does not exist, the capital asset pricing model can be used in empirical work only if it is transformed into an equation that relates realized variables. The following stochastic process generating period-by-period security returns is suggested (see Fama, 1976):

$$R_{it} = c_{1t} + c_{2t}b_{it} + e_{it}$$

where

$i = 1, 2, \ldots, N.$

$R_{it} =$ the rate of return on security i during period t.

$c_{1t}, c_{2t} =$ variables in the stochastic process which generate security returns. These two variables can vary in a stochastic fashion from period to period, but the expected value of the first variable should be equal to $E(R_z)$ and the expected value of the second one should be equal to $E(R_m) - E(R_z)$.

$b_{it} =$ the relative risk of security i at period t.

$e_{it} =$ a stochastic disturbance term in the return on security i at period t. This term is assumed to have zero mean, to be independent of b_i and uncorrelated across i.

Abnormal returns can be estimated by adopting the following methodology:

Step 1 Estimate the coefficient c_{1t} and c_{2t} by employing the methodology of Fama and MacBeth, 1973.

Step 2 Using the estimates from Step 1 compute the residual or abnormal return of security i at period t as follows:

$$\hat{e}_{it} = R_{it} - \hat{c}_{1t} - \hat{c}_{2t}\hat{b}_{it}$$

Step 3 Compute for each time period prior to and subsequent to the announcement period the average residual across firms.

Step 4 Compute the cumulative average residuals for any time period desired.

Step 5 Examine the statistical significance of the cumulative average residuals.

This methodology is also called the Fama–MacBeth methodology because it was used by Fama and MacBeth in 1973 in an attempt to test the capital asset pricing model. The use of the Fama–MacBeth methodology provides a way of measuring the acquiring firm's performance as a result of a merger, relative to the performance of the market index. In view of this method, the abnormal return of a security in a particular period is equal to the difference between the actual security rate of return and the estimated return predicted from the two-parameter capital asset pricing model.

A time-series methodology using the ex-post form of the CAPM

This methodology uses the ex-post form of the capital asset pricing model (see also Chapter 9) which describes the following security return generating model:

$$R_{it} - R_f = a_i + b_i[R_{mt} - R_f] + u_{it} \tag{17.7}$$

where

$i = 1, 2, \ldots, N$.

N = the number of securities in the market index.

R_{it} = the rate of return on security or portfolio i over period t.

R_{mt} = the rate of return on the market index over period t.

R_f = the risk-free rate over period t.

a_i = a measure of the average level of performance.

b_i = the systematic risk of security i.

u_{it} = A stochastic disturbance term assumed to have zero mean and constant variance. It is also assumed that the disturbance term is independent of $R_{mt} - R_f$ and uncorrelated across i. This term can be interpreted as a measure of abnormal returns of security i in period t.

Abnormal returns can be estimated by following the procedure below.

Step 1 For each security in the sample estimate the coefficients of the regression represented by Equation (17.7) over a period prior to the announcement of the event.

Step 2 Estimate the residuals of security i at period t as follows:

$$\hat{u}_{it} = R_{it} - \hat{a}_i - \hat{b}_i R_{mt} - (1 - \hat{b}_i)R_f$$

Step 3 Compute for each time period prior to and subsequent to the announcement period the average residual across firms.
Step 4 Compute the cumulative average residuals for any time period desired.
Step 5 Examine the statistical significance of the cumulative average residuals.

The use of this methodology provides a way of measuring the acquiring firm's performance as a result of a merger relative to that performance over another time period. The regression coefficients are estimated over a period before the event is announced. These coefficients can be utilized to predict the firm's return from the post-event values of the market return and risk-free rate. The difference between the actual and predicted security return, based on the pre-event estimated regression coefficients, measures the effect of the merger on the shareholder returns.

Figure 17.14 presents a summary of several studies which employed share returns and one of the three methodologies described previously.

Discussion of the empirical evidence on mergers

The results are fairly consistent across different studies in inferring that the shareholders of the target firm earn positive abnormal returns. These returns may be attributable to the (anticipated) premium paid by the acquiring firm which is always above the current market price of the target firm (Haugen and Udell, 1972). Another possible explanation could be the competition among potential acquiring firms which results in a rise in the price of the target firm (Mandelker, 1974).

Similarly, positive abnormal returns to target firms in successful tender offer proposals have been reported by Dodd and Ruback (1977), Kummer and Hoffmeister (1978), Bradley (1980), and Bradley *et al.* (1983). A possible reason given to justify these substantial returns and the premiums paid by the acquiring firms is the market's anticipation of significant improvements in the efficiency of operations of the target firms.

Several studies have found that the shareholders of the target firms experienced average abnormal negative returns before the actual event of the merger or tender offer indicating that, on average, target firms had not been performing up to their potential. A possible suggestion emerging from these studies is that mergers or tender offers provided profitable investment opportunities for the target firms in the sense of securing better management or more efficiency in utilizing the target firms' assets. The reported results appear to be consistent with the 'improved management' hypothesis which asserts that mergers provide a way by which the market system replaces inefficient management (see also Mandelker, 1974; Malatesta, 1983).

The US studies cited in Figure 17.14 are relatively consistent in deducing that the shareholders of the acquiring firms earned positive cumulative abnormal returns over several months before the announcement period of the merger or tender offer. Several explanations have been suggested for these abnormal returns, including the following:

1 Leaks associated with the specific merger or tender offer (Keown and Pinkerton, 1981).
2 Good performance over a period of time encourages firms to expand through mergers (Langetieg, 1978).
3 Managers wish to maximize the firm's size (Mueller, 1969).

(a) A time series methodology using a single or a multi-index model

Author(s)	Country/sample period	Interval/model	Conclusions
Halpern (1973)	USA/1950–65	Monthly rates of return/ a multi-index model	In terms of annualized rates of return, both the acquiring and acquired firms had positive abnormal returns over the period between 7 months before a merger was announced and the date of the announcement
Franks *et al.* (1977)	UK/1955–72	Monthly rates of return/ a single index model and a multi-index model	• The acquiring firms earned small positive abnormal returns 4 months before the completion of a merger • The market begins to anticipate megers at least 3 months, on average, before they were announced • After a merger the combined firms realized net gains from merging within the industry
Firth (1980)	UK/1969–75	Monthly rates of return/ a single index model	• The shareholders of the acquiring firms did not observe abnormal returns in the 12 months before a bid was announced • During the month of a bid the acquiring firms experienced negative returns which were statistically significant • After a bid settles the shareholders of the acquiring firms did not realize any significant return trend

(b) The Fama and MacBeth (1973) methodology

Author(s)	Country/sample period	Interval/model	Conclusions
Mandelker (1974)	USA/1941–62	Monthly rates of return	• On average, the shareholders of the acquiring firms experienced positive but not statistically significant abnormal returns • The share prices of the sample firms at the time of the merger reflect fully all the economic gains expected from the merger. This indicates that the capital market is efficient with respect to information released in merger announcements • On average, the shareholders of the acquired firms earned abnormal positive returns over the 7 months prior to the merger month. These returns were statistically significant for the last 5 months which included the announcement date
Ellert (1976)	USA/1950–72	Monthly rates of return	• On average, the shareholders of the acquiring firms earned large abnormal positive returns over 100 months preceding the filing of anti-merger complaints • The market does not adjust share prices downward in anticipation of mergers' complaints made by antitrust authorities. This shows that the market is efficient with respect to the information conveyed by a Section 7 ruling (such a section forbids business combinations that eliminate competition)
Kummer and Hoffmeister (1978)	USA/1956–74	Monthly rates of return	• On average, the shareholders of the acquiring firms realized positive returns during the period between 24 and 4 months before the tender offer was announced. Also positive returns were realized around and including the month in which the tender offer was announced • There were substantial and positive abnormal returns for the shareholders of the acquired firms during the month of the tender offer announcement
Bradley (1980)	USA/1962–77	Daily rates of return	For the successful tender offers, the shareholders of the acquiring firms realized an excess capital gain within 40 days of the tender offer

(c) A time-series methodology using the ex-post form of the CAPM

Author(s)	Country/sample period	Interval/model	Conclusions
Dodd and Ruback (1977)	USA/1958–76	Monthly rates of return	• On average, the shareholders of the acquiring firms experienced positive abnormal returns before the announcement of the tender offer • For successful tender offers there were small and positive statistically significant returns for the acquiring firm's shareholders during the month of the first public announcement of the tender offer • Target firms of unsuccessful tender offers earned significant positive abnormal returns in the month the offer was announced
Langetieg (1978)	USA/1929–69	Monthly rates of return	• On average, the shareholders of the acquiring firms earned positive excess returns over 60 months before the point when information about the merger was announced • The acquired firms observed a significant gain over the period between 6 months and 1 month before the merger. The gain of acquired firms is substantially higher than for the acquiring firms • After the merger the excess returns (adjusted for control group influence) were not significally different from zero, revealing a normal risk-adjusted return to the shareholders of the combined firms
Malatesta (1983)	USA/1969–74	Monthly rates of return	• On average, the shareholders of the acquiring firms experienced significantly abnormal losses before and well before a merger • The shareholders of the acquired firms observed positive returns 4 months before the announcement of the event • Acquiring firms realized negative abnormal returns after the merger approval announcement
Magenheim and Mueller (1988)	1976–81	Monthly rates of return	• Acquiring firms earned significantly positive abnormal returns over two or three years before the acquisition announcement • Around the event period the returns to the acquiring firms were insignificant • The shareholders of the acquired firms observed positive significant returns during the period between 24 and 4 months before the announcement. The returns during the period between 3 months prior the event and 24 months after the event were insignificant

Figure 17.14. A summary of studies on mergers using financial data

4 Firms establish a record for successful mergers or tender offers and the market reacts in such a way because it is anticipating new successful mergers or tender offers (Bradley, 1986).

The pre-merger results might be viewed as consistent with the 'abnormal gains' hypothesis which asserts that information regarding a forthcoming merger should result in higher returns for the shareholders of the acquiring firms.

The US studies just summarized are also fairly consistent in reporting small and insignificant abnormal returns to acquiring firms at the announcement of the merger event. This seems to be in line with the view that the market is efficient with respect to information on mergers. In other words, the market had anticipated the merger and therefore there was little or no reaction at the time the merger was announced. An alternative explanation for the insignificant returns around the merger announcement is that the market is highly competitive and thus it provides a normal return from investments concerning the purchase of other firms.

However, in the case of tender offers (see for example, Bradley, 1980) where the negotiation period is shorter, the results reveal the existence of positive abnormal returns for the shareholders of the acquiring firms at the announcement period of the tender offer.

Lastly, the studies presented in Figure 17.14 also indicate small and insignificant abnormal returns/losses for the shareholders of the acquiring firms after the merger or tender offer is announced. These results reveal that the shareholders of the acquiring firms earn, on average, a normal return commensurate with the risk involved. Therefore, the results appear to be consistent with the 'perfectly competitive acquisitions market' hypothesis which suggests that in a perfectly competitive market assets with similar risk will have the same expected rates of return.

The findings related to the post-merger returns for the shareholders of the acquiring firms can be interpreted in several ways:

1 The shareholders of the acquiring firms did not realize gains from the mergers because their management overvalued the target firms and paid too much (this is called the Hubris hypothesis and was advanced by Roll, 1986).
2 Managers may not be running the firm in the shareholders' best interest and probably they attempt to increase the firm's growth rather than its value.

Individual studies also dealt with other hypotheses concerning mergers. The 'growth maximization' hypothesis states that managers prefer to maximize the firm's growth rather than to maximize the shareholders' wealth. If this is the case, then the shareholders of the acquiring firms should realize low or negative returns. The findings of positive average residuals for the acquiring firms are not consistent with this hypothesis (for example, see Mandelker, 1974). The 'chain-letter' hypothesis states that investors can be misled by manipulation of accounting numbers at the time of the merger (for example, accountants may not include in the reports to shareholders the asset costs at the time of the acquisition). Mandelker (1974) provided results which were consistent with the 'chain-letter' hypothesis.

In contrast to the US studies, the UK empirical investigations on mergers offer less conclusive results. The empirical evidence provided by Franks *et al.* (1977) are similar to those reported in US studies.

Let us now discuss the results derived from the analysis of unsuccessful tender offers. The empirical findings indicate generally non-positive abnormal returns to the unsuccessful bidders. A possible explanation could be the search and administration costs involved in conducting a tender offer (Bradley, 1980) and the negative reaction of the market in relation to these costs. An alternative explanation is that the market is competitive and reacts negatively to an unsuccessful bidder, because it lost the target firm to another competitor.

The empirical investigations reveal that the target firms of unsuccessful tender offers realize significantly positive returns at the offer announcement and throughout the time required for the market to realize the failure of the offer. If the target firms of unsuccessful tender offers do not receive additional offers in the foreseeable future, then these positive abnormal returns vanish. The positive share price reaction for the target firms at the announcement date can be justified as follows: the target firm had a low share price as compared with the value of its assets and its shares were subsequently revalued as a consequence of the tender offer. The 'monopolistic' hypothesis posits that unsuccessful tender offers should produce negative (or zero) returns for shareholders of both the acquiring and selling firms since the monopoly gains will be lost. The empirical evidence is not consistent with this hypothesis (for example, Dodd and Ruback, 1977), as targets of unsuccessful tender offers earned abnormal positive returns at the event month and normal returns thereafter.

The 'new information' hypothesis states that the revaluation of the target firm's shares is generated by two sources: the actions of the market and the firm's managers in response to new information. There have been a number of studies that are consistent with this hypothesis (for example, Dodd and Ruback, 1977; Bradley, 1980). These studies found that, on average, the target firms of unsuccessful tender offers realized significant increases in their share prices at the announcement date; these prices remain higher than those observed before the announcement date.

In general, we may conclude that, on average, the shareholders of the target firms realize benefits by mergers or tender offers, whereas the empirical results seem to indicate that the shareholders of the acquiring firms earn normal risk-adjusted returns.

Let us finally provide a short discussion about the methodologies used in the studies examining the effects of mergers or tender offers on shareholder returns. In order to provide more suitable models for evaluating the return performance required in the research, several studies employed either the Fama–MacBeth methodology or a time-series methodology using the ex-post form of the capital asset pricing model. Both of these methodologies are based upon the capital asset pricing model and use indices to represent the market portfolio. If, however, the index used is not mean-variance efficient during the study period, then the security return would not be exactly related to its systematic risk and the model would be misspecified. The misspecification biases would be included in the entire matrix of residuals both in and out of the event time periods. In addition, the use of the time-series methodology which employs the Jensen measure of performance receives the criticisms of Roll (1978).

Who gains and who loses from mergers?

Mergers provide substantial gains to the shareholders of the selling firms since most mergers offer premiums over and above the pre-merger values of the selling firms. A premium is even higher if there are two or more competitors attempting to purchase the selling firm. If shares are used for the merger transaction and the motive for the merger is to replace inefficient management or re-allocate the selling firm's resources to more effective uses, then the shareholders of the selling firm also gain. The managers of the selling firms may receive several benefits from successful business combinations such as salary increases, bonuses, and so on. Society gains from mergers in the sense that mergers can be employed to eliminate bad management and re-allocate resources to more efficient uses. Investment bankers, business consultants and lawyers also realize large benefits from mergers.

On the other side of the coin, a successful merger may cause the managers of the

Group	Benefits	Losses
Shareholders of the selling firms	Substantial gains from successful business combinations. Gains from unsuccessful business combinations if their shares are subsequently revalued as a consequence of the merger or tender offer	If the merger is not successful and the firm will not receive additional offers in the foreseeable future, they realize losses
Managers of the buying firms	Usually realize gains from successful business combinations	Possible loss of their job when the firm becomes engaged in unsuccessful mergers or tender offers
Society	It benefits from mergers which are used to eliminate bad management or re-allocate resources to efficient uses	It does not benefit if the managers are making decisions related to mergers at the expense of the shareholders
Shareholders of the buying firms	They do not earn much in market value from mergers	The shareholders realize losses if managers act in a manner inconsistent with their interests
Managers of the selling firms	They lose their jobs	
Other parties such as lawyers and investment bankers	They realize large benefits	

Figure 17.15. Benefits/losses to various groups from business combinations

acquired firm to lose their jobs. In view of the empirical evidence, the shareholders of the buying firms do not earn much in market value from business combinations. Figure 17.15 summarizes the benefits and losses to various groups attributable to business combinations.

Summary

1 *Types of mergers* A merger occurs when the managers and shareholders of two or more previously existing companies agree to combine their companies into one new company. Mergers are classified as horizontal, vertical and conglomerate. A horizontal merger occurs when two or more firms in similar businesses are combined. A vertical merger takes place when a firm is combined with one of its suppliers or one of its customers. A conglomerate merger consists of the combination of two or more firms in unrelated businesses.

2 *Motives for mergers* There are several sensible reasons for mergers including the following: (a) synergy; (b) undervalued assets; (c) agency problems; and (d) securing a good management team. Additionally, there are other frequently given reasons for mergers that are more dubious, for example, diversification and earnings per share effect.

3 *Evaluation of mergers* From the buying firm's viewpoint, a merger is considered as a capital budgeting project. Thus, mergers can be evaluated by using the net present value method. However, the buying firm does not need to conduct a full capital budgeting analysis when it evaluates a merger. Instead, it can estimate the present value of the incremental cash flows created by the merger and

compare it with the bid premium for the selling firm. If the difference between the former and latter is positive, the merger should be accepted as it would increase the value of the buying firm.

4 *Empirical studies on mergers* Empirical studies concerning mergers (or tender offers) in the United States show that the shareholders of the selling firm earn, on average, substantial abnormal returns before the merger. The results with respect to the returns to the buying firm's shareholders are less conclusive. Some empirical studies indicate that the shareholders of the buying firm experience no significant gains or losses and other studies reveal small average gains or losses for the buyer.

Questions for discussion

1 For each term shown below in the largest box provide a definition in your own words. Then check your responses against the definitions included in the chapter.

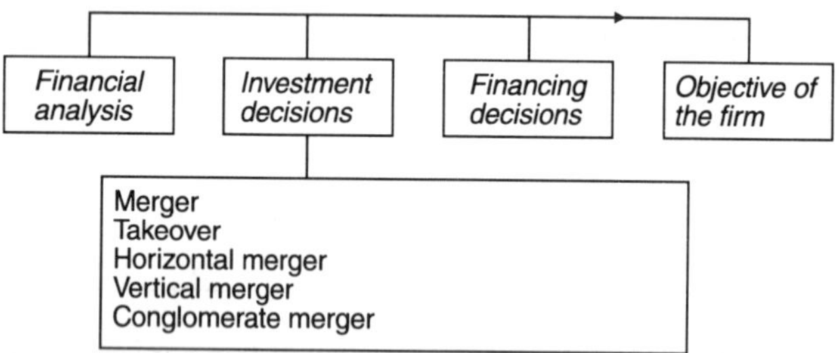

2 Compare and contrast horizontal, vertical and conglomerate mergers. List examples of horizontal, vertical and conglomerate mergers.

3 Discuss each of the following three statements:

(a) 'Synergy is often claimed to be the most common reason for business combinations.'

(b) 'A firm may wish to go the merger route in order to secure a good management team.'

(c) 'Many argue that growth through merger is faster than internal growth.'

4 Evaluate critically and discuss the following statement: 'It is often argued that diversifying into two or more industries provides a common motive for mergers.'

5 'From the acquiring firm's viewpoint, a merger can be evaluated solely by examining the initial effect of the merger on the earnings per share of the combined firm.' Do you agree with this view? Justify your position by using a numerical example.

6 Who benefits from mergers? Are there any losers? Justify your position by also discussing some empirical evidence related to mergers.

7 What are the advantages and disadvantages of the following methods of payment for the acquired firm: (a) paying with cash; and (b) paying with ordinary shares?

8 At the end of a teaching session, the lecturer in financial management gives to the students the following summary statement related to the evaluation of business combinations: 'It is not necessary to conduct a full capital budgeting analysis when we evaluate mergers. Instead a merger can be evaluated

by comparing the present value of the incremental cash flows from the merger with the bid premium for the selling firm'. Provide a full discussion of this statement. Are there any calculation difficulties associated with the evaluation of mergers? Discuss.

9 (a) Consider four different mergers, say A, B, C and D. The diagram below shows the present value of the incremental cash flows created by the merger and the bid premium for each case.

		Present value of the incremental cash flows created by the merger: £2.5 million	£3 million
Premium	£3.5	Merger A: Reject	Merger B:
	£2.8	Merger C:	Merger D:

Fill in your decision related to the acceptance or rejection of mergers B, C and D.

(b) From the viewpoint of the selling firms, which of these four mergers should be accepted?

10 (a) Below you are given four statements related to valuation of mergers. Fill in an appropriate reply by using either the word 'Agree' or the word 'Disagree'.

	Agree	Disagree
From the viewpoint of the acquiring firm, the net present value of the merger decreases as the bid premium increases (other things remain constant).		
If the method of payment for the selling firm is cash, the minimum amount of cash acceptable by the selling firm is lower than its pre-merger market value.		
From the point of view of the selling firm, the net present value of the merger increases as the bid premium increases (other things remain the same).		
If the method of payment for the selling firm is cash, the maximum amount of cash acceptable by the selling firm is higher than its pre-merger market value.		

(b) Discuss in detail each reply given in part (a).

11 Present an analog model summarizing the main points discussed in this chapter.

12 How can spreadsheets be used to facilitate the application of the concepts discussed in this chapter?

Appendix 17A Database statistical functions

A database is an organized collection of pertinent data about a group of items (for example, companies, people, survey results, and so on). A database can be entered in the worksheet itself and can be manipulated by using database commands or statistical functions.

Example 17A.1 Database statistical functions

Figure 17A.1 present a small database containing financial information of 20 quoted UK companies which were engaged in a merger or takeover activity during 1989, both bid price and one month premium are expressed in pence (*source*: *Acquisitions Monthly* and London Business School Risk Measurement Service). Each column in the database is called a field (for example, the columns named Company-Name, Bid-Price, and so on are fields). Each row of information is called a record (for example, the row containing information about Gateway Corp. plc is a record). The first row in the database contains the field names (for example, Company-Name, Bid-Price, and so on).

Databases frequently contain numeric values for which you might want to perform a statistical analysis. 1-2-3 offers seven special database statistical functions. These functions compute statistics about the values in a specified field of the records in the database that match a specified criterion or criteria. A database criterion tells 1-2-3 which records to select from the database when you issue a database command or statistical function. Figure 17A.2 shows the criterion range. In our case the top row of the criterion range includes the field names, while the second and subsequent rows contains two criteria.

Note that each field name in the first row of a criterion range must be identical

	A	B	C	D	E	G
1	A DATABASE OF 20 BIDS FOR UK QUOTED COMPANIES (1989)					
2						
3	Company-Name	Bid-Price	Premium	Beta	Variability	P/E
4	Gateway Corp. plc	230	163	0.900	35	10.5
5	Glass Glover Group	240	170	0.850	39	18.0
6	Hambros Inv Trust plc	311	247	0.880	24	37.8
7	Hunting Petroleum	234	207	0.800	33	10.6
8	Jameson's Chocolates	332	225	0.870	49	20.3
9	Johnstones Paints plc	230	103	0.510	36	14.1
10	Laidlaw Thompson Grp plc	207	140	0.770	36	8.1
11	London Shop plc	340	253	0.670	26	23.6
12	Lorlin Electronics plc	238	133	0.870	49	18.3
13	Microsystem Group	234	225	0.720	33	10.5
14	Northern Engineering Ind	135	134	0.580	28	38.1
15	Personal Computers plc	220	153	0.990	44	12.1
16	Pleasurama Limited	242	200	1.010	31	14.8
17	Polytechnic Electronics	205	165	0.940	50	21.1
18	Ryan International	140	122	0.970	44	10.3
19	Telephone Rentals	340	234	0.990	37	25.5
20	Thermal Scientific plc	222	151	1.060	41	16.4
21	Tyzack (W.A) and Co	210	131	0.880	49	9.7
22	Viking Packaging Grp plc	173	125	0.660	45	9.9
23	Windsmoor plc	127	95	0.930	51	16.3
24		231	169	0.84		

Figure 17A.1. A database of 20 quoted companies

	A	B	C	D	E	G
26	Company Name	Bid Price	Premium	Beta	Variability	P/E
27		1		0		

Figure 17A.2. A criterion range

to the field names included in the first row of the database. The first criterion stored in cell B27 is

```
+B4<350
```

This formula tells 1-2-3 that this criterion applies to the field named 'Bid Price'. Such a criterion formula is stored in cell B27, but 1-2-3 returns the value of 1 indicating that the entry stored in cell B4 is lower than 350. 1-2-3 uses this criterion to test every entry in the field named Bid-Price. Similarly, the second criterion stored in cell D27 uses the following formula:

```
+D4>1
```

In this instance, 1-2-3 returns the value 0 because cell D4 contains a beta value lower than 1. Taking both criteria together we instruct 1-2-3 to choose each record from the database that has in the field named Bid-Price a value lower than 350 and in the field named Beta a value greater than 1.

Figure 17A.3 shows the results from six database functions of 1-2-3. For example, the number of companies that have a bid price lower than 350 pence and a beta greater than 1 is calculated by using the following database function:

```
@DCOUNT(A3..F23,1,A26..F27)
```

where A3..F23 is the database range and A26..F27 is the criterion range. The second argument of the `@DCOUNT` (that is, number 1) tells 1-2-3 on which field to base its calculation (this argument is called field offset). In our case, number 1 is related to the field named 'Bid Price'. All the other database statistical functions have the same form.

	A	B	C	D	E	G
29	Number of Companies	2.00				
30	Minimum	222.00				
31	Maximum	242.00				
32	Average	232.00				
33	Variance	100.00				
34	Standard Deviation	10.00				

Figure 17A.3. Six database statistical functions

Some useful points

1 (Database functions versus ordinary statistical functions) When you work with databases, it is preferable to use the database statistical functions rather than the 1-2-3's ordinary statistical functions because the former can provide faster results. Consider the information provided in Example 17A.1. Suppose you wish now to calculate some statistics for all the firms which have a bid price lower than 350 pence but a beta value greater than 1. If you change only the second criterion (that is, store in cell D27, see Figure 17A.2, the formula `+D4<1`), then 1-2-3 will automatically update the worksheet.

2 (A general point about database functions) Note that the field offset argument 0 instructs 1-2-3 to base the statistical calculations on the entries in the first field, the field offset argument 1 tells 1-2-3 to base the statistical calculations on the second field, and so on.

References and bibliography

Bradley, M. (1980) Interfirm tender offers and the market for corporate control, *Journal of Business*, October, 345–76.

Bradley, M. (1986) The economic consequences of mergers and tender offers, in Stern, J.M. and Chew, D.H., (eds), *Resolution of Corporate Finance*. Basil Blackwell, Oxford.

Bradley, M., Desai, A. and Kim, E.H. (1983) The rationale behind interim tender offers, *Journal of Financial Economics*, April, 183–206.

Copeland, T.E. and Weston, J.F. (1983) *Financial Theory and Corporate Policy*, 2nd edn. Addison-Wesley, Reading, Mass.

Dodd, P. (1980) Mergers proposals, management discretion and stockholder wealth, *Journal of Financial Economics*, **8**, June, 105–37.

Dodd, P. and Ruback, R. (1977) Tender offers and stockholders returns: an empirical analysis, *Journal of Financial Economics*, December, 351–74.

Ellert, J.C. (1976) Mergers, antitrust law enforcement and stockholder returns, *Journal of Finance*, May, 715–32.

Fama, E.F. (1976) *Foundations of Finance*. Basic Books, New York.

Fama, E.F. and MacBeth, J. (1973) Risk, return and equilibrium: empirical test, *Journal of Political Economy*, May, 607–35.

Fama, E.F., Fisher, L., Jensen, M. and Roll, R. (1969) The adjustment of stock prices to new information, *International Economic Review*, February, 1–21.

Firth, M. (1980) Takeovers, shareholders returns, and the theory of the firm, *Quarterly Journal of Economics*, March, 235–60.

Franks, J.R., Broyles, J.E. and Hecht, M.J. (1977) An industry study of the profitability of mergers in the United Kingdom, *Journal of Finance*, December, 1513–25.

Halpern, P.J. (1973) Empirical estimates of the amount and distribution of gains to companies, in mergers, *Journal of Business*, October, 554–75.

Haugen, R.A. and Udell, J.G. (1972) Rates of return to stockholders of acquired companies, *Journal of Financial and Quantitative Analysis*, January, 1387–98.

Hogarty, T. (1970) The profitability of corporate mergers, *Journal of Business*, July, 317–27.

Hong, H.G., Mandelker, G. and Kaplan, R.S. (1978) Pooling vs. purchase: the effects of accounting for mergers on stock prices, *Accounting Review*, **53**, January, 31–47.

Joehnk, M.D. and Nielsen, J.F. (1974) The effects of conglomerate merger activity on systematic risk, *Journal of Financial and Quantitative Analysis*, **9**, March, 215–25.

Kelly, E.M. (1967) *The Profitability of Growth through Mergers*. Pennsylvania State University, University Park, Pa.

Keown, A.J. and Pinkerton, J.M. (1981) Merger announcements and insider trading activity: an empirical investigation, *Journal of Finance*, September 1981, 855–70.

Kummer, D.J. and Hoffmeister, J.F. (1978) Valuation consequences of cash tender offers, *Journal of Finance*, May, 505–16.

Langetieg, T. (1978) An application of a three-factor performance index to measure stockholders gains from merger, *Journal of Financial Economics*, December, 365–83.

Lev, B. (1986a) Observations on the merger phenomenon and a review of the evidence, in: Stern, J.M. and Chew, D.H., Jr (eds), *The Revolution of Corporate Finance*. Basil Blackwell, Oxford, pp. 357–67.

Lewellen, W.G. and Ferri, M.G. (1983) Strategies for the merger game: management and the market, *Financial Management*, Winter, 25–35.

Magenheim, E.B. and Mueller, D.C. (1988) Are acquiring-firm shareholders better off after an aquisition? in: Coffee, J.C., Jr, Lowenstein, L. and Rose-Ackerman, S. (eds), *Knights, Raiders, and Targets: The Impact of Hostile Takeover*. Oxford University Press, pp. 171–93.

Malatesta, P.H. (1983) The wealth effect of merger activity and the objective functions of merging firms, *Journal of Financial Economics*, April, 155–81.

Mandelker, G. (1974) Risk and return: the case of merging firms, *Journal of Financial Economics*, **1** December, 303–35.

Mueller, D.C. (1969) A theory of conglomerate mergers, *Quarterly Journal of Economics*, November, 643–59.

Myers, S.E. (1976) A framework for evaluating mergers, in: *Modern Developments in Financial Management*. Frederick A. Praeger, New York.

Rappaport, A. (1975) Capital budgeting approach to an exchange-of-shares acquisitions, *Mergers and Acquisitions*, **10**, 27–9.

Roll, R. (1978) Ambiguity when performance is measured by the security market line, *Journal of Finance*, September, 1051–69.

Roll, R. (1986) The Hubris hypothesis of corporate takeovers, *Journal of Business*, April, 197–216.

Scott, J.H., Jr. (1977) On the theory of conglomerate mergers, *Journal of Finance*, **32**, September, 1235–50.

Shad, S.R. (1969) The financial realities of mergers, *Harvard Business Review*, **47**, November–December, 133–46.

Shick, R.A. and Jen, F.C. (1974) Merger benefits to shareholders of aquiring firms, *Financial Management*, Winter, 45–53.

Singh, A. (1971) *Takeovers: Their Relevance to the Stock Market and the Theory of the Firm*. Cambridge University Press, Cambridge.

Travlos, N.G. (1987) Corporate takeover bids, methods of payment, and bidding firm's stock returns, *Journal of Finance*, September, 943–63.

Tzoannos, J. and Samuels, J.M. (1972) Mergers and takeovers: the financial characteristics of companies involved, *Journal of Business Finance*, Autumn, 5–16.

Utton, M.A. (1974) On measuring the effects of industrial mergers, *Scottish Journal of Political Economy*, February, 13–28.

Warren, J.H. (1985) *Mergers and Acquisitions: Will You Overpay*? Dow Jones-Irwin, Homewood, Ill.

18 Options

This chapter includes:

- Call and put options
- Profit profiles of call and put options
- Properties of options

In recent years, the popularity of the option markets has increased dramatically. The recent developments in the option markets are summarized as follows:

1973: The Chicago Board Options Exchange opened with calls for 16 shares.
1977: Put options were added.
1978: The European Options Exchange opened in London and Amsterdam.
1982: Foreign currency, interest rate and bond options were added.
1986: Options in stock market indices were added.

The objective of this chapter is to explain call and put options and to present various properties which describe the behaviour of option prices.

Basic concepts, definitions and examples

The concepts described in this chapter are based on the following assumptions:

1. There are no transaction costs of buying or selling any security.
2. There are no taxes.
3. There are no dividend payments on the underlying share during the life of an option.

   Additionally, note that the examples presented in this chapter use closing option prices. Therefore, they ignore the consequences emerging when the last trade in an option and the last trade in the underlying share occur at different times of the day. Finally, the following simplification is made:
4. An option is trading during a day at a price equal to its closing price of that day.

Call options

A call option is a contract between two parties that gives one party the right (and not the obligation) to buy a given number of shares from the other party at a specified price within a predetermined period of time. A call option contract can be fully characterized by the following items:

- Underlying share This is the share in which call options are available.
- Number of shares The number of shares that the option holder has the right to

purchase at a certain price and within a specified period of time (call options are bought and sold in contracts each of which is a unit of 1,000 shares).

- Exercise or striking price This is the price at which the underlying share can be purchased.
- Expiry or expiration date This is the last date at which the right to buy may be exercised. American call options may be exercised at any time on or before the expiry date. European call options may be exercised only at the expiry date. Call options traded via the London Stock Exchange are of the American type.

Example 18.1 The call options of Marks and Spencer plc (20 March 1990)

Figure 18.1 shows actual quotations for the Marks and Spencer calls as reported in the *Financial Times* on 21 March 1990. Call options in Marks and Spencer's shares (and also all other UK options in shares) are available with three possible expiry dates, each separated by three months. The maximum life of a contract is nine months and when it expires a new nine-month option contract is introduced. The expiry date for the Marks and Spencer's April call options (see Figure 18.1) is the 25 April 1990. Call option contracts generally expire on the last Wednesday of the last complete Stock Exchange Account in the expiry month.

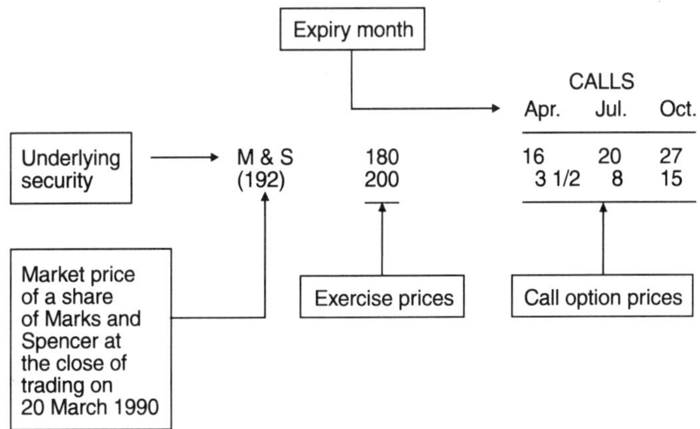

Figure 18.1. A call option in Marks and Spencer's shares

Suppose that Mrs Ruth Jones owns a 180 April call option in Marks and Spencer's shares. This option gives her the right (but not the obligation) to buy from an investor 1,000 shares of Marks and Spencer at 180 pence per share at any time on or before the expiry date (that is, 25 April 1990). Mrs Jones bought the option from Mr Annis in January 1990. Mr Annis owns several hundreds of Marks and Spencer's shares. By selling the option contract, Mr Annis has granted Mrs Jones the right to sell 1,000 shares of Marks and Spencer at 180 pence per share if called upon to do so before 26 April 1990.

The investor who grants the call right (that is, Mr Annis) is known as the writer of the call. The investor who receives the call right (that is, Mrs Jones) is called the buyer or holder of the call. In January 1990, Mr Annis sold the call option to Mrs Jones because he expected that the share price would not increase above 180 pence during the next three months. Mrs Jones bought the call because she anticipated that the firm's share price would rise above 180 pence during the next three months.

At any time, Mrs Jones can take one of the three actions:

1 Exercise the call option by paying the exercise price in return for the Marks and Spencer's shares.
2 Sell the call option at the current market price.
3 Hold the call option until a later time.

At any time, Mr Annis can do one of the following four things:

1 Purchase the contract back from Mrs Jones.
2 Deliver the 1,000 shares of Marks and Spencer for the agreed exercise price in the event that Mrs Jones exercised the option.
3 Find another investor who wished to become the writer of this contract and sell it.
4 Remain the writer of the contract until a later time.

The price of a call (or the call premium) is the fee the option buyer pays to the option seller (the latter could be either the writer or a previous purchaser who now wishes to sell his or her option). Call options are expressed in per-share terms, thus, the actual price can be calculated by multiplying the quoted exercise price by the number of shares reported in the contract. For example, an investor can buy today (that is, 20 March 1990) Marks and Spencer's 3-month, 180 April call option for 16 pence per share, equivalent to £160 for a contract (remember that we assume no transaction costs).

Figure 18.2 presents graphically the Marks and Spencer's (180 April) call option price for the period 16 March 1990 to 9 April 1990. From the graph it can be seen that the option price decreased to a minimum value on 21 March 1990 and increased to a maximum value on 9 April 1990.

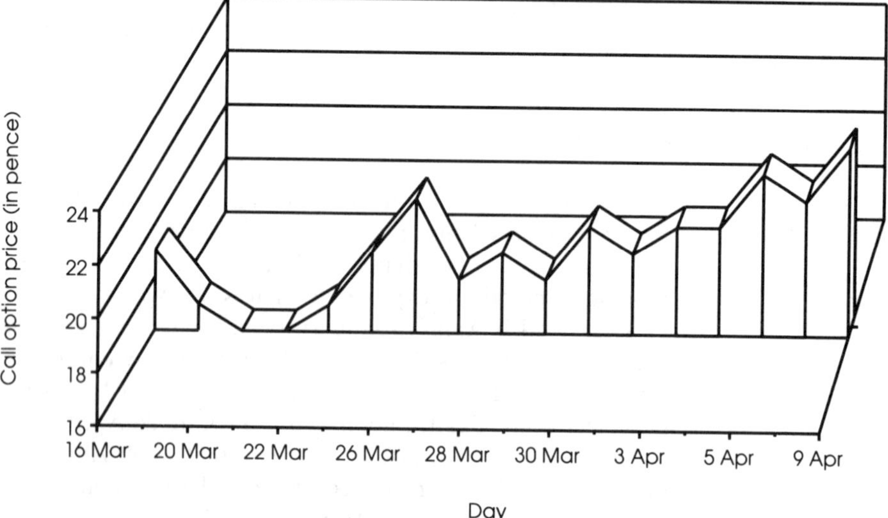

Figure 18.2. The price of a call option in Marks and Spencer's shares (exercise price = 180 pence; expiration 25 March 1990)

Note that the call option contract does not involve the company whose shares are utilized as the underlying security for the contract. A covered call writing is the case where the writer owns the underlying shares. A naked call writing is the case where the writer issues a call option without holding the underlying shares.

Put options

A put option is a contract between two parties that gives one party the right (and not the obligation) to sell a given number of shares to the other party at a specified price within a predetermined period of time. A put contract can be completely characterized (in a similar manner as a call contract) by the following items:

- Underlying share This is the share in which put options are available.
- Number of shares The number of shares that the option holder has the right to sell at a certain price and within a specified period of time (put options are bought and sold in contracts each of which is a unit of 1,000 shares).
- Exercise or striking price This is the price at which the underlying share can be sold.
- Expiry or expiration date This is the last date at which the right to sell may be exercised. American put options may be exercised at any time on or before the expiry date. European put options may be exercised only at the expiry date. Put options traded via the London Stock Exchange are of the American type.

Example 18.2 The put options of Marks and Spencer plc (20 March 1990)

Figure 18.3 presents the put options in Marks and Spencer's shares as published in the *Financial Times* on 21 March 1990. The put options in Marks and Spencer's shares (and also all other UK put options in shares) are available with three possible expiry dates, each separated by three months. As with call options, the maximum life of a put contract is nine months and when it expires a new nine-month option contract is introduced. For example, the April put options in Marks and Spencer's shares expire on 25 April 1990. Put option contracts generally expire on the last Wednesday of the last complete Stock Exchange Account of the expiry month.

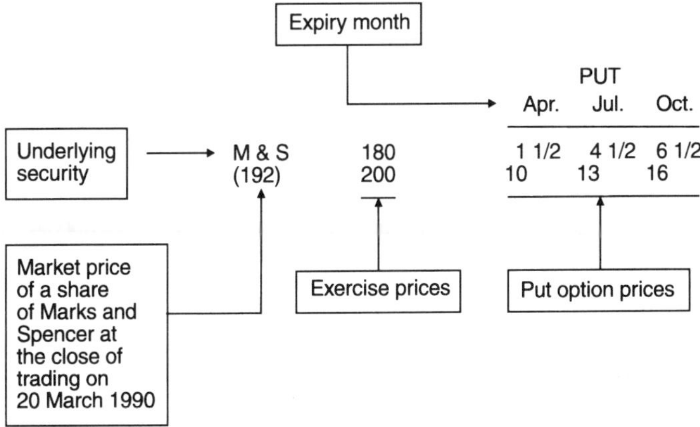

Figure 18.3. A put option in Marks and Spencer's shares

To illustrate more fully the concept of a put option, assume a case where Mrs Ruth Jones owns a 180 April put option in Marks and Spencer's shares. In this case, Mrs Jones has the right (but not the obligation) to sell to an investor 1,000 shares of Marks and Spencer at the stated price of 180 pence per share any time on or before the stated expiry date (that is, 25 April 1990). Mr George Annis sold the option to Mrs Jones in January 1990 and he has the legal obligation to buy from her 1,000 shares of Marks and Spencer at 180 pence per share if called upon to do so before 26 April 1990.

The investor who grants the put right (that is, Mr Annis) is known as the writer of the put. The investor who receives the put right (that is, Mrs Jones) is called the buyer or holder of the put. In January 1990, Mr Annis believed that the share price would not decrease below 180 pence during the next three months. Mrs Jones had a different opinion about the shares of Marks and Spencer; she bought the put in anticipation of a substantial decline in the firm's share price during this time period. At any time, Mrs Jones (Mr Annis) can take similar actions to those discussed in Example 18.1.

The price of a put is usually called the put premium. It is the fee the option buyer pays to the option seller (the latter could be either the writer or a previous purchaser who now wishes to sell his or her option). Put options are reported on a per-share basis, therefore, the actual price can be computed by multiplying the quoted price by the number of shares reported in the contract. For example, the right to sell 1,000 of Marks and Spencer at a price of 180 pence per share before the closing date on 25 April 1990 can be purchased today (that is 20 March 1990) for £15 (remember that we assume no transaction costs).

In the United Kingdom, the London Options Clearing House (LOCH) facilitates trading in options as well as acting as an intermediary guaranteeing all contracts. For example, if an investor wishes to exercise his or her call options, the LOCH uses a computerized system which randomly selects a writer of the required option to deliver the shares. If the writer is unable to deliver the shares, the LOCH guarantees a delivery of the shares.

As with the call option contracts, the put option contracts do not involve the company whose shares are utilized as the underlying security for the contract.

Adjusting the option contract for stock splits

If a firm declares a stock split, then the exercise price of the options in the firm's shares is adjusted accordingly.

Example 18.3 Adjusting the exercise price and number of shares for a stock split

Suppose the exercise price of a call option is 180 pence and the firm the option refers to declares a three-for-two stock split. Then the new exercise price will be 120 pence (that is, 180/1.5). If an investor exercises the call, then the writer is obliged to deliver 1,500 shares (that is, 1,000 × 1.5).

Now assume that the exercise price of a call option is 191 pence and the firm the option refers to declares a three-for-two stock split. Then the exercise price would be $127\frac{3}{8}$ (that is, $191/1.5 = 127.33$; next round the figure to the nearest one-eighth of a point in order to get $127\frac{3}{8}$).

The intrinsic value of an option

The intrinsic value of a call option is defined as zero or the difference between the underlying share price and exercise price, whichever is greater. That is:

$$V_c(S_o, E) = \text{Max}\,(0, S_o - E)$$

where

Max = the larger term between 0 and $S_o - E$.

S_o = the current price of the underlying share.

E = the exercise price of the call option.

Example 18.4 Calculating the intrinsic value of a call option

On 20 March 1990 the price of the shares of Marks and Spencer plc was 192 pence. The exercise prices on the two April 1990 calls were 180 and 200 pence, respectively. Then

$$V_c(192, 180) = \text{Max}\,(0, 192 - 180) = \text{Max}\,(0, 12) = 12$$

$$V_c(192, 200) = \text{Max}\,(0, 192 - 200) = \text{Max}\,(0, -8) = 0$$

Similarly, the intrisic value of a put option is defined as follows:

$$V_p(S_o, E) = \text{Max}\,(0, E - S_o)$$

where

Max = the larger term between 0 and $E - S_o$.

S_o = the current price of the underlying share.

E = the exercise price of the put option.

The price of the underlying share is expected to change during the life of the option and the exercise price is a parameter having a fixed value. From the definition of the intrisic value we may conclude that the intrinsic value of a call (put) option moves in the same (opposite) direction as (from) the underlying share price provided that the latter is greater (lower) than the option's exercise price.

By comparing the underlying share price of an option with its exercise price, we can define the following terms:

- A call (put) option for which the market price of the underlying share is greater (less) than the exercise price of the option is called 'in the money'.
- A call (put) option for which the market price of the underlying share is less than (in excess of) the exercise price of the option is called 'out of the money'.
- A call (put) option for which the market price of the underlying share is equal to the exercise price of the option is called 'at the money'.

Profit profiles of call and put options

The profit from buying (selling) an option (in the absence of transaction costs) depends on the price of the underlying share, the exercise price and the price paid when purchasing (selling) the option. The profit is reported on a per-share basis. The profit obtained from selling an option is the loss incurred from writing the option and vice versa (in this section we will assume that the writer holds the underlying shares).

Profit profiles of call options

The buyer's profit available on a call option can be either profit from trading the call or profit from exercising the call. In the former case, the profit per share can be calculated by simply subtracting the buying price of the option from the price received when selling the option, that is:

Trading profit per share = Selling option price – Buying option price

For example, a buyer of a Marks and Spencer 180 call bought on 2 April 1990 at 19 pence could realize a 3 pence profit per share if the call was sold on 5 April 1990 for 22 pence.

The profit per share obtained from exercising a call option is calculated as the intrinsic value of the option minus the buying price of the option (as we shall see later in this chapter, it is not worth exercising American options before their expiry date). That is:

Profit per share = Intrinsic value – Buying option price

If the share price is at or below the exercise price, the option will expire worthless and the buyer (writer) of the call will realize a loss (profit) equal to the amount paid when purchasing (selling) the option. Conversely, if the share price is above the exercise price the buyer's (writer's) profit is the difference between the intrinsic value and the price of the option paid (received) when purchasing (selling) the option. The maximum loss an option buyer can observe is limited to the buying price of the option. However, he or she has unlimited potential gains.

Example 18.5 The profit profile of a call option

Assume that it is 20 March 1990. The share price of Marks and Spencer is 192 pence and its April 180 call option trades at 16 pence. Consider an investor who buys a Marks and Spencer call at 16 pence, then his or her profit associated with holding the call until the expiry date is related to the underlying share price at the expiry date. Figure 18.4 calculates the investor's profit of holding this call until the expiry date for different prices of the underlying share in the range 156–222 pence. The following function is stored in cell B9

```
IF($C$3>=A9,-$C$4,A9-$C$3-$C$4)
```

In words, if the exercise price, stored in cell C3, is greater than or equal to the underlying share price, stored in cell A9, return the call purchase price as a negative value, otherwise return the following:

share price—exercise price—buying call price

The contents of cell B9 are copied in the range B10 . . B20. Similarly, cell C9 stores the following formula:

```
@IF($C$3>=A9,$C$4,$C$3-A9+$C$4)
```

The profit profile for the call option buyer is illustrated in Figure 18.5.

	A	B	C	D	E	F
1		THE PROFIT PROFILE OF A CALL OPTION				
2		====================================				
3	Exercise Price ------------>		180			
4	Call Price ---------------->		16			
5						
6		Profit per share:				
7	Share Price	Buyer	Seller			
8						
9	156	-16	16			
10	162	-16	16			
11	168	-16	16			
12	174	-16	16			
13	180	-16	16			
14	186	-10	10			
15	192	-4	4			
16	198	2	-2			
17	204	8	-8			
18	210	14	-14			
19	216	20	-20			
20	222	26	-26			
21						

Figure 18.4. The profit associated with a call option for different share prices

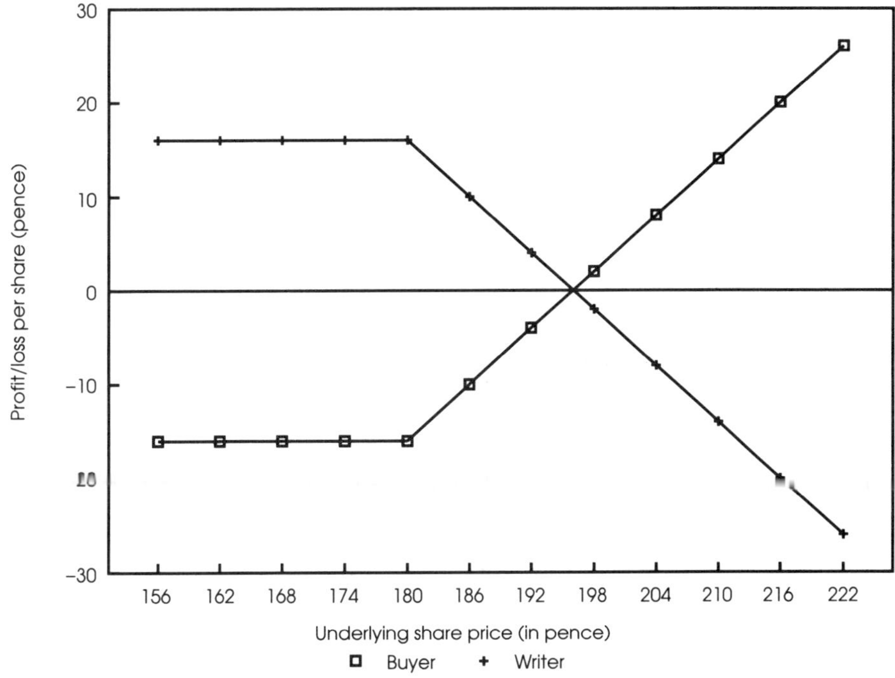

Figure 18.5. The profit profile of a call option (current share price 192 pence)

At the break-even point (that is, the point where the profile line intersects the share price axis) the share price is calculated as follows: $S = 180 + 16 = 196$ pence.

If at the expiry date the share price is below 196 pence, then the call buyer will make a loss. From the viewpoint of the buyer, a call option is a limited liability security, thus, his or her maximum loss will be 16 pence per share. At prices between 180 and 196 pence the buyer will obtain a loss, but if the call is exercised the loss will be less than 16 pence per share. If at expiry date the share price is trading above 196 pence, then the call buyer will realize a profit. For example, for $S = 216$ pence, the buyer's profit will be 20 pence per share. The profits to the call buyer increase with a rise in the underlying share price.

A similar analysis can be conducted to examine the profit obtained from the writer's viewpoint, we assume that the writer owns the shares (see Figure 18.4). Note that the profit obtained from selling the call is the mirror image of the profit incurred from buying the call (ignoring transaction costs). For example, if the share price will be 192 pence, the call buyer will make a loss of 4 pence per share and the call writer will obtain a profit of 4 pence per share (assuming, of course, that the call is exercised). Since the writer's profit from selling a call equals the buyer's loss from buying the call and vice versa, the break-even point of the writer is equal to the break-even point of the buyer and the writer has unlimited potential losses. Figure 18.4 shows also the profit profile for the option writer.

Problems

1 Create the worksheet shown in Figure 18.4.
2 Create Figure 18.5.

The profit profiles associated with call options can be summarized in Figure 18.6.

- *Buyer*
- SELL
Capital gain or loss
- LET EXPIRY
Capital loss
- EXERCISE
Intrisic value—buying call price

Writer

- SELL
Capital loss or gain
- LET EXPIRY
Capital gain
- EXERCISE
Selling call price—intrinsic value

Figure 18.6. Profits to buyers and writers of call options

Profit profiles of put options

The buyer's profit observed from a put option can be either profit from trading the put or profit from exercising the put. In the former case, the profit per share can be computed by simply subtracting the buying price of the option from the price received when selling the option and can be expressed as follows:

Trading profit per share = Selling option price − Buying option price

For example, a buyer of a Marks and Spencer 180 put bought on 2 April 1990 at 1.5 pence would observe a 0.5 pence loss per share if the put was sold on 5 April 1990 for 1 pence.

The profit per share obtained from exercising a put option equals the difference between the intrisic value and the buying price of the option (as we shall see later in this chapter, exercising an American put option before the expiry date could be appropriate). That is:

Profit per share = Intrinsic value – Buying option price

If the share price is at or above the exercise price the option will expire worthless and the buyer (writer) of the put will realize a loss (profit) equal to the amount paid (received) when purchasing (selling) the put. Conversely, if the share price is below the exercise price the buyer (writer) will realize a profit equal to the intrinsic value minus the buying (selling) price of the option. The buyer of a put option has potential limited losses but his or her potential for profit is unlimited.

Example 18.6 The profit profile of a put option

Assume that it is 20 March 1990. The following specifications are given:

- Underlying shares: the shares of Marks and Spencer plc.
- Share price on 20 March 1990: 192 pence.
- April 180 put option price 1.5 pence.

The profits available from holding the above put option depend on the underlying share price (see Figure 18.7).

```
-----------------------------------------------------------------------
        A            B             C             D           E        F
1             THE PROFIT PROFILE OF A PUT OPTION
2             ==================================
3 Exercise Price ------------>              180
4 Call Price ---------------->              1.5
5 ----------------------------------------------------
6                         Profit/loss
7 Share Price         Buyer           Seller
8 ----------------------------------------------------
9             156          22.5          -22.5
10            162          16.5          -16.5
11            168          10.5          -10.5
12            174           4.5           -4.5
13            180          -1.5            1.5
14            186          -1.5            1.5
15            192          -1.5            1.5
16            198          -1.5            1.5
17            204          -1.5            1.5
18            210          -1.5            1.5
19            216          -1.5            1.5
20            222          -1.5            1.5
21 ----------------------------------------------------
-----------------------------------------------------------------------
```

Figure 18.7. The profit associated with a put option for different share prices

We stored in cell B9 the following function:

```
@IF(A9>=$C$3,-$C$4,$C$3-A9-$C$4)
```

In words, if the underlying share price, stored in cell A9, is greater than or equal to the exercise price, stored in cell C3, return the put purchased price as a negative value, otherwise return the following:

exercise price—share price—buying put price

Other profit values are calculated by copying the contents of cell B9 in the range B10..B20.

From the seller's point of view, store the following function in cell C9: `@IF(A9>=$C$3,$C$4,A9-$C$3+$C$4)` and then copy the contents of cell C9 into the range C10..C20.

The relationship between the put option's profit and share price is described graphically in Figure 18.8.

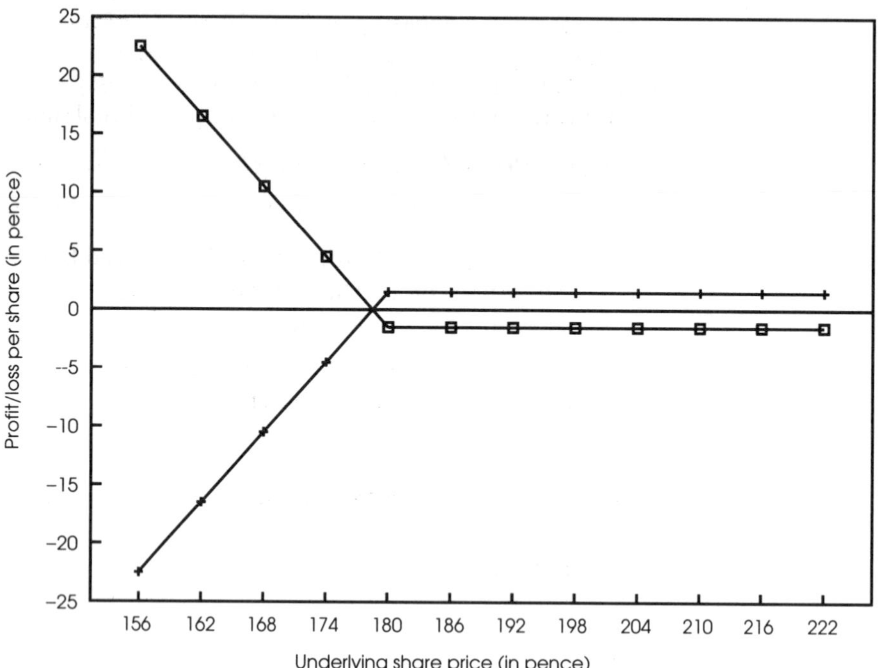

Figure 18.8. The profit profile of a put option (current share price 192 pence)

The break-even share price of the put buyer (that is, the point where the profit line intersects the share price axis) is 178.5 pence (that is 180 – 1.5). The results in Figure 18.8 reveal:

- A loss for a share price greater than 178.5 pence.
- A loss for a share price in the range 178.5–180 pence. If the put is exercised the size of the loss will be less than 1.5 pence.
- A profit for a share price below 178.5 pence. The profits to the put buyer increase with a fall in the underlying share price.

The writer's profit from selling the put is equal to the buyer's loss from buying the put and vice versa. Therefore, the writer breaks even if the share price is 178.5 pence. Figure 18.8 also presents graphically the profit profile from the viewpoint of the put writer.

Problems

1. Set up the worksheet shown in Figure 18.7.
2. Create the graph illustrated in Figure 18.8.

The buyer's and writer's profit profiles associated with a put option are summarized in Figure 18.9.

• *Buyer*

• SELL
Capital gain or loss
• LET EXPIRY
Capital loss
• EXERCISE
Intrisic value—buying put price

Writer

• SELL
Capital loss or gain
• LET EXPIRY
Capital gain
• EXERCISE
Selling put price—intrinsic value

Figure 18.9. Profits to buyers and writers of put options

Properties of options

The price of a call option is dependent upon the following parameters:

- The current price of the underlying share, call it S_o.
- The time to expiry, call it T.
- The exercise price of the option, call it E.

The price of a call option at any point in time before the expiry date can be written as an explicit function of the above three parameters as follows:

$C(S_o, T, E)$

For example, assume that the present date is 20 March 1990, then using the data presented in Example 18.1 we can write for the closing call option price (the 1990 April call option of Marks and Spencer plc expires on 25 April 1990):

$C(192, 36, 180)$

where

192 = the current price of the underlying share.
36 = the number of days before expiration (including the expiry date)
180 = the exercise price of the call option.

As we shall see in the next chapter, other variables, such as the variance of the continuously compounded return on the underlying share and the riskless rate of interest, also influences the price of an option. The call price given by $C(S_o, T, E)$ does not represent the exact option price, but it can be utilized to present several important properties about the option pricing boundary conditions. These properties rely on the assumption that investors are rational.

Properties of call options

Below we will discuss 12 properties related to call options.

Property 1   The price of a call option must be greater than or equal to its intrinsic value

Example 18.7 Illustrating Property 1

Figure 18.10 shows the call prices and calculates the intrinsic values for four different share prices in the range 196–201 pence for an option in Marks and Spencer's shares. For example, the intrinsic value of 16, stored in cell C8, is calculated by using the following function of 1-2-3:

```
@MAX(0,B8-$C$4)
```

In all cases the price of the call option is greater than the option's intrinsic value.

```
          A                B                  C              D
 1 COMPARING THE OPTION PRICE WITH THE OPTION'S INTRINSIC VALUE
 2 ==========================================================
 3
 4 Exercise Price ----------->                     180
 5 ---------------------------------------------------------------
 6 Dare         Share Price (p)       Intrinsic Value (p) Call Price (p)
 7 ---------------------------------------------------------------
 8    02-Apr-90                  196               16            19
 9    04-Apr-90                  197               17            20
10    05-Apr-90                  200               20            22
11    09-Apr-90                  201               21            23
12 ---------------------------------------------------------------
```

Figure 18.10. Option price versus intrinsic value

The difference between the actual option price and its intrinsic value is called the time premium. If the time premium equals zero, then the call option is traded at parity. Note that the option shown in Figure 18.10 is trading above parity.

If the relationship between intrinsic value and call price did not hold, there would be arbitrage opportunities. Assume that the call price on 4 April 1990 was 10 pence, then an investor could proceed as shown in Figure 18.11. This indicates that the investor could obtain unlimited profits at no risk, which is not possible in the real world. This argument validates the property that the price of a call option must be greater than or equal to its intrinsic value.

Figure 18.12 illustrates graphically Property 1 for the period 16 March 1990 to 9 April 1990.

```
          A                B                  C              D
13
14 Share Price ------------------->             197
15 Exercise Price ---------------->             180
16 Number of Shares -------------->           1,000
17 -----------------------------------------------
18                                      (£)
19 Call Cost                                    100
20 Cost of Exercise                           1,800
21
22 Proceeds on Sale                           1,970
23                                -------------------
24 Profit                                        70
25                                ===================
```

Figure 18.11. An arbitrage opportunity

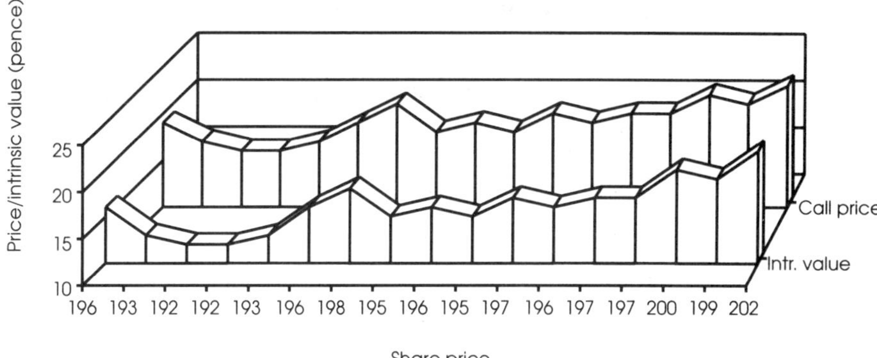

Figure 18.12. Graphic illustration of Property 1 (16 March 1990 to 9 April 1990)

Property 2 The price of a call option is either positive or zero

Property 2 is derived from Property 1 as the intrinsic value of an option can be either positive or zero.

Property 3 Price of a call option on expiry date

On expiry date, the price of a call option is given by:

$$C(S,0,E) = \text{Max}\,(0, S - E)$$

where $S =$ the underlying share price at the expiry date.

Property 4 The percentage charge of a call option price is larger than the percentage change of the underlying share price

Example 18.8 Illustrating Property 4

Let us use once more the call options in Marks and Spencer shares (see Figure 18.13). The results indicate that in percentage terms, the changes in the option price are associated with greater changes in the underlying share price.

	A	B	C	D	E
1	THE CHANGES OF AN OPTION PRICE AND THE UNDERLYING SHARE PRICE				
2					
3					
4					
5	Dare	Call Price (p)	Change	Share Price (p)	Change
6					
7	02-Apr-90	19		196	
8	04-Apr-90	20	5.26%	197	0.51%
9	05-Apr-90	22	10.00%	200	1.52%
10	09-Apr-90	23	4.55%	201	0.50%
11					

Figure 18.13. Calculating percentage price changes

Property 5

If two call options on the same share have the same expiry date, the same underlying share price and different exercise prices, then the price of the call option with the lower exercise price is greater than or equal to the price of the call option with the higher exercise price.

Example 18.9 Illustrating Property 5

Consider two traded options in Marks and Spencer plc shares having exercise prices 180 pence and 200 pence, respectively, and the same expiry date (that is, 25 April 1990)

On 20 April 1990, the price of the underlying share of Marks and Spencer was 192 pence, then we have

$$C(180,0,192) = \text{Max}\,(0,192-180) = 12$$

and

$$C(200,0,192) = \text{Max}\,(0,192-200) = 0$$

Therefore, $C(180,0,192) > C(200,0,192)$.

If the share price was above 200 pence (say 202 pence) then:

$$C(180,0,202) = \text{Max}\,(0,202-180) = 22$$

and

$$C(200,0,202) = \text{Max}\,(0,202-200) = 2$$

Thus, we have $C(180,0,202) > C(200,0,202)$.

Finally, if the Marks and Spencer's share was below 180 pence (say 160 pence) then

$$C(180,0,160) = C(200,0,160) = 0$$

Since the call option with the lower exercise price will be worth at least as much as the call option with the higher exercise price on the expiry date, the price of the former will be at least as great as the price of the latter.

Property 6
If two call options on the same share have the same exercise price, the same underlying share price and different time to expiration, then the price of the option with the longer time to expiration is greater than or equal to the price of the option with the shorter time to expiration.

Example 18.10 Illustrating Property 6

Consider the following information on an April 1990 call option in Marks and Spencer's shares:

On 23 March 1990 → share price 196 pence and call price 19 pence
On 28 March 1990 → share price 196 pence and call price 19 pence
On 20 April 1990 → share price 196 pence and call price 17 pence

Property 7
Consider a call option which expires within a limited time period and has a positive exercise price. Then the underlying share price is greater than or equal to the call option price.

If a call option price was greater than the share price, then investors would purchase the share directly and no one would buy the call option.

Property 8
The price of an American call option is greater than or equal to $\text{Max}\,(0, S_o - E/(1+r))$, where S_o = the current market price of the underlying share, r = the riskless interest rate for the period until the expiry date and E = the option's exercise price.

The boundary conditions on option values are based on the following principle.

> *An investment portfolio (for example, a portfolio comprised of call options and Treasury bills) which has a future series of cash flows at least equal to the series of cash flows of another portfolio should be worth at least as much as this second portfolio.*

This principle is illustrated below.

	Investment outflow	Future cash flow at expiry date	
		$S > E$	$S < E$
Portfolio A			
Buy the call for £C	C	$S - E$	0
Invest £E in Treasury bills	$E/(1+r)$	E	E
TOTAL	$C + E/(1+r)$	S	E
Portfolio B			
Buy shares for S_o	S_o	S	S

Portfolio A is comprised of buying a call option with exercise price of £E at cost of £C and investing in a riskless investment which has a present value of $E/(1+r)$. The future cash flow of portfolio A at the expiry date will be either S (if $S > E$) or E (if $S < E$), where S is the share price at the expiry date. Portfolio B consists only of the underlying share of the call and its cost is equal to the current price of the underlying share. The future cash flow of portfolio B at the expiry date will be equal to the share price at the expiry date. Note that portfolio A's cash outflow is at least equal to the cash outflow associated with portfolio B. Therefore:

$$C + E/(1+r) \geq S_o$$

or equivalently

$$C \geq S_o - E/(1+r)$$

The last inequality is a boundary condition on the call price. Specifically, $S_o - E/(1+r)$ is a lower bound for the value of a call option at any point before the expiry date. At the expiry date the value of the option is equal to $S - E$ (if $S > E$). A call option is a limited liability security and it can not have a negative value. Therefore, we can write:

$$C \geq \text{Max}\,(0, S_o - E/(1+r))$$

Example 18.11 Illustrating Property 8

Consider the following data for a call option in Marks and Spencer's shares:

Current share price:	$S_o = 198$ pence
Current call price:	$C = 21$ pence
Exercise price:	$E = 180$ pence
Riskless interest rate:	$r = 0.16$ per cent
Time before expiry:	$t = 30$ days

Then Max $(0, 198 - 180)/(1 + 0.0016)) = 18.28$ pence.

As we can see the share price of 198 pence is greater than the call price of 21 pence and the latter is greater than the lower price bound of 18.28 pence.

By comparing Properties 1, 7 and 8 we have the following property.

Property 9

Consider an American call option which expires within a limited time period and has a positive exercise price. Then, the following inequalities hold:

$$S_o \geq C(S_o, T, E) \geq \text{Max}\,(0, S_o - E/(1 + r)) \geq \text{Max}\,(0, S_o - E)$$

Example 18.12 Illustrating Property 9

Figure 18.14 presents the value, Max $(0, S_o - E/(1 + r))$ and call price for different prices of the share of Marks and Spencer. It can be seen that the inequality presented in Property 9 is always valid.

	A	B	C	D
1	OPTION PRICE AND INTRINSIC VALUE			
2	=================================			
3	Exercise Price -->	180		
4	Interest rate --->	0.20%		
5	----------------			
6	Share Price	Call Price	MAX(0,So-E/(1+r))	Intrinsic Value
7	----------------			
8	162.00	0.91	0.00	0.00
9	172.00	3.39	0.00	0.00
10	180.00	7.23	0.00	0.00
11	182.00	8.46	2.36	2.00
12	192.00	16.00	12.36	12.00
13	202.00	25.06	22.36	22.00
14	212.00	34.79	32.36	32.00
15	----------------			

Figure 18.14. Illustrating Property 9

The relationships between the share price, call price and `MAX(0,So-E/1+r))` are graphically presented in Figure 18.15 (slight deviations occur due to rounding).

Property 10 An American option should be exercised only at the expiry date

The value of an American option before the expiry date is at least equal to Max $(0, S_o - E/(1 + r))$. In view of Property 9, Max $(0, S_0 - E/(1 + r))$ is greater than $S_o - E$ (that is, the value obtained if the option is exercised). This shows that

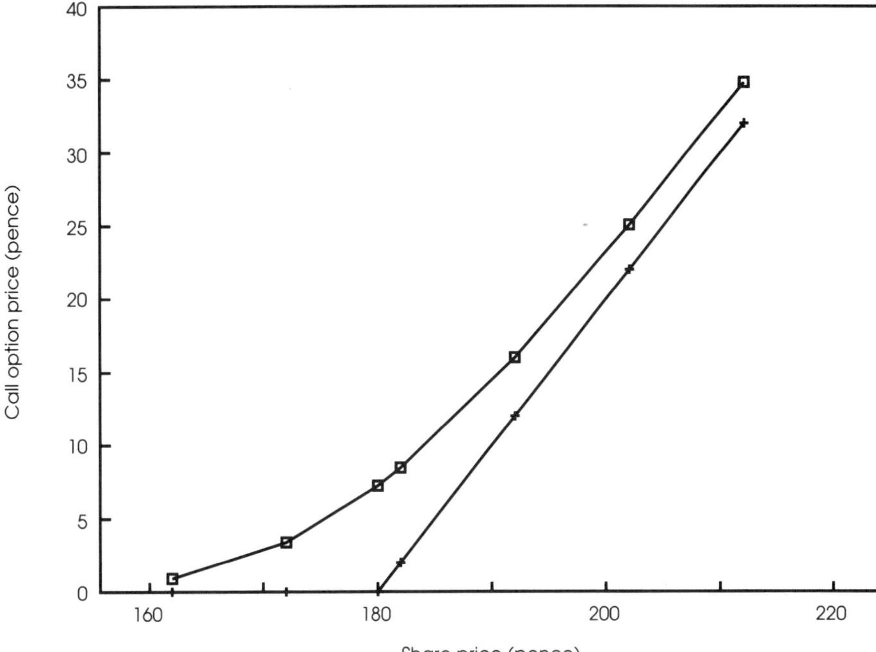

Figure 18.15. A boundary for option prices: the case of the 180 pence April call option on Marks and Spencer's shares

an American option before the expiry date is more valued unexercised than it is exercised; thus, an American option should not be exercised before its expiry date.

From Properties 9 and 10 the following property follows.

Property 11
Consider two call options, one American and one European, which have the same exercise price and expiry date. Then at the expiry date both options have the same price. This price is equal to $\text{Max}\,(0, S - E)$.

Since an American option has all the properties of a European option, and also provides the option buyer the right to exercise before the expiry date, the price of an American option must be at least equal to the price of the European option. Therefore, we have the following property.

Property 12
Consider two call options, one American and one European, which have the same exercise price and expiry date. Then the price of the American call option is greater than or equal to the price of the European call option.

Properties of put options
The call option Properties 1, 2, 4 and 7 are also valid for put options. In addition, we have the following four properties.

Property 13
On expiry date, the price of a put option is given by:

$$P(S, 0, E) = \text{Max}\,(0, E - S)$$

where $S =$ the underlying share price at the expiry date.

Property 14

If two put options on the same share have the same expiry date, the same underlying share price and different exercise prices, then the price of the put option with the lower exercise price is lower than or equal to the price of the put option with the higher exercise price.

Property 15

If two put options on the same share have the exercise price, the same underlying share price and different expiry dates, then the price of the option with the longer time to expiration is greater than or equal to the price of the option with the shorter time to expiration.

Property 16 The put–call parity

Assume the existence of a perfect capital market with no transaction costs and with the same lending and borrowing interest rate. We also consider a European call option and a European put option on the same share having the same exercise price and expiry date. Then the value of the call option is equal to the value of a portfolio comprised of the underlying share, the put option and a loan of $E/(1+r)$ pounds.

Below are shown two portfolios, A and B, which yield the same future cash flows.

	Investment outflow	Future cash flow at expiry date	
		$S > E$	$S \leq E$
Portfolio A			
Buy the put for £P	$-P$	0	$E - S$
Buy the stock for £S_o	$-S_o$	S	S
Borrow £E at interest rate r	$E/(1+r)$	$-E$	$-E$
TOTAL	$-P - S_o + E/(1+r)$	$S - E$	0
Portfolio B			
Buy call	$-C$	$S - E$	0

If the portfolios A and B were associated with different initial outflows, then investors could obtain abnormal profits. For example, if the initial outflow associated with portfolio B was higher than that from portfolio A, then an investor would create a portfolio having a lower initial outflow than that of B and the same future cash flow. This portfolio is comprised of: sell a call, borrow money and buy a put in the underlying share. Since, at equilibrium, the portfolios A and B have equal initial outflows one can write the put-parity equation as follows:

$$C(S_o, T, E) = S_o - E/(1+r) + P(S_o, T, E) \tag{18.1}$$

The last equation is called the put–call parity equation because it relates put and call prices.

Property 17

The price of a European put option is lower than or equal to Max $(0, E/(1+r))$, where $r =$ the riskless interest rate for the period until the expiry date and $E =$ the option's exercise price.

Property 17 is true because Properties 16 and 9 imply:

$$-E/(1+r)+P(S,T,E)=C(S,T,E)-S\leq 0$$

The following property is based upon a similar argument to that utilized to discuss Property 12.

Property 18
Consider two put options, one American and one European, which have the same exercise price and expiry date. Then the price of the American put option is greater than or equal to the price of the European call option.

Property 19
Exercising an American put option before the expiry date may be appropriate.

From Equation (18.1), we have:

$$C(S_o,T,E)-S_o+E/(1+r)=P(S_o,T,E) \qquad (18.2)$$

Equation (18.2) states that the portfolio consisting of the share, a call option, and a loan is identical to pay-off structure to an American put with an exercise price and expiry time the same as that of the call.

If the put option is exercised, then the investor receives a payment of $E-S_o$ (we assume that the exercise price is greater than the underlying share price). The following inequality holds for a small enough share price:

$$C(S_o,T,E)<E(1-1/(1+r))$$

Adding $E-S_o$ on each side of this inequality yields

$$E-S_o+C(S_o,T,E)<E-S_o+E(1-1/(1+r)) \qquad (18.3)$$

Combining Equation (18.2) and inequality (18.3) gives

$$E-S_o>C(S_o,T,E)-S_o+E/(1+r)=P(S_o,T,E)$$

Since $P(S_o,T,E)>P(S,0,E)$, it is better to exercise the put option before its expiry date.

Property 20
Consider an American put option which expires within a limited time period and has a positive exercise price. Then the following inequality holds:

$$\text{Max}\,(0,E-S_o)\leq P(S_o,T,E)$$

Since an American option can be exercised at any time, its price must be greater than or equal to its intrinsic value.

Property 21
Consider an American put and a European put which have the same exercise price and expiry date. Then at the expiry date both options have the same price. This price is equal to $\text{Max}\,(0,E-S)$.

Figure 18.16 summarizes the boundary conditions discussed above.

Call option	Put option
At any time before expiration	*At any time before expiration*
Share price $\geq$ Call price	Put price $\geq$ Intrinsic value
Call price $\geq \text{Max}\,(0, S_o - PV(E))$	Intrinsic value ≥ 0
$\text{Max}\,(0, S_o - PV(E)) \geq$ Intrinsic value	
Intrinsic value ≥ 0	
where $PV(E) = E/(1 + r)$	
At expiry date only	*At expiry date only*
Option value = Intrinsic value	Option value = Intrinsic value

Figure 18.16. A summary of several boundary conditions on options

Summary

1 *Call and put options* Options can be classified as call and put options. Ownership of a call option gives the owner the right (but not the obligation) to purchase from the writer a specified number of shares at a specified price within a predetermined period of time. A put option provides the opposite opportunity, it gives the owner the right (but not the obligation) to sell to the writer a given number of shares at a specified price within a predetermined period of time.

The owner of a call (put) option can exercise his or her rights to buy (sell) the underlying shares, can sell the call (put) option, or can allow his or her rights to expire unused. European options are options that can be exercised only at the expiry date. American options are options that can be exercised at any time on or before their expiry date. Call or put options traded via the London Stock Exchange are of the American type.

2 *Profit profiles of call and put options* Assuming zero transaction costs, the owner of a call option realizes a profit if the selling price of the option is higher than that paid when purchasing (selling) the option. If, at the expiry date, the underlying share price of a call option is lower than the exercise price, the option expires worthless and the owner obtains a loss. If, at the expiry date, the underlying share price of a call option exceeds the exercise price, the owner's profit or loss equals the difference between the option's intrinsic value and the price paid for buying the option. From the owner's point of view, the loss related to a call is limited to the price paid for the call. The profit realized from buying a call is the mirror image of the losses realized from selling the call.

Assuming zero transaction costs, the owner of a put ends up with a profit if the price received from selling the option is higher than that paid when purchasing the option. The profit obtained from holding a put option until the expiry date depends on the share price at the expiry date. If, at the expiry date, the underlying share of a put option is lower than the exercise price, the profit or loss of the owner can be computed by simply subtracting the price of the option from the intrinsic value. If a put option expires worthless, the owner realizes a loss equal to the buying price of the put. For the owner's viewpoint, the losses related to a put are bound by the price paid for the put. Again, the profits of a put owner are the mirror image of the losses of the put writer.

3 *Properties of options* There are several properties associated with options including the following two: (a) it is not optimal to exercise an American call

option before its expiry date (assume that no dividend payments occur during the life of the option); and (b) exercising an American put option before the expiry date may be appropriate (assume that no dividend payments occur during the life of the option).

Questions and discussion

1 For each term shown below provide a definition in your own words. Then check your responses against the definitions included in the chapter.

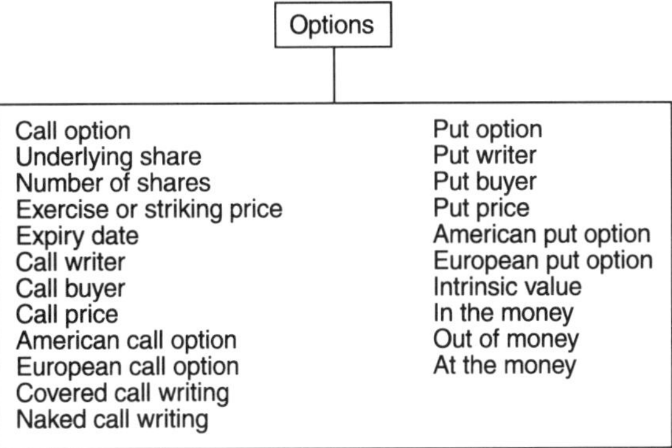

2 Discuss the following information (*source: Financial Times*, 6 December 1990):

		Calls			Puts		
		Jan	Apr	Jul	Jan	Apr	Jul
Boots	300	44	57	63	2 1/2	6 1/2	10
(336)	330	21	34	42	10	14	18
	360	7 1/2	19	26	26	29	31

(**a**) Which call options are out of the money, and which are in the money?
(**b**) Which put options are out of the money, and which are in the money?
(**c**) Which call and put options have zero intrinsic value?
(**d**) Which call and put options have positive intrinsic value?
(**e**) The 360 January options on Boot's shares have zero intrinsic values.

Explain why investors purchase options with zero intrinsic values.

3 'The maximum potential loss a buyer of a call option can realize is limited to his or her initial investment and his or her maximum potential gain is unlimited. However, call writers have limited potential gains and unlimited potential losses.' By using a numerical example discuss this statement verbally and graphically (for your numerical example use a call option of Boots plc given in Question 2).

4 'The maximum potential loss a put owner can realize is limited to his or her initial investment and his or her maximum potential gain is unlimited. However, the maximum potential gain of a put writer is limited and his or her maximum potential loss is unlimited.' By using numerical example discuss this statement verbally and graphically (for your numerical example use a put option of Boots plc given in Question 2).

5 **(a)** Indicate in each of the cases given below whether a gain or a loss is realized. Discuss briefly each answer provided.

	Action: Sell	Let expiry	Exercise
Call buyer			
Call writer			

(b) Similarly, indicate in each of the cases presented below whether a gain or a loss is realized. Be prepared to discuss briefly each answer provided.

	Action: Sell	Let expiry	Exercise
Put buyer			
Put writer			

6 Discuss the following statements:

(a) 'Consider two American call options with the same underlying share, the same expiry date and different exercise prices. Then the price of the call option with the lower exercise price is greater than or equal to the price of the call option with the higher exercise price.'

(b) 'The value of American call options with the same underlying share and the same exercise price increases as time to expiration increases.'

Evaluate these statements by using the data provided in Question 2.

7 Discuss the following statements:

(a) 'Consider two American put options with the same underlying share, the same expiry date and different exercise prices. Then the price of the put option with the lower exercise price is lower than or equal to the price of the put option with the higher exercise price.'

(b) The value of American put options with the same underlying share and the same exercise price increases as time to expiration increases.

Evaluate these statements by using the data provided in Question 2.

8 Discuss with the aid of a numerical example the call–put parity property.

9 Discuss the following option positioning diagram which rates four options on the basis of price and initial time to expiration.

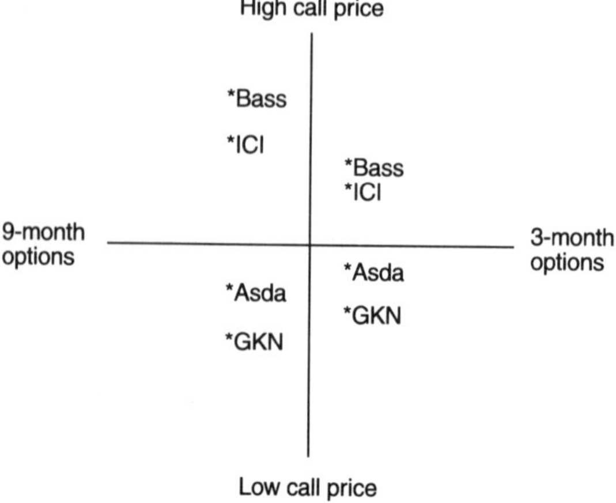

10 **(a)** Consider the following four statements related to options. Fill in the appropriate reply by using either the word 'Agree' or the word 'Disagree'.

	Agree	Disagree
The price of a call option must be greater or equal to its intrinsic value.		
The price of a put option can be lower than zero.		
The percentage change of a call option price is lower than that of the underlying share.		
The percentage change of a put option price is larger than that of the underlying share.		

(b) Discuss in detail each reply given in part (a).

11 **(a)** The shares of GKN are currently quoted at 329 pence (the current day is 6 December 1990). Mr George Maris wishes to purchase four call option contracts of 1,000 shares each. The options have the same expiry date and each has an exercise price of 300 pence. If the investor has only £1,000 to invest, can he afford to purchase the four contracts?

(b) Mr George Annis wants to buy two put option contracts of 1,000 shares each. The underlying security the options are referred to is GKN, while the exercise price of a put option is 360 pence. Also note that both options have the same expiry date and a share of GKN has a current price of 329 pence (the current day is 6 December 1990). Assume that Mr Maris has £500 to invest. Can he afford to purchase the two option contracts?

12 **(a)** Imagine that it is 6 December 1990 and Mr George Annis purchases a call option on Boots plc's shares which expires in January 1990 (assume that the share does not pay dividends during the holding period of the option). Should he exercise his option before its expiry date? Discuss.

(b) On 6 December 1990 Mrs Ruth Kitchin purchased a put option in Boots plc's shares which expires in January 1990 (assume that the share does not pay dividends during the holding period of the option). Is it appropriate to exercise her option before its expiry date? Discuss.

13 Compare and contrast European and American call and put options.

14 Prepare an analog model summarizing the main points discussed in this chapter.

15 How can spreadsheets be used to facilitate the application of the concepts discussed in this chapter?

Appendix 18A The runs test of randomness

A run is simply one or more identical symbols preceded or followed by a different symbol or no symbols at all. For example, consider the weekly rates of return of a share in Marks and Spencer:

Week 1: −0.0733
Week 2: −0.0082
Week 3: 0.0533
Week 4: −0.0237

Designate a negative rate of return by a minus sign (−) and a positive rate of return by a plus sign (+). Then we have the following sequence:

− − + −

The pair − − is a run because it is preceded by no symbol and followed by a symbol that is different to −. Similarly, the single symbol + is a run because it is preceded and followed by the symbol −. Finally, the single symbol − is a run since it is preceded by a different symbol and followed by no symbol. The sequence under consideration has three runs.

A statistical test can be used to examine whether a sequence of symbols is random. Consider a sequence that contains two symbols. We assume that each symbol occurs at least 10 times. Figure 18A.1 summarizes the run test of randomness.

The null and alternative hypotheses are, respectively:

H_0: The sequence of symbols is random.

H_1: The sequence of symbols is not random.

The null hypothesis is rejected if

$$\text{ABS(sample } z) = \text{ABS}\left(\frac{NR - E(R)}{\text{STD}(R)}\right) > \text{critical value of } z$$

where

ABS(sample z) = absolute value of sample z.
NR = number of runs in the sequence.
$E(R)$ = the mean of the sampling distribution of the number of runs:

$$E(R) = \frac{2NM}{N+M} + 1$$

STD(R) = the standard deviation of the sampling distribution of the number of runs:

$$\text{STD}(R) = \sqrt{\frac{2NM(2NM - NR)}{NR^2(NR-1)}}$$

N = number of times one symbol occurs.
M = number of times the other symbol occurs.

Figure 18A.1. A summary of the run test of randomness

Example 18A.1 Applying the runs test of randomness

Figure 18A.2 shows a sample of 27 weekly rates of return for Marks and Spencer's share. We denote a negative return by a minus sign and a positive rate of return by a plus sign. The following function is stored in cell C6:

```
@IF(B6<0,"     -","     +")
```

In words, if cell B6 contains a negative value, return a minus sign, otherwise return a plus sign. The contents of cell C6 are copied in range C7..C32. Since 1-2-3 cannot add symbols, we enter in column D numbers that represent the two signs under consideration. Number 1 represents a minus sign and number 0

```
     A                    B                C     D     E        F           G
 1 RUNS TEST FOR RANDOMNESS FOR THE M&S' WEEKLY RATES OF RETURN
 2 ============================================================
 3 ------------------------------------------------------------
 4    Week       Rate of Return      Symbol   1/0 Number of Runs
 5 ------------------------------------------------------------
 6 12-Sep-89              -0.0317      -       1     1
 7 19-Sep-89              -0.0376      -       1     0
 8 26-Sep-89              -0.0341      -       1     0
 9 03-Oct-89              -0.0200      -       1     0
10 10-Oct-89              -0.0733      -       1     0
11 17-Oct-89              -0.0082      -       1     0
12 24-Oct-89               0.0533      +       0     1
13 31-Oct-89              -0.0237      -       1     1
14 07-Nov-89               0.0314      +       0     1
15 07-Nov-89               0.0103      +       0     0
16 07-Nov-89              -0.0258      -       1     1
17 07-Nov-89               0.0207      +       0     1
18 05-Dec-89               0.0353      +       0     0
19 12-Dec-89              -0.0150      -       1     1
20 19-Dec-89              -0.0203      -       1     0
21 26-Dec-89               0.0102      +       0     1
22 02-Jan-90               0.0349      +       0     0
23 09-Jan-90               0.0337      +       0     0
24 16-Jan-90              -0.0687      -       1     1
25 23-Jan-90              -0.0257      -       1     0
26 30-Jan-90              -0.0157      -       1     0
27 06-Feb-90               0.0764      +       0     1
28 13-Feb-90              -0.0099      -       1     1
29 20-Feb-90               0.0099      +       0     1
30 27-Feb-90               0.0049      +       0     0
31 06-Mar-90              -0.0347      -       1     1
32 13-Mar-90              -0.0360      -       1     0
33                                          -------------
34 Number of negative returns --->         16     13 <-- Number of runs
35 Number of positive returns --->         11
36 Total number of observations ->         27
37
38 Mean -------------->                14.037
39 Variance ------------>               6.036
40 Standard deviation ---->             2.457
41 z value ----------------->          -0.422
                                       =======
```

Figure 18A.2. Calculating the statistic of the runs test for randomness

represents a plus sign. The following function is stored in cell D6:

```
@IF(B6<0,1,0)
```

The contents of cell D6 are copied in the range D7..D32.

The runs are shown in column E. Cell E6 stores the following function:

```
@IF(D6=D5,0,1)
```

In words, if cell D6 contains the same numerical value as the previous cell D5, return 0, otherwise return 1. In this case, the contents of cell E6 are copied in the range E7..E32.

The number of negative returns stored in cell D34 is simply the sum of the values in the range D6..D32. The number of positive returns stored in cell D35 is equal to the sample size minus the number of negative returns. The number of runs stored in cell E34 is equal to the sum of the values in the range E6..E32.

The mean of the sampling distribution of the number of runs would be

$$E(R) = \frac{2(16)(11)}{27} + 1 = 14.037$$

The variance of the sampling distribution of the number of runs is

$$\text{VAR}(R) = \frac{2(16)(11)[2(16)(11) - 13]}{13^2(13-1)} = 58.840$$

Therefore, the standard deviation of the sampling distribution of the number of runs is 7.671. The sample z is calculated as follows:

$$\text{Sample } z = \frac{13.000 - 14.037}{7.671} = -0.1351$$

The critical value of z for a two-tailed test at 5 per cent level of significance is 1.96 (or -1.96). This value can be calculated as follows: $P(-1.96 < z < 1.96) = 2(0.4750) = 0.95$, where 0.4740 is given in the table of areas for the standard normal probability distribution.

Since ABS(-0.1351) = 0.1351 is lower than 1.96, the null hypothesis is accepted. Thus, the sequence of rates of return is random. Stated differently, there is no relationship between successive weekly rates of return of Marks and Spencer for the period under consideration.

References and bibliography

Black, F. (1975) Fact and Fantasy in the Use of Options, *Financial Analyst Journal*, July–August, 36–41, 61–72.

Black, F. and M. Scholes (1973) The Pricing of Options and Corporate Liabilities, *Journal of Political Economy*, May–June, 637–54.

Cox, S. and S. Ross (1976) A Survey of Some New Results in Financial Option Pricing Theory, *Journal of Finance*, 1976, 383–402.

Merton, R.C. (1973) The Theory of Rational Option Pricing, *Bell Journal of Economics and Management Science*, Spring 1973, 141–83.

19 Option valuation models

This chapter includes:

- Black–Scholes valuation model
- Uses of options
- Uses of Black–Scholes valuation model
- Empirical evidence on the option valuation models

In recent years, the rapid growth in the option markets has been accompanied by an increasing amount of research in the area of options valuation and several valuation models have been developed. One procedure used in option valuation is the Black–Scholes model, which expresses the value of an option as a function of five observable variables: the share price; exercise price; time to expiration; the volatility of the underlying share price; and riskless rate of interest. The objective of this chapter is to introduce the Black–Scholes option valuation model as well as to illustrate the sensitivity of option prices to various parameters of the valuation model. Additionally, this chapter discusses some of the empirical tests on the validity of option valuation models.

The Black and Scholes valuation formula

The valuation model (developed by Black and Scholes, 1973) is based upon the following assumptions:

1 The capital market is perfect in the sense that neither transaction costs nor taxes exist; information is freely available to all investors; all securities are infinitely divisible; and no single buyer or seller of securities is large enough to affect their prices.
2 The risk-free rate of return is constant and known throughout the length of the option contract, investors can borrow or lend any amount of money at the risk-free rate of interest.
3 The underlying security does not pay dividends.
4 The underlying security's continuously compounded rate of return follows a normal distribution and it has a constant and known variance over the life of the option contract.
5 The option can be exercised only at the expiry date.
6 Short selling of securities is allowed.

The valuation of call options

According to the Black–Scholes option valuation model, at any point in time a call option can be replicated by a portfolio containing shares of the underlying security some of which are financed with borrowed money. In equilibrium the value of the call option must be equal to the cost of creating the replicating portfolio. If this is not the case, there would be a riskless arbitrage opportunity.

Example 19.1 Creating a portfolio that replicates two call options

Imagine that it is 20 March 1990. A share in Marks and Spencer is currently selling at 192 pence. The exercise price of the April 1990 call option in Marks and Spencer's shares is 180 pence. Assume that the price of Marks and Spencer's shares at the expiry day will be either 168 pence or 193 pence.

Suppose that the current price of the option is £150 (that is, $15 \times 1{,}000/100$). Consider an investor who writes two April call options in Marks and Spencer's shares. In this case, the investor receives £300. Assume that the investor purchases 1,040 shares of Marks and Spencer at 192 pence per share. Such an investment costs £1,996.80 (that is, $1{,}040 \times 192/100$). Therefore, the investor will borrow £1,696.80 to finance his or her investment. Assume that the risk-free rate is 1.19 per cent. From Figure 19.1, we see that the net initial investment of the investor is zero.

If the share price at the expiry date is 168 pence, then the option will expire worthless. In this instance, the investor will hold £1,747.20 worth in shares (that is, $1{,}040 \times 168/100$) and will owe £1,717.0 (that is, $1{,}696.80 \times (1 + 0.0119)$). Thus, his or her profit will be £30.20. If the share price at the expiry date is 193 pence, then his or her profit will also be £30.20 (see Figure 19.1).

We see that in either case there exists the possibility of an arbitrage profit (a profit that is realized at no risk and for no initial investment is known as an arbitrage profit). These opportunities could not last long, and we would expect the option price to adjust towards its equilibrium value of £0.1350735 which is calculated as follows:

$$\frac{£1{,}996.80 - (1{,}747.20)/(1 + 0.0119)}{2} = £135.0735$$

$$(£135.0735) \times (100)/1{,}000 = £0.1350735$$

	A	B	C	D
1	ESTIMATING A CALL OPTION'S VALUE			
2	================================			
3	Current Share Price	£192.00		
4	Exercise Price	£180.00		
5	Possible Share Price 1	£168.00		
6	Possible Share Price 2	£193.00		
7	Risk-Free Rate	1.19%		
8	Number of Shares	1040		
9				
10				
11				
12	Write 2 Call Options	£300.00	£0.00	(£260.00)
13	Buy 1040 Shares	(£1,996.80)	£1,747.20	£2,007.20
14	Borrow at 1.19%	£1,696.80	(£1,717.00)	(£1,717.00)
15		-----------	-----------	-----------
16		£0.00	£30.20	£30.20
17				
18	Write 2 Call Options	£207.10	£0.00	(£260.00)
19	Buy 1040 Shares	(£1,996.80)	£1,747.20	£2,007.20
20	Borrow at 1.19%	£1,726.70	(£1,747.20)	(£1,747.20)
21		-----------	-----------	-----------
22		£0.00	£0.00	£0.00

Figure 19.1. Estimating the value of a call option in Marks and Spencer's shares

The previous calculations are summarized in Figure 19.1.

If the option price is below £0.1350735, then the following strategy will also provide an arbitrage profit: buying two call options, selling short 1,040 shares of Marks and Spencer and placing the proceeds of the transaction into a riskless security.

Problem Create the spreadsheet shown in Figure 19.1.

Note that Example 19.1 is unrealistic because we assigned only two possible values for the underlying share. Additionally, this example did not consider the fact that the stock market operates on a continuous basis during trading hours. However, we could assume a more realistic situation where the option is trading during small intervals of time (for example, every quarter of an hour) and the underlying share price can take on any number of values in a given interval of time. Under these assumptions, it is possible to offer an example that computes the value of a call option in a similar fashion to that illustrated in Example 19.1. In this case, arbitrage opportunities could exist if the option value is different to its fair value.

Black and Scholes (1973) showed that it is possible to construct a portfolio comprised of a written call and an appropriate long position in the underlying security which is riskless for small changes in the security price. Over any instant of time, the portfolio should therefore earn the risk-free rate of return on the net investment in the portfolio position. Consequently, the price of the position in the call and security should be such as to give this risk-free rate of return. Given the security price, this allows the solution for the price of the call.

According to their option valuation model there are five variables that affect the value of a call option: underlying share price; exercise price; time to expiration; risk-free interest rate; and variability of share price. Figure 19.2 summarizes Black–Scholes valuation model.

Definition The option valuation model of Black and Scholes provides a mathematical expression for the value of a call option.

Calculation With the aid of the assumptions presented earlier the equilibrium value of a call option is given by:

$$V_c = S_0 N(d_1) - \mathrm{PV}(E) N(d_2)$$

where

S_0 = the current market price of the underlying share.

$\mathrm{PV}(E)$ = the present value of the exercise price discounted back from the expiry date using continuous discounting.

$N(d_j)$ = probability of drawing a value from a standard normal distribution (that is, a normal distribution with a mean of 0 and an area under the curve of 1) which is less than or equal to d_j, $j = 1, 2$.

Interpretation The first weighted term in the option valuation model is the expected value of an investment of $N(d_1)$ in ordinary shares, while the second weighted term is the present value of the investment's cost (note that the cost occurs only when the option is exercised at maturity). Therefore, the value of the call option is equal to the expected value of the investment of $N(d_1)$ in ordinary shares minus the present value of the cost of the investment if the option is exercised.

Figure 19.2. A summary of the Black–Scholes option valuation model

---

Statistical interpretation of $N(d_j)$

The values d_1 and d_2 are deviations from the mean of a standard normal distribution.

For example, in Figure 19.3 the value of d_1 is taken to be 1.0318. This means that d_1 is 1.0318 standard deviations above the zero mean. Furthermore, $N(1.0318)$ tells us the probability of getting a deviation that is less than or equal to 1.0318. $N(1.0318)$ is represented graphically by the cumulative area from the left tale of the standard normal distribution shown in Figure 19.2 to 1.0318. Similarly if $d_2 = 0.9516$, $N(0.9516)$ is the probability associated with getting a deviation that is less than or equal to 0.9516.

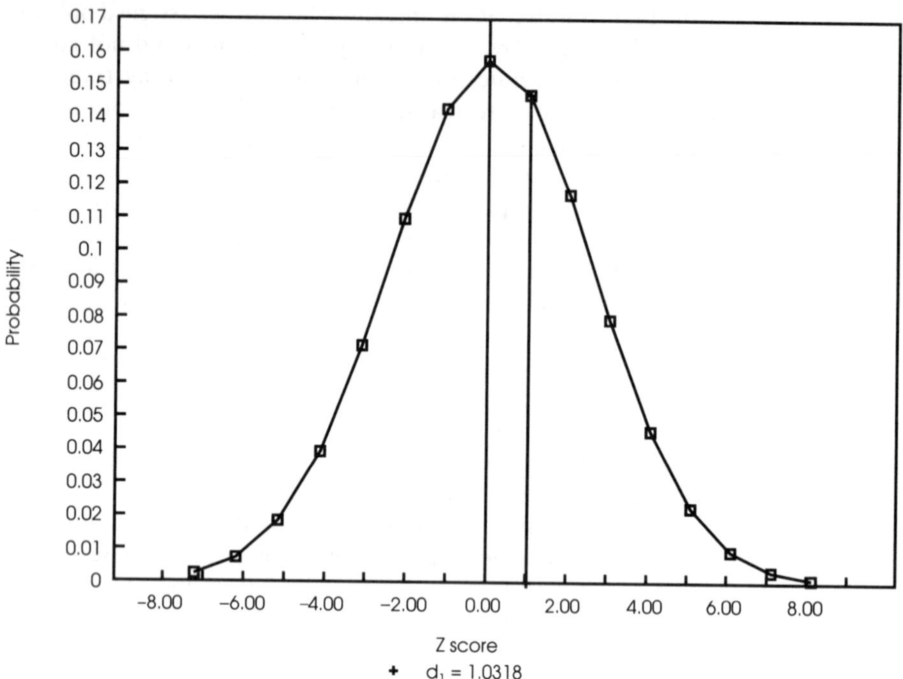

Figure 19.3. Unit normal probability distribution

The values of d_1 and d_2 can be computed as follows:

$$d_1 = \frac{\ln(S_0/E) + (r + \sigma^2/2)T}{\sigma\,\mathrm{SQRT}(T)}$$

and

$$d_2 = \frac{\ln(S_0/E) + (r - \sigma^2/2)T}{\sigma\,\mathrm{SQRT}(T)} = d_1 - 0\,\mathrm{SQRT}(T)$$

where

S_o = the current market price of the underlying share.
E = the exercise price of the option.
r = the (continuously compounded) annual riskless rate of interest.
T = the time remaining before the expiry date expressed as a proportion of a year.
σ = the annualized standard deviation of the underlying security's continuously compounded rate of return.
ln = the natural logarithm operator.
SQRT = the square root operator.

If the cumulative normal probability values of d_1 and d_2 are positive, then they can be calculated as follows:

$N(d_j)$ =	Total area under the left-hand tail of the standard normal distribution (= 0.5)	+	The probability associated with d_j standard deviation above the zero mean (use the standard normal distribution table) j = 1, 2

If d_1 and d_2 are negative, then $N(-d_j) = 1 - N(d_j), j = 1, 2$.

Interpretation of PV(E)

Under continuous compounding the present value of the exercise price can be expressed as follows:

$$\text{PV}(E) = E\text{e}^{-rT}$$

where

e = the natural antilog of 1 (that is, EXP = 2.7128).

e^{-rT} = the factor that discounts the exercise price back from the expiry date, using continuous compounding.

Interpretation of the option valuation formula

The (net) present value of any investment is equal to the present value of all future benefits it is expected to provide over its life span minus the present value of the outflows related to the investment. With no exception a call option is equivalent to a portfolio containing $N(d_1)$ ordinary shares. If the call option is exercised, the cost of this portfolio is equal to the present value of the exercise price discounted back from the expiry date times the probability of exercise. Therefore, the value of a call option is equal to the expected value of the investments in the portfolio of $N(d_1)$ shares minus the cost of this investment.

Example 19.2 Using the Black–Scholes valuation formula to estimate the value of a call option

Imagine that it is 20 March 1990. Marks and Spencer's shares stand at 192 pence and the continuously compounded annual risk-free rate is 15.20 per cent. The exercise price of the April 1990 options in Marks and Spencer's shares is 180 pence, the annualized variance of the underlying security's continuously compounded rate of return is 0.0652 and the option matures in 36 days.

To determine the option price, it is necessary to calculate the values for d_1 and d_2.

$$d_1 = \frac{\ln(192/180) + (0.1520 + 0.0652/2) \times (36/365)}{\text{SQRT}(0.0652)\ \text{SQRT}(36/365)}$$

$$= \frac{0.0645 + 0.0182}{0.0802} = 1.0318$$

and

$$d_2 = 1.0318 - \text{SQRT}(0.0652)\ \text{SQRT}(36/365)$$

$$= 0.9516$$

Next the values of $N(d_1)$ and $N(d_2)$ must be found (see Appendix 19A.1 for the methods used to calculate these values). The two values we seek are:

$$N(d_1) = 0.8489 \approx 0.85$$

$$N(d_2) = 0.8294$$

The present value of the exercise price is

$$180e^{-(0.1520)(0.0986)} = 177.32$$

Finally, we can calculate the call option price as follows:

$$V_c = (192)(0.8489) - (177.32)(0.8294) = 15.92 \text{ pence}$$

The valuation of put options

The Black–Scholes model can also be utilized to value a put option. The formula for the put option's value is:

$$V_p = -SN(-d_1) + \text{PV}(E)N(-d_2)$$

where $N(d_j) + N(-d_j) = 1$

Example 19.3 Using the Black–Scholes valuation formula to estimate the value of a put option

Consider the data presented in Example 19.2. Then

$$V_p = -192(1 - 0.8489) + 177.32(1 - 0.8294) = 1.2395 \text{ pence}$$

Factors influencing option prices

In view of the Black and Scholes option pricing model, there are five factors that influence the value of a call (or put) option:

- The current share price.
- The exercise price.
- The risk-free rate.
- The variance of the underlying share price.
- The time remaining to expiry date.

- Share price The higher is the share price, the larger is the chance that the price of the share will rise above the option's exercise price, everything else being equal. This leads to greater demand (less demand) for calls (puts) which in turn drives their prices up (down).
- Exercise price Consider two options having the same expiry date, the same underlying share and different exercise prices. When the share price increases, the potential profit related to the call (put) option with the lower exercise price is greater (smaller) than the profit for the call option on the higher exercise price. This shows that the potential profits from a call (put) option decrease (increase) as the exercise price increases.
- Risk-free rate An investor can adopt either of the following strategies: invest in shares or place part of his or her money in call options and the remainder in fixed-income securities.

When the interest rates are high, the investor can earn more fixed income by adopting the second strategy. In this instance, the second strategy becomes more attractive and as a result the demand for call options increases. Increasing demand for calls will generally lead to higher prices.

The relationship between a put price and interest rates is negative. If an investor holds both put options and shares, then he or she sacrifices the opportunity to earn some interest. The higher the interest rate the greater the interest sacrificed. Thus, when interest rates rise put option prices decrease.

- The variance of the underlying share price Consider two call options having the same expiry date, the same exercise price and different underlying shares. Assume that the price of the first underlying share is stable while that of the second is extremely volatile. The second option could provide a large profit as there is a high chance for the share price to rise above the exercise price. This and the fact that an option is a limited liability security make the second call option more attractive and the demand for it drives its price up. A similar argument applies for put options.
- Time remaining to expiry date The variance of the distribution of the share returns increases with time (since the standard deviation of price returns increases with the square root of time). In other words, the longer the time remaining before the expiry date, the higher the volatility, everything else being the same. However, the larger is the variance, the greater is the option price, which in turn indicates that the longer the option's life the higher its price.

Figure 19.4 summarizes the relationship between each of these five variables and the call or put option prices.

Variable		Call	Put
Share price	Increases	Increases	Decreases
Exercise price	Increases	Decreases	Increases
Risk-free rate	Increases	Increases	Decreases
Volatility	Increases	Increases	Increases
Time	Increases	Increases	Increases

Figure 19.4. Effects of variables on option price

	A	B	C	D	E	F	G	H
83								
84		Variable	Call	Put		VOLATILITY		
85								
86		0.040	15.245	0.567		0.200		
87		0.060	15.786	1.108		0.245		
88		0.080	16.338	1.659		0.283		
89		0.100	16.876	2.198		0.316		
90		0.120	17.396	2.718		0.346		
91		0.140	17.897	3.218		0.374		
92		0.160	18.378	3.700		0.400		
93		0.180	18.841	4.163		0.424		
94		0.200	19.288	4.610		0.447		
95		0.220	19.720	5.042		0.469		

Figure 19.5. A range of volatilities and their corresponding call/put values

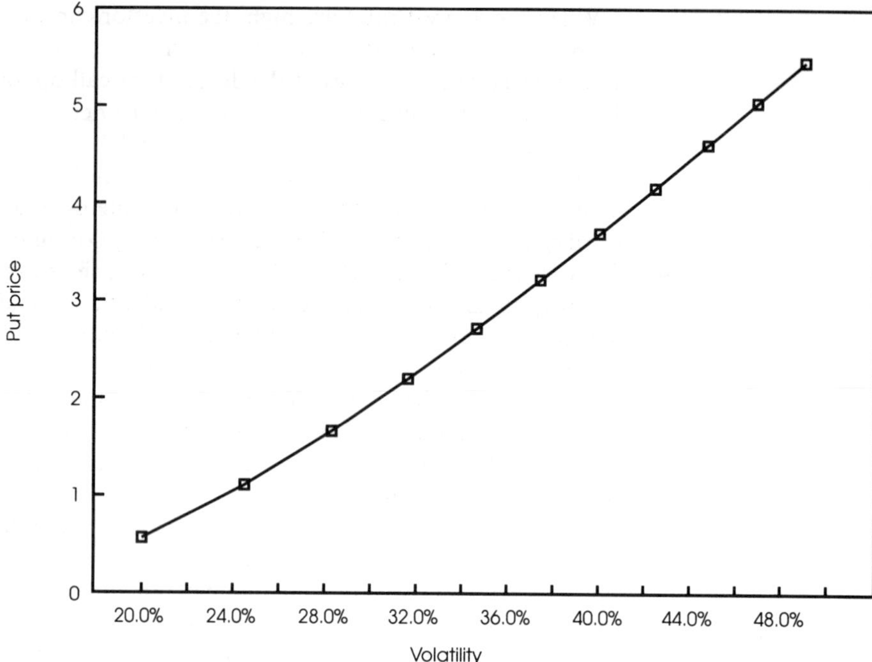

Figure 19.6. Sensitivity of call price to volatility

Example 19.4 Sensitivity of option price to changes in volatility and time to expiration

Call option prices increase as volatility increases, other factors remaining constant (the volatility equals the square root of the variance of the underlying

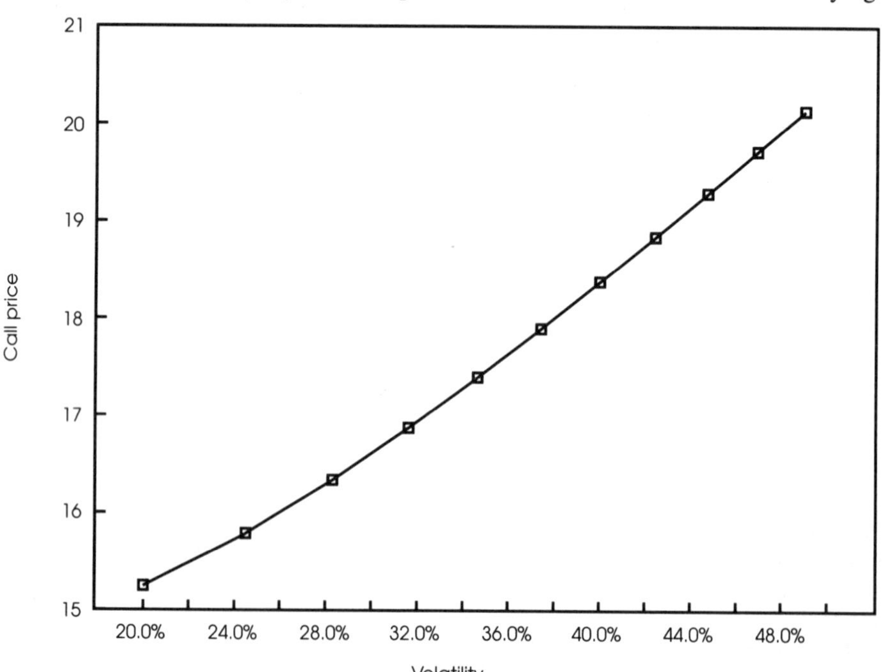

Figure 19.7. Sensitivity of put price to volatility

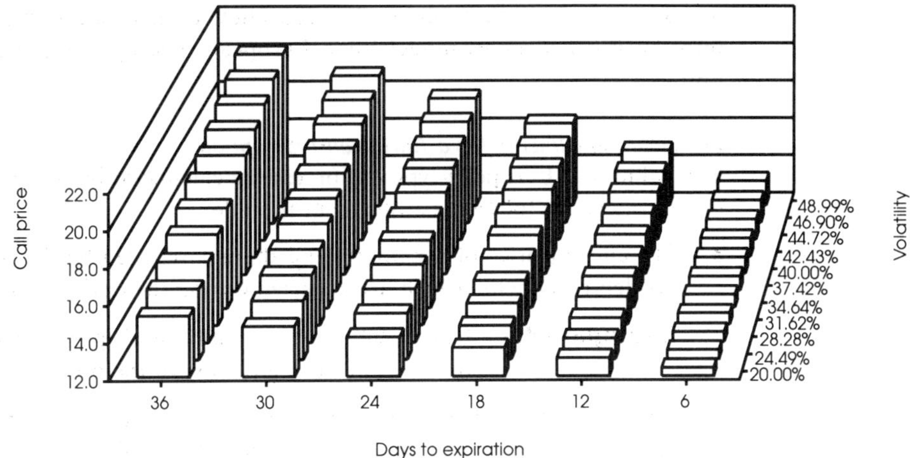

Figure 19.8. Sensitivity of call price to volatility and time to expiration

share's continuously compounded rate of return). Consider the data provided in Example 19.2. Figure 19.5 shows a range of volatility values and its corresponding range of call and put values (other things being the same).

The relationship between the volatility and the call (put) price is illustrated in Figure 19.6 (Figure 19.7). The results presented in this example were derived by using the macro presented in Appendix 19C.

Finally, Figure 19.8 presents graphically the sensitivity of the call price to volatility and days to expiration. It is clear that the call price decreases as time to expiration decreases.

Extensions of the Black–Scholes model

The derivation of the Black–Scholes option valuation model is based upon several unrealistic assumptions. The original Black–Scholes model was extended by relaxing many of its assumptions and the present section discusses several extensions of the model.

Riskless rate of interest

One of the assumptions of the Black–Scholes model is the following: the riskless rate of interest is constant and known throughout the length of the option contract, investors can borrow or lend any amount of money at the risk-free rate. If the interest rate changes from period to period, then calculate the geometric mean of the period-to-period interest changes and use it in the Black–Scholes model. In addition, since the borrowing rate is different from the lending rate, use in the formula the average of the two rates (later in this chapter we briefly discuss a model where the interest rate is stochastic).

Dividends

The original Black–Scholes model assumes that the underlying share of an option does not pay dividends. The model can be expanded for options whose underlying shares declare dividends prior to the expiry date. Let us assume that the dividend payments from the underlying share can be predicted with certainty during the option's life. The discussion that follows illustrates how to incorporate dividend adjustments into the Black–Scholes model for a European-type option and an American-type option.

Dividend adjustments for a European-type option

The value of a European-type option can be calculated by using the Black–Scholes model where the following adjustment is made:

- The current price of the underlying share is reduced by the present value of all dividend payments which are expected during the option's life.

Example 19.5 Calculating a European option's price when two ex-dividend dates occur during the life of the option

Imagine that it is 1 November 1989. Consider a call option in Marks and Spencer's shares which expires on 25 July 1990 and has an exercise price of 180 pence. The current price of the Marks and Spencer share is 188 pence. Assume that the option will be exercised at the expiry date. The share has two ex-dividend dates on 13 November 1989 and on 29 May 1990, respectively. The dividend per share on the first ex-dividend date is expected to be 1.80 pence and on the second 4.45 pence. Consider the following chronological diagram:

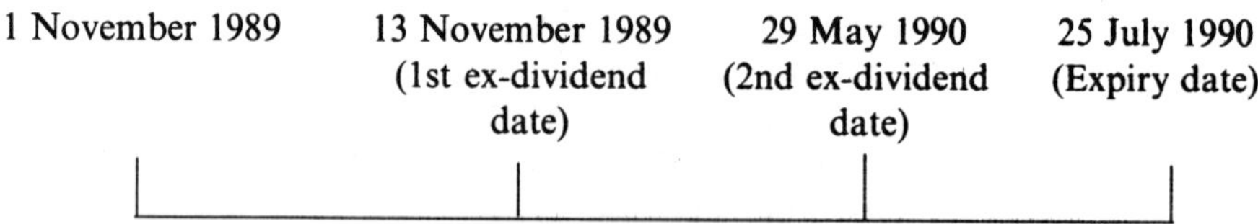

At the assumed continuously compounded risk-free rate of 16.01 per cent, the present value of the dividends is calculated as follows:

$$1.80e^{-(12/365)(0.1601)} + 4.45e^{-(209/365)(0.1601)} = 5.85 \text{ pence}$$

Thus, we use in the Black–Scholes formula a share price of 182.15 pence (that is, 188 pence −5.85 pence). The following data can now be employed in order to calculate the call option price:

Share price → 182.15 pence
Exercise price → 180 pence
Annualized risk-free rate → 16.01 per cent
Variance → 6.52 per cent
Time → 0.7287 (that is, 266/365)

Using the lotus program outlined in Appendix 19A we obtain

$V_c = 28.3382$ pence

Dividend adjustments for an American-type option

The value of an American-type option can be calculated by employing the Black–Scholes model where the following adjustments are simultaneously made:

- The current price of the underlying share is reduced by the present value of all dividends except the final dividend payment which are expected during the option's life (in the United Kingdom there is only the interim dividend payment before the final dividend payment).

- The option period reduces to the ex-dividend date of the final dividend payment.

Example 19.6 Calculating an American option's price when two ex-dividend dates occur during the life of the option

Consider the data given in Example 19.5 and note in the present case that the option can be exercised any time on or before the expiry date. In this instance, two adjustments are required. The first adjustment involves the reduction of the current share price by the present value of the expected interim dividend payment. Thus we have

$$188 - 1.80e^{-(12)(0.1601/365)} = 186.20 \text{ pence}$$

The second adjustment is to reduce the option period to the ex-dividend date of the final dividend payment. In our case, this date is 29 May 1990. We can now calculate the option price by using the following data:

Share price → 186.20 pence
Exercise price → 180 pence
Annualized risk-free rate → 16.01 per cent
Variance → 6.52 per cent
Time → 0.5726 (that is, 209/365)

Once again, using the 1-2-3 macro program outlined in Appendix 19A we obtain

$$V_c = 27.2062 \text{ pence}$$

Black (1975) suggests that the value of the option can be approximated as follows:

$$\text{Value} = \text{Max}\,(27.2062, 28.3382) = 28.3382 \text{ pence}$$

where 28.3382 is the value of the option calculated in Example 19.5.

Below are stated two properties related to the optimal timing of exercising options on dividend-paying shares.

Property 1
Consider a share that pays dividends over the life of a call American option. Then exercising the call option is optimal only at the expiry date (provided that the maximum dividend is less than the interest earned on the exercise price from the ex-dividend date to the expiry date).

Property 2
Consider an American put option on a share when it pays a certain dividend during the life of the option. Then exercising the put option before the expiry date may be appropriate. These properties are proved in Appendix 19D.

Suppose at the time immediately after an ex-dividend date, the put option's exercise price is greater than the underlying share price. Then an investor who owns the underlying shares may exercise his or her option. If the option is not exercised, the price of the option will remain unchanged, then the investor will lose the interest income.

Share price movements

The Black–Scholes model assumes that the distribution of the underlying share's compounded rate of return is normal with constant and known variance. Several models have been developed that attempt to relax this assumption, for example, the constant elasticity variance model (Cox and Ross, 1976a), the jump diffusion model (Merton, 1976) and the stochastic volatility model (Hull and White, 1987). These models are briefly discussed later in the chapter. Finally, note that several attempts have been made to improve the estimated volatility for the Black–Scholes model. For example, Parkison (1980) and Garman and Klass (1980) illustrate that the volatility estimates can be improved by utilizing the opening, high and low share quotes.

Index options

Options on the FT-100 Index began trading on the London Traded Option Market on 3 May 1984. Like share options, index options can be divided into call and put options.

Call index options

A call index option is a contract giving the owner the right (and not the obligation) to purchase an amount of cash at a given price on or before a specified expiry date. On exercise of a FT-100 Index call option the owner will receive a cash amount equal to the difference between the Index value on the day of exercise and the exercise price multiplied by £10.

Example 19.7 Trading or exercising a FT-SE 100 call index option

On 26 July 1989 the closing FT-SE 100 Index price was 2,265 and the price of the 2 September, 150 calls was 162 pence. On 15 August 1989, with the Index increase of 2.7 per cent to 2,326, the option price had jumped 17.28 per cent to 190 pence. If an investor bought this FT-SE Index option on 26 July and sold it on 15 August, he or she would make a profit of £280 (excluding transaction costs). If this option was exercised on 15 August, the investor would make a profit of £140 (excluding transaction costs), the latter is calculated as follows:

```
         A              B              C              D              E
 1 CALCULATING THE PROFIT FROM A FT-SE 100 INDEX CALL OPTION
 2 ===============================================================
 3
 4 Number of Shares ----->              1,000
 5 Exercise Price ------->              2,150
 6
 7 -------------------------------------------------------------------
 8     Date          Index         Call Price       Profit/Loss
 9 -------------------------------------------------------------------
10   26-Jul-89        2,265              162            1,620
11   15-Aug-89        2,326              190            1,900
12                                               ---------------
13            Trading the Option ----->                   280
14            Exercising the Option -->                   140
15                                               ===============
```

Figure 19.9. Determining the profit from a FT-SE 100 Index call option

(2,326 – 2,150)(£10) – £1,620 = £140. This indicates why investors do not exercise options on the FT-SE 100 Index before expiry if the option still has a time value. Figure 19.9 calculates the profit of the investor in both of the above cases.

Put options

A put index option is a contract that gives the owner the right (and not the obligation) to sell an amount of cash at a specified price on or before a specified expiry date. On exercise of a FT-100 Index put option the owner will receive a cash amount equal to the difference between the Index value on the day of exercise and the exercise price multiplied by £10.

Example 19.8 Trading a FT-SE 100 put option

Consider an investor who bought on 20 July 1989, the November FT-SE 100 Index 2,150 put at 22 pence. The closing FT-SE 100 Index price was 2,265. On 15 August 1989, with the Index increase of 2.7 per cent to 2,326, the option price had increased by only 4.55 per cent to 23 pence. If the investor sold this option on 15 August, he or she would receive only £230. In this case his or her profit would be only £10 (excluding transaction costs). The profit of the investor is shown in Figure 19.10.

```
         A              B              C              D          E
 1 CALCULATING THE PROFIT FROM A FT-SE 100 INDEX PUT OPTION
 2 =======================================================
 3
 4 Number of Shares ----->                  1,000
 5 Exercise Price ------->                  2,150
 6
 7 -----------------------------------------------------------------
 8      Date           Index         Call Price       Profit/Loss
 9 -----------------------------------------------------------------
10   26-Jul-89            2,265              22              220
11   15-Aug-89            2,326              23              230
12                                                 ----------------
13              Trading the Option ----->                     10
14                                                 ================
```

Figure 19.10. Determining the profit from a FT-SE 100 Index put option

Share options versus index options

A comparison between share options and index options provides the following differences.

1 With a share option there is an underlying security that the option refers to, while for an index option the underlying asset is a portfolio containing the securities that comprise the index.
2 At any point in time, a share option has three possible expiry dates. Each expiry date is separated by a three-monthly interval and the maximum life of a contract is nine months. Options on FT-100 Index have four different expiry dates each separated by one month and stretching only four months ahead. For example, in January 1990, options on the FT-100 Index were available with expiry dates in January, February, March and April 1990.
3 When an investor exercises a share option, shares are exchanged between buyers

and writers. When a buyer exercises a FT-SE 100 Index option, he or she will receive a cash payment equal to the difference between the exercise price and the index value on the day of exercise, multiplied by £10.

4 Options on shares tend to require a smaller outlay than options on the FT-SE 100 Index. The exercise price of the latter and thus premiums are higher as compared with those related to options on shares.

5 With share options there are cases where investors adopt cover call writing strategies, whereas the latter strategies are not possible with index options.

Foreign currency options

A call (put) option on a foreign currency is a contract giving the right (and not the obligation) to buy (sell) one unit of the foreign currency at a given exchange rate.

Example 19.9 Hedging against foreign currency movements

Suppose it is 8 November 1990. Today the exchange rate for American dollars is $1.9765. An investor has £12,500 and she believes that the pound may drop versus the dollar in three weeks from today. The anticipated short-term decline in the pound can be hedged by buying American dollar put options. Indeed the investor buys a December $1.9554 contract for $312.5. This option gives the right to sell £12,500 at an exchange rate of $1.9554 per £1 at any time on or before the December expiry date.

If the pound falls against the dollar by December, say to $1.9000, the investor's profit can be calculated as follows:

$(1.9554 - 1.9000) \times 12{,}500 - 312.5 = \$380$

If the pound rises against the dollar by December, say to $2.0000, the option will not be exercised, but the investor will realize a profit from the rise of the pound. Her net loss would be given by:

$(2.0000 - 1.9765) \times 12{,}500 - 312.5 = -\$18.75$

Finally, if the pound remains unchanged against the dollar by December, the investor will not exercise the option. In this case, she will obtain a loss of $312.5. This loss could be considered as the amount paid to the writer in order to insure the US dollar value of her money.

The pricing of foreign currency options

Biger and Hull (1983) derived a pricing model for foreign currency options which is based upon the Black–Scholes (1973) methodology. Their analysis assumes perfect foreign exchange markets which operate continuously, and constant domestic and foreign exchange risk-free rates. Biger and Hull's model is summarized in Figure 19.11.

The use of options

This section examines the general uses of options.

Hedging

Hedge strategies can be used by investors to provide partial or full protection

$C = S_0 N(d_1) - PV(E)N(d_2)$

where

$d_1 = [\ln(S_0/E) + (r - r^* + \sigma^2/2)T]/\sigma \, SQRT(T)$

$d_2 = d_1 - \sigma \, SQRT(T)$

In this formula, S_0 is the current spot price of one unit of the foreign currency, E is the exercise price of the option, r is the riskless rate of interest in the home country, r^* is the foreign riskless rate of interest and T is the time remaining before the expiry date expressed as a proportion of a year. The remaining terms are defined similarly as in the general Black and Scholes valuation formula.

Figure 19.11. A valuation formula for currency options

from unfavourable share price changes. Consider an investor with the following strategy:

- Write k calls in a firm's shares each costing £C.
- Buy n shares of the firm each costing £S.

The initial position of the investor is given by:

$$P = kC + nS \qquad (19.1)$$

Our problem is to choose k and n so as to keep the initial position of the investor unchanged, no matter which way the share price moves. If '∂' denotes the change in a variable, then Equation (19.1) yields:

$$\frac{\partial P}{\partial S} = k\frac{\partial C}{\partial S} + n = 0 \qquad (19.2)$$

Rearranging terms in Equation (19.2) gives:

$$\frac{\partial C}{\partial S} = -\frac{n}{k} \qquad (19.3)$$

Using the Black–Scholes option valuation model, one can derive $\partial C/\partial S = -N(\mathrm{d}_1)$. Consequently, we can rewrite Equation (19.3) as

$$\frac{n}{k} = N(\mathrm{d}_1)$$

This ratio is called the hedge ratio and indicates the number of shares which should be purchased for each option in order to protect the investor from changes in the share price.

Example 19.10 Using the hedge ratio

Assume that it is 20 March 1990. The Marks and Spencer share stands at 192 pence. Consider an investor adopting the following investment strategy:

- Write one Marks and Spencer call at 15.93 pence.
- Buy 85 Marks and Spencer shares at 192 pence per share.

Figure 19.12 shows the initial position of the investor and two other cases where the share price of the firm rises by 1 pence and falls by 1 pence, respectively.

The hedge ratio of 0.85 is calculated in Example 19.2. This ratio indicates that 85 shares of Marks and Spencer are utilized to hedge the call. If the share price rises by 1 pence, the option will rise from 15.93 pence to 16.78 pence (that is by 85 pence). In this case, the investor's share value will increase by 85 pence (1 pence for each share bought). These additional funds can be used to purchase the

	A	B	C	D	E
1		USING THE HEDGE RATIO			
2		=====================			
3					
4	Hedge Ratio ------------->	0.85			
5	--				
6	Marks & Spencer Share	1.92		1.92	
7	M&S April Call	0.1593		0.1593	
8					
9					
10	Sell one April Call	159.30		159.30	
11	Buy 85 M&S Shares	163.20		163.20	
12					
13	Marks & Spencer Share	1.93		1.91	
14	M&S April Call	0.1678		0.1508	
15					
16	Buy Back the Call	0.85		0.85	
17	Profit from Share Increase	0.85		0.85	
18		---------		---------	
19		0.00		0.00	

Figure 19.12. Using the hedge ratio

option back. Therefore, if the investor adopts such an investment strategy his or her initial position remains unchanged. Similarly, investors can be protected in cases where the underlying share price decreases (see Figure 19.12).

Problems Consider the data given in Example 19.10.

1 Conduct a sensitivity analysis of the hedge ratio with respect to changes in volatility (the volatility equals the square root of the variance of the underlying share's continuously compounded rate of return).
2 Conduct a sensitivity analysis of the hedge ratio with respect to changes in the expiration time.
3 Conduct a sensitivity analysis of the hedge ratio with respect to changes in volatility and expiration time.

In each of the above cases discuss your results.

Hedge strategies can also be adopted by using options themselves. The hedge ratio indicates the proportion of one option which must be held against another in order to protect the investor from changes in the underlying share price. The hedge ratio between two options can be calculated as in the case explained previously.

$$\frac{n}{k} = \frac{N1(d_1)}{N2(d_1)}$$

where

$N1(d_1)$ = the first option's value of the cumulative standard normal distribution function evaluated at d_1.

$N2(d_1)$ = the second option's value of the cumulative standard normal distribution function evaluated at d_1.

For example, if the hedge ratio (for a January option written against an April option) is 3, the investor can adopt the following investment strategy: write three January options for each April option purchased.

These hedge strategies are appropriate only for short time intervals and small changes in the share price. The hedge ratio must be estimated often, since it changes with the share price, riskless interest rate, volatility and time. Also, if share price increases or decreases dramatically, then these hedge strategies provide only a partial protection.

There are many other hedge strategies that can be used to protect the investor from unfavourable situations. For example:

- An investor can hedge his or her position when anticipating a future share price change, but he or she does not know the direction of the change. Rather than buying the underlying share the investor can simultaneously buy a put and a call with the same exercise price and expiry date. In this case, the maximum loss can be limited to the price paid for purchasing the options.
- Place part of the funds available in call options (that is, purchase call options) and the remainder in government securities. If the underlying share price increases, the investor will benefit by selling his or her options. If the underlying share price is unchanged, a loss is observed but the size of the loss can be partially or totally offset because of the holdings in government securities.
- Managers of well-diversified portfolios (for example, pension fund managers) can buy FT-SE 100 Index options to hedge their portfolios if they believe that the stock market as a whole will decline. If the stock market declines, a manager can offset part (or the whole amount) of the losses by the gains observed from selling put options.
- Foreign currency option strategies can be used by companies to (partially or fully) hedge the risk of the domestic currency declining in value against foreign currencies.

Gearing

Options can be utilized to gear potential returns. Speculators who anticipate that the price of a firm's shares (or the index value) will rise in the near future, can observe potential profits by adopting the following strategy: buy calls in a firm's shares instead of purchasing the shares of the firm directly. If speculators believe that the share price of a firm will decline, then they can buy puts in the firm's shares instead of short selling the shares.

Example 19.11 Geared expected profits through buying FT-SE 100 calls

Suppose that it is 16 November 1990 and an investor expects to receive £25,000 in three weeks time. He believes that within the next two weeks the market will rise substantially and he decides to buy 10 November FT-SE 1000 calls at 98 pence (options on FT-SE 100 are trading at a range of values, but for the sake of the example let us assume that 98 pence is the highest value in the range that existed at 16 November 1990). On 5 December 1990 the call options turn out to trade at 146 pence (assume that 146 pence is the lower price of the range of prices available at that day). Suppose that the investor decides to sell his call options. Figure 19.13 calculates the investor's profit (ignoring transaction costs). The results reveal that the FT-SE 100 Index has risen by 4.41 per cent, whereas the trading in calls yields an expected return of 48.98 per cent.

Figure 19.13.
An example of gearing

	A	B	C	D	E	F
1			GEARING			
2			=======			
3	Number of Calls ------>		10			
4						
5	Date	FT-SE 100	Increase	Call Price	Cash Flow	Increase
6						
7	16-Nov-90	2057		98	9,800	
8	05-Dec-90	2152	4.41%	146	14,600	48.98%
9					------------	
10					4,800	

Reducing the cost of share purchases
Covered call options are utilized by investors in order to reduce the purchasing costs of shares.

Example 19.12 Reducing the cost of share purchases

Suppose it is 20 March 1990. The share price of Marks and Spencer is 192 pence on this date and the call option price is 16 pence. An investor wishes to buy 20,000 Marks and Spencer shares which cost £38,400. This outlay can be reduced to £35,200 by writing today 20 contracts of April 180 Marks and Spencer call option at 16 pence per share (that is, £38,400 – £3,200 = £35,200). Suppose that the share price will be 190 pence on the expiry date (25 April 1990) and the call option will not be exercised, then the investor will realize a profit of £3,200 (ignoring transaction costs). On the other hand, suppose that the option is exercised at the expiry date because the price of the underlying share rose above the exercise price is 180 pence, say at 185 pence. In this instance, the profit of the options' owner is also £2,200 (that is, £3,200 – (£0.05)(20,000)), in this case, we are ignoring transaction costs.

Option pricing theory and the firm's equity
Suppose that a (limited liability) firm has a capital structure that includes both equity and debt. Assume that the debt was recently raised by issuing debentures with a zero coupon rate and the debenture holders will receive an amount of *B* pounds at the maturity date. Since the firm has only two kinds of securities, ordinary shares and debentures, it follows that

$$EQ = V - B$$

where

$EQ =$ the market value of the firm's ordinary shares.
$V =$ the total market value of the firm.
$B =$ the market value of the firm's debt.

This case can be regarded as a call option on the firm's assets which is written by the debenture holders and sold to the firm's shareholders. This call option is completely characterized by the following items:

Underlying security: The value of the firm's assets.
Exercise price: The debt value at the maturity date.
Expiry date: The maturity date of the debt.
Security price on the expiry date: The total value of the firm at that date.

If the firm's value is greater than the value of the debt on the expiry date, the shareholders will exercise their option by paying to the debenture holders the amount of B pounds. After exercising the option, the total value of the equity will be $V1 - B$, where $V1$ = the total value of the firm on the expiry date. On the other hand, if on the expiry date the firm's value is less than the value of the debt, the call option will not be exercised and it will expire worthless. In the latter case, the firm goes into liquidation, the debenture holders get the whole firm and the shareholders receive probably nothing. At the maturity date of the debt the firm's equity can be expressed as follows:

$$C = \text{Max}\,(0, V1 - B)$$

where

Max = the maximum value of 0 and $V1 - B$, whichever is greater.

The debenture holders cannot claim an amount beyond the firm's value because shareholders are liable only to the extent of their investment in the firm.

Example 19.13 Calculating a firm's value of equity using an option approach

GD Fashion plc and RD Computers plc are both financed with equity and debt. GD Fashion's current capital structure consists of £20 million of equity and £10 million of debt, while RD Computers' current capital structure contains £20 million of equity and £30 million of debt. Assume that each firm has £1 shares outstanding. Each share of GD Fashion can be represented as a call option with current value of £2 and exercise price of £1. Likewise, a call option on the RD Computers' assets has a current value of £2 and exercise price of £3. If the total value of GD Fashion is £32 million at the maturity date of its debt, then the value of the equity will be:

$$EQ = \text{Max}\,(0, £32 - £10) = £22 \text{ million}$$

On the other hand, assume that the total value of RD Computers will be £21 million at the maturity date of the debt. In this case, the value of the equity from the shareholders' viewpoint will be:

$$EQ = \text{Max}\,(0, £21 - £30) = 0$$

Figure 19.14 summarizes several trading rules for options.

1. If an option is undervalued buy it. If an option is overvalued sell it.
2. Hedge always your position.
3. Revise often your hedge ratio.
4. It is not optimal to exercise an American call option before its expiry date (assume that no dividend payments occur during the life of the option).
5. It is appropriate to exercise an American call option that pays dividends over its lifetime at the expiry date (provided that the maximum dividend is less than the interest earned on the exercise price from the ex-dividend date to the expiry date).
6. Exercising an American put option before the expiry date may be appropriate (assume that no dividends payments occur during the life of the option).
7. It may be appropriate to exercise an American put option, that pays dividends over its lifetime, before the expiry date (for example, immediately after an ex-dividend date).

Figure 19.14. A summary of trading rules for options

Alternatives to Black–Scholes option valuation model

The Black–Scholes option valuation model relies upon a set of assumptions including the following: (a) the generation process of the underlying share price is a continuous stochastic process which has a constant variance; (b) the interest rate is characterized by constant drifts; and (c) the exercise price of an option is constant. This section describes several models which relax one or more of these three assumptions. The Black–Scholes option valuation model can be applied to a wide range of underlying securities, for example, debt securities. This section also discusses some of these applications.

Merton's stochastic interest-rate model

Merton (1974) developed a model which can be used to value an option when the value of the underlying share and the interest rate are both stochastic. The valuation formula is dependent upon the following factors:

- The share price.
- The exercise price of the option.
- The value of a discount bond that matures at the same time as the option.
- The time before the option's expiry date.
- The volatility of the share price.
- The volatility of bond price.
- The instantaneous correlation between the share and bond prices.

Merton's model for debt

This model views the debt of a firm as a call option, that is, the holder of the firm's debt receives either the amount due on the debentures or the value of the firm, whichever is greater (we assume that the firm's capital structure is comprised only of equity and long-term debt and that the firm's debt will be paid off as a lump sum on a certain maturity date). The model of Merton (1974) is dependent upon the following factors:

- The ratio of the firm's total value to the face value of the debt.
- The amount due to the debenture holders.
- The interest rate.
- The time to maturity of the firm's debt.
- The variance of debt which is a function of the ratio of the firm's total value to the face value of the debt.

Constant elasticity of variance model

Empirical evidence indicates that the variance of share returns decreases as the share price increases. Cox and Ross (1976a) offered a valuation model that uses a standard deviation which is inversely proportional to the underlying share price. Specifically, their model shows that the generation process of share prices through time is stochastic. This process is dependent upon the following:

- The share price.
- The time to expiration.
- A normally distributed stochastic term.

Pure jump model

This model, proposed by Cox and Ross (1975), provides a valuation model when the underlying share price is described by a constant drift, and occasionally it undergoes a jump of a specified size. Their European call option valuation model is dependent upon the following factors (this model assumes that jumps occur according to a continuous-time Poisson process):

- The decline rate of the share price.
- The rate at which jumps occur.
- The jump amplitude.
- The time to expiration.
- The interest rate.
- The share price.
- The exercise price.

Jump diffusion model

Merton (1976) developed a model assuming that share prices can be described as having small, almost continuous movements, except at random times, when they experience sudden jumps. If the size of the proportional jump obeys a normal distribution, then the European call option price is dependent upon the following factors:

- The rate at which jumps happen.
- The average jump size.
- The time to expiration.
- The price derived from the Black–Scholes formula with given estimates for variance and risk-free rate.

Fisher's and Margrabe's stochastic exercise price model

Fisher (1978) and Margrabe (1978) developed a model which can be used to value an option generated when one asset is exchanged for another (for example, the option to exchange a share of one firm with a share of another, where none of the firms uses long-term debt in its capital structure). This model assumes that the exercise price on the call option is stochastic. The variation formula is dependent upon the following factors:

- The current price of the first asset.
- The current price of the second asset.
- The time to expiration.
- The instantaneous proportional variances of the changes in the ratio of price of the first asset to the price of the second asset.
- The instantaneous correlation between the prices of the two assets.

Displaced diffusion model

This model, proposed by Rubinstein (1983), views a firm as having two groups of assets: risky assets which have constant volatility and a riskless asset. The model is dependent upon the following factors (we assume that no dividend payments exists):

- The ratio of the firm's risky assets to total assets.
- The current market value of the share.
- The exercise price.

- The (initial) debt/equity ratio of the firm.
- The variance of the risky assets, which is a function of the ratio of the firm's risky assets to total assets.
- The riskless interest rate.
- The time to expiration.

Stochastic volatility model

Hull and White (1987) developed a model in which the volatility is uncorrelated with the share price. According to their model, the European call price is dependent upon the following:

- The average value of the variance rate.
- The expected Black–Scholes price.
- The probability density function of the average value of the variance rate.

Empirical investigations on option pricing models

The empirical work in the area of options is substantial and can be broadly classified as follows:

1 *Examining the performance of hedge riskless portfolios* Hedge riskless portfolios can be formed by combining options and shares. If an option is overpriced (in the view of the B–S option valuation model), sell the call and purchase an amount of the underlying share equal to the hedge ratio. Conversely, if the option is underpriced, buy the option and sell an amount of shares equal to the hedge ratio. If this strategy does not produce abnormal profits, then the following possible implication emerges: the B–S option valuation model is correct and the option market is efficient. If riskless hedge portfolios produce abnormal profits, then the following possible implication emerges: the B–S option valuation model can be used to yield abnormal profits and the option market is inefficient. The studies using this methodology include Black and Scholes (1973) and Galai (1977).

2 *Investigating possible violations of option pricing boundary conditions* A boundary condition is based on the following principle:

> A portfolio should be worth at least as much as another portfolio if the former has a future series of cash flows at least equal to the series of cash flows of the latter.

If these boundary conditions are violated, then arbitrage opportunities will occur in the option market. Arbitrage gains/losses would imply either the invalidity of the B–S option valuation model or the inefficiency of the option market. There have been several studies which adopted this methodology including the following: Klemkosky and Resnick (1979) and Bodurtha and Courtadon (1986).

3 *Comparing actual option prices with theoretical option prices via a statistical method* A statistical technique can be used to compare actual option prices with theoretical option prices. For example, you can examine the relationship between actual and theoretical option prices by regressing the former against the latter (see Trennepohl, 1981).

Author(s)	Research objective	Conclusions
Black and Scholes (1973)	Uses daily data from the over-the-counter market and investigates whether or not the B–S OVM can be utilized to earn abnormal profits	• Using ex-post estimates of actual variances and returns on the underlying securities and zero transaction costs, the OVM produces, on average, price estimates close to the actual market prices • Utilizing ex-ante variances of the returns and zero transaction costs the B–S OVM could identify overvalued or undervalued options • When transaction costs are used the abnormal profits/losses generated in the case above disappeared
Galai (1977)	Uses daily data from the Chicago Board of Option Exchange and examines whether the B–S OVM can be used to help buy options that are undervalued by the market and sell options that are overvalued	When transaction costs are considered abnormal profits cannot be generated by buying undervalued options and selling overvalued options
Klemkosky and Resnick (1979)	Investigates whether the put–call parity relationship holds in reality	The results presented are consistent with the put–call parity relationship and registered option markets are efficient
Macbeth and Merville (1979)	Examines whether or not the B–S OVM overpriced or underpriced options	• For in-the-money and out-of-the-money options, the B–S OVM yields prices which, on average, deviate significantly from market prices. • Options are mispriced by the B–S formula in the following cases: • Short-term (less than a month) options • Options associated with extremely high volatile prices
Bhattacharya (1980)	Compares actual market prices with the B–S OVM's prices by testing the following hypotheses: —Mathematical structure of the B–S OVM —The estimation of the B–S OVM's parameters —The efficiency of the option market	• In general, the B–S OVM cannot be used to generate abnormal profits • At-the-money options with one day to maturity are overpriced
MacBeth and Merville (1980)	Compares the following: —B–S OVM. —Constant elasticity variance model developed by Cox (1975) and Cox and Ross (1976a)	• The variance of returns decreases as the share price increases • The constant elasticity variance model outperforms the B–S OVM
Trennepohl (1981)	Uses weekly data and investigates how prices derived from the B–S OVM compare with the option market prices	There exist significant deviations between actual prices and model prices

Figure 19.15. Summarizing empirical studies on option valuation models

Rubinstein (1981)	Compares five extensions of the B–S OVM using the following: —A database containing all the reported option trades and quotes over an extremely large sample of observations —Non-parametric statistical tests	• Short-term out-of-the money options are relatively overpriced • The B–S OVM is biased for pricing in-the-money options • Among the five models compared, no model can be superior to the B–S OVM
Whaley (1982)	Examines the consequences of considering dividend adjustments into option valuation models	Using option valuation models that take into consideration dividend adjustments can be useful in removing exercise-price and time-to expiration biases
Geske and Roll (1984)	Investigates whether observed biases are related to the OVM's misspecifications or to the methodology used in the test	• Exercise-price and time-to-expiry biases may be related to the fact that models are tested without taking into account dividend payments • Some of the volatility biases related to the B–S OVM are not caused by the model's misspecifications, but rather by errors associated with the estimation technique for the volatility.
Bodurtha and Courtadon (1986)	Investigates the efficiency of the Philadelphia Stock Exchange foreign currency option market	Under zero transaction costs there are riskless arbitrage opportunities in the foreign currency option market. After transaction costs are considered, the riskless arbitrage profits no longer exist and the market is efficient
Chesney and Scott (1989)	Uses prices of European currency options traded in Geneva and compares the modified B–S OVM (suggested by Biger and Hull, 1983) with a random variance model	• If a constant variance of the return on the foreign exchange rate is utilized, the performance of the revised B–S OVM is poor • If the variance is revised daily then the modified B–S OVM fits the data better than the random variance model • The utilization of the random variance model produces small profits which are offset by the bid–ask spread.

Figure 19.15. (Continued)

Figure 19.15 summarizes several empirical investigations of the option valuation models. The overall conclusion is that the B–S option valuation model (B–S OVM) is supported by most empirical investigations after transaction costs are taken into account.

The non-synchronous problem

Some of the empirical investigations on options (for example, Black and Scholes, 1973; Galai, 1977) used closing option prices in the tests. The appropriate data to use when testing option valuation models should be comprised of synchronous prices (that is, an option price and the corresponding share price must be observed at the same time during the day). In many cases the last option trade occurs before the underlying share stops trading and thus closing option prices (for example, those reported in the press) and closing share prices do not correspond at the same time. Using in tests non-synchronous prices may indicate the existence of arbitrage opportunities and provide misleading conclusions.

Summary

1 *Black–Scholes valuation model* According to the Black–Scholes option valuation model the five factors that determine the price of an option are: (a) the current share price to which the option refers; (b) the exercise price; (c) the risk-free rate; (d) the variance of the underlying share price; and (e) the time remaining to expiry date. When the underlying share pays dividends, American call options cannot be valued by using the original option valuation model. In many cases, adjustments to the original model can be made.

2 *Uses of options* There are a number of specific reasons for purchasing options including the following: (a) hedging, that is, a financial strategy which combines options with shares in order to provide partial or full protection from adverse share price movements; (b) gearing, that is, investing in call (put) options when you anticipate that the price of the underlying share will rise (decline) since the changes in the price of a call (put) option, in percentage terms, will tend to be greater than the changes in the price of the underlying share.

3 *Uses of the Black–Scholes valuation model* The Black–Scholes option valuation model can be employed to value index options. A modified version of the model can also be used to value currency options. The option valuation model can be extended to securities other than call and puts. For example, it can be utilized to calculate the value of the components of a firm's capital structure.

4 *Empirical evidence on the option pricing models* The empirical studies on the Black–Scholes option valuation models discussed in this chapter attempt to investigate the accuracy of the model in predicting actual option prices and to determine whether the model can be used to generate abnormal profits. Most of the studies presented indicate that, on average, the valuation model provides a very good fit to actual option prices. Additionally, when transaction costs are taken into account there is no opportunity for traders to realize abnormal returns. These results are also in line with market efficiency.

Empirical work on options also compares the original Black–Scholes valuation model with several extensions of the model. However, none of these extensions provides results consistently superior to those produced with the aid of the Black–Scholes valuation model. Finally, a part of the empirical research on options attempts to examine whether departures from the Black–Scholes valuation model are attributable to model misspecifications or to statistical errors resulting from the procedures used to estimate the parameters of the model.

Questions for discussion

1 For each term shown below provide a definition in your own words. Then check your responses against the definitions included in the chapter.

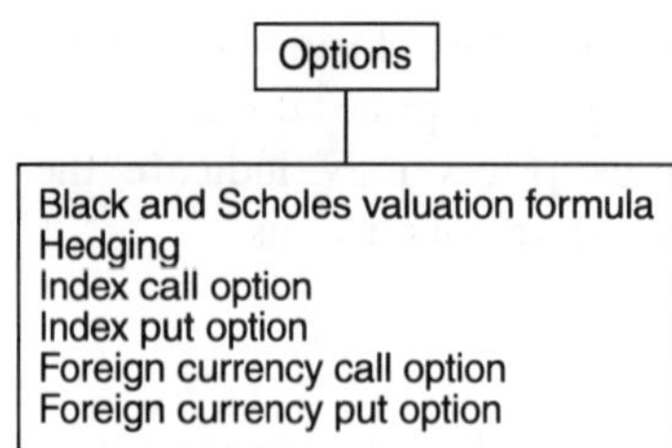

2 Discuss and interpret the Black and Scholes valuation model for call options. Specify the assumptions on which the model is developed.

3 Discuss how the Black–Scholes valuation model can be used to value put options.

4 Consider the following information (*Source*: *Financial Times*, 6 December 1990):

Share	Exercise Price	Price	Intrinsic value
Boots (336)	300	44	36

Discuss why the intrinsic value of each option is different from its price.

5 (**a**) Below you are given five factors that affect the value of a call or put option. Indicate the effect that an increase in each factor has on the call and put price (other things remain the same).

	Effects on: Call	Put
Share price	Increases	
Exercise price		
Risk-free rate		
Volatility		
Time		

(**b**) Discuss in detail each answer provided in part (a).

(**c**) List a number of events which affect either the risk-free rate or the volatility of the underlying share and indicate how each would influence the call and put price (other things being equal).

6 Describe how the Black–Scholes option valuation model can be utilized to calculate the implicit volatility of the underlying share in which options are available.

7 Explain each of the following two statements by using a numerical example:

(**a**) 'Holding a portfolio consisting of a call option and some shares in which the option is available may provide partial or full protection from unfavourable share price changes.'

(**b**) 'One of the most important applications of naked options is their use to gear potential returns.'

8 If the underlying share in which options are available pays dividends before the options' expiry date, discuss how the original Black and Scholes valuation model can be adjusted for a European-type option and an American-type option.

9 Discuss how the option pricing theory can be used to calculate the value of the equity of a firm (assume that the current capital structure of the firm consists of only ordinary shares and debentures, where the latter are associated with zero coupon).

10 Below are shown four alternative combinations in terms of call price and exercise price. For example, the first combination occurs when the call price of an index option increases and the exercise price of the option also increases. How can each combination affect the price of the put index option? Complete the blank boxes in the diagram below by using the word 'Increases' or 'Decreases'.

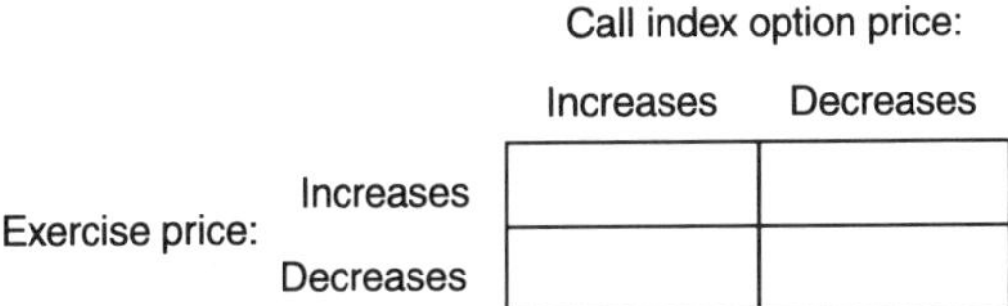

11 Compare and contrast share options and index options.

12 (a) Fill in the blank boxes in the following diagram.

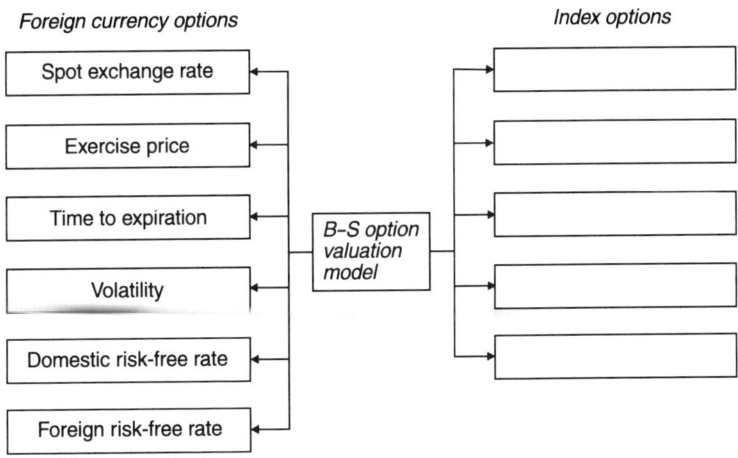

(b) Compare and contrast currency options with index options.

13 Discuss the conclusions related to the empirical evidence presented in this chapter. To what degree is the evidence consistent with the market efficiency of the option market?

14 Prepare an analog model summarizing the main points discussed in this chapter.

15 How can spreadsheets be used to facilitate the application of the concepts discussed in this chapter?

Appendix 19A Calculating $N(d_j)$

Calculating $N(d_j)$ using the normal distribution table

The probability of drawing a value from a standard normal distribution that is less than or equal to d_j can be found by using the standard normal distribution table. If such a probability is not displayed on this table, the linear interpolation method can be used to calculate the required probability as shown in Example 19A.1.

Example 19A.1 Calculating $N(d_j)$ by using the linear interpolation method

In Example 19.2 we found $d_1 = 1.0318$. To calculate $N(d_1)$ follow the steps below.

Step 1 Identify the relevant interpolation interval. In our example, the lowest value of this interval is 1.0300 and the highest value is 1.0400 (1.0300 is calculated by adding the value of 1.0 displayed on the first left column of the standard normal distribution table and the value 0.03 displayed on the top row of the same table; similarly, 1.0400 is calculated by adding the value of 1.0 displayed on the first column of the standard normal distribution table and the value 0.04 displayed on the first row of the same table). Note that 1.0318 lies within the interpolation interval.

Step 2 Apply the linear interpolation formula. That is:

$$0.3485 + \frac{1.0318 - 1.0300}{1.0400 - 1.0300}(0.3508 - 0.3485) = 0.3489$$

where

0.3485 = the probability from the normal distribution table at 1.0300.

0.3508 = the probability from the normal distribution table at 1.0400.

In this case, $N(d_1) = 0.5000 + 0.3489 = 0.8489$. Therefore, the probability of drawing a value from the standard normal distribution that is less than or equal to 1.0318 is 0.8489.

Similarly for $d_2 = 0.9516$ (see also Example 19A.2) we have

$$0.3289 + \frac{0.9516 - 0.9500}{0.9600 - 0.9500}(0.3315 - 0.3289) = 0.3293$$

where

0.3289 = the probability from the normal distribution table at 0.9500.

0.3315 = the probability from the normal distribution table at 0.9600.

In this instance, $N(d_2) = 0.5000 + 0.3293 = 0.8293$

Calculating $N(d_j)$ using a polynomial approximation

$N(d_j)$ can also be estimated by using the polynomial approximation shown in Figure 19A.1.

$$N(d_j) \sim 1 - (1/\text{SQRT}(2\,\text{PI}))\,\text{EXP}\,(-d_j^2/2)\,\text{POL}\,(k_j) \qquad (19A.1)$$

where

$$\text{POL}\,(k_j) = b_1 k_j + b_2 k_j^2 + b_3 k_j^3 + b_4 k_j^4 + b_5 k_j^5 \qquad (19A.2)$$

$j = 1, 2$.
$\sim =$ denotes that the above relationship is an approximation.
SQRT = denotes the square root operator.
PI = 3.1415926.
EXP = the natural antilog of 1 (that is, EXP = 2.7128).
$b_1 = 0.31938153$, $b_2 = -0.356563782$, $b_3 = 1.7814477937$
$b_4 = -1.821255978$, $b_5 = 1.330274429$.
$k_j = 1/(1 + a\text{ABS}(d_j))$, $a = 0.2316419$.

If $d_j < 0$ then $N(d_j)$ can be calculated by using the following approximation:

$$N(d_j) \sim (1/\text{SQRT}(2\,\text{PI}))\,\text{EXP}\,(-d_j^2/2)\,\text{POL}\,(k_j) \qquad (19A.3)$$

Figure 19A.1. Estimating $N(d_j)$ using a polynomial approximation

Example 19A.2 Calculating $N(d_j)$ using a polynomial approximation

The polynomial values are as follows (values are rounded to four decimal points):

For $k_1 = 0.8070$, $\text{POL}(k_1) = 0.6449$

For $k_2 = 0.8193$, $\text{POL}(k_2) = 0.6727$

Finally, the values of $N(d_1)$ and $N(d_2)$ are estimated by utilizing Equation (19A.1). That is:

$$N(1.0318) \sim 1 - (1/\text{SQRT}(6.283185))(\text{EXP}(-(1.0318)\hat{\ }2/2))(0.6449)$$
$$= 0.8489$$

and

$$N(0.9516) \sim 1 - (1/\text{SQRT}(6.283185))(\text{EXP}(-(0.9516)\hat{\ }2/2))(0.6727)$$
$$= 0.8293$$

where $6.283185 = 2 \times (3.1415926)$.

Example 19A.3 Using a Lotus worksheet that calculates $N(d_j)$

Figure 19A.2 presents a worksheet calculating call and put values. The appropriate data is included in the range A5..H9. The value of d_1 (see cell H14) is calculated by using the following formula:

```
(@LN($H$5/$H$6)+$H$9*($H$7+$H$8/2))/(@SQRT($H$8)*@SQRT($H$9))
```

The following formula is used to estimate the value of d_2:

```
+H15-@SQRT(H8)*@SQRT(H9)
```

The absolute values of d_1 and d_2 stored in cells H15 and H18, respectively, are required for calculating the values of the coefficients k_1 and k_2 (see cells E23 and H23).

```
 ------------------------------------------------------------------------------
      A        B          C          D         E        F         G         H
 1               USING THE BLACK-SCHOLES OPTION PRICING MODEL
 2               ============================================
 3                          A S S U M P T I O N S
 4 ------------------------------------------------------------------------
 5 Current price of share                                                 192
 6 Option's exercise price                                                180
 7 Continuously compounded risk-free (%)                               15.20%
 8 Annualised variance of share return (%)                              6.52%
 9 Time before expiration                                              0.0986
10 ========================================================================
11
12                        CALCULATING d1 AND d2
13 ------------------------------------------------------------------------
14                                                        d1 =      1.0318
15 Absolute value of d1 ----------------------->                    1.0318
16
17                                                        d2 =      0.9516
18 Absolute value of d2 ----------------------->                    0.9516
19 ------------------------------------------------------------------------
20
21                      CALCULATING N(d1) and N(d2)
22 ------------------------------------------------------------------------
23 a -->0.231641             k1 -->  0.8070              k2 --> 0.8193
24 ------------------------------------------------------------------------
25                   POLYNOMIAL VALUES FOR:
26     CONSTANTS                k1       k2
27 ------------------------------------------------------------------------
28     1   0.3194          0.2578  0.2617
29     2  -0.3566         -0.2323 -0.2394
30     3   1.7815          0.9366  0.9800
31     4  -1.8213         -0.7728 -0.8209
32     5   1.3303          0.4556  0.4913         N(1.03185) =      0.8489
33                         ----------------       N(0.95166) =      0.8294
34                         0.6449  0.6727
35
36                      CALCULATING CALL AND PUT VALUES
37 ------------------------------------------------------------------------
38                 Call Value --------->         15.9300
39                 Put Value ---------->          1.2516
40 ========================================================================
 ------------------------------------------------------------------------------
```

Figure 19A.2. A worksheet calculating call and put values

The `@IF` function of 1-2-3 is used to estimate the value of $N(1.0318)$, see cell H32:

`@IF(H14>0,Condition1,Condition2)`

where

Condition1 = 1−`@EXP(-H14^2/2)*C34*(1/@SQRT(2*@PI))`

Condition2 = `@EXP(-H14^2/2)*C34*(1/@SQRT(2*@PI))`

Similarly, $N(0.9516)$ is estimated as follows:

`@IF(H17>0,Condition3,Condition4)`

where

Condition3 = 1−`@EXP(-H17^2/2)*D34*(1/@SQRT(2*@PI))`

Condition4 = `@EXP(-H17^2/2)*D34*(1/@SQRT(2*@PI))`

The value of the call is found with the aid of the following formula (see cell F38):

```
+H5*H32-H6*H33/(@EXP(H7*H9))
```

Finally, the value of the put is estimated as follows (see cell F39):

```
-H5*(1-H32)+H6*(1-H33)/@EXP(H7*H9)
```

Note that the difference between the value stored in cell F39 and that calculated in Example 19.3 is due to rounding.

Problem Calculate the value of a call option and a put option assuming the following:

Current price of share	185 pence
Option's exercise price	180 pence
Continuously compounded risk-free	15 per cent
Annualized variance of share return	7 per cent
Time before expiration	0.25

Appendix 19B Implicit volatility

The volatility of a share's logarithmic rates of return can also be estimated by using the observed option price in conjunction with the Black and Scholes equation. This method can be described as follows:

> Given the option price, the current share price, the exercise price, the (continuously compounded) annual riskless interest rate and the time to expiration, calculate the volatility that equates the observed price with the theoretical price.

There is no explicit equation for the variance and the solution to this problem can be derived numerically following the method below:

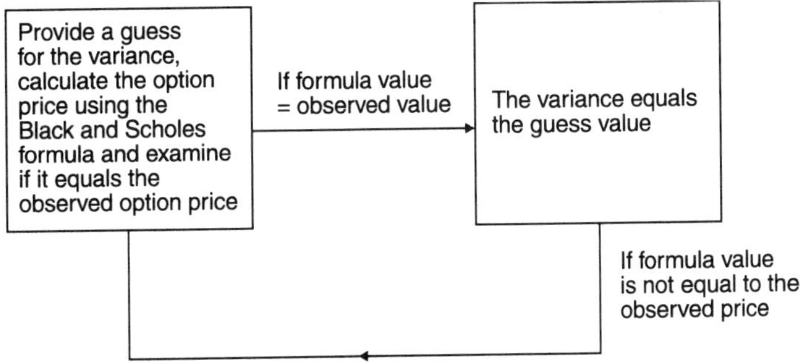

This method can be translated into an iterative mathematical problem which in turn can be solved by using 1-2-3.

Example 19B.1 Calculating the implicit variance using 1-2-3

The macro shown in Figure 19B.1 can be used to estimate the implicit variance of an option. Range A1..H40 calculates the option value employing the Black and Scholes valuation formula (see Example 19A.3). The first part of the macro deals with providing a guess for the variance, if the guess is too low, then 1-2-3 sounds the computer's bell and it asks for another higher guess. The subroutine LOOP calculates the variance by using an iterative procedure. The maximum amount of iterations provided by the macro is 40. This procedure uses different

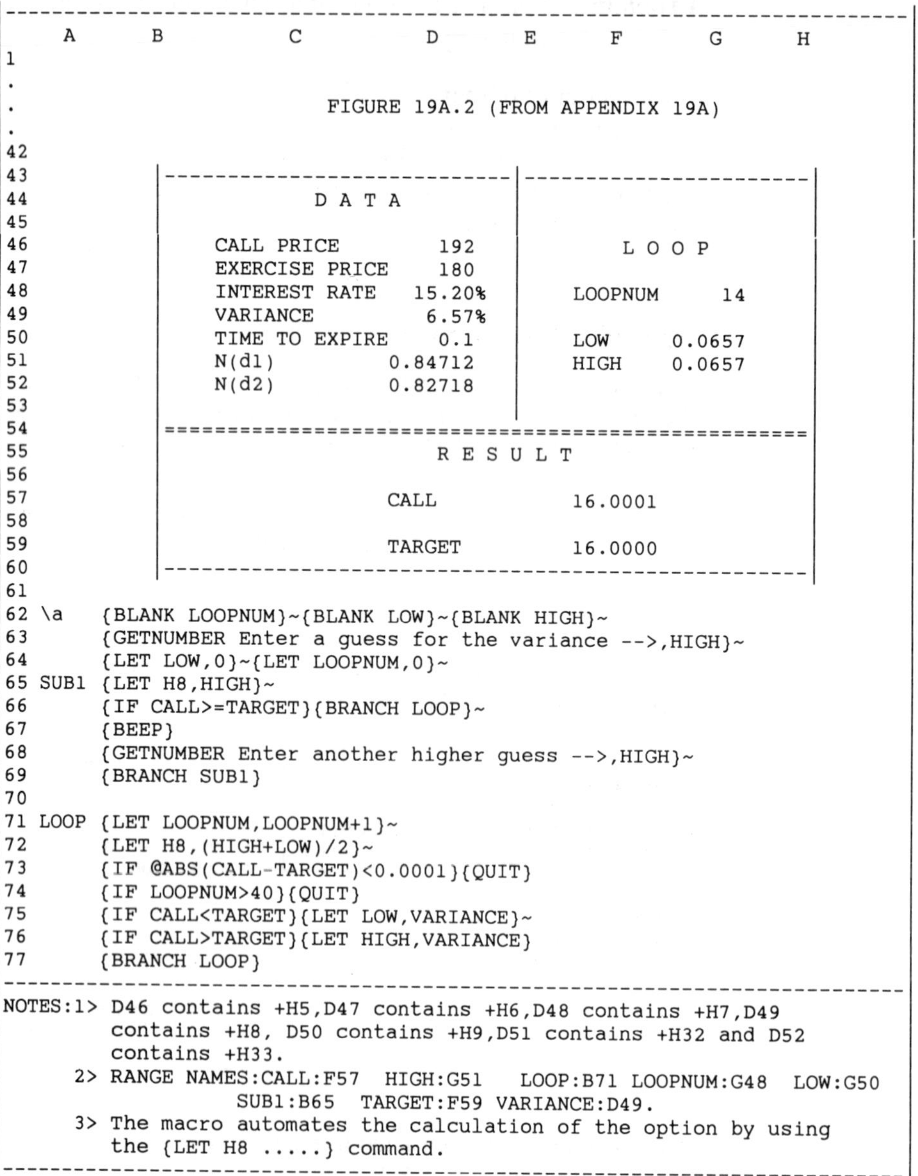

```
      A        B           C                D          E        F          G          H
1
.
.                                    FIGURE 19A.2 (FROM APPENDIX 19A)
.
42
43                -----------------------------|-----------------------
44                            D A T A          |
45                                             |
46                    CALL PRICE          192  |            L O O P
47                    EXERCISE PRICE      180  |
48                    INTEREST RATE    15.20%  |     LOOPNUM        14
49                    VARIANCE          6.57%  |
50                    TIME TO EXPIRE      0.1  |     LOW        0.0657
51                    N(d1)           0.84712  |     HIGH       0.0657
52                    N(d2)           0.82718  |
53                                             |
54                ======================================================
55                                     R E S U L T
56
57                             CALL                  16.0001
58
59                             TARGET                16.0000
60                ------------------------------------------------------
61
62 \a    {BLANK LOOPNUM}~{BLANK LOW}~{BLANK HIGH}~
63       {GETNUMBER Enter a guess for the variance -->,HIGH}~
64       {LET LOW,0}~{LET LOOPNUM,0}~
65 SUB1  {LET H8,HIGH}~
66       {IF CALL>=TARGET}{BRANCH LOOP}~
67       {BEEP}
68       {GETNUMBER Enter another higher guess -->,HIGH}~
69       {BRANCH SUB1}
70
71 LOOP  {LET LOOPNUM,LOOPNUM+1}~
72       {LET H8,(HIGH+LOW)/2}~
73       {IF @ABS(CALL-TARGET)<0.0001}{QUIT}
74       {IF LOOPNUM>40}{QUIT}
75       {IF CALL<TARGET}{LET LOW,VARIANCE}~
76       {IF CALL>TARGET}{LET HIGH,VARIANCE}
77       {BRANCH LOOP}
------------------------------------------------------------------------------
NOTES:1> D46 contains +H5,D47 contains +H6,D48 contains +H7,D49
         contains +H8, D50 contains +H9,D51 contains +H32 and D52
         contains +H33.
      2> RANGE NAMES:CALL:F57  HIGH:G51   LOOP:B71 LOOPNUM:G48  LOW:G50
                    SUB1:B65  TARGET:F59 VARIANCE:D49.
      3> The macro automates the calculation of the option by using
         the {LET H8 .....} command.
```

Figure 19B.1. Calculating the implicit variance for a call option

values for the variance generated by the program and it stops when the option value equals the actual market value (that is, 16 pence).

In the example shown in Figure 19B.1, we use the guess value for the variance of .10. In this case, 14 iterations are required for estimating the implicit variance. The estimate is 6.57 per cent and it is stored in cell D49. Finally, note that the low and high values stored in cells G50 and G51, respectively, are not equal. They appear to be equal because we assign to each cell a fixed format with four decimal points.

Appendix 19C One-way sensitivity analysis of call prices

The macro shown in Figure 19C.1 can be used to examine the sensitivity of call prices to changes in one of the following variables: (a) share price; (b) exercise price; (c) risk-free interest rate; and (d) variance. We assign a name to each of these variables, that is, 'SHARE' for the share price, 'EXE' for the exercise price, 'INT' for the risk-free rate and 'VAR' for the variance. A brief explanation of the macro is given below:

1 The command `{LET LOOPNUM,START}~` enters initially the value 0.04 in cell D79 (the name START is assigned to cell D74 and the name LOOPNUM is assigned to cell D79).
2 The `{GOTO}BEGIN~{RIGHT}{DOWN 3}` moves the cell pointer in cell B83 (the range name BEGIN is assigned to cell A80).
3 The command `/re{RIGHT 3}{END}{DOWN}` erases all previous results.
4 The command `{BRANCH L001}` branches execution of the macro to location B51 (the range name L001 is assigned to cell B51).
5 The command `{LET LOOPNUM,LOOPNUM+STEP}~` starts a loop (the range name STEP is assigned to cell D76).
6 The command `{IF LOOPNUM>=END}{QUIT}` terminates the macro if LOOPNUM > = END (the name END is assigned to cell D75).
7 The formula `+"{LET "&D72&",LOOPNUM}~"` is comprised of three parts: (a) `"{LET "}`; (b) `D72` and (c) `",LOOPNUM}~"`. The outcome of this formula is `{LET VAR,LOOPNUM}~`. The last command enters in cell H8 the value stored in cell D79 (the name VAR is assigned to cell H8).
8 The command `/rvLOOPNUM~~` copies the contents of cell D79 in the current cell.
9 The command `/rvCALL~~` converts the formula stored in cell F38 to its corresponding value and copies the result in the current cell.
10 The command `/rvPUT~~` converts the formula stored in cell F39 to its corresponding value and copies the result in the current cell.
11 The command `{BRANCH LOOP}` branches execution of the macro to location B49 (the range name LOOP is assigned to cell B49).

To produce the results shown in Figure 19C.1 follow the steps below:

Step 1 Type in cell D72 the name of the sensitivity variable (that is VAR).
Step 2 Enter the values 0.04, 0.22, and 0.02 in cells D74, D75 and D76, respectively.
Step 3 Run the macro.

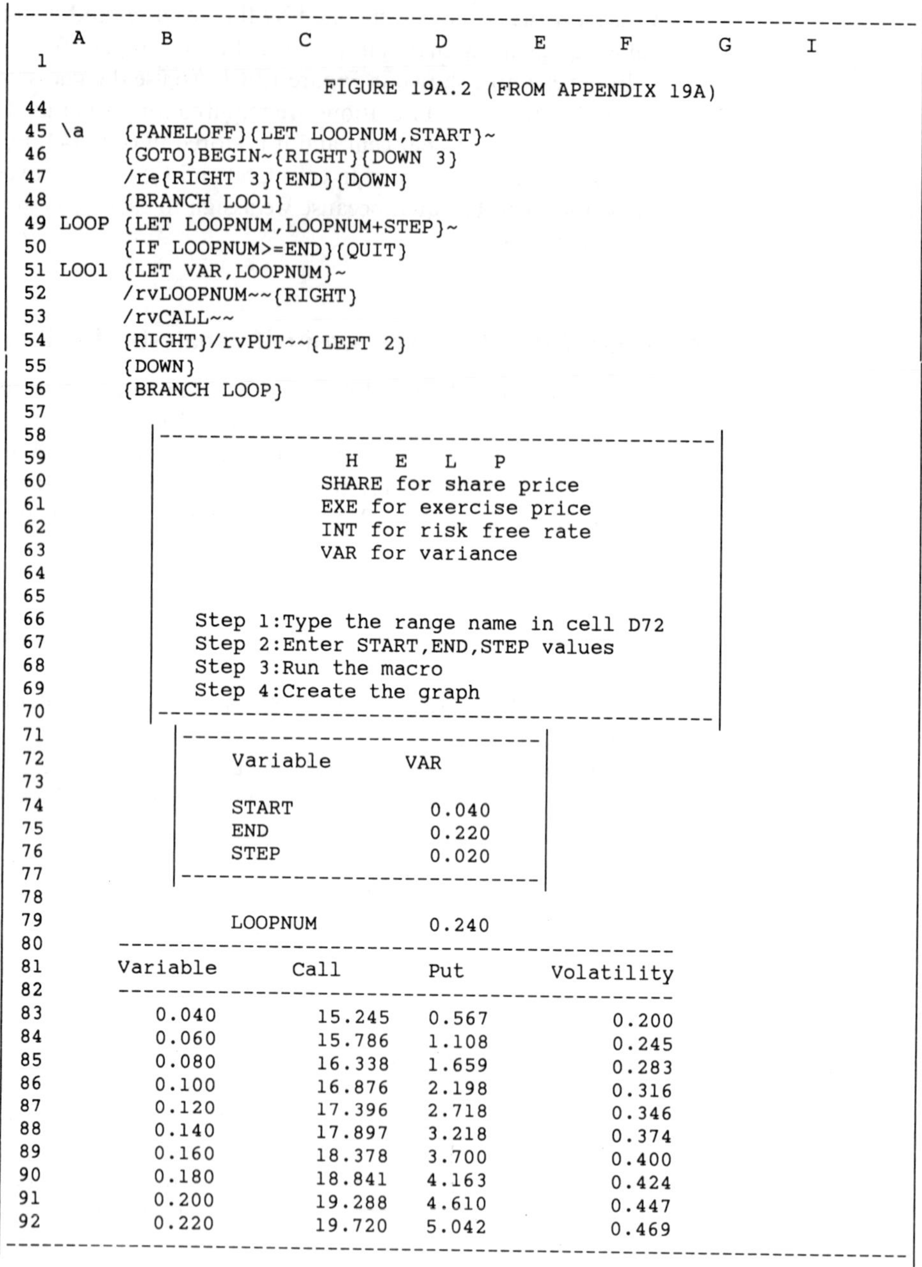

```
     A        B              C              D           E          F            G        I
 1
                                   FIGURE 19A.2 (FROM APPENDIX 19A)
44
45 \a    {PANELOFF}{LET LOOPNUM,START}~
46       {GOTO}BEGIN~{RIGHT}{DOWN 3}
47       /re{RIGHT 3}{END}{DOWN}
48       {BRANCH LOO1}
49 LOOP  {LET LOOPNUM,LOOPNUM+STEP}~
50       {IF LOOPNUM>=END}{QUIT}
51 LOO1  {LET VAR,LOOPNUM}~
52       /rvLOOPNUM~~{RIGHT}
53       /rvCALL~~
54       {RIGHT}/rvPUT~~{LEFT 2}
55       {DOWN}
56       {BRANCH LOOP}
57
58
59                          H   E   L   P
60                          SHARE for share price
61                          EXE for exercise price
62                          INT for risk free rate
63                          VAR for variance
64
65
66            Step 1:Type the range name in cell D72
67            Step 2:Enter START,END,STEP values
68            Step 3:Run the macro
69            Step 4:Create the graph
70
71
72                Variable          VAR
73
74                START               0.040
75                END                 0.220
76                STEP                0.020
77
78
79                LOOPNUM             0.240
80
81        Variable          Call         Put          Volatility
82
83           0.040         15.245       0.567            0.200
84           0.060         15.786       1.108            0.245
85           0.080         16.338       1.659            0.283
86           0.100         16.876       2.198            0.316
87           0.120         17.396       2.718            0.346
88           0.140         17.897       3.218            0.374
89           0.160         18.378       3.700            0.400
90           0.180         18.841       4.163            0.424
91           0.200         19.288       4.610            0.447
92           0.220         19.720       5.042            0.469
```

Figure 19C.1. One-way sensitivity of call and put option prices

Problems

1 Use the macro presented in Figure 19C.1 and conduct a sensitivity analysis of the call price on Marks and Spencer shares with respect to the share price (other things being the same). Produce a graph illustrating your results.

2 Use the macro presented in this example and conduct a sensitivity analysis of the call price on Marks and Spencer shares with respect to the exercise price (other factors remain constant). Produce a graph illustrating your results.

3 Use the macro presented in this example and conduct a sensitivity analysis of the call price on Marks and Spencer shares with respect to the risk-free rate of interest (other things remain the same). Produce a graph illustrating your results.

Appendix 19D Proving properties 1 and 2

Proving property 1

Consider the following diagram which shows three chronological events related to an American call option.

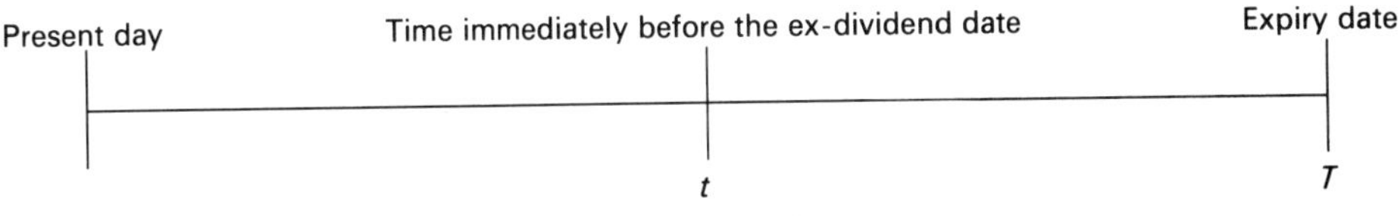

If the dividend payment (call it d) is sacrificed and the option held until the expiry date, then its current value can be represented as follows:

$$\text{Max}\,(0, S_0 - \text{PV}(E) - \text{PV}(d))$$

where

S_0 = the current market price of the underlying share.
PV(E) = the present value of the exercise price (Ee^{-rT}).
PV(d) = the present value of the dividend payment (de^{-rt}).

If $S_0 - \text{PV}(E) - \text{PV}(d) > S_0 - Ee^{-rt}$

then we can produce

$$E(e^{-rt} - e^{-rT}) > de^{-rt}$$

or equivalently

$$E(e^{-rt} - e^{-rt}e^{-r(T-t)}) > de^{-rt} \qquad (19D.1)$$

After simplifying equal terms Equation (19D.1) gives

$$E(1 - e^{-r(T-t)}) > d$$

This inequality shows that if the dividend payment is less than the interest earned on the exercise price from the ex-dividend date to the expiry date, early exercise of an American call option is not appropriate.

Proving property 2

Consider two portfolios A and B. Portfolio A is comprised of a put and portfolio B is comprised of a short position in the underlying share together with $(E + d)$ bonds. The current value of portfolio A is P_0 and the current value of portfolio B is $\text{PV}(E) + \text{PV}(d) - S_0$. To avoid risk-free arbitrage opportunities, one must have:

$$P_0 \geq \text{PV}(E) + \text{PV}(d) - S_0.$$

Appendix 19E Estimating the variance of continuously compounded rates of return

Consider a series of share prices that are collected over a number of T equally spaced periods of time (for example, weeks). For the sake of simplicity, we assume that the share does not pay any dividends during the period under consideration. The continuously compounded rate of return for period t on a given share can be expressed as

$$R_{it} = \ln(S_{it}/S_{it-1})$$

where

$\ln$ = the natural logarithm operator.
S_{it} = the price of the share at the end of period t.
S_{it-1} = the price of the share at the end of period $t-1$.

Assume that the logarithmic rates of return of the share are normally distributed with mean $E(R_i)$ and variance σ_i^2.

The variance of the continuously compounded rate of return required by the Black–Scholes option valuation model can be estimated as follows:

$$s_i^2 = \frac{k}{T-1}\sum_{t=1}^{T}(R_{it} - E(R_i))$$

where

R_{it} = the continuously compounded rate of return for period t on security i.
$E(R_i)$ = the mean return on security i over T periods.
k = a factor required to annualize the variance. For example, with daily data, multiply the variance estimator by 270 (there are approximately 270 working days in a year), with weekly data use 52, and so on.

Example 19E.1 Calculating the volatility of a share of Marks and Spencer (period 5 September 1989–13 March 1990)

The mathematical function `@LN` of 1-2-3 and the `/Copy` command can be used to calculate the weekly logarithmic rates of return associated with a share of Marks and Spencer. Figure 19E.1 shows a spreadsheet presenting the weekly prices for a share of Marks and Spencer. The logarithmic rate of return for the week starting 12 September 1989 can be calculated as follows (see cell C6):

`@LN(B6/B5)` = −0.0317

The variance of the continuously compounded rate of return is calculated by using the following formula (see cell C36):

```
@VAR(C6..C32)*@COUNT(C6..C32)/(@COUNT(C6..C32)-1)
```

where `@COUNT(C6..C32)-1` = 26. When the rates of return are drawn from a population of observations, dividing by $T-1$ (in this case, by 26) provides an unbiased estimate of the population variance. Next multiply the resulting variance by 52 to derive the annualized variance, that is:

`+C36*52` = 0.0652

	A	B	C	D	E	F
1	THE VARIANCE OF M & S SHARE PRICE (PERIOD SEP 5,1989-MARCH 13,1990)					
2						
3	Week	Share Price	LN Changes			
4						
5	05-Sep-89	224.0				
6	12-Sep-89	217.0	-0.0317			
7	19-Sep-89	209.0	-0.0376			
8	26-Sep-89	202.0	-0.0341			
9	03-Oct-89	198.0	-0.0200			
10	10-Oct-89	184.0	-0.0733			
11	17-Oct-89	182.5	-0.0082			
12	24-Oct-89	192.5	0.0533			
13	31-Oct-89	188.0	-0.0237			
14	07-Nov-89	194.0	0.0314			
15	07-Nov-89	196.0	0.0103			
16	07-Nov-89	191.0	-0.0258			
17	07-Nov-89	195.0	0.0207			
18	05-Dec-89	202.0	0.0353			
19	12-Dec-89	199.0	-0.0150			
20	19-Dec-89	195.0	-0.0203			
21	26-Dec-89	197.0	0.0102			
22	02-Jan-90	204.0	0.0349			
23	09-Jan-90	211.0	0.0337			
24	16-Jan-90	197.0	-0.0687			
25	23-Jan-90	192.0	-0.0257			
26	30-Jan-90	189.0	-0.0157			
27	06-Feb-90	204.0	0.0764			
28	13-Feb-90	202.0	-0.0099			
29	20-Feb-90	204.0	0.0099			
30	27-Feb-90	205.0	0.0049			
31	06-Mar-90	198.0	-0.0347			
32	13-Mar-90	191.0	-0.0360			
33						
34						
35		Average	-0.0059			
36		Variance	0.0013			
37		Variance x 52	0.0652			

Figure 19E.1. Calculating the variance of the Marks and Spencer share price (5 September 1989–13 March 1990)

Problem Set up the worksheet shown in Figure 19E.1.

References and bibliography

Bhattacharya, M. (1980) Empirical properties of the Black–Scholes formula under ideal conditions, *Journal of Financial and Quantitative Analysis*, December, 1081–106.

Biger, N. and Hull, J. (1983) The valuation of currency options, *Financial Management*, Spring, 24–8.

Black, F. (1975) Fact and fantasy in the use of options, *Financial Analyst Journal*, July–August, 36–41, 61–72.

Black, F. and Scholes, M. (1973) The pricing of options and corporate liabilities, *Journal of Political Economy*, May–June, 637–54.

Bodurtha, J. and Courtadon, G. (1986) Efficiency tests of foreign currency options market, *Journal of Finance*, March, 151–62.

Chesney, M. and Scott Louis (1989) Pricing European currency options: a comparison of modified Black–Scholes model and a random variance model, *Journal of Financial and Quantitative Analysis*, September, 267–84.

Cox, J. (1975) Notes on option pricing I: Constant elasticity of diffusions, Unpublished draft, Stanford University, September.

Cox, S. and Ross, S. (1975) The pricing of options for jump process, Working Paper No. 2-75, Rodney L. White Center for Financial Research, University of Pennsylvania, April.

Cox, S. and Ross, S. (1976a) The valuation of options for alternative stochastic processes, *Journal of Financial Economics*, March, 145–66.

Cox, S. and Ross, S. (1976b) A survey of some new results in financial option pricing theory, *Journal of Finance*, May, 383–402.

Fisher, S. (1978) Call option pricing when the exercise price is uncertain and the valuation of index bonds, *Journal of Finance*, March, 169–86.

Galai, D. (1977) Tests of market efficiency of the Chicago Board Options Exchange, *Journal of Business*, April, 167–97.

Garman, M. and Klass, M. (1980) On the estimation of security price volatilities from historical data, *Journal of Business*, January, 67–78.

Geske, R. and Roll, R. (1984) On valuing American call options with Black–Scholes valuation formula, *Journal of Finance*, June, 443–55.

Hull, J.C. and White, A. (1987) The pricing of options on assets with stochastic volatility, *Journal of Finance*, June, 281–300.

Klemkosky, R. and Resnick, B. (1979) Put–call parity and market efficiency, *Journal of Finance*, December, 1141–55.

MacBeth, J. and Merville, L. (1979) An empirical examination of the Black–Scholes call option pricing model, *Journal of Finance*, December, 1173–86.

MacBeth, J. and Merville, L. (1980) Tests of Black–Scholes and Cox call option valuation models, *Journal of Finance*, May, 285–300.

Margrabe, W. (1978) The value of an option to exchange one asset for another, *Journal of Finance*, March, 177–86.

Merton, R.C. (1973) The theory of rational option pricing, *Bell Journal of Economics and Management Science*, Spring, 141–83.

Merton, R.C. (1974) On the pricing of corporate debt: the risk structure of interest rates, *Journal of Finance*, May, 449–70.

Merton, R.C. (1976) Option pricing when underlying stock returns are discontinuous, *Journal of Financial Economics*, March, 125–44.

Parkison, M. (1980) The extreme value method for estimating the variance at the rate of return, *Journal of Business*, January, 61–5.

Rubinstein, M. (1981) Nonparametric tests of alternative option pricing models, Working Paper No. 117, University of California, Research Program in Finance.

Rubinstein, M. (1983) Displaced discussion option pricing, *Journal of Finance*, March, 213–17.

Trennepohl, G. (1981) A comparison of listed option premiums and Black and Scholes model prices: 1973–1979, *Journal of Financial Research*, Spring, 11–20.

Whaley, R. (1982) Valuation of American call options on dividend paying stocks: empirical tests, *Journal of Financial Economics*, March, 29–58.

Appendix A A history of spreadsheets and general comparisons

History of spreadsheets

Spreadsheets became popular during the second half of the 1970s. In 1979 Software Arts (owned by Dan Bricklin and Bob Frankston), and Personal Software (owned by Dan Fylstra), launched a package called VisiCalc (an abbreviation for Visible Calculator) at the National Computer Conference. VisiCalc was the first electronic spreadsheet offering several features such as scrolling around the worksheet, using built-in functions and formulae, identifying cells by pointing at them with the cursor, and so on. Since it went on the market hundreds of thousands of VisiCalc packages have been sold. VisiCalc infiltrated business organizations and it became a common fact that spreadsheets were to be used to a greater extent in the future. In the early 1980s Jonathan Sachs and Mitch Kapol worked together on a computer package that was to include three packages in one: a spreadsheet, word processor and graphics. Eventually, the word processor program was substituted by a database program, because databases were easier to write once the skeleton of the spreadsheet had been created. Sachs's package, 1-2-3 Release 1, was introduced in January 1983. Lotus 1-2-3 included three packages in one (hence the name 1-2-3). The three packages are listed below:

1. A spreadsheet (similar to the original 'VisiCalc')
2. A database
3. Graphics

Lotus 1-2-3 offered some new features to the world of spreadsheets such as its speed, its simple menu-driven interface, its macro language and its database. Lotus Release 1A, launched soon afterwards, had drivers which supported hardware devices other than those of an IBM-specific PC and it did not take long for Lotus to become the leading spreadsheet package (early 1983).

In 1985, Lotus Development Corporation made available Lotus 1-2-3 Release 2 providing hardware support, additional commands and new built-in functions. When the Release 2 of Lotus 1-2-3 was originally introduced there were some problems related to compatibility of Releases 1A and 2. Release 2.01 takes care of these compatibility problems.

Lotus Development Corporation offered in the summer of 1989 a new upgrade to Release 2.01, called Release 2.2. This release can be used with 8088 IBM-PC and -XT machines and runs faster the initial loading of the program, several macros, and several menu commands.

Lotus Release 3 became available in June 1989 permitting use of multidimensional worksheets (written in C) and multiple active files. To run it, you have to have an AT or better (that is, a 286 or 386) personal computer with 1 Mb of random access memory. The three-dimensionality has been also extended to the database, providing the new ability to use more than one database at a time. Release 3 also allows you to use external databases (for example, dBASE III), but you need a suitable driver for the database of your choice. Release 3's graphics facilities are greatly improved, but 1-2-3 still has disappointing report presentation.

During the second half of the 1980s there was a wide range of spreadsheet programs on the market, each trying to outdo the others in power and flexibility. The three most popular were, Excel, SuperCalc 5 and Quatro.[1]

Excel was developed by Microsoft Corporation and it runs under all three environments, DOS, OS/2 and Macintosh. It is basically a two-dimensional spreadsheet, but it does have the facility to link cells in different spreadsheets and have multiple files open. Excel runs in MS-DOS under the Microsoft Windows and in OS/2 under the Presentation Manager, implying that the user can easily exchange data among different applications. The graphics of Excel are excellent, with many choices for format and options and its database works well. A disadvantage of the package is its inability to combine charts and spreadsheets. Excel can read and write 1-2-3 worksheets, but it is not completely compatible with 1-2-3.

SuperCalc 5 of Computer Associates International, Inc. offers many of the same facilities as Lotus 1-2-3 Release 3.0. The package offers a multidimensional page linking and also supports links to other spreadsheets (for example, Lotus 1-2-3). SuperCalc 5 can run on an XT machine with 512 K memory. The package also supports an extensive range of graphs and you can create combination graphs or add 3-D prospective. SuperCalc 5 also provides an optional 1-2-3 menu and includes a database management similar to that of Lotus 1-2-3 Release 3.0. Computer Associates can also provide a compatible mainframe version of SuperCalc 5.

Quatro Pro of Borland International, Inc. offers one spreadsheet for all DOS users and it combines the more familiar layout of a standard worksheet with the advantages of a window-driven approach. In a colour monitor, the first thing you notice after retrieving the program is its extensive use of colour. Quatro Pro allows links to be maintained between spreadsheet files and it also allows three-dimensional models to be built up in a single file. One of Quatro Pro's features is that it can load large spreadsheets with relatively limited memory and it can run in 512 Kb on an XT. The package has an excellent range of graphical capabilities, and the facility to

1. The following information was written in 1992 and was valid around that time.

develop a presentation around the graphics. Quatro Pro can read and write 1-2-3 worksheets directly and it is fully compatible with Lotus 1-2-3.

We now discuss several features of four popular spreadsheets, Lotus 1-2-3 (Release 2.2), Excel, SuperCalc 5 and Quatro.

Features and facilities of a spreadsheet

Each of the four spreadsheets discussed in this appendix offers to the user the following features:

1 Ability to interface to other software:
  - (a) exchanging data with other spreadsheet packages;
  - (b) exchanging data with word processing packages;
  - (c) exchanging data with database packages;
  - (d) exchanging data with statistical packages;
  - (e) moving data to graphic packages.

2 Editing abilities:
  - (a) changing cell contents without retyping;
  - (b) coping with cell contents;
  - (c) moving cell contents;
  - (d) inserting new rows or columns;
  - (e) deleting existing rows or columns;
  - (f) manipulating text data.

3 Financial functions (see Figure A.1):
  - (a) present value;
  - (b) future value;
  - (c) net present value;
  - (d) internal rate of return;
  - (e) depreciation functions.

4 Statistical functions (see Figure A.1):
  - (a) summation of values;
  - (b) average of values;
  - (c) minimum value;
  - (d) maximum value;
  - (e) variance of values;
  - (f) standard deviation of values;
  - (g) other (for example, frequency distributions).

5 Other functions (see Figure A.1):
  - (a) mathematical;
  - (b) date;
  - (c) time;
  - (d) logical;
  - (e) string;
  - (f) special;
  - (g) worksheet.

Figure A.1. Number of supported functions for four spreadsheets

Name	Date/time	Financial	Statistical	Math	Logical	String	Other
Excel 2.1	12	13	25	22	7	0	0
Lotus 1-2-3 v2	11	11	7	17	7	19	11
Lotus 1-2-3 v2.2	11	11	7	17	7	19	11
Quatro Pro	12	18	10	19	8	21	25
SuperCalc 5	16	18	15	18	18	16	30

6 Recalculation facilities:
- (a) automatic;
- (b) natural;
- (c) columnwise;
- (d) rowwise;
- (e) manual;
- (f) Iterations.

7 'What if' analysis:
- (a) one-way sensitivity analysis;
- (b) two-way sensitivity analysis.

8 Display facilities:
- (a) numeric formats;
- (b) text formats;
- (c) adjust column widths;
- (d) windows.

9 Manipulation of different files:
- (a) saving files;
- (b) combining files;
- (c) extracting files.

10 Security of models:
- (a) protecting facilities;
- (b) hiding cells.

11 Graphic facilities:
- (a) line;
- (b) bar;
- (c) XY;
- (d) stack-bar;
- (e) pie.

12 Printer features

13 Database facilities

14 Keyboard macros
- (a) recording a sequence of keystrokes and executing it automatically.

15 Command language
- (a) storing repetitive command sequences and executing them automatically.

Invoking and exiting a spreadsheet

We assume that you are using a hard disk and that you are in the directory containing the spreadsheet files. We also assume that your spreadsheet is installed on the hard disk system used. Figure A.2 shows how you can invoke and exit from each of the four spreadsheets discussed in this appendix.

Lotus 1-2-3: (Rel. 2.2)	To invoke the 1-2-3 program type 123 and press the <Enter> key. To exit the 1-2-3 program type /QY and then press the <Enter> key.
Excel:	To invoke the excel program without windows type excel and then press the <Enter> key. To exit the Excel program press <Alt>, F and X.
SuperCalc 5:	To invoke the Supercalc program in black-and-white display type SC5/BW and then press the <Enter> key. To invoke the SuperCalc program in a colour monitor type SC5 and then press the <Enter> key. To exit the SuperCalc program type /QY and then press the <Enter> key.
Quatro:	To invoke the Quatro program type Q and then press the <Enter> key. To exit the Quatro program type /QY and then press the <Enter> key.

Figure A.2. Invoking and exiting a spreadsheet

Entering numbers

A simple rule for entering numbers into any of the four spreadsheets, Lotus 1-2-3, Excel, SuperCalc 5 and Quatro, can be stated below. Numbers can begin with any of the following characters: 0 to 9, a decimal point, a plus sign (+), or a minus sign (−). A number can be also entered in parentheses [( )].

Entering ranges

A range is a rectangular collection of adjacent cells. A range can be a single cell, a single row, a single column, or several rows and columns. A range in Lotus 1-2-3 and Quatro is defined by the cell addresses that specify its corners and is separated by two periods, for example, E1..E1, A1..D1, A1..A10, A1..D10. A range in Excel and SuperCalc 5 separates by a colon (:) the two cell addresses that specify its corners. Here are some example, E1:E1, A1:D1, A1:A10, A1:D10.

Mathematical operators

Mathematical operators are used to indicate arithmetic operations. Each of the four spreadsheets, Lotus 1-2-3, Excel, SuperCalc 5 and Quatro, uses the mathematical operators shown in Figure A.3.

Operator	Meaning
^ (or **)	Exponentiation
+	Addition
−	Subtraction
*	Multiplication
\	Division

Figure A.3. Mathematical operators

Entering numeric formulae that contain cell addresses

The great power and usefulness of a spreadsheet comes from its ability to perform calculations based on formulae you enter into cells. When you enter a numeric formula that contains cell addresses, the spreadsheet stores it in memory and displays the results indicated by the formula. That way, any time the contents of one cell in the formula are changed, the spreadsheet recalculates automatically the new results of the formula. Figure A.4 shows how you can enter a formula in each of the four popular spreadsheets discussed in this appendix.

Lotus 1-2-3: (Rel. 2.2)	Formulae can begin with a plus sign (+) or a left bracket [(]. Examples: `+A1+A2, (A3+A4)^2`
Excel:	Formulae can begin with an equal sign (=) or a left bracket [(]. Examples: `=B1-B4, (B3+B5)*A2`
SuperCalc 5:	Formulae can begin with a plus sign (+) or a left bracket [(]. Examples: `+B3*B6, (D3-B5)/A2`
Quatro:	Formulae can begin with a plus sign (+) or a left bracket [(]. Examples: `+B3*B6/A3, (A1+A2)*A3^2`

Figure A.4. Entering formulae

Entering text

Text consists of groups of letters and special symbols. Labels are simple text entries and they are commonly used for row and column headings, for example, balance sheet, current assets. Each spreadsheet offers a way (or ways) to control label prefixes (see Figure A.5).

Lotus 1-2-3: (Rel. 2.2)	Use the `/Range Label` command.
Excel:	Use the `Format Alignment` command.
SuperCalc 5:	Use the `/Format Entry Text` command.
Quatro:	Use the `/Block Label_Align` command.

Figure A.5. Controlling labels

Function keys

Each spreadsheet uses the function keys [F1] to [F10] for special situations (see Figure A.6).

	Lotus	Excel	SuperCalc 5	Quatro
[F1]	Help	Help	Help	Help
[F2]	Edit	Edit formula bar	Edit	Edit
[F3]	Name	Paste Name	Name	Names
[F4]	Absolute	Absolute	Absolute	Absolute
[F5]	Goto	Goto	Goto	Goto
[F6]	Window	Next/previous panel	Window	Window
[F7]	Query	Formula find next	Tlabels	Query
[F8]	Table	Extend selected cells	Resumes macro executions	Macro
[F9]	Calc	Calculates now	Calc	Calc
[F10]	Graph	Activates menu graph	View graph	Graph

Figure A.6. Function keys

The copy command

One of the main and useful features of a spreadsheet is its ability to replicate the contents of cells from a pre-specified range into another pre-specified range of cells. Figure A.7 shows the appropriate command for each of the four spreadsheets discussed in the present appendix.

Lotus 1-2-3: (Rel. 2.2)	Use the /Copy command.
Excel:	Use the Edit Copy and Edit Paste commands.
SuperCalc 5:	Use the /Copy command.
Quatro:	Use the /Block Copy command.

Figure A.7. Copying the contents of cells

Whenever you copy a formula from one part of a worksheet to another, the addresses of the cells contained in the formula are adjusted automatically to fit the new location. Such a process is known as relative addressing. In many cases, you may wish not to change the address of a cell contained in a formula when the formula is copied. In this instance, you have to create an absolute address, that is, an address that does not change at all when the address is copied. For every worksheet discussed in this chapter, we have the following:

`$A$1` Both row and column address are copied absolutely.
`$A1` Column addresses are copied absolutely with row addresses relatively.
`A$1` Row addresses are copied absolutely with column addresses relatively.

Graphs

Spreadsheet packages allow numeric data to be presented on a computer screen in graphic formats.

Figure A.8 shows the various graph types processed by each of the four spreadsheets discussed in this appendix.

Lotus 1-2-3: (Rel. 2.2)	Line, Bar, XY, Stack-Bar, Pie.
Excel:	Area, Bar, Column, Line, Pie, Scatter, Combination.
SuperCalc 5:	Bar, Pie, Dual, Line, Area, Hi-Lo, X-Y, Radar, Word.
Quatro:	Line, Bar, XY, Stacked Bar, Pie, 3-D Bar, Area, Rotated Bar, Markets, Lines & Markets.

Figure A.8. Types of available graphs

Database facilities

A database is a collection of information organized in a specific format. A record is a collection of information related to a particular item in the database. A field is a single item of information contained in a record. A field name is a label that is used to identify a field.

For example, you can develop a database for the households who borrow funds from a building society in order to purchase a house. In this database each household should occupy a line that can be divided into seven columns: name, married status, salary, funds borrowed, term, interest, payment. For each household the line of information (that is, name, married status, salary, funds borrowed, term, interest, payment) is a record. Each of the columns (that is, name, married status, salary, funds borrowed, term, interest, payment) is a field. The labels, that is, name, married status, salary, funds borrowed, term, interest, payment) are the field names.

A spreadsheet database is nothing more than a worksheet that is organized in a specific format. You can use the spreadsheet's facilities in exactly the same way you use these facilities with any other worksheet. Taking into account this useful feature together with the other specific features of the spreadsheet's databases, the following advantages emerge:

- You can store many kinds of information.
- In many cases a database can be created quickly (for example, using the copy facility).
- You can edit the information in a database quickly.
- You can add or delete records quickly.
- You can manipulate the information in a database quickly and easily.
- You can use database functions or other spreadsheet functions.
- You can load data from ASCII files and other programs (for example, Dbase IV).
- You can improve the appearance of a database (for example, by formatting its entries).
- You can provide graphic presentations of the database fields.
- You can print parts of a database and include them in a financial report.
- You can protect your database.
- You can use macros to automate your database applications.

Spreadsheet databases also offer several disadvantages such as:

- The size of a spreadsheet database is limited by the size of your spreadsheet program and the amount of random access memory in your computer.
- Several database facilities are not as powerful as the facilities available in full database management packages.

Manipulation of matrices

Spreadsheets allow the manipulation of blocks of numeric data with the aid of a special command or a special function (see Figure A.9).

Figure A.9. Commands or functions for matrix manipulation

Lotus 1-2-3: (Rel. 2.2)	Use the `/Data Matrix` command.
Excel:	The following matrix functions exist: `MINVERSE`, produces the inverse of a square matrix; `MMULT`, multiples two matrices; and `MDETERM` produces the determinant of square matrix.
SuperCalc 5:	Use `//Data Matrix` command.
Quatro:	Use `/Advanced Matrix` command.

Regression analysis

Regression analysis determines how one variable is related to one or more other variables. Figure A.10 shows, for each spreadsheet discussed in this appendix, the available command or function that can be utilized to estimate a regression equation.

Figure A.10. Commands or functions for estimating a regression equation

Lotus 1-2-3: (Rel. 2.2)	Use the /Data Regression command.
Excel:	Use the statistical function LINEST.
SuperCalc 5:	Use //Data Analysis Regression command.
Quatro	Use /Advanced Regression command.

Data tables

A really impressive feature of a good spreadsheet is to do sensitivity analysis. A good spreadsheet gets you to provide a sensitivity analysis on one variable (single-variable sensitivity analysis) which can be applied to many formulae. A single variable sensitivity analysis reveals how one variable (for example, sales) changes in response to another variable (for example, number of units sold). A good spreadsheet can also get you to perform a sensitivity analysis on two variables (a two-variable sensitivity analysis), but it can only be applied with regard to one formula. A two-variable sensitivity analysis shows how one variable (for example, debt/equity ratio) changes in response to two variables (for example, debt and equity). Figure A.11 shows the relevant commands.

Figure A.11. A command for sensitivity analysis

Lotus 1-2-3: (Rel. 2.2)	Use the /Data Table command.
Excel:	Use the Data Table command.
SuperCalc 5:	Use //Data Table command.
Quatro:	Use /Advanced What-If command.

Financial functions

The financial functions perform investment calculations. Each of the four worksheets discussed in this chapter provides a family of financial functions (see Figure A.12).

Function	Lotus	Excel	VisiCalc	Quatro
Future value of a stream of periodic, equal payments	@FV	FV	FV	@FV
Present value of a stream of periodic, equal payments	@PV	PV	PV	@PV
Number of periods required for an annuity to reach a given future value	@TERM	NPER	TERM	@TERM
Annuity payment required to pay a loan over a given period	@PMT	PMT	PMT	@PMT
Number of periods for a lump sum to grow to a given future value	@CTERM	—	CTERM	@CTERM
Interest rate required for a lump sum to grow to a given future value	RATE	—	RATE	@RATE
Present value of a stream of periodic cash flows discounted at a fixed rate	@NPV	NPV	NPV	@NPV
Internal rate of return of a stream of periodic cash flows	@IRR	IRR	IRR	@IRR
Depreciation of an asset using the straight-line method	@SLN	SLN	SLN	@SLN
Depreciation of an asset using the double-declining balance method	@DDB	DDB	DDB	@DDB
Depreciation of an asset using the sum-of-the-years method	@SYD	SYD	SYD	@SYD

Figure A.12. Financial functions

Computes the average of a range of values	Lotus @AVG	Excel AVERAGE	VisiCalc AVG	Quatro @AVG
Counts the number of numeric values in a specified range	Lotus @COUNT	Excel COUNT	VisiCalc COUNT	Quatro @COUNT
Computes the sum of values in a specified range	Lotus @SUM	Excel SUM	VisiCalc SUM	Quatro @SUM
Returns the minimum value from a specified range	Lotus @MIN	Excel MIN	VisiCalc MIN	Quatro @MIN
Returns the maximum value from a specified range	Lotus @MAX	Excel MAX	VisiCalc MAX	Quatro @MAX
Returns the variance of values in a specified range	Lotus @VAR	Excel VARP	VisiCalc VAR	Quatro @VAR
Returns the standard deviation of values in a specified range	Lotus @STD	Excel STDEVP	VisiCalc STD	Quatro @STD

Figure A.13. Statistical functions

Statistical functions

The statistical functions perform statistical analysis (see Figure A.13).

References and bibliography

Diacogiannis, P.G. and De Souza, E. (1991) *Lotus 1-2-3 for Finance and Business: A Practical Guide*. Addison-Wesley, Wokingham, UK.

Gobel, D.P. (1988) *Using Quatro*. Que Corporation, Carmel, IN.

Perry, J.T. and Lateer, J.G. (1989) *Using SuperCalc 5*, 2nd edn. Que Corporation, Carmel, IN.

Person, R. and Campbell, M. (1988) *Using Excel: IBM Version*. Que Corporation, Carmel, IN.

Appendix B UK–US equivalent terms

UK term	Equivalent US term
Appropriation account	Statement of retained earnings
Applications of funds	Uses of funds
Consolidated profit and loss account	Income/earnings statement
Creditors	Accounts payable
Debenture	Bond
Debtors	Accounts receivable
Financial year	Fiscal year
Gearing	Leverage
Holding company	Parent company
Issued capital	Stated capital
Reconstruction of a firm	Reorganization of a firm
Ordinary share	Common share
Profit before interest and tax (or taxes)	Earnings before interest and tax (or taxes)
Preference shares	Preferred shares
Stocks	Inventory
Short-term investments	Marketable securities
Sources and application of funds or funds flow statement	Statement of changes in financial position
Trading profit	Operating income/profit

Appendix C Glossary

Accounting rate of return: the average net cash flow over the life span of a project divided by the project's initial investment.

Activity ratios: indicators of how efficiently a firm is utilizing its assets to generate sales.

American option: an option that can be exercised any time on or before the expiry date.

Annual percentage rate: a method that puts investments with different compounding periods into a common basis.

Annuity: a stream of equal periodic payments or receipts.

Annuity due: an annuity in which the payments or receipts occur at the beginning of each period.

Arbitrage pricing model: a multi-factor equilibrium relationship between risk and return. The arbitrage pricing model is based upon a multi-factor index model and the assumption that all portfolios that use no wealth and have zero risk earn a zero expected return.

At the money option: a call option whose exercise price is approximately equal to the current market price of the underlying security.

Beta: the measure of the risk of a security (portfolio) relative to the risk of the market portfolio (proxy).

Book value weights: based on the use of accounting values, they are calculated by dividing the book value of each long-term capital source by the sum of the book values of all the long-term capital sources of the firm.

Breaking point: the point at which a specific cost of capital changes making long term finance more expensive.

Business risk: the portion of a firm's total risk arising from the variability in the firm's expected profits before interest and taxes.

Call option: an option that gives its owner the right to buy a fixed number of shares at a specified price within a specified period of time.

Capital asset pricing model: an equilibrium relationship between risk and return for individual securities or portfolios where the risk is measured by beta.

Capital budgeting: the analysis of the net cash flows of long-term investments providing the optimal allocation of the firm's funds.

Capital market line: an equilibrium relationship between return and risk for efficient portfolios only.

Capital rationing: an implication that a fixed sum of funds is available for investment—usually less than the total outlay of the projects under consideration.

Capital structure: a description of the proportions of the components of the firm's long-term financing (that is, debt and equity).

Cash inflow: an amount equal to the profit after taxes plus non-cash expenses (e.g. depreciation).

Certainty equivalent method: the conversion of a risky stream of cash flows into certain (riskless) flows.

Coefficient of variation (of probable cash flows): the standard deviation of probable cash flows divided by the expected cash flow.

Combined break-even analysis: examination of the relationship between sales, costs and earnings per share; it also determines the number of units sold and their respective selling price which results from a zero earnings per share.

Combined gearing: the utilization of fixed financing costs (for example, interest, preference shares, dividends, and so on) and fixed operating costs (for example, depreciation, indirect labour cost, and so on) to magnify the earnings per share by changes that occur in sales.

Compounding factor: the future value of £1 after *n* periods when interest is compounded at a rate of *r* per cent per period.

Compounding factor (annuity): the future value of a series of *n* equal annual payments £1 when interest is compounded at a rate of *r* per cent per period.

Compound growth rate: the rate at which a stream of cash flows grows over a period of equal intervals (for example, years).

Compound interest: the interest paid on both the principal and the previously accumulated interest.

Compound value: the amount to which a present sum of money or a series of payments will grow over time when compounded at a given rate of interest.

Conglomerate merger: a merger involving two or more firms in unrelated business lines.

Cost of capital: the rate the firm must pay to acquire long-term capital (it is also called the required rate of return).

Cost of debentures: the minimum rate of return investors will accept in order to purchase a firm's debentures.

Cost of ordinary shares: the minimum rate of return investors will accept in order to purchase a firm's ordinary shares.

Cost of reserves: assumed (from the firm's point of view) to be equal to the rate of return shareholders require on the existing ordinary shares of the firm.

Coupon rate: determines the annual amount of interest paid on a debenture par value.

Covariance of security returns: a measure indicating the direction of the relationship between security rates of return.

Cross-sectional analysis: a method providing a comparison of the firm's position at a fixed point in time with other firms or the industry average.

Debenture: a debt obligation offering a fixed income to the holder and having a claim on the firm's earnings before either preference or ordinary shares.

Debenture interest: the interest gained from a debenture is equivalent to its par value multiplied by its coupon rate.

Decision tree: a graphical method of showing in an organized manner all the possible flows generated by an investment project.

Degree of combined gearing: the percentage change in earnings per share with respect to a percentage change of the units sold.

Degree of financial gearing: the percentage change in earnings per share with respect to a percentage change in profit before interest and tax.

Degree of operating gearing: the percentage change in profit before interest and tax with respect to the percentage change in units sold.

Discounting factor: the present value of £1 due to be received n years from now at an interest rate of r.

Discounting factor (annuity): the present value of a series of n equal annual payments of £1 discounted at r per cent for n years.

Discount rate: the rate used to convert future cash flows into present values.

Diversifiable risk: the part of the total security (or portfolio) risk that can be eliminated through diversification.

Diversification: the act of allocating funds in more than one security with the goal of reducing risk.

Dividend: the payment made by a firm to its owners.

Dividend payout ratio: the percentage of the earnings per share distributed to the firm's ordinary shareholders in the form of dividends. It can be found by dividing the firm's dividend per share by its earnings per share.

Effective rate of interest: see Annual percentage rate.

Efficient frontier: see Efficient portfolio set.

Efficient market: a competitive market composed of a large number of investors, which is said to be efficient with respect to a set of information if prices in the market at all times respond fully and quickly to all information in the information set. In an efficient market the intrinsic and market values of an asset are equal.

Efficient market hypothesis: the body of theory around the efficient market concept is called the efficient market hypothesis (EMH).

Efficient portfolio: a portfolio where the maximum expected return is obtained given its standard deviation (variance) of return and the minimum standard deviation (variance) given its expected return.

Efficient portfolio set: the locus of all the efficient portfolios.

European option: an option that can be exercised only at the expiry date.

Exercise price in options: the price per share at which the purchaser of a traded option has the right to buy (or sell) the underlying share from the writer (to the buyer).

Expected cash flow (or mean): the weighted average of the possible outcomes of a probability distribution.

Expiry date: the last date at which an option can be exercised or traded.

Fair game: a set of information on securities available at time t cannot be utilized to earn a return above the actual return at time $t+1$.

Financial break-even analysis: the relationship between profits before interest and tax and earnings per share; it also determines the level of profit before interest and tax which produces a zero earnings per share.

Financial director: in a large firm, he or she is a member of the financial staff who deals with the investment and financing decisions of the firm. In a large firm, the title of treasurer can be compared to the financial director.

Financial forecasting: the process of projecting or estimating the firm's future financial statements.

Financial gearing: the utilization of fixed financing costs (for example, interest, preference shares, dividends, and so on) to magnify the earnings per share by changes that occur in the firm's profit before interest and tax.

Financial lease: one that obligates the lessee to make payments to the lessor throughout the lease period.

Financial risk: the portion of the firm's total risk arising from the additional variability of the expected earnings per share due to the use of financial gearing.

Flat rate: the rate earned by an investment expressed as a percentage of the amount invested.

Flotation costs: costs associated with issuing new shares and debentures.

Future value: the amount of a given payment (or series of payments) will be worth when compounded at a specific interest rate over a given period of time.

Gearing ratios: indicators of the firm's ability to meet its debt obligations.

Government securities: securities issued by the Government for a fixed period of time. They carry a fixed rate of interest and involve virtually no risk.

Horizontal merger: a merger involving two or more firms that have similar business lines.

Hurdle rate: the minimum rate which projects should generate in order to be accepted (that is, the cost of capital or the required rate of return).

In the money option: a call option whose exercise price is below the current market price of the underlying security.

Interest: the price paid for the use of money over a period of time or the price received for lending money over a period of time.

Internal rate of return: the rate of return which (when used as the discount rate) produces a net present value equal to zero.

Intrinsic value: the present value of a security's expected cash flows (for example, dividends, expected market value, and so on) when discounted at the required rate of return.

Intrinsic value of an option: the difference between the exercise price and the price of the underlying security.

Investment opportunity schedule: a graph illustrating possible capital budgeting projects ranked in decreasing order by their internal rate of return. The point of intersection between the weighted marginal cost of capital schedule and the investment opportunity schedule is the discount rate utilized when calculating a project's net present value. This point of intersection is also the hurdle rate utilized in the internal rate of return's decision criterion.

Investment ratios: the firm's potential for being considered as an investment.

Investment value: see Intrinsic value.

Investor's utility: the degree of satisfaction the investor has from making an investment.

Lease: a contract between two parties by which one party allows the use of its assets by the other party for a specified time in return for specified periodic payment.

Liquidity ratios: see Solvency ratios.

Market index: see Market proxy.

Market portfolio: a huge portfolio containing a common fraction of the total market value of each risky security in the market. All risky securities are included in the market portfolio (for example, shares, pensions, art objects, insurance claims and so on).

Market price of the firm's ordinary shares: equal to the present value of the future dividends to the firm's ordinary shareholders and the present value of the market price of the ordinary shares at the period sold.

Market proxy; a portfolio used to represent the whole market of risky securities.

Market-related risk: see Undiversifiable risk.

Market value of a security: the price that can be obtained for the sale of the security.

Market value of a share: the price that can be obtained for the sale of the share.

Market value weights: based on the use of market values, they are calculated by dividing the market value of each long-term capital source by the sum of the market values of all the long-term capital sources of the firm.

Maturity: the length of time before the firm has to redeem its debentures.

Maximum offer price: equivalent to the present value of the expected cash flows (after tax) of the acquired firm (including the initial market value) plus the present value of the incremental cash flows attributable to the merger.

Merger: the combination of two or more firms.

Merger premium: the price paid for a merger above that of its minimum offer price.

Minimum offer price: equivalent to current market value of the acquired firm in the merger.

Minimum variance portfolio: a portfolio which has the lowest variance for a given level of expected return.

Minimum variance portfolio set: the locus of minimum variance portfolios.

Money market: financial markets for the trading of short-term debt instruments (for example, government securities).

Net investment: the initial cash outlay required for the acquisition of an investment project.

Net present value: the sum of all the net cash flows (after tax in present value terms).

Net working capital: the difference between the firm's current assets and its associated current liabilities.

Nominal rate: an interest rate expressed in money terms.

Non-market-related risk: see Diversifiable risk.

Operating break-even analysis: an examination of the relationship between sales, costs and profits before interest and tax; it also determines the number of units sold and their respective selling price which results from a zero profit before interest and tax.

Operating gearing: the utilization of fixed operating costs (for example, depreciation, indirect labour cost, and so on) to magnify the profit before interest and tax by changes that occur in sales.

Operating lease: a short-term lease that can be cancelled by the lessee on short notice.

Option: an option is a contract entitling the holder to buy (or sell) a fixed number of shares at a specified price within a specified period of time.

Option premium: the price paid by the option buyer to the writer.

Ordinary annuity: an annuity in which the payment or receipts occur at the end of each period.

Ordinary dividends: the payments recommended by the board of directors to be distributed to the ordinary shareholders.

Out the money option: a call option whose exercise price is above the current market price of the underlying security.

Payback period: the length of time required by a project to recover its initial cash outlay.

Per cent-of-sales method: projects the sales of the firm, estimates the future expenses, assets and liabilities of the firm as a percentage of the projected sales and uses these percentages to construct the firm's future financial statements.

Perpetuity: an annuity that continues forever.

Portfolio: a collection of two or more securities.

Portfolio analysis: computation of the portfolio efficient portfolio set.

Portfolio expected return: the expected return (or mean) of a portfolio is the average reward that would most likely be gained from investing in the portfolio over a period of time.

Portfolio selection: selection of an efficient portfolio that maximizes the investor's expected utility.

Portfolio standard deviation: the square root of portfolio variance.

Portfolio variance: the variance of a portfolio's return is the average variability of the possible returns around its expected return.

Preference shares: a class of shares that usually pays a fixed dividend which is paid out before ordinary shareholders receive their dividends. Also the preference shareholders are usually entitled to priority over ordinary shareholders on the company's assets in the event of liquidation.

Present value: the value today of a future payment or a series of payments.

Present value of ordinary shareholders' wealth: equal to the number of the firm's ordinary shares times the current market price per ordinary share.

Principal: the initial sum of money borrowed or invested.

Profitability index: is the summation of the yearly cash flows (after tax) in present value terms divided by the initial cash outlay (note that the summation does not include the initial outlay).

Profitability ratios: indicators of the firm's ability to generate profits.

Put option: an option that gives its owner the right to sell a fixed number of shares at a specified price within a specified period of time.

Random walk hypothesis: suggests that security (for example, share) returns (or successive price changes) from one period to the next are independently and identically distributed.

Real rate: a rate adjusted for expected inflation

Required rate of return: the minimum rate of return investors will accept for the use of their funds. The term is another name for the cost of capital and discount rate.

Residual dividend policy: a policy that only pays dividends after all the firm's investment projects have been financed.

Risk-adjusted discount rate: a method of incorporating risk by adjusting the discount rate. It is equal to the risk-free rate plus a risk premium.

Risk averse: investors are generally risk averse if they dislike risk and like larger expected returns, that is, for any level of expected return they prefer the lowest level of risk, and for any level of risk they prefer the highest level of expected return.

Risk-free rate: the rate of return earned by investing in a riskless security (for example, Treasury bills).

Risk premium: the rate of return required in excess to the risk-free rate for additional risk in the investment. The security market line's risk premium is due to the level of systematic risk (as measured by beta).

Risk–return trade-off: a positive relationship between risk and return on investment.

Scrip dividend: a dividend in the form of new ordinary shares rather than cash.

Security: a general name for anything which has a monetary value (for example, shares, debentures, art objects, and so on).

Security analysis: formation of the risk/return characteristics of a specified number of individual securities.

Security expected return: the expected return (or mean) of a security is the average reward that would most likely be gained from investing in the security over a period of time.

Security market line: see Capital asset pricing model.

Security rate of return: the rate of a return of a security is the rate earned by the security over a period of time. The security's rate of return for a period (for example, a year) can be calculated by adding the security's capital gain/loss rate of return for the period to the security's dividend yield for the period.

Security risk: assuming that the probability distribution of security rates of return is normal, the risk of a security in isolation can be measured by the variance (or standard deviation) of the distribution. The variance of a security's rate of return distribution is the average variability of the possible returns around its expected return on the portfolio.

Security risk in a portfolio: the contribution of a security's risk to the risk of a portfolio. The security risk in a portfolio is measured by the covariance between the rate of return on the security and the rate of return on the portfolio.

Semi-strong form of EMH: the capital market is said to be efficient in the semi-strong form if public available information (for example, historical share prices, stock splits, dividends announcements, etc.) cannot be used consistently to earn abnormal profits.

Sensitivity analysis: shows how one variable changes in response to other variables.

Short-selling: occurs when an investor sells shares that he or she does not own, anticipating that the price is going to rise in the near future, at which time he or she buys back at a lower price and returns them to the lender.

Simulation: a risk analysis method that involves utilizing the computer to determine the distribution of an investment project's net present value (or internal rate of return).

Single index model: describes the (linear) relationship between the rates of return on individual securities (or portfolios) and the rates of return on a market index.

Sinking fund: an amount of money that must be deposited every year in order to accumulate a certain lump sum in the future.

Solvency ratios: Indicate the ability of the firm to meet its short-term obligations with cash flows generated from its current assets.

Specific cost of capital: a cost of a component (for example, ordinary shares, preference shares, and so on) in the firm's capital structure.

Specific cost of capital's weight: the proportion of a source of long-term capital in the firm's capital structure.

Standard deviation (of probable cash flows): the square root of variance.

Stream of cash flows: it is a series of payments or receipts.

Striking price: see Exercise price in options.

Strong-form of EMH: the capital market is said to be efficient in the strong form if all information (that is, public or private) cannot be used consistently to earn abnormal profits.

Super-growth payment: a high dividend payment ratio at which surplus earnings per share will be paid out as dividends.

Systematic risk: see Undiversifiable risk.

Theoretical value: the gain of the warrant (that is, the difference between the market value of the ordinary shares and the exercise price of the warrant). It can be found by multiplying the exercise ratio of a warrant by the difference between the ordinary share price and the warrant's exercise price.

Time period: the number of periods during which interest is earned or paid.

Time value in options: the difference between the option premium and the intrinsic price.

Total risk: the total risk of a security (or portfolio) is divided into undiversifiable (or systematic) and diversifiable (or unsystematic) risk.

Total risk of the firm: the sum of the operating and financial risk.

Traded option: see Option.

Traded option contract: shows the minimum number of shares of the underlying security that can be bought or sold.

Trend line: a line that best fits the overall data.

Underlying security: the security in respect of which an option contract has been bought or sold.

Undiversifiable risk: the part of the total security (or portfolio) risk that cannot be eliminated through diversification.

Unincorporated business organizations: business organizations that do not have a separate legal entity from their owners.

Unlimited company: a company that possesses unlimited liability (that is, creditors can claim business and personal assets in settlement of the firm's debts).

Unsystematic risk: see Diversifiable risk.

Valuation model for securities: a model that attempts to identify the factors that influence the value of a security.

Valuation of securities: the process of measuring the value of a security.

Variance (of probable cash flows): the weighted average of the squared deviation of cash flows from the expected cash flow.

Vertical merger: a merger between a firm with one of its suppliers or one of its customers.

Weak form of EMH: the capital market is said to be efficient in the weak form if prices cannot be used consistently to earn abnormal profits.

Weighted average cost of capital: a method calculating the cost of capital by multiplying each specific cost of capital (for example, cost of ordinary shares, preference shares, and so on) by the proportion of that source of long-term capital in the firm's capital structure and adding all the resulting products.

Weighted marginal cost of capital: the cost of using an additional £1 of funds from all the long-term financing sources when many varying cost structures exist.

Weighted marginal cost of capital schedule: a graph illustrating the relationship between the firm's weighted average cost of capital and the level of total new financing.

Working capital: a firm's investment in current assets (for example, stocks, debtors, cash, and so on).

Writer: a person who sells options.

Appendix D Tables

Time value tables

Table D.1 Future value for £1 compounded at r per cent for N periods.
Table D.2 Future value for a £1 annuity compounded at r per cent for N periods.
Table D.3 Present value for £1 discounted at r per cent for N periods.
Table D.4 Present value for a £1 annuity discounted at r per cent for N periods.
Table D.5 Areas under the standardized normal distribution.

Time value tables

	Future value	Present value
	Table D.1	Table D.3
Lump sum	$FV_N = PV(1+r)^N$ where PV = lump sum r = annual compound interest rate N = number of periods	$PV = FV_N/(1+r)^N$ where FV_N = future sum of money r = annual discount interest rate N = number of periods
	Table D.2	Table D.4
Annuity	$FV = CA[(1+r)^N - 1]/r$ where CA = annuity amount r = annual compound interest rate N = number of periods	$PV = CA[1 - (1+r)^{-N}]/r$ where CA = annuity amount r = annual discount interest rate N = number of periods

Table D.1. Future value for £1 compounded at r per cent for N periods: $FV = (1 + r)^N$

Period (N)	Interest rate (r)											
	1%	2%	3%	4%	5%	6%	7%	8%	9%	10%	11%	12%
1	1.010	1.020	1.030	1.040	1.050	1.060	1.070	1.080	1.090	1.100	1.110	1.120
2	1.020	1.040	1.061	1.082	1.103	1.124	1.145	1.166	1.188	1.210	1.232	1.254
3	1.030	1.061	1.093	1.125	1.158	1.191	1.225	1.260	1.295	1.331	1.368	1.405
4	1.041	1.082	1.126	1.170	1.216	1.262	1.311	1.360	1.412	1.464	1.518	1.574
5	1.051	1.104	1.159	1.217	1.276	1.338	1.403	1.469	1.539	1.611	1.685	1.762
6	1.062	1.126	1.194	1.265	1.340	1.419	1.501	1.587	1.677	1.772	1.870	1.974
7	1.072	1.149	1.230	1.316	1.407	1.504	1.606	1.714	1.828	1.949	2.076	2.211
8	1.083	1.172	1.267	1.369	1.477	1.594	1.718	1.851	1.993	2.144	2.305	2.476
9	1.094	1.195	1.305	1.423	1.551	1.689	1.838	1.999	2.172	2.358	2.558	2.773
10	1.105	1.219	1.344	1.480	1.629	1.791	1.967	2.159	2.367	2.594	2.839	3.106
11	1.116	1.243	1.384	1.539	1.710	1.898	2.105	2.332	2.580	2.853	3.152	3.479
12	1.127	1.268	1.426	1.601	1.796	2.012	2.252	2.518	2.813	3.138	3.498	3.896
13	1.138	1.294	1.469	1.665	1.886	2.133	2.410	2.720	3.066	3.452	3.883	4.363
14	1.149	1.319	1.513	1.732	1.980	2.261	2.579	2.937	3.342	3.797	4.310	4.887
15	1.161	1.346	1.558	1.801	2.079	2.397	2.759	3.172	3.642	4.177	4.785	5.474
16	1.173	1.373	1.605	1.873	2.183	2.540	2.952	3.426	3.970	4.595	5.311	6.130
17	1.184	1.400	1.653	1.948	2.292	2.693	3.159	3.700	4.328	5.054	5.895	6.866
18	1.196	1.428	1.702	2.026	2.407	2.854	3.380	3.996	4.717	5.560	6.544	7.690
19	1.208	1.457	1.754	2.107	2.527	3.026	3.617	4.316	5.142	6.116	7.263	8.613
20	1.220	1.486	1.806	2.191	2.653	3.207	3.870	4.661	5.604	6.727	8.062	9.646
21	1.232	1.516	1.860	2.279	2.786	3.400	4.141	5.034	6.109	7.400	8.949	10.804
22	1.245	1.546	1.916	2.370	2.925	3.604	4.430	5.437	6.659	8.140	9.934	12.100
23	1.257	1.577	1.974	2.465	3.072	3.820	4.741	5.871	7.258	8.954	11.026	13.552
24	1.270	1.608	2.033	2.563	3.225	4.049	5.072	6.341	7.911	9.850	12.239	15.179
25	1.282	1.641	2.094	2.666	3.386	4.292	5.427	6.848	8.623	10.835	13.585	17.000
26	1.295	1.673	2.157	2.772	3.556	4.549	5.807	7.396	9.399	11.918	15.080	19.040
27	1.308	1.707	2.221	2.883	3.733	4.822	6.214	7.988	10.245	13.110	16.739	21.325
28	1.321	1.741	2.288	2.999	3.920	5.112	6.649	8.627	11.167	14.421	18.580	23.884
29	1.335	1.776	2.357	3.119	4.116	5.418	7.114	9.317	12.172	15.863	20.624	26.750
30	1.348	1.811	2.427	3.243	4.322	5.743	7.612	10.063	13.268	17.449	22.892	29.960
31	1.361	1.848	2.500	3.373	4.538	6.088	8.145	10.868	14.462	19.194	25.410	33.555
32	1.375	1.885	2.575	3.508	4.765	6.453	8.715	11.737	15.763	21.114	28.206	37.582
33	1.389	1.922	2.652	3.648	5.003	6.841	9.325	12.676	17.182	23.225	31.308	42.092
34	1.403	1.961	2.732	3.794	5.253	7.251	9.978	13.690	18.728	25.548	34.752	47.143
35	1.417	2.000	2.814	3.946	5.516	7.686	10.677	14.785	20.414	28.102	38.575	52.800
36	1.431	2.040	2.898	4.104	5.792	8.147	11.424	15.968	22.251	30.913	42.818	59.136
37	1.445	2.081	2.985	4.268	6.081	8.636	12.224	17.246	24.254	34.004	47.528	66.232
38	1.460	2.122	3.075	4.439	6.385	9.154	13.079	18.625	26.437	37.404	52.756	74.180
39	1.474	2.165	3.167	4.616	6.705	9.704	13.995	20.115	28.816	41.145	58.559	83.081
40	1.489	2.208	3.262	4.801	7.040	10.286	14.974	21.725	31.409	45.259	65.001	93.051
41	1.504	2.252	3.360	4.993	7.392	10.903	16.023	23.462	34.236	49.785	72.151	104.217
42	1.519	2.297	3.461	5.193	7.762	11.557	17.144	25.339	37.318	54.764	80.088	116.723
43	1.534	2.343	3.565	5.400	8.150	12.250	18.344	27.367	40.676	60.240	88.897	130.730
44	1.549	2.390	3.671	5.617	8.557	12.985	19.628	29.556	44.337	66.264	98.676	146.418
45	1.565	2.438	3.782	5.841	8.985	13.765	21.002	31.920	48.327	72.890	109.530	163.988
46	1.580	2.487	3.895	6.075	9.434	14.590	22.473	34.474	52.677	80.180	121.579	183.666
47	1.596	2.536	4.012	6.318	9.906	15.466	24.046	37.232	57.418	88.197	134.952	205.706
48	1.612	2.587	4.132	6.571	10.401	16.394	25.729	40.211	62.585	97.017	149.797	230.391

Table D.1. (cont.)

Period (N)	Interest rate (r) 1%	2%	3%	4%	5%	6%	7%	8%	9%	10%	11%	12%
49	1.628	2.639	4.256	6.833	10.921	17.378	27.530	43.427	68.218	106.719	166.275	258.038
50	1.645	2.692	4.384	7.107	11.467	18.420	29.457	46.902	74.358	117.391	184.565	289.002

Period (N)	Interest rate (r) 13%	14%	15%	16%	17%	18%	19%	20%	21%	22%	23%	24%
1	1.130	1.140	1.150	1.160	1.170	1.180	1.190	1.200	1.210	1.220	1.230	1.240
2	1.277	1.300	1.323	1.346	1.369	1.392	1.416	1.440	1.464	1.488	1.513	1.538
3	1.443	1.482	1.521	1.561	1.602	1.643	1.685	1.728	1.772	1.816	1.861	1.907
4	1.630	1.689	1.749	1.811	1.874	1.939	2.005	2.074	2.144	2.215	2.289	2.364
5	1.842	1.925	2.011	2.100	2.192	2.288	2.386	2.488	2.594	2.703	2.815	2.932
6	2.082	2.195	2.313	2.436	2.565	2.700	2.840	2.986	3.138	3.297	3.463	3.635
7	2.353	2.502	2.660	2.826	3.001	3.185	3.379	3.583	3.797	4.023	4.259	4.508
8	2.658	2.853	3.059	3.278	3.511	3.759	4.021	4.300	4.595	4.908	5.239	5.590
9	3.004	3.252	3.518	3.803	4.108	4.435	4.785	5.160	5.560	5.987	6.444	6.931
10	3.395	3.707	4.046	4.411	4.807	5.234	5.695	6.192	6.727	7.305	7.926	8.594
11	3.836	4.226	4.652	5.117	5.624	6.176	6.777	7.430	8.140	8.912	9.749	10.657
12	4.335	4.818	5.350	5.936	6.580	7.288	8.064	8.916	9.850	10.872	11.991	13.215
13	4.898	5.492	6.153	6.886	7.699	8.599	9.596	10.699	11.918	13.264	14.749	16.386
14	5.535	6.261	7.076	7.988	9.007	10.147	11.420	12.839	14.421	16.182	18.141	20.319
15	6.254	7.138	8.137	9.266	10.539	11.974	13.590	15.407	17.449	19.742	22.314	25.196
16	7.067	8.137	9.358	10.748	12.330	14.129	16.172	18.488	21.114	24.086	27.446	31.243
17	7.986	9.276	10.761	12.468	14.426	16.672	19.244	22.186	25.548	29.384	33.759	38.741
18	9.024	10.575	12.375	14.463	16.879	19.673	22.901	26.623	30.913	35.849	41.523	48.039
19	10.197	12.056	14.232	16.777	19.748	23.214	27.252	31.948	37.404	43.736	51.074	59.568
20	11.523	13.743	16.367	19.461	23.106	27.393	32.429	38.338	45.259	53.358	62.821	73.864
21	13.021	15.668	18.822	22.574	27.034	32.324	38.591	46.005	54.764	65.096	77.269	91.592
22	14.714	17.861	21.645	26.186	31.629	38.142	45.923	55.206	66.264	79.418	95.041	113.574
23	16.627	20.362	24.891	30.376	37.006	45.008	54.649	66.247	80.180	96.889	116.901	140.831
24	18.788	23.212	28.625	35.236	43.297	53.109	65.032	79.497	97.017	118.205	143.788	174.631
25	21.231	26.462	32.919	40.874	50.658	62.669	77.388	95.396	117.391	144.210	176.859	216.542
26	23.991	30.167	37.857	47.414	59.270	73.949	92.092	114.475	142.043	175.936	217.537	268.512
27	27.109	34.390	43.535	55.000	69.345	87.260	109.589	137.371	171.872	214.642	267.570	332.955
28	30.633	39.204	50.066	63.800	81.134	102.967	130.411	164.845	207.965	261.864	329.112	412.864
29	34.616	44.693	57.575	74.009	94.927	121.501	155.189	197.814	251.638	319.474	404.807	511.952
30	39.116	50.950	66.212	85.850	111.065	143.371	184.675	237.376	304.482	389.758	497.913	634.820
31	44.201	58.083	76.144	99.586	129.946	169.177	219.764	284.852	368.423	475.505	612.433	787.177
32	49.947	66.215	87.565	115.520	152.036	199.629	261.519	341.822	445.792	580.116	753.292	976.099
33	56.440	75.485	100.700	134.003	177.883	235.563	311.207	410.186	539.408	707.741	926.550	1210.363
34	63.777	86.053	115.805	155.443	208.123	277.964	370.337	492.224	652.683	863.444	1139.656	1500.850
35	72.069	98.100	133.176	180.314	243.503	327.997	440.701	590.668	789.747	1053.402	1401.777	1861.054
36	81.437	111.834	153.152	209.164	284.899	387.037	524.434	708.802	955.594	1285.150	1724.186	2307.707
37	92.024	127.491	176.125	242.631	333.332	456.703	624.076	850.562	1156.269	1567.883	2120.748	2861.557
38	103.987	145.340	202.543	281.452	389.998	538.910	742.651	1020.675	1399.085	1912.818	2608.520	3548.330
39	117.506	165.687	232.925	326.484	456.298	635.914	883.754	1224.810	1692.893	2333.638	3208.480	4399.930
40	132.782	188.884	267.864	378.721	533.869	750.378	1061.668	1469.772	2048.400	2847.038	3946.430	5455.913
41	150.043	215.327	308.043	439.317	624.626	885.446	1251.484	1763.726	2478.564	3473.386	4854.110	6765.332
42	169.549	245.473	354.250	509.607	730.813	1044.827	1489.266	2116.471	2999.063	4237.531	5970.555	8389.011

Table D.1. (cont.)

Period (*N*)	Interest rate (*r*)											
	13%	14%	15%	16%	17%	18%	19%	20%	21%	22%	23%	24%
43	191.590	279.839	407.387	591.144	855.051	1232.896	1772.227	2539.765	3628.866	5169.788	7343.782	10402.374
44	216.497	319.017	468.495	685.727	1000.410	1454.817	2108.950	3047.718	4390.928	6307.141	9032.852	12898.944
45	244.641	363.679	538.769	795.444	1170.479	1716.684	2509.651	3657.262	5313.023	7694.712	11110.408	15994.690
46	276.445	414.594	619.585	922.715	1369.461	2025.687	2986.484	4388.714	6428.757	9387.549	13665.802	19833.416
47	312.383	472.637	712.522	1070.349	1602.269	2390.311	3553.916	5266.457	7778.796	11452.810	16808.937	24593.436
48	353.992	538.807	819.401	1241.605	1874.655	2820.567	4229.160	6319.749	9412.344	13972.428	20674.992	30495.860
49	398.881	614.239	942.311	1440.262	2193.346	3328.269	5032.701	7583.698	11388.936	17046.362	25430.240	37814.867
50	450.736	700.233	1083.657	1670.704	2566.215	3927.357	5988.914	9100.438	13780.612	20796.561	31279.195	45890.435

Period (*N*)	Interest rate (*r*)											
	25%	26%	27%	28%	29%	30%	31%	32%	33%	34%	35%	36%
1	1.250	1.260	1.270	1.280	1.290	1.300	1.310	1.320	1.330	1.340	1.350	1.360
2	1.563	1.588	1.613	1.638	1.664	1.690	1.716	1.742	1.769	1.796	1.823	1.850
3	1.953	2.000	2.048	2.097	2.147	2.197	2.248	2.300	2.353	2.406	2.460	2.515
4	2.441	2.520	2.601	2.684	2.769	2.856	2.945	3.036	3.129	3.224	3.322	3.421
5	3.052	3.176	3.304	3.436	3.572	3.713	3.858	4.007	4.162	4.320	4.484	4.653
6	3.815	4.002	4.196	4.398	4.608	4.827	5.054	5.290	5.535	5.789	6.053	6.328
7	4.768	5.042	5.329	5.629	5.945	6.275	6.621	6.983	7.361	7.758	8.172	8.605
8	5.960	6.353	6.768	7.206	7.669	8.157	8.673	9.217	9.791	10.395	11.032	11.703
9	7.451	8.005	8.595	9.223	9.893	10.604	11.362	12.166	13.022	13.930	14.894	15.917
10	9.313	10.086	10.915	11.806	12.761	13.786	14.884	16.060	17.319	18.666	20.107	21.647
11	11.642	12.708	13.862	15.112	16.462	17.922	19.498	21.199	23.034	25.012	27.144	29.439
12	14.552	16.012	17.605	19.343	21.236	23.298	25.542	27.983	30.635	33.516	36.644	40.037
13	18.190	20.175	22.359	24.759	27.395	30.288	33.460	36.937	40.745	44.912	49.470	54.451
14	22.737	25.421	28.396	31.691	35.339	39.374	43.833	48.757	54.190	60.182	66.784	74.053
15	28.422	32.030	36.062	40.565	45.587	51.186	57.421	64.359	72.073	80.644	90.158	100.713
16	35.527	40.358	45.799	51.923	58.808	66.542	75.221	84.954	95.858	108.063	121.714	136.969
17	44.409	50.851	58.165	66.461	75.862	86.504	98.540	112.139	127.491	144.804	164.314	186.278
18	55.511	64.072	73.870	85.071	97.862	112.455	129.087	148.024	169.562	194.038	221.824	253.338
19	69.389	80.731	93.815	108.890	126.242	146.192	169.104	195.391	225.518	260.011	299.462	344.540
20	86.736	101.721	119.145	139.380	162.852	190.050	221.527	257.916	299.939	348.414	404.274	468.574
21	108.420	128.169	151.314	178.406	210.080	247.065	290.200	340.449	398.919	466.875	545.769	637.261
22	135.525	161.492	192.168	228.360	271.003	321.184	380.162	449.393	530.562	625.613	736.789	866.674
23	169.407	203.480	244.054	292.300	349.593	417.539	498.012	593.199	705.647	838.321	994.665	1178.677
24	211.758	256.385	309.948	374.144	450.976	542.801	652.396	783.023	938.511	1123.350	1342.797	1603.001
25	264.698	323.045	393.634	478.905	581.759	705.641	854.638	1033.590	1248.220	1505.289	1812.776	2180.081
26	330.872	407.037	499.916	612.998	750.468	917.333	1119.576	1364.339	1660.132	2017.088	2447.248	2964.911
27	413.590	512.867	634.893	784.638	968.104	1192.533	1466.645	1800.927	2207.976	2702.897	3303.785	4032.279
28	516.988	646.212	806.314	1004.336	1248.855	1550.293	1921.305	2377.224	2936.608	3621.882	4460.109	5483.899
29	646.235	814.228	1024.019	1285.550	1611.022	2015.381	2516.909	3137.935	3905.688	4853.323	6021.148	7458.102
30	807.794	1025.927	1300.504	1645.505	2078.219	2619.996	3297.151	4142.075	5194.566	6503.452	8128.550	10143.019
31	1009.742	1292.668	1651.640	2106.246	2680.902	3405.994	4319.268	5467.539	6908.772	8714.626	10973.542	13794.506
32	1262.177	1628.761	2097.583	2695.995	3458.364	4427.793	5658.241	7217.151	9188.667	11677.599	14814.281	18760.528
33	1577.722	2052.239	2663.930	3450.873	4461.290	5756.130	7412.296	9526.639	12220.927	15647.982	19999.280	25514.319
34	1972.152	2585.821	3383.191	4417.118	5755.064	7482.970	9710.108	12575.164	16253.833	20968.296	26999.028	34699.473
35	2465.190	3258.135	4296.653	5653.911	7424.032	9727.860	12720.241	16599.217	21617.598	28097.517	36448.688	47191.284

Table D.1. (cont.)

Period (*N*)	Interest rate (*r*)											
	25%	26%	27%	28%	29%	30%	31%	32%	33%	34%	35%	36%
36	3081.488	4105.250	5456.749	7237.006	9577.002	12646.219	16663.516	21910.966	28751.405	37650.673	49205.728	64180.146
37	3851.860	5172.615	6930.071	9263.367	12354.332	16440.084	21829.206	28922.475	38239.369	50451.902	66427.733	87284.999
38	4814.825	6517.495	8801.190	11857.110	15937.089	21372.109	28596.260	38177.667	50858.361	67605.548	89677.440	118707.6
39	6018.531	8212.044	1[illegible]177.511	15177.101	20558.844	27783.742	37461.100	50394.520	67641.620	90591.434	121064.5	161442.3
40	7523.164	10347.175	14195.439	19426.689	26520.909	36118.865	49074.042	66520.767	89963.354	121392.5	163437.1	219561.6
41	9403.955	13037.441	18028.208	24866.162	34211.973	46954.524	64286.994	87807.412	119651.3	162666.0	220640.1	298603.7
42	11754.944	16427.175	2[illegible]895.824	31828.687	44133.445	61040.882	84215.963	115905.8	159136.2	217972.4	297864.2	406101.1
43	14693.679	20698.241	2[illegible]077.697	40740.720	56932.144	79353.146	110322.9	152995.6	211651.1	292083.0	402116.6	552297.5
44	18367.099	26079.784	3[illegible]928.675	52148.121	73442.466	103159.1	144523.0	201954.2	281496.0	391391.3	542857.5	751124.6
45	22958.874	32860.527	4[illegible]899.417	66749.595	94740.782	134106.8	189325.1	266579.6	374389.7	524464.3	732857.6	1021529.4
46	28698.593	41404.265	5[illegible]562.259	85439.481	122215.6	174338.9	248015.9	351885.1	497938.2	702782.2	989357.7	1389280.0
47	35873.241	52169.373	7[illegible]644.069	109362.5	157658.1	226640.5	324900.9	464488.3	662257.9	941728.1	1335632.9	1889420.8
48	44841.551	65733.410	9[illegible]067.968	139984.0	203379.0	294632.7	425620.2	613124.5	880803.0	1261915.6	1803104.5	2569612.3
49	56051.939	82824.097	12[illegible]006.3	179179.6	262358.9	383022.5	557562.4	809324.4	1171467.9	1690967.0	2434191.0	3494672.7
50	70064.923	104358.4	15[illegible]948.0	229349.9	338443.0	497929.2	730406.8	1068308.2	1558052.4	2265895.7	3286157.9	4752754.9

Table D.2. Future value for a £1 annuity compounded at r per cent for N periods: $FV = [(1 + r)^N - 1]/r$

Period (N)	Interest rate (r) 1%	2%	3%	4%	5%	6%	7%	8%	9%	10%	11%	12%
1	1.000	1.000	1.000	1.000	1.000	1.000	1.000	1.000	1.000	1.000	1.000	1.000
2	2.010	2.020	2.030	2.040	2.050	2.060	2.070	2.080	2.090	2.100	2.110	2.120
3	3.030	3.060	3.091	3.122	3.153	3.184	3.215	3.246	3.278	3.310	3.342	3.374
4	4.060	4.122	4.184	4.246	4.310	4.375	4.440	4.506	4.573	4.641	4.710	4.779
5	5.101	5.204	5.309	5.416	5.526	5.637	5.751	5.867	5.985	6.105	6.228	6.353
6	6.152	6.308	6.468	6.633	6.802	6.975	7.153	7.336	7.523	7.716	7.913	8.115
7	7.214	7.434	7.662	7.898	8.142	8.394	8.654	8.923	9.200	9.487	9.783	10.089
8	8.286	8.583	8.892	9.214	9.549	9.897	10.260	10.637	11.028	11.436	11.859	12.300
9	9.369	9.755	10.159	10.583	11.027	11.491	11.978	12.488	13.021	13.579	14.164	14.776
10	10.462	10.950	11.464	12.006	12.578	13.181	13.816	14.487	15.193	15.937	16.722	17.549
11	11.567	12.169	12.808	13.486	14.207	14.972	15.784	16.645	17.560	18.531	19.561	20.655
12	12.683	13.412	14.192	15.026	15.917	16.870	17.888	18.977	20.141	21.384	22.713	24.133
13	13.809	14.680	15.618	16.627	17.713	18.882	20.141	21.495	22.953	24.523	26.212	28.029
14	14.947	15.974	17.086	18.292	19.599	21.015	22.550	24.215	26.019	27.975	30.095	32.393
15	16.097	17.293	18.599	20.024	21.579	23.276	25.129	27.152	29.361	31.772	34.405	37.280
16	17.258	18.639	20.157	21.825	23.657	25.673	27.888	30.324	33.003	35.950	39.190	42.753
17	18.430	20.012	21.762	23.698	25.840	28.213	30.840	33.750	36.974	40.545	44.501	48.884
18	19.615	21.412	23.414	25.645	28.132	30.906	33.999	37.450	41.301	45.599	50.396	55.750
19	20.811	22.841	25.117	27.671	30.539	33.760	37.379	41.446	46.018	51.159	56.939	63.440
20	22.019	24.297	26.870	29.778	33.066	36.786	40.995	45.762	51.160	57.275	64.203	72.052
21	23.239	25.783	28.676	31.969	35.719	39.993	44.865	50.423	56.765	64.002	72.265	81.699
22	24.472	27.299	30.537	34.248	38.505	43.392	49.006	55.457	62.873	71.403	81.214	92.503
23	25.716	28.845	32.453	36.618	41.430	46.996	53.436	60.893	69.532	79.543	91.148	104.603
24	26.973	30.422	34.426	39.083	44.502	50.816	58.177	66.765	76.790	88.497	102.174	118.155
25	28.243	32.030	36.459	41.646	47.727	54.865	63.249	73.106	84.701	98.347	114.413	133.334
26	29.526	33.671	38.553	44.312	51.113	59.156	68.676	79.954	93.324	109.182	127.999	150.334
27	30.821	35.344	40.710	47.084	54.669	63.706	74.484	87.351	102.723	121.100	143.079	169.374
28	32.129	37.051	42.931	49.968	58.403	68.528	80.698	95.339	112.968	134.210	159.817	190.699
29	33.450	38.792	45.219	52.966	62.323	73.640	87.347	103.966	124.135	148.631	178.397	214.583
30	34.785	40.568	47.575	56.085	66.439	79.058	94.461	113.283	136.308	164.494	199.021	241.333
31	36.133	42.379	50.003	59.328	70.761	84.802	102.073	123.346	149.575	181.943	221.913	271.293
32	37.494	44.227	52.503	62.701	75.299	90.890	110.218	134.214	164.037	201.138	247.324	304.848
33	38.869	46.112	55.078	66.210	80.064	97.343	118.933	145.951	179.800	222.252	275.529	342.429
34	40.258	48.034	57.730	69.858	85.067	104.184	128.259	158.627	196.982	245.477	306.837	384.521
35	41.660	49.994	60.462	73.652	90.320	111.435	138.237	172.317	215.711	271.024	341.590	431.663
36	43.077	51.994	63.276	77.598	95.836	119.121	148.913	187.102	236.125	299.127	380.164	484.463
37	44.508	54.034	66.174	81.702	101.628	127.268	160.337	203.070	258.376	330.039	422.982	543.599
38	45.953	56.115	69.159	85.970	107.710	135.904	172.561	220.316	282.630	364.043	470.511	609.831
39	47.412	58.237	72.234	90.409	114.095	145.058	185.640	238.941	309.066	401.448	523.267	684.010
40	48.886	60.402	75.401	95.026	120.800	154.762	199.635	259.057	337.882	442.593	581.826	767.091
41	50.375	62.610	78.663	99.827	127.840	165.048	214.610	280.781	369.292	487.852	646.827	860.142
42	51.879	64.862	82.023	104.820	135.232	175.951	230.632	304.244	403.528	537.637	718.978	964.359
43	53.398	67.159	85.484	110.012	142.993	187.508	247.776	329.583	440.846	592.401	799.065	1081.083
44	54.932	69.503	89.048	115.413	151.143	199.758	266.121	356.950	481.522	652.641	887.963	1211.813
45	56.481	71.893	92.720	121.029	159.700	212.744	285.749	386.506	525.859	718.905	986.639	1358.230
46	58.046	74.331	96.501	126.871	168.685	226.508	306.752	418.426	574.186	791.795	1096.169	1522.218
47	59.626	76.817	100.397	132.945	178.119	241.099	329.224	452.900	626.863	871.975	1217.747	1705.884
48	61.223	79.354	104.408	139.263	188.025	256.565	353.270	490.132	684.280	960.172	1352.700	1911.590

Table D.2. (Cont.)

Period (*N*)	Interest rate (*r*) 1%	2%	3%	4%	5%	6%	7%	8%	9%	10%	11%	12%
49	62.835	81.941	108.541	145.834	198.427	272.958	378.999	530.343	746.866	1057.190	1502.497	2141.981
50	64.463	84.579	112.797	152.667	209.348	290.336	406.529	573.770	815.084	1163.909	1668.771	2400.018

Period (*N*)	Interest rate (*r*) 13%	14%	15%	16%	17%	18%	19%	20%	21%	22%	23%	24%
1	1.000	1.000	1.000	1.000	1.000	1.000	1.000	1.000	1.000	1.000	1.000	1.000
2	2.130	2.140	2.150	2.160	2.170	2.180	2.190	2.200	2.210	2.220	2.230	2.240
3	3.407	3.440	3.473	3.506	3.539	3.572	3.606	3.640	3.674	3.708	3.743	3.778
4	4.850	4.921	4.993	5.066	5.141	5.215	5.291	5.368	5.446	5.524	5.604	5.684
5	6.480	6.610	6.742	6.877	7.014	7.154	7.297	7.442	7.589	7.740	7.893	8.048
6	8.323	8.536	8.754	8.977	9.207	9.442	9.683	9.930	10.183	10.442	10.708	10.980
7	10.405	10.730	11.067	11.414	11.772	12.142	12.523	12.916	13.321	13.740	14.171	14.615
8	12.757	13.233	13.727	14.240	14.773	15.327	15.902	16.499	17.119	17.762	18.430	19.123
9	15.416	16.085	16.786	17.519	18.285	19.086	19.923	20.799	21.714	22.670	23.669	24.712
10	18.420	19.337	20.304	21.321	22.393	23.521	24.709	25.959	27.274	28.657	30.113	31.643
11	21.814	23.045	24.349	25.733	27.200	28.755	30.404	32.150	34.001	35.962	38.039	40.238
12	25.650	27.271	29.002	30.850	32.824	34.931	37.180	39.581	42.142	44.874	47.788	50.895
13	29.985	32.089	34.352	36.786	39.404	42.219	45.244	48.497	51.991	55.746	59.779	64.110
14	34.883	37.581	40.505	43.672	47.103	50.818	54.841	59.196	63.909	69.010	74.528	80.496
15	40.417	43.842	47.580	51.660	56.110	60.965	66.261	72.035	78.330	85.192	92.669	100.815
16	46.672	50.980	55.717	60.925	66.649	72.939	79.850	87.442	95.780	104.935	114.983	126.011
17	53.739	59.118	65.075	71.673	78.979	87.068	96.022	105.931	116.894	129.020	142.430	157.253
18	61.725	68.394	75.836	84.141	93.406	103.740	115.266	128.117	142.441	158.405	176.188	195.994
19	70.749	78.969	88.212	98.603	110.285	123.414	138.166	154.740	173.354	194.254	217.712	244.033
20	80.947	91.025	102.444	115.380	130.033	146.628	165.418	186.688	210.758	237.989	268.785	303.601
21	92.470	104.768	118.810	134.841	153.139	174.021	197.847	225.026	256.018	291.347	331.606	377.465
22	105.491	120.436	137.632	157.415	180.172	206.345	236.438	271.031	310.781	356.443	408.875	469.056
23	120.205	138.297	159.276	183.601	211.801	244.487	282.362	326.237	377.045	435.861	503.917	582.630
24	136.831	158.659	184.168	213.978	248.808	289.494	337.010	392.484	457.225	532.750	620.817	723.461
25	155.620	181.871	212.793	249.214	292.105	342.603	402.042	471.981	554.242	650.955	764.605	898.092
26	176.850	208.333	245.712	290.088	342.763	405.272	479.431	567.377	671.633	795.165	941.465	1114.634
27	200.841	238.499	283.569	337.502	402.032	479.221	571.522	681.853	813.676	971.102	1159.002	1383.146
28	227.950	272.889	327.104	392.503	471.378	566.481	681.112	819.223	985.548	1185.744	1426.572	1716.101
29	258.583	312.094	377.170	456.303	552.512	669.447	811.523	984.068	1193.513	1447.608	1755.683	2128.965
30	293.199	356.787	434.745	530.312	647.439	790.948	966.712	1181.882	1445.151	1767.081	2160.491	2640.916
31	332.315	407.737	500.957	616.162	758.504	934.319	1151.387	1419.258	1749.632	2156.839	2658.404	3275.736
32	376.516	465.820	577.100	715.747	888.449	1103.496	1371.151	1704.109	2118.055	2632.344	3270.836	4062.913
33	426.463	532.035	664.666	831.267	1040.486	1303.125	1632.670	2045.931	2563.847	3212.460	4024.129	5039.012
34	482.903	607.520	765.365	965.270	1218.368	1538.688	1943.877	2456.118	3103.254	3920.201	4950.678	6249.375
35	546.681	693.573	881.170	1120.713	1426.491	1816.652	2314.214	2948.341	3755.938	4783.645	6090.334	7750.225
36	618.749	791.673	1014.346	1301.027	1669.994	2144.649	2754.914	3539.009	4545.685	5837.047	7492.111	9611.279
37	700.187	903.507	1167.498	1510.191	1954.894	2531.686	3279.348	4247.811	5501.279	7122.197	9216.297	11918.986
38	792.211	1030.998	1343.622	1752.822	2288.225	2988.389	3903.424	5098.373	6657.547	8690.080	11337.045	14780.543
39	896.198	1176.338	1546.165	2034.273	2678.224	3527.299	4646.075	6119.048	8056.632	10602.898	13945.566	18328.873
40	1013.704	1342.025	1779.090	2360.757	3134.522	4163.213	5529.829	7343.858	9749.525	12936.535	17154.046	22728.803
41	1146.486	1530.909	2046.954	2739.478	3668.391	4913.591	6581.496	8813.629	11797.925	15783.573	21100.476	28184.715
42	1296.529	1746.236	2354.997	3178.795	4293.017	5799.038	7832.981	10577.355	14276.489	19256.959	25954.586	34950.047

Table D.2. (Cont.)

Period (*N*)	Interest rate (*r*) 13%	14%	15%	16%	17%	18%	19%	20%	21%	22%	23%	24%
43	1466.078	1991.709	2709.246	3688.402	5023.830	6843.865	9322.247	12693.826	17275.552	23494.490	31925.140	43339.058
44	1657.668	2271.548	3116.633	4279.546	5878.881	8076.760	11094.474	15233.592	20904.418	28664.278	39268.923	53741.432
45	1874.165	2590.565	3585.128	4965.274	6879.291	9531.577	13203.424	18281.310	25295.346	34971.419	48301.775	66640.376
46	2118.807	2954.244	4123.898	5760.718	8049.770	11248.261	15713.075	21938.572	30608.368	42666.131	59412.183	82635.066
47	2395.251	3368.838	4743.482	6683.433	9419.231	13273.948	18699.559	26327.286	37037.126	52053.680	73077.985	102468.482
48	2707.633	3841.475	5456.005	7753.782	11021.500	15664.259	22253.475	31593.744	44815.922	63506.490	89886.922	127061.917
49	3060.626	4380.282	6275.405	8995.387	12896.155	18484.825	26482.636	37913.492	54228.266	77478.917	110561.913	157557.778
50	3459.507	4994.521	7217.716	10435.649	15089.502	21813.094	31515.336	45497.191	65617.202	94525.279	135992.154	195372.644

Period (*N*)	Interest rate (*r*) 25%	26%	27%	28%	29%	30%	31%	32%	33%	34%	35%	36%
1	1.000	1.000	1.000	1.000	1.000	1.000	1.000	1.000	1.000	1.000	1.000	1.000
2	2.250	2.260	2.270	2.280	2.290	2.300	2.310	2.320	2.330	2.340	2.350	2.360
3	3.813	3.848	3.883	3.918	3.954	3.990	4.026	4.062	4.099	4.136	4.173	4.210
4	5.766	5.848	5.931	6.016	6.101	6.187	6.274	6.362	6.452	6.542	6.633	6.725
5	8.207	8.368	8.533	8.700	8.870	9.043	9.219	9.398	9.581	9.766	9.954	10.146
6	11.259	11.544	11.837	12.136	12.442	12.756	13.077	13.406	13.742	14.086	14.438	14.799
7	15.073	15.546	16.032	16.534	17.051	17.583	18.131	18.696	19.277	19.876	20.492	21.126
8	19.842	20.588	21.361	22.163	22.995	23.858	24.752	25.678	26.638	27.633	28.664	29.732
9	25.802	26.940	28.129	29.369	30.664	32.015	33.425	34.895	36.429	38.029	39.696	41.435
10	33.253	34.945	36.723	38.593	40.556	42.619	44.786	47.062	49.451	51.958	54.590	57.352
11	42.566	45.031	47.639	50.398	53.318	56.405	59.670	63.122	66.769	70.624	74.697	78.998
12	54.208	57.739	61.501	65.510	69.780	74.327	79.168	84.320	89.803	95.637	101.841	108.437
13	68.760	73.751	79.107	84.853	91.016	97.625	104.710	112.303	120.439	129.153	138.485	148.475
14	86.949	93.926	101.465	109.612	118.411	127.913	138.170	149.240	161.183	174.065	187.954	202.926
15	109.687	119.347	129.861	141.303	153.750	167.286	182.003	197.997	215.374	234.247	254.738	276.979
16	138.109	151.377	165.924	181.868	199.337	218.472	239.423	262.356	287.447	314.891	344.897	377.692
17	173.636	191.735	211.723	233.791	258.145	285.014	314.645	347.309	383.305	422.954	466.611	514.661
18	218.045	242.585	269.888	300.252	334.007	371.518	413.185	459.449	510.795	567.758	630.925	700.939
19	273.556	306.658	343.758	385.323	431.870	483.973	542.272	607.472	680.358	761.796	852.748	954.277
20	342.945	387.389	437.573	494.213	558.112	630.165	711.376	802.863	905.876	1021.807	1152.210	1298.817
21	429.681	489.110	556.717	633.593	720.964	820.215	932.903	1060.779	1205.814	1370.221	1556.484	1767.391
22	538.101	617.278	708.031	811.999	931.044	1067.280	1223.103	1401.229	1604.733	1837.096	2102.253	2404.651
23	673.626	778.771	900.199	1040.358	1202.047	1388.464	1603.264	1850.622	2135.295	2462.709	2839.042	3271.326
24	843.033	982.251	1144.253	1332.659	1551.640	1806.003	2101.276	2443.821	2840.943	3301.030	3833.706	4450.003
25	1054.791	1238.636	1454.201	1706.803	2002.616	2348.803	2753.672	3226.844	3779.454	4424.380	5176.504	6053.004
26	1319.489	1561.682	1847.836	2185.708	2584.374	3054.444	3608.311	4260.434	5027.673	5929.669	6989.280	8233.085
27	1650.361	1968.719	2347.751	2798.706	3334.843	3971.778	4727.887	5624.772	6687.805	7946.757	9436.528	11197.996
28	2063.952	2481.586	2982.644	3583.344	4302.947	5164.311	6194.532	7425.699	8895.781	10649.654	12740.313	15230.275
29	2580.939	3127.798	3788.958	4587.680	5551.802	6714.604	8115.837	9802.923	11832.389	14271.537	17200.422	20714.173
30	3227.174	3942.026	4812.977	5873.231	7162.824	8729.985	10632.746	12940.859	15738.077	19124.859	23221.570	28172.276
31	4034.968	4967.953	6113.481	7518.735	9241.043	11349.981	13929.897	17082.934	20932.643	25628.312	31350.120	38315.295
32	5044.710	6260.620	7765.121	9624.981	11921.946	14755.975	18249.165	22550.472	27841.415	34342.937	42323.661	52109.801
33	6306.887	7889.382	9862.703	12320.976	15380.310	19183.768	23907.407	29767.623	37030.082	46020.536	57137.943	70870.330
34	7884.609	9941.621	12526.633	15771.849	19841.600	24939.899	31319.703	39294.263	49251.009	61668.518	77137.223	96384.648
35	9856.761	12527.442	15909.824	20188.966	25596.664	32422.868	41029.810	51869.427	65504.842	82636.815	104136.3	131084.1

Table D.2. (Cont.)

Period (*N*)	Interest rate (*r*) 25%	26%	27%	28%	29%	30%	31%	32%	33%	34%	35%	36%
36	12321.952	15785.577	2[illegible]206.477	25842.877	33020.696	42150.729	53750.052	68468.644	87122.440	110734.3	140584.9	178275.4
37	15403.440	19890.828	2[illegible]663.225	33079.883	42597.698	54796.947	70413.568	90379.609	115873.8	148385.0	189790.7	242455.6
38	19255.299	25063.443	3[illegible]593.296	42343.250	54952.030	71237.031	92242.774	119302.1	154113.2	198836.9	256218.4	329740.6
39	24070.124	31580.938	4[illegible]394.486	54200.360	70889.119	92609.141	120839.0	157479.8	204971.6	266422.5	345895.8	448448.1
40	30088.655	39792.982	5[illegible]571.998	69377.460	91447.963	120392.9	158300.1	207874.3	272613.2	357033.9	466960.4	609890.5
41	37611.819	50140.157	6[illegible]767.437	88804.149	117968.9	156511.7	207374.2	274395.0	362576.5	478426.4	630397.5	829452.1
42	47015.774	63177.598	8[illegible]795.645	113670.3	152180.8	203466.3	271661.2	362202.5	482227.8	641092.4	851037.7	1128055.8
43	58770.718	79604.773	1[illegible]691.5	145499.0	196314.3	264507.2	355877.1	478108.2	641364.0	859064.8	1148901.8	1534156.9
44	73464.397	100303.0	1[illegible]769.2	186239.7	253246.4	343860.3	466200.0	631103.9	853015.1	1151147.8	1551018.5	2086454.4
45	91831.496	126382.8	1[illegible]697.8	238387.8	326688.9	447019.4	610723.1	833058.1	1134511.1	1542539.1	2093875.9	2837578.9
46	114790.4	159243.3	2[illegible]597.3	305137.4	421429.7	581126.2	800048.2	1099637.7	1508900.7	2067003.4	2826733.5	3859108.3
47	143489.0	200647.6	2[illegible]159.5	390576.9	543645.3	755465.1	1048064.1	1451522.8	2006839.0	2769785.5	3816091.2	5248388.3
48	179362.2	252817.0	3[illegible]803.6	499939.5	701303.4	982105.6	1372965.0	1916011.1	2669096.9	3711513.6	5151724.2	7137809.2
49	224203.8	318550.4	4[illegible]871.6	639923.5	904682.4	1276738.3	1798585.2	2529135.6	3549899.8	4973429.3	6954828.6	9707421.5
50	280255.7	401374.5	5[illegible]3877.9	819103.1	1167041.3	1659760.7	2356147.6	3338460.0	4721367.8	6664396.2	9389019.7	13202094.2

Table D.3. Present value for £1 discounted at r per cent for N periods: $PV = 1/(1+r)^N$

Period (N)	Interest rate (r)											
	1%	2%	3%	4%	5%	6%	7%	8%	9%	10%	11%	12%
1	0.990	0.980	0.971	0.962	0.952	0.943	0.935	0.926	0.917	0.909	0.901	0.893
2	0.980	0.961	0.943	0.925	0.907	0.890	0.873	0.857	0.842	0.826	0.812	0.797
3	0.971	0.942	0.915	0.889	0.864	0.840	0.816	0.794	0.772	0.751	0.731	0.712
4	0.961	0.924	0.888	0.855	0.823	0.792	0.763	0.735	0.708	0.683	0.659	0.636
5	0.951	0.906	0.863	0.822	0.784	0.747	0.713	0.681	0.650	0.621	0.593	0.567
6	0.942	0.888	0.837	0.790	0.746	0.705	0.666	0.630	0.596	0.564	0.535	0.507
7	0.933	0.871	0.813	0.760	0.711	0.665	0.623	0.583	0.547	0.513	0.482	0.452
8	0.923	0.853	0.789	0.731	0.677	0.627	0.582	0.540	0.502	0.467	0.434	0.404
9	0.914	0.837	0.766	0.703	0.645	0.592	0.544	0.500	0.460	0.424	0.391	0.361
10	0.905	0.820	0.744	0.676	0.614	0.558	0.508	0.463	0.422	0.386	0.352	0.322
11	0.896	0.804	0.722	0.650	0.585	0.527	0.475	0.429	0.388	0.350	0.317	0.287
12	0.887	0.788	0.701	0.625	0.557	0.497	0.444	0.397	0.356	0.319	0.286	0.257
13	0.879	0.773	0.681	0.601	0.530	0.469	0.415	0.368	0.326	0.290	0.258	0.229
14	0.870	0.758	0.661	0.577	0.505	0.442	0.388	0.340	0.299	0.263	0.232	0.205
15	0.861	0.743	0.642	0.555	0.481	0.417	0.362	0.315	0.275	0.239	0.209	0.183
16	0.853	0.728	0.623	0.534	0.458	0.394	0.339	0.292	0.252	0.218	0.188	0.163
17	0.844	0.714	0.605	0.513	0.436	0.371	0.317	0.270	0.231	0.198	0.170	0.146
18	0.836	0.700	0.587	0.494	0.416	0.350	0.296	0.250	0.212	0.180	0.153	0.130
19	0.828	0.686	0.570	0.475	0.396	0.331	0.277	0.232	0.194	0.164	0.138	0.116
20	0.820	0.673	0.554	0.456	0.377	0.312	0.258	0.215	0.178	0.149	0.124	0.104
21	0.811	0.660	0.538	0.439	0.359	0.294	0.242	0.199	0.164	0.135	0.112	0.093
22	0.803	0.647	0.522	0.422	0.342	0.278	0.226	0.184	0.150	0.123	0.101	0.083
23	0.795	0.634	0.507	0.406	0.326	0.262	0.211	0.170	0.138	0.112	0.091	0.074
24	0.788	0.622	0.492	0.390	0.310	0.247	0.197	0.158	0.126	0.102	0.082	0.066
25	0.780	0.610	0.478	0.375	0.295	0.233	0.184	0.146	0.116	0.092	0.074	0.059
26	0.772	0.598	0.464	0.361	0.281	0.220	0.172	0.135	0.106	0.084	0.066	0.053
27	0.764	0.586	0.450	0.347	0.268	0.207	0.161	0.125	0.098	0.076	0.060	0.047
28	0.757	0.574	0.437	0.333	0.255	0.196	0.150	0.116	0.090	0.069	0.054	0.042
29	0.749	0.563	0.424	0.321	0.243	0.185	0.141	0.107	0.082	0.063	0.048	0.037
30	0.742	0.552	0.412	0.308	0.231	0.174	0.131	0.099	0.075	0.057	0.044	0.033
31	0.735	0.541	0.400	0.296	0.220	0.164	0.123	0.092	0.069	0.052	0.039	0.030
32	0.727	0.531	0.388	0.285	0.210	0.155	0.115	0.085	0.063	0.047	0.035	0.027
33	0.720	0.520	0.377	0.274	0.200	0.146	0.107	0.079	0.058	0.043	0.032	0.024
34	0.713	0.510	0.366	0.264	0.190	0.138	0.100	0.073	0.053	0.039	0.029	0.021
35	0.706	0.500	0.355	0.253	0.181	0.130	0.094	0.068	0.049	0.036	0.026	0.019
36	0.699	0.490	0.345	0.244	0.173	0.123	0.088	0.063	0.045	0.032	0.023	0.017
37	0.692	0.481	0.335	0.234	0.164	0.116	0.082	0.058	0.041	0.029	0.021	0.015
38	0.685	0.471	0.325	0.225	0.157	0.109	0.076	0.054	0.038	0.027	0.019	0.013
39	0.678	0.462	0.316	0.217	0.149	0.103	0.071	0.050	0.035	0.024	0.017	0.012
40	0.672	0.453	0.307	0.208	0.142	0.097	0.067	0.046	0.032	0.022	0.015	0.011
41	0.665	0.444	0.298	0.200	0.135	0.092	0.062	0.043	0.029	0.020	0.014	0.010
42	0.658	0.435	0.289	0.193	0.129	0.087	0.058	0.039	0.027	0.018	0.012	0.009
43	0.652	0.427	0.281	0.185	0.123	0.082	0.055	0.037	0.025	0.017	0.011	0.008
44	0.645	0.418	0.272	0.178	0.117	0.077	0.051	0.034	0.023	0.015	0.010	0.007
45	0.639	0.410	0.264	0.171	0.111	0.073	0.048	0.031	0.021	0.014	0.009	0.006
46	0.633	0.402	0.257	0.165	0.106	0.069	0.044	0.029	0.019	0.012	0.008	0.005
47	0.626	0.394	0.249	0.158	0.101	0.065	0.042	0.027	0.017	0.011	0.007	0.005
48	0.620	0.387	0.242	0.152	0.096	0.061	0.039	0.025	0.016	0.010	0.007	0.004

Table D.3. (Cont.)

Period (N)	Interest rate (r)											
	1%	2%	3%	4%	5%	6%	7%	8%	9%	10%	11%	12%
49	0.614	0.379	0.235	0.146	0.092	0.058	0.036	0.023	0.015	0.009	0.006	0.004
50	0.608	0.372	0.228	0.141	0.087	0.054	0.034	0.021	0.013	0.009	0.005	0.003

Period (N)	Interest rate (r)											
	13%	14%	15%	16%	17%	18%	19%	20%	21%	22%	23%	24%
1	0.8850	0.8772	0.8696	0.8621	0.8547	0.8475	0.8403	0.8333	0.8264	0.8197	0.8130	0.8065
2	0.7831	0.7695	0.7561	0.7432	0.7305	0.7182	0.7062	0.6944	0.6830	0.6719	0.6610	0.6504
3	0.6931	0.6750	0.6575	0.6407	0.6244	0.6086	0.5934	0.5787	0.5645	0.5507	0.5374	0.5245
4	0.6133	0.5921	0.5718	0.5523	0.5337	0.5158	0.4987	0.4823	0.4665	0.4514	0.4369	0.4230
5	0.5428	0.5194	0.4972	0.4761	0.4561	0.4371	0.4190	0.4019	0.3855	0.3700	0.3552	0.3411
6	0.4803	0.4556	0.4323	0.4104	0.3898	0.3704	0.3521	0.3349	0.3186	0.3033	0.2888	0.2751
7	0.4251	0.3996	0.3759	0.3538	0.3332	0.3139	0.2959	0.2791	0.2633	0.2486	0.2348	0.2218
8	0.3762	0.3506	0.3269	0.3050	0.2848	0.2660	0.2487	0.2326	0.2176	0.2038	0.1909	0.1789
9	0.3329	0.3075	0.2843	0.2630	0.2434	0.2255	0.2090	0.1938	0.1799	0.1670	0.1552	0.1443
10	0.2946	0.2697	0.2472	0.2267	0.2080	0.1911	0.1756	0.1615	0.1486	0.1369	0.1262	0.1164
11	0.2607	0.2366	0.2149	0.1954	0.1778	0.1619	0.1476	0.1346	0.1228	0.1122	0.1026	0.0938
12	0.2307	0.2076	0.1869	0.1685	0.1520	0.1372	0.1240	0.1122	0.1015	0.0920	0.0834	0.0757
13	0.2042	0.1821	0.1625	0.1452	0.1299	0.1163	0.1042	0.0935	0.0839	0.0754	0.0678	0.0610
14	0.1807	0.1597	0.1413	0.1252	0.1110	0.0985	0.0876	0.0779	0.0693	0.0618	0.0551	0.0492
15	0.1599	0.1401	0.1229	0.1079	0.0949	0.0835	0.0736	0.0649	0.0573	0.0507	0.0448	0.0397
16	0.1415	0.1229	0.1069	0.0930	0.0811	0.0708	0.0618	0.0541	0.0474	0.0415	0.0364	0.0320
17	0.1252	0.1078	0.0929	0.0802	0.0693	0.0600	0.0520	0.0451	0.0391	0.0340	0.0296	0.0258
18	0.1108	0.0946	0.0808	0.0691	0.0592	0.0508	0.0437	0.0376	0.0323	0.0279	0.0241	0.0208
19	0.0981	0.0829	0.0703	0.0596	0.0506	0.0431	0.0367	0.0313	0.0267	0.0229	0.0196	0.0168
20	0.0868	0.0728	0.0611	0.0514	0.0433	0.0365	0.0308	0.0261	0.0221	0.0187	0.0159	0.0135
21	0.0768	0.0638	0.0531	0.0443	0.0370	0.0309	0.0259	0.0217	0.0183	0.0154	0.0129	0.0109
22	0.0680	0.0560	0.0462	0.0382	0.0316	0.0262	0.0218	0.0181	0.0151	0.0126	0.0105	0.0088
23	0.0601	0.0491	0.0402	0.0329	0.0270	0.0222	0.0183	0.0151	0.0125	0.0103	0.0086	0.0071
24	0.0532	0.0431	0.0349	0.0284	0.0231	0.0188	0.0154	0.0126	0.0103	0.0085	0.0070	0.0057
25	0.0471	0.0378	0.0304	0.0245	0.0197	0.0160	0.0129	0.0105	0.0085	0.0069	0.0057	0.0046
26	0.0417	0.0331	0.0264	0.0211	0.0169	0.0135	0.0109	0.0087	0.0070	0.0057	0.0046	0.0037
27	0.0369	0.0291	0.0230	0.0182	0.0144	0.0115	0.0091	0.0073	0.0058	0.0047	0.0037	0.0030
28	0.0326	0.0255	0.0200	0.0157	0.0123	0.0097	0.0077	0.0061	0.0048	0.0038	0.0030	0.0024
29	0.0289	0.0224	0.0174	0.0135	0.0105	0.0082	0.0064	0.0051	0.0040	0.0031	0.0025	0.0020
30	0.0256	0.0196	0.0151	0.0116	0.0090	0.0070	0.0054	0.0042	0.0033	0.0026	0.0020	0.0016
31	0.0226	0.0172	0.0131	0.0100	0.0077	0.0059	0.0046	0.0035	0.0027	0.0021	0.0016	0.0013
32	0.0200	0.0151	0.0114	0.0087	0.0066	0.0050	0.0038	0.0029	0.0022	0.0017	0.0013	0.0010
33	0.0177	0.0132	0.0099	0.0075	0.0056	0.0042	0.0032	0.0024	0.0019	0.0014	0.0011	0.0008
34	0.0157	0.0116	0.0086	0.0064	0.0048	0.0036	0.0027	0.0020	0.0015	0.0012	0.0009	0.0007
35	0.0139	0.0102	0.0075	0.0055	0.0041	0.0030	0.0023	0.0017	0.0013	0.0009	0.0007	0.0005
36	0.0123	0.0089	0.0065	0.0048	0.0035	0.0026	0.0019	0.0014	0.0010	0.0008	0.0006	0.0004
37	0.0109	0.0078	0.0057	0.0041	0.0030	0.0022	0.0016	0.0012	0.0009	0.0006	0.0005	0.00035
38	0.0096	0.0069	0.0049	0.0036	0.0026	0.0019	0.0013	0.0010	0.0007	0.0005	0.0004	0.00028
39	0.0085	0.0060	0.0043	0.0031	0.0022	0.0016	0.0011	0.0008	0.0006	0.0004	0.00031	0.00023
40	0.0075	0.0053	0.0037	0.0026	0.0019	0.0013	0.0010	0.0007	0.0005	0.0004	0.00025	0.00018
41	0.0067	0.0046	0.0032	0.0023	0.0016	0.0011	0.0008	0.0006	0.0004	0.0003	0.00021	0.00015
42	0.0059	0.0041	0.0028	0.0020	0.0014	0.0010	0.0007	0.0005	0.00033	0.00024	0.00017	0.00012

Table D.3. (Cont.)

Period (N)	Interest rate (r)											
	13%	14%	15%	16%	17%	18%	19%	20%	21%	22%	23%	24%
43	0.0052	0.0036	0.0025	0.0017	0.0012	0.0008	0.0006	0.0004	0.00028	0.00019	0.00014	0.00010
44	0.0046	0.0031	0.0021	0.0015	0.0010	0.0007	0.0005	0.00033	0.00023	0.00016	0.00011	0.00008
45	0.0041	0.0027	0.0019	0.0013	0.0009	0.0006	0.0004	0.00027	0.00019	0.00013	0.00009	0.00006
46	0.0036	0.0024	0.0016	0.0011	0.0007	0.0005	0.00033	0.00023	0.00016	0.00011	0.00007	0.00005
47	0.0032	0.0021	0.0014	0.0009	0.0006	0.00042	0.00028	0.00019	0.00013	0.00009	0.00006	0.00004
48	0.0028	0.0019	0.0012	0.0008	0.00053	0.00035	0.00024	0.00016	0.00011	0.00007	0.00005	0.00003
49	0.0025	0.0016	0.0011	0.0007	0.00046	0.00030	0.00020	0.00013	0.00009	0.00006	0.00004	0.00003
50	0.0022	0.0014	0.0009	0.0006	0.00039	0.00025	0.00017	0.00011	0.00007	0.00005	0.00003	0.00002

Period (N)	Interest value (r)											
	25%	26%	27%	28%	29%	30%	31%	32%	33%	34%	35%	36%
1	0.8000	0.7937	0.7874	0.7813	0.7752	0.7692	0.7634	0.7576	0.7519	0.7463	0.7407	0.7353
2	0.6400	0.6299	0.6200	0.6104	0.6009	0.5917	0.5827	0.5739	0.5653	0.5569	0.5487	0.5407
3	0.5120	0.4999	0.4882	0.4768	0.4658	0.4552	0.4448	0.4348	0.4251	0.4156	0.4064	0.3975
4	0.4096	0.3968	0.3844	0.3725	0.3611	0.3501	0.3396	0.3294	0.3196	0.3102	0.3011	0.2923
5	0.3277	0.3149	0.3027	0.2910	0.2799	0.2693	0.2592	0.2495	0.2403	0.2315	0.2230	0.2149
6	0.2621	0.2499	0.2383	0.2274	0.2170	0.2072	0.1979	0.1890	0.1807	0.1727	0.1652	0.1580
7	0.2097	0.1983	0.1877	0.1776	0.1682	0.1594	0.1510	0.1432	0.1358	0.1289	0.1224	0.1162
8	0.1678	0.1574	0.1478	0.1388	0.1304	0.1226	0.1153	0.1085	0.1021	0.0962	0.0906	0.0854
9	0.1342	0.1249	0.1164	0.1084	0.1011	0.0943	0.0880	0.0822	0.0768	0.0718	0.0671	0.0628
10	0.1074	0.0992	0.0916	0.0847	0.0784	0.0725	0.0672	0.0623	0.0577	0.0536	0.0497	0.0462
11	0.0859	0.0787	0.0721	0.0662	0.0607	0.0558	0.0513	0.0472	0.0434	0.0400	0.0368	0.0340
12	0.0687	0.0625	0.0568	0.0517	0.0471	0.0429	0.0392	0.0357	0.0326	0.0298	0.0273	0.0250
13	0.0550	0.0496	0.0447	0.0404	0.0365	0.0330	0.0299	0.0271	0.0245	0.0223	0.0202	0.0184
14	0.0440	0.0393	0.0352	0.0316	0.0283	0.0254	0.0228	0.0205	0.0185	0.0166	0.0150	0.0135
15	0.0352	0.0312	0.0277	0.0247	0.0219	0.0195	0.0174	0.0155	0.0139	0.0124	0.0111	0.0099
16	0.0281	0.0248	0.0218	0.0193	0.0170	0.0150	0.0133	0.0118	0.0104	0.0093	0.0082	0.0073
17	0.0225	0.0197	0.0172	0.0150	0.0132	0.0116	0.0101	0.0089	0.0078	0.0069	0.0061	0.0054
18	0.0180	0.0156	0.0135	0.0118	0.0102	0.0089	0.0077	0.0068	0.0059	0.0052	0.0045	0.0039
19	0.0144	0.0124	0.0107	0.0092	0.0079	0.0068	0.0059	0.0051	0.0044	0.0038	0.0033	0.0029
20	0.0115	0.0098	0.0084	0.0072	0.0061	0.0053	0.0045	0.0039	0.0033	0.0029	0.0025	0.0021
21	0.0092	0.0078	0.0066	0.0056	0.0048	0.0040	0.0034	0.0029	0.0025	0.0021	0.0018	0.0016
22	0.0074	0.0062	0.0052	0.0044	0.0037	0.0031	0.0026	0.0022	0.0019	0.0016	0.0014	0.0012
23	0.0059	0.0049	0.0041	0.0034	0.0029	0.0024	0.0020	0.0017	0.0014	0.0012	0.0010	0.0008
24	0.0047	0.0039	0.0032	0.0027	0.0022	0.0018	0.0015	0.0013	0.0011	0.0009	0.0007	0.0006
25	0.0038	0.0031	0.0025	0.0021	0.0017	0.0014	0.0012	0.0010	0.0008	0.0007	0.0006	0.0005
26	0.0030	0.0025	0.0020	0.0016	0.0013	0.0011	0.0009	0.0007	0.0006	0.0005	0.0004	0.0003
27	0.0024	0.0019	0.0016	0.0013	0.0010	0.0008	0.0007	0.0006	0.0005	0.0004	0.0003	0.000248
28	0.0019	0.0015	0.0012	0.0010	0.0008	0.0006	0.0005	0.0004	0.000341	0.0003	0.000224	0.000182
29	0.0015	0.0012	0.0010	0.0008	0.0006	0.0005	0.0004	0.0003	0.000256	0.000206	0.000166	0.000134
30	0.0012	0.0010	0.0008	0.0006	0.0005	0.0004	0.0003	0.000241	0.000193	0.000154	0.000123	0.000099
31	0.0010	0.0008	0.0006	0.0005	0.0004	0.0003	0.000232	0.000183	0.000145	0.000115	0.000091	0.000072
32	0.0008	0.0006	0.0005	0.0004	0.0003	0.000226	0.000177	0.000139	0.000109	0.000086	0.000068	0.000053
33	0.0006	0.0005	0.0004	0.0003	0.000224	0.000174	0.000135	0.000105	0.000082	0.000064	0.000050	0.000039
34	0.0005	0.0004	0.0003	0.000226	0.000174	0.000134	0.000103	0.000080	0.000062	0.000048	0.000037	0.000029
35	0.0004	0.0003	0.0002	0.000177	0.0001	0.000103	0.000079	0.000060	0.000046	0.000036	0.000027	0.000021

Table D.3. (Cont.)

Period (*N*)	Interest value (*r*)											
	25%	26%	27%	28%	29%	30%	31%	32%	33%	34%	35%	36%
36	0.000325	0.000244	0.000183	0.000138	0.000104	0.000079	0.000060	0.000046	0.000035	0.000027	0.000020	0.000016
37	0.000260	0.000193	0.000144	0.000108	0.000081	0.000061	0.000046	0.000035	0.000026	0.000020	0.000015	0.000011
38	0.000208	0.000153	0.000114	0.000084	0.000063	0.000047	0.000035	0.000026	0.000020	0.000015	0.000011	0.000008
39	0.000166	0.000122	0.000089	0.000066	0.000049	0.000036	0.000027	0.000020	0.000015	0.000011	0.000008	0.000006
40	0.000133	0.000097	0.000070	0.000051	0.000038	0.000028	0.000020	0.000015	0.000011	0.000008	0.000006	0.000005
41	0.000106	0.000077	0.000055	0.000040	0.000029	0.000021	0.000016	0.000011	0.000008	0.000006	0.000005	0.000003
42	0.000085	0.000061	0.000044	0.000031	0.000023	0.000016	0.000012	0.000009	0.000006	0.000005	0.000003	0.0000025
43	0.000068	0.000048	0.000034	0.000025	0.000018	0.000013	0.000009	0.000007	0.000005	0.0000034	0.0000025	0.0000018
44	0.000054	0.000038	0.000027	0.000019	0.000014	0.000010	0.000007	0.000005	0.000004	0.0000026	0.0000018	0.0000013
45	0.000044	0.000030	0.000021	0.000015	0.000011	0.000007	0.000005	0.000004	0.000003	0.0000019	0.0000014	0.0000010
46	0.000034	0.000024	0.000017	0.000012	0.000008	0.000006	0.000004	0.000003	0.0000020	0.0000014	0.0000010	0.0000007
47	0.000028	0.000019	0.000013	0.000009	0.000006	0.000004	0.000003	0.0000022	0.0000015	0.0000011	0.0000007	0.0000005
48	0.000022	0.000015	0.000010	0.000007	0.000005	0.0000034	0.0000023	0.0000016	0.0000011	0.0000008	0.0000006	0.0000004
49	0.000018	0.000012	0.000008	0.000006	0.000004	0.0000026	0.0000018	0.0000012	0.0000009	0.0000006	0.0000004	0.0000003
50	0.000014	0.000010	0.000006	0.000004	0.000003	0.0000020	0.0000014	0.0000009	0.0000006	0.0000004	0.0000003	0.0000002

Table D.4. Present value for a £1 annuity discounted at r per cent for N periods: $PV = [1 - (1 + r)^{-N}]/r$

Period (N)	Interest rate (r)											
	1%	2%	3%	4%	5%	6%	7%	8%	9%	10%	11%	12%
1	0.990	0.980	0.971	0.962	0.952	0.943	0.935	0.926	0.917	0.909	0.901	0.893
2	1.970	1.942	1.913	1.886	1.859	1.833	1.808	1.783	1.759	1.736	1.713	1.690
3	2.941	2.884	2.829	2.775	2.723	2.673	2.624	2.577	2.531	2.487	2.444	2.402
4	3.902	3.808	3.717	3.630	3.546	3.465	3.387	3.312	3.240	3.170	3.102	3.037
5	4.853	4.713	4.580	4.452	4.329	4.212	4.100	3.993	3.890	3.791	3.696	3.605
6	5.795	5.601	5.417	5.242	5.076	4.917	4.767	4.623	4.486	4.355	4.231	4.111
7	6.728	6.472	6.230	6.002	5.786	5.582	5.389	5.206	5.033	4.868	4.712	4.564
8	7.652	7.325	7.020	6.733	6.463	6.210	5.971	5.747	5.535	5.335	5.146	4.968
9	8.566	8.162	7.786	7.435	7.108	6.802	6.515	6.247	5.995	5.759	5.537	5.328
10	9.471	8.983	8.530	8.111	7.722	7.360	7.024	6.710	6.418	6.145	5.889	5.650
11	10.368	9.787	9.253	8.760	8.306	7.887	7.499	7.139	6.805	6.495	6.207	5.938
12	11.255	10.575	9.954	9.385	8.863	8.384	7.943	7.536	7.161	6.814	6.492	6.194
13	12.134	11.348	10.635	9.986	9.394	8.853	8.358	7.904	7.487	7.103	6.750	6.424
14	13.004	12.106	11.296	10.563	9.899	9.295	8.745	8.244	7.786	7.367	6.982	6.628
15	13.865	12.849	11.938	11.118	10.380	9.712	9.108	8.559	8.061	7.606	7.191	6.811
16	14.718	13.578	12.561	11.652	10.838	10.106	9.447	8.851	8.313	7.824	7.379	6.974
17	15.562	14.292	13.166	12.166	11.274	10.477	9.763	9.122	8.544	8.022	7.549	7.120
18	16.398	14.992	13.754	12.659	11.690	10.828	10.059	9.372	8.756	8.201	7.702	7.250
19	17.226	15.678	14.324	13.134	12.085	11.158	10.336	9.604	8.950	8.365	7.839	7.366
20	18.046	16.351	14.877	13.590	12.462	11.470	10.594	9.818	9.129	8.514	7.963	7.469
21	18.857	17.011	15.415	14.029	12.821	11.764	10.836	10.017	9.292	8.649	8.075	7.562
22	19.660	17.658	15.937	14.451	13.163	12.042	11.061	10.201	9.442	8.772	8.176	7.645
23	20.456	18.292	16.444	14.857	13.489	12.303	11.272	10.371	9.580	8.883	8.266	7.718
24	21.243	18.914	16.936	15.247	13.799	12.550	11.469	10.529	9.707	8.985	8.348	7.784
25	22.023	19.523	17.413	15.622	14.094	12.783	11.654	10.675	9.823	9.077	8.422	7.843
26	22.795	20.121	17.877	15.983	14.375	13.003	11.826	10.810	9.929	9.161	8.488	7.896
27	23.560	20.707	18.327	16.330	14.643	13.211	11.987	10.935	10.027	9.237	8.548	7.943
28	24.316	21.281	18.764	16.663	14.898	13.406	12.137	11.051	10.116	9.307	8.602	7.984
29	25.066	21.844	19.188	16.984	15.141	13.591	12.278	11.158	10.198	9.370	8.650	8.022
30	25.808	22.396	19.600	17.292	15.372	13.765	12.409	11.258	10.274	9.427	8.694	8.055
31	26.542	22.938	20.000	17.588	15.593	13.929	12.532	11.350	10.343	9.479	8.733	8.085
32	27.270	23.468	20.389	17.874	15.803	14.084	12.647	11.435	10.406	9.526	8.769	8.112
33	27.990	23.989	20.766	18.148	16.003	14.230	12.754	11.514	10.464	9.569	8.801	8.135
34	28.703	24.499	21.132	18.411	16.193	14.368	12.854	11.587	10.518	9.609	8.829	8.157
35	29.409	24.999	21.487	18.665	16.374	14.498	12.948	11.655	10.567	9.644	8.855	8.176
36	30.108	25.489	21.832	18.908	16.547	14.621	13.035	11.717	10.612	9.677	8.879	8.192
37	30.800	25.969	22.167	19.143	16.711	14.737	13.117	11.775	10.653	9.706	8.900	8.208
38	31.485	26.441	22.492	19.368	16.868	14.846	13.193	11.829	10.691	9.733	8.919	8.221
39	32.163	26.903	22.808	19.584	17.017	14.949	13.265	11.879	10.726	9.757	8.936	8.233
40	32.835	27.355	23.115	19.793	17.159	15.046	13.332	11.925	10.757	9.779	8.951	8.244
41	33.500	27.799	23.412	19.993	17.294	15.138	13.394	11.967	10.787	9.799	8.965	8.253
42	34.158	28.235	23.701	20.186	17.423	15.225	13.452	12.007	10.813	9.817	8.977	8.262
43	34.810	28.662	23.982	20.371	17.546	15.306	13.507	12.043	10.838	9.834	8.989	8.270
44	35.455	29.080	24.254	20.549	17.663	15.383	13.558	12.077	10.861	9.849	8.999	8.276
45	36.095	29.490	24.519	20.720	17.774	15.456	13.606	12.108	10.881	9.863	9.008	8.283
46	36.727	29.892	24.775	20.885	17.880	15.524	13.650	12.137	10.900	9.875	9.016	8.288
47	37.354	30.287	25.025	21.043	17.981	15.589	13.692	12.164	10.918	9.887	9.024	8.293
48	37.974	30.673	25.267	21.195	18.077	15.650	13.730	12.189	10.934	9.897	9.030	8.297

Table D.4. (Cont.)

Period (*N*)	Interest rate (*r*) 1%	2%	3%	4%	5%	6%	7%	8%	9%	10%	11%	12%
49	38.588	31.052	25.502	21.341	18.169	15.708	13.767	12.212	10.948	9.906	9.036	8.301
50	39.196	31.424	25.730	21.482	18.256	15.762	13.801	12.233	10.962	9.915	9.042	8.304

Period (*N*)	Interest rate (*r*) 13%	14%	15%	16%	17%	18%	19%	20%	21%	22%	23%	24%
1	0.885	0.877	0.870	0.862	0.855	0.847	0.840	0.833	0.826	0.820	0.813	0.806
2	1.668	1.647	1.626	1.605	1.585	1.566	1.547	1.528	1.509	1.492	1.474	1.457
3	2.361	2.322	2.283	2.246	2.210	2.174	2.140	2.106	2.074	2.042	2.011	1.981
4	2.974	2.914	2.855	2.798	2.743	2.690	2.639	2.589	2.540	2.494	2.448	2.404
5	3.517	3.433	3.352	3.274	3.199	3.127	3.058	2.991	2.926	2.864	2.803	2.745
6	3.998	3.889	3.784	3.685	3.589	3.498	3.410	3.326	3.245	3.167	3.092	3.020
7	4.423	4.288	4.160	4.039	3.922	3.812	3.706	3.605	3.508	3.416	3.327	3.242
8	4.799	4.639	4.487	4.344	4.207	4.078	3.954	3.837	3.726	3.619	3.518	3.421
9	5.132	4.946	4.772	4.607	4.451	4.303	4.163	4.031	3.905	3.786	3.673	3.566
10	5.426	5.216	5.019	4.833	4.659	4.494	4.339	4.192	4.054	3.923	3.799	3.682
11	5.687	5.453	5.234	5.029	4.836	4.656	4.486	4.327	4.177	4.035	3.902	3.776
12	5.918	5.660	5.421	5.197	4.988	4.793	4.611	4.439	4.278	4.127	3.985	3.851
13	6.122	5.842	5.583	5.342	5.118	4.910	4.715	4.533	4.362	4.203	4.053	3.912
14	6.302	6.002	5.724	5.468	5.229	5.008	4.802	4.611	4.432	4.265	4.108	3.962
15	6.462	6.142	5.847	5.575	5.324	5.092	4.876	4.675	4.489	4.315	4.153	4.001
16	6.604	6.265	5.954	5.668	5.405	5.162	4.938	4.730	4.536	4.357	4.189	4.033
17	6.729	6.373	6.047	5.749	5.475	5.222	4.990	4.775	4.576	5.391	4.219	4.059
18	6.840	6.467	6.128	5.818	5.534	5.273	5.033	4.812	4.608	4.419	4.243	4.080
19	6.938	6.550	6.198	5.877	5.584	5.316	5.070	4.843	4.635	4.442	4.263	4.097
20	7.025	6.623	6.259	5.929	5.628	5.353	5.101	4.870	4.657	4.460	4.279	4.110
21	7.102	6.687	6.312	5.973	5.665	5.384	5.127	4.891	4.675	4.476	4.292	4.121
22	7.170	6.743	6.359	6.011	5.696	5.410	5.149	4.909	4.690	4.488	4.302	4.130
23	7.230	6.792	6.399	6.044	5.723	5.432	5.167	4.925	4.703	4.499	4.311	4.137
24	7.283	6.835	6.434	6.073	5.746	5.451	5.182	4.937	4.713	4.507	4.318	4.143
25	7.330	6.873	6.464	6.097	5.766	5.467	5.195	4.948	4.721	4.514	4.323	4.147
26	7.372	6.906	6.491	6.118	5.783	5.480	5.206	4.956	4.728	4.520	4.328	4.151
27	7.409	6.935	6.514	6.136	5.798	5.492	5.215	4.964	4.734	4.524	4.332	4.154
28	7.441	6.961	6.534	6.152	5.810	5.502	5.223	4.970	4.739	4.528	4.335	4.157
29	7.470	6.983	6.551	6.166	5.820	5.510	5.229	4.975	4.743	4.531	4.337	4.159
30	7.496	7.003	6.566	6.177	5.829	5.517	5.235	4.979	4.746	4.534	4.339	4.160
31	7.518	7.020	6.579	6.187	5.837	5.523	5.239	4.982	4.749	4.536	4.341	4.161
32	7.538	7.035	6.591	6.196	5.844	5.528	5.243	4.985	4.751	4.538	4.342	4.162
33	7.556	7.048	6.600	6.203	5.849	5.532	5.246	4.988	4.753	4.539	4.343	4.163
34	7.572	7.060	6.609	6.210	5.854	5.536	5.249	4.990	4.755	4.540	4.344	4.164
35	7.586	7.070	6.617	6.215	5.858	5.539	5.251	4.992	4.756	4.541	4.345	4.164
36	7.598	7.079	6.623	6.220	5.862	5.541	5.253	4.993	4.757	4.542	4.345	4.165
37	7.609	7.087	6.629	6.224	5.865	5.543	5.255	4.994	4.758	4.543	4.346	4.165
38	7.618	7.094	6.634	6.228	5.867	5.545	5.256	4.995	4.759	4.543	4.346	4.165
39	7.627	7.100	6.638	6.231	5.869	5.547	5.257	4.996	4.759	4.544	4.346	4.166
40	7.634	7.105	6.642	6.233	5.871	5.548	5.258	4.997	4.760	4.544	4.347	4.166
41	7.641	7.110	6.645	6.236	5.873	5.5493	5.2590	4.9972	4.7600	4.5441	4.3469	4.1661
42	7.647	7.114	6.648	6.238	5.874	5.5502	5.2596	4.9976	4.7603	4.5444	4.3471	4.1662

Table D.4. (Cont.)

Period (*N*)	Interest rate (*r*)											
	13%	14%	15%	16%	17%	18%	19%	20%	21%	22%	23%	24%
43	7.652	7.117	6.650	6.239	5.875	5.5510	5.2602	4.9980	4.7606	4.5446	4.3472	4.1663
44	7.657	7.120	6.652	6.241	5.876	5.5517	5.2607	4.9984	4.7508	4.5447	4.3473	4.1663
45	7.661	7.123	6.654	6.242	5.877	5.5523	5.2611	4.9986	4.7610	4.5449	4.3474	4.1664
46	7.664	7.126	6.656	6.2432	5.8781	5.5528	5.2614	4.9989	4.7612	4.5450	4.3475	4.1665
47	7.668	7.128	6.657	6.2442	6.8787	5.5532	5.2617	4.9991	4.7613	4.5451	4.3476	4.1665
48	7.671	7.130	6.659	6.2450	5.8792	5.5536	5.2619	4.9992	4.7614	4.5451	4.3476	4.1665
49	7.673	7.131	6.660	6.2457	5.8797	5.5539	5.2621	4.9993	4.7615	4.5452	4.3477	4.1666
50	7.675	7.133	6.661	6.2463	5.8801	5.5541	5.2623	4.9995	4.7616	4.5452	4.3477	4.1666

Period (*N*)	Interest rate (*r*)											
	25%	26%	27%	28%	29%	30%	31%	32%	33%	34%	35%	36%
1	0.8000	0.7937	0.7874	0.7813	0.7752	0.7692	0.7634	0.7576	0.7519	0.7463	0.7407	0.7353
2	1.4400	1.4235	1.4074	1.3916	1.3761	1.3609	1.3461	1.3315	1.3172	1.3032	1.2894	1.2760
3	1.9520	1.9234	1.8956	1.8684	1.8420	1.8161	1.7909	1.7663	1.7423	1.7188	1.6959	1.6735
4	2.3616	2.3202	2.2800	2.2410	2.2031	2.1662	2.1305	2.0957	2.0618	2.0290	1.9969	1.9658
5	2.6893	2.6351	2.5827	2.5320	2.4830	2.4356	2.3897	2.3452	2.3021	2.2604	2.2200	2.1807
6	2.9514	2.8850	2.8210	2.7594	2.7000	2.6427	2.5875	2.5342	2.4828	2.4331	2.3852	2.3388
7	3.1611	3.0833	3.0087	2.9370	2.8682	2.8021	2.7386	2.6775	2.6187	2.5620	2.5075	2.4550
8	3.3289	3.2407	3.1564	3.0758	2.9986	2.9247	2.8539	2.7860	2.7208	2.6582	2.5982	2.5404
9	3.4631	3.3657	3.2728	3.1842	3.0997	3.0190	2.9419	2.8681	2.7976	2.7300	2.6653	2.6033
10	3.5705	3.4648	3.3644	3.2689	3.1781	3.0915	3.0091	2.9304	2.8553	2.7836	2.7150	2.6495
11	3.6564	3.5435	3.4365	3.3351	3.2388	3.1473	3.0604	2.9776	2.8987	2.8236	2.7519	2.6834
12	3.7251	3.6059	3.4933	3.3868	3.2859	3.1903	3.0995	3.0133	2.9314	2.8534	2.7792	2.7084
13	3.7801	3.6555	3.5381	3.4272	3.3224	3.2233	3.1294	3.0404	2.9559	2.8757	2.7994	2.7268
14	3.8241	3.6949	3.5733	3.4587	3.3507	3.2487	3.1522	3.0609	2.9744	2.8923	2.8144	2.7403
15	3.8593	3.7261	3.6010	3.4834	3.3726	3.2682	3.1696	3.0764	2.9883	2.9047	2.8255	2.7502
16	3.8874	3.7509	3.6228	3.5026	3.3896	3.2832	3.1829	3.0882	2.9987	2.9140	2.8337	2.7575
17	3.9099	3.7705	3.6400	3.5177	3.4028	3.2948	3.1931	3.0971	3.0065	2.9209	2.8398	2.7629
18	3.9279	3.7861	3.6536	3.5294	3.4130	3.3037	3.2008	3.1039	3.0124	2.9260	2.8443	2.7668
19	3.9424	3.7985	3.6642	3.5386	3.4210	3.3105	3.2067	3.1090	3.0169	2.9299	2.8476	2.7697
20	3.9539	3.8083	3.6726	3.5458	3.4271	3.3158	3.2112	3.1129	3.0202	2.9327	2.8501	2.7718
21	3.9631	3.8161	3.6792	3.5514	3.4319	3.3198	3.2147	3.1158	3.0227	2.9349	2.8519	2.7734
22	3.9705	3.8223	3.6844	3.5558	3.4356	3.3230	3.2173	3.1180	3.0246	2.9365	2.8533	2.7746
23	3.9764	3.8273	3.6885	3.5592	3.4384	3.3254	3.2193	3.1197	3.0260	2.9377	2.8543	2.7754
24	3.9811	3.8312	3.6918	3.5619	3.4406	3.3272	3.2209	3.1210	3.0271	2.9386	2.8550	2.7760
25	3.9849	3.8342	3.6943	3.5640	3.4423	3.3286	3.2220	3.1220	3.0279	2.9392	2.8556	2.7765
26	3.9879	3.8367	3.6963	3.5656	3.4437	3.3297	3.2229	3.1227	3.0825	2.9397	2.8560	2.7768
27	3.9903	3.8387	3.6979	3.5669	3.4447	3.3305	3.2236	3.1233	3.0289	2.9401	2.8563	2.7771
28	3.9923	3.8402	3.6991	3.5679	3.4455	3.3312	3.2241	3.1237	3.0293	2.9404	2.8565	2.7773
29	3.9938	3.8414	3.7001	3.5687	3.4461	3.3317	3.2245	3.1240	3.0295	2.9406	2.8567	2.7774
30	3.9950	3.8424	3.7009	3.5693	3.4466	3.3321	3.2248	3.1242	3.0297	2.9407	2.8568	2.7775
31	3.9960	3.8432	3.7015	3.5697	3.4470	3.3324	3.2251	3.1244	3.0299	2.9408	2.8569	2.7776
32	3.9968	3.8438	3.7019	3.5701	3.4473	3.3326	3.2252	3.1246	3.0300	2.9409	2.8569	2.7776
33	3.9975	3.8443	3.7023	3.5704	3.4475	3.3328	3.2254	3.1247	3.0301	2.9410	2.8570	2.7777
34	3.9980	3.8447	3.7026	3.5706	3.4477	3.3329	3.2255	3.1248	3.0301	2.9410	2.8570	2.7777
35	3.9984	3.8450	3.7028	3.5708	3.4478	3.3330	3.2256	3.1248	3.0302	2.9411	2.8571	2.7777
36	3.9987	3.8452	3.7030	3.5709	3.4479	3.3331	3.2256	3.1249	3.0302	2.9411	2.8571	2.7777

Table D.4. (Cont.)

Period (N)	Interest rate (r)											
	25%	26%	27%	28%	29%	30%	31%	32%	33%	34%	35%	36%
37	3.9990	3.8454	3.7032	3.5710	3.4480	3.3331	3.2257	3.1249	3.0302	2.9411	2.8571	2.7777
38	3.9992	3.8456	3.7033	3.5711	3.4481	3.3332	3.2257	3.1249	3.0302	2.9411	2.8571	2.7778
39	3.9993	3.8457	3.7034	3.5712	3.4481	3.3332	3.2257	3.1249	3.0303	2.9411	2.8571	2.7778
40	3.9995	3.8458	3.7034	3.5712	3.4481	3.3332	3.2257	3.1250	3.0303	2.9412	2.8571	2.7778
41	3.9996	3.8459	3.7035	3.5713	3.4482	3.3333	3.2258	3.1250	3.0303	2.9412	2.8571	2.7778
42	3.9997	3.8459	3.7035	3.5713	3.4482	3.3333	3.2258	3.1250	3.0303	2.9412	2.8571	2.7778
43	3.9997	3.8460	3.7036	3.5713	3.4482	3.3333	3.2258	3.1250	3.0303	2.9412	2.8571	2.7778
44	3.9998	3.8460	3.7036	3.5714	3.4482	3.3333	3.2258	3.1250	3.0303	2.9412	2.8571	2.7778
45	3.9998	3.8460	3.7036	3.5714	3.4482	3.3333	3.2258	3.1250	3.0303	2.9412	2.8571	2.7778
46	3.9999	3.8461	3.7036	3.5714	3.4482	3.3333	3.2258	3.1250	3.0303	2.9412	2.8571	2.7778
47	3.9999	3.8461	3.7037	3.5714	3.4483	3.3333	3.2258	3.1250	3.0303	2.9412	2.8571	2.7778
48	3.9999	3.8461	3.7037	3.5714	3.4483	3.3333	3.2258	3.1250	3.0303	2.9412	2.8571	2.7778
49	3.9999	3.8461	3.7037	3.5714	3.4483	3.3333	3.2258	3.1250	3.0303	2.9412	2.8571	2.7778
50	3.9999	3.8461	3.7037	3.5714	3.4483	3.3333	3.2258	3.1250	3.0303	2.9412	2.8571	2.7778

Table D.5. Areas under the standardized normal distribution

z	0.00	0.01	0.02	0.03	0.04	0.05	0.06	0.07	0.08	0.09
0.0	0.0000	0.0040	0.0080	0.0120	0.0160	0.0199	0.0239	0.0279	0.0319	0.0359
0.1	0.0398	0.0438	0.0478	0.0517	0.0557	0.0596	0.0636	0.0675	0.0714	0.0753
0.2	0.0793	0.0832	0.0871	0.0910	0.0948	0.0987	0.1026	0.1064	0.1103	0.1141
0.3	0.1179	0.1217	0.1255	0.1293	0.1331	0.1368	0.1406	0.1443	0.1480	0.1517
0.4	0.1554	0.1591	0.1628	0.1664	0.1700	0.1736	0.1772	0.1808	0.1844	0.1879
0.5	0.1915	0.1950	0.1985	0.2019	0.2054	0.2088	0.2123	0.2157	0.2190	0.2224
0.6	0.2257	0.2291	0.2324	0.2357	0.2389	0.2422	0.2454	0.2486	0.2517	0.2549
0.7	0.2580	0.2611	0.2642	0.2673	0.2704	0.2734	0.2764	0.2794	0.2823	0.2852
0.8	0.2881	0.2910	0.2939	0.2967	0.2995	0.3023	0.3051	0.3078	0.3106	0.3133
0.9	0.3159	0.3186	0.3212	0.3238	0.3264	0.3289	0.3315	0.3340	0.3365	0.3389
1.0	0.3413	0.3438	0.3461	0.3485	0.3508	0.3531	0.3554	0.3577	0.3599	0.3621
1.1	0.3643	0.3665	0.3686	0.3708	0.3729	0.3749	0.3770	0.3790	0.3810	0.3830
1.2	0.3849	0.3869	0.3888	0.3907	0.3925	0.3944	0.3962	0.3980	0.3997	0.4015
1.3	0.4032	0.4049	0.4066	0.4082	0.4099	0.4115	0.4131	0.4147	0.4162	0.4177
1.4	0.4192	0.4207	0.4222	0.4236	0.4251	0.4265	0.4279	0.4292	0.4306	0.4319
1.5	0.4332	0.4345	0.4357	0.4370	0.4382	0.4394	0.4406	0.4418	0.4429	0.4441
1.6	0.4452	0.4463	0.4474	0.4484	0.4495	0.4505	0.4515	0.4525	0.4535	0.4545
1.7	0.4554	0.4564	0.4573	0.4582	0.4591	0.4599	0.4608	0.4616	0.4625	0.4633
1.8	0.4641	0.4649	0.4656	0.4664	0.4671	0.4678	0.4686	0.4693	0.4699	0.4706
1.9	0.4713	0.4719	0.4726	0.4732	0.4738	0.4744	0.4750	0.4756	0.4761	0.4767
2.0	0.4772	0.4778	0.4783	0.4788	0.4793	0.4798	0.4803	0.4808	0.4812	0.4817
2.1	0.4821	0.4826	0.4830	0.4834	0.4838	0.4842	0.4846	0.4850	0.4854	0.4857
2.2	0.4861	0.4864	0.4868	0.4871	0.4875	0.4878	0.4881	0.4884	0.4887	0.4890
2.3	0.4893	0.4896	0.4898	0.4901	0.4904	0.4906	0.4909	0.4911	0.4913	0.4916
2.4	0.4918	0.4920	0.4922	0.4925	0.4927	0.4929	0.4931	0.4932	0.4934	0.4936
2.5	0.4938	0.4940	0.4941	0.4943	0.4945	0.4946	0.4948	0.4949	0.4951	0.4952
2.6	0.4953	0.4955	0.4956	0.4957	0.4959	0.4960	0.4961	0.4962	0.4963	0.4964
2.7	0.4965	0.4966	0.4967	0.4968	0.4969	0.4970	0.4971	0.4972	0.4973	0.4974
2.8	0.4974	0.4975	0.4976	0.4977	0.4977	0.4978	0.4979	0.4979	0.4980	0.4981
2.9	0.4981	0.4982	0.4982	0.4983	0.4984	0.4984	0.4985	0.4895	0.4986	0.4986
3.0	0.4987	0.4987	0.4987	0.4988	0.4988	0.4989	0.4989	0.4989	0.4990	0.4990

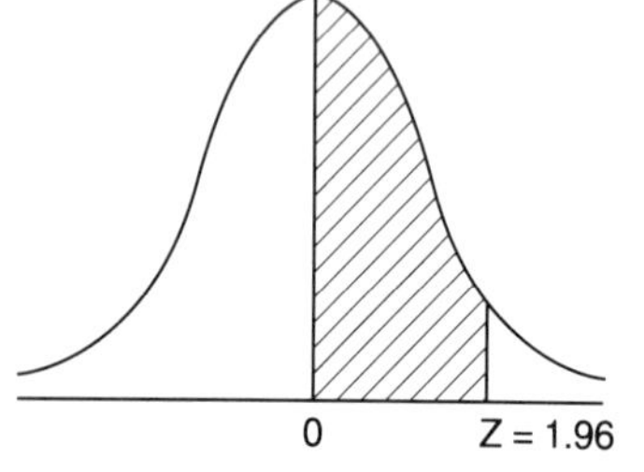

1. For $z = 1.96$, shaded area is 0.4750 out of the total area of 1.0000. Stating it differently, the probability that z has a value greater than or equal to zero and lower than or equal to 1.96 is 47.50 per cent.
2. Since the standardized normal distribution is symmetrical about $z = 0$, the area of the left-hand tail is equal to the area of the right-hand tail. For example, if $z = -1.96$, then the probability that z has a value greater than or equal to -1.96 and lower than or equal to zero is 47.50 per cent.
3. Since the standardized normal distribution is symmetrical about $z = 0$ and the total area under the curve is equal to 1, then the area on each side of the mean is equal to 0.5000.

Appendix E Statistical references

Cohen, L. and Holliday, M. (1982) *Statistics for Social Scientists: An Introductory Text with Computer Programs in BASIC*. Harper & Row, London.

Gujarati, D.N. (1988) *Basic Econometrics*, 2nd edn. McGraw-Hill, New York.

Hey, J.D. (1974) *Statistics in Economics*. Martin Robertson & Co., London.

Makridakis, S., Wheelwright, S.C. and McGee, V.E. (1983) *Forecasting: Methods and Applications*, 2nd edn. John Wiley, New York.

Salvatore D. (1982) *Statistics and Econometrics. Schaum's Outline Series in Economics*. McGraw-Hill, New York.

Taylor, P. and Dunning, D. (1977) *Statistics for Business: A Course Unit Approach*. Polytech Publishers, Stockport.

Index

Accounting model, 94
Accounting period, 94–5
Accounting profit, 141
Accruals management, 411–12
Accrued interest, 444
Activity ratios, 104
Advanced corporation tax (ACT), 185
Agency costs, 33
Agency problem, 33, 660
Aggressive policy, 374
Alternative hypothesis, 562–5
Amortization, 96
Analog models, 1–3
  characteristics, 2
  use in financial management, 1–2
Annual percentage rate (APR), 74
  calculation from monthly interest rate, 74
  calculation of bank loan from flat rate of loan, 75–6
Annuity, 57
Annuity due, 58
Annuity investment, number of periods related to, 78
Arbitrage pricing model, 331–6
  two-factor, 333–4
Arbitrage pricing theory, 335
Arithmetic mean, 83–4
Asset pricing models, 314–69
Asset value method, 497–8
Average rate of return (ARR), 150–1
  calculation, 151
  decision criterion for, 150
  definition, 151
  evaluation of method, 151

Bad debts, 390
Balance sheet, 98–101
  alternative format, 123
Baumol's EQQ model, 380–4
Beta, 320–2
  estimation, 356–8
Beta/return relationship, 329–31
Bimodal, 85
Black and Scholes option valuation model, 719–24
  alternatives to, 738–40
  calculation, 721
  definition, 721
  extensions of, 727–30
  interpretation, 721, 723
  use to estimate value of call option, 723
  use to estimate value of put option, 724
Book value method, 496–7
Book value weights versus market value weights, 541
Break points:
  for ordinary shares, 544
  in marginal cost of capital, 543–4
British depreciation system, 187
Building societies, investment opportunities, 72–4
Business organizations in private sector, 38
Business risk, 573–5
  factors influencing, 575

Call index options, 730–1
Call options, 692–4
  factors influencing, 724–7
  intrinsic value, 696–7
  profit profiles, 698–700
  properties of, 703–9
  valuation of, 719–21
Call prices, one-way sensitivity analysis of, 751–3
Capital allowances, 187
Capital asset pricing model (CAPM), 314, 320–1, 354, 679–80
  and cost of capital, 553–4
  empirical evidence, 326–9
  testing, 329–33
  two-factor, 324–6
  versus single index model, 363–4
Capital budgeting, 135–92
  basic concepts, 135–7
  decisions, 135–7
  definitions, 135–7
  evaluation methods, 169
  methods, 146–64
  methods used in practice, 180–2
  process of, 135
  stages of process, 137–8
Capital budgeting projects, 135
  classification, 136
  contingent, 136

Capital budgeting project (*contd*)
  expansion, 136
  independent, 136
  mutually exclusive, 136
  regulatory, 136
  replacement, 136
Capital employed, 22
Capital gains, 495
Capital loss, 495
Capital market line, 316–19, 323–4, 353–4
Capital rationing, 202–6
  multi-period problem, 204–6
  single-period problem, 202–3
  two-period problem, 203–4
Capital structure, 529, 531
Capital structure theories, 583–607
  Modigliani–Miller approach, 590–3
    with corporation tax, 596–602
    with corporation tax and personal taxes, 601–7
  net income approach, 584–7
  net operating income approach, 587–90
  traditional approach, 593–6
  with no taxes, 584–96
  with taxes, 596–607
Cash discount period, 393
Cash discounts, 389, 393
Cash flow statement, 113–17
Cash flows, 28
  and inflation, 194–8
Cash inflow, 139
Cash management, 379–86
Cash outflow, 139
Cash payments, 95
Cash receipts, 95
Certainty, 218–19
Certainty equivalent coefficient (CEC), 223, 224, 252–3
Certainty equivalent method, 223
  application, 224
  calculation, 223
  definition, 223
  evaluation, 224–5
  interpretation, 223
  versus risk-adjustment discount rate method, 253
Certainty equivalent net cash flow (CENCF), 223
Class frequency, 43
Class mark, 45
Clientele effect, 632–3
Clientele theory, 633
Closing creditors, 95
Closing debtors, 95
Coefficient of variation, 267, 271
Collection policies, 389, 395–8
Combined gearing, 579–83
  calculation, 579
  definition, 579
  degree of, 579–80, 612
  interpretation, 579
Combined risk, 583
Companies limited by shares, 39
Compensating balance, 415
Complete ignorance, 219
Compound annual rate of growth of earnings per share (EPS), 77
Compound value interest factors, 52, 53
Confidence intervals, 491
  estimates for means, 491–2
  for population's simple regression coefficients, 615–17
  for standard deviations, 527–8
Conservative policy, 374
Consistency, 460
Constant dividend payout ratio policy, 633
Constant elasticity of variance model, 738
Constant growth dividend valuation model, 503
Constant growth valuation model, 516–18
Constraints in linear programming, 209
Consumer Price Index (CPI), 452
Consumption combinations, 172–5
Consumption selection, 175
Continuous compounding and discounting, 66–7
Continuous random variable, 254
Controller, 32
Corporation tax, 96, 185–8, 596, 640
  cost of capital with, 599–601
  cost of equity under, 614–15
Correlation coefficient, 214–17, 649–50
  of rates of return, 269–71
Cost-balancing models, 380–6
Cost of capital, 529–66
  and CAPM, 553–4
  basic concepts, 529–32
  calculation of, 549–58
  decision rule using, 531
  definitions, 529–32
  empirical evidence on, 558–9
  with corporation tax, 599–601
Cost of capital (*see also* Weighted average cost of capital)
Cost of goods sold, 95
Coupon interest rate, 430
Covariance between two variables, 188–91
Covariance matrix, 306
Covariance of rates of return, 268–9, 271
Covariance vector, 307
Credit analysis, 398
Credit costs, 407–11
Credit period, 389, 392–3, 407
Credit policy, 389–98
Credit standards, 389–92
Credit terms, 392–5
Creditor management, 406–7
Creditors, 95
Critical value, 564
Cross-sectional analysis, 102–4
'Cum div', 444
Current assets, 22, 99, 373

Current assets/total assets (CA/TA) ratio, 373, 377
Current liabilities, 22, 99, 373
Current liabilities/total liabilities ratio, 373
Current liabilities turnover, 373
Current ratio, 93

Database facilities, 763–4
Database statistical functions, 688–90
Debenture certificate, 430
Debentures, 40, 429–41
 after-tax cost of, 535
 basic concepts, 430–1
 definitions, 430–1
 determining cost of, 532–5
 examples, 430–1
 intrinsic value, 431
 present value, 431–4
 price sensitivity, 447–52
 returns on investments, 434–5
 risks on investments in, 463–6
 valuation of, 431–4
 volatility and duration, 485–7
Debt:
 bad, 390
 cost of, 550
 Merton's model for, 738
Debt/equity ratio, 640
Debt securities, valuation of, 429
Debtor accounts, 396
Debtor finance, 389
Debtors, 95
 management, 389
Decision-making process:
 example, 8–10
 modelling approach, 4, 7–8
 quantitative, 8
Decision trees, 244–7
 evaluation of method, 247
Default risk, 465
Degree of combined gearing, 579–80, 612
Degree of financial gearing, 575–8, 612
Degree of operating gearing, 571–2, 611
Degrees of freedom, 128
Depreciation, 96, 116
 allowances, 640
 British system, 187
 methods, 123–6
Direct lease, 198
Discount interest policy, 414–15
Discount period, 407
Discount rate, 60–1
Discounted cash flow methods, 182
Discounted payback, 149–50
Discrete random variable, 254
Dispersion measures, 85
Displaced diffusion model, 739–40
Diversification, 661
 across industries, 282–4
 effects, 298–300
Dividend adjustments:
 for American-type option, 728–9
 for European-type option, 728
Dividend–irrelevance theory, 623–6, 629, 631, 632, 648
Dividend payout ratio, 620, 622
 and retention rate, 508–10
Dividend policy, 619–55
 basic concepts, 619–22
 comparison of theories, 629–31
 definitions, 619–22
 empirical evidence, 641–3
 example, 620–2
 factors influencing, 638–41, 643
 factors related to shareholders' requirements, 640
 forms of, 633–8
 general views with respect to, 645
 legal constraints, 640–1
 Lintner's model on, 634–6
 reasons for paying dividends, 641–2
 summary of theories, 632
 theories, 623–31, 648–9
Dividend–relevance theory, 625–6, 629, 631, 648–9
Dividend signalling approach, 631–2
Dividend valuation method, 498–502
Dividend valuation model:
 T-year, 500
 two-year, 499–500
Dividends, 495
 present value of, 526–7
Dividends per share, 620, 621
 statistical analysis, 649–50
Double-declining balance depreciation method, 124
Double exponential smoothing, 132–4
Duration:
 and debenture volatility, 485–7
 calculation, 481
 definition, 481
 interpretation, 481
 properties of, 483
 sensitivity to changes in redemption yield and coupon rate, 483
 sensitivity to changes in term to maturity and coupon rate, 483–5, 489–90
Duration of a project, 163–4
 calculation, 163, 164
 definition, 163
 interpretation, 163

Earnings per share (EPS), 620, 621
 compound annual rate of growth of, 77
 in valuation of mergers, 670–5
Economic order quantity (EOQ) model, 399–406
 extensions, 402–6
Efficiency, 460

Efficient frontier, 277–8, 281–2
Efficient market hypothesis:
  empirical tests, 342–9
  forms of, 336–42
Endowment assurance contract, maturity value of, 77
Equity, 494
  cost of, 550, 561–2
    methods of determining, 555–8
  cost under corporation and personal taxes, 614
Estimation, 460–2
Estimator, 460
Excel, 758
Exchange ratio, 664–5
'Ex-div', 444
Expected rate of return, 261
Expected return, 271, 306
Expected utility, 173
Expected value of random variable, 254
Expenses, 96, 139, 143
External finance:
  ability of raising, 639–40
  cost of raising, 640

F-test, 130
Fair game, 340
Fama–MacBeth methodology, 678–9
Filter rules, 344
Financial analysis, 92–134
  and planning, 21
  basic concepts, 92–104
  definitions, 92–104
  example, 93, 97
Financial break-even analysis, 576–7
Financial data, 92
Financial director, role of, 32
Financial forecasting, 117–20
Financial gearing, 575–8
  calculation, 575
  definition, 575
  degree of, 575–8, 612
  interpretation, 575
  properties of degree, 577–8
Financial lease, 198
Financial management:
  basic assumptions, 22
  decisions of, 22
  disciplines involved, 31–2
  evolution, 29–30
  framework, 29
  functions of, 2–3, 21
  nature of, 21
  objective of, 23
  role of, 21–47
  theory of, 23
Financial ratios, 92, 102–13
  analysis evaluation, 110–13
  calculations, 109
Financial risk, 104, 582–3
  factors influencing, 582
Financial statements, 92–4
  relationship of, 102
Financing decisions, 21, 23
First-mortgage debentures, 430
Fisher and Margrabe's stochastic exercise price model, 739
Fisher separation theorem, 179–80
Fisher theory, 169–80
Fixed assets, 22, 98–9
Flotation costs, 530, 534, 538, 630
Forecasting sales, 131–4
Foreign currency options, 732
  pricing of, 732
Forward interest rates, 471–3
Frequency distributions, 42
  example, 43
  graphical representation, 45–7
  measures describing, 82
Frequency polygon, 45
FT-100 Index call option, 730
FT-100 Index put option, 731
Future value, 49–60, 69–78
  annuity, 57–8
  annuity due, 58
  single payment, 50–2
    under continuous compounding, 81–2
  uneven stream of payments, 55–7

Gearing, 567–83, 735
  and value of firm, 605
  tax advance of, 606
  (*see also* Combined gearing; Financial gearing; Operating gearing)
Gearing ratios, 105–6
Gilt-edged securities, 441–5
  comparing, 444–5
Graph of normal distribution, 255
Gross profit/loss, 95
Growth, 660
Growth opportunities, 517
Growth rate in dividends per share, 508–16

Hedge ratio, 733–5
Hedge riskless portfolios, 740
Hedging, 732–5
Histogram, 45
Historical weights, 539–40
Hypothesis testing, 562

Iconic models, 1
Identity matrix, 301
Implicit variance, 750–1
Implicit volatility, 749
Imputation system, 185
Income policy, 641

Incorporated business organizations, 39
Index-linked savings certificates, 72
Index options, 730–2
  versus share options, 731–2
Indifference curves, 173, 175, 290, 291, 307–10
Indifference map, 174, 176
Inefficient market proxy, 561–2
Inflation, 193–8, 640
  and future cash flows, 194–8
  and interest rates, 194, 452–6
  measuring, 452–4
  rate of, 453
Inflation risk, 464
Initial investment, 139–41
Intangible asset, 96
Interest, 49, 96
Interest forgone, 444
Interest rate risk, 464
Interest rates:
  and inflation, 194, 452–6
  nominal, 454–6
  real, 454–6
  term structure of, 466
Interest yield, 443, 445
Internal rate of return, 155–60
  calculation, 156–7
  decision criterion for, 157
  definition, 156
  evaluation method, 158
  modified, 160
  multiple, 159
  undetermined, 159
Investment decisions, 21, 23
Investment opportunities, 639
Investment opportunities schedule, 547–9
Investment ratios, 107–9
Investor's preference, 171–4

Jump diffusion model, 739

Kurtosis, 89
Kurtosis coefficient, 89, 90

Lease–buy decision, 198–201
Leasing, 198–202
  advantages and disadvantages, 201–2
Leptokurtic curve, 89
Lessee, 198
Lessor, 198
Limited liability business organization, 41
Linear interpolation method, 746
Linear programming, 209–14
  constraints in, 209
Linear regression analysis, 131–2
Lintner's model on dividend policy, 634–6
  statistical analysis, 653
Liquidity position, 639
Liquidity preference hypothesis, 474–6
Liquidity ratios, 103–4
Liquidity risk, 465
Loan amortization, 65
Long-term decisions, 22
Long-term loans, 99
Lotus 1-2-3, 757
Lower class limit, 45

Mainstream corporation tax (MCT), 185
Management team, 660
Marginal cost of capital, 542–9
  break points in, 543–4
Marginal rate of substitution, 174
Market anomalies, 346–7
Market segmentation hypothesis, 476–7
Market value method, 496
Market value weights versus book value weights, 541
Marketable securities, 386–9
  characteristics of, 387
  management models, 388–9
  portfolio, 388
  yield on, 387–8
Markowitz analysis, 358–9
Markowitz diversification, 274
Markowitz model, 315
Mathematical models:
  structure, 6
  use in financial management, 3–10
  utilization in financial analysis, 17–20
Matrix, 300–5
  dimension of, 301
  inversion, 303–4
  multiplication, 302–3
  notation, 305–7
  special, 301
Maturity risk, 465
Maturity value of endowment assurance contract, 77
Mean–standard deviation efficient frontier, 289
Mean–standard deviation indifference curves, 307–10
Median, 84–5
Mergers, 656–91
  basic concepts, 656–8
  cash payments, 662–4, 670
  conglomerate, 658
  definitions, 656–8
  earnings per share in valuation, 670–5
  empirical evidence on, 680–4
  evaluating, 661–75
  examples, 656–8, 662–9
  Fama–MacBeth methodology, 678–9
  gains and losses in, 684–5
  horizontal, 658
  methodological issues, 675–85
  motives for, 658–61
  paying with shares, 664–8, 670
  post-merger value, 669–70

  pre-merger value, 669–70
  studies using accounting data, 675
  studies using share returns, 675–7
  synergy as motivation for, 658
  time-series methodology using ex-post form of CAPM, 679–80
  time-series methodology using single or multi-index model, 677–80
  vertical, 658
Merton's model for debt, 738
Merton's stochastic interest-rate model, 738
Mesokurtic curve, 89
Miller–Orr model, 384–6
Miller's corporate tax argument, 605–6
Mode, 85
Models, 1–20
Modified efficient frontier, 284–9
Modified internal rate of return, 160–3
  calculation, 163
  definition, 163
  interpretation, 163
Modigliani–Miller approach, 590–3
  with corporation tax, 596–602
  with corporation tax and personal tax, 601–7
Monopolies and Mergers Commission (MMC), 549
Mortgage, monthly payment, 69–71
Mortgage debentures, 430
Moving average, 132–3
Moving average rules, 344
Multimodal, 85
Multiple linear regression analysis, 364–6
  with three independent variables, 364–6

Naive diversification, 282–4
Naive forecasting method, 510–11
National savings certificates, 71–2
Net cash flow (NCF), 139
  estimating, 142–5
Net fixed assets, 98–9
Net operating (or trading) profit/loss, 96
Net present value (NPV), 151–3, 180
  calculation, 151, 152–3
  decision criterion, 153
  definition, 151
  evaluation of method, 153
  interpretation, 151
  with infinite replicated cash flows, 168
    calculation, 168
    definition, 168
    interpretation, 168
Net present value (NPV) distribution:
  characteristics of, 226
  expected value of, 226
  standard deviation, 227–8
Net present value/payback period method, 220
Net profit, 139
Net working capital, 371, 374

Nominal discount rate, 194
Non-annual compounding and discounting, 65
Normal distribution, 254, 255
  graph, 255
  table, 746
Null hypothesis, 562–5
Number of periods related to annuity investment, 78

Objective function, 209
Objective of the firm in practice, 33–4
Ogive, 45
One-stage supernormal growth dividend valuation model, 504–6
One-tailed test, 564
One-way sensitivity analysis of call prices, 751–3
Opening creditors, 95
Opening debtors, 95
Opening stock, 95
Operating break-even analysis, 569–71
  evaluation, 573
Operating expenses, 95
Operating gearing, 567
  calculation, 568
  definition, 568
  degree of, 611
  interpretation, 568
  properties of degree, 571–2
Optimal capital budget, 547–9
Option contract for stock splits, 696
Option markets, developments in, 692
Option prices:
  factors influencing, 724–7
  non-synchronous, 742–3
  synchronous, 742
Option pricing:
  and firm's equity, 736–7
  boundary conditions, 740
  empirical investigations on models, 740–3
Option valuation models, 719–56
Options, 692–718
  basic concepts, 692–7
  definitions, 692–7
  examples, 692–7
  general uses of, 732–7
  intrinsic value, 696–7
  profit from buying or selling, 697–702
  properties of, 703–11
Ordinary annuity, 57
Ordinary share, intrinsic value, 501
Ordinary shareholders' wealth maximization objective, 23
Ordinary shares, 40, 494–528
  basic concepts, 494–5
  break point for, 544
  cost of, 536–8
  current intrinsic value, 499
  definitions, 494–5

Ordinary shares (*contd*)
  intrinsic value, 503
  valuation of, 495–508
  valuation of unquoted company, 518–21
Organizational chart, 32

Par value, 430, 494
Partnership, 39
Payback period (PB), 146–50, 181, 182
  decision criterion for, 147
  evaluation of method, 148–9
Pension payment calculation, 77–8
Per-cent-of-sales method, 117–20
Perfect correlation, 214
Perfect market, 349
Periodic interest rate, 54
Perpetual debenture, 434
Perpetuity, 65
Personal tax, cost of equity under, 614–15
Pivot element, 211
Pivot operation, 211
Platykurtic curve, 89
Point estimate, 460
Polynomial approximation, 746–7
Population, 422
Portfolio:
  analysis, 260, 271, 284–9
  definition, 272
  diversification, 259
    benefits from, 359–62
    single index model, 359
  rate of return, 271–2
  selection, 258, 260, 279, 289
Portfolio risk, 274–5, 298–300
Portfolio theory, 258–313, 314
  assumptions, 259
  basic concepts, 258–60
  definitions, 258–60
Portfolio variance, 280, 281
Preference shares, 40
  cost of, 535–6
  valuation of, 456–7
Preferred habitat hypothesis, 479–81
Present value, 60–79, 723
  annuity, 63–4
  annuity due, 64
  perpetuity, 65
  single payment, 61
  uneven stream of payments, 61–3
  use in practice, 69–78
Price/earnings (P/E) exchange ratio, 673
Price/earnings ratio, 498, 516–18
Principal, 49
Private limited company, 39
Private sector, business organizations in, 38
Probability, 225, 254
Probability distribution method, 225–32
  calculation, 226
  definition, 226
  evaluation, 232
  for rates of return, 264
  interpretation, 226
  ranking projects using, 228–30
Problem-solving:
  modelling approach, 4, 5–7
  quantitative, 8
Production opportunity set, 170–1
  under perfect capital markets, 176–9
Profit after tax (PAT), 97, 378
Profit and loss account statement, 94–8
Profit estimation, 141–2
Profit/loss before interest and tax (PBIT), 96, 376, 567
Profit maximization, 26–8
Profitability index:
  calculation, 154
  decision criterion for, 155
  definition, 154
  interpretation, 154
Profitability ratios, 106–7
Public limited company (plc), 39
Purchases, 95
Pure jump model, 738–9
Put index options, 731
Put options, 695–6
  factors influencing, 724–7
  intrinsic value, 697
  profit profiles, 700–2
  properties of, 709–11
  valuation of, 724

Quantity discounts, 406
Quatro Pro, 758

Random variable, 254
Random walk, 340–2
Randomness, runs test of, 715–18
Range, 86
Ranking of mutually exclusive projects, 164–9
Ranking projects using probability distribution method, 228–30
Rates of return:
  calculation, 296
  correlation coefficient of, 269–71
  covariance of, 268–9, 271
  on investments, 639
  standard deviation of, 267, 271
  variance of, 266–7
Real discount rate, 194
Redemption date, 430
Redemption yield, 435–41, 445
  approximation formula, 438–40
  determinants of, 463–93
  sensitivity to changes in number of years to maturity, 437

Regression analysis, 765
Regression coefficients, 127–8
Reinvestment rate risk, 465–6
Required rate of return (RRR), 60–1, 537
Reserves, cost of, 538–9
Residual dividend policy, 637–8
Retained earnings statement, 101–2
Retention ratio, 620, 622
Return on current assets (ROCA) ratio, 378
Return on fixed assets (ROFA) ratio, 378
Revenues, 96, 139, 143
Risk, 27–8, 219
  and weighted average cost of capital, 542
  assessment methods used in practice, 247–8
  incorporation into capital budgeting decisions, 218–57
  indirect methods of dealing with, 221
  informal methods of dealing with, 220–1
  on investments in debentures, 463–6
Risk-adjustment discount rate method, 221–3
  versus certainty equivalent method, 253
Risk-return characteristics of two-security portfolio, 273
Risk-return relationship, 549
Risk-return trade-off, 374–8
Roll's critique, 329–33
R-squared, 129
Runs, definition, 345
Runs tests, 345, 715–18

Safety stocks, 403–5
Sale and leaseback, 198
Salvage value, 125
Sample, 422
Sample variance, 461
Sampling methods, 422–7
Scrip dividends, 647
Second-mortgage debentures, 430
Security:
  analysis, 260–70
  definition, 258
  risk-return characteristics, 259
Security market line, 323–4
Semi-strong form of efficiency, 338–9, 345–6
Sensitivity analysis, 232–8, 384, 622, 626, 765
  evaluation, 238
  single variable, 232–3
  supernormal valuation model, 507
  two-variable, 233
Sensitivity table, 383
Serial correlation tests, 342–5
Share capital, 39
Share certificate, 494
Share market price factors, 28–9
Share options versus index options, 731–2
Share price information, 521–3
Share price movements, 730
Share purchases, reducing cost of, 736
Share split, 647
Short-term borrowing:
  cost of, 413–16
  management of, 412–13
Short-term decisions, 22
Short-term interest earned, 373
Significance level, 564
Simple averages method, 511–12
Simple interest policy, 413
Simple linear regression analysis, 126–31
Simple linear regression trend method, 513–14
Simple random sampling, 423–4
Simplex method of linear programming, 209–14
Simulation analysis, 238–43
  evaluation, 242–3
  steps required, 238–42
Single index model, 355–64
  uses of, 356
  versus capital asset pricing model, 363–4
Single linear dividend growth model, 650–2
Single moving average method, 512–13
Single-period rate of return:
  calculation, 260
  definition, 260
  interpretation, 260
  mathematical representation, 261
Single proprietorship, 38
Sinking fund, 59
Skewness, 88
Skewness coefficient, 89
Slack variables, 209
Social responsibility, 25
Solvency ratios, 103, 104
Specific cost of capital, 529, 532–9
Spot rates, 446–7
Spreadsheet-based financial modelling, 10–20
  advantages of, 17–18
  example, 11–16
  phases of, 10–11
  utilization in financial analysis, 17–20
Spreadsheets:
  copy command, 763
  entering numbers, 761
  entering numeric formulae, 762
  entering ranges, 761
  entering text, 762
  exiting, 761
  features and facilities of, 759–60
  financial functions, 765–6
  function keys, 762
  graphs, 763
  history of, 757–9
  invoking, 761
  manipulation of matrices, 764
  mathematical operators, 761
  regression analysis, 765
  sensitivity analysis, 765
  statistical functions, 767

Stable per-share dividends policy, 633
Standard deviation, 88
  confidence intervals for, 527–8
  of net present value distribution, 227–8
  of probability distribution, 255
  of rate of return, 267, 271, 297, 307
Standard error:
  of coefficients, 129–30
  of *Y*-estimate, 128–9
Standard normal probability distribution (SNPD), 256
Statistical inference, 460–2, 562
Statistical measures, 82–91
Statistical population, 422
Stochastic variable, 254
Stochastic volatility model, 740
Stock splits, 647
  option contract for, 696
Stocks management, 398–9
Straight-line depreciation method, 123
Strong form efficiency, 339–40, 346
Studentized range test, 310–12
Subjective method of dealing with risk, 220
Subjective probability, 254
Sum-of-the-year's-digits depreciation method, 125–6
SuperCalc 5, 758
Symmetric matrix, 301
Synergistic financial economies, 659–60
Synergistic operating economies, 658–9
Synergy as motivation for mergers, 658
Systematic risk, 281
Systematic sampling, 424–7

T-period valuation model, 502
t-statistic, 564
t-test, 130
Target weights, 541
Tax credit coefficient, 186
Tax-differential theory, 627–9, 631
Term structure of interest rates, 466
Time period, 49
Time series analysis, 109
Time value of money, 27, 48–91
Total capital and reserves, 99
Total risk, 581–2
Transaction costs, 630
Transpose matrix, 304–5
Treasurer, 32
Trend analysis, 109
Trend forecast method, 131
Turnover, 94–5
Two-stage supernormal growth dividend valuation model, 506–7
Two-tailed test, 564

Unbiased expectations hypothesis, 469
Unbiasedness, 460
Uncertainty, 219
Undervalued assets, 660
Unimodal, 85
Unincorporated business organizations, 38
Unit vector, 305
Unsystematic risk, 281, 361–2
Upper class limit, 45

Valuation ratio, 660
Variable interest policy, 414
Variance, 86–7, 254
  of continuously compounded rates of return, 754
  of rate of return, 266–7, 274, 307
Vectors, 305
VisiCalc, 757

Weak form efficiency, 338, 342–5
Wealth maximization, 26
Weighted average cost of capital, 530, 539–42, 550–3
  advantages and disadvantages, 541
  and risk, 542
Weighted marginal cost of capital, schedule, 544–5
Working capital, 370–428
  basic concepts, 371
  definitions, 371
  importance of management, 372
  policy, 372
Working capital ratios, 373–4
Writing-down allowances, 187

Yield curves, 466–8, 477–8

Zero growth dividend valuation model, 502–3